THE SCOUTING NOTEBOOK 2000

Produced by STATS, Inc.
(Sports Team Analysis and Tracking Systems, Inc.)

John Dewan, Don Zminda
and Jim Callis, Editors

Statistics by STATS, Inc.

STATS
PUBLISHING

The photographs which appear in THE SCOUTING NOTEBOOK 2000 were furnished individually by the 30 teams that comprise Major League Baseball. Their cooperation is gratefully acknowledged: Anaheim Angels, Baltimore Orioles, Boston Red Sox, Chicago White Sox, Cleveland Indians, Detroit Tigers, Kansas City Royals, Minnesota Twins, New York Yankees, Oakland Athletics, Seattle Mariners, Tampa Bay Devil Rays, Texas Rangers, Toronto Blue Jays, Arizona Diamondbacks, Atlanta Braves, Chicago Cubs, Cincinnati Reds, Colorado Rockies, Florida Marlins, Houston Astros, Los Angeles Dodgers, Milwaukee Brewers, Montreal Expos, New York Mets, Philadelphia Phillies, Pittsburgh Pirates, St. Louis Cardinals, San Diego Padres and San Francisco Giants. Thanks also to Steve Moore, who provided our Tim Hudson photo.

Cover by Ben Frobig

Cover photos by Tony Inzerillo (Randy Johnson) and Scott Jordan Levy (Derek Jeter)

First Edition: January, 2000

ISBN 1-884064-74-4

Acknowledgments

The largest and most labor-intensive annual published by STATS, Inc. is *The Scouting Notebook*. The countless hours invested during the fall months produce a volume of work in which we all are proud. Thanks to all who had a hand in our efforts.

STATS CEO John Dewan and President Alan Leib will lead us into the next millennium. Helping them stay on course is Jennifer Manicki, who provides invaluable assistance to both of them. Two vice presidents, Sue Dewan and Bob Meyerhoff, play critical roles in our company's future, directing our Research & Development/Special Projects teams. Sue works with Jim Osborne and Andy Tumpowsky. Bob teams with Athan Arvanitis and Joe Sclafani.

The statistics you find in *The Scouting Notebook* were gathered by our Data Collection Department. Allan Spear heads the group, which includes Jeremy Alpert, Michelle Blanco, Jeff Chernow, Mike Hammer, Derek Kenar, Tony Largo, Jon Passman, Jeff Schinski, Matt Senter, Bill Stephens and Joe Stillwell. With a vast reporter network making statistical collection possible, Jeff Chernow oversaw the compilation of MLB data during the 1999 season.

Then the Publishing Products Department took over, under the direction of our own vice president, Don Zminda. Jim Callis oversaw the production of this book, coordinating writers, executing final edits and tons of decisions, and still taking time to compose the minor league prospect evaluations. As he has for most of the 1990s, Chuck Miller continues to give STATS annuals their distinctive look. Jim Henzler ably writes and manipulates programs for this and all other Publishing Products books. Yours truly wrote the "Other Players" sections for each team, and shared in editing and fact-checking responsibilities with Tony Nistler and part-timers Taylor Bechtold and Marc Carl .

Getting the word out about *The Scouting Notebook* and all other STATS Publishing ventures depends on Marc Elman and his promotions group. Marc works with Ben Frobig, Mike Janosi, Antoinette Kelly and Mike Sarkis. Ben is our graphics man, who integrated photos and charts into the text, as well as designed the Y2K edition's cover with a new flair.

The Commercial Products, Fantasy, Interactive Products and Sales departments are key components of the STATS family. Vincent Smith heads our Commercial Products staff, which includes Ethan D. Cooperson, Dan Matern and David Pinto. Steve Byrd oversees the Fantasy Department, which consists of Bill Burke, Jim Corelis, Dan Ford, Stefan Kretschmann, Walter Lis, Marc Moeller, Mike Mooney, Oscar Palacios, Jim Pollard, Corey Roberts, Eric Robin, Jeff Smith, Yingmin Wang and Rick Wilton. Rick provided much-needed assistance with editing and fact-checking. Michael Canter leads an active Interactive group that includes Dave Carlson, Jake Costello, Will McCleskey, Tim Moriarty, Dean Peterson, Pat Quinn, John Sasman, Meghan Sheehan, Morris Srinivasan and Nick Stamm. Jim Capuano directs a Sales team comprised of Greg Kirkorsky and Jake Stein.

Our Financial/Administrative/Human Resources/Legal Department keeps the office running smoothly and efficiently at our Morton Grove, Ill., home. Howard Lanin oversees the financial details with assistance from Kim Bartlett and Betty Moy. Susan Zamechek assists in finance and watches over the administrative aspects that keep the office functional. Tracy Lickton is in charge of human resources while Carol Savier aids with legal matters. Art Ashley provides programming support throughout the building.

—Thom Henninger

The Scouting Staff

The scouting reports on each team's ballpark, manager and significant players were written by the following people, in conjunction with our editors:

Anaheim Angels	Josh Boyd *STATS, Inc.*
Baltimore Orioles	Rick Wilton *STATS, Inc.*
Boston Red Sox	Peter Gammons *ESPN/Baseball America*
Chicago White Sox	Phil Rogers *Chicago Tribune/ Baseball America*
Cleveland Indians	Paul Hoynes *Cleveland Plain Dealer*
Detroit Tigers	Pat Caputo *Oakland (Mich.) Press/ Baseball America*
Kansas City Royals	Marc Bowman *STATS, Inc.*
Minnesota Twins	John Sickels *STATS, Inc.*
New York Yankees	Tom Keegan *New York Post*
Oakland Athletics	Lawr Michaels *CREATiVESPORTS*
Seattle Mariners	David Schoenfield *ESPN.com*
Tampa Bay Devil Rays	Marc Topkin *St. Petersburg Times/ Baseball America*
Texas Rangers	Phil Rogers *Chicago Tribune/ Baseball America*
Toronto Blue Jays	Mike Mittleman *STATS, Inc.*
Arizona Diamondbacks	Ed Price *Tribune Newspapers (Mesa, Ariz.)*
Atlanta Braves	Bill Ballew *Baseball America*
Chicago Cubs	Mat Olkin *Baseball Weekly*
Cincinnati Reds	Peter Pascarelli *ESPN*
Colorado Rockies	Tracy Ringolsby *Rocky Mountain News (Denver)/Baseball America*
Florida Marlins	Mike Berardino *The Sun-Sentinel (Fort Lauderdale)/Baseball America*
Houston Astros	David Rawnsley *Baseball America*
Los Angeles Dodgers	Don Hartack *STATS, Inc.*
Milwaukee Brewers	Mat Olkin *Baseball Weekly*
Montreal Expos	Mat Olkin *Baseball Weekly*
New York Mets	Mat Olkin *Baseball Weekly*
Philadelphia Phillies	Tony Blengino *Diamond Library*
Pittsburgh Pirates	John Perrotto *Beaver County (Pa.) Times/ Baseball America*
St. Louis Cardinals	Peter Pascarelli *ESPN*
San Diego Padres	Mat Olkin *Baseball Weekly*
San Francisco Giants	David Rawnsley *Baseball America*

The minor league prospect reports were written by yours truly, and I'd like to thank the player-development personnel who were willing to discuss their teams' farm systems. *Baseball America's* David Rawnsley was a big help at filling in some blanks. The "Other Anaheim Angels," etc., were written by Thom Henninger.

I'd also like to offer my personal thanks to my family. My wife Ann, sons A.J. and Ryan and daughter Elizabeth gave me the support I needed to get through the arduous process of putting this book together, though I apparently worked so much that A.J. feared that I would have to work on Christmas. Thankfully, I did not.

—Jim Callis

Table of Contents

As the New York Yankees celebrate their 25th World Series championship of the century, the fans of Chicago's baseball teams are left to imagine what a ticker-tape parade would be like. This book is dedicated to those fans, like myself, who have endured 173 consecutive seasons (91 for the Cubs, 82 for the White Sox) without a world champion. Let's hope the new century will finally bring the next generation of Chicago fans a winner.

—Walter Lis

Foreword

by Karl Ravech
Host of ESPN's "Baseball Tonight"

Under the new agreement between ESPN and Major League Baseball, ESPN will provide somewhere in the vicinity of a million hours of coverage of the greatest game in the world (actually more than 800 hours a year). Anyone who believes that we would undertake such a task without *The Scouting Notebook* also is likely to tell you that taking Randy Johnson deep is as easy as stepping into the batter's box, lefthanded no less.

It is easy to see how valuable a tool this book can be to those who need instant information about a player's tendencies. Very little is left to the imagination as even the intangibles, such as a player's ability to hit or pitch in the clutch, are included in the concise summaries.

Understanding that we all now live in the information age, it is incumbent on those of us who deliver the news, sports or otherwise to be ahead of the curve. If not, we strike out in the viewers' eyes, and once that happens, getting back into the game is extremely difficult.

The staff of *The Scouting Notebook* reads like an all-star lineup. They are the men who cover the teams day-in and day-out, and their access to the players and scouts coupled with STATS' extensive insight and experience, give the reader a real feel for the players, the teams and the organizations.

As host of "Baseball Tonight," I am required to eat, drink and sleep baseball. *The Scouting Notebook* doesn't taste very good but it is filled with every item even the most discriminating fan could ask for. I don't do a show without it.

Introduction

Welcome to the sixth edition of *The Scouting Notebook*. This is the 11th annual book of scouting reports that STATS, Inc. has created. We get several prominent baseball analysts and have them give us detailed reports on every major league player who saw significant action last season. Our scouting staff includes some of the top baseball minds around, such as Peter Gammons, Peter Pascarelli, David Rawnsley, Tracy Ringolsby and Phil Rogers. Marc Bowman, Paul Hoynes and John Perrotto have contributed to all 11 books.

This is an encyclopedia of contemporary major league baseball. We tell you about the strengths and weaknesses of hundreds of players. Our analysis extends beyond major league players, too, covering each club's top minor league prospects. We study the statistics and we talk to the scouts. We look for the true ability that may have been exaggerated or obscured by the hype.

The Ballparks

The book reports on each club's ballpark. We detail how each stadium affects hitters, pitchers and fielders in general, as well as which players it helps and hurts the most. We also project what the park will do to rookies and other newcomers in 2000. We provide vital statistics for each park, such as its dimensions, capacity, elevation, playing surface and the amount of foul territory.

We also present our trademark park indexes, with which readers of our *Major League Handbook* are familiar. In a variety of statistical categories, we show how the home team and its opponents performed at the park and on the road. Interleague games aren't included. By comparing the overall totals at the park and on the road, we get a measure of the stadium's impact. We divide the home totals by the road totals and multiply by 100 to get the park index. An index of greater than 100 shows that the park favors a particular statistic, while an index of less than 100 means the opposite.

Most of the indexes are calculated on a per-at-bat basis. Runs, hits, errors and infield errors are figured on a per-game basis. For most parks, we present data for both 1999 and the last three years overall. If the park's configuration has changed since the end of the 1997 season, we present the data for the different setups separately.

Most of the abbreviations are common, with these exceptions:

E-Infield: Infield errors.

LHB-Avg: Batting average by lefthanded hitters.

LHB-HR: Home runs by lefthanded hitters.

RHB-Avg: Batting average by righthanded hitters.

RHB-HR: Home runs by righthanded hitters.

We also list any indexes in which the park ranked in the top or bottom three in its league in 1999.

The Managers

On these pages, we analyze each manager's strengths and weaknesses, style and strategy, and outlook for 2000. We present his 1999 and career managerial record, and we also show how often he used starting pitchers on various days of rest. We compare his use and the performance of his starters to the league average.

We also provide statistical breakdowns detailing his handling of his pitching staff and his use of strategies like the sacrifice, the hit-and-run and defensive substitutions. To qualify for the rankings, a manager had to have his team for at least 100 games in 1999. Some of the terms listed in the statistics and rankings sections may be unfamiliar. They include:

Hit & Run Success %: The percentage of hit-and-runs resulting in baserunner advancement with no double play.

Platoon Pct.: Frequency that the manager gets his hitters the platoon advantage (lefty vs. righty and vice versa). Switch-hitters always are considered to have the advantage.

Defensive Subs: The number of straight defensive substitutions with the team leading by four runs or fewer.

High-Pitch Outings: The number of times a manager's starting pitchers threw more than 120 pitches in a ballgame.

Quick/Slow Hooks: A Quick Hook occurs when a pitcher is removed after having pitched less than six innings and given up three runs or fewer. A Slow Hook occurs when a pitcher works more than nine innings, allows seven or more runs, or his total innings and runs equal 13 or more.

First-Batter Platoon Percentage: The percentage of times the managers' relievers had a platoon advantage over the first hitter they faced (lefty vs. lefty, righty vs. righty).

Mid-Inning Changes: The number of times the manager changed pitchers in the middle of an inning.

Pitchouts with a Runner Moving: The number of times the opposition was running when the manager called a pitchout.

Sacrifice Bunt Percentage: The percentage of bunts resulting in sacrifices or hits with runners on.

Starting Lineups Used: Based on batting order, 1-8 for National Leaguers, 1-9 for American Leaguers.

2+ Pitching Changes in Low-Scoring Games: The number of times a manager used at least three pitchers in a game in which his team allowed two runs or fewer.

The Players

For each major league team, we give extensive reports on 22 players. Twelve of them get a full page of scouting information, while 10 receive half-page reports. Because we like to get this book into your hands as soon as possible, players are listed with their 1999 clubs. We keep abreast of postseason transactions, and all player moves that took place through December 20, 1999, are noted. If you can't find a particular player, check the detailed index in the back.

Pages for primary players have two columns. The left column provides an in-depth report by an analyst. The right column contains statistical information:

Position: The first position shown is the player's most common position in 1999. Positions at which he played 10 or more games also are shown. For pitchers, SP stands for starting pitcher and RP for relief pitcher.

Bats and Throws: L stands for lefthanded, R stands for righthanded, and B stands for both (switch-hitter).

Ht: Height.

Wt: Weight.

Opening Day Age: This is the player's age on March 29, 2000.

Born: Birthdate and birthplace.

ML Seasons: This number indicates the number of different major league seasons in which the player has appeared. For example, if a player was called up to play in September in each of the last three seasons, the number shown would be 3. This is different from major league service, which is used to determine arbitration and free-agency eligibility.

Overall Statistics: These are traditional major league statistics for the player's 1999 season and his career.

Where He Hits The Ball

For every major league game in 1999, STATS reporters entered into our computers every ball hit into play. They kept track of the type of batted balls—grounders, flyballs, popups, line drives and bunts—as well as the distance each ball traveled. Direction was tracked by dividing the field into 26 "wedges" projecting out from home plate. Distance was measured in 10-foot increments outward from home plate.

Below are the hitting diagrams for righthanded-hitting Sammy Sosa. The chart on the left shows where Sosa hit the ball against lefthanders, while the chart on the right shows what he did against righties.

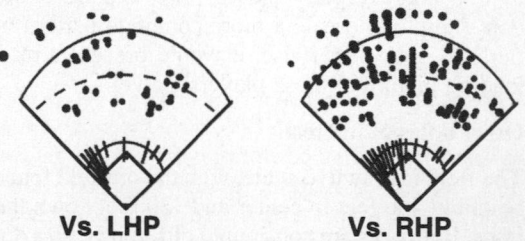

Vs. LHP   Vs. RHP

In the diagrams, groundballs and short line drives are shown by the lines of various lengths in the infield. The longer the line, the more groundballs and line drives were hit in that direction. As you can see from the charts above, when Sosa hits liners and grounders through the infield, he tends to pull the ball sharply. Playing infielders on the left side a few extra steps toward the left-field line probably steals some hits from him.

In the outfield, batted balls are shown by dots. The bigger the dot, the more balls that were hit to that area. The dotted line in the outfield is 300 feet away from home plate, a rough approximation of typical outfield defensive positions. Taking another look at Sosa, when he drives the ball for distance, he sprays it to all fields. Against southpaws, he clearly turns on the ball for his longest shots.

A lot of experimentation went into producing the hitting diagrams. When we first started, we tried to show every single batted ball that was put into play by each player. We found that the charts became very cluttered for everyday players, so we began experimenting with trying to show only the most meaningful information. When all was said and done, here's what we ended up with:

a. Popups and bunts are excluded. We excluded popups because 95 percent of these are caught regardless of how fielders are positioned. We excluded bunts because defensing a bunt is an entirely different strategy primarily used against a select number of players or in specific situations.

b. For groundballs, we excluded only the rare isolated point. For most players, almost all of their grounders are shown.

c. For everyday players, we excluded isolated points in the outfield. If a player hit only one ball in a given area and had no other batted balls in the vicinity all season, we exclude it because it doesn't give a true indication of a tendency.

d. For non-everyday players, we expanded the data sample to create a more complete pattern of outfield dots. Otherwise, it would present a misleading picture of these players' power.

Other notes of interest:

The field is drawn to scale, with the outfield fence reaching 400 feet in center and 330 feet down the lines. Ballparks are configured differently, so a dot inside of the fence might have been a home run. Similarly, a dot outside the fence might actually have been in play.

Line drives under 170 feet are part of the infield. We give responsibility for short liners to the infielders.

No distinction is made between hits and outs.

How Often He Throws Strikes

Our STATS reporters also tracked every pitch thrown in a major league game in 1999. The pitching graphs show how often the hurler throws strikes in different situations. Our data shows most pitchers will toss a strike between 40 and 80 percent of the time. Therefore we've constructed the chart to represent the 40-80 percent range.

The strike count includes swinging strikes, taken strikes, foul balls and balls put in play. Though not all batted balls come on pitches thrown within the strike zone, our theory is that most are and the ones that aren't would be difficult to judge. Our charts reflect these assumptions.

The charts are broken into four categories. *All Pitches* is straightforward, as is *First Pitch*. We define *Ahead* as counts with more strikes than balls. *Behind* includes counts with more balls than strikes. The appropriate league average is shown in each chart.

Below are the 1999 league averages. The National League threw a slightly higher percentage of strikes than the American League, as it has in all 10 years we have tracked this.

Strike Percentage by League — 1999		
	American	National
All Pitches	61.2%	61.7%
First Pitch	56.0%	56.2%
Ahead in the Count	58.9%	60.8%
Behind in the Count	66.0%	65.4%

1999 Situational Stats

There are eight situational breakdowns for every primary player. *Home* and *Road* show performance in his home ballpark and on the road. *First Half* and *Scnd Half* show performance before and after the 1999 All-Star break. For hitters, *LHP* and *RHP* show how the player hit against lefthanders and righthanders. For pitchers, *LHB* and *RHB* show how the opposition lefthanders and righthanders hit against the pitcher. *Sc Pos* shows batting or pitching performance with runners in scoring position. *Clutch* shows batting or pitching performance in clutch situations, defined as the seventh inning or later with the batting team ahead by one run, tied or with the tying run on base, at bat or on deck. Our definition is consistent with save situations.

1999 Rankings

This section shows how the player ranked in his league and among his teammates. Because of space considerations, we omitted some of the less interesting rankings when a player placed high in numerous categories.

We include many less traditional categories. The Definitions and Qualifications section below provides details for these statistics.

Definitions and Qualifications

The following are definitions and qualifications for the Major League Leaders and Rankings.

Definitions:

Times on Base — Hits plus walks plus hit-by-pitch.

Ground/Fly Ratio — Groundballs hit divided by the total of flyballs and popups hit. Bunts and line drives are excluded.

Runs/Times on Base — Runs scored divided by times on base.

Clutch — A player's batting average in the late innings of close games, defined as the seventh inning or later with the batting team ahead by one run, tied or with the tying run on base, at bat or on deck.

Bases Loaded — A player's batting average in bases-loaded situations.

GDP per GDP situation — Groundball double plays divided by groundball double-play situations, defined as a man on first base with less than two out.

Percentage of Pitches Taken — The percentage of pitches a player lets go by without swinging.

Percentage Swings Put In Play — The percentage of swings resulting in a batted ball into fair territory or a foul-ball out.

Run Support per Nine Innings — The number of runs scored for a pitcher while he was pitching, scaled to a nine-inning figure.

Baserunners per Nine Innings — The total of hits, walks and hit batsmen allowed per nine innings.

Strikeout/Walk Ratio — Strikeouts divided by walks.

Stolen-Base Percentage Allowed — Stolen bases divided by stolen-base attempts.

Save Percentage — Saves divided by save opportunities. Save opportunities include saves plus blown saves.

Blown Saves — A blown save is charged any time a pitcher enters a game in a save situation and loses the lead. A save situation is defined as any time a reliever enters the game with a lead, isn't the pitcher of record and either a) pitches at least one inning with a lead of no more than three runs; b) enters the game with the potential tying run on base, at bat or on deck; or c) pitches effectively for at least three innings.

Holds — A hold is given to a pitcher when he enters a game in a save situation and is removed before the end of the game while maintaining his team's lead. The pitcher must retire at least one batter to get a hold.

Percentage of Inherited Runners Scored — Percentage of runners already on base when a pitcher enters a game that he allows to score.

First Batter Efficiency — The batting average allowed by a reliever to the first batter he faces in a game.

Qualifications:

In order to be ranked, a player had to qualify with a minimum number of opportunities, as follows:

Batters

Batting average, slugging percentage, on-base percentage, home run frequency, ground/fly ratio, runs scored per time reached base and pitches seen per plate appearance — 3.1 plate appearances per team game

Percentage of pitches taken, lowest percentage of swings that missed and percentage of swings put into play — 9.26 pitches seen per team game

Percentage of extra bases taken as a runner — .09 opportunities to advance per team game

Stolen-base percentage — .12 stolen-base attempts per team game

Runners in scoring position — .62 plate appearances with runners in scoring position per team game

Clutch — .31 plate appearances in the clutch per team game

Bases loaded — .06 plate appearances with the bases loaded per team game

GDP per GDP situation — .31 plate appearances in GDP situations per team game

BA vs. LHP — .77 plate appearances against lefthanders per team game

BA vs. RHP — 2.33 plate appearances against righthanders per team game

BA at home — 1.55 plate appearances at home per team game

BA on the road — 1.55 plate appearances on the road per team game

Leadoff on-base percentage — .93 plate appearances in the No. 1 lineup spot per team game

Cleanup slugging percentage — .93 plate appearances in the No. 4 lineup spot per team game

BA on 3-1 count — .06 plate appearances with a 3-1 count per team game

BA with 2 strikes — .62 plate appearances with two strikes per team game

BA on 0-2 count — .12 plate appearances with an 0-2 count per team game

BA on 3-2 count — .12 plate appearances with a 3-2 count per team game

Pitchers

Earned run average, run support per nine innings, baserunners per nine innings, batting average allowed, slugging percentage allowed, on-base percentage allowed, home runs per nine innings, strikeouts per nine innings, strikeout/walk ratio, stolen-base percentage allowed, GDPs per nine innings, pitches thrown per batter and ground/fly ratio against — one inning per team game

Winning percentage — .09 decisions per team game

GDPs induced per GDP situation — .19 batters faced in GDP situations per team game

BA allowed, runners in scoring position — .77 batters faced with runners in scoring position per team game

ERA at home — .5 innings at home per team game

ERA on the road — .5 innings on the road per team game

BA vs. LHB — .77 lefthanders faced per team game

BA vs. RHB — 1.39 righthanders faced per team game

Relievers

ERA, batting average allowed, baserunners per nine innings, strikeouts per nine innings — .31 relief innings per team game

Save percentage — .12 save opportunities per team game

Percentage of inherited runners scoring — .19 inherited runners per team game

First batter efficiency — .25 games in relief per team game

Fielders

Percentage caught stealing by catchers — .43 stolen-base attempts per team game

Fielding percentage — .62 games at a position per team game (.19 chances per team game for pitchers)

Other Players

Some players didn't play enough to merit a full- or half-page essay, and aren't young enough or good enough to deserve a prospect report. But they did play in the majors last year, so we give them a brief evaluation. Following the half-page reports for each team, you'll find a page devoted to these part-timers under the heading "Other Anaheim Angels," etc. Each player gets a short summary and his 2000 Outlook is graded as follows:

A — Should be an important contributor.
B — Should play most of the season in the majors and contribute.
C — Unlikely to play much in the majors or contribute much if he does.
D — Unlikely to play in the majors.

Minor League Prospects

We present two pages of minor league prospects for each team. Former *Baseball America* managing editor Jim Callis spoke directly to player-development personnel with each major league team and also looked beyond athletic tools by analyzing statistics. Each club has eight featured prospects. We try to include most of the top phenoms, but our primary emphasis is on advanced players with the best chance of contributing in the majors in 2000.

For featured prospects who are hitters and played in Double-A or Triple-A in 1999, we include major league equivalencies. Developed by Bill James, the MLE translates minor league statistics into major league numbers. It does this by making a series of adjustments for a player's home ballpark, his league, his level of competition and his future major league home park.

We also include an organizational overview for each team. We tell you which clubs are the best and worst at developing talent, and we tell you why. In addition, we summarize another half-dozen or so notable prospects per team in a section called "Others to Watch."

Where we mention that managers voted a player as the best in a specific category in his league, our source is *Baseball America*.

Major League Leaders

After the team sections, we provide a complete listing of Major League Leaders. The top three players in each category are shown for the American and National Leagues. You'll notice a STATS flavor to these leaders. Not only do we show the leaders for the common categories such as batting average, home runs and ERA, but you'll also find less traditional categories like steals of third and total pitches thrown.

Stars, Bums and Sleepers

This section tells you what to expect from each player in 2000: whether they'll improve, decline, remain consistent or come out of nowhere to surprise.

Jim Callis' Top 50 Prospects

The book closes with Jim Callis' ranking of the top 50 prospects in the game. All players who haven't exceeded the rookie limits of 130 at-bats or 50 innings pitched in the major leagues are eligible.

American League Players

Edison International Field

Offense

The primary distinguishing features of Edison International Field are the Disneyesque rock formations and geysers beyond the center-field wall, and the 18-foot scoreboard along the right-field wall. Since it was reconfigured prior to the 1998 season, the Ed has been a very neutral park in most respects. Interestingly, it reduced home runs by lefthanded hitters by 24 percent in 1998, then boosted lefty homers by 41 percent last year, the top mark in the American League. It remains to be seen how this will play out, but the park could have a profound effect on lefty hitters Garret Anderson, Jim Edmonds, Darin Erstad and Mo Vaughn.

Defense

Edison International Field has little effect on the Angels' sound defense. The grass and infield dirt are well maintained, preventing unruly bounces and errors. There isn't an abundance of foul territory, and the short five-foot fences in the outfield corners result in a high total of ground-rule doubles. The walls can present some tricky caroms, but their proximity can turn triples into doubles if the outfielder makes a good play.

Who It Helps The Most

None of Anaheim's hitters was particularly helped or hurt by the Ed in 1999. In the last two years, Ken Hill has a 3.73 ERA at home compared to a 6.67 mark on the road.

Who It Hurts The Most

In his first full season, Troy Glaus hit 17 of his 29 homers away from Anaheim. None of the pitchers has been harmed by Edison International Field.

Rookies & Newcomers

The Angels will be breaking in several pitchers in the next couple of seasons, starting with Ramon Ortiz and Jarrod Washburn, followed by Brian Cooper and Seth Etherton. There's no evidence to suggest that their development will be affected by their home ballpark.

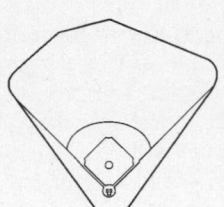

Dimensions: LF-330, LCF-396, CF-408, RCF-370, RF-330

Capacity: 45,050

Elevation: 160 feet

Surface: Grass

Foul Territory: Average

Park Factors

1999 Season

| | Home Games | | | Away Games | | | |
	Angels	Opp	Total	Angels	Opp	Total	Index
G	72	72	144	72	72	144	—
Avg	.252	.269	.261	.260	.267	.263	99
AB	2357	2499	4856	2521	2349	4870	100
R	314	377	691	333	351	684	101
H	595	671	1266	655	628	1283	99
2B	104	131	235	118	118	236	100
3B	13	10	23	7	15	22	105
HR	70	90	160	74	65	139	115
BB	235	288	523	217	277	494	106
SO	440	394	834	473	394	867	96
E	50	41	91	41	52	93	98
E-Infield	43	33	76	37	43	80	95
LHB-Avg	.270	.265	.267	.267	.257	.263	102
LHB-HR	37	45	82	38	21	59	141
RHB-Avg	.234	.271	.255	.252	.274	.264	97
RHB-HR	33	45	78	36	44	80	97

1998-1999

| | Home Games | | | Away Games | | | |
	Angels	Opp	Total	Angels	Opp	Total	Index
G	145	145	290	145	145	290	—
Avg	.258	.263	.261	.270	.270	.270	97
AB	4802	5021	9823	5152	4798	9950	99
R	641	739	1380	712	696	1408	98
H	1240	1321	2561	1391	1296	2687	95
2B	229	277	506	282	273	555	92
3B	30	20	50	15	26	41	124
HR	118	172	290	155	129	284	103
BB	458	580	1038	452	563	1015	104
SO	887	921	1808	947	850	1797	102
E	98	98	196	88	106	194	101
E-Infield	83	83	166	81	87	168	99
LHB-Avg	.276	.262	.269	.277	.268	.273	99
LHB-HR	62	76	138	82	49	131	105
RHB-Avg	.240	.264	.253	.264	.271	.268	95
RHB-HR	56	96	152	73	80	153	102

1999 Rankings (American League)

- Highest LHB home-run factor
- Third-highest walk factor

Mike Scioscia

1999 Season

Just two months after resigning as the manager of the Dodgers' Triple-A Albuquerque affiliate to pursue options outside of the organization, Mike Scioscia was rewarded with the Angels' managerial job. A former All-Star catcher with Los Angeles, Scioscia retired as a player in 1994. His resumé also includes two years as the bench coach for the Dodgers under Bill Russell and a managerial assignment in the Arizona Fall League.

Offense

Of his many tasks at hand, Scioscia will have to impress upon Anaheim hitters the importance of plate discipline. Last season, the Angels ranked dead last in baseball with an uninspiring .322 on-base percentage. Scioscia calls his offense a sleeping giant waiting to awaken and believes it will flourish if his sluggers can stay off the disabled list. If he follows the lead of his Dodgers manager, Tommy Lasorda, and Russell, Scioscia will be aggressive and try to force the action. His Albuquerque team led the Pacific Coast League in sacrifice bunts and ranked second in steal attempts. The Angels haven't had a dynamic basestealing threat in years, and they still need a true tablesetter atop the order.

Pitching & Defense

After catching in the big leagues for 15 years, Scioscia knows how to handle a pitching staff. It will be interesting to see if he works his starters as hard as Lasorda did, but he should know better. Faced with the loss of Chuck Finley and no budget increase on the horizon, Scioscia will have to rely on inexperienced pitchers such as Ramon Ortiz and Jarrod Washburn to develop in a hurry. Anaheim's underrated relief corps will help take some of the pressure off of the starters.

2000 Outlook

His predecessor Terry Collins was a strict disciplinarian who ultimately divided the clubhouse. Scioscia will take the other extreme, enforcing few rules in order to create a relaxed environment. That may not resolve all of the Angels' internal conflicts, but they are bound to improve on their chaotic 1999 season, making Scioscia look good.

Born: 11/27/58 in Upper Darby, PA

Playing Experience: 1980-1992, LA

Managerial Experience: 0 seasons
Pronunciation: SO-shuh

Manager Statistics

Year	Team, Lg	W	L	Pct	GB	Finish
1999		—	—	—	—	—
0 Seasons		—	—	—	—	—

1999 Starting Pitchers by Days Rest

	<=3	4	5	6+
Angels Starts	—	—	—	—
Angels ERA	—	—	—	—
AL Avg Starts	2	82	47	21
AL ERA	6.83	4.98	4.72	5.62

1999 Situational Stats

	Mike Scioscia	AL Average
Hit & Run Success %	—	35.3
Stolen Base Success %	—	68.0
Platoon Pct.	—	56.7
Defensive Subs	—	22
High-Pitch Outings	—	15
Quick/Slow Hooks	—	18/18
Sacrifice Attempts	—	52

1999 Rankings (American League)

- Did not manage in the majors last year

Garret Anderson

Position: CF/LF
Bats: L **Throws:** L
Ht: 6' 3" **Wt:** 215

Opening Day Age: 27
Born: 6/30/72 in Los Angeles, CA
ML Seasons: 6

1999 Season

Garret Anderson and Troy Glaus were the only Anaheim regulars able to avoid the disabled list last year. Anderson maintained his consistent output throughout the club's turmoil and was voted the Angels' 1999 Most Valuable Player by his teammates. He was hampered by nerve damage in his left foot, but Anderson never complained and led Anaheim in batting average, hits and doubles while reaching a career high in home runs.

Hitting

A smooth-swinging lefty, Anderson stays back and adjusts well to offspeed offerings, ripping balls into the gaps. He always has been able to hit lefties and righties alike, lacing line drives to all fields. Anderson isn't a selective batter, drawing a mere 34 walks last year, but he makes consistent contact. He muscled up for a career-high 21 homers, yanking most of them to right field off righthanders, but that's still below-average production for a left fielder.

Baserunning & Defense

Anderson exhibited his versatility when he covered all three outfield positions when injuries sidelined Tim Salmon and Jim Edmonds, spending more time in center than usual. Anderson glides in the outfield with his deceptive speed covering the gaps, and he displays a strong and accurate throwing arm. The sore foot that bothered him for most of the season hindered him on the bases. He succeeded in just three of seven stolen-base attempts and never has been much of a threat.

2000 Outlook

In October, Anderson had surgery to release a trapped nerve in his foot. He's expected to recover fully by spring training. The Angels picked up his option for 2000 at $3.25 million, and once again will market his career .300 average and reasonable salary as they search for starting pitching. Though he's consistent at the plate, his home-run power and RBI ability are below average for a left fielder.

Overall Statistics

	G	AB	R	H	D	T	HR	RBI	SB	BB	SO	Avg	OBP	Slg
1999	157	620	88	188	36	2	21	80	3	34	81	.303	.336	.469
Career	728	2860	355	858	165	15	72	393	34	139	382	.300	.331	.444

Where He Hits the Ball

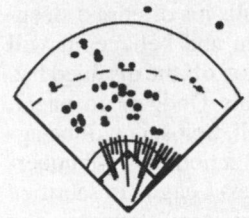

Vs. LHP

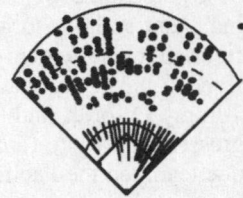

Vs. RHP

1999 Situational Stats

	AB	H	HR	RBI	Avg		AB	H	HR	RBI	Avg
Home	299	88	10	37	.294	LHP	161	45	3	23	.280
Road	321	100	11	43	.312	RHP	459	143	18	57	.312
First Half	339	99	14	43	.292	Sc Pos	160	41	2	51	.256
Scnd Half	281	89	7	37	.317	Clutch	95	25	2	7	.263

1999 Rankings (American League)

- 2nd in lowest batting average with the bases loaded (.000)
- 3rd in fielding percentage in center field (.991) and lowest cleanup slugging percentage (.439)
- Led the Angels in batting average vs. righthanded pitchers, slugging percentage vs. righthanded pitchers (.505), on-base percentage vs. righthanded pitchers (.348), batting average, at-bats, runs scored, hits, singles, doubles, total bases (291), sacrifice flies (6), intentional walks (8), times on base (222), plate appearances (660), batting average at home and games played
- Led AL center fielders in doubles

Tim Belcher

Position: SP
Bats: R **Throws:** R
Ht: 6' 3" **Wt:** 225

Opening Day Age: 38
Born: 10/19/61 in Sparta, OH
ML Seasons: 13

1999 Season

After signing a two-year free-agent deal worth $10.2 million, Tim Belcher was expected to add veteran influence and stability to the Anaheim rotation. Instead, he rapidly declined into the Angels' biggest disappointment of the year. A broken finger interrupted his campaign in June, and Belcher finished the season on the disabled list with a strained right forearm. His six victories were his lowest total ever for a full major league season.

Pitching

The key to Belcher's success always has been his ability to keep hitters off balance by changing speeds and spotting his pitches. But his command went from solid to below average last year and he became vulnerable, as reflected by the 27 home runs and 6.73 ERA he allowed. Belcher was acquired with a proven track record of eating innings, but after three consecutive 200-inning seasons he didn't even average six innings per start. He delivers a vast assortment of pitches with varied speeds and movement, with his velocity peaking in the high 80s.

Defense

Belcher does a great job of thwarting runners with varied pickoff moves and a quick release to home. Just two of the nine basestealers who tested him last year were able to outsmart him. A fluid delivery leaves him in good shape for fielding, and he has a reputation as a competent defender.

2000 Outlook

Belcher is on the downside of his career, and it remains uncertain whether he'll be able to resurrect himself once again. He had surgery in December to repair a muscle tear in his forearm, and he could miss most or all of spring training. A poised veteran, he does have a history of coming back whenever he's counted out. But this isn't good news for the Angels, who may have to use Belcher as their No. 1 starter following the departure of Chuck Finley.

Overall Statistics

	W	L	Pct.	ERA	G	GS	Sv	IP	H	BB	SO	HR	Ratio
1999	6	8	.429	6.73	24	24	0	132.1	168	46	52	27	1.62
Career	142	135	.513	4.12	385	364	5	2402.0	2378	838	1497	256	1.34

How Often He Throws Strikes

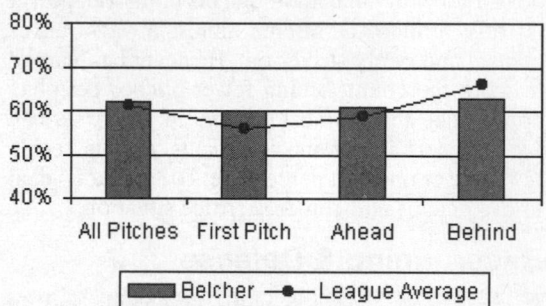

1999 Situational Stats

	W	L	ERA	Sv	IP		AB	H	HR	RBI	Avg
Home	3	3	6.06	0	65.1	LHB	276	86	13	49	.312
Road	3	5	7.39	0	67.0	RHB	258	82	14	44	.318
First Half	5	6	6.53	0	91.0	Sc Pos	126	42	6	63	.333
Scnd Half	1	2	7.19	0	41.1	Clutch	29	6	1	2	.207

1999 Rankings (American League)

- 6th in highest batting average allowed with runners in scoring position
- 9th in highest batting average allowed vs. lefthanded batters
- Led the Angels in home runs allowed

Gary DiSarcina

1999 Season

When Gary DiSarcina was struck by an errant bat which broke his left forearm on the first day of spring training, the Angels began to unravel. The heart and soul of the Anaheim clubhouse, DiSarcina was out until the end of June. He wasn't able to get his bat going until September, far too late to salvage a lost season. Overall, it was his worst offensive performance ever.

Hitting

The forearm injury that cost him the first half of the season effectively robbed DiSarcina of his ability to drive the ball into the gaps. His nine extra-base hits last year aren't an accurate indication of what he can do with the bat, though his home-run power is truly limited. DiSarcina almost always makes contact and rarely strikes out. He never has learned to work the count, seeing fewer pitches per plate appearance than almost anyone in the American League. His impatience accounts for his feeble .291 career on-base percentage. DiSarcina is ideal to use in a hit-and-run or sacrifice situation.

Baserunning & Defense

A throwback shortstop with sure hands and an accurate arm, DiSarcina displays deceiving range with the help of correct positioning and sound instincts. He can make tough plays up the middle and in the hole, and is the quarterback of Anaheim's infield. His dismal offensive season did carry over into the field, as his fielding percentage dropped to a career-low .963. As a runner, DiSarcina makes up for a lack of speed with his intelligence. He's capable of stealing 8-10 bases per year.

2000 Outlook

The Angels are happy with DiSarcina's steady play in the field, but his lack of plate discipline prevents him from improving much offensively. He does a lot of the little things it takes to win, but he has posted decent offensive numbers in only two of the past five seasons. When healthy in a good lineup, DiSarcina should thrive hitting fastballs at the bottom of the order.

Position: SS
Bats: R **Throws:** R
Ht: 6' 2"   **Wt:** 205

Opening Day Age: 32
Born: 11/19/67 in Malden, MA
ML Seasons: 11
Pronunciation: dee-sar-SEE-nuh

Overall Statistics

	G	AB	R	H	D	T	HR	RBI	SB	BB	SO	Avg	OBP	Slg
1999	81	271	32	62	7	1	1	29	2	15	32	.229	.273	.273
Career	1074	3706	438	951	184	20	27	344	47	153	303	.257	.291	.339

Where He Hits the Ball

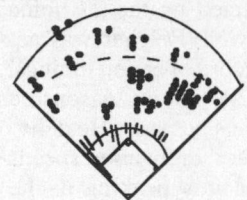 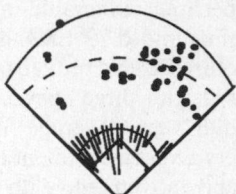

Vs. LHP   **Vs. RHP**

1999 Situational Stats

	AB	H	HR	RBI	Avg		AB	H	HR	RBI	Avg
Home	149	32	1	20	.215	LHP	60	12	0	5	.200
Road	122	30	0	9	.246	RHP	211	50	1	24	.237
First Half	53	14	0	8	.264	Sc Pos	68	21	0	27	.309
Scnd Half	218	48	1	21	.220	Clutch	42	8	0	5	.190

1999 Rankings (American League)

- 2nd in lowest batting average on an 0-2 count (.042)
- 7th in errors at shortstop (15)
- 10th in sacrifice bunts (9)
- Led the Angels in bunts in play (13) and sacrifice bunts (9)

Jim Edmonds

1999 Season

Jim Edmonds was another victim of the injury bug that bit the Angels in 1999. He tore the labrum in his right shoulder while weightlifting, needed surgery and didn't play his first game until August. He spent the remainder of the season trying to rediscover his swing after the long layoff. He said he never quite felt comfortable at the plate.

Hitting

When he's healthy—which isn't very often—Edmonds is a dangerous power hitter who can leave the yard in any direction. He stands upright at the plate and gets his bat through the strike zone very quickly. He looks for pitches up and over the plate to hit hard into the gaps. Edmonds does most of his damage against righthanders. He has performed respectably against lefthanders in the past, but batted only .190 with no homers against them in 1999.

Baserunning & Defense

Edmonds won Gold Gloves for his center-field play in 1997 and 1998, but he wasn't his normal full-tilt, headlong-diving, crash-into-the-wall self last year when he returned from shoulder surgery. He makes excellent reads off the bat and takes perfect angles on balls hit in the alleys. He also makes strong and accurate throws. Edmonds isn't blessed with great speed, but his instincts make him effective on the bases. He's aggressive and runs hard, though he has been successful on just over half of his career steal attempts.

2000 Outlook

Edmonds has been the focus of trade rumors in recent years, and he believes that former Anaheim GM Bill Bavasi was the only team executive in his corner. The Angels picked up the $4.5 million option on his contract for 2000, and his talent and affordable contract should be sufficient bait to finally bring the team the frontline starting pitcher it craves. New Anaheim GM Bill Stoneman has been charged with remaking the club this offseason, and it would be a surprise if Edmonds were to return.

Position: CF
Bats: L **Throws:** L
Ht: 6' 1" **Wt:** 218

Opening Day Age: 29
Born: 6/27/70 in Fullerton, CA
ML Seasons: 7

Overall Statistics

	G	AB	R	H	D	T	HR	RBI	SB	BB	SO	Avg	OBP	Slg
1999	55	204	34	51	17	2	5	23	5	28	45	.250	.339	.426
Career	709	2644	464	768	161	12	121	408	26	274	558	.290	.359	.498

Where He Hits the Ball

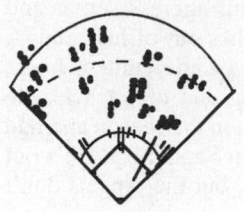 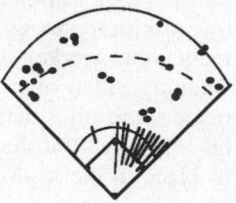

Vs. LHP   **Vs. RHP**

1999 Situational Stats

	AB	H	HR	RBI	Avg		AB	H	HR	RBI	Avg
Home	117	30	3	15	.256	LHP	63	12	0	5	.190
Road	87	21	2	8	.241	RHP	141	39	5	18	.277
First Half	0	0	0	0	-	Sc Pos	35	7	0	11	.200
Scnd Half	204	51	5	23	.250	Clutch	32	3	0	1	.094

1999 Rankings (American League)

- 8th in batting average on a 3-1 count (.600)
- Led the Angels in batting average on a 3-1 count (.600)

Darin Erstad

1999 Season

On the verge of stardom, Darin Erstad labored through a frustrating year-long slump. After an All-Star campaign in 1998, the No. 1 overall pick in the 1995 draft posted a .683 on-base plus slugging percentage, fourth-lowest among American League regulars. To make matters worse, Erstad went on the disabled list in August when his spikes caught in the dirt on a swing, straining a ligament in his right knee.

Hitting

Throughout his first two big league seasons, Erstad smoked line drives into the gaps. The Angels thought home-run power would follow. But last year Erstad often was befuddled at the plate, as pitchers took advantage of his aggressiveness and forced him to swing at pitches out of his zone. A meticulous worker, Erstad spends endless hours studying video of his swing and of pitchers. He made some adjustments late in the season and had his best month of the year in September. He's out of place in the leadoff role, but the Angels don't have an alternative.

Baserunning & Defense

Whether he's on the bases or in the field, the down-and-dirty Erstad goes 100 MPH, 100 percent of the time. He has developed into a very good first baseman, making spectacular leaping catches and accurate throws on double plays. In the outfield, he has above-average range and a strong arm, and he didn't make an error in 69 games last season. He has good speed, but didn't put himself in many basestealing situations in 1999.

2000 Outlook

There are no long-term concerns about Erstad's poor 1999 season. Anaheim has tried to trade Garret Anderson and Jim Edmonds for some much-needed starting pitching, but other teams have made it clear they prefer Erstad. With a healthy Mo Vaughn expected to be back at first base on a daily basis, Erstad will shift back to his natural position of left field in 2000. Given his work ethic, there's no reason Erstad can't regain his All-Star form.

Position: 1B/LF
Bats: L **Throws:** L
Ht: 6' 2" **Wt:** 210

Opening Day Age: 25
Born: 6/4/74 in Jamestown, ND
ML Seasons: 4

Overall Statistics

	G	AB	R	H	D	T	HR	RBI	SB	BB	SO	Avg	OBP	Slg
1999	142	585	84	148	22	5	13	53	13	47	101	.253	.308	.374
Career	471	1869	301	527	100	13	52	232	59	158	293	.282	.339	.433

Where He Hits the Ball

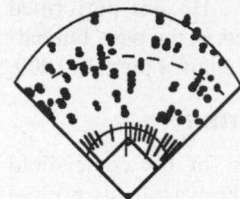 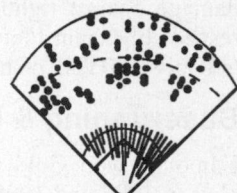

Vs. LHP   **Vs. RHP**

1999 Situational Stats

	AB	H	HR	RBI	Avg		AB	H	HR	RBI	Avg
Home	282	74	7	23	.262	LHP	157	43	5	19	.274
Road	303	74	6	30	.244	RHP	428	105	8	34	.245
First Half	349	93	7	31	.266	Sc Pos	130	34	1	39	.262
Scnd Half	236	55	6	22	.233	Clutch	90	25	5	13	.278

1999 Rankings (American League)

- 5th in lowest on-base percentage vs. lefthanded pitchers (.310)
- Led the Angels in highest groundball/flyball ratio (1.6), stolen-base percentage (65.0), highest percentage of extra bases taken as a runner (64.0), triples, stolen bases, caught stealing (7) and GDPs (16)
- Led AL first basemen in highest groundball/flyball ratio (1.6), stolen-base percentage (65.0), on-base percentage for a leadoff hitter (.321), highest percentage of extra bases taken as a runner (64.0) and bunts in play (4)

Chuck Finley

Position: SP
Bats: L **Throws:** L
Ht: 6' 6" **Wt:** 226

Opening Day Age: 37
Born: 11/26/62 in
Monroe, LA
ML Seasons: 14

Anaheim

1999 Season

Chuck Finley again anchored the Angels rotation after the club was unable to lure a premier free agent in the offseason. Anaheim tried to trade Finley to a contender before the July 31 deadline, but his veto rights and impending free agency didn't help matters. The tall lefthander recorded the third 200-strikeout season of his career and logged more than 200 innings for the eighth time.

Pitching

With Randy Johnson gone from the American League, Finley has become the Junior Circuit's most dominant lefty. He hasn't lost an ounce of effectiveness and can carve up a lineup with his patented one-two fastball-splitter punch. At 37, Finley still can get his heater into the low 90s while working both sides of the plate. He disguises his sharp splitter with the same over-the-top release point as his fastball, forcing hitters to chase balls down in the dirt. He also regained command of his curveball, making him tough on lefties once again. Finley throws a ton of pitches and has shown some signs of a tired arm in recent seasons, but he usually has rebounded to finish with a flourish.

Defense

Finley has been regarded as a poor fielder throughout his career, and last year was no different. He's a big man who doesn't move very swiftly on grounders or toward first base. While he owns a good pickoff move, Finley is slow to the plate because of his leg kick and basestealers take advantage. He also uncorked 15 wild pitches last year, giving runners an extra edge.

2000 Outlook

At the end of 1999, the only two players with longer tenures with their teams were Cal Ripken Jr. and Tony Gwynn. But the franchise's winningest pitcher ever won't return to Anaheim for a 15th season. Finley signed a three-year, $27 million contract with the Indians in December. He should back Bartolo Colon as the Tribe's No. 2 starter.

Overall Statistics

	W	L	Pct.	ERA	G	GS	Sv	IP	H	BB	SO	HR	Ratio
1999	12	11	.522	4.43	33	33	0	213.1	197	94	200	23	1.36
Career	165	140	.541	3.72	436	379	0	2675.0	2544	1118	2151	254	1.37

How Often He Throws Strikes

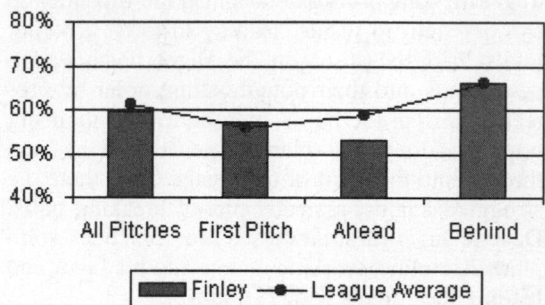

1999 Situational Stats

	W	L	ERA	Sv	IP			AB	H	HR	RBI	Avg
Home	4	4	4.56	0	98.2	LHB		158	37	3	16	.234
Road	8	7	4.32	0	114.2	RHB		643	160	20	83	.249
First Half	5	9	5.66	0	109.2	Sc Pos		185	48	5	74	.259
Scnd Half	7	2	3.13	0	103.2	Clutch		69	11	0	5	.159

1999 Rankings (American League)

- 1st in wild pitches (15)
- 2nd in strikeouts and most strikeouts per nine innings (8.4)
- 3rd in pitches thrown (3,613), lowest slugging percentage allowed (.386) and runners caught stealing (13)
- Led the Angels in ERA, wins, losses, innings pitched, hits allowed, batters faced (913), walks allowed, strikeouts, wild pitches (15), pitches thrown (3,613), winning percentage, highest strikeout/walk ratio (2.1), lowest batting average allowed (.246), lowest slugging percentage allowed (.386), lowest on-base percentage allowed (.330) and highest groundball/flyball ratio allowed (1.4)

Troy Glaus

1999 Season

With high expectations placed upon his shoulders, Troy Glaus gave a glimpse of the future by showcasing his tremendous power potential. However, the third overall pick in the 1997 draft also exposed a few weaknesses and sometimes showed his inexperience during his first full major league season. Following a hot start, Glaus found himself on the brink of being demoted when pitchers adjusted and held him to a .130 batting average in May. He hit just .244 after that, but still launched 29 home runs for the season.

Hitting

Glaus feasts on fastballs, especially when he's able to get his long arms extended. On the flip side, he can get tied up inside, leading to lofty strikeout totals. Prior to last season, the Angels had hoped to ease Glaus into their potent batting order by protecting him in the No. 7 spot. Injuries to their big boppers foiled that plan, however, and he was thrown into the heart of the lineup. Once there, he struggled against a steady diet of breaking balls. Despite his 143 strikeouts, Glaus practices solid plate discipline, working counts into his favor and leading the Angels with 71 walks.

Baserunning & Defense

Glaus could develop into a Gold Glover with his defensive work at the hot corner. A shortstop at UCLA, he has outstanding reactions and the range to make tough plays. He's already superb at charging a slow roller, barehanding the ball and firing a strike to first base. On the basepaths, Glaus is athletic but doesn't possess enough speed to be a factor.

2000 Outlook

The Angels believe Glaus tired toward the end of a long and sometimes trying 1999 season. He now should have an idea of what it takes to hold up physically and mentally throughout a 162-game schedule. If Anaheim can keep him lower in the order, Glaus rapidly could blossom into a home-grown franchise cornerstone, a la Tim Salmon.

Position: 3B
Bats: R **Throws:** R
Ht: 6' 5" **Wt:** 225

Opening Day Age: 23
Born: 8/3/76 in Tarzana, CA
ML Seasons: 2
Pronunciation: GLOSS

Overall Statistics

	G	AB	R	H	D	T	HR	RBI	SB	BB	SO	Avg	OBP	Slg
1999	154	551	85	132	29	0	29	79	5	71	143	.240	.331	.450
Career	202	716	104	168	38	0	30	102	6	86	194	.235	.320	.413

Where He Hits the Ball

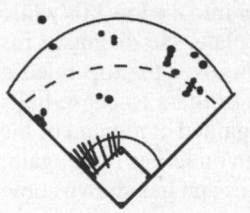 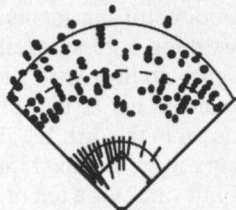

Vs. LHP   **Vs. RHP**

1999 Situational Stats

	AB	H	HR	RBI	Avg		AB	H	HR	RBI	Avg
Home	263	64	12	42	.243	LHP	116	25	5	17	.216
Road	288	68	17	37	.236	RHP	435	107	24	62	.246
First Half	296	69	15	40	.233	Sc Pos	138	32	10	51	.232
Scnd Half	255	63	14	39	.247	Clutch	84	18	0	9	.214

1999 Rankings (American League)

- 2nd in lowest batting average vs. lefthanded pitchers and lowest batting average
- 3rd in strikeouts and lowest batting average on the road
- 4th in errors at third base (19)
- 5th in fielding percentage at third base (.954) and lowest batting average at home
- Led the Angels in most pitches seen per plate appearance (4.03), fewest GDPs per GDP situation (7.4%), walks, strikeouts and pitches seen (2,541)
- Led AL third basemen in fewest GDPs per GDP situation (7.4%)

Ken Hill

1999 Season

Ken Hill's second full season in Anaheim was no better than his first, as the skills of the former All-Star continued to erode. Injuries plagued his 1998 season, and his bad luck carried over into 1999, when he made two trips to the disabled list. He ultimately was banished to the bullpen after returning in September from his second stint on the DL. Hill finished with just four victories, his lowest total since establishing himself in the majors 10 years earlier.

Pitching

Hill's control problems have been his biggest enemy, and his dead-even strikeout-walk ratio last year clearly illustrates his struggles. For years, there have been questions about his stamina, as his velocity inexplicably fluctuates from a powerful 94 MPH all the way down into the 80s. Faulty mechanics and 11 years of mileage have taken their toll. He still offers a potentially effective package that includes a forkball, slider and changeup, but his body no longer cooperates. His first stint on the DL was for inflammation in his surgically repaired elbow, and the second trip was for a strained groin and abdominal muscle.

Defense

Hill doesn't make much of an attempt to combat the running game. Basestealers ran at will last year, swiping 21 bags in 26 attempts. He's a dependable if unspectacular fielder who hasn't made an error since 1996.

2000 Outlook

Hill voiced his displeasure last year when he was demoted to the bullpen and then placed on the DL against his wishes. He didn't feel he was treated fairly, and also claimed racism played a part in the Angels' decisions. The team can't be too pleased that it will pay him $5.6 million in 2000. He'll probably get the chance to start again, but the only way he can silence his critics is to prove his arm is sound.

Position: SP
Bats: R **Throws:** R
Ht: 6' 2" **Wt:** 214

Opening Day Age: 34
Born: 12/14/65 in Lynn, MA
ML Seasons: 12

Overall Statistics

	W	L	Pct.	ERA	G	GS	Sv	IP	H	BB	SO	HR	Ratio
1999	4	11	.267	4.77	26	22	0	128.1	129	76	76	14	1.60
Career	112	100	.528	3.90	309	298	0	1884.0	1821	788	1129	142	1.38

How Often He Throws Strikes

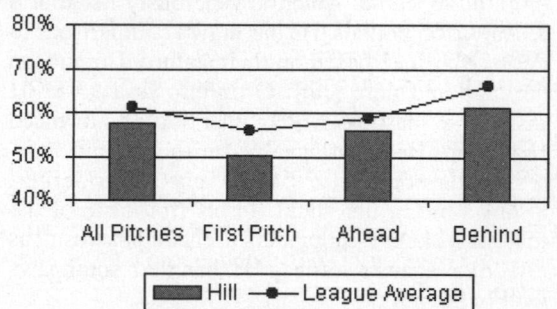

1999 Situational Stats

	W	L	ERA	Sv	IP		AB	H	HR	RBI	Avg
Home	3	7	3.92	0	78.0	LHB	246	59	7	32	.240
Road	1	4	6.08	0	50.1	RHB	232	70	7	29	.302
First Half	3	8	5.58	0	90.1	Sc Pos	129	29	0	43	.225
Scnd Half	1	3	2.84	0	38.0	Clutch	29	10	0	3	.345

1999 Rankings (American League)

- 2nd in lowest winning percentage
- 5th in lowest batting average allowed with runners in scoring position
- 6th in lowest batting average allowed vs. lefthanded batters
- 10th in stolen bases allowed (21)
- Led the Angels in losses, stolen bases allowed (21), lowest batting average allowed vs. lefthanded batters and lowest batting average allowed with runners in scoring position

Ramon Ortiz

Position: SP
Bats: R **Throws:** R
Ht: 6' 0" **Wt:** 165

Opening Day Age: 23
Born: 5/23/76 in Las Matas Cotui, Dominican Republic
ML Seasons: 1
Pronunciation: or-TEEZ

1999 Season

Ramon Ortiz led the minor leagues with 225 strike-outs in 1997, then fractured his elbow while pitching in Double-A the following season. It was a terrible blow to an organization lacking in prospects, especially pitchers, but Ortiz erased all concerns with a strong rebound in 1999. He tore up Double-A and pitched well in Triple-A, earning nine starts with Anaheim. Ortiz allowed just three runs in 15 innings over his first two major league outings, then struggled with his control and got pounded after that.

Pitching

Ortiz generates eye-popping power that belies his diminutive frame, which is generously listed at 6 feet and 165 pounds. He has drawn comparisons to Pedro Martinez based on their stature, Dominican heritage and pure stuff. Ortiz throws a 95-MPH fastball, a sharp 85-MPH slider and an advanced changeup. He's unflappable on the mound, possessing the confidence to throw any of his offerings at any time in the count. In his first taste of the majors, he kept righthanders in check but wasn't as effective against lefties. He handled southpaws well in the minors.

Defense

Ortiz has lots of energy. He comes off the mound like a cat and didn't make an error in 10 big league chances. He's average in terms of controlling the running game.

2000 Outlook

The Angels envision Ortiz leading their staff for their next decade. With Chuck Finley leaving, Tim Belcher coming off forearm surgery and Ken Hill falling apart, Ortiz could emerge as their No. 1 starter as early as this year. The organization might want to monitor his workload more carefully. He regularly has worked plenty of innings in pro ball and winter leagues, and wasn't kept on a pitch count in Anaheim. Care must be taken to not jeopardize a pitcher with this gifted an arm.

Overall Statistics

	W	L	Pct.	ERA	G	GS	Sv	IP	H	BB	SO	HR	Ratio
1999	2	3	.400	6.52	9	9	0	48.1	50	25	44	7	1.55
Career	2	3	.400	6.52	9	9	0	48.1	50	25	44	7	1.55

How Often He Throws Strikes

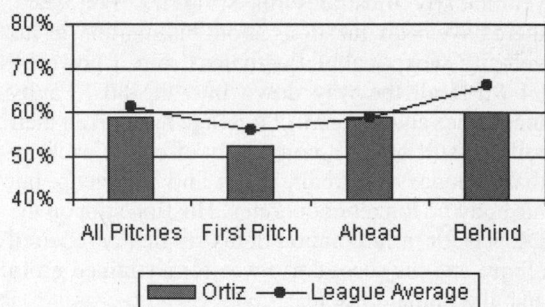

1999 Situational Stats

	W	L	ERA	Sv	IP		AB	H	HR	RBI	Avg
Home	1	1	6.95	0	22.0	LHB	99	29	6	27	.293
Road	1	2	6.15	0	26.1	RHB	90	21	1	5	.233
First Half	0	0	-	0	0.0	Sc Pos	37	16	3	25	.432
Scnd Half	2	3	6.52	0	48.1	Clutch	5	2	0	0	.400

1999 Rankings (American League)
- 3rd in balks (2)
- Led the Angels in balks (2)

Troy Percival

1999 Season

From Opening Day until the beginning of August, Troy Percival was virtually unhittable, yielding 18 hits in 39.2 innings while striking out 41. Then the flamethrower blew six of his next 13 save opportunities and watched his ERA balloon to 7.79 during that period. Overall, opponents managed just a .186 average against him, but he was touched up for a career-worst nine homers before being shut down in September with a sore shoulder.

Pitching

With his dynamic mid-90s heat and intense demeanor, Percival can be one of the nastiest pitchers in the game. Even during his slump, which he called the low point of his career, he was bringing it at 95 MPH. He may have been tipping off his curveball and changeup, which, coupled with his sore shoulder, could have led to his ineffectiveness. When he's right, Percival's command is sharp and he's as tough to hit as anyone in the American League.

Defense

Like many closers, Percival pays little attention to basestealers. They usually succeed against him, but rarely test him because he's usually pitching with the game on the line. The powerful force Percival exerts on every pitch doesn't make him an ideal fielder. It's difficult to put bunts into play against his explosive fastball, so he's spared from making many tough plays.

2000 Outlook

Percival needed surgery in October to shave bone spurs and clean up the labrum in his aching right shoulder. He's expected to be in prime condition by the start of spring training. The Angels would be hopeless without Percival, who is one of the few sure things on their roster for 2000. He'll hope to reverse a trend that has seen his ERA rise in each of his five major league seasons.

Position: RP
Bats: R **Throws:** R
Ht: 6' 3" **Wt:** 230

Opening Day Age: 30
Born: 8/9/69 in Fontana, CA
ML Seasons: 5

Overall Statistics

	W	L	Pct.	ERA	G	GS	Sv	IP	H	BB	SO	HR	Ratio
1999	4	6	.400	3.79	60	0	31	57.0	38	22	58	9	1.05
Career	14	22	.389	2.95	306	0	139	323.2	198	138	411	34	1.04

How Often He Throws Strikes

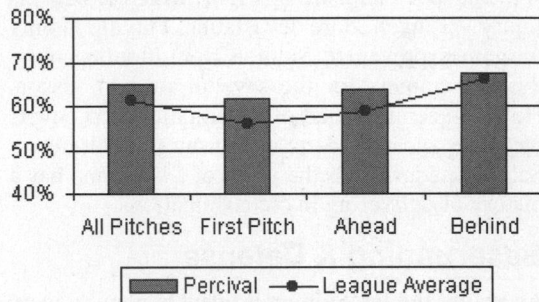

Percival —●— League Average

1999 Situational Stats

	W	L	ERA	Sv	IP		AB	H	HR	RBI	Avg
Home	4	3	3.94	14	29.2	LHB	112	24	5	25	.214
Road	0	3	3.62	17	27.1	RHB	92	14	4	9	.152
First Half	2	2	2.18	23	33.0	Sc Pos	48	14	3	27	.292
Scnd Half	2	4	6.00	8	24.0	Clutch	167	31	8	31	.186

1999 Rankings (American League)

- 3rd in blown saves (8) and lowest batting average allowed in relief (.186)
- 4th in relief losses (6) and lowest save percentage (79.5)
- 5th in save opportunities (39)
- 6th in saves and fewest baserunners allowed per nine innings in relief (9.9) and most strikeouts per nine innings in relief (9.2)
- 10th in games finished (50)
- Led the Angels in saves, games finished (50), save opportunities (39), save percentage (79.5), blown saves (8), relief losses (6), lowest batting average allowed in relief (.186), fewest baserunners allowed per nine innings in relief (9.9) and most strikeouts per nine innings in relief (9.2)

Tim Salmon

1999 Season

Eager to start 1999 with a bang after an injury-plagued 1998 campaign, Tim Salmon again joined the ranks of the Angels' wounded when he sprained his left wrist in May. Before the injury, which sidelined him for almost two months, Salmon appeared to be destined for his first All-Star Game, hitting a robust .347 with seven home runs. He came back before he was fully healthy and batted just .236-10-44 in the second half.

Hitting

Batting out of a slight crouch, Salmon is a disciplined power hitter who can drive the ball over the fence to all fields. He generates his pop with explosive bat speed and strong wrists, which is why his injury was even more devastating. Playing in only 98 games prevented Salmon from clouting more than 20 homers for the seventh straight season. He's an accomplished offspeed hitter who covers the plate and pounds pitches from the belt down. Salmon understands the value of a walk and has a history of delivering in clutch situations.

Baserunning & Defense

As a right fielder, Salmon is adept at coming in on liners. In fact, he jammed his wrist on one of his patented feet-first sliding catches. Injuries have prevented him from playing up to his full capabilities in the field in the last two years, however. When healthy, he displays above-average mobility and a strong, accurate throwing arm. In a half-season's worth of action last year, Salmon gunned down seven runners. He has good instincts on the bases with average speed, but isn't much of a threat to steal. He has been caught stealing more than he has succeeded in the majors.

2000 Outlook

One of the Angels' few certainties for 2000 is that Salmon will be back in right field and in the heart of the order. A fan favorite for his consistent effort and productivity, Salmon still is in the prime of his career. He batted .296-33-129 in his last fully healthy year, and could duplicate those numbers if he can avoid further injuries.

Position: RF
Bats: R **Throws:** R
Ht: 6' 3" **Wt:** 241

Opening Day Age: 31
Born: 8/24/68 in Long Beach, CA
ML Seasons: 8
Pronunciation: SAM-men

Overall Statistics

	G	AB	R	H	D	T	HR	RBI	SB	BB	SO	Avg	OBP	Slg
1999	98	353	60	94	24	2	17	69	4	63	82	.266	.372	.490
Career	955	3483	608	1015	195	14	196	660	29	579	820	.291	.393	.524

Where He Hits the Ball

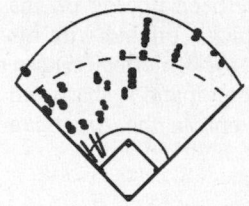
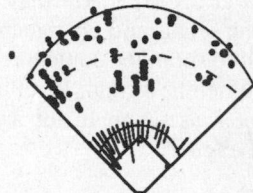

Vs. LHP   **Vs. RHP**

1999 Situational Stats

	AB	H	HR	RBI	Avg		AB	H	HR	RBI	Avg
Home	192	47	7	29	.245	LHP	73	22	2	15	.301
Road	161	47	10	40	.292	RHP	280	72	15	54	.257
First Half	95	33	7	25	.347	Sc Pos	101	28	7	53	.277
Scnd Half	258	61	10	44	.236	Clutch	55	13	4	14	.236

1999 Rankings (American League)

- 5th in lowest batting average on an 0-2 count (.048)
- 7th in errors in right field (4)
- 9th in lowest cleanup slugging percentage (.519)
- Led the Angels in batting average with the bases loaded (.429), cleanup slugging percentage (.519) and sacrifice flies (6)

Mo Vaughn

1999 Season

The string of bad luck that followed the Angels all season long was epitomized by the image of Mo Vaughn falling into the dugout and spraining his ankle in the first inning of his first regular-season game with the Angels. Expectations were sky-high after he signed a six-year, $80 million contract as a free agent, and the pressure was on Vaughn to immediately carry the Angels to the promised land. He came with a reputation as a team leader, and despite the clubhouse turmoil he didn't disappoint. But considering he's a former Most Valuable Player who annually competed for leadership in the triple-crown categories while with the Red Sox, Vaughn's offensive numbers were a letdown.

Hitting

No player presents more of an intimidating presence in the batter's box than Vaughn. The massive lefthanded slugger hovers over the plate, daring pitchers to test him on the inner half. He obliterates fastballs and has become a disciplined hitter who is able to stay back on offspeed deliveries. He became more of a pull hitter after leaving Fenway Park, where he enjoyed taking outside pitches over the Green Monster. His ankle injury inhibited him for most of the summer, creating awkward, off-balance swings. By taking away the inside of the plate, Vaughn gives lefthanders nightmares, but his production versus righthanders suffered last year.

Baserunning & Defense

Already a lumbering baserunner, Vaughn became even less effective on the bases after his ankle injury. At first base, he's relatively agile for a man of his size, but he commits a lot of errors on grounders and low throws. His ankle limited him to just 72 games at first base.

2000 Outlook

Vaughn says the only thing he regrets about his initial season in Anaheim was falling in the dugout, and he remains upbeat about his future with the Angels. His September surge should be a preview of what a healthy Mo Vaughn can bring to the table, as he finally looked comfortable launching moon shots over Edison Field's 18-foot right-field wall.

Position: 1B/DH
Bats: L **Throws:** R
Ht: 6' 1" **Wt:** 245

Opening Day Age: 32
Born: 12/15/67 in Norwalk, CT
ML Seasons: 9
Nickname: The Hit Dog

Overall Statistics

	G	AB	R	H	D	T	HR	RBI	SB	BB	SO	Avg	OBP	Slg
1999	139	524	63	147	20	0	33	108	0	54	127	.281	.358	.508
Career	1185	4352	691	1312	219	10	263	860	28	573	1081	.301	.390	.538

Where He Hits the Ball

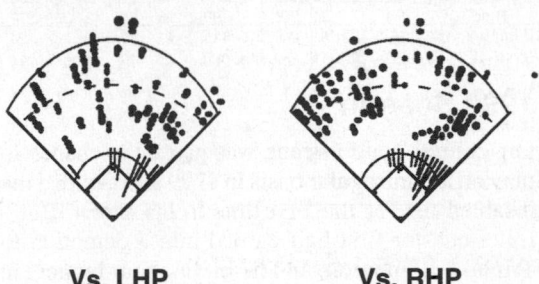

Vs. LHP   **Vs. RHP**

1999 Situational Stats

	AB	H	HR	RBI	Avg			AB	H	HR	RBI	Avg
Home	252	67	16	55	.266		LHP	152	51	11	48	.336
Road	272	80	17	53	.294		RHP	372	96	22	60	.258
First Half	268	77	17	56	.287		Sc Pos	132	46	13	78	.348
Scnd Half	256	70	16	52	.273		Clutch	71	20	4	20	.282

1999 Rankings (American League)

- 8th in on-base percentage vs. lefthanded pitchers (.433)
- 9th in slugging percentage vs. lefthanded pitchers (.599) and hit by pitch (11)
- 10th in batting average vs. lefthanded pitchers and strikeouts
- Led the Angels in slugging percentage, on-base percentage, HR frequency (15.9 ABs per HR), batting average with runners in scoring position, batting average vs. lefthanded pitchers, slugging percentage vs. lefthanded pitchers (.599), on-base percentage vs. lefthanded pitchers (.433), home runs, RBI and hit by pitch (11)
- Led AL first basemen in batting average with runners in scoring position

Todd Greene

Position: DH/RF/C
Bats: R **Throws:** R
Ht: 5'10" **Wt:** 208

Opening Day Age: 28
Born: 5/8/71 in Augusta, GA
ML Seasons: 4

Overall Statistics

	G	AB	R	H	D	T	HR	RBI	SB	BB	SO	Avg	OBP	Slg
1999	97	321	36	78	20	0	14	42	1	12	63	.243	.275	.436
Career	189	595	72	147	31	0	26	82	5	25	119	.247	.281	.430

1999 Situational Stats

	AB	H	HR	RBI	Avg		AB	H	HR	RBI	Avg
Home	142	28	7	18	.197	LHP	95	24	2	16	.253
Road	179	50	7	24	.279	RHP	226	54	12	26	.239
First Half	233	56	12	31	.240	Sc Pos	85	19	3	29	.224
Scnd Half	88	22	2	11	.250	Clutch	46	10	1	3	.217

1999 Season

Oft-injured Todd Greene was given the chance to play on a semiregular basis in 1999 and avoided the disabled list for the first time in his career. But a roller-coaster first half earned him a demotion to Triple-A Edmonton, and he hit just four homers in the final four months.

Hitting, Baserunning & Defense

Greene comes out of his shoes swinging for the fences at the first fastball he sees. Pitchers have made adjustments to him, and now he must counter. He'll have to learn to wait on breaking pitches and lay off pitches in the dirt. A lack of strike-zone judgment has haunted Greene throughout his young career. He's a hard-nosed runner without great wheels. Greene split time last year between DH, right field and catcher. He has limited range as an outfielder and is raw behind the plate. Shoulder injuries have weakened his throwing arm.

2000 Outlook

When he's healthy, Greene shows flashes of the tape-measure power that will continue to earn him opportunities with the Angels. He wants to catch, but his defensive deficiencies may relegate him to a full-time DH role before too long.

Shigetoshi Hasegawa

Position: RP
Bats: R **Throws:** R
Ht: 5'11" **Wt:** 171

Opening Day Age: 31
Born: 8/1/68 in Kobe, Japan
ML Seasons: 3
Pronunciation:
shig-eh-TOE-shee
hos-eh-GAH-wa

Overall Statistics

	W	L	Pct.	ERA	G	GS	Sv	IP	H	BB	SO	HR	Ratio
1999	4	6	.400	4.91	64	1	2	77.0	80	34	44	14	1.48
Career	15	16	.484	3.93	175	8	7	291.0	284	112	200	42	1.36

1999 Situational Stats

	W	L	ERA	Sv	IP		AB	H	HR	RBI	Avg
Home	2	3	5.63	0	40.0	LHB	113	31	3	13	.274
Road	2	3	4.14	2	37.0	RHB	177	49	11	33	.277
First Half	1	3	4.17	0	45.1	Sc Pos	79	21	3	30	.266
Scnd Half	3	3	5.97	2	31.2	Clutch	78	24	5	17	.308

1999 Season

Shigetoshi Hasegawa emerged as a valuable commodity setting up Troy Percival in 1998, but he didn't pitch with the same effectiveness last year. Appearing in more than 60 games for the second straight season, Hasegawa saw his ERA skyrocket from 3.14 to 4.91.

Pitching & Defense

Hasegawa studies hitters and situations, but he was less precise with his pitches last year than in the past. He uses a slight stutter in his windup to add to his diverse arsenal. He'll bring his fastball in the upper 80s with cutting and sinking action. An excellent changeup is his out pitch, and when he's sharp he keeps hitters guessing on location and speed. Hasegawa pounces off the mound to field grounders and hasn't committed an error since his rookie campaign. A quick pickoff move and a slide step prevent runners from stealing bases.

2000 Outlook

A groundball pitcher, Hasegawa needs to have sharp command to succeed. He isn't a prototypical setup man, but he can deceive hitters with his offspeed junk before Percival comes in throwing gas. The Angels again will use Hasegawa in that role.

Jeff Huson

Position: 2B/SS
Bats: L **Throws:** R
Ht: 6' 3" **Wt:** 180

Opening Day Age: 35
Born: 8/15/64 in Scottsdale, AZ
ML Seasons: 11

Overall Statistics

	G	AB	R	H	D	T	HR	RBI	SB	BB	SO	Avg	OBP	Slg
1999	97	225	21	59	7	1	0	18	10	16	27	.262	.307	.302
Career	757	1749	223	411	58	12	8	139	62	178	219	.235	.305	.296

1999 Situational Stats

	AB	H	HR	RBI	Avg		AB	H	HR	RBI	Avg
Home	115	36	0	13	.313	LHP	11	2	0	0	.182
Road	110	23	0	5	.209	RHP	214	57	0	18	.266
First Half	100	25	0	5	.250	Sc Pos	60	14	0	16	.233
Scnd Half	125	34	0	13	.272	Clutch	43	13	0	5	.302

1999 Season

Anaheim signed journeyman Jeff Huson as an insurance policy after their anticipated 1999 starting second baseman, Justin Baughman, broke his leg in winter ball. Huson played sparingly until second baseman Randy Velarde was traded to Oakland in July.

Hitting, Baserunning & Defense

A light-hitting lefty with a slashing line-drive swing, Huson rarely provides extra-base hits. He's an intelligent baserunner who uses instincts rather than speed on the bases. He picked his spots wisely last year, swiping 10 bags in 11 tries. Huson's versatility has kept him around through the years, and last season he filled in admirably at first base, second base, shortstop, third base and even left field, committing a total of five errors in his various roles.

2000 Outlook

The Angels were the fourth team in four years for Huson, and he once again is a free agent who has glove, will travel. He wasn't offered arbitration but should catch on somewhere as a role player.

Al Levine

Position: RP
Bats: L **Throws:** R
Ht: 6' 3" **Wt:** 180

Opening Day Age: 31
Born: 5/22/68 in Park Ridge, IL
ML Seasons: 4
Pronunciation: luh-VEEN

Overall Statistics

	W	L	Pct.	ERA	G	GS	Sv	IP	H	BB	SO	HR	Ratio
1999	1	1	.500	3.39	50	1	0	85.0	76	29	37	13	1.24
Career	3	5	.375	4.44	121	1	0	188.2	201	68	90	24	1.43

1999 Situational Stats

	W	L	ERA	Sv	IP		AB	H	HR	RBI	Avg
Home	0	0	2.74	0	49.1	LHB	120	28	5	14	.233
Road	1	1	4.29	0	35.2	RHB	188	48	8	30	.255
First Half	1	0	3.00	0	42.0	Sc Pos	90	22	2	31	.244
Scnd Half	0	1	3.77	0	43.0	Clutch	28	9	1	5	.321

1999 Season

After spending much of the past three seasons shuttling back and forth between the majors and Triple-A with the White Sox and Rangers, Al Levine finally found his niche in the Anaheim bullpen. He was claimed off waivers from Texas in April and became one of the Angels' most trusted middle relievers.

Pitching & Defense

A former starter in the minors, Levine can withstand a heavy workload. He uses a lot of motion with his arms and legs to throw hitters off, and releases his sinker-slider arsenal from a deceptive three-quarters delivery. His fastball gets into the high 80s, but it's the sink that makes the pitch effective. The bottom also falls out of his very good changeup. Levine demonstrates sound command and his slider keeps lefties in check, but he's susceptible to the longball. Levine is nothing special in the field and does an average job of holding runners.

2000 Outlook

Levine's perseverance in the minors may finally have paid off. He's best suited for middle relief and will stay in that role unless the Angels become desperate for starters.

Orlando Palmeiro

Position: LF/RF/DH
Bats: L **Throws:** L
Ht: 5'11" **Wt:** 175

Opening Day Age: 31
Born: 1/19/69 in Hoboken, NJ
ML Seasons: 5
Pronunciation: pall-MARE-oh

Overall Statistics

	G	AB	R	H	D	T	HR	RBI	SB	BB	SO	Avg	OBP	Slg
1999	109	317	46	88	12	1	1	23	5	39	30	.278	.364	.331
Career	323	723	102	202	27	6	1	59	12	85	66	.279	.361	.337

1999 Situational Stats

	AB	H	HR	RBI	Avg		AB	H	HR	RBI	Avg
Home	147	41	0	9	.279	LHP	35	7	0	2	.200
Road	170	47	1	14	.276	RHP	282	81	1	21	.287
First Half	203	54	1	15	.266	Sc Pos	66	18	0	22	.273
Scnd Half	114	34	0	8	.298	Clutch	58	12	0	3	.207

1999 Season

A prototypical backup outfielder, Orlando Palmeiro is able to answer the manager's call at any time, never complains about his lack of playing time and produces when inserted into the lineup. Given the opportunity to play in a career-high 109 games, Palmeiro responded with a scrappy and consistent performance.

Hitting, Baserunning & Defense

Palmeiro injects energy at the top of the lineup with his hard-nosed brand of baseball. He's a line-drive, opposite-field hitter who makes contact and draws walks. He battles pitchers deep into the count, shortening up and fouling off pitches before slapping the ball the other way. He is very tough to put away with two strikes, though his approach generates little power. Palmeiro hustles on the bases without blinding speed. He played all three outfield positions but is primarily a left fielder by trade. He doesn't have a strong arm, but his throws are accurate.

2000 Outlook

Palmeiro accepts his role and thrives in it. He can't hit lefties and doesn't have enough power to be an everyday player, but he should continue to fulfill his purpose as a reserve for the Angels.

Mark Petkovsek

Position: RP
Bats: R **Throws:** R
Ht: 6'0" **Wt:** 195

Opening Day Age: 34
Born: 11/18/65 in Beaumont, TX
ML Seasons: 7
Pronunciation: pet-KY-zik

Overall Statistics

	W	L	Pct.	ERA	G	GS	Sv	IP	H	BB	SO	HR	Ratio
1999	10	4	.714	3.47	64	0	1	83.0	85	21	43	6	1.28
Career	41	24	.631	4.53	271	40	3	552.1	608	171	285	60	1.41

1999 Situational Stats

	W	L	ERA	Sv	IP		AB	H	HR	RBI	Avg
Home	6	3	3.59	0	42.2	LHB	124	30	1	12	.242
Road	4	1	3.35	1	40.1	RHB	192	55	5	39	.286
First Half	8	2	1.81	1	44.2	Sc Pos	95	29	2	43	.305
Scnd Half	2	2	5.40	0	38.1	Clutch	147	38	2	21	.259

1999 Season

Acquired in the offseason in a trade for minor league catcher Matt Garrick, Mark Petkovsek proved to be quite a steal. He developed into the Angels' most reliable workhorse in the middle innings. After spending most of his career as a swingman for the Cardinals, Petkovsek appeared in a career-high 64 games last year.

Pitching & Defense

Petkovsek survives by locating his sinking 87-MPH fastball and deceiving hitters with an excellent changeup. The crafty righthander varies speeds and throws strikes, depending primarily on his ability to paint the corners and induce groundballs to remain effective. He'll mix in a curveball to keep hitters off balance. The running movement on his pitches makes life tougher on lefties than righties. He's an average fielder and has improved drastically at keeping basestealers at bay.

2000 Outlook

The Angels were extremely pleased with Petkovsek's contributions. He has secured his role with Anaheim and will be expected to repeat his performance again this year.

Andy Sheets

Position: SS
Bats: R **Throws:** R
Ht: 6' 2" **Wt:** 180

Opening Day Age: 28
Born: 11/19/71 in Baton Rouge, LA
ML Seasons: 4

Overall Statistics

	G	AB	R	H	D	T	HR	RBI	SB	BB	SO	Avg	OBP	Slg
1999	87	244	22	48	10	0	3	29	1	14	59	.197	.236	.275
Career	254	637	89	138	26	3	14	76	12	52	196	.217	.275	.333

1999 Situational Stats

	AB	H	HR	RBI	Avg		AB	H	HR	RBI	Avg
Home	111	21	3	16	.189	LHP	70	15	2	7	.214
Road	133	27	0	13	.203	RHP	174	33	1	22	.190
First Half	199	41	3	26	.206	Sc Pos	52	10	1	25	.192
Scnd Half	45	7	0	3	.156	Clutch	41	10	0	6	.244

1999 Season

When Gary DiSarcina was injured on the first day of spring training, the Angels didn't have a replacement lined up to step in. They traded Phil Nevin to San Diego for Andy Sheets in a four-player deal, a move that backfired. Sheets batted .197 and spent time in Triple-A while Nevin crushed a career-high 24 home runs for the Padres.

Hitting, Baserunning & Defense

After a decent start, Sheets hit .179 in May and June before his playing time vanished. He never has learned to take pitches and draw walks, and he strikes out too much. He has shown decent power in the past, but Sheets puts the ball in the air too frequently and is an easy victim when he falls behind in the count. He does offer versatility with his arm and glove and is capable of playing all four infield positions. He's an average baserunner and a skilled bunter.

2000 Outlook

Sheets can offer some value to a major league team as a reserve, but he must boost his production. Another year below the Mendoza Line could spell an end to his big league career. The Angels certainly weren't impressed, cutting Sheets loose in December by not offering him a contract.

Steve Sparks ⟨Knuckleballer⟩

Position: SP
Bats: R **Throws:** R
Ht: 6' 0" **Wt:** 180

Opening Day Age: 34
Born: 7/2/65 in Tulsa, OK
ML Seasons: 4
Nickname: Sparky

Overall Statistics

	W	L	Pct.	ERA	G	GS	Sv	IP	H	BB	SO	HR	Ratio
1999	5	11	.313	5.42	28	26	0	147.2	165	82	73	21	1.67
Career	27	33	.450	5.08	103	86	0	567.0	608	278	280	71	1.56

1999 Situational Stats

	W	L	ERA	Sv	IP		AB	H	HR	RBI	Avg
Home	4	7	6.11	0	70.2	LHB	280	82	9	38	.293
Road	1	4	4.79	0	77.0	RHB	307	83	12	51	.270
First Half	4	5	4.68	0	90.1	Sc Pos	149	42	6	67	.282
Scnd Half	1	6	6.59	0	57.1	Clutch	28	7	0	3	.250

1999 Season

Knuckleballer Steve Sparks pitched his way into Anaheim's rotation after making surprising contributions to the staff a year earlier. He was able to resurrect his career after having Tommy John surgery in 1997. Despite hurling a pair of two-hitters and a three-hitter, Sparks's 1999 season was defined by inconsistent outings. His campaign ended with a torn rotator cuff in September.

Pitching & Defense

Sparks tosses his dancing knuckler a little harder than most knuckleballers. Last year, his knuckler too often was flat and hittable. His command also was shaky, which didn't help. Sparks will try to sneak his low-80s fastball by hitters, but he can't survive when his knuckler isn't on. Like most flutterballers Sparks is an easy target for basestealers, and he also advances runners with wild pitches and passed balls. He made three errors last year, but he's normally not a liability with his glove.

2000 Outlook

Sparks was designated for assignment in October and the Angels figure to look elsewhere to fill holes in their rotation. Because he doesn't count on velocity to be effective, a full recovery from his rotator-cuff injury is likely.

Matt Walbeck

Position: C
Bats: B **Throws:** R
Ht: 5'11" **Wt:** 206

Opening Day Age: 30
Born: 10/2/69 in
Sacramento, CA
ML Seasons: 7

Overall Statistics

	G	AB	R	H	D	T	HR	RBI	SB	BB	SO	Avg	OBP	Slg
1999	107	288	26	69	8	1	3	22	2	26	46	.240	.308	.306
Career	548	1739	183	418	68	4	21	187	13	120	281	.240	.290	.320

1999 Situational Stats

	AB	H	HR	RBI	Avg		AB	H	HR	RBI	Avg
Home	138	28	1	6	.203	LHP	64	17	0	5	.266
Road	150	41	2	16	.273	RHP	224	52	3	17	.232
First Half	183	46	3	13	.251	Sc Pos	79	17	1	19	.215
Scnd Half	105	23	0	9	.219	Clutch	58	16	0	2	.276

1999 Season

After the Angels traded Phil Nevin to the Padres at the end of spring training, Matt Walbeck assumed the bulk of the catching workload. The light-hitting receiver's .614 on-base plus slugging percentage ranked last among starting American League catchers. His playing time dwindled along with his batting average in the final months of the season.

Hitting, Baserunning & Defense

The switch-hitting Walbeck doesn't strike fear in pitchers, as he collected only 12 extra-base hits last year. He's weaker from the left side of the plate, though he delivered all three of his homers last year batting lefthanded. Walbeck earns his paycheck behind the plate. He has an accurate throwing arm, a quick release and a good reputation for handling his staff. His lack of speed limits him on the bases.

2000 Outlook

The Angels anticipated using Walbeck in more of a reserve role when they acquired him, but he has played in 108 and 107 games, respectively, in the past two seasons. They're looking for a catcher who can give them more production and relegate Walbeck to a backup.

Jarrod Washburn

Position: SP
Bats: L **Throws:** L
Ht: 6' 1" **Wt:** 200

Opening Day Age: 25
Born: 8/13/74 in
LaCrosse, WI
ML Seasons: 2

Overall Statistics

	W	L	Pct.	ERA	G	GS	Sv	IP	H	BB	SO	HR	Ratio
1999	4	5	.444	5.25	16	10	0	61.2	61	26	39	6	1.41
Career	10	8	.556	4.91	31	21	0	135.2	131	53	87	17	1.36

1999 Situational Stats

	W	L	ERA	Sv	IP		AB	H	HR	RBI	Avg
Home	3	3	4.95	0	40.0	LHB	51	11	1	5	.216
Road	1	2	5.82	0	21.2	RHB	183	50	5	23	.273
First Half	0	0	7.36	0	3.2	Sc Pos	46	15	1	20	.326
Scnd Half	4	5	5.12	0	58.0	Clutch	13	5	0	1	.385

1999 Season

Jarrod Washburn went 6-3 as a rookie in 1998, but a miserable spring training landed him in Triple-A for the first three months of last season. While there, he spent time on the disabled list with an abdominal strain. He was called up to Anaheim twice, joining the rotation for good in August.

Pitching & Defense

Washburn works quickly and aggressively. He features a fastball that reaches the low 90s, a sharp slider, an occasional curveball and a changeup that he throws to both sides of the plate. He struggles with his command at times and is still learning to mix his pitches and set up hitters. Basestealers have succeeded against Washburn because his pickoff move is weak for a lefthander. He has played flawless defense in his first two big league seasons.

2000 Outlook

Washburn closed out the Angels' horrific season with 8.2 shutout innings against Texas, making a strong bid for a rotation spot this spring. Anaheim doesn't have any sure things among its starting pitchers, and he and Ramon Ortiz are the best the minor league system has to offer.

Other Anaheim Angels

Juan Alvarez (Pos: LHP, Age: 26)

	W	L	Pct.	ERA	G	GS	Sv	IP	H	BB	SO	HR	Ratio
1999	0	1	.000	3.00	8	0	0	3.0	1	4	4	0	1.67
Career	0	1	.000	3.00	8	0	0	3.0	1	4	4	0	1.67

Alvarez' control is his strength. He did OK in his big league test, facing a lefty or two at a time in a specialist role. 2000 Outlook: B

Justin Baughman (Pos: 2B, Age: 25, Bats: R)

	G	AB	R	H	D	T	HR	RBI	SB	BB	SO	Avg	OBP	Slg
1999							Did Not Play							
Career	63	196	24	50	9	1	1	20	10	6	36	.255	.277	.327

The Angels were ready to turn over second base to him a year ago, but Baughman sustained multiple leg fractures in Mexican winter ball. He missed all of 1999 and now must show he can hit. 2000 Outlook: C

Steve Decker (Pos: C, Age: 34, Bats: R)

	G	AB	R	H	D	T	HR	RBI	SB	BB	SO	Avg	OBP	Slg
1999	28	63	5	15	6	0	0	5	0	13	9	.238	.372	.333
Career	263	688	60	152	21	2	13	72	2	76	124	.221	.299	.314

Decker resurfaced in the majors after a two-year absence, bouncing between Triple-A and Anaheim in 1999. He didn't display any magic in Disneyland. 2000 Outlook: C

Mike Fyhrie (Pos: RHP, Age: 30)

	W	L	Pct.	ERA	G	GS	Sv	IP	H	BB	SO	HR	Ratio
1999	0	4	.000	5.05	16	7	0	51.2	61	21	26	8	1.59
Career	0	5	.000	5.50	18	7	0	54.0	65	24	26	8	1.65

Fyhrie was stellar in 18 Triple-A starts in 1999. His debut in Anaheim wasn't as good, but another opportunity awaits him. 2000 Outlook: C

Bret Hemphill (Pos: C, Age: 28, Bats: B)

	G	AB	R	H	D	T	HR	RBI	SB	BB	SO	Avg	OBP	Slg
1999	12	21	3	3	0	0	0	2	0	4	4	.143	.269	.143
Career	12	21	3	3	0	0	0	2	0	4	4	.143	.269	.143

Hemphill turned in a good half season at Triple-A before debuting with the Angels in July. He didn't play much, but he's a decent defensive catcher on a team weak at the position. 2000 Outlook: C

Mike Holtz (Pos: LHP, Age: 27)

	W	L	Pct.	ERA	G	GS	Sv	IP	H	BB	SO	HR	Ratio
1999	2	3	.400	8.06	28	0	0	22.1	26	15	17	3	1.84
Career	10	12	.455	4.31	177	0	3	125.1	123	64	117	11	1.49

Holtz has been dominant at the Triple-A level the last two years, but when he has been in Anaheim, he hasn't been able to duplicate his fine 1997 season. Getting his curveball over has been a big problem. 2000 Outlook: B

Matt Luke (Pos: 1B, Age: 29, Bats: L)

	G	AB	R	H	D	T	HR	RBI	SB	BB	SO	Avg	OBP	Slg
1999	18	30	4	9	0	0	3	6	0	2	10	.300	.344	.600
Career	123	269	39	65	12	1	15	40	2	19	70	.242	.293	.461

Luke produced lots of power and strikeouts during his first big league exposure with the Dodgers in 1998. The Angels recalled him last June, but then a ribcage injury sidelined him. He signed a minor league contract with the Brewers in December. 2000 Outlook: B

Mike Magnante (Pos: LHP, Age: 34)

	W	L	Pct.	ERA	G	GS	Sv	IP	H	BB	SO	HR	Ratio
1999	5	2	.714	3.38	53	0	0	69.1	68	29	44	2	1.40
Career	22	28	.440	4.10	332	19	3	494.0	528	191	296	33	1.46

Magnante answered a solid 1997 season with a so-so '98, but he looked more like the stud of '97 last summer. He had a 1.72 ERA in the second half before signing a two-year, $2 million contract with the Athletics as a free agent. 2000 Outlook: A

Jack McDowell (Pos: RHP, Age: 34)

	W	L	Pct.	ERA	G	GS	Sv	IP	H	BB	SO	HR	Ratio
1999	0	4	.000	8.05	4	4	0	19.0	31	5	12	4	1.89
Career	127	87	.593	3.85	277	265	0	1889.0	1854	606	1311	173	1.30

McDowell's string of arm problems and surgical procedures forced Anaheim to give up on him. He was released in August after four bad starts that left him talking about retirement. 2000 Outlook: D

Steve Mintz (Pos: RHP, Age: 31)

	W	L	Pct.	ERA	G	GS	Sv	IP	H	BB	SO	HR	Ratio
1999	0	0	-	3.60	3	0	0	5.0	8	2	2	1	2.00
Career	1	2	.333	6.66	17	0	0	24.1	34	14	9	5	1.97

After a decade in the minors and a solid 1999 in the bullpen at Double-A and Triple-A, Mintz earned his second taste of the majors in September. He opted for free agency a month later. 2000 Outlook: C

Ben Molina (Pos: C, Age: 25, Bats: R)

	G	AB	R	H	D	T	HR	RBI	SB	BB	SO	Avg	OBP	Slg
1999	31	101	8	26	5	0	1	10	0	6	6	.257	.312	.337
Career	33	102	8	26	5	0	1	10	0	6	6	.255	.309	.333

Charlie O'Brien's release in early August opened the door for Molina, who was OK in his brief audition. There isn't much in his minor league hitting numbers that says he'll be any better than OK. 2000 Outlook: C

Charlie O'Brien (Pos: C, Age: 38, Bats: R)

	G	AB	R	H	D	T	HR	RBI	SB	BB	SO	Avg	OBP	Slg
1999	27	62	3	6	0	0	1	4	0	1	12	.097	.136	.145
Career	791	2213	215	489	118	4	55	259	1	207	347	.221	.303	.352

After being an important part-time player for years, O'Brien experienced a lost season in 1999. He went down with a ligament tear in his right foot in June, and was released by the Angels when he returned. 2000 Outlook: C

Lou Pote (Pos: RHP, Age: 28)

	W	L	Pct.	ERA	G	GS	Sv	IP	H	BB	SO	HR	Ratio
1999	1	1	.500	2.15	20	0	3	29.1	23	12	20	1	1.19
Career	1	1	.500	2.15	20	0	3	29.1	23	12	20	1	1.19

After pitching OK as a starter at Triple-A Edmonton in 1999, Pote made a fairly smooth transition to the Anaheim bullpen. He even got three saves after Troy Percival was injured. 2000 Outlook: B

Chris Pritchett (Pos: 1B, Age: 30, Bats: L)

	G	AB	R	H	D	T	HR	RBI	SB	BB	SO	Avg	OBP	Slg
1999	20	45	3	7	1	0	1	2	1	2	9	.156	.188	.244
Career	56	138	16	32	3	1	3	11	3	6	28	.232	.262	.333

Pritchett has earned tons of frequent-flyer miles between Triple-A and Anaheim the last two years, but he didn't do as well in the majors in 1999 as he did in '98. He signed with the Phillies after the season. 2000 Outlook: C

Scott Schoeneweis (Pos: LHP, Age: 26)

	W	L	Pct.	ERA	G	GS	Sv	IP	H	BB	SO	HR	Ratio
1999	1	1	.500	5.49	31	0	0	39.1	47	14	22	4	1.55
Career	1	1	.500	5.49	31	0	0	39.1	47	14	22	4	1.55

Schoeneweis had been one of Anaheim's better prospects, but he appeared shell-shocked as a reliever in the majors. Normally a starter, he's a four-pitch pitcher who tops out at 92 MPH. 2000 Outlook: C

Dave Silvestri (Pos: 2B, Age: 32, Bats: R)

	G	AB	R	H	D	T	HR	RBI	SB	BB	SO	Avg	OBP	Slg
1999	3	11	0	1	1	0	0	1	0	0	1	.091	.091	.182
Career	181	336	42	68	12	3	6	36	4	56	96	.202	.315	.310

Silvestri keeps surfacing in the bigs, but his major league stays are growing shorter and he's 2-for-29 over the last three seasons. His power is fading, though he hits well enough to earn promotions. 2000 Outlook: C

Tim Unroe (Pos: RF, Age: 29, Bats: R)

	G	AB	R	H	D	T	HR	RBI	SB	BB	SO	Avg	OBP	Slg
1999	27	54	5	13	2	0	1	6	0	4	16	.241	.305	.333
Career	75	90	13	21	3	0	3	11	2	10	30	.233	.317	.367

Unroe bounced between Triple-A and Anaheim before earning a July release from the Angels. His years of Triple-A success never led to a big league role. 2000 Outlook: C

Reggie Williams (Pos: RF, Age: 33, Bats: B)

	G	AB	R	H	D	T	HR	RBI	SB	BB	SO	Avg	OBP	Slg
1999	30	63	8	14	1	2	1	6	2	5	21	.222	.286	.349
Career	88	136	22	34	3	3	2	14	5	15	45	.250	.331	.360

Williams pounded the ball in Triple-A and earned a May promotion. He fanned four times in four at-bats in his second game with Anaheim, and it was all downhill from there. 2000 Outlook: C

Anaheim Angels Minor League Prospects

Organization Overview:

Seven of the Angels' regular position players, their No. 1 starter and their closer in 1999 all were homegrown products. The downside is that there has been little influx of new talent in Anaheim during the past few seasons, something that won't change with the utter lack of quantity or quality in the system. The team is paying for scrimping in scouting and player development. Last summer, it pulled all its scouts off the road in July. And with the Angels underachieving season after season, there's some question as to whether the players they've signed and nurtured have what it takes to win. Team president Tony Tavares fired GM Bill Bavasi and several veteran scouts after the season, and farm director Jeff Parker and scouting director Bob Fontaine resigned. New GM Bill Stoneman inherits a mess.

Mike Colangelo

Position: OF   **Opening Day Age:** 23
Bats: R **Throws:** R   **Born:** 10/22/76 in
Ht: 6' 1" **Wt:** 185   Teaneck, NJ

Recent Statistics

	G	AB	R	H	D	T	HR	RBI	SB	BB	SO	Avg
1999 AA Erie	28	109	24	37	10	3	1	13	3	14	22	.339
1999 AAA Edmonton	26	105	13	38	7	1	0	9	2	13	18	.362
1999 AL Anaheim	1	2	0	1	0	0	0	0	0	1	0	.500
1999 MLE	54	202	29	63	13	2	0	17	3	19	41	.312

Colangelo signed late after being drafted in 1997's 21st round out of George Mason, but to say he made up for lost time is an understatement. He needed just 442 at-bats before reaching the majors last June, catching the Angels' attention by hitting .346 along the way. He went 1-for-2 in his major league debut, then tore ligaments in his left thumb in an outfield collision with Reggie Williams and was knocked out for the year. Colangelo also missed half of 1998 with an ankle injury. He is best suited for left field, but his gap power may not be enough to win an everyday job at that position unless he continues to produce gaudy batting averages.

Brian Cooper

Position: P   **Opening Day Age:** 25
Bats: R **Throws:** R   **Born:** 8/19/74 in
Ht: 6' 1" **Wt:** 185   Hollywood, CA

Recent Statistics

	W	L	ERA	G	GS	Sv	IP	H	R	BB	SO	HR
1999 AA Erie	10	5	3.30	22	22	0	158.0	146	61	29	143	17
1999 AAA Edmonton	2	1	3.77	5	5	0	31.0	30	17	10	32	0
1999 AL Anaheim	1	1	4.88	5	5	0	27.2	23	15	18	15	3

There couldn't have been anyone happier than Brian Cooper when Anaheim switched its Double-A affiliate from Midland to Erie last year. Midland is one of the minors' most treacherous parks for a pitcher, and Cooper got rocked to the tune of a 7.13 ERA and 35 homers in 1998. In Erie a year later, he cut both of those figures by better than half and used his performance as a springboard to the majors. A 1995 fourth-round pick out of the University of Southern California, Cooper throws four pitches (fastball, curveball, slider, changeup) for strikes. He can get his fastball up to 93-94 MPH, but he has more movement and is more effective at 90-91 MPH. He's durable too, leading the minors with six complete games last year. Cooper will get a chance to fill one of Anaheim's several rotation openings in spring training.

Jeff DaVanon

Position: OF   **Opening Day Age:** 26
Bats: B **Throws:** R   **Born:** 12/8/73 in San
Ht: 6' 0" **Wt:** 185   Diego, CA

Recent Statistics

	G	AB	R	H	D	T	HR	RBI	SB	BB	SO	Avg
1999 AA Midland	100	374	87	128	29	11	11	60	18	53	68	.342
1999 AAA Edmonton	34	132	35	43	8	3	6	19	11	20	27	.326
1999 AL Anaheim	7	20	4	4	0	1	1	4	0	2	7	.200
1999 MLE	134	474	86	139	29	9	11	55	18	44	98	.293

Of the three players acquired in the July 29 trade that dispatched Omar Olivares and Randy Velarde to Oakland, DaVanon was the first to reach the majors for the Angels. He hit .250 in his first three seasons after being drafted in the 26th round in 1995 out of San Diego State, then surged to .336 and .338 the last two years. The latter figure led all minor league switch-hitters in 1999. The son of former major league infielder Jerry DaVanon, Jeff has occasional power, good on-base ability and above-average speed. He doesn't have enough pop to play in left or right field, however, and he doesn't have the range to play center on an everyday basis. He projects as a fourth outfielder, albeit a versatile and productive one.

Jason Dewey

Position: C   **Opening Day Age:** 22
Bats: R **Throws:** R   **Born:** 4/18/77 in
Ht: 6' 1" **Wt:** 200   Syracuse, NY

Recent Statistics

	G	AB	R	H	D	T	HR	RBI	SB	BB	SO	Avg
1998 A Lk Elsinore	111	391	64	115	30	3	15	66	8	66	118	.294
1999 AA Erie	40	139	17	31	7	0	4	14	0	17	50	.223
1999 A Lk Elsinore	66	242	48	78	23	0	10	31	0	30	62	.322

In their 39 years of existence, the Angels have had just three All-Star backstops, none since Lance Parrish in 1990. Their system offers little hope, with the possible exception of Dewey. He struggled in Double-A last year but has pounded the ball everywhere else. A 26th-round draft-and-follow in 1996 out of Indian River (Fla.) Community College, he was primarily a first baseman before turning pro. Dewey still has plenty of work to do defensively. He has a strong arm, but his receiving skills and throwing accuracy leave a lot to be desired. Dewey will need at least two more years in the minors.

Seth Etherton

Position: P   **Opening Day Age:** 23
Bats: R **Throws:** R   **Born:** 10/17/76 in
Ht: 6' 1" **Wt:** 200   Laguna Beach, CA

Recent Statistics

	W	L	ERA	G	GS	Sv	IP	H	R	BB	SO	HR
1998 AA Midland	1	5	6.14	9	7	0	48.1	57	36	12	35	9
1999 AA Erie	10	10	3.27	24	24	0	167.2	153	72	43	153	14
1999 AAA Edmonton	0	2	5.48	4	4	0	21.1	25	13	6	19	7

Etherton's faith in himself paid off when he turned down a $75,000 offer from the Cardinals to sign as a ninth-round pick in 1997. After leading NCAA Division I in strikeouts and pitching the University of Southern California to the College World Series championship, he got $1 million more as the Angels' 1998 first-round choice. Etherton's best attributes are his changeup, command and makeup. His fastball is nothing special but he spots it very well, and he also throws a curveball. Etherton was drafted highly because he was thought to be close to being ready for the majors, and the Angels were right. He should make his big league debut by midseason.

Elpidio Guzman

Position: OF   **Opening Day Age:** 21
Bats: L **Throws:** L   **Born:** 2/24/79 in Santo
Ht: 6' 2" **Wt:** 165   Domingo, Dom. Rep.

Recent Statistics

	G	AB	R	H	D	T	HR	RBI	SB	BB	SO	Avg
1998 R Butte	69	299	70	99	16	5	9	61	40	24	44	.331
1999 A Cedar Rapds	130	526	74	144	26	13	4	48	52	41	84	.274

Anaheim has a shortage of exciting athletes in its system, with Guzman one of the rare exceptions. He was one of the last players signed out of the Angels' academy in the Dominican Republic before they shut it down. Guzman is extremely fast, getting from the left side of the plate to first base in 3.9-4.0 seconds. He translates his speed into stolen bases and plays a very good center field. He also has a significant amount of as-yet-untapped raw power. He needs to improve his pitch selection, though he makes fairly good contact. He has been brought along slowly thus far, and his major league ETA is 2002.

Norm Hutchins

Position: OF   **Opening Day Age:** 24
Bats: B **Throws:** L   **Born:** 11/20/75 in White
Ht: 5' 11" **Wt:** 198   Plains, NY

Recent Statistics

	G	AB	R	H	D	T	HR	RBI	SB	BB	SO	Avg
1998 AA Midland	89	394	74	123	20	10	10	50	32	14	84	.312
1998 AAA Vancouver	7	29	4	6	0	0	1	3	1	2	9	.207
1999 AAA Edmonton	126	521	80	130	27	6	7	51	25	40	127	.250
1999 MLE	126	499	60	108	21	5	5	38	17	30	133	.216

Compared to Devon White since signing as a 1994 second-round pick, Hutchins is more of a tease than a prospect. He simply doesn't know how to use his tools. He has tremendous speed and some power, but has yet to be an effective offensive player. He has a long swing and tries to hit too many home runs, resulting in low batting averages and horrid strikeout-walk ratios. He's not even a prolific or effective basestealer because he hasn't learned how to make reads or get good jumps. Hutchins will need to mature mentally and physically if he's going to have much of a major league career.

Scot Shields

Position: P   **Opening Day Age:** 24
Bats: R **Throws:** R   **Born:** 7/22/75 in Fort
Ht: 6' 1" **Wt:** 175   Lauderdale, FL

Recent Statistics

	W	L	ERA	G	GS	Sv	IP	H	R	BB	SO	HR
1998 A Cedar Rapds	6	5	3.65	58	0	7	74.0	62	33	29	81	5
1999 A Lk Elsinore	10	3	2.52	24	9	1	107.1	91	37	39	113	1
1999 AA Erie	4	4	2.89	10	10	0	74.2	57	26	26	81	10

A mere 38th-round pick out of Lincoln Memorial (Tenn.) University in 1997, Shields hasn't let his poor draft pedigree hold him back. He succeeded as a reliever in his first two pro seasons, then won 14 games in his first taste as a starter last year to run his career record to 27-14, 2.95 with 336 strikeouts in 308 innings. He can't overpower hitters with his fastball-slider combination, so he doesn't try to. And he doesn't just throw strikes, he throws quality strikes and keeps his pitches down in the zone. Shields also has lots of life if not velocity on his pitches, and he's deceptive. The Angels need starters, so he could get a look sometime in 2000.

Others to Watch

Lefthander **Doug Bridges** (23) led the minors with 18 victories last year, but it's still a bit early to get excited. He was old for Class-A, where he earned all his wins, and his stuff is below average. His best pitch is his curveball. . . Anaheim was desperate for a second baseman last year and gave 36 starts to **Trent Durrington** (24). While he provides speed and defense, his bat is too weak for him to play regularly. . . Righthander **Steve Green** (22) was Canada's best pitcher at the 1999 Pan American Games, not allowing an earned run in 10 innings against power-house Cuba. He has a 92-MPH fastball and led the minors with four shutouts last year. . . Outfielder **Nathan Haynes** (20), acquired in the Omar Olivares-Randy Velarde trade with Oakland, plays to his strength, which is speed. He made major strides at the plate in 1999 after returning from hernia surgery, keeping the ball on the ground and showing much improved plate discipline. . . Venezuelan righthander **Francisco Rodriguez** (18) signed for $900,000, representing a rare burst of aggression for the Angels in the Latin American market. He was rated the top prospect in the Rookie-level Pioneer League, showing a mid-90s fastball and a very hard slider. . . The Angels grabbed righthander **Derrick Turnbow** (22) from the Phillies in December's major league Rule 5 draft. He throws a 91-94 MPH fastball with late life, and his curveball and changeup also could become above-average pitches.

Oriole Park at Camden Yards

Offense

When Oriole Park at Camden Yards was unveiled in 1992, it was expected to become one of the American League's top home-run parks. But that hasn't become the case, as it ranks seventh among the league's 14 current parks over the past three seasons. It's only 318 feet down the right-field line, but there's a 25-foot wall that's tough to clear. The ball just doesn't carry well in right field, though Camden Yards continues to be a good park for righthanded sluggers.

Defense

The infield grass is cut higher in Baltimore than in most American League parks. The tall grass slows down grounders for the infielders and benefits pitchers who keep the ball down in the strike zone. Though the ballpark isn't symmetrical, it rarely yields strange outfield caroms.

Who It Helps The Most

Though it seems made to order for him, Camden Yards did little to help (or hurt) Albert Belle last year. The player who gets the biggest boost is Scott Erickson, who keeps the ball on the ground and has gone 36-23 in Baltimore. The Orioles' veteran infielders, especially Delino DeShields and Cal Ripken, would be exposed more if the grass wasn't as tall.

Who It Hurts The Most

Brady Anderson hit 63 points higher on the road than at home last season. Over the last four years, 66 of his 110 homers have come away from Camden Yards. B.J. Surhoff has established career highs in homers in each of the last two seasons, but hit just 18 of his 50 longballs in Baltimore.

Rookies & Newcomers

DH Harold Baines returned as a free agent, and he has a .315 career average at Camden Yards. Mike Trombley will be glad to have left the Metrodome, while another bullpen pickup, Chuck McElroy, will miss Shea Stadium a bit. Lefthander Matt Riley, the club's top prospect, surrendered four homers in 8.1 innings in Baltimore last September, though he was tired and not at his best.

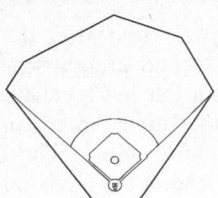

Dimensions: LF-333, LCF-364, CF-410, RCF-373, RF-318

Capacity: 48,876

Elevation: 20 feet

Surface: Grass

Foul Territory: Average

Park Factors

1999 Season

	Home Games			Away Games			Index
	Orioles	Opp	Total	Orioles	Opp	Total	
G	72	72	144	72	72	144	—
Avg	.277	.264	.270	.272	.276	.274	99
AB	2429	2511	4940	2562	2362	4924	100
R	370	360	730	375	387	762	96
H	672	663	1335	698	652	1350	99
2B	126	97	223	139	142	281	79
3B	8	14	22	11	16	27	81
HR	85	92	177	92	96	188	94
BB	270	292	562	273	287	560	100
SO	394	459	853	408	420	828	103
E	43	45	88	41	46	87	101
E-Infield	39	39	78	40	39	79	99
LHB-Avg	.282	.248	.264	.283	.285	.284	93
LHB-HR	36	36	72	47	48	95	78
RHB-Avg	.273	.277	.275	.265	.268	.266	103
RHB-HR	49	56	105	45	48	93	110

1997-1999

	Home Games			Away Games			Index
	Orioles	Opp	Total	Orioles	Opp	Total	
G	217	217	434	220	220	440	—
Avg	.272	.258	.265	.274	.270	.272	97
AB	7268	7525	14793	7807	7335	15142	99
R	1070	1000	2070	1171	1059	2230	94
H	1975	1939	3914	2136	1981	4117	96
2B	341	323	664	446	399	845	80
3B	19	30	49	30	49	79	63
HR	277	242	519	272	244	516	103
BB	762	757	1519	855	808	1663	93
SO	1194	1479	2673	1263	1392	2655	103
E	120	120	240	130	144	274	89
E-Infield	102	107	209	111	115	226	94
LHB-Avg	.276	.249	.262	.282	.276	.279	94
LHB-HR	128	96	224	139	112	251	92
RHB-Avg	.268	.264	.266	.267	.265	.266	100
RHB-HR	149	146	295	133	132	265	113

1999 Rankings (American League)

- Third-highest RHB home-run factor
- Lowest double factor
- Second-lowest LHB home-run factor
- Third-lowest LHB batting-average factor

Mike Hargrove

1999 Season

Former manager Ray Miller was fired after the Orioles underachieved for the second straight season. Mike Hargrove met the same fate in Cleveland despite winning his fifth consecutive American League Central title. His failure to win a World Series and a blown two-game lead in the Division Series against the Red Sox led to his demise.

Offense

Despite having the game's most potent offense at his disposal with the Indians, Hargrove invested heavily in one-run strategies. No AL manager attempted more steals or sacrifice bunts than he did in 1999. He won't be able to run as much with the Orioles, who have far less speed than his former club. Hargrove prefers to go with a set lineup rather than platooning. He's not afraid to give playing time to talented young players, as he did with Richie Sexson last year.

Pitching & Defense

Hargrove benefited from a strong bullpen for most of his tenure in Cleveland. Indians relievers were plagued by injuries during the past two seasons, exposing a lack of quality starters. Hargrove uses relievers as much as any manager in the game, but he'll have to shape up a Baltimore bullpen that performed horribly in 1999. He'll gamble with intentional walks, a strategy that backfired when Troy O'Leary hit two homers after free passes to Nomar Garciaparra in the deciding Game 5 of the Division Series. Hargrove's teams play fundamentally sound defense.

2000 Outlook

Hargrove is easier on his players than Miller was, and that's the main reason he was hired. Baltimore's rotation will be the best he has had to work with. Because most of the key Orioles have long-term contracts, Hargrove isn't expected to make many changes. He got along well with the difficult Albert Belle when both were with Cleveland. Hargrove will oversee an aging team that might be disbanded if it doesn't make a run at the playoffs this season.

Born: 10/26/49 in Perryton, TX

Playing Experience: 1974-1985, Tex, Cle, SD

Managerial Experience: 9 seasons
Nickname: Grover

Manager Statistics

Year	Team, Lg	W	L	Pct	GB	Finish
1999	Cleveland, AL	97	65	.599	—	1st Central
9 Seasons		721	591	.550	—	—

1999 Starting Pitchers by Days Rest

	<=3	4	5	6+
Indians Starts	1	82	47	23
Indians ERA	23.14	4.73	5.20	5.91
AL Avg Starts	2	82	47	21
AL ERA	6.83	4.98	4.72	5.62

1999 Situational Stats

	Mike Hargrove	AL Average
Hit & Run Success %	37.3	35.3
Stolen Base Success %	74.6	68.0
Platoon Pct.	66.3	56.7
Defensive Subs	22	22
High-Pitch Outings	15	15
Quick/Slow Hooks	17/21	18/18
Sacrifice Attempts	82	52

1999 Rankings (American League)

- 1st in stolen base attempts (197), steals of third base (28), double steals (9), sacrifice bunt attempts (82), intentional walks (36), relief appearances (466) and one-batter pitcher appearances (47)
- 2nd in stolen-base percentage (74.6%) and steals of second base (119)
- 3rd in sacrifice-bunt percentage (87.8%) and first-batter platoon percentage (66.3%)

Brady Anderson

1999 Season

After a slump-ridden 1998, Brady Anderson started slowly once again. But he rallied to have a strong season, especially in July and August. He was as healthy as he had been in years and continued to be one of the most powerful and effective leadoff hitters in the game.

Hitting

No longer bothered by back, neck and rib problems, Anderson got his strength back and was able to pull all but three of his home runs last year. He once again was able to turn on inside fastballs. He also refined his approach, taking outside breaking balls to the opposite field more often. Rather than weakly pulling offspeed stuff to the right side of the infield, Anderson drove it to center. He continues to hang over the plate, leading the American League in hit by pitches for the third time in four years.

Baserunning & Defense

With his legs healthy again, Anderson was able to steal more bases than he had since 1992, when he set his career high with 53. During spring training he worked on improving his jumps at first base, and his 84 percent success rate was his best in nine years. Anderson had another solid season in center field. His instincts and speed give him good range, and he committed only one error in 1999. His only defensive weakness is a below-average arm that has registered just six assists in the last three years.

2000 Outlook

Health is the key for Anderson. While it was encouraging that he stayed injury free in 1999, he'll be hard pressed to repeat those numbers. A drop in power and stolen bases seems likely. He'll continue to play center field for Baltimore until prospect Eugene Kingsale proves he can play at the major league level.

Position: CF
Bats: L **Throws:** L
Ht: 6' 1" **Wt:** 202

Opening Day Age: 36
Born: 1/18/64 in Silver Spring, MD
ML Seasons: 12

Overall Statistics

	G	AB	R	H	D	T	HR	RBI	SB	BB	SO	Avg	OBP	Slg
1999	150	564	109	159	28	5	24	81	36	96	105	.282	.404	.477
Career	1528	5483	919	1431	296	64	182	661	283	790	987	.261	.365	.438

Where He Hits the Ball

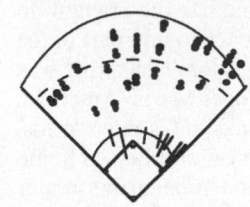
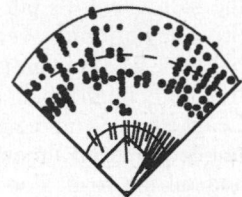

Vs. LHP   **Vs. RHP**

1999 Situational Stats

	AB	H	HR	RBI	Avg		AB	H	HR	RBI	Avg
Home	269	67	10	31	.249	LHP	93	22	4	20	.237
Road	295	92	14	50	.312	RHP	471	137	20	61	.291
First Half	311	85	12	45	.273	Sc Pos	110	31	2	54	.282
Scnd Half	253	74	12	36	.292	Clutch	76	18	2	12	.237

1999 Rankings (American League)

- 1st in on-base percentage for a leadoff hitter (.408), fielding percentage in center field (.997) and hit by pitch (24)
- 3rd in batting average with the bases loaded (.526)
- Led the Orioles in on-base percentage, most pitches seen per plate appearance (3.84), fewest GDPs per GDP situation (5.1%), batting average with the bases loaded (.526), on-base percentage for a leadoff hitter (.408), on-base percentage vs. righthanded pitchers (.416), highest percentage of extra bases taken as a runner (55.0), highest percentage of pitches taken (60.0), steals of third (4), runs scored, stolen bases and hit by pitch (24)

Albert Belle

1999 Season

Following two seasons with the White Sox, Albert Belle exercised a contract option to explore other offers. He signed with the Orioles for five years and $65 million, then lapsed into the same pattern that dogged him in Chicago. Belle started slowly while his team underachieved, then heated up during a meaningless second half, while his off-field demeanor continued to ire fans and the media. He hit .258-9-31 as Baltimore buried itself with a 19-31 start, and padded his statistics by batting .357-8-30 after August 31.

Hitting

Belle is still one of the most fearsome hitters in the game, making consistently hard contact. He'll hit the ball where it's pitched and has the strength to drive any offering over the fence to any part of the ballpark. The conventional wisdom last spring was that Belle might challenge Roger Maris' American League home-run record thanks to Camden Yards, but he produced almost identical numbers at home and on the road. For the first time in his major league career, Belle walked more times than he struck out.

Baserunning & Defense

Power hitters aren't supposed to be basestealers, but Belle breaks the mold. He stole 17 bases in 20 attempts last year, mostly because of his aggressive nature rather than pure speed. Playing in right field for the first time since his rookie season, Belle worked hard to improve his defense. His career-high 17 assists tied for the AL lead among right fielders, and his .985 fielding percentage was his best since 1993. The Orioles just wanted him to provide average defense and not be a liability, and Belle delivered.

2000 Outlook

Only Hall of Famers Jimmie Foxx (12) and Lou Gehrig (nine) can surpass Belle's eight consecutive seasons with at least 30 homers and 100 RBI. But in today's era of offense, Belle is going to be a disappointment if he doesn't provide at least 40 homers and 130 RBI. That won't be difficult if he can get off to a strong start in 2000.

Position: RF
Bats: R **Throws:** R
Ht: 6' 2" **Wt:** 225

Opening Day Age: 33
Born: 8/25/66 in Shreveport, LA
ML Seasons: 11

Overall Statistics

	G	AB	R	H	D	T	HR	RBI	SB	BB	SO	Avg	OBP	Slg
1999	161	610	108	181	36	1	37	117	17	101	82	.297	.400	.541
Career	1398	5294	903	1569	352	20	358	1136	88	631	893	.296	.372	.573

Where He Hits the Ball

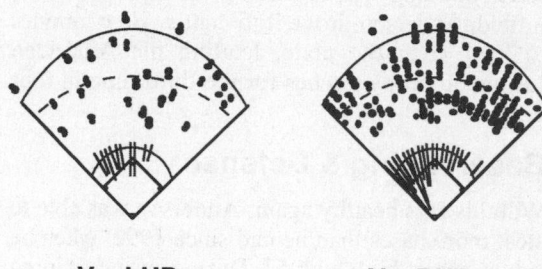

Vs. LHP   **Vs. RHP**

1999 Situational Stats

	AB	H	HR	RBI	Avg		AB	H	HR	RBI	Avg
Home	299	91	19	60	.304	LHP	98	36	11	27	.367
Road	311	90	18	57	.289	RHP	512	145	26	90	.283
First Half	322	87	18	53	.270	Sc Pos	174	51	14	86	.293
Scnd Half	288	94	19	64	.326	Clutch	83	23	5	14	.277

1999 Rankings (American League)

- 1st in slugging percentage vs. lefthanded pitchers (.776) and on-base percentage vs. lefthanded pitchers (.508)
- 2nd in games played
- 3rd in fielding percentage in right field (.985), walks and intentional walks (15)
- Led the Orioles in slugging percentage, HR frequency (16.5 ABs per HR), stolen-base percentage (85.0), batting average on a 3-1 count (.652), cleanup slugging percentage (.541), slugging percentage vs. lefthanded pitchers (.776), slugging percentage vs. righthanded pitchers (.496), on-base percentage vs. lefthanded pitchers (.508), home runs, RBI, walks, intentional walks (15) and times on base (289)

Mike Bordick

Position: SS
Bats: R **Throws:** R
Ht: 5'11" **Wt:** 175

Opening Day Age: 34
Born: 7/21/65 in Marquette, MI
ML Seasons: 10

1999 Season

Mike Bordick spent the entire offseason in a vigorous workout program designed to keep him healthy and strong. He played in all but two of Baltimore's games and showed that the offensive gains he made in 1998 were no fluke by having an even better year. Bordick also was consistent throughout the season, and many observers felt he deserved to win the Gold Glove that went to Omar Vizquel.

Hitting

Bordick no longer chops down on the ball to generate groundballs. These days, he's more of a line-drive hitter. His conditioning program has given him the strength to drive balls into the gaps for extra-base hits. He used to struggle to turn on inside fastballs, but his increased strength has made that less of a problem. Bordick's major league-best .402 average against lefthanders in 1999 far surpassed his previous performances against southpaws, and was accomplished by taking outside pitches to right field more often. He remains one of the better bunters in the American League.

Baserunning & Defense

Bordick uses quickness more than pure speed to steal bases. He reads pitchers well and gets good jumps. His workouts also have improved his shortstop defense. He has more range than ever before, especially to his left, and turns the double play better than ever. Bordick has a very strong arm, and he excels at taking slow rollers on the run and making accurate throws.

2000 Outlook

Bordick enters the last season of his three-year contract with Baltimore at the top of his game, both at the plate and in the field. His improvement as a hitter the past two seasons has been a bonus for the Orioles, who signed him for his defense.

Overall Statistics

	G	AB	R	H	D	T	HR	RBI	SB	BB	SO	Avg	OBP	Slg
1999	160	631	93	175	35	7	10	77	14	54	102	.277	.334	.403
Career	1287	4248	480	1098	177	24	51	426	68	366	542	.258	.322	.347

Where He Hits the Ball

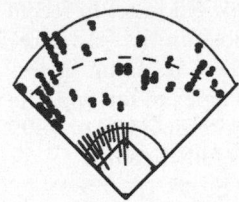

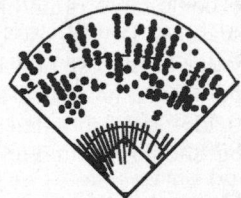

Vs. LHP   **Vs. RHP**

1999 Situational Stats

	AB	H	HR	RBI	Avg		AB	H	HR	RBI	Avg
Home	302	75	3	40	.248	LHP	107	43	3	23	.402
Road	329	100	7	37	.304	RHP	524	132	7	54	.252
First Half	348	96	6	35	.276	Sc Pos	175	44	2	64	.251
Scnd Half	283	79	4	42	.279	Clutch	94	27	3	12	.287

1999 Rankings (American League)

- 1st in batting average vs. lefthanded pitchers and fielding percentage at shortstop (.989)
- 2nd in GDPs (25)
- 3rd in at-bats, sacrifice flies (10) and games played
- 5th in on-base percentage vs. lefthanded pitchers (.472) and lowest on-base percentage vs. righthanded pitchers (.304)
- Led the Orioles in highest groundball/flyball ratio (1.1), batting average vs. lefthanded pitchers, bunts in play (13), triples, sacrifice bunts (8), sacrifice flies (10) and GDPs (25)
- Led AL shortstops in batting average vs. lefthanded pitchers, at-bats, sacrifice flies (10), GDPs (25) and games played (160)

Will Clark

1999 Season

When Texas signed Will Clark as a free agent in 1993, it forced Rafael Palmeiro's exodus to Baltimore. Five years later, the Orioles were shocked to lose Palmeiro to the Rangers as a free agent and settled on Clark as his replacement. Though Clark came cheaper at two years and $11 million, his signing didn't work out as Baltimore hoped. He got off to a fast start in April before bone chips in his left elbow started to hinder his swing. He did his best to play through the pain, but gave up in late August when he couldn't even straighten his elbow.

Hitting

Because of his age and elbow problems, Clark has become more of an opposite-field hitter in recent seasons. Two elbow operations in the past three years have cost him bat speed, resulting in less power and more line-drive singles to the opposite field. Clark struggled against lefthanders in 1999 but should rebound once he's fully healthy.

Baserunning & Defense

Clark is an intelligent but slow baserunner. He's an average first baseman who makes the routine plays but rarely the spectacular ones. He struggles at times with bunts toward first base and slowly hit groundballs. His arm strength has been diminished by his elbow injuries, but he still makes accurate throws. Clark works well with catcher Charles Johnson, who likes to throw behind the runner at first base.

2000 Outlook

Clark had successful elbow surgery to remove the bone chips and is expected to be ready for spring training. He struggled with scar tissue after his first elbow operation in 1996, and can be expected to do so again. He has topped 20 homers just once in the past eight seasons, unacceptable production for a first baseman. He may start getting more of his at-bats at DH this season.

Position: 1B
Bats: L **Throws:** L
Ht: 6' 1" **Wt:** 200

Opening Day Age: 36
Born: 3/13/64 in New Orleans, LA
ML Seasons: 14
Nickname: The Thrill

Overall Statistics

	G	AB	R	H	D	T	HR	RBI	SB	BB	SO	Avg	OBP	Slg
1999	77	251	40	76	15	0	10	29	2	38	42	.303	.395	.482
Career	1846	6746	1108	2040	410	45	263	1135	62	868	1121	.302	.381	.493

Where He Hits the Ball

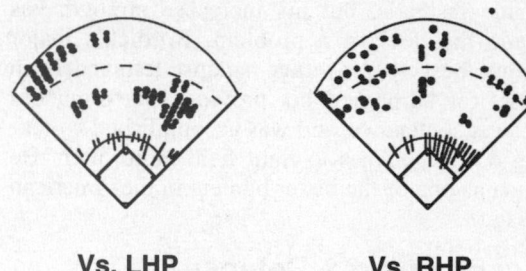

Vs. LHP   **Vs. RHP**

1999 Situational Stats

	AB	H	HR	RBI	Avg		AB	H	HR	RBI	Avg
Home	115	35	5	10	.304	LHP	52	10	0	3	.192
Road	136	41	5	19	.301	RHP	199	66	10	26	.332
First Half	167	52	7	23	.311	Sc Pos	71	21	0	16	.296
Scnd Half	84	24	3	6	.286	Clutch	41	12	1	2	.293

1999 Rankings (American League)

- Did not rank near the top or bottom in any category

Delino DeShields

1999 Season

On a team of overpriced underachievers, Delino DeShields was one of the bigger disappointments. Signed to a three-year, $12.5 million contract as a free agent to replace the departed Roberto Alomar, DeShields didn't make his Orioles debut until mid-April after breaking his left thumb in spring training. He also lost time to a hamstring injury, back spasms and quadriceps trouble, and generally was unproductive when he played.

Hitting

DeShields developed some gap power while with St. Louis the previous two seasons, but it wasn't evident in Baltimore. His injuries took their toll on his strength and swing, and he no longer could drive the ball. As he has added pop, he has bunted less often. DeShields started pulling outside pitches weakly to second base when his back spasms started to hinder his swing. After playing nine seasons in the National League, he made a quick adjustment to the tighter American League strike zone.

Baserunning & Defense

DeShields still has the speed to take an extra base, but his injuries have reduced his desire to steal bases. He established career lows in steals, attempts (19) and success rate (58 percent) in 1999. He has slightly above-average range at second base, but he clearly has lost a step. His weak arm hurts him at times because he still gets to balls up the middle, but he often can't get enough on the throw to complete the play.

2000 Outlook

The Orioles didn't expect DeShields to match Alomar's production, but they also didn't expect him to fall as short as he did. If DeShields struggles this spring or is hurt again, Jerry Hairston Jr. is waiting in the wings to take over the second-base job. Baltimore wouldn't mind trading DeShields, both to save money and clear room for Hairston, but that will be a difficult task.

Position: 2B
Bats: L **Throws:** R
Ht: 6' 1" **Wt:** 175

Opening Day Age: 31
Born: 1/15/69 in Seaford, DE
ML Seasons: 10
Pronunciation: duh-LINE-oh

Overall Statistics

	G	AB	R	H	D	T	HR	RBI	SB	BB	SO	Avg	OBP	Slg
1999	96	330	46	87	11	2	6	34	11	37	52	.264	.339	.364
Career	1271	4721	713	1272	178	63	62	428	393	605	864	.269	.353	.373

Where He Hits the Ball

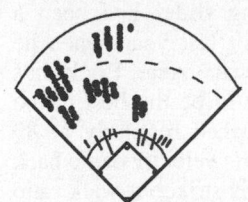
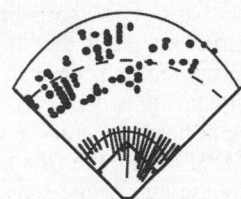

Vs. LHP   **Vs. RHP**

1999 Situational Stats

	AB	H	HR	RBI	Avg		AB	H	HR	RBI	Avg
Home	145	38	4	18	.262	LHP	41	7	1	3	.171
Road	185	49	2	16	.265	RHP	289	80	5	31	.277
First Half	190	52	4	18	.274	Sc Pos	76	20	1	26	.263
Scnd Half	140	35	2	16	.250	Clutch	49	14	2	8	.286

1999 Rankings (American League)

- 8th in errors at second base (10)
- Led the Orioles in caught stealing (8)
- Led AL second basemen in fewest GDPs per GDP situation (6.7%)

Scott Erickson

Position: SP
Bats: R **Throws:** R
Ht: 6' 4" **Wt:** 230

Opening Day Age: 32
Born: 2/2/68 in Long Beach, CA
ML Seasons: 10

1999 Season

Scott Erickson's season can best be described as hot and cold. In the first half of the season, he struggled with his command and went 4-8, 6.06. Former manager Ray Miller attributed Erickson's problems to his efforts to quicken his delivery in order to combat basestealers. Erickson went back to his old style after the All-Star break and went 11-4, 3.50. At times, he even outpitched Mike Mussina.

Pitching

Erickson continued to be a durable starter, logging his fourth straight season of 220 or more innings. But signs of trouble were on the horizon all season. His strikeouts were noticeably down from prior seasons. His sharp-breaking slider had been a strikeout pitch, but it wasn't last year, when he struggled to keep it in the strike zone. Erickson's sinker, considered by many to be the best in the American League, was clocked regularly at 89 MPH during the first half. His velocity came back by the end of the season. His strikeout-walk ratio was nearly even, which often presages a decline.

Defense

Erickson does a very poor job of holding baserunners because of his deliberate move to home plate. He worked on adding a slide step, but it only detracted from his pitching. With Charles Johnson behind the plate, Erickson wasn't the easy mark he had been in the past. He's slow to get off the mound to field his position, especially to the third-base side.

2000 Outlook

Erickson has won 60 games in four seasons as an Oriole and has considerable value as an innings eater. If he can regain his command, there's no reason to believe that he won't continue to maintain his performance or improve it in 2000. His declining strikeout-walk ratio is a concern and will be watched closely in the early stages of the year, however.

Overall Statistics

	W	L	Pct.	ERA	G	GS	Sv	IP	H	BB	SO	HR	Ratio
1999	15	12	.556	4.81	34	34	0	230.1	244	99	106	27	1.49
Career	130	108	.546	4.27	310	306	0	2013.2	2154	697	1111	177	1.42

How Often He Throws Strikes

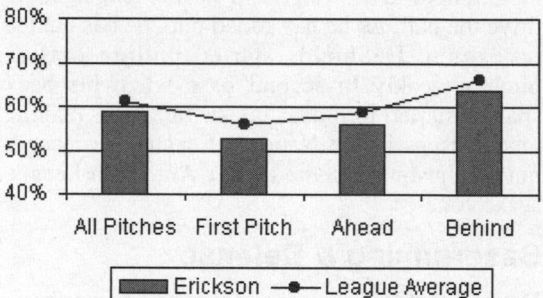

1999 Situational Stats

	W	L	ERA	Sv	IP		AB	H	HR	RBI	Avg
Home	7	4	4.49	0	106.1	LHB	440	119	14	62	.270
Road	8	8	5.08	0	124.0	RHB	432	125	13	57	.289
First Half	4	8	6.06	0	117.1	Sc Pos	203	55	6	91	.271
Scnd Half	11	4	3.50	0	113.0	Clutch	58	12	3	6	.207

1999 Rankings (American League)

- 1st in shutouts (3), batters faced (995), walks allowed, GDPs induced (41) and highest groundball/flyball ratio allowed (2.8)
- 2nd in complete games (6), innings pitched, hits allowed, pitches thrown (3,716), most GDPs induced per GDP situation (20.9%), games started, lowest strikeout/walk ratio (1.1) and fewest strikeouts per nine innings (4.1)
- Led the Orioles in losses, complete games (6), shutouts (3), innings pitched, hits allowed, batters faced (995), walks allowed, hit batsmen (11), wild pitches (10), pitches thrown (3,716), GDPs induced (41), highest groundball/flyball ratio allowed (2.8), most GDPs induced per GDP situation (20.9%) and games started

Charles Johnson

Position: C
Bats: R **Throws:** R
Ht: 6' 2" **Wt:** 220

Opening Day Age: 28
Born: 7/20/71 in Fort Pierce, FL
ML Seasons: 6

1999 Season

The first-ever amateur draft pick by the Marlins, Charles Johnson joined the Dodgers in the Mike Piazza trade in May 1998. Seven months later, he and Roger Cedeno were swapped to the Mets for Todd Hundley, and Johnson was immediately sent on to the Orioles for Armando Benitez. Johnson was a major improvement over Baltimore's previous catcher, Chris Hoiles, batting a personal-best .251 with 16 homers and his usual Gold Glove-caliber defense. Catching in a career-high 135 game took its toll as his bat was much less potent after the All-Star break.

Hitting

Inside pitches continue to plague Johnson because he can't extend his arms. American League pitchers soon learned to exploit this weakness by pounding him with fastballs. Sometimes his swing becomes too long, which makes him susceptible to offspeed and breaking pitches. After shortening his swing in May and becoming more productive, Johnson slumped in June when he became pull-conscious. He switched to a lighter bat in September and hit .299 in the final month.

Baserunning & Defense

Johnson is an extremely slow runner who has gone 1-for-7 in major league stolen-base attempts. He won Gold Gloves in each of his four National League seasons, and the only better catcher in the AL is Ivan Rodriguez, who might be the best defensive backstop ever. Johnson calls a good game and works well with pitchers. No one blocks balls in the dirt better than he does, and his arm and release are second only to Rodriguez'. Johnson springs out with surprising quickness on bunts in front of the plate.

2000 Outlook

Johnson should be in the prime of his career. He has shown flashes of greater offensive potential, but prolonged slumps have hindered his growth. He would be a perennial All-Star if he could hit more consistently. Rodriguez is Johnson's only superior as a catcher, and no one else really approaches the quality of their defense.

Overall Statistics

	G	AB	R	H	D	T	HR	RBI	SB	BB	SO	Avg	OBP	Slg
1999	135	426	58	107	19	1	16	54	0	55	107	.251	.340	.413
Career	613	2013	224	479	92	4	79	255	1	247	511	.238	.324	.405

Where He Hits the Ball

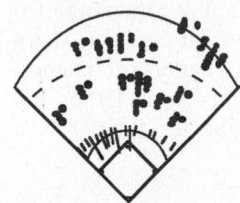 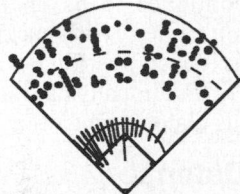

Vs. LHP   **Vs. RHP**

1999 Situational Stats

	AB	H	HR	RBI	Avg		AB	H	HR	RBI	Avg
Home	196	52	8	25	.265	LHP	62	22	3	9	.355
Road	230	55	8	29	.239	RHP	364	85	13	45	.234
First Half	233	61	13	35	.262	Sc Pos	116	28	3	36	.241
Scnd Half	193	46	3	19	.238	Clutch	69	20	2	11	.290

1999 Rankings (American League)

- 1st in lowest batting average vs. righthanded pitchers
- 3rd in highest percentage of runners caught stealing as a catcher (36.7)
- 4th in lowest batting average on the road and lowest percentage of extra bases taken as a runner (26.2)
- 7th in lowest batting average on an 0-2 count (.053)
- 9th in errors at catcher (5)
- Led the Orioles in strikeouts
- Led AL catchers in walks and strikeouts

Mike Mussina

1999 Season

For a second consecutive season, Mike Mussina struggled during April before getting untracked in May. He attributed the slow start to cold weather and his inability to get a feel for his curveball. He recovered to lead the Orioles in wins, strikeouts and ERA. In August, he was hit by a line drive that resulted in a huge bruise on his pitching shoulder, but it didn't land him on the disabled list.

Pitching

Mussina's fastball was clocked at 95 MPH most of the season and he kept excellent control of it. His biggest improvement in 1999 was keeping the ball in the park. Mussina allowed only 16 home runs, his lowest total for a full season. His cut fastball continues to be an important weapon against lefthanders. His knuckle-curve isn't quite as sharp as it once was, but it still keeps batters off balance. He traditionally has fared better against lefties, but his platoon splits were negligible last year.

Defense

Mussina has a unique deep bend in his delivery, but it doesn't hinder his ability to control the running game. He has a terrific spin move that keeps basestealers honest, and he tied for the American League lead last season by permitting a measly 44 percent stolen-base success rate. Winner of four straight Gold Gloves, Mussina gets off the mound as quickly as anyone. His error last year was his first since 1995.

2000 Outlook

Mussina continues to be the ace of the Baltimore staff, a Cy Young Award contender and a perennial 20-win candidate. His mechanics are solid and his arm is sound as he continues in the prime of his career. He's in the final season of a three-year, $21 million extension he signed in 1997, so Mussina has extra motivation to post the best season of his career.

Position: SP
Bats: B **Throws:** R
Ht: 6' 2" **Wt:** 185

Opening Day Age: 31
Born: 12/8/68 in Williamsport, PA
ML Seasons: 9
Pronunciation: myoo-SEE-nuh
Nickname: Moose

Overall Statistics

	W	L	Pct.	ERA	G	GS	Sv	IP	H	BB	SO	HR	Ratio
1999	18	7	.720	3.50	31	31	0	203.1	207	52	172	16	1.27
Career	136	66	.673	3.50	254	254	0	1772.0	1659	421	1325	182	1.17

How Often He Throws Strikes

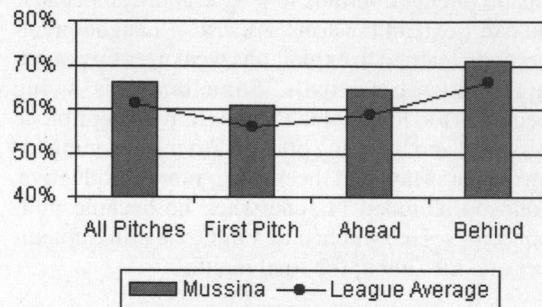

1999 Situational Stats

	W	L	ERA	Sv	IP		AB	H	HR	RBI	Avg
Home	10	3	3.22	0	89.1	LHB	365	98	7	36	.268
Road	8	4	3.71	0	114.0	RHB	408	109	9	39	.267
First Half	11	4	3.70	0	129.0	Sc Pos	184	42	4	58	.228
Scnd Half	7	3	3.15	0	74.1	Clutch	73	21	1	8	.288

1999 Rankings (American League)

- 2nd in wins, lowest stolen-base percentage allowed (44.4) and fewest home runs allowed per nine innings (.71)
- 3rd in ERA, winning percentage, highest strikeout/walk ratio (3.3) and fewest baserunners allowed per nine innings (11.5)
- Led the Orioles in ERA, wins, strikeouts, winning percentage, highest strikeout/walk ratio (3.3), lowest batting average allowed (.268), lowest slugging percentage allowed (.411), lowest on-base percentage allowed (.312), lowest stolen-base percentage allowed (44.4), fewest baserunners allowed per nine innings (11.5), most run support per nine innings (6.8) and most strikeouts per nine innings (7.6)

Sidney Ponson

1999 Season

The Orioles have developed few players in recent years, so they took great pride in Sidney Ponson's 1999 performance. He was as effective as any Baltimore starter during the first half, though he ran out of gas in September en route to working 70 innings more than he had in any previous pro season. His six complete games were one off the American League lead. Though Ponson set a franchise record by allowing 35 homers, he was one of the biggest highlights of Baltimore's disappointing season.

Pitching

Ponson throws a 92-MPH fastball, a nasty slider and a curveball that drops off the table. As he tired, his fastball dipped to 87-90 MPH and he didn't spot it as well. His slider also flattened out later in the year. Poor location led to the barrage of homers. Ponson worked on improving his changeup throughout the season, with mixed results.

Defense

Ponson needs to get in better shape, but he fields his position adequately. He was slow to cover first base early in the year, but he handled that responsibility better as the season progressed. His move to first base continues to be erratic, resulting in poor throws at times. But he worked well with catcher Charles Johnson in controlling the running game, giving up just 12 steals in 26 attempts.

2000 Outlook

The Orioles want Ponson to focus on his offseason conditioning, hoping he'll lose 10-15 pounds and improve his stamina. He declined to remain in Baltimore and use the team's personal trainer, deciding instead to work out in his native Aruba. If he can accomplish what the team wants, Ponson should be able to work deeper into his starts and better maintain his velocity. He already has displayed the ability to change speeds to set up his fastball, a positive sign. Ponson isn't far away from being an above-average starter and may get there this season.

Position: SP
Bats: R **Throws:** R
Ht: 6' 1" **Wt:** 225

Opening Day Age: 23
Born: 11/2/76 in Noord, Aruba
ML Seasons: 2
Pronunciation: pawn-SONE

Overall Statistics

	W	L	Pct.	ERA	G	GS	Sv	IP	H	BB	SO	HR	Ratio
1999	12	12	.500	4.71	32	32	0	210.0	227	80	112	35	1.46
Career	20	21	.488	4.93	63	52	1	345.0	384	122	197	54	1.47

How Often He Throws Strikes

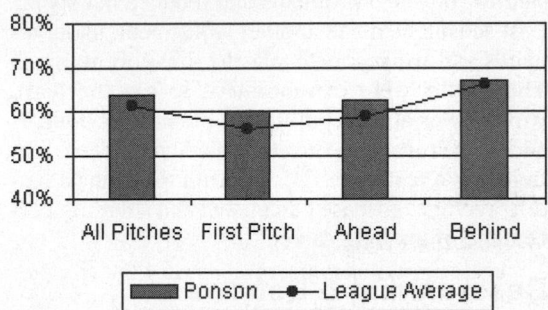

1999 Situational Stats

	W	L	ERA	Sv	IP		AB	H	HR	RBI	Avg
Home	7	6	4.68	0	127.0	LHB	393	114	18	42	.290
Road	5	6	4.77	0	83.0	RHB	412	113	17	67	.274
First Half	7	6	4.10	0	112.0	Sc Pos	176	49	9	76	.278
Scnd Half	5	6	5.42	0	98.0	Clutch	68	13	2	4	.191

1999 Rankings (American League)

- 1st in runners caught stealing (14)
- 2nd in complete games (6) and home runs allowed
- 3rd in lowest stolen-base percentage allowed (46.2) and most home runs allowed per nine innings (1.50)
- 4th in fewest strikeouts per nine innings (4.8)
- 5th in lowest strikeout/walk ratio (1.4)
- 6th in highest slugging percentage allowed (.468) and lowest groundball/flyball ratio allowed (1.0)
- 10th in innings pitched
- Led the Orioles in losses, complete games (6), home runs allowed, fewest pitches thrown per batter (3.67) and runners caught stealing (14)

Cal Ripken Jr.

Position: 3B
Bats: R **Throws:** R
Ht: 6' 4" **Wt:** 220

Opening Day Age: 39
Born: 8/24/60 in Havre de Grace, MD
ML Seasons: 19
Nickname: Junior

1999 Season

The legend of Cal Ripken Jr. took another leap forward in 1999. His baseball obituary was being written when he went on the disabled list for the first time in his career in late April. He delayed surgery to relieve the pain in his lower back, the result of a narrowing of the nerve area in his spinal cord. Then he raised his batting average from .243 in late May to .340 before he finally went under the knife in late September. He finished the year nine hits shy of 3,000.

Hitting

Throughout the course of his career, Ripken has made numerous changes in his stance to compensate for physical problems and reduced bat speed. Last season he made another adjustment, using his hands and arms more to take the stress off his back. The results were extraordinary, to say the least. Ripken was able to pull inside pitches for doubles and home runs while hitting outside pitches to right field. As a result, he finished with the highest batting average, on-base percentage and slugging percentage of his long career.

Baserunning & Defense

Ripken uses his experience on the basepaths, making him a savvy if slow baserunner. He is not a threat to steal. His mobility at third base was reduced by his back problems. He struggled to go to the line, and charging grounders hit in front of him became more difficult as the season wore on. His arm strength remains solid, allowing him to make tough throws when needed. Without back problems, Ripken is an above-average third baseman.

2000 Outlook

Ripken's determination will serve him well as he recovers from surgery to release the pressure on nerves in his lower back. Initial reports suggested that his condition wasn't as severe as thought before the operation. Still, he has a long road to recovery that might last into spring training. During the 1999 season he proved he should never be counted out, and that goes for 2000 as well.

Overall Statistics

	G	AB	R	H	D	T	HR	RBI	SB	BB	SO	Avg	OBP	Slg
1999	86	332	51	113	27	0	18	57	0	13	31	.340	.368	.584
Career	2790	10765	1561	2991	571	44	402	1571	36	1080	1205	.278	.344	.451

Where He Hits the Ball

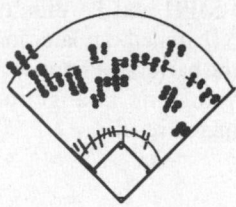

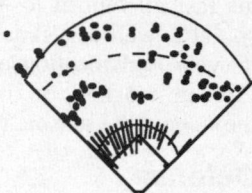

Vs. LHP   **Vs. RHP**

1999 Situational Stats

	AB	H	HR	RBI	Avg		AB	H	HR	RBI	Avg
Home	150	53	12	30	.353	LHP	49	16	2	5	.327
Road	182	60	6	27	.330	RHP	283	97	16	52	.343
First Half	230	72	12	38	.313	Sc Pos	90	30	5	38	.333
Scnd Half	102	41	6	19	.402	Clutch	54	16	1	5	.296

1999 Rankings (American League)

- 6th in batting average on a 3-2 count (.375)
- 8th in errors at third base (13)
- 9th in most GDPs per GDP situation (18.2%)
- Led the Orioles in batting average on a 3-2 count (.375)
- Led AL third basemen in batting average on a 3-2 count (.375)

B.J. Surhoff

Position: LF/DH
Bats: L **Throws:** R
Ht: 6' 1" **Wt:** 200

Opening Day Age: 35
Born: 8/4/64 in Bronx, NY
ML Seasons: 13

1999 Season

B.J. Surhoff enrolled in the same offseason program that allowed Mike Bordick to have his best season ever, and the results were positive for Surhoff as well. He played in every Orioles game and set career highs in almost every category. Surhoff was much more productive before the All-Star break than after.

Hitting

Surhoff made a smooth transition from the sixth spot in the lineup in 1998 to the third slot last season. He hits the ball to all fields, making him difficult to pitch to and an ideal candidate for the No. 3 role. His wrists and swing still are quick enough to turn on fastballs inside, even from lefthanders. He hits most of his homers off fastballs. Surhoff showed improvement last season in his approach to offspeed pitches, staying back on the ball better and going to the opposite field more often. As a result, he hit a career-high .327 with newfound power against lefthanders.

Baserunning & Defense

Surhoff was once a threat for double-digit stolen bases, but those days are behind him. His experience helps compensate for what he has lost in pure speed. He'll steal a base if the opportunity is there but won't force the issue. For someone who didn't play the outfield regularly before 1997, Surhoff does a creditable job. His range is unremarkable in left field, but he rarely makes errors. He charges groundballs well and makes strong and accurate throws to all bases, leading American League left fielders with 16 assists in 1999. He still can play third base in an emergency situation.

2000 Outlook

Surhoff will remain Baltimore's No. 3 hitter and left fielder. His professional attitude and work ethic should continue to keep him at the top of his game, and he shows no signs of declining at the plate or in the field.

Overall Statistics

	G	AB	R	H	D	T	HR	RBI	SB	BB	SO	Avg	OBP	Slg
1999	162	673	104	207	38	1	28	107	5	43	78	.308	.347	.492
Career	1716	6195	809	1738	323	36	146	893	117	482	621	.281	.331	.415

Where He Hits the Ball

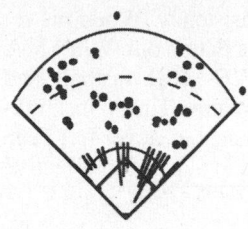 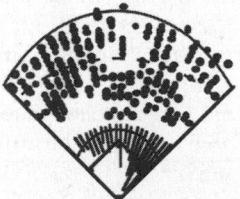

Vs. LHP   **Vs. RHP**

1999 Situational Stats

	AB	H	HR	RBI	Avg		AB	H	HR	RBI	Avg
Home	322	102	9	47	.317	LHP	159	52	7	36	.327
Road	351	105	19	60	.299	RHP	514	155	21	71	.302
First Half	370	123	20	71	.332	Sc Pos	195	52	9	84	.267
Scnd Half	303	84	8	36	.277	Clutch	103	34	5	19	.330

1999 Rankings (American League)

- 1st in at-bats and games played
- 2nd in hits and plate appearances (727)
- 4th in batting average on an 0-2 count (.333)
- 6th in singles
- 8th in batting average with two strikes (.264) and total bases (331)
- 10th in sacrifice flies (8)
- Led the Orioles in batting average in the clutch, batting average vs. righthanded pitchers, batting average on an 0-2 count (.333), batting average with two strikes (.264), batting average, at-bats, hits, singles, doubles, total bases (331), pitches seen (2,681), plate appearances (727), batting average at home and games played

Mike Timlin

1999 Season

The Orioles surprised many baseball observers by signing the inconsistent Mike Timlin to a four-year, $16 million contract last offseason. He lost nine games and tied for the American League lead in blown saves with nine, symptomatic of a disastrous Baltimore bullpen. There were some positives, however. Timlin converted 17 of his final 18 save opportunites and was excellent in the final two months.

Pitching

Timlin has yet to put together a complete, effective season. In 1997 he pitched well in the first half, while the past two seasons have seen his best work come after the All-Star break. Erratic mechanics are the reason for his inconsistency. When his release point drops, his pitches flatten out. When he's on, his combination of a 93-MPH fastball and sharp slider are almost unhittable. Timlin has tinkered with a changeup at times, but never has been able to master the arm speed to make it an effective pitch.

Defense

Timlin has a decent move to first base and keeps baserunners at bay with a quick delivery. He tends to fall off slightly to the first-base side of the mound, making him vulnerable to bunts toward third base. He makes up for that minor flaw by being aggressive in fielding his position, though he committed a career-high three errors in 1999.

2000 Outlook

When Timlin is pitching well, he's near the top of the closer class in the AL. His history suggests he can't perform at that level for an entire season. He'll open 2000 as the Orioles' closer, though the team has an alternative after signing free agent Mike Trombley to a three-year, $7.75 million contract. If Timlin doesn't get the job done, Baltimore won't be as patient as it was a year ago.

Position: RP
Bats: R **Throws:** R
Ht: 6' 4" **Wt:** 210

Opening Day Age: 34
Born: 3/10/66 in Midland, TX
ML Seasons: 9

Overall Statistics

	W	L	Pct.	ERA	G	GS	Sv	IP	H	BB	SO	HR	Ratio
1999	3	9	.250	3.57	62	0	27	63.0	51	23	50	9	1.17
Career	32	36	.471	3.53	463	3	99	561.1	526	211	450	45	1.31

How Often He Throws Strikes

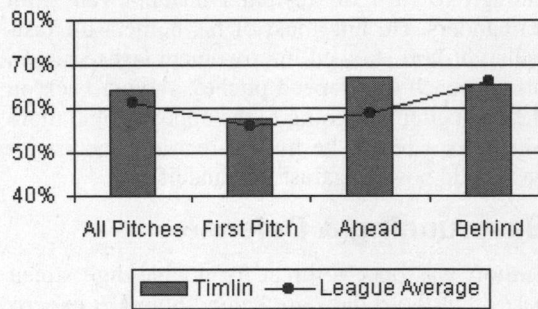

Timlin — League Average

1999 Situational Stats

	W	L	ERA	Sv	IP		AB	H	HR	RBI	Avg
Home	3	6	4.09	13	33.0	LHB	108	21	4	17	.194
Road	0	3	3.00	14	30.0	RHB	123	30	5	18	.244
First Half	3	8	5.06	9	37.1	Sc Pos	64	16	5	30	.250
Scnd Half	0	1	1.40	18	25.2	Clutch	155	35	6	24	.226

1999 Rankings (American League)

- 1st in blown saves (9) and lowest save percentage (75.0)
- 2nd in relief losses (9)
- 5th in errors at pitcher (3)
- Led the Orioles in saves, games finished (52), save opportunities (36), save percentage (75.0), blown saves (9), lowest batting average allowed in relief with runners on base (.220), relief ERA (3.57), relief losses (9), relief innings (63.0) and fewest baserunners allowed per nine innings in relief (11.3)

Rich Amaral

Position: RF/CF/DH/LF
Bats: R **Throws:** R
Ht: 6' 0" **Wt:** 175

Opening Day Age: 37
Born: 4/1/62 in Visalia, CA
ML Seasons: 9
Pronunciation: AM-ur-all

Overall Statistics

	G	AB	R	H	D	T	HR	RBI	SB	BB	SO	Avg	OBP	Slg
1999	91	137	21	38	8	1	0	11	9	15	20	.277	.348	.350
Career	697	1728	295	480	81	9	11	153	106	169	269	.278	.345	.354

1999 Situational Stats

	AB	H	HR	RBI	Avg		AB	H	HR	RBI	Avg
Home	73	22	0	8	.301	LHP	73	25	0	4	.342
Road	64	16	0	3	.250	RHP	64	13	0	7	.203
First Half	83	25	0	10	.301	Sc Pos	38	7	0	11	.184
Scnd Half	54	13	0	1	.241	Clutch	26	2	0	2	.077

1999 Season

Signed to a two-year contract as a free agent, Rich Amaral provided the Orioles with steady backup play at all three outfield positions and as an emergency infielder. His playing time dropped off noticeably the last six weeks of the season.

Hitting, Baserunning & Defense

Amaral continued to make solid contact but provided little production last year, hitting to all fields with no power. He struggled against righthanders for the first time since 1994, and he played almost solely against southpaws down the stretch. Amaral used experience and speed to his advantage on the basepaths, though he had a mediocre year stealing bases. Defensively, his speed allows him to cover the gaps, but he has a below-average arm.

2000 Outlook

The end of Amaral's career is in sight. The Orioles want to get younger, and it's not impossible that they would decide to just eat the final year of his contract. His speed and versatility might earn him another two or three seasons as a bit player.

Jeff Conine

Position: 1B/DH
Bats: R **Throws:** R
Ht: 6' 1" **Wt:** 220

Opening Day Age: 33
Born: 6/27/66 in Tacoma, WA
ML Seasons: 9
Pronunciation: COH-nine

Overall Statistics

	G	AB	R	H	D	T	HR	RBI	SB	BB	SO	Avg	OBP	Slg
1999	139	444	54	129	31	1	13	75	0	30	40	.291	.335	.453
Career	987	3395	434	973	186	17	119	551	11	343	667	.287	.351	.457

1999 Situational Stats

	AB	H	HR	RBI	Avg		AB	H	HR	RBI	Avg
Home	218	69	7	42	.317	LHP	93	26	5	15	.280
Road	226	60	6	33	.265	RHP	351	103	8	60	.293
First Half	229	66	7	36	.288	Sc Pos	125	41	2	60	.328
Scnd Half	215	63	6	39	.293	Clutch	85	25	0	17	.294

1999 Season

Three days before opening their season, the Orioles traded Chris Fussell to the Royals for Jeff Conine. They wanted Conine to serve in a DH platoon with Harold Baines, but his ability to play first base proved valuable in the wake of Will Clark's injury-plagued season.

Hitting, Baserunning & Defense

A pull hitter earlier in his career, Conine has started to hit the ball to all fields, though his homers still come to left-center and center field. He also is making more contact than he has in the past. Conine has below-average speed but makes few mistakes on the basepaths. He rarely makes an error on routine plays, though his range at first base is limited. He seldom plays in the outfield anymore.

2000 Outlook

A free agent, Conine re-signed with the Orioles for two years and $5.75 million. He'll probably share the DH job with Harold Baines and fill in at first if Clark gets hurt again. Conine has matured as a hitter, even if his power has decreased somewhat with age.

Mike Figga

Claimed By
DEVIL RAYS

Jerry Hairston Jr.

Position: C
Bats: R **Throws:** R
Ht: 6' 0" **Wt:** 200

Opening Day Age: 29
Born: 7/31/70 in Tampa, FL
ML Seasons: 3

Position: 2B
Bats: R **Throws:** R
Ht: 5'10" **Wt:** 175

Opening Day Age: 23
Born: 5/29/76 in Naperville, IL
ML Seasons: 2

Overall Statistics

	G	AB	R	H	D	T	HR	RBI	SB	BB	SO	Avg	OBP	Slg
1999	43	86	12	19	4	0	1	5	0	2	27	.221	.236	.302
Career	46	94	13	20	4	0	1	5	0	2	31	.213	.227	.287

1999 Situational Stats

	AB	H	HR	RBI	Avg		AB	H	HR	RBI	Avg
Home	47	6	0	3	.128	LHP	11	2	0	0	.182
Road	39	13	1	2	.333	RHP	75	17	1	5	.227
First Half	27	5	0	1	.185	Sc Pos	28	3	0	4	.107
Scnd Half	59	14	1	4	.237	Clutch	6	2	0	0	.333

Overall Statistics

	G	AB	R	H	D	T	HR	RBI	SB	BB	SO	Avg	OBP	Slg
1999	50	175	26	47	12	1	4	17	9	11	24	.269	.323	.417
Career	56	182	28	47	12	1	4	17	9	11	25	.258	.311	.401

1999 Situational Stats

	AB	H	HR	RBI	Avg		AB	H	HR	RBI	Avg
Home	94	23	1	6	.245	LHP	27	9	1	3	.333
Road	81	24	3	11	.296	RHP	148	38	3	14	.257
First Half	58	19	2	5	.328	Sc Pos	46	11	1	12	.239
Scnd Half	117	28	2	12	.239	Clutch	24	5	0	2	.208

1999 Season

The Yankees didn't have a role for Mike Figga, but because he was out of options they kept him on the roster as a little-used third-string catcher. When New York needed to promote Tony Tarasco, they waived Figga, who had appeared in two games without getting an at-bat. Baltimore claimed him and used him sparingly.

Hitting, Baserunning & Defense

In his brief major league career, Figga has been overmatched at the plate and hasn't been able to make consistent contact. He has 98 home runs in 633 minor league games but has yet to display that power in the majors. Figga has little strike-zone judgment, so that doesn't enhance his chances to hit. Like most catchers, he is a below-average baserunner. He has fair mechanics behind the plate and an average arm.

2000 Outlook

Figga was claimed on waivers by the Devil Rays in November, but they designated him for assignment in December. Free agent Greg Myers, signed by Baltimore to a two-year contract worth approximately $1 million, becomes Charles Johnson's backup.

1999 Season

With the offseason signing of Delino DeShields, Jerry Hairston expected to spend the season at Triple-A Rochester. When DeShields went down with a leg injury, Hairston was promoted and performed well. The Orioles were impressed with his solid defensive play and maturity. He's the fourth member of his family and third generation to reach the major leagues.

Hitting, Baserunning & Defense

Though he entered 1999 with just 742 professional at-bats, Hairston already knows how to work counts. He hits line drives to all fields and has decent pop for a middle infielder. Hairston has average speed and good first-step quickness that allows him to steal a base on occasion. A converted shortstop, he has very good range at second base, especially to his right. His arm is above average and he turns double plays with authority.

2000 Outlook

The Orioles liked what Hairston showed last season, and he's clearly their second baseman of the future. But he won't start this year unless they can trade DeShields. Hairston came home early from winter ball in Venezuela with a slight tear in his left shoulder, though he's not expected to need surgery.

Doug Johns

Position: RP
Bats: R **Throws:** L
Ht: 6' 2" **Wt:** 195

Opening Day Age: 32
Born: 12/19/67 in South Bend, IN
ML Seasons: 4

Overall Statistics

	W	L	Pct.	ERA	G	GS	Sv	IP	H	BB	SO	HR	Ratio
1999	6	4	.600	4.47	32	5	0	86.2	81	25	50	9	1.22
Career	20	22	.476	5.13	114	47	2	386.0	420	152	180	44	1.48

1999 Situational Stats

	W	L	ERA	Sv	IP		AB	H	HR	RBI	Avg
Home	4	3	4.18	0	51.2	LHB	87	12	2	14	.138
Road	2	1	4.89	0	35.0	RHB	240	69	7	32	.288
First Half	2	1	4.91	0	25.2	Sc Pos	78	22	3	33	.282
Scnd Half	4	3	4.28	0	61.0	Clutch	45	13	2	8	.289

1999 Season

Recalled in May, Doug Johns initially was used in short relief stints. Later in the season, he proved more effective in a limited starting role. He pitched very well in September, supporting his preference to be a starter.

Pitching & Defense

Johns is a finesse pitcher who does a good job of changing speeds on his breaking ball. He likes to spot his fastball on the outer half of the plate. When he's pitching well, he can work his fastball inside against righthanders, keeping them from leaning over the plate. When his control is off, Johns is unable to keep hitters off stride. His move to first base has improved to the point where it's above average. He's a capable fielder.

2000 Outlook

Johns' job description for 2000 is uncertain. He dominated lefthanders last season and could take over the lefty setup role from Arthur Rhodes, a free agent. Johns pitched better as a starter, though he won't have an opening in the rotation if Matt Riley makes the club. It's most likely that Johns will shuttle between roles.

Jason Johnson

Position: SP
Bats: R **Throws:** R
Ht: 6' 6" **Wt:** 220

Opening Day Age: 26
Born: 10/27/73 in Santa Barbara, CA
ML Seasons: 3

Overall Statistics

	W	L	Pct.	ERA	G	GS	Sv	IP	H	BB	SO	HR	Ratio
1999	8	7	.533	5.46	22	21	0	115.1	120	55	71	16	1.52
Career	10	12	.455	5.56	38	34	0	181.1	204	83	110	27	1.58

1999 Situational Stats

	W	L	ERA	Sv	IP		AB	H	HR	RBI	Avg
Home	2	3	5.05	0	46.1	LHB	215	52	8	33	.242
Road	6	4	5.74	0	69.0	RHB	235	68	8	30	.289
First Half	1	3	5.93	0	44.0	Sc Pos	128	35	2	40	.273
Scnd Half	7	4	5.17	0	71.1	Clutch	3	0	0	0	.000

1999 Season

The Orioles acquired Jason Johnson from the Devil Rays on March 30 for outfield prospect Danny Clyburn. Johnson was recalled in May and served as the No. 5 starter. He pitched well in four September starts, providing hope that he'll emerge during the 2000 season.

Pitching & Defense

Johnson has nice raw stuff but is far from being a polished pitcher. His fastball can be overpowering but still is inconsistent. He also needs to tighten his curveball and refine his changeup. Johnson has been more effective versus lefthanders than righthanders during his brief major league career. Because of his size, he struggles to get off the mound to field his position. His delivery to the plate is slow, allowing basestealers to succeed in 17 of 18 attempts last year.

2000 Outlook

The Orioles believe Johnson will develop into a power pitcher as he fills out. For 2000, they'll hope he can fill the fourth slot in the rotation. He's a favorite of the organization, so he'll be given plenty of chances to succeed.

Jesse Orosco

Position: RP
Bats: R **Throws:** L
Ht: 6' 2" **Wt:** 205

Opening Day Age: 42
Born: 4/21/57 in Santa Barbara, CA
ML Seasons: 20
Pronunciation: oh-ROSS-koh

Overall Statistics

	W	L	Pct.	ERA	G	GS	Sv	IP	H	BB	SO	HR	Ratio
1999	0	2	.000	5.34	65	0	1	32.0	28	20	35	5	1.50
Career	84	75	.528	3.03	1090	4	141	1216.0	970	538	1103	101	1.24

1999 Situational Stats

	W	L	ERA	Sv	IP		AB	H	HR	RBI	Avg
Home	0	1	4.32	0	16.2	LHB	63	17	3	15	.270
Road	0	1	6.46	1	15.1	RHB	54	11	2	11	.204
First Half	0	2	7.58	0	19.0	Sc Pos	49	10	4	25	.204
Scnd Half	0	0	2.08	1	13.0	Clutch	56	16	3	15	.286

1999 Season

Jesse Orosco finished the season with more appearances than any other pitcher in major league history. He struggled with some minor arm problems the first half of the season. Once he was healthy, Orosco returned to the form that has made him one of the best situational lefthanders in baseball.

Pitching & Defense

Orosco's best pitch is his slider, and he's effective as long as he keeps it at hitters' knees. He improved his ability to turn his fastball over against lefthanders, though he still struggled with the pitch most of the season. Orosco also has a backdoor curve that he uses to get righthanders out. He's an average fielder. His motion to first base is below average and he doesn't hold runners well.

2000 Outlook

Orosco looked like he was at the end of his career when he carried a 7.58 ERA into the All-Star break. He bounced back and was untouchable in the season's final three months, guaranteeing him work for at least one more season. He'll return to his first major league club, the Mets, after a December trade for Chuck McElroy. McElroy could replace Arthur Rhodes as Baltimore's primary lefty reliever.

Jeff Reboulet

Position: 3B/2B/SS
Bats: R **Throws:** R
Ht: 6' 0" **Wt:** 175

Opening Day Age: 35
Born: 4/30/64 in Dayton, OH
ML Seasons: 8
Pronunciation: REB-uh-lay

Overall Statistics

	G	AB	R	H	D	T	HR	RBI	SB	BB	SO	Avg	OBP	Slg
1999	99	154	25	25	4	0	0	4	1	33	29	.162	.317	.188
Career	727	1524	206	362	65	2	14	139	17	203	261	.238	.330	.310

1999 Situational Stats

	AB	H	HR	RBI	Avg		AB	H	HR	RBI	Avg
Home	73	12	0	3	.164	LHP	51	12	0	2	.235
Road	81	13	0	1	.160	RHP	103	13	0	2	.126
First Half	106	20	0	3	.189	Sc Pos	41	6	0	4	.146
Scnd Half	48	5	0	1	.104	Clutch	22	9	0	2	.409

1999 Season

Hampered by foot, hamstring and quadriceps injuries, Jeff Reboulet endured easily his worst season in the major leagues. Serving as a backup at second base, third base and shortstop, he provided adequate defense but next to no offense.

Hitting, Baserunning & Defense

Reboulet was able to work counts and draw more walks than strikeouts last year, making his .162 batting average and utter lack of power more disappointing. His bat speed has slowed considerably, and he simply can't handle fastballs in on his hands. He has below-average speed and is not a threat to steal. Defensively, Reboulet gets by with experience and smooth footwork, overcoming his lack of range and an average arm. He's beginning to struggle at turning the pivot on double plays.

2000 Outlook

Reboulet was a solid clubhouse presence and a reliable utility player for the Orioles, but his age and declining skills at the plate and in the field worked against him. Baltimore traded him to Kansas City in December for a player to be named later.

Al Reyes

Position: RP
Bats: R **Throws:** R
Ht: 6' 1" **Wt:** 206

Opening Day Age: 28
Born: 4/10/71 in San Cristobal, Dominican Republic
ML Seasons: 5
Pronunciation: RAY-ess

Overall Statistics

	W	L	Pct.	ERA	G	GS	Sv	IP	H	BB	SO	HR	Ratio
1999	4	3	.571	4.52	53	0	0	65.2	50	41	67	9	1.39
Career	12	7	.632	4.23	154	0	2	191.1	164	101	184	26	1.39

1999 Situational Stats

	W	L	ERA	Sv	IP		AB	H	HR	RBI	Avg
Home	2	2	3.86	0	39.2	LHB	86	15	3	19	.174
Road	2	1	5.54	0	26.0	RHB	147	35	6	29	.238
First Half	2	0	4.25	0	36.0	Sc Pos	70	18	3	39	.257
Scnd Half	2	3	4.85	0	29.2	Clutch	93	24	5	19	.258

1999 Season

Al Reyes started the season with the Brewers before being dealt to the Orioles on July 21 for Rocky Coppinger. Reyes worked mainly as a middle reliever for both teams and struggled with his control.

Pitching & Defense

Reyes continues to struggle with inconsistent pitching mechanics, which lead to bouts of wildness. He doesn't throw as hard now as he did before having elbow problems. He still relies on a hard slider, but it isn't as sharp as it once was. His changeup is below average and he has lost confidence in it, refusing to throw it very often. Reyes' inability to change speeds greatly reduces his effectiveness. His fielding and ability to hold baserunners are both average.

2000 Outlook

Reyes is a solid short reliever at times. But an inability to maintain his arm angle and develop an offspeed pitch have led to frustrating periods of ineffectiveness. The Orioles lack bullpen depth, so he'll be back in 2000.

Arthur Rhodes

Position: RP
Bats: L **Throws:** L
Ht: 6' 2" **Wt:** 205

Opening Day Age: 30
Born: 10/24/69 in Waco, TX
ML Seasons: 9

Overall Statistics

	W	L	Pct.	ERA	G	GS	Sv	IP	H	BB	SO	HR	Ratio
1999	3	4	.429	5.43	43	0	3	53.0	43	45	59	9	1.66
Career	43	36	.544	4.86	238	61	9	622.1	575	316	579	79	1.43

1999 Situational Stats

	W	L	ERA	Sv	IP		AB	H	HR	RBI	Avg
Home	1	0	5.33	0	25.1	LHB	68	14	1	9	.206
Road	2	4	5.53	3	27.2	RHB	127	29	8	23	.228
First Half	3	4	6.19	3	36.1	Sc Pos	53	13	3	25	.245
Scnd Half	0	0	3.78	0	16.2	Clutch	82	18	4	14	.220

1999 Season

Arthur Rhodes missed a golden opportunity last May to seize Baltimore's closer job when Mike Timlin faltered. Rhodes continued to show promise, but he frustrated the Orioles with his inconsistency. His season was cut short late in the year, when a finger injury kept him from gripping the baseball properly.

Pitching & Defense

Rhodes has one of the better fastballs among American League lefthanders, topping out at 96 MPH. He uses it high in the strike zone to overpower hitters, though that approach also leaves him vulnerable to home runs. Rhodes also throws a curveball and has added a much-needed changeup, though he still must learn to vary his speeds more effectively. He doesn't handle the running game or his fielding responsibilities particularly well. Bunts on the first-base side of the mound give him trouble.

2000 Outlook

Rhodes entered the free-agent market as the most talented lefthanded reliever available. The Orioles would like to have him back. But the Yankees reportedly offered Rhodes a four-year contract worth $11 million, making it unlikely that he'll return to Baltimore.

Other Baltimore Orioles

Ricky Bones (Pos: RHP, Age: 30)

	W	L	Pct.	ERA	G	GS	Sv	IP	H	BB	SO	HR	Ratio
1999	0	3	.000	5.98	30	2	0	43.2	59	19	26	7	1.79
Career	57	75	.432	4.86	258	164	1	1137.0	1257	404	464	154	1.46

After posting a 1.62 ERA in April for the Orioles, Bones unraveled. He spent time on the disabled list with a tired arm in July, and Baltimore released him in August. 2000 Outlook: C

Jim Corsi (Pos: RHP, Age: 38)

	W	L	Pct.	ERA	G	GS	Sv	IP	H	BB	SO	HR	Ratio
1999	1	3	.250	4.34	36	0	0	37.1	40	20	22	6	1.61
Career	22	24	.478	3.25	368	1	7	481.1	450	191	290	33	1.33

Corsi had pitched respectably since the 1994 labor dispute until his game fell apart early in 1999. The Red Sox released him in June, but he pitched well for the Orioles in August until a bad hamstring sidelined him. 2000 Outlook: B

Tommy Davis (Pos: C, Age: 26, Bats: R)

	G	AB	R	H	D	T	HR	RBI	SB	BB	SO	Avg	OBP	Slg
1999	5	6	0	1	0	0	0	0	0	0	2	.167	.167	.167
Career	5	6	0	1	0	0	0	0	0	0	2	.167	.167	.167

Davis hasn't been able to match his success at Triple-A in 1997, when he batted .304-15-62. He came close last year before his callup, and a major rebuilding in Baltimore might mean a job. 2000 Outlook: C

Mike Fetters (Pos: RHP, Age: 35)

	W	L	Pct.	ERA	G	GS	Sv	IP	H	BB	SO	HR	Ratio
1999	1	0	1.000	5.81	27	0	0	31.0	35	22	22	5	1.84
Career	19	33	.365	3.62	422	6	85	539.2	537	248	373	42	1.45

Fetters' best years were from 1994-97, and there's no sign that the good times will return. An elbow strain was part of the problem last year. He signed a minor league contract with the Dodgers in December. 2000 Outlook: C

Jesse Garcia (Pos: SS, Age: 26, Bats: R)

	G	AB	R	H	D	T	HR	RBI	SB	BB	SO	Avg	OBP	Slg
1999	17	29	6	6	0	0	2	2	0	2	3	.207	.258	.414
Career	17	29	6	6	0	0	2	2	0	2	3	.207	.258	.414

Garcia had a 53-2 record as a Golden Gloves boxer, but he offers little punch at the plate. He could stick with the Orioles as a utilityman after they traded Jeff Reboulet. 2000 Outlook: C

Scott Kamieniecki (Pos: RHP, Age: 35)

	W	L	Pct.	ERA	G	GS	Sv	IP	H	BB	SO	HR	Ratio
1999	2	4	.333	4.95	43	3	2	56.1	52	29	39	4	1.44
Career	50	55	.476	4.45	198	138	3	917.2	942	404	496	96	1.47

A bad hamstring shelved Kamieniecki in April, and he didn't last four innings in his first two starts in May. He endured a trip to Rochester and landed in the Orioles pen. It was a second straight lost season, though it earned him a two-year, $3.8 million contract from Cleveland. 2000 Outlook: C

Doug Linton (Pos: RHP, Age: 35)

	W	L	Pct.	ERA	G	GS	Sv	IP	H	BB	SO	HR	Ratio
1999	1	4	.200	5.95	14	8	0	59.0	69	25	31	14	1.59
Career	17	20	.459	5.86	105	35	0	296.1	353	121	199	48	1.60

Except for three good starts in September, Linton wasn't effective as a starter or reliever in 1999. That's pretty much the story for each of his six major league seasons and most of his Triple-A work as well. Baltimore released him in December. 2000 Outlook: C

Derrick May (Pos: DH, Age: 31, Bats: L)

	G	AB	R	H	D	T	HR	RBI	SB	BB	SO	Avg	OBP	Slg
1999	26	49	5	13	0	0	4	12	0	4	6	.265	.315	.510
Career	797	2200	244	596	103	10	52	310	30	156	254	.271	.319	.398

May has earned a callup from Triple-A in each of the last two seasons, but he hasn't done enough in the bigs to resume his major league career. At most he would be a pinch-hitter or part-time DH. 2000 Outlook: C

Baltimore Orioles Minor League Prospects

Organization Overview:

The Orioles system is on the rebound after falling apart in the early 1990s, though owner Peter Angelos' infatuation with free agents may block prospects from getting much of an opportunity. When free agents Rafael Palmeiro and Roberto Alomar departed after the 1998 season, the club signed Will Clark and Delino DeShields to shortsighted deals instead of giving opportunities to Calvin Pickering and Jerry Hairston Jr. Rather than wait for Armando Benitez to blossom, they traded him in a deal for Charles Johnson. Baltimore already has one of the top catching prospects in the game in Jayson Werth, and watched its bullpen fall apart while Benitez helped pitch the Mets to the playoffs. The Orioles had a chance to restock their system with seven of the first 50 picks in the 1999 draft, and the early returns on their choices were positive.

Brian Falkenborg

Position: P
Bats: R **Throws:** R
Ht: 6' 6" **Wt:** 187

Opening Day Age: 22
Born: 1/18/78 in Newport Beach, CA

Recent Statistics

	W	L	ERA	G	GS	Sv	IP	H	R	BB	SO	HR
1999 R Orioles	1	0	2.00	3	2	0	9.0	6	2	3	11	0
1999 AA Bowie	3	6	3.78	16	16	0	83.1	77	40	36	77	11
1999 AL Baltimore	0	0	0.00	2	0	0	3.0	2	0	2	1	0

Though Falkenborg hasn't been able to pitch a complete season since 1997, he reached the major leagues last year at age 21. Baltimore's top pick (second round) in the 1996 draft, he throws strikes with an above-average curveball and a 90-91 MPH fastball that bores in on the fists of righthanders. Because he's a skinny 6-foot-6, he projects to add more velocity in the future. Elbow problems have caused Falkenborg to miss half of each of the last two seasons, though the Orioles believe he'll be fine in the future. They'd like him to be healthy enough to pitch a full season in Triple-A.

Ryan Minor

Position: 3B
Bats: R **Throws:** R
Ht: 6' 7" **Wt:** 225

Opening Day Age: 26
Born: 1/5/74 in Canton, OH

Recent Statistics

	G	AB	R	H	D	T	HR	RBI	SB	BB	SO	Avg
1999 AAA Rochester	101	383	56	98	24	1	21	67	3	37	119	.256
1999 AL Baltimore	46	124	13	24	7	0	3	10	1	8	43	.194
1999 MLE	101	372	47	87	20	0	18	57	2	30	126	.234

Minor has tremendous raw potential, though for now he's best knows as the answer to a trivia question: Who replaced Cal Ripken Jr. in the lineup on the night his consecutive-games streak ended? Minor lasted until the 33rd round of the 1996 draft because he was a basketball star at the University of Oklahoma and had NBA aspira-

tions. The Orioles persuaded him to play baseball full-time, and they've been intrigued by his powerful bat. But his inexperience after focusing on hoops in college has held him back. He has yet to master the strike zone or learn how to make adjustments at the plate, essentially making him an all-or-nothing hitter. Defensively, he has the arm (rated the best among Triple-A International League infielders), first-step quickness and hands of a prototypical third baseman. The best-case scenario is that Minor will develop into a Matt Williams, though he needs to start making strides because he's already 26.

Gabe Molina

Position: P
Bats: R **Throws:** R
Ht: 5' 11" **Wt:** 190

Opening Day Age: 24
Born: 5/3/75 in Denver, CO

Recent Statistics

	W	L	ERA	G	GS	Sv	IP	H	R	BB	SO	HR
1999 AAA Rochester	2	2	3.14	45	0	18	57.1	45	22	23	58	3
1999 AL Baltimore	1	2	6.65	20	0	0	23.0	22	19	16	14	4

Baltimore's bullpen situation deteriorated so quickly last year that, for a brief time in July, Molina got a look at closer despite having very little experience above Double-A. A 21st-round pick in 1996 from Arizona State, he has breezed through the minors, posting a 2.89 ERA and 285 strikeouts in 240 innings while allowing just 181 hits and 12 homers. He has a very quick arm action, delivering 92-94 MPH fastballs and wicked sliders. He struggled in the majors, mainly because he didn't challenge hitters and pitched from behind in the count. This season Molina should make the Orioles, who still see him as a future closer.

Calvin Pickering

Position: 1B
Bats: L **Throws:** L
Ht: 6' 5" **Wt:** 283

Opening Day Age: 23
Born: 9/29/76 in St. Thomas, Virgin Islands

Recent Statistics

	G	AB	R	H	D	T	HR	RBI	SB	BB	SO	Avg
1999 AAA Rochester	103	372	63	106	20	0	16	63	1	60	99	.285
1999 AL Baltimore	23	40	4	5	1	0	1	5	0	11	16	.125
1999 MLE	103	359	53	93	17	0	13	53	0	50	104	.259

Coming off a monster season in Double-A, Calvin Pickering easily could have matched the 10 homers and 29 RBI that the Orioles paid Will Clark $5.5 million to deliver. A 35th-round pick in 1995, Pickering combines explosive power with fine plate discipline, making him a legitimate middle-of-the-order threat. He shows some agility at first base but has had some throwing problems. Arizona Fall League observers were disappointed by his weight, which has soared to 300 pounds in the past, and his lackluster work ethic. He probably will start the year in Triple-A after the Orioles signed Harold Baines and Jeff Conine to DH.

51

Matt Riley

Position: P   **Opening Day Age:** 20
Bats: L **Throws:** L   **Born:** 8/2/79 in Antioch,
Ht: 6' 1" **Wt:** 205   CA

Recent Statistics

	W	L	ERA	G	GS	Sv	IP	H	R	BB	SO	HR
1999 A Frederick	3	2	2.61	8	8	0	51.2	34	19	14	58	5
1999 AA Bowie	10	6	3.22	20	20	0	125.2	113	53	42	131	13
1999 AL Baltimore	0	0	7.36	3	3	0	11.0	17	9	13	6	4

Riley didn't sign after getting drafted in the third round in 1997, but the Orioles retained his rights and signed him for $750,000 after he spent a season at Sacramento (Calif.) City College. He immediately became the organization's top pitching prospect and capped 1999, his first full pro season, by making his major league debut shortly after his 20th birthday. He throws a 95-MPH fastball and a hard overhand curveball with the same motion, so hitters have no idea what's coming. Riley also has a decent changeup and good command. He'll begin this year in Triple-A and should be a frontline starter in Baltimore in the near future.

B.J. Ryan

Position: P   **Opening Day Age:** 24
Bats: L **Throws:** L   **Born:** 12/28/75 in
Ht: 6' 6" **Wt:** 230   Bossier City, LA

Recent Statistics

	W	L	ERA	G	GS	Sv	IP	H	R	BB	SO	HR
1999 AA Chattanooga	2	1	2.59	35	0	6	41.2	33	13	17	46	1
1999 AAA Indianapols	1	0	4.00	11	0	0	9.0	9	4	3	12	0
1999 AAA Rochester	0	0	2.51	11	0	1	14.1	8	4	4	20	2
1999 NL Cincinnati	0	0	4.50	1	0	0	2.0	4	1	1	1	0
1999 AL Baltimore	1	0	2.95	13	0	0	18.1	9	6	12	28	0

Baltimore owner Peter Angelos had blocked trades of impending free agents for prospects in the past, but permitted former GM Frank Wren to send Juan Guzman to the Reds for Ryan and Jacobo Sequea at last year's trading deadline. A 17th-round pick in 1998 out of the University of Southwestern Louisiana, Ryan reached the majors after just 90 pro innings and was untouchable in Baltimore. He's very deceptive, turning his back to the plate before delivering a 91-92 MPH fastball or a slider. He generally throws strikes and has a very resilient arm. If Arthur Rhodes signs elsewhere, the Orioles will need Ryan to become the top lefty in their bullpen.

John Stephens

Position: P   **Opening Day Age:** 20
Bats: R **Throws:** R   **Born:** 11/15/79 in
Ht: 6' 1" **Wt:** 175   Sydney, Australia

Recent Statistics

	W	L	ERA	G	GS	Sv	IP	H	R	BB	SO	HR
1998 A Delmarva	1	2	2.60	6	6	0	34.2	25	11	13	40	3
1999 A Delmarva	10	8	3.22	28	27	0	170.1	148	75	36	217	10

Stephens may be the first pitcher ever to lead the minor leagues in strikeouts with an 81-82 MPH fastball. He also has an excellent changeup and a very good overhand curveball, and what makes him so tough is that he throws all three pitches with the same delivery. They arrive at the plate at different speeds and with different movements, and hitters often can't pull the trigger until it's too late. Stephens' career was in jeopardy after he dove for a bunt and pinched a nerve in his neck in 1998, cutting off the blood flow to his arm, but he proved he was fine last year. It's very difficult to project how his stuff will hold up as he moves up the system, but he's so polished and poised at age 20 that it's hard to bet against him.

Jayson Werth

Position: C   **Opening Day Age:** 20
Bats: R **Throws:** R   **Born:** 5/20/79 in
Ht: 6' 6" **Wt:** 191   Springfield, IL

Recent Statistics

	G	AB	R	H	D	T	HR	RBI	SB	BB	SO	Avg
1998 A Delmarva	120	408	71	108	20	3	8	53	21	50	92	.265
1998 AA Bowie	5	19	2	3	2	0	0	1	1	2	6	.158
1999 A Frederick	66	236	41	72	10	1	3	30	16	37	37	.305
1999 AA Bowie	35	121	18	33	5	1	1	11	7	17	26	.273

Scouts have compared Werth to a young Dale Murphy, the standard by which young catching prospects are judged. Werth already hits for average and controls the strike zone. He has shown little power thus far, but projects to develop significantly more pop as he fills out. Extremely athletic for a catcher, Werth has stolen 52 bases in 63 attempts as a pro and is very mobile behind the plate. He doesn't have the strongest arm, but combats baserunners with a quick release and accuracy. A 1997 first-round pick, he's from a family that includes three former major leaguers: grandfather Ducky Schofield, uncle Dick Schofield and stepfather Dennis Werth. The Orioles may need Jayson to catch for them in 2001 if Charles Johnson leaves as a free agent.

Others to Watch

First baseman **Rick Elder** (20) offers tremendous lefthanded power potential and a good eye. In 60 games in Rookie and Class-A ball last year, he hit .299 with 14 homers and 42 walks. . . The Orioles still have a righthander named **Juan Guzman** (22) after trading the major league version to the Reds. This one is a converted catcher with a 95-MPH fastball, and he has 134 strikeouts in 124.1 Class-A innings in 1999, his first full year as a pitcher. . . Outfielder **Eugene Kingsale** (23) always has had plenty of speed, but last year he added some strength. He hit the ball harder than ever and stayed healthy, though he'll have to continue to improve offensively. . . In **Luis Matos** (21) and 1997 first-round picks **Darnell McDonald** (21) and **Ntema Ndungidi** (20), the Orioles have three tools outfielders who spent much of last season in Class-A. A pure center fielder, Matos has the best overall skills and has been compared to a young Moises Alou. McDonald and Ndungidi are corner guys who have been mediocre at the plate. . . Righthander **Jacobo Sequea** (18) was part of the trade that sent the other Juan Guzman to the Reds last July. Sequea has a 94-MPH fastball and a potentially above-average curve.

Fenway Park

Offense

Fenway Park still boosts batting averages, but now it's a fairly neutral park in terms of scoring and the toughest place to homer in the American League. Both the Green Monster in left field and the vast amount of territory in right-center make it a good doubles park. Fenway benefits pitchers more than usual during the cooler months of April and May.

Defense

The outfield has all kinds of intricacies to maneuver through. Playing the 37-foot wall in left is a special skill, and then there's that nook in center, all that open space in right-center and the odd-shaped right-field corner. As a result, strikeout and groundball pitchers have much more success than flyball pitchers.

Who It Helps the Most

Two newcomers to Boston's lineup in 1999, Brian Daubach and Jose Offerman, hit 43 and 61 points better, respectively, at Fenway Park than on the road. In his first year as a regular, Jason Varitek batted 94 points higher in Boston than elsewhere. Reliever Derek Lowe, one of the game's most extreme groundball pitchers, posted a 2.01 ERA and allowed only one homer at Fenway last year.

Who It Hurts the Most

Mike Stanley has hit just 24 of his 63 Red Sox homers at Fenway Park. As a rookie, Trot Nixon smashed 12 of his 15 homers and slugged 103 points better away from Boston. The departed Pat Rapp never got the hang of pitching at Fenway, going 2-4, 6.15, compared to 4-3, 2.39 on the road.

Rookies & Newcomers

Carl Everett must be excited to leave the Astrodome, a pitchers' park that's the toughest place to homer in the National League. Wilton Veras, the heir apparent at third base, struggled during his brief exposure to Fenway Park last year. Mound prospects such as Jin Ho Cho, Tomokazu Ohka, Juan Pena will need to keep their pitches down in Boston.

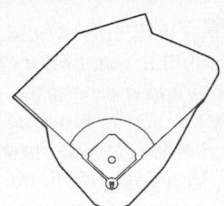

Dimensions: LF-310, LCF-379, CF-420, RCF-380, RF-302

Capacity: 33,871

Elevation: 21 feet

Surface: Grass

Foul Territory: Small

Park Factors

1999 Season

	Home Games			Away Games			
	Red Sox	Opp	Total	Red Sox	Opp	Total	Index
G	72	72	144	72	72	144	—
Avg	.292	.253	.272	.274	.245	.260	105
AB	2413	2497	4910	2553	2389	4942	99
R	403	311	714	363	306	669	107
H	704	632	1336	700	585	1285	104
2B	159	128	287	145	120	265	109
3B	18	9	27	19	8	27	101
HR	68	64	132	89	73	162	82
BB	275	199	474	272	215	487	98
SO	389	531	920	428	481	909	102
E	68	48	116	40	45	85	136
E-Infield	56	42	98	39	31	70	140
LHB-Avg	.294	.262	.278	.265	.251	.258	108
LHB-HR	34	18	52	47	33	80	66
RHB-Avg	.289	.246	.267	.281	.239	.262	102
RHB-HR	34	46	80	42	40	82	98

1997-1999

	Home Games			Away Games			
	Red Sox	Opp	Total	Red Sox	Opp	Total	Index
G	217	217	434	220	220	440	—
Avg	.295	.263	.279	.276	.260	.268	104
AB	7409	7663	15072	7879	7347	15226	100
R	1182	1013	2195	1140	1044	2184	102
H	2186	2016	4202	2172	1907	4079	104
2B	500	426	926	439	362	801	117
3B	50	31	81	51	28	79	104
HR	236	192	428	281	227	508	85
BB	760	685	1445	732	751	1483	98
SO	1316	1500	2816	1386	1354	2740	104
E	180	136	316	143	141	284	113
E-Infield	159	116	275	131	109	240	116
LHB-Avg	.304	.274	.288	.272	.268	.270	107
LHB-HR	110	72	182	140	97	237	78
RHB-Avg	.288	.254	.271	.279	.253	.266	102
RHB-HR	126	120	246	141	130	271	92

1999 Rankings (American League)

- Highest error factor
- Highest infield-error factor
- Second-highest batting-average factor
- Second-highest LHB batting-average factor
- Third-highest run factor
- Lowest home-run factor
- Lowest LHB home-run factor

Boston

Jimy Williams

1999 Season

There was little doubt that Jimy Williams would win American League Manager of the Year honors. To get 94 regular-season victories and reach the AL Championship Series with only one starter winning more than 10 games was remarkable. Despite running a playoff club two years in a row, Williams still manages as if he's teaching in the Florida State League. His players completely trust him because they know he'll never give any of them up to either the media or the front office.

Offense

Though the Red Sox lost Mo Vaughn's power, Williams avoided little ball in 1999 because his team lacked speed. No AL team tried fewer stolen-base attempts, and only Oakland's Art Howe put the hit-and-run on less than the Boston skipper. And only Howe's club produced a higher success rate with the hit-and-run. Williams will call for a bunt on occasion, and he likes to platoon. He's a hunch manager who eschews the book, allowing batters to swing 3-and-0 or putting together odd lineups geared to get every one of his position players feeling as if they were contributors.

Pitching & Defense

Williams and pitching coach Joe Kerrigan are hands-on in the dugout, controlling the game with detailed preparations, called pitches and pitchouts. Their 75 pitchouts were more than any other two AL teams combined. With only Pedro Martinez as a regular starter, Williams ranked first in the league in quick hooks. He protected his ace as well, giving Martinez the majority of his starts with at least five days of rest. Boston led the AL in saves of four-plus outs, partially a function of using eight different closers after Tom Gordon was injured.

2000 Outlook

There have been small philosophical differences between Williams and GM Dan Duquette, but their relationship seems stronger than ever. Williams once again will take care with Martinez, and he'll also make sure key position players Nomar Garciaparra and Jason Varitek get plenty of rest. Then he'll manage according to what he's given, as he would have in the Florida State League.

Born: 10/04/43 in Santa Maria, CA

Playing Experience: 1966-1967, StL

Managerial Experience: 7 seasons

Manager Statistics

Year	Team, Lg	W	L	Pct	GB	Finish
1999	Boston, AL	94	68	.580	4.0	2nd East
7 Seasons		545	463	.540	—	—

1999 Starting Pitchers by Days Rest

	<=3	4	5	6+
Red Sox Starts	2	63	54	32
Red Sox ERA	9.45	3.60	4.18	4.78
AL Avg Starts	2	82	47	21
AL ERA	6.83	4.98	4.72	5.62

1999 Situational Stats

	Jimy Williams	AL Average
Hit & Run Success %	48.3	35.3
Stolen Base Success %	63.2	68.0
Platoon Pct.	61.8	56.7
Defensive Subs	9	22
High-Pitch Outings	13	15
Quick/Slow Hooks	32/8	18/18
Sacrifice Attempts	47	52

1999 Rankings (American League)

- 1st in steals of home plate (2), pitchouts (75), pitchouts with a runner moving (22), quick hooks (32) and 2+ pitching changes in low-scoring games (33)
- 2nd in hit-and-run percentage (48.3%) and saves with over 1 inning pitched (17)
- 3rd in fewest caught stealings of second base (35)

Brian Daubach

1999 Season

There was a time in early August when New Englanders gleefully pointed out that Brian Daubach was outproducing the departed Mo Vaughn. Signed as a minor league free agent after nine seasons in the bushes, Daubach provided the Red Sox with some much-needed lefthanded power. He came up big in August, homering seven times and driving in 27 runs as Boston made a push for the playoffs. He faded horribly in September and October, however.

Hitting

Daubach has some undeniable strengths. He's a dead lowball hitter and doesn't miss many low fastballs. He's a prototypical Fenway Park hitter, a lefty who can put the ball in the air off or over the Green Monster. Adept at fouling off good fastballs, he's one of the best Red Sox at wearing out a pitcher with a long at-bat. He has a good eye and is very patient, though he'll tee off on the first pitch if it's to his liking. When he put the first pitch in play last year, he batted .391. Daubach also hung in well against lefthanders.

Baserunning & Defense

As a first baseman, Daubach works hard, has decent hands and can start the 3-6-3 double play. He got some time in left field as well, though that experiment was short-lived. He'll spend his career as a first baseman and DH. Daubach doesn't bring any speed to the Boston lineup.

2000 Outlook

Pitchers learned to bust Daubach up and in with fastballs by the end of last season. After his slow finish, he'll have to make adjustments of his own to maintain his role as a semi-regular first baseman and DH. Whether he'll stick in the No. 3 hole in the lineup remains to be seen.

Position: 1B/DH
Bats: L **Throws:** R
Ht: 6' 1" **Wt:** 201

Opening Day Age: 28
Born: 2/11/72 in Belleville, IL
ML Seasons: 2
Pronunciation: DAW-back

Overall Statistics

	G	AB	R	H	D	T	HR	RBI	SB	BB	SO	Avg	OBP	Slg
1999	110	381	61	112	33	3	21	73	0	36	92	.294	.360	.562
Career	120	396	61	115	34	3	21	76	0	37	97	.290	.357	.551

Where He Hits the Ball

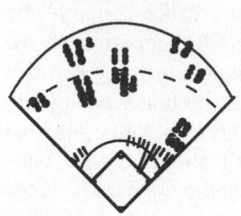

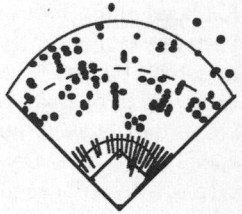

Vs. LHP **Vs. RHP**

1999 Situational Stats

	AB	H	HR	RBI	Avg		AB	H	HR	RBI	Avg
Home	180	57	11	42	.317	LHP	44	12	1	9	.273
Road	201	55	10	31	.274	RHP	337	100	20	64	.297
First Half	180	54	9	33	.300	Sc Pos	105	34	6	48	.324
Scnd Half	201	58	12	40	.289	Clutch	41	8	3	9	.195

1999 Rankings (American League)

- 6th in errors at first base (8)
- Led the Red Sox in fewest GDPs per GDP situation (5.2%)

Boston

Nomar Garciaparra

1999 Season

It didn't seem to matter that Nomar Garciaparra was bothered by an assortment of injuries that included hamstring, groin and quad ailments. He still produced 42 doubles and 27 homers in just 135 games, hitting .393 in the final month to win his first American League batting title. Garciaparra was valiant during the postseason, overcoming a bruised right wrist to hit .406 with four homers and nine RBI in nine games.

Hitting

For all of the gyrations, twitches and ceremony that go into a Garciaparra at-bat, when it comes time to pull the trigger he's as still as Joe DiMaggio and Paul Molitor. Garciaparra swings at pitches over his head and a foot out of the strike zone, yet he perfectly centers each swing. Pitchers rarely throw a fastball by him. There have been many theories on trying to pitch around him, such as making him chase bad pitches, but his great balance and bat speed make him very difficult to game plan. Garciaparra doesn't get cheated at the plate, as he takes a lot of cuts and makes consistent contact. He uses the entire field and can take a pitch that appears inches from the catcher's glove and deposit it into the right-field corner.

Baserunning & Defense

Garciaparra's unique defensive style is best described as shortstop on the run. Because of his great soccer footwork, he likes to make plays on the go and throw across his body. Few shortstops can match his range of daring. Garciaparra tends to try to throw everything at 93 MPH. He's not the quickest shortstop when it comes to turning double plays. He's a solid baserunner with above-average speed, and he can steal a base when needed.

2000 Outlook

Garciaparra and Pedro Martinez aren't just the two best players on the Red Sox. They're also the club's heart and soul. Garciaparra seems destined to earn an MVP Award before long.

Position: SS
Bats: R **Throws:** R
Ht: 6' 0" **Wt:** 180

Opening Day Age: 26
Born: 7/23/73 in Whittier, CA
ML Seasons: 4
Pronunciation: NO-mar gar-see-uh-PARR-uh

Overall Statistics

	G	AB	R	H	D	T	HR	RBI	SB	BB	SO	Avg	OBP	Slg
1999	135	532	103	190	42	4	27	104	14	51	39	.357	.418	.603
Career	455	1907	347	615	125	26	96	340	53	123	207	.322	.367	.566

Where He Hits the Ball

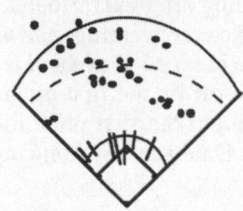

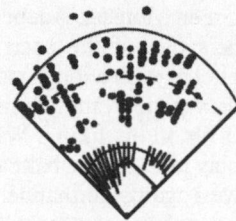

Vs. LHP   **Vs. RHP**

1999 Situational Stats

	AB	H	HR	RBI	Avg		AB	H	HR	RBI	Avg
Home	296	112	14	67	.378	LHP	110	44	9	32	.400
Road	236	78	13	37	.331	RHP	422	146	18	72	.346
First Half	276	101	14	57	.366	Sc Pos	148	52	9	76	.351
Scnd Half	256	89	13	47	.348	Clutch	65	25	3	10	.385

1999 Rankings (American League)

- 1st in batting average and batting average at home
- Led the Red Sox in slugging percentage, on-base percentage, HR frequency (19.7 ABs per HR), batting average with runners in scoring position, batting average in the clutch, batting average vs. lefthanded pitchers, batting average vs. righthanded pitchers, batting average on an 0-2 count (.280), cleanup slugging percentage (.608), slugging percentage vs. lefthanded pitchers (.764), slugging percentage vs. righthanded pitchers (.562), on-base percentage vs. lefthanded pitchers (.476), on-base percentage vs. righthanded pitchers (.403), batting average on a 3-2 count (.389), batting average and hits

Darren Lewis

1999 Season

Darren Lewis might have the worst swing in the major leagues, and his offensive production in 1999 was down from his career-best numbers of the previous year. But hard work, desire and defense have made him an important part of a Red Sox team that has reached the playoffs the last two years. In Lewis' defense, he slumped badly after injuring his left wrist August 14.

Hitting

Lewis' bat drags through the strike zone as if it's going through molten lava, and many of his hits are bloops over infielders' heads. But hard work, including hours with his laptop studying opposing pitchers, has kept him going. Lewis tries to bang the ball up the middle and he tries to keep the ball on the ground. He's a good bunter, both for hits and for sacrifices. He's always willing to give himself up and advance baserunners with groundballs to the right side. Lewis' slow bat sometimes forces him to identify pitches at the last instant and poke them to the right side, but he doesn't swing and miss often.

Baserunning & Defense

Jimy Williams believes that Lewis is the player who got the rest of the Red Sox to buy into the manager's teachings about defense. Though Lewis started only 88 games in center field, his teammates thought he should have won a Gold Glove. His lifetime .995 fielding percentage is the best in major league history among outfielders with at least 1,000 games. Lewis has good range and takes excellent routes to balls. While his arm is below average, he gets rid of balls quickly and tries to hit cutoff men. He's a fine baserunner but not a high-percentage basestealer.

2000 Outlook

Boston's trade for Carl Everett probably spells the end of Lewis' days as an everyday player for the Red Sox. But he'll still be a valuable part of the team, offering quality defense and possibly platooning with Trot Nixon in right field.

Position: CF/RF
Bats: R **Throws:** R
Ht: 6' 0" **Wt:** 190

Opening Day Age: 32
Born: 8/28/67 in Berkeley, CA
ML Seasons: 10

Boston

Overall Statistics

	G	AB	R	H	D	T	HR	RBI	SB	BB	SO	Avg	OBP	Slg
1999	135	470	63	113	14	6	2	40	16	45	52	.240	.311	.309
Career	1117	3568	538	891	113	35	24	306	231	366	444	.250	.325	.321

Where He Hits the Ball

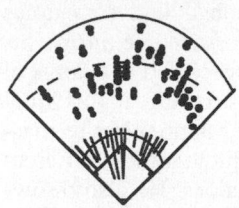 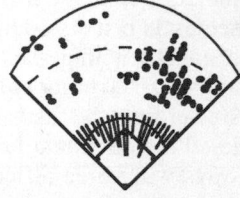

Vs. LHP　　　　**Vs. RHP**

1999 Situational Stats

	AB	H	HR	RBI	Avg		AB	H	HR	RBI	Avg
Home	210	49	1	18	.233	LHP	140	32	1	14	.229
Road	260	64	1	22	.246	RHP	330	81	1	26	.245
First Half	261	68	2	21	.261	Sc Pos	149	31	1	37	.208
Scnd Half	209	45	0	19	.215	Clutch	52	16	1	3	.308

1999 Rankings (American League)

- 2nd in sacrifice bunts (14), lowest slugging percentage vs. lefthanded pitchers (.279), lowest slugging percentage vs. righthanded pitchers (.321) and lowest on-base percentage vs. lefthanded pitchers (.270)
- 3rd in lowest slugging percentage, lowest HR frequency (235.0 ABs per HR) and lowest batting average
- 5th in bunts in play (29), lowest stolen-base percentage (61.5), lowest batting average with runners in scoring position and lowest batting average vs. lefthanded pitchers
- Led the Red Sox in highest groundball/flyball ratio (1.8), stolen-base percentage (61.5), bunts in play (29) and sacrifice bunts (14)

1999 Season

Pedro Martinez may have had the best season in the American League since World War II. In baseball's highest-scoring season since 1936, Martinez' 2.07 ERA was 2.79 runs better than the American League average and 1.37 better than his closest AL competitor, David Cone. Cone's perfect game notwithstanding, Martinez threw the game of the year when he fired a 17-strikeout one-hitter against the Yankees in September. He won his second Cy Young Award and might have won the MVP if not for a couple of short-sighted writers who refused to vote for a pitcher.

Pitching

Martinez has the best stuff in baseball. His stuff includes a 92-98 MPH fastball that sometimes seems as if it's skidding across ice. He throws his changeup with perfect arm speed and at a range of angles, so no hitter knows it's coming. It's 15 MPH slower than the fastball, and Martinez has so mastered the pitch that he can throw it three different ways with three different actions. He also throws his curveball from several different arm angles, and the curve devastated lefthanders in the second half. When Martinez hurt his back in the Division Series, he started throwing cut fastballs from all sorts of arm angles and pitched 13 scoreless, two-hit innings against the Indians and Yankees.

Defense

A decent fielder, Martinez is quick around the mound and has good instincts. His windup, though, makes him an easy target to run on. Though one AL scout claims that he documented Martinez throwing 95 MPH on all five slide steps he tried in one game, he did allow 21 steals in 31 attempts.

2000 Outlook

It's hard to believe now that Red Sox GM Dan Duquette was ripped two years ago for letting Roger Clemens get away as a free agent, then trading for Martinez and handing him a six-year, $75 million contract. That deal is a bargain in the current market, and Martinez is indisputably the best pitcher in the game.

Position: SP
Bats: R **Throws:** R
Ht: 5'11" **Wt:** 170

Opening Day Age: 28
Born: 10/25/71 in Manoguayabo, Dominican Republic
ML Seasons: 8

Overall Statistics

	W	L	Pct.	ERA	G	GS	Sv	IP	H	BB	SO	HR	Ratio
1999	23	4	.852	2.07	31	29	0	213.1	160	37	313	9	0.92
Career	107	50	.682	2.83	249	182	3	1359.1	1050	410	1534	107	1.07

How Often He Throws Strikes

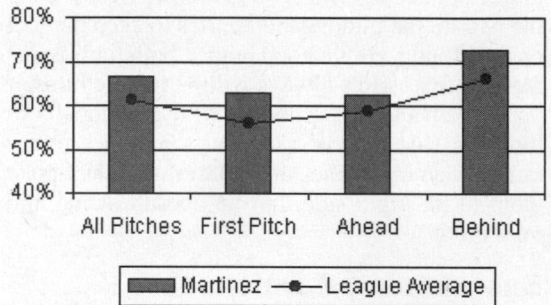

1999 Situational Stats

	W	L	ERA	Sv	IP		AB	H	HR	RBI	Avg
Home	13	2	2.22	0	117.2	LHB	414	92	4	27	.222
Road	10	2	1.88	0	95.2	RHB	366	68	5	24	.186
First Half	15	3	2.10	0	132.2	Sc Pos	167	34	0	41	.204
Scnd Half	8	1	2.01	0	80.2	Clutch	67	9	0	3	.134

1999 Rankings (American League)

- 1st in ERA, wins, strikeouts, winning percentage, highest strikeout/walk ratio (8.5), lowest batting average allowed (.205), lowest slugging percentage allowed (.288), lowest on-base percentage allowed (.248), fewest baserunners allowed per nine innings (8.7), most strikeouts per nine innings (13.2), ERA on the road, lowest batting average allowed vs. righthanded batters and fewest home runs allowed per nine innings (.38)
- Led the Red Sox in ERA, wins, complete games (5), innings pitched, batters faced (835), hit batsmen (9), strikeouts, wild pitches (6), pitches thrown (3,326), winning percentage, highest strikeout/walk ratio (8.5), lowest batting average allowed (.205) and ERA at home

Trot Nixon

1999 Season

At first glance, Trot Nixon had a mediocre rookie season. Fifteen homers and 52 RBI aren't good enough for a corner outfielder in an American League, where they offer counseling to anyone who doesn't knock in 90 runs. But as one GM said at season's end, "Never underestimate the value of a player who always wants to be better and plays the game right every day, which is why you don't want to sell Trot short." Clearly, Red Sox manager Jimy Williams never sold him short, even after Nixon batted .105 in April. Williams' patience paid off in the second half, when Nixon batted .296-12-33 and slugged .587.

Hitting

Back problems caused Nixon to lose his stroke for nearly three minor league seasons, but he slowly has rediscovered it. In the first half last year, he had too many defensive swings and hit too many balls on the ground. As the season went along, Nixon began to heed batting coach Jim Rice's advice to get the ball into the air more consistently. At times Nixon looked like the line-drive hitter who uses the whole field that he was projected to be. He's a dogged competitor who usually doesn't waste an at-bat. Nixon got just 43 at-bats against lefties and batted .116 against them last year, but because he hangs in and can go the other way, there's no reason to think he won't hit them.

Baserunning & Defense

Nixon plays a solid right field. He runs good routes to flyballs and will cut off balls down the line. He has a quick release and an above-average arm. Nixon's speed was more of a factor in the outfield than on the bases in 1999, but he has the wheels to register steals in double digits.

2000 Outlook

Nixon's second-half strides are a sign that the Red Sox should get more production from him in 2000. The trade for Carl Everett could mean that the Sox will platoon Darren Lewis with Nixon.

Position: RF
Bats: L **Throws:** L
Ht: 6' 2"   **Wt:** 200

Opening Day Age: 25
Born: 4/11/74 in Durham, NC
ML Seasons: 3

Overall Statistics

	G	AB	R	H	D	T	HR	RBI	SB	BB	SO	Avg	OBP	Slg
1999	124	381	67	103	22	5	15	52	3	53	75	.270	.357	.472
Career	139	412	72	112	24	5	15	52	4	54	79	.272	.354	.464

Where He Hits the Ball

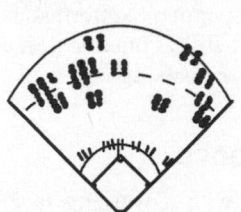

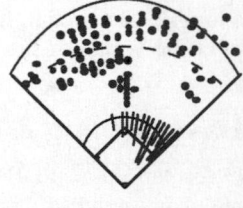

Vs. LHP   **Vs. RHP**

1999 Situational Stats

	AB	H	HR	RBI	Avg		AB	H	HR	RBI	Avg
Home	190	54	3	18	.284	LHP	43	5	1	2	.116
Road	191	49	12	34	.257	RHP	338	98	14	50	.290
First Half	192	47	3	19	.245	Sc Pos	104	23	2	32	.221
Scnd Half	189	56	12	33	.296	Clutch	49	13	3	8	.265

1999 Rankings (American League)
- 1st in lowest batting average with the bases loaded (0.000) and lowest fielding percentage in right field (.968)
- 2nd in errors in right field (7)
- 10th in sacrifice flies (8)
- Led the Red Sox in sacrifice flies (8)

Boston

Jose Offerman

1999 Season

Faced with the pressure of being Boston's only free-agent signing in the wake of Mo Vaughn's departure, Jose Offerman opened the season with six straight multihit games. He ranked second among American League leadoff hitters in on-base percentage, scored 107 runs and led the AL in triples. Except for an abysmal .165 stretch from mid-June to mid-July, Offerman hit .323 the rest of the year.

Hitting

Offerman has impressive bat speed that helps him deliver some power from the top of order. He remains productive from both sides of the plate. He walked 96 times in 1999, the second straight year he set a career high in that department. Offerman is a tough out who will foul off strikes until he gets a pitch he wants or the pitcher gives up and walks him.

Baserunning & Defense

Offerman came to Boston with a warning label about his defense, and his shortcomings led to a brief benching in late July. For the most part, he plays grounders passably, though he sometimes sits back and allows balls to play him. On the other hand, he's in a class right below Roberto Alomar in tracking flyballs into the outfield. Turning the double play has been problematic, because he has a long throwing motion and lacks quick feet. While Offerman is an intelligent hitter and runs the bases well, he's not an effective basestealer. Manager Jimy Williams often used the hit-and-run or bunt to advance him.

2000 Outlook

In the midst of the firestorm over the loss of Vaughn and the $26 million signing of Offerman, Boston GM Dan Duquette said that Offerman would replace Vaughn's on-base percentage. That set off alternate howls of derision and criticism from New England media and fans alike, but Duquette was right. Offerman gave the Red Sox the productive leadoff hitter they lacked. In an era when productive leadoff hitters might be more difficult to find than cleanup hitters, that meant something.

Position: 2B/DH
Bats: B **Throws:** R
Ht: 6' 0" **Wt:** 190

Opening Day Age: 31
Born: 11/8/68 in San Pedro de Macoris, Dominican Republic
ML Seasons: 10

Overall Statistics

	G	AB	R	H	D	T	HR	RBI	SB	BB	SO	Avg	OBP	Slg
1999	149	586	107	172	37	11	8	69	18	96	79	.294	.391	.435
Career	1143	4145	610	1162	186	62	30	381	157	564	661	.280	.366	.377

Where He Hits the Ball

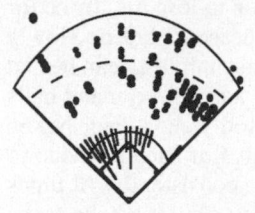 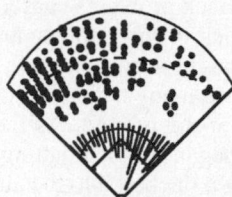

Vs. LHP   **Vs. RHP**

1999 Situational Stats

	AB	H	HR	RBI	Avg		AB	H	HR	RBI	Avg
Home	283	92	5	36	.325	LHP	138	37	3	18	.268
Road	303	80	3	33	.264	RHP	448	135	5	51	.301
First Half	341	93	3	35	.273	Sc Pos	140	39	2	58	.279
Scnd Half	245	79	5	34	.322	Clutch	70	22	0	10	.314

1999 Rankings (American League)

- 1st in triples
- 2nd in on-base percentage for a leadoff hitter (.406)
- 3rd in caught stealing (12) and lowest fielding percentage at second base (.975)
- Led the Red Sox in most pitches seen per plate appearance (3.90), batting average with the bases loaded (.500), on-base percentage for a leadoff hitter (.406), highest percentage of extra bases taken as a runner (55.1), highest percentage of pitches taken (61.6), runs scored, triples, stolen bases, caught stealing (12), walks, times on base (270), pitches seen (2,702) and plate appearances (693)

Troy O'Leary

1999 Season

Claimed off waivers from the Brewers in 1995, Troy O'Leary has become one of Boston's most trusted assets. The big payoff came in 1999, when he had a career year and reached the 100-RBI mark for the first time. In the last three seasons, O'Leary's homers have increased from 15 to 23 to 28; his extra-base hits from 51 to 67 to 68; his RBI from 80 to 83 to 103. He catapulted the Red Sox into the American League Championship Series by twice following intentional walks to Nomar Garciaparra with home runs in Game 5 of the Division Series.

Hitting

Fenway Park is perfect for O'Leary. He stays back and drives balls to the opposite field when he has to, taking full advantage of The Wall. O'Leary uses the entire field when he swings at fastballs. If he's sitting on a pitch and gets it, he'll pull it for power. O'Leary has become a dangerous breaking-ball hitter. He was outstanding last year against lefthanders, batting .346. Power pitchers try to dominate him up in the strike zone and on the inner half. But those periods have decreased each year.

Baserunning & Defense

Not only has O'Leary improved at the plate, he also has made himself a good defensive left fielder. He has learned to play angles and run good routes to balls in the gap. His arm strength is below average but he aggressively charges balls and gets rid of throws quickly. While O'Leary is an adequate runner, he's not a basestealer.

2000 Outlook

Batting behind Garciaparra in the lineup, O'Leary is a key cog in Boston's offense. It will be interesting to see if he can boost his numbers yet again in 2000. He has two seasons remaining on a four-year, $16.5 million contract.

Position: LF
Bats: L **Throws:** L
Ht: 6' 0" **Wt:** 200

Opening Day Age: 30
Born: 8/4/69 in Compton, CA
ML Seasons: 7
Nickname: Yum-Yum

Overall Statistics

	G	AB	R	H	D	T	HR	RBI	SB	BB	SO	Avg	OBP	Slg
1999	157	596	84	167	36	4	28	103	1	56	91	.280	.343	.495
Career	766	2709	384	768	167	28	93	406	12	217	434	.283	.338	.469

Where He Hits the Ball

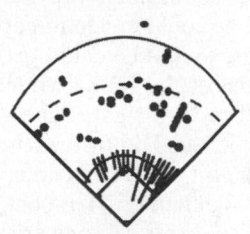

Vs. LHP   **Vs. RHP**

1999 Situational Stats

	AB	H	HR	RBI	Avg		AB	H	HR	RBI	Avg
Home	304	88	13	60	.289	LHP	156	54	4	31	.346
Road	292	79	15	43	.271	RHP	440	113	24	72	.257
First Half	327	97	17	58	.297	Sc Pos	178	58	5	75	.326
Scnd Half	269	70	11	45	.260	Clutch	79	20	4	18	.253

1999 Rankings (American League)

- 2nd in fielding percentage in left field (.993)
- 6th in GDPs (21)
- 7th in batting average vs. lefthanded pitchers
- Led the Red Sox in home runs, at-bats, GDPs (21) and games played
- Led AL left fielders in slugging percentage, batting average vs. lefthanded pitchers, on-base percentage vs. lefthanded pitchers (.415) and GDPs (21)

Boston

Bret Saberhagen

1999 Season

Despite enduring three stints on the disabled list with shoulder and foot injuries, Bret Saberhagen pitched many a huge game for the Red Sox and finished second on the club with 10 victories. By the time Boston reached the postseason, however, this experienced money pitcher could barely throw. He was hammered in three postseason starts, and when it was over Saberhagen faced a third major operation on his shoulder.

Pitching

Early in the season when Saberhagen was strong, he was hitting 92 MPH with some consistency, but the wear and tear on that shoulder took its toll. In several second-half starts, he had to dabble with his curveball and anything else he could create to get through two or three innings, so that he could get loose and get his fastball out of the 82-84 MPH range and closer to 90. When he's right, Saberhagen is the consummate pitcher. His fastball is straight, but he's able to paint it on either corner against both lefthanders and righthanders. His consistent command of the fastball is his calling card, as he walked just 11 in 119 innings in 1999. He also has uncanny control of a terrific changeup, and he'll throw an occasional slider.

Defense

Saberhagen was a high school phenom as a shortstop, and his athleticism and fielding ability make him close to a fifth infielder. He covers first base quickly and keeps runners close. Because he holds the ball well and is quick to the plate, he allowed only five steals in 1999 and has given up just 17 in his last four seasons.

2000 Outlook

A November procedure on Saberhagen's shoulder revealed a partial tear of the rotator cuff—instead of a less-serious fraying of the cuff—and that puts his 2000 season and career at risk. Clearly Saberhagen won't be ready in the spring, and the road back won't be an easy one. Of course, he has made it back before.

Position: SP
Bats: R **Throws:** R
Ht: 6' 1" **Wt:** 200

Opening Day Age: 35
Born: 4/11/64 in Chicago Heights, IL
ML Seasons: 15

Overall Statistics

	W	L	Pct.	ERA	G	GS	Sv	IP	H	BB	SO	HR	Ratio
1999	10	6	.625	2.95	22	22	0	119.0	122	11	81	11	1.12
Career	166	115	.591	3.33	396	368	1	2547.2	2433	471	1705	215	1.14

How Often He Throws Strikes

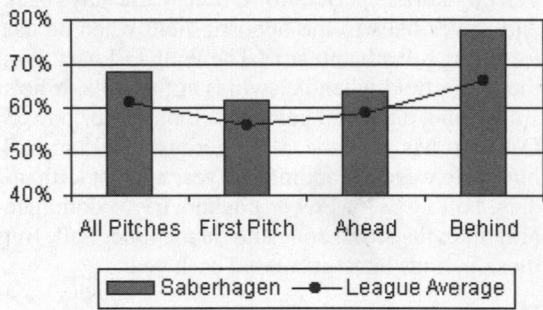

1999 Situational Stats

	W	L	ERA	Sv	IP		AB	H	HR	RBI	Avg
Home	4	5	2.49	0	65.0	LHB	210	58	3	15	.276
Road	6	1	3.50	0	54.0	RHB	251	64	8	25	.255
First Half	6	2	2.31	0	62.1	Sc Pos	99	25	4	31	.253
Scnd Half	4	4	3.65	0	56.2	Clutch	10	4	0	2	.400

1999 Rankings (American League)

- 10th in winning percentage

Mike Stanley

1999 Season

The term "professional" applies to Mike Stanley at the plate, in the field and in the clubhouse. When he struggled through a .206 July, there was speculation that his bat was slowing. Stanley even was benched for a while, only to come back and hit .333 the last five weeks of the season to lead the Red Sox into the playoffs.

Hitting

Stanley is a situational master. He looks for certain pitches and drives them when he gets them. He has enough power to hit fastballs out of the park to center and right-center, and he turns on breaking balls. He tries to get the ball in the air. Stanley always has hit lefties well, slugging .559 against them the last five seasons. He'll sometimes chase fastballs out of the strike zone and go through periods where he struggles against breaking balls from righthanders. He fights in every at-bat and last season posted a .393 on-base percentage, a key factor in maintaining rallies.

Baserunning & Defense

There was a time when teams considered Stanley a DH and occasional third catcher, a position he left because of chronic shoulder problems. Through determination and hard work, he has made himself a decent first baseman. He has good hands and starts the 3-6-3 double play better than most righthanded throwers. Though Stanley's range is limited, he's very sound on pop flies and moving back along the right-field line. He has the speed of a catcher, but is a very intelligent baserunner who seldom overestimates his ability to get around the bases.

2000 Outlook

Stanley is Boston's primary first baseman and part-time DH heading into 2000. As long as he continues to demonstrate that age hasn't taken its toll on his bat speed, he'll remain in the lineup.

Position: 1B/DH
Bats: R **Throws:** R
Ht: 6' 0" **Wt:** 205

Opening Day Age: 36
Born: 6/25/63 in Ft. Lauderdale, FL
ML Seasons: 14

Boston

Overall Statistics

	G	AB	R	H	D	T	HR	RBI	SB	BB	SO	Avg	OBP	Slg
1999	136	427	59	120	22	0	19	72	0	70	94	.281	.393	.466
Career	1377	3940	592	1071	208	7	173	656	13	608	864	.272	.372	.460

Where He Hits the Ball

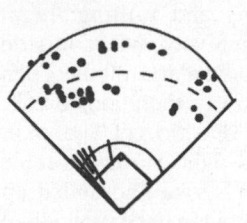

Vs. LHP

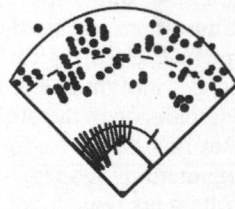

Vs. RHP

1999 Situational Stats

	AB	H	HR	RBI	Avg		AB	H	HR	RBI	Avg
Home	216	56	8	33	.259	LHP	126	38	8	22	.302
Road	211	64	11	39	.303	RHP	301	82	11	50	.272
First Half	260	72	13	45	.277	Sc Pos	125	34	8	56	.272
Scnd Half	167	48	6	27	.287	Clutch	55	13	2	9	.236

1999 Rankings (American League)

- 1st in lowest fielding percentage at first base (.988) and lowest percentage of extra bases taken as a runner (22.2)
- 4th in errors at first base (11) and lowest ground-ball/flyball ratio (0.7)
- 5th in lowest cleanup slugging percentage (.467)
- 9th in hit by pitch (11)
- Led the Red Sox in hit by pitch (11) and strike-outs

John Valentin

1999 Season

In the playoffs, John Valentin looked like the player who had 27 homers and 102 RBI in 1995. But for most of the 1999 season, Valentin played as if he were wounded, and he was. He spent two stints on the disabled list with post-concussion syndrome after a beaning and tendinitis in his left knee, and played just 113 games.

Hitting

Batting coach Jim Rice believed that Valentin got into bad habits last year with a crouch that forced him to hit the ball while standing up, which earned him the talk-show nickname of "Johnny Popup." When he's right, Valentin will hit fastballs a number of ways—sometimes inside-outing inside pitches, sometimes turning and pulling them, sometimes going the other way with outside pitches. He'll try to take advantage of the open spaces in right-center in Fenway, then hook breaking balls up in the air in the direction of The Wall. But in 1999 he seldom was right. He had trouble maintaining his right-center stroke and ended up rolling his wrists over, resulting in easy groundball outs.

Baserunning & Defense

When healthy, Valentin is a solid, underrated defensive third baseman. In 1998, he went 65 games without an error. He has the hands of a former shortstop and knows the limits of his arm. His knee problems cut down on his range, giving him problems charging balls and sometimes causing offline throws because of his altered footwork. His knee bothered him so much that he has become one of the slowest runners in the American League.

2000 Outlook

In November, Valentin finally had his ailing left knee arthroscoped, an operation that may or may not restart a stalled career. He maintains that he couldn't hit or set to throw correctly for all of 1999 because of his knee ailment, so perhaps 2000 will be his renaissance. If he stumbles, prospect Wilton Veras will put some pressure on Valentin at third base.

Position: 3B
Bats: R **Throws:** R
Ht: 6' 0" **Wt:** 185

Opening Day Age: 33
Born: 2/18/67 in Mineola, NY
ML Seasons: 8
Pronunciation: VAL-en-tin
Nickname: Val

Overall Statistics

	G	AB	R	H	D	T	HR	RBI	SB	BB	SO	Avg	OBP	Slg
1999	113	450	58	114	27	1	12	70	0	40	68	.253	.315	.398
Career	961	3614	582	1022	263	17	118	521	47	430	474	.283	.362	.463

Where He Hits the Ball

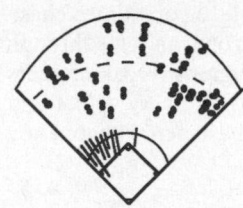
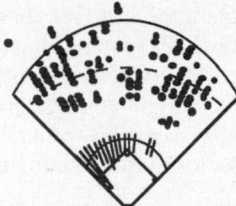

Vs. LHP   **Vs. RHP**

1999 Situational Stats

	AB	H	HR	RBI	Avg		AB	H	HR	RBI	Avg
Home	238	60	5	41	.252	LHP	94	26	0	4	.277
Road	212	54	7	29	.255	RHP	356	88	12	66	.247
First Half	274	70	7	44	.255	Sc Pos	119	35	5	57	.294
Scnd Half	176	44	5	26	.250	Clutch	59	15	1	11	.254

1999 Rankings (American League)

- 4th in fielding percentage at third base (.954)
- 6th in lowest on-base percentage vs. righthanded pitchers (.307)
- 7th in errors at third base (14)
- 8th in lowest batting average
- 9th in lowest groundball/flyball ratio (0.8)
- 10th in sacrifice flies (8), lowest on-base percentage, lowest batting average vs. righthanded pitchers and lowest batting average at home
- Led the Red Sox in sacrifice flies (8)

Jason Varitek

1999 Season

After seeing Jason Varitek blossom in the second half of 1999, it's hard to imagine Red Sox GM Dan Duquette making a better trade than the one that sent Heathcliff Slocumb to Seattle for Derek Lowe and Varitek in July 1997. With platoon partner Scott Hatteberg sidelined by bone chips in his elbow, Varitek played regularly for the first time in the major leagues. By the end of last season, virtually everyone in the American League realized that he's second only to Pudge Rodriguez among Junior Circuit backstops.

Hitting

Coming out of Georgia Tech, Varitek had a long, looping aluminum-bat swing, and the two-year process to get him signed and playing professionally may have set him back. But Varitek is very smart and an attentive listener, and he shortened his stroke. In 1999, he batted for a higher average from the right side and showed more power from the left. Red Sox coaches believe he has such leg-drive potential that once he's completed the progression from an arm hitter to a leg hitter, he'll have tape-measure power. Varitek will chase high fastballs and low breaking balls at times.

Baserunning & Defense

Varitek's catching is the reason he's one of the most valued members of the Red Sox. He studies the opposition and his own pitchers, and he works hard to get on the same wavelength with his battery-mates. He's an improved receiver who blocks pitches and is willing to take the statistical beating of handling Tim Wakefield's knuckleball. Varitek steals a base or two each year, but his baserunning is more about hustle than speed.

2000 Outlook

Varitek is one of Boston's clubhouse leaders, and the club thinks his ceiling is 35 homers and 100-plus RBIs. If he approaches the improvement he made in 1999, he'll become a star.

Position: C
Bats: B **Throws:** R
Ht: 6' 2" **Wt:** 220

Opening Day Age: 27
Born: 4/11/72 in Rochester, MN
ML Seasons: 3
Pronunciation: VARE-ih-tek

Overall Statistics

	G	AB	R	H	D	T	HR	RBI	SB	BB	SO	Avg	OBP	Slg
1999	144	483	70	130	39	2	20	76	1	46	85	.269	.330	.482
Career	231	705	101	187	52	2	27	109	3	63	130	.265	.324	.460

Where He Hits the Ball

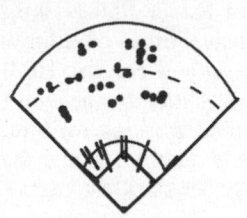

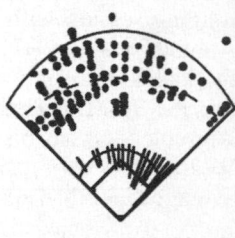

Vs. LHP   **Vs. RHP**

1999 Situational Stats

	AB	H	HR	RBI	Avg		AB	H	HR	RBI	Avg
Home	248	78	12	45	.315	LHP	103	29	3	19	.282
Road	235	52	8	31	.221	RHP	380	101	17	57	.266
First Half	259	63	9	31	.243	Sc Pos	120	27	2	48	.225
Scnd Half	224	67	11	45	.299	Clutch	70	19	3	15	.271

1999 Rankings (American League)

- 1st in errors at catcher (11) and lowest batting average on the road
- 4th in lowest fielding percentage at catcher (.990)
- 6th in lowest percentage of extra bases taken as a runner (29.8)
- 9th in doubles
- 10th in sacrifice flies (8)
- Led the Red Sox in sacrifice flies (8)
- Led AL catchers in doubles and games played (144)

Boston

Tim Wakefield

Position: RP/SP
Bats: R **Throws:** R
Ht: 6' 2" **Wt:** 210

Opening Day Age: 33
Born: 8/2/66 in Melbourne, FL
ML Seasons: 7

1999 Season

When the Red Sox took Tim Wakefield off their American League Championship Series roster, manager Jimy Williams offered his knuckleballer this apology: "We wouldn't be here without you." Wakefield began and ended the regular season as a starter. In between, he moved into the closer role and had 15 saves in 18 opportunities to keep the Red Sox in the race. Still, it was hardly Wakefield's best season. He went just 5-9, 5.86 as a starter.

Pitching

There were several theories as to why Wakefield didn't succeed with his trademark knuckleball in 1999. One was that he lost the feel of his delivery, which means he probably will need another spring-training session with Hall of Famer Phil Niekro. Another was that Wakefield sometimes overthrew the knuckler, losing movement and control. He'll mix in a 78-MPH fastball and a slider, but he won't win unless he has his flutterball working for him. Wakefield is very resilient and durable, though he averaged less than six innings per start last year.

Defense

Wakefield is a solid fielder but must learn to cope with runners. Obviously, basestealers are a problem for any knuckleballer. But Wakefield, a converted first baseman, is athletic and has a good slide step, so there's no reason why he should have allowed 35 stolen bases in 41 attempts last year. Those steals sometimes unnerved Wakefield, who isn't blessed with extraordinary self-confidence.

2000 Outlook

The Pirates cast aside Wakefield after a 6-11 season in 1993, and he's coming off another 6-11 campaign. While he was invaluable as a closer role last season, it's critical that he re-establish himself as a starter this spring, especially with Bret Saberhagen's status uncertain. Wakefield has rebounded before and there's no reason he can't do so again.

Overall Statistics

	W	L	Pct.	ERA	G	GS	Sv	IP	H	BB	SO	HR	Ratio
1999	6	11	.353	5.08	49	17	15	140.0	146	72	104	19	1.56
Career	79	67	.541	4.34	216	171	15	1184.2	1172	506	770	150	1.42

How Often He Throws Strikes

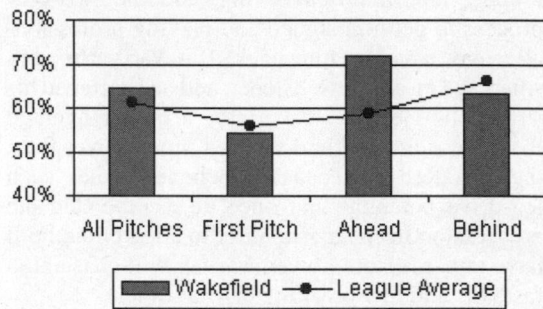

Wakefield — League Average

1999 Situational Stats

	W	L	ERA	Sv	IP		AB	H	HR	RBI	Avg
Home	2	6	4.04	9	69.0	LHB	229	65	7	33	.284
Road	4	5	6.08	6	71.0	RHB	319	81	12	46	.254
First Half	3	7	5.14	10	77.0	Sc Pos	155	41	7	61	.265
Scnd Half	3	4	5.00	5	63.0	Clutch	89	19	3	10	.213

1999 Rankings (American League)

- 2nd in stolen bases allowed (35)
- 5th in lowest winning percentage
- Led the Red Sox in saves, walks allowed and stolen bases allowed (35)

Rod Beck

Position: RP
Bats: R **Throws:** R
Ht: 6' 1" **Wt:** 235

Opening Day Age: 31
Born: 8/3/68 in
Burbank, CA
ML Seasons: 9
Nickname: Shooter

Overall Statistics

	W	L	Pct.	ERA	G	GS	Sv	IP	H	BB	SO	HR	Ratio
1999	2	5	.286	5.93	43	0	10	44.0	50	18	25	5	1.55
Career	26	37	.413	3.20	540	0	260	587.1	540	131	499	68	1.14

1999 Situational Stats

	W	L	ERA	Sv	IP		AB	H	HR	RBI	Avg
Home	1	2	8.10	5	20.0	LHB	77	22	1	9	.286
Road	1	3	4.13	5	24.0	RHB	96	28	4	19	.292
First Half	2	4	10.54	7	13.2	Sc Pos	39	13	1	20	.333
Scnd Half	0	1	3.86	3	30.1	Clutch	89	28	2	18	.315

1999 Season

Coming off a heroic 51-save season, Rod Beck opened 1999 as the Cubs' closer. He missed two months after having bone chips removed from his elbow in May, and was traded to Boston on August 31 for Mark Guthrie and Cole Liniak. He pitched very well in September, but gave up a killing homer to Bernie Williams in the 10th inning of the American League Championship Series opener.

Pitching & Defense

Beck's fastball returned to 87-88 MPH by the end of last season. He likes to get ahead in the count, then get hitters to chase his splitter out of the strike zone. Most batters sit on his fastball and hope for a mistake. Beck has the toughness and guile to get by with mediocre stuff. He's a decent if slow fielder who doesn't stifle the running game very well.

2000 Outlook

With Tom Gordon sidelined, it's possible that the Red Sox will let Derek Lowe do the dirty work in the seventh and eighth innings and close games with Beck. It's also possible that American League lineups are too deep and the ballparks too small for him.

Rheal Cormier

Position: RP
Bats: L **Throws:** L
Ht: 5'10" **Wt:** 187

Opening Day Age: 32
Born: 4/23/67 in
Moncton, Canada
ML Seasons: 8
Pronunciation: RAY-al KOR-mee-ay

Overall Statistics

	W	L	Pct.	ERA	G	GS	Sv	IP	H	BB	SO	HR	Ratio
1999	2	0	1.000	3.69	60	0	0	63.1	61	18	39	4	1.25
Career	40	39	.506	4.14	229	108	0	778.0	832	166	464	77	1.28

1999 Situational Stats

	W	L	ERA	Sv	IP		AB	H	HR	RBI	Avg
Home	1	0	3.90	0	30.0	LHB	96	19	1	18	.198
Road	1	0	3.51	0	33.1	RHB	152	42	3	13	.276
First Half	1	0	4.24	0	34.0	Sc Pos	82	19	2	28	.232
Scnd Half	1	0	3.07	0	29.1	Clutch	76	17	1	7	.224

1999 Season

Rheal Cormier underwent complex elbow surgery in 1997 and pitched a grand total of 10 Triple-A innings the following year before signing a minor league deal with the Red Sox. Used cautiously by manager Jimy Williams, Cormier gradually regained both his velocity and the tight rotation on his breaking ball. He was one of the American League's most effective lefthanded relievers and a big reason Boston made it all the way to the American League Championship Series.

Pitching & Defense

Cormier throws a hard sinker and a tight slider, and he uses a splitter against righthanders. He paints the outside corner against lefties, holding them last year to a .198 average and just six walks in 103 plate appearances. He induces doubles plays with his sinker. Cormier is an agile fielder and has a decent move to first base.

2000 Outlook

Cormier clearly has found a niche in the Boston bullpen in 2000. The Red Sox should get a lot of mileage out of him if he remains healthy.

Rich Garces

Position: RP
Bats: R **Throws:** R
Ht: 6' 0" **Wt:** 215

Opening Day Age: 28
Born: 5/18/71 in
Maracay, Venezuela
ML Seasons: 7
Nickname: El Sapo
Pronunciation:
GARR-suss

Overall Statistics

	W	L	Pct.	ERA	G	GS	Sv	IP	H	BB	SO	HR	Ratio
1999	5	1	.833	1.55	30	0	2	40.2	25	18	33	1	1.06
Career	9	7	.563	3.43	135	0	5	178.1	150	104	160	15	1.42

1999 Situational Stats

	W	L	ERA	Sv	IP		AB	H	HR	RBI	Avg
Home	3	1	1.50	1	24.0	LHB	66	13	0	2	.197
Road	2	0	1.62	1	16.2	RHB	80	12	1	5	.150
First Half	0	0	0.00	0	1.1	Sc Pos	40	5	0	6	.125
Scnd Half	5	1	1.60	2	39.1	Clutch	45	6	0	2	.133

1999 Season

By the time baseball finally ended in New England in mid-October, Rich Garces had become a cult hero. Promoted from Triple-A in July, he quickly became one of the American League's most effective setup men. Garces was used in any inning to shut down rallies, keep games close and give the Red Sox a chance to win.

Pitching & Defense

Recurring elbow problems hurt Garces' effectiveness in both 1997 and '98, but he has regained the stuff that once made him the Twins' best prospect. He can reach 92-93 MPH with his fastball. When effective, his curveball has a hard, nasty bite, and he uses a splitter as his strikeout pitch when he gets ahead in the count. He can be used against both lefthanders and righthanders. Garces' weight restricts his mobility in the field, and he's easy to run on.

2000 Outlook

The Red Sox will start the season without closer Tom Gordon, so they hope that Garces can carry over his success from 1999. If his elbow holds up, that shouldn't be a problem.

Scott Hatteberg

Position: C
Bats: L **Throws:** R
Ht: 6' 1" **Wt:** 205

Opening Day Age: 30
Born: 12/14/69 in
Salem, OR
ML Seasons: 5

Overall Statistics

	G	AB	R	H	D	T	HR	RBI	SB	BB	SO	Avg	OBP	Slg
1999	30	80	12	22	5	0	1	11	0	18	14	.275	.410	.375
Career	268	802	108	221	52	2	23	98	0	104	144	.276	.362	.431

1999 Situational Stats

	AB	H	HR	RBI	Avg		AB	H	HR	RBI	Avg
Home	42	12	1	8	.286	LHP	15	4	0	2	.267
Road	38	10	0	3	.263	RHP	65	18	1	9	.277
First Half	25	4	0	3	.160	Sc Pos	22	9	0	10	.409
Scnd Half	55	18	1	8	.327	Clutch	6	2	0	0	.333

1999 Season

Scott Hatteberg lost his grip on the lefthanded-hitting half of the Boston catching job in 1999. An elbow ailment led to two trips on the disabled list and eventual surgery to repair nerve damage, allowing Jason Varitek to become the club's full-time backstop.

Hitting, Baserunning & Defense

Hatteberg has an uppercut swing that utilizes all of Fenway Park. He might drive a ball off The Wall or jerk a pitch into the seats down the short right-field line. He's very patient and walks almost as much as he strikes out. Defensively, Hatteberg's strong suit has been his work with pitchers. His ability to block pitches and his throwing arm have been average, and his arm will be called into question after his surgery. He doesn't run well.

2000 Outlook

Hatteberg was rehabbing his elbow while Varitek was producing a breakout season. The question is whether Hatteberg can re-establish himself as a catcher with a significant role in Boston. To his credit, he hit .327 in 55 at-bats upon returning in mid-August, but becoming a regular eventually may require a relocation.

Butch Huskey

Position: DH/LF/RF/1B
Bats: R **Throws:** R
Ht: 6' 3" **Wt:** 244

Opening Day Age: 28
Born: 11/10/71 in
Anadarko, OK
ML Seasons: 6

Overall Statistics

	G	AB	R	H	D	T	HR	RBI	SB	BB	SO	Avg	OBP	Slg
1999	119	386	62	109	15	0	22	77	3	34	65	.282	.338	.492
Career	533	1771	219	475	77	4	77	291	20	123	321	.268	.313	.447

1999 Situational Stats

	AB	H	HR	RBI	Avg			AB	H	HR	RBI	Avg
Home	184	57	9	39	.310	LHP		110	36	9	29	.327
Road	202	52	13	38	.257	RHP		276	73	13	48	.264
First Half	242	72	15	49	.298	Sc Pos		115	34	8	56	.296
Scnd Half	144	37	7	28	.257	Clutch		46	10	2	7	.217

1999 Season

In search of some righthanded power, the Red Sox took a flyer on Butch Huskey at the trading deadline, picking him up from Seattle for minor league lefthander Rob Ramsay. Huskey pounded lefthanders and finished with respectable numbers, though he slumped in September.

Hitting, Baserunning & Defense

Huskey is a classic mistake hitter. He'll hammer mediocre fastballs and hanging breaking balls, and he can turn on inside pitches from lefthanders. Righthanders bust him inside with hard stuff, then get him to chase bad breaking balls away. Huskey isn't a burner or a basestealer, but he can go first to third once he gets up a head of speed. His athleticism is underrated. Huskey isn't a drawback in the outfield and has a good arm, but his poor hands cost him as a first baseman.

2000 Outlook

If Huskey got more playing time, he might learn to use the whole field and become a productive everyday player. But he has been much more productive against lefties than righties, so he may be slotted as a platoon player.

Derek Lowe

Position: RP
Bats: R **Throws:** R
Ht: 6' 6" **Wt:** 200

Opening Day Age: 26
Born: 6/1/73 in
Dearborn, MI
ML Seasons: 3

Overall Statistics

	W	L	Pct.	ERA	G	GS	Sv	IP	H	BB	SO	HR	Ratio
1999	6	3	.667	2.63	74	0	15	109.1	84	25	80	7	1.00
Career	11	18	.379	4.00	157	19	19	301.1	284	90	209	23	1.24

1999 Situational Stats

	W	L	ERA	Sv	IP			AB	H	HR	RBI	Avg
Home	5	0	2.01	8	53.2	LHB		181	42	4	22	.232
Road	1	3	3.23	7	55.2	RHB		223	42	3	21	.188
First Half	0	2	3.04	4	56.1	Sc Pos		109	22	1	36	.202
Scnd Half	6	1	2.21	11	53.0	Clutch		211	45	4	28	.213

1999 Season

Derek Lowe was Boston's second-most valuable pitcher last year. The Red Sox used him whenever the game was on the line, whether it was the second inning or the ninth. Lowe's 109.1 innings led all relievers, his 2.63 ERA was remarkable, and he had 22 holds and 15 saves. Many of his saves required more than one inning of work.

Pitching & Defense

Lowe has three above-average pitches: a sinker, curveball and change. His sinker is as good as it gets. It has hard, boring action and is nearly impossible to put into the air. By the end of the season, he could throw his curveball in any count, and it buckles hitters' knees. Batters have trouble picking up his changeup. Lowe is adequate defensively but doesn't control the running game very well.

2000 Outlook

Catcher Jason Varitek thinks Lowe could be a 20-game winner, but because of age and injuries in Boston's bullpen, he'll begin 2000 as a reliever. The Red Sox probably will let Lowe do most of the dirty work and let Rod Beck handle the easy ninth-inning saves.

Boston

Ramon Martinez

Position: SP
Bats: B **Throws:** R
Ht: 6' 4" **Wt:** 184

Opening Day Age: 32
Born: 3/22/68 in Santo Domingo, Dominican Republic
ML Seasons: 12

Overall Statistics

	W	L	Pct.	ERA	G	GS	Sv	IP	H	BB	SO	HR	Ratio
1999	2	1	.667	3.05	4	4	0	20.2	14	8	15	2	1.06
Career	125	78	.616	3.44	270	266	0	1752.1	1532	712	1329	150	1.28

1999 Situational Stats

	W	L	ERA	Sv	IP		AB	H	HR	RBI	Avg
Home	1	1	3.60	0	10.0	LHB	33	6	1	3	.182
Road	1	0	2.53	0	10.2	RHB	40	8	1	4	.200
First Half	0	0	-	0	0.0	Sc Pos	17	2	1	5	.118
Scnd Half	2	1	3.05	0	20.2	Clutch	4	1	0	0	.250

1999 Season

Boston signed Ramon Martinez to a minor league contract in March, knowing he would miss at least the first half after having rotator-cuff surgery in June 1998. He didn't make it back until September. His first two starts were brief and rocky, but he wrapped up the regular season with two impressive wins over Baltimore. Behind his younger brother Pedro, Ramon was Boston's second-best starter in the postseason.

Pitching & Defense

By the time the playoffs rolled around, Martinez had his fastball back into the 90s. It's a pitch he has to have, and it's very effective because of its sharp tailing action. He also works with a solid changeup and an average slurve. There's nothing special about his defensive work, but Martinez is adequate when fielding the ball and holding runners.

2000 Outlook

His work in September and October suggests the Red Sox will benefit greatly from having both Martinezes at the front of their 2000 rotation. Ramon should survive the difficulties of pitching in Fenway Park, especially if the velocity on his fastball reaches the mid-90s as he regains arm strength.

Kent Mercker

Position: SP
Bats: L **Throws:** L
Ht: 6' 2" **Wt:** 200

Opening Day Age: 32
Born: 2/1/68 in Dublin, OH
ML Seasons: 11

Overall Statistics

	W	L	Pct.	ERA	G	GS	Sv	IP	H	BB	SO	HR	Ratio
1999	8	5	.615	4.80	30	23	0	129.1	148	64	81	16	1.64
Career	62	58	.517	4.20	345	143	19	1021.0	1005	459	683	105	1.43

1999 Situational Stats

	W	L	ERA	Sv	IP		AB	H	HR	RBI	Avg
Home	4	4	5.12	0	82.2	LHB	135	40	2	15	.296
Road	4	1	4.24	0	46.2	RHB	375	108	14	60	.288
First Half	2	4	5.87	0	61.1	Sc Pos	127	38	5	55	.299
Scnd Half	6	1	3.84	0	68.0	Clutch	14	7	1	2	.500

1999 Season

Kent Mercker recovered from an awful start to pitch decently in the Cardinals rotation before being traded to the Red Sox on August 24 for a pair of fringe prospects. He pitched well in two starts for Boston before pulling a ribcage muscle that sidelined him for most of September. He returned in time to win the wild-card clincher on September 29, but fared poorly in two postseason starts.

Pitching & Defense

Unlike most lefties, Mercker can touch the low 90s with a fastball that he can cut or sink. He mixes in a solid curveball and changeup, which gives him a decent arsenal. Still, batters have hit .301 against Mercker the last two seasons. Control problems have been a chronic concern. He's a so-so fielder and permitted just three steals in 12 attempts in 1999.

2000 Outlook

Mercker won't return to Boston after he declared free agency and the club didn't offer him arbitration. His numbers usually aren't pretty, but he has won enough in recent years to keep teams interested in him. He's a fourth or fifth starter at best.

Pat Rapp

Position: SP/RP
Bats: R **Throws:** R
Ht: 6' 3" **Wt:** 215

Opening Day Age: 32
Born: 7/13/67 in
Jennings, LA
ML Seasons: 8

Overall Statistics

	W	L	Pct.	ERA	G	GS	Sv	IP	H	BB	SO	HR	Ratio
1999	6	7	.462	4.12	37	26	0	146.1	147	69	90	13	1.48
Career	56	67	.455	4.46	197	181	0	1043.1	1096	529	637	95	1.56

1999 Situational Stats

	W	L	ERA	Sv	IP		AB	H	HR	RBI	Avg
Home	2	4	6.15	0	67.1	LHB	289	76	6	33	.263
Road	4	3	2.39	0	79.0	RHB	270	71	7	29	.263
First Half	2	5	5.17	0	71.1	Sc Pos	146	35	2	45	.240
Scnd Half	4	2	3.12	0	75.0	Clutch	16	4	0	0	.250

1999 Season

Signed to a one-year, $1.2 million contract as a free agent, Pat Rapp finished second to Pedro Martinez in games started for the Red Sox. Though he didn't make the Division Series roster, Rapp's 4.36 ERA as a starter was well below the American League average, and his ERA after the All-Star break was 3.12.

Pitching & Defense

Rapp throws mostly cutters, and he also has a running fastball and a decent curveball. He's able to get the cutter in on lefthanders so they hit him no better than righthanders. He keeps the ball down and gets a lot of groundballs. Rapp gets into trouble when his delivery gets out of sync. He's not athletic, so fielding his position is sometimes a problem. He's slow to the plate and baserunners took advantage last season.

2000 Outlook

The Red Sox chose not to pick up Rapp's $3 million option for 2000, making him a free agent. While he doesn't work deep into games and inconsistency has kept him from putting together a big season, he's still valuable because he eats innings.

Brian Rose

Position: SP
Bats: R **Throws:** R
Ht: 6' 3" **Wt:** 215

Opening Day Age: 24
Born: 2/13/76 in New
Bedford, MA
ML Seasons: 3

Overall Statistics

	W	L	Pct.	ERA	G	GS	Sv	IP	H	BB	SO	HR	Ratio
1999	7	6	.538	4.87	22	18	0	98.0	112	29	51	19	1.44
Career	8	10	.444	5.58	31	27	0	138.2	160	45	72	28	1.48

1999 Situational Stats

	W	L	ERA	Sv	IP		AB	H	HR	RBI	Avg
Home	4	0	4.47	0	50.1	LHB	191	42	6	13	.220
Road	3	6	5.29	0	47.2	RHB	209	70	13	44	.335
First Half	4	2	3.77	0	59.2	Sc Pos	106	30	5	41	.283
Scnd Half	3	4	6.57	0	38.1	Clutch	14	2	1	1	.143

1999 Season

Called up from Triple-A on May 19 with the Boston staff in chaos, Brian Rose threw seven shutout innings against the Yankees. Rose went 4-0, 1.47 in his first seven starts, then hit the wall. He went 3-6, 7.47 the rest of the season, which included another four weeks in the minors.

Pitching & Defense

Rose has basic stuff: an 88-90 MPH fastball, a slider, an occasional curveball and a changeup. He'll throw the change in any count in any situation, and that was the pitch that made him so good in his first month around the American League. Even when he hit the skids, his changeup was an out pitch against lefthanders. Rose ran out of gas and tried to compensate by overthrowing, which compromised the outstanding command he demonstrated early in the season. He needs to work on fielding and controlling the running game.

2000 Outlook

The Red Sox still believe that Rose can be a No. 3 starter. His detractors think he's just Dave Eiland in a Boston cap, an OK pitcher who lacks an above-average pitch to get him out of trouble.

Other Boston Red Sox

Damon Buford (**Pos**: CF, **Age**: 29, **Bats**: R)

	G	AB	R	H	D	T	HR	RBI	SB	BB	SO	Avg	OBP	Slg
1999	91	297	39	72	15	2	6	38	9	21	74	.242	.294	.367
Career	514	1273	205	309	66	6	36	162	52	122	289	.243	.312	.389

After a productive 1998 as a part-timer (.282-10-42), Buford's average dropped 40 points in '99. The Cubs traded Manny Alexander to Boston in December to get Buford, whom they'll start in center. 2000 Outlook: B

Kirk Bullinger (**Pos**: RHP, **Age**: 30)

	W	L	Pct.	ERA	G	GS	Sv	IP	H	BB	SO	HR	Ratio
1999	0	0	-	4.50	4	0	0	2.0	2	2	0	0	2.00
Career	1	0	1.000	8.00	12	0	0	9.0	16	2	2	1	2.00

In the last five seasons, Bullinger hasn't posted an overall ERA above 2.36 in the high minors. He earned 25 saves and had a 1.81 ERA between Double-A and Triple-A in '99. Now he's a free agent. 2000 Outlook: C

Bryce Florie (**Pos**: RHP, **Age**: 29)

	W	L	Pct.	ERA	G	GS	Sv	IP	H	BB	SO	HR	Ratio
1999	4	1	.800	4.65	41	5	0	81.1	94	35	65	8	1.59
Career	20	19	.513	4.32	225	29	1	435.2	431	217	354	40	1.49

After working primarily as a starter in Detroit during the second half of 1998, Florie opened with a start and a win in '99. Then he was back in the pen and was traded to Boston in July. 2000 Outlook: B

Chad Fonville (**Pos**: 2B, **Age**: 29, **Bats**: B)

	G	AB	R	H	D	T	HR	RBI	SB	BB	SO	Avg	OBP	Slg
1999	3	2	1	0	0	0	0	0	1	2	0	.000	.500	.000
Career	226	546	80	133	10	2	0	31	30	45	77	.244	.302	.269

Fonville is an excellent defensive player who managed to stick in the bigs during the mid-1990s because of his glove. In the high minors, he never has hit higher than .253, and he has absolutely no power. 2000 Outlook: C

Jeff Frye (**Pos**: 2B, **Age**: 33, **Bats**: R)

	G	AB	R	H	D	T	HR	RBI	SB	BB	SO	Avg	OBP	Slg
1999	41	114	14	32	3	0	1	12	2	14	11	.281	.362	.333
Career	487	1654	243	483	110	10	13	163	49	164	207	.292	.358	.394

For a second straight season, Frye's left knee sidelined him for a long stretch. He had surgery in mid-June and returned on September 1. He hit when he was healthy, so he's in the mix for playing time. 2000 Outlook: B

Tom Gordon (**Pos**: RHP, **Age**: 32)

	W	L	Pct.	ERA	G	GS	Sv	IP	H	BB	SO	HR	Ratio
1999	0	2	.000	5.60	21	0	11	17.2	17	12	24	2	1.64
Career	104	96	.520	4.15	444	203	71	1645.0	1516	807	1431	133	1.41

A tender elbow sidelined Gordon in April. He returned in May, but the pain forced a shutdown in June. The Bosox said he didn't need an operation, but he had Tommy John surgery and probably will miss this entire season. 2000 Outlook: D

Kip Gross (**Pos**: RHP, **Age**: 35)

	W	L	Pct.	ERA	G	GS	Sv	IP	H	BB	SO	HR	Ratio
1999	0	2	.000	7.82	11	1	0	12.2	15	8	9	3	1.82
Career	7	7	.500	3.70	71	11	0	143.1	159	64	78	12	1.56

After five seasons in Japan, Gross made his first major league appearance since 1993. It was a rocky return and a broken hand sidelined him in May. He finished 1999 in Triple-A and was released. 2000 Outlook: C

Creighton Gubanich (**Pos**: C, **Age**: 28, **Bats**: R)

	G	AB	R	H	D	T	HR	RBI	SB	BB	SO	Avg	OBP	Slg
1999	18	47	4	13	2	1	1	11	0	3	13	.277	.346	.426
Career	18	47	4	13	2	1	1	11	0	3	13	.277	.346	.426

After Scott Hatteberg went down with a bad elbow, Gubanich bounced between Triple-A and Boston in 1999. He hit for average with little power at both locales. He has signed with Milwaukee. 2000 Outlook: C

Tim Harikkala (**Pos**: RHP, **Age**: 28)

	W	L	Pct.	ERA	G	GS	Sv	IP	H	BB	SO	HR	Ratio
1999	1	1	.500	6.23	7	0	0	13.0	15	6	7	0	1.62
Career	1	2	.333	9.15	9	1	0	20.2	26	9	9	2	1.69

Harikkala is 22-37, 5.06 in five Triple-A seasons. He's a control pitcher who wasn't any more successful at Triple-A Pawtucket or in Boston in 1999 than he was in four Pacific Coast League seasons. 2000 Outlook: C

Reggie Jefferson (**Pos**: DH, **Age**: 31, **Bats**: L)

	G	AB	R	H	D	T	HR	RBI	SB	BB	SO	Avg	OBP	Slg
1999	83	206	21	57	13	1	5	17	0	17	54	.277	.338	.422
Career	680	2123	285	637	131	11	72	300	2	146	451	.300	.349	.474

Jefferson's 1999 season began with a stint on the disabled list with a lower back strain. He hit well when he returned, but played less as the year wore on. He's a free agent looking for a new home. 2000 Outlook: B

Lou Merloni (**Pos**: SS, **Age**: 28, **Bats**: R)

	G	AB	R	H	D	T	HR	RBI	SB	BB	SO	Avg	OBP	Slg
1999	43	126	18	32	7	0	1	13	0	8	16	.254	.307	.333
Career	82	222	28	59	13	0	2	28	1	15	36	.266	.322	.351

Once again Merloni benefited from injuries to Jeff Frye, getting promoted when Frye was sidelined in mid-June. But Merloni doesn't have much pop and his glove is average. He was sold to Japan's Yokohama BayStars in November. 2000 Outlook: D

Jon Nunnally (**Pos**: DH, **Age**: 28, **Bats**: L)

	G	AB	R	H	D	T	HR	RBI	SB	BB	SO	Avg	OBP	Slg
1999	10	14	4	4	1	0	0	1	0	0	6	.286	.286	.357
Career	316	811	146	204	42	11	40	119	16	129	213	.252	.356	.478

Nunnally's 1999 season began with a trade from Cincinnati to Boston for minor league righthander Pat Flury, and ended with a November trade from the Red Sox to the Mets for Jermaine Allensworth. In between, Nunnally hit .267-23-76 with 85 walks and 26 steals in Triple-A. 2000 Outlook: B

Mark Portugal (Pos: RHP, Age: 37)

	W	L	Pct.	ERA	G	GS	Sv	IP	H	BB	SO	HR	Ratio
1999	7	12	.368	5.51	31	27	0	150.1	179	41	79	28	1.46
Career	109	95	.534	4.03	346	283	5	1826.1	1813	607	1134	209	1.33

Portugal's ERA has been creeping upward in recent seasons, and he's now giving up more hits than innings pitched. He considered retirement when he struggled early in 1999, and the Red Sox cut him in September. 2000 Outlook: C

Donnie Sadler (Pos: SS, Age: 24, Bats: R)

	G	AB	R	H	D	T	HR	RBI	SB	BB	SO	Avg	OBP	Slg
1999	49	107	18	30	5	1	0	4	2	5	20	.280	.313	.346
Career	107	231	39	58	9	5	3	19	6	11	48	.251	.293	.372

Sadler hadn't done much in the high minors prior to 1999, but he hit .291 and boosted his power in Triple-A last summer. Then he hit .321 in his second '99 stint with the Sox, beginning in July. 2000 Outlook: B

Marino Santana (Pos: RHP, Age: 27)

	W	L	Pct.	ERA	G	GS	Sv	IP	H	BB	SO	HR	Ratio
1999	0	0	-	15.75	3	0	0	4.0	8	3	4	3	2.75
Career	0	0	-	7.94	10	0	0	11.1	17	11	14	4	2.47

Santana has turned in incredible back-to-back seasons in Triple-A ball, but he was bounced around in three July appearances with Boston. He became a free agent at the end of the season. 2000 Outlook: C

John Wasdin (Pos: RHP, Age: 27)

	W	L	Pct.	ERA	G	GS	Sv	IP	H	BB	SO	HR	Ratio
1999	8	3	.727	4.12	45	0	2	74.1	66	18	57	14	1.13
Career	27	21	.563	5.01	175	38	2	443.2	457	136	281	74	1.34

Wasdin began 1999 in Triple-A, but came up after posting a 2.12 ERA in five April starts. Except for rough spots when he was hurting with a forearm strain in July, he came up big in the Sox pen. 2000 Outlook: B

Lenny Webster (Pos: C, Age: 35, Bats: R)

	G	AB	R	H	D	T	HR	RBI	SB	BB	SO	Avg	OBP	Slg
1999	22	50	1	6	1	0	0	4	0	10	7	.120	.290	.140
Career	548	1369	151	351	70	2	33	171	1	134	195	.256	.327	.383

After Webster's career year with Baltimore in 1998, a May ankle injury cost him seven weeks. While he was out, the O's picked up Mike Figga and soon released Webster. Boston then signed and cut him. 2000 Outlook: B

Bob Wolcott (Pos: RHP, Age: 26)

	W	L	Pct.	ERA	G	GS	Sv	IP	H	BB	SO	HR	Ratio
1999	0	0	-	8.10	4	0	0	6.2	8	3	2	1	1.65
Career	16	21	.432	5.86	66	58	0	325.2	391	113	178	62	1.55

In the late 1990s, Wolcott was a teammate of Tim Harikkala in the Pacific Coast League, and he struggled as much as Harikkala did. Wolcott fared better in Triple-A, but no better in Boston. 2000 Outlook: C

Boston

Boston Red Sox Minor League Prospects

Organization Overview:

Since the end of the 1997 season, the Red Sox have used their farm system to produce trade fodder. They have dealt prospects Tony Armas Jr., Adam Everett, Matt Kinney, Cole Liniak, Greg Miller, Peter Munro, Carl Pavano and Robert Ramsay—all of whom were held in high regard by Boston at some point—in deals for veterans Rod Beck, Carl Everett, Butch Huskey, Pedro Martinez, Mike Stanley and Greg Swindell. Thus far, each of those trades has worked out for the Sox, though they have stripped the system of depth. During the same period, the only homegrown products who have played significant roles in Boston have been Trot Nixon and Brian Rose. The Red Sox work the Far East as hard as any organization, perhaps to the detriment of their budget for the amateur draft.

Jin Ho Cho

Position: P		**Opening Day Age:** 24
Bats: R **Throws:** R		**Born:** 8/16/75 in Jun Ju
Ht: 6' 3" **Wt:** 207		City, Korea

Recent Statistics

	W	L	ERA	G	GS	Sv	IP	H	R	BB	SO	HR
1999 AAA Pawtucket	9	3	3.45	17	17	0	109.2	99	46	29	80	12
1999 AL Boston	2	3	5.72	9	7	0	39.1	45	26	8	16	7

Ten Koreans played with major league organizations last year, and the Red Sox had four of them. A member of Korea's 1996 Olympic team, Cho signed in March 1998 and reached Boston just four months later. He has a fastball that can reach 92 MPH, a splitter, a slider and a changeup. His best attribute is his control, which was rated the best in the Triple-A International League last year. Big league hitters have touched Cho for 11 homers in 58 innings, so he'll have to learn the difference between throwing strikes and throwing quality strikes. The Red Sox have openings in their rotation, and he's a prime candidate to fill one.

Michael Coleman

Position: OF		**Opening Day Age:** 24
Bats: R **Throws:** R		**Born:** 8/16/75 in
Ht: 5' 11" **Wt:** 207		Nashville, TN

Recent Statistics

	G	AB	R	H	D	T	HR	RBI	SB	BB	SO	Avg
1999 AAA Pawtucket	115	467	95	125	29	2	30	74	14	51	128	.268
1999 AL Boston	2	5	1	1	0	0	0	0	0	1	0	.200
1999 MLE	115	453	74	111	28	1	23	57	9	39	134	.245

A former tailback recruit of the University of Alabama, Coleman may be the best athlete in the system. He also may have had the worst attitude, which led to a suspension in July 1999 and subsequent counseling. Scouts thought he looked more relaxed in 1999, and it showed, as he increased his home-run output in Triple-A from 14 to 30. Outside of his strength, he hasn't translated his physical gifts into baseball skills. His plate discipline isn't the best, so he hasn't hit for average, and while he has good speed, he hasn't been a basestealer. An 18th-round pick in 1994, he does have above-average range and arm strength for a center fielder. Coleman might make the Red Sox this year, but his chances of starting were negated when Boston dealt for Carl Everett.

Sun Kim

Position: P		**Opening Day Age:** 22
Bats: R **Throws:** R		**Born:** 9/4/77 in Inchon,
Ht: 6' 2" **Wt:** 180		Korea

Recent Statistics

	W	L	ERA	G	GS	Sv	IP	H	R	BB	SO	HR
1998 A Sarasota	12	8	4.82	26	24	0	153.0	159	88	40	132	18
1999 AA Trenton	9	8	4.89	26	26	0	149.0	160	86	44	130	16

Most of Boston's upper-level pitching prospects don't project as anything better than a No. 3 starter, but Kim is the exception. He had a storied amateur career, helping pitch Korea to the 1994 World Junior Championships and becoming the youngest player ever to represent his nation in the Olympics two years later. He throws a 92-94 MPH fastball, though he tends to miss with it high in the strike zone, which can lead to home runs. He's going to try to add a two-seamer to go with his four-seamer, and his curveball, slider and changeup still need some tinkering. Like his countryman Cho, Kim has very good control but must throw a higher quality of strikes. He'll begin 2000 in Triple-A and could factor in Boston's rotation later in the year.

Steve Lomasney

Position: C		**Opening Day Age:** 22
Bats: R **Throws:** R		**Born:** 8/29/77 in
Ht: 6' 0" **Wt:** 185		Melrose, MA

Recent Statistics

	G	AB	R	H	D	T	HR	RBI	SB	BB	SO	Avg
1999 A Sarasota	55	189	35	51	10	0	8	28	5	26	57	.270
1999 AA Trenton	47	151	24	37	6	0	12	31	7	31	44	.245
1999 AL Boston	1	2	0	0	0	0	0	0	0	0	2	.000

Since Dan Duquette took over as GM in 1994, Boston began emphasizing New England talent in the annual amateur draft. The Red Sox took Lomasney out of nearby Peabody, Mass., in 1995's fifth round and convinced him to forego a Boston College football scholarship. He since has emerged as an all-around catching prospect. He should produce 15-20 homers per season, hit for a decent average and draw a few walks. A good athlete for a catcher, Lomasney runs OK and moves well behind the plate. He has above-average arm strength and threw out two basestealers in his major league debut last September. He needs to improve against breaking stuff and use the entire field more often, but Lomasney is only a year away from being able to contribute in Boston.

Tomokazu Ohka

Position: P **Opening Day Age:** 24
Bats: R **Throws:** R **Born:** 3/18/76 in Kyoto,
Ht: 6' 1" **Wt:** 179 Japan

Recent Statistics

	W	L	ERA	G	GS	Sv	IP	H	R	BB	SO	HR
1999 AA Trenton	8	0	3.00	12	12	0	72.0	63	26	25	53	9
1999 AAA Pawtucket	7	0	1.58	12	12	0	68.1	60	17	11	63	5
1999 AL Boston	1	2	6.23	8	2	0	13.0	21	12	6	8	2

Besides Korea, the Red Sox also have made significant inroads in Japan. There were 11 Japanese players in major league organizations in 1999, and Boston was the only club with three of them. The Red Sox purchased Ohka from Japan's Yokohama BayStars in December 1998, and he had an impressive U.S. debut. He went a combined 15-0 in Double-A and Triple-A, pitched in the inaugural Futures Games and reached Boston by midseason. He's aggressive with his 88-92 MPH fastball, which has late sinking, boring action. He also throws an average splitter and changeup, and an inconsistent slider. Ohka will get a chance to make the Red Sox this spring.

Juan Pena

Position: P **Opening Day Age:** 22
Bats: R **Throws:** R **Born:** 6/27/77 in Santo
Ht: 6' 5" **Wt:** 211 Domingo, Dom. Rep.

Recent Statistics

	W	L	ERA	G	GS	Sv	IP	H	R	BB	SO	HR
1999 R Red Sox	0	0	0.00	1	1	0	2.0	0	0	0	4	0
1999 A Sarasota	0	1	7.11	2	2	0	6.1	12	6	0	5	0
1999 AAA Pawtucket	4	2	4.13	10	10	0	48.0	44	28	13	61	8
1999 AL Boston	2	0	0.69	2	2	0	13.0	9	1	3	15	0

Pena might already have cemented a spot for himself in the Boston rotation had shoulder tendinitis not halted his big league debut after two starts last May. He went on the disabled list, then tried pitching in Triple-A only to have his shoulder flare up again. A 27th-round pick in 1995 out of Miami-Dade Community College Wolfson, Pena threw harder in Boston (88-91 MPH) than he did in the minors (87-88 MPH). His fastball has very nice sink, and he also throws a curveball and changeup. He has good command of both sides of the plate. Pena is expected to compete for a starting job in spring training.

Dernell Stenson

Position: 1B **Opening Day Age:** 21
Bats: L **Throws:** L **Born:** 6/17/78 in
Ht: 6' 1" **Wt:** 230 LaGrange, GA

Recent Statistics

	G	AB	R	H	D	T	HR	RBI	SB	BB	SO	Avg
1998 AA Trenton	138	505	90	130	21	1	24	71	5	84	135	.257
1999 R Red Sox	6	23	2	5	0	0	2	7	0	3	5	.217
1999 AAA Pawtucket	121	440	64	119	28	2	18	82	2	55	119	.270
1999 MLE	121	427	50	106	27	1	13	64	1	43	124	.248

Stenson was rated the top hitting prospect in the Triple-A International League in 1999, just as he was the year before in the Double-A Eastern League. A 1996 third-round pick, he has a short stroke with loft, giving him power to all fields. Stenson also has solid plate discipline and should hit for average. He doesn't offer much else, however. He's a below-average runner, and didn't help himself by getting heavier in 1999. And his conversion from the outfield was a disaster, as he led all minor league first basemen with 34 errors. If everything comes together for Stenson at the plate, the Red Sox won't miss Mo Vaughn.

Wilton Veras

Position: 3B **Opening Day Age:** 22
Bats: R **Throws:** R **Born:** 1/19/78 in
Ht: 6' 2" **Wt:** 186 Montecristy, Dom. Rep.

Recent Statistics

	G	AB	R	H	D	T	HR	RBI	SB	BB	SO	Avg
1999 AA Trenton	116	474	65	133	23	2	11	75	7	23	55	.281
1999 AL Boston	36	118	14	34	5	1	2	13	0	5	14	.288
1999 MLE	116	463	53	122	22	1	8	61	4	16	58	.263

Veras' time in Boston is near. John Valentin faded badly and Triple-A third-base prospect Cole Liniak was traded to the Cubs in 1999. Scouts are divided on how good Veras can become. Those who like him point to his ability to hit the fastball and his strong arm, and project him as a possible 25-homer hitter. Those who don't point to his long swing and lack of selectivity, and see him as more of a cripple hitter who will feast only on mistakes. Veras' second season in Double-A actually wasn't as good as his first, though he was rated the Eastern League's best defensive third baseman. And he did have his moments in Boston.

Others to Watch

Rick Asadoorian (19), Boston's first-round pick in June, signed for a club-record $1.7255 million. His power and arm strength remind the Red Sox of Dwight Evans, and he also runs well. . . DH **Morgan Burkhart** (28) played four years in independent ball and won three straight MVP Awards in the Frontier League before signing with the Red Sox. In his first year in Organized Ball, he led the high Class-A Florida State league in homers (23) despite playing in just 68 games, and ranked seventh in the minors with an overall total of 35. . . **David Eckstein** (25) is an overachiever who has succeeded wherever he has played, despite lacking an above-average tool. He's a career .308 hitter as a pro, he can steal bases with his smarts and he was rated the best defensive second baseman in the Double-A Eastern League last year. . . Lefthander **Casey Fossum** (22), a 1999 supplemental first-round pick, has a 90-93 MPH fastball, a hard curveball and a fine changeup. With that kind of stuff, he could move quickly. . . Lefthander **Wilfredo Ledezma** (19) is further away than Fossum but might develop better stuff. Ledezma already throws 90-92 MPH and has a good feel for a curveball and changeup. . . Righthander **Jeff Taglienti** (24) has a 2.88 ERA and 189 strikeouts in 162.1 pro innings. He throws an 89-94 MPH fastball from a low three-quarters delivery.

Comiskey Park

Offense

Comiskey Park has been a tough place to hit since it opened in 1991, largely because of its pitcher-friendly dimensions and cold weather. Over the last three seasons, it has decreased scoring by 5 percent and home runs by 7 percent. During that period, Comiskey ranks second only to Fenway Park among American League parks in reducing homers by lefthanded hitters. Righties are more immune to the power outage. Attendance has fallen off drastically, but the young White Sox do a good job ignoring generally unfriendly conditions.

Defense

Not to say that groundskeeper Roger Bossard is a perfectionist, but he tore up one of the American League's best infields last October to put down a completely new surface. It should be a treasure by the middle of the season but the grass may need some time to grow in the spring. The raw early-season weather can make Comiskey a tough place for fielders.

Who It Helps The Most

Comiskey Park has become a security blanket for White Sox pitchers, who can't wait to get back home after getting hit hard on the road. It has been especially kind to lefthander Mike Sirotka. As bad as he has been, Jaime Navarro has much better numbers pitching at Comiskey than on the road over the last three years.

Who It Hurts The Most

While Frank Thomas hates the new Comiskey, he's hit only seven more home runs on the road than at home over the last four years. His batting average does suffer as his drives die in the gaps, especially early in the season. Ray Durham has been a much better hitter on the road than at home, for both power and average.

Rookies & Newcomers

Comiskey could be the best place in the league to break in new pitchers, and the Sox have Kip Wells, Aaron Myette and Jon Garland on the way. Rising hitters such as McKay Christensen, Joe Crede, Jason Dellaero, Josh Paul and Brian Simmons won't enjoy it as much.

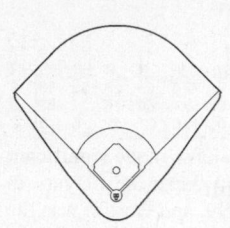

Dimensions: LF-347, LCF-375, CF-400, RCF-375, RF-347

Capacity: 44,321

Elevation: 595 feet

Surface: Grass

Foul Territory: Average

Park Factors

1999 Season

| | Home Games | | | Away Games | | | |
	White Sox	Opp	Total	White Sox	Opp	Total	Index
G	72	72	144	72	72	144	—
Avg	.272	.281	.277	.278	.285	.282	98
AB	2423	2597	5020	2569	2447	5016	100
R	333	377	710	359	391	750	95
H	660	730	1390	715	698	1413	98
2B	119	125	244	149	125	274	89
3B	18	3	21	14	13	27	78
HR	71	93	164	72	92	164	100
BB	217	254	471	222	283	505	93
SO	337	421	758	383	416	799	95
E	56	52	108	54	61	115	94
E-Infield	49	41	90	46	51	97	93
LHB-Avg	.254	.272	.263	.276	.303	.289	91
LHB-HR	17	44	61	29	41	70	89
RHB-Avg	.286	.288	.287	.280	.272	.276	104
RHB-HR	54	49	103	43	51	94	108

1997-1999

| | Home Games | | | Away Games | | | |
	White Sox	Opp	Total	White Sox	Opp	Total	Index
G	221	221	442	216	216	432	—
Avg	.275	.273	.274	.273	.282	.277	99
AB	7304	7827	15131	7700	7368	15068	98
R	1089	1161	2250	1102	1206	2308	95
H	2012	2133	4145	2099	2075	4174	97
2B	382	408	790	388	392	780	101
3B	50	33	83	43	32	75	110
HR	231	253	484	237	282	519	93
BB	753	764	1517	724	819	1543	98
SO	1083	1315	2398	1250	1225	2475	96
E	173	148	321	186	173	359	87
E-Infield	145	119	264	159	141	300	86
LHB-Avg	.269	.279	.274	.274	.294	.284	96
LHB-HR	58	117	175	82	128	210	85
RHB-Avg	.281	.268	.274	.271	.272	.272	101
RHB-HR	173	136	309	155	154	309	98

1999 Rankings (American League)

- Third-highest RHB batting-average factor
- Lowest walk factor
- Third-lowest double factor
- Third-lowest strikeout factor
- Third-lowest LHB batting-average factor

Jerry Manuel

1999 Season

After a feel-good first season on the job, Jerry Manuel experienced a trying year without veterans Robin Ventura and Albert Belle. Their departure put more focus on two-time MVP Frank Thomas, and he responded with the worst year of his career. Manuel's communication skills were challenged by the stubbornly proud Thomas. He questioned Manuel's desire to have him play more at first base and waited until September before giving hitting coach Von Joshua a chance to help him regain his missing power. Manuel and Thomas clashed over Thomas' unwillingness to play at less than 100 percent, and Thomas' season-ending ankle surgery raised questions as to who was to blame.

Offense

Manuel is a believer in putting runners in motion, bunting and doing anything possible to manufacture runs. But that belief was put to the test with Belle and Ventura elsewhere. The difficulty creating runs left Manuel wondering about the importance of big boppers in the American League. The bigger problem for the White Sox was their lack of discipline at the plate. They ranked next-to-last in the AL in walks and 11th in on-base percentage. For Manuel to put pressure on his opponents, he first must have men on base.

Pitching & Defense

Manuel has been beside himself for two years about the number of four- and five-out innings the White Sox allow. He and his coaching staff do what they can to emphasize the need to improve fielding, but it will take a personnel overhaul—not a manager's willpower—to change the fundamentally flawed club. The Sox will start with the left side of their infield, where Ventura was badly missed last year. Manuel has been a resourceful handler of pitchers, getting good results from a bullpen without a proven lefthander for two years.

2000 Outlook

Manuel has established a solid reputation without having a winning season. He's under no visible pressure from ownership. The Sox need at least one more year on training wheels before being ready to start taking themselves seriously.

Born: 12/23/53 in Hahira, Georgia

Playing Experience: 1975-1982, Det, Mon, SD

Managerial Experience: 2 seasons
Pronucnciation: MAN-you-ell

Manager Statistics

Year	Team, Lg	W	L	Pct	GB	Finish
1999	Chicago, AL	75	86	.466	21.5	2nd Central
2 Seasons		155	168	.477	—	—

1999 Starting Pitchers by Days Rest

	<=3	4	5	6+
White Sox Starts	2	73	43	34
White Sox ERA	5.40	5.37	4.93	5.48
AL Avg Starts	2	82	47	21
AL ERA	6.83	4.98	4.72	5.62

1999 Situational Stats

	Jerry Manuel	AL Average
Hit & Run Success %	32.2	35.3
Stolen Base Success %	68.8	68.0
Platoon Pct.	57.7	56.7
Defensive Subs	39	22
High-Pitch Outings	9	15
Quick/Slow Hooks	21/26	18/18
Sacrifice Attempts	69	52

1999 Rankings (American League)

- 1st in slow hooks (26)
- 2nd in sacrifice bunt attempts (69) and defensive substitutions (39)

Chicago (AL)

Mike Caruso

1999 Season

There were smirks all around the White Sox organization in 1998 about those who questioned whether Mike Caruso could make the jump from Class-A to the big leagues. By the end of Caruso's disappointing sophomore season in 1999, even Sox GM Ron Schueler was citing the lack of education the shortstop had received on his way to Comiskey Park. Caruso's repeated mental mistakes and errors on routine grounders led to two weeklong benchings in the second half.

Hitting

Caruso is a slap hitter who depends on his quickness to get on base. His effectiveness is limited by his inability to work the count and draw walks. He has a short, quick swing but chases too many pitches outside the strike zone, especially those off the outside of the plate. He hasn't learned to hit good breaking pitches but gets plenty of fastballs because of the lack of respect pitchers have for him. Caruso has very little power and his .280 on-base percentage in 1999 was the lowest among American League qualifiers. He's a very good bunter.

Baserunning & Defense

Caruso's play at shortstop improved marginally over his rookie season, largely because he didn't suffer through the arm troubles that contributed to his 35 errors in 1998. He has good range and reasonable fundamentals, but isn't the on-field quarterback teams want at shortstop. While Caruso is a speedy runner, he has yet to become a good basestealer. He led the AL by being caught 14 times in 1999, when he stole just 12 bases.

2000 Outlook

The fading golden boy of the White Flag trade could get some remedial time in Triple-A this season, but the greater likelihood is that Caruso will share time with a veteran. His biggest challenge could from former first-round pick Jason Dellaero, whom the Sox hope soon will be ready to establish himself as the everyday shortstop.

Position: SS
Bats: L **Throws:** R
Ht: 6' 1" **Wt:** 172

Opening Day Age: 22
Born: 5/27/77 in Queens, NY
ML Seasons: 2
Nickname: Slappy

Overall Statistics

	G	AB	R	H	D	T	HR	RBI	SB	BB	SO	Avg	OBP	Slg
1999	136	529	60	132	11	4	2	35	12	20	36	.250	.280	.297
Career	269	1052	141	292	28	10	7	90	34	34	74	.278	.305	.343

Where He Hits the Ball

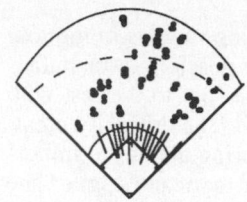 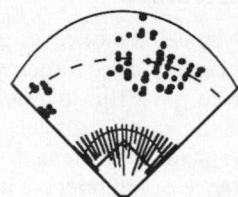

Vs. LHP   **Vs. RHP**

1999 Situational Stats

	AB	H	HR	RBI	Avg		AB	H	HR	RBI	Avg
Home	260	58	0	18	.223	LHP	109	29	0	6	.266
Road	269	74	2	17	.275	RHP	420	103	2	29	.245
First Half	306	79	1	21	.258	Sc Pos	140	31	1	33	.221
Scnd Half	223	53	1	14	.238	Clutch	73	21	1	6	.288

1999 Rankings (American League)

- 1st in caught stealing (14), lowest slugging percentage, lowest on-base percentage, lowest HR frequency (264.5 ABs per HR), lowest stolen-base percentage (46.2%), fewest pitches seen per plate appearance (3.13), lowest slugging percentage vs. righthanded pitchers (.295), lowest on-base percentage vs. righthanded pitchers (.272), lowest fielding percentage at shortstop (.957) and highest percentage of swings put into play (56.6%)
- Led the White Sox in sacrifice bunts (11), caught stealing (14), highest groundball/flyball ratio (2.1), fewest GDPs per GDP situation (5.8%) and lowest percentage of swings that missed (9.5%)

Ray Durham

1999 Season

After agreeing to a four-year, $20 million contract in February, Ray Durham displayed the same inconsistencies that once made the White Sox debate whether to offer him salary arbitration or trade him. He did show some leadership skills, which the Sox badly need. While he contributed to his team's continuing defensive inadequacies, Durham had another good year at the plate. His speed helped him score a team-high 109 runs, and his .373 on-base percentage was a career high.

Hitting

Hitting coach Von Joshua has made the switch-hitting Durham better from the right side, which makes opposing managers less likely to bring in a lefthander to face him late in games. He works the count from both sides of the plate but has struck out at least 100 times two years in a row. After a power surge in 1998, Durham regressed a little last year. Not only was his extra-base hit total down, but he also hit just .237 with men in scoring position.

Baserunning & Defense

Five years into his big league career, Durham remains a defensive liability at second base. He has surprisingly little range for an excellent athlete, almost never making plays going to his right, and is average at best on the double-play pivot. He set a career high with 19 errors last year. Durham is a speedy runner and good basestealer. Scouts consider him one of the best American Leaguers in scoring from first on doubles.

2000 Outlook

Durham is valuable as the leadoff man in a dangerous, if young, lineup. He appears settled in at second base, but his below-average play there leads to ongoing speculation about a possible shift to center field. It isn't likely the Sox will do anything that drastic because Chris Singleton established himself in center, and other prospects are coming behind him. There's no guarantee Durham will play second for the three years left on his contract, but in the short term a second All-Star season isn't out of the question.

Position: 2B
Bats: B **Throws:** R
Ht: 5' 8" **Wt:** 180

Opening Day Age: 28
Born: 11/30/71 in Charlotte, NC
ML Seasons: 5

Overall Statistics

	G	AB	R	H	D	T	HR	RBI	SB	BB	SO	Avg	OBP	Slg
1999	153	612	109	181	30	8	13	60	34	73	105	.296	.373	.435
Career	747	2909	488	808	152	32	60	296	151	296	484	.278	.348	.414

Where He Hits the Ball

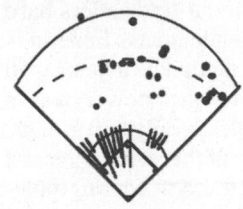 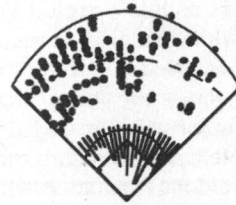

Vs. LHP   **Vs. RHP**

1999 Situational Stats

	AB	H	HR	RBI	Avg		AB	H	HR	RBI	Avg
Home	297	86	7	29	.290	LHP	136	41	3	13	.301
Road	315	95	6	31	.302	RHP	476	140	10	47	.294
First Half	342	102	9	38	.298	Sc Pos	135	32	4	46	.237
Scnd Half	270	79	4	22	.293	Clutch	81	27	4	13	.333

1999 Rankings (American League)
- 2nd in pitches seen (2,827), errors at second base (19), lowest fielding percentage at second base (.974) and highest percentage of extra bases taken as a runner (71.9%)
- 5th in triples
- Led the White Sox in runs scored, singles, triples, stolen bases, times on base (258), strikeouts, pitches seen (2,827), plate appearances (694), most pitches seen per plate appearance (4.07), on-base percentage for a leadoff hitter (.377), on-base percentage vs. lefthanded pitchers (.396), steals of third (2) and highest percentage of extra bases taken as a runner (71.9%)
- Led AL second basemen in highest percentage of extra bases taken as a runner (71.9%)

Brook Fordyce

1999 Season

A spring-training trade with the Reds for minor league pitcher Jake Meyer gave Brook Fordyce the chance to become a regular. After playing behind Todd Hundley and Eddie Taubensee, Fordyce thrived in the land of opportunity that is Comiskey Park. He wound up with more at-bats than he had been given in his four seasons with the Mets and Reds, and surprisingly became one of the American League's best No. 9 hitters.

Hitting

No one saw this coming. A career .237 hitter, the long-time backup catcher threatened to hit .300 for the first time since 1990, when he was in Class-A. Fordyce has holes in his long swing, but AL pitchers couldn't exploit them. He hit lefthanders hard while hanging in against righthanders. Fordyce's bat speed is nothing special, though he adjusts well against breaking pitches. His gap power was a major surprise, with 25 doubles in only 333 at-bats. He has a good understanding of the strike zone and seldom expands it when men are in scoring position.

Baserunning & Defense

Fordyce's handling of pitchers and solid play behind the plate drew the attention of White Sox scouts. He often had played as a late-inning replacement for Taubensee in Cincinnati. But Fordyce was not as good as advertised defensively. He has an average arm and is often slow getting rid of the ball on steal attempts. He was successful throwing out only 22 percent of basestealers, the third-worst ratio in the AL. Fordyce runs like a catcher.

2000 Outlook

The Sox were pleased with Fordyce last year, and signed him to a two-year, $1.5 million contract in November. Still, he could become a midseason bargaining chip if prospect Josh Paul gets off to a good start. As last season went along, manager Jerry Manuel seemed more comfortable using rookie Mark Johnson to handle the young pitching staff. For Fordyce to maintain his position, he'll have to make defensive strides while continuing to show .300-15-75 potential at the plate.

Position: C
Bats: R **Throws:** R
Ht: 6' 1" **Wt:** 185

Opening Day Age: 29
Born: 5/7/70 in New London, CT
ML Seasons: 5

Overall Statistics

	G	AB	R	H	D	T	HR	RBI	SB	BB	SO	Avg	OBP	Slg
1999	105	333	36	99	25	1	9	49	2	21	48	.297	.343	.459
Career	217	584	52	159	41	1	13	72	4	44	92	.272	.325	.413

Where He Hits the Ball

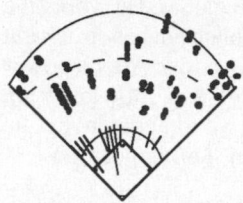
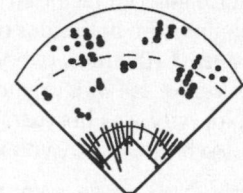

Vs. LHP   **Vs. RHP**

1999 Situational Stats

	AB	H	HR	RBI	Avg		AB	H	HR	RBI	Avg
Home	155	47	5	23	.303	LHP	93	31	4	18	.333
Road	178	52	4	26	.292	RHP	240	68	5	31	.283
First Half	184	57	5	24	.310	Sc Pos	84	25	2	35	.298
Scnd Half	149	42	4	25	.282	Clutch	58	19	0	7	.328

1999 Rankings (American League)

- 1st in lowest fielding percentage at catcher (.987)
- 3rd in errors at catcher (8)
- Led AL catchers in fewest GDPs per GDP situation (9.4%) and batting average in the clutch

Bob Howry

Position: RP
Bats: L **Throws:** R
Ht: 6' 5" **Wt:** 220

Opening Day Age: 26
Born: 8/4/73 in Phoenix, AZ
ML Seasons: 2

1999 Season

In his first full season in the big leagues, Bob Howry established himself as a closer. He went through the usual growing pains en route to 28 saves in 34 opportunities. He twice seemed close to losing the closer's job but rebounded from alarming stretches in May and August. Howry struggled with his control at times but proved that his fastball is good enough on most nights.

Pitching

There are few subtleties with Howry. He's comfortable standing on the mound and challenging fastball hitters with fastballs. In one memorable showdown, he and Mark Grace went at it for 12 pitches at Wrigley Field before Grace finally doubled off the right-field wall. Howry could have made Grace look silly with an offspeed pitch, but he instead threw one 96-MPH fastball after another. Hitters can sit on that fastball, which lacks movement when Howry gets it up. The Sox continue working with Howry in hopes he'll learn to throw his curveball or changeup for strikes, but are willing to live with his fastball. It's as effective against lefthanders as righthanders.

Defense

Howry would seem to be an easy target for basestealers as he has a pedestrian pickoff move. But teams rarely try to run on him, perhaps because his pitches get to the plate quickly. Howry is a maximum-effort pitcher who's slow off the mound. He could help himself by flagging down a few more grounders.

2000 Outlook

Now that he's entrenched in the closer's job, Howry could get as many as 40 saves if the White Sox can improve enough to finish with a winning record. Late-inning relief pitching should be the least of their concerns with Howry and setup man Keith Foulke.

Overall Statistics

	W	L	Pct.	ERA	G	GS	Sv	IP	H	BB	SO	HR	Ratio
1999	5	3	.625	3.59	69	0	28	67.2	58	38	80	8	1.42
Career	5	6	.455	3.39	113	0	37	122.0	95	57	131	15	1.25

How Often He Throws Strikes

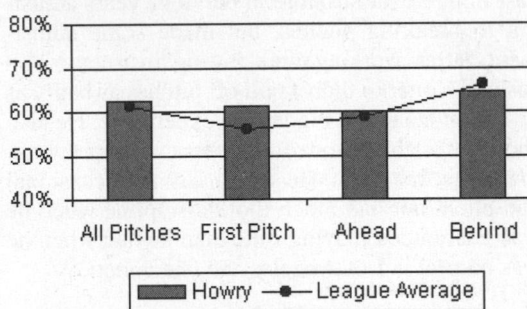

1999 Situational Stats

	W	L	ERA	Sv	IP		AB	H	HR	RBI	Avg
Home	3	2	4.98	16	34.1	LHB	133	30	3	19	.226
Road	2	1	2.16	12	33.1	RHB	120	28	5	10	.233
First Half	2	1	3.67	13	34.1	Sc Pos	64	11	1	17	.172
Scnd Half	3	2	3.51	15	33.1	Clutch	153	32	5	19	.209

1999 Rankings (American League)

- 2nd in first batter efficiency (.121) and most strikeouts per 9 innings in relief (10.6)
- 5th in lowest batting average allowed in relief with runners in scoring position (.172)
- 6th in lowest save percentage (82.4%)
- 8th in games finished (54) and blown saves (6)
- 9th in saves
- 10th in save opportunities (34)
- Led the White Sox in saves, games finished (54), save opportunities (34), save percentage (82.4%), blown saves (6), first batter efficiency (.121) and most strikeouts per 9 innings in relief (10.6)

Chicago (AL)

Paul Konerko

1999 Season

Since being named *Baseball America*'s 1997 Minor League Player of the Year, Paul Konerko has been traded twice. Like the Dodgers, the Reds failed to translate Konerko's minor league resumé into big league success. After obtaining him in a deal for center fielder Mike Cameron, the White Sox were able to guarantee Konerko 500 at-bats. He responded as scouts always had insisted he would.

Hitting

Konerko is a large man with a relatively small swing and power to all fields. His short, quick stroke makes it tough for pitchers to sneak fastballs past him. He had trouble in previous years adjusting to breaking pitches, but made some adjustments after working with hitting instructor Von Joshua. Konerko didn't pull off pitches as badly as he had in his initial big league experience. He also showed the ability to work pitchers, seldom swinging at the first pitch. He still chases the occasional bad pitch, but had much more discipline when he was guaranteed playing time than he had when he was on trial in Los Angeles and Cincinnati.

Baserunning & Defense

Konerko isn't a Gold Glove candidate, but was more than adequate at first base and a definite upgrade from Frank Thomas. Konerko is a reliable fielder but doesn't get to a lot of groundballs, leaving a large hole between him and second baseman Ray Durham. Though Konerko has played third base and left field, first is his home. He really clogs the bases with his sundial-like speed.

2000 Outlook

Konerko worked his way up the batting order a year ago, finishing as the No. 5 hitter behind Thomas and Magglio Ordonez. The Sox would like to obtain another productive lefthanded bat, which would allow them to drop Konerko and Carlos Lee to sixth and seventh, respectively. The Sox believe they can get 30 homers and 100 RBI out of Konerko.

Position: 1B/DH
Bats: R **Throws:** R
Ht: 6' 3" **Wt:** 211
Opening Day Age: 24
Born: 3/5/76 in Providence, RI
ML Seasons: 3
Pronunciation: kuh-NER-koh

Overall Statistics

	G	AB	R	H	D	T	HR	RBI	SB	BB	SO	Avg	OBP	Slg
1999	142	513	71	151	31	4	24	81	1	45	68	.294	.352	.511
Career	223	737	92	199	35	4	31	110	1	62	110	.270	.328	.455

Where He Hits the Ball

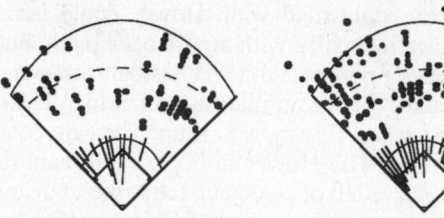

Vs. LHP   Vs. RHP

1999 Situational Stats

	AB	H	HR	RBI	Avg		AB	H	HR	RBI	Avg
Home	259	84	16	41	.324	LHP	116	37	5	23	.319
Road	254	67	8	40	.264	RHP	397	114	19	58	.287
First Half	234	66	11	31	.282	Sc Pos	136	38	7	55	.279
Scnd Half	279	85	13	50	.305	Clutch	73	21	4	12	.288

1999 Rankings (American League)

- 8th in most GDPs per GDP situation (18.3%)
- 9th in GDPs (19)
- Led the White Sox in slugging percentage, batting average with the bases loaded (.375), batting average vs. lefthanded pitchers, slugging percentage vs. lefthanded pitchers (.509) and batting average at home

Carlos Lee

1999 Season

No one ever doubted that Carlos Lee could hit, and the baby-faced Panamanian showed why in his rookie season. He was promoted from Triple-A in early May, homered in his first game and stayed in the lineup the rest of the season. He ended the year hitting .302-20-104 between Charlotte and Chicago.

Hitting

Lee has one of the sweetest swings of any righthander in the game. He generates tremendous bat speed but will have to improve his strike-zone judgment. Big league hurlers got him out on pitches that he had been used to hitting hard or fouling off. His measly total of 13 walks was as unexpected as it was disappointing. Ditto for his increased strikeout totals. Lee isn't afraid of big situations and will be dangerous once he truly becomes comfortable in his new surroundings.

Baserunning & Defense

Lee was a valued prospect as a third baseman, but was shifted to the outfield in advance of Joe Crede's expected arrival at third base in 2000. Lee only had dabbled in the outfield before the Sox made the switch a week before he was promoted to the big leagues. He showed average range and made most of the routine plays in left, but was an easy target for speedy baserunners. His arm strength was below average, and he was slow to develop an outfielder's release. Lee is a good athlete and has above-average speed for a big man, but manager Jerry Manuel rarely runs with him.

2000 Outlook

The White Sox see Lee as an exciting part of their lineup, even if they aren't sold on his fielding skills. He should hit behind Frank Thomas and Magglio Ordonez, but could drop in the lineup if Manuel finds a lefthanded hitter to break up the string of righthanded sluggers.

Position: LF/DH
Bats: R **Throws:** R
Ht: 6' 2" **Wt:** 220

Opening Day Age: 23
Born: 6/20/76 in Aguadulce, Panama
ML Seasons: 1

Overall Statistics

	G	AB	R	H	D	T	HR	RBI	SB	BB	SO	Avg	OBP	Slg
1999	127	492	66	144	32	2	16	84	4	13	72	.293	.312	.463
Career	127	492	66	144	32	2	16	84	4	13	72	.293	.312	.463

Where He Hits the Ball

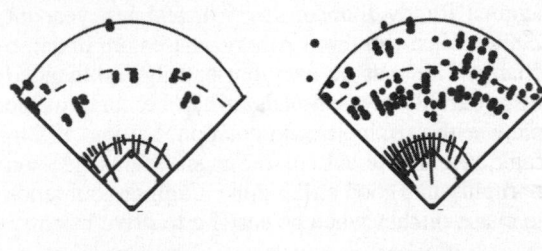

Vs. LHP   **Vs. RHP**

1999 Situational Stats

	AB	H	HR	RBI	Avg		AB	H	HR	RBI	Avg
Home	245	79	10	47	.322	LHP	93	28	3	9	.301
Road	247	65	6	37	.263	RHP	399	116	13	75	.291
First Half	216	64	4	36	.296	Sc Pos	140	40	6	71	.286
Scnd Half	276	80	12	48	.290	Clutch	65	22	4	11	.338

1999 Rankings (American League)

- 4th in lowest fielding percentage in left field (.981)
- 6th in errors in left field (4)
- 8th in lowest percentage of pitches taken (48.4%)
- 9th in lowest on-base percentage
- Led the White Sox in batting average in the clutch
- Led AL left fielders in batting average at home

Greg Norton

Position: 3B/1B
Bats: B **Throws:** R
Ht: 6' 1" **Wt:** 205

Opening Day Age: 27
Born: 7/6/72 in San Lendro, CA
ML Seasons: 4
Nickname: Nawton

1999 Season

Robin Ventura's departure allowed Greg Norton to move from first base to third base, his natural position. While Norton had his moments and continued to develop a cult following at Comiskey Park, it was a trying season. He was inconsistent both in the field and at the plate, failing to produce enough runs to offset his frequent errors. He was healthy all season but got only 113 starts, as manager Jerry Manuel often turned to Craig Wilson, a steadier fielder, as the year progressed.

Hitting

The switch-hitting Norton has a knack for hitting tough pitchers yet is unable to deliver reliably against lesser ones. He had a two-homer game against Randy Johnson in 1998 and last year hit .389 against the three American League division champs. He was an easy out batting righthanded last year and pressed badly when he came to the plate with men in scoring position, batting .175 to rank last in the AL in those situations. Norton normally has good strike-zone judgment but tends to chase pitches when he's trying to drive in runs.

Baserunning & Defense

Norton topped AL third basemen with 25 errors last year and also lacked range. His arm is average and his throws are often wild. He has played all four infield spots in the big leagues, doing a good job as a semiregular at first base in 1998. He is a below-average runner who ties Manuel's hands when he's on base.

2000 Outlook

Norton is a strong presence in the clubhouse and has a future with the team, even if it's not as an everyday player. He could open the season platooning with the righthanded-hitting Wilson at third base, and is likely to be supplanted by rising prospect Joe Crede by the All-Star break.

Overall Statistics

	G	AB	R	H	D	T	HR	RBI	SB	BB	SO	Avg	OBP	Slg
1999	132	436	62	111	26	0	16	50	4	69	93	.255	.358	.424
Career	266	792	109	196	45	4	27	90	7	101	184	.247	.334	.417

Where He Hits the Ball

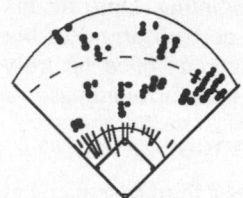

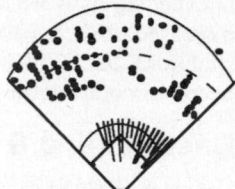

Vs. LHP   **Vs. RHP**

1999 Situational Stats

	AB	H	HR	RBI	Avg		AB	H	HR	RBI	Avg
Home	207	44	5	15	.213	LHP	74	15	0	3	.203
Road	229	67	11	35	.293	RHP	362	96	16	47	.265
First Half	264	60	11	30	.227	Sc Pos	114	20	2	29	.175
Scnd Half	172	51	5	20	.297	Clutch	60	16	4	9	.267

1999 Rankings (American League)

- 1st in lowest batting average with runners in scoring position, errors at third base (25) and lowest fielding percentage at third base (.922)
- 9th in lowest batting average
- 10th in most pitches seen per plate appearance (4.06)
- Led AL third basemen in highest groundball/flyball ratio (1.5), most pitches seen per plate appearance (4.06) and batting average on a 3-1 count (.533)

Magglio Ordonez

Position: RF
Bats: R **Throws:** R
Ht: 6' 0" **Wt:** 200

Opening Day Age: 26
Born: 1/28/74 in
Caracas, Venezuela
ML Seasons: 3
Pronunciation:
or-DOAN-yez

1999 Season

Few players have made as many big leaps in the last three years as Magglio Ordonez. Any team could have had him for $50,000 in the Rule 5 draft before the 1997 season, but by 1999 he was an All-Star. He followed up an excellent rookie season with an even better encore, leading the White Sox with 30 homers and 117 RBI. Ordonez was an asset in right field while developing into the team's most reliable run producer.

Hitting

Ordonez has a short, quick swing that draws comparisons to Edgar Martinez. He has shown the ability to adjust to almost all pitches and is a difficult hitter to put away. When he gets himself out by chasing bad pitches, it's usually when the bases are empty and he's trying to find the seats. Ordonez swings at the first pitch a lot, frequently doing damage. He got deeper into counts last season than in 1998, but it was mostly the result of pitchers being more careful with him than they were when he was hitting behind Albert Belle and Robin Ventura.

Baserunning & Defense

Ordonez doesn't have an exceptionally strong arm, but he's an accurate thrower who can make opponents pay for running on him. He has very good range in right field and is willing to crash into walls. He has average speed but manager Jerry Manuel doesn't mind running him.

2000 Outlook

Ordonez can't be counted on to repeat as an All-Star, but his production from the cleanup spot is one of the surest things in Chicago's lineup. There's no reason why he shouldn't hit 25 homers and drive in 100 runs. If opponents don't pay attention to him, he'll steal 20 bases as well.

Overall Statistics

	G	AB	R	H	D	T	HR	RBI	SB	BB	SO	Avg	OBP	Slg
1999	157	624	100	188	34	3	30	117	13	47	64	.301	.349	.510
Career	323	1228	182	361	65	5	48	193	23	77	125	.294	.338	.472

Where He Hits the Ball

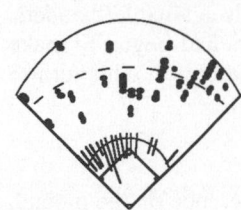
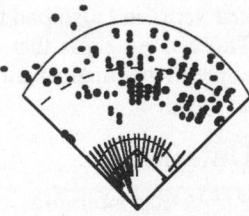

Vs. LHP **Vs. RHP**

1999 Situational Stats

	AB	H	HR	RBI	Avg		AB	H	HR	RBI	Avg
Home	294	89	16	50	.303	LHP	103	33	3	15	.320
Road	330	99	14	67	.300	RHP	521	155	27	102	.298
First Half	337	112	18	68	.332	Sc Pos	185	59	9	89	.319
Scnd Half	287	76	12	49	.265	Clutch	83	22	2	17	.265

1999 Rankings (American League)

- 2nd in fielding percentage in right field (.991)
- 3rd in GDPs (24)
- 4th in batting average on a 3-1 count (.667)
- Led the White Sox in home runs, at-bats, hits, total bases (318), RBI, GDPs (24), HR frequency (20.8 ABs per HR), batting average on a 3-1 count (.667), cleanup slugging percentage (.521), slugging percentage vs. righthanded pitchers (.516), batting average on a 3-2 count (.326), batting average with two strikes (.258), bunts in play (3), games played and steals of third (2)
- Led AL right fielders in at-bats, singles, GDPs (24), highest groundball/flyball ratio (1.6) and batting average on a 3-1 count (.667)

Jim Parque

1999 Season

Jim Parque was the first player from the 1997 draft to reach the majors, and when he went 7-5 as a rookie in 1998, no one doubted his worthiness. In 1999, he went winless in his last 13 starts after beginning the year 9-6. He pitched hurt after bruising his left thumb in late July.

Pitching

Parque's best weapon is his brainpower. Despite his small build, he throws a sneaky quick fastball that can hit 92-93 MPH and he has a full array of pitches. He goes to the mound with a plan for attacking hitters and seldom strays from it. His best pitch is his changeup, but hitters often sat on it last year. He gave up a surprising number of home runs last year, and also had trouble against lefthanders. Those were signs that hitters had begun to make adjustments against him, and now it's his turn to answer.

Defense

Parque has an impressive presence on the mound, always taking an aggressive posture. He's a good athlete and moves around well, fielding his position with Gold Glove potential. He gobbles up comebackers, sometimes roaming far from the mound to get a glove on a ball. He's reasonably quick to the plate but needs to vary his pickoff moves. Good baserunners appeared to time him last year.

2000 Outlook

While it probably shouldn't be, this is a critical season for Parque. His career ERA is higher than expected after his first 50 starts, but the Sox must understand that Parque has been getting his education at the big league level. He made only 21 starts between UCLA and Comiskey Park. Parque should be approaching the time when he's viewed as a finished product. He showed more potential in the minors than he has delivered the last two seasons.

Position: SP
Bats: L **Throws:** L
Ht: 5'11" **Wt:** 165

Opening Day Age: 24
Born: 2/8/76 in Norwalk, CA
ML Seasons: 2
Pronunciation: par-KAY

Overall Statistics

	W	L	Pct.	ERA	G	GS	Sv	IP	H	BB	SO	HR	Ratio
1999	9	15	.375	5.13	31	30	0	173.2	210	79	111	23	1.66
Career	16	20	.444	5.12	52	51	0	286.2	345	128	188	37	1.65

How Often He Throws Strikes

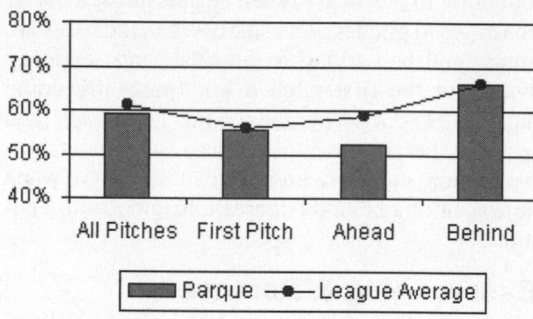

1999 Situational Stats

	W	L	ERA	Sv	IP		AB	H	HR	RBI	Avg
Home	6	7	4.47	0	94.2	LHB	157	51	5	24	.325
Road	3	8	5.92	0	79.0	RHB	545	159	18	75	.292
First Half	9	6	3.94	0	105.0	Sc Pos	180	50	4	75	.278
Scnd Half	0	9	6.95	0	68.2	Clutch	12	5	1	1	.417

1999 Rankings (American League)

- 2nd in losses, pickoff throws (200), highest on-base percentage allowed (.374) and most baserunners allowed per 9 innings (15.5)
- 3rd in balks (2) and highest batting average allowed (.299)
- 5th in least run support per 9 innings (4.7)
- 6th in highest ERA, lowest strikeout/walk ratio (1.4) and highest walks per 9 innings (4.1)
- 9th in hit batsmen (10)
- 10th in most pitches thrown per batter (3.90)
- Led the White Sox in losses, balks (2), pickoff throws (200), runners caught stealing (7), most GDPs induced per 9 innings (0.8) and most strikeouts per 9 innings (5.8)

Chris Singleton

1999 Season

After arriving from the Yankees in an unheralded minor league trade, Chris Singleton was given the last spot on the bench when Brian Simmons was injured at the end of spring training. Singleton spent April on the bench before emerging as a Rookie of the Year candidate with his contributions in center field and at the plate. He hit for the cycle on July 6, the first rookie to achieve the feat in 14 years. Singleton's humility along the way made his story even more enjoyable.

Hitting

Singleton built his impressive offensive numbers around some of baseball's best lefty-vs.-lefty stats. He showed the ability to hit fastballs from lefties the first time around the league, then hung in just as well on breaking balls throughout the summer. This didn't seem like a guy who batted .277 over six minor league seasons. A line-drive hitter, Singleton can put the ball into the seats when he really connects. He makes consistent contact, striking out only once every 11 at-bats. His biggest shortcoming is his lack of patience, as he drew just 22 walks last year.

Baserunning & Defense

Singleton proved to be an above-average fielder as his confidence increased throughout the season. He spent most of the year playing center and also can play the corners. He has good range and isn't afraid of the wall. His arm is average and accurate. He's a good runner and dangerous basestealer who succeeded on 80 percent of his stolen-base attempts.

2000 Outlook

Before Singleton's emergence, the White Sox had McKay Christensen penciled in as their center fielder of the future. Don't bet on Singleton giving away his squatter's rights on the position any time soon. He has shown the ability to persevere in an overcrowded outfield.

Position: CF/LF
Bats: L **Throws:** L
Ht: 6' 2"   **Wt:** 195

Opening Day Age: 27
Born: 8/15/72 in Martinez, CA
ML Seasons: 1

Overall Statistics

	G	AB	R	H	D	T	HR	RBI	SB	BB	SO	Avg	OBP	Slg
1999	133	496	72	149	31	6	17	72	20	22	45	.300	.328	.490
Career	133	496	72	149	31	6	17	72	20	22	45	.300	.328	.490

Where He Hits the Ball

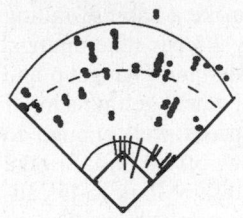

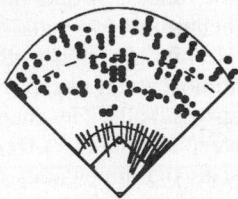

Vs. LHP   **Vs. RHP**

1999 Situational Stats

	AB	H	HR	RBI	Avg		AB	H	HR	RBI	Avg
Home	230	64	5	26	.278	LHP	76	31	3	15	.408
Road	266	85	12	46	.320	RHP	420	118	14	57	.281
First Half	237	75	7	39	.316	Sc Pos	110	38	2	49	.345
Scnd Half	259	74	10	33	.286	Clutch	74	17	0	8	.230

1999 Rankings (American League)

- 4th in fielding percentage in center field (.989)
- 5th in fewest pitches seen per plate appearance (3.25)
- 6th in errors in center field (4)
- 7th in lowest percentage of pitches taken (47.0%)
- 9th in lowest on-base percentage vs. righthanded pitchers (.309)
- Led the White Sox in stolen-base percentage (80.0%), batting average with runners in scoring position and batting average on the road

Chicago (AL)

Mike Sirotka

1999 Season

While not many people outside Chicago noticed, Mike Sirotka put together one of the best seasons by a lefthanded starter in the majors. His first-half ERA (3.20) merited consideration for the All-Star Game, but the White Sox hadn't gotten him enough wins for the trip to Fenway Park. Sirotka was remarkably consistent in his second full major league season. He led the Sox in innings and easily could have won 15-plus games.

Pitching

Sirotka has Jamie Moyer's command with a little better velocity. He can hit 90 MPH but is too smart to try to get his fastball past most hitters. His cut fastball breaks bats when righthanders swing for the fences. Sirotka doesn't make a habit of falling behind hitters, walking only 2.5 per nine innings. He hits his spots with a slider and changeup and almost always keeps the ball down, getting a lot of groundballs. He changes speeds well enough to keep righthanders from teeing off on him. Sirotka uses the dimensions of Comiskey Park to his advantage, pitching more effectively at home than on the road.

Defense

Fielding is the last piece of the puzzle for Sirotka. He needs to improve his reactions when the ball is hit to or in front of him. Teams run on him more than they do most lefthanders, succeeding on 13 of 20 attempts last year.

2000 Outlook

Financial security won't be an issue. The White Sox rewarded Sirotka with a multiyear contract at midseason, and there's no reason to think that he won't earn all his money. With a similar performance and more run support, he should get more recognition and perhaps a spot on the All-Star team. Sirotka might be the most tradeable asset the Sox have, but he has the savvy to become a leader for one of the youngest staffs in the majors.

Position: SP
Bats: L **Throws:** L
Ht: 6' 1" **Wt:** 200

Opening Day Age: 28
Born: 5/13/71 in Chicago, IL
ML Seasons: 5
Pronunciation: sir-ROT-kuh

Overall Statistics

	W	L	Pct.	ERA	G	GS	Sv	IP	H	BB	SO	HR	Ratio
1999	11	13	.458	4.00	32	32	0	209.0	236	57	125	24	1.40
Career	30	32	.484	4.51	93	79	0	513.1	600	138	307	63	1.44

How Often He Throws Strikes

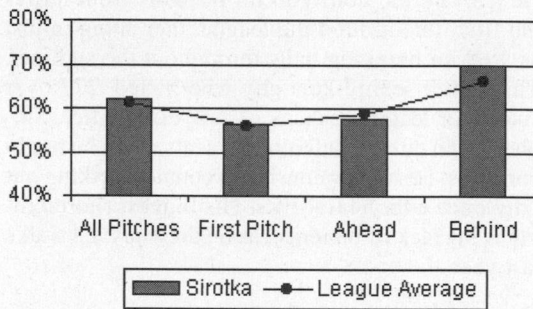

1999 Situational Stats

	W	L	ERA	Sv	IP		AB	H	HR	RBI	Avg
Home	7	7	3.60	0	110.0	LHB	188	50	7	27	.266
Road	4	6	4.45	0	99.0	RHB	647	186	17	76	.287
First Half	7	8	3.20	0	112.1	Sc Pos	197	54	4	74	.274
Scnd Half	4	5	4.93	0	96.2	Clutch	54	17	2	6	.315

1999 Rankings (American League)

- 1st in lowest fielding percentage at pitcher (.879)
- 2nd in errors at pitcher (4)
- Led the White Sox in ERA, complete games (3), innings pitched, hits allowed, batters faced (909), strikeouts, pitches thrown (3,374), runners caught stealing (7), highest strikeout/walk ratio (2.2), lowest slugging percentage allowed (.418), lowest on-base percentage allowed (.327), highest groundball/flyball ratio allowed (1.4), lowest stolen-base percentage allowed (65.0%), fewest baserunners allowed per 9 innings (12.7), fewest home runs allowed per 9 innings (1.03), walks per 9 innings (2.5), ERA at home and ERA on the road

Frank Thomas

1999 Season

Frank Thomas arrived in spring training carrying less weight and the best intentions to bounce back from an awful performance in 1998, but wound up digging himself a bigger hole in a year marked by injury and frequent misunderstandings with manager Jerry Manuel. They clashed over Thomas' growing reluctance to play first base and unwillingness to play when he was less than 100 percent, with Thomas' drop in power numbers an underlying reason for Manuel's disappointment. Thomas finished with career-worst totals in home runs and RBI.

Hitting

Like Austin Powers, Thomas has lost his mojo. He has seen the size of his strike zone increase and the respect of opposing pitchers drop in the last two years. After being busted inside regularly in 1998, Thomas has backed way off the plate and seems content to take pitches over the middle of the plate to right field for singles. He has a hard time pulling pitches into the seats. Thomas still does a good job working counts, but doesn't do as much when he's ahead in the count as in past years. He'll get himself out in big situations.

Baserunning & Defense

While Thomas never has moved well in the field, he was a valuable first baseman early in his career, providing a huge target for infielders to throw to. But now he gets embarrassed by his errors and prefers the safety of the DH spot. He played only 50 games in the field last year, displaying absolutely no range. With no speed to match, he clogs the bases when he gets on.

2000 Outlook

For the second winter in a row, there's talk that the White Sox would like to trade their franchise player. But with his contract having $66.7 million guaranteed through the year 2006, he has become immovable. It seems unlikely that he'll become an All-Star again. Thomas' contract contains a diminished-performance clause that could cause a clash with management and possibly open a window of free agency for him after 2001.

Position: DH/1B
Bats: R **Throws:** R
Ht: 6' 5" **Wt:** 270

Opening Day Age: 31
Born: 5/27/68 in Columbus, GA
ML Seasons: 10
Nickname: Big Hurt

Overall Statistics

	G	AB	R	H	D	T	HR	RBI	SB	BB	SO	Avg	OBP	Slg
1999	135	486	74	148	36	0	15	77	3	87	66	.305	.414	.471
Career	1371	4892	968	1564	317	10	301	1040	28	1076	741	.320	.440	.573

Where He Hits the Ball

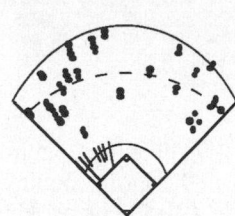 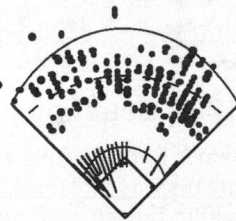

Vs. LHP   **Vs. RHP**

1999 Situational Stats

	AB	H	HR	RBI	Avg		AB	H	HR	RBI	Avg
Home	252	78	9	42	.310	LHP	75	19	3	7	.253
Road	234	70	6	35	.299	RHP	411	129	12	70	.314
First Half	316	102	12	57	.323	Sc Pos	137	38	4	66	.277
Scnd Half	170	46	3	20	.271	Clutch	62	20	1	13	.323

1999 Rankings (American League)

- 5th in intentional walks (13)
- 6th in highest percentage of pitches taken (62.0%)
- 10th in sacrifice flies (8)
- Led the White Sox in batting average, doubles, sacrifice flies (8), walks, intentional walks (13), hit by pitch (9), on-base percentage, batting average vs. righthanded pitchers, on-base percentage vs. righthanded pitchers (.419) and highest percentage of pitches taken (62.0%)
- Led designated hitters in doubles, hit by pitch (9) and lowest percentage of swings that missed (12.2%)

Chicago (AL)

James Baldwin

Position: SP
Bats: R **Throws:** R
Ht: 6' 3" **Wt:** 235

Opening Day Age: 28
Born: 7/15/71 in
Southern Pines, NC
ML Seasons: 5

Overall Statistics

	W	L	Pct.	ERA	G	GS	Sv	IP	H	BB	SO	HR	Ratio
1999	12	13	.480	5.10	35	33	0	199.1	219	81	123	34	1.51
Career	48	41	.539	5.19	138	121	0	742.0	800	290	508	101	1.47

1999 Situational Stats

	W	L	ERA	Sv	IP		AB	H	HR	RBI	Avg
Home	5	8	5.73	0	97.1	LHB	419	114	16	55	.272
Road	7	5	4.50	0	102.0	RHB	368	105	18	50	.285
First Half	4	9	6.62	0	100.2	Sc Pos	187	46	6	68	.246
Scnd Half	8	4	3.56	0	98.2	Clutch	35	5	0	1	.143

1999 Season

James Baldwin followed his 1998 blueprint, pitching his way into the doghouse in the spring months before finishing strong after the All-Star break. He managed double figures in victories for his fourth consecutive season and missed his preseason goal of 200 innings by only two outs.

Pitching & Defense

Baldwin came to the big leagues with a devastating curveball but hasn't developed command with his other pitches, including a fastball that tends to straighten out and get hit hard. His velocity is inconsistent and he gives up a lot of home runs when his pitches get up in the strike zone. Baldwin's athleticism hasn't translated into being a reliable fielder. In 742 career innings, most with runners all over the bases, he never has started a double play. He's not a factor in controlling the running game.

2000 Outlook

Before Baldwin went 8-4 in the second half, there was almost no chance that the White Sox would offer him arbitration. He pitched well enough to merit an estimated $3 million salary, but once again needs to deliver on his fading potential.

Carlos Castillo

Position: RP
Bats: R **Throws:** R
Ht: 6' 2" **Wt:** 250

Opening Day Age: 24
Born: 4/21/75 in
Boston, MA
ML Seasons: 3
Pronunciation:
cas-TEE-oh

Overall Statistics

	W	L	Pct.	ERA	G	GS	Sv	IP	H	BB	SO	HR	Ratio
1999	2	2	.500	5.71	18	2	0	41.0	45	14	23	10	1.44
Career	10	7	.588	5.03	109	6	1	207.2	207	82	130	36	1.39

1999 Situational Stats

	W	L	ERA	Sv	IP		AB	H	HR	RBI	Avg
Home	1	1	7.71	0	21.0	LHB	77	25	6	16	.325
Road	1	1	3.60	0	20.0	RHB	87	20	4	8	.230
First Half	—	—	—	—	—	Sc Pos	45	11	2	15	.244
Scnd Half	2	2	5.71	0	41.0	Clutch	5	2	0	0	.400

1999 Season

Carlos Castillo rocketed through the minors and reached Chicago at age 21, but he hasn't been able to stick. He began 1999 in Triple-A and didn't surface in the majors until late July. He pitched decently in relief but was bombed in two starts.

Pitching & Defense

Castillo has the stuff to be an effective starter, especially on a team that has been looking for rotation fodder as much as the White Sox. He throws in the low 90s and his slider at times is a very good second pitch. But he has yet to figure out that it's important to not just throw strikes, but quality strikes. He leaves too many hittable pitches in the zone, which is why he allowed 10 homers in 41 innings last year. He doesn't do a very good job of fielding or holding runners.

2000 Outlook

The White Sox are moving several pitching prospects through their system in a hurry, so Castillo may be facing his last chance to start for Chicago this spring. That is, if he hasn't already. His lack of improvement and lack of condition are disheartening.

Keith Foulke

Position: RP
Bats: R **Throws:** R
Ht: 6' 0" **Wt:** 200

Opening Day Age: 27
Born: 10/19/72 in Ellsworth AFB, SD
ML Seasons: 3
Pronunciation: FOLK

Overall Statistics

	W	L	Pct.	ERA	G	GS	Sv	IP	H	BB	SO	HR	Ratio
1999	3	3	.500	2.22	67	0	9	105.1	72	21	123	11	0.88
Career	10	10	.500	3.98	148	8	13	244.0	211	64	234	33	1.13

1999 Situational Stats

	W	L	ERA	Sv	IP		AB	H	HR	RBI	Avg
Home	2	2	2.19	5	53.1	LHB	186	34	6	15	.183
Road	1	1	2.25	4	52.0	RHB	198	38	5	14	.192
First Half	1	2	3.04	3	53.1	Sc Pos	94	15	2	16	.160
Scnd Half	2	1	1.38	6	52.0	Clutch	217	43	8	19	.198

1999 Season

The annual Elias free-agent rankings, flawed as they may be, rated Keith Foulke as the top reliever in the American League after the 1999 season. A struggling fifth starter for the Giants before joining the White Sox in the White Flag trade of 1997, Foulke has become an excellent setup man. He made a quick recovery from surgery to remove a bone spur from his shoulder in August 1998.

Pitching & Defense

Pedro Martinez may be the only AL pitcher with a better changeup. Foulke disguises his perfectly, seldom has trouble throwing it for strikes and gets a screwball action on it that makes it run in on righthanders. The change also keeps lefthanders at bay, and he sets it up by spotting a below-average fastball. Foulke keeps runners close and is an aggressive fielder, though he sometimes tries to do too much with grounders.

2000 Outlook

Foulke once again will be a key man for the White Sox. His presence is vital as the organization continues to integrate kids into the pitching staff. There could come a time when Foulke's ability gets him another chance as a starter.

Mark Johnson

Position: C
Bats: L **Throws:** R
Ht: 6' 0" **Wt:** 185

Opening Day Age: 24
Born: 9/12/75 in Wheat Ridge, CO
ML Seasons: 2

Overall Statistics

	G	AB	R	H	D	T	HR	RBI	SB	BB	SO	Avg	OBP	Slg
1999	73	207	27	47	11	0	4	16	3	36	58	.227	.344	.338
Career	80	230	29	49	11	2	4	17	3	37	66	.213	.325	.330

1999 Situational Stats

	AB	H	HR	RBI	Avg		AB	H	HR	RBI	Avg
Home	104	25	2	8	.240	LHP	36	9	1	2	.250
Road	103	22	2	8	.214	RHP	171	38	3	14	.222
First Half	101	19	4	9	.188	Sc Pos	50	7	1	13	.140
Scnd Half	106	28	0	7	.264	Clutch	23	5	0	2	.217

1999 Season

Mark Johnson established himself as a tough and heady presence behind the plate while backing up regular catcher Brook Fordyce. Johnson quietly played for at least a month with a tear in his left shoulder, an injury that required surgery and ended his season in late September.

Hitting, Baserunning & Defense

Johnson hardly strikes fear into anyone at the plate. He seems smaller than his listed size and uses his diminished strike zone to his advantage. He maintained a respectable on-base percentage while hitting .227 last year. He isn't intimidated by anything, including lefthanders. White Sox pitchers like throwing to him, largely because of his emphasis on defense. The one flaw in his receiving skills last year was a large number of passed balls. His arm is average but he has a quick release. Johnson is a below-average runner who will steal a base when teams forget about him.

2000 Outlook

A former first-round pick, Johnson should stick with the White Sox in the next few years. If fellow prospect Josh Paul shows he can hit, the Sox likely will trade Fordyce and go with a homegrown platoon.

Jeff Liefer

Position: 1B/LF
Bats: L **Throws:** R
Ht: 6' 3" **Wt:** 195

Opening Day Age: 25
Born: 8/17/74 in Fontana, CA
ML Seasons: 1
Pronunciation: LEAF-err

Overall Statistics

	G	AB	R	H	D	T	HR	RBI	SB	BB	SO	Avg	OBP	Slg
1999	45	113	8	28	7	1	0	14	2	8	28	.248	.295	.327
Career	45	113	8	28	7	1	0	14	2	8	28	.248	.295	.327

1999 Situational Stats

	AB	H	HR	RBI	Avg		AB	H	HR	RBI	Avg
Home	57	13	0	10	.228	LHP	8	1	0	2	.125
Road	56	15	0	4	.268	RHP	105	27	0	12	.257
First Half	97	23	0	12	.237	Sc Pos	29	9	0	12	.310
Scnd Half	16	5	0	2	.313	Clutch	19	5	0	3	.263

1999 Season

A shortage of lefthanded hitters prompted the White Sox to break camp with Jeff Liefer on the roster. It proved to be a mistake, as the 1995 first-round pick needed more at-bats than he got on the bench. His lost power returned after he went to Triple-A and played regularly.

Hitting, Baserunning & Defense

Liefer is normally a patient hitter with good power, but he couldn't show those skills when he was starting only once a week. His swing gets a little long, making him susceptible to breaking balls. He was drafted as a third baseman but has moved all over the field after injuring his shoulder. He no longer throws well and is a below-average defender at first base and in the outfield corners. He also has below-average speed.

2000 Outlook

Liefer appears ready for the big leagues, but is in danger of being crowded out of the picture once again. His best shot at playing appears to be in a first-base platoon with Paul Konerko, who could get some playing time in left field or at third base.

Sean Lowe

Position: RP
Bats: R **Throws:** R
Ht: 6' 2" **Wt:** 205

Opening Day Age: 29
Born: 3/29/71 in Dallas, TX
ML Seasons: 3

Overall Statistics

	W	L	Pct.	ERA	G	GS	Sv	IP	H	BB	SO	HR	Ratio
1999	4	1	.800	3.67	64	0	0	95.2	90	46	62	10	1.42
Career	4	6	.400	5.02	74	5	0	118.1	128	61	72	13	1.60

1999 Situational Stats

	W	L	ERA	Sv	IP		AB	H	HR	RBI	Avg
Home	2	0	3.72	0	46.0	LHB	134	35	5	19	.261
Road	2	1	3.62	0	49.2	RHB	210	55	5	32	.262
First Half	3	0	2.83	0	54.0	Sc Pos	108	28	3	41	.259
Scnd Half	1	1	4.75	0	41.2	Clutch	40	9	2	6	.225

1999 Season

After making a poor impression on Cardinals manager Tony La Russa, Sean Lowe strongly considered joining his father in the trucking business before a minor league trade sent him from St. Louis to Chicago. The former first-round pick opened the year as a long reliever but was used in more important situations as the year progressed.

Pitching & Defense

There's nothing fancy about Lowe. He's a standard sinker-slider pitcher who throws his sinker about 90 percent of the time. He has to get ahead of hitters to be effective. His control was much better last year than it had been in cameos with St. Louis the previous two seasons. He gets a lot of groundballs when he's on. Lowe moves slowly on the mound, but is an average fielder with a very good pickoff move.

2000 Outlook

Considering his history as a minor league starter, the White Sox could give Lowe a chance to join the starting rotation in spring training. His durability makes him a valuable part of a bullpen, so Chicago may leave him there.

Jaime Navarro

Position: SP
Bats: R **Throws:** R
Ht: 6' 4" **Wt:** 250

Opening Day Age: 32
Born: 3/27/68 in
Bayamon, Puerto Rico
ML Seasons: 11
Pronunciation:
JAY-mee nuh-VARR-oh

Overall Statistics

	W	L	Pct.	ERA	G	GS	Sv	IP	H	BB	SO	HR	Ratio
1999	8	13	.381	6.09	32	27	0	159.2	206	71	74	29	1.73
Career	116	120	.492	4.62	349	302	2	2022.0	2259	667	1097	205	1.45

1999 Situational Stats

	W	L	ERA	Sv	IP		AB	H	HR	RBI	Avg
Home	4	6	5.31	0	83.0	LHB	327	118	17	58	.361
Road	4	7	6.93	0	76.2	RHB	332	88	12	50	.265
First Half	6	8	5.31	0	95.0	Sc Pos	175	55	11	81	.314
Scnd Half	2	5	7.24	0	64.2	Clutch	36	9	0	2	.250

1999 Season

News flash: Jaime Navarro did *not* have the highest ERA in the American League last year for the first time in three seasons. But the round mound of getting taken downtown nevertheless got bounced out of the White Sox rotation for the second year in a row. His one lasting value has been as an innings-eater, but that total dropped for the third year in a row.

Pitching & Defense

Navarro's strength remains a two-seam fastball. But his inability to throw other pitches for strikes, a characteristic that often has him barking at umpires, creates too many fastball counts. His lack of quality offspeed stuff gets him pounded by lefthanders and gives him trouble putting hitters away. Navarro doesn't help himself in the field and does a terrible job holding runners on base.

2000 Outlook

The White Sox would have dumped Navarro long ago if anyone wanted him. This is the last year of the foolish four-year, $20 million contract that GM Ron Schueler gave him, and manager Jerry Manuel has no plans to use Navarro as a starter if Schueler can't move him in a garbage-for-garbage trade.

Bill Simas

Position: RP
Bats: L **Throws:** R
Ht: 6' 3" **Wt:** 235

Opening Day Age: 28
Born: 11/28/71 in
Hanford, CA
ML Seasons: 5
Pronunciation:
SEE-muss

Overall Statistics

	W	L	Pct.	ERA	G	GS	Sv	IP	H	BB	SO	HR	Ratio
1999	6	3	.667	3.75	70	0	2	72.0	73	32	41	6	1.46
Career	16	16	.500	3.92	248	0	23	270.2	263	127	216	30	1.44

1999 Situational Stats

	W	L	ERA	Sv	IP		AB	H	HR	RBI	Avg
Home	0	2	4.05	1	33.1	LHB	124	32	1	18	.258
Road	6	1	3.49	1	38.2	RHB	154	41	5	35	.266
First Half	2	2	3.99	2	38.1	Sc Pos	94	29	4	48	.309
Scnd Half	4	1	3.48	0	33.2	Clutch	114	28	2	20	.246

1999 Season

The emergence of Bob Howry cost Bill Simas a chance to be the White Sox' closer, but Simas and Keith Foulke formed one of the American League's better combinations of righthanded setup men. Simas isn't considered especially durable but set a new career high with 72.2 innings.

Pitching & Defense

Simas is a classic fastball-sinker reliever who isn't afraid to challenge hitters. He hasn't maintained consistent velocity on his fastball in recent years, becoming less of a strikeout pitcher. Batters tend to lift Simas' pitches, accounting for a high total of both home runs and flyouts. He'll groove pitches when he's behind in the count, so he must throw strikes. While Simas is a large man, he's actually a very good fielder. He could pay more attention to baserunners, however.

2000 Outlook

Simas' status as a four-year player could extend his salary beyond what the White Sox are willing to pay a middle reliever. It wouldn't be a surprise if the Sox included Simas in a deal for a shortstop or lefthanded hitter. He should be an effective big league reliever for years to come.

John Snyder

Position: SP
Bats: R **Throws:** R
Ht: 6' 3" **Wt:** 200

Opening Day Age: 25
Born: 8/16/74 in Southfield, MI
ML Seasons: 2

Overall Statistics

	W	L	Pct.	ERA	G	GS	Sv	IP	H	BB	SO	HR	Ratio
1999	9	12	.429	6.68	25	25	0	129.1	167	49	67	27	1.67
Career	16	14	.533	5.93	40	39	0	215.2	263	72	119	41	1.55

1999 Situational Stats

	W	L	ERA	Sv	IP		AB	H	HR	RBI	Avg
Home	5	5	5.65	0	65.1	LHB	266	79	13	46	.297
Road	4	7	7.73	0	64.0	RHB	271	88	14	49	.325
First Half	7	6	5.81	0	79.0	Sc Pos	126	45	10	70	.357
Scnd Half	2	6	8.05	0	50.1	Clutch	11	1	0	0	.091

1999 Season

Who knows what to make of John Snyder? A mid-level prospect, Snyder opened eyes by going 7-2 with the White Sox at the end of the 1998 season, then went 6-1, 2.00 in his first seven starts last year. But Snyder pitched his way back to Triple-A in June and never recovered his early form. He had bone chips removed from his elbow in September, and the Sox hope that explains his sudden fall.

Pitching & Defense

When Snyder was on his game, he hit his spots and used his sinker and changeup to get outs without dominating hitters. His fastball is one of the more pedestrian on the Sox staff, seldom hitting 90 MPH. He got into trouble by pitching behind in the count and not getting his sinker down. Snyder is an above-average fielder and holds runners OK.

2000 Outlook

Snyder won't be rushed if he needs extra time to recover from surgery. He'll be hard-pressed to win the fifth starter's job in spring training, but will earn another look if he pitches well at Triple-A.

Craig Wilson

Position: 3B/SS
Bats: R **Throws:** R
Ht: 6' 0" **Wt:** 185

Opening Day Age: 29
Born: 9/3/70 in Chicago, IL
ML Seasons: 2

Overall Statistics

	G	AB	R	H	D	T	HR	RBI	SB	BB	SO	Avg	OBP	Slg
1999	98	252	28	60	8	1	4	26	1	23	22	.238	.301	.325
Career	111	299	42	82	13	1	7	36	2	26	28	.274	.330	.395

1999 Situational Stats

	AB	H	HR	RBI	Avg		AB	H	HR	RBI	Avg
Home	104	18	0	7	.173	LHP	70	20	1	5	.286
Road	148	42	4	19	.284	RHP	182	40	3	21	.220
First Half	86	23	2	9	.267	Sc Pos	58	18	3	22	.310
Scnd Half	166	37	2	17	.223	Clutch	44	6	1	4	.136

1999 Season

After four years at Kansas State and six in the minor leagues, Craig Wilson didn't mind the view from the White Sox bench at all. He didn't get much playing time until late July, and improved the team's fielding while contributing offensively once he got his chance.

Hitting, Baserunning & Defense

Wilson sometimes seems overmatched against big league pitching, getting blown away by both fastballs and quality breaking pitches. He's a singles hitter with outstanding strike-zone judgment, and he can drive the ball when pitchers get behind and groove strikes. Wilson is a natural shortstop, but lacks the range to be a long-term option there. He has developed into a utilityman and is especially reliable at third base. Wilson would be more valuable off the bench if he had speed, but he's a below-average runner.

2000 Outlook

Wilson's approach and selflessness make him popular with both management and teammates. He could get a chance to platoon with Greg Norton at third base until prospect Joe Crede takes over at the hot corner.

Other Chicago White Sox

Jeff Abbott (**Pos**: LF, **Age**: 27, **Bats**: R)

	G	AB	R	H	D	T	HR	RBI	SB	BB	SO	Avg	OBP	Slg
1999	17	57	5	9	0	0	2	6	1	5	12	.158	.222	.263
Career	125	339	46	87	15	1	15	49	4	14	46	.257	.281	.440

A pure hitter with a .336 lifetime mark in the minors, Abbott impressed the Sox in 1998, when he hit .279 with 12 homers. But a bad start in '99 doomed him to Triple-A Charlotte. 2000 Outlook: B

Chad Bradford (**Pos**: RHP, **Age**: 25)

	W	L	Pct.	ERA	G	GS	Sv	IP	H	BB	SO	HR	Ratio
1999	0	0	-	19.64	3	0	0	3.2	9	5	0	1	3.82
Career	2	1	.667	4.98	32	0	1	34.1	36	12	11	1	1.40

A submariner, Bradford posted a 1.94 ERA in Triple-A in both 1998 and 1999. He was effective with the Sox in '98, but didn't have it in three '99 outings. He became a free agent in October. 2000 Outlook: B

Joe Davenport (**Pos**: RHP, **Age**: 24)

	W	L	Pct.	ERA	G	GS	Sv	IP	H	BB	SO	HR	Ratio
1999	0	0	-	0.00	3	0	0	1.2	1	2	0	0	1.80
Career	0	0	-	0.00	3	0	0	1.2	1	2	0	0	1.80

Davenport pitched adequately at Double-A Birmingham in 1999, earning a brief callup in July and September. He is young and probably isn't ready, so he's likely to spend the 2000 season in the minors. 2000 Outlook: C

Scott Eyre (**Pos**: LHP, **Age**: 27)

	W	L	Pct.	ERA	G	GS	Sv	IP	H	BB	SO	HR	Ratio
1999	1	1	.500	7.56	21	0	0	25.0	38	15	17	6	2.12
Career	8	13	.381	5.56	65	28	0	192.2	214	110	126	41	1.68

The Sox put Eyre in their rotation after a solid 1997 season at Double-A Birmingham. He wasn't ready and Eyre has struggled ever since, although his numbers at Triple-A in '99 suggest a rebound. 2000 Outlook: C

Darrin Jackson (**Pos**: LF/CF, **Age**: 36, **Bats**: R)

	G	AB	R	H	D	T	HR	RBI	SB	BB	SO	Avg	OBP	Slg
1999	73	149	22	41	9	1	4	16	4	3	20	.275	.288	.430
Career	960	2629	311	676	114	15	80	317	43	131	480	.257	.293	.403

Jackson provided a classy clubhouse presence and helped mentor surprising rookie Chris Singleton. Jackson retired in November to join the Sox' television broadcast booth. 2000 Outlook: D

David Lundquist (**Pos**: RHP, **Age**: 26)

	W	L	Pct.	ERA	G	GS	Sv	IP	H	BB	SO	HR	Ratio
1999	1	1	.500	8.59	17	0	0	22.0	28	12	18	3	1.82
Career	1	1	.500	8.59	17	0	0	22.0	28	12	18	3	1.82

After posting good numbers in the high minors in 1998, Lundquist made the Sox last spring. He struggled for two months before a demotion to Triple-A Charlotte. The Royals claimed him off waivers in October. 2000 Outlook: C

Jesus Pena (**Pos**: LHP, **Age**: 25)

	W	L	Pct.	ERA	G	GS	Sv	IP	H	BB	SO	HR	Ratio
1999	0	0	-	5.31	26	0	0	20.1	21	23	20	3	2.16
Career	0	0	-	5.31	26	0	0	20.1	21	23	20	3	2.16

Pena had an impressive second season at Double-A Birmingham in 1999, and the Sox recalled him in August. He may have been in over his head, but the Sox are desperate for lefthanded relief help. He figures to be back for more before too long. 2000 Outlook: C

Todd Rizzo (**Pos**: LHP, **Age**: 28)

	W	L	Pct.	ERA	G	GS	Sv	IP	H	BB	SO	HR	Ratio
1999	0	2	.000	6.75	3	0	0	1.1	4	3	2	0	5.25
Career	0	2	.000	12.38	12	0	0	8.0	16	9	5	0	3.13

Rizzo hasn't been impressive in three Triple-A seasons, and he lost twice in three relief appearances with the Sox in July. Rizzo became a free agent at the end of the 1999 campaign. 2000 Outlook: C

Liu Rodriguez (**Pos**: 2B/SS, **Age**: 23, **Bats**: B)

	G	AB	R	H	D	T	HR	RBI	SB	BB	SO	Avg	OBP	Slg
1999	39	93	8	22	2	2	1	12	0	12	11	.237	.343	.333
Career	39	93	8	22	2	2	1	12	0	12	11	.237	.343	.333

His strength is his defense, as Rodriguez doesn't hit for power but does draw some walks. He filled in for an injured Ray Durham in 1999. 2000 Outlook: C

Tanyon Sturtze (**Pos**: RHP, **Age**: 29)

	W	L	Pct.	ERA	G	GS	Sv	IP	H	BB	SO	HR	Ratio
1999	0	0	-	0.00	1	1	0	6.0	4	2	2	0	1.00
Career	2	1	.667	7.49	18	6	0	51.2	67	26	27	10	1.80

Sturtze had his best Triple-A season in five tries in 1999. He was 9-4 with 107 strikeouts in 104.1 innings, suggesting he may be able to fool major league hitters. Can he duplicate 1999's success? 2000 Outlook: C

Bryan Ward (**Pos**: LHP, **Age**: 28)

	W	L	Pct.	ERA	G	GS	Sv	IP	H	BB	SO	HR	Ratio
1999	0	1	.000	7.55	40	0	0	39.1	63	11	35	10	1.88
Career	1	3	.250	5.83	68	0	1	66.1	93	18	52	14	1.67

Ward earned a callup in July 1998 with a good first half after a conversion to relief. He pitched OK but didn't get lefties out. In '99 he didn't get anybody out, and Ward became a free agent in October. He signed a minor league deal with the Phillies. 2000 Outlook: C

Chicago (AL)

Chicago White Sox Minor League Prospects

Organization Overview:

The White Sox aren't ready to challenge the Indians for American League Central supremacy, but their rebuilding plan is progressing nicely. In the last two years, Chicago has given regular jobs to homegrown products Mark Johnson, Carlos Lee, Greg Norton, Magglio Ordonez, Jim Parque and Mike Sirotka. During the same time, they've given six young players acquired in trades their first shot at prime-time duty: Mike Caruso, Bobby Howry, Paul Konerko, Sean Lowe, Chris Singleton and John Snyder. The Sox remain optimistic about most of those players, and have a bevy of players in the upper minors ready for their turn. They also had four first-round picks in the 1999 draft and used those to restock their pitching supply.

McKay Christensen

Position: OF
Bats: L **Throws:** L
Ht: 5' 11" **Wt:** 180

Opening Day Age: 24
Born: 8/14/75 in Upland, CA

Recent Statistics

	G	AB	R	H	D	T	HR	RBI	SB	BB	SO	Avg
1999 AA Birmingham	75	293	53	85	8	6	3	28	18	31	46	.290
1999 AAA Charlotte	1	4	0	1	0	0	0	0	1	0	0	.250
1999 AL Chicago	28	53	10	12	1	0	1	6	2	4	7	.226
1999 MLE	76	287	45	76	7	4	2	24	13	22	48	.265

Teams can't blow a first-round draft pick much worse than the Angels did with Christensen. Drafting sixth overall in 1994 and in desperate need of a shortstop, the Halos passed on Nomar Garciaparra because Christensen, who was set to go on a two-year Mormon mission, was much cheaper to sign. Then they sent Christensen to the White Sox in the ill-fated Jim Abbott trade of 1995. Now he's blossomed into a potential .300 hitter with leadoff skills, including speed, and Southern League managers voted him the Double-A circuit's most exciting player in 1999. He's also a flashy center fielder with an average arm. Chris Singleton and Brian Simmons are ahead of Christensen, so he'll probably spend most of 2000 in Triple-A.

Joe Crede

Position: 3B
Bats: R **Throws:** R
Ht: 6' 3" **Wt:** 195

Opening Day Age: 21
Born: 4/26/78 in Jefferson City, MO

Recent Statistics

	G	AB	R	H	D	T	HR	RBI	SB	BB	SO	Avg
1998 A Winston-Sal	137	492	92	155	32	3	20	88	9	53	98	.315
1999 AA Birmingham	74	291	37	73	14	1	4	42	2	22	47	.251
1999 MLE	74	284	32	66	12	0	3	36	1	16	49	.232

Dissatisfied with Greg Norton's inconsistency and Carlos Lee's glove, the White Sox are looking forward to the day when Joe Crede will take over at third base. That could happen as early as Opening Day. A 1996 fifth-round pick, Crede nearly won the high Class-A Carolina League triple crown in 1998 despite a painful bone spur in his right big toe. The pain worsened and affected his hitting last year until he had season-ending surgery in July. He projects as a .300 hitter with 20-plus homers per season, and managers named him the best defensive third baseman in the Double-A Southern League. If Crede has a big spring training, he'll probably win Chicago's third-base job.

Jason Dellaero

Position: SS
Bats: B **Throws:** R
Ht: 6' 2" **Wt:** 195

Opening Day Age: 23
Born: 12/17/76 in Mt. Kisco, NY

Recent Statistics

	G	AB	R	H	D	T	HR	RBI	SB	BB	SO	Avg
1999 A Winston-Sal	54	184	22	41	13	0	2	19	9	18	59	.223
1999 AA Birmingham	81	272	40	73	13	3	10	44	6	14	76	.268
1999 AL Chicago	11	33	1	3	0	0	0	2	0	1	13	.091
1999 MLE	81	264	34	65	11	2	7	38	4	10	80	.246

Though he was drafted in 1997's first round, Dellaero has just a .238 average to show for three pro seasons. His best tool by far is his arm, which was rated the best in the high Class-A Carolina League (where he also was named the top defensive shortstop) and Double-A Southern League in 1999. Dellaero's arm may be the best of any shortstop in baseball, though he relies on it too much and sometimes lets hops play him. He also has some power, but he negates it by overcommitting on fastballs and swinging at just about everything. The White Sox are tiring of Mike Caruso at shortstop, but Dellaero will have to prove he can hit before they give him the job.

Jon Garland

Position: P
Bats: R **Throws:** R
Ht: 6' 6" **Wt:** 205

Opening Day Age: 20
Born: 9/27/79 in Valencia, CA

Recent Statistics

	W	L	ERA	G	GS	Sv	IP	H	R	BB	SO	HR
1998 A Rockford	4	7	5.03	19	19	0	107.1	124	69	45	70	11
1998 A Hickory	1	4	5.40	5	5	0	26.2	36	20	13	19	2
1999 A Winston-Sal	5	7	3.33	19	19	0	119.0	109	57	39	84	7
1999 AA Birmingham	3	1	4.38	7	7	0	39.0	39	22	18	27	4

In one of the biggest heists in recent memory, the White Sox extracted 1997 first-round pick Garland from the crosstown Cubs for Matt Karchner in mid-1998. Karchner has been either ineffective or injured ever since, while Garland finished last season with a dominating Triple-A World Series performance that had onlookers comparing his stuff to Kevin Brown's. Featuring an extremely heavy 90-93 MPH sinker, he surrendered just 11 homers in 158 innings last year. His curve is his second pitch, and he's refining a changeup and slider. Garland likely will pitch in Triple-A this season and could make his major league debut before he turns 21.

Aaron Myette

Position: P
Bats: R **Throws:** R
Ht: 6' 4" **Wt:** 195

Opening Day Age: 22
Born: 9/26/77 in New
Westminster, Canada

Recent Statistics

	W	L	ERA	G	GS	Sv	IP	H	R	BB	SO	HR
1999 AA Birmingham	12	7	3.66	28	28	0	164.2	138	76	77	135	19
1999 AL Chicago	0	2	6.32	4	3	0	15.2	17	11	14	11	2

With six first-round picks in 1997, the White Sox landed 40 percent of their future rotation. Lefthander Jim Parque was the first player from that draft to reach the majors when he did so in 1998, and Myette debuted last September. Signed out of Central Arizona Junior College, he likes to pitch inside with a 91-94 MPH fastball. He was the toughest pitcher to hit in the Southern League last year, permitting batters a .225 average, and also led the Double-A circuit by drilling 15 batters. His slider gives him a second above-average offering. Barring a horrid spring training, Myette probably will open the season in Chicago.

Josh Paul

Position: C
Bats: R **Throws:** R
Ht: 6' 1" **Wt:** 185

Opening Day Age: 24
Born: 5/19/75 in
Evanston, IL

Recent Statistics

	G	AB	R	H	D	T	HR	RBI	SB	BB	SO	Avg
1999 AA Birmingham	93	319	47	89	19	3	4	42	6	29	68	.279
1999 AL Chicago	6	18	2	4	1	0	0	1	0	0	4	.222
1999 MLE	93	310	40	80	17	2	3	36	4	21	72	.258

Paul broke the hamate bone in his right wrist in 1997, a year after signing as a second-round pick out of Vanderbilt, and since then he hasn't hit like the White Sox have hoped. That doesn't mean they still don't have high hopes for him. They continue to love his athleticism, leadership and receiving skills. Paul is extremely quick for a catcher, getting from the right side of the plate to first base in 4.1 seconds, and moves very well behind the plate. His arm is good, and Chicago still believes he'll hit for average with gap power and 10-15 homers per season. He'll try to recapture that form in Triple-A this year, and will push for a regular big league job if he does.

Brian Simmons

Position: OF
Bats: B **Throws:** R
Ht: 6' 2" **Wt:** 190

Opening Day Age: 26
Born: 9/4/73 in Lebanon,
PA

Recent Statistics

	G	AB	R	H	D	T	HR	RBI	SB	BB	SO	Avg
1999 AAA Charlotte	78	285	53	77	14	0	10	44	8	37	60	.270
1999 AL Chicago	54	126	14	29	3	3	4	17	4	9	30	.230
1999 MLE	78	274	42	66	11	0	7	35	5	29	61	.241

Simmons would have opened 1999 as Chicago's center fielder had he not cut his hand on a headfirst slide late in spring training. Instead, he went on the disabled list and watched Chris Singleton claim the job before he could return. A 1995 second-round pick from the University of Michigan, Simmons can hit in the .270s with some power from both sides of the plate, though sometimes he gets too pull-conscious batting righthanded. He's a very good center fielder with above-average speed and arm strength. He must wait for Singleton to cool off before getting another shot, but Simmons has a better future.

Kip Wells

Position: P
Bats: R **Throws:** R
Ht: 6' 3" **Wt:** 196

Opening Day Age: 22
Born: 4/21/77 in
Houston, TX

Recent Statistics

	W	L	ERA	G	GS	Sv	IP	H	R	BB	SO	HR
1999 A Winston-Sal	5	6	3.57	14	14	0	85.2	78	39	34	95	4
1999 AA Birmingham	8	2	2.94	11	11	0	70.1	49	24	31	44	5
1999 AL Chicago	4	1	4.04	7	7	0	35.2	33	17	15	29	2

Chicago's 1998 first-round pick, Wells didn't sign until the White Sox handed him $1.495 million that December. Despite the delay in starting his career, he reached the majors less than eight months later. The Baylor product throws in the low 90s with a deceptive delivery that doesn't allow hitters to pick up the ball until it's too late. He also has a nasty curveball that was rated the best breaking pitch in the Carolina League, and he also was named the high Class-A circuit's top prospect. His changeup is a good third pitch. Wells won four of his seven major league starts, and it's unlikely he'll return to the minors.

Others to Watch

Righthander **Lorenzo Barcelo** (22) missed much of 1999 after reconstructive elbow surgery, but got his fastball up to 93-94 MPH upon his return and should get stronger. He could be the best player received in the infamous White Flag trade with the Giants in 1997. . . Righthander **Pat Daneker** (24), a fifth-round pick, could give the Sox three starters from the 1997 draft. He's a sinker-slider pitcher whose control was rated the best in the Double-A Southern League. . . Righthander **Josh Fogg** (23) earned the same honor in the high Class-A Carolina League. He has three average pitches and projects as a possible fifth starter. . . The second of Chicago's four 1999 first-round picks, righthander **Matt Ginter** (22) has an 92-95 MPH and an 85-88 MPH slider that's impossible to hit when he drives it down in the strike zone. Several team envisioned Ginter as a future closer, but he'll remain a starter for now. . . **Aaron Rowand** (22) was named the best batting prospect in the Carolina League. He hits for power and average, and he's an athletic right fielder with a strong arm. . . Righthander **Jason Stumm** (18) was the Sox' top 1999 draft choice. He throws a tick harder than Ginter and has been clocked as high as 98 MPH, though his secondary pitches need work.

Jacobs Field

Offense

Hitters flourish in Jacobs Field. The Indians, the first team to score 1,000 runs since the 1950 Red Sox, batted .298 at home last year. Since the ballpark opened in 1994, the Tribe never has hit lower than .287 at home. There's a short porch down the left- and right-field lines, and the 19-foot wall in left field can turn sure outs into extra-base hits. The Jake probably is overrated as a home-run park because the Tribe has so many sluggers. Over the last three years, the park has been neutral in terms of favoring home runs.

Defense

The infield once was considered among the game's best. However, a change in the dirt had Gold Glovers Roberto Alomar and Omar Vizquel complaining about bad hops because there was such inconsistency between the thick infield grass and hard infield dirt. Speed is needed to cover center field, and the left and right fielders must be ready to challenge the wall because so many balls are hit to the warning track and beyond.

Who It Helps The Most

Vizquel has hit 22 points better at the Jake over the last five years than he has on the road. In his first full season, Richie Sexson hit 18 of his 31 homers in Cleveland.

Who It Hurts The Most

Kenny Lofton seems obsessed with swinging for the Jake's right-field wall and his average has suffered. He hit 58 points higher on the road last year. Relievers Ricky Rincon and Paul Shuey have had problems here.

Rookies & Newcomers

Lefthander Chuck Finley, who signed a three-year deal worth $27 million, will have to contend with a left-center power alley that's 26 feet closer to the plate than the one in Anaheim. He's 2-2, 2.66 in six career starts at the Jake. Having pitched for the Cuban national team, Danys Baez is accustomed to the pressure he'll face at Jacobs Field.

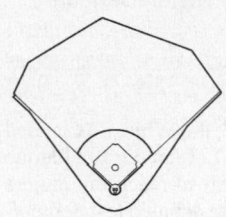

Dimensions: LF-325, LCF-370, CF-405, RCF-375, RF-325

Capacity: 42,865

Elevation: 660 feet

Surface: Grass

Foul Territory: Small

Park Factors

1999 Season

	Home Games			Away Games			
	Indians	Opp	Total	Indians	Opp	Total	Index
G	72	72	144	72	72	144	—
Avg	.297	.278	.287	.283	.260	.272	106
AB	2433	2581	5014	2568	2399	4967	101
R	451	405	856	466	355	821	104
H	723	717	1440	728	623	1351	107
2B	127	153	280	158	122	280	99
3B	15	11	26	14	16	30	86
HR	96	98	194	89	77	166	116
BB	326	282	608	333	271	604	100
SO	473	527	1000	488	458	946	105
E	55	57	112	36	58	94	119
E-Infield	43	43	86	30	47	77	112
LHB-Avg	.293	.273	.283	.285	.258	.273	104
LHB-HR	40	50	90	41	35	76	115
RHB-Avg	.301	.282	.291	.282	.261	.271	107
RHB-HR	56	48	104	48	42	90	117

1997-1999

	Home Games			Away Games			
	Indians	Opp	Total	Indians	Opp	Total	Index
G	220	220	440	216	216	432	—
Avg	.290	.279	.284	.274	.267	.270	105
AB	7413	7846	15259	7663	7285	14948	100
R	1258	1162	2420	1206	1065	2271	105
H	2153	2188	4341	2097	1945	4042	105
2B	407	441	848	445	372	817	102
3B	41	31	72	36	47	83	85
HR	280	256	536	286	247	533	99
BB	909	815	1724	880	783	1663	102
SO	1337	1527	2864	1439	1358	2797	100
E	163	166	329	125	154	279	116
E-Infield	126	130	256	104	129	233	108
LHB-Avg	.296	.286	.291	.273	.271	.272	107
LHB-HR	127	132	259	130	112	242	104
RHB-Avg	.286	.272	.279	.275	.263	.269	104
RHB-HR	153	124	277	156	135	291	94

1999 Rankings (American League)

- Highest batting-average factor
- Highest hit factor
- Highest RHB batting-average factor
- Second-highest error factor
- Second-highest RHB home-run factor
- Third-highest home-run factor
- Third-highest strikeout factor
- Third-highest infield-error factor

Charlie Manuel

1999 Season

After finishing his sixth year as Cleveland's hitting coach, Charlie Manuel replaced Mike Hargrove as manager on October 15, four days after the Indians lost the Division Series to Boston. Manuel has been with the Indians as a hitting coach or minor league manager since 1988. He managed the Tribe's Triple-A teams in Colorado Springs and Charlotte from 1990-93.

Offense

Manuel, who has never managed in the big leagues, knows offense. Last year the Indians became the first team in franchise history and baseball's first in 39 years to score 1,000 runs. He has worked successfully with all kind of hitters, but now must run the whole show. In the minors, he liked to play for big innings early and then play situational baseball in the late innings of tight games.

Pitching & Defense

As a coach, Manuel believed in getting close to his hitters. Now he's going to have to do the same with his pitchers. He selected veteran Dick Pole as pitching coach and will rely on him heavily. In the minors, Manuel often stayed with starters through some rocky early innings. He figures to stay with the same approach in Cleveland because his offense will give him a chance to win, even after being put in a deep hole. Manuel might be at a disadvantage in the bullpen because the Indians could enter the season without a dominant closer. Defensively, Manuel is in good hands with Roberto Alomar and Omar Vizquel in the middle infield.

2000 Outlook

Manuel is popular with the players, but he'll have to show them he wasn't given the job because the front office believes it can manipulate him. Manuel has a good reputation among the players as a motivator. He'll need it because the stakes keep getting higher every year in Cleveland. Hargrove won 97 games last year and lost his job. After winning five straight American League Central titles, the Indians won't be satisfied with anything less than a World Series championship.

Born: 1/4/44 in North Fork, WV

Playing Experience: 1969-1975, Min, LA

Managerial Experience: 0 seasons
Pronunciation: MAN-you-ull

Manager Statistics

Year	Team, Lg	W	L	Pct	GB	Finish
1999		—	—	—	—	—
0 Seasons		—	—	—	—	—

1999 Starting Pitchers by Days Rest

	<=3	4	5	6+
Indians Starts	—	—	—	—
Indians ERA	—	—	—	—
AL Avg Starts	2	82	47	21
AL ERA	6.83	4.98	4.72	5.62

1999 Situational Stats

	Charlie Manuel	AL Average
Hit & Run Success %	—	35.3
Stolen Base Success %	—	68.0
Platoon Pct.	—	56.7
Defensive Subs	—	22
High-Pitch Outings	—	15
Quick/Slow Hooks	—	18/18
Sacrifice Attempts	—	52

1999 Rankings (American League)
- Did not manage in the majors last year

Cleveland

Roberto Alomar

1999 Season

Happy and completely healthy for the first time in three seasons, Roberto Alomar re-emerged as one of baseball's best players. Making his Indians' debut after signing a four-year, $32 million free-agent contract prior to the season, he became the first player in franchise history to top 100 runs, 20 homers, 100 RBI and 30 steals in the same season. He set a club record for a switch-hitter with 24 homers and 120 RBI, while reaching 2,000 hits on September 22. Alomar won his eighth Gold Glove and third Silver Slugger.

Hitting

Traditionally a stronger hitter lefthanded, Alomar batted .338 righthanded last year. He was a .267 career hitter righthanded coming into the season. The majority of his power still comes from the left side, where he has great whip at the end of his swing. Alomar still can be fooled by high and tight fastballs, but he consistently hits the ball where it's pitched. While setting career highs in walks and strikeouts in 1999, he balanced the lineup from the No. 3 hole with his bunting, situational hitting and power. He saw more pitches than any player in the league.

Baserunning & Defense

Alomar had everything working last year. His 37 steals were his most since 1993 and helped him lead the American League in runs. Defensively, he teamed with shortstop Omar Vizquel to give the Indians the most exciting double-play combination in the game. Alomar has great range to his left and right and has a strong enough arm to make relay throws from the outfield and turn double plays. His sidearm flick throws to first and second base sometimes caught his new teammates off guard.

2000 Outlook

The Indians need Alomar to repeat his MVP-type season this year. He brought a focus to the club, directing its attention toward the postseason. They need to get back to the World Series, and so does Alomar.

Position: 2B
Bats: B **Throws:** R
Ht: 6' 0" **Wt:** 185

Opening Day Age: 32
Born: 2/5/68 in Ponce, Puerto Rico
ML Seasons: 12
Pronunciation: AL-uh-mar
Nickname: Robby

Overall Statistics

	G	AB	R	H	D	T	HR	RBI	SB	BB	SO	Avg	OBP	Slg
1999	159	563	138	182	40	3	24	120	37	99	96	.323	.422	.533
Career	1722	6611	1117	2007	372	58	151	829	377	758	796	.304	.375	.446

Where He Hits the Ball

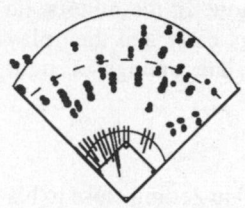 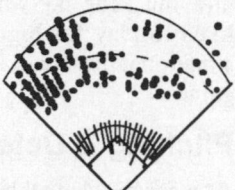

Vs. LHP   **Vs. RHP**

1999 Situational Stats

	AB	H	HR	RBI	Avg		AB	H	HR	RBI	Avg
Home	282	94	12	60	.333	LHP	145	49	6	21	.338
Road	281	88	12	60	.313	RHP	418	133	18	99	.318
First Half	321	104	12	60	.324	Sc Pos	176	69	10	99	.392
Scnd Half	242	78	12	60	.322	Clutch	80	28	3	23	.350

1999 Rankings (American League)

- 1st in fielding percentage at second base (.992), runs scored, sacrifice flies (13) and pitches seen (2,946)
- 2nd in stolen-base percentage (86.0) and batting average with runners in scoring position
- 3rd in steals of third (6)
- Led the Indians in stolen-base percentage (86.0), batting average with runners in scoring position, batting average on a 3-1 count (.500), runs scored, doubles, sacrifice flies (13), times on base (288), pitches seen (2,946), plate appearances (694) and games played
- Led AL second basemen in batting average, home runs, slugging percentage, on-base percentage and stolen bases

Dave Burba

1999 Season

Quick, who pitched more innings last year, Dave Burba or Cy Young Award winner Pedro Martinez? The answer is Burba, 220 to 213.1. Burba had his second straight 15-victory season, continuing to save GM John Hart from criticism for sending Sean Casey to Cincinnati for the big righthander just before Opening Day in 1998. Burba went 8-3 in his last 15 starts, including winning six straight decisions. Burba came down with a strained right forearm late in the season.

Pitching

Burba is a power pitcher who fell in love with his splitter last year. The 83-85 MPH pitch helped him set a career high in strikeouts, but it put undue strain on his right forearm and prevented him from throwing his curveball late in the season. Burba throws two- and four-seam fastballs that reach as high as 92-94 MPH, along with a curve and changeup. He throws way too many fat pitches, allowing 60 homers over the last two years. His composure needs work as well. When Burba starts getting hit, he gets mad and loses concentration.

Defense

Burba has trouble getting his large body in position to field. He hasn't had an errorless season since 1995. He pays close attention to the running game, with 15 of 27 basestealers getting thrown out against him last year.

2000 Outlook

Burba is a tinkerer. He works hard on his mechanics between starts. The Indians want him to reduce such work so he'll still be strong late in the season. He has come down with a sore forearm in September the last two seasons. Last year it was disastrous because he had to leave Game 3 in the Division Series with a 1-0 lead and the Tribe ahead in the series 2-0. Boston rallied to win the next three games.

Position: SP
Bats: R **Throws:** R
Ht: 6' 4" **Wt:** 240
Opening Day Age: 33
Born: 7/7/66 in Dayton, OH
ML Seasons: 10

Overall Statistics

	W	L	Pct.	ERA	G	GS	Sv	IP	H	BB	SO	HR	Ratio
1999	15	9	.625	4.25	34	34	0	220.0	211	96	174	30	1.40
Career	79	64	.552	4.23	344	152	1	1170.0	1123	515	920	138	1.40

How Often He Throws Strikes

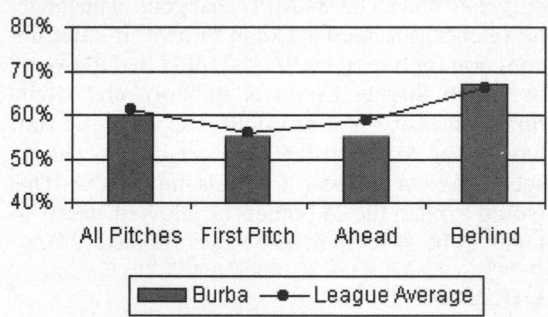

1999 Situational Stats

	W	L	ERA	Sv	IP		AB	H	HR	RBI	Avg
Home	6	5	4.10	0	127.1	LHB	379	85	13	36	.224
Road	9	4	4.47	0	92.2	RHB	452	126	17	67	.279
First Half	7	5	4.56	0	118.1	Sc Pos	189	56	5	70	.296
Scnd Half	8	4	3.90	0	101.2	Clutch	50	11	1	2	.220

1999 Rankings (American League)

- 2nd in walks allowed, wild pitches (13) and games started
- 3rd in lowest batting average allowed vs. lefthanded batters
- 4th in innings pitched, pitches thrown (3,602) and runners caught stealing (12)
- 5th in batters faced (940) and strikeouts
- Led the Indians in innings pitched, batters faced (940), home runs allowed, walks allowed, strikeouts, wild pitches (13), pitches thrown (3,602), pickoff throws (74), GDPs induced (20), lowest stolen-base percentage allowed (55.6), most strikeouts per nine innings (7.1), ERA at home, games started and runners caught stealing (12)

Bartolo Colon

1999 Season

The Indians spent most of the last decade looking for a No. 1 starter. Their search ended last year with the emergence of Bartolo Colon. He won 18 games, the most by a Tribe pitcher since 1988, and was one of seven American League starters to have an ERA less than 4.00. Unlike 1998, when he wore down in the second half, Colon went 11-2, 2.60 after the All-Star break. He dominated Boston in Game 1 of the Division Series, but allowed seven runs in one inning in Game 4 on three days' rest.

Pitching

Colon consistently throws between 95-100 MPH. He throws two- and four-seam fastballs, a hard curveball and an 83-84 MPH changeup. The longer he pitches, the harder Colon throws. It's not uncommon for him to hit 98-100 MPH in the seventh or eighth inning. Colon is stubborn and would throw all fastballs if he could. The coaching staff has to nag him constantly to get him to change speeds. When he doesn't, he gets into trouble. That would explain the 24 homers he allowed, nearly as many as he gave up in 1997-98 combined (27).

Defense

Colon has made eight errors in three years. He has trouble with balls hit right back at him. He gets off the mound quickly and his throws to first are hard. He hadn't focused much on runners in the past, but last year just nine of 16 basestealers succeeded against him.

2000 Outlook

The Indians have a potential 20-game winner in Colon, but they need to take care of him. Last year they limited his pitch count in the first half, and it paid dividends. Colon still needs to mature physically and mentally. He reported to spring training 20 pounds overweight last year and his collapse in Game 4 of the Division Series showed he's still not there yet. The signing of Chuck Finley should take some pressure off Colon.

Position: SP
Bats: R **Throws:** R
Ht: 6' 0" **Wt:** 225

Opening Day Age: 24
Born: 5/24/75 in Altamira, Dominican Republic
ML Seasons: 3
Pronunciation: bar-TOE-loh ko-LONE

Overall Statistics

	W	L	Pct.	ERA	G	GS	Sv	IP	H	BB	SO	HR	Ratio
1999	18	5	.783	3.95	32	32	0	205.0	185	76	161	24	1.27
Career	36	21	.632	4.17	82	80	0	503.0	497	200	385	51	1.39

How Often He Throws Strikes

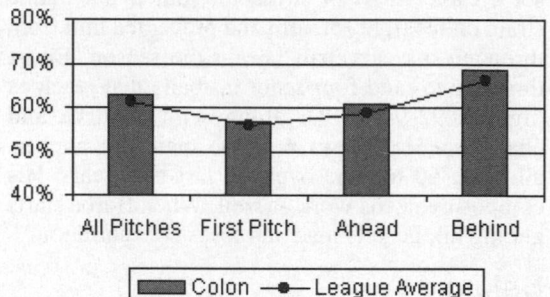

1999 Situational Stats

	W	L	ERA	Sv	IP		AB	H	HR	RBI	Avg
Home	9	2	4.12	0	102.2	LHB	368	94	14	46	.255
Road	9	3	3.78	0	102.1	RHB	398	91	10	39	.229
First Half	7	3	5.35	0	101.0	Sc Pos	167	41	5	60	.246
Scnd Half	11	2	2.60	0	104.0	Clutch	35	8	0	1	.229

1999 Rankings (American League)

- 1st in most pitches thrown per batter (4.05)
- 2nd in wins, winning percentage and most run support per nine innings (7.5)
- Led the Indians in ERA, wins, winning percentage, lowest batting average allowed (.242), lowest slugging percentage allowed (.398), lowest on-base percentage allowed (.314), fewest baserunners allowed per nine innings (11.8), most run support per nine innings (7.5), ERA on the road, lowest batting average allowed vs. righthanded batters, lowest batting average allowed with runners in scoring position and fewest home runs allowed per nine innings (1.05)

Travis Fryman

1999 Season

Before coming to Cleveland, Travis Fryman averaged 153 games a year in his six full seasons with Detroit. But in two years with the Tribe, he has averaged just 116. Last year Fryman played 85 games because he tore the posterior cruciate ligament in his right knee on July 3. In 1998, he was slowed by back problems. The gritty Fryman returned to the lineup September 2, wearing a brace on his knee. He got hot toward the end of the month and started all five games at third base in the Division Series.

Hitting

Fryman is a good fastball hitter. The harder a pitcher throws, the better he likes it. He has problems with sliders and changeups away when he's behind in the count. He's a pull hitter with decent power to left-center and center field. Fryman's main problem is a lack of selectivity. He never has struck out less than 100 times in a full big league season, and for his career he has averaged 2.4 strikeouts for every walk.

Baserunning & Defense

When he first returned to third in September, Fryman moved like he had a wooden leg. His throwing was questionable because he wasn't confident about pushing off his right leg. Through hard work, Fryman was playing decent defense by the time the postseason started. Fryman's baserunning also suffered. An intelligent runner when healthy, he was slowed considerably by the brace. Still, he continued to slide into second base so hard to break up double plays that he bent his knee brace at least once.

2000 Outlook

Fryman didn't have surgery on his knee because team doctors said it wouldn't do any good. This season will be a big test as to how much game Fryman still has left. Fryman balances a locker room full of big egos in Cleveland. But what the Indians really need him to do is play 145 games and hit 20-25 homers from the bottom of the order.

Position: 3B
Bats: R **Throws:** R
Ht: 6' 1" **Wt:** 195

Opening Day Age: 31
Born: 3/25/69 in Lexington, KY
ML Seasons: 10

Overall Statistics

	G	AB	R	H	D	T	HR	RBI	SB	BB	SO	Avg	OBP	Slg
1999	85	322	45	82	16	2	10	48	2	25	57	.255	.309	.410
Career	1327	5176	726	1418	278	33	187	823	70	459	1113	.274	.333	.449

Where He Hits the Ball

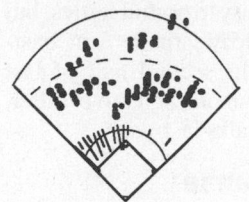 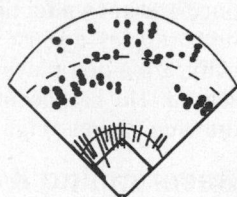

Vs. LHP   **Vs. RHP**

1999 Situational Stats

	AB	H	HR	RBI	Avg		AB	H	HR	RBI	Avg
Home	148	34	6	26	.230	LHP	66	18	2	13	.273
Road	174	48	4	22	.276	RHP	256	64	8	35	.250
First Half	243	63	8	42	.259	Sc Pos	94	28	6	41	.298
Scnd Half	79	19	2	6	.241	Clutch	51	11	1	5	.216

1999 Rankings (American League)

- 7th in lowest batting average with the bases loaded (.091)

David Justice

1999 Season

David Justice's 1999 season was one of extremes. He was very good in the first half, hitting .302-17-67, and mediocre in the second half, batting .261-4-21. Justice drove in five runs in three different games during the season, but homered just twice in his final 126 at-bats.

Hitting

Despite his size, Justice is not a big home-run hitter. He has had 21 homers and 88 RBI in each of the last two seasons. He has a pretty lefthanded swing, but it can get jumbled quickly. If he stays back and keeps his stride strong and balanced, he can drive balls into the gaps and out of the park. Justice has problems with breaking balls away. He once was known for his ability to pound lefties, but his struggles against southpaws made him basically a platoon player in the second half of last season. He has become a more selective hitter, drawing a career-high 94 walks last year.

Baserunning & Defense

In 1999 Justice managed to avoid most of the injuries that hounded him his first two years in Cleveland, and he started 88 games in the outfield after spending most of 1998 as a DH. He plays a decent left field, charging balls well and reaching most drives in the gap. Justice has an above-average arm, but doesn't go to the line well. With the exception of running through the occasional stop sign at third base, Justice runs the bases intelligently if not swiftly.

2000 Outlook

Justice went into the winter thinking he and his $7 million a year contract would be traded. He didn't endear himself to fans by sitting out the final game of the Division Series with a stiff neck. If he's still on the club in spring training, he'll compete with Richie Sexson, Jacob Cruz and Alex Ramirez for playing time in left field and as the DH.

Position: LF/DH/RF
Bats: L **Throws:** L
Ht: 6' 3" **Wt:** 200

Opening Day Age: 33
Born: 4/14/66 in Cincinnati, OH
ML Seasons: 11

Overall Statistics

	G	AB	R	H	D	T	HR	RBI	SB	BB	SO	Avg	OBP	Slg
1999	133	429	75	123	18	0	21	88	1	94	90	.287	.413	.476
Career	1235	4322	728	1223	215	19	235	799	46	702	759	.283	.382	.505

Where He Hits the Ball

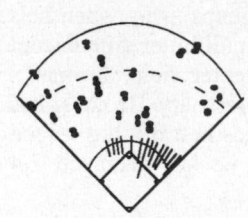
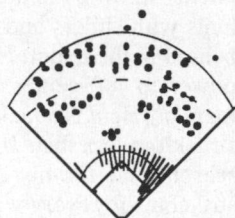

Vs. LHP   **Vs. RHP**

1999 Situational Stats

	AB	H	HR	RBI	Avg		AB	H	HR	RBI	Avg
Home	223	68	11	44	.305	LHP	101	25	5	19	.248
Road	206	55	10	44	.267	RHP	328	98	16	69	.299
First Half	268	81	17	67	.302	Sc Pos	122	35	6	66	.287
Scnd Half	161	42	4	21	.261	Clutch	64	16	5	12	.250

1999 Rankings (American League)

- 7th in intentional walks (11)
- 8th in lowest percentage of extra bases taken as a runner (31.1)
- 9th in on-base percentage vs. righthanded pitchers (.431)
- 10th in errors in left field (3)
- Led the Indians in highest groundball/flyball ratio (1.4)
- Led AL left fielders in on-base percentage, batting average with the bases loaded (.412), on-base percentage vs. righthanded pitchers (.431) and intentional walks (11)

Kenny Lofton

1999 Season

Kenny Lofton had a great season for two months. He was hitting .340 at the end of May when his game shut down. By the All-Star break, his average had dropped to .305. Then he strained his right hamstring on July 27, and didn't return to the lineup full-time until September 13. Lofton barely ended the year above .300. To complete a disappointing season, he separated his left shoulder in Game 5 of the Division Series, an injury which required major surgery after the season.

Hitting

Four years ago, the lefthanded-hitting Lofton was a marvel. He hit for average, drove the ball into the gaps, bunted, stole bases and hit the occasional homer. Now his skills are fading. Lofton is at his best when he bunts and hits line drives. Pitchers work him away with breaking balls and pound him inside with fastballs. He wastes countless at-bats by turning high fastballs into harmless flyballs to the warning track.

Baserunning & Defense

Lofton had 24 steals when he injured his right hamstring. The man who led the American League in steals five times stole one base the rest of the year. While making his sixth All-Star Game appearance, Lofton said he no longer was interested in stealing bases because basestealers get overlooked. Defensively, Lofton has a good arm but overthrows the cutoff man too much. He covers the gaps well, though he doesn't go straight back or come in on balls as well as he did when he was winning Gold Gloves.

2000 Outlook

Lofton's injury to his throwing shoulder puts his immediate future in doubt. A MRI revealed a torn rotator cuff, and he underwent surgery on December 14. He's expected to be out until at least the All-Star break. If he can play in 2000, Lofton needs an attitude adjustment. He needs to start bunting and stealing again. The Indians need to monitor him as well, resting him when he goes into his mental and physical slumps. Until he returns, they'll try to replace him with Jacob Cruz and Dave Roberts.

Position: CF
Bats: L **Throws:** L
Ht: 6' 0" **Wt:** 190

Opening Day Age: 32
Born: 5/31/67 in East Chicago, IN
ML Seasons: 9

Overall Statistics

	G	AB	R	H	D	T	HR	RBI	SB	BB	SO	Avg	OBP	Slg
1999	120	465	110	140	28	6	7	39	25	79	84	.301	.405	.432
Career	1096	4379	852	1356	212	60	63	412	433	537	590	.310	.384	.429

Where He Hits the Ball

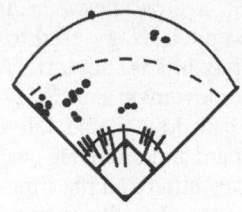

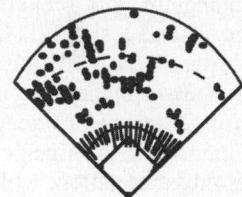

Vs. LHP   **Vs. RHP**

1999 Situational Stats

	AB	H	HR	RBI	Avg		AB	H	HR	RBI	Avg
Home	235	64	1	14	.272	LHP	116	26	0	5	.224
Road	230	76	6	25	.330	RHP	349	114	7	34	.327
First Half	328	100	6	27	.305	Sc Pos	105	23	1	29	.219
Scnd Half	137	40	1	12	.292	Clutch	67	12	0	5	.179

1999 Rankings (American League)

- 1st in lowest slugging percentage vs. lefthanded pitchers (.259)
- 3rd in on-base percentage for a leadoff hitter (.404)
- 4th in lowest batting average vs. lefthanded pitchers
- 5th in fielding percentage in center field (.989)
- Led the Indians in batting average on an 0-2 count (.294), on-base percentage for a leadoff hitter (.404) and highest percentage of extra bases taken as a runner (59.4)
- Led AL center fielders in most pitches seen per plate appearance (3.97), batting average on an 0-2 count (.294) and highest percentage of pitches taken (61.1)

Cleveland

Charles Nagy

Position: SP
Bats: L **Throws:** R
Ht: 6' 3" **Wt:** 200

Opening Day Age: 32
Born: 5/5/67 in Fairfield, CT
ML Seasons: 10
Pronunciation: NAG-ee

1999 Season

Charles Nagy won 15 or more games for the fifth straight season last year, joining Greg Maddux as the only other pitcher with that long of an active streak. Nagy made the All-Star team for the third time, but missed a chance to set a career high in victories when he went 0-2 in his last three starts. He won Game 2 of the Division Series, but pitched poorly in Game 5.

Pitching

The durable Nagy, who has made 184 straight starts without missing a turn, pitched with shoulder pain in the first half. It took its toll after the All-Star break, when he won only six games. He throws a sinking fastball, breaking ball, splitter and changeup. His breaking ball, a cross between a curve and a slider, is his best pitch. Nagy used to throw 88-91 MPH but he rarely hits 90 now. He's a finesse pitcher, relying on movement and location. Nagy has to keep the ball down, especially against lefties, or he gets hit hard and often. He has a long arm action, which gives hitters ample time to pick up the ball if he doesn't make adjustments in his delivery to hide it.

Defense

Nagy fields his position well. He hustles to first and led Tribe pitchers in total fielding chances last year. He never has controlled the running game. Just five of the 18 basestealers who tested him last year were thrown out. Nagy prefers to concentrate on throwing strikes.

2000 Outlook

It's clear by now that Nagy isn't a No. 1 starter. What the Indians need him to do is stabilize the middle of the rotation and put together a consistent year. If he does that, he could win 20 games. Nagy, working on a streak of four straight seasons of 200-plus innings, needs to be watched closely this year so he stays strong in the second half.

Overall Statistics

	W	L	Pct.	ERA	G	GS	Sv	IP	H	BB	SO	HR	Ratio
1999	17	11	.607	4.95	33	32	0	202.0	238	59	126	26	1.47
Career	121	86	.585	4.20	268	266	0	1766.1	1924	529	1143	182	1.39

How Often He Throws Strikes

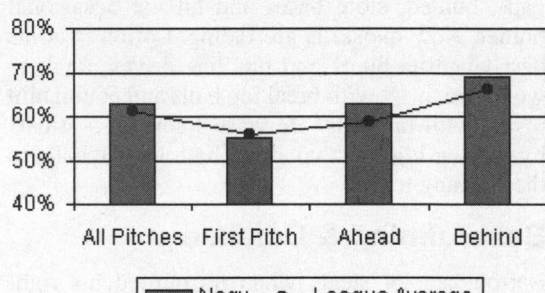

1999 Situational Stats

	W	L	ERA	Sv	IP		AB	H	HR	RBI	Avg
Home	8	6	4.94	0	102.0	LHB	402	130	11	61	.323
Road	9	5	4.95	0	100.0	RHB	411	108	15	50	.263
First Half	11	4	4.43	0	103.2	Sc Pos	202	63	4	81	.312
Scnd Half	6	7	5.49	0	98.1	Clutch	26	8	2	4	.308

1999 Rankings (American League)

- 2nd in fewest pitches thrown per batter (3.49)
- 4th in highest groundball/flyball ratio allowed (1.8), most run support per nine innings (7.0) and highest batting average allowed vs. lefthanded batters
- 5th in wins, hits allowed and highest batting average allowed (.293)
- Led the Indians in losses, hits allowed, GDPs induced (20), highest strikeout/walk ratio (2.1), highest groundball/flyball ratio allowed (1.8), fewest pitches thrown per batter (3.49) and fewest walks per nine innings (2.6)

Manny Ramirez

1999 Season

If Manny Ramirez isn't the best run producer in baseball, he's close. He drove in 165 runs last season, the most in the big leagues in 61 years, despite missing 15 games. He had 96 RBI in 78 games at the All-Star break. In a three-game series against Toronto in September, Ramirez drove in 11 runs, including eight in one contest. He finished tied for third in the MVP voting with teammate Roberto Alomar.

Hitting

Ramirez can handle almost any kind of pitch when it's on the plate. He's a power hitter with a high-average swing. In four of the last five years, he has batted .308 or better. What sets Ramirez apart is his ability to hit for power to all fields. Using a fluid weight shift and a smooth swing, he can drive inside pitches and breaking balls away out of the park. Ramirez changed his stance late in the season, pointing his left foot inward like teammate Harold Baines. In the postseason, Ramirez went 1-for-18 as Boston jammed him with fastballs.

Baserunning & Defense

It's doubtful that Ramirez ever will be an all-around player. But he's no longer clueless on the bases. He goes from first to third aggressively and knows he's not a basestealer. He takes long strides in right field, which gives the impression that he's not hustling. He has soft hands, which allow him to catch the ball in seemingly awkward positions, especially when he's coming in or going toward the foul line. He has a strong, accurate arm.

2000 Outlook

Ramirez is a free agent after this season. He's 27, which means he's entering his prime years. His market value is $15 million to $17 million a year. Tribe GM John Hart said he probably would play out the year with Ramirez and then try to re-sign him or let him walk away.

Position: RF
Bats: R **Throws:** R
Ht: 6' 0" **Wt:** 205

Opening Day Age: 27
Born: 5/30/72 in Santo Domingo, Dominican Republic
ML Seasons: 7

Overall Statistics

	G	AB	R	H	D	T	HR	RBI	SB	BB	SO	Avg	OBP	Slg
1999	147	522	131	174	34	3	44	165	2	96	131	.333	.442	.663
Career	849	3031	573	932	203	9	198	682	27	455	663	.307	.399	.576

Where He Hits the Ball

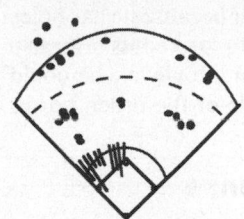

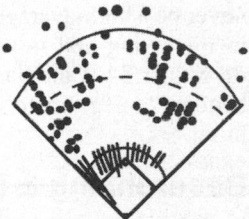

Vs. LHP   **Vs. RHP**

1999 Situational Stats

	AB	H	HR	RBI	Avg		AB	H	HR	RBI	Avg
Home	254	79	21	73	.311	LHP	115	44	8	38	.383
Road	268	95	23	92	.354	RHP	407	130	36	127	.319
First Half	303	101	25	96	.333	Sc Pos	189	73	17	126	.386
Scnd Half	219	73	19	69	.333	Clutch	68	18	3	17	.265

1999 Rankings (American League)

- 1st in slugging percentage, HR frequency (11.9 ABs per HR), cleanup slugging percentage (.667) and RBI
- Led the Indians in slugging percentage, on-base percentage, HR frequency (11.9 ABs per HR), batting average with the bases loaded (.500), batting average vs. lefthanded pitchers, cleanup slugging percentage (.667), slugging percentage vs. lefthanded pitchers (.687), slugging percentage vs. righthanded pitchers (.656), on-base percentage vs. lefthanded pitchers (.493), batting average, home runs, total bases (346), RBI and hit by pitch (13)
- Led AL right fielders in slugging percentage, on-base percentage, batting average and RBI

Cleveland

Richie Sexson

1999 Season

Richie Sexson figured he'd be lucky to get 300 at-bats after he lost the DH job to Wil Cordero in spring training. When Cordero broke his left wrist June 8, a door opened for Sexson. He made 53 starts at first base, 40 in left field, 21 at DH and one in right field. He ended the year with 479 at-bats, and 45 percent of his hits went for extra bases. In one game, he drove in five runs in one inning.

Hitting

At 6-foot-7, Sexson has a big strike zone. Pitchers pound him inside with fastballs, but when he's balanced properly, he has a short, quick swing with power. When he's off balance, he swings too hard and can't catch up to inside fastballs. Sexson might never be a high-average hitter because he has holes in his swing and is prone to strikeouts. He also drew just 34 walks last year. However, he could become a legitimate middle-of-the-order power hitter.

Baserunning & Defense

Sexson is no sprinter, but he did lead the Indians with seven triples. He already is an accomplished first baseman, but with Jim Thome ahead of him, Sexson has had to move to the outfield. First base is by far Sexson's best position. He has good range going to the line, scoops low throws and makes a good target. He's a better left fielder than right fielder and moves well for a big man. He has a strong but erratic arm and often throws to the wrong base.

2000 Outlook

Former manager Mike Hargrove said Sexson reminded him of a young Mark McGwire. Whether Sexson has McGwire-like power is unproven, but there's no doubt he could turn into a player who annually hits 30-40 homers and drives in 100-plus runs with consistent playing time. The Indians have to find a regular spot in the lineup for Sexson at first base, DH or left field.

Position: 1B/LF/DH
Bats: R **Throws:** R
Ht: 6' 7" **Wt:** 210

Opening Day Age: 25
Born: 12/29/74 in Portland, OR
ML Seasons: 3

Overall Statistics

	G	AB	R	H	D	T	HR	RBI	SB	BB	SO	Avg	OBP	Slg
1999	134	479	72	122	17	7	31	116	3	34	117	.255	.305	.514
Career	188	664	101	179	31	8	42	151	4	40	161	.270	.314	.530

Where He Hits the Ball

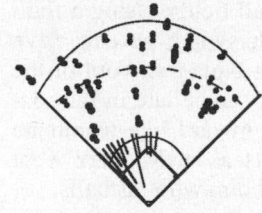 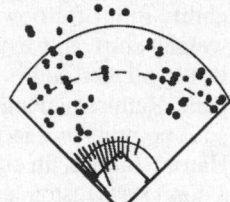

Vs. LHP   **Vs. RHP**

1999 Situational Stats

	AB	H	HR	RBI	Avg		AB	H	HR	RBI	Avg
Home	244	64	18	60	.262	LHP	137	38	11	35	.277
Road	235	58	13	56	.247	RHP	342	84	20	81	.246
First Half	253	62	15	54	.245	Sc Pos	160	41	9	87	.256
Scnd Half	226	60	16	62	.265	Clutch	79	21	7	20	.266

1999 Rankings (American League)

- 5th in lowest on-base percentage
- 8th in errors at first base (7) and lowest batting average on the road
- 9th in triples and GDPs (19)
- 10th in slugging percentage vs. lefthanded pitchers (.584), sacrifice flies (8) and lowest batting average
- Led the Indians in triples and GDPs (19)
- Led AL left fielders in home runs, RBI, sacrifice flies (8) and strikeouts

Jim Thome

Position: 1B/DH
Bats: L **Throws:** R
Ht: 6' 4" **Wt:** 245

Opening Day Age: 29
Born: 8/27/70 in Peoria, IL
ML Seasons: 9
Pronunciation: TOE-mee

1999 Season

All-or-nothing Jim Thome led the American League in both strikeouts and walks last year, the first player to do that since Mickey Mantle in 1958. Thome set a club record with 171 strikeouts, while becoming the first lefthanded hitter to have four straight seasons with 30-plus homers for the Tribe. He was hitting .240 on June 11, but hit 25 homers and drove in 79 runs in his last 95 games. He hit four homers in the Division Series to give him a career total of 16, third-most in postseason history.

Hitting

Thome is a contradiction. He has a big swing, which makes him easy to strike out. But he's conservative when it comes to swinging at bad pitches. Because he works the count well, pitchers throw him changeups and breaking balls when they're behind in the count. That led to a lot of strikeouts last year because Thome kept waiting for fastballs. Finally, he adjusted and started hitting the offspeed pitches up the middle and to left-center. Thome has frightening power, but his big swing may have led to the back spasms that plagued him last year.

Baserunning & Defense

Since moving from third to first base in 1997, Thome has been a DH in waiting. Through hard work in the offseason, he bulked up to 245 pounds. While the extra muscle helped his power, it hurt his range at first. With smooth-fielding Richie Sexson pushing for playing time, Thome must lose weight to improve his agility or move to DH. Thome has an average arm and runs well for his size.

2000 Outlook

The Indians think the adjustment Thome made on breaking balls last year can make him a consistent 40-homer hitter. They also think he could bat .300 again if he reduces his strikeouts and studies opposing pitchers more. He hasn't reached that level since 1996.

Overall Statistics

	G	AB	R	H	D	T	HR	RBI	SB	BB	SO	Avg	OBP	Slg
1999	146	494	101	137	27	2	33	108	0	127	171	.277	.426	.540
Career	916	3077	609	883	181	16	196	579	16	646	882	.287	.412	.547

Where He Hits the Ball

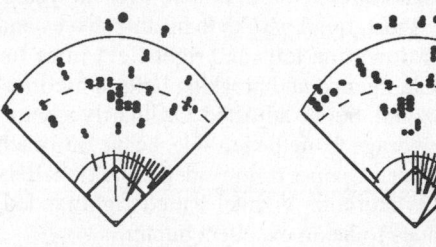

Vs. LHP   **Vs. RHP**

1999 Situational Stats

	AB	H	HR	RBI	Avg		AB	H	HR	RBI	Avg
Home	238	67	19	52	.282	LHP	134	32	6	29	.239
Road	256	70	14	56	.273	RHP	360	105	27	79	.292
First Half	258	73	14	50	.283	Sc Pos	142	47	9	74	.331
Scnd Half	236	64	19	58	.271	Clutch	75	16	2	9	.213

1999 Rankings (American League)

- 1st in walks and strikeouts
- 3rd in most pitches seen per plate appearance (4.29) and on-base percentage vs. righthanded pitchers (.448)
- 4th in fewest GDPs per GDP situation (4.4%) and fielding percentage at first base (.994)
- 5th in intentional walks (13)
- Led the Indians in most pitches seen per plate appearance (4.29), fewest GDPs per GDP situation (4.4%), on-base percentage vs. righthanded pitchers (.448), highest percentage of pitches taken (61.9), walks, intentional walks (13) and strikeouts
- Led AL first basemen in on-base percentage and most pitches seen per plate appearance (4.29)

Cleveland

Omar Vizquel

1999 Season

Omar Vizquel always wanted to hit .300. Last year he did and then some, finishing with the sixth-highest batting average in the American League. Known for his defense, Vizquel set career highs in average, hits, doubles, RBI, on-base percentage and slugging percentage. His 112 runs were the second-most ever scored by a Cleveland shortstop. In the midst of all that offense, he won his seventh straight Gold Glove.

Hitting

Sandwiched between leadoff man Kenny Lofton and No. 3 hitter Roberto Alomar, the switch-hitting Vizquel blossomed last year. He laid off the high fastballs that had given him trouble over the years. He used a short, quick stroke to hit line drives and push balls down the left- and right-field lines for doubles. Changeups and breaking balls sometimes fooled Vizquel, but he adjusted. Ordinarily a better hitter for average from the left side, he hit .333 each way last year. Against righthanded knuckleballers like Tim Wakefield, Vizquel batted righthanded. He continues to be an excellent bunter.

Baserunning & Defense

Bothered by a quadriceps injury in April, Vizquel didn't have one of his better defensive seasons. He made 15 errors, including five in the first month. That didn't discourage him from using his trademark barehanded grab-and-throw on bouncers. He and Alomar made highlight plays in the middle of the infield almost every night. Vizquel has worked hard to become a good basestealer since coming to Cleveland in 1994. His judgment hasn't always been the best, but last year he finished second in the league with 42 steals while getting tossed out just nine times.

2000 Outlook

At $3 million a year through 2002, Vizquel is one of baseball's best bargains. He asked to restructure part of the contract after the 1998 season and the Indians refused. Vizquel was expected to make the same request after last season, which may lead to him being traded.

Position: SS
Bats: B **Throws:** R
Ht: 5' 9" **Wt:** 170

Opening Day Age: 32
Born: 4/24/67 in Caracas, Venezuela
ML Seasons: 11
Pronunciation: viz-KELL

Overall Statistics

	G	AB	R	H	D	T	HR	RBI	SB	BB	SO	Avg	OBP	Slg
1999	144	574	112	191	36	4	5	66	42	65	50	.333	.397	.436
Career	1464	5196	734	1429	223	33	34	449	238	495	504	.275	.338	.350

Where He Hits the Ball

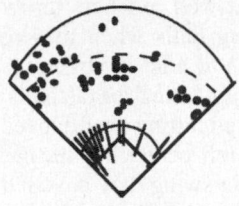 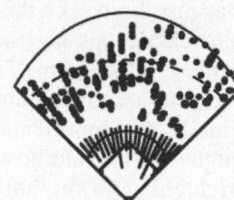

Vs. LHP   **Vs. RHP**

1999 Situational Stats

	AB	H	HR	RBI	Avg		AB	H	HR	RBI	Avg
Home	273	98	3	35	.359	LHP	147	49	1	15	.333
Road	301	93	2	31	.309	RHP	427	142	4	51	.333
First Half	293	96	3	38	.328	Sc Pos	145	49	4	60	.338
Scnd Half	281	95	2	28	.338	Clutch	78	31	2	13	.397

1999 Rankings (American League)

- 1st in steals of third (13) and sacrifice bunts (17)
- 2nd in batting average in the clutch, bunts in play (45) and stolen bases
- 3rd in singles and batting average at home
- Led the Indians in batting average in the clutch, batting average vs. righthanded pitchers, batting average with two strikes (.262), bunts in play (45), steals of third (13), at-bats, hits, singles, sacrifice bunts (17), stolen bases, caught stealing (9) and batting average at home
- Led AL shortstops in stolen-base percentage (82.4), batting average in the clutch, highest percentage of pitches taken (58.7), steals of third (13), sacrifice bunts (17) and stolen bases

Jaret Wright

1999 Season

Branded a headhunter by the American League, Jaret Wright was suspended once and called on the carpet by league president Dr. Gene Budig after hitting Tony Clark in the head. Wright spent all of last season under the microscope. It didn't help that he went on the disabled list twice after the All-Star break with a strained muscle behind his right shoulder. Wright gave up six runs in 2.1 innings in his last regular-season start, costing him a spot in the playoff rotation.

Pitching

Somewhere beneath all the mechanical changes that Wright went through last year is the power pitcher the Indians need. But how do they rediscover him? He needs more than just his 94-96 MPH fastball. Former pitcher coach Phil Regan worked with Wright on throwing a curveball and changeup, but he has little feel for the finesse part of his craft. Wright's mechanics were changed so many times last year that no one knew how or what he was supposed to look like by the end of the season. The only thing that was clear is that the pitcher who started the seventh game of the 1997 World Series as a rookie needed help.

Defense

Slow and overweight, Wright hurt himself defensively last year. He made three errors and couldn't catch a ball back through the middle to save his life. He's only fair at stopping the running game.

2000 Outlook

The Indians told Wright that he'd come to spring training as the fifth starter. They were challenging the ultra-competitive Wright to get in shape, stop running the streets at night and to take his profession seriously. They made it clear he could be traded if the right deal came along.

Position: SP
Bats: R **Throws:** R
Ht: 6' 2" **Wt:** 230

Opening Day Age: 24
Born: 12/29/75 in Anaheim, CA
ML Seasons: 3

Overall Statistics

	W	L	Pct.	ERA	G	GS	Sv	IP	H	BB	SO	HR	Ratio
1999	8	10	.444	6.06	26	26	0	133.2	144	77	91	18	1.65
Career	28	23	.549	5.08	74	74	0	416.2	432	199	294	49	1.51

How Often He Throws Strikes

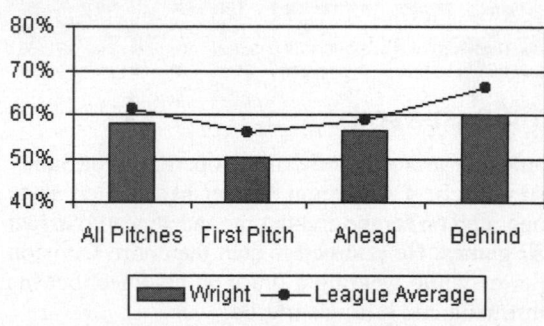

1999 Situational Stats

	W	L	ERA	Sv	IP		AB	H	HR	RBI	Avg
Home	3	5	5.90	0	58.0	LHB	255	75	10	44	.294
Road	5	5	6.19	0	75.2	RHB	264	69	8	37	.261
First Half	7	5	6.09	0	99.0	Sc Pos	129	39	5	64	.302
Scnd Half	1	5	5.97	0	34.2	Clutch	10	6	0	1	.600

1999 Rankings (American League)

- 2nd in lowest fielding percentage at pitcher (.903)
- 5th in errors at pitcher (3)

Cleveland

Sandy Alomar Jr.

Position: C
Bats: R **Throws:** R
Ht: 6' 5" **Wt:** 220

Opening Day Age: 33
Born: 6/18/66 in
Salinas, Puerto Rico
ML Seasons: 12
Pronunciation:
AL-uh-mar

Overall Statistics

	G	AB	R	H	D	T	HR	RBI	SB	BB	SO	Avg	OBP	Slg
1999	37	137	19	42	13	0	6	25	0	4	23	.307	.322	.533
Career	896	3073	373	845	179	6	86	417	22	152	349	.275	.314	.421

1999 Situational Stats

	AB	H	HR	RBI	Avg		AB	H	HR	RBI	Avg
Home	70	23	4	12	.329	LHP	34	12	2	7	.353
Road	67	19	2	13	.284	RHP	103	30	4	18	.291
First Half	82	26	3	16	.317	Sc Pos	36	9	2	18	.250
Scnd Half	55	16	3	9	.291	Clutch	20	4	1	4	.200

1999 Season

Another season, another knee operation for Sandy Alomar Jr. The veteran catcher had his left knee operated on for the eighth time and appeared in just 37 games. He returned to start the entire Division Series while wearing a brace on his knee, but his throwing and hitting suffered.

Hitting, Baserunning & Defense

A notoriously impatient hitter who drew only four walks last year, Alomar fares best when he tries to drive the ball up the middle or to right field. He has power, but he's more of a gap hitter who has gone pull-crazy the last few years. Alomar calls a good game, but threw out just four of 31 basestealers in 1999 because the knee injuries have hurt his quickness and agility.

2000 Outlook

Alomar, who faced a ninth surgery on his left knee during the offseason, was trying to avoid it with weight loss and conditioning. The Indians picked up his option for 2000, and manager Charlie Manuel believes he's still capable of hitting .300 with 20 homers. Alomar has to prove he can stay healthy enough to catch 100 games.

Harold Baines

Signed By
ORIOLES

Position: DH
Bats: L **Throws:** L
Ht: 6' 2" **Wt:** 195

Opening Day Age: 41
Born: 3/15/59 in St. Michaels, MD
ML Seasons: 20

Overall Statistics

	G	AB	R	H	D	T	HR	RBI	SB	BB	SO	Avg	OBP	Slg
1999	135	430	62	134	18	1	25	103	1	54	48	.312	.387	.533
Career	2702	9541	1270	2783	474	49	373	1583	34	1018	1375	.292	.358	.469

1999 Situational Stats

	AB	H	HR	RBI	Avg		AB	H	HR	RBI	Avg
Home	211	65	13	51	.308	LHP	53	16	3	17	.302
Road	219	69	12	52	.315	RHP	377	118	22	86	.313
First Half	220	76	19	63	.345	Sc Pos	122	45	9	82	.369
Scnd Half	210	58	6	40	.276	Clutch	58	19	6	25	.328

1999 Season

Harold Baines was acquired from Baltimore on August 27, in a waiver deal for minor league pitchers Juan Aracena and Jimmy Hamilton. Always a professional hitter, he singled home two runs in a 2-1 victory over Tampa Bay in his first at-bat with the Indians. He finished the year with 103 RBI, joining Dave Winfield as the only 40-year-olds ever to top 100.

Hitting, Baserunning & Defense

Baines is strictly a DH. He can't run and never was seen wearing a glove in the 28 regular-season games he played with the Indians. He can handle lefties, but he has more power against righthanders and is usually used as a platoon player. He stands deep in the box and uses a fluid swing to crush pitches down in the strike zone. Curveballs will fool him, but he makes adjustments quickly.

2000 Outlook

The Indians liked Baines, but he went back to the Orioles as expected after the season, signing a one-year, $2 million contract. He'd like to stick around long enough to get 3,000 hits. Baines is 217 hits shy of that milestone, which means he's about two years away. Cleveland has no shortage of DH candidates.

Wil Cordero

Position: LF/DH
Bats: R **Throws:** R
Ht: 6' 2" **Wt:** 200

Opening Day Age: 28
Born: 10/3/71 in Mayaguez, Puerto Rico
ML Seasons: 8
Pronunciation: cor-DAIR-oh

Overall Statistics

	G	AB	R	H	D	T	HR	RBI	SB	BB	SO	Avg	OBP	Slg
1999	54	194	35	58	15	0	8	32	2	15	37	.299	.364	.500
Career	773	2833	406	791	174	13	79	368	44	199	497	.279	.333	.433

1999 Situational Stats

	AB	H	HR	RBI	Avg		AB	H	HR	RBI	Avg
Home	103	32	3	16	.311	LHP	55	14	2	6	.255
Road	91	26	5	16	.286	RHP	139	44	6	26	.317
First Half	152	48	5	26	.316	Sc Pos	64	19	1	23	.297
Scnd Half	42	10	3	6	.238	Clutch	32	13	3	8	.406

1999 Season

Wil Cordero came to spring training on a $500,000 make-good contract and ended up beating out prospect Richie Sexson for the DH job. Overweight and troubled by spousal-abuse charges in 1997 and 1998, Cordero found peace in Cleveland. He was hitting .316 when he broke his left wrist making a catch in left field on June 8. He needed surgery and didn't return until September 8.

Hitting, Baserunning & Defense

Cordero makes hard contact and crushes low fastballs. He's a professional hitter who can hit breaking balls and changeups into right field. He has power, but he's best when he hits line drives. Cordero made 29 starts in left field, where he's adequate with a below-average arm. He played first and third base in spring training, but never appeared at those positions during the season.

2000 Outlook

The Indians liked Cordero, but they're top-heavy with outfielders. He signed a three-year, $9 million contract with the Pirates in December. Pittsburgh looks for him to provide depth, but he could get a lot of playing time if he hits like he did in 1999.

Einar Diaz

Position: C
Bats: R **Throws:** R
Ht: 5'10" **Wt:** 165

Opening Day Age: 27
Born: 12/28/72 in Chiriqui, Panama
ML Seasons: 4

Overall Statistics

	G	AB	R	H	D	T	HR	RBI	SB	BB	SO	Avg	OBP	Slg
1999	119	392	43	110	21	1	3	32	11	23	41	.281	.328	.362
Career	145	448	52	122	23	1	5	42	11	26	45	.272	.320	.362

1999 Situational Stats

	AB	H	HR	RBI	Avg		AB	H	HR	RBI	Avg
Home	181	59	2	18	.326	LHP	94	20	2	7	.213
Road	211	51	1	14	.242	RHP	298	90	1	25	.302
First Half	212	57	2	21	.269	Sc Pos	99	31	1	29	.313
Scnd Half	180	53	1	11	.294	Clutch	46	9	0	1	.196

1999 Season

Rookie Einar Diaz reinvented himself last year. The Indians thought the converted third baseman would never be more than a backup catcher, but when Sandy Alomar Jr. went down with a knee injury in May, Diaz went behind the plate and proved he could catch every day. The Indians went 63-45 in his 108 starts.

Hitting, Baserunning & Defense

Diaz is a free swinger who can handle any pitch above the knees. Sinkers and curveballs below the knees give him problems. He's a singles hitter who could someday hit 10-15 homers a year. Diaz has a strong arm and quick feet. Despite a 1-for-14 start throwing out basestealers in 1999, his 34.5 percent success rate ranked fifth in the American League. Diaz' 11 steals were the most by a Tribe catcher since 1934.

2000 Outlook

Built low to the ground, Diaz is the Tribe's catcher of the future. The Indians like his toughness, durability and enthusiasm. He'll never be a force with the bat, but should hit enough to play as often as needed.

Cleveland

Mike Jackson

Position: RP
Bats: R **Throws:** R
Ht: 6' 2" **Wt:** 225

Opening Day Age: 35
Born: 12/22/64 in
Houston, TX
ML Seasons: 14

Overall Statistics

	W	L	Pct.	ERA	G	GS	Sv	IP	H	BB	SO	HR	Ratio
1999	3	4	.429	4.06	72	0	39	68.2	60	26	55	11	1.25
Career	53	61	.465	3.26	835	7	138	1017.2	801	414	905	101	1.19

1999 Situational Stats

	W	L	ERA	Sv	IP		AB	H	HR	RBI	Avg
Home	3	3	4.33	16	35.1	LHB	130	31	2	6	.238
Road	0	1	3.78	23	33.1	RHB	129	29	9	27	.225
First Half	3	2	4.58	19	39.1	Sc Pos	62	11	3	20	.177
Scnd Half	0	2	3.38	20	29.1	Clutch	156	36	5	19	.231

1999 Season

Mike Jackson delivered his second straight productive season as a closer, saving 39 games in 43 chances. A converted setup man, Jackson pitched with shoulder and elbow problems early in the year, and his ERA suffered as a result.

Pitching, Defense & Hitting

Jackson uses a fastball to set up his slider. He doesn't throw as hard as he once did, which may explain why he gave up 11 homers in 1999, as opposed to four in 1998. But his fastball is still in the 89-94 MPH range. Jackson always has been tough against righthanders, but he has improved dramatically against lefties during the last two years. He does a decent job of holding runners, but doesn't move well off the mound because of bad knees.

2000 Outlook

One of the best bargains in baseball during his three-year stay with the Indians, Jackson agreed to a contract with the Cardinals this past winter only to fail their physical. The Phillies then signed him to a one-year, $3 million contract, which also includes plenty of incentives and two option years. He'll serve as Philadelphia's closer, while Paul Shuey may take over that role in Cleveland.

Steve Karsay

Position: RP
Bats: R **Throws:** R
Ht: 6' 3" **Wt:** 209

Opening Day Age: 28
Born: 3/24/72 in
Flushing, NY
ML Seasons: 5
Pronunciation:
CAR-say

Overall Statistics

	W	L	Pct.	ERA	G	GS	Sv	IP	H	BB	SO	HR	Ratio
1999	10	2	.833	2.97	50	3	1	78.2	71	30	68	6	1.28
Career	17	20	.459	4.52	97	40	1	312.2	343	107	221	34	1.44

1999 Situational Stats

	W	L	ERA	Sv	IP		AB	H	HR	RBI	Avg
Home	4	1	1.80	0	40.0	LHB	134	28	2	11	.209
Road	6	1	4.19	1	38.2	RHB	153	43	4	23	.281
First Half	7	1	2.63	1	54.2	Sc Pos	77	16	1	27	.208
Scnd Half	3	1	3.75	0	24.0	Clutch	88	23	1	11	.261

1999 Season

It took Steve Karsay four years to completely recover from ligament-transplant surgery on his right elbow. He made it all the way back last year as a setup man. He was 8-1 in August when the Indians decided to make him a starter. Karsay won his first two starts before straining a flexor tendon in his right elbow and going on the disabled list. He and the Indians bullpen were never the same.

Pitching & Defense

Before straining his forearm, Karsay was consistently throwing between 95-98 MPH. His combination of an overpowering fastball and hard curveball made him one of the most dominant setup men in the American League. He also throws a splitter and changeup, but rarely used them in relief. Karsay isn't a great fielder but does a good job holding runners.

2000 Outlook

After the season Karsay had surgery to remove bone chips from his right elbow. His days as a starter are probably over. With former Tribe closer Mike Jackson signing with the Phillies, Karsay has been mentioned as a candidate. He's excited about the opportunity, but his durability remains questionable.

Steve Reed

Position: RP
Bats: R **Throws:** R
Ht: 6' 2" **Wt:** 212

Opening Day Age: 34
Born: 3/11/66 in Los Angeles, CA
ML Seasons: 8

Overall Statistics

	W	L	Pct.	ERA	G	GS	Sv	IP	H	BB	SO	HR	Ratio
1999	3	2	.600	4.23	63	0	0	61.2	69	20	44	10	1.44
Career	33	23	.589	3.62	480	0	16	527.1	473	173	403	71	1.23

1999 Situational Stats

	W	L	ERA	Sv	IP		AB	H	HR	RBI	Avg
Home	2	0	3.86	0	30.1	LHB	87	23	7	19	.264
Road	1	2	4.60	0	31.1	RHB	155	46	3	29	.297
First Half	3	1	3.22	0	36.1	Sc Pos	70	21	4	38	.300
Scnd Half	0	1	5.68	0	25.1	Clutch	66	20	2	14	.303

1999 Season

Injuries keep following reliever Steve Reed. After having the second half of his 1998 season ruined by a blood clot in his right wrist, Reed was hurt last year by a strep infection and a sore right elbow. He scratched his left elbow on a clubhouse pillar in May and missed a week with an infection that left him weak for the rest of the first half. He missed 11 games in September because of a sore elbow.

Pitching & Defense

Reed relies on the movement of his pitches and the deception in his three-quarters delivery. His best pitch is an 84-86 MPH sinker, and he also throws a slider and changeup. He usually dominates righthanders, but last year they hit .297 against him. He's an average fielder and controls the running game pretty well.

2000 Outlook

Reed needs to have a healthy season to re-establish himself as a quality reliever. The Indians still are upset at him for not telling them that his elbow still hurt in the postseason. He'd benefit from a more defined role in the bullpen, but he has to earn it.

Ricky Rincon

Position: RP
Bats: L **Throws:** L
Ht: 5'10" **Wt:** 188

Opening Day Age: 29
Born: 4/13/70 in Veracruz, Mexico
ML Seasons: 3
Pronunciation: rin-CONE

Overall Statistics

	W	L	Pct.	ERA	G	GS	Sv	IP	H	BB	SO	HR	Ratio
1999	2	3	.400	4.43	59	0	0	44.2	41	24	30	6	1.46
Career	6	13	.316	3.50	181	0	18	169.2	142	77	165	17	1.29

1999 Situational Stats

	W	L	ERA	Sv	IP		AB	H	HR	RBI	Avg
Home	1	1	5.40	0	25.0	LHB	73	17	3	11	.233
Road	1	2	3.20	0	19.2	RHB	92	24	3	9	.261
First Half	0	1	4.74	0	19.0	Sc Pos	55	10	0	12	.182
Scnd Half	2	2	4.21	0	25.2	Clutch	67	13	1	7	.194

1999 Season

Acquired from the Pirates in November 1998 to be the final piece to the Indians bullpen, Ricky Rincon was a disappointment. While the guy he was traded for, Brian Giles, blossomed as a power-hitting center fielder, Rincon struggled in his first year in the American League.

Pitching & Defense

Rincon is a sinker-slider pitcher who didn't adapt to the matchup style of relief pitching in the AL. He was used to working an inning or two at a time, not a batter or two. He also was hampered early in the year by a sore elbow. When the Indians finally started letting him pitch in one-inning segments, he allowed just three earned runs in his final 16 regular-season appearances. Rincon, who can hit 91 MPH with his sinker, doesn't field his position well, but holds runners close.

2000 Outlook

The Indians must figure out how to use Rincon, while the pocket-sized lefthander needs to pitch like he did for the Pirates in 1997 and 1998. With Paul Assenmacher gone, the Indians need Rincon to be a strong lefthanded presence in the bullpen.

Cleveland

Paul Shuey Future Closer

Position: RP
Bats: R **Throws:** R
Ht: 6' 3" **Wt:** 215

Opening Day Age: 29
Born: 9/16/70 in Lima, OH
ML Seasons: 6
Pronunciation: SHOO-ey

Overall Statistics

	W	L	Pct.	ERA	G	GS	Sv	IP	H	BB	SO	HR	Ratio
1999	8	5	.615	3.53	72	0	6	81.2	68	40	103	8	1.32
Career	22	16	.579	4.01	218	0	19	249.1	228	136	272	26	1.46

1999 Situational Stats

	W	L	ERA	Sv	IP		AB	H	HR	RBI	Avg
Home	5	3	4.43	5	44.2	LHB	139	31	3	20	.223
Road	3	2	2.43	1	37.0	RHB	166	37	5	22	.223
First Half	5	4	4.09	4	44.0	Sc Pos	76	21	1	31	.276
Scnd Half	3	1	2.87	2	37.2	Clutch	174	43	5	31	.247

1999 Season

Paul Shuey drove Indians fans to distraction last year. He was the first Cleveland reliever to strike out more than 100 batters since Sid Monge in 1979, but he also blew six of 12 save opportunities. Shuey won a career-high eight games but allowed 48 percent of his inherited runners to score. In April, he made his seventh career trip to the disabled list, this time with a hamstring injury.

Pitching & Defense

Shuey has three strong pitches. He throws a 94-97 MPH fastball, a hard-breaking curveball and a diving splitter. The problem was he overthrew the splitter and constantly was burned by it. He gave up eight homers, most coming off hanging splitters in crucial late-inning situations.

2000 Outlook

The Indians used their 1992 first-round pick on Shuey with the idea of someday making him their closer. It has taken a long time, but this could be the year he gets the job. There's no doubt he has the stuff, though he needs to overcome his inconsistency in the strike zone and his history of chronic leg problems.

Enrique Wilson

Position: 3B/SS/2B
Bats: B **Throws:** R
Ht: 5'11" **Wt:** 170

Opening Day Age: 24
Born: 7/27/75 in Santo Domingo, Dominican Republic
ML Seasons: 3

Overall Statistics

	G	AB	R	H	D	T	HR	RBI	SB	BB	SO	Avg	OBP	Slg
1999	113	332	41	87	22	1	2	24	5	25	41	.262	.310	.352
Career	150	437	56	121	28	1	4	37	7	29	51	.277	.320	.373

1999 Situational Stats

	AB	H	HR	RBI	Avg		AB	H	HR	RBI	Avg
Home	162	45	1	14	.278	LHP	110	28	1	5	.255
Road	170	42	1	10	.247	RHP	222	59	1	19	.266
First Half	165	51	1	15	.309	Sc Pos	84	19	0	19	.226
Scnd Half	167	36	1	9	.216	Clutch	52	12	1	5	.231

1999 Season

Utility infielder Enrique Wilson had a busy season. He filled in at shortstop in April when Omar Vizquel had a strained quadriceps muscle. He moved to third in July when Travis Fryman injured his right knee. He made 47 starts at third, 21 at shortstop and five at second base. After hitting .309 before the All-Star break, Wilson wore down in the second half. A jammed left thumb in late July hurt him at the plate.

Hitting, Baserunning & Defense

The switch-hitting Wilson is a line-drive hitter with just a touch of power. He hits for a higher average and for more power lefthanded. He's a shortstop by trade and has a strong arm, though he sometimes makes wild throws. He can steal bases, but has been a lot less aggressive in the majors than in the minors.

2000 Outlook

The Indians like Wilson because he can play short and second without a major drop in performance if Vizquel or Roberto Alomar needs a break. Wilson needs to get stronger so he holds up better over the course of the season.

Paul Assenmacher (Pos: LHP, Age: 39)

	W	L	Pct.	ERA	G	GS	Sv	IP	H	BB	SO	HR	Ratio
1999	2	1	.667	8.18	55	0	0	33.0	50	17	29	6	2.03
Career	61	44	.581	3.53	884	1	56	855.2	817	315	807	73	1.32

After not posting an ERA above 3.55 dating back to 1993, Assenmacher had the wheels come off in '99. Another Tribe pitcher pushing 40, Assenmacher was cut loose after five years in Cleveland. 2000 Outlook: C

Carlos Baerga (Pos: 3B/2B, Age: 31, Bats: B)

	G	AB	R	H	D	T	HR	RBI	SB	BB	SO	Avg	OBP	Slg
1999	55	137	10	33	1	0	3	10	2	10	24	.241	.300	.314
Career	1280	4807	659	1400	246	17	124	686	52	253	511	.291	.330	.427

Baerga hasn't had a productive season or been in shape for a few years now. A free agent, he may have seen his career end when he tore up his knee playing winter ball. 2000 Outlook: C

Jim Brower (Pos: RHP, Age: 27)

	W	L	Pct.	ERA	G	GS	Sv	IP	H	BB	SO	HR	Ratio
1999	3	1	.750	4.56	9	2	0	25.2	27	10	18	8	1.44
Career	3	1	.750	4.56	9	2	0	25.2	27	10	18	8	1.44

Brower's first Triple-A season was no better than average, but he pitched OK in Cleveland. He debuted with four scoreless outings in relief, and the numbers aren't bad if you take away his one bad start. 2000 Outlook: C

Jolbert Cabrera (Pos: CF, Age: 27, Bats: R)

	G	AB	R	H	D	T	HR	RBI	SB	BB	SO	Avg	OBP	Slg
1999	30	37	6	7	1	0	0	0	3	1	8	.189	.231	.216
Career	31	39	6	7	1	0	0	0	3	1	9	.179	.220	.205

After posting career highs in batting (.318) and homers (10) in Triple-A in 1998, Cabrera made the Tribe to open last season. He didn't play or hit much before a June demotion. 2000 Outlook: C

Tom Candiotti (Pos: RHP, Age: 42)

	W	L	Pct.	ERA	G	GS	Sv	IP	H	BB	SO	HR	Ratio
1999	4	6	.400	7.32	18	13	0	71.1	86	30	41	14	1.63
Career	151	164	.479	3.73	451	410	0	2725.0	2662	883	1735	250	1.30

A torn fingernail and knee tendinitis hampered Candiotti before he was let go by Oakland in June. The Indians signed him, but he was cut loose after two horrible outings in late July. He may be done. 2000 Outlook: D

Rich DeLucia (Pos: RHP, Age: 35)

	W	L	Pct.	ERA	G	GS	Sv	IP	H	BB	SO	HR	Ratio
1999	0	1	.000	6.75	6	0	0	9.1	13	9	7	4	2.36
Career	38	51	.427	4.62	320	49	7	624.0	590	299	502	91	1.42

Rather than pay DeLucia $700,000 for 1999, the Angels released him in March. He signed with the Indians, but was shipped off to Triple-A in late May and never returned. 2000 Outlook: C

Dwight Gooden (Pos: RHP, Age: 35)

	W	L	Pct.	ERA	G	GS	Sv	IP	H	BB	SO	HR	Ratio
1999	3	4	.429	6.26	26	22	0	115.0	127	67	88	18	1.69
Career	188	107	.637	3.46	403	396	1	2695.2	2445	910	2238	187	1.24

Gooden may have had his worst season in 1999, then became a free agent. He once looked like a lock for the Hall of Fame, but now just reaching 200 wins will be a struggle. 2000 Outlook: C

Chris Haney (Pos: LHP, Age: 31)

	W	L	Pct.	ERA	G	GS	Sv	IP	H	BB	SO	HR	Ratio
1999	0	2	.000	4.69	13	4	0	40.1	43	16	22	3	1.46
Career	38	52	.422	5.10	171	125	0	793.2	891	275	427	92	1.47

After his release by the Dodgers in spring training, Haney inked with the Indians and bounced between Triple-A and Cleveland. He wasn't particularly effective, but the Tribe offered arbitration. 2000 Outlook: C

Tyler Houston (Pos: 3B/C, Age: 29, Bats: L)

	G	AB	R	H	D	T	HR	RBI	SB	BB	SO	Avg	OBP	Slg
1999	113	276	28	62	10	1	10	30	1	31	78	.225	.302	.377
Career	359	869	90	223	36	3	24	118	7	62	193	.257	.305	.388

Houston impressed the Cubs with his pop, earning a fair bit of playing time in Chicago in 1998 and '99. He was dealt to Cleveland in August for minor league righthander Richard Negrette, but didn't produce much to cap off a so-so season. The Tribe non-tendered him in December, making him a free agent. 2000 Outlook: B

Mark Langston (Pos: LHP, Age: 39)

	W	L	Pct.	ERA	G	GS	Sv	IP	H	BB	SO	HR	Ratio
1999	2	3	.333	5.25	25	5	0	61.2	69	29	43	9	1.59
Career	179	158	.531	3.97	457	428	0	2962.2	2723	1289	2464	311	1.35

Langston hasn't recorded an ERA below last year's 5.25 since 1996. That didn't stop the Indians from signing him to a minor league deal for this season. 2000 Outlook: C

Jesse Levis (Pos: C, Age: 31, Bats: L)

	G	AB	R	H	D	T	HR	RBI	SB	BB	SO	Avg	OBP	Slg
1999	10	26	0	4	0	0	0	3	0	1	6	.154	.214	.154
Career	307	621	60	159	21	1	3	57	2	73	59	.256	.337	.308

Tampa Bay released Levis in July, and Cleveland, looking for alternatives to Einar Diaz and Pat Borders with Sandy Alomar Jr. disabled, picked him up. He was sent down in August and became a free agent. 2000 Outlook: C

Tom Martin (Pos: LHP, Age: 29)

	W	L	Pct.	ERA	G	GS	Sv	IP	H	BB	SO	HR	Ratio
1999	0	1	.000	8.68	6	0	0	9.1	13	3	8	2	1.71
Career	6	5	.545	4.84	75	0	2	80.0	94	38	53	7	1.65

Martin pitched well as a Houston rookie in 1997, but since then has spent more time on the disabled list than in the pen. He had shoulder surgery last April and didn't pitch for Cleveland until August. 2000 Outlook: C

Cleveland

Jim Poole (Pos: LHP, Age: 33)

	W	L	Pct.	ERA	G	GS	Sv	IP	H	BB	SO	HR	Ratio
1999	2	1	.667	4.71	54	0	1	36.1	50	18	22	3	1.87
Career	21	12	.636	4.11	408	0	4	352.1	355	152	248	36	1.44

Dissatisfaction with Paul Assenmacher inspired Cleveland to sign Poole after his release by the Phillies. Poole was sent down to Triple-A after struggling. The aging vet has signed a minor league deal with Detroit. 2000 Outlook: C

Jason Rakers (Pos: RHP, Age: 26)

	W	L	Pct.	ERA	G	GS	Sv	IP	H	BB	SO	HR	Ratio
1999	0	0	-	4.50	1	0	0	2.0	2	1	0	1	1.50
Career	0	0	-	6.00	2	0	0	3.0	2	4	0	1	2.00

Rakers hasn't been especially impressive in Triple-A the last two seasons, and he quickly pulled a groin muscle after an August recall. The Royals claimed him off waivers in November. 2000 Outlook: C

Dave Roberts (Pos: CF, Age: 27, Bats: L)

	G	AB	R	H	D	T	HR	RBI	SB	BB	SO	Avg	OBP	Slg
1999	41	143	26	34	4	0	2	12	11	9	16	.238	.281	.308
Career	41	143	26	34	4	0	2	12	11	9	16	.238	.281	.308

With Kenny Lofton out for much of the first half of 2000, Roberts may be the Tribe's top candidate to play center. He's fast and draws some walks, but playing every day in the bigs may be too much to ask. 2000 Outlook: B

Dave Stevens (Pos: RHP, Age: 30)

	W	L	Pct.	ERA	G	GS	Sv	IP	H	BB	SO	HR	Ratio
1999	0	0	-	10.00	5	0	0	9.0	10	8	6	1	2.00
Career	15	16	.484	5.95	181	6	21	248.0	293	131	166	47	1.71

Once viewed as Minnesota's closer of the future, Stevens now battles for a major league job. He pitched well in Triple-A, then gave up runs in four of five outings in Cleveland and was gone. 2000 Outlook: C

Chris Turner (Pos: C, Age: 31, Bats: R)

	G	AB	R	H	D	T	HR	RBI	SB	BB	SO	Avg	OBP	Slg
1999	12	21	3	4	0	0	0	0	1	1	8	.190	.227	.190
Career	121	290	40	69	13	2	3	29	5	26	68	.238	.303	.328

Turner came up from Triple-A when Sandy Alomar Jr. was injured in May, but he was back in Buffalo a month later. He never returned. 2000 Outlook: C

Paul Wagner (Pos: RHP, Age: 32)

	W	L	Pct.	ERA	G	GS	Sv	IP	H	BB	SO	HR	Ratio
1999	1	0	1.000	4.15	3	0	0	4.1	5	3	0	0	1.85
Career	29	45	.392	4.83	160	84	3	598.2	640	255	452	64	1.49

Wagner was impressive in his first three Triple-A starts in April but didn't show much in three outings with Cleveland. He was back in Triple-A in May and never returned. He's a free agent. 2000 Outlook: C

Mark Whiten (Pos: LF, Age: 33, Bats: B)

	G	AB	R	H	D	T	HR	RBI	SB	BB	SO	Avg	OBP	Slg
1999	8	25	2	4	1	0	1	4	0	3	4	.160	.250	.320
Career	934	3097	463	802	128	20	105	422	78	375	710	.259	.341	.415

A stress fracture in his right foot sidelined Whiten until mid-June, and he was sent to Triple-A in early July. When the Indians wanted him in August, he was on the Triple-A disabled list. 2000 Outlook: C

Cleveland Indians Minor League Prospects

Organization Overview:

During the 1990s, the Indians signed and developed five key members of their current club: Bartolo Colon, Manny Ramirez, Richie Sexson, Paul Shuey and Jaret Wright. That's one fewer than the number of promising players they signed but casted off. Cleveland probably wishes it could reverse the trades involving all six, especially David Bell for Joey Cora, Danny Graves and others for John Smiley, Steve Kline for Jeff Juden and Mitch Meluskey for Buck McNabb. Dave Burba has been an effective starter for the Tribe, but he cost Sean Casey, one of the finest young hitters in the National League. And while the Indians used Paul Byrd as part of a deal for Jeromy Burnitz, they traded Burnitz for Kevin Seitzer. Cleveland had a lot of success in the past decade, both on the field and in player development. But its failure to produce enough pitching to win a World Series is beginning to haunt the franchise, and it cost manager Mike Hargrove his job.

Danys Baez

Position: P **Opening Day Age:** 22
Bats: R **Throws:** R **Born:** 9/10/77 in Pinar
Ht: 6' 3" **Wt:** 225 del Rio, Cuba

Recent Statistics

	W	L	ERA	G GS Sv	IP	H	R	BB	SO	HR
1999				Did Not Play						

The Indians finished second to the Yankees in the bidding for Orlando Hernandez, which may have cost the Tribe a World Series championship or two. Still looking to add a frontline starter, Cleveland was determined not to fall short again when Baez went on the market last fall. After defecting from the Cuban national team at the Pan American Games in August, he signed with the Indians for four years and $14.5 million in November. Baez throws his fastball in the low to mid-90s, and also has a hard curve. He needs to improve his splitter and changeup. Baez is expected to start 2000 in Cleveland's rotation, and the combination of his age (which may be as high as 25) and stuff gives him the highest ceiling of any of the Cuban pitchers who have defected.

Russ Branyan

Position: 3B **Opening Day Age:** 24
Bats: L **Throws:** R **Born:** 12/19/75 in
Ht: 6' 3" **Wt:** 195 Warner Robins, GA

Recent Statistics

	G	AB	R	H	D	T	HR	RBI	SB	BB	SO	Avg
1999 AAA Buffalo	109	395	51	82	11	1	30	67	8	52	187	.208
1999 AL Cleveland	11	38	4	8	2	0	1	6	0	3	19	.211
1999 MLE	109	387	42	74	10	0	25	56	6	43	196	.191

Branyan has the best raw power of any player in the minors, and his strikeout feats are perhaps more legen-

dary. He went through an 0-for-43 slump that included 27 strikeouts last year and led the minors with 187 whiffs in just 395 at-bats. A 1994 seventh-round pick, he has 149 homers in 537 minor league contests, which translates into 45 per 162 games. Branyan will have to learn to recognize pitches and tone down his swing at least a little, but there's no question he's exciting when he steps into the batter's box. He draws a healthy number of walks, runs OK and has a strong arm at third base. Only time will tell if he'll be more than a Rob Deer.

Jamie Brown

Position: P **Opening Day Age:** 22
Bats: R **Throws:** R **Born:** 3/31/77 in
Ht: 6' 2" **Wt:** 205 Meridian, MS

Recent Statistics

	W	L	ERA	G GS Sv	IP	H	R	BB	SO	HR
1998 A Kinston	11	9	3.81	27 27 0	172.2	162	91	44	148	12
1998 AA Akron	1	0	2.57	1 1 0	7.0	5	2	1	5	1
1999 AA Akron	5	9	4.57	23 23 0	138.0	140	72	39	98	11
1999 AAA Buffalo	1	0	5.40	1 0 0	5.0	8	4	1	2	0

Brown went 22-11 in his first two years as a pro, then hit the wall in Double-A last season. He still has an above-average fastball and changeup, and he continued to throw strikes, but his lack of an effective breaking pitch was his undoing. He's working on a hard curveball that will decide his ultimate success. A 21st-round pick in 1996, Brown signed after a season at Meridian (Miss.) Community College. The Indians still think he can be a major league starter, but their offseason signings of Danys Baez and Chuck Finley certainly don't help Brown's chances.

Jacob Cruz

Position: OF **Opening Day Age:** 27
Bats: L **Throws:** L **Born:** 1/28/73 in Oxnard,
Ht: 6' 0" **Wt:** 179 CA

Recent Statistics

	G	AB	R	H	D	T	HR	RBI	SB	BB	SO	Avg
1999 AAA Buffalo	54	202	29	55	7	2	7	31	4	21	39	.272
1999 AL Cleveland	32	88	14	29	5	1	3	17	0	5	13	.330

One of John Hart's better and most underrated trades as Indians GM was the June 1998 deal that sent Shawon Dunston, Jose Mesa and Alvin Morman to San Francisco for Cruz and Steve Reed. Reed has been an effective middle reliever for Cleveland, while Cruz may pick up part of the slack in center field in 2000, with Kenny Lofton expected to miss at least half the season. A 1994 supplemental first-round pick from Arizona State, Cruz will hit for average and has gap power. He's an average runner with an above-average arm, and he can do a solid job at any of the three outfield positions. He'd likely be starting for the Giants if they hadn't given him away.

Cleveland

John McDonald

Position: SS   **Opening Day Age:** 25
Bats: R **Throws:** R   **Born:** 9/24/74 in New
Ht: 5' 11" **Wt:** 175   London, CT

Recent Statistics

	G	AB	R	H	D	T	HR	RBI	SB	BB	SO	Avg
1999 AA Akron	55	226	31	67	12	0	1	26	7	19	26	.296
1999 AAA Buffalo	66	237	30	75	12	1	0	25	6	11	23	.316
1999 AL Cleveland	18	21	2	7	0	0	0	0	0	0	3	.333
1999 MLE	121	451	52	130	22	0	0	43	9	23	51	.288

McDonald's defensive skills are so outstanding that Cleveland placed him on its 40-man roster after he batted .230 in Double-A in 1998. He rewarded their confidence by improving at the plate, hitting .308 last year after altering his swing to hit more grounders. A 12th-round pick in 1996 out of Providence College, his range, hands and arm make him an impact shortstop. He has been rated the Double-A Eastern League's best defensive shortstop for two years running. McDonald will have to continue to hit, but even if he does he won't supplant Omar Vizquel.

Scott Morgan

Position: OF   **Opening Day Age:** 26
Bats: R **Throws:** R   **Born:** 7/19/73 in
Ht: 6' 7" **Wt:** 230   Westlake, CA

Recent Statistics

	G	AB	R	H	D	T	HR	RBI	SB	BB	SO	Avg
1998 AA Akron	119	456	95	134	31	4	25	89	4	56	124	.294
1999 AA Akron	88	344	72	97	26	2	26	70	6	38	96	.282
1999 AAA Buffalo	48	171	32	44	9	0	8	31	2	18	38	.257
1999 MLE	136	503	89	129	32	1	28	87	5	43	141	.256

For all of Russ Branyan's power, he has outhomered Morgan by just an 86-84 margin during the last three years. Branyan has battled wrist injuries, but Morgan has big-time pop. He was the sixth man on the Gonzaga basketball team that won the West Coast Conference championship in 1995, the same year Cleveland drafted him in the seventh round. After years of battling back problems, Morgan was healthy last season. He clubbed 34 homers, the ninth-highest total in the minors, and was rated the best power hitter in the Double-A Eastern League. He walks a little and strikes out a lot. He's a good athlete, but a below-average arm relegates him to left field. Morgan will spend most of 2000 in Triple-A.

Danny Peoples

Position: 1B   **Opening Day Age:** 25
Bats: R **Throws:** R   **Born:** 1/20/75 in Round
Ht: 6' 1" **Wt:** 207   Rock, TX

Recent Statistics

	G	AB	R	H	D	T	HR	RBI	SB	BB	SO	Avg
1998 AA Akron	60	222	30	62	19	0	8	32	1	29	61	.279
1999 AA Akron	127	494	75	124	23	3	21	78	2	55	142	.251
1999 MLE	127	485	66	115	22	2	18	69	1	41	152	.237

A 1996 first-round pick out of the University of Texas, Peoples has spent most of his time as a pro either getting hurt or striking out. He has been fully healthy for just two of his four pro seasons, though he did play a career-high 127 games in 1999. Peoples has very good bat speed and raw power, but he also has a long swing that has resulted in 384 whiffs in 343 games. Shoulder, back and knee injuries have turned him from a third baseman to a left fielder to a first baseman. Peoples can drive the ball a long way, but it's hard to imagine him beating out Jim Thome in Cleveland.

Alex Ramirez

Position: OF   **Opening Day Age:** 25
Bats: R **Throws:** R   **Born:** 10/3/74 in
Ht: 5' 11" **Wt:** 190   Caracas, Venezuela

Recent Statistics

	G	AB	R	H	D	T	HR	RBI	SB	BB	SO	Avg
1999 AAA Buffalo	75	305	50	93	20	2	12	50	5	17	52	.305
1999 AL Cleveland	48	97	11	29	6	1	3	18	1	3	26	.299
1999 MLE	75	296	41	84	18	1	9	41	3	14	54	.284

The Indians have an abundance of qualified outfielders in the majors and upper minors. Ramirez may be the best of the prospects, because he has 30-homer potential and the rest of his tools are all average. The bad news is that his 34-homer season in 1998 prompted Cleveland to trade Brian Giles to Pittsburgh for Ricky Rincon. Though he has a quick bat, Ramirez will have to overcome his aversion to walk in order to hit for average. He also needs to work on his defense. Ramirez will factor into Cleveland's mix at left field and DH in 2000. At worst, he'll provide the Indians with power off the bench.

Others to Watch

Righthander **J.D. Brammer** (25) has a 5.24 ERA in four pro seasons, yet Cleveland envisions him as a bullpen contributor in the mold of Eric Plunk. Brammer has an above-average fastball and a power curve. . . A surprise addition to the Tribe's postseason roster, righthander **Sean DePaula** (26) was the club's best reliever in the American League Division Series. He has three above-average pitches: an untouchable splitter, a 91-93 MPH sinker and a hard curveball. . . Righthander **Ryan Drese** (23) was projected as the ace of the 1996 U.S. Olympic team before elbow problems ruined him for most of three years. Healthy again, he has recovered his 94-MPH fastball and nasty slider. . . In 1997, righthander **Tim Drew** (21) and his older brother J.D. became the first siblings to go in the first round of the same draft. Tim led the high Class-A Carolina League with 13 victories last year, showing a nice slider and a lively 90-MPH fastball. . . Righthander **David Riske** (23) was the hardest minor league reliever to hit in 1999, limiting opponents to a .113 average. He's more deceptive than overpowering, and he got rocked for an 8.36 ERA in 12 big league appearances. . . Lefthander **C.C. Sabathia** (19) is the organization's best hope for a homegrown No. 1 starter. He's quite raw, but few southpaws can match his fastball, which is a consistent 92-94 MPH and has touched 97.

Comerica Park

Offense

A goal of Detroit GM Randy Smith has been to make Detroit more like a National League team. The move from the bandbox dimensions of Tiger Stadium to Comerica Park will make that possible. Tiger Stadium teams were plodding and homer-dependent, but Comerica is more pitcher-friendly. Though the prevailing wind will blow out to left, it will be 345 feet to the left-field wall, and 398 to the left-center power alley. It's likely that Comerica will cut down on homers while increasing doubles and triples.

Defense

Comerica's outfield is much bigger than that of Tiger Stadium, so Detroit's flychasers will need very good range. Tiger Stadium's grass was long and ate up groundballs. New manager Phil Garner will have the final say about the height of Comerica's grass.

Who It Helps the Most

Juan Encarnacion could flourish at Comerica because he's a line-drive hitter who covers a lot of ground in the outfield. Tony Clark seems to do his best work in bigger parks, where he isn't tempted to pull the ball. Brian Moehler was hurt badly by Tiger Stadium and should benefit from the move.

Who It Hurts the Most

Bobby Higginson liked the short right-field porch at Tiger Stadium and also lacks outfield range. In his first season with Detroit, Dean Palmer hit 24 of his 38 homers at home, so he'll miss the old digs. If the infield grass is shorter, Deivi Cruz' lack of range at shortstop will be exposed.

Rookies & Newcomers

Last season, two-time American League MVP Juan Gonzalez said he didn't want to be traded to Detroit after learning of Comerica Park's spacious left-center field. Then he was traded to Detroit. The organization's best prospects are sluggers Javier Cardona, Robert Fick, Eric Munson and Chris Wakeland. Their power production almost assuredly would have been higher at Tiger Stadium than it will be at Comerica.

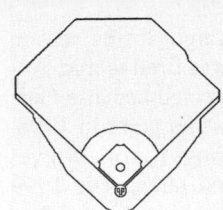

Dimensions: LF-345, LCF-398, CF-420, RCF-380, RF-330

Capacity: 42,000

Elevation: 585 feet

Surface: Grass

Foul Territory: Average

Park Factors

1999 Season (Tiger Stadium)

	Home Games			Away Games			
	Tigers	Opp	Total	Tigers	Opp	Total	Index
G	72	72	144	71	71	142	—
Avg	.262	.268	.265	.262	.285	.273	97
AB	2391	2505	4896	2458	2381	4839	100
R	347	388	735	310	402	712	102
H	627	672	1299	643	678	1321	97
2B	121	121	242	140	127	267	90
3B	19	14	33	11	10	21	155
HR	102	108	210	78	85	163	127
BB	213	259	472	189	252	441	106
SO	457	435	892	452	402	854	103
E	33	59	92	59	40	99	92
E-Infield	23	52	75	43	31	74	100
LHB-Avg	.265	.277	.272	.272	.299	.287	95
LHB-HR	38	58	96	32	51	83	116
RHB-Avg	.261	.261	.261	.256	.272	.263	99
RHB-HR	64	50	114	46	34	80	140

1997-1999 (Tiger Stadium)

	Home Games			Away Games			
	Tigers	Opp	Total	Tigers	Opp	Total	Index
G	217	217	434	219	219	438	—
Avg	.258	.265	.262	.265	.284	.274	96
AB	7210	7612	14822	7721	7380	15101	99
R	1035	1134	2169	983	1182	2165	101
H	1863	2014	3877	2043	2093	4136	95
2B	337	362	699	446	385	831	86
3B	46	42	88	37	49	86	104
HR	268	297	565	217	235	452	127
BB	718	783	1501	618	785	1403	109
SO	1444	1326	2770	1463	1255	2718	104
E	136	182	318	149	125	274	117
E-Infield	109	154	263	116	105	221	120
LHB-Avg	.266	.268	.267	.272	.293	.283	94
LHB-HR	126	135	261	105	123	228	120
RHB-Avg	.253	.262	.258	.260	.276	.267	96
RHB-HR	142	162	304	112	112	224	135

1999 Rankings (American League/Tiger Stadium)

- Highest home-run factor
- Highest RHB home-run factor
- Second-highest triple factor
- Third-lowest batting-average factor
- Third-lowest hit factor

Phil Garner

1999 Season

In the midst of his seventh straight losing season with Milwaukee, Phil Garner was fired in mid-August. The change wasn't unexpected because Garner was nearly canned at the same point in 1998. Garner's Brewers were poster boys for small-revenue teams short on payroll and talent. His 1999 club was typical of those during his regime, playing close to .500 in late July before the bottom fell out. The Tigers ignored a Major League Baseball mandate to recruit minority applicants, and didn't fire incumbent Larry Parrish until Garner agreed to a four-year, $4 million contract.

Offense

Garner came to Detroit claiming that he's not tied to any one style of play and will fit his strategies to his players. That's a good thing, because the Tigers are much different than the Brewers. Detroit has power hitters, something Milwaukee lacked. As a result, he was aggressive on-the bases with the Brewers. When Parrish tried to do the same with the Tigers last year, his players continually ran themselves out of innings.

Pitching & Defense

Garner will be more accustomed to the type of pitching staff he inherits in Detroit. He has a deep and talented bullpen but a young and uncertain rotation. After overworking starters early in his managerial tenure, Garner did a 180 and now has a quick hook. That's good news for pitchers such as Jeff Weaver and Dave Borkowski. He values defense, though the Tigers aren't strong up the middle with the exception of catcher Brad Ausmus. Garner likes to make defensive substitutions in the late innings.

2000 Outlook

At the press conference in which he was hired, Garner got a closeup look at the tension surrounding the Tigers. Reporters aggressively questioned owner Mike Ilitch, president John McHale Jr. and GM Randy Smith about the franchise's failures, and Ilitch walked out at one point. Garner had one winning season in eight years in Milwaukee. The Tigers had two winning seasons in the 1990s. It's a marriage of two parties looking for redemption.

Born: 4/30/49 in Jefferson City, TN

Playing Experience: 1973-1988, Oak, Pit, Hou, LA, SF

Managerial Experience: 8 seasons
Nickname: Scrap Iron

Manager Statistics

Year	Team, Lg	W	L	Pct	GB	Finish
1999	Milwaukee, NL	52	60	.464	15.0	5th Central
8 Seasons		563	617	.477	—	—

1999 Starting Pitchers by Days Rest

	<=3	4	5	6+
Brewers Starts	4	63	23	14
Brewers ERA	3.63	5.31	5.07	5.94
NL Avg Starts	3	81	48	21
NL ERA	4.84	4.53	4.72	4.98

1999 Situational Stats

	Phil Garner	NL Average
Hit & Run Success %	28.3	33.6
Stolen Base Success %	70.7	70.2
Platoon Pct.	56.6	55.2
Defensive Subs	5	25
High-Pitch Outings	4	13
Quick/Slow Hooks	13/16	16/15
Sacrifice Attempts	85	89

(Garner managed 112 games in 1999)

1999 Rankings (National League)
- 1st in fewest caught stealings of second base (18), pitchouts (57) and pitchouts with a runner moving (16)
- 2nd in squeeze plays (9)

Brad Ausmus

1999 Season

After playing for two playoff teams with the Astros, Brad Ausmus returned to the Tigers in January. Houston wanted to cut some salary, and Detroit was happy to oblige, parting with five spare parts in exchange for Ausmus and C.J. Nitkowski. Ausmus made the All-Star team for the first time in 1999, en route to reaching career bests in home runs and RBI. He also maintained his status as one of the game's top defensive catchers.

Hitting

Ausmus is a contact hitter on a team of strikeout kings. He's capable of getting down a bunt and can be used to hit-and-run. Rarely does Ausmus turn on the ball and hit it with great authority, but he'll drive a ball up the gap now and then. One thing Ausmus did very well last year was hit in clutch situations. As smart at the plate as he is behind it, Ausmus will look for a pitch in a given situation and make something of it when he gets it. As a result, he hit considerably better with runners on base than he did with nobody on.

Baserunning & Defense

Ausmus runs exceptionally well for a catcher. He had six triples and 12 stolen bases in 1999 and goes from home to first very well for a righthanded hitter. He also is a smart baserunner who uses good judgment when it comes time to take an extra base. Ausmus is flexible, which helps him present a low target behind the plate. He frames pitches well and calls a solid game. Pitchers like throwing to him. His arm strength is slightly above average at best, but his release is among the quickest in the game and his throws are consistently accurate.

2000 Outlook

Ausmus is the ideal player for the young Tigers. He has several years remaining yet is experienced enough to lead his teammates. He's one of the few Detroit players to have played on winning teams, and that shows in his ability to produce in tough situations.

Position: C
Bats: R **Throws:** R
Ht: 5'11" **Wt:** 195

Opening Day Age: 30
Born: 4/14/69 in New Haven, CT
ML Seasons: 7
Pronunciation: AHHS-muss

Overall Statistics

	G	AB	R	H	D	T	HR	RBI	SB	BB	SO	Avg	OBP	Slg
1999	127	458	62	126	25	6	9	54	12	51	71	.275	.365	.415
Career	763	2485	322	652	112	17	41	248	63	248	428	.262	.334	.371

Where He Hits the Ball

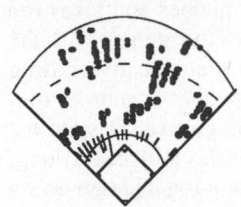
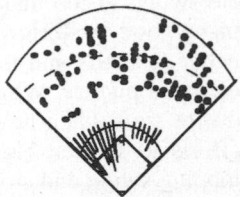

Vs. LHP　　　**Vs. RHP**

1999 Situational Stats

	AB	H	HR	RBI	Avg		AB	H	HR	RBI	Avg
Home	234	68	5	27	.291	LHP	72	19	0	8	.264
Road	224	58	4	27	.259	RHP	386	107	9	46	.277
First Half	242	67	7	34	.277	Sc Pos	113	32	1	43	.283
Scnd Half	216	59	2	20	.273	Clutch	59	19	2	9	.322

1999 Rankings (American League)

- 1st in fielding percentage at catcher (.998)
- 3rd in lowest stolen-base percentage (57.1)
- 6th in hit by pitch (14)
- Led the Tigers in on-base percentage, most pitches seen per plate appearance (3.96), batting average on a 3-1 count (.524) and batting average at home
- Led AL catchers in on-base percentage, most pitches seen per plate appearance (3.96), on-base percentage vs. righthanded pitchers (.367), highest percentage of pitches taken (60.7), triples, hit by pitch (14) and pitches seen (2,086)

Detroit

Tony Clark

1999 Season

Tony Clark has developed the bad habit of starting poorly when his team needs him the most, then finishing strongly when his team is hopelessly out of contention. Last year he had eight homers and 38 RBI in the first half, when he spent time on the disabled list with a shoulder strain. After the All-Star break, he produced 23 homers and 61 RBI. His season totals were about average for an everyday first baseman. Clark's only quick start came during his rookie year of 1997.

Hitting

Clark has enormous power and is capable of hitting the ball as far as anyone in organized baseball. Yet he hasn't quite been able to harness all that power. He swings at too many bad pitches and takes too many good ones. He struggles to catch up with the better fastballs and isn't all that effective hitting offspeed pitches. What Clark does is murder mediocre stuff when he's in his groove. Despite his efforts to shorten his stroke, he still has a long, looping swing and strikes out a lot. Though he's a natural righthanded hitter, he's more consistent and has better pop from the left side.

Baserunning & Defense

Clark didn't have a good season at first base in 1998, taking a step back from the improvement he made the season before. In 1999 he got back on track again. For Clark, that means making the play on routine groundballs and digging out a throw in the dirt now and then. Signed as an outfielder, Clark tracks pop flies well, particularly those hit over his head or down the right-field line. Clark has below-average speed and plays it station to station as much as possible on the bases.

2000 Outlook

Club officials debate Clark's merits as much as any Tigers player. His raw ability is unquestioned and he has been productive since reaching the majors to stay midway through the 1996 season. The problem is that he usually comes through when it's too late.

Position: 1B/DH
Bats: B **Throws:** R
Ht: 6' 7" **Wt:** 245

Opening Day Age: 27
Born: 6/15/72 in Newton, KS
ML Seasons: 5

Overall Statistics

	G	AB	R	H	D	T	HR	RBI	SB	BB	SO	Avg	OBP	Slg
1999	143	536	74	150	29	0	31	99	2	64	133	.280	.361	.507
Career	586	2195	329	603	113	4	127	402	6	257	562	.275	.351	.503

Where He Hits the Ball

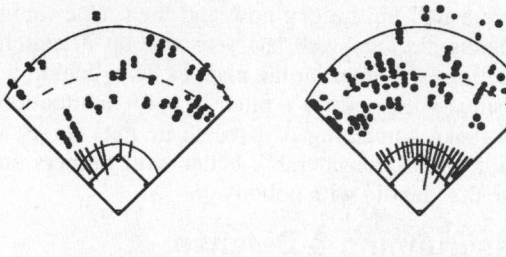

Vs. LHP   **Vs. RHP**

1999 Situational Stats

	AB	H	HR	RBI	Avg		AB	H	HR	RBI	Avg
Home	249	65	12	50	.261	LHP	107	28	7	19	.262
Road	287	85	19	49	.296	RHP	429	122	24	80	.284
First Half	258	62	8	38	.240	Sc Pos	132	42	11	70	.318
Scnd Half	278	88	23	61	.317	Clutch	73	28	5	22	.384

1999 Rankings (American League)

- 3rd in lowest percentage of extra bases taken as a runner (25.6)
- 4th in batting average in the clutch, lowest cleanup slugging percentage (.456) and lowest fielding percentage at first base (.992)
- 5th in errors at first base (10)
- 6th in strikeouts
- Led the Tigers in batting average with runners in scoring position, batting average in the clutch, batting average with the bases loaded (.364), batting average vs. righthanded pitchers, slugging percentage vs. righthanded pitchers (.510), on-base percentage vs. righthanded pitchers (.375), hits, walks, intentional walks (7) and times on base (220)

Deivi Cruz

1999 Season

Deivi Cruz was a much better player in 1999 than he was the year before, when he never fully recovered from a fractured left ankle. Healthy from the start of last season, he played in 155 games and nearly doubled his home-run output from the previous two seasons combined. Cruz also raised his batting average to a career-high .284. He hit .238-0-4 through May 31, then batted .299-13-54 afterward.

Hitting

Prior to last season, Cruz was able to hit even the best fastballs when he was ahead in the count and knew they were coming. Last season, he started hitting offspeed pitches as well. He still isn't a good breaking-ball hitter, but he's not an easy mark like he was early in his career. He lays off breaking pitches more often, though his lack of patience at the plate is astounding. Cruz walked just 12 times in 518 at-bats last season. He's a good bunter who can be used to hit-and-run.

Baserunning & Defense

Cruz had above-average speed early in his minor league career, but a knee injury and the ankle fracture have robbed him of it. He's a below-average runner, especially for a shortstop. He stole one base in five attempts last season. Defensively, Cruz has sure hands and one of the strongest infield throwing arms in the game. He's particularly effective throwing to home or third base as a relay man. His range is limited, however, and he doesn't get to a lot of balls that other major league shortstops do.

2000 Outlook

The jury is still out on Cruz. His improvement as a hitter, his ability to make the routine play and his throwing arm are positive. His lack of speed and range and his inability to draw walks are negatives. In an era when so much more is expected of a shortstop than ever before, the Tigers must decide whether they can win with him.

Position: SS
Bats: R **Throws:** R
Ht: 6' 0" **Wt:** 184
Opening Day Age: 24
Born: 11/6/75 in Nizao de Bani, Dominican Republic
ML Seasons: 3
Pronunciation: DAY-vee

Overall Statistics

	G	AB	R	H	D	T	HR	RBI	SB	BB	SO	Avg	OBP	Slg
1999	155	518	64	147	35	0	13	58	1	12	57	.284	.302	.427
Career	437	1408	151	370	83	3	20	143	7	39	167	.263	.284	.369

Where He Hits the Ball

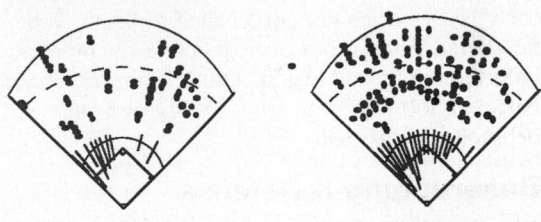

Vs. LHP　　　　　**Vs. RHP**

1999 Situational Stats

	AB	H	HR	RBI	Avg		AB	H	HR	RBI	Avg
Home	241	67	9	35	.278	LHP	93	27	1	10	.290
Road	277	80	4	23	.289	RHP	425	120	12	48	.282
First Half	250	67	3	17	.268	Sc Pos	120	31	3	43	.258
Scnd Half	268	80	10	41	.299	Clutch	62	16	1	13	.258

1999 Rankings (American League)

- 1st in batting average on a 3-2 count (.438)
- 2nd in fielding percentage at shortstop (.983), sacrifice bunts (14) and fewest pitches seen per plate appearance (3.14)
- 4th in lowest on-base percentage, lowest on-base percentage vs. righthanded pitchers (.298) and lowest percentage of pitches taken (46.0)
- Led the Tigers in highest groundball/flyball ratio (1.6), batting average on a 3-2 count (.438), batting average, singles, doubles, sacrifice bunts (14) and games played
- Led AL shortstops in batting average on a 3-2 count (.438)

Detroit

Damion Easley

Position: 2B/SS
Bats: R **Throws:** R
Ht: 5'11" **Wt:** 185

Opening Day Age: 30
Born: 11/11/69 in New York, NY
ML Seasons: 8

1999 Season

Damion Easley's statistics suggest he posted a decent if not spectacular season. In truth, it was a disappointing year for a player expected to take his game up a notch. Detroit GM Randy Smith viewed Easley as a key part of the club's nucleus, a quiet but effective team leader expected to produce in the clutch. But Easley struggled mightily last season in crucial situations.

Hitting

Easley is strong and has a lot of power for a middle infielder. A key asset is his well-balanced stance. He'll murder a fastball if he gets ahead in the count and can look for one. His problems stem from an inability to hit breaking pitches. In clutch situations early last year, he got curveballed to death. When he started leaning out over the plate for breaking balls, he got busted inside. That left him caught in between, too far out in front of offspeed stuff and behind good fastballs.

Baserunning & Defense

Each season Easley gets a little steadier with the glove. There was a time when his hands and movements were stiff, but he has become more fluid. He has above-average range and rarely boots routine grounders. Easley turns the double play well and continues to plug away in the field, regardless of how he's doing at the plate. Easley lifts a lot of weights and has bulked up through the years, which has cost him quickness. He stole 11 bases last season, down from 28 in 1997.

2000 Outlook

Given his raw tools and the fact he's in the prime of his career, Easley is counted on to produce more than he did in 1999, especially in terms of RBI. Pitchers obviously have adjusted to Easley. It's time for him to respond with some modifications of his own.

Overall Statistics

	G	AB	R	H	D	T	HR	RBI	SB	BB	SO	Avg	OBP	Slg
1999	151	549	83	146	30	1	20	65	11	51	124	.266	.346	.434
Career	826	2836	401	732	155	11	86	353	81	265	519	.258	.334	.411

Where He Hits the Ball

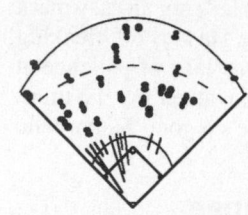 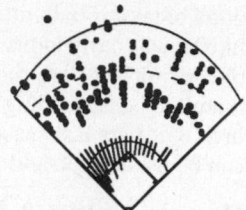

Vs. LHP   **Vs. RHP**

1999 Situational Stats

	AB	H	HR	RBI	Avg		AB	H	HR	RBI	Avg
Home	265	71	12	30	.268	LHP	86	25	4	9	.291
Road	284	75	8	35	.264	RHP	463	121	16	56	.261
First Half	307	78	10	42	.254	Sc Pos	133	25	3	42	.188
Scnd Half	242	68	10	23	.281	Clutch	76	19	3	6	.250

1999 Rankings (American League)

- 2nd in fielding percentage at second base (.989) and lowest batting average with runners in scoring position
- 3rd in hit by pitch (19)
- Led the Tigers in sacrifice flies (6), hit by pitch (19) and GDPs (15)
- Led AL second basemen in strikeouts

Juan Encarnacion

Position: LF/CF
Bats: R **Throws:** R
Ht: 6' 3" **Wt:** 187

Opening Day Age: 24
Born: 3/8/76 in Las Matas de Faran, Dominican Republic
ML Seasons: 3
Pronunciation: en-car-NAH-see-own

1999 Season

In his first full season in the major leagues, Juan Encarnacion did some things very well. He had 55 extra-base hits and he stole 33 bases. He showed everyone that he indeed is a five-tool player. Ah, but he also walked just 14 times in 538 plate appearances and made errors at some of the most inopportune times. His season ended a couple weeks early when he was beaned by Kansas City's Blake Stein, fracturing his cheekbone.

Hitting

To Encarnacion, the word "walk" is as vile as any other four-letter word. He has no patience whatsoever at the plate. Because he holds his bat high above his head in an upright position, Encarnacion often is worked high and tight. But he hits that pitch surprisingly well and he does OK against offspeed stuff. That is, if he waits out the pitcher and gets a strike. When he does connect, Encarnacion hits the ball exceptionally hard on a line to all fields.

Baserunning & Defense

When he goes from first to third or second to home, Encarnacion runs with the grace of a Bernie Williams. He's a long strider with exceptional speed, especially after he gets going. He was caught stealing 12 times last year because he doesn't get good jumps or read pitchers well. Defensively, Encarnacion was a disappointment while mostly playing left field last season. He has an extraordinary arm, yet he often muscles up and makes poor throws. He also made a habit of dropping routine flyballs, which was extremely disheartening for his struggling team. He doesn't break back well on balls hit directly over his head.

2000 Outlook

Encarnacion fascinates scouts because of his tools, yet frustrates his coaches and club officials because of his maddening inconsistencies. He's either very good or awful, with little middle ground. Developing consistency is the obvious key to his future. Laying off bad pitches would be a good start in that direction.

Overall Statistics

	G	AB	R	H	D	T	HR	RBI	SB	BB	SO	Avg	OBP	Slg
1999	132	509	62	130	30	6	19	74	33	14	113	.255	.287	.450
Career	183	706	95	191	40	11	27	100	43	24	156	.271	.304	.473

Where He Hits the Ball

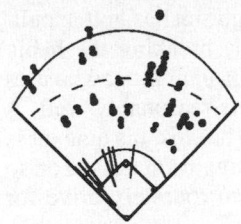

Vs. LHP

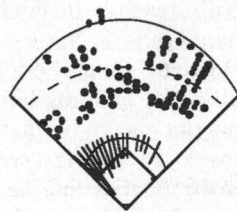

Vs. RHP

1999 Situational Stats

	AB	H	HR	RBI	Avg		AB	H	HR	RBI	Avg
Home	250	54	6	32	.216	LHP	95	25	5	18	.263
Road	259	76	13	42	.293	RHP	414	105	14	56	.254
First Half	288	78	9	40	.271	Sc Pos	115	31	4	53	.270
Scnd Half	221	52	10	34	.235	Clutch	69	22	3	14	.319

1999 Rankings (American League)

- 1st in lowest fielding percentage in left field (.970)
- 2nd in errors in left field (7), lowest on-base percentage vs. righthanded pitchers (.280) and lowest batting average at home
- 3rd in caught stealing (12), lowest on-base percentage and lowest percentage of pitches taken (45.5)
- 5th in steals of third (5)
- 9th in stolen bases
- 10th in fewest pitches seen per plate appearance (3.43)
- Led the Tigers in stolen-base percentage (73.3), steals of third (5), stolen bases and caught stealing (12)

Bobby Higginson

Position: RF/DH
Bats: L **Throws:** R
Ht: 5'11" **Wt:** 195

Opening Day Age: 29
Born: 8/18/70 in Philadelphia, PA
ML Seasons: 5

1999 Season

Bobby Higginson signed a four-year, $16 million contract in January 1998 and hasn't been the same player since. He experienced a slight decline in 1998, then took a nosedive last year. He had his worst season since his rookie year in 1995 and at one point was benched for three games by former Detroit manager Larry Parrish. He was hindered during the second half by a sprained right toe, spending a month on the disabled list and ending his season by opting for surgery in mid-September.

Hitting

Higginson used to do a good job of covering the entire plate, but he covered none of it last season. He even had trouble teeing off on low, inside fastballs, his favorite pitch. Higginson has gotten pull-happy and is having trouble breaking the habit. When he's at his best, he's a patient hitter who uses all fields and hits lefthanders reasonably well. A major concern is whether he has lost his quickness inside, because last season Higginson missed on so many pitches that he used to routinely drive for extra-base hits.

Baserunning & Defense

Higginson has below-average speed for an outfielder. He's not an effective baserunner, often getting thrown out while being overly aggressive, and he isn't a basestealing threat. A corner outfielder who played mostly in right last season, Higginson has below-average range. He has had a lot of outfield assists in his career, but his arm is more accurate than strong and he's slow getting to grounders. For the most part, Higginson is sure-handed on the balls he can reach.

2000 Outlook

Higginson needs to recapture the hunger that catapulted him from a lightly regarded prospect to a solid big leaguer. Despite his relative youth, the knock on him is that he already is starting to lose his tools. It's no secret that the Tigers would like to trade him.

Overall Statistics

	G	AB	R	H	D	T	HR	RBI	SB	BB	SO	Avg	OBP	Slg
1999	107	377	51	90	18	0	12	46	4	64	66	.239	.351	.382
Career	671	2385	373	660	137	14	104	356	31	324	425	.277	.364	.477

Where He Hits the Ball

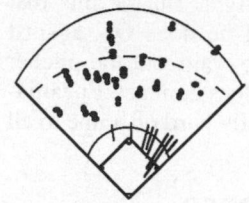
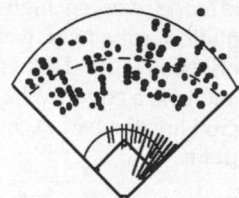

Vs. LHP   **Vs. RHP**

1999 Situational Stats

	AB	H	HR	RBI	Avg		AB	H	HR	RBI	Avg
Home	193	49	8	30	.254	LHP	83	22	2	10	.265
Road	184	41	4	16	.223	RHP	294	68	10	36	.231
First Half	299	73	9	36	.244	Sc Pos	97	26	4	34	.268
Scnd Half	78	17	3	10	.218	Clutch	47	9	1	2	.191

1999 Rankings (American League)

- 1st in fewest GDPs per GDP situation (2.1%)
- 10th in highest percentage of pitches taken (61.8)
- Led the Tigers in fewest GDPs per GDP situation (2.1%), highest percentage of pitches taken (61.8) and walks
- Led AL right fielders in fewest GDPs per GDP situation (2.1%)

Gabe Kapler

1999 Season

The Tigers originally planned for Gabe Kapler to begin the season in Triple-A, but he played so well during spring training that former manager Larry Parrish couldn't justify sending him down. With Brian Hunter still Detroit's regular center fielder, Kapler saw little action before heading to Triple-A on April 13. Hunter soon was traded to Seattle to accomodate Kapler, who slumped for most of the season.

Hitting

Kapler has an impressive build and has appeared on the cover of fitness magazines. His strength in the weight room translates into home runs. He hit 18 longballs as a rookie despite struggling in other areas of hitting, and has the potential to do much more. Kapler is extremely pull-conscious, and veteran pitchers exploited that flaw repeatedly last season. He doesn't strike out much and will take a walk.

Baserunning & Defense

In 1998, Kapler set a Southern League record with 146 RBI for Double-A Jacksonville. Detroit officials became so enamored with him that they started seeing things in his tools that scouts from other organizations did not, such as above-average speed. Kapler is an average runner who will steal an occasional base. He doesn't cover enough ground to play center field regularly in the majors, but his range is solid for right field. He also has an accurate and fairly strong arm.

2000 Outlook

In retrospect, Kapler was rushed to the major leagues before he was ready. He would have benefited from a few more months in the minor leagues and the lessons he learned last season were painful. However, he's a former 57th-round draft pick with a lot of grit and self-confidence. He was a key player for the Rangers in the November trade in which they sent Juan Gonzalez, Danny Patterson and Gregg Zaun to Detroit for Frank Catalanotto, Francisco Cordero, Bill Haselman, Kapler, Justin Thompson and Alan Webb. Kapler will play right field in Texas. Learning to hit the ball where it's pitched is the key to his development.

Position: CF/RF
Bats: R **Throws:** R
Ht: 6' 2" **Wt:** 208

Opening Day Age: 24
Born: 8/31/75 in Hollywood, CA
ML Seasons: 2
Pronunciation: KAP-ler

Overall Statistics

	G	AB	R	H	D	T	HR	RBI	SB	BB	SO	Avg	OBP	Slg
1999	130	416	60	102	22	4	18	49	11	42	74	.245	.315	.447
Career	137	441	63	107	22	5	18	49	13	43	78	.243	.310	.438

Where He Hits the Ball

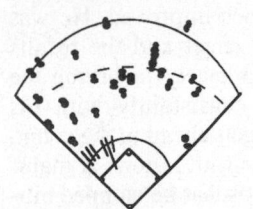 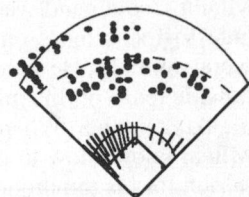

Vs. LHP   **Vs. RHP**

1999 Situational Stats

	AB	H	HR	RBI	Avg		AB	H	HR	RBI	Avg
Home	219	66	12	29	.301	LHP	75	21	4	11	.280
Road	197	36	6	20	.183	RHP	341	81	14	38	.238
First Half	218	53	12	32	.243	Sc Pos	97	22	3	30	.227
Scnd Half	198	49	6	17	.247	Clutch	52	10	5	6	.192

1999 Rankings (American League)

- 3rd in lowest batting average vs. righthanded pitchers
- 4th in lowest fielding percentage in center field (.985)
- 6th in errors in center field (4)
- 7th in lowest on-base percentage vs. righthanded pitchers (.307)
- 9th in lowest batting average with the bases loaded (.100)

Detroit

129

Dave Mlicki

1999 Season

Squeezed out of the Dodgers rotation after they signed Kevin Brown, Dave Mlicki opened the year in the Los Angeles bullpen before being traded to Detroit in April, with reliever Mel Rojas and cash in exchange for three so-so pitching prospects. Mlicki took to his new surroundings by winning a career-high 14 games, including eight in a row beginning in August.

Pitching

Mlicki has four major league-caliber pitches. He relies more on his fastball and curveball than his slider and changeup. His fastball usually registers in the lows 90s and is even more effective because of its sinking action. During his winning streak, Mlicki's command was much improved. He was able to focus more on the target and the results were stunning. He gained a knack for hitting the outside part of the plate consistently with his breaking pitches. When he gets ahead in the count, Mlicki knows how to tinker with hitters. A major reason for his turnaround was that he stopped nibbling early in the count and began to put more trust in his ability.

Defense

Mlicki doesn't field his position well. He has poor range and made three errors last season for a woeful .919 fielding percentage. Mlicki also is easy on baserunners. He doesn't have much of a pickoff move and he's slow getting the ball to home plate out of the set position.

2000 Outlook

Mlicki's late-season surge earned him a three-year, $15.5 million contract from the Tigers. With the trade of Justin Thompson to Texas, Mlicki may be Detroit's No. 1 starter. He'll be counted on to set an example and chew up innings, but he'll have to prove he's more than just an eight-start wonder.

Position: SP
Bats: R **Throws:** R
Ht: 6' 4" **Wt:** 205

Opening Day Age: 31
Born: 6/8/68 in Cleveland, OH
ML Seasons: 7
Pronunciation: mah-LICK-ee

Overall Statistics

	W	L	Pct.	ERA	G	GS	Sv	IP	H	BB	SO	HR	Ratio
1999	14	13	.519	4.61	33	31	0	199.0	219	72	120	25	1.46
Career	45	48	.484	4.25	182	127	1	859.2	890	320	623	106	1.41

How Often He Throws Strikes

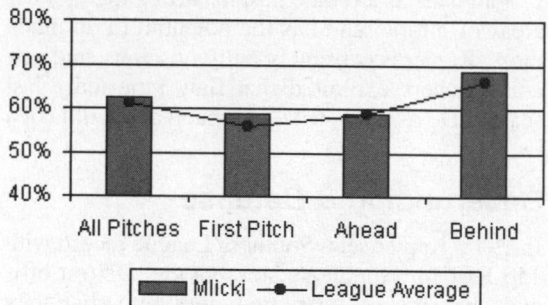

Legend: Mlicki — League Average

1999 Situational Stats

	W	L	ERA	Sv	IP		AB	H	HR	RBI	Avg
Home	7	6	4.63	0	105.0	LHB	355	98	13	51	.276
Road	7	7	4.60	0	94.0	RHB	433	121	12	49	.279
First Half	4	9	5.31	0	100.0	Sc Pos	196	47	5	71	.240
Scnd Half	10	4	3.91	0	99.0	Clutch	69	18	3	8	.261

1999 Rankings (American League)

- 3rd in hit batsmen (12)
- 4th in lowest fielding percentage at pitcher (.917)
- 5th in errors at pitcher (3)
- Led the Tigers in ERA (4.60), wins (14), complete games (2), walks allowed (70), strikeouts (119), pickoff throws (163), GDPs induced (18), winning percentage (.538), lowest batting average allowed (.276), lowest slugging percentage allowed (.437), lowest on-base percentage allowed (.344), fewest pitches thrown per batter (3.62), ERA at home (4.63), lowest batting average allowed vs. lefthanded batters (.272), lowest batting average allowed with runners in scoring position (.241) and runners caught stealing (7)

Brian Moehler

Position: SP
Bats: R **Throws:** R
Ht: 6' 3" **Wt:** 235

Opening Day Age: 28
Born: 12/31/71 in Rockingham, NC
ML Seasons: 4
Pronunciation: MOE-lur

1999 Season

Brian Moehler went 3-2, 3.94 in his first five starts in 1999. During his sixth outing, umpire Larry Barnett discovered a dime-sized piece of sandpaper attached to the thumb of Moehler's glove hand. Moehler was suspended for 10 days by the American League and wasn't the same pitcher afterward, going 7-14, 5.26.

Pitching

Moehler isn't overpowering, usually sitting at 89-90 MPH with his fastball. It does have good sink, and he maintained that movement after the suspension. He moves the ball around the strike zone well and changes speeds effectively. Dating back to his days in the minors, Moehler has been more effective against righthanders than lefthanders. He leans on his cut fastball to get lefties out. He's not especially durable and generally is good for six innings per start.

Defense

Moehler slipped last season in his ability to hold runners and field his position. He wasn't as solid in those areas as he was during his first two seasons in the major leagues. His range on the mound wasn't good and he stopped paying attention to basestealers. An improvement in those areas is expected because he has proven capable in the past.

2000 Outlook

A lot has been put on Moehler's shoulders in recent years. The Tigers have good, young arms, but they haven't developed quickly or they've been injured or painfully inconsistent. That's made Moehler the lone constant. He has made 31 or more starts and won 10 or more games each of the last three seasons. Ideally, he'd be a No. 3 or 4 starter, but the trade of Justin Thompson to Texas means that Moehler and Dave Mlicki will have to anchor the Detroit rotation.

Overall Statistics

	W	L	Pct.	ERA	G	GS	Sv	IP	H	BB	SO	HR	Ratio
1999	10	16	.385	5.04	32	32	0	196.1	229	59	106	22	1.47
Career	35	42	.455	4.50	98	98	0	603.1	658	184	328	75	1.40

How Often He Throws Strikes

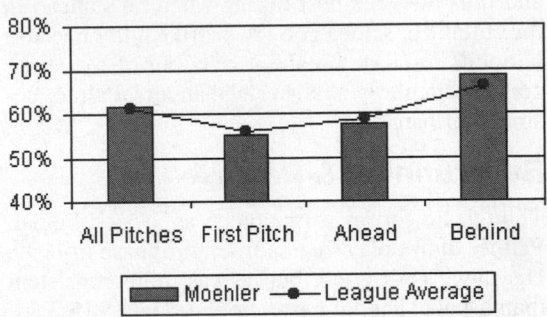

1999 Situational Stats

	W	L	ERA	Sv	IP		AB	H	HR	RBI	Avg
Home	6	10	5.46	0	115.1	LHB	392	116	15	58	.296
Road	4	6	4.44	0	81.0	RHB	388	113	7	41	.291
First Half	7	9	4.70	0	107.1	Sc Pos	183	54	4	73	.295
Scnd Half	3	7	5.46	0	89.0	Clutch	54	17	2	4	.315

1999 Rankings (American League)

- 1st in losses
- 2nd in shutouts (2) and highest stolen-base percentage allowed (81.8)
- 4th in highest batting average allowed (.294) and least run support per nine innings (4.5)
- 5th in fewest strikeouts per nine innings (4.9)
- Led the Tigers in losses, complete games (2), shutouts (2), innings pitched, hits allowed, batters faced (859), pitches thrown (3,160), stolen bases allowed (18), highest groundball/flyball ratio allowed (1.6), fewest baserunners allowed per nine innings (13.5), fewest walks per nine innings (2.7), ERA on the road, games started and fewest home runs allowed per nine innings (1.01)

Dean Palmer

1999 Season

Dean Palmer signed a five-year, $35 million contract as a free agent, and he lived up to it in his first season in Detroit. He tied his career best with 38 home runs and reached 100 RBI for the third time in his career. On the downside, Palmer slumped terribly in July and August, when the Tigers struggled the most.

Hitting

Palmer has an exceptionally live bat and his home runs are rarely cheap. A free swinger, he doesn't get cheated at the plate but also strikes out in bunches. He's an all-or-nothing hitter who, for all his power, doesn't hit a lot of doubles. Palmer loves fastballs and thus does his best hitting when he's ahead in the count. He's not a good two-strike hitter because he tends to chase breaking balls out of the strike zone, particularly against righthanders. Palmer destroys lefthanders.

Baserunning & Defense

Though he carries a reputation as a poor fielder, Palmer didn't play that badly at third base in 1999. His range isn't good, but he was more consistent than usual at handling routine plays. His .945 fielding percentage was an improvement from his .920 mark in Kansas City the previous year. Palmer's best defensive tool is his arm, which is average in strength and usually on target. He doesn't make hopeless throws, electing instead to hold onto the ball. Most of his errors come when he botches grounders. He's slow afoot and not a particularly smart baserunner.

2000 Outlook

Palmer was one of the few Tigers to meet expectations last year. He also leads by example, knowing how to grind his way through even the most difficult situations. He runs hot and cold at the plate, but he's consistent in terms of preparation. Since returning from a ruptured left biceps in 1995, he has averaged 34 homers and 103 RBI per season.

Position: 3B
Bats: R **Throws:** R
Ht: 6' 1" **Wt:** 210

Opening Day Age: 31
Born: 12/27/68 in Tallahassee, FL
ML Seasons: 10

Overall Statistics

	G	AB	R	H	D	T	HR	RBI	SB	BB	SO	Avg	OBP	Slg
1999	150	560	92	147	25	2	38	100	3	57	153	.263	.339	.518
Career	1125	4064	624	1035	196	13	235	701	40	399	1094	.255	.325	.483

Where He Hits the Ball

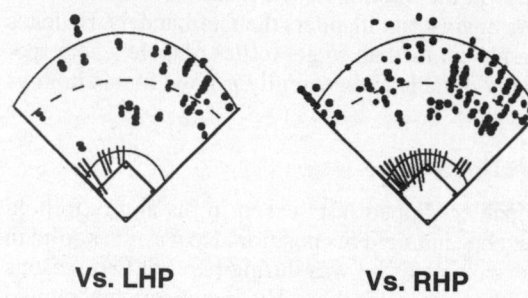

Vs. LHP   **Vs. RHP**

1999 Situational Stats

	AB	H	HR	RBI	Avg		AB	H	HR	RBI	Avg
Home	265	70	24	51	.264	LHP	100	39	10	24	.390
Road	295	77	14	49	.261	RHP	460	108	28	76	.235
First Half	312	85	22	58	.272	Sc Pos	145	38	5	56	.262
Scnd Half	248	62	16	42	.250	Clutch	78	15	6	19	.192

1999 Rankings (American League)

- 2nd in strikeouts and lowest batting average vs. righthanded pitchers
- 4th in errors at third base (19) and lowest fielding percentage at third base (.945)
- Led the Tigers in slugging percentage, HR frequency (14.7 ABs per HR), cleanup slugging percentage (.540), highest percentage of extra bases taken as a runner (48.1), home runs, at-bats, runs scored, total bases (290), RBI, strikeouts, pitches seen (2,455) and plate appearances (631)
- Led AL third basemen in slugging percentage, HR frequency (14.7 ABs per HR), cleanup slugging percentage (.540), home runs, runs scored, RBI, hit by pitch (10) and strikeouts

Justin Thompson

Position: SP
Bats: L **Throws:** L
Ht: 6' 4" **Wt:** 215

Opening Day Age: 27
Born: 3/8/73 in San Antonio, TX
ML Seasons: 4

1999 Season

Justin Thompson had suffered a significant injury in four of the previous six years, and 1999 added to his litany of physical problems. He went on the disabled list in August and had surgery to repair a torn labrum in his left shoulder a month later. The operation brought an end to the worst season of Thompson's major league career.

Pitching

The last two years, Thompson hasn't been the same pitcher who went 15-11, 3.02 in 1997. Back then he had four above-average major league pitches—two- and four-seam fastballs, a changeup and a curveball—and he could throw them consistently for strikes. Following that season, he had arthroscopic surgery to clean out bone spurs and loose deposits in his left elbow. It was supposed to be a minor procedure, but he hasn't thrown as well since. His fastball is down from 93-94 MPH to 91-92, his curveball isn't nearly as sharp and his command is inconsistent. There still are nights when Thompson dominates, but they're less frequent. His changeup remains a top-notch pitch, though it's much more effective when he has his good fastball.

Defense

Thompson isn't athletic and doesn't field his position well. He's not surehanded, doesn't move quickly off the mound and is shaky when required to cover first base. Thompson's delivery to the plate is deliberate. He doesn't hold baserunners well, though he has improved his move to first.

2000 Outlook

Coming off shoulder surgery, Thompson should return to full strength early this season. Only 27, he has few peers among major league lefthanders when he's healthy. He was a key player in the Juan Gonzalez trade with Texas. With a better team behind him, he's a possiblity for 20 wins if he can avoid injuries. Given his track record, that's a big "if."

Overall Statistics

	W	L	Pct.	ERA	G	GS	Sv	IP	H	BB	SO	HR	Ratio
1999	9	11	.450	5.11	24	24	0	142.2	152	59	83	24	1.48
Career	36	43	.456	3.98	101	101	0	647.0	629	235	427	71	1.34

How Often He Throws Strikes

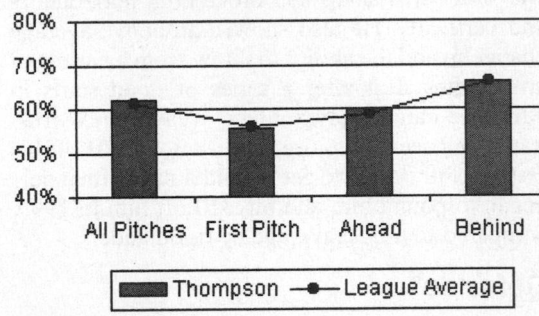

1999 Situational Stats

	W	L	ERA	Sv	IP		AB	H	HR	RBI	Avg
Home	5	5	5.63	0	62.1	LHB	112	30	4	21	.268
Road	4	6	4.71	0	80.1	RHB	443	122	20	56	.275
First Half	8	8	4.57	0	110.1	Sc Pos	115	23	6	50	.200
Scnd Half	1	3	6.96	0	32.1	Clutch	38	9	2	6	.237

1999 Rankings (American League)

- Did not rank near the top or bottom in any category

Jeff Weaver

1999 Season

When the Tigers selected Jeff Weaver with the 14th overall pick in the 1998 draft, they expected him to move fast. But he caught them by surprise, making it to Detroit after six minor league starts. He took the American League by storm, going 6-2, 2.89 in his first nine outings. When hitters adjusted, he didn't, losing 12 of his final 15 decisions and posting an 8.29 ERA after the All-Star break.

Pitching

Weaver came to the major leagues with an impressive menu of pitches. His fastball was clocked consistently at 94 MPH with a lot of movement, and he was throwing it over the plate consistently. His slider was sharp and broke both horizontally and vertically. He also showed an above-average changeup and the ability to throw from a variety of arm angles. But after a series of good starts in which he came away winless, Weaver grew frustrated and seemed to tire. He lost 3-4 MPH off his fastball and started to get his slider up. Lefthanders began to pound him and hit .310 off him in 1999, compared to a .236 average by righthanders.

Defense

Weaver is an outstanding athlete who also served as a DH at Fresno State. He went 2-for-4 in interleague play last year and showed exceptional speed on the bases. He's an outstanding fielder, but like a lot of young pitchers he needs to improve at combating basestealers. He has a quick pickoff move, but sometimes concentrates on pitching so much that he forgets about runners.

2000 Outlook

Weaver is potentially the best starter developed by the Tigers since Jack Morris. To reach that level, he'll need to control his emotions better and develop a pitch to get lefties out. He worked on a cut fastball late last season, and that may be the answer. As long as Weaver doesn't bomb in spring training, he should be Detroit's No. 3 starter in 2000.

Position: SP
Bats: R **Throws:** R
Ht: 6' 5" **Wt:** 200

Opening Day Age: 23
Born: 8/22/76 in Northridge, CA
ML Seasons: 1

Overall Statistics

	W	L	Pct.	ERA	G	GS	Sv	IP	H	BB	SO	HR	Ratio
1999	9	12	.429	5.55	30	29	0	163.2	176	56	114	27	1.42
Career	9	12	.429	5.55	30	29	0	163.2	176	56	114	27	1.42

How Often He Throws Strikes

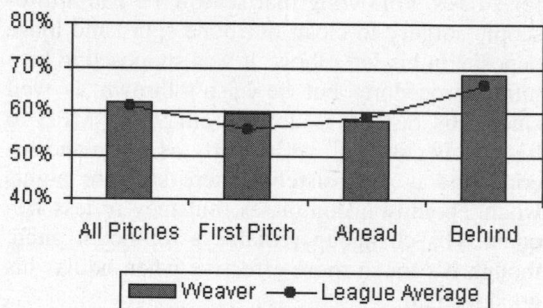

1999 Situational Stats

	W	L	ERA	Sv	IP		AB	H	HR	RBI	Avg
Home	4	8	5.34	0	87.2	LHB	358	111	20	71	.310
Road	5	4	5.80	0	76.0	RHB	276	65	7	26	.236
First Half	6	5	3.84	0	100.2	Sc Pos	140	46	4	65	.329
Scnd Half	3	7	8.29	0	63.0	Clutch	37	12	4	5	.324

1999 Rankings (American League)

- 1st in hit batsmen (17)
- 3rd in highest slugging percentage allowed (.478)
- 4th in highest ERA
- 5th in lowest batting average allowed vs. righthanded batters and most home runs allowed per nine innings (1.48)
- Led the Tigers in hit batsmen (17), GDPs induced (18), highest strikeout/walk ratio (2.0), lowest stolen-base percentage allowed (50.0), most run support per nine innings (5.6), most strikeouts per nine innings (6.3), most GDPs induced per GDP situation (14.2%) and lowest batting average allowed vs. righthanded batters

Matt Anderson (Future Closer)

Position: RP
Bats: R **Throws:** R
Ht: 6' 4" **Wt:** 200

Opening Day Age: 23
Born: 8/17/76 in
Louisville, KY
ML Seasons: 2

Overall Statistics

	W	L	Pct.	ERA	G	GS	Sv	IP	H	BB	SO	HR	Ratio
1999	2	1	.667	5.68	37	0	0	38.0	33	35	32	8	1.79
Career	7	2	.778	4.39	79	0	0	82.0	71	66	76	11	1.67

1999 Situational Stats

	W	L	ERA	Sv	IP		AB	H	HR	RBI	Avg
Home	1	0	6.98	0	19.1	LHB	56	13	7	19	.232
Road	1	1	4.34	0	18.2	RHB	86	20	1	14	.233
First Half	1	1	6.08	0	23.2	Sc Pos	40	10	3	24	.250
Scnd Half	1	0	5.02	0	14.1	Clutch	27	10	3	8	.370

1999 Season

The No. 1 overall pick in the 1997 draft, Matt Anderson seemed headed for a solid sophomore season last year, carrying a 2.17 ERA into late May. Then he gave up 11 earned runs in his next three innings and was demoted to Triple-A. He didn't pitch well in the minors or after rejoining the Tigers in mid-August.

Pitching & Defense

Anderson is one of the hardest throwers in the game, working in the high 90s and sometimes hitting triple digits. As he struggled with his mechanics last season, he didn't throw as consistently hard as he did in 1998. When he loses command of his fastball, Anderson often lets up to gain control, grooves pitches and gets shelled. He holds his slider like a knuckle-curve and throws it in the upper 80s without much command. Anderson is a below-average fielder but holds runners well.

2000 Outlook

Faced with his first real stretch of failure last season, Anderson couldn't snap out of it. With the trade of Francisco Cordero to Texas, he's Detroit's unquestioned closer of the future if he can straighten himself out.

Willie Blair

Position: RP/SP
Bats: R **Throws:** R
Ht: 6' 1" **Wt:** 185

Opening Day Age: 34
Born: 12/18/65 in
Paintsville, KY
ML Seasons: 10

Overall Statistics

	W	L	Pct.	ERA	G	GS	Sv	IP	H	BB	SO	HR	Ratio
1999	3	11	.214	6.85	39	16	0	134.0	169	44	82	29	1.59
Career	49	76	.392	4.94	362	118	4	1093.1	1215	369	670	147	1.45

1999 Situational Stats

	W	L	ERA	Sv	IP		AB	H	HR	RBI	Avg
Home	2	2	5.09	0	70.2	LHB	275	89	13	44	.324
Road	1	9	8.81	0	63.1	RHB	274	80	16	47	.292
First Half	1	7	7.01	0	69.1	Sc Pos	139	42	9	63	.302
Scnd Half	2	4	6.68	0	64.2	Clutch	40	14	0	5	.350

1999 Season

Any hopes that Willie Blair would recapture the magic that made him a 16-game winner for Detroit two years earlier were dashed in a hurry. Traded back to the Tigers by the Mets for Joe Randa, Blair was 1-5, 8.80 at the end of May.

Pitching & Defense

Blair has little margin for error. His fastball is usually around 90 MPH, but it's straight and he must locate it almost perfectly to be effective. He threw a little harder when he had his big season in 1997. Blair's slider is an effective pitch, though only when he has precise control. Not very athletic, Blair is a mediocre fielder who is poor at holding runners on base.

2000 Outlook

Given a choice, Blair would prefer to be used as a starter. But if he has a future in the game, it will be as a reliever. His ERA was 4.10 out of the bullpen last year, compared to 8.63 in the rotation. Blair has one year remaining on the three-year, $11.5 million contract given to him by the Diamondbacks.

Doug Brocail

Position: RP
Bats: L **Throws:** R
Ht: 6' 5" **Wt:** 235

Opening Day Age: 32
Born: 5/16/67 in
Clearfield, PA
ML Seasons: 8
Pronunciation:
broh-KALE

Overall Statistics

	W	L	Pct.	ERA	G	GS	Sv	IP	H	BB	SO	HR	Ratio
1999	4	4	.500	2.52	70	0	2	82.0	60	25	78	7	1.04
Career	23	32	.418	3.85	289	42	5	512.1	507	176	362	55	1.33

1999 Situational Stats

	W	L	ERA	Sv	IP		AB	H	HR	RBI	Avg
Home	2	1	2.04	1	39.2	LHB	141	30	5	14	.213
Road	2	3	2.98	1	42.1	RHB	150	30	2	16	.200
First Half	2	2	2.72	2	46.1	Sc Pos	69	15	0	20	.217
Scnd Half	2	2	2.27	0	35.2	Clutch	168	34	2	16	.202

1999 Season

Few have noticed, but Doug Brocail has emerged as one of the top setup men in the American League. He has turned in three consecutive solid seasons, leading AL relievers last year by allowing just a .178 average with runners on base. He also ranked among the league's best in holds (23), relief ERA and opponent batting average (.206) in relief during his finest season to date.

Pitching & Defense

Completely recovered from the arm problems that hindered him early in his career, Brocail touched 97 MPH a couple of times last season. He backs up his fastball with a knuckle-curve, which he uses like most pitchers use a slider. Brocail also has a decent slider and a usable changeup in case his main pitches aren't working. He's an excellent fielder who is difficult to bunt on. He's extraordinarily quick to home plate and has an excellent pickoff move.

2000 Outlook

One of the few Detroit pitchers who has made significant progress during the last three years, Brocail has emerged as a bullpen fixture. He has also become a team leader, setting a fine example for young pitchers with his mental toughness.

Frank Catalanotto

Traded To RANGERS

Position: 1B/2B/3B
Bats: L **Throws:** R
Ht: 6' 0" **Wt:** 195

Opening Day Age: 25
Born: 4/27/74 in
Smithtown, NY
ML Seasons: 3
Pronunciation:
cat-uh-lah-NOT-toh

Overall Statistics

	G	AB	R	H	D	T	HR	RBI	SB	BB	SO	Avg	OBP	Slg
1999	100	286	41	79	19	0	11	35	3	15	49	.276	.327	.458
Career	202	525	66	147	34	2	17	63	6	30	95	.280	.329	.450

1999 Situational Stats

	AB	H	HR	RBI	Avg		AB	H	HR	RBI	Avg
Home	156	35	6	16	.224	LHP	26	7	0	1	.269
Road	130	44	5	19	.338	RHP	260	72	11	34	.277
First Half	177	49	7	26	.277	Sc Pos	63	13	0	19	.206
Scnd Half	109	30	4	9	.275	Clutch	48	15	4	10	.313

1999 Season

Frank Catalanotto had another steady season as a backup infielder. He hit for roughly the same average as his first full season in the majors while nearly doubling his home-run output.

Hitting, Baserunning & Defense

Catalanotto has a classic, smooth lefthanded stroke. After much hard work in the weight room and the batting cage, he has started to drive the ball. He can pull inside pitches, but is at his best sending shots into gaps. Catalanotto is impatient, swinging at bad pitches and walking infrequently. His lack of defensive skills may prevent him from winning a regular major league job. He lacks range and doesn't have soft hands. His best position is second base, and he also can play first and third. Catalanotto doesn't run well.

2000 Outlook

Catalanotto is best suited for the role he's played the last two seasons, getting 200-300 at-bats and providing an occasional offensive boost. His bat is the reason he's in the majors. Now that he's been dealt to Texas in the Juan Gonzalez trade, Catalanotto could compete for the second-base job after Mark McLemore left as a free agent.

Karim Garcia

Position: RF/LF
Bats: L **Throws:** L
Ht: 6' 0" **Wt:** 172

Opening Day Age: 24
Born: 10/29/75 in
Ciudad Obregon, Mexico
ML Seasons: 5
Pronunciation:
kuh-REEM

Overall Statistics

	G	AB	R	H	D	T	HR	RBI	SB	BB	SO	Avg	OBP	Slg
1999	96	288	38	69	10	3	14	32	2	20	67	.240	.288	.441
Career	238	681	83	152	20	11	24	83	7	44	164	.223	.268	.391

1999 Situational Stats

	AB	H	HR	RBI	Avg		AB	H	HR	RBI	Avg
Home	140	30	4	9	.214	LHP	38	11	1	5	.289
Road	148	39	10	23	.264	RHP	250	58	13	27	.232
First Half	128	28	4	11	.219	Sc Pos	66	11	4	19	.167
Scnd Half	160	41	10	21	.256	Clutch	32	4	1	1	.125

1999 Season

The Tigers traded Luis Gonzalez to the Diamond-backs for Karim Garcia in December 1998, then watched while Gonzalez had a career year and Garcia was a disappointment. Garcia did display power with 14 homers, some of them tape-measure shots, in 288 at-bats, but he did little else.

Hitting, Baserunning & Defense

Garcia likes to put on a power show during batting practice when he would be better served to work on hitting the ball to all fields. He's capable of doing that without sacrificing his power, but he seems intent on trying to pull the ball. When he comes up with runners in scoring position, Garcia tends to get overanxious and swing at a lot of bad pitches. He hustles in the outfield and on the bases, though he has limited quickness and lacks fluidity. He does have a strong arm.

2000 Outlook

The days when Garcia was considered one of base-ball's top prospects are long gone. He has above-average power and that's about it. It's unlikely that he'll start for the Tigers.

Bill Haselman

Traded To RANGERS

Position: C
Bats: R **Throws:** R
Ht: 6' 3" **Wt:** 223

Opening Day Age: 33
Born: 5/25/66 in Long
Branch, NJ
ML Seasons: 9
Pronunciation:
HASS-ul-mun

Overall Statistics

	G	AB	R	H	D	T	HR	RBI	SB	BB	SO	Avg	OBP	Slg
1999	48	143	13	39	8	0	4	14	2	10	26	.273	.320	.413
Career	407	1101	134	282	63	3	35	141	9	80	211	.256	.308	.414

1999 Situational Stats

	AB	H	HR	RBI	Avg		AB	H	HR	RBI	Avg
Home	69	21	2	7	.304	LHP	39	12	1	4	.308
Road	74	18	2	7	.243	RHP	104	27	3	10	.260
First Half	89	27	4	10	.303	Sc Pos	39	6	1	9	.154
Scnd Half	54	12	0	4	.222	Clutch	14	5	0	1	.357

1999 Season

Bill Haselman expected to play regularly after signing a two-year, $1.75 million contract as a free agent in December. But a month later, the Tigers traded for Brad Ausmus and gave Ausmus the starting job. Haselman produced when given the chance to play, especially early in the season.

Hitting, Baserunning & Defense

Haselman is a better hitter than he is a defender. He has a relatively live bat and would hit 20-25 homers if he played every day. He hammers fastballs up and over the heart of the plate. Haselman hits lefthanders much better than righthanders. Defensively, his strength is calling a good game, and pitchers respond to him. But Haselman is a below-average receiver with little arm strength. He doesn't run well.

2000 Outlook

Disappointed because of his lack of playing time, Haselman asked Detroit GM Randy Smith to trade him early last season. He got his wish in November when he joined the Rangers for the third time, as part of the nine-player Juan Gonzalez trade. Haselman will get even fewer at-bats behind Ivan Rodriguez. Greg Zaun, part of the deal with Texas, will fill Haselman's role in Detroit.

Detroit

Gregg Jefferies

Position: DH
Bats: B **Throws:** R
Ht: 5'10" **Wt:** 185

Opening Day Age: 32
Born: 8/1/67 in
Burlingame, CA
ML Seasons: 13
Nickname: Puggsly

Overall Statistics

	G	AB	R	H	D	T	HR	RBI	SB	BB	SO	Avg	OBP	Slg
1999	70	205	22	41	8	0	6	18	3	13	11	.200	.258	.327
Career	1424	5378	743	1554	292	27	124	649	196	456	338	.289	.344	.422

1999 Situational Stats

	AB	H	HR	RBI	Avg		AB	H	HR	RBI	Avg
Home	106	20	5	11	.189	LHP	47	7	1	3	.149
Road	99	21	1	7	.212	RHP	158	34	5	15	.215
First Half	174	36	5	16	.207	Sc Pos	49	9	0	11	.184
Scnd Half	31	5	1	2	.161	Clutch	27	3	0	0	.111

1999 Season

After signing with Detroit as a free agent, Gregg Jefferies had a nightmare season. A lifetime .289 hitter, Jefferies literally had trouble getting the ball out of the infield. He made the weak groundout his own personal art form.

Hitting, Baserunning & Defense

In the past, Jefferies made consistent contact and was a tough out in the defining moments that decide ballgames. He was none of the above in 1999. He had trouble hitting any type of pitching, his bat was slow and he looked totally bewildered at the plate. There was a time when Jefferies ran well, but he didn't look as quick last season. Used almost exclusively as a DH by Detroit, he's an awkward outfielder who doesn't get good jumps on balls and has a well below-average arm.

2000 Outlook

Is Jefferies washed up at age 32? He certainly looked like it last season. He's due to make $6 million this year, and it's a lock that Detroit won't pick up his option for 2001. If he has another season like 1999, he could be out of baseball faster than anyone possibly could have expected.

Todd Jones

Position: RP
Bats: L **Throws:** R
Ht: 6' 3" **Wt:** 230

Opening Day Age: 31
Born: 4/24/68 in
Marietta, GA
ML Seasons: 7

Overall Statistics

	W	L	Pct.	ERA	G	GS	Sv	IP	H	BB	SO	HR	Ratio
1999	4	4	.500	3.80	65	0	30	66.1	64	35	64	7	1.49
Career	28	24	.538	3.55	392	0	128	466.2	412	231	419	37	1.38

1999 Situational Stats

	W	L	ERA	Sv	IP		AB	H	HR	RBI	Avg
Home	3	2	3.86	14	32.2	LHB	130	38	4	17	.292
Road	1	2	3.74	16	33.2	RHB	117	26	3	14	.222
First Half	1	3	4.66	12	36.2	Sc Pos	70	13	1	21	.186
Scnd Half	3	1	2.73	18	29.2	Clutch	159	39	3	19	.245

1999 Season

After starting slowly and drawing the ire of Detroit fans, Todd Jones pitched some of the best baseball of his career during the second half. He went 3-1, 2.73 after the All-Star break, converting 18 of 20 save opportunities.

Pitching & Defense

From a strictly mechanical standpoint, Jones is a study in how not to throw a baseball. He has poor balance as he goes through his motion, forcing his arm to catch up with his body at the last instant. He throws in the low to mid-90s with good movement, and it's difficult for hitters to pick up the ball because of his awkward delivery. Jones became more effective when he developed a slider during the second half of 1999. He's a good fielder but has problems holding runners.

2000 Outlook

There was a time when the Tigers were looking to unload Jones, but not any longer. Top closer prospect Francisco Cordero was traded to Texas in the Juan Gonzalez deal and Matt Anderson, the No. 1 pick in the 1997 draft, struggled mightily a year ago. Jones's slider should extend his tenure as Detroit's closer for a while longer.

Masao Kida

Position: RP
Bats: R **Throws:** R
Ht: 6' 3" **Wt:** 210

Opening Day Age: 31
Born: 9/12/68 in Tokyo, Japan
ML Seasons: 1
Pronunciation: muh-SOW KEY-duh

Overall Statistics

	W	L	Pct.	ERA	G	GS	Sv	IP	H	BB	SO	HR	Ratio
1999	1	0	1.000	6.26	49	0	1	64.2	73	30	50	6	1.59
Career	1	0	1.000	6.26	49	0	1	64.2	73	30	50	6	1.59

1999 Situational Stats

	W	L	ERA	Sv	IP		AB	H	HR	RBI	Avg
Home	1	0	5.89	1	36.2	LHB	111	31	3	21	.279
Road	0	0	6.75	0	28.0	RHB	142	42	3	24	.296
First Half	1	0	5.32	1	44.0	Sc Pos	78	24	3	40	.308
Scnd Half	0	0	8.27	0	20.2	Clutch	21	7	0	1	.333

1999 Season

Given a two-year, $3 million contract as a free agent from Japan's Orix Blue Wave, Masao Kida wasn't as effective as the Tigers anticipated. When put in a key relief role in early April, he was hit very hard. He was moved to a mopup role and stayed there for the remainder of the year.

Pitching & Defense

Kida consistently tops 90 MPH, but his fastball is straight as an arrow. He doesn't have a breaking ball or a changeup he can throw with any degree of effectiveness. Despite being a 10-year veteran of the Japanese major leagues, Kida has surprisingly little feel for pitching. When he gets in trouble, he stays in trouble. He's a poor fielder, but he's quick to the plate and has a decent pickoff move.

2000 Outlook

Unless he manages to develop some secondary pitches, Kida's career in the U.S. major leagues will be short. Based on the way he pitched last season, it's unlikely that Detroit will trust him with much responsibility in 2000.

Luis Polonia

Position: DH/LF/RF
Bats: L **Throws:** L
Ht: 5' 8" **Wt:** 160

Opening Day Age: 35
Born: 12/10/64 in Santiago, Dominican Republic
ML Seasons: 11

Overall Statistics

	G	AB	R	H	D	T	HR	RBI	SB	BB	SO	Avg	OBP	Slg
1999	87	333	46	108	21	8	10	32	17	16	32	.324	.357	.526
Career	1262	4496	680	1322	175	65	29	375	309	340	511	.294	.344	.381

1999 Situational Stats

	AB	H	HR	RBI	Avg		AB	H	HR	RBI	Avg
Home	182	63	8	23	.346	LHP	23	5	1	3	.217
Road	151	45	2	9	.298	RHP	310	103	9	29	.332
First Half	130	46	3	15	.354	Sc Pos	60	20	0	21	.333
Scnd Half	203	62	7	17	.305	Clutch	41	11	2	4	.268

1999 Season

After spending two seasons in the Mexican League, where he batted .377 and .381, Luis Polonia signed a minor league contract with the Tigers. He hit .323 in 42 Triple-A games before being recalled on May 26. Polonia had his best offensive season ever, filling Detroit's leadoff hole and taking at-bats away from the disappointing Gregg Jefferies.

Hitting, Baserunning & Defense

Polonia was fed a steady diet of breaking balls in Mexico, allowing him to become a much better hitter. He still isn't patient and draws far fewer walks than is ideal for a leadoff man. As he has gotten older, Polonia has developed more power. His 10 home runs in 1999 were one more than he totaled in his previous seven major league seasons. Polonia isn't as fast as he once was, but he's still a threat to steal whenever he reaches base. He's a below-average outfielder who lacks arm strength.

2000 Outlook

Polonia showed enough last year to warrant a one-year, $1.3 million contract from Detroit after declaring his free agency in November. There are glaring holes in his game, particularly defensively, but he still has a lot to offer.

Detroit

Other Detroit Tigers

Gabe Alvarez (Pos: DH, Age: 26, Bats: R)

	G	AB	R	H	D	T	HR	RBI	SB	BB	SO	Avg	OBP	Slg
1999	22	53	5	11	3	0	2	4	0	3	9	.208	.250	.377
Career	80	252	21	57	14	0	7	33	1	21	74	.226	.289	.365

Alvarez has hit 41 homers in Triple-A the last two seasons, but a big swing and offspeed stuff have been his undoing with the Tigers. 2000 Outlook: C

Kimera Bartee (Pos: CF, Age: 27, Bats: R)

	G	AB	R	H	D	T	HR	RBI	SB	BB	SO	Avg	OBP	Slg
1999	41	77	11	15	1	3	0	3	3	9	20	.195	.279	.286
Career	220	397	67	90	12	5	4	32	35	34	134	.227	.289	.312

Bartee enjoyed his finest Triple-A season in 1999, but he hasn't been above the Mendoza Line in either of the last two seasons with Detroit. He was dealt to Cincinnati in December. 2000 Outlook: C

Will Brunson (Pos: LHP, Age: 30)

	W	L	Pct.	ERA	G	GS	Sv	IP	H	BB	SO	HR	Ratio
1999	1	0	1.000	6.00	17	0	0	12.0	18	6	9	3	2.00
Career	1	1	.500	5.71	27	0	0	17.1	23	9	11	3	1.85

An adequate Triple-A pitcher for a few years, Brunson has struggled in his major league auditions. He signed with Oakland after the season. 2000 Outlook: C

Nelson Cruz (Pos: RHP, Age: 27)

	W	L	Pct.	ERA	G	GS	Sv	IP	H	BB	SO	HR	Ratio
1999	2	5	.286	5.67	29	6	0	66.2	74	23	46	11	1.46
Career	2	7	.222	5.90	48	6	0	93.0	103	32	69	17	1.45

Cruz got hot early in the season, going 7-1 with a 2.73 ERA for Triple-A Toledo. He couldn't bring the same magic to Detroit's rotation, but he pitched much better out of the bullpen in the second half. 2000 Outlook: B

Luis Garcia (Pos: SS, Age: 24, Bats: R)

	G	AB	R	H	D	T	HR	RBI	SB	BB	SO	Avg	OBP	Slg
1999	8	9	0	1	1	0	0	0	0	0	2	.111	.111	.222
Career	8	9	0	1	1	0	0	0	0	0	2	.111	.111	.222

Garcia hasn't shown much pop or patience in two Triple-A seasons. The Tigers released him in November. 2000 Outlook: C

Beiker Graterol (Pos: RHP, Age: 25)

	W	L	Pct.	ERA	G	GS	Sv	IP	H	BB	SO	HR	Ratio
1999	0	1	.000	15.75	1	1	0	4.0	4	4	2	3	2.00
Career	0	1	.000	15.75	1	1	0	4.0	4	4	2	3	2.00

Graterol has had only nominal success at the Triple-A level. He was removed from the 40-man roster in November. 2000 Outlook: C

Seth Greisinger (Pos: RHP, Age: 24)

	W	L	Pct.	ERA	G	GS	Sv	IP	H	BB	SO	HR	Ratio
1999					Did Not Play								
Career	6	9	.400	5.12	21	21	0	130.0	142	48	66	17	1.46

After a rocky debut with the Tigers in 1998, Greisinger endured a lost '99 season when he underwent Tommy John surgery in mid-June. The former first-round pick won't pitch until midseason this year. 2000 Outlook: C

Erik Hiljus (Pos: RHP, Age: 27)

	W	L	Pct.	ERA	G	GS	Sv	IP	H	BB	SO	HR	Ratio
1999	0	0	-	5.19	6	0	0	8.2	7	5	1	2	1.38
Career	0	0	-	5.19	6	0	0	8.2	7	5	1	2	1.38

Hiljus was hard to hit at Double-A and Triple-A in 1999, allowing just 54 hits and 21 walks in 76.2 innings while fanning 101. He wasn't invincible in Detroit, but he'll be back. 2000 Outlook: C

Felipe Lira (Pos: RHP, Age: 27)

	W	L	Pct.	ERA	G	GS	Sv	IP	H	BB	SO	HR	Ratio
1999	0	0	-	10.80	2	0	0	3.1	7	2	3	2	2.70
Career	21	38	.356	5.22	106	72	1	470.2	516	184	294	72	1.49

After an extended trial in Detroit's rotation during the mid-1990s, Lira has spent most of the last two years starting in Triple-A. 2000 Outlook: C

Jose Macias (Pos: 2B, Age: 26, Bats: B)

	G	AB	R	H	D	T	HR	RBI	SB	BB	SO	Avg	OBP	Slg
1999	5	4	2	1	0	0	1	2	0	0	1	.250	.250	1.000
Career	5	4	2	1	0	0	1	2	0	0	1	.250	.250	1.000

Macias is a switch-hitter who has shown patience at the plate until 1999, when he spent his first season at Triple-A and played briefly with the Tigers. He has got some pop and fields well. 2000 Outlook: C

C.J. Nitkowski (Pos: LHP, Age: 27)

	W	L	Pct.	ERA	G	GS	Sv	IP	H	BB	SO	HR	Ratio
1999	4	5	.444	4.30	68	7	0	81.2	63	45	66	11	1.32
Career	11	18	.379	5.50	142	33	3	258.2	268	141	177	33	1.58

Nitkowski looked good in a few September starts, fueling a possible return to the rotation. 2000 Outlook: B

Willis Roberts (Pos: RHP, Age: 24)

	W	L	Pct.	ERA	G	GS	Sv	IP	H	BB	SO	HR	Ratio
1999	0	0	-	13.50	1	0	0	1.1	3	0	0	0	2.25
Career	0	0	-	13.50	1	0	0	1.1	3	0	0	0	2.25

Walks have been a problem for Roberts in the high minors. He survived one rough outing against the Twins in July. 2000 Outlook: C

Sean Runyan (Pos: LHP, Age: 25)

	W	L	Pct.	ERA	G	GS	Sv	IP	H	BB	SO	HR	Ratio
1999	0	1	.000	3.38	12	0	0	10.2	9	3	6	2	1.13
Career	1	5	.167	3.54	100	0	1	61.0	56	31	45	9	1.43

After leading the AL in games pitched in 1998, Runyan needed arthroscopic shoulder surgery at season's end. His troubles continued in '99, leading to rotator-cuff surgery in July. 2000 Outlook: C

Jason Wood (Pos: 3B, Age: 30, Bats: R)

	G	AB	R	H	D	T	HR	RBI	SB	BB	SO	Avg	OBP	Slg
1999	27	44	5	7	1	0	1	8	0	2	13	.159	.196	.250
Career	40	68	11	15	3	0	2	9	0	5	18	.221	.274	.353

A career minor league infielder with some pop, Wood broke his left forearm in the spring. He was recalled in June, but didn't make much contact. He signed with the Pirates after the season. 2000 Outlook: C

Detroit Tigers Minor League Prospects

Organization Overview:

The Tigers won *Baseball America's* prestigious Organization of the Year Award in 1997, but little has gone right since then. After getting on the verge of contention when they jumped from 53 wins in 1996 to 79 a year later, they've gone 134-189 the past two seasons. Desperate to make a splash when the club opens Comerica Park in 2000, beleaguered GM Randy Smith sent Justin Thompson, Detroit's only creditable starter, and Francisco Cordero and Gabe Kapler, two of the organization's best young players, to Texas in a nine-player trade for Juan Gonzalez. If Gonzalez leaves as a free agent after this season, that deal could come back to bite the Tigers as much as Smith's last nine-player swap, which cost them Jose Lima and Daryle Ward.

Dave Borkowski

Position: P
Bats: R **Throws:** R
Ht: 6' 1" **Wt:** 200
Opening Day Age: 23
Born: 2/7/77 in Detroit, MI

Recent Statistics

	W	L	ERA	G	GS	Sv	IP	H	R	BB	SO	HR
1999 AAA Toledo	6	8	3.50	19	19	0	126.0	119	59	43	94	16
1999 AL Detroit	2	6	6.10	17	12	0	76.2	86	58	40	50	10

Borkowski plowed through the minors after signing as an 11th-round pick in 1995, going 51-30 before making his major league debut last July at age 22. He struggled mightily with Detroit, but two strong starts at the end of September gave him something to build on. His velocity dropped in 1998 but returned last year, as his hard sinker consistently registered 91-93 MPH. He has a decent curveball and slider, and also has a changeup he doesn't trust enough. Borkowski will need to improve his secondary pitches before he succeeds in the majors. The Tigers will have at least two openings in their rotation entering spring training, and he'll be in the running to fill one.

Javier Cardona

Position: C
Bats: R **Throws:** R
Ht: 6' 1" **Wt:** 185
Opening Day Age: 24
Born: 9/15/75 in Santurce, Puerto Rico

Recent Statistics

	G	AB	R	H	D	T	HR	RBI	SB	BB	SO	Avg
1998 AA Jacksnville	46	163	31	54	16	1	4	40	0	15	29	.331
1998 AAA Toledo	47	162	12	31	4	0	5	16	0	9	32	.191
1999 AA Jacksnville	108	418	84	129	31	0	26	92	4	46	69	.309
1999 MLE	108	396	61	107	25	0	21	67	2	28	73	.270

Cardona's career seemed to stall at the end of 1998, when he hit .191 in Triple-A. In five seasons after signing as a 1994 23rd-round pick out of Lincoln Land (Ill.) Junior College, he had batted .266 with 23 homers. But he broke through last year, leading the Double-A Southern League in homers and slugging percentage (.569). Cardona also showed improved control of the strike zone and contin-

ued to play solid defense. His arm has average strength and good accuracy, and he moves well behind the plate. With major league incumbent Brad Ausmus coming off an All-Star season, the Tigers can afford to give Cardona a full season in Triple-A this year.

Robert Fick

Position: 1B-C
Bats: L **Throws:** R
Ht: 6' 1" **Wt:** 189
Opening Day Age: 26
Born: 3/15/74 in Torrance, CA

Recent Statistics

	G	AB	R	H	D	T	HR	RBI	SB	BB	SO	Avg
1999 R Tigers	3	9	2	3	1	0	0	2	1	2	0	.333
1999 A W Michigan	3	11	2	3	0	0	0	0	1	2	0	.273
1999 AAA Toledo	14	48	11	15	0	1	2	8	1	8	5	.313
1999 AL Detroit	15	41	6	9	0	0	3	10	1	7	6	.220

Fick lost almost the entire 1999 season after dislocating his left shoulder in a spring-training "B" game, requiring surgery to repair a chronic condition. The injury contributed to ending thoughts of Fick as a regular big league catcher, but his defense was mediocre and his strength was offense anyway. A 1996 fifth-round pick out of Cal State Northridge, he has batted .316 with 105 doubles and 43 homers in 337 pro games. He hits line drives to all fields, has pull power and knows the strike zone. For now his career highlight is hitting a grand slam in the final game at Tiger Stadium, but Detroit thinks bigger things are in store for him. Fick broke into pro ball as a first baseman and could serve the Tigers there in 2000 if Tony Clark is traded. If not, he's in line to be the regular DH.

Brandon Inge

Position: C
Bats: R **Throws:** R
Ht: 5' 11" **Wt:** 185
Opening Day Age: 22
Born: 5/19/77 in Lynchburg, VA

Recent Statistics

	G	AB	R	H	D	T	HR	RBI	SB	BB	SO	Avg
1998 A Jamestown	51	191	24	44	10	1	8	29	8	17	53	.230
1999 A W Michigan	100	352	54	86	25	2	9	46	15	39	87	.244

Inge jump-started his career after last season with a dynamic performance in the California Fall League, where he won MVP honors after batting a league-best .407. A shortstop at Virginia Commonwealth University, Inge converted to catcher after being drafted in the second round in 1998. While he took quickly to the position switch, showing a very strong arm and fine athleticism behind the plate, Inge's offense suffered. He batted .239 before breaking out in the CFL. The Tigers envision him becoming Brad Ausmus with more power, and Inge's 6.9-second speed in the 60-yard-dash is a nice bonus. He'll start 2000 in high Class-A and could move up quickly if he continues to hit. The presence of Ausmus and Javier Cardona ahead of him mean that Inge won't have to be rushed.

Detroit

141

Eric Munson

Position: 1B-DH	**Opening Day Age:** 22
Bats: L **Throws:** R	**Born:** 10/3/77 in San
Ht: 6' 3" **Wt:** 220	Diego, CA

Recent Statistics

	G	AB	R	H	D	T	HR	RBI	SB	BB	SO	Avg
1999 A Lakeland	2	6	0	2	0	0	0	1	0	1	1	.333
1999 A W Michigan	67	252	42	67	16	1	14	44	3	37	47	.266

The third overall pick in the 1999 draft, Munson received a $6.75 million major league contract that included a $3.5 million bonus. Though he played just 67 games for full-season Class-A West Michigan, Munson led the club with 14 homers. *Baseball America* rated him the best pure hitter, best power hitter and closest player to being ready for the majors among college prospects last year. He's willing to draw a walk and he'll become even more dangerous when he stops being so pull-conscious. Munson was a catcher at the University of Southern California and has a strong arm, but the Tigers have good organizational depth behind the plate with Brad Ausmus, Javier Cardona and Brandon Inge. They're more concerned with getting Munson's bat to the majors, and they'll play him at first base or DH. He could reach Detroit this year, especially if Tony Clark is traded.

Adam Pettyjohn

Position: P	**Opening Day Age:** 22
Bats: R **Throws:** L	**Born:** 6/11/77 in
Ht: 6' 3" **Wt:** 190	Phoenix, AZ

Recent Statistics

	W	L	ERA	G	GS	Sv	IP	H	R	BB	SO	HR
1998 A Jamestown	2	2	2.86	4	4	0	22.0	21	10	4	24	0
1998 A W Michigan	4	2	1.97	8	8	0	50.1	46	15	9	64	3
1999 A Lakeland	3	4	3.77	9	9	0	59.2	62	35	11	51	2
1999 AA Jacksnville	9	5	4.69	20	20	0	126.2	134	75	35	92	13

The Tigers made a wise pick when they took Jeff Weaver in the first round of the 1998 draft, and they scored again when they took another Fresno State pitcher one round later. Pettyjohn reached Double-A early last season, making Detroit comfortable in including fellow lefthander Alan Webb in the Juan Gonzalez trade. Pettyjohn's strong suits are his curveball and his command of an 88-89 MPH fastball. His primary goal in Triple-A this season will be to improve his changeup. Pettyjohn projects as a No. 3-5 starter.

Victor Santos

Position: P	**Opening Day Age:** 23
Bats: R **Throws:** R	**Born:** 10/2/76 in San
Ht: 6' 3" **Wt:** 175	Pedro de Macoris, D.R.

Recent Statistics

	W	L	ERA	G	GS	Sv	IP	H	R	BB	SO	HR
1998 AAA Toledo	1	2	11.05	5	3	0	14.2	24	22	10	12	5
1998 A Lakeland	5	2	2.51	16	15	1	100.1	88	38	24	74	9
1998 AA Jacksnville	4	2	4.17	6	6	0	36.2	40	20	15	37	2
1999 AA Jacksnville	12	6	3.49	28	28	0	173.0	150	86	58	146	16

A nondrafted free agent, Santos pitched in high Class-A ball for parts of three seasons before establishing himself in Double-A in 1999. He led the Southern League in strikeouts while winning in double figures for the third straight season. Santos has two primary pitches, an 89-93 MPH fastball and a splitter. He also uses a slider and a changeup. He helps himself by throwing strikes and keeping the ball in the ballpark. Santos is ticketed for a full year in Triple-A, but he isn't far from being able to help a Tigers team that's hungry for starters.

Chris Wakeland

Position: OF	**Opening Day Age:** 25
Bats: L **Throws:** L	**Born:** 6/15/74 in
Ht: 6' 0" **Wt:** 185	Huntington Beach, CA

Recent Statistics

	G	AB	R	H	D	T	HR	RBI	SB	BB	SO	Avg
1998 A Lakeland	131	487	82	147	26	5	18	89	19	66	111	.302
1999 R Tigers	4	14	2	1	0	0	0	1	0	0	4	.071
1999 A Lakeland	4	17	3	7	1	0	0	7	1	0	0	.412
1999 AA Jacksnville	55	212	42	68	16	3	13	36	6	35	53	.321
1999 MLE	55	200	30	56	13	2	10	26	3	21	56	.280

A .300 hitter since signing as a 15th-round pick from Oregon State in 1996, Wakeland was enjoying his best pro year when he sprained his left wrist and broke his hamate bone last June. He has a quick, compact stroke that produces line drives and opposite-field power, and he was rated the Double-A Southern League's best batting prospect in a midseason survey of managers. After his injury, he came back and hit .356 in the Arizona Fall League. Wakeland has average speed and arm strength, and last year showed improvement as a right fielder. He'll spend 2000 in Triple-A and could become an even bigger threat if he develops pull power.

Others to Watch

Righthander **Nate Cornejo** (20) has the stuff to have a longer major league career than his father Mardie, who pitched 25 games for the 1978 Mets. Nate throws a 90-94 MPH sinker and a good curveball. . . Outfielder **Richard Gomez** (22) hit .303 and led the Class-A Midwest League with 66 stolen bases last season. He also has raw power and an athletic body that reminds the Tigers of Bo Jackson's. . . Righthander **Kris Keller** (22) touched 98 MPH last year while saving eight games and fanning 87 in 77 innings at Class-A West Michigan. He has been compared to a young John Wetteland. . . Acquired from the Red Sox in a trade for Bryce Florie last July, lefthander **Mike Maroth** (22) won 14 games and reached Double-A in 1999, his first full pro season. He has a good changeup and can reach 92 MPH with his fastball. . . Righthander **Fernando Rodney** (19) may ease the loss of Francisco Cordero in the Juan Gonzalez trade. Rodney's fastball hit 98 MPH in his pro debut last year, 5 MPH harder than Cordero was at the same stage of his career. . . Like Rodney, shortstop **Ramon Santiago** (18) is a Dominican who opened eyes when he broke into pro ball in 1999. He's a very polished defender who hit .326 and stole 25 bases in 47 games, most in Rookie ball.

Ewing M. Kauffman Stadium

Offense

Shortening the outfield fences prior to the 1996 season has turned Kauffman Stadium into a hitters' park. Over the last three years, it has had the second-highest home-run index, as well as the third-highest run and batting average indices. The park features good sight lines, which reduce strikeout totals. The only negative from a hitter's standpoint is that Kauffman Stadium cuts down on doubles.

Defense

The lofty reputation of the Kauffman grounds crew is well earned. The grass surface is always in immaculate condition. A large outfield expanse means an outfield trio with good range is critical. Corner outfielders who fail to get to balls down the line may find them scooting past and hugging the outfield wall as it curves around towards the bullpens.

Who It Helps The Most

The breakthrough seasons of Jermaine Dye and Mike Sweeney were fueled in part by Kaufmann Stadium. Jeremy Giambi is a pronounced ground-ball hitter, but he hit 204 points higher at home. Mark Quinn didn't miss a beat when stepping into The K from the Triple-A Pacific Coast League. Surprisingly, Jose Rosado gave up two-thirds of his homers on the road. Blake Stein's ERA was 2.91 in Kansas City and 7.99 elsewhere.

Who It Hurts The Most

Kauffman Stadium is no longer the pitcher's friend it used to be. Pitchers must be careful of the park's new longball tendencies, and to their credit most of Kansas City's hurlers were in 1999. Fleet-footed, slashing, line-drive hitters used to rule this ballyard, but the new dimensions now diminish their talents. Johnny Damon would have been better off with the old configuration.

Rookies & Newcomers

Mark Quinn's slugging skills will be enhanced in Kansas City. Dan Reichert will enjoy pitching in Kauffman Stadium if he can keep the ball on the ground as he has done in the minors. Chris Fussell and Orber Moreno will find the park less friendly.

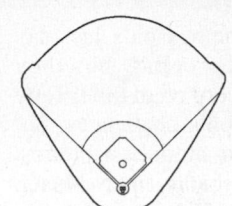

Dimensions: LF-330, LCF-375, CF-400, RCF-375, RF-330

Capacity: 40,625

Elevation: 750 feet

Surface: Grass

Foul Territory: Average

Park Factors

1999 Season

	Home Games			Away Games			
	Royals	Opp	Total	Royals	Opp	Total	Index
G	71	71	142	72	72	144	—
Avg	.288	.284	.286	.273	.279	.276	104
AB	2451	2511	4962	2524	2412	4936	102
R	387	373	760	356	415	771	100
H	707	712	1419	688	672	1360	106
2B	119	104	223	134	112	246	90
3B	28	17	45	16	12	28	160
HR	71	81	152	65	95	160	95
BB	231	273	504	240	292	532	94
SO	387	344	731	428	389	817	89
E	49	62	111	61	59	120	94
E-Infield	38	51	89	51	49	100	90
LHB-Avg	.287	.305	.297	.272	.276	.274	108
LHB-HR	16	37	53	15	45	60	83
RHB-Avg	.289	.266	.278	.273	.280	.276	101
RHB-HR	55	44	99	50	50	100	102

1997-1999

	Home Games			Away Games			
	Royals	Opp	Total	Royals	Opp	Total	Index
G	217	217	434	217	217	434	—
Avg	.272	.283	.278	.265	.275	.270	103
AB	7419	7796	15215	7628	7296	14924	102
R	1048	1221	2269	1013	1143	2156	105
H	2015	2208	4223	2021	2008	4029	105
2B	332	349	681	393	362	755	88
3B	71	45	116	41	26	67	170
HR	212	273	485	181	257	438	109
BB	733	746	1479	668	829	1497	97
SO	1241	1216	2457	1406	1284	2690	90
E	146	154	300	152	162	314	96
E-Infield	120	129	249	129	139	268	93
LHB-Avg	.276	.289	.283	.270	.273	.272	104
LHB-HR	57	113	170	42	108	150	109
RHB-Avg	.269	.279	.274	.262	.276	.269	102
RHB-HR	155	160	315	139	149	288	109

1999 Rankings (American League)
- Highest triple factor
- Highest LHB batting-average factor
- Third-highest batting-average factor
- Lowest strikeout factor
- Second-lowest walk factor
- Third-lowest infield-error factor

Tony Muser

1999 Season

A questionable rainout on the season's last day helped the Royals avoid the cellar, but they couldn't escape their worst record of all time. Tony Muser met most of the season's challenges, but individual successes failed to produce victories. The overall results reflected badly upon Muser. The club lost several games painfully in late innings because an awful bullpen never got straightened out.

Offense

Muser's background as a hitting coach showed as the Royals' offense exploded for a club-record 856 runs. That's even more impressive, considering none of the regulars was an everyday player at his position for Kansas City in 1998. Muser's lineups remained simple with speed at the top (sometimes at the expense of on-base percentage) and power in the middle. He preferred to sacrifice instead of pinch-hitting for his lighter-hitting middle infielders. He likes to put runners in motion, using the stolen base and the hit-and-run more than most American League managers.

Pitching & Defense

Muser showed confidence in his young starters, letting them try to work out of jams. However, his bullpen blew 30 saves in 59 tries, so his tactics were understandable. Muser stood by closer Jeff Montgomery long after others would have abandoned him. When he finally did turn to other options, they also failed miserably. Muser managed to improve the infield defense appreciably without cost to the offense. He shifted Mike Sweeney to first base and was willing to live with Chad Kreuter's weak bat because it meant improved catching. Despite all the maneuvering, the Royals allowed a club-record 921 runs.

2000 Outlook

Despite poor results in the standings, Muser received a contract extension. He's overseen an influx of young players that could pay off in a couple of years. After fixing the bullpen in his first full season, he'll have to focus on that area again, facing the new challenge of not having a set closer.

Born: 8/1/47 in Los Angeles, CA

Playing Experience: 1969-1978, Bos, CWS, Bal, Mil

Managerial Experience: 3 seasons

Manager Statistics

Year	Team, Lg	W	L	Pct	GB	Finish
1999	Kansas City, AL	64	97	.398	32.5	4th Central
3 Seasons		167	234	.416	—	—

1999 Starting Pitchers by Days Rest

	<=3	4	5	6+
Royals Starts	2	82	44	23
Royals ERA	11.88	4.80	4.54	6.56
AL Avg Starts	2	82	47	21
AL ERA	6.83	4.98	4.72	5.62

1999 Situational Stats

	Tony Muser	AL Average
Hit & Run Success %	34.7	35.3
Stolen Base Success %	76.5	68.0
Platoon Pct.	47.5	56.7
Defensive Subs	12	22
High-Pitch Outings	21	15
Quick/Slow Hooks	16/12	18/18
Sacrifice Attempts	69	52

1999 Rankings (American League)

- 1st in stolen-base percentage (76.5%), steals of second base (122) and fewest caught stealings of third base (2)
- 2nd in sacrifice bunt attempts (69), hit-and-run attempts (101) and starts with over 120 pitches (21)
- 3rd in intentional walks (28)

Carlos Beltran

Position: CF
Bats: B **Throws:** R
Ht: 6' 0" **Wt:** 175

Opening Day Age: 22
Born: 4/24/77 in Manati, Puerto Rico
ML Seasons: 2

Kansas City

1999 Season

The Royals worried they might be overextending by jumping Carlos Beltran directly from Double-A Wichita to a full-time center field job in the majors. Their worries were unfounded. Beltran had one of the most productive rookie seasons ever, becoming the first player to produce 100 runs and 100 RBI in his debut since Boston's Fred Lynn in 1975—when Lynn was named the American League's Most Valuable Player. Beltran's emergence, which culminated with the AL Rookie of the Year Award, was the most enjoyable part of an otherwise disappointing Royals season.

Hitting

A very aggressive hitter, Beltran turned around a number of fastballs when pitchers challenged him early in the year. He seemed to wilt a bit in the August heat, then rebounded with a fine September even while hurlers tried to pitch around him more often. Beltran generates his power from a sweet, lightning-quick swing. The only weakness in his offense is overanxiousness, which leads him to chase pitches and get overly pull-conscious.

Baserunning & Defense

Beltran is a five-tool player. Besides hitting for average and power, he has good speed, above-average range and an accurate arm. Beltran stole 27 bases in 35 tries while showing fine natural instincts on the basepaths. Though he committed 12 errors last season, he stole a number of homers with perfectly timed leaps at the fence. He also finished right behind teammate Jermaine Dye for the AL lead in outfield assists, gunning down 16 baserunners.

2000 Outlook

The Royals are clearly building their team around youngsters like Beltran and Carlos Febles. After a trial batting leadoff, Beltran will remain in the club's No. 3 spot, where the full range of his offensive talents can come to the fore. One of the best young talents in baseball, he'll get even better once he develops more plate discipline.

Overall Statistics

	G	AB	R	H	D	T	HR	RBI	SB	BB	SO	Avg	OBP	Slg
1999	156	663	112	194	27	7	22	108	27	46	123	.293	.337	.454
Career	170	721	124	210	32	10	22	115	30	49	135	.291	.336	.455

Where He Hits the Ball

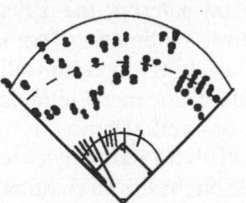

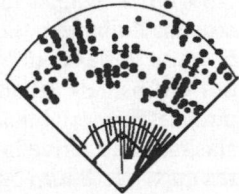

Vs. LHP **Vs. RHP**

1999 Situational Stats

	AB	H	HR	RBI	Avg		AB	H	HR	RBI	Avg
Home	336	94	12	55	.280	LHP	132	36	7	19	.273
Road	327	100	10	53	.306	RHP	531	158	15	89	.298
First Half	377	114	12	59	.302	Sc Pos	173	53	6	83	.306
Scnd Half	286	80	10	49	.280	Clutch	87	22	3	22	.253

1999 Rankings (American League)

- 1st in errors in center field (12)
- 2nd in at-bats and lowest fielding percentage in center field (.971)
- 3rd in sacrifice flies (10) and plate appearances (723)
- 7th in hits and singles
- 9th in triples, fewest pitches seen per plate appearance (3.40) and lowest on-base percentage for a leadoff hitter (.336)
- 10th in lowest percentage of pitches taken (49.1%)
- Led the Royals in at-bats, runs scored, singles, sacrifice flies (10), caught stealing (8), strikeouts, plate appearances (723) and slugging percentage vs. lefthanded pitchers (.500)

Johnny Damon

1999 Season

For the fourth straight season, Johnny Damon showed across-the-board improvement. Asked to take on leadoff duties, Damon posted several personal bests while leading the Royals to their most productive offensive season ever. Mired in a .169 slump through the first three weeks of the season, Damon went on a 16-game hitting streak immediately after the birth of his twins, his first children. Damon hit .323 over the next five months before losing the last two weeks of the season to a strained ribcage muscle.

Hitting

Damon developed the patience to take a few more pitches, which produced dramatic results. A career .239 hitter against lefthanders entering the 1999 season, he batted .329 against southpaws. That's because lefties couldn't induce him to get himself out on inside fastballs, and he got more hittable pitches from righthanders as well. Damon is a slashing, line-drive hitter with extra-base power to the gaps. He'll turn on inside pitches from righties.

Baserunning & Defense

Damon can fly. His excellent speed shows on the bases and in the outfield. He makes aggressive use of his wheels to take an extra base as a runner, and he stole 36 bases in 42 tries last year, his best-ever performance in both steals and steal percentage. Though he usually can outrun his mistakes, Damon still doesn't read balls well off the bat. A below-average arm remains his biggest flaw and consigned him to left field when rookie Carlos Beltran took over in center last year.

2000 Outlook

The Royals' most difficult offseason decision will be how to make Damon's blossoming big-revenue talent fit into their small-revenue budget. Destined for a significant raise via arbitration, Damon might well be traded for budgetary purposes. The willingness of Kansas City to pay him will be indicative of its interest in keeping its young team together.

Position: LF
Bats: L **Throws:** L
Ht: 6' 2" **Wt:** 190

Opening Day Age: 26
Born: 11/5/73 in Fort Riley, KS
ML Seasons: 5
Pronunciation: DAY-mun

Overall Statistics

	G	AB	R	H	D	T	HR	RBI	SB	BB	SO	Avg	OBP	Slg
1999	145	583	101	179	39	9	14	77	36	67	50	.307	.379	.477
Career	644	2402	368	680	114	37	49	264	110	210	290	.283	.342	.423

Where He Hits the Ball

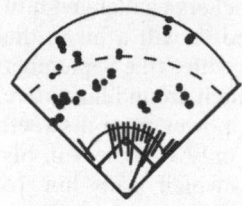 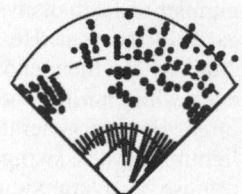

Vs. LHP   **Vs. RHP**

1999 Situational Stats

	AB	H	HR	RBI	Avg		AB	H	HR	RBI	Avg
Home	294	88	5	39	.299	LHP	140	46	1	20	.329
Road	289	91	9	38	.315	RHP	443	133	13	57	.300
First Half	352	105	8	48	.298	Sc Pos	145	46	2	59	.317
Scnd Half	231	74	6	29	.320	Clutch	76	24	2	13	.316

1999 Rankings (American League)

- 2nd in triples
- 3rd in stolen-base percentage (85.7%)
- 4th in fielding percentage in left field (.987)
- 5th in highest percentage of extra bases taken as a runner (66.7%)
- Led the Royals in triples, stolen bases, walks, intentional walks (5), stolen-base percentage (85.7%), fewest GDPs per GDP situation (10.2%), batting average with runners in scoring position, batting average vs. lefthanded pitchers, on-base percentage for a leadoff hitter (.371), on-base percentage vs. lefthanded pitchers (.370), on-base percentage vs. righthanded pitchers (.382), steals of third (2) and highest percentage of extra bases taken as a runner (66.7%)

Jermaine Dye

1999 Season

In his first two seasons after joining the Royals in a 1997 trade with the Braves for Michael Tucker, Jermaine Dye played in just 135 games because of a series of leg injuries. When in the lineup, he did little to endear himself to his new team. Then he broke out in 1999, more than doubling his career totals in most power-hitting categories while finishing with the second-most RBI in Kansas City history.

Hitting

Patience at the plate gave Johnny Damon better on-base ability and Jermaine Dye a whole new lease on life as a hitter. Dye overcame his tendency to lash out at the first hittable pitch and his quick, powerful bat took over from there. However, he still will chase high pitches and can be jammed with inside fastballs. Despite his high RBI count, Dye didn't hit especially well with runners in scoring position. When baserunners are in motion, Dye gets slightly distracted from hitting.

Baserunning & Defense

Dye has average speed but doesn't do well on the bases. He runs tentatively and is caught more often than not when trying to steal. Dye makes much better use of his quickness in right field, where his range is among the best in the majors. He always gets a good read on flyballs and owns a strong, accurate arm. Dye tied for the American League lead with 17 outfield assists in 1999.

2000 Outlook

The Royals acted quickly to retain their big RBI bat. Two weeks after the season ended, they signed Dye to a two-year, $6.1 million contract. He's just coming into his own as a power hitter, and the club hopes he can become a fixture in right field and the middle of the order.

Position: RF
Bats: R **Throws:** R
Ht: 6' 4" **Wt:** 220

Opening Day Age: 26
Born: 1/28/74 in Vacaville, CA
ML Seasons: 4

Overall Statistics

	G	AB	R	H	D	T	HR	RBI	SB	BB	SO	Avg	OBP	Slg
1999	158	608	96	179	44	8	27	119	2	58	119	.294	.354	.526
Career	391	1377	178	373	79	9	51	201	7	94	283	.271	.317	.452

Where He Hits the Ball

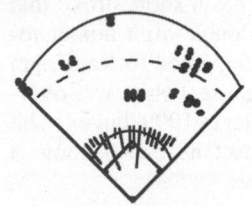

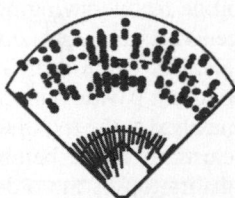

Vs. LHP   **Vs. RHP**

1999 Situational Stats

	AB	H	HR	RBI	Avg		AB	H	HR	RBI	Avg
Home	299	92	15	57	.308	LHP	101	27	5	18	.267
Road	309	87	12	62	.282	RHP	507	152	22	101	.300
First Half	328	99	17	66	.302	Sc Pos	189	48	6	80	.254
Scnd Half	280	80	10	53	.286	Clutch	87	15	2	10	.172

1999 Rankings (American League)

- 2nd in doubles
- 4th in fielding percentage in right field (.984)
- 5th in triples, errors in right field (6) and bunts in play (6)
- 7th in lowest cleanup slugging percentage (.497)
- 8th in games played
- 9th in RBI
- 10th in lowest batting average in the clutch
- Led the Royals in home runs, doubles, total bases (320), RBI, pitches seen (2,517), slugging percentage, HR frequency (22.5 ABs per HR), batting average with the bases loaded (.400), slugging percentage vs. righthanded pitchers (.531), bunts in play (6) and games played
- Led AL right fielders in triples

Carlos Febles

1999 Season

When the Royals turned over their entire infield in 1999, it was their defense that improved the most. Carlos Febles made a large contribution to that success. In addition to helping the Royals post their second-best double play total ever, Febles also enjoyed a good season at the plate. Despite losing nearly a month to a dislocated finger and sore shoulder, Febles had a fine campaign worthy of Rookie-of-the-Year consideration.

Hitting

Febles is still learning to hit in the majors. After he hit .286 before the All-Star break, pitchers adjusted better than he did, leading to a .205 average afterward. Once he fell behind in the count, Febles was prone to overswinging. He has a short stroke that generates enough pop for double-digit homer totals. His gap power is ideally suited to Kauffman Stadium's wide outfield expanse. Febles was overmatched at the top of the order in 1999, but once he learns to make better contact he can become a quality top-of-the-order hitter.

Baserunning & Defense

A smooth fielder, Febles plays deep at second base, permitting him outstanding range in all directions. He also works the double play pivot well. His primary fielding deficiency is a tendency to try to make impossible plays, resulting in occasional throwing errors. Febles is a speedy baserunner who is just beginning to learn how to steal bases. Eventually he should be capable of swiping 40 in a full season.

2000 Outlook

The Royals look to Febles as an anchor for their infield defense. If he makes expected progress as a hitter, they'll find a place for him near the top of their batting order, too. Febles has star potential and is one of the cornerstones of Kansas City's future.

Position: 2B
Bats: R **Throws:** R
Ht: 5'11" **Wt:** 170

Opening Day Age: 23
Born: 5/24/76 in El Seybo, Dominican Republic
ML Seasons: 2
Pronunciation: FAY-bless

Overall Statistics

	G	AB	R	H	D	T	HR	RBI	SB	BB	SO	Avg	OBP	Slg
1999	123	453	71	116	22	9	10	53	20	47	91	.256	.336	.411
Career	134	478	76	126	23	11	10	55	22	51	98	.264	.344	.421

Where He Hits the Ball

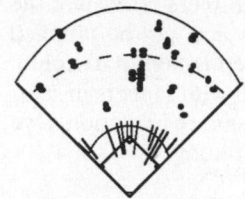 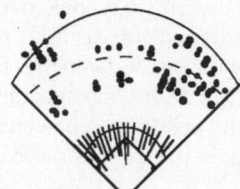

Vs. LHP   **Vs. RHP**

1999 Situational Stats

	AB	H	HR	RBI	Avg		AB	H	HR	RBI	Avg
Home	200	50	5	29	.250	LHP	97	27	2	12	.278
Road	253	66	5	24	.261	RHP	356	89	8	41	.250
First Half	287	82	6	35	.286	Sc Pos	129	34	3	44	.264
Scnd Half	166	34	4	18	.205	Clutch	56	16	2	13	.286

1999 Rankings (American League)

- 1st in highest groundball/flyball ratio (2.5)
- 2nd in triples
- 4th in sacrifice bunts (12) and errors at second base (14)
- 5th in lowest fielding percentage at second base (.979)
- 7th in stolen-base percentage (83.3%)
- 8th in highest percentage of extra bases taken as a runner (62.2%)
- Led the Royals in triples, sacrifice bunts (12), highest groundball/flyball ratio (2.5), most pitches seen per plate appearance (3.82) and highest percentage of pitches taken (59.0%)
- Led AL second basemen in sacrifice bunts (12) and highest groundball/flyball ratio (2.5)

Jeremy Giambi

Position: DH/1B
Bats: L **Throws:** L
Ht: 6' 0" **Wt:** 205

Opening Day Age: 25
Born: 9/30/74 in San Jose, CA
ML Seasons: 2
Pronunciation: gee-AHM-bee

1999 Season

Jeremy Giambi led the minor leagues in batting with a .372 average in 1998 and was expected to start for the Royals last season. But a nagging hamstring injury sidelined him for most of April, and he didn't get called up for good until June. He started slowly in Kansas City before batting .321 in September.

Hitting

Giambi's bat is his only productive tool. He has an extremely quick swing and can make productive contact with almost any pitch. A line-drive hitter, he has hit 32 homers in 131 Triple-A games, but his home-run power may have been inflated by the Pacific Coast League and the ballpark in Omaha. He may never be more than a moderate longball threat in the majors. Giambi was too aggressive at times as a rookie, frequently getting himself out on bad pitches. Once he settled down, he performed much better.

Baserunning & Defense

Giambi is barely adequate on the basepaths, and his defense is poor enough to cost him playing time. Had he but worked harder to shift from left field, where he was a poor fielder with an adequate arm, he would have been given the first-base job almost by default when Jeff King suddenly retired in May. Instead, he worked on his hitting and often appeared confused and out of place at first base in the majors.

2000 Outlook

Though Giambi was highly touted after tearing up the minors in 1998, the window of opportunity might not be open for him for long. The Royals were disappointed that he couldn't handle first-base defense, and he may already be typecast as a DH. The September emergence of Mark Quinn gives Kansas City another DH candidate. Giambi should hit for average, but his power production ultimately will determine how much he'll play in the majors.

Overall Statistics

	G	AB	R	H	D	T	HR	RBI	SB	BB	SO	Avg	OBP	Slg
1999	90	288	34	82	13	1	3	34	0	40	67	.285	.373	.368
Career	108	346	40	95	17	1	5	42	0	51	76	.275	.368	.373

Where He Hits the Ball

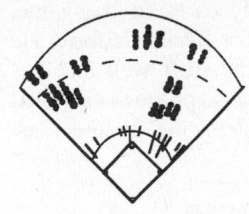
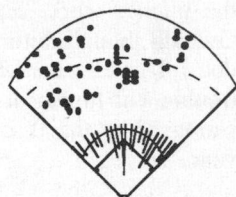

Vs. LHP   **Vs. RHP**

1999 Situational Stats

	AB	H	HR	RBI	Avg		AB	H	HR	RBI	Avg
Home	156	59	2	24	.378	LHP	48	14	0	6	.292
Road	132	23	1	10	.174	RHP	240	68	3	28	.283
First Half	109	30	1	13	.275	Sc Pos	81	21	1	30	.259
Scnd Half	179	52	2	21	.291	Clutch	49	8	1	5	.163

1999 Rankings (American League)

- 7th in lowest batting average in the clutch
- 9th in batting average on a 3-1 count (.571)
- Led the Royals in intentional walks (5) and batting average on a 3-1 count (.571)
- Led designated hitters in batting average on a 3-1 count (.571)

Chad Kreuter

1999 Season

Signed as a free agent from the Angels, Chad Kreuter emerged from spring training with the lion's share of the Royals' catching duties. An outstanding May boosted his average to .278, but he batted .167 after the All-Star break to slip back to his normal level. He wore down late in the season and played less frequently as Kansas City tried other options. Throughout the year, Kreuter provided steady management of the Royals' young pitching staff.

Hitting

Kreuter is a low-average hitter with a bit of power, though not nearly enough to make up for his lack of contact. He's a patient hitter who likes to make the pitcher work, especially early in the game. Overall, though, hitting is not Kreuter's forte. He doesn't handle hard breaking stuff well and has trouble with high heat. Kreuter is prone to extended slumps, like the 0-for-38 streak he endured last year.

Baserunning & Defense

An adept backstop, Kreuter handles a pitching staff very well and does a good job of blocking pitches in the dirt. Those are the traits that won him the catching job in the first place. Kreuter is as hard-nosed as they come, always ready to block the plate. He nearly died because of internal bleeding after such a collision with current teammate Johnny Damon in 1996. Kreuter has average arm strength and is extremely accurate. He's strictly a station-to-station baserunner.

2000 Outlook

"Have mitt, will travel" could be Kreuter's motto. His one-year stint with the Royals was purely a stopgap measure, and he became a free agent after the season. On a good team he'd be a backup, but a young club could use him more often because of his expertise at handling a pitching staff.

Position: C
Bats: B **Throws:** R
Ht: 6' 2" **Wt:** 200

Opening Day Age: 35
Born: 8/26/64 in Greenbrae, CA
ML Seasons: 12
Pronunciation: CREW-ter

Overall Statistics

	G	AB	R	H	D	T	HR	RBI	SB	BB	SO	Avg	OBP	Slg
1999	107	324	31	73	15	0	5	35	0	34	65	.225	.309	.318
Career	743	1989	228	469	93	7	40	217	3	253	460	.236	.325	.350

Where He Hits the Ball

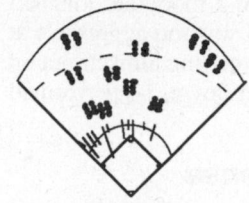 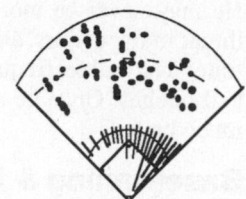

Vs. LHP **Vs. RHP**

1999 Situational Stats

	AB	H	HR	RBI	Avg		AB	H	HR	RBI	Avg
Home	165	38	2	22	.230	LHP	43	12	2	5	.279
Road	159	35	3	13	.220	RHP	281	61	3	30	.217
First Half	216	55	4	29	.255	Sc Pos	87	17	0	28	.195
Scnd Half	108	18	1	6	.167	Clutch	59	10	0	6	.169

1999 Rankings (American League)

- 3rd in lowest batting average with runners in scoring position
- 5th in most GDPs per GDP situation (19.8%) and fielding percentage at catcher (.994)
- 9th in lowest batting average in the clutch
- Led AL catchers in batting average with the bases loaded (.385)

Joe Randa

Position: 3B
Bats: R **Throws:** R
Ht: 5'11" **Wt:** 190

Opening Day Age: 30
Born: 12/18/69 in Milwaukee, WI
ML Seasons: 5
Nickname: The Joker

1999 Season

Traded back to his original organization by the Mets for minor league outfielder Juan LeBron, Joe Randa duplicated his slow start of 1998. He entered June with a .254 batting average before interleague play invigorated him. He hit .442 to earn American League Player of the Month honors for July, and finished the season with a .341 average after May. It was his best season ever as Randa shattered career bests for batting average, runs, hits, doubles, homers and RBI.

Hitting

Despite a few too many strikeouts for a hitter who lacks serious power, Randa is a productive big league hitter. Randa has begun to pull the ball a little more for power, but mostly he'll hit the ball where it's pitched, slashing liners to all parts of the park. He's not usually as streaky as he was in 1999, though he often starts slowly. His career average after April 30 is .301.

Baserunning & Defense

Randa has the tools for the hot corner. He has quick reflexes and above-average range for a third sacker. He occasionally will get into a throwing funk, accumulating the bulk of his season's errors in a short span. Randa is an average baserunner. He lacks the raw speed to steal many bases each season, but he does a good job taking the extra base and rarely runs into outs.

2000 Outlook

Randa's high-average hitting and defense are a good fit for the young Royals. Because he's not a dangerous power threat, Randa also fits the club's meager budget. He's not a big star, but he's a solid regular who again will play a crucial role in Kansas City.

Overall Statistics

	G	AB	R	H	D	T	HR	RBI	SB	BB	SO	Avg	OBP	Slg
1999	156	628	92	197	36	8	16	84	5	50	80	.314	.363	.473
Career	564	1938	248	562	110	20	39	246	30	164	278	.290	.348	.428

Where He Hits the Ball

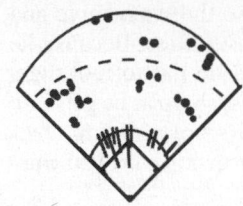
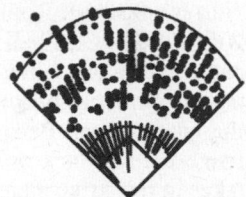

Vs. LHP   **Vs. RHP**

1999 Situational Stats

	AB	H	HR	RBI	Avg		AB	H	HR	RBI	Avg
Home	316	101	7	47	.320	LHP	101	36	1	10	.356
Road	312	96	9	37	.308	RHP	527	161	15	74	.306
First Half	341	109	9	41	.320	Sc Pos	181	52	4	68	.287
Scnd Half	287	88	7	43	.307	Clutch	87	28	2	13	.322

1999 Rankings (American League)

- 3rd in errors at third base (22)
- 5th in at-bats, triples and lowest fielding percentage at third base (.952)
- Led the Royals in hits, times on base (250), batting average in the clutch and highest percentage of swings put into play (52.3%)
- Led AL third basemen in at-bats, runs scored, hits, singles, triples, total bases (297), times on base (250), plate appearances (689), batting average on the road, games played (156), lowest percentage of swings that missed (13.1%) and highest percentage of swings put into play (52.3%)

Jose Rosado

1999 Season

Jose Rosado returned to his 1996 form, consistently keeping the Royals in games while compiling the best ERA of any American League lefthander. If not for spotty run support, his 10-14 record could have been reversed. After Kevin Appier was dealt to Oakland at the trade deadline, Rosado was pushed to the front of the rotation. Though he continued to pitch well, he's not a true No. 1 starter.

Pitching

Rosado added some velocity to his fastball in 1999, reaching the low 90s consistently. That added to his strength: changing speeds. His changeup is especially effective when he gets ahead in the count with his fastball. Rosado also throws a curve and will use a cut fastball against lefties. Because he can't overpower hitters, Rosado has to fool them instead. His stuff becomes less sharp as he gets into the late innings. Because he's not afraid to challenge batters, he's prone to making critical mistakes in the strike zone.

Defense

With runners on base, Rosado works at a glacial pace. It has the effect of freezing runners, and he tied for the AL lead by limiting basestealers to a 44.4 percent success rate. But his deliberate style also hurts the defense behind him and disrupts his pitching rhythm. His pickoff move is merely average. Rosado seems distracted after his delivery. He's sometimes out of position, fails to cover a base or doesn't back up throws.

2000 Outlook

Kansas City can't afford to sign a quality veteran starter, so Rosado will headline the rotation again. He's one of the best southpaws in the AL, though his lack of run support and the team's also-ran status make him a well-kept secret.

Position: SP
Bats: L **Throws:** L
Ht: 6' 0" **Wt:** 185

Opening Day Age: 25
Born: 11/9/74 in Jersey City, NJ
ML Seasons: 4
Pronunciation: ro-SAH-doh

Overall Statistics

	W	L	Pct.	ERA	G	GS	Sv	IP	H	BB	SO	HR	Ratio
1999	10	14	.417	3.85	33	33	0	208.0	197	72	141	24	1.29
Career	35	43	.449	4.21	120	107	1	692.2	686	228	469	82	1.32

How Often He Throws Strikes

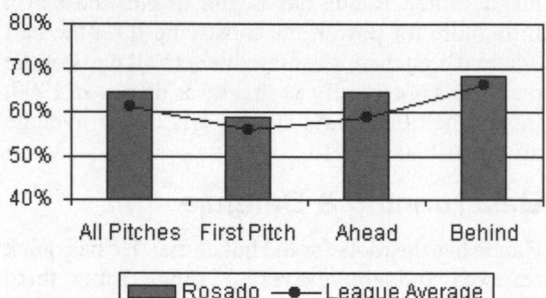

1999 Situational Stats

	W	L	ERA	Sv	IP		AB	H	HR	RBI	Avg
Home	5	4	3.48	0	88.0	LHB	149	36	6	21	.242
Road	5	10	4.13	0	120.0	RHB	644	161	18	68	.250
First Half	5	6	3.01	0	113.2	Sc Pos	169	42	5	65	.249
Scnd Half	5	8	4.87	0	94.1	Clutch	60	14	1	5	.233

1999 Rankings (American League)

- 1st in lowest stolen-base percentage allowed (44.4%)
- 4th in losses, complete games (5) and lowest slugging percentage allowed (.390)
- 5th in ERA and ERA at home
- Led the Royals in ERA, wins, losses, games started, complete games (5), strikeouts, wild pitches (9), pitches thrown (3,413), highest strikeout/walk ratio (2.0), lowest batting average allowed (.248), lowest slugging percentage allowed (.390), lowest on-base percentage allowed (.313), lowest stolen-base percentage allowed (44.4%), fewest baserunners allowed per 9 innings (11.9) and fewest home runs allowed per 9 innings (1.04)

Rey Sanchez

1999 Season

The Royals signed Rey Sanchez as a free agent from the Giants in order to steady their infield defense and provide a mentor for young second baseman Carlos Febles. Sanchez gave them everything they asked while also contributing more than expected at the plate. Only a partially torn hamstring slowed Sanchez. Even then, he refused to go on the disabled list and played through the late-season injury. Sanchez set career bests in batting average, runs scored, RBI and stolen bases.

Hitting

An impatient singles hitter, Sanchez has a short stroke. He'll slap the first hittable pitch on the ground toward a hole in the infield. He's also a good bunter and can hit behind baserunners. Sanchez lacks power and can be overmatched by hard throwers. He does hit well with runners in scoring position and is significantly better against lefthanders. Because of his poor plate discipline, Sanchez fits best at the bottom of a batting order.

Baserunning & Defense

Though he has decent speed, Sanchez isn't an especially successful basestealer. He will run into some outs on the bases and doesn't always use his speed wisely. Sanchez is a steady fielder who can play second base or shortstop equally well. He has average range and a strong arm, and he's adept at the double-play pivot.

2000 Outlook

Sanchez wanted a chance to prove he could be a productive starting shortstop in the majors, and he did that in 1999. He became a free agent, and the Royals re-signed him for two years and $4.6 million.

Position: SS
Bats: R **Throws:** R
Ht: 5' 9" **Wt:** 170

Opening Day Age: 32
Born: 10/5/67 in Rio Piedras, Puerto Rico
ML Seasons: 9
Pronunciation: RAY SAN-chezz

Overall Statistics

	G	AB	R	H	D	T	HR	RBI	SB	BB	SO	Avg	OBP	Slg
1999	134	479	66	141	18	6	2	56	11	22	48	.294	.329	.370
Career	875	2768	316	755	122	16	11	225	33	139	303	.273	.312	.340

Where He Hits the Ball

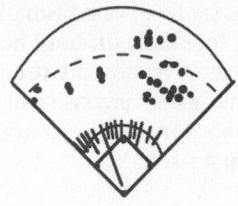 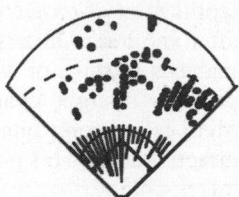

Vs. LHP   **Vs. RHP**

1999 Situational Stats

	AB	H	HR	RBI	Avg		AB	H	HR	RBI	Avg
Home	240	64	1	28	.267	LHP	95	31	0	8	.326
Road	239	77	1	28	.322	RHP	384	110	2	48	.286
First Half	281	75	2	34	.267	Sc Pos	139	41	1	51	.295
Scnd Half	198	66	0	22	.333	Clutch	67	18	0	4	.269

1999 Rankings (American League)

- 2nd in lowest HR frequency (239.5 ABs per HR) and highest groundball/flyball ratio (2.3)
- 3rd in fewest pitches seen per plate appearance (3.17) and fielding percentage at shortstop (.982)
- 6th in lowest slugging percentage and lowest percentage of pitches taken (47.0%)
- 7th in sacrifice bunts (10), lowest slugging percentage vs. righthanded pitchers (.362) and batting average on a 3-2 count (.367)
- 8th in lowest percentage of swings that missed (10.0%)
- 10th in batting average on the road
- Led the Royals in batting average on the road and lowest percentage of swings that missed (10.0%)

Blake Stein

1999 Season

Two years after being included in a trade-deadline deal for Mark McGwire, Blake Stein was a key component in another July 31 swap, this time with the Athletics for Kevin Appier. Stein assumed Appier's spot in the Kansas City rotation. Seven of his first eight starts were quality starts, but he was bombed in his last three outings and ended up with only one win in 11 starts for the Royals.

Pitching

Stein pitches like a 6-foot-7, 228-pounder looks like he should: hard. He reaches the low 90s with two- and four-seam fastballs and also mixes in a slider. His stuff tends to rise in the strike zone, making Stein an extreme flyball pitcher. He also works a lot of long counts as he feeds one fastball after another to hitters, who foul them off until he makes a mistake or walks them. His best offspeed pitch, a straight change, has been inconsistent. Stein is a strong pitcher who doesn't lose much effectiveness as his pitch count rises.

Defense

Stein has a slow delivery and is slower still to field his position. He has a decent pickoff move and is persistent in paying attention to runners, but those with the patience to wait him out can steal successfully.

2000 Outlook

Toward the end of 1999, Stein talked a lot about focus. Focus again will be a prime directive for him as he enters what could be a make-or-break season. The Royals expect him to pitch near the top of their rotation, though he has yet to demonstrate the consistent command needed to succeed in that role.

Position: SP
Bats: R **Throws:** R
Ht: 6' 7" **Wt:** 228

Opening Day Age: 26
Born: 8/3/73 in McComb, MS
ML Seasons: 2

Overall Statistics

	W	L	Pct.	ERA	G	GS	Sv	IP	H	BB	SO	HR	Ratio
1999	1	2	.333	4.56	13	12	0	73.0	65	47	47	11	1.53
Career	6	11	.353	5.67	37	32	0	190.1	182	118	136	33	1.58

How Often He Throws Strikes

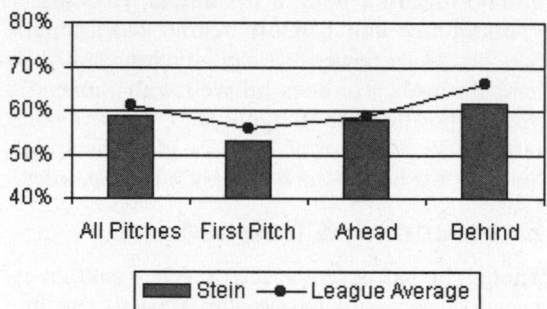

1999 Situational Stats

	W	L	ERA	Sv	IP		AB	H	HR	RBI	Avg
Home	1	0	2.12	0	46.2	LHB	133	34	6	18	.256
Road	0	2	8.89	0	26.1	RHB	137	31	5	18	.226
First Half	0	0	-	0	0.0	Sc Pos	63	17	3	23	.270
Scnd Half	1	2	4.56	0	73.0	Clutch	24	4	1	2	.167

1999 Rankings (American League)

- Did not rank near the top or bottom in any category

Jeff Suppan

1999 Season

Emerging as one of the Royals' most consistent starters, Jeff Suppan enjoyed a breakthrough season. He set personal bests in every category and finally seemed fully recovered from his 1996 elbow injury. He pitched at least five innings in all but four of his 32 starts and gave his club a chance to win almost every time out. Suppan met every expectation the Royals had for him and helped settle the club's uncertain rotation.

Pitching

Suppan works with an easy delivery that makes his 90-MPH fastball look quicker. He uses his fastball to setup his offspeed stuff. His sharp-breaking curveball is a superior pitch, especially against righthanders. Suppan's fosh changeup is an effective two-strike pitch that induces groundballs. He also throws a slider. Not overpowering, Suppan succeeds by painting the edges of the strike zone. Though he's durable over the course of the season, Suppan wears down during a game. Opponents batted .298 with a .490 slugging percentage after he reached the 75-pitch mark in games last year.

Defense

Reliance on an offspeed repertoire and a deliberate delivery puts Suppan at a disadvantage against baserunners. They stole 19 bases against him in 25 tries in 1999. His move to first base is average. A shaky fielder, he's slow to react to grounders and often looks unsure on his throws to the bases.

2000 Outlook

Suppan will hold down a spot at the front of Kansas City's rotation again. The Royals need him to take the ball every fifth day and give them a competitive outing. They'd be happy if he merely repeated his 1999 performance.

Position: SP
Bats: R **Throws:** R
Ht: 6' 2" **Wt:** 210

Opening Day Age: 25
Born: 1/2/75 in Oklahoma City, OK
ML Seasons: 5
Pronunciation: soo-PAWN

Overall Statistics

	W	L	Pct.	ERA	G	GS	Sv	IP	H	BB	SO	HR	Ratio
1999	10	12	.455	4.53	32	32	0	208.2	222	62	103	28	1.36
Career	20	25	.444	5.26	88	75	0	445.0	511	138	253	60	1.46

How Often He Throws Strikes

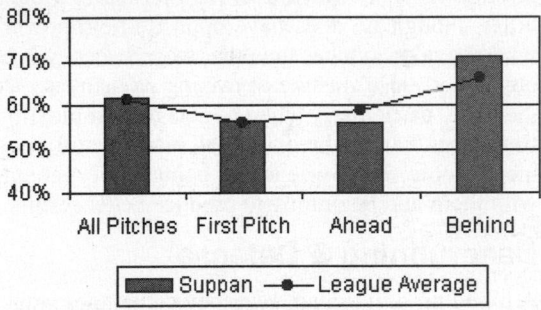

Suppan — League Average

1999 Situational Stats

	W	L	ERA	Sv	IP		AB	H	HR	RBI	Avg
Home	6	7	4.69	0	109.1	LHB	402	104	17	42	.259
Road	4	5	4.35	0	99.1	RHB	408	118	11	59	.289
First Half	4	5	3.86	0	119.0	Sc Pos	181	51	7	71	.282
Scnd Half	6	7	5.42	0	89.2	Clutch	32	14	1	5	.438

1999 Rankings (American League)

- 3rd in fewest strikeouts per 9 innings (4.4)
- 5th in GDPs induced (26)
- Led the Royals in wins, innings pitched, hits allowed, batters faced (887), home runs allowed, pickoff throws (121), stolen bases allowed (19), GDPs induced (26), highest groundball/flyball ratio allowed (1.6), fewest pitches thrown per batter (3.62), most run support per 9 innings (5.7), most GDPs induced per 9 innings (1.1), fewest walks per 9 innings (1.1), most GDPs induced per GDP situation (15.8%) and lowest batting average allowed vs. lefthanded batters

Mike Sweeney

1999 Season

The surprising May retirement of Jeff King provided the Royals with a solution as to what to do with Mike Sweeney. Wanting to get his bat into their lineup but not wanting to deal with his atrocious catching, they shifted him to first base. He played regularly and blossomed into a productive middle-of-the-order hitter. In a breakthrough season, Sweeney had a 25-game hitting streak and a 13-game RBI skein, the latter tying a 58-year-old American League record.

Hitting

An aggressive first-ball, fastball hitter, Sweeney has a line-drive stroke which generates power through its sheer quickness. He's primarily a pull hitter, though he does have opposite-field power when he takes pitches the other way. Sweeney is a quick study. He's astute at making adjustments at the plate, particularly when he gets regular playing time. Righthanded breaking-ball pitchers still give him trouble, but Sweeney is being more patient with them and beginning to produce better results.

Baserunning & Defense

A plodding baserunner, Sweeney sometimes wanders into outs on the bases. Despite the switch to first base, Sweeney remains a below-average defensive player. His .9811 fielding percentage was the worst for a first baseman with 600 chances since Cesar Cedeno's .9807 mark 20 years earlier. Though he made visible progress over the course of the season, Sweeney is still a mechanical first baseman who's not adept at scooping low throws and is sometimes out of position on grounders.

2000 Outlook

Last year's sudden emergence merely confirmed what the Royals had suspected all along. Sweeney can be a productive, high-average hitter if he plays regularly. He might even add some more power as he remains in the middle of their order as either a first baseman or DH.

Position: 1B/DH
Bats: R **Throws:** R
Ht: 6' 2" **Wt:** 215

Opening Day Age: 26
Born: 7/22/73 in Orange, CA
ML Seasons: 5

Overall Statistics

	G	AB	R	H	D	T	HR	RBI	SB	BB	SO	Avg	OBP	Slg
1999	150	575	101	185	44	2	22	102	6	54	48	.322	.387	.520
Career	380	1266	187	363	80	2	41	192	12	113	140	.287	.353	.450

Where He Hits the Ball

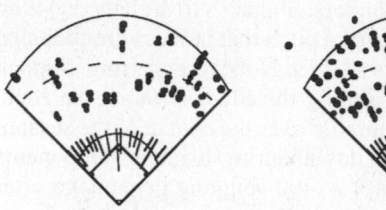

Vs. LHP	Vs. RHP

1999 Situational Stats

	AB	H	HR	RBI	Avg		AB	H	HR	RBI	Avg
Home	289	97	10	49	.336	LHP	100	35	4	18	.350
Road	286	88	12	53	.308	RHP	475	150	18	84	.316
First Half	295	94	11	58	.319	Scr Pos	175	55	6	80	.314
Scnd Half	280	91	11	44	.325	Clutch	78	16	0	9	.205

1999 Rankings (American League)

- 2nd in doubles
- 3rd in errors at first base (12)
- 4th in batting average with two strikes (.284)
- 6th in GDPs (21)
- 8th in batting average on an 0-2 count (.300) and cleanup slugging percentage (.546)
- 9th in batting average at home
- Led the Royals in batting average, doubles, hit by pitch (10), GDPs (21), on-base percentage, batting average vs. righthanded pitchers, batting average on an 0-2 count (.300), cleanup slugging percentage (.546), batting average at home and batting average with two strikes (.284)
- Led AL first basemen in batting average, hits, singles, doubles and GDPs (21)

Sal Fasano

Position: C
Bats: R **Throws:** R
Ht: 6' 2" **Wt:** 230

Opening Day Age: 28
Born: 8/10/71 in
Chicago, IL
ML Seasons: 4
Pronunciation:
fuh-SAH-noh

Overall Statistics

	G	AB	R	H	D	T	HR	RBI	SB	BB	SO	Avg	OBP	Slg
1999	23	60	11	14	2	0	5	16	0	7	17	.233	.373	.517
Career	161	457	56	100	16	0	20	67	2	32	110	.219	.304	.385

1999 Situational Stats

	AB	H	HR	RBI	Avg		AB	H	HR	RBI	Avg
Home	37	9	2	9	.243	LHP	8	3	1	2	.375
Road	23	5	3	7	.217	RHP	52	11	4	14	.212
First Half	0	0	0	0	-	Sc Pos	19	4	1	8	.211
Scnd Half	60	14	5	16	.233	Clutch	2	0	0	0	.000

1999 Season

After sharing Kansas City's catching job in 1998, Sal Fasano spent most of 1999 at Triple-A Omaha, drilling 21 homers in 88 games. Recalled in September, he played regularly for the Royals. He showed power in his short stint and provided his usual above-average defense.

Hitting, Baserunning & Defense

Like many reserve catchers, Fasano isn't much of a hitter. His looping swing provides power but also hinders his ability to make contact. Fasano is a slow baserunner, even for a catcher. When he's in the lineup, it's for his defense. Several young Royals pitchers believe Fasano provides a superior target. He uses his knowledge of a pitcher's strengths and weaknesses to call a good game. Fasano has a quick release and accurate arm.

2000 Outlook

Though incumbent Chad Kreuter seems destined to leave as a free agent and Mike Sweeney has moved from behind the plate, Fasano probably won't be Kansas City's regular catcher this year. He doesn't appear to be a favorite of the Royals who signed free agent Brian Johnson for $550,000 plus incentives. It also remains to be seen whether Fasano's power surge was only a fluke.

Chris Fussell

Position: RP
Bats: R **Throws:** R
Ht: 6' 2" **Wt:** 200

Opening Day Age: 23
Born: 5/19/76 in
Oregon, OH
ML Seasons: 2
Pronunciation:
FUSS-sul

Overall Statistics

	W	L	Pct.	ERA	G	GS	Sv	IP	H	BB	SO	HR	Ratio
1999	0	5	.000	7.39	17	8	2	56.0	72	36	37	9	1.93
Career	0	6	.000	7.54	20	10	2	65.2	83	45	45	10	1.95

1999 Situational Stats

	W	L	ERA	Sv	IP		AB	H	HR	RBI	Avg
Home	0	1	8.39	1	24.2	LHB	95	30	4	21	.316
Road	0	4	6.61	1	31.1	RHB	124	42	5	21	.339
First Half	0	4	8.44	0	32.0	Sc Pos	69	23	2	31	.333
Scnd Half	0	1	6.00	2	24.0	Clutch	24	6	0	1	.250

1999 Season

The pitching-strapped Orioles decided they needed Jeff Conine's veteran bat, so they shipped Chris Fussell to Kansas City on the eve of the season. Fussell spent six weeks in Triple-A before joining the rotation in May. After going 0-4 in seven starts, he returned to the minors before rejoining the Royals in August, pitching mostly in relief the rest of the way.

Pitching & Defense

Opponents hit .329 off Fussell in the majors last year, but his stuff isn't the problem. He throws an above-average fastball, a curveball, slider and changeup. Rather than trust his stuff, he nibbles at the plate and falls behind hitters, who often take advantage. He also runs up pitch counts quickly, so he's not more than a six-inning starter. Fussell is a shaky fielder who made three errors in 11 big league chances last year. Runners also took liberties against him, stealing nine bases in 11 tries.

2000 Outlook

Few pitching staffs are more unsettled than the Royals, so Fussell probably will get another shot in the rotation. He needs to pitch more aggressively if he wants to stay off the Kansas City-Omaha shuttle.

Alvin Morman

Position: RP
Bats: R **Throws:** L
Ht: 6' 3" **Wt:** 210

Opening Day Age: 31
Born: 1/6/69 in Rockingham, NC
ML Seasons: 4

Overall Statistics

	W	L	Pct.	ERA	G	GS	Sv	IP	H	BB	SO	HR	Ratio
1999	2	4	.333	4.05	49	0	1	53.1	66	23	31	6	1.67
Career	6	7	.462	4.79	176	0	3	142.2	161	75	98	21	1.65

1999 Situational Stats

	W	L	ERA	Sv	IP		AB	H	HR	RBI	Avg
Home	2	2	4.11	1	30.2	LHB	92	27	2	10	.293
Road	0	2	3.97	0	22.2	RHB	123	39	4	19	.317
First Half	1	1	3.91	0	25.1	Sc Pos	65	16	0	23	.246
Scnd Half	1	3	4.18	1	28.0	Clutch	31	12	2	7	.387

1999 Season

Entering 1999, Alvin Morman had pitched for three teams in three seasons, compiling a 5.24 ERA. Signed as a free agent after the Giants declined to offer him a contract, he began the year in Triple-A before getting called up in late April. Besides a rough August, Morman pitched decently as a lefty specialist.

Pitching & Defense

There's nothing particularly notable about Morman's pitching, with the exception of his deceptive delivery. He mixes a high-80s fastball with average offspeed stuff. He doesn't have the stuff to survive more than once through a batting order, if that long. Morman's role is to get lefthanders out, but they batted .293 against him in 1999. He's not very resilient, struggling when he pitches on consecutive days and usually fading after the All-Star break. Though Morman isn't quick to the plate, his pickoff move nailed three runners last year. He's steady defensively.

2000 Outlook

Morman has no competition for his job in Kansas City. He'll remain the Royals' lefthanded specialist, as much by default as on merit.

Brad Rigby

Position: RP
Bats: R **Throws:** R
Ht: 6' 6" **Wt:** 214

Opening Day Age: 26
Born: 5/14/73 in Milwaukee, WI
ML Seasons: 2

Overall Statistics

	W	L	Pct.	ERA	G	GS	Sv	IP	H	BB	SO	HR	Ratio
1999	4	6	.400	5.06	49	0	0	83.2	102	31	36	11	1.59
Career	5	13	.278	4.96	63	14	0	161.1	194	53	70	25	1.53

1999 Situational Stats

	W	L	ERA	Sv	IP		AB	H	HR	RBI	Avg
Home	1	3	5.35	0	35.1	LHB	163	57	5	32	.350
Road	3	3	4.84	0	48.1	RHB	174	45	6	30	.259
First Half	3	4	4.55	0	55.1	Sc Pos	105	35	2	50	.333
Scnd Half	1	2	6.04	0	28.1	Clutch	59	17	2	13	.288

1999 Season

Brad Rigby had his moments as an Athletics rookie in 1997, but shoulder problems and ineffectiveness kept him out of the big leagues the following year. He bounced back and spent almost all of 1999 in the majors, though he was converted from a starter to a reliever. After joining Kansas City in a trade-deadline deal for Kevin Appier, Rigby had a 7.17 ERA and allowed six homers in 21.1 innings.

Pitching & Defense

Rigby uses his 6-foot-6 frame to generate a low-90s fastball and a hard slider. He also throws a curveball and changeup. He's not a strikeout pitcher, so he has to keep the ball down to succeed. Too often he leaves his hard stuff up in the strike zone and gets pounded. Because of recurring back problems, Rigby hasn't been able to pitch more than a couple of innings at a time. He gets shelled when he doesn't get plenty of rest after an outing.

2000 Outlook

The Royals bullpen was a disaster area in 1999 and Rigby will be one of a cast of thousands the club will try in 2000. He'll get a chance to pitch in just about every bullpen role except closer.

Jose Santiago

Position: RP
Bats: R **Throws:** R
Ht: 6' 3" **Wt:** 215

Opening Day Age: 25
Born: 11/5/74 in
Fajardo, Puerto Rico
ML Seasons: 3

Overall Statistics

	W	L	Pct.	ERA	G	GS	Sv	IP	H	BB	SO	HR	Ratio
1999	3	4	.429	3.42	34	0	2	47.1	46	14	15	7	1.27
Career	3	4	.429	3.50	40	0	2	54.0	57	16	18	7	1.35

1999 Situational Stats

	W	L	ERA	Sv	IP		AB	H	HR	RBI	Avg
Home	1	2	2.74	0	23.0	LHB	81	17	2	8	.210
Road	2	2	4.07	2	24.1	RHB	102	29	5	24	.284
First Half	2	3	3.89	2	39.1	Sc Pos	65	14	3	25	.215
Scnd Half	1	1	1.13	0	8.0	Clutch	66	19	2	12	.288

1999 Season

One of the few bright spots in an otherwise dreadful Royals bullpen, Jose Santiago had a fine half-season in short relief. He collected the first wins and saves of his career and usually displayed good command. Santiago struggled in June before being sidelined with a sore trapezious muscle for nearly the entire second half.

Pitching & Defense

Santiago works almost exclusively with a mid-90s fastball. The heater is difficult to hit and he throws it hard enough to use high in the strike zone. He has struggled to add a second pitch, though he has had some success with a slider. Because Santiago relies on his fastball so much, batters sit on it and swing at the first strike they see. Santiago has yet to make a major league error and both runners who tried to steal on him in 1999 were gunned down.

2000 Outlook

The Royals need a closer in the wake of Jeff Montgomery's retirement. Santiago is expected to battle Orber Moreno for the job in spring training. At worst, Santiago will be the primary setup man.

Scott Service

Position: RP
Bats: R **Throws:** R
Ht: 6' 6" **Wt:** 240

Opening Day Age: 33
Born: 2/26/67 in
Cincinnati, OH
ML Seasons: 9

Overall Statistics

	W	L	Pct.	ERA	G	GS	Sv	IP	H	BB	SO	HR	Ratio
1999	5	5	.500	6.09	68	0	8	75.1	87	42	68	13	1.71
Career	18	17	.514	4.74	264	1	14	325.0	328	145	326	42	1.46

1999 Situational Stats

	W	L	ERA	Sv	IP		AB	H	HR	RBI	Avg
Home	4	2	5.57	4	42.0	LHB	118	40	7	25	.339
Road	1	3	6.75	4	33.1	RHB	178	47	6	37	.264
First Half	3	3	5.98	3	49.2	Sc Pos	97	31	2	46	.320
Scnd Half	2	2	6.31	5	25.2	Clutch	138	48	8	34	.348

1999 Season

Though he collected a career-high eight saves, 1999 was the worst big league season of Scott Service's career. Expected to reprise his successful setup role from 1998, Service instead often let the game slip away before getting it to the closer. When he was tried as the finisher, Service was equally bad, blowing nearly half of his 15 save chances.

Pitching & Defense

Service throws two pitches hard: a low-90s fastball and a slider. He'll occasionally mix in a splitter or a changeup, but he primarily just tries to throw the ball past the few hitters he's asked to face in each outing. Control has been a problem for Service. He has a durable arm and is able to pitch effectively on consecutive days. Despite permitting 10 steals in 11 tries last year, Service had been effective against the running game in the past. As a fielder he's slow and lumbering, but surehanded.

2000 Outlook

Just when it appeared that Service finally had made it to the majors to stay, he left himself having to battle a host of younger prospects to win a bullpen job. He must prove himself again before getting the ball late in close games.

Tim Spehr

Position: C
Bats: R **Throws:** R
Ht: 6' 2" **Wt:** 200

Opening Day Age: 33
Born: 7/2/66 in Excelsior Springs, MO
ML Seasons: 8
Pronunciation: SPEER

Overall Statistics

	G	AB	R	H	D	T	HR	RBI	SB	BB	SO	Avg	OBP	Slg
1999	60	155	26	32	7	0	9	26	1	22	47	.206	.324	.426
Career	363	556	76	110	31	1	19	72	9	67	153	.198	.298	.360

1999 Situational Stats

	AB	H	HR	RBI	Avg		AB	H	HR	RBI	Avg
Home	72	13	4	11	.181	LHP	48	7	2	5	.146
Road	83	19	5	15	.229	RHP	107	25	7	21	.234
First Half	80	16	3	15	.200	Sc Pos	43	7	4	17	.163
Scnd Half	75	16	6	11	.213	Clutch	19	6	0	1	.316

1999 Season

Tim Spehr made the Royals as a nonroster player in spring training. He spent the whole year on the major league roster, serving as the second-string catcher. Though he slumped during the second half, Spehr filled his reserve role well and established career highs in several hitting categories, including nearly doubling his previous homer total.

Hitting, Baserunning & Defense

Though he's coming off his best offensive season, Spehr remains a poor hitter. He doesn't make good contact, usually hits for an abysmal average and has marginal power. Spehr especially has trouble against lefthanders. He's a below-average baserunner whose sole positive is his above-average defense. Spehr handles pitchers so well that starters request his services. He has an accurate arm and usually controls the running game well, though opponents stole 35 bases in 40 tries against him last year.

2000 Outlook

Spehr is a journeyman reserve who has overcome cancer and a broken wrist. Getting to play more regularly allowed him to display the range of his limited talents and will help extend his career for a few more years. A free agent, he'll probably do so elsewhere.

Larry Sutton

Signed By
CARDINALS

Position: 1B
Bats: L **Throws:** L
Ht: 6' 0" **Wt:** 185

Opening Day Age: 29
Born: 5/14/70 in West Covina, CA
ML Seasons: 3

Overall Statistics

	G	AB	R	H	D	T	HR	RBI	SB	BB	SO	Avg	OBP	Slg
1999	43	102	14	23	6	0	2	15	1	13	17	.225	.308	.343
Career	181	481	52	119	22	2	9	65	4	47	75	.247	.314	.358

1999 Situational Stats

	AB	H	HR	RBI	Avg		AB	H	HR	RBI	Avg
Home	48	13	2	11	.271	LHP	7	1	1	4	.143
Road	54	10	0	4	.185	RHP	95	22	1	11	.232
First Half	97	21	2	15	.216	Sc Pos	23	8	1	14	.348
Scnd Half	5	2	0	0	.400	Clutch	14	5	0	1	.357

1999 Season

Larry Sutton began 1999 as a semi-regular, serving as a fourth outfielder, part-time first baseman and occasional DH. After he struggled at the plate and spent time on the disabled list with a sore elbow, Sutton was demoted to Triple-A. He didn't return until September.

Hitting, Baserunning & Defense

A patient contact hitter, Sutton has only occasional power and he doesn't hit for a useful average. He has shown a flair for hitting in key situations, though his career average as a pinch-hitter is a mere .178. His ability to contribute off the bench is an asset. Sutton has average speed and runs the bases intelligently. He's adept at first base and both outfield corners. He has decent range and an accurate arm.

2000 Outlook

Kansas City removed Sutton from its 40-man roster in October, and he opted for free agency. His timely hitting and defensive versatility landed him a one-year contract with the Cardinals.

Makoto Suzuki

Position: RP/SP
Bats: R **Throws:** R
Ht: 6' 3" **Wt:** 195

Opening Day Age: 24
Born: 5/31/75 in Kobe, Japan
ML Seasons: 3

Overall Statistics

	W	L	Pct.	ERA	G	GS	Sv	IP	H	BB	SO	HR	Ratio
1999	2	5	.286	6.79	38	13	0	110.0	124	64	68	16	1.71
Career	3	7	.300	7.00	45	18	0	137.2	160	81	88	19	1.75

1999 Situational Stats

	W	L	ERA	Sv	IP		AB	H	HR	RBI	Avg
Home	1	1	7.46	0	56.2	LHB	222	63	7	38	.284
Road	1	4	6.08	0	53.1	RHB	212	61	9	43	.288
First Half	0	3	8.47	0	56.1	Sc Pos	138	38	6	65	.275
Scnd Half	2	2	5.03	0	53.2	Clutch	13	4	1	3	.308

1999 Season

Traded from the Mariners to the Mets in June, Makoto Suzuki never pitched for New York before being claimed on waivers by the Royals. He was merely mediocre in Kansas City after being atrocious in several trials in Seattle.

Pitching & Defense

Suzuki regularly hits the mid-90s with his fastball, though he less regularly throws it for strikes. His offspeed pitches, a slider and a splitter, haven't been especially useful. Suzuki took a little off his fastball and threw more strikes with the Royals, though his strikeout rate also declined significantly. Hitters have succeeded against Suzuki early in at-bats by swinging at the first hittable fastball. After elbow and shoulder problems early in his career, Suzuki is still building his arm strength. As a starter, he usually tires after five innings. Suzuki is a tentative fielder with a below-average pickoff move.

2000 Outlook

Suzuki is still quite young and the Royals view him as a project. They hope to harness his lively fastball and try him as a back-of-the-rotation starter this year. He also could be used in long relief.

Jay Witasick

Position: SP
Bats: R **Throws:** R
Ht: 6' 4" **Wt:** 210

Opening Day Age: 27
Born: 8/28/72 in Baltimore, MD
ML Seasons: 4
Pronunciation: wih-TA-sick

Overall Statistics

	W	L	Pct.	ERA	G	GS	Sv	IP	H	BB	SO	HR	Ratio
1999	9	12	.429	5.57	32	28	0	158.1	191	83	102	23	1.73
Career	11	16	.407	5.72	59	31	0	209.1	253	109	151	39	1.73

1999 Situational Stats

	W	L	ERA	Sv	IP		AB	H	HR	RBI	Avg
Home	4	6	4.95	0	80.0	LHB	307	99	11	45	.322
Road	5	6	6.20	0	78.1	RHB	322	92	12	47	.286
First Half	3	6	6.98	0	77.1	Sc Pos	149	50	5	67	.336
Scnd Half	6	6	4.22	0	81.0	Clutch	22	9	0	2	.409

1999 Season

Jay Witasick began the season in the Royals bullpen, then moved into the rotation at the end of April. Though he struggled initially, Witasick gradually got stronger. He finished the season as one of Kansas City's most effective starters, allowing more than three earned runs just once over the last two months.

Pitching & Defense

Primarily a power pitcher, Witasick works mostly with a mid-90s fastball, which often comes in high and straight to hitters. His offspeed pitches, a knuckle-curve and a changeup, are inconsistent. He flashes them mostly to keep hitters from sitting on his fastball. Stamina had been a problem for Witasick in the past, but he showed an ability to pitch deep into games late in 1999. He's adequate with the glove but doesn't hold runners well.

2000 Outlook

The Royals have talked about shifting Witasick into their now-vacant closer spot because he has the fastball for the role. But they also need starters, so they may let him build on his success. Either way, an important role awaits Witasick.

Brian Barber (**Pos**: RHP, **Age**: 27)

	W	L	Pct.	ERA	G	GS	Sv	IP	H	BB	SO	HR	Ratio
1999	1	3	.250	9.64	8	3	1	18.2	31	10	7	6	2.20
Career	5	8	.385	6.77	26	16	1	93.0	111	45	59	15	1.68

Once a hard-throwing prospect with a bright future, Barber is now a finesse pitcher, thanks to injuries. He had a solid Triple-A season in 1998, but never has had success in the majors. The Indians signed him to a minor league deal after the season. 2000 Outlook: C

Tim Byrdak (**Pos**: LHP, **Age**: 26)

	W	L	Pct.	ERA	G	GS	Sv	IP	H	BB	SO	HR	Ratio
1999	0	3	.000	7.66	33	0	1	24.2	32	20	17	5	2.11
Career	0	3	.000	7.52	36	0	1	26.1	37	20	18	6	2.16

A finesse pitcher, Byrdak has been a stud in relief in Triple-A the last two years, posting an ERA of 2.45 in 1998 and a 1.81 mark in '99. That has yet to translate into big league success, however. 2000 Outlook: B

Lance Carter (**Pos**: RHP, **Age**: 25)

	W	L	Pct.	ERA	G	GS	Sv	IP	H	BB	SO	HR	Ratio
1999	0	1	.000	5.06	6	0	0	5.1	3	3	3	2	1.13
Career	0	1	.000	5.06	6	0	0	5.1	3	3	3	2	1.13

Carter turned in a remarkable season as the closer at Double-A Wichita, posting a 0.78 ERA and fanning 77 in 69.2 innings. That earned him a September callup and a long look next spring. 2000 Outlook: C

Jed Hansen (**Pos**: 2B, **Age**: 27, **Bats**: R)

	G	AB	R	H	D	T	HR	RBI	SB	BB	SO	Avg	OBP	Slg
1999	49	79	16	16	1	0	3	5	0	10	32	.203	.289	.329
Career	87	176	27	45	7	1	4	19	3	23	64	.256	.342	.375

Hansen hit a combined 27 homers in Triple-A in 1997 and '98, and he hit well in his Kansas City debut in '97. But Hansen still doesn't make enough contact and the Royals have Carlos Febles. San Diego picked up Hansen on waivers this fall. 2000 Outlook: C

Ray Holbert (**Pos**: SS/2B, **Age**: 29, **Bats**: R)

	G	AB	R	H	D	T	HR	RBI	SB	BB	SO	Avg	OBP	Slg
1999	34	100	14	28	3	0	0	5	7	8	20	.280	.330	.310
Career	112	198	28	44	5	1	2	11	11	18	49	.222	.291	.288

Holbert spent the second half of the 1999 season in the majors, his longest stay since '95. He also did his best hitting this time, but handling defensive duties in the infield is his ticket to stay. 2000 Outlook: C

Jeff King (**Pos**: 1B, **Age**: 35, **Bats**: R)

	G	AB	R	H	D	T	HR	RBI	SB	BB	SO	Avg	OBP	Slg
1999	21	72	14	17	2	0	3	11	2	15	10	.236	.385	.389
Career	1201	4262	600	1091	222	18	154	709	75	442	584	.256	.324	.425

King didn't wait until the end of the season. After a two-week stint on the disabled list with a bad back, the first pick in the June 1986 draft announced in late May that his heart wasn't in it and he was retiring. 2000 Outlook: D

Scott Leius (**Pos**: 1B, **Age**: 34, **Bats**: R)

	G	AB	R	H	D	T	HR	RBI	SB	BB	SO	Avg	OBP	Slg
1999	37	74	8	15	1	0	1	10	1	4	8	.203	.244	.257
Career	557	1536	214	375	63	10	28	172	16	161	236	.244	.316	.353

While he continues to be a dependable defensive replacement, Leius hasn't produced much offensively since he stroked 14 homers for Minnesota in 1994. His '99 season ended in July with a dislocated shoulder. 2000 Outlook: C

Mendy Lopez (**Pos**: 2B, **Age**: 25, **Bats**: R)

	G	AB	R	H	D	T	HR	RBI	SB	BB	SO	Avg	OBP	Slg
1999	7	20	2	8	0	1	0	3	0	0	5	.400	.429	.500
Career	81	226	20	58	10	3	1	18	5	12	45	.257	.299	.341

Lopez inherited the shortstop job when Felix Martinez self-destructed in 1998. Then the Royals signed Rey Sanchez before the 1999 season. Lopez had his best minor league season at Triple-A in '99, so he may be back. 2000 Outlook: B

Felix Martinez (**Pos**: SS, **Age**: 25, **Bats**: B)

	G	AB	R	H	D	T	HR	RBI	SB	BB	SO	Avg	OBP	Slg
1999	6	7	1	1	0	0	0	0	0	0	0	.143	.143	.143
Career	56	123	11	19	2	2	0	8	3	11	29	.154	.230	.203

Martinez was handed the Royals' shortstop job in 1998, but lost it with poor hitting and fielding—and his reckless behavior. He gets to start anew after the Phillies picked him up on waivers. 2000 Outlook: C

Terry Mathews (**Pos**: RHP, **Age**: 35)

	W	L	Pct.	ERA	G	GS	Sv	IP	H	BB	SO	HR	Ratio
1999	2	1	.667	4.38	24	1	1	39.0	44	17	19	4	1.56
Career	22	21	.512	4.25	324	5	10	421.2	429	180	300	50	1.44

Does Mathews have nine lives? He was released by Baltimore in July 1998 and resurfaced in Kansas City in '99. After spending July on the disabled list with a rotator cuff strain, the Royals cut him. 2000 Outlook: C

Jeff Montgomery (**Pos**: RHP, **Age**: 38)

	W	L	Pct.	ERA	G	GS	Sv	IP	H	BB	SO	HR	Ratio
1999	1	4	.200	6.84	49	0	12	51.1	72	21	27	7	1.81
Career	46	52	.469	3.27	700	1	304	868.2	785	296	733	81	1.24

After 13 seasons in the majors, during which he accumulated 304 saves, Montgomery announced his retirement in the final days of the 1999 campaign. 2000 Outlook: D

Dan Murray (**Pos**: RHP, **Age**: 26)

	W	L	Pct.	ERA	G	GS	Sv	IP	H	BB	SO	HR	Ratio
1999	0	0	-	7.84	5	0	0	10.1	13	6	9	4	1.84
Career	0	0	-	7.84	5	0	0	10.1	13	6	9	4	1.84

Following a good Double-A season in 1998, Murray wasn't as impressive at Triple-A or with the Mets last summer. He was traded to the Royals in September, where more opportunities await him. 2000 Outlook: C

Marc Pisciotta (Pos: RHP, Age: 29)

	W	L	Pct.	ERA	G	GS	Sv	IP	H	BB	SO	HR	Ratio
1999	0	2	.000	8.64	8	0	0	8.1	9	10	3	1	2.28
Career	4	5	.444	4.24	75	0	0	80.2	73	58	55	6	1.62

Everything went right in 1997, when Pisciotta excelled as a closer at Triple-A Iowa and pitched well in 24 games with the Cubs. That has been his only solid season in five years. 2000 Outlook: C

Scott Pose (Pos: LF/DH, Age: 33, Bats: L)

	G	AB	R	H	D	T	HR	RBI	SB	BB	SO	Avg	OBP	Slg
1999	86	137	27	39	3	0	0	12	6	21	22	.285	.377	.307
Career	155	265	46	66	7	1	0	20	9	32	37	.249	.329	.283

A career minor leaguer, Pose got his longest major league audition in 1999. It also was his most productive, but at his age the best Pose can hope for is a reserve role. 2000 Outlook: C

Ken Ray (Pos: RHP, Age: 25)

	W	L	Pct.	ERA	G	GS	Sv	IP	H	BB	SO	HR	Ratio
1999	1	0	1.000	8.74	13	0	0	11.1	23	6	0	2	2.56
Career	1	0	1.000	8.74	13	0	0	11.1	23	6	0	2	2.56

Ray was part of a gifted crew of young starters at Class-A Rockford in 1994, expected to be Kansas City's future. But he never put it together in the high minors and his big league debut wasn't impressive. 2000 Outlook: C

Steve Scarsone (Pos: SS/1B, Age: 33, Bats: R)

	G	AB	R	H	D	T	HR	RBI	SB	BB	SO	Avg	OBP	Slg
1999	46	68	2	14	5	0	0	6	1	9	24	.206	.295	.279
Career	350	830	103	198	44	4	20	86	7	70	266	.239	.302	.373

In 1995 Scarsone hit .266 with 11 homers for the Giants, but hasn't been productive at the plate since then. After he bounced between Triple-A and Kansas City in '99, the Royals released him in September. 2000 Outlook: D

Joe Vitiello (Pos: 1B, Age: 29, Bats: R)

	G	AB	R	H	D	T	HR	RBI	SB	BB	SO	Avg	OBP	Slg
1999	13	41	4	6	1	0	1	4	0	2	9	.146	.222	.244
Career	205	565	57	133	26	1	21	83	2	63	142	.235	.322	.396

Vitiello looked like a hitter on the verge of major league success in 1994, but he didn't hit for average or power with the Royals. He rekindled his major league dream by hitting .318-28-98 in Triple-A in 1999, then signed a minor league contract with the Padres in November. 2000 Outlook: C

Derek Wallace (Pos: RHP, Age: 28)

	W	L	Pct.	ERA	G	GS	Sv	IP	H	BB	SO	HR	Ratio
1999	0	1	.000	3.24	8	0	0	8.1	7	5	5	2	1.44
Career	2	4	.333	3.82	27	0	3	33.0	36	19	20	4	1.67

Wallace looked like the Mets' closer of the future in 1996 after a great year at Norfolk, but an aneurysm discovered in his right arm the next spring halted his progress. He still could be a decent reliever. 2000 Outlook: C

Don Wengert (Pos: RHP, Age: 30)

	W	L	Pct.	ERA	G	GS	Sv	IP	H	BB	SO	HR	Ratio
1999	0	1	.000	9.25	11	1	0	24.1	41	5	10	6	1.89
Career	14	29	.326	5.74	146	44	3	412.2	524	146	215	69	1.62

Wengert showed promise in 1995, but he hasn't posted an ERA below 4.50 since then—in the minors or the majors. He made the Royals out of spring training, but quickly pitched himself out of a job. The Astros gave him a minor league deal in November. 2000 Outlook: C

Kansas City Royals Minor League Prospects

Organization Overview:

Though the Royals went 64-97 in 1999, finishing with the worst record in franchise history, the year was a success on the player-development front. Homegrown products Johnny Damon and Mike Sweeney finally played as well as Kansas City had hoped, and they were joined in the lineup by American League Rookie of the Year Carlos Beltran and leadoff hitter of the future Carlos Febles. Two more rookies, Jeremy Giambi and Mark Quinn, batted better than .300 in September. In the minors, potential stars Dee Brown and Orber Moreno showed that they're very close to being ready, and there's a whole wave of pitching on the way to Kansas City. As bad as the big league club was, at least there's legitimate hope for the future.

Jeff Austin

Position: P
Bats: R **Throws:** R
Ht: 6' 0" **Wt:** 185

Opening Day Age: 23
Born: 10/19/76 in San Bernardino, CA

Recent Statistics

	W	L	ERA	G	GS	Sv	IP	H	R	BB	SO	HR
1999 A Wilmington	7	2	3.77	18	18	0	112.1	108	52	39	97	10
1999 AA Wichita	3	1	4.46	6	6	0	34.1	40	19	11	21	1

When the Royals picked fourth in 1998, it marked their highest selection ever in the amateur draft. They chose Austin, who won *Baseball America's* College Player of the Year award at Stanford, then endured an eight-month holdout before signing him for a club-record $2.7 million. Making his pro debut last season, he was as good as advertised. Austin showed an 88-92 MPH fastball with nice movement, a curveball that's his best pitch and a changeup. He has good command and held up well at Wichita, one of the best hitters' parks in Double-A. A tender elbow sidelined him briefly in August, but he was fine in the Arizona Fall League. Austin will start 2000 in Triple-A and could reach Kansas City after the All-Star break.

Dee Brown

Position: OF
Bats: L **Throws:** R
Ht: 6' 0" **Wt:** 215

Opening Day Age: 22
Born: 3/27/78 in Bronx, NY

Recent Statistics

	G	AB	R	H	D	T	HR	RBI	SB	BB	SO	Avg
1999 A Wilmington	61	221	49	68	10	2	13	46	20	44	56	.308
1999 AA Wichita	65	235	58	83	14	3	12	56	10	35	41	.353
1999 AL Kansas City	12	25	1	2	0	0	0	0	0	2	7	.080
1999 MLE	65	223	44	71	11	2	9	42	6	22	41	.318

In 1974, the Royals spent their first-round pick on University of Maryland-bound running back Willie Wilson. Twenty-two years later they used another first-rounder on a Terrapins tailback recruit, and it looks like they scored big again with Brown. After hitting 23 homers in his first two-and-a-half pro seasons, he smashed 25 in 1999 at age 21. A well-rounded offensive player, he also hits for average (.331 last year), draws walks and steals bases. He was voted the No. 2 prospect in the high Class-A Carolina League (where he was also named the best power prospect and most exciting player) and Double-A Texas League. His only shortcoming is a weak arm, which relegates him to left field. He's a year away from Kansas City, and the Royals may trade Johnny Damon to save money and open a spot for Brown.

Jeremy Dodson

Position: OF
Bats: L **Throws:** R
Ht: 6' 2" **Wt:** 200

Opening Day Age: 22
Born: 5/3/77 in Sherman, TX

Recent Statistics

	G	AB	R	H	D	T	HR	RBI	SB	BB	SO	Avg
1998 A Spokane	69	268	56	90	19	5	9	59	8	25	59	.336
1999 AA Wichita	133	452	63	116	20	1	21	58	9	51	95	.257
1999 MLE	133	435	47	99	16	0	15	44	5	32	96	.228

Kansas City challenged Dodson by skipping him past two Class-A teams and promoting him from short-season ball to Double-A for his first pro season. Though he struggled, he still looks like a potential steal, considering he was just a seventh-round pick out of Baylor in 1998. Dodson has the quickest bat in the system, quicker even than Dee Brown's, and his outfield arm was rated the best in the Texas League last year. He also has above-average power and average speed. Dodson may not be ready until 2001, but he could provide an alternative in right field should Jermaine Dye become too expensive for the Royals.

Chad Durbin

Position: P
Bats: R **Throws:** R
Ht: 6' 1" **Wt:** 175

Opening Day Age: 22
Born: 12/3/77 in Spring Valley, IL

Recent Statistics

	W	L	ERA	G	GS	Sv	IP	H	R	BB	SO	HR
1999 AA Wichita	8	10	4.64	28	27	0	157.0	154	88	49	122	20
1999 AL Kansas City	0	0	0.00	1	0	0	2.1	1	0	1	3	0

Durbin gave a sneak preview of one of the game's best changeups when he made his major league debut on September 26 and held the Tigers scoreless for 2.1 innings. It's just one example of how advanced the 1996 third-round pick is for his age. He also does a fine job of throwing strikes and keeping the ball down in the zone. Durbin also has a 90-91 MPH fastball and a hard curve. He excelled in the Arizona Fall League after the season, leading all pitchers with a 0.75 ERA. He should be able to help the Royals by the end of 2000.

Chris George

Position: P
Bats: L **Throws:** L
Ht: 6' 1" **Wt:** 165

Opening Day Age: 20
Born: 9/16/79 in
Houston, TX

Recent Statistics

	W	L	ERA	G	GS	Sv	IP	H	R	BB	SO	HR
1998 R Royals	0	1	2.87	5	4	0	15.2	14	9	4	10	1
1999 A Wilmington	9	7	3.60	27	27	0	145.0	142	65	53	142	8

As precocious as Chad Durbin may be, he pales in comparison to George, who's two years younger. Nearly everyone who watches George comes away impressed at how advanced he is. A 1998 supplemental first-round pick, George's best pitch is his straight changeup. He regularly throws 89-90 MPH, though he has touched 93-94 and is young enough to add more velocity. His third pitch is a curveball that needs some polishing. Durbin has a smooth delivery and fine command. He could use a full year at both Double-A and Triple-A, though it would be no surprise if he accelerated that timetable.

Orber Moreno

Position: P
Bats: R **Throws:** R
Ht: 6' 2" **Wt:** 190

Opening Day Age: 22
Born: 4/27/77 in
Caracas, Venezuela

Recent Statistics

	W	L	ERA	G	GS	Sv	IP	H	R	BB	SO	HR
1999 AAA Omaha	3	1	2.10	16	0	4	25.2	17	6	4	30	2
1999 R Royals	0	0	0.00	1	1	0	1.0	0	0	0	1	0
1999 AL Kansas City	0	0	5.63	7	0	0	8.0	4	5	6	7	1

Jeff Montgomery's retirement and the wretched state of the Kansas City bullpen have combined to leave a gaping hole at closer. Moreno should be the man to fill it, providing he has recovered from the biceps tendinitis and shoulder soreness that aborted his big league debut last season shortly after it began. Since becoming a reliever in 1998, Moreno has posted a 2.21 ERA and yielded just five homers in 102 innings. His primary pitch is a mid-90s fastball, and he'll also show hitters a slider and a changeup. Moreno tried to overthrow once reaching the majors, which led to uncharacteristic wildness and his arm problems. The Royals expect him to be ready for spring training.

Mark Quinn

Position: OF
Bats: R **Throws:** R
Ht: 6' 1" **Wt:** 175

Opening Day Age: 25
Born: 5/21/74 in La
Mirada, CA

Recent Statistics

	G	AB	R	H	D	T	HR	RBI	SB	BB	SO	Avg
1999 AAA Omaha	107	428	67	154	27	0	25	84	7	28	69	.360
1999 AL Kansas City	17	60	11	20	4	1	6	18	1	4	11	.333
1999 MLE	107	408	52	134	23	0	19	66	4	21	68	.328

Quinn announced his arrival in the majors like few others had before him, becoming the fourth player in big league history to homer twice in his first game when he went deep twice against the Angels on September 14. An 11th-round pick in 1995 out of Rice, he hit six homers in 17 games for Kansas City, capping a season in which he won the Triple-A Pacific Coast League batting title and raised his career average as a pro to .329. Quinn has a very odd stance, stepping in the bucket and leaving himself wide open, yet he still can drive the ball to the opposite field. PCL managers rated him the league's best defensive outfielder even though he plays in left, and he has a strong arm. This spring, Quinn and Jeremy Giambi will compete for an everyday job, probably at DH.

Dan Reichert

Position: P
Bats: R **Throws:** R
Ht: 6' 3" **Wt:** 175

Opening Day Age: 23
Born: 7/12/76 in
Monterey, CA

Recent Statistics

	W	L	ERA	G	GS	Sv	IP	H	R	BB	SO	HR
1999 AAA Omaha	9	2	3.71	17	17	0	111.2	92	51	50	123	9
1999 AL Kansas City	2	2	9.08	8	8	0	36.2	48	38	32	20	2

Considered something of a signability pick when the Royals drafted him seventh overall out of Pacific in 1997, Reichert reached the big leagues less than two years after he signed. He didn't have the easiest of paths to the majors, losing an alarming amount of weight early in 1998 before he was diagnosed with diabetes. He has two tough pitches, a 90-92 MPH fastball with outstanding sink and a mid-80s slider that chews up hitters. He needs to develop his changeup and believe in the pitch. Reichert got rocked with Kansas City, particularly by lefthanders, because he wasn't as aggressive and didn't get ahead in the count like he had in the minors. He cracked his pitching elbow when he was drilled by a line drive in August, but should be fine by spring training.

Others to Watch

Armed with a mid-90s fastball and a high-80s slider, righthander **Junior Guerrero** (20) ranked among minor league leaders last year with a 2.31 ERA and 10.46 strikeouts per nine innings. . . First baseman **Ken Harvey** (22) won the 1999 NCAA Division I batting championship with a .478 average for Nebraska, then won the short-season Northwest League batting title with a .397 mark. . . Kansas City loaded up on pitching with six of the first 60 picks in the 1999 draft. Righthander **Mike MacDougal** (23), a first-rounder with a wicked mid-90s sinker, fanned 57 hitters in 46.1 Northwest League innings. . . **Paul Phillips** (22) is an athletic catcher who had a lackluster year with the bat in Double-A. If he can get stronger, he eventually might fill a position that has been a weakness at the major league level. . . Righthander **Kyle Snyder** (22) was the Royals' top 1999 draft pick and the seventh choice overall. He has three quality pitches: a fastball that has hit 96-97 MPH, a hard slider and a devastating changeup. . . **Goefrey Tomlinson** (23) is a center fielder with some speed and leadoff potential. He rebounded from a so-so Double-A season to hit .304 in the Arizona Fall League.

Hubert H. Humphrey Metrodome

Offense

Considered a state-of-the-art facility when it opened in 1982, the Metrodome is now an anachronism, made obsolete by the building of all-grass, baseball-only parks with luxury suites. This makes the Dome even more unique than it was a few years ago. Lefties can reach the short porch in right field easily, but the big outfield in left cuts down on home runs while increasing doubles and triples substantially. Foul territory is restricted, which helps all hitters, and the bouncy artificial turf makes ground-rule doubles rather frequent.

Defense

The off-white roof continues to be the park's most distinctive feature, affecting several games each year by causing inexperienced fielders to lose balls in the ceiling. Despite frequent attempts to fix the problem, glare from the lights compounds this difficulty. The infield turf is fast, but hops are usually consistent and predictable.

Who It Helps The Most

Righthanded gap hitters such as Chad Allen fare well when they shoot for the power alley in left field. Lefthanded sluggers who pull the ball down the right-field line and over the football seats, such as Corey Koskie, also find the Dome to their liking.

Who It Hurts The Most

Righthanded hitters like Ron Coomer and Terry Steinbach find that flyballs don't carry well if pulled too much. The quirks of the park are difficult for most young pitchers and fielders to deal with until they gain experience.

Rookies & Newcomers

Righthander Jason Ryan struggled in Minnesota in 1999, surrendering six homers in 21 innings. He'll have to adapt better this season. Lefthander J.C. Romero, who got a brief taste last year, will benefit from the deep outfield in left. The next hitter to arrive should be catcher Matt LeCroy, who has considerable power to all fields.

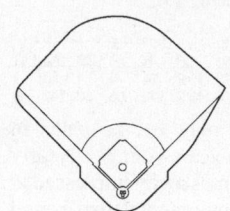

Dimensions: LF-343, LCF-385, CF-408, RCF-367, RF-327

Capacity: 48,678

Elevation: 815 feet

Surface: Turf

Foul Territory: Small

Park Factors

1999 Season

	Home Games			Away Games			
	Twins	Opp	Total	Twins	Opp	Total	Index
G	72	72	144	72	72	144	—
Avg	.264	.281	.273	.252	.279	.266	103
AB	2422	2618	5040	2468	2396	4864	104
R	307	403	710	278	349	627	113
H	639	736	1375	623	669	1292	106
2B	144	171	315	114	115	229	133
3B	18	16	34	8	18	26	126
HR	39	97	136	50	82	132	99
BB	232	242	474	215	205	420	109
SO	440	439	879	437	389	826	103
E	53	48	101	34	53	87	116
E-Infield	40	42	82	27	50	77	106
LHB-Avg	.256	.281	.267	.248	.270	.257	104
LHB-HR	15	51	66	25	25	50	124
RHB-Avg	.273	.281	.278	.258	.285	.273	102
RHB-HR	24	46	70	25	57	82	84

1997-1999

	Home Games			Away Games			
	Twins	Opp	Total	Twins	Opp	Total	Index
G	220	220	440	217	217	434	—
Avg	.271	.282	.277	.259	.284	.271	102
AB	7512	7992	15504	7580	7328	14908	103
R	1004	1190	2194	960	1112	2072	104
H	2037	2257	4294	1961	2080	4041	105
2B	424	481	905	368	405	773	113
3B	52	54	106	41	47	88	116
HR	138	270	408	175	253	428	92
BB	715	681	1396	659	625	1284	105
SO	1370	1337	2707	1320	1185	2505	104
E	142	155	297	133	161	294	100
E-Infield	115	129	244	104	146	250	96
LHB-Avg	.272	.284	.278	.250	.290	.269	103
LHB-HR	60	138	198	72	95	167	114
RHB-Avg	.270	.281	.276	.266	.280	.273	101
RHB-HR	78	132	210	103	158	261	77

1999 Rankings (American League)

- Highest run factor
- Highest double factor
- Highest walk factor
- Second-highest hit factor
- Third-highest error factor
- Third-highest LHB home-run factor
- Third-lowest RHB home-run factor

Tom Kelly

1999 Season

Tom Kelly seemed more comfortable last season in his role as a teacher for a young club than he had in years past. The Twins finished with the worst record in baseball in 1999, but in some ways the season has to be considered a success. The club won just 18 games in April and May, but then the pitching gelled and the Twins played close to .500 ball for three months. The mound corps remained decent during a 7-21 collapse in September.

Offense

In this age of high-octane offense, it's hard to believe exactly how bad the Twins' hitting attack was last year. Dearth of power was a big problem, but the club also lacked a true leadoff hitter and didn't get enough people on base. Kelly tried to overcome his team's shortcomings with the use of one-run strategies such as the hit-and-run, and as usual he encouraged his players to be aggressive on the bases. He bunted a bit more last year than he did in the past, but it isn't his favorite play and never will be. Kelly will platoon, particularly with youngsters, and usually keeps his entire roster involved.

Pitching & Defense

The development of young pitchers Eric Milton and Joe Mays gives cause for optimism. Kelly will pull anyone but Brad Radke or Milton at the first sign of trouble, and he always has done a good job keeping his pitchers healthy. Defense is an obsession with Kelly. Players must have a sound glove to get into the everyday lineup.

2000 Outlook

Despite the club's 1999 performance, Kelly is on solid ground and has the longest tenure of any manager with his current team. The key for 2000 will be finding more hitting to go with the improved pitching staff. The stadium situation remains a sore spot for the franchise, and the long-term future of the club depends on finding a way to increase revenues.

Born: 8/15/50 in Graceville, MN

Playing Experience: 1975, Min

Managerial Experience: 14 seasons

Manager Statistics

Year	Team, Lg	W	L	Pct	GB	Finish
1999	Minnesota, AL	63	97	.394	33.0	5th Central
14 Seasons		986	1074	.478	—	—

1999 Starting Pitchers by Days Rest

	<=3	4	5	6+
Twins Starts	3	91	42	15
Twins ERA	4.00	5.36	4.13	6.78
AL Avg Starts	2	82	47	21
AL ERA	6.83	4.98	4.72	5.62

1999 Situational Stats

	Tom Kelly	AL Average
Hit & Run Success %	25.9	35.3
Stolen Base Success %	66.3	68.0
Platoon Pct.	67.7	56.7
Defensive Subs	30	22
High-Pitch Outings	6	15
Quick/Slow Hooks	20/13	18/18
Sacrifice Attempts	46	52

1999 Rankings (American League)

- 1st in hit-and-run attempts (108), starting lineups used (152) and pinch-hitters used (165)
- 2nd in stolen base attempts (178), squeeze plays (5) and starts on three days rest (3)
- 3rd in steals of home plate (1), double steals (6), mid-inning pitching changes (220), saves with over 1 inning pitched (13) and one-batter pitcher appearances (41)

Chad Allen

1999 Season

After his mediocre 1998 season at Double-A New Britian, not much was expected of Chad Allen in 1999. He came to spring training hoping for a reserve role, then promptly set a club record with 35 spring hits and won the left-field job. He struggled at times, but won over the team and the fans with his hard-nosed style of play. He was streaky and played better in the first half before the pitchers adjusted to him, but overall it was a nice year.

Hitting

Allen is a good athlete who hits out of an open stance. He's strong, but like most Twins hitter he has a line-drive rather than a lofting swing. Allen hangs in well against righthanders but shows more power against southpaws. He tends to get himself into trouble by swinging at pitches outside the strike zone, especially hard sliders. Allen has the natural ability to get much better with the bat, but needs to be more patient. He took extra batting practice frequently to work on his deficiencies.

Baserunning & Defense

Allen has good natural speed, which he magnifies by being very aggressive on the bases, almost to the point of recklessness. He missed signs several times in crucial situations, which isn't the way to win the heart of manager Tom Kelly. Allen has an average arm and good range. He puts in maximum effort going after balls but sometimes makes careless errors.

2000 Outlook

The Twins were pleased with Allen in 1999 and will give him plenty of playing time again in 2000. He's already done more in the majors than he did in the minors, but big league outfielders today have to hit much more than Allen did last year to be considered effective.

Position: LF
Bats: R **Throws:** R
Ht: 6' 1" **Wt:** 195

Opening Day Age: 25
Born: 2/6/75 in Dallas, TX
ML Seasons: 1

Overall Statistics

	G	AB	R	H	D	T	HR	RBI	SB	BB	SO	Avg	OBP	Slg
1999	137	481	69	133	21	3	10	46	14	37	89	.277	.330	.395
Career	137	481	69	133	21	3	10	46	14	37	89	.277	.330	.395

Where He Hits the Ball

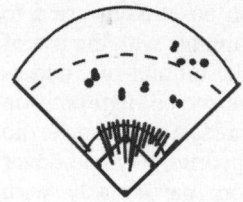 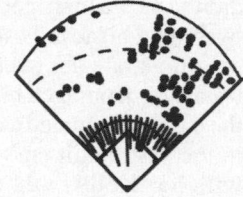

Vs. LHP   **Vs. RHP**

1999 Situational Stats

	AB	H	HR	RBI	Avg		AB	H	HR	RBI	Avg
Home	222	63	4	25	.284	LHP	116	35	3	9	.302
Road	259	70	6	21	.270	RHP	365	98	7	37	.268
First Half	272	80	6	25	.294	Sc Pos	109	27	1	34	.248
Scnd Half	209	53	4	21	.254	Clutch	72	24	1	10	.333

1999 Rankings (American League)

- 2nd in errors in left field (7) and lowest fielding percentage in left field (.975)
- 4th in highest percentage of extra bases taken as a runner (69.0%)
- 6th in lowest batting average with the bases loaded (.091)
- 9th in lowest slugging percentage, highest groundball/flyball ratio (1.8) and lowest slugging percentage vs. righthanded pitchers (.386)
- 10th in lowest stolen-base percentage (66.7%)
- Led the Twins in runs scored, HR frequency (48.1 ABs per HR), highest groundball/flyball ratio (1.8) and batting average vs. lefthanded pitchers

Ron Coomer

Position: 1B/3B
Bats: R **Throws:** R
Ht: 5'11" **Wt:** 206

Opening Day Age: 33
Born: 11/18/66 in Chicago, IL
ML Seasons: 5

Minnesota

1999 Season

Ron Coomer once again saw considerable action for the Twins in 1999, providing their main source of power. He split time at third base with rookie Corey Koskie, played first base frequently when rookie Doug Mientkiewicz was struggling and also saw some action at DH. As the season progressed, Coomer was worn down by a variety of nagging injuries, including bruised cartilage in his left knee that ended his season a few days early.

Hitting

Coomer is one of the strongest Twins but isn't a tremendous power hitter. Hitting out of a slightly open stance, his swing is tailored for the line drive rather than the home run. He's most effective against lefthanders and would be more productive as a platoon player than as a regular. Coomer hits the ball hard and low, making him a good candidate for the double play. Sliders on the outer part of the plate give him trouble, especially if he's set on pulling the ball. Coomer was slightly more patient last year, but his on-base percentage is still too low.

Baserunning & Defense

Coomer is one of the slowest players in the American League. He hustles and runs hard, but his body will only go so fast. His career high in steals is four, and he's a station-to-station runner. A corner infielder, Coomer is quite good at first base and more than adequate at third. His range and mobility at either position are somewhat limited, but he has soft hands and a strong arm, and seldom makes an error. His fundamentals are sound, which makes him a favorite of manager Tom Kelly.

2000 Outlook

As the Twins work more young players into the lineup, Coomer's playing time will decrease gradually. His ability to play the corner positions well and to provide a spark of offense makes him a useful player to have around, though he doesn't hit enough to be a mainstay with a contending team.

Overall Statistics

	G	AB	R	H	D	T	HR	RBI	SB	BB	SO	Avg	OBP	Slg
1999	127	467	53	123	25	1	16	65	2	30	69	.263	.307	.424
Career	536	1853	219	520	92	6	61	282	11	96	267	.281	.314	.436

Where He Hits the Ball

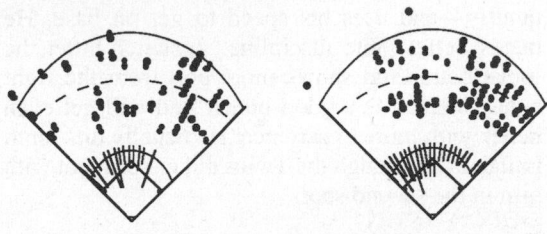

Vs. LHP   **Vs. RHP**

1999 Situational Stats

	AB	H	HR	RBI	Avg		AB	H	HR	RBI	Avg
Home	229	61	6	29	.266	LHP	115	32	5	15	.278
Road	238	62	10	36	.261	RHP	352	91	11	50	.259
First Half	284	80	11	37	.282	Sc Pos	123	33	3	43	.268
Scnd Half	183	43	5	28	.235	Clutch	73	23	2	10	.315

1999 Rankings (American League)

- 2nd in lowest cleanup slugging percentage (.394)
- Led the Twins in home runs and slugging percentage vs. lefthanded pitchers (.470)

Cristian Guzman

Position: SS
Bats: B **Throws:** R
Ht: 6' 0" **Wt:** 188

Opening Day Age: 22
Born: 3/21/78 in Santo Domingo, Dominican Republic
ML Seasons: 1
Pronunciation: GOOZ-mahn

1999 Season

Acquired from the Yankees in 1998 along with Eric Milton in the Chuck Knoblauch trade, Cristian Guzman earned his way onto the roster with a solid spring training, especially with his glovework. Guzman's bat was very weak early in the year, but he did better in the second half before hitting .148 in September.

Hitting

Guzman is a terrific athlete but not much of a hitter. He moves around at the plate, perhaps too much for his own good, and shows little power. He likes to slap balls around the infield—his groundball/fly-ball ratio of 3.15 would have led the American League had he had enough plate appearances to qualify—and uses his speed to get on base. He needs better plate discipline. A switch-hitter, he looks better and shows more pop from the right side. Guzman is a good bunter and will get even better with more experience. He usually hits ninth in the order, though the Twins did experiment with him in the second spot.

Baserunning & Defense

Guzman is a good example of how raw speed and basestealing ability aren't the same thing. He runs like the wind, but has trouble reading pitchers and is caught making mistakes on the bases far too often. Those mistakes can be corrected with experience. Defensively, Guzman has above-average range, soft hands and a very strong arm. He gets sloppy on routine plays and appears more comfortable playing defense on natural grass than he does on turf. Of course, that's a problem in the Metrodome.

2000 Outlook

Though Guzman's raw potential has made him a favorite of manager Tom Kelly, his lack of offensive production is a major problem for the team. Guzman's glove will be excellent once he plays more. He must hit better to hold off Luis Rivas, a shortstop prospect who also has a good glove and offers more with the bat.

Overall Statistics

	G	AB	R	H	D	T	HR	RBI	SB	BB	SO	Avg	OBP	Slg
1999	131	420	47	95	12	3	1	26	9	22	90	.226	.267	.276
Career	131	420	47	95	12	3	1	26	9	22	90	.226	.267	.276

Where He Hits the Ball

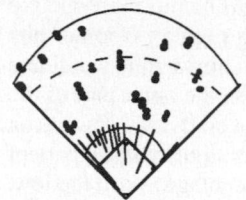

Vs. LHP

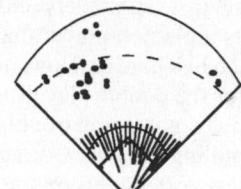

Vs. RHP

1999 Situational Stats

	AB	H	HR	RBI	Avg		AB	H	HR	RBI	Avg
Home	209	51	1	13	.244	LHP	115	34	1	8	.296
Road	211	44	0	13	.209	RHP	305	61	0	18	.200
First Half	221	49	1	16	.222	Sc Pos	109	23	0	24	.211
Scnd Half	199	46	0	10	.231	Clutch	45	9	0	1	.200

1999 Rankings (American League)

- 2nd in errors at shortstop (24) and lowest fielding percentage at shortstop (.959)
- 5th in lowest percentage of pitches taken (46.6%)
- 6th in fewest GDPs per GDP situation (4.9%) and lowest batting average with runners in scoring position
- 8th in lowest slugging percentage vs. lefthanded pitchers (.400)
- 10th in batting average on a 3-1 count (.571)
- Led the Twins in sacrifice bunts (7), fewest GDPs per GDP situation (4.9%) and batting average on a 3-1 count (.571)
- Led AL shortstops in fewest GDPs per GDP situation (4.9%) and batting average on a 3-1 count (.571)

LaTroy Hawkins

1999 Season

LaTroy Hawkins entered the 1999 campaign with a new two-year contract, hoping to build on the steady progress he made in 1998. It didn't happen. He was terrible out of the gate, posting a 7.84 ERA in the first half. He improved in July and August, but fell back into bad habits and was crushed in September. Hawkins remains an enigma, obviously talented but dogged by inconsistency.

Pitching

Arm strength isn't the problem for Hawkins. His fastball has been timed as high as 95 MPH, though it lacks movement at that speed and is more effective in the 90-92 MPH range. Hawkins has experimented with different grips on the pitch, but still has trouble establishing consistent control of it. He frequently leaves fastballs up in the strike zone, where they get pounded. His secondary offerings are a curveball, slider, splitter and changeup. All have potential, but some observers think his arsenal is too diverse and that he would be better off concentrating on improving one or two offerings. Hawkins has good mechanics and a durable arm. He tends to work slowly when in a jam, which just makes his problems worse by lulling his fielders to sleep.

Defense

A former basketball player, Hawkins is tall, athletic and mobile. He has improved against the running game, and does a decent job cutting it off for a tall righthander. His move to first has improved noticeably the past two seasons. Hawkins is an adequate fielder.

2000 Outlook

Minnesota has been exceptionally patient with Hawkins and will give him one more season to get straightened out. He continues to show flashes of strong pitching, but his career record is now 26-44, 6.16.

Position: SP
Bats: R **Throws:** R
Ht: 6' 5" **Wt:** 204

Opening Day Age: 27
Born: 12/21/72 in Gary, IN
ML Seasons: 5

Minnesota

Overall Statistics

	W	L	Pct.	ERA	G	GS	Sv	IP	H	BB	SO	HR	Ratio
1999	10	14	.417	6.66	33	33	0	174.1	238	60	103	29	1.71
Career	26	44	.371	6.16	99	98	0	521.1	680	189	299	86	1.67

How Often He Throws Strikes

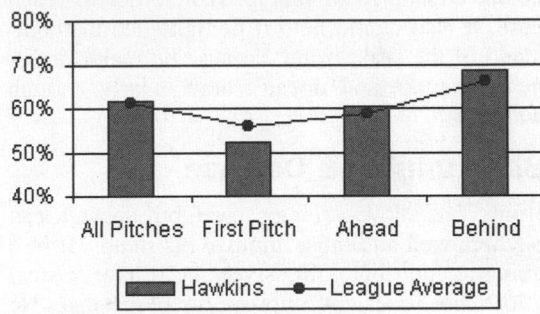

1999 Situational Stats

	W	L	ERA	Sv	IP		AB	H	HR	RBI	Avg
Home	3	9	8.36	0	85.0	LHB	342	106	18	63	.310
Road	7	5	5.04	0	89.1	RHB	394	132	11	52	.335
First Half	5	8	7.84	0	90.2	Sc Pos	179	54	7	77	.302
Scnd Half	5	6	5.38	0	83.2	Clutch	23	8	1	3	.348

1999 Rankings (American League)

- 1st in highest ERA, highest batting average allowed (.323), highest slugging percentage allowed (.507), least run support per 9 innings (4.0) and highest ERA at home
- 2nd in highest batting average allowed vs. righthanded batters
- 3rd in highest on-base percentage allowed (.373) and most baserunners allowed per 9 innings (15.4)
- 4th in losses and most home runs allowed per 9 innings (1.50)
- 5th in hits allowed
- Led the Twins in losses, home runs allowed and wild pitches (9)

Torii Hunter

1999 Season

A 1993 first-round pick, Hunter hit a soft .259 in six minor league seasons before winning Minnesota's center-field job with a strong spring training. After batting .227 in the first two months of the season, he eventually was delegated to a platoon role, sharing time in center field with Jacque Jones. Hunter took well to part-time action, showing a much stronger bat against lefthanders.

Hitting

A terrific athlete, Hunter is very strong but doesn't have a power swing. He does best when he keeps his stroke short and struggles when he becomes pull-conscious. He needs to do a better job of taking advantage of his speed in order to reach base. It also would help if he tightened his command of the strike zone, because he makes infrequent contact and doesn't draw nearly enough walks.

Baserunning & Defense

Hunter has above-average speed, but doesn't read pitchers well and must improve his jumps. If he's going to contribute offensively, he'll have to steal a lot more bases and improve his percentage. He also has to eliminate a tendency to miss signs and make sloppy decisions on the bases, which doesn't endear him to manager Tom Kelly. Hunter's defense is excellent and he's the best outfielder in the organization. He has terrific range and a strong, accurate arm.

2000 Outlook

Hunter won't be a star but is a legitimate big leaguer. His glovework and ability to hit southpaws will keep him in the majors for a long time as a fourth outfielder. He has the physical ability to be better than that, but never has made the adjustments that would make him an effective offensive player. If Chad Allen falters, it's possible that Hunter might get another shot at playing regularly.

Position: CF/LF/RF
Bats: R **Throws:** R
Ht: 6' 2" **Wt:** 205

Opening Day Age: 24
Born: 7/18/75 in Pine Bluff, AR
ML Seasons: 3

Overall Statistics

	G	AB	R	H	D	T	HR	RBI	SB	BB	SO	Avg	OBP	Slg
1999	135	384	52	98	17	2	9	35	10	26	72	.255	.309	.380
Career	142	401	52	102	18	2	9	37	10	28	78	.254	.309	.377

Where He Hits the Ball

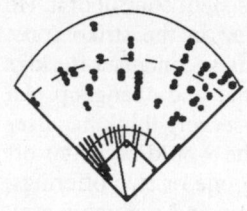 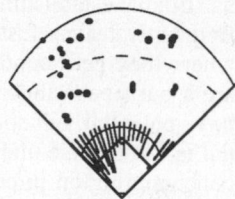

Vs. LHP **Vs. RHP**

1999 Situational Stats

	AB	H	HR	RBI	Avg		AB	H	HR	RBI	Avg
Home	179	43	2	18	.240	LHP	112	33	2	12	.295
Road	205	55	7	17	.268	RHP	272	65	7	23	.239
First Half	238	55	6	22	.231	Sc Pos	97	23	1	23	.237
Scnd Half	146	43	3	13	.295	Clutch	48	10	1	6	.208

1999 Rankings (American League)

- 2nd in fielding percentage in center field (.996)
- 9th in lowest slugging percentage vs. lefthanded pitchers (.402)

Jacque Jones

Position: CF/RF
Bats: L **Throws:** L
Ht: 5'10" **Wt:** 175

Opening Day Age: 24
Born: 4/25/75 in San Diego, CA
ML Seasons: 1

1999 Season

A star at the University of Southern California and a member of the 1996 U.S. Olympic Team, Jacque Jones was expected to challenge for the center-field job in spring training. He played poorly and was sent to the minors, not to be recalled until June. Once he arrived, Jones had a sound rookie season.

Hitting

Jones came to the majors with a long swing, and he would dive out over the plate and occasionally jam himself. By the end of the season, his swing was shorter and more controlled. He has power, especially to the opposite field, and usually puts good wood on the ball, relying on quick wrists and bat speed rather than a picture-perfect swing. Jones will hit for average and has 20-homer potential. He isn't a wild swinger, but he needs to work the count more effectively to get the most out of his ability, especially if he stays at the top of the order.

Baserunning & Defense

Jones runs very well but doesn't have great technique on the bases. He won't be a big stolen-base threat until he improves his ability to read pitchers. His arm is fairly strong and accurate, and his range in the outfield is very good. By the end of the year, he was more comfortable tracking balls in the difficult Metrodome, where the ceiling can give players problems. With time, Jones should be a very good center fielder.

2000 Outlook

Jones will see plenty of action in 2000 and if he gets the chance, he may see full-time rather than platoon duty. He irritated the coaching staff a few times with a happy-go-lucky attitude, but he's generally regarded as a hard worker. He's well on his way to a fine career.

Overall Statistics

	G	AB	R	H	D	T	HR	RBI	SB	BB	SO	Avg	.OBP	Slg
1999	95	322	54	93	24	2	9	44	3	17	63	.289	.329	.460
Career	95	322	54	93	24	2	9	44	3	17	63	.289	.329	.460

Where He Hits the Ball

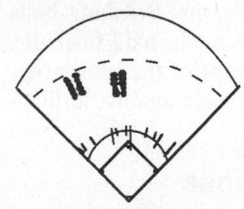

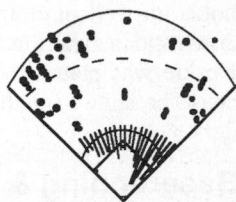

Vs. LHP   **Vs. RHP**

1999 Situational Stats

	AB	H	HR	RBI	Avg		AB	H	HR	RBI	Avg
Home	161	43	5	21	.267	LHP	36	8	1	8	.222
Road	161	50	4	23	.311	RHP	286	85	8	36	.297
First Half	113	33	2	14	.292	Sc Pos	76	21	3	35	.276
Scnd Half	209	60	7	30	.287	Clutch	48	14	0	6	.292

1999 Rankings (American League)

- 4th in errors in center field (5)
- 5th in lowest on-base percentage for a leadoff hitter (.314)

Corey Koskie

1999 Season

In an otherwise disappointing season for Minnesota hitters, rookie third baseman Corey Koskie was a breath of fresh air. He hit over .300 in every month except May, showed excellent power potential and earned the respect of the coaching staff with his willingness to work hard and improve. Of all the rookies who debuted with the Twins, Koskie did the most to solidify his place on the team.

Hitting

Koskie is a strong lefthanded hitter with a conventional style at the plate. He can pull for power but also is willing to go to the opposite field, as he's quite capable of driving the ball in any direction. He's reasonably patient, makes decent contact and holds up well in clutch situations. Breaking balls down and in give him trouble, but he nails fastballs. Koskie was platooned for most of the season because he shows much less power against lefthanders.

Baserunning & Defense

Koskie is a big guy and not a fast runner. Like many products of the Twins system, he's extremely aggressive and will move up whenever an extra base presents itself. At the beginning of the year, Koskie looked rough with the glove at third base, but he worked hard on improving his footwork. By the end of the year, he proved he could handle the position. Koskie also spent some time in the outfield but didn't look comfortable there.

2000 Outlook

Koskie did little wrong in 1999, hitting well, improving his fielding and impressing the coaches with his work ethic. His place in the lineup is assured for 2000. In the long term, he faces a challenge from prospect Michael Cuddyer at third base. Koskie's bat should ensure him a job, perhaps at first base.

Position: 3B/RF/DH
Bats: L **Throws:** R
Ht: 6' 3" **Wt:** 217

Opening Day Age: 26
Born: 6/28/73 in Anola, Canada
ML Seasons: 2
Pronunciation: KOSS-kee

Overall Statistics

	G	AB	R	H	D	T	HR	RBI	SB	BB	SO	Avg	OBP	Slg
1999	117	342	42	106	21	0	11	58	4	40	72	.310	.387	.468
Career	128	371	44	110	21	0	12	60	4	42	82	.296	.373	.450

Where He Hits the Ball

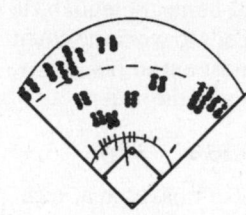
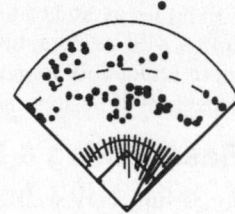

Vs. LHP   **Vs. RHP**

1999 Situational Stats

	AB	H	HR	RBI	Avg		AB	H	HR	RBI	Avg
Home	169	61	4	32	.361	LHP	45	12	0	5	.267
Road	173	45	7	26	.260	RHP	297	94	11	53	.316
First Half	186	57	7	34	.306	Sc Pos	106	37	3	46	.349
Scnd Half	156	49	4	24	.314	Clutch	51	18	1	5	.353

1999 Rankings (American League)
- 10th in batting average with runners in scoring position
- Led the Twins in batting average in the clutch
- Led AL third basemen in batting average in the clutch

Matt Lawton

1999 Season

The Twins hoped that Matt Lawton would build on his solid 1998 season and establish himself as a minor star in 1999. He looked good in April, hitting .299, but slumped in May, then missed most of June after being beaned. The injury fractured two bones in his right eye socket. Lawton returned in July, but had just six extra-base hits in the second half.

Hitting

When Lawton is right, he's a very patient hitter who can drive pitches to the opposite field for power. He appeared too passive after his injury. Even when he got ahead in the count, he couldn't make pitchers pay. Pitches that he whacked for extra bases in 1998 became foul balls or grounders last year. Lawton handles lefthanders well, and is one of the few players in the Twins lineup that manager Tom Kelly seldom platoons. He makes contact and is a decent hit-and-run artist.

Baserunning & Defense

Blessed with good speed, Lawton has matured into one of the most effective baserunners that the Twins possess. He steals bases at an excellent percentage and is adept at moving up whenever possible. Lawton's work with the glove is considerably better than it was when he first reached the majors. His range is above average and he's reasonably reliable. He has an average and accurate arm, and Minnesota is comfortable playing him in right field.

2000 Outlook

Lawton denied that there was anything wrong when he returned from the beaning, but he didn't look like the same player after the injury. He'll be in the lineup every day again in 2000 after signing a one-year deal worth $2 million. He's still in his prime, so a rebound is likely.

Position: RF/LF
Bats: L **Throws:** R
Ht: 5'10" **Wt:** 186

Opening Day Age: 28
Born: 11/3/71 in Gulfport, MS
ML Seasons: 5

Minnesota

Overall Statistics

	G	AB	R	H	D	T	HR	RBI	SB	BB	SO	Avg	OBP	Slg
1999	118	406	58	105	18	0	7	54	26	57	42	.259	.353	.355
Career	512	1735	268	458	94	11	49	245	54	254	226	.264	.367	.416

Where He Hits the Ball

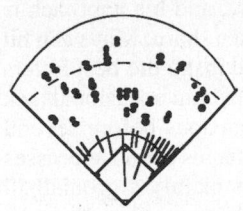 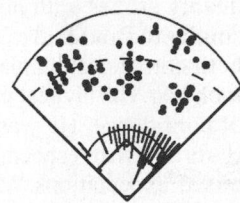

Vs. LHP   **Vs. RHP**

1999 Situational Stats

	AB	H	HR	RBI	Avg		AB	H	HR	RBI	Avg
Home	206	56	2	25	.272	LHP	100	29	2	15	.290
Road	200	49	5	29	.245	RHP	306	76	5	39	.248
First Half	202	53	5	26	.262	Sc Pos	103	27	2	47	.262
Scnd Half	204	52	2	28	.255	Clutch	71	16	1	20	.225

1999 Rankings (American League)

- 1st in stolen-base percentage (86.7%)
- 4th in lowest fielding percentage in right field (.980) and highest percentage of swings put into play (55.3%)
- Led the Twins in sacrifice flies (7), stolen bases, walks, intentional walks (7), stolen-base percentage (86.7%), batting average with the bases loaded (.500), bunts in play (4), highest percentage of pitches taken (60.1%), lowest percentage of swings that missed (10.1%) and highest percentage of swings put into play (55.3%)
- Led AL right fielders in stolen bases, stolen-base percentage (86.7%) and highest percentage of swings put into play (55.3%)

Joe Mays

1999 Season

Joe Mays' development was one of the biggest surprises of the 1999 season. A minor leaguer with a mixed track record and no experience above Double-A, Mays earned a job in the bullpen with a strong spring-training performance. He was adequate in relief, then moved into the rotation in mid-June after other pitchers failed. His best start was a complete-game shutout of the Cubs on July 17.

Pitching

Mays works with a 90-MPH fastball that he usually throws for strikes. His curveball and changeup are also solid pitches, and he's adept at changing speeds and keeping hitters off balance. He throws quality strikes with his curve, and his approach is similar to Brad Radke's. When sharp, Mays can hit both corners of the plate and make the best hitters look lost. His biggest problem is an occasional lack of confidence. He was too anxious before several starts last year, especially after his initial successes raised expectations. Mays is mainly a groundball pitcher, though he gives up homers when he overthrows and leaves his pitches up in the strike zone. He works rapidly and adjusted to the Metrodome more quickly than most young pitchers.

Defense

Mays will make routine plays, but like most young pitchers he needs more experience to improve as a fielder. His move to first isn't very good, but his delivery is fairly quick and he isn't overly vulnerable to the stolen base.

2000 Outlook

Barring a spring-training collapse, expect Mays to be in the rotation again in 2000. He won't be sneaking up on teams this year and he may not live up to his 1999 season, especially if he doesn't maintain his faith in himself.

Position: RP/SP
Bats: B **Throws:** R
Ht: 6' 1" **Wt:** 185

Opening Day Age: 24
Born: 12/10/75 in Flint, MI
ML Seasons: 1

Overall Statistics

	W	L	Pct.	ERA	G	GS	Sv	IP	H	BB	SO	HR	Ratio
1999	6	11	.353	4.37	49	20	0	171.0	179	67	115	24	1.44
Career	6	11	.353	4.37	49	20	0	171.0	179	67	115	24	1.44

How Often He Throws Strikes

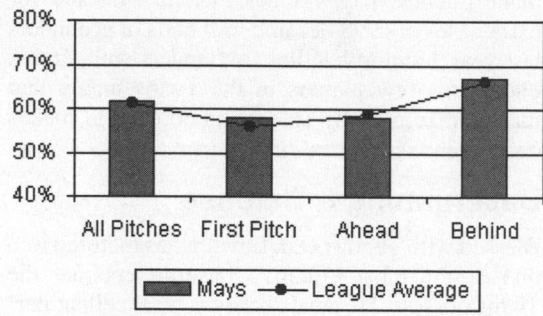

1999 Situational Stats

	W	L	ERA	Sv	IP		AB	H	HR	RBI	Avg
Home	4	6	4.13	0	102.1	LHB	322	82	15	43	.255
Road	2	5	4.72	0	68.2	RHB	342	97	9	46	.284
First Half	1	3	4.80	0	75.0	Sc Pos	154	41	6	65	.266
Scnd Half	5	8	4.03	0	96.0	Clutch	55	23	1	5	.418

1999 Rankings (American League)

- 2nd in least run support per 9 innings (4.1)
- 5th in lowest winning percentage
- 8th in most home runs allowed per 9 innings (1.26)
- 9th in highest groundball/flyball ratio allowed (1.5)
- 10th in highest stolen-base percentage allowed (70.6%)
- Led the Twins in walks allowed, highest groundball/flyball ratio allowed (1.5) and lowest batting average allowed vs. lefthanded batters

Eric Milton

1999 Season

It was a tale of two seasons for Eric Milton. His performance in the first part of the season was similar to his 1998 rookie campaign: inconsistent but promising. In the second half, Milton realized he belonged in the major leagues and started pitching with much more confidence. He was excellent from late June on, and punctuated his season with a 13-strikeout no-hitter against the Angels on September 11.

Pitching

A prize prospect acquired from the Yankees in the Chuck Knoblauch trade, Milton put everything together in 1999. His fastball is usually in the low 90s and tops out at 94 MPH, and he has learned to get more movement on the pitch. His curveball was much sharper last year, and the Twins have worked with him on improving his slider. He struggled against lefties in 1998, but the improvement of his breaking stuff last year solved that problem. Milton also has a solid changeup that he'll use at any point in the count. A flyball pitcher susceptible to the home run, Milton increased his strikeout rate last year while cutting his walks. He has had twinges of elbow and shoulder pain throughout his career, so the Twins must watch his innings and pitch counts carefully.

Defense

Milton is a good athlete, but he made three errors last year and must improve his handling of bunts and infield situations. He should get better with experience. He has a very good move to first base and is solid at controlling the running game.

2000 Outlook

Milton established himself as one of the best young pitchers in the American League in 1999, drawing comparisons to Frank Viola. If Milton gets more run support this season, his record should begin to reflect his true ability.

Position: SP
Bats: L **Throws:** L
Ht: 6' 3" **Wt:** 220

Opening Day Age: 24
Born: 8/4/75 in State College, PA
ML Seasons: 2

Minnesota

Overall Statistics

	W	L	Pct.	ERA	G	GS	Sv	IP	H	BB	SO	HR	Ratio
1999	7	11	.389	4.49	34	34	0	206.1	190	63	163	28	1.23
Career	15	25	.375	5.01	66	66	0	378.2	385	133	270	53	1.37

How Often He Throws Strikes

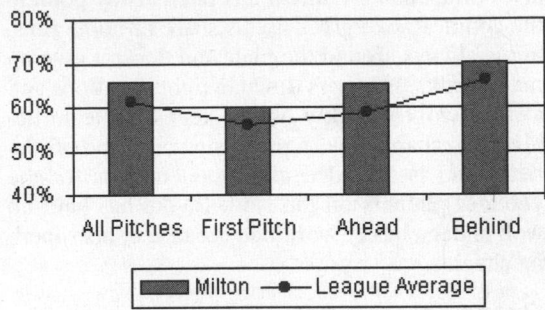

1999 Situational Stats

	W	L	ERA	Sv	IP			AB	H	HR	RBI	Avg
Home	4	5	3.61	0	104.2	LHB		154	39	7	19	.253
Road	3	6	5.40	0	101.2	RHB		629	151	21	78	.240
First Half	3	8	5.17	0	102.2	Sc Pos		144	45	9	70	.313
Scnd Half	4	3	3.82	0	103.2	Clutch		35	6	0	4	.171

1999 Rankings (American League)

- 1st in lowest groundball/flyball ratio allowed (0.6)
- 2nd in games started, shutouts (2), lowest on-base percentage allowed (.299), fewest baserunners allowed per 9 innings (11.2) and fewest GDPs induced per 9 innings (0.4)
- 4th in complete games (5)
- 5th in lowest batting average allowed (.243), lowest stolen-base percentage allowed (50.0%) and errors at pitcher (3)
- Led the Twins in games started, complete games (5), shutouts (2), strikeouts, pitches thrown (3,377), pickoff throws (64), runners caught stealing (6) and lowest batting average allowed (.243)

Brad Radke

1999 Season

His record doesn't reflect it, but Brad Radke was one of the best pitchers in the American League in 1999. His ERA ranked fourth in the circuit, and he continued to draw the attention of contending clubs, hoping to convince the Twins to trade him. Minnesota is reluctant to part with its ace, especially because his contract is affordable.

Pitching

Radke's fastball is a tick above average, in the 90-91 MPH range on most nights. He throws the pitch to spots and can hit the black in a Maddux-like manner when he is sharp. His second pitch is an excellent changeup. His curveball and slider are also solid, and he'll throw any pitch at any point in the count. Radke gives up his share of home runs, but is always around the plate and doesn't give up many walks. He bears down in tight situations and always works quickly, which keeps the team behind him sharp. He is a professional on and off the field, and is regarded as a good mentor for the younger pitchers on the staff. Radke has held up well under a heavy workload because of his superb mechanics.

Defense

A sound athlete, Radke has made just one error in his entire career. He moves around the infield well and seldom makes a mistake or error in judgment. His move to first base is adequate, though far from outstanding. He relies mainly on quick work to control baserunners.

2000 Outlook

The Twins picked up the 2000 option on Radke's contract for $3.5 million, a bargain in today's market. He's the only thing close to a No. 1 starter on the staff. Radke would be a perennial 15-20 game winner on a contending club, but has expressed a desire to spend his career in Minnesota. The Twins will certainly oblige if the money works out.

Position: SP
Bats: R **Throws:** R
Ht: 6' 2" **Wt:** 188

Opening Day Age: 27
Born: 10/27/72 in Eau Claire, WI
ML Seasons: 5

Overall Statistics

	W	L	Pct.	ERA	G	GS	Sv	IP	H	BB	SO	HR	Ratio
1999	12	14	.462	3.75	33	33	0	218.2	239	44	121	28	1.29
Career	66	68	.493	4.30	164	163	0	1085.0	1141	239	664	151	1.27

How Often He Throws Strikes

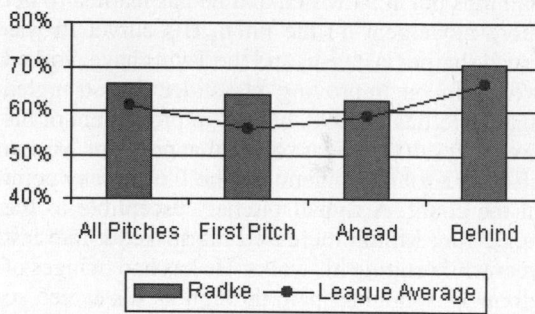

1999 Situational Stats

	W	L	ERA	Sv	IP		AB	H	HR	RBI	Avg
Home	5	7	4.36	0	95.0	LHB	456	128	14	53	.281
Road	7	7	3.27	0	123.2	RHB	399	111	14	41	.278
First Half	6	7	3.66	0	118.0	Sc Pos	178	44	10	68	.247
Scnd Half	6	7	3.84	0	100.2	Clutch	66	15	0	5	.227

1999 Rankings (American League)

- 3rd in fewest pitches thrown per batter (3.53), least run support per 9 innings (4.3), walks per 9 innings (1.8) and ERA on the road
- 4th in ERA, losses and hits allowed
- 5th in fewest baserunners allowed per 9 innings (11.7)
- Led the Twins in ERA, wins, losses, innings pitched, hits allowed, batters faced (910), stolen bases allowed (13), runners caught stealing (6), GDPs induced (22), winning percentage, highest strikeout/walk ratio (2.8), fewest pitches thrown per batter (3.53), fewest home runs allowed per 9 innings (1.15), most GDPs induced per 9 innings (0.9), walks per 9 innings (1.8) and ERA on the road

Todd Walker

Position: 2B/DH
Bats: L **Throws:** R
Ht: 6' 0" **Wt:** 181

Opening Day Age: 26
Born: 5/25/73 in
Bakersfield, CA
ML Seasons: 4

Minnesota

1999 Season

After challenging for the American League batting title in 1998, Todd Walker looked like a franchise cornerstone. His 1999 season was a different story. Though he batted better than .300 in May, June and July, he both started and finished slowly to wind up with disappointing overall numbers. His power didn't develop as anticipated, and his batting average dropped from .316 to .279.

Hitting

Walker has one of the purest strokes around. He keeps his swing short and sharp, is very adept at lashing liners all over the field and will pull the ball for power occasionally. At his best, he's quite patient and shows few weaknesses. Walker attributed his slumps to bad luck, though his timing appeared off to outside observers and Twins coaches felt his swing was getting too long. He continues to have trouble against lefthanders, leading to frequent platooning. Walker struggled with runners in scoring position last year, perhaps because he was trying too hard to overcome the team's lack of offense. He needs to relax in clutch situations and let his talent work for him.

Baserunning & Defense

Walker runs well. He isn't a blazer, but gets down the line in good time and is a very smart baserunner. He usually gets good jumps on a pitcher, and like most Twins, he's very aggressive at taking the extra base. Minnesota manager Tom Kelly has been critical of Walker's defense and frequently uses defensive subs to cover for him in the late innings. Walker never will win a Gold Glove, mainly because of limited range. He's reasonably reliable, however, and his fielding percentage was safely above the league average last year.

2000 Outlook

Walker should be entering his peak seasons. He has vowed to stick closely with a weight-training program this winter to increase his strength and agility. He remains a very intriguing player with star potential.

Overall Statistics

	G	AB	R	H	D	T	HR	RBI	SB	BB	SO	Avg	OBP	Slg
1999	143	531	62	148	37	4	6	46	18	52	83	.279	.343	.397
Career	363	1297	170	373	91	8	21	130	46	114	191	.288	.344	.419

Where He Hits the Ball

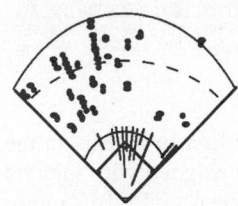
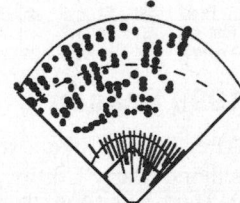

Vs. LHP   **Vs. RHP**

1999 Situational Stats

	AB	H	HR	RBI	Avg		AB	H	HR	RBI	Avg
Home	260	67	4	23	.258	LHP	101	18	1	10	.178
Road	271	81	2	23	.299	RHP	430	130	5	36	.302
First Half	312	87	4	26	.279	Sc Pos	134	31	1	38	.231
Scnd Half	219	61	2	20	.279	Clutch	80	22	4	18	.275

1999 Rankings (American League)

- 3rd in highest percentage of extra bases taken as a runner (70.7%)
- 5th in fielding percentage at second base (.984)
- Led the Twins in batting average, at-bats, hits, singles, doubles, triples, total bases (211), caught stealing (10), times on base (201), pitches seen (2,250), plate appearances (586), slugging percentage, on-base percentage, most pitches seen per plate appearance (3.84), batting average vs. righthanded pitchers, on-base percentage for a leadoff hitter (.368), slugging percentage vs. righthanded pitchers (.430), on-base percentage vs. righthanded pitchers (.368), batting average on a 3-2 count (.294), batting average at home and batting average on the road

Marty Cordova

Position: DH/RF
Bats: R **Throws:** R
Ht: 6' 0" **Wt:** 206

Opening Day Age: 30
Born: 7/10/69 in Las Vegas, NV
ML Seasons: 5
Pronunciation: core-DOE-vuh

Overall Statistics

	G	AB	R	H	D	T	HR	RBI	SB	BB	SO	Avg	OBP	Slg
1999	124	425	62	121	28	3	14	70	13	48	96	.285	.365	.464
Career	628	2322	336	643	139	14	79	385	52	233	498	.277	.348	.451

1999 Situational Stats

	AB	H	HR	RBI	Avg		AB	H	HR	RBI	Avg
Home	216	70	9	35	.324	LHP	102	21	2	11	.206
Road	209	51	5	35	.244	RHP	323	100	12	59	.310
First Half	257	74	8	41	.288	Sc Pos	115	33	4	53	.287
Scnd Half	168	47	6	29	.280	Clutch	72	20	3	14	.278

1999 Season

After looking like a star his first two years in the majors, Marty Cordova was plagued with injuries in 1997 and 1998. This was especially frustrating for the Twins because they had given Cordova a three-year contract. He was healthier in 1999 and played better, but Minnesota would have preferred to trade him.

Hitting, Baserunning & Defense

In an attempt to quicken his bat, Cordova opened up his stance slightly in 1999. He has become mainly a line-drive, gap hitter who did most of his damage in the friendly Metrodome. Injuries have reduced his speed, though he still can steal a base when called upon to do so. A chronically sore rotator cuff limited Cordova's outfield play in 1999. His arm strength and accuracy are far from what they were three years ago, and his range has declined as well.

2000 Outlook

The Twins let Cordova go at the end of the year and don't expect him back. His bat is decent, but his decline as an outfielder makes him difficult to employ in any role but DH.

Brent Gates

Position: 3B/2B
Bats: B **Throws:** R
Ht: 6' 1" **Wt:** 190

Opening Day Age: 30
Born: 3/14/70 in Grand Rapids, MI
ML Seasons: 7

Overall Statistics

	G	AB	R	H	D	T	HR	RBI	SB	BB	SO	Avg	OBP	Slg
1999	110	306	40	78	13	2	3	38	1	34	56	.255	.328	.340
Career	685	2329	268	616	119	11	25	279	18	225	349	.264	.327	.357

1999 Situational Stats

	AB	H	HR	RBI	Avg		AB	H	HR	RBI	Avg
Home	177	44	2	24	.249	LHP	115	32	2	23	.278
Road	129	34	1	14	.264	RHP	191	46	1	15	.241
First Half	174	50	2	24	.287	Sc Pos	81	19	1	33	.235
Scnd Half	132	28	1	14	.212	Clutch	59	12	0	8	.203

1999 Season

Manager Tom Kelly likes having fundamentally sound veteran players on the bench, and Brent Gates fit the bill in 1999. Seeing considerable action at second and third base spelling Todd Walker and rookie Corey Koskie, Gates played particularly well in May and June. He slumped in the second half to finish with numbers almost identical to what he did in 1998.

Hitting, Baserunning & Defense

A switch-hitter who's more effective against lefthanders, Gates' plan is to punch liners through the infield. He has very little power and only average patience, making his overall offensive contribution rather slim. He bunts decently and can execute the hit-and-run. Gates' speed is average and he isn't a threat to steal. He works hard and knows his fundamentals, which makes him a sound defensive player. He doesn't really have the arm for third base but is reliable. Gates made no errors in 46 games at second base.

2000 Outlook

The Twins dropped Gates from the 40-man roster at the end of the season. The same thing happened last year before he returned to Minnesota. That scenario may play out again.

Eddie Guardado

Position: RP
Bats: R **Throws:** L
Ht: 6' 0" **Wt:** 194

Opening Day Age: 29
Born: 10/2/70 in Stockton, CA
ML Seasons: 7
Pronunciation: gwar-DAH-doe

Overall Statistics

	W	L	Pct.	ERA	G	GS	Sv	IP	H	BB	SO	HR	Ratio
1999	2	5	.286	4.50	63	0	2	48.0	37	25	50	6	1.29
Career	18	34	.346	5.22	368	25	9	436.1	457	188	356	64	1.48

1999 Situational Stats

	W	L	ERA	Sv	IP		AB	H	HR	RBI	Avg
Home	2	1	4.23	2	27.2	LHB	74	13	2	9	.176
Road	0	4	4.87	0	20.1	RHB	93	24	4	19	.258
First Half	2	2	4.50	0	22.0	Sc Pos	53	13	2	20	.245
Scnd Half	0	3	4.50	2	26.0	Clutch	84	16	4	12	.190

1999 Season

Everyday Eddie Guardado once again did yeoman's work as the primary lefthanded option out of the Twins bullpen. In the past he was able to handle a heavy workload, but a strained ulnar ligament in his elbow landed him on the disabled list in May. His elbow flared up again in late July and August, reducing his control.

Pitching & Defense

Guardado uses a 92-MPH fastball that seems to get a bit faster every year. His curveball has sharp movement, and the combination of the two is very tough on lefthanders. Guardado holds his own against righthanders, but is vulnerable to the longball against them if he hangs his curve. Pressure situations don't scare him, and he has adjusted well to conditions at the Metrodome. Guardado has a quick delivery, which keeps runners in check even though he doesn't have much of a move to first base. He fields his position adequately.

2000 Outlook

One of the more unappreciated players in the American League, Guardado is highly valued by the Twins. He can pitch and Minnesota will hold onto him as long as possible.

Denny Hocking

Position: SS/2B/LF/RF/CF
Bats: B **Throws:** R
Ht: 5'10" **Wt:** 183

Opening Day Age: 29
Born: 4/2/70 in Torrance, CA
ML Seasons: 7

Overall Statistics

	G	AB	R	H	D	T	HR	RBI	SB	BB	SO	Avg	OBP	Slg
1999	136	386	47	103	18	2	7	41	11	22	54	.267	.307	.378
Career	445	1056	137	253	46	9	13	96	23	72	187	.240	.288	.337

1999 Situational Stats

	AB	H	HR	RBI	Avg		AB	H	HR	RBI	Avg
Home	199	44	2	26	.221	LHP	128	31	3	14	.242
Road	187	59	5	15	.316	RHP	258	72	4	27	.279
First Half	201	55	2	20	.274	Sc Pos	85	30	2	34	.353
Scnd Half	185	48	5	21	.259	Clutch	68	16	0	5	.235

1999 Season

Denny Hocking entered the year as the Twins' primary utility infielder. He saw action on a nearly regular basis, playing all four infield positions and even the outfield on occasion. He was used as a defensive sub and pinch-runner, and sometimes platooned with Todd Walker. The extra playing time seemed to agree with him, and Hocking had the best year of his career.

Hitting, Baserunning & Defense

Hocking has a compact swing that produces gap shots and line drives. He showed more pop last year than in the past, and appeared much more confident and comfortable at the plate. His lack of patience is still a problem, however. Blessed with very good speed, Hocking was more aggressive on the bases last year, but still needs work on reading pitchers. His fielding is both excellent and versatile. Though his best position is probably second base, he can handle any assignment well, making just three errors all year.

2000 Outlook

Twins manager Tom Kelly loves to have a flexible fielder on his bench. Expect to see Hocking on the Minnesota roster for years to come.

Mike Lincoln

Position: SP
Bats: R **Throws:** R
Ht: 6' 2" **Wt:** 211

Opening Day Age: 24
Born: 4/10/75 in
Carmichael, CA
ML Seasons: 1

Overall Statistics

	W	L	Pct.	ERA	G	GS	Sv	IP	H	BB	SO	HR	Ratio
1999	3	10	.231	6.84	18	15	0	76.1	102	26	27	11	1.68
Career	3	10	.231	6.84	18	15	0	76.1	102	26	27	11	1.68

1999 Situational Stats

	W	L	ERA	Sv	IP		AB	H	HR	RBI	Avg
Home	3	6	5.96	0	51.1	LHB	162	58	6	26	.358
Road	0	4	8.64	0	25.0	RHB	156	44	5	25	.282
First Half	3	9	6.35	0	73.2	Sc Pos	76	22	2	33	.289
Scnd Half	0	1	20.25	0	2.2	Clutch	5	2	0	1	.400

1999 Season

Lincoln led the Double-A Eastern League with 15 victories in 1998, then earned the fourth spot in Minnesota's rotation in spring training, more with his poise than his Grapefruit League performance. A sore shoulder bothered him in May, and he was sent down for good in July.

Pitching & Defense

In the minors, Lincoln succeeded by throwing three pitches for strikes and keeping them down, inducing groundballs. He continued to put the ball over the plate with the Twins, perhaps to his own detriment, as opponents hit .321 off him. Batters teed off, knowing he'd come at them with less-than-overpowering stuff. He has an 87-89 MPH fastball, a nice curveball and a changeup. He didn't make an error in 17 chances and is extremely tough to run on. Only three basestealers tested him, and two were gunned down.

2000 Outlook

Though he had bone spurs removed from his elbow in September, Lincoln should be ready to go in spring training. Whether he'll resurface in the big league rotation remains to be seen. He really needs to find a way to get lefthanders out after they batted .358 with a .605 slugging percentage against him during his rookie season.

Doug Mientkiewicz

Position: 1B
Bats: L **Throws:** R
Ht: 6' 2" **Wt:** 193

Opening Day Age: 25
Born: 6/19/74 in
Toledo, OH
ML Seasons: 2
Pronunciation:
mint-KAY-vich

Overall Statistics

	G	AB	R	H	D	T	HR	RBI	SB	BB	SO	Avg	OBP	Slg
1999	118	327	34	75	21	3	2	32	1	43	51	.229	.324	.330
Career	126	352	35	80	22	3	2	34	2	47	54	.227	.323	.324

1999 Situational Stats

	AB	H	HR	RBI	Avg		AB	H	HR	RBI	Avg
Home	158	35	0	17	.222	LHP	39	10	0	8	.256
Road	169	40	2	15	.237	RHP	288	65	2	24	.226
First Half	203	48	1	23	.236	Sc Pos	77	15	0	25	.195
Scnd Half	124	27	1	9	.218	Clutch	57	17	0	3	.298

1999 Season

Doug Mientkiewicz won the Twins' first-base job in spring training, pushing aside disappointing David Ortiz and tempting the club with Mark Grace-like potential. Mientkiewicz hit .280 in April with 10 doubles, and impressed the coaching staff with his fundamentals and fielding ability. After hitting a home run in early May, Mientkiewicz fell into bad habits in an attempt to hit for more power. The results were disastrous.

Hitting, Baserunning & Defense

When he was going good, Mientkiewicz showed a compact, line-drive swing that sprayed hits to all fields. When he tried to hit for power, his swing got long and he fell apart. He's patient at the plate and makes contact. He didn't steal much last year, but usually makes sound baserunning decisions and has decent speed. Mientkiewicz is a superb first baseman with fine range, a strong arm and very soft, quick hands.

2000 Outlook

The Twins were happy with Mientkiewicz' glove last year, but were dissatisfied with his bat. He enters spring training with a tenuous hold on a roster spot. First basemen don't play if they can't hit.

David Ortiz

Position: DH
Bats: L **Throws:** L
Ht: 6' 4" **Wt:** 230

Opening Day Age: 24
Born: 11/18/75 in Santo Domingo, Dominican Republic
ML Seasons: 3
Pronunciation: or-TEEZ

Overall Statistics

	G	AB	R	H	D	T	HR	RBI	SB	BB	SO	Avg	OBP	Slg
1999	10	20	1	0	0	0	0	0	0	5	12	.000	.200	.000
Career	111	347	58	93	23	0	10	52	1	46	103	.268	.358	.421

1999 Situational Stats

	AB	H	HR	RBI	Avg		AB	H	HR	RBI	Avg
Home	11	0	0	0	.000	LHP	2	0	0	0	.000
Road	9	0	0	0	.000	RHP	18	0	0	0	.000
First Half	0	0	0	0	-	Sc Pos	5	0	0	0	.000
Scnd Half	20	0	0	0	.000	Clutch	8	0	0	0	.000

1999 Season

David Ortiz lost Minnesota's first-base job in spring training when he was massively outplayed with the glove by Doug Mientkiewicz, and Ortiz hit so poorly that he couldn't even earn the DH role. He hit .315 with 30 homers in Triple-A, but hurt his knee in the Pacific Coast League playoffs and saw only limited action for the Twins in September.

Hitting, Baserunning & Defense

Ortiz is extremely strong and has well above-average pull power. He swings too hard at times, messing up his mechanics and lengthening his swing. Manager Tom Kelly was particularly concerned about Ortiz' sloppy defense in the spring. Ortiz never will be more than adequate with the glove and likely will be a full-time DH in the future. He's no threat to steal and can be careless on the bases.

2000 Outlook

Ortiz will head to spring training with a good chance to make the roster as the DH. He must prove that he can make adjustments at the plate in order to regain the confidence of the coaching staff.

Mike Trombley

Position: RP
Bats: R **Throws:** R
Ht: 6' 2" **Wt:** 204

Opening Day Age: 32
Born: 4/14/67 in Springfield, MA
ML Seasons: 8
Pronunciation: TROM-blee

Overall Statistics

	W	L	Pct.	ERA	G	GS	Sv	IP	H	BB	SO	HR	Ratio
1999	2	8	.200	4.33	75	0	24	87.1	93	28	82	15	1.39
Career	30	33	.476	4.46	360	36	34	641.2	658	243	525	88	1.40

1999 Situational Stats

	W	L	ERA	Sv	IP		AB	H	HR	RBI	Avg
Home	2	3	4.04	9	42.1	LHB	146	35	4	13	.240
Road	0	5	4.60	15	45.0	RHB	196	58	11	39	.296
First Half	2	5	3.38	13	58.2	Sc Pos	100	25	3	37	.250
Scnd Half	0	3	6.28	11	28.2	Clutch	185	47	7	30	.254

1999 Season

Mike Trombley entered the season as the Twins' primary setup man, then became the closer after the trade of Rick Aguilera to the Cubs. After taking the job, Trombley struggled in July, but generally proved he could handle the role, saving 24 games in 30 opportunities.

Pitching & Defense

Trombley's fastball reaches 90 MPH only occasionally, so it's his complementary pitches that make him effective. He has one of the best split-finger pitches in the American League, and also has an effective curve. Trombley does best when he keeps the ball down, and his control is usually sound. His arm is very durable. He doesn't have a strong move to first base, but is an excellent fielder who hasn't committed an error in four years.

2000 Outlook

The Twins were happy with the job Trombley did. A free agent, he wanted to return to Minnesota, but the club's financial situation precluded that when the Orioles offered him a three-year, $7.75 million contract. On most clubs he'd be a good setup man, but Trombley could emerge as a closer again in Baltimore's troubled bullpen.

Minnesota

Javier Valentin

Position: C
Bats: B **Throws:** R
Ht: 5'10" **Wt:** 192

Opening Day Age: 24
Born: 9/19/75 in
Manati, Puerto Rico
ML Seasons: 3
Pronunciation:
val-en-TEEN

Overall Statistics

	G	AB	R	H	D	T	HR	RBI	SB	BB	SO	Avg	OBP	Slg
1999	78	218	22	54	12	1	5	28	0	22	39	.248	.313	.381
Career	137	387	34	88	19	2	8	46	0	33	72	.227	.286	.349

1999 Situational Stats

	AB	H	HR	RBI	Avg		AB	H	HR	RBI	Avg
Home	114	34	2	17	.298	LHP	63	20	1	8	.317
Road	104	20	3	11	.192	RHP	155	34	4	20	.219
First Half	144	38	3	20	.264	Sc Pos	60	12	0	20	.200
Scnd Half	74	16	2	8	.216	Clutch	36	7	0	1	.194

1999 Season

In his second season as Terry Steinbach's caddy, Javier Valentin performed much better than he had in 1998. He played particularly well in June, seeing regular action when Steinbach was injured.

Hitting, Baserunning & Defense

A switch-hitter, Valentin does considerably better batting righthanded. He's more patient from the right side and is less prone to overswinging. A strong man, Valentin showed power in the low minors but hasn't shown much in the majors. He runs like a catcher and is no threat to steal. His defense is very good. Valentin has above-average arm strength and a quick release. He blocks balls well and moves quickly behind the plate. The Twins like the way he works with pitchers.

2000 Outlook

Once a highly regarded prospect, Valentin will get first crack at the starting job behind the plate. He'll have to hold off more powerful hitters from the minor leagues in the long run, and might end up as a career backup.

Bob Wells

Position: RP
Bats: R **Throws:** R
Ht: 6' 0" **Wt:** 200

Opening Day Age: 33
Born: 11/1/66 in
Yakima, WA
ML Seasons: 6

Overall Statistics

	W	L	Pct.	ERA	G	GS	Sv	IP	H	BB	SO	HR	Ratio
1999	8	3	.727	3.81	76	0	1	87.1	79	28	44	8	1.23
Career	30	15	.667	5.17	225	21	3	422.2	458	151	262	67	1.44

1999 Situational Stats

	W	L	ERA	Sv	IP		AB	H	HR	RBI	Avg
Home	4	2	2.91	1	52.2	LHB	121	30	3	15	.248
Road	4	1	5.19	0	34.2	RHB	202	49	5	34	.243
First Half	4	1	3.81	0	54.1	Sc Pos	111	22	4	40	.198
Scnd Half	4	2	3.82	1	33.0	Clutch	110	32	1	15	.291

1999 Season

Bob Wells pitched poorly with the Mariners in 1998, and his career looked over. Looking for cheap veteran help, the Twins gave him a chance as a mopup man. He pitched well, and by the end of the season was one of the mainstays of the bullpen. He tied for the American League lead in appearances in by far the best season of his career.

Pitching & Defense

Wells' overall stuff is average. His fastball has just adequate velocity and movement, but he throws it for strikes and mixes it effectively with his breaking ball and changeup. His control is good, which it has to be because he isn't overpowering. Wells isn't the best athlete in the world and won't win any awards for his glovework. He does have a quick delivery and holds runners well.

2000 Outlook

Minnesota had to be happy with the solid bargain-basement performance they got from Wells last year. It isn't the first time that manager Tom Kelly and pitching coach Dick Such have revived the career of a veteran pitcher. The Twins would like to have Wells back if they can afford him.

Other Minnesota Twins

Hector Carrasco (Pos: RHP, **Age**: 30)

	W	L	Pct.	ERA	G	GS	Sv	IP	H	BB	SO	HR	Ratio
1999	2	3	.400	4.96	39	0	1	49.0	48	18	35	3	1.35
Career	19	29	.396	3.99	333	0	13	414.2	389	211	321	24	1.45

A hard thrower often mentioned as a potential closer, Carrasco rarely has shown the command to succeed in the majors. A circulatory problem in his right arm last spring kept him from building on a good second half in '98. 2000 Outlook: B

Midre Cummings (Pos: RF, **Age**: 28, **Bats**: L)

	G	AB	R	H	D	T	HR	RBI	SB	BB	SO	Avg	OBP	Slg
1999	16	38	1	10	0	0	1	9	2	3	7	.263	.310	.342
Career	318	831	96	208	45	8	16	92	8	72	155	.250	.311	.381

Once a promising Twins prospect, Cummings disappointed three organizations before returning and doing his best hitting in years. Several outfield prospects cloud his future in Minnesota. 2000 Outlook: C

Cleatus Davidson (Pos: 2B, **Age**: 23, **Bats**: B)

	G	AB	R	H	D	T	HR	RBI	SB	BB	SO	Avg	OBP	Slg
1999	12	22	3	3	0	0	0	3	2	0	4	.136	.136	.136
Career	12	22	3	3	0	0	0	3	2	0	4	.136	.136	.136

Speed is his greatest asset, as Davidson hasn't hit for average or power as a minor leaguer. Nor has he reached base effectively. 2000 Outlook: C

Chris Latham (Pos: LF, **Age**: 26, **Bats**: B)

	G	AB	R	H	D	T	HR	RBI	SB	BB	SO	Avg	OBP	Slg
1999	14	22	1	2	0	0	0	3	0	0	13	.091	.083	.091
Career	63	138	19	21	2	0	1	9	4	13	57	.152	.222	.188

Latham's stats have improved steadily in four years at Triple-A Salt Lake, but he hasn't converted that progress into big league success. His one asset is speed, but his .222 OBP in the majors neutralizes his wheels. Minnesota traded him to Colorado for minor league righthander Scott Randall in December. 2000 Outlook: C

Travis Miller (Pos: LHP, **Age**: 27)

	W	L	Pct.	ERA	G	GS	Sv	IP	H	BB	SO	HR	Ratio
1999	2	2	.500	2.72	52	0	0	49.2	55	16	40	3	1.43
Career	4	11	.267	5.67	86	14	0	147.2	189	59	104	18	1.68

Miller pitched decently in 1998, and he continued to improve as a situational reliever last summer. He was a bit lucky stranding runners, but he pitched well enough to keep his job. 2000 Outlook: B

Dan Perkins (Pos: RHP, **Age**: 25)

	W	L	Pct.	ERA	G	GS	Sv	IP	H	BB	SO	HR	Ratio
1999	1	7	.125	6.54	29	12	0	86.2	117	43	44	14	1.85
Career	1	7	.125	6.54	29	12	0	86.2	117	43	44	14	1.85

Perkins improved dramatically in his second seasons at high Class-A and Double-A, but he hardly had any Triple-A experience before arriving in Minnesota in 1999. He probably should be at Triple-A Salt Lake this year. 2000 Outlook: C

Rob Radlosky (Pos: RHP, **Age**: 26)

	W	L	Pct.	ERA	G	GS	Sv	IP	H	BB	SO	HR	Ratio
1999	0	1	.000	12.46	7	0	0	8.2	15	4	3	7	2.19
Career	0	1	.000	12.46	7	0	0	8.2	15	4	3	7	2.19

Radlosky pitched as well at Triple-A Salt Lake as any pitcher in the system. That didn't translate into success during a midseason callup, but Twins fans will see more of Radlosky before long. 2000 Outlook: B

Gary Rath (Pos: LHP, **Age**: 27)

	W	L	Pct.	ERA	G	GS	Sv	IP	H	BB	SO	HR	Ratio
1999	0	1	.000	11.57	5	1	0	4.2	6	5	1	1	2.36
Career	0	1	.000	11.25	8	1	0	8.0	9	7	5	2	2.00

Rath hasn't recorded a strong season in five years of Triple-A ball, but the Twins gave him an audition in June after Rick Aguilera was traded. It's hard to imagine him succeeding if he can't do it at Triple-A. 2000 Outlook: C

Mark Redman (Pos: LHP, **Age**: 26)

	W	L	Pct.	ERA	G	GS	Sv	IP	H	BB	SO	HR	Ratio
1999	1	0	1.000	8.53	5	1	0	12.2	17	7	11	3	1.89
Career	1	0	1.000	8.53	5	1	0	12.2	17	7	11	3	1.89

Despite a 5.05 ERA, Redman was the winningest pitcher at Triple-A Salt Lake in 1999. But major league clubs had their way with him in four of five major league appearances. 2000 Outlook: C

Benj Sampson (Pos: LHP, **Age**: 24)

	W	L	Pct.	ERA	G	GS	Sv	IP	H	BB	SO	HR	Ratio
1999	3	2	.600	8.11	30	4	0	71.0	107	34	56	17	1.99
Career	4	2	.667	6.83	35	6	0	88.1	117	40	72	17	1.78

Sampson was one of a number of young kids who wasn't ready to pitch in Minnesota but did. He pitched better in a 1998 September callup than he had in Triple-A, but that didn't carry over last year. 2000 Outlook: C

Terry Steinbach (Pos: C, **Age**: 38, **Bats**: R)

	G	AB	R	H	D	T	HR	RBI	SB	BB	SO	Avg	OBP	Slg
1999	101	338	35	96	16	4	4	42	2	38	54	.284	.358	.391
Career	1546	5369	638	1453	273	21	162	745	23	418	938	.271	.326	.420

After a 14-year career that included a World Series title in Oakland and three All-Star Game selections, Steinbach retired in November. 2000 Outlook: D

Minnesota Twins Minor League Prospects

Organization Overview:

The Twins may be the poster boys for the struggles of small-revenue teams, suffering through seven consecutive losing seasons, but they have moved plenty of players through their system to Minnesota. Granted, they've had more openings for youngsters than richer clubs, but the Twins do deserve credit for establishing Chad Allen, Cristian Guzman, Torii Hunter, Jacque Jones, Corey Koskie, Joe Mays, Eric Milton and Todd Walker as regulars in the lineup or rotation over the last two years. They consistently draft well even if they can't always sign their picks, and may have landed a banner crop in 1997 with prospects Michael Cuddyer, Matthew LeCroy, Mike Restovich and late-round find J.C. Romero.

Michael Cuddyer

Position: 3B
Bats: R **Throws:** R
Ht: 6' 2" **Wt:** 202

Opening Day Age: 21
Born: 3/27/79 in Norfolk, VA

Recent Statistics

		G	AB	R	H	D	T	HR	RBI	SB	BB	SO	Avg
1998 A Fort Wayne		129	497	82	137	37	7	12	81	16	61	107	.276
1999 A Fort Myers		130	466	87	139	24	4	16	82	14	76	91	.298

A year after failing to sign 1996 first-round pick Travis Lee, the Twins almost lost out on Cuddyer, their 1997 first-rounder, before finally landing him for $1.85 million. He made his pro debut at shortstop in 1998 before moving to the hot corner last year, when he earned recognition as the best defensive third baseman in the high Class-A Florida State League. Even better, he's an extremely advanced hitter for his age. His power, ability to hit for average, willingness to take a walk, strong arm and enthusiasm remind Minnesota of Scott Rolen. Cuddyer is moving quickly through the minors and could reach the Twin Cities in the second half of 2001.

Matthew LeCroy

Position: C
Bats: R **Throws:** R
Ht: 6' 2" **Wt:** 225

Opening Day Age: 24
Born: 12/13/75 in Belton, SC

Recent Statistics

		G	AB	R	H	D	T	HR	RBI	SB	BB	SO	Avg
1998 A Fort Wayne		64	225	33	62	17	1	9	40	0	34	45	.276
1998 A Fort Myers		51	200	32	61	9	1	12	51	2	21	35	.305
1998 AAA Salt Lake		3	13	2	4	1	0	2	4	0	0	7	.308
1999 A Fort Myers		89	333	54	93	20	1	20	69	0	42	51	.279
1999 AAA Salt Lake		29	119	23	36	4	1	10	30	0	5	22	.303

Power always has been the calling card for LeCroy, who led all minor league catchers with 30 homers in 1999. One of four 1996 U.S. Olympians drafted by the Twins, he was a supplemental first-round pick in 1997. He'll take a walk and makes good contract for a slugger, so he should hit for a decent average as well. Whether he'll be an offensive force at catcher or merely a productive first baseman or DH remains to be seen. LeCroy is making steady progress behind the plate and has a solid arm, but he needs to improve his footwork, release and receiving skills. He'll spend most of this season in Triple-A trying to do just that.

Kyle Lohse

Position: P
Bats: R **Throws:** R
Ht: 6' 2" **Wt:** 190

Opening Day Age: 21
Born: 10/4/78 in Chico, CA

Recent Statistics

		W	L	ERA	G	GS	Sv	IP	H	R	BB	SO	HR
1998 A Rockford		13	8	3.22	28	26	0	170.2	158	76	45	121	8
1999 A Daytona		5	3	2.89	9	9	0	53.0	48	21	16	41	4
1999 A Fort Myers		2	3	5.18	7	7	0	41.2	47	28	9	33	5
1999 AA New Britain		3	4	5.89	11	11	0	70.1	87	49	23	41	9

Acquired in the Rick Aguilera trade with the Cubs, Lohse has a higher ceiling than Jason Ryan, who accompanied him in the deal. A 29th-round draft-and-follow who signed in 1997 after a year at Butte (Calif.) Junior College, Lohse features a hard slider and also throws an average fastball and a straight changeup. He has an idea of how to pitch, throwing strikes to both sides of the plate. He wasn't quite ready for Double-A at age 20 last season, so he'll have to prove himself at that level this year. Minnesota's rotation is in shambles, and Lohse might be able to help in 2001.

Michael Restovich

Position: OF
Bats: R **Throws:** R
Ht: 6' 4" **Wt:** 233

Opening Day Age: 21
Born: 1/3/79 in Rochester, MN

Recent Statistics

		G	AB	R	H	D	T	HR	RBI	SB	BB	SO	Avg
1998 R Elizabethtn		65	242	68	86	20	1	13	64	5	54	58	.355
1998 A Fort Wayne		11	45	9	20	5	2	0	6	0	4	12	.444
1999 A Quad City		131	493	91	154	30	6	19	107	7	74	100	.312

The Twins probably found the future heart of their order when they took Michael Cuddyer, Matthew LeCroy and Restovich with their first three draft picks in 1997. A second-round selection, Restovich is the likely cleanup hitter of the group. He was named MVP of the Rookie-level Appalachian League in his pro debut in 1998, then slugged his way through the Class-A Midwest League last year. Like Cuddyer, he already has established that he can hit for power and average while drawing a healthy amount of walks. Restovich runs OK on the bases, though he lumbers a little bit in right field after making the conversion from third base. The Twins aren't pushing him quite as quickly as Cuddyer, so Restovich's ETA is 2002.

Juan Rincon

Position: P
Bats: R **Throws:** R
Ht: 5' 11" **Wt:** 187

Opening Day Age: 21
Born: 1/23/79 in
Maracaibo, Venezuela

Recent Statistics

	W	L	ERA	G	GS	Sv	IP	H	R	BB	SO	HR
1998 A Fort Wayne	6	4	3.83	37	13	6	96.1	84	51	54	74	6
1999 A Quad City	14	8	2.92	28	28	0	163.1	146	67	66	153	8

The Twins haven't mined Latin America as profitably as other teams. The only Latins with regular roles on their 1999 club, Hector Carrasco and Cristian Guzman, were signed by the Mets and Yankees, respectively. However, Minnesota may have a gem in Rincon, a Venezuelan who led the Class-A Midwest League in strikeouts last year, also ranking second in wins and third in ERA. For now he's purely a power guy, throwing a 94-MPH fastball and hard curveball. As he moves up the ladder, he'll need to develop his changeup and command. No Twins pitching prospect has as high a ceiling.

Luis Rivas

Position: SS
Bats: R **Throws:** R
Ht: 5' 10" **Wt:** 175

Opening Day Age: 20
Born: 8/30/79 in La
Guaira, Venezuela

Recent Statistics

	G	AB	R	H	D	T	HR	RBI	SB	BB	SO	Avg
1998 A Fort Myers	126	463	58	130	21	5	4	51	34	14	75	.281
1999 AA New Britain	132	527	78	134	30	7	7	49	31	41	92	.254
1999 MLE	132	513	64	120	28	5	5	40	22	29	100	.234

Rivas is another Venezuelan who may reverse the Twins' trend of not developing Latin American prospects. Since making his pro debut at age 16, he has been the youngest regular in his league three times in four seasons, including 1999, when he played in the Double-A Eastern League at age 19. His best tool is his speed, which gives him range at shortstop and makes him a basestealing threat. He also has a strong arm. Because he's been rushed, he hasn't hit much or drawn many walks, but Minnesota projects him as a future .270 hitter. Rivas would do well to repeat Double-A and focus on his hitting, and he's at least two years away.

J.C. Romero

Position: P
Bats: B **Throws:** L
Ht: 5' 11" **Wt:** 193

Opening Day Age: 23
Born: 6/4/76 in Rio
Piedras, Puerto Rico

Recent Statistics

	W	L	ERA	G	GS	Sv	IP	H	R	BB	SO	HR
1999 AA New Britain	4	4	3.40	36	1	7	53.0	51	25	34	53	6
1999 AAA Salt Lake	4	1	3.20	15	0	1	19.2	18	11	14	20	1
1999 AL Minnesota	0	0	3.72	5	0	0	9.2	13	4	0	4	0

The biggest surprise to make the Pan American Games team that qualified the United States for the 2000 Olympics, Romero earned a win against powerful Cuba during the tournament. A 21st-round pick in 1997, he has very good stuff for a lefthander. With a fastball that can reach 92-93 MPH and a hard slider, he has averaged more than a strikeout per inning as a pro. The Twins aren't sure whether he'll eventually be a starter, closer or setup man. Romero likely will start 2000 in Triple-A and could push for a second-half promotion.

Jason Ryan

Position: P
Bats: B **Throws:** R
Ht: 6' 3" **Wt:** 185

Opening Day Age: 24
Born: 1/23/76 in Long
Branch, NJ

Recent Statistics

	W	L	ERA	G	GS	Sv	IP	H	R	BB	SO	HR
1999 AA West Tenn	5	0	1.41	8	7	0	44.2	29	12	15	53	1
1999 AA New Britain	2	4	4.80	8	8	0	50.2	48	29	24	42	6
1999 AAA Salt Lake	4	4	5.13	9	9	0	54.1	57	36	24	34	8
1999 AL Minnesota	1	4	4.87	8	8	0	40.2	46	23	17	15	9

A 1994 ninth-round pick by the Cubs, Ryan reached Double-A at age 18 in his debut and pitched well in high Class-A the following year, then struggled for the next three seasons. He stopped hanging pitches in the strike zone and finally rebounded in 1999, which earned him a ticket to Minnesota in the Rick Aguilera trade. Ryan's forte is throwing four pitches (fastball, curveball, slider, changeup) for strikes. When he does that he succeeds, though his margin for error is slight. He finished last season by making eight starts for the Twins and could make their thin rotation in 2000.

Others to Watch

Outfielder **B.J. Garbe** (19) was rated the best athlete and best pure hitter among high school prospects by *Baseball America* before the Twins selected him fifth overall in the 1999 draft. He's a legit five-tool player who also showed a 92-94 MPH fastball as a pitcher. . . In this decade, just nine players had a 20-homer season at Double-A New Britain, a notorious pitchers' park. Six of them have reached the majors. First basemen **Steve Hacker** (25) and **Tommy Peterman** (24) became the eighth and ninth last year, though they offer little more than power. . . Outfielder **Bobby Kielty** (23) wasn't drafted in 1998, then went out and led the prestigious Cape Cod League in hitting, earning him a $500,000 bonus to sign with the Twins. A pulled hamstring and allergies to oak pollen cut short his debut in 1999, but he did show power from both sides of the plate while batting .294-13-43 in 69 games at Class-A Quad City. . . Acquired in the 1998 Greg Swindell trade with Boston, righthander **Matt Kinney** (23) missed much of last season after having bone chips removed from his elbow. When healthy, he can hit 93-94 MPH and has a tough slider. . . **A.J. Pierzynski** (23) may be the best all-around catching prospect in the system, but he didn't help his cause by slumping offensively and defensively in 1999. The Twins have other backstop options, so he needs to turn himself around quickly. . . Second baseman **Ruben Salazar** (22) was a bit old for the Rookie-level Appalachian League, but his .401 average was certainly eye-catching and earned him league MVP honors.

Yankee Stadium

Offense

There was a time when Yankee Stadium's right-field dimensions made it a launching pad for lefthanded hitters. After the construction of so many hitter-friendly ballparks, the Stadium's right-field distances are the norm. The left-center dimensions—399 to the alley, a.k.a. Death Valley—are what make the Stadium atypical. It's now the best pitchers' park in the American League, suppressing scoring more than any other over the last three seasons. During the same period, only Fenway Park and SkyDome have been stingier in terms of homers.

Defense

The infield grass is cut taller than at most parks, which slows balls down and enables infielders to get to grounders that might shoot through to the outfield elsewhere. It pays to play the better corner outfielder in left field rather than right, because there's so much ground out there to patrol.

Who It Helps The Most

Generally speaking, lefthanded hitters and pitchers fare better at Yankee Stadium than righties do. Lefty slugger Darryl Strawberry, as much because of the way he feeds off the New York crowds as the dimensions being suited to his swing, consistently performs better at Yankee Stadium than on the road. The same is true of southpaw starter Andy Pettitte. Righty Roger Clemens, who always has liked the atmosphere at Yankee Stadium, went 9-5, 3.56 in the Bronx last year, compared to 5-5, 6.20 away from home.

Who It Hurts The Most

For reasons that aren't apparent, first baseman Tino Martinez always has hit with more power on the road than at Yankee Stadium. He has hit more road homers in each of his four seasons with the Yankees, and 79 of his 125 homers have come away from the Bronx during that time.

Rookies & Newcomers

Rookie lefthander Ed Yarnall will surrender a high percentage of flyballs because he throws high fastballs. Death Valley will help him out considerably.

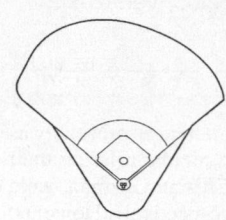

Dimensions: LF-318, LCF-399, CF-408, RCF-385, RF-314

Capacity: 57,545

Elevation: 55 feet

Surface: Grass

Foul Territory: Average

Park Factors

1999 Season

| | Home Games | | | Away Games | | | |
	Yankees	Opp	Total	Yankees	Opp	Total	Index
G	72	72	144	72	72	144	—
Avg	.271	.239	.255	.294	.267	.281	91
AB	2388	2473	4861	2578	2420	4998	97
R	362	280	642	437	353	790	81
H	647	592	1239	759	645	1404	88
2B	118	114	232	151	117	268	89
3B	12	10	22	20	16	36	63
HR	76	63	139	95	75	170	84
BB	325	259	584	309	249	558	108
SO	451	509	960	431	492	923	107
E	56	40	96	45	42	87	110
E-Infield	44	35	79	36	33	69	114
LHB-Avg	.259	.242	.250	.309	.268	.289	87
LHB-HR	37	33	70	50	41	91	79
RHB-Avg	.282	.237	.259	.282	.265	.274	94
RHB-HR	39	30	69	45	34	79	89

1997-1999

| | Home Games | | | Away Games | | | |
	Yankees	Opp	Total	Yankees	Opp	Total	Index
G	215	215	430	222	222	444	—
Avg	.287	.247	.266	.290	.265	.278	96
AB	7240	7463	14703	8049	7511	15560	98
R	1164	868	2032	1355	1001	2356	89
H	2075	1841	3916	2335	1987	4322	94
2B	390	350	740	450	363	813	96
3B	36	30	66	46	39	85	82
HR	231	192	423	281	224	505	89
BB	895	671	1566	944	746	1690	98
SO	1253	1551	2804	1397	1460	2857	104
E	143	131	274	137	176	313	90
E-Infield	119	116	235	109	145	254	96
LHB-Avg	.283	.250	.267	.296	.275	.287	93
LHB-HR	119	90	209	154	107	261	86
RHB-Avg	.290	.245	.266	.285	.257	.271	98
RHB-HR	112	102	214	127	117	244	92

1999 Rankings (American League)

- Highest strikeout factor
- Second-highest walk factor
- Second-highest infield-error factor
- Lowest batting-average factor
- Lowest run factor
- Lowest hit factor
- Lowest LHB batting-average factor
- Second-lowest triple factor
- Second-lowest home-run factor
- Third-lowest double factor
- Third-lowest LHB home-run factor
- Third-lowest RHB batting-average factor

Joe Torre

1999 Season

Manager Joe Torre was diagnosed with prostate cancer on March 10. He underwent surgery March 18 and was back in the dugout exactly two months later, making his return at Fenway Park. When Torre returned to the Yankees, so did tranquility. There were no more controversies with owner George Steinbrenner. The Yankees finished the season 98-64, 16 games worse than in 1998. But they were even better than 1998 during the postseason, going 11-1 and suffering their lone loss at the hands of Cy Young Award winner Pedro Martinez.

Offense

Torre prefers the hit-and-run or the stolen base to giving up an out with a bunt. He encourages his hitters to take a patient approach at the plate, work pitchers for deep counts and wear out the starters so the bullpens can be reached sooner. As a rule, Torre likes to stay with a set lineup rather than move hitters up and down in the order because of platoon matchups. Paul O'Neill batted .190 against lefties but still batted third against all types of pitching for most of the year.

Pitching & Defense

Unless he sees a starter losing his stuff, Torre generally lets him work his way out of trouble. Relievers like working for him because he defines their roles and doesn't get them up and down several times without bringing them into the game. He's very careful not to overwork pitchers and is liberal with extra rest when he thinks one of his hurlers needs it.

2000 Outlook

Steinbrenner routinely refers to Torre as the best manager he ever has had. Torre's players would have difficulty imagining a better one. He treats them like adults and is there for them when they need a father figure. Troubled Darryl Strawberry, welcomed back to the team by Torre, broke down and cried when he tried to thank Torre at the Yankees' victory parade.

Born: 7/18/40 in Brooklyn, NY

Playing Experience: 1960-1977, Atl, StL, NYM

Managerial Experience: 18 seasons

Pronunciation: TOAR-ee

Manager Statistics

Year	Team, Lg	W	L	Pct	GB	Finish
1999	New York, AL	77	49	.611	—	1st East
18 Seasons		1273	1236	.507	—	—

1999 Starting Pitchers by Days Rest

	<=3	4	5	6+
Yankees Starts	0	64	46	14
Yankees ERA	0.00	4.92	3.44	4.85
AL Avg Starts	2	82	47	21
AL ERA	6.83	4.98	4.72	5.62

1999 Situational Stats

	Joe Torre*	AL Average
Hit & Run Success %	36.6	35.3
Stolen Base Success %	64.3	68.0
Platoon Pct.	63.0	56.7
Defensive Subs	10	22
High-Pitch Outings	26	15
Quick/Slow Hooks	10/6	18/18
Sacrifice Attempts	31	52

* Torre managed the Yankees for 126 games

1999 Rankings (American League)

- 1st in starts with over 120 pitches (26)
- 3rd in steals of home plate (1)

Scott Brosius

1999 Season

The 1998 World Series MVP, Scott Brosius understandably had difficulty staying 100 percent focused on baseball in 1999. His father died in September after a prolonged illness that had Brosius leaving the team to visit him. His production at the plate slipped, but he remained a solid contributor to the Yankees, particularly with the glove.

Hitting

Brosius so often seems to be involved in late-inning heroics because he crushes fastballs. The better the fastball, the better he hits it, which is why he does so well against one-pitch closers. He remains a sucker for sliders that drift way off the plate and toward the dirt. He also has trouble making contact against lefties. He batted .194 against southpaws in 1999, though 10 of his 21 hits were homers.

Baserunning & Defense

An instinctive baserunner with average speed, Brosius will steal a base if pitchers don't keep him honest. He deservedly won his first Gold Glove in 1999. He has terrific range in both directions and can make strong, accurate throws even when off balance and rushed. Nobody is quicker on a slow roller than Brosius, who has that play down to an art form.

2000 Outlook

Brosius might never have another season like the one he had in 1998, which earned him a three-year, $15.75 million contract from the Yankees. But they don't need him to have another year like that. They would settle for something between his efforts the last two seasons. He stands a good chance of finishing his contract as the Yankees' regular third baseman, but after that he likely will play elsewhere as New York looks to get younger. The Yankees have several infield prospects on the way.

Position: 3B
Bats: R **Throws:** R
Ht: 6' 1" **Wt:** 202

Opening Day Age: 33
Born: 8/15/66 in Hillsboro, OR
ML Seasons: 9
Pronunciation: BRO-shus

Overall Statistics

	G	AB	R	H	D	T	HR	RBI	SB	BB	SO	Avg	OBP	Slg
1999	133	473	64	117	26	1	17	71	9	39	74	.247	.307	.414
Career	891	2991	430	770	155	6	112	418	54	269	543	.257	.324	.426

Where He Hits the Ball

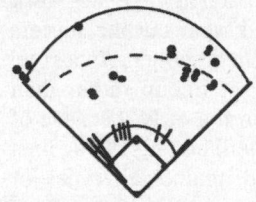
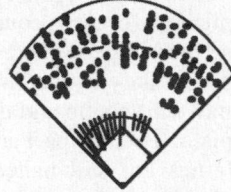

Vs. LHP   **Vs. RHP**

1999 Situational Stats

	AB	H	HR	RBI	Avg		AB	H	HR	RBI	Avg
Home	215	51	4	26	.237	LHP	108	21	10	23	.194
Road	258	66	13	45	.256	RHP	365	96	7	48	.263
First Half	261	67	9	36	.257	Sc Pos	117	33	5	55	.282
Scnd Half	212	50	8	35	.236	Clutch	64	10	1	9	.156

1999 Rankings (American League)

- 1st in fielding percentage at third base (.962)
- 4th in lowest batting average
- 5th in lowest batting average in the clutch
- 6th in lowest on-base percentage and lowest groundball/flyball ratio (0.8)
- 7th in sacrifice flies (9)
- 8th in errors at third base (13)
- 10th in lowest slugging percentage vs. righthanded pitchers (.389) and lowest batting average on the road
- Led AL third basemen in steals of third (2), sacrifice flies (9) and stolen bases

Roger Clemens

1999 Season

Roger Clemens joined New York in spring training in a blockbuster trade with Toronto that cost the Yankees Homer Bush, Graeme Lloyd and David Wells. Coming off back-to-back Cy Young Awards, Clemens was merely mediocre, even while running his American League-record winning streak to 20. He even spent time on the disabled list with a hamstring strain. His age, injury and the pressure of pitching in New York all were responsible for his struggles. Clemens did pitch brilliantly in winning the World Series clincher against the Braves, but that couldn't erase all the frustration from an otherwise-disappointing first year in pinstripes.

Pitching

Clemens continued to send radar guns up to 95 MPH, but he didn't locate any of his pitches well. He tended to pitch defensively, showing too much respect for hitters. Instead of challenging them with hard stuff, Clemens too often nibbled at the corners. As a result, he fell behind hitters, ran deep counts and ran out of gas. His splitter didn't have the same nasty, late drop to it that it had in the past.

Defense

Though nicknamed The Rocket, Clemens isn't particularly quick to the plate and he does only an OK job of holding runners. Though he isn't the most nimble pitcher, he finishes his delivery in correct fielding position and does a solid job defensively.

2000 Outlook

Clemens tried so hard to impress everyone in his first season with the Yankees that he ended up thinking too much on the mound. He fell away from an aggressive gameplan and let things snowball when he didn't get off to a strong start. Expectations of his own and others won't be as high in his second season in the Bronx. He won't be counted on as the ace. History suggests that when the pressure eases, Clemens responds with better performances.

Position: SP
Bats: R **Throws:** R
Ht: 6' 4" **Wt:** 230

Opening Day Age: 37
Born: 8/4/62 in Dayton, OH
ML Seasons: 16
Nickname: Rocket

Overall Statistics

	W	L	Pct.	ERA	G	GS	Sv	IP	H	BB	SO	HR	Ratio
1999	14	10	.583	4.60	30	30	0	187.2	185	90	163	20	1.47
Career	247	134	.648	3.04	480	479	0	3462.1	2917	1102	3316	234	1.16

How Often He Throws Strikes

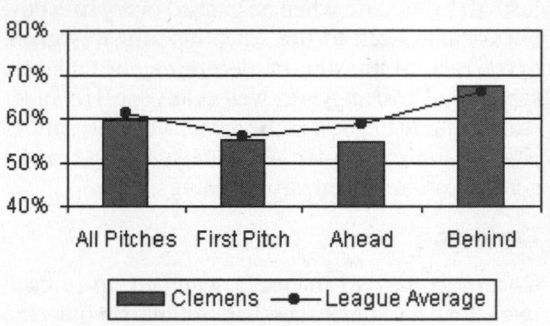

1999 Situational Stats

	W	L	ERA	Sv	IP		AB	H	HR	RBI	Avg
Home	9	5	3.56	0	113.2	LHB	365	96	6	38	.263
Road	5	5	6.20	0	74.0	RHB	343	89	14	52	.259
First Half	8	3	4.70	0	88.0	Sc Pos	175	44	4	66	.251
Scnd Half	6	7	4.52	0	99.2	Clutch	55	15	0	3	.273

1999 Rankings (American League)

- 2nd in most pitches thrown per batter (4.05) and most walks per nine innings (4.3)
- 5th in walks allowed, most strikeouts per nine innings (7.8) and runners caught stealing (11)
- 6th in lowest slugging percentage allowed (.394) and ERA at home
- 8th in fewest home runs allowed per nine innings (.96) and highest on-base percentage allowed (.350)
- 9th in strikeouts and lowest batting average allowed (.261)
- 10th in least run support per nine innings (4.9)
- Led the Yankees in walks allowed, wild pitches (8), lowest stolen-base percentage allowed (60.7) and runners caught stealing (11)

New York (AL)

David Cone

1999 Season

On an afternoon that started with Don Larsen throwing out the ceremonial first pitch to Yogi Berra on Yogi Berra Day, David Cone pitched the third perfect game in Yankees history. The whole season wasn't as storybook as that day, however. Cone showed signs of aging but remained extremely effective when given extra rest. A big-game pitcher who is at his best in the clutch, Cone again came through for the Yankees in the postseason.

Pitching

Cone throws two different fastballs, two curveballs, a slider, a splitter and a cutter. His 92-MPH fastball lost its life when he pitched every fifth day, but it came back to life when his arm was given extra rest. A master of deception, he changes speeds and arm angles as well as anyone. His slider still is among the best in the game, while his splitter is another big out pitch. When rested, Cone can be counted on for seven strong innings.

Defense

Cone becomes so intensely wrapped up in each pitch that he sometimes has trouble flipping the switch to defense after the pitch has been hit. He tends to rush when fielding groundballs. Cone also gets so locked in on hitters that he can lose track of baserunners. He throws over to first more often than in the past, but he's not difficult to steal against.

2000 Outlook

Every year there are forecasts that Cone's right arm will fall off, but when the 1999 season ended he said he felt much better than he had a year ago at the same time. Adamant in his belief that he deserved a two-year contract but wanting to stay with the Yankees, Cone re-signed as a free agent for one year and $12 million. When he's healthy, there aren't many pitchers who rank ahead of him, particularly in big games.

Position: SP
Bats: L **Throws:** R
Ht: 6' 1" **Wt:** 190

Opening Day Age: 37
Born: 1/2/63 in Kansas City, MO
ML Seasons: 14

Overall Statistics

	W	L	Pct.	ERA	G	GS	Sv	IP	H	BB	SO	HR	Ratio
1999	12	9	.571	3.44	31	31	0	193.1	164	90	177	21	1.31
Career	180	102	.638	3.19	390	361	1	2590.0	2144	985	2420	212	1.21

How Often He Throws Strikes

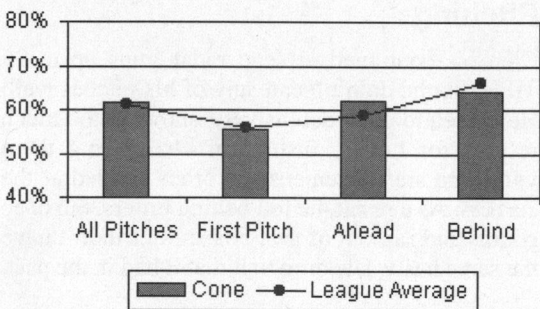

Cone ——— League Average

1999 Situational Stats

	W	L	ERA	Sv	IP		AB	H	HR	RBI	Avg
Home	6	5	1.90	0	104.0	LHB	360	88	15	46	.244
Road	6	4	5.24	0	89.1	RHB	355	76	6	34	.214
First Half	9	4	2.86	0	113.1	Sc Pos	171	34	5	57	.199
Scnd Half	3	5	4.28	0	80.0	Clutch	26	7	1	3	.269

1999 Rankings (American League)

- 1st in ERA at home and lowest batting average allowed with runners in scoring position
- 2nd in ERA, lowest batting average allowed (.229) and lowest slugging percentage allowed (.375)
- 3rd in most strikeouts per nine innings (8.2), lowest batting average allowed vs. righthanded batters and most walks per nine innings (4.2)
- Led the Yankees in ERA, walks allowed, hit batsmen (11), strikeouts, stolen bases allowed (22), lowest batting average allowed (.229), lowest slugging percentage allowed (.375), most strikeouts per nine innings (8.2), ERA at home and lowest batting average allowed vs. lefthanded batters

Orlando Hernandez

1999 Season

In his first full season in the big leagues, Orlando Hernandez was the best pitcher on the Yankees. A great big-game pitcher, El Duque was one of the top starters in the American League and the biggest bargain in baseball. Manager Joe Torre made him the Game 1 starter in the playoffs and Hernandez responded to that responsibility with dominance. He's Exhibit A in building the case that smart decisions, not big-market advantages, are most responsible for New York winning three World Series in four years. Hernandez has two years remaining on a four-year, $6.6 million contract. A player of his abilities would command $10 million to $12 million annually in today's free-agent market.

Pitching

Hernandez evokes memories of Hall of Fame pitcher Juan Marichal because he has command of a wide variety of pitches that he can deliver at different speeds from many different arm slots. He can drop down to sidearm to throw wicked sliders and curveballs. His fastball has excellent movement, and when it's thrown at 88 MPH, it appears to the hitters to be more like 95 MPH because he hides the ball so well with his high leg kick. Because he uses so many different arm slots, Hernandez' mechanical flaws can be difficult to detect and can lead to slumps. When his delivery is off kilter, his pitches flatten out and can result in home runs.

Defense

Extremely athletic, Hernandez is so quick and agile that he ought to be considered for the Gold Glove. He instinctively makes the right plays defensively and his mind is as quick as his reflexes. He also does a decent job of holding runners.

2000 Outlook

On a staff that had two former Cy Young Award winners (Roger Clemens, David Cone) and one former Cy Young Award runner-up (Andy Pettitte), Hernandez established himself as the bona fide ace. A 20-win campaign is well within his capabilities, as is a Cy Young Award.

Position: SP
Bats: R **Throws:** R
Ht: 6' 2" **Wt:** 210

Opening Day Age: 34
Born: 10/11/65 in Villa Clara, Cuba
ML Seasons: 2
Pronunciation: her-NAN-dezz
Nickname: El Duque

New York (AL)

Overall Statistics

	W	L	Pct.	ERA	G	GS	Sv	IP	H	BB	SO	HR	Ratio
1999	17	9	.654	4.12	33	33	0	214.1	187	87	157	24	1.28
Career	29	13	.690	3.72	54	54	0	355.1	300	139	288	35	1.24

How Often He Throws Strikes

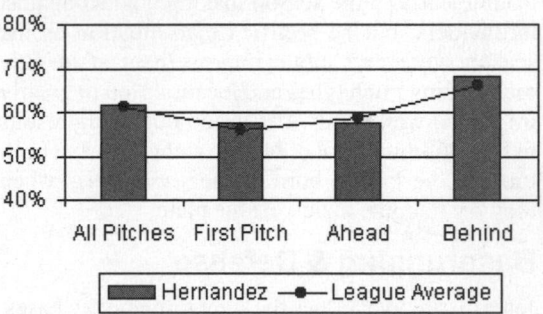

Hernandez —●— League Average

1999 Situational Stats

	W	L	ERA	Sv	IP		AB	H	HR	RBI	Avg
Home	7	4	3.96	0	97.2	LHB	432	118	15	63	.273
Road	10	5	4.24	0	116.2	RHB	369	69	9	29	.187
First Half	10	6	3.95	0	118.1	Sc Pos	176	45	4	65	.256
Scnd Half	7	3	4.31	0	96.0	Clutch	51	11	0	4	.216

1999 Rankings (American League)

- 2nd in lowest batting average allowed vs. righthanded batters
- 3rd in lowest batting average allowed (.233), lowest groundball/flyball ratio allowed (0.8) and fewest GDPs induced per nine innings (0.5)
- 4th in lowest on-base percentage allowed (.311)
- 5th in wins, pitches thrown (3,548) and lowest slugging percentage allowed (.392)
- Led the Yankees in wins, complete games (2), innings pitched, batters faced (910), pitches thrown (3,548), winning percentage, lowest on-base percentage allowed (.311), fewest baserunners allowed per nine innings (11.8), ERA on the road, lowest batting average allowed vs. righthanded batters and games started

Derek Jeter

1999 Season

Derek Jeter has the look of a perennial MVP candidate. He gets a little better every year, and 1999 was no exception. He was in the race for the batting title, showed solid power growth and continued to improve in all areas, thanks largely to an all-business attitude. His effort, both physically and mentally, set a professional tone for others with less ability to follow.

Hitting

Jeter's development as a hitter was evident in every statistical area. He made significant strides in batting average, slugging percentage and on-base percentage. Jeter still strikes out too often and had trouble early in the season making contact against lefthanders, but he rectified that situation as the season wore on. Subtle improvement at quickly recognizing pitch types and locations led to greatly improved walk totals. His inside-out swing results in him dumping a lot of balls to right field, but he'll turn on the ball to burn pitchers who miss when they try to come inside off the plate.

Baserunning & Defense

Jeter instinctively does the right thing on the bases. His effort is second to none, as he never assumes an out, always goes full blast down the line and forever looks to take the extra base. He does an excellent job at keeping abreast of the strength and accuracy of outfielders' arms. Defensively, he has excellent range, an arm that is as accurate as it is strong and the mind for positioning the hitters. Jeter makes the play in the hole as well as anybody and studies baserunners closely enough to know when to rush his throws and when to take his time.

2000 Outlook

The Yankees wouldn't trade Jeter straight up for any player in baseball. He rates straight A's as far as mental and physical preparation and performance. Because he's a player who very rarely makes a mental mistake and who always hustles, Jeter will continue to be better than just his numbers, which are getting better all the time.

Position: SS
Bats: R **Throws:** R
Ht: 6' 3" **Wt:** 195

Opening Day Age: 25
Born: 6/26/74 in Pequannock, NJ
ML Seasons: 5
Pronunciation: JEE-ter

Overall Statistics

	G	AB	R	H	D	T	HR	RBI	SB	BB	SO	Avg	OBP	Slg
1999	158	627	134	219	37	9	24	102	19	91	116	.349	.438	.552
Career	638	2537	486	807	122	31	63	341	86	273	473	.318	.389	.465

Where He Hits the Ball

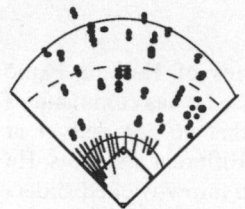 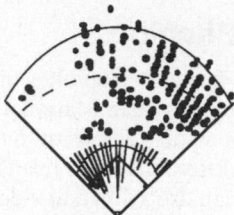

Vs. LHP   **Vs. RHP**

1999 Situational Stats

	AB	H	HR	RBI	Avg		AB	H	HR	RBI	Avg
Home	313	103	15	62	.329	LHP	124	35	5	18	.282
Road	314	116	9	40	.369	RHP	503	184	19	84	.366
First Half	334	124	14	60	.371	Sc Pos	155	56	6	75	.361
Scnd Half	293	95	10	42	.324	Clutch	76	24	4	16	.316

1999 Rankings (American League)

- 1st in batting average vs. righthanded pitchers, batting average on an 0-2 count (.368), on-base percentage vs. righthanded pitchers (.455), hits, times on base (322) and plate appearances (739)
- 2nd in batting average, runs scored, singles and triples
- 3rd in on-base percentage
- Led the Yankees in slugging percentage, on-base percentage, batting average with runners in scoring position, batting average in the clutch, batting average vs. righthanded pitchers, batting average on an 0-2 count (.368), slugging percentage vs. righthanded pitchers (.577), on-base percentage vs. righthanded pitchers (.455) and highest percentage of extra bases taken as a runner (60.3)

Chuck Knoblauch

1999 Season

Offensively, Chuck Knoblauch was extremely close to being the player the Yankees thought they were getting when they traded for him before the 1998 season. He scrapped his way to a .393 on-base percentage, showed some pop and ran the bases well. Defensively, he went in the opposite direction, committing 26 errors, many on simple throws to first base.

Hitting

After a 1998 season in which he became too home run-conscious and hit far too many balls in the air, Knoblauch returned to spraying line drives, taking walks and sticking his body in front of pitches to get on base. He also went back to hitting more balls into the gaps. Ideally suited for the leadoff spot in the order, he crowds the plate and hits from a crouch. To further annoy pitchers, Knoblauch disrupts their rhythm by stepping out after every pitch to unfasten and fasten his batting gloves. The high fastball is the one pitch he'll chase.

Baserunning & Defense

Knoblauch's throwing woes, which surfaced in 1998 and then vanished, returned with a vengeance in 1999. It got to the point that manager Joe Torre replaced Knoblauch with Luis Sojo in the late innings of playoff games. By the end of the season, Knoblauch no longer was in denial about the problem. He worked hard at curing it by taking extra groundballs during batting practice, but it remains an issue worth watching heading into 2000. On the bases, he continues to be a steady threat to steal, though his 28 steals were his fewest since his rookie year of 1991.

2000 Outlook

Even if he doesn't conquer his throwing problems, Knoblauch will do more things to help the Yankees win than he does to cause them to lose. His second season with New York was better than his first, and there's reason to believe his third will be as good or better than his second. His somewhat uptight personality makes him less than a perfect fit for New York, but he gradually is growing more comfortable with all the pressures.

Position: 2B
Bats: R **Throws:** R
Ht: 5' 9" **Wt:** 170

Opening Day Age: 31
Born: 7/7/68 in Houston, TX
ML Seasons: 9
Pronunciation: NOB-lock
Nickname: Knobby

Overall Statistics

	G	AB	R	H	D	T	HR	RBI	SB	BB	SO	Avg	OBP	Slg
1999	150	603	120	176	36	4	18	68	28	83	57	.292	.393	.454
Career	1313	5145	950	1533	271	59	78	523	335	672	580	.298	.388	.419

Where He Hits the Ball

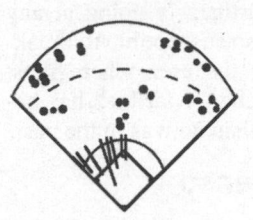
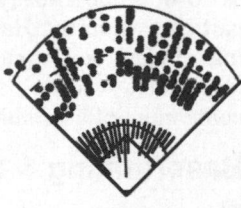

Vs. LHP   **Vs. RHP**

1999 Situational Stats

	AB	H	HR	RBI	Avg		AB	H	HR	RBI	Avg
Home	300	88	11	34	.293	LHP	114	31	4	17	.272
Road	303	88	7	34	.290	RHP	489	145	14	51	.297
First Half	307	82	5	27	.267	Sc Pos	115	36	3	48	.313
Scnd Half	296	94	13	41	.318	Clutch	73	23	1	10	.315

1999 Rankings (American League)

- 1st in errors at second base (26) and lowest fielding percentage at second base (.963)
- 2nd in hit by pitch (21)
- 4th in on-base percentage for a leadoff hitter (.393) and pitches seen (2,784)
- 5th in batting average on a 3-2 count (.377) and plate appearances (715)
- Led the Yankees in stolen-base percentage (75.7), most pitches seen per plate appearance (3.89), on-base percentage for a leadoff hitter (.393), slugging percentage vs. lefthanded pitchers (.491), batting average on a 3-2 count (.377), highest percentage of pitches taken (60.3), steals of third (3), stolen bases, hit by pitch (21) and pitches seen (2,784)

New York (AL)

195

Tino Martinez

1999 Season

Tino Martinez led the Yankees in home runs, scored 95 times and drove in 105 runs, yet he was tough on himself for leaving too many runners on base. His defense remained an asset and his quiet yet friendly personality made him a favorite in the clubhouse. He remains among the least talked about, most productive Yankees, though he never went on a tear in 1999.

Hitting

Martinez continues to crowd the plate, which makes him crave fastballs high and away. The book on him used to be to throw breaking pitches away, and that strategy still works when he's slumping. How he handles those pitches is the best barometer as to how the streaky Martinez is going at any particular moment. He's also susceptible to breaking pitches down and in, the area where most lefthanders want to be pitched. Martinez has become more of a pull hitter than he was in the past.

Baserunning & Defense

The slowest regular on New York's roster, Martinez knows his limitations and runs the bases wisely. He enjoyed another strong season in the field despite having unspectacular range. What he lacks in mobility, he makes up for with a very accurate arm, which makes him very adept at starting the 3-6-3 double play. He saves infielders errors by scooping balls out of the dirt and is able to leave the bag to corral wayward throws. He makes all the routine plays look, well, routine.

2000 Outlook

Even though he's a private person playing in a fishbowl, Martinez enjoys New York and likes the fit of pinstripes. He very much would like to remain a Yankee for the rest of his career. How big a season he has in 2000 could go a long way toward determining whether he gets to fulfill that wish. First baseman Nick Johnson, one of the top hitting prospects in the minors, is only a year away from joining the Yankees.

Position: 1B
Bats: L **Throws:** R
Ht: 6' 2" **Wt:** 210

Opening Day Age: 32
Born: 12/7/67 in Tampa, FL
ML Seasons: 10

Overall Statistics

	G	AB	R	H	D	T	HR	RBI	SB	BB	SO	Avg	OBP	Slg
1999	159	589	95	155	27	2	28	105	3	69	86	.263	.341	.458
Career	1157	4205	615	1156	225	11	213	798	13	471	638	.275	.347	.486

Where He Hits the Ball

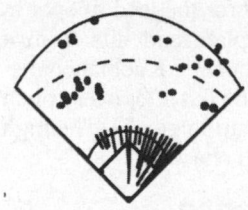 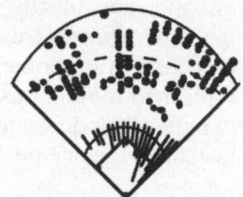

Vs. LHP   **Vs. RHP**

1999 Situational Stats

	AB	H	HR	RBI	Avg		AB	H	HR	RBI	Avg
Home	286	65	7	38	.227	LHP	180	47	7	31	.261
Road	303	90	21	67	.297	RHP	409	108	21	74	.264
First Half	325	91	14	54	.280	Sc Pos	173	49	9	77	.283
Scnd Half	264	64	14	51	.242	Clutch	76	19	3	11	.250

1999 Rankings (American League)

- 2nd in fielding percentage at first base (.995)
- 4th in lowest batting average at home
- 5th in games played
- 7th in lowest on-base percentage vs. lefthanded pitchers (.315)
- 8th in errors at first base (7) and lowest batting average on an 0-2 count (.065)
- Led the Yankees in HR frequency (21.0 ABs per HR), home runs and games played (159)
- Led AL first basemen in batting average on a 3-2 count (.339), at-bats, caught stealing (4) and games played

Paul O'Neill

1999 Season

It was a season that appeared to mark the beginning of a decline for a great Yankee. Even so, Paul O'Neill drove in 110 runs and played his usual strong defense. He still was an important cog in the New York machine, but he no longer performed at an All-Star level. Opponents no longer dreaded seeing him come up in a big spot.

Hitting

O'Neill reverted to early-career form against lefthanders, struggling mightily against them and batting just .190. Southpaws with decent breaking pitches ate him up in short order. Pitchers of all varieties can get him out when they locate the ball up and in, but he remains a serious power threat on balls down and in. He didn't hit outside pitches with his usual authority, another sign of decline.

Baserunning & Defense

Pitchers did a much better job of watching O'Neill last year, and he didn't have the same success at picking pitches to run on as he enjoyed in the past. O'Neill was thrown out nine times in 20 stolen-base attempts. He still has enough speed to take the extra base. He also remains among the most fundamentally sound right fielders in the game. His throwing mechanics are flawless and his arm strength has stood the test of time.

2000 Outlook

Manager Joe Torre has a special affection for O'Neill, which might delay his necessary move downward from the No. 3 spot in the order. Torre has too much respect for O'Neill, whose option was renewed for $6.5 million, to consider platooning him if he continues to struggle against lefties. A possible scenario would have O'Neill batting third against righthanders, seventh against lefties and taking one day off a week against a tough southpaw. O'Neill has hinted at retiring after this season. If he does, he's sure to go out in style.

Position: RF
Bats: L **Throws:** L
Ht: 6' 4" **Wt:** 215

Opening Day Age: 37
Born: 2/25/63 in Columbus, OH
ML Seasons: 15

Overall Statistics

	G	AB	R	H	D	T	HR	RBI	SB	BB	SO	Avg	OBP	Slg
1999	153	597	70	170	39	4	19	110	11	66	89	.285	.353	.459
Career	1774	6242	885	1809	392	20	242	1099	105	793	1017	.290	.368	.475

Where He Hits the Ball

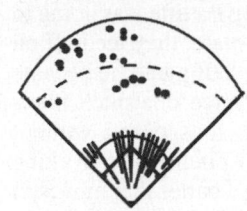
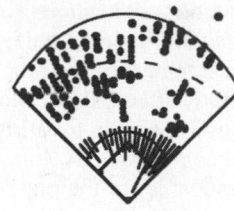

Vs. LHP   **Vs. RHP**

1999 Situational Stats

	AB	H	HR	RBI	Avg		AB	H	HR	RBI	Avg
Home	292	74	9	50	.253	LHP	158	30	3	26	.190
Road	305	96	10	60	.315	RHP	439	140	16	84	.319
First Half	313	92	10	55	.294	Sc Pos	197	52	6	88	.264
Scnd Half	284	78	9	55	.275	Clutch	78	16	2	13	.205

1999 Rankings (American League)

- 1st in errors in right field (8), lowest batting average vs. lefthanded pitchers and lowest on-base percentage vs. lefthanded pitchers (.246)
- 2nd in lowest stolen-base percentage (55.0) and lowest fielding percentage in right field (.974)
- 3rd in sacrifice flies (10), GDPs (24) and lowest slugging percentage vs. lefthanded pitchers (.297)
- 9th in doubles
- Led the Yankees in doubles, sacrifice flies (10) and GDPs (24)
- Led AL right fielders in caught stealing (9) and GDPs (24)

Andy Pettitte

Position: SP
Bats: L **Throws:** L
Ht: 6' 5" **Wt:** 225

Opening Day Age: 27
Born: 6/15/72 in Baton Rouge, LA
ML Seasons: 5
Pronunciation: PET-it

1999 Season

It was a tale of two seasons for perennial big winner Andy Pettitte. The first half was terrible, while the second half was much better. The Yankees thought long and hard about trading him, but decided against it, in large part because manager Joe Torre wanted to keep him. Finally knowing he wasn't going anywhere played a key role in helping Pettitte to relax and return to his winning ways. His biggest victory came in Game 4 of the American League Championship Series against the Red Sox.

Pitching

Pettitte became too enamored with his cut fastball last year and in turn became too predictable when facing righthanders. Knowing Pettitte was going to stay on the inner half of the plate, they teed off on him. Once he used the outer half again he became more effective. He doesn't have one pitch that's good enough to allow him to succeed without changing speeds, mixing his pitches and working both sides of the plate. With a cutter that moves in to righthanders and a sinking fastball and changeup that move away, he keeps hitters off stride.

Defense

Pettitte has one of the game's best moves to first base. So why do runners continue to get picked off instead of staying grounded at first? Because he's slow to the plate and can be stolen on if the baserunner guesses right. As difficult as it is to steal second on him because of his great move, he's easy prey for stealing third. Pettitte continues to flash remarkable agility for a pitcher of his size, once again logging a considerable number of assists while playing virtually error-free ball.

2000 Outlook

Pettitte is among the AL's most durable pitchers and consistently can be counted on for 200 innings and 15 victories. He can do even better than that if he goes an entire season without grabbing too often for his security blanket, a cut fastball he originally learned from Yankees minor league pitching coordinator Billy Connors.

Overall Statistics

	W	L	Pct.	ERA	G	GS	Sv	IP	H	BB	SO	HR	Ratio
1999	14	11	.560	4.70	31	31	0	191.2	216	89	121	20	1.59
Career	81	46	.638	3.92	165	158	0	1044.1	1087	376	709	85	1.40

How Often He Throws Strikes

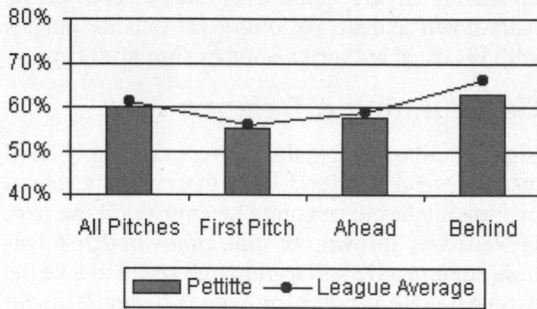

1999 Situational Stats

	W	L	ERA	Sv	IP		AB	H	HR	RBI	Avg
Home	8	5	4.22	0	102.1	LHB	149	41	8	29	.275
Road	6	6	5.24	0	89.1	RHB	598	175	12	62	.293
First Half	5	7	5.59	0	93.1	Sc Pos	194	49	7	69	.253
Scnd Half	9	4	3.84	0	98.1	Clutch	42	14	0	2	.333

1999 Rankings (American League)

- 1st in pickoff throws (213)
- 2nd in highest groundball/flyball ratio allowed (2.1)
- 3rd in GDPs induced (28)
- 4th in lowest strikeout/walk ratio (1.4)
- 5th in highest on-base percentage allowed (.364), most baserunners allowed per nine innings (14.5) and most walks per nine innings (4.2)
- Led the Yankees in losses, hits allowed, pickoff throws (213), GDPs induced (28), highest groundball/flyball ratio allowed (2.1), most GDPs induced per GDP situation (16.1%) and fewest home runs allowed per nine innings (.94)

Jorge Posada

Position: C
Bats: B **Throws:** R
Ht: 6' 2" **Wt:** 205

Opening Day Age: 28
Born: 8/17/71 in
Santurce, Puerto Rico
ML Seasons: 5
Pronunciation:
HOR-hay poh-SOD-uh

1999 Season

After an encouraging 1998 season, Jorge Posada regressed as a hitter and as a receiver. He finished 1999 with an unacceptable 17 passed balls, an indication of wandering concentration. He was hitting .210 at the All-Star break, but bounced back to hit .285 in the second half. Rather than turn Joe Girardi into an overpriced relic, Posada instead accentuated Girardi's value to the Yankees.

Hitting

Pitchers recognized that the way to mess with Posada's timing and turn him into a groundball machine is to change speeds on him. Busting him inside with fastballs and getting him to chase slop away was an effective way to handle him, particularly when he batted from the left side. Posada gets around on good fastballs and has nice power.

Baserunning & Defense

Posada runs better than some catchers and has a cannon for an arm. Excessive passed-ball totals are an indication that he didn't work as hard at his trade as he did when he was first converted from the infield. A humble man at heart, Posada should learn from his mistakes and turn himself back into a solid receiver. Pitchers like the way he calls a game.

2000 Outlook

At the very least, the Yankees would like to see Posada revert to his 1998 form. He didn't come into last season prepared and had a terrible first half, but regained a measure of respect with a decent second half. Girardi's departure via free agency means that Posada will play regularly for the first time in the majors. If he duplicates his hitting and receiving problems of a year ago, the Yankees will find themselves questioning whether he's their long-range solution behind the plate.

Overall Statistics

	G	AB	R	H	D	T	HR	RBI	SB	BB	SO	Avg	OBP	Slg
1999	112	379	50	93	19	2	12	57	1	53	91	.245	.341	.401
Career	292	939	136	237	54	2	35	145	2	131	222	.252	.345	.426

Where He Hits the Ball

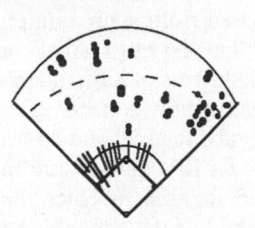 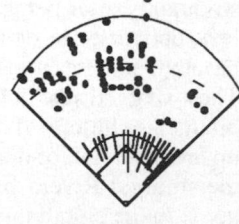

Vs. LHP   **Vs. RHP**

1999 Situational Stats

	AB	H	HR	RBI	Avg		AB	H	HR	RBI	Avg
Home	168	37	4	18	.220	LHP	99	30	4	18	.303
Road	211	56	8	39	.265	RHP	280	63	8	39	.225
First Half	200	42	9	34	.210	Sc Pos	130	32	2	41	.246
Scnd Half	179	51	3	23	.285	Clutch	71	20	4	17	.282

1999 Rankings (American League)

- 5th in lowest percentage of runners caught stealing as a catcher (21.9)
- 9th in errors at catcher (5)

New York (AL)

Mariano Rivera

1999 Season

Mariano Rivera established himself as the best closer in baseball with another terrific regular season. He limited hitters to a .176 batting average and allowed just two home runs in 69 innings. He succeeded in 45 of 49 regular-season save opportunities, including his final 22, and didn't allow a run over his final 28 appearances. He was even better in the postseason, winning twice and collecting six saves in eight scoreless appearances. He earned World Series MVP honors while lowering his career postseason ERA to 0.38 in 47.1 innings.

Pitching

Clocked at 96 MPH, Rivera's fastball seems more like 100 MPH to hitters because it jumps on them so quickly after being released from such a quiet, lazy delivery. He delivers the best cut fastball in baseball and uses it to break the bats of lefthanders. They slugged just .171 against him in 1999. The pitch takes hitters off his regular fastball and opens up the outer half of the plate for Rivera. A starter in the minors, Rivera has the stamina to enter the game in the eighth inning and still have plenty left for the final frame. He doesn't need to throw many pitches in the bullpen in order to get ready.

Defense

Rivera is as good a fielder among pitchers as there is in the game. He pounces on groundballs with remarkable quickness. He sometimes shags flyballs in center field during batting practice and supplies enough evidence to suggest that if he were an outfielder by trade, he would be a Gold Glove candidate. Rivera isn't good at checking basestealers, but he doesn't allow enough runners to worry about that flaw.

2000 Outlook

One of the most consistent performers in baseball, Rivera is primed for another dominant season. Manager Joe Torre has done a terrific job of getting maximum results out of Rivera with a minimum workload. Torre doesn't have him warm up unless he knows he's going to bring Rivera into the game.

Position: RP
Bats: R **Throws:** R
Ht: 6' 2" **Wt:** 170

Opening Day Age: 30
Born: 11/29/69 in Panama City, Panama
ML Seasons: 5

Overall Statistics

	W	L	Pct.	ERA	G	GS	Sv	IP	H	BB	SO	HR	Ratio
1999	4	3	.571	1.83	66	0	45	69.0	43	18	52	2	0.88
Career	26	13	.667	2.58	266	10	129	376.2	300	119	337	22	1.11

How Often He Throws Strikes

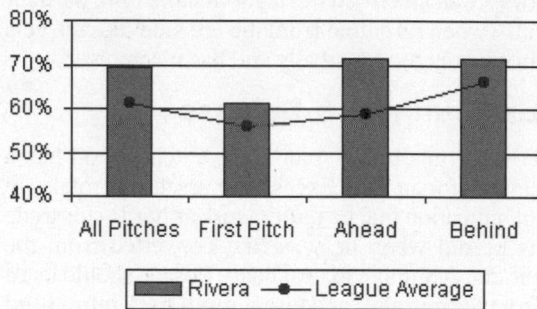

1999 Situational Stats

	W	L	ERA	Sv	IP		AB	H	HR	RBI	Avg
Home	2	2	2.48	20	32.2	LHB	140	20	1	8	.143
Road	2	1	1.24	25	36.1	RHB	105	23	1	9	.219
First Half	2	2	2.29	23	35.1	Sc Pos	49	10	1	15	.204
Scnd Half	2	1	1.34	22	33.2	Clutch	165	34	2	16	.206

1999 Rankings (American League)

- 1st in saves, save percentage (91.8), first batter efficiency (.048) and relief ERA (1.83)
- 2nd in save opportunities (49) and lowest batting average allowed in relief (.176)
- 3rd in games finished (63) and fewest baserunners allowed per nine innings in relief (8.3)
- Led the Yankees in saves, games finished (63), save opportunities (49), save percentage (91.8), first batter efficiency (.048), lowest batting average allowed in relief with runners on base (.198), relief ERA (1.83), lowest batting average allowed in relief (.176) and fewest baserunners allowed per nine innings in relief (8.3)

Bernie Williams

Position: CF
Bats: B **Throws:** R
Ht: 6' 2" **Wt:** 205

Opening Day Age: 31
Born: 9/13/68 in San Juan, Puerto Rico
ML Seasons: 9

1999 Season

He may have slipped some in center field, but Bernie Williams was able to overcome shoulder woes to turn in another terrific season at the plate. There was sentiment from several areas of the organization that the Yankees overpaid Williams by signing him to a seven-year, $87.5 million contract during the offseason, but that lessened as he showed what he can do with the bat. Several huge contracts doled out by other major league owners also helped to diminish the sticker shock.

Hitting

Among hitters who have plus power, there might not be a tougher out in baseball than Williams. The book on how to pitch to him is forever changing. Last year, he was a better hitter from the left side than the right. Part of that disparity could be attributed to a left shoulder injury that impaired his swing from the right side, while part of it was the cumulative effect of facing far more righthanders than lefthanders over the years. He's not a good hitter—he's a great one.

Baserunning & Defense

Attempts to turn the fleet Williams into a bona fide basestealer finally have been abandoned. It just isn't going to happen. He doesn't have natural baserunning instincts and must think where others simply react. He covers so much ground with long, graceful strides that he's as fast as anyone once he gets going. Defensively, he didn't have anything close to a Gold Glove season, though he won his third straight. He tends to break in the wrong direction and doesn't get especially quick breaks because he's flat-footed. Williams has the speed to compensate for most of those mistakes, but he doesn't have a strong arm.

2000 Outlook

The Yankees can expect more of the same All-Star production from Williams, a hitter who can deliver the single when needed, the extra-base hit when the situation calls for it and the clutch home run. If he just has a typical Bernie Williams season, he again will rank among the most efficient hitters in the majors.

Overall Statistics

	G	AB	R	H	D	T	HR	RBI	SB	BB	SO	Avg	OBP	Slg
1999	158	591	116	202	28	6	25	115	9	100	95	.342	.435	.536
Career	1096	4269	754	1298	241	44	151	681	106	595	679	.304	.389	.487

Where He Hits the Ball

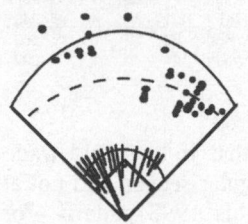
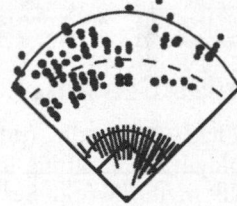

Vs. LHP   **Vs. RHP**

1999 Situational Stats

	AB	H	HR	RBI	Avg		AB	H	HR	RBI	Avg
Home	285	96	11	48	.337	LHP	165	49	5	22	.297
Road	306	106	14	67	.346	RHP	426	153	20	93	.359
First Half	330	111	13	52	.336	Sc Pos	185	64	8	89	.346
Scnd Half	261	91	12	63	.349	Clutch	74	23	4	15	.311

1999 Rankings (American League)

- 1st in batting average with the bases loaded (.583) and intentional walks (17)
- 2nd in batting average vs. righthanded pitchers, on-base percentage vs. righthanded pitchers (.451) and times on base (303)
- 3rd in batting average with two strikes (.298), batting average and hits
- Led the Yankees in highest groundball/flyball ratio (1.8), batting average with the bases loaded (.583), batting average vs. lefthanded pitchers, cleanup slugging percentage (.524), on-base percentage vs. lefthanded pitchers (.393), batting average with two strikes (.298), RBI, caught stealing (10), walks, intentional walks (17) and batting average at home

Chad Curtis

Position: LF/DH
Bats: R **Throws:** R
Ht: 5'10" **Wt:** 185

Opening Day Age: 31
Born: 11/6/68 in
Marion, IN
ML Seasons: 8

Overall Statistics

	G	AB	R	H	D	T	HR	RBI	SB	BB	SO	Avg	OBP	Slg
1999	96	195	37	51	6	0	5	24	8	43	35	.262	.398	.369
Career	1058	3567	576	941	167	15	90	403	202	459	584	.264	.350	.395

1999 Situational Stats

	AB	H	HR	RBI	Avg		AB	H	HR	RBI	Avg
Home	80	18	0	9	.225	LHP	74	22	1	6	.297
Road	115	33	5	15	.287	RHP	121	29	4	18	.240
First Half	129	28	4	16	.217	Sc Pos	52	13	0	19	.250
Scnd Half	66	23	1	8	.348	Clutch	24	7	1	4	.292

1999 Season

Chad Curtis told friends that if he could trade playing a lot during the regular season and not at all in the World Series—his 1998 pattern—for playing less in the regular season and getting to appear in the Fall Classic, he would make that deal. That's exactly how things panned out for him. In his only World Series start, Curtis homered twice, a nice finish to an otherwise forgettable year.

Hitting, Baserunning & Defense

Curtis gave the Yankees someone to play center in case of an injury to Bernie Williams, and he filled in capably at the other two outfield positions as well. But he's strictly a strong-armed reserve at this point. He brings a power hitter's mentality to the plate without the power to justify it. He has trouble with sliders and is better suited to playing solely against lefthanders. His limited playing time gave him few opportunities to flash his aggressiveness on the basepaths.

2000 Outlook

While Curtis served as a useful backup for the Yankees, he was dealt to Texas for minor league righthanders Brandon Knight and Sam Marsonek. New York's purpose was twofold: to ease the left-field logjam in New York and cut costs. Curtis will have a similar role in Texas.

Joe Girardi

Position: C
Bats: R **Throws:** R
Ht: 5'11" **Wt:** 200

Opening Day Age: 35
Born: 10/14/64 in
Peoria, IL
ML Seasons: 11
Pronunciation:
jeh-RAR-dee

Overall Statistics

	G	AB	R	H	D	T	HR	RBI	SB	BB	SO	Avg	OBP	Slg
1999	65	209	23	50	16	1	2	27	3	10	26	.239	.271	.354
Career	987	3278	365	885	151	23	26	343	42	207	457	.270	.316	.354

1999 Situational Stats

	AB	H	HR	RBI	Avg		AB	H	HR	RBI	Avg
Home	101	23	1	9	.228	LHP	49	9	0	4	.184
Road	108	27	1	18	.250	RHP	160	41	2	23	.256
First Half	114	24	0	8	.211	Sc Pos	49	18	0	24	.367
Scnd Half	95	26	2	19	.274	Clutch	16	4	0	0	.250

1999 Season

Joe Girardi was supposed to be relegated to backup duty by Jorge Posada, but Girardi was too good defensively and ended up catching almost 40 percent of the time. His offensive decline continued, though he still delivered in key situations.

Hitting, Baserunning & Defense

Girardi can get around on fastballs, but he can be baited into pounding sinkers into the ground. He grounded into 16 double plays in just 209 at-bats last year. He also has trouble handling good sliders. He runs the bases well for a catcher, routinely takes the extra base and rarely makes a mental error. He has worked hard to become better than average at blocking balls in the dirt and still combines a plus arm with a quick release.

2000 Outlook

Manager Joe Torre successfully lobbied to have Girardi's contract option picked up for 1999, but the Yankees bid goodbye to Girardi as a free agent after the season. He wanted more playing time, not less, and will start for the Cubs, who signed him for three years and $5.5 million.

Hideki Irabu

Position: SP
Bats: R **Throws:** R
Ht: 6' 4" **Wt:** 240

Opening Day Age: 30
Born: 5/5/69 in Hyogo, Japan
ML Seasons: 3
Pronunciation: hih-DECK-ee ee-ROB-oo

Overall Statistics

	W	L	Pct.	ERA	G	GS	Sv	IP	H	BB	SO	HR	Ratio
1999	11	7	.611	4.84	32	27	0	169.1	180	46	133	26	1.33
Career	29	20	.592	4.80	74	64	0	395.2	397	142	315	68	1.36

1999 Situational Stats

	W	L	ERA	Sv	IP		AB	H	HR	RBI	Avg
Home	6	5	4.55	0	83.0	LHB	363	104	16	49	.287
Road	5	2	5.11	0	86.1	RHB	312	76	10	41	.244
First Half	6	3	4.15	0	89.0	Sc Pos	156	40	5	63	.256
Scnd Half	5	4	5.60	0	80.1	Clutch	7	3	1	4	.429

1999 Season

For the second year in a row, Hideki Irabu was much better in the first half of the season than the second half. His lackluster work ethic and poor conditioning results in subpar stamina for a 162-game season.

Pitching & Defense

Irabu's devastating splitter and 95-MPH fastball give him the stuff to be a big winner. But the minute he runs into tough times, he doesn't have the confidence or mental toughness to carry him through. He begins to doubt himself and works the fringes of the strike zone instead of trusting his pitches. He thinks major league hitters are better than they are and pays the price by too often falling behind in the count. Irabu does little to slow the running game, and his lack of work ethic and conditioning come back to haunt him in the field.

2000 Outlook

Growing tired of being teased by his talent only to be disappointed by his late-season dropoffs, the Yankees would love to trade Irabu and hand his rotation spot to prospect Ed Yarnall. If they keep Irabu, they might exile him to the bullpen at the first sign of regression.

Ricky Ledee

Position: LF
Bats: L **Throws:** L
Ht: 6' 1" **Wt:** 160

Opening Day Age: 26
Born: 11/22/73 in Ponce, Puerto Rico
ML Seasons: 2
Pronunciation: luh-DAY

Overall Statistics

	G	AB	R	H	D	T	HR	RBI	SB	BB	SO	Avg	OBP	Slg
1999	88	250	45	69	13	5	9	40	4	28	73	.276	.346	.476
Career	130	329	58	88	18	7	10	52	7	35	102	.267	.335	.456

1999 Situational Stats

	AB	H	HR	RBI	Avg		AB	H	HR	RBI	Avg
Home	131	37	4	16	.282	LHP	39	11	2	4	.282
Road	119	32	5	24	.269	RHP	211	58	7	36	.275
First Half	66	16	2	10	.242	Sc Pos	67	21	3	33	.313
Scnd Half	184	53	7	30	.288	Clutch	38	11	1	5	.289

1999 Season

Ricky Ledee shook off a slow start to produce a solid second half, but he still didn't convince the Yankees that he's their long-term solution in left field. He struck out too often and wasn't aggressive enough to suit the tastes of New York's brass.

Hitting, Baserunning & Defense

Ledee has the potential to hit for both power and average. He can handle lefthanders, though he still is pinch-hit for in key situations against southpaws. He must improve at the art of recognizing and staying back on offspeed pitches in order to reduce his strikeouts. A streaky outfielder whose concentration can drift, he nevertheless has a strong, fairly accurate arm. Ledee has yet to translate his decent speed into a significant number of stolen bases.

2000 Outlook

If he can assert himself and maintain confidence through good times and bad, Ledee could win the left-field job outright. But if that doesn't happen early in the season, chances are it won't ever happen with the Yankees. At that point, Ledee most likely would be moved to another organization where he could play daily and continue to develop.

New York (AL)

Jim Leyritz

Position: 1B/C/DH
Bats: R **Throws:** R
Ht: 5'11" **Wt:** 220

Opening Day Age: 36
Born: 12/27/63 in
Lakewood, OH
ML Seasons: 10
Pronunciation: LAY-ritz
Nickname: The King

Overall Statistics

	G	AB	R	H	D	T	HR	RBI	SB	BB	SO	Avg	OBP	Slg
1999	81	200	25	47	9	1	8	26	0	28	54	.235	.339	.410
Career	838	2412	320	643	106	2	88	375	7	323	555	.267	.365	.422

1999 Situational Stats

	AB	H	HR	RBI	Avg		AB	H	HR	RBI	Avg
Home	107	26	4	14	.243	LHP	88	21	5	15	.239
Road	93	21	4	12	.226	RHP	112	26	3	11	.232
First Half	134	32	8	21	.239	Sc Pos	60	13	2	19	.217
Scnd Half	66	15	0	5	.227	Clutch	35	8	2	7	.229

1999 Season

Jim Leyritz didn't hit much for the Yankees after joining them in a July trade with the Padres for pitching prospect Geraldo Padua. Once the postseason rolled around, it was the same old Leyritz. As if for old time's sake, he homered in the World Series against the Braves.

Hitting, Baserunning & Defense

Leyritz doesn't handle righthanders as well as in the past and is moving toward platoon duty. For the first time in his career, he had trouble catching up with the game's hardest throwers last year. Only a catcher on an emergency basis at this stage of his career, Leyritz serves as a backup first baseman and a part-time DH. His speed and defensive ability are negligible.

2000 Outlook

There was a time when Leyritz griped if he wasn't playing on a full-time basis, but he's a reserve now and accepts that role without complaint. After re-signing for one year and $1.25 million, he'll probably open 2000 platooning at DH with Darryl Strawberry. If Leyritz doesn't hit better than he did last season for New York, he'll have trouble keeping that job.

Ramiro Mendoza

Position: RP
Bats: R **Throws:** R
Ht: 6' 2" **Wt:** 170

Opening Day Age: 27
Born: 6/15/72 in Los
Santos, Panama
ML Seasons: 4

Overall Statistics

	W	L	Pct.	ERA	G	GS	Sv	IP	H	BB	SO	HR	Ratio
1999	9	9	.500	4.29	53	6	3	123.2	141	27	80	13	1.36
Career	31	22	.585	4.27	145	46	6	440.2	509	95	252	42	1.37

1999 Situational Stats

	W	L	ERA	Sv	IP		AB	H	HR	RBI	Avg
Home	2	6	4.76	1	51.0	LHB	231	66	10	37	.286
Road	7	3	3.96	2	72.2	RHB	265	75	3	26	.283
First Half	3	5	4.76	3	75.2	Sc Pos	124	35	3	45	.282
Scnd Half	6	4	3.56	0	48.0	Clutch	119	36	3	16	.303

1999 Season

Possibly because he felt let down that he still hasn't been given the opportunity to win a job in New York's rotation, Ramiro Mendoza didn't have as efficient a season as he did in 1998. He got it together in the postseason, however, and had a stellar American League Championship Series against the Red Sox.

Pitching & Defense

When Mendoza is on, his devastating sinker has been likened by Joe Girardi to that of Greg Maddux. Mendoza also has an effective changeup. When he drops his arm, his pitches stay flat and get pounded, so he needs to be reminded constantly to maintain sound mechanics. Extremely nimble afoot, he fields his position well and does a sound job of checking the running game.

2000 Outlook

Mendoza likely will start 2000 in the bullpen but could move into the rotation if needed. He would be a starter for most teams, but has to stand in line on the deepest pitching staff in baseball. Manager Joe Torre repeatedly has fought the idea of including Mendoza in trades, even though other clubs are forever asking for him.

Jeff Nelson

Position: RP
Bats: R **Throws:** R
Ht: 6' 8" **Wt:** 235

Opening Day Age: 33
Born: 11/17/66 in Baltimore, MD
ML Seasons: 8

Overall Statistics

	W	L	Pct.	ERA	G	GS	Sv	IP	H	BB	SO	HR	Ratio
1999	2	1	.667	4.15	39	0	1	30.1	27	22	35	2	1.62
Career	27	28	.491	3.41	461	0	17	485.2	420	242	489	35	1.36

1999 Situational Stats

	W	L	ERA	Sv	IP		AB	H	HR	RBI	Avg
Home	2	0	2.55	0	17.2	LHB	34	8	1	5	.235
Road	0	1	6.39	1	12.2	RHB	76	19	1	14	.250
First Half	1	1	5.74	0	15.2	Sc Pos	45	10	0	15	.222
Scnd Half	1	0	2.45	1	14.2	Clutch	46	11	0	10	.239

1999 Season

Jeff Nelson missed much of the season because of elbow problems that required surgery in June. He was his normal effective self after his return and pitched five scoreless innings in the postseason.

Pitching & Defense

Nelson's sidearm slider is among the widest breaking pitches in baseball and serves as a tremendous strikeout pitch. He tends to fall in love with it, though, which can lead him to fall behind in the count. The pitch has such a big break that umpires can have difficulty calling it and he sometimes gets squeezed. The Yankees have urged him to throw more fastballs through the years, but he sometimes lacks confidence when he tries to bring the heat. Stealing bases against him isn't difficult, and he never will be a candidate for a Gold Glove.

2000 Outlook

As long as his elbow remains fit, Nelson figures to keep his job as the righthanded setup man to Mariano Rivera. In terms of pure stuff, there aren't many non-closer relievers who can match Nelson.

Shane Spencer

Position: LF/RF
Bats: R **Throws:** R
Ht: 5'11" **Wt:** 210

Opening Day Age: 28
Born: 2/20/72 in Key West, FL
ML Seasons: 2

Overall Statistics

	G	AB	R	H	D	T	HR	RBI	SB	BB	SO	Avg	OBP	Slg
1999	71	205	25	48	8	0	8	20	0	18	51	.234	.301	.390
Career	98	272	43	73	14	0	18	47	0	23	63	.268	.328	.518

1999 Situational Stats

	AB	H	HR	RBI	Avg		AB	H	HR	RBI	Avg
Home	94	24	2	9	.255	LHP	83	24	5	8	.289
Road	111	24	6	11	.216	RHP	122	24	3	12	.197
First Half	107	26	6	12	.243	Sc Pos	42	9	0	12	.214
Scnd Half	98	22	2	8	.224	Clutch	24	7	1	2	.292

1999 Season

Illness, including food poisoning and an irregular heartbeat, left Shane Spencer on the outside looking in for most of the season. When he did play, he struck out too often, walked too rarely, didn't play particularly well in the outfield and regressed in the eyes of the Yankees' front office. It was a far cry from his stunning 1998 heroics.

Hitting, Baserunning & Defense

Spencer has trouble laying off high fastballs and lacks patience in general at the plate. His playing time was so sparse in 1999 that when he did play, he was too anxious to prove he should be in the lineup more often. He has good raw power but makes infrequent contact. His speed and arm are below average, and he doesn't track flyballs particularly well in left field.

2000 Outlook

When he was left off the World Series roster, Spencer groused that he would like to be traded to another organization if New York did not plan on playing him. If the Yankees thought they could get something of value in return, they would be happy to accommodate his wishes.

Mike Stanton

Position: RP
Bats: L **Throws:** L
Ht: 6' 1" **Wt:** 215

Opening Day Age: 32
Born: 6/2/67 in
Houston, TX
ML Seasons: 11

Overall Statistics

	W	L	Pct.	ERA	G	GS	Sv	IP	H	BB	SO	HR	Ratio
1999	2	2	.500	4.33	73	1	0	62.1	71	18	59	5	1.43
Career	35	29	.547	3.99	611	1	65	597.1	564	227	491	57	1.32

1999 Situational Stats

	W	L	ERA	Sv	IP		AB	H	HR	RBI	Avg
Home	1	0	2.20	0	32.2	LHB	90	23	2	15	.256
Road	1	2	6.67	0	29.2	RHB	156	48	3	18	.308
First Half	1	2	4.60	0	31.1	Sc Pos	82	22	3	31	.268
Scnd Half	1	0	4.06	0	31.0	Clutch	111	34	4	21	.306

1999 Season

Mike Stanton had a streaky season, having trouble getting hitters out in April, July and September, and ranking among baseball's best lefthanded relievers the rest of the year. He battled through back troubles and led the Yankees with 73 appearances.

Pitching & Defense

When he's on his game, Stanton can throw four pitches—fastball, curveball, slider and changeup—for strikes. When he's off, he can throw four pitches for balls. He must pitch often to remain effective. When he goes too long between appearances, his pitches rise in the strike zone, begging to be creamed, and he has trouble throwing strikes. Stanton has the ideal makeup for the late innings and for pitching in New York because he lets criticism roll off his back. His delivery leaves him in less than ideal fielding position, but he holds the running game in check.

2000 Outlook

The Yankees could have justified letting Stanton walk as a free agent. But the club knows it needs him in the bullpen as the lefthanded setup man to Mariano Rivera. He got a three-year, $7.35 million contract in November.

Darryl Strawberry

Position: DH
Bats: L **Throws:** L
Ht: 6' 6" **Wt:** 215

Opening Day Age: 38
Born: 3/12/62 in Los
Angeles, CA
ML Seasons: 17
Nickname: Straw

Overall Statistics

	G	AB	R	H	D	T	HR	RBI	SB	BB	SO	Avg	OBP	Slg
1999	24	49	10	16	5	0	3	6	2	17	16	.327	.500	.612
Career	1583	5418	898	1401	256	38	335	1000	221	816	1352	.259	.357	.505

1999 Situational Stats

	AB	H	HR	RBI	Avg		AB	H	HR	RBI	Avg
Home	18	6	1	2	.333	LHP	6	3	1	1	.500
Road	31	10	2	4	.323	RHP	43	13	2	5	.302
First Half	0	0	0	0	-	Sc Pos	14	3	0	2	.214
Scnd Half	49	16	3	6	.327	Clutch	8	4	0	1	.500

1999 Season

In a microcosm of his career, Darryl Strawberry was productive and solid in the clutch when he played but had his season abbreviated because of off-the-field mistakes. Coming back from colon cancer, Strawberry pleaded no contest to charges of solicitation and possession of a small amount of cocaine. Suspended until August, he rejoined the Yankees in September and hit with authority.

Hitting, Baserunning & Defense

Strawberry drew a crucial walk from Greg Maddux in Game 1 of the World Series, proof that even the top pitchers treat him with great care. He still gets around on the best of fastballs and punishes mistakes with great power. Strawberry runs the bases wisely and can steal a base when his degenerating left knee permits. Primarily a DH, he can appear in the outfield once or twice a week without embarrassing himself.

2000 Outlook

New York didn't hesitate to pick up the $750,000 option on Strawberry's contract. His knee remains a concern, but there's no question that there's still a lot of life left in his bat. If he can stay healthy, the Yankees are confident he can be a productive platoon DH against righthanders.

Other New York Yankees

Clay Bellinger (**Pos**: 3B, **Age**: 31, **Bats**: R)

	G	AB	R	H	D	T	HR	RBI	SB	BB	SO	Avg	OBP	Slg
1999	32	45	12	9	2	0	1	2	1	1	10	.200	.217	.311
Career	32	45	12	9	2	0	1	2	1	1	10	.200	.217	.311

Bellinger has been playing Triple-A ball since 1993. He finally got a cup of coffee in New York in 1999, playing five positions. 2000 Outlook: C

Mike Buddie (**Pos**: RHP, **Age**: 29)

	W	L	Pct.	ERA	G	GS	Sv	IP	H	BB	SO	HR	Ratio
1999	0	0	-	4.50	2	0	0	2.0	3	0	1	1	1.50
Career	4	1	.800	5.56	26	2	0	43.2	49	13	21	6	1.42

Buddie has gone 20-8 with a 2.75 ERA in three seasons of Triple-A relief work. He hasn't done as well in the Bronx. 2000 Outlook: C

Chili Davis (**Pos**: DH, **Age**: 40, **Bats**: B)

	G	AB	R	H	D	T	HR	RBI	SB	BB	SO	Avg	OBP	Slg
1999	146	476	59	128	25	1	19	78	4	73	100	.269	.366	.445
Career	2436	8673	1240	2380	424	30	350	1372	142	1194	1698	.274	.360	.451

Just two months shy of his 40th birthday, Davis retired with 350 home runs and three World Series rings. Departing with World Series championships in his final two seasons was sweet. 2000 Outlook: D

Todd Erdos (**Pos**: RHP, **Age**: 26)

	W	L	Pct.	ERA	G	GS	Sv	IP	H	BB	SO	HR	Ratio
1999	0	0	-	3.86	4	0	0	7.0	5	4	4	2	1.29
Career	2	0	1.000	5.16	17	0	0	22.2	27	9	17	3	1.59

Erdos was a closer in the minors in the three seasons leading up to 1999, but he wasn't as effective in Triple-A last summer. He pitched OK in New York. 2000 Outlook: C

Tony Fossas (**Pos**: LHP, **Age**: 42)

	W	L	Pct.	ERA	G	GS	Sv	IP	H	BB	SO	HR	Ratio
1999	0	0	-	36.00	5	0	0	1.0	6	1	0	1	7.00
Career	17	24	.415	3.90	567	0	7	415.2	434	180	324	39	1.48

The 1999 season may have been the last hurrah for Fossas, too. Failing to make the Rangers in the spring, he hooked up with the Yankees briefly in May, but was sent down after five appearances. 2000 Outlook: D

Jason Grimsley (**Pos**: RHP, **Age**: 32)

	W	L	Pct.	ERA	G	GS	Sv	IP	H	BB	SO	HR	Ratio
1999	7	2	.778	3.60	55	0	1	75.0	66	40	49	7	1.41
Career	25	27	.481	5.12	156	68	2	501.0	516	303	332	42	1.63

After a two-year absence from the majors, Grimsley made the Yankees in the spring and stuck. He struggled with his control for stretches in the middle of the season, but pitched adequately. 2000 Outlook: C

Jeff Juden (**Pos**: RHP, **Age**: 29)

	W	L	Pct.	ERA	G	GS	Sv	IP	H	BB	SO	HR	Ratio
1999	0	1	.000	1.59	2	1	0	5.2	5	3	9	1	1.41
Career	27	32	.458	4.81	147	76	0	533.0	510	247	441	73	1.42

Juden's reputation for being uncoachable may have something to do with him being on six teams in four years. The Yanks gave him a brief look, but he allowed nine runs (eight unearned) in two games. 2000 Outlook: C

Jeff Manto (**Pos**: 3B, **Age**: 35, **Bats**: R)

	G	AB	R	H	D	T	HR	RBI	SB	BB	SO	Avg	OBP	Slg
1999	18	33	5	6	0	0	1	2	0	13	15	.182	.413	.273
Career	282	708	95	160	33	2	30	93	3	95	182	.226	.325	.405

Because of his power, Manto manages to surface each season. He hasn't stayed long enough to get 100 major league at-bats since 1996. 2000 Outlook: C

Dan Naulty (**Pos**: RHP, **Age**: 30)

	W	L	Pct.	ERA	G	GS	Sv	IP	H	BB	SO	HR	Ratio
1999	1	0	1.000	4.38	33	0	0	49.1	40	22	25	8	1.26
Career	5	5	.500	4.54	130	0	5	160.2	137	77	119	24	1.33

Naulty turned in his best effort since his rookie year in 1996. He was better in the first half and was sent to Triple-A briefly in August. The Yankees traded him to the Dodgers for minor league first baseman Nick Leach in December. 2000 Outlook: B

Luis Sojo (**Pos**: 3B/2B, **Age**: 34, **Bats**: R)

	G	AB	R	H	D	T	HR	RBI	SB	BB	SO	Avg	OBP	Slg
1999	49	127	20	32	6	0	2	16	1	4	17	.252	.275	.346
Career	711	2187	262	572	83	11	29	215	25	103	164	.262	.297	.349

Sojo provided infield help at second and third base when regulars missed time due to injury. After his third season in New York, he became a free agent. 2000 Outlook: B

Tony Tarasco (**Pos**: LF, **Age**: 29, **Bats**: L)

	G	AB	R	H	D	T	HR	RBI	SB	BB	SO	Avg	OBP	Slg
1999	14	31	5	5	2	0	0	3	1	3	5	.161	.229	.226
Career	397	910	136	217	41	5	28	103	37	98	158	.238	.313	.387

Tarasco earned a reputation for not listening to coaches in 1995, when he played well for the Expos but didn't make adjustments during a second-half fade. He hasn't hit well in brief trials since then, and will play in Japan next year. 2000 Outlook: D

Jay Tessmer (**Pos**: RHP, **Age**: 28)

	W	L	Pct.	ERA	G	GS	Sv	IP	H	BB	SO	HR	Ratio
1999	0	0	-	14.85	6	0	0	6.2	16	4	3	1	3.00
Career	1	0	1.000	8.22	13	0	0	15.1	20	8	9	2	1.83

Tessmer is a sidearmer who's much more deceptive than overpowering. He has been dominant at Double-A and below, ordinary at higher levels. 2000 Outlook: B

Allen Watson (**Pos**: LHP, **Age**: 29)

	W	L	Pct.	ERA	G	GS	Sv	IP	H	BB	SO	HR	Ratio
1999	6	3	.667	3.51	38	4	1	77.0	72	35	64	13	1.39
Career	51	55	.481	4.90	189	137	1	870.0	949	333	569	133	1.47

Watson was traded from the Mets to the Mariners in June, then hooked up with the Yankees after Seattle released him 10 days later. He pitched well, earning a two-year, $3 million contract. 2000 Outlook: B

New York Yankees Minor League Prospects

Organization Overview:

Not only have the Yankees won three of the last four World Series, they also have the best collection of talent in the minor leagues. While it's true that owner George Steinbrenner has an open checkbook, New York generally spends its money wisely. Mainstays Derek Jeter, Andy Pettitte, Jorge Posada, Mariano Rivera and Bernie Williams all were signed and developed by the Yankees, who are about two years away from being able to win with a purely homegrown lineup, if they so desired. No organization can match their depth of infielders, which includes Drew Henson, D'Angelo Jimenez, Nick Johnson and Alfonso Soriano in the upper minors.

Ryan Bradley

Position: P | **Opening Day Age:** 24
Bats: R **Throws:** R | **Born:** 10/26/75 in
Ht: 6' 4" **Wt:** 226 | Covina, CA

Recent Statistics

	W	L	ERA	G	GS	Sv	IP	H	R	BB	SO	HR
1998 A Tampa	7	4	2.38	32	11	7	94.2	59	29	30	112	5
1998 AA Norwich	2	0	1.44	3	3	0	25.0	8	4	8	25	1
1998 AAA Columbus	0	1	6.19	3	3	0	16.0	15	13	13	12	4
1999 AAA Columbus	5	12	6.21	29	24	0	145.0	163	112	73	118	28

A 1997 supplemental first-round pick, Bradley reached New York and won his big league debut just 14 months after he signed. Then he completely fell apart last season. A reliever at Arizona State, he became a full-time starter in 1999 and didn't adapt. He added a four-seam fastball that stayed up in the strike zone and got hammered, and his control also suffered. Restored to the bullpen in the Arizona Fall League, he went back to throwing a low-90s two-seamer with good sink and an above-average splitter. Bradley probably will start 2000 in Triple-A, and he'd be a potential closer in an organization that didn't include Mariano Rivera.

Drew Henson

Position: 3B | **Opening Day Age:** 20
Bats: R **Throws:** R | **Born:** 2/13/80 in San
Ht: 6' 5" **Wt:** 220 | Diego, CA

Recent Statistics

	G	AB	R	H	D	T	HR	RBI	SB	BB	SO	Avg
1998 R Yankees	10	38	5	12	3	0	1	2	0	3	9	.316
1999 A Tampa	69	254	37	71	12	0	13	37	3	26	71	.280

If not for his scholarship to play quarterback for the University of Michigan, Henson would have been among the first players selected in the 1998 draft. Undaunted, New York drafted him in the third round and signed him for a $2 million bonus that escalates to $4 million if he commits full-time to baseball in the future. If he does, the Yankees think he'll be one of the best third basemen baseball has seen in a while. With just 10 games of prior pro experience, Henson showed big-time power in the high Class-A Florida State League. He's an athletic third baseman with the feet, hands and arm scouts like at the position. His worst tool is his speed, but even that grades out as average. If he ever gives up football, his baseball future is unlimited.

D'Angelo Jimenez

Position: SS | **Opening Day Age:** 22
Bats: B **Throws:** R | **Born:** 12/21/77 in Santo
Ht: 6' 0" **Wt:** 160 | Domingo, Dom. Rep.

Recent Statistics

	G	AB	R	H	D	T	HR	RBI	SB	BB	SO	Avg
1999 AAA Columbus	126	526	97	172	32	5	15	88	26	59	75	.327
1999 AL New York	7	20	3	8	2	0	0	4	0	3	4	.400
1999 MLE	126	499	73	145	26	3	11	66	18	43	77	.291

With all the hype surrounding Alfonso Soriano, the fact that Jimenez may be the Yankees' best shortstop prospect is often overlooked. All of his tools are average or better, except for his power, and he generates a surprising number of doubles and homers for a slender middle infielder. He led all minor league shortstops by hitting .327 last year, draws a reasonable amount of walks and makes contact. Jimenez runs very well, though he has yet to become an accomplished basestealer. Defensively, he was rated the best defensive shortstop in the Triple-A International League. Of course, neither he nor Soriano will supplant Derek Jeter in New York. Jimenez also has played second and third base, and he'll serve the Yankees as a utilityman this season.

Nick Johnson

Position: 1B | **Opening Day Age:** 21
Bats: L **Throws:** L | **Born:** 9/19/78 in
Ht: 6' 3" **Wt:** 220 | Sacramento, CA

Recent Statistics

	G	AB	R	H	D	T	HR	RBI	SB	BB	SO	Avg
1998 A Tampa	92	303	69	96	14	1	17	58	1	68	76	.317
1999 AA Norwich	132	420	114	145	33	5	14	87	8	123	88	.345
1999 MLE	132	404	95	129	29	3	11	72	5	86	93	.319

When Johnson signed as a 1996 third-round pick, the Yankees envisioned him blossoming into a Mark Grace-type player. Instead, he has become one of the best all-around hitters in the minors and should be better than Grace. The nephew of former All-Star Larry Bowa, Johnson won the Double-A Eastern League batting title in 1999 and led the minors in walks (123), hit by pitches (37) and on-base percentage (.525). He has gained 25 pounds since signing and should develop above-average home-run power. Though he was rated the Eastern League's best defensive first baseman, he committed a league-high 20 errors, many when he got caught in between hops on grounders. He can correct that flaw by being more aggressive. Tino Martinez' contract expires after this season, and the guess is that they'll decline his 2001 option so they can give his job to Johnson.

Donzell McDonald

Position: OF
Bats: B **Throws:** R
Ht: 5' 11" **Wt:** 165

Opening Day Age: 25
Born: 2/20/75 in Long Beach, CA

Recent Statistics

	G	AB	R	H	D	T	HR	RBI	SB	BB	SO	Avg
1998 AA Norwich	134	495	80	125	20	7	6	36	35	55	127	.253
1998 A Tampa	5	18	6	6	1	2	0	2	2	2	7	.333
1999 AA Norwich	137	533	95	145	19	10	4	33	54	90	110	.272
1999 MLE	137	516	79	128	16	6	3	27	37	62	115	.248

Forced to repeat Double-A in 1999, McDonald got back in good standing with the Yankees by showing them what they wanted: improved on-base percentage, better selectivity and more stolen bases. A 22nd-round pick out of Yavapai (Ariz.) Junior College in 1995, he's the older brother of Orioles outfield prospect Darnell McDonald. Donzell still has work to do offensively. He plays a nice center field, and his upside is as a Lance Johnson with 10-12 homers per year.

Jackson Melian

Position: OF
Bats: R **Throws:** R
Ht: 6' 2" **Wt:** 190

Opening Day Age: 20
Born: 1/7/80 in Barcelona, Venezuela

Recent Statistics

	G	AB	R	H	D	T	HR	RBI	SB	BB	SO	Avg
1998 A Greensboro	135	467	66	119	18	2	8	45	15	41	120	.255
1999 A Tampa	128	467	65	132	17	13	6	61	11	49	98	.283

A raw athlete who holds the Venezuelan national record for the 50-meter freestyle in swimming, Melian has legitimate 30-30 potential. His 1999 numbers don't seem impressive, but they indeed were for a 19-year-old in a high Class-A league with huge ballparks. Melian also had to recover from the tragic death of his parents, who were killed in an automobile accident while driving to see him play in 1998. The Yankees believe he'll continue to develop as a hitter, and his speed, center-field range and arm are all beyond reproach.

Alfonso Soriano

Position: SS
Bats: R **Throws:** R
Ht: 6' 1" **Wt:** 160

Opening Day Age: 22
Born: 1/7/78 in San Pedro de Macoris, D.R.

Recent Statistics

	G	AB	R	H	D	T	HR	RBI	SB	BB	SO	Avg
1999 AA Norwich	89	361	57	110	20	3	15	68	24	32	67	.305
1999 R Yankees	5	19	7	5	2	0	1	5	0	1	3	.263
1999 AAA Columbus	20	82	8	15	5	1	2	11	1	5	18	.183
1999 AL New York	9	8	2	1	0	0	1	1	0	0	3	.125
1999 MLE	109	427	53	109	21	2	13	64	17	25	89	.255

Soriano signed out of the Dominican with the Hiroshima Toyo Carp, then "retired" in 1998 to become a free agent, then signed with the Yankees for $3.1 million. Making his U.S. pro debut in 1999, he was named MVP of the inaugural Futures Game as well as the most exciting player in the Double-A Eastern League. Though he's just 160 pounds, he's wiry strong and generates power with tremendous bat speed. Soriano is a free swinger who will

need to show more selectivity to fit in with New York. He runs well but scouts are divided as to whether he has the quickness to play shortstop. That's a moot point because Derek Jeter isn't going anywhere. Soriano's arm and bat are good enough for any infield position. He'll spend most of 2000 in Triple-A.

Ed Yarnall

Position: P
Bats: L **Throws:** L
Ht: 6' 3" **Wt:** 234

Opening Day Age: 24
Born: 12/4/75 in Lima, PA

Recent Statistics

	W	L	ERA	G	GS	Sv	IP	H	R	BB	SO	HR
1999 AAA Columbus	13	4	3.47	23	23	0	145.1	136	61	57	146	5
1999 AL New York	1	0	3.71	5	2	0	17.0	17	8	10	13	1

In a trade reminiscent of the bully picking on the littlest kid on the schoolyard, the Yankees traded Mike Lowell to the Marlins in February for three pitchers: Mark Johnson, Todd Noel and Yarnall. A 1996 third-round pick out of Louisiana State who joined Florida in the Mike Piazza trade two years later, Yarnall was named the most valuable pitcher in the Triple-A International League in 1999. He has a very deceptive delivery that doesn't allow hitters to pick up his sneaky 90-92 MPH or his slider. He throws strikes and surrendered just six homers in 162.1 innings last year. Yarnall pitched well enough in the majors that the Yankees would love to trade Hideki Irabu to create room in their rotation.

Others to Watch

Using a 93-95 MPH fastball and a power slider, righthander **Craig Dingman** (26) posted a 1.57 ERA and 90-12 strikeout-walk ratio in Double-A last year. He could be a quality setup man. . . New York restocked its pitching with a couple of early-round 1999 draft picks, lefthander **Alex Graman** (22) and righthander **David Walling** (21). A third-rounder, Graman has a 90-93 MPH fastball, and his curveball and splitter also will become above-average pitches. Walling, a first-rounder who reminds the Yankees of Orlando Hernandez without the breaking ball, has an 88-93 MPH fastball and a tremendous changeup. . . Third baseman **Donny Leon** (23) is stuck behind the Yankees' deep crop of infielders, but he did hit .302 with power from both sides of the plate in Double-A last season. He also has a strong arm. . . The Yankees say that righthander **Todd Noel** (21) has the best arm of any pitcher they've had since Brien Taylor, the No. 1 pick in the 1991 draft. He's still raw, but his 95-96 MPH fastball was rated the best in the high Class-A Florida State League. . . **Willy Mo Pena** (18) originally signed with the Marlins and then the Mets, but the commissioner's office ruled both contracts invalid. Signed by the Yankees for $3.7 million in April, he's a five-tool center fielder with tremendous speed and power. . . **Juan Rivera** (21) is New York's right fielder of the future. He has both the power and the arm to make an impact at that position.

New York (AL)

209

Network Associates Coliseum

Offense

Since the formerly cavernous facility was enclosed in 1996, flyballs have carried much better at the refurbished Network Associates Coliseum. However, the park still depresses scoring and home runs. Over the past three years, the only places that have had a harsher effect on runs have been Yankee Stadium and Seattle's new Safeco Field. The Coliseum has a huge amount of foul territory, turning balls that would be out of play in other parks into outs.

Defense

The Coliseum infield is natural grass and slows down groundballs, and the same is true of the outfield. Starting in midsummer, shadows often fall across the plate, making pitches difficult to pick up as they come out of the sun. The right side of the infield and outfield also are sunny, making tracking flyballs an adventure at times.

Who It Helps The Most

Kevin Appier certainly benefited from his trade to Oakland. After joining the Athletics, his ERA was 2.91 at the Coliseum and 10.66 on the road. Jeremy Giambi has hit better at home throughout his career, and batted .353 with 17 homers in Oakland in 1999. Eric Chavez showed more power at the Coliseum than elsewhere as a rookie.

Who It Hurts The Most

Young slugger Ben Grieve has been more effective on the road. Matt Stairs had enjoyed more success at the Coliseum until last year, when 23 of his 38 homers came away from Oakland. None of the team's pitchers has been adversely affected by his ballpark.

Rookies & Newcomers

The Coliseum is a nice place to break in young pitchers, and prospects Chad Harville, Mark Mulder and Barry Zito all should join Oakland sometime in 2000. The Athletics' hitting prospects all are at least a year away.

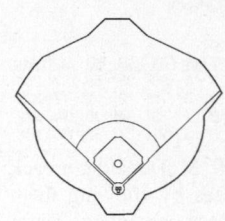

Dimensions: LF-330, LCF-362, CF-400, RCF-362, RF-330

Capacity: 43,012

Elevation: 25 feet

Surface: Grass

Foul Territory: Large

Park Factors

1999 Season

	Home Games			Away Games			
	Athletics	Opp	Total	Athletics	Opp	Total	Index
G	72	72	144	72	72	144	—
Avg	.267	.263	.265	.258	.292	.275	96
AB	2377	2529	4906	2542	2473	5015	98
R	402	355	757	404	417	821	92
H	634	664	1298	657	721	1378	94
2B	127	140	267	128	151	279	98
3B	12	11	23	7	18	25	94
HR	93	67	160	113	80	193	85
BB	320	251	571	355	246	601	97
SO	447	421	868	542	422	964	92
E	58	59	117	50	54	104	113
E-Infield	47	50	97	42	45	87	111
LHB-Avg	.269	.272	.271	.267	.274	.270	100
LHB-HR	53	28	81	69	29	98	82
RHB-Avg	.265	.253	.259	.250	.307	.279	93
RHB-HR	40	39	79	44	51	95	88

1997-1999

	Home Games			Away Games			
	Athletics	Opp	Total	Athletics	Opp	Total	Index
G	218	218	436	218	218	436	—
Avg	.261	.277	.270	.257	.292	.275	98
AB	7263	7789	15052	7645	7485	15130	99
R	1073	1143	2216	1120	1245	2365	94
H	1899	2160	4059	1968	2189	4157	98
2B	367	442	809	406	448	854	95
3B	29	34	63	20	64	84	75
HR	256	226	482	262	258	520	93
BB	884	757	1641	935	809	1744	95
SO	1400	1266	2666	1664	1244	2908	92
E	167	158	325	172	154	326	100
E-Infield	136	135	271	141	125	266	102
LHB-Avg	.277	.283	.280	.275	.290	.282	99
LHB-HR	133	108	241	128	107	235	99
RHB-Avg	.248	.273	.261	.243	.295	.268	97
RHB-HR	123	118	241	134	151	285	88

1999 Rankings (American League)

- Lowest RHB batting-average factor
- Second-lowest strikeout factor
- Third-lowest batting-average factor
- Third-lowest run factor
- Third-lowest hit factor
- Third-lowest home-run factor

Art Howe

1999 Season

Rebuilding can be a frustrating task, but Art Howe's four years of patience in Oakland are coming to fruition. Working with a growing number of excellent young players—with a few solid free-agent pickups and vets mixed in—Howe guided general manager Billy Beane's assemblage to the fifth-best record in the American League. The Athletics showed a 13-game improvement over their 1998 performance.

Offense

The Athletics started slowly, but wound up wielding one of the more potent offenses in the game last year. Up and down the system, patience and selectivity at the plate have been stressed, and the lessons paid off as the team placed first in the league in walks, second in home runs and fourth in on-base percentage. Howe has been criticized for being too predictable, always going by the book and relying on his cache of statistics to set lineups and substitutes. Whatever his methods, they certainly worked in 1999 and should leave little room for concern, let alone criticism.

Pitching & Defense

With assistance from pitching coach Rick Peterson, Oakland's pitching was much improved in 1999, particularly in the bullpen. Howe's easy-going style diffused pressure from his pitching staff, which faced an unexpected pennant race. The Athletics stayed close deep into games, allowing their offense and relievers to turn contests in question into victories. On defense, the team suffered mostly from youth and inexperience. Howe has been patient with young players like Miguel Tejada when they initially struggled in the field. That has helped build the confidence of his young players.

2000 Outlook

Howe will try to guide "Beane's Babies" to post-season play for the first time since 1992. The Athletics are loaded with young talent and have more excellent prospects on the way. Despite contending in 1999, Oakland wasn't ready for the playoffs. That may change in 2000.

Born: 12/15/46 in Pittsburgh, PA

Playing Experience: 1974-1985, Pit, Hou, StL

Managerial Experience: 9 seasons

Manager Statistics

Year	Team, Lg	W	L	Pct	GB	Finish
1999	Oakland, AL	87	75	.537	8.0	2nd West
9 Seasons		696	762	.477	—	—

1999 Starting Pitchers by Days Rest

	<=3	4	5	6+
Athletics Starts	0	91	38	23
Athletics ERA	0.00	5.48	3.55	5.21
AL Avg Starts	2	82	47	21
AL ERA	6.83	4.98	4.72	5.62

1999 Situational Stats

	Art Howe	AL Average
Hit & Run Success %	49.1	35.3
Stolen Base Success %	65.4	68.0
Platoon Pct.	62.4	56.7
Defensive Subs	56	22
High-Pitch Outings	5	15
Quick/Slow Hooks	12/18	18/18
Sacrifice Attempts	53	52

1999 Rankings (American League)

- 1st in fewest caught stealings of second base (32), hit-and-run success percentage (49.1%), defensive substitutions (56), mid-inning pitching changes (234) and saves with over 1 inning pitched (19)
- 2nd in sacrifice-bunt percentage (88.7%), pitchouts (43), pitchouts with a runner moving (11), intentional walks (32), one-batter pitcher appearances (44) and 2+ pitching changes in low-scoring games (30)
- 3rd in pinch-hitters used (144)

Oakland

Kevin Appier

Position: SP
Bats: R **Throws:** R
Ht: 6' 2" **Wt:** 200

Opening Day Age: 32
Born: 12/6/67 in
Lancaster, CA
ML Seasons: 11
Pronunciation:
APE-ee-er

1999 Season

Just a year removed from shoulder surgery, Kevin Appier was surrounded by trade rumors even before he joined the Royals in spring training. He handled the distraction like the pro he is, and eventually was traded to the Athletics for young pitchers Jeff D'Amico, Brad Rigby and Blake Stein. Appier didn't pitch as well as Oakland hoped, but he did go 7-5 to finish with 16 victories, the second-highest total of his career.

Pitching

In the past, Appier was known for his aggressive nature and an arsenal that included two- and four-seam fastballs, a splitter and a hard slider. While he topped 200 innings in 1999, he generally pitched in the high 80s rather than in his accustomed low 90s. His slider also wasn't as sharp, and hitters were able to look for his tough splitter more often. Because the quality of Appier's stuff has slipped, he no longer dominates righthanders. He also struggled once he reached 75 pitches last year, which hadn't been a problem in the past.

Defense

Appier's exaggerated motion reduces his ability to cover balls hit toward the left side of the diamond. He's very surehanded and makes plays on balls he can reach. He tries to hold runners, but his reliance on the splitter makes him easy prey for basestealers. Appier got little support from Oakland's catchers in that regard.

2000 Outlook

Considering that he made just three starts in 1998, last year had to be considered a success for Appier. The Athletics are good at protecting their pitchers' arms, which will help him. They picked up his option for $5.2 million, anticipating that he'll regain the form that once made him one of the best starters in the American League.

Overall Statistics

	W	L	Pct.	ERA	G	GS	Sv	IP	H	BB	SO	HR	Ratio
1999	16	14	.533	5.17	34	34	0	209.0	230	84	131	27	1.50
Career	121	94	.563	3.54	293	281	0	1889.1	1726	657	1504	143	1.26

How Often He Throws Strikes

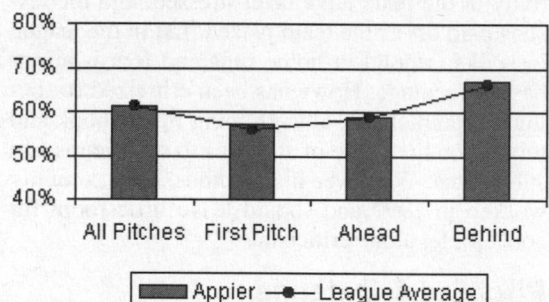

1999 Situational Stats

	W	L	ERA	Sv	IP		AB	H	HR	RBI	Avg
Home	10	5	3.80	0	123.0	LHB	411	122	11	48	.297
Road	6	9	7.12	0	86.0	RHB	412	108	16	65	.262
First Half	8	7	4.95	0	120.0	Sc Pos	216	65	8	91	.301
Scnd Half	8	7	5.46	0	89.0	Clutch	30	14	1	10	.467

1999 Rankings (American League)

- 1st in highest ERA on the road (7.12)
- 2nd in games started (34)
- 4th in losses (14)
- 5th in highest ERA (5.17)
- 6th in batters faced (926) and stolen bases allowed (24)
- 7th in highest stolen-base percentage allowed (72.7%)
- 8th in wild pitches (10)
- 9th in wins (16), hits allowed (230), lowest strikeout/walk ratio (1.6), fewest pitches thrown per batter (3.66) and most baserunners allowed per 9 innings (13.8)
- 10th in highest slugging percentage allowed (.448) and lowest ERA at home (3.80)

Eric Chavez

1999 Season

Baseball America's 1998 Minor League Player of the Year, Eric Chavez was the Opening Day third sacker for the Athletics last year at age 21. He did little in the first half of the season, then started to sting the ball before going on the disabled list for a month in late August with a torn plantar fascia in his right foot.

Hitting

A natural hitter, Chavez has terrific hand-eye coordination and a quick bat, which give him good power to the gaps and beyond. He's a line-drive hitter who is comfortable taking outside pitches to the opposite field. Chavez still has some trouble with inside fastballs, and his strike-zone judgment is promising yet needs work. Lefthanders give him trouble, especially hard throwers. He's a diligent worker, so he should improve as he learns the pitchers around the American League.

Baserunning & Defense

Chavez has above-average speed for a third baseman, though it may be compromised by his foot woes. He won't steal much but is aggressive enough to take extra bases. His glovework at third base is solid, though his reactions sometimes are slow. He moves better to his right than to his left, and is average at charging bunts and rollers. His throws to first are strong but sail on him from time to time.

2000 Outlook

Chavez' much-anticipated arrival didn't live up to expectations, but it would be unfair to say his rookie season was a disappointment. His second-half improvement was a very good sign, and if he continues to progress he quickly will become the top third baseman in the American League. He's still young and inexperienced, so he'll probably experience some travails in 2000.

Position: 3B
Bats: L **Throws:** R
Ht: 6' 0" **Wt:** 204

Opening Day Age: 22
Born: 12/7/77 in Los Angeles, CA
ML Seasons: 2

Overall Statistics

	G	AB	R	H	D	T	HR	RBI	SB	BB	SO	Avg	OBP	Slg
1999	115	356	47	88	21	2	13	50	1	46	56	.247	.333	.427
Career	131	401	53	102	25	3	13	56	2	49	61	.254	.336	.429

Where He Hits the Ball

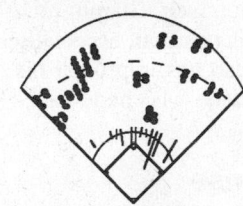
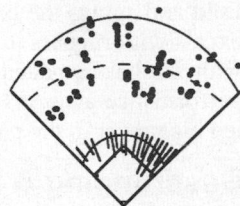

Vs. LHP   **Vs. RHP**

1999 Situational Stats

	AB	H	HR	RBI	Avg		AB	H	HR	RBI	Avg
Home	179	45	8	28	.251	LHP	49	9	0	3	.184
Road	177	43	5	22	.243	RHP	307	79	13	47	.257
First Half	214	49	7	26	.229	Sc Pos	82	18	1	30	.220
Scnd Half	142	39	6	24	.275	Clutch	42	12	2	6	.286

1999 Rankings (American League)

- 2nd in fielding percentage at third base (.961)
- 10th in lowest batting average with runners in scoring position
- Led the Athletics in batting average with the bases loaded (.462)

Oakland

Jason Giambi

1999 Season

His numbers had shown steady improvement since 1995, and in 1999 Jason Giambi turned in a career year. For the first time in his five major league seasons, Giambi topped .300, 30 homers, 100 walks and a .400 on-base percentage. After hitting just .231 in June, he batted .363 in July and .404 in August. Not only did he hit .361 with 72 RBI in the second half, he also used his leadership skills to push his young teammates to the brink of postseason play.

Hitting

An intelligent hitter who remembers what pitchers have thrown to him in different situations, Giambi makes the most of every at-bat. He uses the entire field and sprays the ball with power. Giambi now excels with runners in scoring position, especially with the bases loaded. He also has improved his performance against lefthanders, who had shackled his power in the past.

Baserunning & Defense

Not known for his speed on the bases, Giambi is a hard worker who gets the most out of his abilities. His hustle takes him from first to third on a single and brings him home from second on most hits to the gaps and corners. Giambi improved his glovework a lot during his second full season as Oakland's first sacker, cutting his error total in half from 1998 to 1999. Improving his defense is an ongoing project.

2000 Outlook

Giambi is a key component of a young team on the brink of contending for a number of years. His numbers should continue to improve, and he's capable of a 40-homer season and an American League batting crown. An MVP Award isn't out of the question, either.

Position: 1B/DH
Bats: L **Throws:** R
Ht: 6' 3" **Wt:** 235

Opening Day Age: 29
Born: 1/8/71 in West Covina, CA
ML Seasons: 5
Pronunciation: gee-AHM-bee

Overall Statistics

	G	AB	R	H	D	T	HR	RBI	SB	BB	SO	Avg	OBP	Slg
1999	158	575	115	181	36	1	33	123	1	105	106	.315	.422	.553
Career	647	2368	384	700	152	4	106	418	5	320	423	.296	.381	.497

Where He Hits the Ball

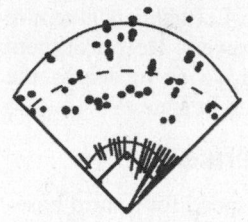

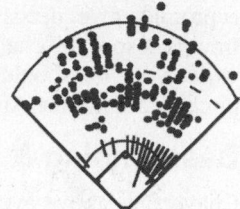

Vs. LHP   **Vs. RHP**

1999 Situational Stats

	AB	H	HR	RBI	Avg		AB	H	HR	RBI	Avg
Home	278	98	17	61	.353	LHP	181	51	8	37	.282
Road	297	83	16	62	.279	RHP	394	130	25	86	.330
First Half	306	84	15	51	.275	Sc Pos	163	51	10	89	.313
Scnd Half	269	97	18	72	.361	Clutch	72	19	2	9	.264

1999 Rankings (American League)

- 2nd in walks
- 3rd in times on base (293), pitches seen (2,818) and fielding percentage at first base (.995)
- 5th in batting average at home
- Led the Athletics in batting average, runs scored, hits, singles, doubles, total bases (318), RBI, sacrifice flies (8), walks, intentional walks (6), times on base (293), pitches seen (2,818), plate appearances (695), on-base percentage, batting average with runners in scoring position, batting average in the clutch, batting average vs. righthanded pitchers, slugging percentage vs. righthanded pitchers (.586), on-base percentage vs. righthanded pitchers (.440), batting average at home and batting average on the road

Ben Grieve

Position: LF
Bats: L **Throws:** R
Ht: 6' 4" **Wt:** 230

Opening Day Age: 23
Born: 5/4/76 in
Arlington, TX
ML Seasons: 3
Pronunciation:
GREEVE

1999 Season

Big things were expected of Ben Grieve following his Rookie-of-the-Year campaign in 1998. Thus it was shocking to find Grieve hitting .131 with just 11 RBI six weeks into the 1999 season. His early struggles caused manager Art Howe to sit Grieve against lefthanders for a stretch, before a string of multihit games in late May turned the tide. From May 20 on, Grieve batted .303-25-75, setting a personal high for homers while stabilizing the middle of the formidable Athletics lineup.

Hitting

Grieve is as even-keeled as a hitter can be. During his protracted slump, he worked hard to get out of the funk but didn't let it alter his demeanor. His swing is a thing of beauty, generating impressive power to all fields. Already a selective hitter, Grieve will rank among the American League's best once he learns the pitchers and stays back consistently on breaking pitches. He struggled all season against lefthanders, especially those who threw good breaking balls on the outside corner. By the time he masters southpaws, he should be a complete hitter.

Baserunning & Defense

In exchange for that beautiful swing, Grieve has been saddled with slow feet and slow reactions in the field. In 1999 he moved from right field to left, where he's less of a liability, but he doesn't get much of a jump on the ball regardless of where he plays. His arm is adequate, especially in left. Grieve was successful in four of four basestealing attempts, proving he knows his limitations and knows how to exploit them.

2000 Outlook

Grieve's 1999 probably was an anomaly. A repeat of his 1999 numbers, though, while below expectations, still would be very good for a 23-year-old. He soon should begin posting .300-30-100 seasons on an annual basis.

Overall Statistics

	G	AB	R	H	D	T	HR	RBI	SB	BB	SO	Avg	OBP	Slg
1999	148	486	80	129	21	0	28	86	4	63	108	.265	.358	.481
Career	327	1162	186	326	68	2	49	199	6	161	256	.281	.376	.469

Where He Hits the Ball

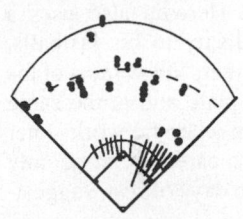

Vs. LHP

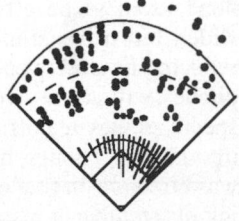

Vs. RHP

1999 Situational Stats

	AB	H	HR	RBI	Avg		AB	H	HR	RBI	Avg
Home	243	62	13	43	.255	LHP	109	17	3	13	.156
Road	243	67	15	43	.276	RHP	377	112	25	73	.297
First Half	248	63	11	38	.254	Sc Pos	137	34	8	56	.248
Scnd Half	238	66	17	48	.277	Clutch	44	6	1	2	.136

1999 Rankings (American League)

- 3rd in lowest batting average in the clutch and highest fielding percentage in left field (.987)
- 9th in highest percentage of pitches taken (61.9%)
- 10th in errors in left field (3)
- Led the Athletics in GDPs (17), highest ground-ball/flyball ratio (1.4) and highest percentage of swings put into play (45.1%)
- Led AL left fielders in home runs, HR frequency (17.4 ABs per HR) and slugging percentage vs. righthanded pitchers (.544)

Oakland

Gil Heredia

1999 Season

Before 1999, Gil Heredia had spent parts of seven seasons in the major leagues, none as a full-time starter. A strong showing at the end of 1998 and in spring training earned him a spot in Oakland's rotation, and he never relinquished it. He established several personal bests and was particularly effective in July and August, going 8-0 in 11 starts to fuel the Athletics' wild-card run.

Pitching

Heredia proves that excellent control can be a substitute for velocity. He tops out in the mid- to high 80s, throwing four different fastballs: a two-seamer, four-seamer, cutter and splitter. When he's on, he mixes those pitches well. When he struggles, none seem to be effective. Heredia also uses a slider, but it has similar velocity to his fastballs, reducing its effectiveness. Hitters know most of his pitches will arrive over the plate and at the same speed, so they tee off on him when he works later into games. Though he had a career year, he only was effective on five or more days of rest, suggesting his stamina is suspect.

Defense

Possessed with a quick delivery and nice move to first, Heredia keeps basestealers at bay. Just 11 of 21 succeeded on his watch in 1999, and he picked off two others. He handles bunts adequately, though he occasionally is slow to cover first base and makes more than his share of errors.

2000 Outlook

Eligible for arbitration, Heredia re-signed for two years and $2.35 million. Much of his success was a result of the opportunity provided by the Athletics and the approach they take with their pitchers. Though he has little room for improvement, Heredia is a good fit as the No. 3 starter in Oakland.

Position: SP
Bats: R **Throws:** R
Ht: 6' 1" **Wt:** 221

Opening Day Age: 34
Born: 10/26/65 in Nogales, AZ
ML Seasons: 8
Pronunciation: her-RAY-dee-uh

Overall Statistics

	W	L	Pct.	ERA	G	GS	Sv	IP	H	BB	SO	HR	Ratio
1999	13	8	.619	4.81	33	33	0	200.1	228	34	117	22	1.31
Career	35	32	.522	4.38	211	78	4	645.2	721	126	398	64	1.31

How Often He Throws Strikes

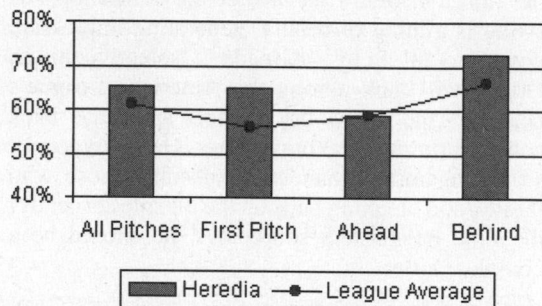

1999 Situational Stats

	W	L	ERA	Sv	IP		AB	H	HR	RBI	Avg
Home	5	3	4.61	0	80.0	LHB	409	117	7	43	.286
Road	8	5	4.94	0	120.1	RHB	398	111	15	57	.279
First Half	5	5	5.51	0	99.2	Sc Pos	180	60	4	73	.333
Scnd Half	8	3	4.11	0	100.2	Clutch	39	18	2	8	.462

1999 Rankings (American League)

- 1st in fewest pitches thrown per batter (3.40) and walks per 9 innings (1.5)
- 2nd in highest strikeout/walk ratio (3.4)
- Led the Athletics in ERA, wins, games started, innings pitched, hits allowed, batters faced (852), home runs allowed, pitches thrown (2,893), runners caught stealing (10), winning percentage, highest strikeout/walk ratio (3.4), lowest batting average allowed (.283), lowest slugging percentage allowed (.441), lowest on-base percentage allowed (.318), highest groundball/flyball ratio allowed (1.6), lowest stolen-base percentage allowed (52.4%), fewest pitches thrown per batter (3.40), fewest baserunners allowed per 9 innings (12.1) and most run support per 9 innings (6.2)

Ramon Hernandez

1999 Season

Ramon Hernandez made his major league debut in late June when Mike Macfarlane went on the disabled list with a sprained thumb. Hernandez played so well that he displaced starter A.J. Hinch, who was sent to Triple-A when Macfarlane returned. While a knee injury sidelined him for most of August, Hernandez was productive when he got regular playing time in early July and September.

Hitting

Blessed with great mechanics, Hernandez has an excellent knowledge of the strike zone and is a good two-strike hitter. He drills line drives to all fields and possesses untapped power. When his swing gets long at times, pitchers can blow fastballs by Hernandez. With his power potential and ability to make contact, he presents intriguing offensive abilities at a key defensive position. Hernandez excelled in situational hitting as a rookie, batting .389 with runners in scoring position and .375 in the clutch.

Baserunning & Defense

Hernandez runs like a typical catcher, which is to say not well at all. Behind the plate, he has decent arm strength but has been bothered by chronic elbow pain that limited him to DH duties for most of 1998. He threw out 24 percent of basestealers for Oakland, a slightly better rate than Hinch's. Hernandez struggles to block some balls in the dirt and his footwork needs improvement if he's to be a full-time catcher.

2000 Outlook

Hernandez likely will open 2000 as Oakland's starting catcher. He'll have to continue to fend off Hinch, but Hernandez has hit much better than Hinch in the majors. Interestingly, Hinch has a significantly better track record in the minors. Hernandez' offensive skills ultimately will determine how much he plays.

Position: C
Bats: R **Throws:** R
Ht: 6' 0" **Wt:** 227

Opening Day Age: 23
Born: 5/20/76 in Caracas, Venezuela
ML Seasons: 1

Overall Statistics

	G	AB	R	H	D	T	HR	RBI	SB	BB	SO	Avg	OBP	Slg
1999	40	136	13	38	7	0	3	21	1	18	11	.279	.363	.397
Career	40	136	13	38	7	0	3	21	1	18	11	.279	.363	.397

Where He Hits the Ball

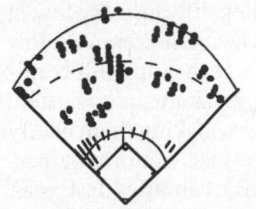
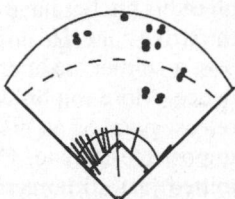

Vs. LHP   **Vs. RHP**

1999 Situational Stats

	AB	H	HR	RBI	Avg		AB	H	HR	RBI	Avg
Home	70	23	1	15	.329	LHP	42	15	3	12	.357
Road	66	15	2	6	.227	RHP	94	23	0	9	.245
First Half	39	12	2	8	.308	Sc Pos	36	14	1	18	.389
Scnd Half	97	26	1	13	.268	Clutch	16	6	0	5	.375

1999 Rankings (American League)

- 7th in errors at catcher (6)

Oakland

Tim Hudson

1999 Season

The Athletics tried to restock their pitching supply in the 1997 draft, when they spent eight of their first nine picks on hurlers. Little did they realize that the last of those pitchers, sixth-round choice Tim Hudson, would be the first to reach Oakland and that he would dominate when he got there. In his major league debut on June 8, Hudson struck out 11 in five innings. He went 11-2 in 21 starts, all but establishing himself as the Athletics' ace. Two of his victories came against 1999 Cy Young Award winners Randy Johnson and Pedro Martinez in head-to-head matchups.

Pitching

Hudson doesn't have overwhelming raw stuff, but all of his pitches have excellent life and stay low in the strike zone. He throws a heavy sinker in the low 90s, a splitter, a slider and a changeup with confidence. More important, he maintains a consistent release point on all his pitches, making them nearly impossible to read. Counting the minors, he permitted just 10 homers in 203.1 innings last year. Hudson also keeps hitters off balance by changing speeds on his splitter. He isn't afraid to claim his share of the plate.

Defense

Hudson gets off the mound quickly and handles his defensive responsibilities well. His move to first base is improving and should be above average in time. While his motion to the plate can be slow, American League runners didn't run wild on him.

2000 Outlook

Hudson heads into 2000 as one of the more promising young pitchers in the game. The only thing he seems to need is a little work on controlling his emotions better while he's on the mound. Having Kevin Appier as a veteran to lean on will help him.

Position: SP
Bats: R **Throws:** R
Ht: 6' 0" **Wt:** 160

Opening Day Age: 24
Born: 7/14/75 in Columbus, GA
ML Seasons: 1

Overall Statistics

	W	L	Pct.	ERA	G	GS	Sv	IP	H	BB	SO	HR	Ratio
1999	11	2	.846	3.23	21	21	0	136.1	121	62	132	8	1.34
Career	11	2	.846	3.23	21	21	0	136.1	121	62	132	8	1.34

How Often He Throws Strikes

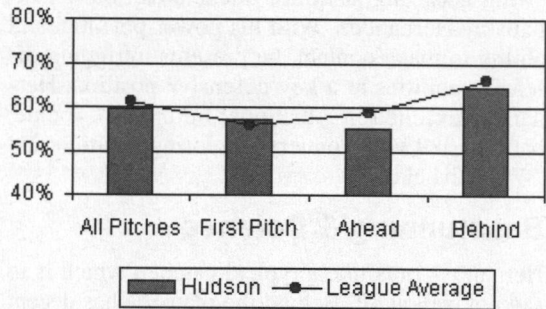

1999 Situational Stats

	W	L	ERA	Sv	IP		AB	H	HR	RBI	Avg
Home	5	1	3.29	0	65.2	LHB	265	62	4	22	.234
Road	6	1	3.18	0	70.2	RHB	246	59	4	24	.240
First Half	5	1	2.09	0	47.1	Sc Pos	116	21	3	22	.181
Scnd Half	6	1	3.84	0	89.0	Clutch	34	4	0	1	.118

1999 Rankings (American League)

- 5th in lowest batting average allowed vs. lefthanded batters
- Led the Athletics in strikeouts, stolen bases allowed (14) and lowest batting average allowed vs. lefthanded batters

John Jaha

Position: DH
Bats: R **Throws:** R
Ht: 6' 1" **Wt:** 224

Opening Day Age: 33
Born: 5/27/66 in Portland, OR
ML Seasons: 8
Pronunciation: JAH-hah

1999 Season

After a 1998 season during which he suffered through his usual assortment of ailments and lost his confidence at the plate with the Brewers, John Jaha signed a minor league deal with the Athletics for $850,000. He discovered he had made the team just prior to breaking camp, then turned in a monster year. He got off to a great start and remained healthy enough to play in 140 games for the first time since 1996, slumping only briefly in August. His 35 homers and 111 RBI almost doubled his combined totals from the previous two seasons.

Hitting

Jaha is a disciplined hitter who used his selectivity to his advantage in 1999 after falling behind in the count too often the year before. He generates good power to the gaps, especially to right-center field, because he stays on top of breaking pitches. Conversely, he gets in trouble with inside pitches, as his propensity to pull creates a lot of foul balls and flyouts. When Jaha is in a groove, his homers are hit to all fields while his singles and doubles are pulled. He hits lefthanders for a better average, but shows more power against righties.

Baserunning & Defense

Because of his fragile health, Jaha's aggressiveness on the basepaths has been limited. He struggles to score from second base on singles hit to center and left field. Though he only played eight games in the field last year, he had no miscues in 46 chances at first base. Because his playing time in the field has been greatly reduced in recent years, his range has declined and he struggles with bunts.

2000 Outlook

The Athletics gave Jaha a two-year contract as soon as the 1999 season ended, ensuring his spot at DH in a productive lineup if he stays healthy. This offseason marked his first surgery-free winter in several years.

Overall Statistics

	G	AB	R	H	D	T	HR	RBI	SB	BB	SO	Avg	OBP	Slg
1999	142	457	93	126	23	0	35	111	2	101	129	.276	.414	.556
Career	781	2633	454	709	122	5	140	477	35	391	633	.269	.371	.479

Where He Hits the Ball

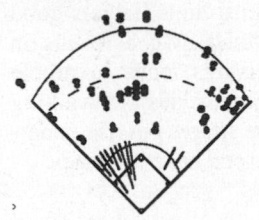 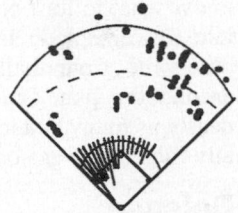

Vs. LHP   **Vs. RHP**

1999 Situational Stats

	AB	H	HR	RBI	Avg		AB	H	HR	RBI	Avg
Home	230	66	18	63	.287	LHP	129	41	11	29	.318
Road	227	60	17	48	.264	RHP	328	85	24	82	.259
First Half	234	67	19	56	.286	Sc Pos	142	40	13	80	.282
Scnd Half	223	59	16	55	.265	Clutch	52	13	4	13	.250

1999 Rankings (American League)

- 1st in most pitches seen per plate appearance (4.38) and highest percentage of pitches taken (67.1%)
- 3rd in walks
- 5th in slugging percentage vs. lefthanded pitchers (.643)
- Led the Athletics in strikeouts, slugging percentage, HR frequency (13.1 ABs per HR), most pitches seen per plate appearance (4.38), batting average vs. lefthanded pitchers, cleanup slugging percentage (.563), slugging percentage vs. lefthanded pitchers (.643), on-base percentage vs. lefthanded pitchers (.451) and highest percentage of pitches taken (67.1%)

Omar Olivares

1999 Season

Omar Olivares did exactly what the Athletics hoped for when they acquired him and Randy Velarde from the Angels on July 29 in exchange for minor leaguers Jeff DaVanon, Nathan Haynes and Elvin Nina. Olivares went 7-2 in 12 starts for Oakland, finishing the year with a career-high 15 victories. However, he was far less effective in the second half. His ERA was 5.28 after the All-Star break, compared to 3.28 before.

Pitching

Olivares' strength is changing speeds. Though his fastball reaches the low 90s on occasion, the key is mixing in breaking balls that he'll throw anywhere from the low 70s to the mid-80s. Hitters never know what to look for against him. He gets good late movement on his fastball, which results in plenty of groundballs. Olivares tends to nibble around the plate, and succeeds despite walking nearly as many batters as he strikes out. He generally runs out of gas once he reaches 90 pitches.

Defense

Olivares has two very good moves to first base, allowing him to keep baserunners close, and his delivery is quick to the plate. Just 12 of 19 basestealers succeeded against him last season, despite the lack of a strong defensive catcher on either team he played for. Olivares covers groundballs and bunts equally well on both sides of the mound, and is diligent about covering first base.

2000 Outlook

Olivares is Oakland's highest priority among its free agents, but it may be difficult to re-sign him. He could price himself out of Oakland during an offseason in which the demand for free agents outweighs the supply. He had little success before 1998, so the bottom could drop out quickly.

Position: SP
Bats: R **Throws:** R
Ht: 6' 1" **Wt:** 205

Opening Day Age: 32
Born: 7/6/67 in Mayaguez, Puerto Rico
ML Seasons: 10
Pronunciation: oh-lih-VARE-es

Overall Statistics

	W	L	Pct.	ERA	G	GS	Sv	IP	H	BB	SO	HR	Ratio
1999	15	11	.577	4.16	32	32	0	205.2	217	81	85	19	1.45
Career	67	69	.493	4.36	283	201	3	1373.2	1421	583	727	132	1.46

How Often He Throws Strikes

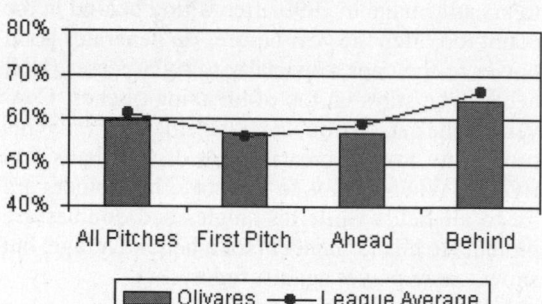

1999 Situational Stats

	W	L	ERA	Sv	IP		AB	H	HR	RBI	Avg
Home	7	4	3.71	0	97.0	LHB	392	103	12	53	.263
Road	8	7	4.56	0	108.2	RHB	393	114	7	45	.290
First Half	8	6	3.28	0	115.1	Sc Pos	188	54	2	74	.287
Scnd Half	7	5	5.28	0	90.1	Clutch	56	11	2	5	.196

1999 Rankings (American League)

- 1st in lowest strikeout/walk ratio (1.0) and fewest strikeouts per 9 innings (3.7)
- 2nd in GDPs induced (31) and most GDPs induced per 9 innings (1.4)
- 4th in fewest home runs allowed per 9 innings (.83)
- 5th in pickoff throws (166), fewest pitches thrown per batter (3.55) and errors at pitcher (3)
- 7th in complete games (4) and most GDPs induced per GDP situation (17.5%)
- 9th in ERA at home (3.71)
- 10th in wins (15)

Matt Stairs

1999 Season

A main cog in the Athletics' offensive machine, Matt Stairs cracked the 30-homer barrier for the first time in his career while also producing career highs in extra-base hits, total bases and walks. His strikeouts also reached new heights, and his power surge came with a significant dip in batting average. He hit just .228 through June and July, the heart of the season, which led to his career-low .258 mark for a full major league campaign.

Hitting

Stairs swings from the heels, and when he connects, pitchers are in trouble. He has tremendous power but sometimes concentrates too much on pulling the ball. While he can do so effectively, he's a better hitter when he's spraying the ball all over the field. Not only did his overall average dip in 1999, his mark against lefthanders plummeted from .280 the year before to .236.

Baserunning & Defense

After a stringent offseason conditioning program, Stairs came into camp in 1999 in the best shape of his life. With deceptive speed buried in his squat body, Stairs nearly scored 100 runs and hit a career-high three triples last year. He didn't have as much success stealing bases, getting nailed seven times in nine tries. He doesn't read pitchers well. Stairs made a career-high 139 appearances in the outfield, almost solely in right, and played solid defense. He has good instincts and an impressive arm.

2000 Outlook

Stairs fits in well with the Athletics, providing power and flexibility in the batting order at a reasonable salary. He had an at-bat in every spot in the order but first and eighth. Signed through 2000 with a club option for 2001, Stairs is poised for a few more strong years. The Athletics are top-heavy in lefthanded power, so it isn't inconceivable that he might be swapped for pitching.

Position: RF
Bats: L **Throws:** R
Ht: 5' 9" **Wt:** 217

Opening Day Age: 32
Born: 2/27/68 in Saint John, Canada
ML Seasons: 7

Overall Statistics

	G	AB	R	H	D	T	HR	RBI	SB	BB	SO	Avg	OBP	Slg
1999	146	531	94	137	26	3	38	102	2	89	124	.258	.366	.533
Career	547	1669	276	465	93	6	102	328	14	228	322	.279	.367	.525

Where He Hits the Ball

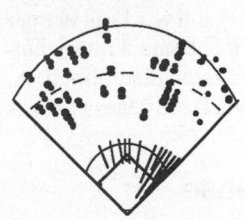
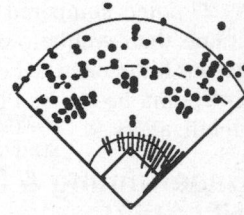

Vs. LHP **Vs. RHP**

1999 Situational Stats

	AB	H	HR	RBI	Avg		AB	H	HR	RBI	Avg
Home	256	64	15	44	.250	LHP	165	39	8	26	.236
Road	275	73	23	58	.265	RHP	366	98	30	76	.268
First Half	279	68	17	50	.244	Sc Pos	147	36	10	65	.245
Scnd Half	252	69	21	52	.274	Clutch	64	15	5	11	.234

1999 Rankings (American League)

- 1st in lowest cleanup slugging percentage (.393)
- 4th in highest percentage of pitches taken (64.4%)
- 5th in most pitches seen per plate appearance (4.24) and lowest fielding percentage in right field (.981)
- 6th in errors in right field (5) and bunts in play (5)
- 7th in lowest batting average vs. lefthanded pitchers
- 8th in home runs, HR frequency (14.0 ABs per HR) and lowest batting average at home
- Led the Athletics in home runs, caught stealing (7), intentional walks (6), fewest GDPs per GDP situation (5.4%) and bunts in play (5)
- Led AL right fielders in highest percentage of pitches taken (64.4%)

Miguel Tejada

1999 Season

Regarded as one of the best shortstop prospects in the game, Miguel Tejada showed why in his first full major league season. His 84 RBI set an Oakland record for shortstops, and his 21 homers were just one shy of Bert Campaneris' standard. Tejada homered three times in one game against the Dodgers on June 11 and was especially hot in August, helping the Athletics stay close in the wild-card race.

Hitting

An aggressive hitter with solid power, Tejada isn't troubled by breaking pitches. He must learn to use the entire field and be more selective. He made strides in 1999, improving his on-base percentage by 27 points compared to 1998 and working deeper counts than ever before. He'll become a more dangerous hitter once he becomes more disciplined. At this point, he has had limited effectiveness versus righthanders.

Baserunning & Defense

Blessed with excellent speed, Tejada can be a terror on the basepaths, but he also can run into outs and has yet to become a prolific or effective basestealer. If he can improve his reads and jumps, he should be able to steal 20-30 bases each season. On defense, Tejada's quickness helps him get to balls, though he often falls victim to poor decisions after he does. He was steadier than in 1998, so that's a good sign.

2000 Outlook

With the steady improvement in his numbers over the last three seasons, it's clear that Tejada's skills are growing as he gains confidence and experience. It also helps that Tejada will continue to play alongside a steady and disciplined second baseman, Randy Velarde. That should keep Tejada in the game mentally, and his strong skills set should take over from there.

Position: SS
Bats: R **Throws:** R
Ht: 5' 9" **Wt:** 188

Opening Day Age: 23
Born: 5/25/76 in Bani, Dominican Republic
ML Seasons: 3
Pronunciation: mee-GHEL teh-HAH-duh

Overall Statistics

	G	AB	R	H	D	T	HR	RBI	SB	BB	SO	Avg	OBP	Slg
1999	159	593	93	149	33	4	21	84	8	57	94	.251	.325	.427
Career	290	1057	156	254	56	7	34	139	15	87	202	.240	.308	.403

Where He Hits the Ball

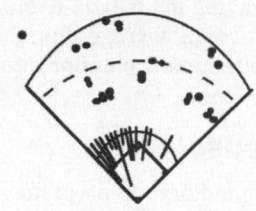 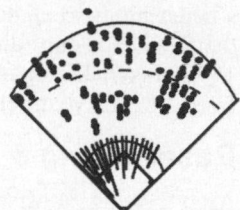

Vs. LHP   **Vs. RHP**

1999 Situational Stats

	AB	H	HR	RBI	Avg		AB	H	HR	RBI	Avg
Home	290	79	12	42	.272	LHP	140	38	4	20	.271
Road	303	70	9	42	.231	RHP	453	111	17	64	.245
First Half	319	83	8	34	.260	Sc Pos	144	34	6	57	.236
Scnd Half	274	66	13	50	.241	Clutch	64	8	2	9	.125

1999 Rankings (American League)

- 1st in lowest batting average in the clutch
- 2nd in lowest batting average on the road
- 4th in errors at shortstop (21)
- 5th in lowest batting average vs. righthanded pitchers, lowest fielding percentage at shortstop (.973) and games played
- 6th in lowest batting average
- 10th in sacrifice bunts (9) and lowest on-base percentage vs. righthanded pitchers (.312)
- Led the Athletics in at-bats, triples, sacrifice bunts (9), caught stealing (7), games played, steals of third (2) and highest percentage of extra bases taken as a runner (56.1%)

Randy Velarde

Position: 2B
Bats: R **Throws:** R
Ht: 6' 0" **Wt:** 200

Opening Day Age: 37
Born: 11/24/62 in Midland, TX
ML Seasons: 13
Pronunciation: vuh-LARR-dee

1999 Season

After missing most of the previous two seasons with elbow, shoulder and forearm injuries, Randy Velarde managed to stay healthy in 1999. He appeared in a career-high 156 games and had his best offensive season in his 13th year in the majors. Traded by the Angels to the Athletics along with Omar Olivares on July 29, Velarde hit .333 in Oakland and more than replaced the injured Tony Phillips in the lineup. He assumed a leadership role and solidified the infield with his steady, focused approach to the game.

Hitting

Velarde is a professional hitter who uses the entire field. He's adept at inside-outing pitches to right field. Still, he hit almost all of his home runs this past season to left and left-center. Inside fastballs no longer tie up Velarde, as he has learned to pull them for power. His control of the strike zone has improved as he has gotten older.

Baserunning & Defense

A fine baserunner, Velarde scored 105 runs, had seven triples and stole 24 bases—all testaments that he still has plenty of speed and knowledge on the basepaths. He makes the routine plays at second base, but his range is diminished. He struggles at times with balls up the middle. His surgically repaired arm has rebounded and once again has average strength.

2000 Outlook

Because they valued his presence both on the field and in the clubhouse, the Athletics re-signed Velarde to a two-year deal soon after the season ended. Whether he can repeat his wonderful 1999 season is a question, but he still should rank among the more productive second sackers in the American League. Velarde has an intense workout regiment, which keeps him in good shape and should mitigate his past injury problems.

Overall Statistics

	G	AB	R	H	D	T	HR	RBI	SB	BB	SO	Avg	OBP	Slg
1999	156	631	105	200	25	7	16	76	24	70	98	.317	.390	.455
Career	1002	3284	479	911	164	21	77	364	60	360	640	.277	.353	.410

Where He Hits the Ball

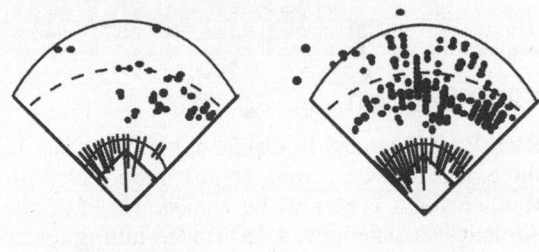

Vs. LHP   **Vs. RHP**

1999 Situational Stats

	AB	H	HR	RBI	Avg		AB	H	HR	RBI	Avg
Home	300	93	8	31	.310	LHP	141	49	4	20	.348
Road	331	107	8	45	.323	RHP	490	151	12	56	.308
First Half	319	99	7	41	.310	Sc Pos	132	42	3	51	.318
Scnd Half	312	101	9	35	.324	Clutch	79	29	2	9	.367

1999 Rankings (American League)

- 1st in singles (152)
- 3rd in at-bats (631)
- 4th in hits (200) and errors at second base (14)
- 6th in pitches seen (2,763) and highest percentage of extra bases taken as a runner (66.2%)
- Led the Athletics in stolen bases (11), batting average on a 3-1 count (.500), batting average on an 0-2 count (.368), batting average on a 3-2 count (.381), batting average with two strikes (.274) and steals of third (2)
- Led AL second basemen in at-bats (631), hits (200), singles (152), GDPs (19), batting average vs. lefthanded pitchers (.348), on-base percentage vs. lefthanded pitchers (.446) and batting average on the road (.323)

Rich Becker

Position: CF/LF/RF
Bats: L **Throws:** L
Ht: 5'10" **Wt:** 193

Opening Day Age: 28
Born: 2/1/72 in Aurora, IL
ML Seasons: 7

Overall Statistics

	G	AB	R	H	D	T	HR	RBI	SB	BB	SO	Avg	OBP	Slg
1999	129	264	36	68	8	2	6	26	8	58	81	.258	.395	.371
Career	674	1942	286	501	86	12	37	204	64	283	529	.258	.354	.372

1999 Situational Stats

	AB	H	HR	RBI	Avg		AB	H	HR	RBI	Avg
Home	116	33	5	14	.284	LHP	19	3	0	2	.158
Road	148	35	1	12	.236	RHP	245	65	6	24	.265
First Half	84	20	3	7	.238	Sc Pos	57	13	1	19	.228
Scnd Half	180	48	3	19	.267	Clutch	46	9	0	4	.196

1999 Season

Rich Becker landed in Oakland, his fifth team in three seasons, via a mid-August trade with Milwaukee for a player to be named. He gave the Athletics an experienced, lefthanded-hitting center fielder to platoon with Ryan Christenson. Becker also batted .279 as a pinch-hitter last year, connecting for 12 hits with five RBI.

Hitting, Baserunning & Defense

Displaying occasional power, Becker is a gap-to-gap hitter. He's patient but often takes too many pitches. He continues to struggle with high, inside pitches and with lefthanders. Because of his troubles versus southpaws, Becker has been labeled a strict platoon player. He's capable of stealing 20-plus bases over the course of a full season, but he doesn't justify enough playing time to make that happen. That speed helps him get to balls in the outfield. His arm isn't strong, but it's accurate.

2000 Outlook

With center-field prospects Mario Encarnacion and Terrence Long getting closer to the majors, Oakland decided not to tender Becker a contract. His best bet is catching on as a platoon player or a fourth outfielder.

Ryan Christenson

Position: CF
Bats: R **Throws:** R
Ht: 6' 0" **Wt:** 191

Opening Day Age: 26
Born: 3/28/74 in Redlands, CA
ML Seasons: 2

Overall Statistics

	G	AB	R	H	D	T	HR	RBI	SB	BB	SO	Avg	OBP	Slg
1999	106	268	41	56	12	1	4	24	7	38	58	.209	.305	.306
Career	223	638	97	151	34	3	9	64	12	74	164	.237	.314	.342

1999 Situational Stats

	AB	H	HR	RBI	Avg		AB	H	HR	RBI	Avg
Home	120	29	2	11	.242	LHP	93	28	3	16	.301
Road	148	27	2	13	.182	RHP	175	28	1	8	.160
First Half	130	25	2	13	.192	Sc Pos	73	16	1	21	.219
Scnd Half	138	31	2	11	.225	Clutch	28	4	0	0	.143

1999 Season

After outplaying Jason McDonald in 1998 and retaining the center-field job coming out of spring training, Ryan Christenson never got untracked at the plate. Sent to Triple-A in mid-April, he returned in late May, only to go 1-for-25 at the plate. His season was a disappointment.

Hitting, Baserunning & Defense

A line-drive hitter with decent power, Christenson is a hard worker who needs to become more consistent at the plate. Sometimes he overswings rather than simply relying on his ability, which results in a lack of contact. Despite good speed, he's not much of a basestealer. His wheels serve him better in center, where he gets good jumps and outruns flyballs. His arm is solid.

2000 Outlook

The Athletics believe Christenson has a higher upside than McDonald, whom they outrighted in October. And when they didn't offer Rich Becker a contract, Christenson became their starting center fielder by default. He hit 141 points higher against lefthanders than righthanders in 1999, and a similar performance in 2000 would stick him with a platoon tag he might never shed. If he doesn't step up his play, Oakland could turn to prospects Mario Encarnacion and Terrence Long.

A.J. Hinch

Position: C
Bats: R **Throws:** R
Ht: 6' 1" **Wt:** 207

Opening Day Age: 25
Born: 5/15/74 in
Waverly, IA
ML Seasons: 2

Overall Statistics

	G	AB	R	H	D	T	HR	RBI	SB	BB	SO	Avg	OBP	Slg
1999	76	205	26	44	4	1	7	24	6	11	41	.215	.260	.346
Career	196	542	60	122	14	1	16	59	9	41	130	.225	.283	.343

1999 Situational Stats

	AB	H	HR	RBI	Avg		AB	H	HR	RBI	Avg
Home	101	22	3	11	.218	LHP	49	11	1	3	.224
Road	104	22	4	13	.212	RHP	156	33	6	21	.212
First Half	143	29	3	12	.203	Sc Pos	52	11	2	18	.212
Scnd Half	62	15	4	12	.242	Clutch	13	2	0	1	.154

1999 Season

A.J. Hinch, who sailed through college and the minors hitting everything in sight, stalled in his first major league trial in 1998. A rebound was expected last year, but Hinch slumped even more and was sent to Triple-A Vancouver twice in the second half. By year's end, Ramon Hernandez had stolen Hinch's title as the Athletics' backstop of the future.

Hitting, Baserunning & Defense

Hinch hit .328 in the minors before reaching Oakland, but has struggled with offspeed pitches in the majors. When he's on, he's an effective gap hitter who makes contact. His defense has been disappointing as well, as he has thrown out just 23 percent of basestealers in his two big league seasons and committed 10 passed balls in 73 games last year. His leadership skills are formidable. Hinch does have good speed, especially for a catcher.

2000 Outlook

Hernandez more than held his own at the plate and his defensive skills were at least equal to Hinch's, so Hinch goes into 2000 as a backup. If he struggles, he'll likely earn another trip to the minors or a trade.

Jason Isringhausen

Position: RP
Bats: R **Throws:** R
Ht: 6' 3" **Wt:** 210

Opening Day Age: 27
Born: 9/7/72 in
Brighton, IL
ML Seasons: 4
Pronunciation:
IS-ring-how-zin
Nickname: Izzy

Overall Statistics

	W	L	Pct.	ERA	G	GS	Sv	IP	H	BB	SO	HR	Ratio
1999	1	4	.200	4.73	33	5	9	64.2	64	34	51	9	1.52
Career	18	22	.450	4.49	80	52	9	359.0	382	160	245	31	1.51

1999 Situational Stats

	W	L	ERA	Sv	IP		AB	H	HR	RBI	Avg
Home	1	0	2.25	5	32.0	LHB	113	25	4	10	.221
Road	0	4	7.16	4	32.2	RHB	135	39	5	23	.289
First Half	1	2	6.21	1	29.0	Sc Pos	67	17	2	25	.254
Scnd Half	0	2	3.53	8	35.2	Clutch	34	8	1	5	.235

1999 Season

After a long run of arm trouble with the Mets, Jason Isringhausen got a new lease on life when he was included in the Billy Taylor trade on July 31. A former starter moving to an unfamiliar role with an unfamiliar team, he didn't allow a run in his first seven relief appearances with the Athletics and converted all eight of his save opportunities.

Pitching & Defense

A pure power pitcher, Isringhausen throws hard sliders, curves and changeups to go with a fastball that clocks in near 97 MPH. Frequent injuries and lost time have compromised the impressive command he displayed as a rookie in 1995. His control must improve if he's to excel as a closer. Isringhausen makes the routine plays in the field. His delivery to the plate is slow, and his pickoff move is average at best.

2000 Outlook

On an up-and-coming team with no set closer, Isringhausen goes into 2000 as the leading candidate to finish ballgames. Veteran Doug Jones was brought back mainly for insurance and to assist in Isringhausen's development.

Oakland

Doug Jones

Position: RP
Bats: R **Throws:** R
Ht: 6' 2" **Wt:** 224

Opening Day Age: 42
Born: 6/24/57 in Covina, CA
ML Seasons: 15

Overall Statistics

	W	L	Pct.	ERA	G	GS	Sv	IP	H	BB	SO	HR	Ratio
1999	5	5	.500	3.55	70	0	10	104.0	106	24	63	10	1.25
Career	65	77	.458	3.26	792	4	301	1055.0	1069	229	855	80	1.23

1999 Situational Stats

	W	L	ERA	Sv	IP		AB	H	HR	RBI	Avg
Home	4	1	3.00	5	57.0	LHB	204	52	5	28	.255
Road	1	4	4.21	5	47.0	RHB	193	54	5	25	.280
First Half	1	2	3.58	3	60.1	Sc Pos	114	29	1	42	.254
Scnd Half	4	3	3.50	7	43.2	Clutch	197	60	5	32	.305

1999 Season

Looking for bullpen help, the Athletics signed Doug Jones as a free agent. He performed well and even was promoted to closer following the trade of Billy Taylor to the Mets. After Jones faltered in August, Oakland turned to Jason Isringhausen to finish games.

Pitching & Defense

Jones relies on varying the speed of his one pitch, a changeup, to get hitters out. For the most part, it works. He keeps the ball around the plate, rarely walking anyone. He needs to work often to maintain his touch but struggles when asked to pitch on consecutive days. Jones' motion to the plate is quick, though his utter lack of velocity allows basestealers to get good jumps. He fields his position adequately.

2000 Outlook

Jones was signed to a one-year contract in November as an insurance policy in case Isringhausen struggles. Jones really shouldn't be more than a setup man, so it won't be a good sign for the Athletics if they ask him to close. Though his margin for error is tiny, he continues to hang on.

T.J. Mathews

Position: RP
Bats: R **Throws:** R
Ht: 6' 1" **Wt:** 214

Opening Day Age: 30
Born: 1/19/70 in Belleville, IL
ML Seasons: 5

Overall Statistics

	W	L	Pct.	ERA	G	GS	Sv	IP	H	BB	SO	HR	Ratio
1999	9	5	.643	3.81	50	0	3	59.0	46	20	42	9	1.12
Career	29	22	.569	3.38	270	0	15	319.2	275	122	273	33	1.24

1999 Situational Stats

	W	L	ERA	Sv	IP		AB	H	HR	RBI	Avg
Home	7	3	3.26	2	30.1	LHB	95	22	5	18	.232
Road	2	2	4.40	1	28.2	RHB	119	24	4	17	.202
First Half	6	3	3.89	1	34.2	Sc Pos	60	17	4	29	.283
Scnd Half	3	2	3.70	2	24.1	Clutch	118	27	6	22	.229

1999 Season

Rediscovering the form that made the Athletics insist he be included in the Mark McGwire trade with the Cardinals in 1997, T.J. Mathews posted a 1.42 ERA during a stellar April. He suffered from arm and shoulder problems over the next three months, but bounced back with a strong August before needing elbow surgery to remove bone spurs at the end of the season.

Pitching & Defense

A hard thrower, Mathews uses two- and four-seam fastballs that hit the low 90s. He also throws a splitter and slider. His pitches have a lot of late movement, and he's able to vertically expand his strike zone to keep hitters off balance. He's a fly-ball pitcher, which makes him more effective at the spacious confines of Network Associates Coliseum. Mathews is an average fielder but is slow to the plate, allowing basestealers to get good jumps.

2000 Outlook

Mathews is expected to be ready by the start of training camp and will be brought along slowly. Based on his prior experience, he appears better suited for a setup role than the closer job. Oakland signed him to a two-year, $3.25 million deal in November.

Jason McDonald

Position: CF/LF/RF
Bats: B **Throws:** R
Ht: 5' 7" **Wt:** 190

Opening Day Age: 28
Born: 3/20/72 in Modesto, CA
ML Seasons: 3

Overall Statistics

	G	AB	R	H	D	T	HR	RBI	SB	BB	SO	Avg	OBP	Slg
1999	100	187	26	39	2	1	3	8	6	25	48	.209	.310	.278
Career	248	598	98	145	22	5	8	38	29	88	130	.242	.345	.336

1999 Situational Stats

	AB	H	HR	RBI	Avg		AB	H	HR	RBI	Avg
Home	96	23	0	1	.240	LHP	54	12	1	4	.222
Road	91	16	3	7	.176	RHP	133	27	2	4	.203
First Half	126	28	1	6	.222	Sc Pos	37	5	1	6	.135
Scnd Half	61	11	2	2	.180	Clutch	23	3	0	2	.130

1999 Season

After losing his starting spot to injury following a frightening outfield collision with Rickey Henderson in 1998, Jason McDonald didn't even make the Athletics out of spring training. He bounced between Triple-A Vancouver and Oakland three times and was far less productive than he had been in two previous stints with the Athletics.

Hitting, Baserunning & Defense

McDonald is a good fastball hitter, but he chases breaking pitches and tries to play a power game he's not suited for. He's one of Oakland's fastest baserunners, though his effectiveness stealing bases dropped off last year. A former infielder, McDonald handles himself well in center, charging balls with the mentality of an infielder. He also can play an adequate second base if called upon. His arm is average in terms of strength and accuracy.

2000 Outlook

McDonald has the tools to be a good leadoff hitter or a valuable bench player. After a subpar 1999 performance, his biggest hurdle is finding a team that will give him 400 at-bats. That isn't likely to happen in Oakland after he was outrighted off the 40-man roster in October.

Tony Phillips

Position: 2B/CF/LF/RF
Bats: B **Throws:** R
Ht: 5'10" **Wt:** 175

Opening Day Age: 40
Born: 4/25/59 in Atlanta, GA
ML Seasons: 18

Overall Statistics

	G	AB	R	H	D	T	HR	RBI	SB	BB	SO	Avg	OBP	Slg
1999	106	406	76	99	24	4	15	49	11	71	94	.244	.362	.433
Career	2161	7617	1300	2023	360	50	160	819	177	1319	1499	.266	.374	.389

1999 Situational Stats

	AB	H	HR	RBI	Avg		AB	H	HR	RBI	Avg
Home	196	45	5	25	.230	LHP	92	18	0	3	.196
Road	210	54	10	24	.257	RHP	314	81	15	46	.258
First Half	328	80	13	41	.244	Sc Pos	78	16	4	33	.205
Scnd Half	78	19	2	8	.244	Clutch	45	10	3	9	.222

1999 Season

Following a 1998 to forget, Tony Phillips used free agency to return to Oakland, where his big league career started in 1982. He provided the savvy and leadership the improving Athletics needed, playing aggressively at second base and center field until breaking his left leg in August.

Hitting, Baserunning & Defense

Phillips is a tireless worker who's fundamentally sound. He uses the whole field and handles off-speed pitches with aplomb, though high fastballs get the better of him. He has moderate power and a knack for getting on base. Phillips is an aggressive baserunner who can steal and take an extra base. He's a competent fielder at nearly every position, though his style of play sometimes leads to miscues and he has a weak arm. He hits better when he plays the outfield.

2000 Outlook

With the Athletics re-signing Randy Velarde to play second base, Phillips' time in Oakland is over. A free agent, he offers versatility, leadership and some speed and power.

Oakland

Olmedo Saenz

Position: 3B/1B
Bats: R **Throws:** R
Ht: 6' 0" **Wt:** 185

Opening Day Age: 29
Born: 10/8/70 in Chitre
Herrera, Panama
ML Seasons: 2
Pronunciation: SIGNS

Overall Statistics

	G	AB	R	H	D	T	HR	RBI	SB	BB	SO	Avg	OBP	Slg
1999	97	255	41	70	18	0	11	41	1	22	47	.275	.363	.475
Career	102	269	43	72	18	1	11	41	1	22	52	.268	.353	.465

1999 Situational Stats

	AB	H	HR	RBI	Avg		AB	H	HR	RBI	Avg
Home	121	32	8	28	.264	LHP	111	33	3	16	.297
Road	134	38	3	13	.284	RHP	144	37	8	25	.257
First Half	153	40	3	23	.261	Sc Pos	80	15	2	30	.188
Scnd Half	102	30	8	18	.294	Clutch	34	8	4	11	.235

1999 Season

Another of general manager Billy Beane's free-agent gems, Olmedo Saenz made the club after a red-hot spring. He was effective as a platoon player while super-prospect Eric Chavez adjusted to big league pitching, and as a starter down the stretch after Chavez went down with a foot injury. Saenz improved over the course of the season, batting .294 and stroking eight of his 11 homers in the second half.

Hitting, Baserunning & Defense

A focused player, Saenz takes his game preparation seriously. That makes him as good off the bench as he is as a starter. He's a gap hitter with plus power, and he can go the opposite way when appropriate. Saenz hits fastballs well and holds his own against breaking pitches. Saenz isn't a burner, but he'll take an extra base. His glovework around first base is better than at third. He needs to improve at both positions.

2000 Outlook

Saenz could start at third base for some big league teams. He'll probably see a little more playing time in 2000, filling in at both infield corners and DH. The Athletics love his work ethic.

Scott Spiezio

Position: 2B/3B/1B
Bats: B **Throws:** R
Ht: 6' 2" **Wt:** 225

Opening Day Age: 27
Born: 9/21/72 in Joliet,
IL
ML Seasons: 4
Pronunciation:
SPEE-zee-oh

Overall Statistics

	G	AB	R	H	D	T	HR	RBI	SB	BB	SO	Avg	OBP	Slg
1999	89	247	31	60	24	0	8	33	0	29	36	.243	.324	.437
Career	359	1220	149	305	73	5	33	156	10	121	171	.250	.318	.399

1999 Situational Stats

	AB	H	HR	RBI	Avg		AB	H	HR	RBI	Avg
Home	122	28	3	16	.230	LHP	70	16	1	7	.229
Road	125	32	5	17	.256	RHP	177	44	7	26	.249
First Half	127	24	2	14	.189	Sc Pos	61	13	1	24	.213
Scnd Half	120	36	6	19	.300	Clutch	28	3	0	1	.107

1999 Season

Injuries sidetracked Scott Spiezio in both 1997 and '98, but it was his bat that cost him a spot in the Oakland lineup last year. He hit .189 in 127 at-bats before a mid-June demotion to Triple-A Vancouver that gave the second-base job to Tony Phillips. Spiezio hit .300-6-19 after he was recalled on July 26, filling in adeptly at first, second and third base.

Hitting, Baserunning & Defense

Spiezio is an aggressive hitter and a heady player, but that doesn't always translate into production. He's a good first-ball, fastball hitter who has developing power, but he must use the opposite field more often. Spiezio can play all four infield positions. While he doesn't have the quickest feet or greatest range, he has very sure hands. Once a decent basestealer, Spiezio has been slowed since tearing up his left knee in 1998.

2000 Outlook

Oakland declined to offer Spiezio a contract for 2000. He'll find a job, but it won't be as an everyday player.

Other Oakland Athletics

Buddy Groom (Pos: LHP, Age: 34)

	W	L	Pct.	ERA	G	GS	Sv	IP	H	BB	SO	HR	Ratio
1999	3	2	.600	5.09	76	0	0	46.0	48	18	32	1	1.43
Career	15	18	.455	5.14	409	15	8	408.1	478	176	262	42	1.60

Groom is a fixture in the Oakland bullpen. Once again he proved effective against lefthanders, and once again he'll be called upon to fill that specialist role. 2000 Outlook: B

Jimmy Haynes (Pos: RHP, Age: 27)

	W	L	Pct.	ERA	G	GS	Sv	IP	H	BB	SO	HR	Ratio
1999	7	12	.368	6.34	30	25	0	142.0	158	80	93	21	1.68
Career	26	34	.433	5.75	106	85	1	522.2	594	278	379	69	1.67

A highly regarded pitching prospect who was impressive in his 1995 debut, Haynes hasn't been very effective since then. He was dealt to Milwaukee in a four-team Winter Meetings trade that brought pitching prospect Justin Miller to Oakland. 2000 Outlook: B

Kevin Jarvis (Pos: RHP, Age: 30)

	W	L	Pct.	ERA	G	GS	Sv	IP	H	BB	SO	HR	Ratio
1999	0	1	.000	11.57	4	1	0	14.0	28	6	11	6	2.43
Career	12	19	.387	6.62	85	40	1	299.0	392	115	165	57	1.70

Framing an OK season at Triple-A Vancouver were two horrible outings in April and two more ugly ones during the last week of the season. Jarvis still is trying to beat his best single-season ERA of 5.70. 2000 Outlook: D

Tim Kubinski (Pos: LHP, Age: 28)

	W	L	Pct.	ERA	G	GS	Sv	IP	H	BB	SO	HR	Ratio
1999	0	0	-	5.84	14	0	0	12.1	14	5	7	3	1.54
Career	0	0	-	5.76	25	0	0	25.0	26	11	17	5	1.48

Kubinski turned in his best Triple-A season in 1999, posting a 3.44 ERA and allowing just two homers in the Pacific Coast League. His success at Vancouver didn't translate into success with the A's. 2000 Outlook: C

Mike Macfarlane (Pos: C, Age: 35, Bats: R)

	G	AB	R	H	D	T	HR	RBI	SB	BB	SO	Avg	OBP	Slg
1999	81	226	24	55	17	0	4	31	0	13	52	.243	.282	.372
Career	1164	3602	458	906	221	17	129	514	12	295	700	.252	.322	.430

Macfarlane has hit .243 in each of the last two seasons, and he's been near 35 RBI for the last three campaigns. That's about as much production as you can expect from him this season. 2000 Outlook: B

Ron Mahay (Pos: LHP, Age: 28)

	W	L	Pct.	ERA	G	GS	Sv	IP	H	BB	SO	HR	Ratio
1999	2	0	1.000	1.86	6	1	1	19.1	8	3	15	2	0.57
Career	6	1	.857	2.69	63	1	2	70.1	53	29	51	7	1.17

Acquired off waivers from Boston in the days before the season started, Mahay spent 1999 at Triple-A Vancouver before returning in September. He pitched well, retiring 21 straight batters in one stretch. 2000 Outlook: B

Greg McMichael (Pos: RHP, Age: 33)

	W	L	Pct.	ERA	G	GS	Sv	IP	H	BB	SO	HR	Ratio
1999	1	1	.500	5.08	36	0	0	33.2	35	20	21	6	1.63
Career	31	29	.517	3.21	438	0	53	507.0	471	189	445	39	1.30

While McMichael doesn't throw hard, his pinpoint control allowed him to close for Atlanta in 1993 and '94. His command has slipped, and shoulder trouble in '99 made him even less effective. 2000 Outlook: B

Frank Menechino (Pos: SS, Age: 29, Bats: R)

	G	AB	R	H	D	T	HR	RBI	SB	BB	SO	Avg	OBP	Slg
1999	9	9	0	2	0	0	0	0	0	0	4	.222	.222	.222
Career	9	9	0	2	0	0	0	0	0	0	4	.222	.222	.222

Menechino enjoyed his best Triple-A season in 1999, batting .309 with 31 doubles, 15 homers, 73 walks and a .397 OBP. He's a decent second baseman who could win a bench job with the A's. 2000 Outlook: B

Mike Oquist (Pos: RHP, Age: 31)

	W	L	Pct.	ERA	G	GS	Sv	IP	H	BB	SO	HR	Ratio
1999	9	10	.474	5.37	28	24	0	140.2	158	64	89	18	1.58
Career	25	31	.446	5.46	133	79	0	555.0	623	243	351	73	1.56

Oquist was squeezed out of Oakland's rotation by Kevin Appier and Omar Olivares following the club's late-season trades. He'll try to hook on with the Tigers, who signed him in November. 2000 Outlook: C

Tim Raines (Pos: LF, Age: 40, Bats: B)

	G	AB	R	H	D	T	HR	RBI	SB	BB	SO	Avg	OBP	Slg
1999	58	135	20	29	5	0	4	17	4	26	17	.215	.337	.341
Career	2353	8694	1548	2561	419	112	168	964	807	1290	938	.295	.385	.427

Lupus caused the kidney inflammation that ended Raines' 1999 season in July. A free agent, he may have a hard time finding a job this year. 2000 Outlook: C

Jorge Velandia (Pos: 2B, Age: 25, Bats: R)

	G	AB	R	H	D	T	HR	RBI	SB	BB	SO	Avg	OBP	Slg
1999	63	48	4	9	1	0	0	2	2	2	13	.188	.235	.208
Career	85	81	4	13	3	0	0	2	2	3	21	.160	.200	.198

Velandia has hit for average with almost no power in the minors. He has struggled in the majors, and an ankle injury ended his season in August. 2000 Outlook: C

Luis Vizcaino (Pos: RHP, Age: 22)

	W	L	Pct.	ERA	G	GS	Sv	IP	H	BB	SO	HR	Ratio
1999	0	0	-	5.40	1	0	0	3.1	3	3	2	1	1.80
Career	0	0	-	5.40	1	0	0	3.1	3	3	2	1	1.80

Vizcaino reached Triple-A and Oakland for the first time in 1999. He wasn't dominant, so a full year in Triple-A may be in order. 2000 Outlook: C

Tim Worrell (Pos: RHP, Age: 32)

	W	L	Pct.	ERA	G	GS	Sv	IP	H	BB	SO	HR	Ratio
1999	2	2	.500	4.15	53	0	0	69.1	69	34	62	6	1.49
Career	20	32	.385	4.46	239	49	4	528.1	529	206	403	58	1.39

After playing for three teams in 1998, Worrell had a solid season last year. His only downside was allowing too many inherited runners to score. 2000 Outlook: B

Oakland

Oakland Athletics Minor League Prospects

Organization Overview:

The Athletics competed for the American League wild-card berth despite a $22 million payroll, and the future is only going to get brighter. Oakland led all teams by placing 13 players on *Baseball America's* minor league Top 10 Prospects lists, and also earned the magazine's 1999 Organization of the Year award. In the past two years, impact players Eric Chavez, Ben Grieve, Tim Hudson and Miguel Tejada have established themselves in the majors. Pitchers Chad Harville, Mark Mulder and Barry Zito should follow in 2000, and a group of hitters led by Mario Encarnacion and Adam Piatt should be ready the next season. In recent years, no team has spent its money more wisely than the Athletics, in terms of both major league talent and amateur signings.

Mario Encarnacion

Position: OF
Bats: R **Throws:** R
Ht: 6' 2" **Wt:** 187

Opening Day Age: 22
Born: 9/24/77 in Bani, Dominican Republic

Recent Statistics

	G	AB	R	H	D	T	HR	RBI	SB	BB	SO	Avg
1998 AA Huntsville	110	357	70	97	15	2	15	61	11	60	123	.272
1999 AA Midland	94	353	69	109	21	4	18	71	9	47	86	.309
1999 AAA Vancouver	39	145	18	35	5	0	3	17	5	6	44	.241
1999 MLE	133	473	63	119	21	2	13	64	9	31	135	.252

A product of Oakland's fertile academy in the Dominican Republic, Encarnacion has the best all-around tools in the system. He's still polishing his skills, but he should hit for power and average once he tightens his strike zone. His speed currently surpasses his basestealing instincts, and he plays a fine center field with a right-field caliber arm. Encarnacion needs a full season in Triple-A before battling Terrence Long to win the long-term job in center for Oakland.

Chad Harville

Position: P
Bats: R **Throws:** R
Ht: 5' 9" **Wt:** 180

Opening Day Age: 23
Born: 9/16/76 in Selmer, TN

Recent Statistics

	W	L	ERA	G	GS	Sv	IP	H	R	BB	SO	HR
1999 AA Midland	2	0	2.01	17	0	7	22.1	13	6	9	35	1
1999 AAA Vancouver	1	0	1.75	22	0	11	25.2	24	5	11	36	0
1999 AL Oakland	0	2	6.91	15	0	0	14.1	18	11	10	15	2

Harville's calling card is his fastball, which was rated the best in the Double-A Texas League and the Triple-A Pacific Coast League last season. Because he's short and delivers a high-90s fastball, he has been likened to a righthanded Billy Wagner on several occasions. A 1997 second-round pick from the University of Memphis, Harville has 216 strikeouts and just 148 hits allowed in 169.2 pro innings. His second pitch is a nasty slider that reaches the high 80s. The biggest concern with Harville is a maximum-effort delivery that seemingly puts strain on his arm, but he has stayed healthy thus far. He also could use some more movement on his fastball and more depth on his slider. Jason Isringhausen will get the first shot to close for Oakland this year, with Harville next in line.

Brett Laxton

Position: P
Bats: L **Throws:** R
Ht: 6' 2" **Wt:** 205

Opening Day Age: 26
Born: 10/5/73 in Stratford, NJ

Recent Statistics

	W	L	ERA	G	GS	Sv	IP	H	R	BB	SO	HR
1999 AAA Vancouver	13	8	3.46	25	25	0	161.1	158	68	49	112	8
1999 AL Oakland	0	1	7.45	3	2	0	9.2	12	12	7	9	1

Laxton seemed destined for stardom in 1993, when he pitched Louisiana State to a College World Series title by striking out 16 Wichita State batters in the championship game. He also edged a Tennessee first baseman/lefthander named Todd Helton for *Baseball America's* Freshman of the Year award. Then Laxton endured so many arm problems that he lasted until the 24th round of the 1996 draft. His stuff has bounced back—he has a low-90s fastball and a slider, both with tremendous life—though he usually needs about 30 pitches in a game before he settles into a groove. The son of former big league pitcher Bill Laxton, Brett sharply upgraded his command last year, except during a brief major league stint. He'll get a chance to make Oakland's rotation in spring training.

Terrence Long

Position: OF
Bats: L **Throws:** L
Ht: 6' 1" **Wt:** 190

Opening Day Age: 24
Born: 2/29/76 in Montgomery, AL

Recent Statistics

	G	AB	R	H	D	T	HR	RBI	SB	BB	SO	Avg
1999 AAA Norfolk	78	304	41	99	20	4	7	47	14	23	41	.326
1999 AAA Vancouver	40	154	16	38	6	2	2	21	7	10	29	.247
1999 NL New York	3	3	0	0	0	0	0	0	0	0	2	.000
1999 MLE	118	439	45	118	21	3	6	54	14	26	72	.269

When the Athletics traded Kenny Rogers to the Mets last July for Long and minor league lefthander Leo Vasquez, Oakland GM Billy Beane touted Long's 30-30 potential. A 1994 first-round pick, Long slumped after joining the A's Triple-A Vancouver affiliate, but rallied to win Triple-A World Series MVP honors by batting .400 with 10 RBI in five games. He has improved his hitting dramatically in the last two seasons, though his power is still more potential than reality and he needs to be more selective. Long also must learn how to apply his speed better, both offensively and defensively. His arm was rated the best among International League outfielders last year. Oakland may turn to Long quickly if Ryan Christenson disappoints.

Mark Mulder

Position: P   **Opening Day Age:** 22
Bats: L **Throws:** L   **Born:** 8/5/77 in South
Ht: 6' 6" **Wt:** 200   Holland, IL

Recent Statistics

	W	L	ERA	G	GS	Sv	IP	H	R	BB	SO	HR
1999 AAA Vancouver	6	7	4.06	22	22	0	128.2	152	69	31	81	13

The second overall pick in the 1998 draft, Mulder signed late for a club-record $3.2 million and didn't debut until 1999. The Michigan State product was at his best in big games. Mulder worked six innings of one-run ball against Mexico in the Pan American Games semifinals, a must-win game that qualified Team USA for the Sydney Olympics. He twirled a shutout in the final game of the Pacific Coast League playoffs, then won the Triple-A World Series finale. He has command of four pitches: a low-90s fastball that tails away from righthanders, a cut fastball, a big overhand curve and an effective changeup. Mulder's numbers aren't overwhelming because his velocity decreased to the mid-80s before returning to its normal level by season's end. If he has a good spring training, he could open the year in Oakland's rotation.

Jose Ortiz

Position: SS   **Opening Day Age:** 22
Bats: R **Throws:** R   **Born:** 6/13/77 in Santo
Ht: 5' 9" **Wt:** 160   Domingo, Dom. Rep.

Recent Statistics

	G	AB	R	H	D	T	HR	RBI	SB	BB	SO	Avg
1998 AA Huntsville	94	354	70	98	24	2	6	55	22	48	63	.277
1999 AAA Vancouver	107	377	66	107	29	2	9	45	13	29	50	.284
1999 MLE	107	370	61	100	27	1	8	42	10	26	51	.270

Another product of Oakland's Dominican academy, Ortiz is the club's second baseman of the future. He has nice offensive potential for a middle infielder, with a sound swing and surprising power. He makes good contact and has average speed, though he could walk more often. Ortiz has played mostly shortstop in the minors, but he won't dethrone Miguel Tejada in Oakland. His hands and arm are solid. Randy Velarde is signed though 2001, so the Athletics can afford to be patient with Ortiz.

Adam Piatt

Position: 3B   **Opening Day Age:** 24
Bats: R **Throws:** R   **Born:** 2/8/76 in Chicago,
Ht: 6' 2" **Wt:** 195   IL

Recent Statistics

	G	AB	R	H	D	T	HR	RBI	SB	BB	SO	Avg
1998 A Modesto	133	500	91	144	40	3	20	107	20	80	99	.288
1999 AA Midland	129	476	128	164	48	3	39	135	7	93	101	.345
1999 AAA Vancouver	6	18	1	4	1	0	0	3	0	6	2	.222
1999 MLE	135	460	88	134	39	2	25	95	4	58	108	.291

Convinced that power was his ticket to the majors, Piatt became too pull-conscious early in his career. He abandoned that approach midway through the 1998 season, when he had a paltry three homers in high-A ball. He hit 17 homers in the second half, then exploded in 1999. The 1997 eighth-round pick from Mississippi State became the second player in 104 seasons to win the Double-A Texas League triple crown, and led the minors in runs, RBI, total bases (340) and extra-base hits (91). He's a complete hitter with no holes in his swing. He also has a discriminating batting eye and average speed. Piatt has worked to improve at third base, though he probably won't push Eric Chavez off the hot corner. A more likely scenario is that Piatt will spend 2000 in Triple-A, then play for Oakland as a left fielder, first baseman or DH.

Barry Zito

Position: P   **Opening Day Age:** 21
Bats: L **Throws:** L   **Born:** 5/13/78 in Las
Ht: 6' 4" **Wt:** 205   Vegas, NV

Recent Statistics

	W	L	ERA	G	GS	Sv	IP	H	R	BB	SO	HR
1999 A Visalia	3	0	2.45	8	8	0	40.1	21	13	22	62	3
1999 AA Midland	2	1	4.91	4	4	0	22.0	22	15	11	29	1
1999 AAA Vancouver	1	0	1.50	1	1	0	6.0	5	1	2	6	0

The ninth overall pick in the 1999 draft, Zito reached Triple-A 84 days after signing for $1.59 million. Pitching for three teams at three levels, he went a combined 6-1, 3.16 wiith 97 strikeouts and just 48 hits allowed in 68.1 innings. His curveball devastates hitters and he also has an 89-91 MPH fastball, above-average velocity for a lefthander. His changeup will be an effective third pitch once he stops telegraphing it by slowing down his delivery. While he was at the University of Southern California, *Baseball America* rated him the college prospect with the best command. Oakland is committed to giving Zito a full season in Triple-A, but if he pitches as well as he did in 1999, it will be hard to avoid promoting him.

Others to Watch

Blue-collar outfielder **Eric Byrnes** (24) won the high Class-A California League batting title with a .337 average. He'll need to add some power. . . Though he was the only 18-year-old pitcher to spend all of 1999 in high-A ball, righthander **Jesus Colome** (19) fanned nearly a batter per inning. His fastball, which has reached 100 MPH, was rated the best in the Cal League. His slider has touched 92 MPH. . . Shortstop **Josue Espada** (24) temporarily was lost to the Twins in the 1998 major league Rule 5 draft, but returned to Oakland when he couldn't stick with Minnesota. He has more speed and draws more walks than Jose Ortiz, but Ortiz is a far stronger hitter. . . Second baseman **Esteban German** (21) has the skills of a prototypical leadoff man. Though he played the full season in high-A ball at age 20, he hit .311 with 107 runs, 102 walks and 40 stolen bases in 1999. . . First baseman **Jason Hart** (22) led the Cal League with 48 doubles and 105 RBI. He could have a monster year in 2000 at Midland, one of the best hitters' parks in Double-A. . . Catcher **Miguel Olivo** (21) had one of his throws to second base last year clocked at 90 MPH—without a windup. His bat is as powerful as his arm.

Safeco Field

Offense

After the All-Star break, the Mariners moved into new Safeco Field, a $500 million gem of a ballpark with real grass and a retractable roof. Hitters were complaining about its pitcher-friendly dimensions before they even played their first game. Ken Griffey Jr. kept whining even though his home-run rate proved slightly better than at the Kingdome last season. Overall, Safeco did cut offensive production, but that was mostly due to the effects on batting average, not homers. The paint used on the hitting background was too glossy and will be redone, so batting averages should go up in 2000.

Defense

It will be much easier to play defense at Safeco Field, with its perfectly manicured grass. The spongy Kingdome turf and tricky right-field wall made it a difficult outfield to play. With larger power alleys, a good defensive center fielder may prove vital in Safeco. Infielders did complain that the fence behind home plate was too low, allowing the ball to blend in too easily with white T-shirts.

Who It Helps The Most

Early on, it looks like Safeco Field will favor pitchers, but there's not enough data to know for sure. Beyond favoring all pitchers, it could be particularly beneficial to power pitchers. Indeed, Freddy Garcia thrived during the second half in his new home, while Gil Meche posted a 3.50 ERA at home, 6.18 on the road.

Who It Hurts The Most

Righthanded hitters with warning-track power didn't fare well at Safeco. David Bell and Russ Davis hit just two home runs each at Safeco.

Rookies & Newcomers

Free-agent first baseman John Olerud, who signed for three years and $20 million, might lose a little off his batting average but should hit more homers than he did at Shea Stadium. Safeco won't help free-agent role players Stan Javier and Mark McLemore. All-time Japanese saves leader Kazuhiro Sasaki, who got a two-year deal for $8 million, should be able to use his nasty splitter to keep the ball in the park.

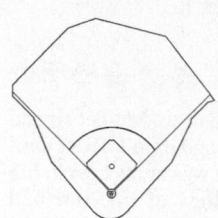

Dimensions: LF-331, LCF-390, CF-405, RCF-386, RF-326

Capacity: 47,145

Elevation: -2 feet

Surface: Grass

Foul Territory: Average

Park Factors

1999 Season (Safeco Field)

	Home Games			Away Games			Index
	Mariners	Opp	Total	Mariners	Opp	Total	
G	36	36	72	33	33	66	—
Avg	.243	.247	.245	.253	.289	.270	91
AB	1155	1224	2379	1144	1119	2263	96
R	159	159	318	146	172	318	92
H	281	302	583	289	323	612	87
2B	45	57	102	56	67	123	79
3B	3	5	8	4	10	14	54
HR	41	42	83	46	28	74	107
BB	142	131	273	119	139	258	101
SO	255	242	497	263	178	441	107
E	21	20	41	27	23	50	75
E-Infield	17	17	34	22	21	43	72
LHB-Avg	.254	.211	.229	.240	.296	.272	84
LHB-HR	20	13	33	12	15	27	118
RHB-Avg	.239	.269	.253	.258	.284	.269	94
RHB-HR	21	29	50	34	13	47	100

1997-1999 (Kingdome)

	Home Games			Away Games			Index
	Mariners	Opp	Total	Mariners	Opp	Total	
G	182	182	364	184	184	368	—
Avg	.283	.275	.279	.278	.278	.278	100
AB	6212	6505	12717	6573	6265	12838	100
R	1030	1009	2039	1043	975	2018	102
H	1761	1786	3547	1826	1743	3569	100
2B	372	410	782	334	364	698	113
3B	23	20	43	31	29	60	72
HR	290	237	527	288	203	491	108
BB	714	699	1413	625	659	1284	111
SO	1215	1392	2607	1216	1183	2399	110
E	117	105	222	157	125	282	80
E-Infield	102	94	196	136	104	240	83
LHB-Avg	.282	.287	.285	.275	.304	.289	99
LHB-HR	110	105	215	116	90	206	104
RHB-Avg	.284	.267	.276	.280	.264	.272	101
RHB-HR	180	132	312	172	113	285	111

1999 Rankings (American League)

- Highest strikeout factor
- Second-highest home-run factor
- Second-highest LHB home-run factor
- Lowest batting-average factor
- Lowest hit factor
- Lowest double factor
- Lowest triple factor
- Lowest error factor
- Lowest infield-error factor
- Lowest LHB batting-average factor
- Second-lowest run factor
- Second-lowest RHB batting-average factor

Lou Piniella

1999 Season

Lou Piniella's Mariners were expected to contend for the American League West title, but slow starts by Jeff Fassero and Jamie Moyer and an injury to Alex Rodriguez quickly doomed the club's chances. The bullpen was better than in previous years but still full of leaks, and by midseason the team threw in the towel. With three rookies in the rotation, Piniella accepted the team's fate and gave his young starters a chance to prove themselves.

Offense

Under Piniella, the Mariners have been the prototype of the American League style: slow, station-to-station baseball while waiting for the three-run home run. They produced the league's best offense in 1996 and 1997, but aging and declining talent turned the Mariners into a mediocre offensive club in 1999. Piniella's adjustment was to acquire a speed player in Brian Hunter, whom Piniella kept batting leadoff until September even though Hunter had the second-worst on-base percentage in the AL. That showed unusual patience for Piniella, who's never shy about benching anybody not named Buhner, Griffey, Martinez or Rodriguez.

Pitching & Defense

Piniella much prefers veteran pitchers, so he was a bit out of his element in handling a young staff. While Freddy Garcia thrived, Piniella let him run up some very high pitch counts, including an absurd 137-pitch outing in September. Sweet Lou is not so sweet to young pitchers, a reputation known by Seattle's minor leaguers. That helps explain why the Mariners ran through 28 pitchers, including 16 rookies. With Seattle, Piniella usually has gone for offense over defense, with Hunter a rare exception.

2000 Outlook

The Mariners entered the offseason in a state of flux. Ken Griffey Jr. asked for a trade and the team didn't know what to do with Alex Rodriguez. The only sure thing was a potentially very good starting rotation that led the AL in ERA after the All-Star break. If Safeco Field proves to be a pitchers' park, Piniella and the Mariners will have to adjust their offensive approach.

Born: 8/28/43 in Tampa, FL

Playing Experience: 1964-1984, Bal, Cle, KC, NYY

Managerial Experience: 13 seasons
Pronunciation: pih-NEL-luh
Nickname: Sweet Lou

Manager Statistics

Year	Team, Lg	W	L	Pct	GB	Finish
1999	Seattle, AL	79	83	.488	16.0	3rd West
13 Seasons		1019	949	.518	—	—

1999 Starting Pitchers by Days Rest

	<=3	4	5	6+
Mariners Starts	2	79	47	21
Mariners ERA	8.03	4.74	4.55	5.13
AL Avg Starts	2	82	47	21
AL ERA	6.83	4.98	4.72	5.62

1999 Situational Stats

	Lou Piniella	AL Average
Hit & Run Success %	30.5	35.3
Stolen Base Success %	74.3	68.0
Platoon Pct.	46.0	56.7
Defensive Subs	30	22
High-Pitch Outings	21	15
Quick/Slow Hooks	22/20	18/18
Sacrifice Attempts	49	52

1999 Rankings (American League)

- 1st in steals of home plate (2) and starts with over 140 pitches (1)
- 2nd in steals of third base (18), double steals (8), quick hooks (22) and starts with over 120 pitches (21)
- 3rd in stolen-base percentage (74.3%), steals of second base (110), squeeze plays (4), pitchouts (31), pitchouts with a runner moving (10) and starting lineups used (130)

Seattle

David Bell

1999 Season

Acquired late in the 1998 season from Cleveland for Joey Cora, David Bell was expected to be Seattle's backup at second base and third base. When rookie Carlos Guillen blew out his right knee in the season's fifth game, Bell became the everyday second baseman. He stormed out of the gate with 13 home runs through May, but slowed down after that when he was moved up into the first two slots in the order.

Hitting

When Bell was hitting seventh and lower early in the season, he thrived off all the meaty fastballs he saw. He had 177 at-bats in the lower three spots in the order, where he hit .311 with six home runs. He received the majority of his at-bats in the No. 2 slot, but hit just .239 there. He saw more breaking pitches, and that proved to be his weakness. He definitely looks to pull fastballs. Twenty of his 21 home runs went to left field and left-center, and the other went to center field.

Baserunning & Defense

Bell isn't the fastest guy around, but displayed slightly above-average range in the field. He melded well with Alex Rodriguez and the pair developed into a smooth double-play combination. Bell came up as a third baseman and has a strong arm for a second baseman, allowing him to make some tough plays from behind second. He did commit 17 errors, more because of concentration lapses than poor hands. Like many of the Mariners, Bell isn't particularly fast or aggressive on the basepaths.

2000 Outlook

Bell's season was a nice surprise for the Mariners, particularly his power output. Whether he can maintain that production at Safeco Field, where he hit just two homers after the move, remains to be seen. Seattle will keep Bell at second base and move Guillen to third base, after letting Russ Davis walk instead of paying the salary he would earn in arbitration.

Position: 2B
Bats: R **Throws:** R
Ht: 5'10" **Wt:** 175

Opening Day Age: 27
Born: 9/14/72 in Cincinnati, OH
ML Seasons: 5

Overall Statistics

	G	AB	R	H	D	T	HR	RBI	SB	BB	SO	Avg	OBP	Slg
1999	157	597	92	160	31	2	21	78	7	58	90	.268	.331	.432
Career	458	1459	174	374	81	8	35	167	10	109	230	.256	.308	.395

Where He Hits the Ball

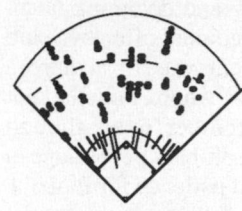
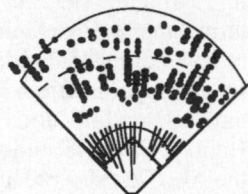

Vs. LHP   **Vs. RHP**

1999 Situational Stats

	AB	H	HR	RBI	Avg		AB	H	HR	RBI	Avg
Home	293	77	11	42	.263	LHP	118	26	3	15	.220
Road	304	83	10	36	.273	RHP	479	134	18	63	.280
First Half	326	88	15	53	.270	Sc Pos	129	37	3	54	.287
Scnd Half	271	72	6	25	.266	Clutch	74	19	4	13	.257

1999 Rankings (American League)

- 3rd in lowest batting average vs. lefthanded pitchers and errors at second base (17)
- 4th in lowest on-base percentage for a leadoff hitter (.310), lowest slugging percentage vs. lefthanded pitchers (.347) and lowest fielding percentage at second base (.977)
- 6th in lowest on-base percentage vs. lefthanded pitchers (.311)
- Led the Mariners in on-base percentage for a leadoff hitter (.310), lowest percentage of swings that missed (13.9%) and highest percentage of extra bases taken as a runner (57.1%)

Jay Buhner

1999 Season

For the second straight season, Jay Buhner had a string of injuries and declining numbers. His playing time in April was limited because of offseason elbow surgery, and he later missed most of May and all of June with knee problems. When he returned, he hit just .201 after the All-Star break. He finished with a .222 average and .421 slugging mark, his worst totals since his rookie year in 1988.

Hitting

Buhner still terrorizes lefthanders. He hit .266 and slugged .656 against southpaws in 1999. However, it was a different story against righthanders. Buhner simply couldn't get around on a good fastball and pitchers busted him inside with a high degree of success. Because Buhner always has hit many home runs to right-center, this affected his power totals. An all-or-nothing hitter, Buhner took that description to new extremes in 1999, striking out 100 times in just 266 at-bats. He did draw plenty of walks to push his on-base percentage to a fine .388.

Baserunning & Defense

Surprisingly, Buhner's Tommy John surgery didn't ruin his arm strength. While he no longer possesses his cannon of old, his arm is still average and he picked up seven assists. Buhner takes good routes on flyballs, but he's now extremely slow and lacks range. Because of this, he tends to play a fairly deep right field. Buhner is not only slow on the bases, but also cautious. He hasn't stolen a base since 1993.

2000 Outlook

Buhner has had a decade of fine and underrated play for Seattle. However, injuries and age have taken their toll. The Mariners declined his $6.3 million option for 2000, then brought him back for one year at $1.1 million with another possible $1 million in incentives. He still can hit lefties and get on base, and he could be a tremendous platoon player.

Position: RF
Bats: R **Throws:** R
Ht: 6' 3" **Wt:** 210

Opening Day Age: 35
Born: 8/13/64 in Louisville, KY
ML Seasons: 13
Pronunciation: BYEW-ner
Nickname: Bone

Overall Statistics

	G	AB	R	H	D	T	HR	RBI	SB	BB	SO	Avg	OBP	Slg
1999	87	266	37	59	11	0	14	38	0	69	100	.222	.388	.421
Career	1341	4604	744	1171	211	19	282	878	6	725	1299	.254	.359	.492

Where He Hits the Ball

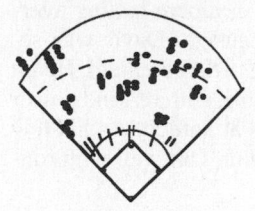

Vs. LHP

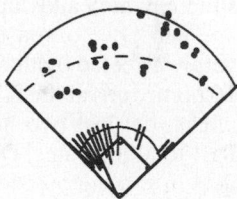

Vs. RHP

1999 Situational Stats

	AB	H	HR	RBI	Avg		AB	H	HR	RBI	Avg
Home	158	30	5	21	.190	LHP	64	17	8	16	.266
Road	108	29	9	17	.269	RHP	202	42	6	22	.208
First Half	82	22	6	18	.268	Sc Pos	68	16	6	29	.235
Scnd Half	184	37	8	20	.201	Clutch	37	8	3	4	.216

1999 Rankings (American League)

- 9th in lowest batting average with the bases loaded (.100)
- 10th in lowest batting average on an 0-2 count (.069)
- Led the Mariners in batting average on a 3-2 count (.306)

Russ Davis

1999 Season

Russ Davis had another season of too many negatives and not enough positives. After making 32 errors in 1998, he reduced that total to 12. He also smacked 17 home runs before the break. The negatives? A .225 average in the first half, just four home runs in the second half and sloth-like reactions in the field. He missed the final two weeks with minor ailments.

Hitting

Davis remains a pure fastball hitter who looks to drive the ball in the alleys. Every pitcher in the American League knows this, so Davis receives a steady diet of breaking pitches and sliders off the plate. He still lacks the discipline to lay off those sliders, which adds up to a mediocre batting average and poor on-base percentage. Davis was severely affected by the move to Safeco Field. He hit 10 home runs at the Kingdome, with its kind power alleys, but just two homers at Safeco. As his low RBI total indicates, Davis didn't hit well with runners in scoring position.

Baserunning & Defense

After a disastrous season in the field in 1998, Davis was determined to improve. He did cut down his errors, but he's not about to win a Gold Glove. He has slow reactions on groundballs and was hesitant making double-play throws to second. He never has had fluid mechanics while making plays on bunts and slow choppers. He does have a strong throwing arm. Davis has average speed, but lacks the instincts to run the bases aggressively and rarely looks to steal.

2000 Outlook

Davis doesn't really hit enough for a third baseman, and he doesn't draw enough walks or hit for a high enough average to offset his lack of true power. Rather than offer him arbitration, the Mariners decided to non-tender Davis and hand third base to Carlos Guillen.

Position: 3B
Bats: R **Throws:** R
Ht: 6' 0" **Wt:** 195

Opening Day Age: 30
Born: 9/13/69 in Birmingham, AL
ML Seasons: 6

Overall Statistics

	G	AB	R	H	D	T	HR	RBI	SB	BB	SO	Avg	OBP	Slg
1999	124	432	55	106	17	1	21	59	3	32	111	.245	.304	.435
Career	479	1633	218	418	90	5	68	235	15	120	425	.256	.310	.442

Where He Hits the Ball

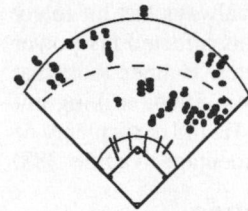

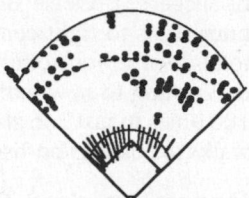

Vs. LHP   **Vs. RHP**

1999 Situational Stats

	AB	H	HR	RBI	Avg		AB	H	HR	RBI	Avg
Home	216	62	12	34	.287	LHP	104	31	8	18	.298
Road	216	44	9	25	.204	RHP	328	75	13	41	.229
First Half	258	58	17	41	.225	Sc Pos	103	23	5	35	.223
Scnd Half	174	48	4	18	.276	Clutch	59	17	3	6	.288

1999 Rankings (American League)

- 3rd in fielding percentage at third base (.959)
- 5th in lowest batting average with the bases loaded (.091)
- 9th in lowest batting average on an 0-2 count (.065)
- 10th in errors at third base (12)
- Led the Mariners in strikeouts and GDPs (13)
- Led AL third basemen in sacrifice bunts (7)

Freddy Garcia

1999 Season

A product of Houston's Venezuelan pipeline, the Mariners acquired Freddy Garcia in the Randy Johnson trade in 1998. Garcia had an impressive rookie season, finishing in the top 10 in the American League in wins, ERA and strikeouts. He didn't miss a start and remained strong down the stretch, going 6-1 his final nine starts and posting a 2.97 ERA after the All-Star break. He went at least five innings in 29 of 33 starts.

Pitching

Big and strong, Garcia has a nice, easy delivery. He's a fastball pitcher who brings it consistently at 93 MPH and sometimes a notch or two higher. Garcia throws both a two-seam and four-seam fastball, and he allowed only 18 home runs, a testament to his velocity and natural movement. He complements his fastballs with a decent curve, which he likes to throw when he's ahead in the count. Garcia also is developing a changeup that improved during the season. His poise was impressive. He pitched out of jams and held hitters to a .202 average with runners in scoring position.

Defense

Like many young fastball pitchers, Garcia isn't adept at holding basestealers. Taking advantage of his slow delivery, they went 26-for-33 against him. Only four AL pitchers allowed more steals. Garcia is a good athlete and displayed surprising agility as a defender.

2000 Outlook

With Garcia, it's not a matter of potential, just refinement. If he sharpens his control, he can become one of the AL's top starters. The biggest concern is the heavy workload he carried as a rookie. He had nine games of 120-plus pitches, and in a meaningless September contest against Baltimore, manager Lou Piniella carelessly left him in to throw 137.

Position: SP
Bats: R **Throws:** R
Ht: 6' 4" **Wt:** 210

Opening Day Age: 23
Born: 10/6/76 in Caracas, Venezuela
ML Seasons: 1

Overall Statistics

	W	L	Pct.	ERA	G	GS	Sv	IP	H	BB	SO	HR	Ratio
1999	17	8	.680	4.07	33	33	0	201.1	205	90	170	18	1.47
Career	17	8	.680	4.07	33	33	0	201.1	205	90	170	18	1.47

How Often He Throws Strikes

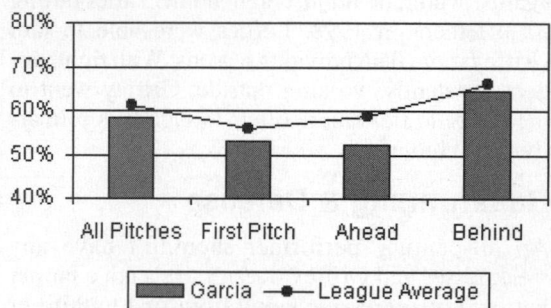

1999 Situational Stats

	W	L	ERA	Sv	IP		AB	H	HR	RBI	Avg
Home	10	5	3.81	0	104.0	LHB	424	108	12	42	.255
Road	7	3	4.35	0	97.1	RHB	355	97	6	40	.273
First Half	9	5	5.15	0	101.1	Sc Pos	218	44	5	63	.202
Scnd Half	8	3	2.97	0	100.0	Clutch	57	16	0	7	.281

1999 Rankings (American League)

- 1st in balks (3)
- 2nd in lowest batting average allowed with runners in scoring position
- 3rd in fewest home runs allowed per 9 innings (.80)
- Led the Mariners in wins, games started, walks allowed, hit batsmen (10), strikeouts, wild pitches (12), balks (3), pitches thrown (3,514), pickoff throws (142), stolen bases allowed (26), winning percentage, lowest batting average allowed (.263), highest groundball/flyball ratio allowed (1.4), most run support per 9 innings (6.3), fewest home runs allowed per 9 innings (.80), most strikeouts per 9 innings (7.6) and ERA at home

Ken Griffey Jr.

1999 Season

Ken Griffey Jr. led the American League in home runs for the third consecutive season while finishing third in RBI and fifth in runs scored. As the Mariners drifted out of the pennant race after the All-Star break, Griffey's numbers tailed off noticeably, much as they did in 1998. He finished the year by getting voted onto baseball's all-century team.

Hitting

The new ballpark was hardly to blame for his failure to hit 56 homers for the third straight year. Griffey hit 14 home runs in 151 at-bats at Safeco, compared to 13 home runs in 144 at-bats at the Kingdome. His struggles came against lefthanders, against whom he hit just eight homers after hitting 21 off them in 1998. Lefties were able to jam Griffey more than previous seasons. With righthanders constantly working outside, Griffey went to the opposite field more often, though he's primarily a pull hitter.

Baserunning & Defense

An all-century performer shouldn't have any weaknesses and Griffey doesn't. He's not a burner but is very aggressive going from first to third or second to home. He also stole a career-high 24 bases in 1999. Defensively, Griffey capped the decade with his 10th consecutive Gold Glove. He makes the occasional spectacular catch and has great instincts. His arm is slightly above average with a quick release. He did make nine errors, several coming on throws that hit a baserunner or weren't caught by his fielder.

2000 Outlook

Griffey can become a free agent after 2000. The Mariners offered him an eight-year deal worth $135 million, but he asked them to trade him instead. They worked out a December deal to send him to the Mets for Armando Benitez, Roger Cedeno and Octavio Dotel. But by that point, Griffey had decided he would approve a trade only to the Reds, who broke off negotiations when the Mariners insisted on Pokey Reese. If Griffey can adjust his swing against lefthanders, there's no reason he shouldn't hit 50 home runs again and perhaps reach .300 for the first time since 1997.

Position: CF
Bats: L **Throws:** L
Ht: 6' 3" **Wt:** 205

Opening Day Age: 30
Born: 11/21/69 in Donora, PA
ML Seasons: 11
Nickname: Junior, The Kid

Overall Statistics

	G	AB	R	H	D	T	HR	RBI	SB	BB	SO	Avg	OBP	Slg
1999	160	606	123	173	26	3	48	134	24	91	108	.285	.384	.576
Career	1535	5832	1063	1742	320	30	398	1152	167	747	984	.299	.380	.569

Where He Hits the Ball

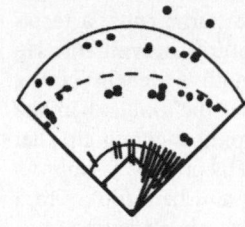
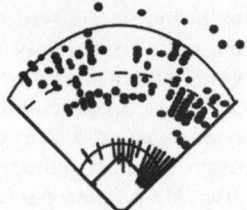

Vs. LHP   **Vs. RHP**

1999 Situational Stats

	AB	H	HR	RBI	Avg		AB	H	HR	RBI	Avg
Home	295	85	27	74	.288	LHP	170	39	8	27	.229
Road	311	88	21	60	.283	RHP	436	134	40	107	.307
First Half	332	103	29	81	.310	Sc Pos	149	51	11	80	.342
Scnd Half	274	70	19	53	.255	Clutch	58	22	4	20	.379

1999 Rankings (American League)

- 1st in home runs and intentional walks (17)
- 2nd in errors in center field (9)
- 3rd in total bases (349), RBI, slugging percentage vs. righthanded pitchers (.640), lowest fielding percentage in center field (.978) and games played
- Led the Mariners in home runs, at-bats, runs scored, hits, total bases (349), RBI, caught stealing (7), intentional walks (17), hit by pitch (7), pitches seen (2,672), plate appearances (706), batting average with runners in scoring position, batting average in the clutch, batting average on an 0-2 count (.286), slugging percentage vs. righthanded pitchers (.640) and games played

John Halama

1999 Season

The player to be named in 1998's Randy Johnson trade, John Halama had put together two excellent campaigns for Houston's Triple-A New Orleans affiliate but couldn't stick with the Astros. Seattle manager Lou Piniella isn't a big fan of finesse pitchers, so Halama began 1999 in the bullpen before earning his way into the rotation. He won his first seven decisions as a starter and finished with a fine 4.22 ERA. He did go 0-5, 4.71 in his last six starts.

Pitching

Though 6-foot-5, Halama is a soft tosser. He relies on a sinking fastball and superb changeup. He also throws a slow curveball that he primarily targets off the plate to keep hitters off stride. Because his fastball is in the mid-80s, Halama relies on location. He works more like Tom Glavine than teammate Jamie Moyer, who isn't afraid to pitch inside. Halama tries to work down and away and usually does that, as witnessed by his 25 double plays. He did tire at the end of the season, but prior to that showed he could work into the seventh or eighth inning.

Defense & Hitting

Halama has a terrific pickoff move and isn't shy about using it. Similar to Andy Pettitte, he'll bring his front leg straight up and not give away his delivery. Baserunners quickly learned and attempted just 12 steals off him, succeeding seven times. Halama isn't the quickest guy off the mound but was solid on balls hit back to him. He started four double plays.

2000 Outlook

Like all control pitchers, Halama will have to prove himself constantly. He gave up 15 homers after the All-Star break as opposed to five before, so hitters made some adjustments the second time around. Halama will have to do the same. He'll begin the year as Seattle's No. 3 or No. 4 starter.

Position: SP/RP
Bats: L **Throws:** L
Ht: 6' 5" **Wt:** 200

Opening Day Age: 28
Born: 2/22/72 in Brooklyn, NY
ML Seasons: 2
Pronunciation: huh-LAH-muh

Overall Statistics

	W	L	Pct.	ERA	G	GS	Sv	IP	H	BB	SO	HR	Ratio
1999	11	10	.524	4.22	38	24	0	179.0	193	56	105	20	1.39
Career	12	11	.522	4.47	44	30	0	211.1	230	69	126	20	1.41

How Often He Throws Strikes

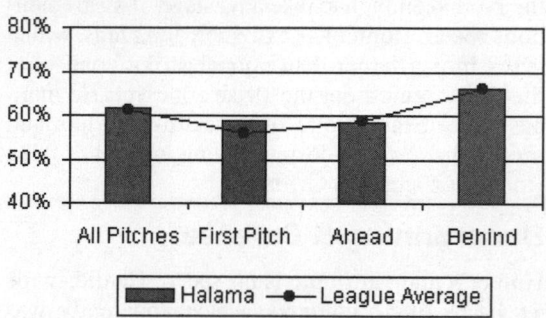

1999 Situational Stats

	W	L	ERA	Sv	IP		AB	H	HR	RBI	Avg
Home	5	5	4.01	0	89.2	LHB	175	50	5	23	.286
Road	6	5	4.43	0	89.1	RHB	510	143	15	57	.280
First Half	7	2	2.89	0	90.1	Sc Pos	156	40	4	54	.256
Scnd Half	4	8	5.58	0	88.2	Clutch	71	16	2	5	.225

1999 Rankings (American League)

- 5th in most GDPs induced per 9 innings (1.3)
- 6th in GDPs induced (25) and fewest pitches thrown per batter (3.61)
- 8th in fewest strikeouts per 9 innings (5.3)
- Led the Mariners in GDPs induced (25), fewest pitches thrown per batter (3.61) and most GDPs induced per 9 innings (1.3)

Seattle

Brian Hunter

1999 Season

The Tigers were all too happy to dump Brian Hunter on the Mariners for two players to be named in late April. The speedy Washington state native became Seattle's everyday left fielder and leadoff hitter. To say he failed would be kind, as Hunter nearly pulled off a unique triple crown. Among major leaguers with 502 plate appearances, he finished last in batting average and next to last in on-base and slugging percentage.

Hitting

Hunter is neither a power hitter nor a contact hitter. He doesn't have the patience required to be even an adequate leadoff man and he doesn't hit the ball on the ground enough to take advantage of his tremendous speed. Hunter has extremely long legs, which gives him a larger-than-normal strike zone—not that he's figured out the strike zone yet. He managed the meager total of 23 extra-base hits and scored just 79 runs despite batting in front of Alex Rodriguez and Ken Griffey Jr.

Baserunning & Defense

Hunter's main attribute is his speed. He did swipe 44 bases in 52 attempts, which apparently was enough to keep him in the lineup. He gets nice leads and can read pitchers. Hunter played center field in Detroit to mixed reviews. With Griffey around, he moved to left field for the first time, which was a bit of an adventure. He took some circuitous routes on flyballs and appeared lost on others. Hunter's speed helps him track down some tough plays, however. He does have a good arm and gunned down 15 runners.

2000 Outlook

Hunter has been a terrible major league hitter the past two seasons. He can steal a base, but even that may not be enough to keep him in the lineup as a regular. Manager Lou Piniella caught on last September, when he demoted Hunter to the No. 9 hole. The Mariners considered non-tendering him but decided to keep him as insurance in case they trade Griffey. Seattle's signings of Stan Javier and Mark McLemore could relegate Hunter to the bench, however.

Position: LF/CF
Bats: R **Throws:** R
Ht: 6' 3" **Wt:** 180

Opening Day Age: 29
Born: 3/5/71 in Portland, OR
ML Seasons: 6

Overall Statistics

	G	AB	R	H	D	T	HR	RBI	SB	BB	SO	Avg	OBP	Slg
1999	139	539	79	125	13	6	4	34	44	37	91	.232	.280	.301
Career	659	2663	386	701	113	23	19	178	221	178	456	.263	.309	.344

Where He Hits the Ball

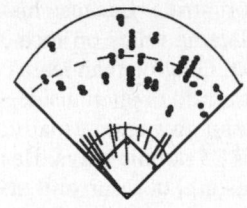

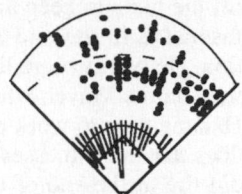

Vs. LHP   **Vs. RHP**

1999 Situational Stats

	AB	H	HR	RBI	Avg		AB	H	HR	RBI	Avg
Home	242	50	0	14	.207	LHP	102	19	0	1	.186
Road	297	75	4	20	.253	RHP	437	106	4	33	.243
First Half	317	85	3	23	.268	Sc Pos	108	26	0	29	.241
Scnd Half	222	40	1	11	.180	Clutch	51	7	0	1	.137

1999 Rankings (American League)

- 1st in lowest batting average (.232), stolen bases (44), steals of third (11), lowest on-base percentage for a leadoff hitter (.285) and lowest batting average at home (.207)
- 2nd in lowest slugging percentage (.301), lowest on-base percentage (.280) and steals of third (11)
- 3rd in lowest slugging percentage vs. righthanded pitchers (.323) and lowest on-base percentage vs. righthanded pitchers (.292)
- Led the Mariners in triples (5), stolen bases (44), highest groundball/flyball ratio (1.9), stolen-base percentage (89.8%), highest percentage of swings put into play (48.9%) and steals of third (11)

Edgar Martinez

1999 Season

Edgar Martinez is a pure hitting machine. His "slow" start meant he hit only .298 in April. After that, it was the same old Edgar. He hit two home runs and scored five runs against the Twins on May 17, then hit three home runs the next night. He batted better than .320 for the fifth straight year and led the American League in on-base percentage. Perhaps the only negative was his failure to drive in 100 runs for the first time since 1994.

Hitting

As always, Martinez has an idea every time he steps into the batter's box. Sometimes he'll lash at the first offering, but he usually waits for his pitch. Martinez has defined himself as a guess hitter who targets a particular pitch. His great eye allows him to avoid pitches just off the plate. He may have a bit of a weakness for hard stuff inside, but he still has the bat speed to turn on it and knock it over the fence. He also destroys mediocre breaking stuff. Despite his age, Martinez stays strong throughout the season. He had the third-highest average in the AL after the All-Star break.

Baserunning & Defense

Martinez dusted the cobwebs off his glove for five games at first base last season. The less he plays in the field, the better, but it's hard to sit him during interleague games. Known as one of the slowest runners in baseball, Martinez is an extremely opportunistic baserunner and swiped seven bases in nine tries in 1999.

2000 Outlook

Martinez was one of the most underrated, consistent players of the 1990s. He won two batting titles, led the AL three times in on-base percentage and hit .300 all eight full seasons he played. The Mariners re-signed Martinez to a one-year deal worth $5.2 million, with an option at the same salary for 2001. He'll bat fourth or fifth and continue to be one of the best bargains in the game.

Position: DH
Bats: R **Throws:** R
Ht: 5'11" **Wt:** 200

Opening Day Age: 37
Born: 1/2/63 in New York, NY
ML Seasons: 13

Overall Statistics

	G	AB	R	H	D	T	HR	RBI	SB	BB	SO	Avg	OBP	Slg
1999	142	502	86	169	35	1	24	86	7	97	99	.337	.447	.554
Career	1387	4876	880	1558	372	14	198	780	40	877	746	.320	.426	.523

Where He Hits the Ball

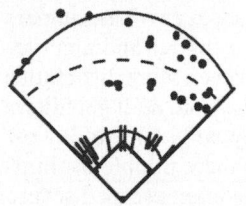 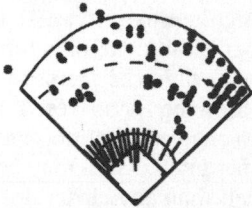

Vs. LHP   **Vs. RHP**

1999 Situational Stats

	AB	H	HR	RBI	Avg		AB	H	HR	RBI	Avg
Home	278	100	12	47	.360	LHP	109	39	10	24	.358
Road	224	69	12	39	.308	RHP	393	130	14	62	.331
First Half	249	78	14	50	.313	Sc Pos	130	38	8	62	.292
Scnd Half	253	91	10	36	.360	Clutch	52	17	1	5	.327

1999 Rankings (American League)

- 1st in on-base percentage
- 2nd in most pitches seen per plate appearance (4.30), batting average at home and lowest percentage of extra bases taken as a runner (22.2%)
- 3rd in slugging percentage vs. lefthanded pitchers (.725), on-base percentage vs. lefthanded pitchers (.478) and highest percentage of pitches taken (64.8%)
- Led the Mariners in batting average, singles, doubles, walks, times on base (272), on-base percentage, most pitches seen per plate appearance (4.30), batting average with the bases loaded (.500), batting average vs. lefthanded pitchers, batting average vs. righthanded pitchers and highest percentage of pitches taken (64.8%)

Seattle

Jose Mesa

1999 Season

Signed as a free agent to a two-year, $6.45 million contract before last season, Jose Mesa seemed an unlikely choice to solve Seattle's notorious bullpen problems. In one regard, he performed fairly well, tying a club record with 33 saves and blowing only five save opportunities. However, closer examination reveals that just seven of those saves came when Mesa had to protect a one-run lead. He also allowed 84 hits in 68.2 innings and barely struck out more hitters than he walked.

Pitching

Mesa's fastball still registers in the mid-90s and has impressive movement at times. However, he often has trouble throwing it for strikes, which leads to a high number of walks and about two baserunners per inning. He also throws a splitter and a curveball, which he seems to have even more difficulties throwing for strikes. When he's on, he'll get hitters to chase the splitter, but they've learned to lay off that pitch. Mesa may create more trouble for himself than any closer does. He often escaped severe damage last year, but his ERA remained high.

Defense

As a fielder, Mesa is fairly immobile, though he snared several line drives last season and started two double plays. He's better at holding runners than most closers, but allowed four steals in six attempts in 1999.

2000 Outlook

Mesa will return as Seattle's closer, making his manager, teammates and fans reach for their antacids. Yes, his save totals were good a year ago, but very few came in tight games. Considering that opponents hit .305 off him—the fourth straight year their average against him has increased—it's a risky proposition that Mesa will hold his job all season. He was impressive with Cleveland in 1995, but Mesa has been dogged by inconsistency throughout his career. The Mariners signed Japanese career saves leader Kazuhiro Sasaki to a two-year, $8 million contract in December. If Mesa struggles again, Seattle won't hesitate to turn to Sasaki.

Position: RP
Bats: R **Throws:** R
Ht: 6' 3" **Wt:** 225

Opening Day Age: 33
Born: 5/22/66 in Azua, Dominican Republic
ML Seasons: 11
Pronunciation: MAY-sa
Nickname: Joe Table

Overall Statistics

	W	L	Pct.	ERA	G	GS	Sv	IP	H	BB	SO	HR	Ratio
1999	3	6	.333	4.98	68	0	33	68.2	84	40	42	11	1.81
Career	54	69	.439	4.35	490	95	137	1016.0	1074	413	644	93	1.46

How Often He Throws Strikes

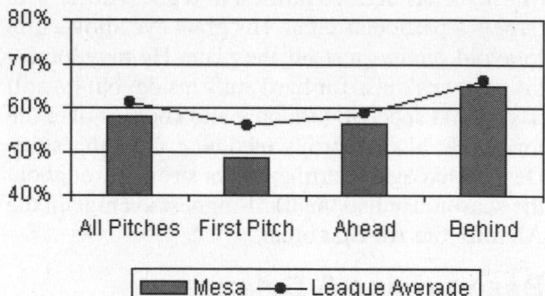

1999 Situational Stats

	W	L	ERA	Sv	IP		AB	H	HR	RBI	Avg
Home	3	3	8.44	16	32.0	LHB	157	52	8	31	.331
Road	0	3	1.96	17	36.2	RHB	118	32	3	14	.271
First Half	0	3	6.94	18	36.1	Sc Pos	96	21	3	34	.219
Scnd Half	3	3	2.78	15	32.1	Clutch	170	43	7	31	.253

1999 Rankings (American League)

- 2nd in most baserunners allowed per 9 innings in relief (16.8)
- 3rd in highest batting average allowed in relief (.305)
- 4th in relief losses (6)
- 5th in saves, games finished (60) and save percentage (86.8%)
- 6th in save opportunities (38)
- 8th in highest relief ERA (4.98)
- 10th in fewest strikeouts per 9 innings in relief (5.5)
- Led the Mariners in games pitched, saves, games finished (60), save opportunities (38), save percentage (86.8%) and lowest percentage of inherited runners scored (31.3%)

Jamie Moyer

1999 Season

Once again, Jamie Moyer pitched as well as any lefthander in the American League. He finished sixth in the league in ERA, third in innings pitched and only David Wells won more games among southpaws. Moyer started slowly, with a 7.64 ERA in five April starts, but went 13-5 the rest of the way. Like most Mariners starters, he benefited from the move into Safeco Field. However, he still posted a better ERA on the road than at home.

Pitching

Moyer is the prototypical crafty lefthander. His fastball rarely tops 85 MPH, but he throws his changeup at any number of speeds: slow, slower and slowest. What makes him so effective is that right when the hitter sits on the changeup, Moyer will bust him inside with a fastball that suddenly looks 95 MPH. He also throws two curveballs, a big sweeper he works on the outside corner to righthanders, and another which turns down and in. Moyer works all areas of the strike zone: up and down, inside and outside. Because he's so efficient with his pitch counts, Moyer can work deep into games.

Defense

Moyer even refined the little aspects of his game last season. He had a terrific year with the glove, recording 47 assists and starting nine double plays, an extremely high total for a pitcher. He probably deserved to win the Gold Glove. Moyer doesn't have the quickest delivery to home, but basestealers were just 9-for-17 against him after going 21-for-25 in 1998.

2000 Outlook

Over the last four seasons, Moyer has gone 59-25, which is why Seattle extended his contract through 2002 by adding a year for $6.5 million. He's 37 years old but in the prime of his career. His strikeout-walk ratio is still excellent, plus he's durable and healthy. Pitching in Safeco Field certainly won't hurt his totals. He also has become the leader of a rotation that featured three rookie starters in 1999. Moyer has been extremely consistent the past few seasons. Look for more of the same: 15 victories and a solid ERA.

Position: SP
Bats: L **Throws:** L
Ht: 6' 0" **Wt:** 170

Opening Day Age: 37
Born: 11/18/62 in Sellersville, PA
ML Seasons: 13

Overall Statistics

	W	L	Pct.	ERA	G	GS	Sv	IP	H	BB	SO	HR	Ratio
1999	14	8	.636	3.87	32	32	0	228.0	235	48	137	23	1.24
Career	118	101	.539	4.21	346	294	0	1928.1	2028	567	1164	221	1.35

How Often He Throws Strikes

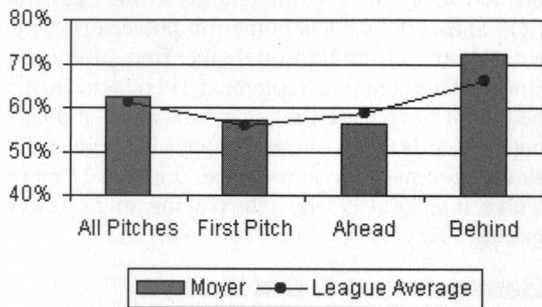

1999 Situational Stats

	W	L	ERA	Sv	IP		AB	H	HR	RBI	Avg
Home	7	6	4.17	0	127.1	LHB	214	50	7	25	.234
Road	7	2	3.49	0	100.2	RHB	666	185	16	68	.278
First Half	8	5	5.05	0	130.0	Sc Pos	177	56	5	68	.316
Scnd Half	6	3	2.30	0	98.0	Clutch	78	15	3	6	.192

1999 Rankings (American League)

- 3rd in innings pitched, batters faced (945) and lowest on-base percentage allowed (.311)
- 4th in fewest baserunners allowed per 9 innings (11.5), fewest walks per 9 innings (1.9), ERA on the road and lowest batting average allowed vs. lefthanded batters
- 5th in highest strikeout/walk ratio (2.9) and fewest home runs allowed per 9 innings (.91)
- Led the Mariners in ERA, complete games (4), innings pitched, hits allowed, batters faced (945), runners caught stealing (8), GDPs induced (25), highest strikeout/walk ratio (2.9), lowest slugging percentage allowed (.394), lowest on-base percentage allowed (.311) and lowest stolen-base percentage allowed (52.9%)

Alex Rodriguez

1999 Season

In the season's second game, Alex Rodriguez tore a ligament in his left knee, which sidelined him for just over a month. Upon his return, he blistered the ball until a 6-for-62 slump at the start of September. Still, he finished with 42 home runs and topped 100 runs and 100 RBI in just 129 games. Midway through the season, he was shifted to the cleanup spot for the first time in his career.

Hitting

Because of his quick hands, Rodriguez has tremendous plate coverage. It's nearly impossible to slip anything past him on the inner half of the plate, and he feasts on fastballs and breaking balls alike. If pitched away, he's willing to go to the opposite field and certainly has home-run power that way. Rodriguez suffered through the first prolonged slump of his career in September. He resorted to his bad habit of chasing breaking balls away and perhaps got a little too homer-happy. Rodriguez did show more patience at the plate, drawing 11 more walks than in 1998 despite playing in 32 fewer games.

Baserunning & Defense

Rodriguez has one of the strongest infield arms in the American League, soft hands, a new grass infield and experience. It all added up to the best defensive year of his career in 1999. He made 4.82 plays per game, the highest of his career and a better total than rivals Nomar Garciaparra or Derek Jeter. Rodriguez is very fluid going to his left, and his strong arm allows him to play a step deeper than other shortstops. Despite the knee injury, he stole 21 bases in 28 attempts. He said he should be able to run more this season.

2000 Outlook

Rodriguez becomes a free agent after 2000 and has made it clear that he'll test the free-agent market, even if the Mariners trade him. Because of his youth and ability, he likely will receive the biggest contract in sports history, perhaps something along the lines of eight years and $200 million.

Position: SS
Bats: R **Throws:** R
Ht: 6' 3" **Wt:** 195

Opening Day Age: 24
Born: 7/27/75 in New York, NY
ML Seasons: 6
Nickname: A-Rod

Overall Statistics

	G	AB	R	H	D	T	HR	RBI	SB	BB	SO	Avg	OBP	Slg
1999	129	502	110	143	25	0	42	111	21	56	109	.285	.357	.586
Career	642	2572	493	791	160	11	148	463	118	210	495	.308	.363	.551

Where He Hits the Ball

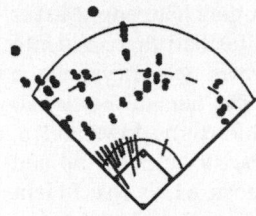

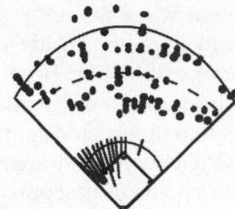

Vs. LHP   **Vs. RHP**

1999 Situational Stats

	AB	H	HR	RBI	Avg		AB	H	HR	RBI	Avg
Home	250	71	20	59	.284	LHP	112	31	7	17	.277
Road	252	72	22	52	.286	RHP	390	112	35	94	.287
First Half	215	68	18	48	.316	Sc Pos	125	36	6	61	.288
Scnd Half	287	75	24	63	.261	Clutch	57	9	3	11	.158

1999 Rankings (American League)

- 2nd in HR frequency (12.0 ABs per HR) and cleanup slugging percentage (.614)
- 5th in home runs, slugging percentage vs. righthanded pitchers (.610) and fielding percentage at shortstop (.977)
- 6th in slugging percentage, most pitches seen per plate appearance (4.13) and lowest batting average in the clutch
- 9th in errors at shortstop (14)
- 10th in sacrifice flies (8) and steals of third (3)
- Led the Mariners in sacrifice flies (8), caught stealing (7), slugging percentage, HR frequency (12.0 ABs per HR) and cleanup slugging percentage (.614)

Dan Wilson

1999 Season

For the third consecutive season, Dan Wilson saw his home runs, RBI and slugging percentage decrease. His numbers in those categories were his lowest since his first season with Seattle in 1994. Wilson was hitting .293 through June, but had knocked in only 21 runs. His batting average dipped noticeably thereafter, though he did have his best month of the season in September, when he hit .303.

Hitting

Wilson changed his hitting approach somewhat in 1999. In the past, he primarily drove the ball up the middle or into right-center, yanking the occasional mistake for a home run. He pulled the ball more often last year, perhaps trying to rediscover some of the power he had in his All-Star season of 1996, when he hit 18 home runs. But this tactic didn't develop any more extra-base authority. Wilson can get overpowered by high-octane heat. He chases outside breaking balls, resulting in a lot of ground-balls to third base and shortstop. In the past, he has hit lefthanders better than righties, but that trend reversed last season.

Baserunning & Defense

Wilson's defense didn't measure up well when compared to backup Tom Lampkin. Both threw out 19 runners, but Lampkin did so in 48 attempts compared to Wilson's 97. Two years ago, Wilson threw out 43 percent of runners, so his arm strength obviously has deteriorated. He still has a quick release and remains excellent at blocking balls in the dirt. Wilson is no turtle on the basepaths and was a perfect 5-for-5 in steals.

2000 Outlook

Wilson may be hitting the wall that most catchers do once they turn 30. His bat speed and defensive skills have declined. The Mariners still decided to bring him back with a three-year, $12.9 million contract. He's a favorite of the front office and catchers are difficult to find.

Position: C
Bats: R **Throws:** R
Ht: 6' 3" **Wt:** 190

Opening Day Age: 31
Born: 3/25/69 in Barrington, IL
ML Seasons: 8

Overall Statistics

	G	AB	R	H	D	T	HR	RBI	SB	BB	SO	Avg	OBP	Slg
1999	123	414	46	110	23	2	7	38	5	29	83	.266	.315	.382
Career	761	2520	274	667	135	9	61	328	18	179	443	.265	.316	.398

Where He Hits the Ball

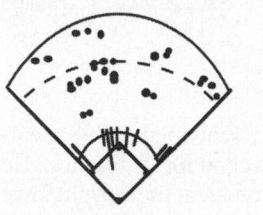
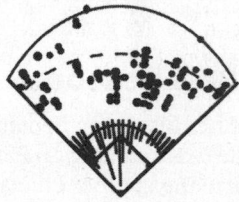

Vs. LHP   **Vs. RHP**

1999 Situational Stats

	AB	H	HR	RBI	Avg		AB	H	HR	RBI	Avg
Home	197	57	3	17	.289	LHP	102	26	1	7	.255
Road	217	53	4	21	.244	RHP	312	84	6	31	.269
First Half	235	66	4	21	.281	Sc Pos	99	26	0	29	.263
Scnd Half	179	44	3	17	.246	Clutch	52	11	0	1	.212

1999 Rankings (American League)

- 1st in lowest percentage of runners caught stealing as a catcher (19.6%)
- 7th in sacrifice bunts (10)
- Led the Mariners in sacrifice bunts (10)
- Led AL catchers in sacrifice bunts (10) and intentional walks (4)

Paul Abbott

Position: RP
Bats: R **Throws:** R
Ht: 6' 3" **Wt:** 195

Opening Day Age: 32
Born: 9/15/67 in Van Nuys, CA
ML Seasons: 6

Overall Statistics

	W	L	Pct.	ERA	G	GS	Sv	IP	H	BB	SO	HR	Ratio
1999	6	2	.750	3.10	25	7	0	72.2	50	32	68	9	1.13
Career	12	10	.545	4.36	62	26	0	208.2	180	122	178	22	1.45

1999 Situational Stats

	W	L	ERA	Sv	IP		AB	H	HR	RBI	Avg
Home	5	1	2.66	0	40.2	LHB	138	22	3	18	.159
Road	1	1	3.66	0	32.0	RHB	121	28	6	18	.231
First Half	0	0	3.55	0	12.2	Sc Pos	60	14	2	27	.233
Scnd Half	6	2	3.00	0	60.0	Clutch	43	3	0	5	.070

1999 Season

After his strong September showing in 1998, Seattle was counting on Paul Abbott for its rotation. He tore the anterior cruciate ligament in his right knee while pitching in Puerto Rico, which got him waived by the Mariners in December 1998, but they re-signed him a month later. He returned just before the All-Star break and pitched well.

Pitching & Defense

Abbott is essentially a two-pitch pitcher, with a fastball in the low 90s and a hard sinker/splitter. He also throws an occasional curve. He proved difficult to hit and was particularly tough against lefthanders. Control problems kept him in the minors for years, and he still loses touch of the strike zone at times. Abbott pays close attention to baserunners and there were only three attempted steals off him. He's a steady fielder.

2000 Outlook

As usual, the Mariners are in desperate need of relievers, so Abbott will be the primary setup man for closer Jose Mesa. He has the versatility to move into the rotation if needed and could even become the closer if Mesa falters.

Rafael Bournigal

Position: SS/2B
Bats: R **Throws:** R
Ht: 5'11" **Wt:** 175

Opening Day Age: 33
Born: 5/12/66 in Azua, Dominican Republic
ML Seasons: 7
Pronunciation: BORE-nuh-gal

Overall Statistics

	G	AB	R	H	D	T	HR	RBI	SB	BB	SO	Avg	OBP	Slg
1999	55	95	16	26	5	0	2	14	0	7	6	.274	.317	.389
Career	365	932	104	234	44	3	4	85	12	59	64	.251	.301	.318

1999 Situational Stats

	AB	H	HR	RBI	Avg		AB	H	HR	RBI	Avg
Home	37	14	2	10	.378	LHP	17	6	1	5	.353
Road	58	12	0	4	.207	RHP	78	20	1	9	.256
First Half	49	16	2	13	.327	Sc Pos	25	9	0	10	.360
Scnd Half	46	10	0	1	.217	Clutch	7	2	0	0	.286

1999 Season

Veteran utilityman Rafael Bournigal began the year at Triple-A Oklahoma with the Rangers before being sold to the Mariners in late April. Replacing the injured Alex Rodriguez, he had two homers and nine RBI in his first six games, then remembered he was Rafael Bournigal. He played sparingly once Rodriguez returned.

Hitting, Baserunning & Defense

Bournigal's hands are as soft as any infielder in the game, as his lifetime .988 fielding percentage attests. He has good range at both shortstop and second base, and a decent throwing arm. He's not flashy, just very solid. At the plate, Bournigal's two home runs equaled his career total. For the most part, he looks to make contact. He's an excellent bunter and hit-and-run man. He didn't attempt to steal last year but has average speed.

2000 Outlook

Bournigal's lifetime on-base and slugging percentages are both higher than Rey Ordonez'. His lifetime fielding percentage also is higher. But Ordonez is considered a star while Bournigal was non-tendered in December. He'll be on somebody's bench in 2000.

Tom Davey

Position: RP
Bats: R **Throws:** R
Ht: 6' 7" **Wt:** 230

Opening Day Age: 26
Born: 9/11/73 in
Garden City, MI
ML Seasons: 1

Overall Statistics

	W	L	Pct.	ERA	G	GS	Sv	IP	H	BB	SO	HR	Ratio
1999	2	1	.667	4.71	45	0	1	65.0	62	40	59	5	1.57
Career	2	1	.667	4.71	45	0	1	65.0	62	40	59	5	1.57

1999 Situational Stats

	W	L	ERA	Sv	IP		AB	H	HR	RBI	Avg
Home	2	0	4.78	0	26.1	LHB	101	27	1	13	.267
Road	0	1	4.66	1	38.2	RHB	147	35	4	24	.238
First Half	1	1	4.70	1	44.0	Sc Pos	99	23	2	32	.232
Scnd Half	1	0	4.71	0	21.0	Clutch	41	12	0	4	.293

1999 Season

Tom Davey began his rookie season in Toronto's bullpen, spent time at Triple-A Syracuse and was traded to Seattle with Steve Sinclair for David Segui in July. The Mariners used him in middle relief, with so-so results.

Pitching & Defense

Davey has an explosive fastball but has been plagued by control problems throughout his career. He struggles with his release point, which is why his fastball can hit 98 MPH at times and dip down to 92 MPH at others. He also has a splitter, giving him the two-pitch arsenal he needs to survive in the bullpen. With Davey, it's all about command. At 6-foot-7, he can be intimidating and fanned nearly a hitter an inning in 1999, but he also walked 40 and hit seven batters in 65 frames. Like most big pitchers, Davey is slow to the plate, but runners went just 5-for-9 in basestealing attempts. He's an erratic fielder.

2000 Outlook

The Mariners hope Davey will play a major role in their bullpen this year and envision him as a future closer. He could inherit that role very soon if he develops any consistency.

Carlos Guillen

Position: SS
Bats: B **Throws:** R
Ht: 6' 1" **Wt:** 180

Opening Day Age: 24
Born: 9/30/75 in
Maracay, Venezuela
ML Seasons: 2
Pronunciation:
GHEE-un

Overall Statistics

	G	AB	R	H	D	T	HR	RBI	SB	BB	SO	Avg	OBP	Slg
1999	5	19	2	3	0	0	1	3	0	1	6	.158	.200	.316
Career	15	58	11	16	1	1	1	8	2	4	15	.276	.323	.379

1999 Situational Stats

	AB	H	HR	RBI	Avg		AB	H	HR	RBI	Avg
Home	19	3	1	3	.158	LHP	7	1	0	1	.143
Road	—	—	—	—	—	RHP	—	—	—	—	—
First Half	19	3	1	3	.158	Sc Pos	4	2	0	2	.500
Scnd Half	—	—	—	—	—	Clutch	—	—	—	—	—

1999 Season

Part of the 1998 Randy Johnson trade, Carlos Guillen won Seattle's second-base job in spring training. In the season's fifth game, he tore the anterior cruciate ligament in his right knee during a rundown, ending his year.

Hitting, Baserunning & Defense

Guillen's bat is his best tool. He's a switch-hitter with power potential, though his offense will be held back until he develops some semblance of strike-zone judgment. He has been dogged by injuries and played just 316 pro games, so he has room to get better with experience. Guillen rose through the Astros system as a shortstop and moved to second once he became a teammate of Alex Rodriguez. He has the range and arm to play any infield position. Before his injury, he had good speed but wasn't a basestealer.

2000 Outlook

The Mariners don't want to risk Guillen's knee on double-play pivots, and they didn't want to pay Russ Davis arbitration money. Thus Seattle will move Guillen to third base in 2000. He has promise but will need some time to adjust to the majors because of his inexperience.

Seattle

Raul Ibanez

Position: RF/LF/1B
Bats: L **Throws:** R
Ht: 6' 2" **Wt:** 200

Opening Day Age: 27
Born: 6/2/72 in
Manhattan, NY
ML Seasons: 4
Pronunciation:
ih-BONN-yez

Overall Statistics

	G	AB	R	H	D	T	HR	RBI	SB	BB	SO	Avg	OBP	Slg
1999	87	209	23	54	7	0	9	27	5	17	32	.258	.313	.421
Career	139	338	38	83	14	2	12	43	5	22	61	.246	.293	.405

1999 Situational Stats

	AB	H	HR	RBI	Avg		AB	H	HR	RBI	Avg
Home	90	22	3	13	.244	LHP	21	5	1	2	.238
Road	119	32	6	14	.269	RHP	188	49	8	25	.261
First Half	60	20	0	4	.333	Sc Pos	63	16	2	18	.254
Scnd Half	149	34	9	23	.228	Clutch	47	10	2	5	.213

1999 Season

Raul Ibanez spent most of his seven pro seasons in the minors before finally sticking in Seattle in 1999. He played mostly in right field early on, then got some action at first base after David Segui was traded.

Hitting, Baserunning & Defense

Ibanez has a nice, quick stroke but never generated a lot of power or hit for a great average in the minors. He did slug nine home runs last year, perhaps suggesting he'll hit for the power the Mariners always have hoped for. He can be a little too aggressive at the plate and will chase fastballs out of the strike zone. Drafted as a catcher, Ibanez had a decent arm until shoulder surgery in 1998. He was adequate in right field but looked out of his element at first base, where he has little experience. He has only average speed but swiped five bases in six attempts in 1999.

2000 Outlook

Ibanez once again will be part of Seattle's bench. He's unlikely to develop into a starter, but a lefthanded hitter who can run a little and play the outfield will have a job.

Tom Lampkin

Position: C
Bats: L **Throws:** R
Ht: 5'11" **Wt:** 195

Opening Day Age: 36
Born: 3/4/64 in
Cincinnati, OH
ML Seasons: 10

Overall Statistics

	G	AB	R	H	D	T	HR	RBI	SB	BB	SO	Avg	OBP	Slg
1999	76	206	29	60	11	2	9	34	1	13	32	.291	.345	.495
Career	558	1208	149	289	52	6	34	154	18	128	169	.239	.321	.377

1999 Situational Stats

	AB	H	HR	RBI	Avg		AB	H	HR	RBI	Avg
Home	102	32	5	21	.314	LHP	27	8	0	4	.296
Road	104	28	4	13	.269	RHP	179	52	9	30	.291
First Half	96	31	4	14	.323	Sc Pos	55	14	0	20	.255
Scnd Half	110	29	5	20	.264	Clutch	41	8	1	8	.195

1999 Season

Seattle native Tom Lampkin returned home as a free agent when he signed a two-year contract worth $1.55 million. He enjoyed a productive year as Dan Wilson's backup. Lampkin hit .291, provided some power and even played solid defense. In fact, he outplayed Wilson both offensively and defensively.

Hitting, Baserunning & Defense

Lampkin has a good approach while hitting. He's a fastball hitter with enough patience to wait for one. He looks to drive the inside pitch but will go up the middle or to the opposite field if necessary. All his power is to right field, and he's been largely ineffective against lefties in his career. Lampkin isn't known for a strong arm, but he had an excellent year throwing out runners, nailing 19 of 48, a much better percentage than Wilson's. Lampkin's mechanics behind the plate are solid and Seattle's young pitchers like throwing to him.

2000 Outlook

With Wilson's skills in apparent decline, Lampkin may have earned himself a little more playing time. He had his best year at the plate in 1999, so some dropoff should be expected there.

John Mabry

Position: RF/3B/1B
Bats: L **Throws:** R
Ht: 6' 4" **Wt:** 210

Opening Day Age: 29
Born: 10/17/70 in Wilmington, DE
ML Seasons: 6
Pronunciation: MAY-bree

Overall Statistics

	G	AB	R	H	D	T	HR	RBI	SB	BB	SO	Avg	OBP	Slg
1999	87	262	34	64	14	0	9	33	2	20	60	.244	.297	.401
Career	631	1981	215	555	109	3	41	233	5	152	346	.280	.332	.400

1999 Situational Stats

	AB	H	HR	RBI	Avg		AB	H	HR	RBI	Avg
Home	130	29	5	16	.223	LHP	28	7	0	2	.250
Road	132	35	4	17	.265	RHP	234	57	9	31	.244
First Half	205	49	8	29	.239	Sc Pos	72	17	1	22	.236
Scnd Half	57	15	1	4	.263	Clutch	32	3	0	2	.094

1999 Season

Signed to a two-year, $3.25 million contract as a free agent after the Cardinals non-tendered him, John Mabry had the same job he had in St. Louis. He filled in at right field, third base and first base, while also serving as a lefthanded pinch-hitter. His season ended in August with a fractured kneecap.

Hitting, Baserunning & Defense

After he hit .307 as a rookie in 1995, Mabry's batting average has declined each season. He has lost control of the strike zone and chased a lot of breaking stuff off the plate in 1999. He has turned into strictly a platoon player. Mabry is adequate in right field, where he has a strong arm. The versatility he provides is nice, but he shouldn't play third base, where his career fielding percentage is .895. He's slow on the bases.

2000 Outlook

Mabry will have a role in 2000 because he bats lefthanded and can play three positions. While he can do many things, he doesn't really do anything particularly well. He no longer resembles the hitter who showed promise in his first two years.

Gil Meche

Position: SP
Bats: R **Throws:** R
Ht: 6' 3" **Wt:** 180

Opening Day Age: 21
Born: 9/8/78 in Lafayette, LA
ML Seasons: 1
Pronunciation: MESH

Overall Statistics

	W	L	Pct.	ERA	G	GS	Sv	IP	H	BB	SO	HR	Ratio
1999	8	4	.667	4.73	16	15	0	85.2	73	57	47	9	1.52
Career	8	4	.667	4.73	16	15	0	85.2	73	57	47	9	1.52

1999 Situational Stats

	W	L	ERA	Sv	IP		AB	H	HR	RBI	Avg
Home	5	2	3.50	0	46.1	LHB	179	43	5	15	.240
Road	3	2	6.18	0	39.1	RHB	129	30	4	22	.233
First Half	0	0	6.14	0	7.1	Sc Pos	60	12	1	20	.200
Scnd Half	8	4	4.60	0	78.1	Clutch	9	3	0	1	.333

1999 Season

Though he hadn't pitched above Class-A before 1999, Gil Meche made his major league debut on July 6 at age 20 and stayed in the rotation the rest of the season. The 1996 first-round pick finished with a kick, going 4-0 with a 3.19 ERA in September.

Pitching & Defense

Meche possesses a legitimate 95-MPH fastball that seems to explode at times. He also has a tight-breaking curveball, excellent mechanics and fine composure. "Freddy Garcia is ahead of him now, but for me Meche is the best-looking young pitcher in the American League," one scout said last year. Meche did have control problems, especially with his curve, and walked more hitters than he struck out, but he was difficult to hit. He knows how to hold baserunners and was flawless in the field.

2000 Outlook

Meche just needs experience and good health. The Mariners have him penciled in as their No. 5 starter and believe he can handle the pressure. He has terrific talent and an electric arm, though he still has a long way to go before becoming a consistent starter.

Seattle

Jose Paniagua

Position: RP
Bats: R **Throws:** R
Ht: 6' 2" **Wt:** 185

Opening Day Age: 26
Born: 8/20/73 in San Jose de Ocoa, Dominican Republic
ML Seasons: 4
Pronunciation: pahn-ee-AH-gwah

Overall Statistics

	W	L	Pct.	ERA	G	GS	Sv	IP	H	BB	SO	HR	Ratio
1999	6	11	.353	4.06	59	0	3	77.2	75	52	74	5	1.64
Career	11	17	.393	4.48	99	14	4	168.2	174	96	125	17	1.60

1999 Situational Stats

	W	L	ERA	Sv	IP		AB	H	HR	RBI	Avg
Home	2	4	5.45	1	34.2	LHB	127	35	3	25	.276
Road	4	7	2.93	2	43.0	RHB	157	40	2	21	.255
First Half	6	8	4.01	1	49.1	Sc Pos	105	28	2	42	.267
Scnd Half	0	3	4.13	2	28.1	Clutch	168	44	3	32	.262

1999 Season

Jose Paniagua was manager Lou Piniella's first choice to enter in tight situations in the seventh and eighth innings, and he performed with mixed results. He was better than most of Seattle's recent middle relievers but also finished with 11 losses, second-highest on the team. He tired by the end of the year and pitched in just five games the final month.

Pitching & Defense

Paniagua is primarily a one-pitch guy, with a hard sinker in the low 90s. It can be an effective pitch, as he allowed only five home runs and induced a high rate of groundballs. However, he can be wild with the pitch and gets in trouble when he uses his four-seam fastball and mediocre slider on a regular basis. While he has a quick delivery to home, Paniagua doesn't pay much attention to baserunners. He's adequate as a fielder.

2000 Outlook

The Mariners showed confidence in Paniagua in 1999 and they expect improvement from him as their top setup man. As with so many pitchers, the key to Paniagua's future will be command of the strike zone.

Frank Rodriguez

Position: RP
Bats: R **Throws:** R
Ht: 6' 0" **Wt:** 210

Opening Day Age: 27
Born: 12/11/72 in Brooklyn, NY
ML Seasons: 5

Overall Statistics

	W	L	Pct.	ERA	G	GS	Sv	IP	H	BB	SO	HR	Ratio
1999	2	4	.333	5.65	28	5	3	73.1	94	30	47	11	1.69
Career	27	38	.415	5.39	154	82	5	598.0	661	255	343	67	1.53

1999 Situational Stats

	W	L	ERA	Sv	IP		AB	H	HR	RBI	Avg
Home	0	1	2.27	2	31.2	LHB	146	47	7	28	.322
Road	2	3	8.21	1	41.2	RHB	153	47	4	24	.307
First Half	2	3	7.54	1	37.0	Sc Pos	88	26	2	38	.295
Scnd Half	0	1	3.72	2	36.1	Clutch	18	8	1	4	.444

1999 Season

Frank Rodriguez still has a good arm and still hasn't had much success in the big leagues. After the Twins finally gave up on Rodriguez in May, the Mariners picked him up on waivers. He started off well, winning two spot starts in June, but his season went downhill from there. He was a primary participant in two brawls, including one that led to a seven-game suspension.

Pitching & Defense

Rodriguez throws a 92-MPH fastball, a slider with good action on it and a curveball. He has the stuff to succeed but never has developed the proper command or pitching instincts. When he falls behind in the count, he tends to lay fastballs right over the plate. His career ERA is now 5.39 in 598 innings, and even though he's 27 time may be running out. An excellent athlete, Rodriguez is quick around the mound and shuts down the running game.

2000 Outlook

Rodriguez simply doesn't fool enough major league hitters. He's still young enough to warrant another chance, and he'll probably get it in Seattle. His best hope is for a long-relief role.

Other Seattle Mariners

Mike Blowers (Pos: 1B, Age: 34, Bats: R)

	G	AB	R	H	D	T	HR	RBI	SB	BB	SO	Avg	OBP	Slg
1999	19	46	2	11	1	0	2	7	0	4	12	.239	.300	.391
Career	761	2300	290	591	116	8	78	365	7	248	610	.257	.329	.416

Released in August by Japan's Hanshin Tigers, Blowers joined the Mariners in September. His low averages of late illustrate his struggles against righthanders, but Seattle needs corner help. 2000 Outlook: C

Mel Bunch (Pos: RHP, Age: 28)

	W	L	Pct.	ERA	G	GS	Sv	IP	H	BB	SO	HR	Ratio
1999	0	0	-	11.70	5	1	0	10.0	20	7	4	3	2.70
Career	1	3	.250	6.84	18	6	0	50.0	62	21	23	14	1.66

Bunch scuffled in the high minors in the four seasons prior to 1999. He went 10-2, 3.10 at Triple-A Tacoma in '99, but that success didn't follow him to Seattle. He'll try again this spring. 2000 Outlook: C

Rafael Carmona (Pos: RHP, Age: 27)

	W	L	Pct.	ERA	G	GS	Sv	IP	H	BB	SO	HR	Ratio
1999	1	0	1.000	7.94	9	0	0	11.1	18	9	0	3	2.38
Career	11	7	.611	4.94	81	4	2	155.0	171	100	96	24	1.75

Carmona was a promising pitching prospect with a good arm, but his career has been sidetracked by injuries. He was recalled in May, but in June he went out for two months with a triceps injury. He was non-tendered in December. 2000 Outlook: C

Ken Cloude (Pos: RHP, Age: 25)

	W	L	Pct.	ERA	G	GS	Sv	IP	H	BB	SO	HR	Ratio
1999	4	4	.500	7.96	31	6	1	72.1	106	46	35	10	2.10
Career	16	16	.500	6.56	71	45	1	278.2	334	152	195	47	1.74

Cloude was a prospect after a strong showing at the end of 1997, but can't really be considered one now. He has two big problems: a straight fastball and an inability to throw strikes. 2000 Outlook: C

Ryan Franklin (Pos: RHP, Age: 27)

	W	L	Pct.	ERA	G	GS	Sv	IP	H	BB	SO	HR	Ratio
1999	0	0	-	4.76	6	0	0	11.1	10	8	6	2	1.59
Career	0	0	-	4.76	6	0	0	11.1	10	8	6	2	1.59

For a third straight season Franklin pitched OK as a starter at Triple-A Tacoma. He was just so-so as a member of the Seattle bullpen. 2000 Outlook: C

Charles Gipson (Pos: 3B/RF, Age: 27, Bats: R)

	G	AB	R	H	D	T	HR	RBI	SB	BB	SO	Avg	OBP	Slg
1999	55	80	16	18	5	2	0	9	3	6	13	.225	.287	.338
Career	99	131	27	30	6	2	0	11	5	11	22	.229	.299	.305

The speedy Gipson can play a few positions, but he doesn't hit enough to utilize his wheels or warrant much attention. It's a mild surprise that he managed seven extra-base hits with the Mariners. 2000 Outlook: C

Giomar Guevara (Pos: SS, Age: 27, Bats: B)

	G	AB	R	H	D	T	HR	RBI	SB	BB	SO	Avg	OBP	Slg
1999	10	12	2	3	2	0	0	2	0	0	2	.250	.250	.417
Career	26	29	6	6	4	0	0	2	1	4	8	.207	.324	.345

For a third straight year Guevara appeared briefly with the M's. He came up when Alex Rodriguez was injured at the start of the season, but by May Guevara was gone. He signed with Detroit. 2000 Outlook: C

Butch Henry (Pos: LHP, Age: 31)

	W	L	Pct.	ERA	G	GS	Sv	IP	H	BB	SO	HR	Ratio
1999	2	0	1.000	5.04	7	4	0	25.0	30	10	15	1	1.60
Career	33	33	.500	3.83	148	91	7	621.0	677	149	345	61	1.33

Henry broke down in the first month of the last two seasons. Knee surgery sidelined him in 1998, and a torn labrum shelved him in '99. He's a big injury risk, and he signed with the Rockies. Ouch. 2000 Outlook: C

Brett Hinchliffe (Pos: RHP, Age: 25)

	W	L	Pct.	ERA	G	GS	Sv	IP	H	BB	SO	HR	Ratio
1999	0	4	.000	8.80	11	4	0	30.2	41	21	14	10	2.02
Career	0	4	.000	8.80	11	4	0	30.2	41	21	14	10	2.02

Hinchliffe had some success in the high minors, but just got shelled in Seattle. Walks had been a problem in the past, and they were a big problem in Seattle. He fared a bit better in relief. 2000 Outlook: C

Ryan Jackson (Pos: 1B, Age: 28, Bats: L)

	G	AB	R	H	D	T	HR	RBI	SB	BB	SO	Avg	OBP	Slg
1999	32	68	4	16	3	0	0	10	3	6	19	.235	.299	.279
Career	143	328	30	81	18	1	5	41	4	26	92	.247	.304	.354

Jackson has hit better than .300 with pop in the high minors. Recalled in August, he started 7-for-17 with a five-game hitting streak, but that was about all Jackson produced. 2000 Outlook: C

Mark Leiter (Pos: RHP, Age: 36)

	W	L	Pct.	ERA	G	GS	Sv	IP	H	BB	SO	HR	Ratio
1999	0	0	-	6.75	2	0	0	1.1	2	0	1	0	1.50
Career	63	72	.467	4.60	315	146	26	1148.1	1173	416	866	149	1.38

Coming off his career year as Philadelphia's closer in 1998, Leiter made two appearances before tearing his rotator cuff. His rehab may carry over into this season. 2000 Outlook: C

Damaso Marte (Pos: LHP, Age: 25)

	W	L	Pct.	ERA	G	GS	Sv	IP	H	BB	SO	HR	Ratio
1999	0	1	.000	9.35	5	0	0	8.2	16	6	3	3	2.54
Career	0	1	.000	9.35	5	0	0	8.2	16	6	3	3	2.54

Desperate for bullpen help, the Mariners tried anyone on their Triple-A Tacoma roster who had a remote chance to contribute in Seattle. Marte took his 5.13 ERA at Tacoma north to Seattle and struggled. 2000 Outlook: C

Seattle

Shane Monahan (**Pos**: LF, **Age**: 25, **Bats**: L)

	G	AB	R	H	D	T	HR	RBI	SB	BB	SO	Avg	OBP	Slg
1999	16	15	3	2	0	0	0	0	0	0	6	.133	.133	.133
Career	78	226	20	53	8	1	4	28	1	8	59	.235	.261	.332

Monahan has shown some gap power in the high minors, but he's a free swinger who doesn't walk. His strikeout-walk ratio is a big liability. 2000 Outlook: C

Aaron Scheffer (**Pos**: RHP, **Age**: 24)

	W	L	Pct.	ERA	G	GS	Sv	IP	H	BB	SO	HR	Ratio
1999	0	0	-	1.93	4	0	0	4.2	6	3	4	0	1.93
Career	0	0	-	1.93	4	0	0	4.2	6	3	4	0	1.93

Scheffer may be the only Triple-A Tacoma hurler who was dominating before he was called up. He fanned 62 batters in 59.2 innings and saved nine games. He may be worth watching in the spring. 2000 Outlook: B

Steve Sinclair (**Pos**: LHP, **Age**: 28)

	W	L	Pct.	ERA	G	GS	Sv	IP	H	BB	SO	HR	Ratio
1999	0	1	.000	6.52	21	0	0	19.1	22	14	18	5	1.86
Career	0	3	.000	5.24	45	0	0	34.1	35	19	26	5	1.57

Sinclair arrived in the deal that moved David Segui to Toronto, and the M's gave him a lengthy audition. He had been solid in Triple-A for two seasons, but he hasn't impressed in the majors. 2000 Outlook: C

Sean Spencer (**Pos**: LHP, **Age**: 24)

	W	L	Pct.	ERA	G	GS	Sv	IP	H	BB	SO	HR	Ratio
1999	0	0	-	21.60	2	0	0	1.2	5	3	2	0	4.80
Career	0	0	-	21.60	2	0	0	1.2	5	3	2	0	4.80

Spencer has made rapid progress in three minor league seasons and pitched well at Triple-A Tacoma in 1999. He was bounced around in two outings with the M's, but in time he may adjust well to the majors. 2000 Outlook: C

Ozzie Timmons (**Pos**: LF, **Age**: 29, **Bats**: R)

	G	AB	R	H	D	T	HR	RBI	SB	BB	SO	Avg	OBP	Slg
1999	26	44	4	5	2	0	1	3	0	4	12	.114	.188	.227
Career	174	364	53	81	17	1	16	47	4	32	75	.223	.286	.407

Timmons slugged 22 doubles and 21 homers in 82 games at Triple-A Tacoma in 1999. Seattle brought him up in mid-July, but he didn't do much coming off the bench. Succeeding in that role is his best shot. Tampa Bay signed him in November. 2000 Outlook: C

Eric Weaver (**Pos**: RHP, **Age**: 26)

	W	L	Pct.	ERA	G	GS	Sv	IP	H	BB	SO	HR	Ratio
1999	0	1	.000	10.61	8	0	0	9.1	14	8	14	2	2.36
Career	2	1	.667	5.68	15	0	0	19.0	19	14	19	3	1.74

Weaver pitched well at Triple-A Tacoma early in 1999 after seven seasons in the Dodgers system. He took a pounding in most of his May outings with Seattle, then missed much of '99 with bone spurs. 2000 Outlook: C

Todd Williams (**Pos**: RHP, **Age**: 29)

	W	L	Pct.	ERA	G	GS	Sv	IP	H	BB	SO	HR	Ratio
1999	0	0	-	4.66	13	0	0	9.2	11	7	7	1	1.86
Career	2	3	.400	5.63	35	0	0	38.1	45	20	19	5	1.70

Williams has been a closer in the high minors for much of the 1990s, but he hasn't succeeded in three major league auditions. He wasn't the answer to Seattle's bullpen woes, but he may get another look. 2000 Outlook: C

Seattle Mariners Minor League Prospects

Organization Overview:

There may be some hope for a Seattle farm system that for years only had No. 1 overall picks Ken Griffey Jr. and Alex Rodriguez to brag about. Part of the problem was that the Mariners traded away most of the quality players they developed, though they reversed that trend in 1998 by getting pitchers Freddy Garcia and John Halama and infielder Carlos Guillen from Houston for Randy Johnson. Rookie righthander Gil Meche went 8-4 and looks like the best pitcher signed by Seattle since it drafted Mike Hampton in 1990. The Mariners have bolstered their international efforts, and new GM Pat Gillick oversaw a productive system while with Toronto. There's little talent in the upper minors, but Seattle did place four players on *Baseball America's* Northwest League Top 10 Prospects list. Help finally is on the way.

Ryan Anderson

Position: P	Opening Day Age: 20
Bats: L Throws: L	Born: 7/12/79 in
Ht: 6' 10" Wt: 215	Southfield, MI

Recent Statistics

	W	L	ERA	G	GS	Sv	IP	H	R	BB	SO	HR
1998 A Wisconsin	6	5	3.23	22	22	0	111.1	86	47	67	152	4
1999 AA New Haven	9	13	4.50	24	24	0	134.0	131	77	86	162	9

The Mariners may not have Randy Johnson any longer, but they do have another 6-foot-10 lefthanded power pitcher. Anderson, a 1997 first-round pick known as Little Unit, may have the highest ceiling of any minor league mound prospect. Pitching in Double-A as a teenager, he led the Eastern League in strikeouts and strikeouts per nine innings (10.88). Along the way, he pitched in the Futures Game, the Double-A All-Star Game and the Pan American Games. Though his curveball was rated the best breaking pitch in the circuit, Anderson's calling card is a mid-90s fastball that has reached 99 MPH. He needs a year to refine his changeup and his control, and then he should be ready for Seattle.

Jermaine Clark

Position: 2B	Opening Day Age: 23
Bats: L Throws: R	Born: 9/29/76 in
Ht: 5' 10" Wt: 175	Berkeley, CA

Recent Statistics

	G	AB	R	H	D	T	HR	RBI	SB	BB	SO	Avg
1998 A Wisconsin	123	448	81	145	24	13	6	55	40	57	64	.324
1999 A Lancaster	126	502	112	158	27	8	6	61	33	58	80	.315

A 1997 fifth-round pick out of the University of San Francisco, Clark has batted .322 in three pro seasons. He has a quick bat, and though he has an unorthodox uppercut and pulls off of pitches, his style works for him. He has a little pop, draws some walks and uses his speed to steal bases. Clark's glove is less intriguing than his bat at this point. He doesn't move very well to his right and needs to improve his double-play pivot. If he can get better defensively, the Mariners could have a sparkplug middle infielder who can bat at the top of the order.

Brian Fuentes

Position: P	Opening Day Age: 24
Bats: L Throws: L	Born: 8/9/75 in Merced,
Ht: 6' 4" Wt: 220	CA

Recent Statistics

	W	L	ERA	G	GS	Sv	IP	H	R	BB	SO	HR
1998 A Lancaster	7	7	4.17	24	22	0	118.2	121	73	81	137	8
1999 AA New Haven	3	3	4.95	15	14	0	60.0	53	36	46	66	5

Though they're both lefthanded, Brian Fuentes couldn't be much more different than Ryan Anderson. While Anderson was a first-round pick, Fuentes was a 25th-rounder in 1995 who signed after a year at Merced (Calif.) Junior College. His stuff is as plain as Anderson's is extraordinary. Fuentes' fastball, curveball and changeup are all average pitches. Yet he has permitted just 281 hits while striking out 382 in 324 pro innings, thanks to a herky-jerky delivery and late movement on his fastball, neither of which lets hitters get comfortable. Shoulder problems limited him to 60 innings in 1999, but he didn't need surgery. After a year in Triple-A to improve his command, Fuentes will get a look from the Mariners.

Joel Pineiro

Position: P	Opening Day Age: 21
Bats: R Throws: R	Born: 9/25/78 in Rio
Ht: 6' 1" Wt: 180	Pedres, Puerto Rico

Recent Statistics

	W	L	ERA	G	GS	Sv	IP	H	R	BB	SO	HR
1998 A Wisconsin	8	4	3.19	16	16	0	96.0	92	40	28	84	8
1998 A Lancaster	2	0	7.80	9	9	0	45.0	58	40	22	48	6
1998 AA Orlando	1	0	5.40	1	1	0	5.0	7	4	2	2	0
1999 AA New Haven	10	15	4.72	28	25	0	166.0	190	105	52	116	18

Pineiro stamped himself as a prospect with a strong performance in Puerto Rico last winter, but his busy offseason also may have contributed to a lackluster 1999. After going 16-6 in his first two pro seasons, he struggled in Double-A and led the Eastern League with 15 losses. Worse, his fastball dipped from the low 90s to the high 80s. A 12th-round pick in 1997 from Edison (Fla.) Community College, he has a very effective curveball and also uses a slider and changeup. Pineiro needs to get stronger and may begin 2000 back in Double-A.

Rob Ramsay

Position: P
Bats: L **Throws:** L
Ht: 6' 5" **Wt:** 230

Opening Day Age: 26
Born: 12/3/73 in
Vancouver, WA

Recent Statistics

	W	L	ERA	G	GS	Sv	IP	H	R	BB	SO	HR
1999 AAA Pawtucket	6	6	5.35	20	20	0	114.1	114	81	36	79	21
1999 AAA Tacoma	4	1	1.08	5	5	0	33.1	20	6	14	37	2
1999 AL Seattle	0	2	6.38	6	3	0	18.1	23	13	9	11	3

When the Mariners fell out of the playoff race last season, they traded Butch Huskey to the Red Sox for Ramsay. A 1996 seventh-round pick out of Washington State, Ramsay had struggled at Triple-A Pawtucket, a strong hitters' park, but thrived after the deal. He was brilliant at Triple-A Tacoma, then impressed Seattle manager Lou Piniella with his fearlessness after a callup. Ramsay's top pitch is a curveball, and he hits his spots with an average fastball and good changeup. He could make the Mariners as a middle reliever/spot starter this year.

Denny Stark

Position: P
Bats: R **Throws:** R
Ht: 6' 2" **Wt:** 210

Opening Day Age: 25
Born: 10/27/74 in
Hicksville, OH

Recent Statistics

	W	L	ERA	G	GS	Sv	IP	H	R	BB	SO	HR
1999 AA New Haven	9	11	4.40	26	26	0	147.1	151	82	62	103	14
1999 AL Seattle	0	0	9.95	5	0	0	6.1	10	8	4	4	0

Stark's career is back on track after he had ankle surgery. . . to correct shoulder trouble. A 1996 fourth-round pick out of the University of Toledo, he was limited to 29.1 innings two years later by arm problems. The cause was ligament damage and bone chips in his ankle, which affected his delivery. Healthy again last season, he showed enough in Double-A to earn a September callup. Stark isn't overpowering, but he's effective when he mixes his fastball, curveball and changeup and throws them for strikes. He'll probably spend most of 2000 in Triple-A.

Jake Weber

Position: OF
Bats: L **Throws:** R
Ht: 5' 11" **Wt:** 188

Opening Day Age: 23
Born: 4/22/76 in
Poughkeepsie, NY

Recent Statistics

	G	AB	R	H	D	T	HR	RBI	SB	BB	SO	Avg.
1998 A Everett	75	275	75	93	20	2	11	52	14	67	42	.338
1999 AA New Haven	136	489	64	125	22	2	11	59	5	66	73	.256
1999 MLE	136	481	63	117	20	1	11	58	3	55	78	.243

Weber is similar to Darren Bragg, another short, gritty outfielder drafted by the Mariners out of the Atlantic Coast Conference. A 1998 sixth-round pick from North Carolina State, Weber's tools are a notch better than Bragg's. Weber spent his first full season in Double-A, which was asking too much. He's a solid all-around player who's better than his 1999 performance would indicate. He'll hit decently for average and power, draw walks and make consistent contact. He runs well, though knee problems that required arthroscopic surgery slowed him last year. He also has the range and arm to play a good right field. Weber would be best served by repeating Double-A for the first half of 2000.

Jordan Zimmerman

Position: P
Bats: R **Throws:** L
Ht: 6' 0" **Wt:** 200

Opening Day Age: 24
Born: 4/28/75 in
Kelowna, Canada

Recent Statistics

	W	L	ERA	G	GS	Sv	IP	H	R	BB	SO	HR
1999 A Everett	0	0	27.00	1	0	0	0.2	3	2	0	1	0
1999 AAA Tacoma	0	0	5.14	9	0	0	7.0	13	4	4	4	1
1999 AA New Haven	1	4	1.08	22	0	2	33.1	26	8	19	33	0
1999 AL Seattle	0	0	7.88	12	0	0	8.0	14	8	4	3	0

While Jeff Zimmerman was captivating the baseball world in 1999, his younger brother overcame four years of health problems to reach the majors as well. A 32nd-round pick in 1994 who signed after a year at Blinn (Texas) Junior College, Jordan didn't debut until 1997 because of a stress fracture in his lower back, then missed much of 1998 with shoulder trouble. Zimmerman threw 93-94 MPH when he signed, and he has most of his velocity back. He also throws a slider and changeup. Though lefties batted .474 off him in the majors, Zimmerman has the stuff to be a very effective southpaw reliever.

Others to Watch

Korean righthander **Cha Baek** (19) signed in 1998 for $1.3 million, a record for a Mariners international signee. Rated the top pitching prospect in the Rookie-level Arizona League in his debut last year, he throws four pitches for strikes, including a 92-94 MPH fastball. . . **Ryan Christianson** (18) was considered the best high school catcher available in the 1999 draft. A first-round pick who signed for $2.1 million, his arm and power are first-rate. . . Managers rated righthander **Chris Mears** (22) the Class-A Midwest League's best pitching prospect in a midseason survey. He has an above-average fastball and succeeds with command and movement. . . Australian outfielder **Chris Snelling** (18) and Christianson were the two youngest players in the Northwest League last year, yet both ranked among the short-season circuit's top five prospects. Snelling is a fiery player with all-around skills, and he hit better than expected. . . **Rafael Soriano** (20) hit .220 in two seasons as a Rookie-level outfielder, then converted to the mound last year and threw 92-94 MPH with a decent slider. In his pitching debut, he allowed just 56 hits and fanned 83 in 75.1 innings at short-season Everett. . . First baseman **Peanut Williams** (22) is a one-dimensional power hitter, but it's quite a dimension. He slammed 28 homers in 304 at-bats last year, most in high-A ball, before breaking his wrist.

Tropicana Field

Offense

After their inaugural season, the Devil Rays discovered that Tropicana Field's outfield distances were about 12 feet shorter than thought. They moved the fences back last year to correct the discrepancy. While the listed dimensions didn't change, Tropicana's park effects certainly did. One of the best hitters' parks in the American League in 1998, it slightly favored pitchers last year. The bigger outfield and raised fences really clamped down on power, though it continued to be a good home-run park for lefties. The bottom line wasn't good, as the Rays were outhit, outhomered and outscored at home by a more pronounced margin in 1999 than in 1998.

Defense

The Rays said from the start that they planned to build with speedy outfielders to cover the large Tropicana Field expanse, and someday they will. But pending a major transaction, the Rays again will struggle to defend their large outfield. The all-dirt basepaths, unique among current artificial turf stadiums, generate a few grumbles but don't have much impact. More of an issue is the quickness of the turf, which exposes players who lack range. The off-white roof and overhead catwalks lead to a handful of lost flyballs each season.

Who It Helps The Most

Fred McGriff prospered even after the fences were moved back, hitting 63 points higher in Tampa Bay, where he drilled 18 of his 32 homers. Among the pitchers, Wilson Alvarez' ERA was 1.72 runs lower at home.

Who It Hurts The Most

Jose Canseco was muted by the Trop. He batted 55 points lower and hit 12 of his 34 homers at home.

Rookies & Newcomers

Vinny Castilla really is going to miss Coors Field, which inflated his righthanded power. That won't happen in Tampa Bay, where free-agent outfielders Greg Vaughn and Gerald Williams also will be affected. Righthander Dan Wheeler struggled in 15.2 innings at Tropicana Field last year, permitting five homers and a 6.89 ERA.

Dimensions: LF-315, LCF-370, CF-404, RCF-370, RF-322

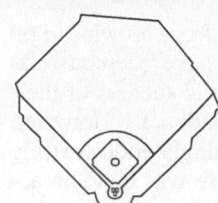

Capacity: 42,531

Elevation: 15 feet

Surface: Turf

Foul Territory: Average

Park Factors

1999 Season

	Home Games			Away Games			
	Devil Rays	Opp	Total	Devil Rays	Opp	Total	Index
G	72	72	144	72	72	144	—
Avg	.270	.286	.278	.281	.279	.280	99
AB	2381	2543	4924	2567	2400	4967	99
R	331	403	734	367	380	747	98
H	642	727	1369	721	670	1391	98
2B	110	160	270	137	122	259	105
3B	10	17	27	14	11	25	109
HR	55	81	136	74	73	147	93
BB	244	290	534	239	320	559	96
SO	456	494	950	463	438	901	106
E	55	43	98	60	50	110	89
E-Infield	48	38	86	50	40	90	96
LHB-Avg	.290	.296	.293	.276	.276	.276	106
LHB-HR	25	38	63	24	37	61	109
RHB-Avg	.257	.278	.267	.284	.282	.283	94
RHB-HR	30	43	73	50	36	86	83

1998 Season

	Home Games			Away Games			
	Devil Rays	Opp	Total	Devil Rays	Opp	Total	Index
G	73	73	146	73	73	146	—
Avg	.256	.266	.261	.268	.256	.262	100
AB	2461	2574	5035	2533	2338	4871	103
R	292	356	648	280	319	599	108
H	630	685	1315	678	599	1277	103
2B	120	131	251	125	104	229	106
3B	16	10	26	23	14	37	68
HR	63	83	146	41	70	111	127
BB	211	280	491	216	304	520	91
SO	469	454	923	504	455	959	93
E	45	55	100	39	45	84	119
E-Infield	40	49	89	38	40	78	114
LHB-Avg	.258	.271	.264	.266	.266	.266	99
LHB-HR	43	31	74	15	30	45	152
RHB-Avg	.253	.263	.259	.269	.249	.259	100
RHB-HR	20	52	72	26	40	66	110

1999 Rankings (American League)

- Second-highest strikeout factor
- Second-lowest RHB batting-average factor
- Second-lowest RHB home-run factor
- Third-lowest walk factor
- Third-lowest error factor

Tampa Bay

Larry Rothschild

1999 Season

The Devil Rays' improvement from 63 wins to 69 under Larry Rothschild may have seemed relatively minor, especially given the success of their expansion brethren, the Diamondbacks. However, considering Tampa Bay's seemingly endless string of injuries, that six-win increase was quite an accomplishment. The Devil Rays were 22-20 in late May before the injuries began to mount, sending them into a 2-16 tailspin from which they never recovered. But taking their cue from Rothschild, the players continued to put out a full effort.

Offense

Rothschild prefers an all-out aggressive approach, but hasn't had all the weapons. He adapted to his team's limitations better in 1999 than in his rookie season as manager, becoming more judicious with basestealing attempts. Ideally, he wants speed at the top and bottom of the order, with power in the middle. After two seasons of having to mix and match at several positions, Rothschild is looking forward to playing more of a set lineup in 2000. He plays more of a National League style than most of his American League counterparts, often calling for bunts and hit-and-runs. He likes to use pinch-hitters but has been restricted by a thin bench.

Pitching & Defense

A former pitcher and pitching coach, Rothschild puts an emphasis on protecting young arms, even in the face of criticism. He led the AL in quick hooks in 1998 and ranked behind only Boston manager Jimy Williams last year. With a star closer in Roberto Hernandez, Rothschild likes to establish roles for the other relievers. As with his offense, he prefers a quick and aggressive defense, and will sacrifice power at some positions to get it.

2000 Outlook

Devil Rays ownership and management have been outspoken in saying that the Rays will be better in 2000. Just getting his full squad back and healthy would be a plus for Rothschild, who also stands to benefit from GM Chuck LaMar's promise to make some major acquisitions. A one-year contract extension through the 2001 season gives Rothschild some security.

Born: 3/12/54 in Chicago, IL

Playing Experience: 1981-1982, Det

Managerial Experience: 2 seasons

Manager Statistics

Year	Team, Lg	W	L	Pct	GB	Finish
1999	Tampa Bay, AL	69	93	.426	29.0	5th East
2 Seasons		132	192	.407	—	—

1999 Starting Pitchers by Days Rest

	<=3	4	5	6+
Devil Rays Starts	1	65	63	20
Devil Rays ERA	3.00	4.41	6.34	6.17
AL Avg Starts	2	82	47	21
AL ERA	6.83	4.98	4.72	5.62

1999 Situational Stats

	Larry Rothschild	AL Average
Hit & Run Success %	37.2	35.3
Stolen Base Success %	59.8	68.0
Platoon Pct.	54.3	56.7
Defensive Subs	37	22
High-Pitch Outings	20	15
Quick/Slow Hooks	22/20	18/18
Sacrifice Attempts	45	52

1999 Rankings (American League)

- 1st in starts with over 140 pitches (1)
- 2nd in starting lineups used (138), quick hooks (22) and relief appearances (453)
- 3rd in defensive substitutions (37)

Wilson Alvarez

1999 Season

Wilson Alvarez had another disappointing season in which he flashed moments of greatness, yet for the most part left coaches and fans wondering what might have been. Two trips to the disabled list with shoulder and triceps inflammation were minor disruptions, but the bigger story was a childish dugout tantrum in June that led to a fine and a stricter training regimen. Alvarez responded with some of his best pitching as a Devil Ray, including a five-game winning streak, but he dropped off again toward the end of the season. He was winless in his final six starts.

Pitching

Alvarez is best when he works off his 92-94 MPH fastball, moving it around the plate and using it to set up his offspeed stuff. But he tends to work backwards, throwing too many breaking pitches early in counts, then falling behind and having to come in with the fastball. That's trouble because hitters attack his heater when they know it's coming, and because he piles up high pitch counts early in games. During his strong second-half run, he established his fastball early and wasn't concerned with strikeouts, letting his fielders do the work. But too often he tends to lose confidence in his stuff and himself rather quickly.

Defense

Athleticism isn't one of Alvarez' assets. He tends to get a glove on balls hit right back at him, but that's about it. His windup doesn't leave him in the best fielding position, and his lack of speed doesn't help. Alvarez' pickoff move is enough to discourage most basestealers. He gave up just two steals in 12 attempts last year.

2000 Outlook

In the first two seasons of his five-year, $35-million contract, Alvarez has gone 15-23 and hasn't shown much of the talent or leadership the Devil Rays were counting on. They hope he saw the relationship between the hard work and his strong second-half run, and that he'll dedicate himself to that type of effort over a full season.

Position: SP
Bats: L **Throws:** L
Ht: 6' 1" **Wt:** 245

Opening Day Age: 30
Born: 3/24/70 in Maracaibo, Venezuela
ML Seasons: 10

Overall Statistics

	W	L	Pct.	ERA	G	GS	Sv	IP	H	BB	SO	HR	Ratio
1999	9	9	.500	4.22	28	28	0	160.0	159	79	128	22	1.49
Career	86	77	.528	3.96	250	224	1	1433.0	1324	708	1074	153	1.42

How Often He Throws Strikes

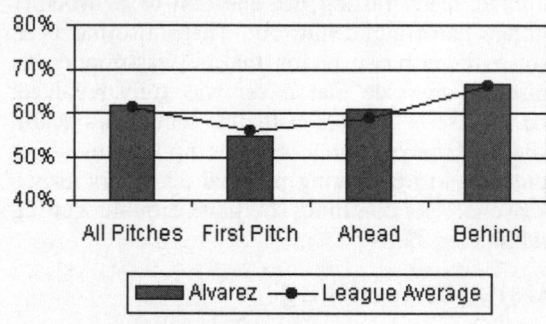

1999 Situational Stats

	W	L	ERA	Sv	IP		AB	H	HR	RBI	Avg
Home	4	2	3.32	0	76.0	LHB	116	32	7	21	.276
Road	5	7	5.04	0	84.0	RHB	495	127	15	57	.257
First Half	4	6	4.83	0	91.1	Sc Pos	152	39	6	57	.257
Scnd Half	5	3	3.41	0	68.2	Clutch	33	6	2	4	.182

1999 Rankings (American League)

- 5th in errors at pitcher (3)
- 6th in GDPs induced (25)
- 8th in runners caught stealing (10) and most GDPs induced per GDP situation (17.0%)
- Led the Devil Rays in wins, strikeouts, winning percentage, most GDPs induced per GDP situation (17.0%), ERA on the road and lowest batting average allowed with runners in scoring position

Rolando Arrojo

1999 Season

After signing for a $7 million bonus in 1997 and setting an expansion record with 14 victories last year, Rolando Arrojo endured a trying sophomore season. A spring-training back injury set him behind, and he never seemed to catch up. Arrojo went 2-5, 7.31 in his first nine starts, then spent seven weeks on the disabled list with shoulder inflammation. He rebounded following his return, going 5-7, 4.08 in his final 15 outings.

Pitching

Arrojo's rookie success was built around a confusing mix of arm angles, pitch combinations and deliveries. But what worked so well in 1998 failed him in 1999, raising the question as to whether hitters had figured him out. There also has been some lingering suspicion that he was tipping his pitches, an issue that never was fully resolved. Arrojo uses a low-90s fastball to set up his sidearm slider as an out pitch. He has no qualms about pitching inside, having plunked 33 hitters in two seasons. He continues to have trouble getting lefthanders out.

Defense & Hitting

Arrojo doesn't have a particularly good pickoff move, but he throws often to first base in order to keep runners close. A veteran of international play with Cuba's national team, he doesn't get rattled easily in the field. His nonchalance, especially in games in which he gets behind early, occasionally costs him.

2000 Outlook

The Rays weren't thrilled with what they saw of Arrojo last year, and dealt him and Aaron Ledesma to Colorado in the four-team Winter Meetings trade that brought Vinny Castilla to Tampa Bay. The Rockies hope they're getting the Arrojo who was so effective in 1998, when he got a steady stream of groundball outs. He'll need to do that again if he hopes to succeed in Coors Field.

Position: SP
Bats: R **Throws:** R
Ht: 6' 4" **Wt:** 220

Opening Day Age: 31
Born: 7/18/68 in Havana, Cuba
ML Seasons: 2
Pronunciation: uh-ROH-ho

Overall Statistics

	W	L	Pct.	ERA	G	GS	Sv	IP	H	BB	SO	HR	Ratio
1999	7	12	.368	5.18	24	24	0	140.2	162	60	107	23	1.58
Career	21	24	.467	4.23	56	56	0	342.2	357	125	259	44	1.41

How Often He Throws Strikes

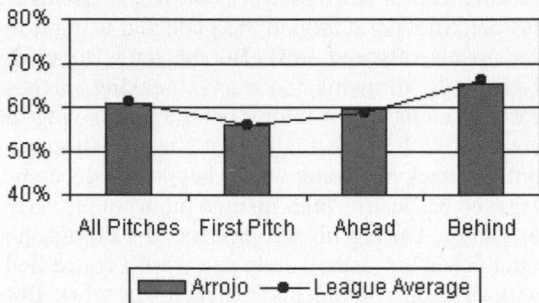

Arrojo — League Average

1999 Situational Stats

	W	L	ERA	Sv	IP		AB	H	HR	RBI	Avg
Home	2	9	5.95	0	84.2	LHB	302	95	16	50	.315
Road	5	3	4.02	0	56.0	RHB	246	67	7	27	.272
First Half	2	5	7.31	0	48.0	Sc Pos	149	40	5	53	.268
Scnd Half	5	7	4.08	0	92.2	Clutch	23	7	0	0	.304

1999 Rankings (American League)

- 2nd in hit batsmen (14)
- 3rd in highest ERA at home
- 8th in lowest winning percentage and highest batting average allowed vs. lefthanded batters
- Led the Devil Rays in home runs allowed and hit batsmen (14)

Miguel Cairo

1999 Season

Miguel Cairo followed up his rookie campaign with a strong sophomore season, firmly establishing himself as an everyday player. He raised his batting average 27 points and sliced his errors nearly in half. But he also endured two trips to the disabled list with hamstring injuries, and he had stretches where his defense was shaky.

Hitting

If nothing else, Cairo gets the bat on the ball. He's one of the toughest American Leaguers to strike out, though he walks far too infrequently for someone who batted leadoff most of the second half last year. Cairo continued to use his unorthodox grip, with his hands spread about three inches apart on the handle. The theory is that the wide grip will help him hit more grounders to take advantage of his speed. It also reduces his slight power, and he still falls into ruts where he hits the ball in the air too much.

Baserunning & Defense

Cairo has excellent speed but still is learning to take full advantage of it. His hamstring injuries restricted him in 1999, but the Rays still want him to become more daring on the bases. As for his defense, they would settle for consistency. He had the third-highest fielding percentage among AL second basemen but made too many careless mistakes, such as breaking late to a base or dropping a throw. He's not flashy but can make the routine plays and an occasional great one.

2000 Outlook

Cairo's 2000 role will be determined by what moves the Rays make or don't make during the winter. If he comes back as the leadoff hitter, he needs to improve his on-base percentage by taking more walks. If he's the No. 2 hitter, he needs to improve his bunting and bat handling. Or he could drop to the bottom of the order, where he might have the opportunity to drive in more runs. Steadying his defense is a must in any case.

Position: 2B
Bats: R **Throws:** R
Ht: 6' 1" **Wt:** 200

Opening Day Age: 25
Born: 5/4/74 in Anaco, Venezuela
ML Seasons: 4
Pronunciation: KY-roh

Overall Statistics

	G	AB	R	H	D	T	HR	RBI	SB	BB	SO	Avg	OBP	Slg
1999	120	465	61	137	15	5	3	36	22	24	46	.295	.335	.368
Career	295	1036	122	288	44	10	8	84	41	52	102	.278	.320	.363

Where He Hits the Ball

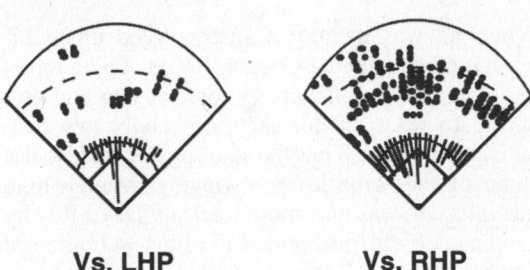

Vs. LHP   **Vs. RHP**

1999 Situational Stats

	AB	H	HR	RBI	Avg		AB	H	HR	RBI	Avg
Home	213	58	1	12	.272	LHP	86	33	0	5	.384
Road	252	79	2	24	.313	RHP	379	104	3	31	.274
First Half	239	75	2	26	.314	Sc Pos	92	23	0	29	.250
Scnd Half	226	62	1	10	.274	Clutch	68	20	0	9	.294

1999 Rankings (American League)

- 3rd in fielding percentage at second base (.986)
- 4th in lowest HR frequency (155.0 ABs per HR)
- 5th in lowest slugging percentage and lowest slugging percentage vs. righthanded pitchers (.354)
- 7th in lowest on-base percentage for a leadoff hitter (.333)
- 9th in errors at second base (9)
- Led the Devil Rays in singles, triples, stolen bases, highest groundball/flyball ratio (1.3), stolen-base percentage (75.9), batting average in the clutch, on-base percentage for a leadoff hitter (.333), highest percentage of extra bases taken as a runner (54.9) and steals of third (2)

Tampa Bay

Jose Canseco

1999 Season

It was a tale of two seasons for Jose Canseco, who accepted an incentive-laden contract from the Devil Rays as a free agent. In the first half he was as dangerous as any American League hitter, batting .276-31-69 in 82 games. But after midseason back surgery and a speedy recovery he was hardly the same, hitting just .287-3-26 in 31 contests. While his back was fine, Canseco fought to get back his timing and to overcome minor hand and leg injuries. He hit his 400th career homer early in the season and later had a streak of homering in 13 consecutive series. He became the first player in history to hit 30-plus homers for four different teams.

Hitting

When he was healthy, Canseco lived up to his reputation as a feared slugger. He sets up on top of the plate, daring pitchers to come at him and preparing to feast on mistakes, especially low fastballs. While he still has the same power, he also has some of the same holes, swinging through high fastballs. He was hurt more than any Devil Ray by Tropicana Field, hitting just 12 of his 34 homers at home.

Baserunning & Defense

The Rays decided early in spring training that their primary goal was to keep Canseco healthy. That meant they would curtail his activity on the bases and limit his exposure in the field. After stealing 29 bases in 1998, Canseco made just three attempts in 1999. He only showed his speed when it was needed to take an extra base. As much fun as everyone, including Canseco, made of his defense, he actually wasn't bad in his six left-field appearances, showing off an above-average arm.

2000 Outlook

It's an old refrain, but Canseco's and Tampa Bay's goal is to keep him in the lineup for a full season. Before his back flared up, he was on pace to challenge Roger Maris' American League home-run record.

Position: DH
Bats: R **Throws:** R
Ht: 6' 4"   **Wt:** 240

Opening Day Age: 35
Born: 7/2/64 in Havana, Cuba
ML Seasons: 15
Pronunciation: can-SAY-co

Overall Statistics

	G	AB	R	H	D	T	HR	RBI	SB	BB	SO	Avg	OBP	Slg
1999	113	430	75	120	18	1	34	95	3	58	135	.279	.369	.563
Career	1713	6472	1093	1728	314	14	431	1309	196	797	1765	.267	.351	.520

Where He Hits the Ball

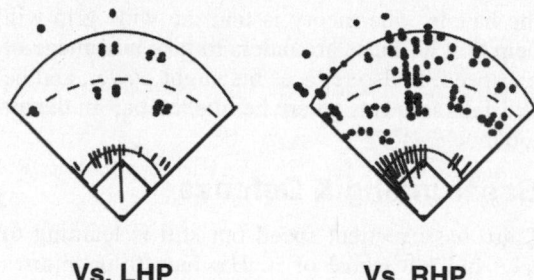

Vs. LHP   **Vs. RHP**

1999 Situational Stats

	AB	H	HR	RBI	Avg			AB	H	HR	RBI	Avg
Home	204	51	12	42	.250		LHP	89	26	8	26	.292
Road	226	69	22	53	.305		RHP	341	94	26	69	.276
First Half	315	87	31	69	.276		Sc Pos	124	27	7	55	.218
Scnd Half	115	33	3	26	.287		Clutch	57	12	2	7	.211

1999 Rankings (American League)

- 3rd in lowest groundball/flyball ratio (0.7)
- 5th in strikeouts and HR frequency (12.6 ABs per HR)
- 8th in lowest batting average with runners in scoring position
- 9th in slugging percentage
- Led the Devil Rays in home runs, strikeouts, GDPs (14), slugging percentage, HR frequency (12.6 ABs per HR), most pitches seen per plate appearance (3.96) and batting average on a 3-1 count (.500)
- Led designated hitters in strikeouts

John Flaherty

1999 Season

The 71-point increase in John Flaherty's batting average from 1998 to 1999 was the largest improvement among American League regulars, and he also set career highs in homers and RBI. His strong all-around play earned him a three-year contract extension in September. And for the second straight year, Tampa Bay beat writers voted Flaherty's the winner of the team's good-guy award.

Hitting

Flaherty succeeded offensively by keeping his approach simple. In 1999 he moved up close to the plate and hit the ball where it was pitched. Sure, he got overmatched at times, but he also had a 13-game hitting streak and four others of at least six games. As impressive a turnaround as Flaherty mounted, he still can do better. He had a surprising vulnerability to lefthanders last season, hitting just .175 against them with four RBI in 80 at-bats. While he ranked second on the Devil Rays behind Fred McGriff with 25 game-tying or go-ahead RBI, Flaherty hit just .271 with runners in scoring position. And he walked just 19 times, accounting for a .310 on-base percentage. Despite his surge to 14 homers, Flaherty is at his best spraying line drives around the park.

Baserunning & Defense

Flaherty's offensive numbers overshadowed a spectacular season behind the plate. He ranked second in the majors by throwing out 38.6 percent of basestealers, trailing only American League MVP Ivan Rodriguez. Flaherty has a strong arm, and fundamental adjustments to his footwork accounted for his fine showing. He blocks balls well and does a good job getting his pitchers through tough innings. As with most catchers, speed is not a strong suit for Flaherty.

2000 Outlook

Flaherty was driven last season to prove he was better than he showed in 1998. Now his focus will be on proving that 1999 wasn't a fluke. He'll benefit if the Devil Rays succeed in adding a power hitter, because he'd be better off batting lower than fifth in the order.

Position: C
Bats: R **Throws:** R
Ht: 6' 1" **Wt:** 200
Opening Day Age: 32
Born: 10/21/67 in New York, NY
ML Seasons: 8
Nickname: Flash

Overall Statistics

	G	AB	R	H	D	T	HR	RBI	SB	BB	SO	Avg	OBP	Slg
1999	117	446	53	124	19	0	14	71	0	19	64	.278	.310	.415
Career	650	2090	199	533	102	2	50	253	7	115	304	.255	.295	.378

Where He Hits the Ball

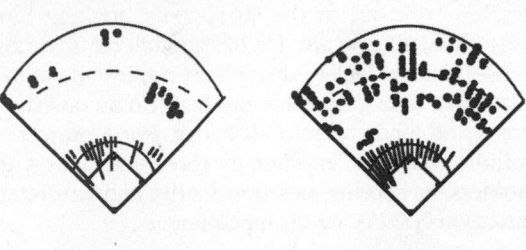

Vs. LHP   **Vs. RHP**

1999 Situational Stats

	AB	H	HR	RBI	Avg		AB	H	HR	RBI	Avg
Home	217	62	3	31	.286	LHP	80	14	1	4	.175
Road	229	62	11	40	.271	RHP	366	110	13	67	.301
First Half	257	71	9	42	.276	Sc Pos	118	32	3	54	.271
Scnd Half	189	53	5	29	.280	Clutch	60	12	1	10	.200

1999 Rankings (American League)

- 2nd in highest percentage of runners caught stealing as a catcher (38.6) and lowest percentage of pitches taken (45.2)
- 3rd in sacrifice flies (10)
- 7th in errors at catcher (6)
- Led the Devil Rays in sacrifice flies (10), GDPs (14) and batting average on a 3-2 count (.318)
- Led AL catchers in sacrifice flies (10) and batting average on a 3-2 count (.318)

Tampa Bay

Jose Guillen

1999 Season

After playing every day for Pittsburgh in 1997 at age 20, Jose Guillen frustrated the Pirates by not improving. In need of catching to replace the injured Jason Kendall, they gave up on Guillen, sending him and Jeff Sparks to Tampa Bay for backstops Joe Oliver and Humberto Cota in mid-July. Guillen joined the Rays after a brief stopover at Triple-A and made a strong first impression, but the same holes the Pirates saw in his game began to surface after a few months. Yet he represents a rare commodity for Tampa Bay, a young major leaguer with star potential.

Hitting

Guillen swings at most everything, including pitches well out of the strike zone, making him very difficult to walk. He has a quick bat and raw power, but his lack of discipline cripples him at the plate. He doesn't hit the ball hard on a consistent basis and tends to get pull-happy. For a projected middle-of-the-order hitter, his career averages with runners in scoring position (.249) and in clutch situations (.225) are disappointments.

Baserunning & Defense

Guillen was considered a plus runner in the minor leagues, but has yet to show that in the majors, totaling just five stolen bases for his career. He made several baserunning gaffes with the Rays, mostly because of a lack of concentration. Guillen is a decent right fielder but doesn't get to as many balls as he should. His big weapon is an extraordinary arm that's the equal of any in the majors. He likes to show off his arm, however, missing cutoff men and making unnecessary throws.

2000 Outlook

The Rays want Guillen to become their everyday right fielder for the next decade. To do so, he'll have to make adjustments at the plate while playing harder and smarter. If it doesn't work out, he'll probably go to Triple-A rather than sit on the bench in the majors.

Position: RF
Bats: R **Throws:** R
Ht: 5'11" **Wt:** 195

Opening Day Age: 23
Born: 5/17/76 in San Cristobal, Dominican Republic
ML Seasons: 3
Pronunciation: GHEE-un

Overall Statistics

	G	AB	R	H	D	T	HR	RBI	SB	BB	SO	Avg	OBP	Slg
1999	87	288	42	73	16	0	3	31	1	20	57	.253	.315	.340
Career	383	1359	160	359	74	7	31	185	5	58	245	.264	.303	.397

Where He Hits the Ball

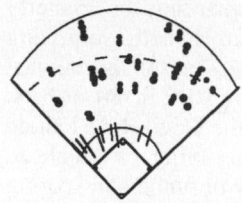

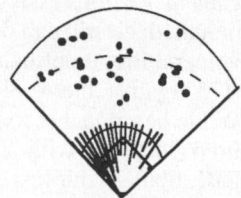

Vs. LHP	Vs. RHP

1999 Situational Stats

	AB	H	HR	RBI	Avg		AB	H	HR	RBI	Avg
Home	150	38	1	15	.253	LHP	79	24	0	8	.304
Road	138	35	2	16	.254	RHP	209	49	3	23	.234
First Half	120	32	1	18	.267	Sc Pos	86	21	0	24	.244
Scnd Half	168	41	2	13	.244	Clutch	47	9	0	1	.191

1999 Rankings (American League)

- Did not rank near the top or bottom in any category

Roberto Hernandez

Position: RP
Bats: R **Throws:** R
Ht: 6' 4" **Wt:** 250

Opening Day Age: 35
Born: 11/11/64 in
Santurce, Puerto Rico
ML Seasons: 9
Pronunciation:
her-NAN-dezz

1999 Season

The only negative concerning Roberto Hernandez' 1999 performance was that more people didn't appreciate it. He was spectacular from start to finish, converting 43 of 47 save opportunities to rank second in the American League behind only Mariano Rivera in save percentage. Hernandez was voted Tampa Bay's MVP and rightly so, given that he had a hand in 45 of the team's 69 victories.

Pitching

Hernandez can be close to unhittable when he has everything working for him, and that was the case many more times than not in 1999. He pushed the radar gun to 100 MPH on several occasions and routinely to 98, and left hitters shaking their heads when he tossed a splitter. Unlike 1998, Hernandez had little trouble with mechanics or control. He ran into difficulty only when he walked a batter early in an inning, or when he couldn't get his fastball over and turned to a slider that at times can be very hittable.

Defense

Hernandez moves pretty well off the mound for a big man, but occasionally gets too excited or out of control on a bunt play. He also has a dangerous habit of trying to snare bouncing balls with his bare hand. He docsn't usually pay much attention to baserunners, preferring to concentrate on the hitter.

2000 Outlook

There really isn't much more Hernandez can do in 2000. The bigger winter question around Tampa Bay was whether the Rays would bring him back or try to capitalize on his career year by trading him for a multiplayer package that could improve the team. If he does come back, anything close to a repeat performance would be more than enough.

Overall Statistics

	W	L	Pct.	ERA	G	GS	Sv	IP	H	BB	SO	HR	Ratio
1999	2	3	.400	3.07	72	0	43	73.1	68	33	69	1	1.38
Career	38	35	.521	3.02	512	3	234	582.0	491	244	570	40	1.26

How Often He Throws Strikes

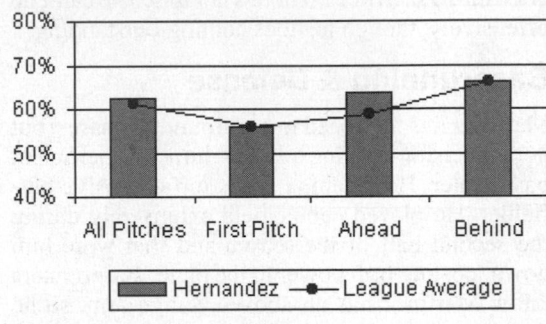

1999 Situational Stats

	W	L	ERA	Sv	IP		AB	H	HR	RBI	Avg
Home	1	3	3.68	22	36.2	LHB	141	34	0	16	.241
Road	1	0	2.45	21	36.2	RHB	137	34	1	13	.248
First Half	1	3	3.72	26	46.0	Sc Pos	86	25	1	28	.291
Scnd Half	1	0	1.98	17	27.1	Clutch	205	49	1	21	.239

1999 Rankings (American League)

- 1st in games finished (66)
- 2nd in saves and save percentage (91.5)
- 3rd in save opportunities (47)
- 7th in games pitched and relief ERA (3.07)
- Led the Devil Rays in games pitched, saves, games finished (66), save opportunities (47), save percentage (91.5), blown saves (4), lowest batting average allowed in relief with runners on base (.226), relief ERA (3.07), lowest batting average allowed in relief (.245) and most strikeouts per nine innings in relief (8.5)

Dave Martinez

1999 Season

The Rays asked a lot of Dave Martinez in 1999 and he gave it to them, starting at all three outfield positions and in seven different spots in the batting order. He hit 28 points higher and showed more power than he did in 1998. Inconsistency was his biggest flaw, as two extended slumps cost him a shot at a .300 season.

Hitting

Martinez has a short, quick lefthanded stroke that produces decent batting averages and gap power. He's willing to give himself up with a bunt or sacrifice fly. He led the Devil Rays with seven bunt singles and ranked among American League leaders with 10 sacrifices. There's not much he can't do offensively, though he does nothing outstanding.

Baserunning & Defense

Martinez has the speed to get around the bases, but poor decision-making renders him an inefficient basestealer. He's Tampa Bay's top defensive outfielder. He played center field extensively during the second half of the season and that wore him down, costing him power at the plate. Baserunners know Martinez has an above-average arm, so he doesn't get many opportunities to showcase it.

2000 Outlook

The Devil Rays feel good about what Martinez did for them in 1999, and made it easy for him to reach the 500 plate appearances he needed to activate his $2 million option for this year. But now they have to figure out what to do with him. They hope Jose Guillen becomes the regular right fielder, and either Quinton McCracken or free-agent signee Gerald Williams will man center. That may mean a return to a super-sub role for Martinez, where he plays all three outfield positions, comes into games as a defensive replacement or pinch-hitter, and is asked to do a lot of things well.

Position: RF/CF
Bats: L **Throws:** L
Ht: 5'10" **Wt:** 190

Opening Day Age: 35
Born: 9/26/64 in New York, NY
ML Seasons: 14

Overall Statistics

	G	AB	R	H	D	T	HR	RBI	SB	BB	SO	Avg	OBP	Slg
1999	143	514	79	146	25	5	6	66	13	60	76	.284	.361	.387
Career	1667	5101	702	1406	208	64	84	513	172	496	776	.276	.341	.391

Where He Hits the Ball

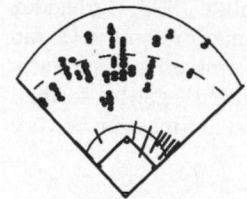 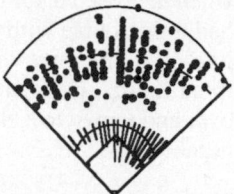

Vs. LHP   **Vs. RHP**

1999 Situational Stats

	AB	H	HR	RBI	Avg		AB	H	HR	RBI	Avg
Home	243	61	2	23	.251	LHP	88	21	1	14	.239
Road	271	85	4	43	.314	RHP	426	125	5	52	.293
First Half	295	85	6	47	.288	Sc Pos	121	37	0	56	.306
Scnd Half	219	61	0	19	.279	Clutch	67	13	0	5	.194

1999 Rankings (American League)

- 7th in sacrifice bunts (10)
- 8th in fewest GDPs per GDP situation (5.1%) and lowest slugging percentage
- 9th in bunts in play (23) and lowest batting average at home
- 10th in lowest HR frequency (85.7 ABs per HR)
- Led the Devil Rays in runs scored, triples, sacrifice bunts (10), batting average on the road, bunts in play (23) and highest percentage of pitches taken (59.6)
- Led AL right fielders in sacrifice bunts (10) and bunts in play (23)

Quinton McCracken

1999 Season

Quinton McCracken's 1999 season came to a painful and abrupt end on May 24, when he jumped into the outfield wall at Tropicana Field and tore the anterior cruciate ligament in his right knee. He sprained the same knee while working out at home prior to spring training and didn't play in his first exhibition game until late March. The loss of McCracken, the club's 1998 MVP, and the subsequent failures of Randy Winn left the Devil Rays with a huge hole in center field.

Hitting

A switch-hitter, McCracken usually bats leadoff for the Rays because of his speed and bat control. He keeps the ball on the ground, though he really doesn't have the patience needed to be a true table-setter. He's at his best when he hits the ball hard and rips line drives into the gaps. Occasionally he gets caught up in flexing his muscles—he played defensive back at Duke—and strikes out too much for a No. 1 hitter. Most of the time, he keeps the ball on the ground to take advantage of his quickness.

Baserunning & Defense

There's always a concern any time a speed player has knee trouble, and that will be an issue with McCracken until he proves otherwise. He once stole 60 bases in a minor league season, but swiped just 19 in 1998 and only six in 11 chances prior to his injury last year. He made huge strides defensively in 1998, learning how to compensate for an average arm with excellent positioning, timing and a quick delivery. He has played well in both center and left field.

2000 Outlook

McCracken must prove that he's able to play at full speed. The Devil Rays decided to hedge their bets, signing free-agent Gerald Williams to a two-year, $5.75 million contract in December. He's expected to compete with McCracken for the center-field job.

Position: LF/CF
Bats: B **Throws:** R
Ht: 5' 9" **Wt:** 173

Opening Day Age: 29
Born: 8/16/70 in Wilmington, NC
ML Seasons: 5
Nickname: Q, Coo Coo

Overall Statistics

	G	AB	R	H	D	T	HR	RBI	SB	BB	SO	Avg	OBP	Slg
1999	40	148	20	37	6	1	1	18	6	14	23	.250	.317	.324
Career	469	1371	216	393	68	15	14	153	70	129	255	.287	.348	.389

Where He Hits the Ball

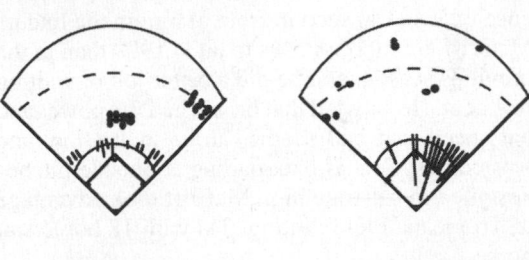

Vs. LHP   **Vs. RHP**

1999 Situational Stats

	AB	H	HR	RBI	Avg		AB	H	HR	RBI	Avg
Home	70	18	1	14	.257	LHP	35	9	0	2	.257
Road	78	19	0	4	.244	RHP	113	28	1	16	.248
First Half	148	37	1	18	.250	Sc Pos	31	11	1	17	.355
Scnd Half	0	0	0	0	-	Clutch	14	3	0	2	.214

1999 Rankings (American League)

- Did not rank near the top or bottom in any category

Fred McGriff

1999 Season

The 1999 version of Fred McGriff was the player the Devil Rays thought they had traded for on the night of the expansion draft, not the impostor who batted .284-19-81 in 1998. After hitting that career low in home runs, he reached 30 homers for the first time in five seasons and drove in 104 runs, the third-highest total of his career.

Hitting

Determined to bounce back, McGriff spent extra time in spring training working to keep his legs strong. At the plate, he showed more patience than he had in years. He drew 86 walks, his highest total since 1992. Though he didn't think it was a big deal, McGriff also seemed to benefit from the presence of Jose Canseco in front of him in the lineup. McGriff got more pitches to hit in 1999 than in the previous season, and he did a better job of waiting for them. He showed that he still had the power and bat speed that had seemed to be in decline, and wasted very few at-bats flailing at outside pitches designed to frustrate him. McGriff took advantage of Tropicana Field, hitting .344 with 18 homers at home.

Baserunning & Defense

Speed never has been part of McGriff's game, and late-season leg troubles reduced him to trotting around the bases. Even when healthy, he looks slower than he is because of his casual style on the bases. McGriff is slipping as a first baseman, committing 13 errors and showing a lack of range in 1999.

2000 Outlook

McGriff re-established himself as an offensive force in 1999, earning a two-year extension with a third-year option that could increase the contract's value to $19 million. McGriff says he wants to be part of a winner, though his hometown Devil Rays aren't close to contention. It's possible that he could get traded to a contender this summer. Cynics wonder if he'll be able to have another strong season without the motivation of a contract drive.

Position: 1B/DH
Bats: L **Throws:** L
Ht: 6' 3" **Wt:** 215

Opening Day Age: 36
Born: 10/31/63 in Tampa, FL
ML Seasons: 14
Nickname: Crime Dog

Overall Statistics

	G	AB	R	H	D	T	HR	RBI	SB	BB	SO	Avg	OBP	Slg
1999	144	529	75	164	30	1	32	104	1	86	107	.310	.405	.552
Career	1897	6786	1094	1946	354	20	390	1192	68	1045	1472	.287	.382	.517

Where He Hits the Ball

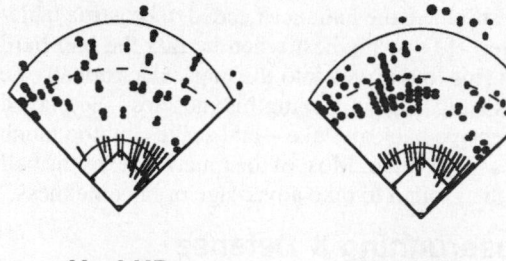

Vs. LHP   **Vs. RHP**

1999 Situational Stats

	AB	H	HR	RBI	Avg		AB	H	HR	RBI	Avg
Home	241	83	18	54	.344	LHP	148	35	8	25	.236
Road	288	81	14	50	.281	RHP	381	129	24	79	.339
First Half	310	99	19	56	.319	Sc Pos	148	48	9	73	.324
Scnd Half	219	65	13	48	.297	Clutch	75	16	0	7	.213

1999 Rankings (American League)

- 2nd in errors at first base (13) and lowest fielding percentage at first base (.989)
- 5th in batting average vs. righthanded pitchers
- Led the Devil Rays in batting average, at-bats, hits, doubles, total bases (292), RBI, walks, intentional walks (11), times on base (251), pitches seen (2,360), plate appearances (620), on-base percentage, batting average with runners in scoring position, batting average with the bases loaded (.500), batting average vs. lefthanded pitchers, batting average vs. righthanded pitchers, cleanup slugging percentage (.554), slugging percentage vs. lefthanded pitchers (.446), slugging percentage vs. righthanded pitchers (.593) and games played

Ryan Rupe

1999 Season

Ryan Rupe made such a strong showing during spring training that the Devil Rays figured they would promote him at some point during the 1999 season. What they didn't know was that it would be as soon as May or that he would do so well. When watching Rupe, it was difficult to remember that he was pitching for Texas A&M the previous spring before being selected in the sixth round of the 1998 draft. He was a tremendous surprise for Tampa Bay.

Pitching

Rupe comes right at hitters with a mid-90s fastball. He's still developing a slider that has the potential to be nasty. But his best pitch is his changeup, which usually leaves hitters shaking their heads and walking back to the bench. What Devils Rays coaches like most of all is Rupe's fierce competitiveness. Tampa Bay was careful to protect its young gem, but he has the potential to be an innings-eater at the front end of the rotation for a long time. He could use some slight adjustments to improve his control.

Defense

Because he is a big, gangly power pitcher, Rupe isn't the smoothest fielder. His intensity also can work against him defensively. He needs to improve at holding runners and making better throws to first, as evidenced by the 20 successful steals in 26 attempts against him in 1999.

2000 Outlook

Assuming just a normal learning curve, Rupe should be markedly better next season, having the benefit of a more relaxed spring training and the knowledge and experience of five months in the majors. With his determination and dedication, the leap could be huge. The only concern is keeping him healthy. He had elbow troubles in college and missed his final three starts last year with a tired arm.

Position: SP
Bats: R **Throws:** R
Ht: 6' 5" **Wt:** 230

Opening Day Age: 24
Born: 3/31/75 in Houston, TX
ML Seasons: 1

Overall Statistics

	W	L	Pct.	ERA	G	GS	Sv	IP	H	BB	SO	HR	Ratio
1999	8	9	.471	4.55	24	24	0	142.1	136	57	97	17	1.36
Career	8	9	.471	4.55	24	24	0	142.1	136	57	97	17	1.36

How Often He Throws Strikes

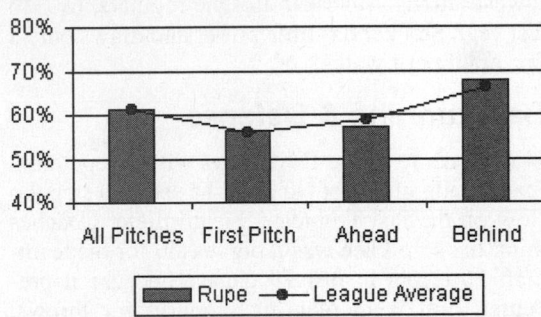

1999 Situational Stats

	W	L	ERA	Sv	IP		AB	H	HR	RBI	Avg
Home	3	6	4.72	0	82.0	LHB	245	64	8	38	.261
Road	5	3	4.33	0	60.1	RHB	292	72	9	34	.247
First Half	4	4	4.77	0	71.2	Sc Pos	131	35	4	55	.267
Scnd Half	4	5	4.33	0	70.2	Clutch	48	12	0	3	.250

1999 Rankings (American League)

- 3rd in hit batsmen (12)
- 5th in errors at pitcher (3)
- 8th in lowest batting average allowed vs. righthanded batters
- Led the Devil Rays in ERA at home, lowest batting average allowed vs. lefthanded batters and lowest batting average allowed vs. righthanded batters

Tampa Bay

Kevin Stocker

1999 Season

Kevin Stocker was off to a good start in proving his disastrous 1998 performance was an aberration, but then his season came to a premature end for the second straight year. In 1998, he was struck on the hand by a pitch and missed the final month. Last season he was bothered by left-knee inflammation starting in July, and underwent season-ending surgery on August 31.

Hitting

Stocker returned to his old hitting style in 1999, choking up on the bat and taking short, aggressive swings. The change was especially relevant from the left side, as he improved from .194 in 1998, the lowest among American League regulars, to .316 last year. Stocker has little power and draws only a fair number of walks.

Baserunning & Defense

Stocker came to the Devil Rays with a reputation for a steady glove, but at times he seems a step too slow on the fast Tropicana Field infield. Coaches think the sore knee was a big reason for his team-high 16 errors in just 79 games, because it prevented him from planting properly for throws. Stocker doesn't have a particularly strong arm either, and occasionally has to rely on bouncing balls off the turf. He's an average runner who never has shown an aptitude for stealing bases.

2000 Outlook

Stocker is expected to be healthy for the start of spring training. He's entering the final year of a contract that will pay him $3.3 million in 1999, and has to prove that he can be the complete player the Rays are seeking at shortstop. If not, they're going to have to start looking quickly for a replacement, perhaps as soon as midseason. It's safe to say that they regret the expansion-draft trade that sent Bobby Abreu to Philadelphia for Stocker.

Position: SS
Bats: B **Throws:** R
Ht: 6' 1"   **Wt:** 180

Opening Day Age: 30
Born: 2/13/70 in Spokane, WA
ML Seasons: 7

Overall Statistics

	G	AB	R	H	D	T	HR	RBI	SB	BB	SO	Avg	OBP	Slg
1999	79	254	39	76	11	2	1	27	9	24	41	.299	.369	.370
Career	736	2430	299	628	104	24	21	224	44	262	460	.258	.340	.347

Where He Hits the Ball

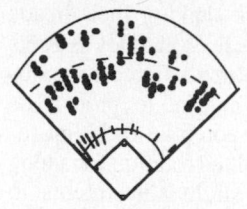
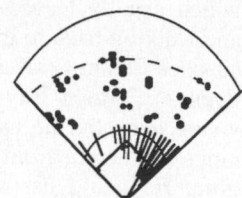

Vs. LHP   **Vs. RHP**

1999 Situational Stats

	AB	H	HR	RBI	Avg		AB	H	HR	RBI	Avg
Home	106	30	1	14	.283	LHP	61	15	0	5	.246
Road	148	46	0	13	.311	RHP	193	61	1	22	.316
First Half	236	72	1	27	.305	Sc Pos	66	21	0	25	.318
Scnd Half	18	4	0	0	.222	Clutch	42	9	0	2	.214

1999 Rankings (American League)

- 6th in errors at shortstop (16)

Mike DiFelice

Position: C
Bats: R **Throws:** R
Ht: 6' 2" **Wt:** 205

Opening Day Age: 30
Born: 5/28/69 in
Philadelphia, PA
ML Seasons: 4
Pronunciation:
dee-fah-LEECE

Overall Statistics

	G	AB	R	H	D	T	HR	RBI	SB	BB	SO	Avg	OBP	Slg
1999	51	179	21	55	11	0	6	27	0	8	23	.307	.346	.469
Career	232	694	54	176	34	4	13	82	1	42	141	.254	.301	.370

1999 Situational Stats

	AB	H	HR	RBI	Avg		AB	H	HR	RBI	Avg
Home	93	23	5	14	.247	LHP	49	14	2	9	.286
Road	86	32	1	13	.372	RHP	130	41	4	18	.315
First Half	76	20	2	14	.263	Sc Pos	48	15	2	22	.313
Scnd Half	103	35	4	13	.340	Clutch	25	6	0	4	.240

1999 Season

Even though his playing time was limited, Mike DiFelice had the best season of his career. He hiked his batting average 77 points and doubled his home-run total from 1998. DiFelice even was stronger than usual behind the plate. The Rays went 28-22 in his starts, 41-71 otherwise.

Hitting, Baserunning & Defense

DiFelice showed better knowledge of the strike zone and didn't seem to be fooled as often last year. At the same time, he developed the ability to drive the ball. DiFelice is slow even for a catcher. His strength is catching and throwing the ball. Even though he'll miss a pitch now and then, his toughness and willingness to throw his body around are appreciated. His arm is strong, and improved mechanics led to him throwing out 16 basestealers in 39 attempts in 1999.

2000 Outlook

The Rays are quite pleased with their catching tandem of John Flaherty and DiFelice. The only problem for DiFelice is that he has little chance of moving out of the backup role after Flaherty signed a three-year contract.

Tony Graffanino

Position: 2B/SS
Bats: R **Throws:** R
Ht: 6' 1" **Wt:** 195

Opening Day Age: 27
Born: 6/6/72 in
Amityville, NY
ML Seasons: 4
Pronunciation:
graf-a-NEEN-oh

Overall Statistics

	G	AB	R	H	D	T	HR	RBI	SB	BB	SO	Avg	OBP	Slg
1999	39	130	20	41	9	4	2	19	3	9	22	.315	.364	.492
Career	270	651	92	158	33	7	15	63	10	63	149	.243	.311	.384

1999 Situational Stats

	AB	H	HR	RBI	Avg		AB	H	HR	RBI	Avg
Home	55	12	0	6	.218	LHP	30	11	0	5	.367
Road	75	29	2	13	.387	RHP	100	30	2	14	.300
First Half	0	0	0	0	-	Sc Pos	28	13	1	16	.464
Scnd Half	130	41	2	19	.315	Clutch	16	9	1	4	.563

1999 Season

Once considered the Braves' second baseman of the future, Tony Graffanino was terrible in 1998 and became expendable when they traded for Bret Boone last offseason. Waived toward the end of spring training, he signed with Tampa Bay and spent four months in Triple-A. Injuries to Miguel Cairo and Kevin Stocker gave Graffanino a chance to play, and he had a strong second half at the plate.

Hitting, Baserunning & Defense

Graffanino is strong for a middle infielder and can do some damage when he gets fastballs to hit. His ability to make contact and draw walks leave something to be desired, however. His speed and range are rather ordinary, but Graffanino has sure hands and makes the plays on what he can reach. Though he saw action at shortstop for Tampa Bay, he's better suited for second base.

2000 Outlook

Graffanino resuscitated his career after his callup, but his long-term future is far from secure. The Devil Rays have Miguel Cairo at second base, so Graffanino will have to keep hitting to stay in the majors as a utilityman.

Tampa Bay

Aaron Ledesma

Traded To ROCKIES

Position: SS/3B/2B
Bats: R **Throws:** R
Ht: 6' 2" **Wt:** 210

Opening Day Age: 28
Born: 6/3/71 in Union City, CA
ML Seasons: 4
Pronunciation: luh-DEZZ-muh

Overall Statistics

	G	AB	R	H	D	T	HR	RBI	SB	BB	SO	Avg	OBP	Slg
1999	93	294	32	78	15	0	0	30	1	14	35	.265	.305	.316
Career	252	714	90	214	36	4	2	73	11	42	102	.300	.342	.370

1999 Situational Stats

	AB	H	HR	RBI	Avg		AB	H	HR	RBI	Avg
Home	158	39	0	16	.247	LHP	65	17	0	7	.262
Road	136	39	0	14	.287	RHP	229	61	0	23	.266
First Half	97	26	0	11	.268	Sc Pos	83	23	0	30	.277
Scnd Half	197	52	0	19	.264	Clutch	51	14	0	4	.275

1999 Season

The 1999 season reconfirmed what the Devil Rays already knew: Aaron Ledesma is a good utility infielder. The problem is, they came to that realization after watching him struggle playing every day at shortstop in the second half, while Kevin Stocker was out with a knee injury. Ledesma missed the first five weeks of the season after hurting his thumb in spring training.

Hitting, Baserunning & Defense

Ledesma brought a .324 career average into 1999, and he hit consistently except for a .178 slump in July. He doesn't offer much in the way of power or speed. Ledesma's main value is his ability to fill in at all four infield positions. His lack of range, however, became painfully apparent when he played shortstop on a regular basis, especially on turf. His arm hasn't been the same since he had shoulder problems while in the minors with the Mets.

2000 Outlook

Ledesma went to Colorado with Rolando Arrojo in the December deal that brought Vinny Castilla to the Devil Rays. He figures to be used in a utility role again, getting most of his time at second base.

Bobby Smith

Position: 3B/2B
Bats: R **Throws:** R
Ht: 6' 3" **Wt:** 190

Opening Day Age: 25
Born: 5/10/74 in Oakland, CA
ML Seasons: 2

Overall Statistics

	G	AB	R	H	D	T	HR	RBI	SB	BB	SO	Avg	OBP	Slg
1999	68	199	18	36	4	1	3	19	4	16	64	.181	.244	.256
Career	185	569	62	138	19	4	14	74	9	50	174	.243	.309	.364

1999 Situational Stats

	AB	H	HR	RBI	Avg		AB	H	HR	RBI	Avg
Home	115	19	1	9	.165	LHP	42	7	0	2	.167
Road	84	17	2	10	.202	RHP	157	29	3	17	.185
First Half	86	13	2	4	.151	Sc Pos	45	12	0	13	.267
Scnd Half	113	23	1	15	.204	Clutch	19	1	0	1	.053

1999 Season

Bobby Smith was the Devil Rays' biggest disappointment in 1999. After a decent rookie season and a strong spring, Smith looked ready to establish himself as the everyday third baseman. Instead, his inconsistent and uninspired play earned him a seat on the bench and then a demotion to Triple-A.

Hitting, Baserunning & Defense

It's still a mystery what went wrong with Smith. His average dropped 95 points and his power disappeared. The same fat pitches that he drove in 1998 became easy outs last season. In one stretch, he was called out looking in six consecutive at-bats. He hit well in Triple-A, so the problems didn't appear to be physical. Smith has a good glove and, despite a herky-jerky motion, a strong arm. He's athletic but not particularly fast on the bases.

2000 Outlook

Smith is at a crossroads in his career. He hoped to win the Rays' third-base job this spring, but Vinny Castilla's arrival put an end to that idea. The best he can hope for now is a utility role.

Paul Sorrento

Position: LF/1B
Bats: L **Throws:** R
Ht: 6' 2" **Wt:** 210

Opening Day Age: 34
Born: 11/17/65 in
Somerville, MA
ML Seasons: 11

Overall Statistics

	G	AB	R	H	D	T	HR	RBI	SB	BB	SO	Avg	OBP	Slg
1999	99	294	40	69	14	1	11	42	1	49	101	.235	.351	.401
Career	1093	3412	454	876	176	5	166	565	8	426	844	.257	.340	.457

1999 Situational Stats

	AB	H	HR	RBI	Avg			AB	H	HR	RBI	Avg
Home	152	34	6	22	.224	LHP		38	11	2	5	.289
Road	142	35	5	20	.246	RHP		256	58	9	37	.227
First Half	149	37	6	22	.248	Sc Pos		86	20	2	30	.233
Scnd Half	145	32	5	20	.221	Clutch		44	12	1	7	.273

1999 Season

Paul Sorrento suffered through a second straight disappointing season with the Devil Rays. He tried hard but couldn't master the switch to playing the outfield, and he struggled at the plate when he did get into the lineup. His sole highlight was a 491-foot homer at Texas, the longest in stadium history.

Hitting, Baserunning & Defense

Sorrento was a wreck at the plate most days, biting at weak offspeed stuff, chasing fastballs out of the zone and missing the handful of pitches he should have been able to handle. While there was no faulting his effort or professionalism, Sorrento proved that as an outfielder he is a pretty good first baseman. He just does not have the speed, agility or arm to play the outfield. He's a non-factor on the bases as well.

2000 Outlook

The Devil Rays declined Sorrento's 2000 option, then didn't offer him arbitration as a free agent, ensuring that he'll play elsewhere this season. He'll look for a team that will allow him to call first base home.

Bubba Trammell

Position: LF/RF
Bats: R **Throws:** R
Ht: 6' 2" **Wt:** 220

Opening Day Age: 28
Born: 11/6/71 in
Knoxville, TN
ML Seasons: 3
Pronunciation:
TRAM-mull

Overall Statistics

	G	AB	R	H	D	T	HR	RBI	SB	BB	SO	Avg	OBP	Slg
1999	82	283	49	82	19	0	14	39	0	43	37	.290	.384	.505
Career	185	605	91	167	42	1	30	87	3	74	117	.276	.354	.498

1999 Situational Stats

	AB	H	HR	RBI	Avg			AB	H	HR	RBI	Avg
Home	146	44	6	20	.301	LHP		66	15	4	9	.227
Road	137	38	8	19	.277	RHP		217	67	10	30	.309
First Half	78	19	4	10	.244	Sc Pos		79	16	3	23	.203
Scnd Half	205	63	10	29	.307	Clutch		34	11	3	6	.324

1999 Season

Bubba Trammell's 1999 season was much like the previous one. He had a rough spring, spent most of the first half in the minors and had a strong second half in the big leagues. His 14 home runs ranked third on the Devil Rays, and he hit .338 over the final month to push his average to .290.

Hitting, Baserunning & Defense

Trammell always has hit with impressive power, especially if a pitcher foolishly leaves a fastball over the plate. And he's learning discipline, totaling more walks than strikeouts for the first time in his pro career in 1999. He's not blessed with blazing speed but can get around the bases when he needs to. Trammell's downfall is his defense. He can't run down balls that aren't hit right at him, though he does have a strong arm.

2000 Outlook

Trammell says all he wants is the chance to play a full season at the big league level. But his defensive shortcomings and the Rays' signings of Greg Vaughn and Gerald Williams make it doubtful that an opportunity will be forthcoming. With Jose Canseco around, DH isn't an option for Trammell.

Rick White

Position: RP
Bats: R **Throws:** R
Ht: 6' 4" **Wt:** 230

Opening Day Age: 31
Born: 12/23/68 in Springfield, OH
ML Seasons: 4

Randy Winn

Position: CF
Bats: B **Throws:** R
Ht: 6' 2" **Wt:** 193

Opening Day Age: 25
Born: 6/9/74 in Los Angeles, CA
ML Seasons: 2

Overall Statistics

	W	L	Pct.	ERA	G	GS	Sv	IP	H	BB	SO	HR	Ratio
1999	5	3	.625	4.08	63	1	0	108.0	132	38	81	8	1.57
Career	13	17	.433	4.07	159	18	6	307.0	343	96	187	28	1.43

1999 Situational Stats

	W	L	ERA	Sv	IP		AB	H	HR	RBI	Avg
Home	4	1	3.91	0	53.0	LHB	188	58	4	29	.309
Road	1	2	4.25	0	55.0	RHB	246	74	4	40	.301
First Half	4	2	4.05	0	60.0	Sc Pos	139	40	2	58	.288
Scnd Half	1	1	4.13	0	48.0	Clutch	26	12	1	6	.462

Overall Statistics

	G	AB	R	H	D	T	HR	RBI	SB	BB	SO	Avg	OBP	Slg
1999	79	303	44	81	16	4	2	24	9	17	63	.267	.307	.366
Career	188	641	95	175	25	13	3	41	35	46	132	.273	.323	.367

1999 Situational Stats

	AB	H	HR	RBI	Avg		AB	H	HR	RBI	Avg
Home	123	34	2	12	.276	LHP	80	19	1	2	.238
Road	180	47	0	12	.261	RHP	223	62	1	22	.278
First Half	288	74	1	20	.257	Sc Pos	74	17	1	21	.230
Scnd Half	15	7	1	4	.467	Clutch	42	10	1	4	.238

1999 Season

Though hardly anyone noticed, Rick White turned in an impressive performance for the Devil Rays, pitching in wherever he was needed. He started a game, pitched long relief and worked some crucial late-inning situations, piling up 108 innings.

Pitching & Defense

White is at his best when he rears back and fires his fastball in the low 90s. He'll mix in sliders, some curveballs and a decent forkball now and then, but the fastball is his forte. As successful as he was in a multitude of roles, he needs to improve his command within the strike zone and do better with inherited runners (30 of 62 scored off him in 1999). He also allowed the first batters he faced in an appearance to bat .400. White is an average fielder and permitted just two steals in eight attempts last year.

2000 Outlook

White's value probably won't ever be as high as it was in 1999. His best shot for continued success this season remains in long relief.

1999 Season

Randy Winn opened 1999 as Tampa Bay's regular center fielder, but couldn't hold onto the job and was demoted twice. A lingering heel injury at the end of the season cost him a shot at redemption.

Hitting, Baserunning & Defense

The Devil Rays hoped that Winn would improve on his promising rookie season, but he regressed. He showed very little patience and didn't make consistent contact. He didn't bunt well or hit the ball on the ground enough. A switch-hitter, he struggled from the right side. Winn did little to take advantage of his electrifying speed, reaching base infrequently and getting caught in nine of 18 steal attempts. While he showed fine range in center, he didn't heed tips on how to quicken his release to compensate for a woefully weak throwing arm.

2000 Outlook

Winn faces a major challenge in rebuilding his stock as a potential starter. His poor 1999 showing led to the signing of free agent Gerald Williams as another option in center field.

Bobby Witt

Position: SP
Bats: R **Throws:** R
Ht: 6' 2" **Wt:** 215

Opening Day Age: 35
Born: 5/11/64 in
Arlington, VA
ML Seasons: 14

Overall Statistics

	W	L	Pct.	ERA	G	GS	Sv	IP	H	BB	SO	HR	Ratio
1999	7	15	.318	5.84	32	32	0	180.1	213	96	123	23	1.71
Career	138	155	.471	4.82	409	388	0	2406.1	2429	1344	1918	242	1.57

1999 Situational Stats

	W	L	ERA	Sv	IP		AB	H	HR	RBI	Avg
Home	4	7	5.73	0	81.2	LHB	363	106	12	56	.292
Road	3	8	5.93	0	98.2	RHB	338	107	11	54	.317
First Half	5	5	5.42	0	98.0	Sc Pos	180	53	6	83	.294
Scnd Half	2	10	6.34	0	82.1	Clutch	29	9	2	5	.310

1999 Season

Signed to a minor league contract in January, Bobby Witt won a job in spring training. He led the Devil Rays with 32 starts and 180.1 innings, but never got on a roll and lost a career-high 15 games.

Pitching & Defense

After being discarded by Texas and St. Louis in 1998, Witt showed that he still had the same stuff from earlier in his career: a lively fastball, a sharp slider and something he calls a split-change. What he didn't have was any consistency. He puts too many runners on base, then gets tentative and pitches from behind in the count, which usually spells disaster. Witt remains in excellent shape and is good at getting to grounders, though he's a bit error-prone. He does a decent job of battling basestealers.

2000 Outlook

Witt became a free agent and the Devil Rays showed that they had no interest in re-signing him when they declined to offer him arbitration. Given his tenacity and durability, some team will give him another chance.

Esteban Yan

Position: RP
Bats: R **Throws:** R
Ht: 6' 4" **Wt:** 230

Opening Day Age: 25
Born: 6/22/74 in
Campina del Seibo,
Dominican Republic
ML Seasons: 4
Pronunciation: YAWN

Overall Statistics

	W	L	Pct.	ERA	G	GS	Sv	IP	H	BB	SO	HR	Ratio
1999	3	4	.429	5.90	50	1	0	61.0	77	32	46	8	1.79
Career	8	9	.471	5.39	121	3	1	168.2	188	83	134	25	1.61

1999 Situational Stats

	W	L	ERA	Sv	IP		AB	H	HR	RBI	Avg
Home	2	2	5.91	0	32.0	LHB	116	36	4	18	.310
Road	1	2	5.90	0	29.0	RHB	120	41	4	21	.342
First Half	2	2	5.03	0	39.1	Sc Pos	86	24	2	32	.279
Scnd Half	1	2	7.48	0	21.2	Clutch	67	28	5	18	.418

1999 Season

Considered one of the jewels of Tampa Bay's expansion draft, Esteban Yan faltered after a fine 1998. The Devil Rays tried him in a variety of relief roles and gave him one start, but nothing turned him around. He went on the disabled list for a month at midseason with bursitis in his shoulder, and finished the season on the sidelines for the same reason.

Pitching & Defense

Yan can be explosive on the mound, unleashing a fastball that can push the mid- to upper 90s and has good movement. He also has a slider and a changeup that are effective when he establishes his fastball. Yan tends to get excited on the mound, which can work to his advantage when things are going well but also can be detrimental in tough situations. He's not the most graceful fielder and doesn't have much of a pickoff move.

2000 Outlook

The Rays asked Yan to avoid winter ball for the first time in his career, hoping the extra rest will keep him strong for the full season. If healthy, he might settle into a late-inning setup role.

Tampa Bay

Other Tampa Bay Devil Rays

Wade Boggs (**Pos**: 3B, **Age**: 41, **Bats**: L)

	G	AB	R	H	D	T	HR	RBI	SB	BB	SO	Avg	OBP	Slg
1999	90	292	40	88	14	1	2	29	1	38	23	.301	.377	.377
Career	2440	9180	1513	3010	578	61	118	1014	24	1412	745	.328	.415	.443

Boggs made dramatic history on August 7, homering off Chris Haney for his 3,000th career hit. His season ended a month later with knee surgery, and he retired after the season. 2000 Outlook: D

Rich Butler (**Pos**: RF, **Age**: 26, **Bats**: L)

	G	AB	R	H	D	T	HR	RBI	SB	BB	SO	Avg	OBP	Slg
1999	7	20	2	3	1	0	0	0	0	2	4	.150	.227	.200
Career	86	251	30	56	5	3	7	22	4	19	44	.223	.280	.351

After starting the 1999 season on the disabled list with a sore Achilles tendon, Butler didn't do much in his second go-round with the Rays. He signed a minor league deal with Seattle in November. 2000 Outlook: C

Mickey Callaway (**Pos**: RHP, **Age**: 24)

	W	L	Pct.	ERA	G	GS	Sv	IP	H	BB	SO	HR	Ratio
1999	1	2	.333	7.45	5	4	0	19.1	30	14	11	2	2.28
Career	1	2	.333	7.45	5	4	0	19.1	30	14	11	2	2.28

Callaway's Triple-A numbers weren't pretty when the Rays came calling in June. A hamstring injury soon landed him on the disabled list. 2000 Outlook: C

Norm Charlton (**Pos**: LHP, **Age**: 37)

	W	L	Pct.	ERA	G	GS	Sv	IP	H	BB	SO	HR	Ratio
1999	2	3	.400	4.44	42	0	0	50.2	49	36	45	4	1.68
Career	47	52	.475	3.67	559	37	96	848.2	756	392	759	65	1.35

Charlton is enrolled in the Bob McClure School of Lefties with Nine Lives, surviving as a lefty specialist beyond the point of effectiveness at which righties no longer are tolerated. The end is near. 2000 Outlook: C

Danny Clyburn (**Pos**: LF, **Age**: 25, **Bats**: R)

	G	AB	R	H	D	T	HR	RBI	SB	BB	SO	Avg	OBP	Slg
1999	28	81	8	16	4	0	3	5	0	7	21	.198	.270	.358
Career	41	109	14	23	4	0	4	8	0	8	33	.211	.271	.358

After a solid Triple-A debut in 1997, Clyburn's numbers have declined at that level since then. He wasn't as good in the majors last year as in 1998, either. 2000 Outlook: C

Mike Duvall (**Pos**: LHP, **Age**: 25)

	W	L	Pct.	ERA	G	GS	Sv	IP	H	BB	SO	HR	Ratio
1999	1	1	.500	4.05	40	0	0	40.0	46	27	18	5	1.83
Career	1	1	.500	4.30	43	0	0	44.0	50	29	19	5	1.80

The Rays were looking for a dependable lefty specialist in the pen, and Duvall didn't succeed when called upon. Three times he came in and walked the only batter he faced. 2000 Outlook: C

Dave Eiland (**Pos**: RHP, **Age**: 33)

	W	L	Pct.	ERA	G	GS	Sv	IP	H	BB	SO	HR	Ratio
1999	4	8	.333	5.60	21	15	0	80.1	98	27	53	8	1.56
Career	10	24	.294	5.48	75	60	0	318.1	388	100	136	38	1.53

Eiland pitched remarkably well at Triple-A in April and May, but found himself on the disabled list with back and hip injuries after his recall. He pitched OK for the Rays and may be back. 2000 Outlook: C

Julio Franco (**Pos**: 1B, **Age**: 38, **Bats**: R)

	G	AB	R	H	D	T	HR	RBI	SB	BB	SO	Avg	OBP	Slg
1999	1	1	0	0	0	0	0	0	0	0	1	.000	.000	.000
Career	1891	7244	1104	2177	335	47	141	981	260	753	1006	.301	.366	.418

After batting .423-14-77 for the Mexico City Tigers in the Mexican League, Franco joined Durham during the Triple-A playoffs before he was promoted to the Rays. Not much major league mileage left. 2000 Outlook: C

Eddie Gaillard (**Pos**: RHP, **Age**: 29)

	W	L	Pct.	ERA	G	GS	Sv	IP	H	BB	SO	HR	Ratio
1999	1	0	1.000	2.08	8	0	0	8.2	12	4	7	1	1.85
Career	2	0	1.000	4.66	30	0	1	36.2	32	17	24	6	1.34

In 1999 Gaillard was the closer at Triple-A Durham, where he posted a 2.89 ERA en route to 26 saves. Major leaguers had an easier time hitting him in September, but he'll get another look after the Reds claimed him off waivers in November. 2000 Outlook: B

David Lamb (**Pos**: SS/2B, **Age**: 24, **Bats**: B)

	G	AB	R	H	D	T	HR	RBI	SB	BB	SO	Avg	OBP	Slg
1999	55	124	18	28	5	1	1	13	0	10	18	.226	.284	.306
Career	55	124	18	28	5	1	1	13	0	10	18	.226	.284	.306

A major league Rule 5 draft selection from Baltimore, Lamb spent the entire 1999 season with the Devil Rays. Early-season injuries to Miguel Cairo and Aaron Ledesma allowed him some playing time. He'll have to earn it now. 2000 Outlook: C

Cory Lidle (**Pos**: RHP, **Age**: 28)

	W	L	Pct.	ERA	G	GS	Sv	IP	H	BB	SO	HR	Ratio
1999	1	0	1.000	7.20	5	1	0	5.0	8	2	4	0	2.00
Career	8	2	.800	3.74	59	3	2	86.2	94	22	58	7	1.34

Lidle had elbow surgery in the spring of 1998, and he made it back to the majors for some September work last year. In 1997, he had had some success as a Mets reliever. 2000 Outlook: B

Albie Lopez (**Pos**: RHP, **Age**: 28)

	W	L	Pct.	ERA	G	GS	Sv	IP	H	BB	SO	HR	Ratio
1999	3	2	.600	4.64	51	0	0	64.0	66	24	37	8	1.41
Career	22	20	.524	5.03	174	31	2	372.0	406	163	272	54	1.53

Lopez wasn't as sharp as he was in 1998, when he posted seven wins and a 2.60 ERA. An oblique muscle injury sidelined him for six weeks in 1999. Still, he managed to pick up 12 holds. He may rebound. 2000 Outlook: B

Terrell Lowery (Pos: CF/LF, Age: 29, Bats: R)

	G	AB	R	H	D	T	HR	RBI	SB	BB	SO	Avg	OBP	Slg
1999	66	185	25	48	15	1	2	17	0	19	53	.259	.330	.384
Career	99	214	29	55	16	1	2	18	1	25	63	.257	.336	.369

Lowery's .335 average at Durham was his best in three Triple-A seasons, though he has fanned at an alarming rate all three years. The whiffs continued with the Rays, but he also showed some pop. 2000 Outlook: C

Jim Mecir (Pos: RHP, Age: 29)

	W	L	Pct.	ERA	G	GS	Sv	IP	H	BB	SO	HR	Ratio
1999	0	1	.000	2.61	17	0	0	20.2	15	14	15	0	1.40
Career	8	8	.500	3.93	138	0	0	183.1	166	82	158	17	1.35

Coming off his career-best 1998 season, Mecir struggled with his control in '99 before falling and breaking his right elbow during batting practice in May. He should return as the primary setup man. 2000 Outlook: A

Jim Morris (Pos: LHP, Age: 36)

	W	L	Pct.	ERA	G	GS	Sv	IP	H	BB	SO	HR	Ratio
1999	0	0	-	5.79	5	0	0	4.2	3	2	3	1	1.07
Career	0	0	-	5.79	5	0	0	4.2	3	2	3	1	1.07

A high school coach, Morris was talked back into pro ball by his players after a 10-year absence from the minor leagues. He pitched briefly in Triple-A before debuting in the bigs. 2000 Outlook: C

Alan Newman (Pos: LHP, Age: 30)

	W	L	Pct.	ERA	G	GS	Sv	IP	H	BB	SO	HR	Ratio
1999	2	2	.500	6.89	18	0	0	15.2	22	9	20	2	1.98
Career	2	2	.500	6.89	18	0	0	15.2	22	9	20	2	1.98

A former Twins prospect, Newman spent two years in independent leagues in the mid-1990s before producing a solid Triple-A season. He wasn't as good in Tampa. 2000 Outlook: C

Herbert Perry (Pos: 3B/1B, Age: 30, Bats: R)

	G	AB	R	H	D	T	HR	RBI	SB	BB	SO	Avg	OBP	Slg
1999	66	209	29	53	10	1	6	32	0	16	42	.254	.331	.397
Career	129	392	54	106	24	2	9	56	2	33	73	.270	.345	.411

There's no doubt Perry can hit, but can he stay healthy? He missed all of the 1997 season and much of 1998, and he was sidelined for six weeks in '99 with a rib muscle injury. Tampa Bay designated him for assignment in December. 2000 Outlook: B

Bryan Rekar (Pos: RHP, Age: 27)

	W	L	Pct.	ERA	G	GS	Sv	IP	H	BB	SO	HR	Ratio
1999	6	6	.500	5.80	27	12	0	94.2	121	41	55	14	1.71
Career	15	24	.385	5.93	74	54	0	334.0	409	118	199	55	1.58

It appeared getting out of Colorado would be Rekar's ticket to success, but he has struggled with injuries and, more importantly, the longball. Many a decent outing has been compromised by gopheritis. 2000 Outlook: C

Julio Santana (Pos: RHP, Age: 26)

	W	L	Pct.	ERA	G	GS	Sv	IP	H	BB	SO	HR	Ratio
1999	1	4	.200	7.32	22	5	0	55.1	66	32	34	10	1.77
Career	10	16	.385	5.72	87	38	0	305.0	358	143	159	44	1.64

A pleasant surprise during the Rays' inaugural season, Santana was awful in 1999. Designated for assignment and dealt to Boston in July, he hit the DL with shoulder tendinitis soon after. 2000 Outlook: C

Tony Saunders (Pos: LHP, Age: 25)

	W	L	Pct.	ERA	G	GS	Sv	IP	H	BB	SO	HR	Ratio
1999	3	3	.500	6.43	9	9	0	42.0	53	29	30	6	1.95
Career	13	24	.351	4.56	62	61	0	345.2	343	204	304	33	1.58

Saunders was looking to build on a promising 1998 performance, but his season ended when the humerus bone in his arm snapped while throwing a pitch on May 26. He should be ready in the spring. 2000 Outlook: B

Jeff Sparks (Pos: RHP, Age: 27)

	W	L	Pct.	ERA	G	GS	Sv	IP	H	BB	SO	HR	Ratio
1999	0	0	-	5.40	8	0	1	10.0	6	12	17	1	1.80
Career	0	0	-	5.40	8	0	1	10.0	6	12	17	1	1.80

Sparks joined the Rays in the July trade that brought Jose Guillen from Pittsburgh. He enjoyed a solid Triple-A season, but he wasn't as effective in the majors. 2000 Outlook: C

Tampa Bay Devil Rays Minor League Prospects

Organization Overview:

While their expansion counterparts, the Diamondbacks, were winning a division title in their second year of existence, the Devil Rays were struggling like most fledgling franchises. Of course, eight members of Arizona's nucleus were signed as free agents, while Tampa Bay is building in a more traditional manner. The Rays don't have as much money as their expansion brethren and are going to need more time. Last year was a success in that they promoted their first truly homegrown players to the majors in former draft picks Mickey Callaway, Ryan Rupe and Dan Wheeler. They also had the No. 1 overall pick in the draft, and secured a franchise cornerstone in Josh Hamilton.

Steve Cox

Position: 1B
Bats: L **Throws:** L
Ht: 6' 4" **Wt:** 225

Opening Day Age: 25
Born: 10/31/74 in Delano, CA

Recent Statistics

	G	AB	R	H	D	T	HR	RBI	SB	BB	SO	Avg
1999 AAA Durham	134	534	107	182	49	4	25	127	3	67	74	.341
1999 AL Tampa Bay	6	19	0	4	1	0	0	0	0	0	2	.211
1999 MLE	134	501	73	149	41	2	18	87	1	45	77	.297

The Devil Rays drafted Cox in the second round of the 1997 expansion draft, but any hopes he had of starting for Tampa Bay ended when the club traded for Fred McGriff immediately after the draft. A 1992 fifth-round pick by the Athletics, he exploded last year, however, winning International League MVP honors after topping the circuit in several categories, including batting average and slugging percentage (.588). The caveat is that it was his third year at the same level, but the Rays see Cox as a fluid hitter who finally got stronger. He's a good athlete for his position, running decently and getting rated as the IL's best defensive first baseman. McGriff continues to present an obstacle, signing a contract through 2001, so Cox worked out in left field in instructional league. He figures to make the Rays as a reserve this year.

Josh Hamilton

Position: OF
Bats: L **Throws:** L
Ht: 6' 4" **Wt:** 200

Opening Day Age: 18
Born: 5/21/81 in Raleigh, NC

Recent Statistics

	G	AB	R	H	D	T	HR	RBI	SB	BB	SO	Avg
1999 R Princeton	56	236	49	82	20	4	10	48	18	13	43	.347
1999 A Hudson Val	16	72	7	14	3	0	0	7	1	1	14	.194

Owners of the No. 1 overall pick in last June's draft, the Devil Rays locked in on Hamilton early. He signed quickly for a draft-record $3.96 million bonus, then was named the top prospect in the Rookie-level Appalachian League. There are five-tool players and then there's

Hamilton, who has solid above-average tools across the board. *Baseball America* ranked his power and arm strength as the best among 1999 high school prospects. He has a tremendously quick bat and will hit for average, though he needs a tad more plate discipline. He can run the 60-yard dash in 6.75 seconds, and projects either as a center or right fielder. Hamilton also had nice potential as a lefthanded pitcher with a 90-92 MPH fastball, but Tampa Bay won't even think about that. He's the club's future No. 3 hitter, perhaps by 2002.

Aubrey Huff

Position: 3B
Bats: L **Throws:** R
Ht: 6' 4" **Wt:** 220

Opening Day Age: 23
Born: 12/20/76 in Marion, OH

Recent Statistics

	G	AB	R	H	D	T	HR	RBI	SB	BB	SO	Avg
1998 A Chston-SC	69	265	38	85	19	1	13	54	3	24	40	.321
1999 AA Orlando	133	491	85	148	40	3	22	78	2	64	77	.301
1999 MLE	133	468	62	125	34	2	17	57	1	39	82	.267

When 1998 No. 1 overall draft pick Pat Burrell had back problems that spring at the University of Miami, teammate Aubrey Huff took over at the hot corner and led the Hurricanes in batting average, homers and RBI. Scouts took note and Tampa Bay drafted Huff in the fifth round. He has done nothing but hit in two years as a pro, leading the Double-A Southern League in extra-base hits (65) in 1999, his first full season. The only other 1998 draftee with better numbers at that level was Burrell. Huff has good plate discipline and makes fine contact for a slugger. He lacks first-step quickness, but the Devil Rays hope his hands and arm will enable him to become an adequate third baseman. The Vinny Castilla trade doesn't help Huff's cause, however.

Jared Sandberg

Position: 3B
Bats: R **Throws:** R
Ht: 6' 3" **Wt:** 185

Opening Day Age: 22
Born: 3/2/78 in Olympia, WA

Recent Statistics

	G	AB	R	H	D	T	HR	RBI	SB	BB	SO	Avg
1998 A Chston-SC	56	191	31	35	11	0	3	25	4	27	76	.183
1998 A Hudson Val	73	271	49	78	15	2	12	54	13	42	76	.288
1999 A St. Pete	136	504	73	139	24	1	22	96	8	51	133	.276

The nephew of Ryne Sandberg, Jared followed up two all-star years in short-season leagues by finishing second in the high Class-A Florida State League home-run race in 1999. A 16th-round pick three years earlier, he has power to all fields. Sandberg won't hit for average until he makes better contact, and he was less patient last season than he had been in the past. He has the potential to be a fine third baseman, as he's athletic and possesses good hands and an average arm. If Aubrey Huff can't cut it at the hot corner, Sandberg will replace him as Tampa Bay's third baseman of the future.

Bobby Seay

Position: P
Bats: L **Throws:** L
Ht: 6' 2" **Wt:** 190

Opening Day Age: 21
Born: 6/20/78 in Sarasota, FL

Recent Statistics

	W	L	ERA	G	GS	Sv	IP	H	R	BB	SO	HR
1998 A Chston-SC	1	7	4.30	15	15	0	69.0	59	40	29	74	10
1999 A St. Pete	2	6	3.00	12	11	0	57.0	56	25	23	45	0
1999 AA Orlando	1	2	7.94	6	6	0	17.0	22	15	15	16	2

Seay has had injury problems since signing for $3 million as the first draft free agent in 1996, and he was bothered by a pinched nerve in his forearm in 1999. When healthy last year, he began to make some strides. He has fine stuff for a lefthander, with a lively low-90s fastball, a very good curveball and a changeup that has potential. Seay keeps the ball in the park, too, permitting just two homers in 74 innings last year. His biggest needs are to develop command and maturity. He'll start 2000 in Double-A and will move quickly once he makes those adjustments.

Jason Standridge

Position: P
Bats: R **Throws:** R
Ht: 6' 4" **Wt:** 205

Opening Day Age: 21
Born: 11/9/78 in Birmingham, AL

Recent Statistics

	W	L	ERA	G	GS	Sv	IP	H	R	BB	SO	HR
1998 R Princeton	4	4	7.00	12	12	0	63.0	82	61	28	47	4
1999 A Chston-SC	9	1	2.02	18	18	0	116.0	80	35	31	84	5
1999 A St. Pete	4	4	3.91	8	8	0	48.1	49	21	20	26	0

The Devil Rays love to sign college football quarterbacks. Doug Johnson and Kenny Kelly started for powerhouses Florida and Miami, respectively, this fall, and they've also taken top recruits from Auburn (Standridge), Fresno State (Marquis Roberts) and Nebraska (Carl Crawford). Standridge, a 1997 first-round pick, is the best prospect of the group. Last year, he led the Class-A South Atlantic League in ERA, threw a no-hitter and was named the circuit's most valuable pitcher and best pitching prospect. Standridge has learned how to pitch, and he's well-armed with a 90-94 MPH fastball, curveball and changeup. He throws strikes, keeps the ball down and has a huge heart. Now on the fast track, Standridge could reach Tampa Bay in 2001.

Dan Wheeler

Position: P
Bats: R **Throws:** R
Ht: 6' 3" **Wt:** 215

Opening Day Age: 22
Born: 12/10/77 in Providence, RI

Recent Statistics

	W	L	ERA	G	GS	Sv	IP	H	R	BB	SO	HR
1999 AA Orlando	3	0	3.26	9	9	0	58.0	56	27	8	53	7
1999 AAA Durham	7	5	4.92	14	14	0	82.1	103	59	25	58	16
1999 AL Tampa Bay	0	4	5.87	6	6	0	30.2	35	20	13	32	7

Wheeler was one of the more obscure pitchers on the U.S. Pan American Games staff that included five first-round picks, but he was the team's best. He threw four perfect innings to beat Mexico in 10 innings in the semifinals, qualifying Team USA for the 2000 Olympics. A 34th-round pick out of Central Arizona Junior College in 1996, Wheeler signed a year later as a draft-and-follow. His best pitch is a tight slider, and he also throws a low-90s fastball and a changeup. He generally throws strikes, though he battled his control in six late-season starts with Tampa Bay in 1999. Nevertheless, the club is counting on him for its rotation this year.

Matt White

Position: P
Bats: R **Throws:** R
Ht: 6' 5" **Wt:** 215

Opening Day Age: 21
Born: 8/13/78 in Waynesboro, PA

Recent Statistics

	W	L	ERA	G	GS	Sv	IP	H	R	BB	SO	HR
1998 A Chston-SC	4	3	3.82	12	12	0	75.1	72	41	21	59	1
1998 A St. Pete	4	8	5.55	17	17	0	95.2	107	70	41	64	10
1999 A St. Pete	9	7	5.18	21	20	0	113.0	125	75	33	92	6

White's performance hasn't lived up to his stuff or the record $10.2 million bonus he received as a draft free agent in 1996. In three pro seasons, the guy who some scouts rated the best high school pitching prospect ever has gone 21-24, 4.74 and hasn't made it past high Class-A. White hasn't been hurt, and he still throws a fastball that can touch 98 MPH, a power curveball and a straight changeup. But his velocity fluctuates, sometimes dropping to 92 MPH, and his fastball has been fairly straight. His delivery is easy for batters to read. While he throws strikes, he doesn't paint the corners and sometimes just lays the ball over the heart of the plate when he falls behind in the count. White still has potential, but the Devil Rays have to be worrying about their investment.

Others to Watch

The Devil Rays drafted **Andrew Beinbrink** (23) in the seventh round last June with the idea of converting him from a third baseman to a catcher. But he has been so impressive at the hot corner that they've left him there, and he hit .339 with power at short-season Hudson Valley. . . Catcher **Toby Hall** (24) was the MVP of the Southern League playoffs after leading Double-A Orlando to the championship. He has a strong arm and projects as an average hitter. . . Righthander **Travis Harper** (23) signed with Boston in 1997, but had his contract voided because he had elbow tendinitis. Healthy since signing with the Devil Rays, he has thrown a 90-93 MPH fastball and had more strikeouts than innings while reaching Double-A. . . **Paul Hoover** (23) is very athletic for a catcher. He's a fluid receiver who steals bases and makes contact, though like Hall he lacks above-average potential at the plate. . . **Kenny Kelly** (21) is a center fielder with a nice combination of power and speed. He's developing slowly, however, because he's also the University of Miami's starting quarterback. . . Shortstop **Ramon Soler** (18) has been compared to Omar Vizquel defensively. Offensively, he's a switch-hitter with speed, though he's still learning to hit.

The Ballpark in Arlington

Offense

The right-field seats at The Ballpark in Arlington can be reached with line drives or seemingly harmless flyballs, which benefits lefthanded power hitters and righthanded hitters who can use the whole field. The left-field power alley is deep, creating a gap that Rangers hitters traditionally exploit. Few American League parks boost triples and home runs as much as The Ballpark. The small amount of foul territory extends at-bats, which also works against pitchers.

Defense

With game-time temperatures often in the 90s and sometimes above 100 degrees, fielders appreciate pitchers who throw strikes and get them back into the dugout quickly. It's remarkable that Ivan Rodriguez makes more than 140 starts behind the plate every year, considering half of those are played under adverse conditions. The large outfield dimensions challenge the left fielder and center fielder, both of whom need good range.

Who It Helps The Most

Rafael Palmeiro put up astounding numbers in his first year at The Ballpark, hitting .325-28-83 in 271 at-bats. Rusty Greer is a similar hitter who also has put up good home numbers with the Rangers. Aaron Sele has excelled in Texas, going 24-10 in 40 career starts there.

Who It Hurts The Most

Juan Gonzalez never thrived at The Ballpark, in part because of his insistence on pulling the ball instead of taking outside pitches toward the right field. Just 14 of his 39 homers last year came in Texas. Rick Helling has trouble keeping the ball in the park at home but has gone 19-12 there.

Rookies & Newcomers

Young outfielders Gabe Kapler and Ruben Mateo would do well to not follow Gonzalez' example. Their power will be surpressed if they don't use the entire field. Whoever winds up in center field will be tested by the deep left-center gap. Justin Thompson is 0-3, 5.01 in four starts at The Ballpark, but he has permitted just two homers in 23.1 innings.

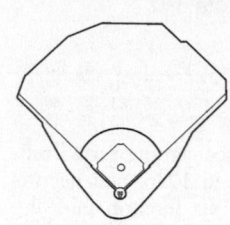

Dimensions: LF-332, LCF-390, CF-400, RCF-381, RF-325

Capacity: 49,166

Elevation: 551 feet

Surface: Grass

Foul Territory: Small

Park Factors

1999 Season

	Home Games			Away Games			
	Rangers	Opp	Total	Rangers	Opp	Total	Index
G	72	72	144	72	72	144	—
Avg	.304	.293	.298	.289	.287	.288	104
AB	2447	2615	5062	2576	2438	5014	101
R	427	407	834	424	355	779	107
H	743	765	1508	744	699	1443	105
2B	132	151	283	145	161	306	92
3B	19	18	37	9	18	27	136
HR	95	99	194	114	68	182	106
BB	278	211	489	259	237	496	98
SO	378	449	827	427	432	859	95
E	52	42	94	49	50	99	95
E-Infield	43	39	82	44	41	85	96
LHB-Avg	.293	.282	.287	.284	.287	.285	101
LHB-HR	48	45	93	47	37	84	119
RHB-Avg	.314	.301	.307	.293	.287	.290	106
RHB-HR	47	54	101	67	31	98	95

1997-1999

	Home Games			Away Games			
	Rangers	Opp	Total	Rangers	Opp	Total	Index
G	218	218	436	218	218	436	—
Avg	.297	.290	.294	.273	.283	.278	106
AB	7480	7893	15373	7733	7359	15092	102
R	1238	1212	2450	1175	1078	2253	109
H	2225	2289	4514	2108	2086	4194	108
2B	418	448	866	421	436	857	99
3B	54	59	113	25	49	74	150
HR	274	263	537	289	208	497	106
BB	769	696	1465	754	713	1467	98
SO	1317	1305	2622	1459	1300	2759	93
E	172	147	319	134	155	289	110
E-Infield	145	117	262	115	130	245	107
LHB-Avg	.297	.289	.293	.272	.280	.276	106
LHB-HR	121	127	248	114	103	217	116
RHB-Avg	.298	.291	.294	.273	.287	.280	105
RHB-HR	153	136	289	175	105	280	98

1999 Rankings (American League)
- Second-highest run factor
- Second-highest RHB batting-average factor
- Third-highest triple factor

Johnny Oates

1999 Season

For the third time in Johnny Oates' five-year tenure, Texas won the American League West, this time with a club-record 95 victories. Such accomplishments should create pride for a franchise that never had been to the playoffs previously, but Oates has been haunted by his inability to win in the postseason. The Yankees swept the Rangers in the Division Series for the second straight year, dropping his postseason record to 1-9.

Offense

Unless the calendar reads October, scoring runs is seldom difficult for Oates' team. He generally sits back and lets the Rangers swing away, rarely employing the sacrifice, hit-and-run or a pinch-hitter. Texas may run less in 2000 after losing two of its top three basestealers, Tom Goodwin and Mark McLemore, to free agency. Hitting instructor Rudy Jaramillo is one of the most underrated coaches in the majors, but he could be forced out if the Rangers lay another postseason egg.

Pitching & Defense

Oates doesn't have a good track record with young starters, and he soon could be tested. The Rangers have a strong group of minor league pitchers headed toward the majors. He relied heavily on rookie relievers Mike Venafro and Jeff Zimmerman last year, and will do so with another (Francisco Cordero) in 2000. He'll lean heavily on a bullpen that's likely to include three lefthanders and four hard-throwing righties, which allows him to exploit platoon matchups. Oates isn't a fan of the intentional walk. He has emphasized defense since coming to Texas, with positive results.

2000 Outlook

Owner Tom Hicks was so exasperated after last year's sweep by the Yankees that he couldn't bring himself to even visit the clubhouse after Game 3. He has sent a clear signal that getting to the playoffs is no longer enough, so look for a major shakeup if the Rangers either fail to repeat as division champs or go down meekly in the playoffs.

Born: 1/21/46 in Sylva, NC

Playing Experience: 1970-1981, Bal, Atl, Phi, LA, NYY

Managerial Experience: 9 seasons

Texas

Manager Statistics

Year	Team, Lg	W	L	Pct	GB	Finish
1999	Texas, AL	95	67	.586	—	1st West
9 Seasons		715	638	.528	—	—

1999 Starting Pitchers by Days Rest

	<=3	4	5	6+
Rangers Starts	4	92	40	18
Rangers ERA	5.82	5.54	4.64	7.13
AL Avg Starts	2	82	47	21
AL ERA	6.83	4.98	4.72	5.62

1999 Situational Stats

	Johnny Oates	AL Average
Hit & Run Success %	31.5	35.3
Stolen Base Success %	67.3	68.0
Platoon Pct.	56.3	56.7
Defensive Subs	7	22
High-Pitch Outings	17	15
Quick/Slow Hooks	18/14	18/18
Sacrifice Attempts	41	52

1999 Rankings (American League)

- 1st in sacrifice-bunt percentage (92.7%), starts on three days rest (4) and first-batter platoon percentage (67.4%)
- 2nd in mid-inning pitching changes (221)
- 3rd in steals of third base (14) and relief appearances (439)

Royce Clayton

1999 Season

Fielding long has been Royce Clayton's calling card, but he's emerging as more of an American League-type shortstop. He's becoming a more productive hitter but not without a cost. He wasn't as reliable in the field as the Rangers anticipated he would be when they signed him to a four-year, $18 million contract after acquiring him in a 1998 trade with St. Louis. Injuries slowed Clayton early in the season but he finished strong, hitting .327 in his last 68 games despite being ridden hard by manager Johnny Oates.

Hitting

Impatience is Clayton's biggest problem as a hitter. He always has struck out a lot and did so more frequently last year, as he seemed infatuated with the idea of hitting home runs. He needs to be reminded about the importance of using the whole field, as his natural tendency is to try to pull everything. Clayton likes the ball down but will chase pitches out of the strike zone. He's a significantly more dangerous hitter against lefthanders.

Baserunning & Defense

Clayton is the kind of shortstop whom pitchers just love. He can go into the hole for grounders and usually has a strong enough arm to get outs after ranging to his right for balls. But he wasn't his normal self after straining a muscle in the back of his shoulder in the third game last season. He seemed worried about the shoulder all season, hurrying throws and muffing grounders that he normally eats up. Though Clayton stole 30-plus bases in consecutive seasons in St. Louis, he's no longer that dangerous as a basestealer. He remains a force to contend with going after the extra base.

2000 Outlook

A winter's rest and continued rehabilitation should be all that Clayton's shoulder needs. If he's healthy, he should improve in the field. He once again will give Oates the kind of hitter that AL teams need at the bottom of the lineup. If there were questions about Clayton handling the heat in Texas, he answered them last year.

Position: SS
Bats: R **Throws:** R
Ht: 6' 0" **Wt:** 185

Opening Day Age: 30
Born: 1/2/70 in Burbank, CA
ML Seasons: 9

Overall Statistics

	G	AB	R	H	D	T	HR	RBI	SB	BB	SO	Avg	OBP	Slg
1999	133	465	69	134	21	5	14	52	8	39	100	.288	.346	.445
Career	1064	3863	476	1004	183	34	56	385	161	291	724	.260	.313	.368

Where He Hits the Ball

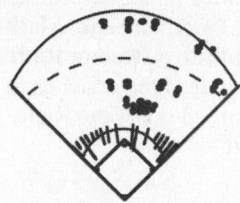 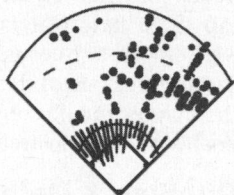

Vs. LHP   **Vs. RHP**

1999 Situational Stats

	AB	H	HR	RBI	Avg		AB	H	HR	RBI	Avg
Home	210	65	6	23	.310	LHP	98	30	5	23	.306
Road	255	69	8	29	.271	RHP	367	104	9	29	.283
First Half	208	51	4	16	.245	Sc Pos	112	29	2	36	.259
Scnd Half	257	83	10	36	.323	Clutch	54	20	0	1	.370

1999 Rankings (American League)

- 1st in errors at shortstop (25) and highest percentage of extra bases taken as a runner (78.6)
- 3rd in lowest fielding percentage at shortstop (.961)
- 5th in highest groundball/flyball ratio (2.0)
- 7th in batting average in the clutch
- 10th in sacrifice bunts (9)
- Led the Rangers in highest groundball/flyball ratio (2.0), highest percentage of extra bases taken as a runner (78.6) and sacrifice bunts (9)
- Led AL shortstops in highest percentage of extra bases taken as a runner (78.6)

Juan Gonzalez

Texas

1999 Season

For the first time in a long time, Juan Gonzalez played in the shadows. The two-time MVP had a solid year but wasn't as productive as teammates Rafael Palmeiro and Ivan Rodriguez. While Gonzalez hit a career-best .326, all of his other offensive numbers were down. Injuries, often a problem, were a factor again. He missed 18 games with a strained hamstring and a jammed thumb.

Hitting

Though he never has changed as a hitter, Gonzalez remains dangerous. He can't lay off outside breaking balls, though he somehow gets enough strikes to do damage. He always has looked to pull the ball. Despite the favorable right-field dimensions of The Ballpark in Arlington, Gonzalez hit just six homers that way last year. He'll cut down his swing with two strikes, but poor judgment still leaves him with twice as many strikeouts as walks.

Baserunning & Defense

Gonzalez never has been a complete player but does possess a strong throwing arm. His muscle-bound body makes it tough for him to get off accurate throws if he has to move laterally to get to a ball. He's a decent right fielder, though he rarely makes plays on balls in front of him. He has average speed but is ultra-cautious, almost never taking a chance on the bases.

2000 Outlook

Unwilling to pay what it would cost to retain Gonzalez as a free agent after the 2000 season, the Rangers traded him and spare parts Danny Patterson and Greg Zaun to the Tigers in November. In exchange, they received Frank Catalanotto, Bill Haselman, Gabe Kapler, Justin Thompson and prospects Francisco Cordero and Alan Webb. The consensus was that Texas GM Doug Melvin fleeced Detroit counterpart Randy Smith. It will be a surprise if Gonzalez puts together a big season with the Tigers, who need him to revive their offense and become a drawing card. He's leery of the dimensions at new Comerica Park, which features a deep power alley in left-center, and never has been comfortable in the spotlight. Kapler will take over right field in Texas.

Position: RF/DH
Bats: R **Throws:** R
Ht: 6' 3" **Wt:** 220

Opening Day Age: 30
Born: 10/16/69 in Vega Baja, Puerto Rico
ML Seasons: 11
Nickname: Igor

Overall Statistics

	G	AB	R	H	D	T	HR	RBI	SB	BB	SO	Avg	OBP	Slg
1999	144	562	114	183	36	1	39	128	3	51	105	.326	.378	.601
Career	1248	4831	791	1421	282	19	340	1075	21	344	947	.294	.343	.572

Where He Hits the Ball

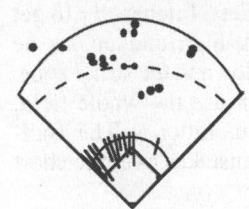
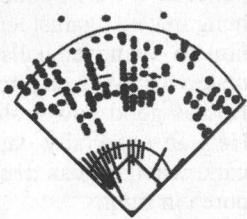

Vs. LHP   **Vs. RHP**

1999 Situational Stats

	AB	H	HR	RBI	Avg		AB	H	HR	RBI	Avg
Home	271	87	14	58	.321	LHP	114	39	9	23	.342
Road	291	96	25	70	.330	RHP	448	144	30	105	.321
First Half	309	97	24	79	.314	Sc Pos	173	51	12	90	.295
Scnd Half	253	86	15	49	.340	Clutch	62	20	3	13	.323

1999 Rankings (American League)

- 2nd in sacrifice flies (12) and lowest ground-ball/flyball ratio (0.7)
- 4th in slugging percentage and cleanup slugging percentage (.601)
- 5th in fielding percentage in right field (.983) and RBI
- Led the Rangers in batting average vs. lefthanded pitchers, cleanup slugging percentage (.601), slugging percentage vs. lefthanded pitchers (.632) and sacrifice flies (12)
- Led AL right fielders in batting average in the clutch, batting average vs. righthanded pitchers, sacrifice flies (12) and batting average at home

Rusty Greer

1999 Season

Like some little-noticed piston in an engine, Rusty Greer quietly drives the Rangers' offense. He handled the move to the No. 3 spot in the lineup, driving the ball when needed and showing a willingness to take walks and put the bat in the hands of Juan Gonzalez or Rafael Palmeiro. Greer reached 100 runs and RBI for the second consecutive season. The negatives were a slippage in defense and a seeming allergy to base hits in the postseason.

Hitting

Greer has good bat speed and is a smart hitter. He generally has good strike-zone judgment and the patience to work counts in his favor. He always has hung in well against lefthanders. Pitchers try to get him to swing at balls waist-high and up, as he makes his living on pitches down in the strike zone. He has good power and will use the whole field. He's an especially dangerous hitter at The Ballpark, where he can deposit mistakes over the short porch in right.

Baserunning & Defense

Greer never has gotten good jumps in left field but he has compensated with his ability to react to the ball. He wasn't nearly as successful making sliding and lunging catches last season. There was some speculation about his eyesight after he bruised a retina in September when he walked into the middle of a game of catch between teammates. Greer has an average arm and can put his throws on the money, making it a risky proposition to run on him. Greer can play first in an emergency. He has enough speed to steal bases but was too smart to risk an out with Gonzalez and Palmeiro hitting behind him.

2000 Outlook

Greer is a career .309 hitter, but his average has dropped three years in a row. If that progression continues, he'll hit below .300 for the first time since 1995. His outfield play already has slipped, and Greer may have reached the point in his career where he starts going backward.

Position: LF
Bats: L **Throws:** L
Ht: 6' 0" **Wt:** 195

Opening Day Age: 31
Born: 1/21/69 in Fort Rucker, AL
ML Seasons: 6

Overall Statistics

	G	AB	R	H	D	T	HR	RBI	SB	BB	SO	Avg	OBP	Slg
1999	147	556	107	167	41	3	20	101	2	96	67	.300	.405	.493
Career	809	2991	516	923	192	20	103	503	25	422	445	.309	.393	.489

Where He Hits the Ball

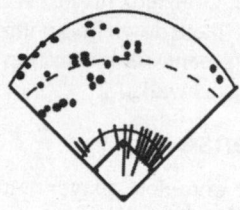

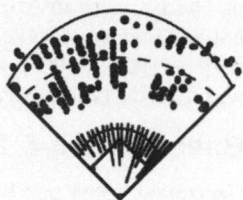

Vs. LHP   **Vs. RHP**

1999 Situational Stats

	AB	H	HR	RBI	Avg		AB	H	HR	RBI	Avg
Home	258	82	10	57	.318	LHP	124	35	3	24	.282
Road	298	85	10	44	.285	RHP	432	132	17	77	.306
First Half	317	85	7	50	.268	Sc Pos	153	50	5	73	.327
Scnd Half	239	82	13	51	.343	Clutch	62	17	1	7	.274

1999 Rankings (American League)

- 4th in errors in left field (5)
- 5th in doubles and lowest fielding percentage in left field (.983)
- 7th in most pitches seen per plate appearance (4.13) and pitches seen (2,731)
- 9th in walks
- Led the Rangers in most pitches seen per plate appearance (4.13), on-base percentage vs. lefthanded pitchers (.411), doubles, hit by pitch (5) and pitches seen (2,731)
- Led AL left fielders in most pitches seen per plate appearance (4.13), batting average vs. righthanded pitchers, runs scored, doubles, walks, times on base (268) and pitches seen (2,731)

Rick Helling

1999 Season

Style points don't count a lot for Rick Helling. The former University of North Dakota linebacker is all about results, and he added to his reputation as a workhorse by turning in a productive season despite seldom having his best stuff. He led Texas in starts, innings and complete games. Along the way, he raised his career victory total to 44, breaking Lynn Sheldon's record for wins by a North Dakota native.

Pitching

Problems with his changeup forced Helling to become basically a two-pitch pitcher. He normally throws at least a dozen changeups per game, but he all but abandoned the pitch after losing command of it early in the season. A lesser competitor would have crumbled after such a critical desertion, but not Helling. He found a way to win while throwing only an 88-MPH fastball and a curveball, which is his best pitch. He did it by continuing to attack hitters, even if he seldom had them off balance. Helling tried to get high fastballs past hitters, which partially explains why he allowed 41 home runs, tops in the majors last year and the most ever off a Rangers pitcher.

Defense

Helling is an excellent athlete and does a good job fielding his position. He gets into great fielding position and handles comebackers and tappers well. He can be slow to the plate, but that seems to be true with every pitcher who works with Ivan Rodriguez.

2000 Outlook

Helling returns for another season at the front of the Texas rotation. He'll spend spring training working as hard as possible to regain confidence in his changeup, and he should be better than ever if he gets the hang of it. If not, look for pitching coach Dick Bosman to give him a third pitch so he doesn't experience a repeat of 1999. It was admirable that Helling got through the crisis, but his effectiveness won't last for long if he remains a two-pitch pitcher.

Position: SP
Bats: R **Throws:** R
Ht: 6' 3" **Wt:** 220

Opening Day Age: 29
Born: 12/15/70 in Devils Lake, ND
ML Seasons: 6

Overall Statistics

	W	L	Pct.	ERA	G	GS	Sv	IP	H	BB	SO	HR	Ratio
1999	13	11	.542	4.84	35	35	0	219.1	228	85	131	41	1.43
Career	44	34	.564	4.71	132	102	0	679.0	661	274	466	110	1.38

How Often He Throws Strikes

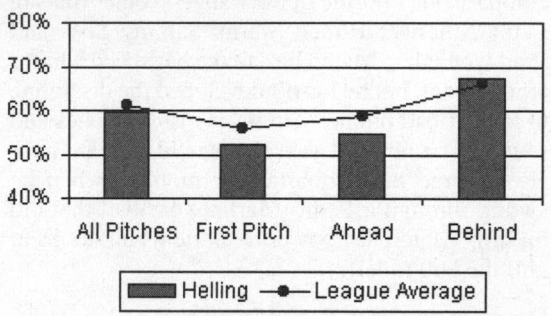

1999 Situational Stats

	W	L	ERA	Sv	IP		AB	H	HR	RBI	Avg
Home	6	4	4.76	0	104.0	LHB	401	105	20	50	.262
Road	7	7	4.92	0	115.1	RHB	436	123	21	62	.282
First Half	6	7	4.64	0	116.1	Sc Pos	170	38	8	63	.224
Scnd Half	7	4	5.07	0	103.0	Clutch	39	12	4	9	.308

1999 Rankings (American League)

- 1st in home runs allowed, pitches thrown (3,814), games started, runners caught stealing (14) and most home runs allowed per nine innings (1.68)
- Led the Rangers in losses, complete games (3), innings pitched, batters faced (943), home runs allowed, walks allowed, wild pitches (8), pitches thrown (3,814), stolen bases allowed (13), lowest batting average allowed (.272), lowest on-base percentage allowed (.340), lowest stolen-base percentage allowed (48.1), fewest baserunners allowed per nine innings (13.1), ERA on the road, lowest batting average allowed vs. righthanded batters, lowest batting average allowed with runners in scoring position, games started and runners caught stealing (14)

Ruben Mateo

1999 Season

The table was set for Ruben Mateo to have a dramatic impact, but the five-tool prospect couldn't dodge the injury problems that bothered him in previous seasons. After arriving from Triple-A, Mateo had to deal with a pulled groin and a broken hamate bone in his left wrist, with the latter injury ending his season on August 4. While he could have been starting in the postseason, Mateo ended the year shagging flies in instructional league.

Hitting

There's no missing Mateo when he's taking batting practice. The ball jumps off his bat, prompting comparisons to some of the Rangers' other finds in Latin America: Ruben Sierra, Sammy Sosa and Juan Gonzalez. Mateo has all the bat speed a hitter would want, but he hasn't developed the discipline to lay off bad pitches. He loves inside pitches and fouled off a few last year that would have hit him. He suffered one embarrassing moment when he swung through a Pedro Martinez fastball that did hit him. Mateo has power to all fields but looks to pull the ball to left.

Baserunning & Defense

Mateo has one of those rare arms that makes fans cheer during pregame practice. He throws laser beams, though he often misses his target. He forces the action with his arm, sometimes allowing the trail runners to take an extra base. He has good range in the outfield, whether playing center field or right. He has very good speed but probably will need a year or two to become a dangerous baserunner in the big leagues.

2000 Outlook

Mateo will replace Tom Goodwin in center field, though some in the organization think his long-term position will be right field. If he can stay healthy, Mateo will contend for the American League Rookie of the Year Award.

Position: CF
Bats: R **Throws:** R
Ht: 6' 0" **Wt:** 170

Opening Day Age: 22
Born: 2/10/78 in San Cristobal, Dominican Republic
ML Seasons: 1
Pronunciation: MUH-tay-oh

Overall Statistics

	G	AB	R	H	D	T	HR	RBI	SB	BB	SO	Avg	OBP	Slg
1999	32	122	16	29	9	1	5	18	3	4	28	.238	.268	.451
Career	32	122	16	29	9	1	5	18	3	4	28	.238	.268	.451

Where He Hits the Ball

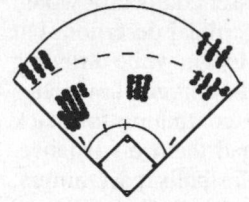
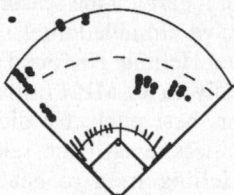

Vs. LHP   **Vs. RHP**

1999 Situational Stats

	AB	H	HR	RBI	Avg		AB	H	HR	RBI	Avg
Home	65	20	2	12	.308	LHP	20	7	1	4	.350
Road	57	9	3	6	.158	RHP	102	22	4	14	.216
First Half	45	8	3	6	.178	Sc Pos	36	10	1	12	.278
Scnd Half	77	21	2	12	.273	Clutch	14	3	1	3	.214

1999 Rankings (American League)

- Did not rank near the top or bottom in any category

Mark McLemore

1999 Season

For years Mark McLemore has played all out on bad knees, and the wear was painfully evident in 1999. The veteran second baseman was a step slower after another round of rehab for his third of three knee surgeries since 1997. McLemore nevertheless contributed with his steady play in the field, intelligent approach at the plate and terrific leadership in the clubhouse.

Hitting

At one time McLemore was a troublesome hitter from both sides of the plate, but he now builds his stats strictly from the left side. He's patient from both sides of the plate, finishing three of the last four years with more walks than strikeouts. McLemore's bat has slowed down recently, making it possible to throw fastballs past him. His limited power comes almost exclusively from the left side, and he just tries to put the ball in play as a righthander. Manager Johnny Oates used him as his leadoff man in 63 of the last 68 games in 1999, but McLemore probably would be better hitting at the bottom of the order.

Baserunning & Defense

McLemore remains reliable at second base, going 46 games without an error in one stretch last year. He doesn't have the range he once did, though he maintains a strong arm and an alert presence. He's a versatile athlete who last year made his first starts in the outfield since 1995. Oates insists that McLemore would have been the Rangers' best defensive outfielder if he had played there regularly. McLemore is a decent baserunner, but isn't the threat he was before his knees became a constant problem.

2000 Outlook

The Rangers appreciated McLemore's contributions but declined to pursue him as a free agent. He put on 20 pounds in the first three months after the season, and Seattle insisted on putting a weight clause in his one-year contract, which could be worth $3 million if he makes all his incentives. The Mariners may start McLemore at a variety of positions and bat him leadoff. Luis Alicea is the frontrunner to take over for McLemore in Texas.

Position: 2B
Bats: B **Throws:** R
Ht: 5'11" **Wt:** 207

Opening Day Age: 35
Born: 10/4/64 in San Diego, CA
ML Seasons: 14

Texas

Overall Statistics

	G	AB	R	H	D	T	HR	RBI	SB	BB	SO	Avg	OBP	Slg
1999	144	566	105	155	20	7	6	45	16	83	79	.274	.363	.366
Career	1289	4406	676	1142	170	33	34	413	180	585	654	.259	.345	.336

Where He Hits the Ball

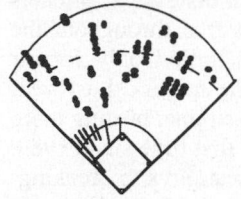 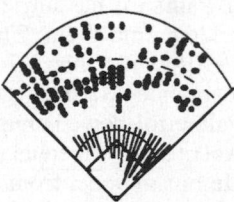

Vs. LHP   **Vs. RHP**

1999 Situational Stats

	AB	H	HR	RBI	Avg		AB	H	HR	RBI	Avg
Home	279	85	2	26	.305	LHP	104	17	1	4	.163
Road	287	70	4	19	.244	RHP	462	138	5	41	.299
First Half	289	79	4	22	.273	Sc Pos	126	31	0	38	.246
Scnd Half	277	76	2	23	.274	Clutch	65	16	1	9	.246

1999 Rankings (American League)

- 2nd in highest percentage of pitches taken (64.9)
- 3rd in batting average on an 0-2 count (.360)
- 4th in lowest slugging percentage
- 5th in lowest batting average on the road
- 6th in fielding percentage at second base (.983)
- 7th in errors at second base (12)
- 8th in lowest HR frequency (94.3 ABs per HR)
- 9th in triples and lowest stolen-base percentage (66.7)
- 10th in sacrifice bunts (9)
- Led the Rangers in batting average on an 0-2 count (.360), on-base percentage for a leadoff hitter (.363), bunts in play (16), highest percentage of pitches taken (64.9), triples and sacrifice bunts (9)

Rafael Palmeiro

1999 Season

Five years after awkward negotiations forced him out of Texas, Rafael Palmeiro returned as an even better hitter than the guy who went away. Signed to a five-year, $45 million contract as a free agent, he merged the line-drive hitting of his youth with his midcareer power surge to become a truly wondrous force. He finished August with a shot at the Triple Crown and ended the year with totals worthy of MVP consideration. Palmeiro did this all after having two knee surgeries in the spring. His play in the field was limited, but he had no trouble making the transition to DH. He also provided leadership in the clubhouse.

Hitting

If Palmeiro has any holes in his swing, pitchers seldom find them. That was true throughout the 1990s, when his 1,747 hits trailed only former teammate Mark Grace in the majors. Last year Palmeiro showed unusual discipline, posting more walks than strikeouts for the first time since 1989. He hits anyone, from high-heat guys to breaking-ball pitchers. He's one of the American League's few true pull hitters, always looking to jerk a pitch toward Texas' short porch in right field. Palmeiro set a club record with 28 home runs at The Ballpark in Arlington.

Baserunning & Defense

In an utter travesty, Palmeiro somehow won his third consecutive Gold Glove despite being limited to 28 games at first base in 1999. He'll have to prove himself if he returns to the field on a full-time basis. He does a good job scooping throws but never has had much range at first. Palmeiro's mobility is likely to be limited by a knee brace, but he should regain some of the speed he lost last year.

2000 Outlook

The only question is whether Palmeiro will play first base or DH for the Rangers. Either way, it should be another big offensive year for the prodigal son. Palmeiro has averaged 41 home runs over the last five years, and could be ready to make a run at 50.

Position: DH/1B
Bats: L **Throws:** L
Ht: 6' 0" **Wt:** 190

Opening Day Age: 35
Born: 9/24/64 in Havana, Cuba
ML Seasons: 14
Pronunciation: pall-MARE-oh
Nickname: Raffy

Overall Statistics

	G	AB	R	H	D	T	HR	RBI	SB	BB	SO	Avg	OBP	Slg
1999	158	565	96	183	30	1	47	148	2	97	69	.324	.420	.630
Career	1940	7281	1157	2158	426	33	361	1227	86	832	906	.296	.369	.513

Where He Hits the Ball

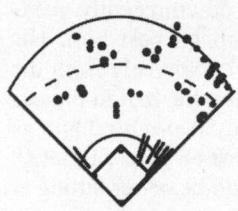
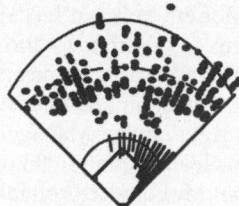

Vs. LHP   **Vs. RHP**

1999 Situational Stats

	AB	H	HR	RBI	Avg		AB	H	HR	RBI	Avg
Home	271	88	28	83	.325	LHP	146	40	11	40	.274
Road	294	95	19	65	.323	RHP	419	143	36	108	.341
First Half	310	110	22	76	.355	Sc Pos	162	58	11	98	.358
Scnd Half	255	73	25	72	.286	Clutch	75	31	8	27	.413

1999 Rankings (American League)

- 1st in batting average in the clutch, slugging percentage vs. righthanded pitchers (.656) and lowest groundball/flyball ratio (0.6)
- 2nd in slugging percentage, home runs, total bases (356) and RBI
- 3rd in HR frequency (12.0 ABs per HR)
- Led the Rangers in slugging percentage, on-base percentage, HR frequency (12.0 ABs per HR), batting average with runners in scoring position, batting average in the clutch, batting average vs. righthanded pitchers, slugging percentage vs. righthanded pitchers (.656), on-base percentage vs. righthanded pitchers (.444), home runs, total bases (356), RBI, walks, intentional walks (14), times on base (283) and games played

Ivan Rodriguez

Position: C
Bats: R **Throws:** R
Ht: 5' 9" **Wt:** 205

Opening Day Age: 28
Born: 11/30/71 in Vega Baja, Puerto Rico
ML Seasons: 9
Nickname: Pudge

Texas

1999 Season

Few catchers can match the all-around season Ivan Rodriguez had in 1999, when he won the American League Most Valuable Player Award. While hitting for the highest average by an AL catcher since Bill Dickey batted .362 in 1936, Rodriguez became the first Junior Circuit backstop to have 30 homers, 100 runs and 100 RBI in the same season. He also stole 25 bases, just nine fewer than he permitted behind the plate.

Hitting

Rodriguez has a short, quick swing that allows him to be a dangerous hitter despite terrible strike-zone judgment. He not only swings at pitches he should lay off, especially those low and outside, but also sprays them around the park. He somehow gets the bat on some really bad pitches, hitting into a ton of double plays. He grounded into 31 last year, the most in the AL in 15 years. Rodriguez' home-run total was higher than expected but no fluke. He had raised the bar for three consecutive years, though he never before had topped 21.

Baserunning & Defense

Only the boldest managers and basestealers challenge Rodriguez' arm, which has earned him eight consecutive Gold Gloves. While he threw out 53 percent of runners attempting to steal last year, former Detroit manager Larry Parrish said Rodriguez could have gunned down 90 percent if the Texas pitching staff wasn't unusually slow to the plate. His ability to make snap throws behind baserunners forces them to be cautious and cuts down the number of extra bases taken against the Rangers. Rodriguez eliminated the one weakness in his game last season, allowing only one passed ball. He's unusually quick on the bases for a catcher, but gets overaggressive and runs into too many outs.

2000 Outlook

Rodriguez has tremendous wear on his 28-year-old body, but the Rangers believe he was fresher last September because he finally stopped playing winter ball. He'll have a hard time improving on his 1999 performance, but once again should give Texas the most complete catcher in the game.

Overall Statistics

	G	AB	R	H	D	T	HR	RBI	SB	BB	SO	Avg	OBP	Slg
1999	144	600	116	199	29	1	35	113	25	24	64	.332	.356	.558
Career	1169	4443	649	1333	261	20	144	621	60	237	571	.300	.337	.465

Where He Hits the Ball

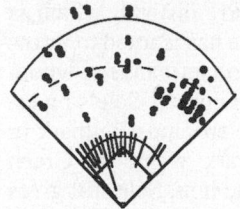 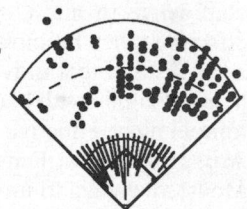

Vs. LHP   **Vs. RHP**

1999 Situational Stats

	AB	H	HR	RBI	Avg			AB	H	HR	RBI	Avg
Home	305	109	12	58	.357		LHP	114	37	6	20	.325
Road	295	90	23	55	.305		RHP	486	162	29	93	.333
First Half	302	89	15	49	.295		Sc Pos	164	50	10	79	.305
Scnd Half	298	110	20	64	.369		Clutch	81	23	7	13	.284

1999 Rankings (American League)

- 1st in highest percentage of runners caught stealing as a catcher (52.8), GDPs (32) and lowest percentage of pitches taken (40.9)
- 3rd in caught stealing (12)
- Led the Rangers in batting average with two strikes (.258), batting average, at-bats, runs scored, hits, singles, caught stealing (12), GDPs (32) and batting average at home
- Led AL catchers in slugging percentage, HR frequency (17.1 ABs per HR), highest groundball/flyball ratio (2.0), stolen-base percentage (67.6), batting average vs. righthanded pitchers, batting average on an 0-2 count (.259), slugging percentage vs. righthanded pitchers (.570) and batting average with two strikes (.258)

Aaron Sele

1999 Season

While the Red Sox have gone to the playoffs two years in a row since foolishly trading Aaron Sele, they might have gone farther if they had held on to him. He has come into his own since moving to Texas. Only Pedro Martinez can top Sele's total of 37 victories in 1998-99. He started slowly last season but finished strong, going 10-3, 4.08 after the All-Star break. The Rangers deserve some credit for his success, however, averaging 7.5 runs in his starts last year.

Pitching

An overhand curveball is Sele's calling card, but it's hardly the only reason he has pitched well with the Rangers. Every year Sele seems to gain more confidence in his 87-89 MPH fastball, which is effective when he spots it. He has learned to throw a cut fastball that moves in on lefthanders, whom he also battles with backdoor curves. Sele's repertoire is more effective at the spacious Ballpark in Arlington than at Fenway Park, where the Green Monster seemed to intimidate him. Sele still gives up a lot of hits but does a good job minimizing the damage. He ranked third in the American League in strikeouts in 1999.

Defense

Sele does an average job fielding his position. He moves fairly well for a big man but has slow reactions on comebackers. Sele will miss Ivan Rodriguez if he leaves Texas, as he's slow to the plate and lacks a strong pickoff move.

2000 Outlook

In a weak year for free agents, Sele was the cream of the pitching class. He seemed wise to turn down attempts by the Rangers to sign him to an extension, preferring to take his chances in a market bigger in demand than supply. Texas may be able to re-sign him after trading Juan Gonzalez and losing Todd Zeile.

Position: SP
Bats: R **Throws:** R
Ht: 6' 5" **Wt:** 220

Opening Day Age: 29
Born: 6/25/70 in Golden Valley, NM
ML Seasons: 7
Pronunciation: SEE-lee

Overall Statistics

	W	L	Pct.	ERA	G	GS	Sv	IP	H	BB	SO	HR	Ratio
1999	18	9	.667	4.79	33	33	0	205.0	244	70	186	21	1.53
Career	75	53	.586	4.45	174	174	0	1039.2	1143	423	831	95	1.51

How Often He Throws Strikes

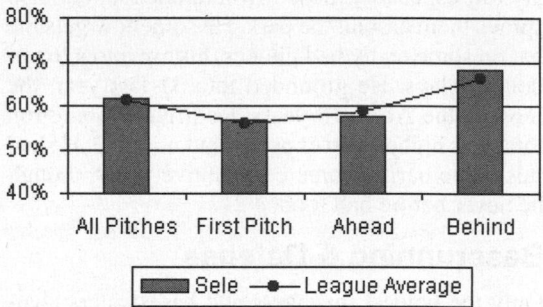

1999 Situational Stats

	W	L	ERA	Sv	IP		AB	H	HR	RBI	Avg
Home	11	5	4.69	0	124.2	LHB	399	114	11	56	.286
Road	7	4	4.93	0	80.1	RHB	435	130	10	48	.299
First Half	8	6	5.51	0	101.1	Sc Pos	220	57	6	75	.259
Scnd Half	10	3	4.08	0	103.2	Clutch	22	7	0	5	.318

1999 Rankings (American League)

- 2nd in wins, shutouts (2) and hits allowed
- 3rd in hit batsmen (12), strikeouts, highest groundball/flyball ratio allowed (1.9) and most run support per nine innings (7.5)
- Led the Rangers in ERA, wins, shutouts (2), hits allowed, hit batsmen (12), strikeouts, winning percentage, highest strikeout/walk ratio (2.7), lowest slugging percentage allowed (.447), highest groundball/flyball ratio allowed (1.9), fewest pitches thrown per batter (3.76), most run support per nine innings (7.5), most strikeouts per nine innings (8.2), fewest walks per nine innings (3.1), ERA at home and fewest home runs allowed per nine innings (.92)

Lee Stevens

Position: 1B
Bats: L **Throws:** L
Ht: 6' 4" **Wt:** 235

Opening Day Age: 32
Born: 7/10/67 in Kansas City, MO
ML Seasons: 7

1999 Season

When Mike Simms tore his Achilles tendon in spring training, Texas GM Doug Melvin looked for another righthanded-hitting platoon partner for Lee Stevens. But Stevens made that concern moot, working with hitting coach Rudy Jaramillo to improve his approach against lefthanders, who owned him in 1998. Stevens wound up hitting .304 against southpaws and set career highs in just about every category. Injuries to Rafael Palmeiro forced Stevens to move from first base to DH, and he excelled in the field.

Hitting

Stevens is tremendously streaky. When he's on, he's a low-ball hitter with power to all fields. When he's off, he gets himself out by swinging at pitches in the dirt. He especially chases splitters out of the strike zone. He strikes out too much, but can drive the ball all over the park when he makes contact. Stevens has a knack for preparing well in spring training and then coming out swinging in April. He hit .354 with eight homers in the first month last season, and 21 of his 68 longballs during the last five season have come in April.

Baserunning & Defense

Stevens always has been a good first baseman, but he played better than ever in the field, perhaps because he was out there almost every day. He has good range and soft hands, along with perhaps the best arm among American League first baseman. He's especially good at starting double plays. Stevens also can play the corner positions in the outfield without hurting his team. The one consistent downside with him is his lack of speed.

2000 Outlook

While the Rangers have been delighted with Stevens since bringing him back from Japan, he no longer is a bargain. Performance and arbitration have sent his salary climbing, and he'd pull in more in arbitration this winter than Texas wants to pay a DH. While the trade of Juan Gonzalez provided some financial relief, Stevens could be another victim of owner Tom Hicks' desire to keep the payroll at about $70 million.

Overall Statistics

	G	AB	R	H	D	T	HR	RBI	SB	BB	SO	Avg	OBP	Slg
1999	146	517	76	146	31	1	24	81	2	52	132	.282	.344	.485
Career	621	1983	253	522	110	10	82	304	6	169	481	.263	.319	.453

Where He Hits the Ball

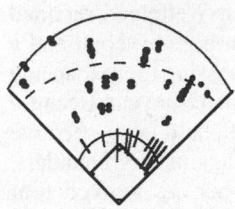
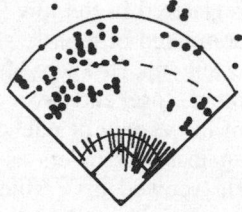

Vs. LHP   **Vs. RHP**

1999 Situational Stats

	AB	H	HR	RBI	Avg		AB	H	HR	RBI	Avg
Home	269	74	10	38	.275	LHP	102	31	4	23	.304
Road	248	72	14	43	.290	RHP	415	115	20	58	.277
First Half	270	77	14	48	.285	Sc Pos	127	32	3	51	.252
Scnd Half	247	69	10	33	.279	Clutch	69	18	4	16	.261

1999 Rankings (American League)

- 5th in fielding percentage at first base (.994)
- 6th in errors at first base (8)
- 7th in batting average on a 3-1 count (.643) and strikeouts
- 9th in GDPs (19)
- 10th in intentional walks (10)
- Led the Rangers in strikeouts
- Led AL first basemen in batting average on a 3-1 count (.643) and GDPs (19)

John Wetteland

1999 Season

John Wetteland proved his elite status last year, putting together an All-Star season despite not being 100 percent. Offseason elbow surgery and a spring-training ankle injury robbed Wetteland of his normal velocity, but he adjusted well enough to set a Texas record with 43 saves. His ERA was 4.89 in late July, but he brought it down by more than a run before season's end. He converted 17 straight chances as the Rangers rolled to the American League West title.

Pitching

Wetteland always has had quality pitches to complement his fastball, and he needed them last year. Instead of its usual 96 MPH, his heater more often registered in the low 90s. But Wetteland retained command of a nasty sinker, a big curveball and a changeup. He keeps hitters guessing more than any other closer and never more than last year. Because of his variety of pitches, Wetteland is as effective against lefthanders as he is against righthanders. He showed his resiliency when he worked four games in three days last September.

Defense

Wetteland is a poor fielder. He cost himself a couple of games with misplays in July. Like most Rangers pitchers, he has become lazy while working with Ivan Rodriguez. Wetteland is slow to the plate and does a poor job of keeping runners close, but with Rodriguez behind the plate few steals are attempted.

2000 Outlook

Barring injury, Wetteland will become the Rangers' all-time save leader before the All-Star break. He has 116 saves in three years, 18 short of Jeff Russell's club record. Wetteland is a good bet for his fifth 40-plus save season, a feat accomplished only by Dennis Eckersley. Wetteland's four-year contract with the Rangers expires after this season. Their interest in re-signing him will depend on the development of Francisco Cordero, a product of the Juan Gonzalez trade who they believe will be their future closer.

Position: RP
Bats: R **Throws:** R
Ht: 6' 2" **Wt:** 215

Opening Day Age: 33
Born: 8/21/66 in San Mateo, CA
ML Seasons: 11
Pronunciation: WET-land

Overall Statistics

	W	L	Pct.	ERA	G	GS	Sv	IP	H	BB	SO	HR	Ratio
1999	4	4	.500	3.68	62	0	43	66.0	67	19	60	9	1.30
Career	42	40	.512	2.82	556	17	296	705.0	549	228	751	63	1.10

How Often He Throws Strikes

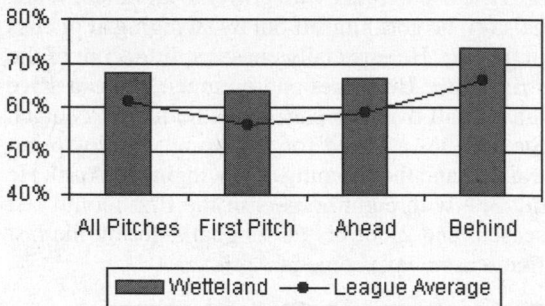

Wetteland —●— League Average

1999 Situational Stats

	W	L	ERA	Sv	IP		AB	H	HR	RBI	Avg
Home	3	3	4.41	23	34.2	LHB	136	36	4	16	.265
Road	1	1	2.87	20	31.1	RHB	120	31	5	14	.258
First Half	2	3	3.96	26	36.1	Sc Pos	63	13	0	18	.206
Scnd Half	2	1	3.34	17	29.2	Clutch	179	43	6	22	.240

1999 Rankings (American League)

- 1st in save opportunities (50)
- 2nd in saves
- 4th in blown saves (7)
- 6th in games finished (59) and save percentage (86.0)
- Led the Rangers in saves, games finished (59), save opportunities (50), save percentage (86.0), blown saves (7) and most strikeouts per nine innings in relief (8.2)

Todd Zeile

Position: 3B
Bats: R **Throws:** R
Ht: 6' 1" **Wt:** 200

Opening Day Age: 34
Born: 9/9/65 in Van Nuys, CA
ML Seasons: 11
Pronunciation: ZEAL

1999 Season

During a trading spree at midseason in 1998, Todd Zeile was one of three veterans acquired by the Rangers. Seen as a stopgap necessitated by the trading of Fernando Tatis, Zeile has contributed more to the Rangers than the other two players, Royce Clayton and Todd Stottlemyre. Zeile gave manager Johnny Oates a dangerous hitter to put behind Rafael Palmeiro, helping Palmeiro get pitches to hit. Zeile finished 1999 with his most RBI in six years and has helped Texas win consecutive American League West titles.

Hitting

Zeile is about as streaky as they come. When he's locked in, he's a tough out. But if he's out of sync, he'll get himself out by taking strikes and chasing balls. Zeile seems to become especially focused in big situations, not only hitting .301 with men in scoring position last year, but also going 13-for-24 with the bases loaded, including two grand slams. His swing can get long, but he works counts and takes advantage of hanging breaking pitches.

Baserunning & Defense

On a Rangers team full of slow runners, Zeile would have a hard time beating anyone in a sprint. He often has trouble scoring from second base on singles and goes from first to third only on hits to right field. Zeile is limited defensively. He makes the spectacular play on occasion at third base, but it was no fluke that he committed the most errors by an AL third baseman (25) last year. He figures to be adequate at first base, where he'll play in 2000.

2000 Outlook

The Rangers hoped to re-sign Zeile after his contract expired, offering him a three-year deal worth $16 million. He accepted the deal, then stunned Texas hours later when he took a three-year, $18 million contract from the Mets, who will use him to replace John Olerud at first base. Unless Texas signs a free agent, prospect Mike Lamb might jump from Double-A to the majors.

Overall Statistics

	G	AB	R	H	D	T	HR	RBI	SB	BB	SO	Avg	OBP	Slg
1999	156	588	80	172	41	1	24	98	1	56	94	.293	.354	.488
Career	1473	5345	722	1430	287	17	183	805	47	654	863	.268	.347	.430

Where He Hits the Ball

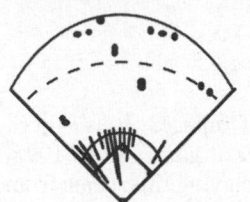
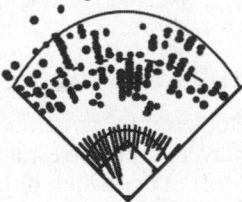

Vs. LHP   **Vs. RHP**

1999 Situational Stats

	AB	H	HR	RBI	Avg		AB	H	HR	RBI	Avg
Home	297	84	13	51	.283	LHP	117	34	3	22	.291
Road	291	88	11	47	.302	RHP	471	138	21	76	.293
First Half	316	90	11	47	.285	Sc Pos	173	52	7	80	.301
Scnd Half	272	82	13	51	.301	Clutch	76	20	3	10	.263

1999 Rankings (American League)

- 1st in errors at third base (25)
- 2nd in batting average with the bases loaded (.542)
- 3rd in lowest fielding percentage at third base (.940)
- 5th in doubles
- 8th in GDPs (20)
- Led the Rangers in batting average with the bases loaded (.542) and doubles
- Led AL third basemen in batting average with the bases loaded (.542), slugging percentage vs. righthanded pitchers (.503), on-base percentage vs. lefthanded pitchers (.378), highest percentage of pitches taken (61.7), doubles, GDPs (20), pitches seen (2,656) and games played (156)

Luis Alicea

Position: 2B/3B
Bats: B **Throws:** R
Ht: 5' 9" **Wt:** 176

Opening Day Age: 34
Born: 7/29/65 in
Santurce, Puerto Rico
ML Seasons: 10
Pronunciation:
ah-la-SAY-ya

Overall Statistics

	G	AB	R	H	D	T	HR	RBI	SB	BB	SO	Avg	OBP	Slg
1999	68	164	33	33	10	0	3	17	2	28	32	.201	.316	.317
Career	995	2807	394	712	140	39	36	304	70	386	459	.254	.348	.370

1999 Situational Stats

	AB	H	HR	RBI	Avg		AB	H	HR	RBI	Avg
Home	62	10	0	4	.161	LHP	62	18	1	5	.290
Road	102	23	3	13	.225	RHP	102	15	2	12	.147
First Half	97	16	0	6	.165	Sc Pos	52	6	0	12	.115
Scnd Half	67	17	3	11	.254	Clutch	22	2	1	3	.091

1999 Season

Bothered by wrist and calf injuries, Luis Alicea played in his fewest number of games since 1994. Most of the switch-hitter's playing time came from the right side of the plate in a second-base platoon with Mark McLemore. Alicea's batting average dropped 73 points from the year before.

Hitting, Baserunning & Defense

Alicea was much better hitting righthanded than lefthanded in 1999. He was hardly feared from either side. As his playing time went down, he chased more pitches. He was much easier to strike out last season than usual, and some scouts said Alicea had lost bat speed. His injuries cost him some range, which is his best asset defensively. Alicea is erratic and has trouble turning the double play. He can play third base and the outfield, but has a below-average arm. He stole 22 bases in 1997 but has just six in the last two years combined.

2000 Outlook

Alicea re-signed with the Rangers as a free agent for one year and $750,000. McLemore's departure makes Alicea the leading candidate to start at second base, though trade acquisition Frank Catalanotto or free-agent pickup Edwin Diaz could figure into the mix if Alicea slumps again.

John Burkett

Position: SP
Bats: R **Throws:** R
Ht: 6' 3" **Wt:** 215

Opening Day Age: 35
Born: 11/28/64 in New
Brighton, PA
ML Seasons: 11
Pronunciation: BURK-it

Overall Statistics

	W	L	Pct.	ERA	G	GS	Sv	IP	H	BB	SO	HR	Ratio
1999	9	8	.529	5.62	30	25	0	147.1	184	46	96	18	1.56
Career	119	101	.541	4.31	319	308	1	1940.0	2116	482	1238	182	1.34

1999 Situational Stats

	W	L	ERA	Sv	IP		AB	H	HR	RBI	Avg
Home	6	4	7.64	0	68.1	LHB	307	86	7	31	.280
Road	3	4	3.87	0	79.0	RHB	292	98	11	55	.336
First Half	2	4	5.65	0	63.2	Sc Pos	133	45	6	65	.338
Scnd Half	7	4	5.59	0	83.2	Clutch	12	5	0	1	.417

1999 Season

John Burkett was bothered by bursitis in his right shoulder early in the season and lost his spot in the Rangers' starting rotation in May. He pitched better after getting back into the rotation in late June and his first winning season since 1993, but nevertheless, it was the worst of his 10-year career.

Pitching & Defense

Never a hard thrower, Burkett now has games when he can't hit 85 MPH with his fastball. He compensates with a slow curve that's a good pitch when he gets it over. When he pitched well late in the year, he had enough arm strength to use his fastball to set up his changeup. He always throws strikes but is very hittable. Burkett never has been a good fielder. He's slow to the plate and to first base, a flaw that might present problems when someone other than Ivan Rodriguez is catching him.

2000 Outlook

Texas declined Burkett's $4.2 million option for 2000 and didn't offer him arbitration, so he won't be back. His relatively strong finish (9-5, 4.82 over his last 19 starts) should be enough to attract some attention.

Tim Crabtree

Position: RP
Bats: R **Throws:** R
Ht: 6' 4" **Wt:** 220

Opening Day Age: 30
Born: 10/13/69 in Jackson, MI
ML Seasons: 5

Overall Statistics

	W	L	Pct.	ERA	G	GS	Sv	IP	H	BB	SO	HR	Ratio
1999	5	1	.833	3.46	68	0	0	65.0	71	18	54	4	1.37
Career	19	10	.655	3.75	253	0	3	290.1	311	105	218	19	1.43

1999 Situational Stats

	W	L	ERA	Sv	IP		AB	H	HR	RBI	Avg
Home	3	1	3.40	0	39.2	LHB	98	22	1	10	.224
Road	2	0	3.55	0	25.1	RHB	156	49	3	27	.314
First Half	4	1	3.62	0	32.1	Sc Pos	88	27	1	34	.307
Scnd Half	1	0	3.31	0	32.2	Clutch	95	31	2	15	.326

1999 Season

For the second year in a row, Tim Crabtree was a valuable member of the Texas bullpen. He served as the primary setup man for John Wetteland early in the season, when manager Johnny Oates was easing in rookie Jeff Zimmerman, and again later in the season after Zimmerman cooled off. Crabtree strung together 16 consecutive scoreless appearances in April and May, which was the club record until Zimmerman outdid him in June and July.

Pitching & Defense

Few pitchers throw harder than Crabtree, who can reach 98 MPH. He complements his fastball with a hard slider but doesn't change speeds a lot. His fastball sinks when he takes something off it, and he also can blow it by hitters up in the strike zone. He needs to pitch inside more to righthanders. For a reliever, Crabtree isn't particularly resilient. He's a good fielder and improved his pickoff move last year.

2000 Outlook

Crabtree will open the season as the third righthander in the Rangers bullpen. If Francisco Cordero, acquired in the Juan Gonzalez trade, is as good as Texas believes he will be, Crabtree could become trade bait by midseason.

Jeff Fassero

Position: SP/RP
Bats: L **Throws:** L
Ht: 6' 1" **Wt:** 195

Opening Day Age: 37
Born: 1/5/63 in Springfield, IL
ML Seasons: 9
Pronunciation: fuh-SAIR-oh

Overall Statistics

	W	L	Pct.	ERA	G	GS	Sv	IP	H	BB	SO	HR	Ratio
1999	5	14	.263	7.20	37	27	0	156.1	208	83	114	35	1.86
Career	92	83	.526	3.81	366	194	10	1465.1	1439	507	1229	146	1.33

1999 Situational Stats

	W	L	ERA	Sv	IP		AB	H	HR	RBI	Avg
Home	3	6	6.81	0	76.2	LHB	140	38	3	26	.271
Road	2	8	7.57	0	79.2	RHB	515	170	32	102	.330
First Half	4	9	6.89	0	109.2	Sc Pos	195	63	10	88	.323
Scnd Half	1	5	7.91	0	46.2	Clutch	31	8	1	6	.258

1999 Season

For the fifth time in six years, Jeff Fassero served as his team's Opening Day starter, working Seattle's opener. But that was where the similarities between 1999 and previous seasons stopped. Fassero's 7.20 ERA was the highest among pitchers with 150 innings since Jim Walkup's 7.36 in 1937. An August trade to Texas for a player to be named provided Fassero a chance to turn himself around, but he didn't pitch well enough to make the Rangers' postseason rotation.

Pitching & Defense

Fassero may have been affected by surgery to remove bone chips from his elbow after the 1998 season. He threw in the 90s for much of the year but consistently lacked command of his offspeed pitches, including his forkball. Fassero is a good fielder but can be distracted by baserunners, leading to countless pickoff throws.

2000 Outlook

Fassero gambled and lost by going to free agency. He won't get a big deal and may have to earn a job in spring training. He could be a pleasant surprise for someone, as he'll be two years removed from his surgery and should benefit from an offseason of rest.

Tom Goodwin

Position: CF
Bats: L **Throws:** R
Ht: 6' 1" **Wt:** 175

Opening Day Age: 31
Born: 7/27/68 in
Fresno, CA
ML Seasons: 9

Overall Statistics

	G	AB	R	H	D	T	HR	RBI	SB	BB	SO	Avg	OBP	Slg
1999	109	405	63	105	12	6	3	33	39	40	61	.259	.324	.341
Career	794	2602	431	714	83	23	12	172	252	241	405	.274	.338	.338

1999 Situational Stats

	AB	H	HR	RBI	Avg		AB	H	HR	RBI	Avg
Home	200	52	1	18	.260	LHP	61	16	0	4	.262
Road	205	53	2	15	.259	RHP	344	89	3	29	.259
First Half	212	51	1	12	.241	Sc Pos	94	20	1	27	.213
Scnd Half	193	54	2	21	.280	Clutch	42	11	0	2	.262

1999 Season

Tom Goodwin was leading the American League in stolen bases when he pulled a hip flexor muscle in June, and he never recovered. He opened the year as Texas' leadoff man but finished it in the No. 9 spot as his on-base percentage dropped 54 points from his solid 1998 season.

Hitting, Baserunning & Defense

Goodwin is a slap hitter who can't catch up to good fastballs. He makes a living off loopers and groundballs to the left side. Goodwin is a good bunter but has a hard time bunting for hits because of the way teams play him. Despite having the most steals in the majors over the last five years, Goodwin is more of a Herb Washington than a Lou Brock. He steals bases with sheer speed, not the ability to get good jumps. He has very good range in center field but his arm is brutal.

2000 Outlook

Texas let Goodwin leave as a free agent so it could hand center field to Ruben Mateo, one of the game's best prospects. Goodwin hooked up with the Rockies, who gave him a three-year contract worth $10.75 million.

Roberto Kelly

Position: CF/RF/LF
Bats: R **Throws:** R
Ht: 6' 2" **Wt:** 198

Opening Day Age: 35
Born: 10/1/64 in
Panama City, Panama
ML Seasons: 13
Nickname: Gray

Overall Statistics

	G	AB	R	H	D	T	HR	RBI	SB	BB	SO	Avg	OBP	Slg
1999	87	290	41	87	17	1	8	37	6	21	57	.300	.355	.448
Career	1327	4772	683	1387	240	30	123	584	235	316	856	.291	.338	.431

1999 Situational Stats

	AB	H	HR	RBI	Avg		AB	H	HR	RBI	Avg
Home	145	47	4	16	.324	LHP	95	34	2	14	.358
Road	145	40	4	21	.276	RHP	195	53	6	23	.272
First Half	156	49	4	24	.314	Sc Pos	79	18	2	28	.228
Scnd Half	134	38	4	13	.284	Clutch	45	13	1	8	.289

1999 Season

Few fourth outfielders do a better job than Roberto Kelly. He reached .300 for the third time in the last four years while playing all three outfield positions well. Kelly got most of his playing time in center field, where his performance against lefthanders forced manager Johnny Oates to consider platooning him with Tom Goodwin.

Hitting, Baserunning & Defense

Kelly's free-swinging style limits his effectiveness. He managed only 29 walks in two years with the Rangers. But he's a dangerous hitter, especially against lefties. He has the ability to turn on inside pitches and likes the ball down. Kelly makes the plays in all three outfield spots, with center field perhaps his best position. His arm is fair at best and has been slipping, which hurts him as a right fielder. He's an average baserunner.

2000 Outlook

After Kelly became a free agent, the Rangers found a new fourth outfielder by trading minor league righthanders Brandon Knight and Sam Marsonek to the Yankees for Chad Curtis. Kelly would be a good pickup for any team. He understands the mental routine needed to stay sharp when playing two or three times a week.

Esteban Loaiza

Position: SP/RP
Bats: R **Throws:** R
Ht: 6' 3" **Wt:** 205

Opening Day Age: 28
Born: 12/31/71 in Tijuana, Mexico
ML Seasons: 5
Pronunciation: low-EYE-zuh

Overall Statistics

	W	L	Pct.	ERA	G	GS	Sv	IP	H	BB	SO	HR	Ratio
1999	9	5	.643	4.56	30	15	0	120.1	128	40	77	10	1.40
Career	39	39	.500	4.76	140	116	0	713.0	811	222	424	87	1.45

1999 Situational Stats

	W	L	ERA	Sv	IP		AB	H	HR	RBI	Avg
Home	6	2	4.54	0	71.1	LHB	214	55	1	25	.257
Road	3	3	4.59	0	49.0	RHB	252	73	9	32	.290
First Half	0	1	7.31	0	28.1	Sc Pos	136	38	3	48	.279
Scnd Half	9	4	3.72	0	92.0	Clutch	25	13	1	5	.520

1999 Season

Esteban Loaiza lost Texas' fifth starter's job to journeyman Mike Morgan in spring training and broke his right hand when he slammed it in a car door in May. Those two events provided some shock therapy that resulted in a more focused Loaiza emerging in the second half, when he was one of the Rangers' two best starters.

Pitching & Defense

Loaiza throws easy heat, with a fastball that was consistently around 95 MPH in August and September. He also has a hard slider and a changeup. Control rarely is a problem. In the past, Loaiza lacked the ability to pitch in trouble. A bloop here, a bleeder there, and little hits would snowball into big innings. But he didn't surrender nearly as many big innings last year. Loaiza is an average fielder who does a good job holding runners on base.

2000 Outlook

The Rangers hope Loaiza can retain the confidence he gained last year, when his 3.83 ERA as a starter was the best on the Rangers. If not, they'll continue to regret parting with Warren Morris to get Loaiza in a 1998 trade.

Mike Munoz

Position: RP
Bats: L **Throws:** L
Ht: 6' 2" **Wt:** 198

Opening Day Age: 34
Born: 7/12/65 in Baldwin Park, CA
ML Seasons: 11
Pronunciation: MOON-yohz

Overall Statistics

	W	L	Pct.	ERA	G	GS	Sv	IP	H	BB	SO	HR	Ratio
1999	2	1	.667	3.93	56	0	1	52.2	52	18	27	5	1.33
Career	18	19	.486	5.10	446	0	11	360.1	397	171	239	33	1.58

1999 Situational Stats

	W	L	ERA	Sv	IP		AB	H	HR	RBI	Avg
Home	1	1	3.77	0	28.2	LHB	100	29	3	17	.290
Road	1	0	4.13	1	24.0	RHB	98	23	2	8	.235
First Half	1	0	3.41	1	34.1	Sc Pos	50	13	2	22	.260
Scnd Half	1	1	4.91	0	18.1	Clutch	36	9	1	6	.250

1999 Season

Cyberspace wasn't kind to Mike Munoz. The lefty reliever helped Texas win the American League West but wasn't available for the playoffs after dropping a computer monitor on his right foot. It was a disappointing end to a solid season for Munoz, whose 3.93 ERA was his lowest since 1994.

Pitching & Defense

Munoz is a lefty specialist who spots an underwhelming fastball and a changeup to keep hitters off balance. He throws the change a lot against righthanders, and held them to a .235 batting average in 1999. Though he worked 3.1 innings in one outing last year, there are questions about his durability. Munoz is an above-average fielder who isn't afraid to cut down the lead runner. He holds runners well.

2000 Outlook

Munoz became a free agent and re-signed with Texas for one year and $750,000, plus a club option for 2001. The preliminary plan is to have him work alongside fellow southpaws Mike Venafro and Matt Perisho in a bullpen built around righthanded fireballers.

Mike Venafro

Position: RP
Bats: L **Throws:** L
Ht: 5'10" **Wt:** 180

Opening Day Age: 26
Born: 8/2/73 in Takoma Park, MD
ML Seasons: 1
Pronunciation: VEN-ah-froh

Overall Statistics

	W	L	Pct.	ERA	G	GS	Sv	IP	H	BB	SO	HR	Ratio
1999	3	2	.600	3.29	65	0	0	68.1	63	22	37	4	1.24
Career	3	2	.600	3.29	65	0	0	68.1	63	22	37	4	1.24

1999 Situational Stats

	W	L	ERA	Sv	IP		AB	H	HR	RBI	Avg
Home	1	1	3.22	0	36.1	LHB	114	22	1	14	.193
Road	2	1	3.38	0	32.0	RHB	137	41	3	26	.299
First Half	2	1	2.84	0	38.0	Sc Pos	89	29	2	38	.326
Scnd Half	1	1	3.86	0	30.1	Clutch	57	16	1	12	.281

1999 Season

Promoted from Triple-A on April 22, Mike Venafro eventually became Texas' top southpaw setup man. The former 29th-round draft choice racked up the second-most appearances on the staff while finishing with the lowest ERA among American League lefthanded relievers.

Pitching & Defense

At 5-foot-10, Venafro doesn't intimidate anyone. But his fastball is sneaky quick, hitting 90 MPH with regularity. His curveball and changeup are both quality pitches, making him especially tough on lefthanders. Just ask Ken Griffey Jr., who fanned twice against Venafro, once with the bases loaded. Venafro showed his durability by making 71 appearances overall, including six in Triple-A. He's an excellent athlete who fields his position well. His pickoff move shuts down the running game.

2000 Outlook

Like fellow rookie reliever Jeff Zimmerman, Venafro tired late in the season. He shouldn't have that problem the second time around. Venafro once again will serve as the last lefty used out of the bullpen. His workload could decrease if the Rangers keep two other southpaws in their bullpen, which is the tentative plan.

Jeff Zimmerman

Surprise

Position: RP
Bats: R **Throws:** R
Ht: 6' 1" **Wt:** 200

Opening Day Age: 27
Born: 8/9/72 in Kelowna, Canada
ML Seasons: 1

Overall Statistics

	W	L	Pct.	ERA	G	GS	Sv	IP	H	BB	SO	HR	Ratio
1999	9	3	.750	2.36	65	0	3	87.2	50	23	67	9	0.83
Career	9	3	.750	2.36	65	0	3	87.2	50	23	67	9	0.83

1999 Situational Stats

	W	L	ERA	Sv	IP		AB	H	HR	RBI	Avg
Home	5	1	2.28	2	43.1	LHB	146	23	6	13	.158
Road	4	2	2.44	1	44.1	RHB	156	27	3	19	.173
First Half	8	0	0.86	1	52.1	Sc Pos	72	13	0	20	.181
Scnd Half	1	3	4.58	2	35.1	Clutch	170	30	4	19	.176

1999 Season

After beginning his pro career in France and the independent Northern League, Jeff Zimmerman showed that all he needed was an opportunity. He earned a trip to the All-Star Game in his rookie season, throwing nothing but zeroes for much of the summer. He set a Rangers record with 26 straight scoreless appearances between May 25 and August 2, and his streak of 29.2 scoreless innings was the longest in the majors in 1999.

Pitching & Defense

Zimmerman combines a 93-94 MPH fastball with a devastating slider. His fastball has natural screwball action, and his slider was untouchable until he tired in the second half. He held opponents to a .166 batting average, including a .106 mark before the All-Star break. Zimmerman is average at fielding and holding runners.

2000 Outlook

The Rangers hope that a winter's rest is all Zimmerman needs to once again overpower hitters. He'll remain as the primary setup man for John Wetteland, though there are some in the organization who believe Zimmerman could be effective as a starter.

Other Texas Rangers

Mark Clark (Pos: RHP, Age: 31)

	W	L	Pct.	ERA	G	GS	Sv	IP	H	BB	SO	HR	Ratio
1999	3	7	.300	8.60	15	15	0	74.1	103	34	44	17	1.84
Career	71	66	.518	4.48	207	189	0	1202.1	1298	343	712	144	1.36

Clark was off to a terrible start when a sore elbow sidelined him in June. The elbow may have been a key factor in his poor performance, and it kept him out for the rest of the season. 2000 Outlook: B

Scarborough Green (Pos: CF, Age: 25, Bats: R)

	G	AB	R	H	D	T	HR	RBI	SB	BB	SO	Avg	OBP	Slg
1999	18	13	4	4	0	0	0	0	0	1	2	.308	.357	.308
Career	38	44	9	7	0	0	0	1	0	3	7	.159	.213	.159

Green bounced between Triple-A Oklahoma and Texas all season long. He didn't hit much in Oklahoma and didn't play much in Texas. Flight 2000 for Oklahoma City is now boarding. 2000 Outlook: C

Eric Gunderson (Pos: LHP, Age: 34)

	W	L	Pct.	ERA	G	GS	Sv	IP	H	BB	SO	HR	Ratio
1999	0	0	-	7.20	11	0	0	10.0	20	2	6	1	2.20
Career	8	10	.444	4.89	248	5	2	222.2	259	82	135	29	1.53

Gunderson has had just two decent years in the majors during the 1990s, but hey, he's lefthanded. After battling a shoulder ailment for nearly all of 1999, he's a free agent looking for a new team. 2000 Outlook: C

Jonathan Johnson (Pos: RHP, Age: 25)

	W	L	Pct.	ERA	G	GS	Sv	IP	H	BB	SO	HR	Ratio
1999	0	0	-	15.00	1	0	0	3.0	9	2	3	0	3.67
Career	0	0	-	11.05	2	1	0	7.1	14	7	6	0	2.86

This former first-round draft pick has struggled as a pro. Johnson bombed at Double-A and Triple-A in 1999, so he'll try to rebound in the spring. 2000 Outlook: C

Mike Morgan (Pos: RHP, Age: 40)

	W	L	Pct.	ERA	G	GS	Sv	IP	H	BB	SO	HR	Ratio
1999	13	10	.565	6.24	34	25	0	140.0	184	48	61	25	1.66
Career	134	180	.427	4.19	477	406	3	2598.2	2734	872	1310	251	1.39

The Rangers scored at least six runs in 13 of Morgan's 25 starts, so it's not that surprising that he won 13 games despite a 6.24 ERA. He was pulled from the rotation in August, and now he's a free agent. 2000 Outlook: C

Danny Patterson (Pos: RHP, Age: 29)

	W	L	Pct.	ERA	G	GS	Sv	IP	H	BB	SO	HR	Ratio
1999	2	0	1.000	5.67	53	0	0	60.1	77	19	43	5	1.59
Career	14	11	.560	4.26	170	0	3	200.2	221	64	150	19	1.42

After an impressive rookie season in 1997, Patterson had shoulder surgery in 1998 and hasn't been the same. He moves to Detroit courtesy of the Juan Gonzalez deal. 2000 Outlook: B

Jon Shave (Pos: SS, Age: 32, Bats: R)

	G	AB	R	H	D	T	HR	RBI	SB	BB	SO	Avg	OBP	Slg
1999	43	73	10	21	4	0	0	9	1	5	17	.288	.350	.342
Career	79	160	20	46	9	0	1	21	3	8	35	.288	.326	.363

Shave filled in on the left side of the Texas infield, and he hit adequately without power. The Rangers waived him at season's end. 2000 Outlook: B

Scott Sheldon (Pos: 3B, Age: 31, Bats: R)

	G	AB	R	H	D	T	HR	RBI	SB	BB	SO	Avg	OBP	Slg
1999	2	1	0	0	0	0	0	0	0	0	0	.000	.000	.000
Career	22	41	2	8	0	0	1	3	0	2	12	.195	.250	.268

After batting .311 with 28 homers at Triple-A Oklahoma, giving him 57 longballs there in two seasons, Sheldon was recalled in September but barely played. 2000 Outlook: C

Mike Simms (Pos: 1B, Age: 33, Bats: R)

	G	AB	R	H	D	T	HR	RBI	SB	BB	SO	Avg	OBP	Slg
1999	4	2	0	1	0	0	0	0	0	0	1	.500	.500	.500
Career	330	660	92	163	33	1	36	121	4	69	175	.247	.323	.464

Simms had a career year in 1998 as a pinch-hitter and part-time player, batting .296-16-46. He lost a chance to build on his success when a torn Achilles kept him out all year. He's signed for 2000. 2000 Outlook: B

Gregg Zaun (Pos: C, Age: 28, Bats: B)

	G	AB	R	H	D	T	HR	RBI	SB	BB	SO	Avg	OBP	Slg
1999	43	93	12	23	2	1	1	12	1	10	7	.247	.314	.323
Career	307	777	90	183	38	6	13	90	9	101	111	.236	.325	.350

Zaun has backed up Charles Johnson and Ivan Rodriguez in recent years. He went to Detroit in the Juan Gonzalez deal and will back up Brad Ausmus this year. 2000 Outlook: B

Texas Rangers Minor League Prospects

Organization Overview:

Not only have the last four years seen the Rangers' first three postseason appearances in franchise history, but they've also marked a rejuvenation of the Texas farm system. Homegrown rookies Ruben Mateo, Mike Venafro and Jeff Zimmerman made contributions to the club's American League West title in 1999. Third baseman Mike Lamb and a number of pitchers could play significant roles this season. The Rangers had a strong draft in June, adding pitchers Aaron Harang, Colby Lewis and Nick Regilio, all of whom dominated the Rookie-level Appalachian League, and hitters Hank Blalock and Kevin Mench, both of whom topped .350 in the lower minors. They also added pitching prospects Francisco Cordero and Alan Webb via the Juan Gonzalez trade with Detroit in November. Last season represented a nice rebound from two missteps in 1998, when Texas traded Warren Morris to the Pirates and failed to sign third-round pick Barry Zito, who's now on the verge of making the Athletics.

Francisco Cordero

Position: P　　　　**Opening Day Age:** 22
Bats: R **Throws:** R　　**Born:** 8/11/77 in Santo
Ht: 6' 2" **Wt:** 200　　Domingo, Dom. Rep.

Recent Statistics

	W	L	ERA	G	GS	Sv	IP	H	R	BB	SO	HR
1999 AA Jacksnville	4	1	1.38	47	0	27	52.1	35	9	22	58	3
1999 AL Detroit	2	2	3.32	20	0	0	19.0	19	7	18	19	2

Cordero missed almost all of 1998 with a stress fracture in a bone near his pitching elbow, then made a triumphant return last year before the Tigers sent him to the Rangers in the Juan Gonzalez trade. One of the best relief prospects in the game, Cordero will join John Wetteland and Jeff Zimmerman to give the Texas bullpen three power righthanders, all with the ability to close. Cordero has two devastating pitches, a 95-97 MPH fastball that can touch 99, and a slider. He even has a good changeup, though he mostly uses it for show, and he has the composure needed to nail down a ninth-inning lead. Though Detroit still has a top-notch bullpen prospect in Matt Anderson, it will rue trading Cordero.

Doug Davis

Position: P　　　　**Opening Day Age:** 24
Bats: R **Throws:** L　　**Born:** 9/21/75 in
Ht: 6' 3" **Wt:** 185　　Sacramento, CA

Recent Statistics

	W	L	ERA	G	GS	Sv	IP	H	R	BB	SO	HR
1999 AA Tulsa	4	4	2.42	12	12	0	74.1	65	26	25	79	9
1999 AAA Oklahoma	7	0	3.00	13	11	0	78.0	77	27	31	74	4
1999 AL Texas	0	0	33.75	2	0	0	2.2	12	10	0	3	3

Though he's far from overpowering, Davis led the high Class-A Florida State League in strikeouts in 1998 be-

fore rocketing to the majors for two relief appearances in 1999. A 10th-round pick in 1996 out of the City College of San Francisco, he has three average pitches: a fastball, curveball and changeup. Davis' deceptive motion and his ability to mix his pitches have allowed him to go 33-16, 2.82 as a pro, with 454 strikeouts in 420.2 innings. He may need some more time in Triple-A, but he should be part of the Rangers staff before long.

Kelly Dransfeldt

Position: SS　　　　**Opening Day Age:** 24
Bats: R **Throws:** R　　**Born:** 4/16/75 in Joliet, IL
Ht: 6' 2" **Wt:** 195

Recent Statistics

	G	AB	R	H	D	T	HR	RBI	SB	BB	SO	Avg
1999 AAA Oklahoma	102	359	55	85	21	2	10	44	6	24	108	.237
1999 AL Texas	16	53	3	10	1	0	1	5	0	3	12	.189
1999 MLE	102	353	48	79	19	1	8	38	4	21	112	.224

Dransfeldt had a breakthrough season in 1998, batting .289 with 27 homers and 112 RBI, excellent numbers for a shortstop. Though he didn't hit with the same authority in Triple-A last year, he provided solid defense for Texas when Royce Clayton was injured in May. A 1996 fourth-round pick from the University of Michigan, Dransfeldt's best tool is his power. He has shortened his swing, though he still has some holes and isn't patient enough. Rated the Pacific Coast League's top defensive shortstop, he has a strong arm and nice range. Dransfeldt isn't set to take Clayton's job in 2000, but it's possible he could beat out Luis Alicea at second base or factor into the mix to replace the departed Todd Zeile at third.

Ryan Glynn

Position: P　　　　**Opening Day Age:** 25
Bats: R **Throws:** R　　**Born:** 11/1/74 in
Ht: 6' 3" **Wt:** 195　　Portsmouth, VA

Recent Statistics

	W	L	ERA	G	GS	Sv	IP	H	R	BB	SO	HR
1999 AAA Oklahoma	6	2	3.39	16	16	0	90.1	81	46	36	55	7
1999 AL Texas	2	4	7.24	13	10	0	54.2	71	46	35	39	10

Though he has been a pro for five seasons, Glynn doesn't have much mileage on his arm. He divided his time between the outfield and the mound at the Virginia Military Institute, before being drafted in 1995's fourth round. He continued to work toward his college degree after signing, so he didn't pitch full-time until 1997. Like most of Texas' upper-level pitching prospects, Glynn has good command of a diverse repertoire. His best pitch is his slider, and he also has a 90-92 MPH fastball, a curveball and a changeup. The Rangers envision him developing into a steady presence in the middle of a rotation, like a John Burkett in his prime. Glynn could make the Texas rotation in spring training.

Mike Lamb

Position: 3B
Bats: L **Throws:** R
Ht: 6' 1" **Wt:** 185
Opening Day Age: 24
Born: 8/9/75 in West Covina, CA

Recent Statistics

	G	AB	R	H	D	T	HR	RBI	SB	BB	SO	Avg
1998 A Charlotte	135	536	83	162	35	3	9	93	18	45	63	.302
1999 AA Tulsa	137	544	98	176	51	5	21	100	4	53	65	.324
1999 AAA Oklahoma	2	2	0	1	0	0	0	0	0	1	0	.500
1999 MLE	139	536	88	167	48	4	20	90	2	40	68	.312

Lamb has done nothing but hit since signing as a 1997 seventh-round pick out of Cal State Fullerton, and he may get the opportunity to do so in Texas after Todd Zeile stunned the club by reneging on a three-year, $16 million offer. Lamb has hit .317 as a pro and really blossomed in 1999, when he was the Rangers' minor league player of the year. His power came on, as he led the Double-A Texas League with 51 doubles and hit 21 homers, three more than in his first two seasons combined. He's solid defensively as well, and was rated the Texas League's best defensive third baseman. Lamb hit .343 in the Arizona Fall League, further convincing the Rangers that he could handle the jump from Double-A.

Corey Lee

Position: P
Bats: B **Throws:** L
Ht: 6' 2" **Wt:** 180
Opening Day Age: 25
Born: 12/26/74 in Raleigh, NC

Recent Statistics

	W	L	ERA	G	GS	Sv	IP	H	R	BB	SO	HR
1999 AA Tulsa	8	5	4.44	22	22	0	127.2	132	76	44	121	11
1999 AAA Oklahoma	3	0	2.03	4	4	0	26.2	21	6	8	25	2
1999 AL Texas	0	1	27.00	1	0	0	1.0	2	3	1	0	1

When he first reached Double-A in 1998, Lee nibbled at the plate to an extreme. He allowed hitters to bat just .206, the lowest mark among Double-A starters, but also led the Texas League with 102 walks. Though his record and ERA changed little last year, the Rangers were pleased that he changed his approach. Though Lee gave up more hits, he had more confidence in his stuff and his control was much improved. A 1996 supplemental first-round pick from North Carolina State, he gets outs with his curveball. He also throws an 88-90 MPH fastball, a slider and a changeup. After some Triple-A seasoning, Lee could join the Texas rotation.

Matt Perisho

Position: P
Bats: L **Throws:** L
Ht: 6' 0" **Wt:** 190
Opening Day Age: 24
Born: 6/8/75 in Burlington, IA

Recent Statistics

	W	L	ERA	G	GS	Sv	IP	H	R	BB	SO	HR
1999 AAA Oklahoma	15	7	4.61	27	27	0	156.1	160	86	78	150	14
1999 AL Texas	0	0	2.61	4	1	0	10.1	8	3	2	17	0

The Angels don't have many prospects, so it's inexplicable that they would have traded Perisho to the Rangers for minor league infielder Mike Bell in October 1997. Perisho had surgery to repair small tears in his labrum and rotator cuff midway through his first season in the Texas system, then bounced back last year to lead the Triple-A Pacific Coast League in victories. A 1993 third-round pick, Perisho sets up hitters with a 90-92 MPH fastball and finishes them off with a changeup. He also has an average curveball. He threw extremely well in four major league appearances last year, and the Rangers plan on using him as one of three lefties in their bullpen.

Alan Webb

Position: P
Bats: L **Throws:** L
Ht: 6' 0" **Wt:** 165
Opening Day Age: 20
Born: 9/26/79 in Las Vegas, NV

Recent Statistics

	W	L	ERA	G	GS	Sv	IP	H	R	BB	SO	HR
1998 A W Michigan	10	7	2.93	27	27	0	172.0	110	69	58	202	9
1999 AA Jacksnville	9	9	4.95	26	22	0	140.0	140	88	64	88	17

Webb may have been the least-known player in the Juan Gonzalez trade with Detroit, but he was a nice bonus. A 1997 fourth-round pick, he has grown three inches and added about 3 MPH to his fastball since signing, and those trends could continue because he's only 20. After dominating the Class-A Midwest League in his first full season, he handled a jump to a Double-A hitters' park in 1999 well, considering he was still a teenager. Webb features an outstanding curveball, a very good changeup and an 88-90 MPH fastball. He didn't challenge enough hitters last year, so a return trip to Double-A could do wonders for his confidence.

Others to Watch

First baseman **Shawn Gallagher** (23), the 1998 MVP in the high Class-A Florida State League, continued to hit for average and power in Double-A last year. He didn't endear himself to the Rangers, however, when he dislocated his left shoulder playing paintball and was sidelined for a month. . . In his first season as a full-time third baseman, **Jason Grabowski** (23) was rated the FSL's best infield arm. He also has the makings of a complete hitter. . . Righthander **Travis Hughes** (21) thrived after moving from the bullpen to the rotation in 1999, his first full pro season. Using an above-average fastball, he went 11-7, 2.81 with 150 strikeouts in 157 innings at Class-A Savannah. . . Righthander **Danny Kolb** (25) can throw in the mid-90s, but he has learned that he's more effective when he throws 92-94 MPH and lets his fastball run in on righthanders. He could make the Texas bullpen in spring training. . . First baseman **Carlos Pena** (21), a 1998 first-round pick, could become a Mark Grace with more power. Pena batted .255 with 18 homers in the spacious ballparks of the FSL, and managers named him the league's best defensive first baseman. . . **Jason Romano** (20) is the Rangers' second baseman of the future. He hit .312 with 54 extra-base hits and 34 steals in the FSL. A converted third baseman, Texas dreams of him turning into a Craig Biggio.

SkyDome

Offense

SkyDome is a fairly neutral park. It's most noticeable effects are on doubles and homers. Since 1997 in the American League, only Fenway Park has cut down more on homers. Power is muted by the long distances in the alleys, both of which extend 375 feet from the plate. Conversely, SkyDome ranks third in how much it has increased doubles. The slick artifical turf turns hard-hit liners into two-base hits. Batters benefit when the retractable roof is closed, eliminating swirling winds coming off Lake Ontario.

Defense

The artificial turf yields truer hops than grass and cuts down on errors to a degree, but it also makes it tougher for slower fielders to catch up with see-ing-eye grounders. Speedy outfielders are a must in SkyDome because balls scoot quickly through the gaps. The springy underpadding also can turn lazy flyballs into doubles if they drop and bounce over the outfielder's outstretched glove. The ample protective padding on the 10-foot wall gives outfielders a chance to occasionally steal a homer.

Who It Helps The Most

Homer Bush, who has good speed and hits down on the ball, is helped both offensively and defensively by the fast infield. Young pitchers Kelvim Escobar and Roy Halladay have performed significantly better in Toronto, where their mistakes become long flyouts rather than home runs.

Who It Hurts The Most

Any home-run hitter is going to be affected by SkyDome. Shawn Green didn't fare too badly in his final season with the Blue Jays, hitting 20 of his 42 homers in Toronto. Carlos Delgado, however, led the AL with 27 road homers while going deep just 17 times at home. Tony Batista's lack of range hurts him at shortstop.

Rookies & Newcomers

Raul Mondesi probably will lose some homers but have significant gains in doubles and RBI after trading Dodger Stadium for SkyDome. Vernon Wells' speed and ability to make contact will benefit him in Toronto if he wins the center-field job.

Dimensions: LF-328, LCF-375, CF-400, RCF-375, RF-328

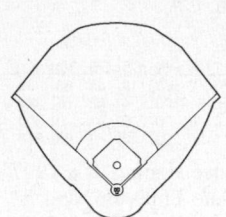

Capacity: 51,000

Elevation: 300 feet

Surface: Turf

Foul Territory: Average

Park Factors

1999 Season

| | Home Games | | | Away Games | | | |
	Blue Jays	Opp	Total	Blue Jays	Opp	Total	Index
G	72	72	144	72	72	144	—
Avg	.278	.287	.283	.285	.277	.281	101
AB	2426	2582	5008	2593	2436	5029	100
R	380	417	797	420	358	778	102
H	674	741	1415	738	675	1413	100
2B	156	172	328	151	119	270	122
3B	6	10	16	7	18	25	64
HR	86	88	174	105	87	192	91
BB	248	268	516	267	259	526	99
SO	470	450	920	477	449	926	100
E	46	30	76	42	52	94	81
E-Infield	41	26	67	38	44	82	82
LHB-Avg	.271	.304	.288	.274	.262	.269	107
LHB-HR	60	43	103	66	31	97	100
RHB-Avg	.284	.272	.278	.294	.287	.291	96
RHB-HR	26	45	71	39	56	95	79

1997-1999

| | Home Games | | | Away Games | | | |
	Blue Jays	Opp	Total	Blue Jays	Opp	Total	Index
G	217	217	434	221	221	442	—
Avg	.265	.259	.262	.264	.274	.269	97
AB	7222	7643	14865	7791	7436	15227	99
R	1062	1014	2076	1076	1078	2154	98
H	1912	1977	3889	2060	2034	4094	97
2B	434	446	880	410	397	807	112
3B	39	30	69	31	50	81	87
HR	241	218	459	275	264	539	87
BB	770	730	1500	705	799	1504	102
SO	1442	1506	2948	1526	1502	3028	100
E	158	118	276	127	171	298	94
E-Infield	132	97	229	108	145	253	92
LHB-Avg	.275	.258	.266	.271	.273	.272	98
LHB-HR	127	99	226	139	124	263	85
RHB-Avg	.257	.259	.258	.260	.274	.266	97
RHB-HR	114	119	233	136	140	276	89

1999 Rankings (American League)

- Second-highest double factor
- Third-highest LHB batting-average factor
- Lowest RHB home-run factor
- Second-lowest error factor
- Second-lowest infield-error factor
- Third-lowest triple factor

Jim Fregosi

1999 Season

Hired abruptly during spring training after Tim Johnson was fired, manager Jim Fregosi returned to the dugout after a two-year absence. Fregosi instilled professionalism and a calm discipline to a team that sorely needed both. The end result proved disappointing, however, as Toronto finished with four less wins than the previous year. The Blue Jays did recapture their fan base by contending for the wild card for most of the season.

Offense

Fregosi possesses an acute baseball mind. He's excellent at allowing a team to showcase its strengths, rather than trying to transform it into something it isn't. While the Blue Jays led the league in attempted steals in 1998, Fregosi cut back on the stolen-base attempts and relied more on power from the middle of the order. He's a student of batter-pitcher matchups and platoon advantages. Fregosi works well with young players but keeps his distance emotionally.

Pitching & Defense

Fregosi gets mixed reviews when it comes to handling his pitching staff, because Toronto's starting rotation underachieved all season long. The starters' 5.14 ERA increased by a full run over the season before. That's partly the result of Fregosi's patience, as he often allowed struggling starters the chance to pitch out of trouble. He champions successful young pitchers, as he did with Roy Halladay and Billy Koch. Fregosi was determined to establish roles for all of his relievers. He's always cognizant of late-inning defensive adjustments.

2000 Outlook

Any time a new manager is brought into an unfamiliar situation and is asked to work with coaches he didn't hire, it's a tough proposition. To Fregosi's credit, he handled it extremely well. Still, he reminded people why he wore out his welcome in Philadelphia when he got into two bar fights and never tempered his frankness. For 2000, he has his own coaching staff and no excuses. Nothing short of a winning season will be acceptable, even though the budget has been reduced significantly.

Born: 4/04/42 in San Francisco, California

Playing Experience: 1961-1978, Ana, NYM, Tex, Pit

Managerial Experience: 14 seasons

Manager Statistics

Year	Team, Lg	W	L	Pct	GB	Finish
1999	Toronto, AL	84	78	.519	14.0	3rd East
14 Seasons		945	1016	.482	—	—

1999 Starting Pitchers by Days Rest

	<=3	4	5	6+
Blue Jays Starts	1	92	45	17
Blue Jays ERA	9.00	5.40	4.63	4.83
AL Avg Starts	2	82	47	21
AL ERA	6.83	4.98	4.72	5.62

1999 Situational Stats

	Jim Fregosi	AL Average
Hit & Run Success %	31.1	35.3
Stolen Base Success %	71.3	68.0
Platoon Pct.	58.8	56.7
Defensive Subs	6	22
High-Pitch Outings	7	15
Quick/Slow Hooks	14/23	18/18
Sacrifice Attempts	41	52

1999 Rankings (American League)

- 1st in fewest caught stealings of third base (2)
- 3rd in sacrifice-bunt percentage (87.8%) and slow hooks (23)

Tony Batista

1999 Season

Dissatisfied with his defense and in need of a lefthanded setup man, the Diamondbacks traded Tony Batista and John Frascatore for Dan Plesac. Arizona would like to have that one back, because it still doesn't have a shortstop and Batista finished the season with 31 homers and 100 RBI. He helped turn around a Blue Jays team that had gone 7-16 between losing Alex Gonzalez and acquiring Batista.

Hitting

Batista is a free swinger who employs one of the most unusual batting stances in the game. He stands completely open to the pitcher with both feet parallel along the back line of the batter's box. When the pitcher begins his windup, the righthanded-hitting Batista moves his left foot and twists his torso into a traditional stance while the ball is in flight. He murders low fastballs and gives himself a chance for a home run with any inside pitch he can pull with his big uppercut swing. American League pitchers undoubtedly will work him with more outside breaking stuff in 2000. Batista feasted mainly on lefthanders in 1998, but improved and hammered all types of pitching last season.

Baserunning & Defense

Batista has decent speed but doesn't steal bases because of difficulty reading pitchers. As a shortstop, Batista has average skills with the glove and doesn't cover a lot of ground. He does have a very quick release, which overcomes the lack of velocity on his throws.

2000 Outlook

Batista's power surge helped ignite the Toronto offense, which will rely on him even more after an offseason spent reducing payroll. With a healthy Alex Gonzalez able to return to shortstop, Batista may move to third base. First base and the outfield also could be possibilities.

Position: SS
Bats: R **Throws:** R
Ht: 6' 0" **Wt:** 190

Opening Day Age: 26
Born: 12/9/73 in Puerto Plata, Dominican Republic
ML Seasons: 4
Pronunciation: bah-TEESE-tah

Overall Statistics

	G	AB	R	H	D	T	HR	RBI	SB	BB	SO	Avg	OBP	Slg
1999	142	519	77	144	30	1	31	100	4	38	96	.277	.330	.518
Career	390	1238	183	333	66	5	59	184	14	89	228	.269	.321	.473

Where He Hits the Ball

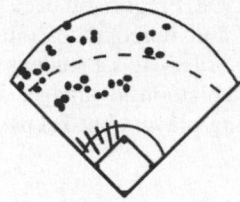 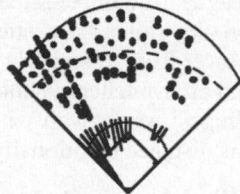

Vs. LHP   Vs. RHP

1999 Situational Stats

	AB	H	HR	RBI	Avg		AB	H	HR	RBI	Avg
Home	241	67	10	37	.278	LHP	110	31	6	20	.282
Road	278	77	21	63	.277	RHP	409	113	25	80	.276
First Half	244	65	15	43	.266	Sc Pos	155	48	10	75	.310
Scnd Half	275	79	16	57	.287	Clutch	84	26	4	15	.310

1999 Rankings (American League)

- 6th in batting average on an 0-2 count (.313)
- Led the Blue Jays in batting average on an 0-2 count (.313)

Homer Bush

1999 Season

Homer Bush has been a secondary player in two major trades, joining the Yankees in the Hideki Irabu deal with the Padres, then coming to the Blue Jays last spring in the Roger Clemens-David Wells blockbuster. Second base had been a void in Toronto since Roberto Alomar left, and Bush got off to an inauspicious start when he went on the disabled list in mid-April with a torn ligament in his right index finger. When he returned a month later, he surprised everyone with a superb year.

Hitting

Bush batted .320 in 1999 because he understands and utilizes his assets, chiefly his speed. He makes contact with a level swing, which produces a lot of low liners and hard-hit groundballs. Bush has the wheels to turn routine grounders into base hits. He was used most of the time as a No. 9 hitter, but also can handle the No. 2 spot as well with his fine bat control. Bush will never be considered good lead-off material until he shows more selectivity and learns to take a walk. His power is mainly limited to occasional doubles.

Baserunning & Defense

Bush is a legitimate threat to steal 40 or more bases each year. He has great instincts and rarely gets caught. If he improves his on-base percentage, he could challenge for the American League lead. Though Bush played some shortstop for Toronto on an emergency basis, his home is at second base because of a less-than-powerful arm. Bush has good range and hands, and he turns the double-play pivot well.

2000 Outlook

The Blue Jays' problems at second base have ended, presuming that Bush can continue to hit .300 and play solid defense. Though not particularly flashy, he gets the job done. He'll probably continue to be used at the bottom of the order.

Position: 2B/SS
Bats: R **Throws:** R
Ht: 5'10" **Wt:** 175

Opening Day Age: 27
Born: 11/12/72 in East St Louis, IL
ML Seasons: 3

Overall Statistics

	G	AB	R	H	D	T	HR	RBI	SB	BB	SO	Avg	OBP	Slg
1999	128	485	69	155	26	4	5	55	32	21	82	.320	.353	.421
Career	183	567	88	186	29	4	6	63	38	26	101	.328	.362	.425

Where He Hits the Ball

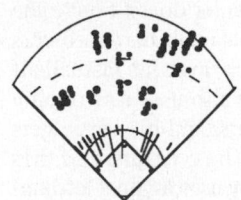 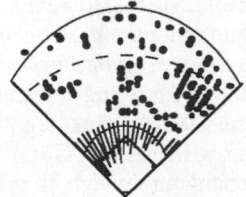

Vs. LHP **Vs. RHP**

1999 Situational Stats

	AB	H	HR	RBI	Avg		AB	H	HR	RBI	Avg
Home	234	76	2	32	.325	LHP	76	28	1	12	.368
Road	251	79	3	23	.315	RHP	409	127	4	43	.311
First Half	206	59	1	25	.286	Sc Pos	126	42	0	47	.333
Scnd Half	279	96	4	30	.344	Clutch	66	25	0	8	.379

1999 Rankings (American League)

- 1st in batting average on a 3-1 count (.833)
- 3rd in highest groundball/flyball ratio (2.2)
- 4th in fielding percentage at second base (.984)
- 6th in batting average in the clutch
- 7th in lowest HR frequency (97.0 ABs per HR) and steals of third (4)
- 9th in errors at second base (9)
- 10th in stolen bases and stolen-base percentage (80.0%)
- Led the Blue Jays in triples, sacrifice bunts (8), highest groundball/flyball ratio (2.2), stolen-base percentage (80.0%), batting average in the clutch, batting average on a 3-1 count (.833) and steals of third (4)

Chris Carpenter

1999 Season

While not yet anointed Toronto's ace, Chris Carpenter undoubtedly was the Blue Jays' best starter for the first two months of last season. Despite being placed on the 15-day disabled list in mid-June with elbow inflammation, Carpenter came back to post a 3.24 ERA prior to the All-Star break. The elbow worsened later in the season, however, causing him to be shelved for good in early September.

Pitching

Carpenter's success at this early stage of his career can be traced to his effective control of a variety of pitches. He can come at hitters hard with both a two-seam and four-seam fastball, the latter clocked at 95 MPH. However, Carpenter doesn't have the late movement on his heat that other hard throwers generate, and hitters can catch up to his fastballs if they're looking for them. He also uses a swooping curveball against righthanders, and his curve gets groundballs. Carpenter has improved his changeup, which he primarily uses against lefthanders. He usually keeps the ball down and is tough to take out of the park.

Defense

Considering that none of Toronto's catchers has a strong arm, it's a tribute to Carpenter that just nine runners attempted to steal on him in 1999 and only three succeeded. He has an extremely quick spin move to first base and virtually no wasted motion in his delivery to the plate. He's a decent fielder.

2000 Outlook

Carpenter had surgery last September to remove a bone spur and chips from his elbow. The Blue Jays expect him at full strength for spring training. He'll be the club's No. 1 starter if David Wells is traded, and if Wells stays Carpenter still will inherit that role soon enough. If Carpenter can improve his location, he'll join the ranks of the elite pitchers in the game.

Position: SP
Bats: R **Throws:** R
Ht: 6' 6" **Wt:** 215

Opening Day Age: 24
Born: 4/27/75 in Exeter, NH
ML Seasons: 3

Overall Statistics

	W	L	Pct.	ERA	G	GS	Sv	IP	H	BB	SO	HR	Ratio
1999	9	8	.529	4.38	24	24	0	150.0	177	48	106	16	1.50
Career	24	22	.522	4.52	71	61	0	406.1	462	146	297	41	1.50

How Often He Throws Strikes

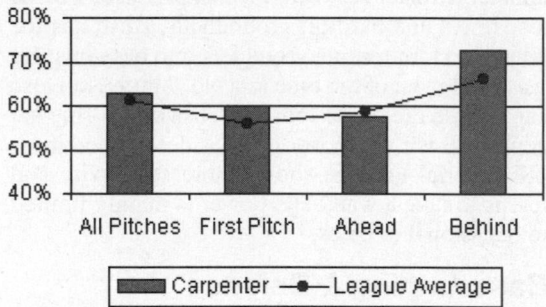

| Carpenter | League Average |

1999 Situational Stats

	W	L	ERA	Sv	IP		AB	H	HR	RBI	Avg
Home	4	4	4.54	0	77.1	LHB	278	83	11	33	.299
Road	5	4	4.21	0	72.2	RHB	324	94	5	36	.290
First Half	6	5	3.24	0	94.1	Sc Pos	160	38	4	50	.238
Scnd Half	3	3	6.31	0	55.2	Clutch	31	12	2	4	.387

1999 Rankings (American League)

- 7th in complete games (4)
- 8th in lowest batting average allowed with runners in scoring position
- 10th in wild pitches (9)
- Led the Blue Jays in wild pitches (9) and lowest batting average allowed with runners in scoring position

Carlos Delgado

Position: 1B
Bats: L **Throws:** R
Ht: 6' 3" **Wt:** 225

Opening Day Age: 27
Born: 6/25/72 in Aguadilla, Puerto Rico
ML Seasons: 7
Pronunciation: del-GAH-doh

Toronto

1999 Season

Finishing tied for third in the American League in home runs and RBI, Carlos Delgado continued to establish himself as one of the premier power hitters in the game. He set career highs in both categories and also surpassed the century mark in runs scored for the first time. Delgado's numbers would have been even better had his season not ended September 23, when he fouled a pitch off his right leg and broke his tibia.

Hitting

Delgado is just entering his prime. If Toronto wasn't one of the toughest home-run parks in the AL, he might have won the longball title, as he led the league with 27 road homers. He has enormous power to all fields and can hit the ball out to any part of any ballpark. His biggest gain in 1999 came against lefthanders, who no longer were able to keep him in check. Delgado generally hits in the .270 range, and while he strikes out a lot he also draws walks.

Baserunning & Defense

Delgado's defense came under a microscope this season after the Jays acquired accomplished first baseman David Segui, but manager Jim Fregosi continued to play Delgado in the field. He doesn't have first-step quickness around the bag and committed a league-high 14 errors. He often appears to lack concentration in the field. Delgado is an adequate baserunner, but nothing more.

2000 Outlook

Eligible to become a free agent after this season, Delgado stated that he wouldn't re-sign with Toronto. The Blue Jays faced the same dilemma with Shawn Green, whom they dealt to the Dodgers, and trading Delgado was their next order of business. But after John Olerud signed for three years and $20 million with Seattle, Delgado's price tag came down. He agreed to a three-year, $36 million deal with Toronto that will allow him to demand a trade after the 2000 season. Even is his address eventually changes, his power production won't.

Overall Statistics

	G	AB	R	H	D	T	HR	RBI	SB	BB	SO	Avg	OBP	Slg
1999	152	573	113	156	39	0	44	134	1	86	141	.272	.377	.571
Career	667	2332	378	622	157	6	149	467	5	313	624	.267	.361	.531

Where He Hits the Ball

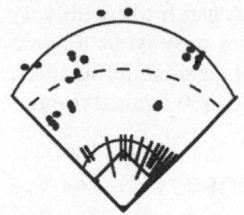

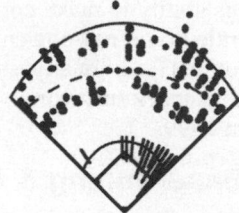

Vs. LHP **Vs. RHP**

1999 Situational Stats

	AB	H	HR	RBI	Avg		AB	H	HR	RBI	Avg
Home	284	77	17	58	.271	LHP	152	47	12	33	.309
Road	289	79	27	76	.273	RHP	421	109	32	101	.259
First Half	344	84	21	77	.244	Sc Pos	195	51	12	94	.262
Scnd Half	229	72	23	57	.314	Clutch	79	26	9	21	.329

1999 Rankings (American League)

- 1st in errors at first base (14)
- 3rd in home runs, RBI and lowest fielding percentage at first base (.990)
- 4th in hit by pitch (15) and strikeouts
- 5th in cleanup slugging percentage (.577)
- Led the Blue Jays in home runs, RBI, sacrifice flies (7), walks, hit by pitch (15), strikeouts, pitches seen (2,713), HR frequency (13.0 ABs per HR), most pitches seen per plate appearance (3.98), cleanup slugging percentage (.577), slugging percentage vs. lefthanded pitchers (.605), on-base percentage vs. lefthanded pitchers (.416) and highest percentage of pitches taken (58.0%)
- Led AL first basemen in home runs, total bases (327), RBI and hit by pitch (15)

Tony Fernandez

1999 Season

After a scintillating first three months in which he consistently flirted with a .400 average, Tony Fernandez hit just .251 the rest of the way. Routinely rested by manager Jim Fregosi at least once a week throughout most of the season, Fernandez developed a few nagging injuries related to his knee and neck, which reduced his playing time even more down the stretch.

Hitting

Fernandez continues to be a consummate contact hitter from both sides of the plate, with his Rod Carew batting style of open stances and level swings. He's not an overly patient hitter, but he does not go down on strikes very often because of his ability to make contact. A gap hitter with very little home-run power, he was miscast as a No. 5 hitter. Traditionally stronger against lefthanders, Fernandez surprisingly batted .330 against righties in 1999.

Baserunning & Defense

Fernandez hasn't been a threat to steal since the early 1990s, when he swiped 20 or more bases most seasons. He made just 13 attempts last year and looked uninterested in trying to get a read on pitchers. He also can look foolish on the basepaths because he too often disregards signs. Fernandez never before had played third base for a full season, and his inexperience showed with 18 errors and limited range.

2000 Outlook

The Blue Jays will let Fernandez walk as a free agent. Their priority is to find a way to keep Tony Batista in their infield, and third base is a possible spot for him. Fernandez is past his prime defensively and lacks the power to be a DH, so he probably will have to accept a part-time role.

Position: 3B
Bats: B **Throws:** R
Ht: 6' 2" **Wt:** 195

Opening Day Age: 37
Born: 6/30/62 in San Pedro de Macoris, Dominican Republic
ML Seasons: 16
Nickname: Gadget Man

Overall Statistics

	G	AB	R	H	D	T	HR	RBI	SB	BB	SO	Avg	OBP	Slg
1999	142	485	73	159	41	0	6	75	6	77	62	.328	.427	.449
Career	2082	7788	1046	2240	410	92	92	829	245	682	767	.288	.347	.399

Where He Hits the Ball

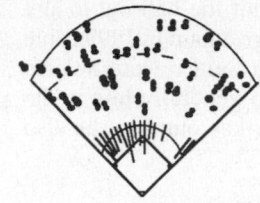 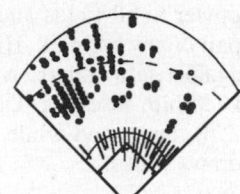

Vs. LHP   **Vs. RHP**

1999 Situational Stats

	AB	H	HR	RBI	Avg		AB	H	HR	RBI	Avg
Home	239	84	5	49	.351	LHP	143	46	1	22	.322
Road	246	75	1	26	.305	RHP	342	113	5	53	.330
First Half	288	107	5	59	.372	Sc Pos	138	55	1	69	.399
Scnd Half	197	52	1	16	.264	Clutch	61	21	0	12	.344

1999 Rankings (American League)

- 1st in batting average with runners in scoring position
- Led the Blue Jays in batting average, intentional walks (11), on-base percentage, batting average with runners in scoring position, batting average with the bases loaded (.500), batting average vs. lefthanded pitchers, batting average vs. righthanded pitchers, on-base percentage vs. righthanded pitchers (.447), batting average on a 3-2 count (.361), batting average at home, batting average with two strikes (.267) and highest percentage of extra bases taken as a runner (61.9%)
- Led AL third basemen in highest percentage of extra bases taken as a runner (61.9%)

Darrin Fletcher

Position: C
Bats: L **Throws:** R
Ht: 6' 2" **Wt:** 200

Opening Day Age: 33
Born: 10/3/66 in Elmhurst, IL
ML Seasons: 11

1999 Season

In his second season as Toronto's No. 1 catcher, Darrin Fletcher enhanced every part of his game and carved out personal bests in just about every offensive category. He managed to do so despite spending all of May on the disabled list with eye lacerations he received in a freak batting-practice incident. He hit a foul off the top of the batting cage, and the ball ricocheted back into his face.

Hitting

Fletcher continues to be a quality hitter against righthanders and a weakling against southpaws. He's primarily a pull hitter with a slight uppercut swing. He decided to go for the fences more last year, rather than spraying the ball to all fields as he did in 1998. Fletcher can look as good as any hitter in the American League when he works a count in his favor, but he gets very defensive otherwise. He's very tough to strike out but also too reluctant to take a free pass.

Baserunning & Defense

The knock against Fletcher throughout his career always has been his defense. The truth is, he's good at making plays in the field, protecting the plate and throwing accurately to first on bunts. But he had his worst year ever in terms of receiving, allowing 10 passed balls, and once again ranked near the bottom of the AL in throwing out basestealers. Fletcher runs like a typical catcher and hasn't attempted a steal since 1997.

2000 Outlook

The Blue Jays love Fletcher's lefthanded bat and are prepared to overlook his defensive deficiencies. They picked up his 2000 option for $2.5 million, and because they lack catching depth in the upper minors, the Jays likely will try to sign him to a longer deal. He's clearly established as the club's top backstop.

Overall Statistics

	G	AB	R	H	D	T	HR	RBI	SB	BB	SO	Avg	OBP	Slg
1999	115	412	48	120	26	0	18	80	0	26	47	.291	.339	.485
Career	944	2943	290	793	169	7	90	447	1	207	298	.269	.322	.423

Where He Hits the Ball

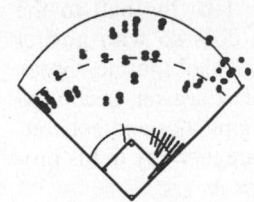

Vs. LHP

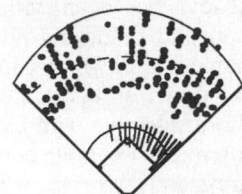

Vs. RHP

1999 Situational Stats

	AB	H	HR	RBI	Avg		AB	H	HR	RBI	Avg
Home	194	58	10	39	.299	LHP	79	18	7	26	.228
Road	218	62	8	41	.284	RHP	333	102	11	54	.306
First Half	192	58	9	37	.302	Sc Pos	118	37	5	60	.314
Scnd Half	220	62	9	43	.282	Clutch	57	17	4	17	.298

1999 Rankings (American League)

- 2nd in fielding percentage at catcher (.997)
- Led the Blue Jays in GDPs (16), lowest percentage of swings that missed (14.2%) and highest percentage of swings put into play (48.8%)
- Led AL catchers in highest percentage of swings put into play (48.8%)

Shawn Green

Traded To DODGERS

Position: RF
Bats: L **Throws:** L
Ht: 6' 4" **Wt:** 200

Opening Day Age: 27
Born: 11/10/72 in Des Plaines, IL
ML Seasons: 7

1999 Season

Shawn Green became a complete five-tool player in 1999. He once again improved his power, taking a quantum leap past his breakout season the year before. Green also topped .300 for the first time, earned his first All-Star Game selection and won his first Gold Glove.

Hitting

Green's rapid climb to become one of the American League's best all-around hitters is attributable to his ability to overcome a former weakness: hitting southpaws. He used to bail out against southpaws but corrected that problem in 1999. He employs a wide-open stance while still covering the outside part of the plate with his long arms. He always has been willing to take the ball to the opposite field, and now he does so with greater home-run power because of added muscle. Green cut down on his strikeouts last season, becoming more selective with breaking pitches and generating more favorable counts, another key to his progress.

Baserunning & Defense

In 1998, Green became the first Blue Jay to enjoy a 30-30 season. He didn't run as much last year, but he continued to show a good blend of speed and instincts, stealing successfully 74 percent of the time. Green played a near-flawless right field, making only one error after committing seven in 1998. He has a strong arm, although his accuracy seemed to decline a bit last season when he recorded only five assists, compared to 14 the year before.

2000 Outlook

Carlos Delgado and Green were the cornerstones on the Blue Jays' future, but their pending free agency after 2000 was something Toronto decided it couldn't afford. Green and second-base prospect Jorge Nunez were traded to Los Angeles for Raul Mondesi, who'll take over for Green in right, and lefthanded reliever Pedro Borbon. Green quickly signed a six-year, $84 million contract with the Dodgers. Mondesi is under contract through 2003, and will cost the Jays $7.5 million less than Green will get over the same period.

Overall Statistics

	G	AB	R	H	D	T	HR	RBI	SB	BB	SO	Avg	OBP	Slg
1999	153	614	134	190	45	0	42	123	20	66	117	.309	.384	.588
Career	716	2513	402	718	164	15	119	376	76	206	510	.286	.344	.505

Where He Hits the Ball

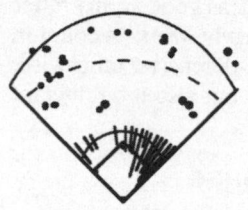

Vs. LHP

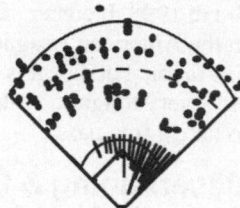

Vs. RHP

1999 Situational Stats

	AB	H	HR	RBI	Avg		AB	H	HR	RBI	Avg
Home	289	82	20	60	.284	LHP	164	46	8	39	.280
Road	325	108	22	63	.332	RHP	450	144	34	84	.320
First Half	318	104	25	70	.327	Sc Pos	175	48	12	83	.274
Scnd Half	296	86	17	53	.291	Clutch	92	23	6	12	.250

1999 Rankings (American League)

- 1st in doubles, total bases (361) and fielding percentage in right field (.997)
- 2nd in runs scored
- 4th in slugging percentage vs. righthanded pitchers (.618) and batting average on the road
- 5th in home runs and slugging percentage
- Led the Blue Jays in at-bats, runs scored, hits, doubles, total bases (361), times on base (267), plate appearances (696), slugging percentage, slugging percentage vs. righthanded pitchers (.618), batting average on the road and games played
- Led AL right fielders in runs scored, hits, doubles, total bases (361), pitches seen (2,671) and steals of third (3)

Pat Hentgen

Traded To
CARDINALS

Position: SP
Bats: R **Throws:** R
Ht: 6' 2" **Wt:** 195

Opening Day Age: 31
Born: 11/13/68 in Detroit, MI
ML Seasons: 9
Pronunciation: HENT-gen

1999 Season

Over the past two seasons, former Cy Young Award winner Pat Hentgen has been trying to stave off mediocrity. He has gone 23-23, able to rekindle only brief flashes of his former greatness. For the first time since becoming a full-time starter in 1993, Hentgen averaged less than six innings per outing in 1999. Despite his first losing record in three seasons, Hentgen finished with a decent second-half ERA of 3.79.

Pitching

Hentgen used to be a premier power pitcher, but some scouts believe his four-seam fastball has lost some juice because of his chronically tender shoulder. He averages 91 MPH with the four-seamer these days, down from 94 MPH in his heyday. He still uses his trademark cut fastball against lefthanders, but he's too predictable and doesn't locate his cutter as well as he once did. Hentgen likes to throw his hard stuff high in the strike zone, but that makes him more vulnerable to homers because he can't blow away hitters any longer. He also throws a roundhouse curve and a circle change.

Defense

Hentgen has good mobility handling bunts and covering first base. He made a career-high three errors in 1999 but still is a good fielder. Hentgen is adept at holding runners with a quick delivery to the plate, and he gives his catcher a decent chance to throw out basestealers because he usually throws hard stuff.

2000 Outlook

The Blue Jays essentially gave Hentgen to the Cardinals in November, trading him for a backup catcher (Alberto Castillo), situational lefty reliever (Lance Painter) and a nondescript minor league righthander (Matt DeWitt). But for a team looking to trim payroll and having Roy Halladay ready to replace Hentgen, Toronto cut a $6.6 million salary without weakening its rotation. Hentgen still has some mileage left in him, but he needs to transform himself into more of a finesse pitcher. He showed progress in doing so during a few late-season starts.

Toronto

Overall Statistics

	W	L	Pct.	ERA	G	GS	Sv	IP	H	BB	SO	HR	Ratio
1999	11	12	.478	4.79	34	34	0	199.0	225	65	118	32	1.46
Career	105	76	.580	4.14	252	222	0	1555.2	1587	557	995	191	1.38

How Often He Throws Strikes

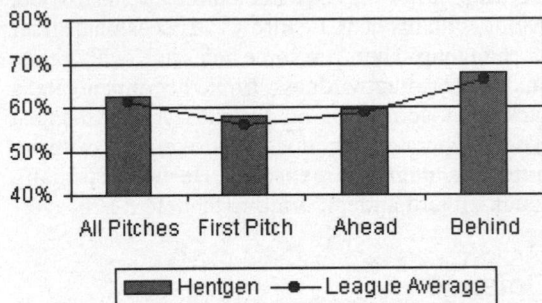

1999 Situational Stats

	W	L	ERA	Sv	IP		AB	H	HR	RBI	Avg
Home	5	6	6.83	0	89.2	LHB	395	121	18	60	.306
Road	6	6	3.13	0	109.1	RHB	392	104	14	46	.265
First Half	6	6	5.75	0	101.2	Sc Pos	182	57	7	71	.313
Scnd Half	5	6	3.79	0	97.1	Clutch	35	11	1	7	.314

1999 Rankings (American League)

- 2nd in games started, highest ERA at home and lowest ERA on the road
- 5th in home runs allowed, highest slugging percentage allowed (.474) and errors at pitcher (3)
- 6th in most home runs allowed per 9 innings (1.45) and lowest fielding percentage at pitcher (.925)
- 9th in highest batting average allowed (.286) and highest stolen-base percentage allowed (70.8%)
- 10th in fewest strikeouts per 9 innings (5.3)
- Led the Blue Jays in ERA, losses, games started, home runs allowed, pickoff throws (125), ERA on the road and lowest batting average allowed vs. righthanded batters

Billy Koch

1999 Season

The fourth overall pick in the 1996 draft, Billy Koch blew out his elbow three starts into his pro career a year later, requiring Tommy John surgery. He came back stronger than ever in 1998. When the Blue Jays decided last May that they didn't have a suitable closer, they turned to Koch, who never had relieved as a pro. He was equal to the task, establishing an American League rookie record with 31 saves in 35 tries.

Pitching

Koch may have the hardest fastball in the major leagues, reaching 101 MPH at times and averaging in the upper 90s. It's apparent that he didn't lose anything after having his elbow reconstructed. Along with his heat, he throws an occasional slider or changeup. There are some holes in Koch's game, such as periodic wildness, limited command and a lack of movement on his fastball. Despite the heat Koch generates, he doesn't strike out as many hitters as might be expected. He was especially tough on lefthanders, limiting them to a .209 average.

Defense

Koch is extremely agile coming off the mound, covering first base or charging a bunt as quickly as anyone. Despite his hard stuff, basestealers were more daring against him than most other closers, swiping seven bases in nine tries. Koch has a high leg kick and his delivery is not always smooth, which allows experienced runners to get sizable jumps.

2000 Outlook

The Blue Jays were pleasantly surprised to find out how poised Koch was despite being an inexperienced closer in his first season in the majors. He'll need to refine his control and recognize that hitters are sitting on his fastball. After the All-Star break, his ERA zoomed from 1.34 to 5.70. If he can make some refinements, he'll be able to thrive in his new role.

Position: RP
Bats: R **Throws:** R
Ht: 6' 3" **Wt:** 218

Opening Day Age: 25
Born: 12/14/74 in Rockville Center, NY
ML Seasons: 1
Pronunciation: KOTCH

Overall Statistics

	W	L	Pct.	ERA	G	GS	Sv	IP	H	BB	SO	HR	Ratio
1999	0	5	.000	3.39	56	0	31	63.2	55	30	57	5	1.34
Career	0	5	.000	3.39	56	0	31	63.2	55	30	57	5	1.34

How Often He Throws Strikes

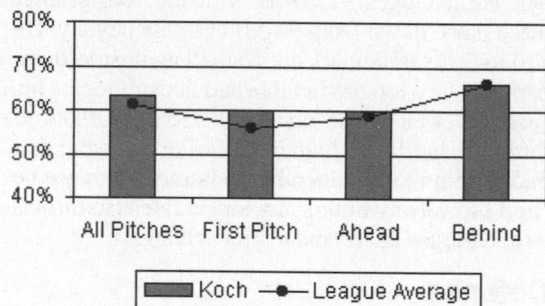

1999 Situational Stats

	W	L	ERA	Sv	IP		AB	H	HR	RBI	Avg
Home	0	3	5.01	13	32.1	LHB	115	24	3	12	.209
Road	0	2	1.72	18	31.1	RHB	119	31	2	13	.261
First Half	0	0	1.34	14	33.2	Sc Pos	70	13	1	19	.186
Scnd Half	0	5	5.70	17	30.0	Clutch	162	40	4	23	.247

1999 Rankings (American League)

- 4th in save percentage (88.6%)
- 6th in saves
- 8th in save opportunities (35)
- 10th in lowest batting average allowed in relief with runners in scoring position (.186) and relief ERA (3.39)
- Led the Blue Jays in saves, games finished (48), save opportunities (35), save percentage (88.6%), most GDPs induced per GDP situation (15.6%), lowest batting average allowed in relief with runners in scoring position (.186) and lowest batting average allowed in relief (.235)

David Segui

1999 Season

David Segui's tenure in Seattle lasted just a year and a half, as he was traded to Toronto for relievers Tom Davey and Steve Sinclair on July 28. Segui continued to be as consistent as ever, batting close to .300 most of the year, but with limited power for a first baseman. Typically, Segui also loses time to injuries and 1999 was no exception. He played just 31 games for the Blue Jays because he broke a bone in his right hand 10 days after the trade, when he took a liner off his glove.

Hitting

An accomplished switch-hitter, Segui generally makes contact and takes what a pitcher gives him by driving the ball to all fields. He hits the majority of his home runs while batting lefthanded, off breaking pitches down and in. From the right side, he looks more for offspeed pitches away, which he dumps into right field. That approach prevents strikeouts but diminishes his power potential. Another reason for his lack of home runs is that Segui will shorten his swing whenever he falls behind in the count, sometimes even after going 0-1.

Baserunning & Defense

Segui often is mentioned as the best fielding first baseman in the game, and his fielding percentage usually ranks among the league leaders. He made just one error in 1998 and four last season. In addition to his sure glove, he has a very good throwing arm and works the 3-6-3 double play as well as anyone. As far as baserunning, Segui contributes very little. He has had a couple of knee operations and doesn't take risks.

2000 Outlook

The primary reason Seattle traded Segui at the deadline was his pending free agency. The Blue Jays needed an extra bat while they were chasing a wild-card berth. They offered him arbitration only to get draft picks as compensation when he signed elsewhere as a free agent, but he stunned the Jays by accepting it. With Carlos Delgado signed to a three-year extension, Toronto has no clear role for Segui.

Position: 1B/DH
Bats: B **Throws:** L
Ht: 6' 1" **Wt:** 202

Opening Day Age: 33
Born: 7/19/66 in Kansas City, KS
ML Seasons: 10
Pronunciation: suh-GHEE

Overall Statistics

	G	AB	R	H	D	T	HR	RBI	SB	BB	SO	Avg	OBP	Slg
1999	121	440	57	131	27	3	14	52	1	40	60	.298	.355	.468
Career	1113	3603	498	1028	207	13	102	487	15	380	460	.285	.352	.435

Where He Hits the Ball

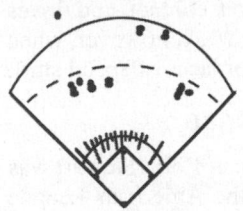
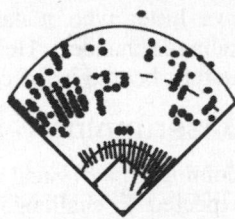

Vs. LHP   **Vs. RHP**

1999 Situational Stats

	AB	H	HR	RBI	Avg		AB	H	HR	RBI	Avg
Home	193	53	5	24	.275	LHP	70	19	1	4	.271
Road	247	78	9	28	.316	RHP	370	112	13	48	.303
First Half	298	88	9	34	.295	Sc Pos	118	31	2	37	.263
Scnd Half	142	43	5	18	.303	Clutch	53	19	2	9	.358

1999 Rankings (American League)

- 4th in lowest batting average on a 3-1 count (.000)
- 10th in batting average in the clutch (.358)
- Led AL first basemen in batting average on the road (.316)

Shannon Stewart

1999 Season

Shannon Stewart continued his rapid development as Toronto's leadoff man, climbing over the .300 batting mark and scoring more than 100 runs in just his second full season. Stewart's primary responsibility of setting the table was fulfilled with a .371 on-base percentage. Though he avoided the disabled list, Stewart played only 13 games in September because of an ankle injury.

Hitting

A slashing hitter, Stewart has better-than-average pop for a leadoff man. He can turn on a high, inside fastball and reach the left-field bleachers. Stewart strokes numerous liners and seeing-eye ground-balls, then burns up the basepaths. He's an aggressive hitter who makes good contact and loves facing lefthanders. He's still weak, however, when he falls behind in the count or faces offspeed stuff.

Baserunning & Defense

Coming off a 51-steal season in 1998, Stewart was expected to challenge for the American League lead last year. That didn't happen, as he dropped to 37. New manager Jim Fregosi had his players run far less frequently than predecessor Tim Johnson did. Stewart also was hampered by knee and ankle problems during the second half of the season. When healthy, he's one of the fastest players in the game. He has the range and instincts to be a top-notch center fielder, but his arm is so weak that he's relegated to left field.

2000 Outlook

The Blue Jays are extremely comfortable with the progress made by Stewart, an accomplished leadoff man on the verge of entering his prime. His contact skills and consistency at the plate virtually assure another productive offensive season. His steal totals could shoot up again if he's fully healthy and Fregosi turns him loose.

Position: LF
Bats: R **Throws:** R
Ht: 6' 1" **Wt:** 205

Opening Day Age: 26
Born: 2/25/74 in Cincinnati, OH
ML Seasons: 5

Overall Statistics

	G	AB	R	H	D	T	HR	RBI	SB	BB	SO	Avg	OBP	Slg
1999	145	608	102	185	28	2	11	67	37	59	83	.304	.371	.411
Career	352	1347	221	388	71	12	23	147	101	151	193	.288	.370	.410

Where He Hits the Ball

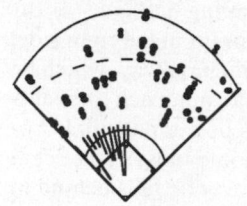
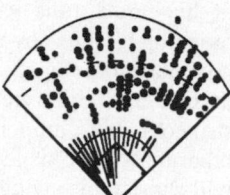

Vs. LHP   **Vs. RHP**

1999 Situational Stats

	AB	H	HR	RBI	Avg		AB	H	HR	RBI	Avg
Home	298	86	4	34	.289	LHP	103	38	1	12	.369
Road	310	99	7	33	.319	RHP	505	147	10	55	.291
First Half	366	111	8	43	.303	Sc Pos	123	43	4	57	.350
Scnd Half	242	74	3	24	.306	Clutch	88	32	1	14	.364

1999 Rankings (American League)

- 1st in caught stealing (14)
- 3rd in lowest fielding percentage in left field (.980)
- 4th in singles, stolen bases and errors in left field (5)
- 5th in on-base percentage for a leadoff hitter (.377)
- Led the Blue Jays in singles, stolen bases, caught stealing (14) and on-base percentage for a leadoff hitter (.377)
- Led AL left fielders in singles, caught stealing (14), batting average with runners in scoring position, batting average in the clutch, on-base percentage for a leadoff hitter (.377) and batting average on the road

David Wells

Position: SP
Bats: L **Throws:** L
Ht: 6' 4" **Wt:** 225

Opening Day Age: 36
Born: 5/20/63 in Torrance, CA
ML Seasons: 13
Nickname: Boomer

1999 Season

After a six-year hiatus in which he established himself as one of the premier lefthanded starters in the game, David Wells returned to Toronto via a blockbuster spring-training trade that sent five-time Cy Young Award winner Roger Clemens to the New York Yankees. Though Wells wasn't happy about leaving New York, he worked as hard as ever. Working a career-high 231.2 innings, he won at least 16 games for the third straight season.

Pitching

First and foremost a location pitcher, Wells is known for pinpoint accuracy and allowing very few bases on balls. He also induces a lot of grounders because of a heavy, downward-breaking curveball that he can throw consistently for strikes. He generally reaches the low 90s with his fastball and mixes in an effective changeup. He wasn't dominant in 1999, primarily because he seemed to lose stamina once he hit the sixth inning. Wells became much too ordinary from the stretch position with runners on base and no longer proved to be poison to lefthanders. Though his strikeout-to-walk ratio remained excellent, he allowed too many hits, which swelled his ERA.

Defense

Wells is a good fielder who moves quickly off the mound for a big man. He's smart and knows when and where he needs to back up a base. However, he seemed to lose concentration with respect to holding runners on. He gave up 37 steals in 46 tries, which is horrendous for a lefthander. No American Leaguer permitted more swipes.

2000 Outlook

The Blue Jays locked up Wells through the 2001 season, rewarding him last June with a two-year, $16 million extension that will be worth $23.75 million if they pick up his 2002 option. At age 36, Wells figures to hold his value for at least a couple more years because his mechanics and control remain superb. Toronto will have to play better defense behind Wells if management expects him to perform like he did for the Yankees in 1997-98.

Overall Statistics

	W	L	Pct.	ERA	G	GS	Sv	IP	H	BB	SO	HR	Ratio
1999	17	10	.630	4.82	34	34	0	231.2	246	62	169	32	1.33
Career	141	99	.588	4.05	444	274	13	2077.0	2076	507	1410	250	1.24

How Often He Throws Strikes

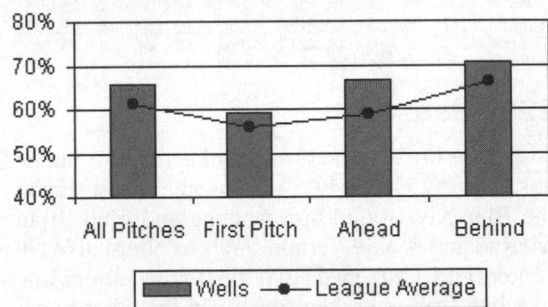

1999 Situational Stats

	W	L	ERA	Sv	IP		AB	H	HR	RBI	Avg
Home	8	6	4.29	0	121.2	LHB	156	46	6	30	.295
Road	9	4	5.40	0	110.0	RHB	751	200	26	90	.266
First Half	9	6	5.13	0	124.2	Sc Pos	212	58	6	77	.274
Scnd Half	8	4	4.46	0	107.0	Clutch	95	30	4	16	.316

1999 Rankings (American League)

- 1st in complete games (7), innings pitched, hits allowed and stolen bases allowed (37)
- 2nd in games started and batters faced (987)
- 3rd in highest stolen-base percentage allowed (80.4%)
- Led the Blue Jays in wins, games started, complete games (7), innings pitched, hits allowed, batters faced (987), home runs allowed, strikeouts, pitches thrown (3,499), stolen bases allowed (37), GDPs induced (19), winning percentage, highest strikeout/walk ratio (2.7), lowest batting average allowed (.271), lowest slugging percentage allowed (.438), lowest on-base percentage allowed (.320) and highest groundball/flyball ratio allowed (1.3)

Jose Cruz

Position: CF
Bats: B **Throws:** R
Ht: 6' 0" **Wt:** 195

Opening Day Age: 25
Born: 4/19/74 in Arroyo, Puerto Rico
ML Seasons: 3

Overall Statistics

	G	AB	R	H	D	T	HR	RBI	SB	BB	SO	Avg	OBP	Slg
1999	106	349	63	84	19	3	14	45	14	64	91	.241	.358	.433
Career	315	1096	177	271	52	7	51	155	32	162	307	.247	.342	.447

1999 Situational Stats

	AB	H	HR	RBI	Avg		AB	H	HR	RBI	Avg
Home	187	50	8	28	.267	LHP	80	22	2	10	.275
Road	162	34	6	17	.210	RHP	269	62	12	35	.230
First Half	250	56	9	29	.224	Sc Pos	93	24	3	30	.258
Scnd Half	99	28	5	16	.283	Clutch	50	14	0	7	.280

1999 Season

Jose Cruz hit 26 homers as a rookie in 1997, but he has hit just 25 in the two seasons since. Last season the Blue Jays found him wanting and tried Brian McRae and rookie Vernon Wells as alternatives in center field. Cruz made two trips to the minors, one to rehab from a broken finger and the other to get out of a slump.

Hitting, Baserunning & Defense

The best that can be said of Cruz' hitting skills is that he's very selective. A switch-hitter, he has power from both sides but hits better and makes more contact batting righthanded. He has great difficulty reading offspeed pitches. Cruz is a good basestealer who's both fast and quick off the mark. He covers plenty of ground in center field but his arm is below average.

2000 Outlook

Though Cruz still has potential, time is running out on him in Toronto. He may have to settle for a part-time role unless he's traded. There would be no shortage of teams willing to give Cruz a chance to turn it around.

Kelvim Escobar

Position: SP
Bats: R **Throws:** R
Ht: 6' 1" **Wt:** 195

Opening Day Age: 23
Born: 4/11/76 in La Guaira, Venezuela
ML Seasons: 3

Overall Statistics

	W	L	Pct.	ERA	G	GS	Sv	IP	H	BB	SO	HR	Ratio
1999	14	11	.560	5.69	33	30	0	174.0	203	81	129	19	1.63
Career	24	16	.600	4.84	82	40	14	284.2	303	135	237	25	1.54

1999 Situational Stats

	W	L	ERA	Sv	IP		AB	H	HR	RBI	Avg
Home	6	5	4.80	0	86.1	LHB	348	97	10	54	.279
Road	8	6	6.57	0	87.2	RHB	346	106	9	44	.306
First Half	8	6	5.93	0	101.2	Sc Pos	186	56	4	74	.301
Scnd Half	6	5	5.35	0	72.1	Clutch	19	6	0	2	.316

1999 Season

For the first time in his three major league seasons, Kelvim Escobar was a full-time starter. He managed to post a winning record and ranked third on the club in innings pitched, but his wildness led to high pitch counts and ruined his ERA.

Pitching & Defense

A starter in the minors, Escobar was converted to a closer when he first came up in 1997. He was quite successful because of his blistering 96-MPH fastball and tough splitter. The transition back to starter hasn't worked as well because he has lost command of his curveball and changeup. When he struggles to establish his breaking stuff, Escobar falls behind in the count, relies on his fastball and gets smoked. Escobar is a basestealer's dream. He's inattentive and has a slow motion to the plate. He's an average fielder at best.

2000 Outlook

The trade of Pat Hentgen to the Cardinals likely cemented Escobar's place in the rotation. Before the deal, there was a chance that Roy Halladay would have supplanted him. Escobar has the stuff to be a big winner if he regains control of his offspeed pitches.

John Frascatore

Position: RP
Bats: R **Throws:** R
Ht: 6' 1" **Wt:** 210

Opening Day Age: 30
Born: 2/4/70 in
Queens, NY
ML Seasons: 5
Pronunciation:
fras-kuh-TORE-ee

Overall Statistics

	W	L	Pct.	ERA	G	GS	Sv	IP	H	BB	SO	HR	Ratio
1999	8	5	.615	3.73	59	0	1	70.0	73	21	37	11	1.34
Career	17	13	.567	3.74	202	5	1	281.2	288	108	167	32	1.41

1999 Situational Stats

	W	L	ERA	Sv	IP		AB	H	HR	RBI	Avg
Home	4	0	2.87	0	31.1	LHB	102	25	3	13	.245
Road	4	5	4.42	1	38.2	RHB	163	48	8	33	.294
First Half	4	4	3.98	0	43.0	Sc Pos	83	19	3	31	.229
Scnd Half	4	1	3.33	1	27.0	Clutch	96	27	4	18	.281

1999 Season

Picked up by the Blue Jays along with shortstop Tony Batista in a lopsided midseason trade for reliever Dan Plesac, John Frascatore excelled in his American League debut. In 33 appearances as a middle man, he earned seven victories and six holds.

Pitching & Defense

Though Frascatore throws hard, he lacks the stuff to close games. His 92-MPH fastball is fairly straight. He tries to make that pitch look faster by mixing in a good curveball and a hard-breaking slider. He doesn't blow away hitters and registers few strikeouts. He's unflappable enough to be unfazed by late-inning pressure situations. Frascatore is a good fielder but is very easy to run on.

2000 Outlook

The Blue Jays were ecstatic about their acquisition of Frascatore and the righthanded depth he added to the bullpen. If Paul Quantrill falters, Frascatore could replace him as Toronto's top setup man.

Alex Gonzalez

Position: SS
Bats: R **Throws:** R
Ht: 6' 0" **Wt:** 200

Opening Day Age: 26
Born: 4/8/73 in Miami, FL
ML Seasons: 6

Overall Statistics

	G	AB	R	H	D	T	HR	RBI	SB	BB	SO	Avg	OBP	Slg
1999	38	154	22	45	13	0	2	12	4	16	23	.292	.370	.416
Career	595	2095	260	504	116	13	51	205	63	171	496	.241	.303	.381

1999 Situational Stats

	AB	H	HR	RBI	Avg		AB	H	HR	RBI	Avg
Home	73	18	1	6	.247	LHP	41	11	1	3	.268
Road	81	27	1	6	.333	RHP	113	34	1	9	.301
First Half	154	45	2	12	.292	Sc Pos	42	12	1	10	.286
Scnd Half	0	0	0	0	-	Clutch	28	9	1	2	.321

1999 Season

Alex Gonzalez appeared in just 38 games before his season was aborted in June by arthroscopic surgery to repair a torn labrum. Before he went out, Gonzalez was hitting much better than he ever had as Toronto's starting shortstop.

Hitting, Baserunning & Defense

After struggling to make consistent contact during his first four full years in the American League, Gonzalez shortened his swing and went after balls earlier in the count. That approach worked for him, and he also was more willing to take a walk. Always considered one of the better defensive shortstops in the AL, Gonzalez had a cannon for an arm before his shoulder injury. He runs well and could steal as many as 30 bases in a season if he can keep his on-base percentage as high as he did in 1999.

2000 Outlook

The Blue Jays traded for Tony Batista to fill in for Gonzalez, and Batista bashed 26 homers in 98 games. Gonzalez could return to short with Batista moving to a position he's better suited for. The Jays also could accept less defense, keeping Batista at short and trading Gonzalez.

Willie Greene

Position: DH
Bats: L **Throws:** R
Ht: 5'11" **Wt:** 192
Opening Day Age: 28
Born: 9/23/71 in Milledgeville, GA
ML Seasons: 8

Overall Statistics

	G	AB	R	H	D	T	HR	RBI	SB	BB	SO	Avg	OBP	Slg
1999	81	226	22	46	7	0	12	41	0	20	56	.204	.266	.394
Career	550	1603	220	386	61	10	76	270	13	224	408	.241	.333	.434

1999 Situational Stats

	AB	H	HR	RBI	Avg		AB	H	HR	RBI	Avg
Home	128	29	8	28	.227	LHP	20	3	0	1	.150
Road	98	17	4	13	.173	RHP	206	43	12	40	.209
First Half	106	21	5	19	.198	Sc Pos	72	16	1	25	.222
Scnd Half	120	25	7	22	.208	Clutch	43	14	3	13	.326

1999 Season

After being cast off by the Orioles last winter, Willie Greene signed with the Blue Jays in an attempt to shore up their DH spot. He didn't respond well to what amounted to less than a part-time role and had his worst season in the majors.

Hitting, Baserunning & Defense

Greene's only asset is a quick bat that sometimes puts a real charge into the ball. Making enough contact always has been a problem for him, though he does draw a good number of walks. Greene can handle fastballs on the inner half, so he rarely sees those pitches. Instead, he's easily fooled with off-speed breaking stuff. Greene is an adequate baserunner. He also rarely played the field for Toronto, but can fill in at third base or the outfield. His arm is solid.

2000 Outlook

Toronto removed Greene from its 40-man roster shortly after the season ended. The Blue Jays will look elsewhere for a solution to their DH woes. He's still young enough to get another shot, but his career will be in jeopardy if he struggles mightily again.

Roy Halladay

Position: SP/RP
Bats: R **Throws:** R
Ht: 6'6" **Wt:** 205
Opening Day Age: 22
Born: 5/14/77 in Denver, CO
ML Seasons: 2
Pronunciation: HOWL-luh-day

Overall Statistics

	W	L	Pct.	ERA	G	GS	Sv	IP	H	BB	SO	HR	Ratio
1999	8	7	.533	3.92	36	18	1	149.1	156	79	82	19	1.57
Career	9	7	.563	3.75	38	20	1	163.1	165	81	95	21	1.51

1999 Situational Stats

	W	L	ERA	Sv	IP		AB	H	HR	RBI	Avg
Home	6	5	3.00	0	90.0	LHB	296	81	7	33	.274
Road	2	2	5.31	1	59.1	RHB	282	75	12	44	.266
First Half	6	3	3.58	1	88.0	Sc Pos	153	39	6	62	.255
Scnd Half	2	4	4.40	0	61.1	Clutch	24	7	0	0	.292

1999 Season

The next bright pitching star on the horizon in Toronto is Roy Halladay, who passed every test last season. He handled work as a long reliever and spot starter, and he even provided occasional late-inning heroics. Halladay strained a pectoral muscle in late September and was shut down for the remainder of the season.

Pitching & Defense

Halladay has enormous physical tools, starting with his 6-foot-6 frame and high-grade athleticism that produces outstanding mechanics. His four-seam fastball has been clocked as high as 97 MPH, and he can buckle a righthander's knees with a knuckle-curve. Halladay prefers to work a cut fastball or hard slider in on lefthanders. He also is working on a circle change. He needs to cut down on his walks, and he doesn't accumulate as many strikeouts as his stuff would warrant. Halladay is a good fielder and keeps runners honest.

2000 Outlook

The Pat Hentgen trade cleared an obvious spot for Halladay in the Toronto rotation. Once he puts all of his considerable gifts together, he projects as an ace.

Joey Hamilton

Position: SP
Bats: R **Throws:** R
Ht: 6' 4" **Wt:** 230

Opening Day Age: 29
Born: 9/9/70 in
Statesboro, GA
ML Seasons: 6
Nickname: Big Daddy

Overall Statistics

	W	L	Pct.	ERA	G	GS	Sv	IP	H	BB	SO	HR	Ratio
1999	7	8	.467	6.52	22	18	0	98.0	118	39	56	13	1.60
Career	62	52	.544	4.09	168	160	0	1032.2	1030	382	695	93	1.37

1999 Situational Stats

	W	L	ERA	Sv	IP		AB	H	HR	RBI	Avg
Home	2	5	8.27	0	49.0	LHB	207	72	5	32	.348
Road	5	3	4.78	0	49.0	RHB	189	46	8	33	.243
First Half	1	5	8.57	0	49.1	Sc Pos	111	35	3	51	.315
Scnd Half	6	3	4.44	0	48.2	Clutch	19	5	1	2	.263

1999 Season

Toronto traded Woody Williams and two young players to San Diego last winter for Joey Hamilton, then gave Hamilton a three-year contract worth $17 million. It may have been the most disappointing offseason transaction in the game. Hamilton was shut down twice with a sore shoulder and got shelled when he took the mound.

Pitching & Defense

Hamilton has an impressive array of pitches that includes a 92-MPH sinking fastball, a splitter he uses as an out pitch, a decent slider and a changeup. Hamilton became easy prey for lefthanders after his injury, when he lost velocity and his breaking stuff flattened out. Hamilton isn't a well-conditioned athlete. He's slow coming off the mound and commits plenty of errors. His quick delivery keeps basestealers honest.

2000 Outlook

Hamilton had shoulder surgery in September and is expected to be 100 percent by spring training. The Blue Jays need him to rebound if they're to contend for the playoffs.

Graeme Lloyd

Position: RP
Bats: L **Throws:** L
Ht: 6' 7" **Wt:** 234

Opening Day Age: 32
Born: 4/9/67 in
Geelong, Victoria,
Australia
ML Seasons: 7

Overall Statistics

	W	L	Pct.	ERA	G	GS	Sv	IP	H	BB	SO	HR	Ratio
1999	5	3	.625	3.63	74	0	3	72.0	68	23	47	11	1.26
Career	16	22	.421	3.62	366	0	11	358.0	351	107	198	37	1.28

1999 Situational Stats

	W	L	ERA	Sv	IP		AB	H	HR	RBI	Avg
Home	4	1	3.03	2	35.2	LHB	108	29	6	17	.269
Road	1	2	4.21	1	36.1	RHB	164	39	5	19	.238
First Half	5	3	2.98	3	42.1	Sc Pos	60	13	3	23	.217
Scnd Half	0	0	4.55	0	29.2	Clutch	149	35	7	23	.235

1999 Season

Traded from the Yankees to Toronto last February as part of the Roger Clemens-David Wells deal, Graeme Lloyd later allowed Toronto to use Dan Plesac in a trade for Tony Batista. Lloyd's 74 appearances were a career high, but they took a toll on his numbers later in the season.

Pitching & Defense

Lloyd's role in Toronto was expanded to full-fledged setup man, as opposed to the one- or two-batter specialist he was in New York. He has a 93-MPH, two-seam fastball with good sinking action, a tough slider and a decent curveball. He fared well with that assortment, facing more righthanded hitters than ever last season. Despite his large frame, he seemed to wear down from the extra workload in the last month of the season. Lloyd is a surehanded fielder with a good pickoff move.

2000 Outlook

Lloyd declared his free agency as the Blue Jays were trying to reduce their payroll. A good indication that they wouldn't try to re-sign him came in November, when they got lefthanded relievers Pedro Borbon and Lance Painter in trades two days apart. Lloyd struck it rich in Montreal, landing a three-year contract worth $9 million.

Toronto

Brian McRae

Position: CF/DH
Bats: B **Throws:** R
Ht: 6' 0" **Wt:** 195

Opening Day Age: 32
Born: 8/27/67 in Bradenton, FL
ML Seasons: 10

Overall Statistics

	G	AB	R	H	D	T	HR	RBI	SB	BB	SO	Avg	OBP	Slg
1999	134	403	47	88	17	2	12	48	2	57	86	.218	.327	.360
Career	1354	5114	734	1336	264	58	103	532	196	488	824	.261	.331	.396

1999 Situational Stats

	AB	H	HR	RBI	Avg		AB	H	HR	RBI	Avg
Home	174	33	6	20	.190	LHP	91	23	1	9	.253
Road	229	55	6	28	.240	RHP	312	65	11	39	.208
First Half	263	61	8	31	.232	Sc Pos	109	21	5	38	.193
Scnd Half	140	27	4	17	.193	Clutch	58	12	0	5	.207

1999 Season

Traded by the Mets and the Rockies in a nine-day span in July and August, Brian McRae also lost his status as an everyday player by the end of the season. Picked up by Toronto for a player to be named, McRae hit just .195 for the Jays and was benched in favor of rookie Vernon Wells.

Hitting, Baserunning & Defense

The switch-hitting McRae has declined offensively since 1995, with the exception of an upturn in 1998. He doesn't hit the ball with authority any longer, especially from the left side. He'll work counts patiently and take more walks than he did in the past. McRae still is one of the better range rovers in the game despite knee problems that have slowed him down. He doesn't have much of an arm, but his overall prowess makes up for it. McRae's stolen-base skills also have eroded, as he was caught seven times in nine tries last year.

2000 Outlook

The Blue Jays won't re-sign McRae as a free agent. He has slipped so far that he may have to sign a minor league contract and prove himself all over again.

Paul Quantrill

Position: RP
Bats: L **Throws:** R
Ht: 6' 1" **Wt:** 180

Opening Day Age: 31
Born: 11/3/68 in London, Canada
ML Seasons: 8
Pronunciation: KWON-trill

Overall Statistics

	W	L	Pct.	ERA	G	GS	Sv	IP	H	BB	SO	HR	Ratio
1999	3	2	.600	3.33	41	0	0	48.2	53	17	28	5	1.44
Career	39	57	.406	3.91	382	64	15	770.2	898	225	450	83	1.46

1999 Situational Stats

	W	L	ERA	Sv	IP		AB	H	HR	RBI	Avg
Home	0	2	3.91	0	25.1	LHB	69	18	3	9	.261
Road	3	0	2.70	0	23.1	RHB	119	35	2	19	.294
First Half	1	1	2.40	0	15.0	Sc Pos	47	16	1	21	.340
Scnd Half	2	1	3.74	0	33.2	Clutch	66	23	3	15	.348

1999 Season

Paul Quantrill's 1999 campaign didn't begin until mid-June because of an offseason snowmobiling accident in which he broke his right leg. The absence of Toronto's key setup man left its bullpen in disarray, and his performance slipped a notch from his previous two seasons.

Pitching & Defense

Quantrill has been one of the most reliable setup men in the game. He normally has good control, and his hard, 92-MPH sinker yields plenty of groundballs. He also uses a tight slider, primarily against righthanders, and he'll show a changeup to lefthanders. He lacked command this past season, which forced him to throw more pitches and work from behind in the count more than usual. Quantrill fields his position well and isn't easy to steal on. He has good instincts and a quick move to first.

2000 Outlook

Quantrill once again will be counted on to be a workhorse in the setup role. He averaged 80 appearances in his two seasons before the injury, and the Jays need him to regain his form of 1998, when he led the American League with 27 holds.

Other Toronto Blue Jays

John Bale (**Pos**: LHP, **Age**: 25)

	W	L	Pct.	ERA	G	GS	Sv	IP	H	BB	SO	HR	Ratio
1999	0	0	-	13.50	1	0	0	2.0	2	2	4	1	2.00
Career	0	0	-	13.50	1	0	0	2.0	2	2	4	1	2.00

After pitching brilliantly at Double-A Knoxville in 1999, Bale absorbed a rough initiation from Cleveland in the final days of the season. He may need some time in Triple-A, but he'll be back. 2000 Outlook: C

Geronimo Berroa (**Pos**: DH, **Age**: 35, **Bats**: R)

	G	AB	R	H	D	T	HR	RBI	SB	BB	SO	Avg	OBP	Slg
1999	22	62	11	12	3	0	1	6	0	9	15	.194	.315	.290
Career	755	2475	377	684	113	8	101	377	19	272	502	.276	.349	.451

In 1999 Berroa bounced between Toronto, Triple-A Syracuse and the disabled list. The Jays let him go in August when he returned from a pulled oblique muscle. 2000 Outlook: D

Pat Borders (**Pos**: C, **Age**: 36, **Bats**: R)

	G	AB	R	H	D	T	HR	RBI	SB	BB	SO	Avg	OBP	Slg
1999	12	34	3	9	0	1	1	6	0	1	5	.265	.286	.412
Career	1001	3046	266	779	155	12	67	327	6	149	506	.256	.291	.380

Borders hasn't been a regular since 1994, but he manages to keep his major league career alive. He has been with seven different teams over the last five seasons, and he'll probably find another one. 2000 Outlook: C

Kevin Brown (**Pos**: C, **Age**: 26, **Bats**: R)

	G	AB	R	H	D	T	HR	RBI	SB	BB	SO	Avg	OBP	Slg
1999	2	9	1	4	2	0	0	1	0	0	3	.444	.444	.667
Career	61	128	20	35	9	1	3	18	0	11	36	.273	.333	.430

Brown's major league debut in 1998 was respectable, but he barely saw the majors in '99. At Triple-A Syracuse, Brown continued to fan at an alarming rate while batting .258-13-51 in 88 games. 2000 Outlook: C

Jacob Brumfield (**Pos**: CF/LF, **Age**: 34, **Bats**: R)

	G	AB	R	H	D	T	HR	RBI	SB	BB	SO	Avg	OBP	Slg
1999	80	187	29	45	8	4	2	20	1	19	44	.241	.306	.358
Career	568	1575	260	404	91	14	32	162	74	137	290	.257	.318	.393

Brumfield made the Dodgers out of spring training, but they released him a month later. He hooked on with Toronto again and has been re-signed for this season. 2000 Outlook: C

Rob Butler (**Pos**: DH, **Age**: 29, **Bats**: L)

	G	AB	R	H	D	T	HR	RBI	SB	BB	SO	Avg	OBP	Slg
1999	8	7	1	1	0	0	0	1	0	0	0	.143	.250	.143
Career	109	218	32	53	13	2	0	21	3	19	28	.243	.309	.321

Rich Butler's twin brother hasn't shown enough pop or speed in the high minors to sustain a major league career. He's had four brief stays in the majors during the 1990s and time is running out. 2000 Outlook: D

Mark Dalesandro (**Pos**: C, **Age**: 31, **Bats**: R)

	G	AB	R	H	D	T	HR	RBI	SB	BB	SO	Avg	OBP	Slg
1999	16	27	3	5	0	0	0	1	1	0	2	.185	.207	.185
Career	78	129	17	31	7	0	3	17	1	3	14	.240	.259	.364

His .299 mark in 67 at-bats in 1998 was a solid year for this career minor leaguer. Dalesandro dropped below the Mendoza line in '99 and faced minor league free agency once again. 2000 Outlook: C

Curtis Goodwin (**Pos**: CF/LF, **Age**: 27, **Bats**: L)

	G	AB	R	H	D	T	HR	RBI	SB	BB	SO	Avg	OBP	Slg
1999	91	165	15	38	6	1	0	9	2	13	41	.230	.285	.279
Career	431	1014	129	251	38	4	3	56	66	87	221	.248	.307	.302

The Cubs and Jays took a chance that Goodwin might complement his defensive prowess by getting on base enough to utilize his speed. Days after the Jays claimed him on waivers in August, he retired. 2000 Outlook: D

Craig Grebeck (**Pos**: 2B, **Age**: 35, **Bats**: R)

	G	AB	R	H	D	T	HR	RBI	SB	BB	SO	Avg	OBP	Slg
1999	34	113	18	41	7	0	0	10	0	15	13	.363	.443	.425
Career	663	1706	200	445	96	8	16	162	4	201	232	.261	.342	.355

Grebeck collected a career-high 301 at-bats in 1998, when Toronto didn't have a regular second baseman. Homer Bush arrived in '99. Still, Grebeck hit .363 with a .443 on-base percentage in 113 at-bats. 2000 Outlook: B

Dave Hollins (**Pos**: DH, **Age**: 33, **Bats**: B)

	G	AB	R	H	D	T	HR	RBI	SB	BB	SO	Avg	OBP	Slg
1999	27	99	12	22	5	0	2	6	0	5	22	.222	.260	.333
Career	967	3324	577	867	166	17	112	482	47	463	682	.261	.359	.422

Hollins did little for the Blue Jays, who released him in June. He did hit .317-8-33 at Triple-A Charlotte for the White Sox, who may give him a look. 2000 Outlook: B

John Hudek (**Pos**: RHP, **Age**: 33)

	W	L	Pct.	ERA	G	GS	Sv	IP	H	BB	SO	HR	Ratio
1999	0	2	.000	8.44	20	0	0	21.1	33	15	20	3	2.25
Career	10	15	.400	4.43	194	0	29	201.1	176	123	206	29	1.49

Despite a good second half with the Reds in 1998, Hudek was traded for Mark Wohlers in April and released by the Braves in July. He wasn't effective anywhere, including Toronto. The Jays released him in October. 2000 Outlook: C

Pat Kelly (**Pos**: 2B, **Age**: 32, **Bats**: R)

	G	AB	R	H	D	T	HR	RBI	SB	BB	SO	Avg	OBP	Slg
1999	37	116	17	31	7	0	6	20	0	10	23	.267	.318	.483
Career	681	1988	253	495	109	11	36	217	61	145	425	.249	.307	.369

While Kelly rebounded to put up respectable numbers at the plate in 1999, Homer Bush made him expandable. The Jays released him in June and Kelly didn't resurface. 2000 Outlook: C

Patrick Lennon (Pos: LF, **Age**: 31, **Bats**: R)

	G	AB	R	H	D	T	HR	RBI	SB	BB	SO	Avg	OBP	Slg
1999	9	29	3	6	2	0	1	6	0	2	12	.207	.281	.379
Career	91	189	25	50	14	1	2	22	0	27	59	.265	.359	.381

The 14-year minor league vet hit .290-27-95 in Triple-A in 1998 and .287-30-83 at that level in '99, but he didn't show enough in six major league cups of coffee to stick. 2000 Outlook: C

Eric Ludwick (Pos: RHP, **Age**: 28)

	W	L	Pct.	ERA	G	GS	Sv	IP	H	BB	SO	HR	Ratio
1999	0	0	.000	27.00	1	0	0	1.0	3	2	0	0	5.00
Career	2	10	.167	8.35	31	12	0	74.1	104	44	60	19	1.99

Taken in the 1999 major league Rule 5 draft by the Tigers and traded to the Blue Jays, Ludwick returned to the Marlins after one disastrous outing in Toronto. Then he signed a minor league deal with Milwaukee in December. 2000 Outlook: C

Norberto Martin (Pos: 2B, **Age**: 33, **Bats**: R)

	G	AB	R	H	D	T	HR	RBI	SB	BB	SO	Avg	OBP	Slg
1999	9	27	3	6	2	0	0	0	0	4	4	.222	.364	.296
Career	354	880	116	245	32	6	7	89	23	35	123	.278	.306	.352

The versatile Martin was a valuable reserve for the White Sox in the mid-1990s, but he hasn't been very effective since leaving Chicago two years ago. He became a free agent and signed a minor league deal with the Brewers. 2000 Outlook: C

Mike Matheny (Pos: C, **Age**: 29, **Bats**: R)

	G	AB	R	H	D	T	HR	RBI	SB	BB	SO	Avg	OBP	Slg
1999	57	163	16	35	6	0	3	17	0	12	37	.215	.271	.307
Career	502	1335	116	306	62	4	22	145	6	69	289	.229	.277	.331

Matheny didn't hit for Toronto, but he still excelled at handling pitchers and their offerings from the mound. The Jays released him in November, and the Cardinals signed him for $800,000. 2000 Outlook: B

Willis Otanez (Pos: 3B/1B, **Age**: 26, **Bats**: R)

	G	AB	R	H	D	T	HR	RBI	SB	BB	SO	Avg	OBP	Slg
1999	71	207	28	49	11	0	7	24	0	15	46	.237	.293	.391
Career	74	212	28	50	11	0	7	24	0	15	48	.236	.291	.387

After hitting .285-27-100 in Triple-A in 1998, Otanez was plucked off waivers from Baltimore in May. He struggled as expected, but lit it up against Cleveland, hitting .345-3-6 in 29 at-bats. He was designated for assignment in December after David Segui accepted arbitration. 2000 Outlook: B

Nerio Rodriguez (Pos: RHP, **Age**: 27)

	W	L	Pct.	ERA	G	GS	Sv	IP	H	BB	SO	HR	Ratio
1999	0	1	.000	13.50	2	0	0	2.0	2	2	2	2	2.00
Career	4	6	.400	6.49	29	7	0	68.0	76	34	36	7	1.62

A former catcher, Rodriguez made a big splash as a hard-throwing pitcher in 1995. His last two years have been a struggle, though, as he hasn't established his offspeed stuff and his command. 2000 Outlook: C

Mike Romano (Pos: RHP, **Age**: 28)

	W	L	Pct.	ERA	G	GS	Sv	IP	H	BB	SO	HR	Ratio
1999	0	0	-	11.81	3	0	0	5.1	8	5	3	1	2.44
Career	0	0	-	11.81	3	0	0	5.1	8	5	3	1	2.44

Romano pitched OK at Triple-A Syracuse in 1999, but he's walked 211 hitters in 399.2 innings there over three seasons. He walked five in five rough-and-tumble innings with Toronto in September. 2000 Outlook: C

Anthony Sanders (Pos: LF, **Age**: 26, **Bats**: R)

	G	AB	R	H	D	T	HR	RBI	SB	BB	SO	Avg	OBP	Slg
1999	3	7	1	2	1	0	0	2	0	0	2	.286	.286	.429
Career	3	7	1	2	1	0	0	2	0	0	2	.286	.286	.429

After a 26-homer season in Double-A in 1997, Sanders hasn't been able to put it together in Triple-A in two straight seasons. With high strikeout numbers and a low average, his star is falling. 2000 Outlook: C

Paul Spoljaric (Pos: LHP, **Age**: 29)

	W	L	Pct.	ERA	G	GS	Sv	IP	H	BB	SO	HR	Ratio
1999	2	5	.286	6.26	42	5	0	73.1	85	39	73	10	1.69
Career	8	17	.320	5.48	182	12	4	267.2	266	158	272	37	1.58

Despite good stuff, Spoljaric has been traded three times in two years. Seattle, Philadelphia and Toronto all tried him as a starter with disastrous results. He flourished in relief for the Jays in 1999, then joined the Cardinals in the Pat Hentgen trade. 2000 Outlook: B

Chris Woodward (Pos: SS, **Age**: 23, **Bats**: R)

	G	AB	R	H	D	T	HR	RBI	SB	BB	SO	Avg	OBP	Slg
1999	14	26	1	6	1	0	0	2	0	2	6	.231	.276	.269
Career	14	26	1	6	1	0	0	2	0	2	6	.231	.276	.269

Woodward is a steady fielder who had his best year with the bat in 1999 in Triple-A. That earned him two callups, but he's not a long-range prospect. 2000 Outlook: C

Toronto Blue Jays Minor League Prospects

Organization Overview:

Though the Blue Jays began slashing payroll this offseason, they're in no danger of becoming the Expos. Few teams, if any, have drafted better than Toronto has in the 1990s, and even after the dollars-dictated trade of Shawn Green, the Jays still have plenty of young talent in the majors and throughout the minors. As a result, they should be able to contend for at least a wild-card berth with a mid-market budget. The big league club has a fine pitching nucleus in Chris Carpenter, Kelvim Escobar, Roy Halladay and Billy Koch, all of whom are 25 or younger. Toronto's system is deep in up-the-middle prospects, led by Vernon Wells.

Brent Abernathy

Position: 2B
Bats: R **Throws:** R
Ht: 6' 1" **Wt:** 185

Opening Day Age: 22
Born: 9/23/77 in Atlanta, GA

Recent Statistics

	G	AB	R	H	D	T	HR	RBI	SB	BB	SO	Avg
1998 A Dunedin	124	485	85	159	36	1	3	65	35	44	38	.328
1999 AA Knoxville	136	577	108	168	42	1	13	62	34	55	47	.291
1999 MLE	136	550	79	141	37	0	9	45	23	34	50	.256

Abernathy is a righthanded-hitting version of Pittsburgh's Warren Morris, and at four years younger he's further developed than Morris was at the same age. Named the nation's top high school athlete in 1996, when he was also a second-round pick, Abernathy has a career .308 average as a pro. In 1999, he led the Double-A Southern League in runs and hits while increasing his home-run power significantly. He runs well, has very good instincts and will be an acceptable defender. Homer Bush is flashier, but Abernathy will be a better offensive player and could challenge for Bush's job in 2001.

Clayton Andrews

Position: P
Bats: R **Throws:** L
Ht: 6' 0" **Wt:** 175

Opening Day Age: 21
Born: 5/15/78 in Dunedin, FL

Recent Statistics

	W	L	ERA	G	GS	Sv	IP	H	R	BB	SO	HR
1998 A Hagerstown	10	7	2.28	27	26	0	162.0	112	59	46	193	7
1999 AA Knoxville	10	8	3.93	25	25	0	132.2	143	85	69	93	13
1999 AAA Syracuse	0	1	7.80	3	3	0	15.0	10	14	13	9	5

Named the most valuable pitcher in the Class-A South Atlantic League in 1998, Andrews skipped a level last season and wasn't nearly as dominant in Double-A. A 1996 third-round pick, he has a fastball that averages 91 MPH, good velocity for a lefthander, a power curveball and a promising changeup. He's a fierce competitor who sometimes gets a bit too aggressive. If everything comes together for Andrews, he could be a poor man's Mike Hampton. It's also possible that the Blue Jays may use him as a lefthanded setup man.

Gary Glover

Position: P
Bats: R **Throws:** R
Ht: 6' 5" **Wt:** 205

Opening Day Age: 23
Born: 12/3/76 in Cleveland, OH

Recent Statistics

	W	L	ERA	G	GS	Sv	IP	H	R	BB	SO	HR
1999 AA Knoxville	8	2	3.56	13	13	0	86.0	70	39	27	77	5
1999 AAA Syracuse	4	6	5.19	14	14	0	76.1	93	50	35	57	10
1999 AL Toronto	0	0	0.00	1	0	0	1.0	0	0	1	0	0

Glover may have the best arm in the Jays system, though he's needed time to adjust to each level as he has risen through the minors. A 15th-round pick in 1994, his career 31-55 record belies the quality of his stuff. He averages 93-95 MPH with his fastball and has a hard slider, a curveball and a changeup. He posted his first winning record in six seasons in 1999, as he began to make progress in controlling his fastball and developing a consistent delivery. He projects as a major league starter, but may get a look as a long reliever in spring training.

Joe Lawrence

Position: 3B
Bats: R **Throws:** R
Ht: 6' 2" **Wt:** 190

Opening Day Age: 23
Born: 2/13/77 in Lake Charles, LA

Recent Statistics

	G	AB	R	H	D	T	HR	RBI	SB	BB	SO	Avg
1998 A Dunedin	125	454	102	140	31	6	11	44	15	105	88	.308
1999 AA Knoxville	70	250	52	66	16	2	7	24	7	56	48	.264
1999 MLE	70	239	38	55	14	1	5	17	4	35	51	.230

Lawrence moved from shortstop to third base in 1999, and the Blue Jays were about to try him as a catcher when he slipped on a wet base and tore ligaments in his ankle, ending his season. A 1996 first-round pick, Lawrence's excellent eye at the plate—he has 161 walks in 195 games over the last two seasons—should translate into a healthy batting average, and he could eventually develop above-average power. His strong arm suits him well at third base, and it would be a huge bonus if he could develop into a catcher. He'll be valuable at either position when he's ready sometime in 2001.

John Sneed

Position: P
Bats: L **Throws:** R
Ht: 6' 6" **Wt:** 235

Opening Day Age: 23
Born: 6/30/76 in Houston, TX

Recent Statistics

	W	L	ERA	G	GS	Sv	IP	H	R	BB	SO	HR
1998 A Hagerstown	16	2	2.56	27	27	0	161.2	123	59	58	210	9
1999 A Dunedin	11	2	3.45	21	20	0	125.1	107	53	36	143	10
1999 AA Knoxville	3	1	5.08	6	6	0	28.1	33	17	21	28	2

Sneed lasted until the 22nd round of the 1997 draft after pitching sparingly his last two years at Texas A&M, and all he's done ever since is dominate. He has gone 36-6, 2.81 as a pro, allowing just 305 hits and striking out 460 in 385 innings. Sneed throws a very heavy 91-94 MPH fastball, sometimes relying on it too much at the expense of his slider and changeup. He was rated the best pitching prospect in the high Class-A Florida State League in a midseason survey of managers, then got a taste of Double-A at season's end. If his secondary pitches don't develop, Sneed could become a Jeff Nelson-type reliever. He may get a look from the Blue Jays after the All-Star break this year.

Andy Thompson

Position: OF
Bats: R **Throws:** R
Ht: 6' 3" **Wt:** 210

Opening Day Age: 24
Born: 10/8/75 in Oconomowoc, WI

Recent Statistics

	G	AB	R	H	D	T	HR	RBI	SB	BB	SO	Avg
1998 AA Knoxville	125	481	74	137	33	2	14	88	8	54	69	.285
1999 AA Knoxville	67	254	56	62	16	3	15	53	7	34	55	.244
1999 AAA Syracuse	62	229	42	67	17	2	16	42	5	21	45	.293
1999 MLE	129	467	78	113	30	3	23	76	8	39	105	.242

Thompson slid until the 23rd round of the 1994 draft because of signability questions, but received a $355,000 bonus, the equivalent of late-first-round money at the time, because of his prodigious power potential. Then he went out and hit just 46 homers in 502 games over his first four pro seasons. His career at a crossroads, Thompson changed his swing on his own. No longer trying to muscle every pitch out of the ballpark, he responded with 31 homers in 1999 and was rated the best power prospect in the Double-A Southern League. He has reasonable plate discipline for a power hitter, and took to a move from third base to left field. Toronto may have an opening at DH in 2000, and Thompson would be a candidate to fill it.

Vernon Wells

Position: OF
Bats: R **Throws:** R
Ht: 6' 1" **Wt:** 210

Opening Day Age: 21
Born: 12/8/78 in Shreveport, LA

Recent Statistics

	G	AB	R	H	D	T	HR	RBI	SB	BB	SO	Avg
1999 A Dunedin	70	265	43	91	16	2	11	43	13	26	34	.343
1999 AA Knoxville	26	106	18	36	6	2	3	17	6	12	15	.340
1999 AAA Syracuse	33	129	20	40	8	1	4	21	5	10	22	.310
1999 AL Toronto	24	88	8	23	5	0	1	8	1	4	18	.261
1999 MLE	59	225	30	66	12	1	5	30	8	15	39	.293

No prospect took a bigger leap forward in 1999 than Wells, who was named the No. 1 prospect in three minor leagues while going from high Class-A to the majors at age 20. When the Blue Jays drafted him fifth overall in 1997, the industry buzz was that he went that early only because he was willing to sign quickly for a relatively inexpensive $1.6 million. Two years later, he's arguably the best position-player prospect in the game. He's a legitimate five-tool player who is learning to drive the ball and steal bases. He's a very good center fielder with a very strong arm. Though Toronto made him its everyday center fielder while contending for the wild card last September, Wells would benefit from a half-season in Triple-A to polish his game.

Kevin Witt

Position: 1B-OF
Bats: L **Throws:** R
Ht: 6' 4" **Wt:** 200

Opening Day Age: 24
Born: 1/5/76 in High Point, NC

Recent Statistics

	G	AB	R	H	D	T	HR	RBI	SB	BB	SO	Avg
1999 AAA Syracuse	114	421	72	117	24	3	24	71	0	64	109	.278
1999 AL Toronto	15	34	3	7	1	0	1	5	0	2	9	.206
1999 MLE	114	410	63	106	23	2	20	62	0	56	114	.259

A 1994 first-round pick, Witt has taken to first base after previously playing shortstop and third base. Power is his best tool and he hits southpaws very well for a lefthanded hitter. Witt altered his swing early in 1999 with poor results, but corrected his mechanics and was generating his usual bat speed by season's end. He hits for a decent average and has increased his walk total in each of his six pro seasons. Witt could wind up in a platoon with Andy Thompson at DH this year in Toronto. Witt would have been in line for more playing time had Carlos Delgado been traded, as initially was expected.

Others to Watch

Casey Blake (26), rated the best defensive third baseman in the Triple-A International League in 1999, saw his batting average drop to .245 from .357 the year before. He should rebound and also has power and a strong arm. He could start for Toronto or serve in a reserve role in 2000. . . **Cesar Izturis** (20) is a polished shortstop. A switch-hitter, he hit .308 and stole 32 bases for high Class-A Dunedin as a teenager. . . Right behind Izturis on the organization depth chart is **Felipe Lopez** (19), the eighth overall pick in the 1998 draft. He's also a switch-hitter and flashy shortstop, though his skills are currently more raw than Izturis' . . . Righthander **Peter Munro** (24), acquired in the 1998 Mike Stanley trade with Boston, uses three pitches, including an 89-92 MPH fastball. A starter in the minors, he has relieved in the majors for Toronto. . . Catcher **Josh Phelps** (21) led the Florida State League with a .562 slugging percentage despite his youth and home ballpark, one of the toughest in the high Class-A circuit. He's a solid catch-and-throw guy who calls a good game, and he has worked diligently to improve his foot speed. . . **Mike Young** (23) was chosen as the Florida State League's best defensive shortstop over Izturis, but yielded the position to his teammate and moved to second base by the end of the year. Young makes good contact, has gap power and steals bases.

National League Players

Bank One Ballpark

Offense

Though it has the second-highest elevation among major league parks, Bank One Ballpark has little overall effect on scoring. The 24-foot-high wall in center field is difficult to clear, but the deep center field and tricky right-field corner make it a good triples park. Scoring goes up when the retractable roof is open, thanks to the warm desert air.

Defense

Shorter fences in left and right field allow outfielders to take home runs away. The team still is trying to master growing grass in a building that is mostly closed off from sunlight. Early and late in the season, the field can have some dead spots in the outfield that can create bad hops. The Bermuda grass currently in use lends itself to large divots, such as on a golf fairway. Picnic-area overhangs on both sides of the center-field wall can create tough caroms and tough calls for umpires. The center fielder has more ground to cover than in most National League parks, making speed essential for the position.

Who It Helps The Most

Jay Bell's power is mostly from left field to the line, and he takes advantage of Bank One's dimensions. Travis Lee has hit for a much higher average at home in two seasons. BOB cuts down on homers, so it has benefited Brian Anderson, who's vulnerable to the longball.

Who It Hurts The Most

Luis Gonzalez, Damian Miller and Tony Womack all have hit significantly better away from Arizona since joining the Diamondbacks. Both pitchers signed as free agents from the Cardinals, Andy Benes and Todd Stottlemyre, didn't pitch well at Bank One last season.

Rookies & Newcomers

The Diamondbacks aren't expected to have any significant new faces playing prominent roles in 2000. Their biggest offseason move was the signing of Russ Springer. Erubiel Durazo, who provided electrifying offense in the final two months last year, tore the cover off the ball at home and on the road.

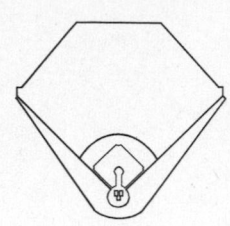

Dimensions: LF-330, LCF-374, CF-407, RCF-374, RF-334

Capacity: 48,500

Elevation: 1090 feet

Surface: Grass

Foul Territory: Average

Park Factors

1999 Season

	Home Games			Away Games			
	D'backs	Opp	Total	D'backs	Opp	Total	Index
G	75	75	150	72	72	144	—
Avg	.279	.250	.264	.277	.249	.263	100
AB	2534	2620	5154	2591	2432	5023	99
R	407	304	711	415	307	722	95
H	707	656	1363	717	606	1323	99
2B	129	126	255	131	109	240	104
3B	31	22	53	14	11	25	207
HR	93	74	167	100	85	185	88
BB	266	229	495	268	253	521	93
SO	447	534	981	511	546	1057	90
E	39	60	99	57	45	102	93
E-Infield	33	49	82	50	36	86	92
LHB-Avg	.282	.250	.271	.288	.257	.276	98
LHB-HR	45	18	63	45	23	68	92
RHB-Avg	.275	.250	.260	.265	.246	.254	102
RHB-HR	48	56	104	55	62	117	86

1998-1999

	Home Games			Away Games			
	D'backs	Opp	Total	D'backs	Opp	Total	Index
G	148	148	296	148	148	296	—
Avg	.268	.257	.262	.254	.257	.255	103
AB	4977	5185	10162	5167	4905	10072	101
R	708	655	1363	701	686	1387	98
H	1333	1331	2664	1312	1260	2572	104
2B	228	249	477	247	227	474	100
3B	54	41	95	33	21	54	174
HR	159	155	314	173	174	347	90
BB	484	417	901	504	520	1024	87
SO	958	926	1884	1145	986	2131	88
E	81	107	188	100	103	203	93
E-Infield	67	88	155	81	79	160	97
LHB-Avg	.269	.258	.264	.263	.264	.264	100
LHB-HR	70	45	115	75	50	125	92
RHB-Avg	.267	.256	.261	.244	.253	.249	105
RHB-HR	89	110	199	98	124	222	88

1999 Rankings (National League)

- Highest triple factor
- Third-highest RHB batting-average factor
- Second-lowest walk factor
- Third-lowest strikeout factor
- Third-lowest RHB home-run factor

Buck Showalter

1999 Season

Working with a much different roster than in Arizona's expansion year, Buck Showalter loosened the reins somewhat. The veteran players were allowed to grow facial hair, for example, and for the most part policed themselves. On the field, Showalter was able to use more consistent lineups. Fortified by free-agent signings, the Diamondbacks became the first expansion team to reach the playoffs in their second season.

Offense

Once he decided upon his regulars last year, Showalter stayed with them with only occasional days off. He relied on a typically built lineup: speed (Tony Womack) leading off, someone who can handle the bat (Jay Bell) batting second, the team's best hitter (Luis Gonzalez) third and the club's top slugger (Matt Williams) cleanup. Arizona scored more runs than any National League team, more via power than speed, though Womack led the league in steals. Showalter uses hit-and-run plays and pinch-hitters less often than most managers.

Pitching & Defense

Only six pitchers started games for Arizona last year, with Brian Anderson filling in for Todd Stottlemyre and Armando Reynoso. Other than Randy Johnson, Diamondbacks pitchers weren't allowed to run up high pitch counts, and Johnson's arm was protected for most of the second half. Once Matt Mantei arrived as closer, Showalter was consistent in his use of setup men: Gregg Olson and Bobby Chouinard from the right side and Dan Plesac and Greg Swindell from the left. Showalter sacrificed some defense for offense, playing Womack at shortstop against lefthanders during the second half to get Bernard Gilkey's bat in right field.

2000 Outlook

Showalter likely will keep his veterans in the same roles. Several of his players had career years in 1999, so defending the NL West title will be tough. Showalter's biggest decisions appear to be how to preserve Johnson for the long haul and how to get first basemen Erubiel Durazo and Travis Lee into the lineup. It appears that Lee will play right field and Womack will move to short.

Born: 5/23/56 in DeFuniak, Florida

Playing Experience: No major league experience

Managerial Experience: 6 seasons

Arizona

Manager Statistics

Year	Team, Lg	W	L	Pct	GB	Finish
1999	Arizona, NL	100	62	.617	—	1st West
6 Seasons		478	427	.528	—	—

1999 Starting Pitchers by Days Rest

	<=3	4	5	6+
Diamondbacks Starts	0	84	46	26
Diamondbacks ERA	0.00	3.33	4.13	4.64
NL Avg Starts	3	81	48	21
NL ERA	4.84	4.53	4.72	4.98

1999 Situational Stats

	Buck Showalter	NL Average
Hit & Run Success %	33.8	33.6
Stolen Base Success %	77.8	70.2
Platoon Pct.	62.7	55.2
Defensive Subs	17	25
High-Pitch Outings	25	13
Quick/Slow Hooks	9/12	16/15
Sacrifice Attempts	75	89

1999 Rankings (National League)

- 1st in starts with over 140 pitches (2)
- 2nd in stolen-base percentage (77.8%), steals of home plate (2), squeeze plays (9) and starts with over 120 pitches (25)
- 3rd in sacrifice-bunt percentage (86.7%)

Jay Bell

1999 Season

Moved to second base late in 1998, Jay Bell turned in one of the best offensive performances ever for that position in 1999. Rogers Hornsby, Davey Johnson and Ryne Sandberg are the only second baseman who ever hit more homers in a year than Bell's 38. He also had a combined 244 runs and RBI, a total exceeded by just five second basemen this century: Hall of Famers Charlie Gehringer, Hornsby, Nap Lajoie and Jackie Robinson, plus Roberto Alomar. Bell's home and road splits were close, so his monster season wasn't the product of Bank One Ballpark.

Hitting

Bell is an excellent mistake hitter who belts middle-of-the-plate fastballs or hanging breaking balls. He's also one of the most patient hitters in the National League, willing to go deep in the count especially when a basestealer such as Tony Womack is on first. Bell displayed an improved ability to pull pitches last year, as 28 of his 38 homers were hit left of center field. He also showed a knack for fouling off tough outside pitches while waiting for something he could handle.

Baserunning & Defense

Once a Gold Glove shortstop, Bell led National League second basemen in errors last year. His arm is fine, but his hands are weak. His miscues usually come on balls he bobbles or fails to come up with. His range to his right isn't as strong as it was during his shortstop days, though he makes the plays to his left. He has learned to turn the double play capably. Bell's speed is now average at best and he steals only infrequently.

2000 Outlook

With three years left on his contract and a no-trade clause, Bell is entrenched as Arizona's second baseman. Whether he can repeat his career year seems doubtful. But he certainly has learned to hit for power and should continue to pile up walks and strikeouts. Expect a power dropoff as pitchers give his bat more respect.

Position: 2B
Bats: R **Throws:** R
Ht: 6' 0" **Wt:** 184
Opening Day Age: 34
Born: 12/11/65 in Eglin AFB, FL
ML Seasons: 14

Overall Statistics

	G	AB	R	H	D	T	HR	RBI	SB	BB	SO	Avg	OBP	Slg
1999	151	589	132	170	32	6	38	112	7	82	132	.289	.374	.557
Career	1681	6240	963	1677	338	60	162	732	84	691	1229	.269	.344	.420

Where He Hits the Ball

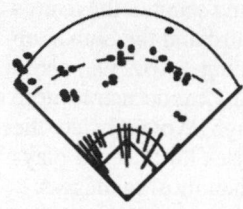 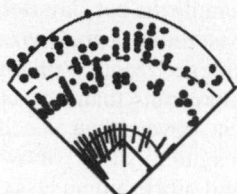

Vs. LHP	Vs. RHP

1999 Situational Stats

	AB	H	HR	RBI	Avg		AB	H	HR	RBI	Avg
Home	293	89	21	67	.304	LHP	168	57	12	38	.339
Road	296	81	17	45	.274	RHP	421	113	26	74	.268
First Half	343	98	24	65	.286	Sc Pos	143	44	7	71	.308
Scnd Half	246	72	14	47	.293	Clutch	93	26	6	15	.280

1999 Rankings (National League)

- 1st in most pitches seen per plate appearance (4.39), errors at second base (22), pitches seen (3,023) and lowest fielding percentage at second base (.968)
- 2nd in on-base percentage vs. lefthanded pitchers (.479) and runs scored
- 3rd in sacrifice flies (9)
- Led the Diamondbacks in slugging percentage, HR frequency (15.5 ABs per HR), most pitches seen per plate appearance (4.39), batting average vs. lefthanded pitchers, batting average on an 0-2 count (.314), slugging percentage vs. lefthanded pitchers (.661), on-base percentage vs. lefthanded pitchers (.479) and highest percentage of pitches taken (60.3)

Andy Benes

1999 Season

No longer asked to be the ace of the Arizona rotation, Andy Benes slumped early last year. He really struggled to protect leads. He led at some point in nine of his 12 losses, and he had a 5.67 ERA in innings in which he took the mound with a lead. He did prove to be fairly reliable in the second half of the season, though overall it was the worst year of his career.

Pitching

Benes has four pitches; a fastball, curveball, slider and changeup. His fastball has dropped to 91-92 MPH, and he also has lost some movement and command with the pitch. That slippage contributed to the career-high 34 homers he allowed in 1999. His mechanics were inconsistent last year, which flattened out his slider. He also is hurt by his reluctance to change speeds. He continues to handle lefthanders and righthanders equally well.

Defense & Hitting

Benes has an average move to first base, but his deliberate delivery allows baserunners to get good jumps against him. He fields bunts to both sides of the mound and covers first base adequately, though his error totals have risen in recent seasons. Benes helps himself at the plate. He can pull an inside fastball down the left-field line on occasion and has six career home runs. He's also one of the better bunting pitchers in the game.

2000 Outlook

Benes had a player option for $6 million for 2000 but opted instead for free agency. He should have plenty of innings left in his arm, and his endurance and repertoire make him an attractive commodity. That said, he still has to prove he can be counted on as a top-of-the-rotation starter. Because this year's free-agent pool is weak in quality starters, he'll be in demand.

Position: SP
Bats: R **Throws:** R
Ht: 6' 6" **Wt:** 245

Opening Day Age: 32
Born: 8/20/67 in Evansville, IN
ML Seasons: 11
Pronunciation: BENN-ess
Nickname: Big Train, Rain Man

Overall Statistics

	W	L	Pct.	ERA	G	GS	Sv	IP	H	BB	SO	HR	Ratio
1999	13	12	.520	4.81	33	32	0	198.1	216	82	141	34	1.50
Career	131	119	.524	3.79	328	324	1	2135.0	2001	729	1721	219	1.28

How Often He Throws Strikes

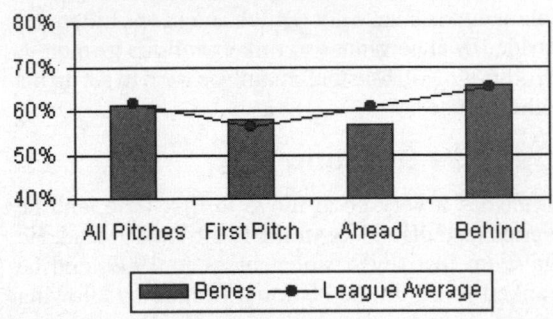

1999 Situational Stats

	W	L	ERA	Sv	IP		AB	H	HR	RBI	Avg
Home	6	8	5.53	0	94.1	LHB	366	100	14	52	.273
Road	7	4	4.15	0	104.0	RHB	425	116	20	56	.273
First Half	5	9	5.51	0	111.0	Sc Pos	194	47	5	63	.242
Scnd Half	8	3	3.92	0	87.1	Clutch	39	8	1	5	.205

1999 Rankings (National League)

- 3rd in home runs allowed
- 5th in pickoff throws (167), highest ERA at home and most home runs allowed per nine innings (1.54)
- 7th in most run support per nine innings (6.3)
- 9th in wild pitches (10), most pitches thrown per batter (3.81), fewest GDPs induced per nine innings (0.5) and lowest fielding percentage at pitcher (.933)
- 10th in stolen bases allowed (21)
- Led the Diamondbacks in losses, hits allowed, home runs allowed, walks allowed and wild pitches (10)

Arizona

Omar Daal

Position: SP
Bats: L **Throws:** L
Ht: 6' 3" **Wt:** 195

Opening Day Age: 28
Born: 3/1/72 in Maracaibo, Venezuela
ML Seasons: 7
Pronunciation: DOLL

1999 Season

For the first time, Omar Daal entered a season with a multiyear contract and the knowledge he would be a starter. He responded by proving his breakthrough 1998 was no fluke. He was consistent through the first five months, then was roughed up in September, perhaps because he pitched a career-high 214.2 innings. Daal also set a personal best with 16 victories, double his previous high.

Pitching

Coached by Luis Tiant in the Dodgers system, Daal uses a similar back-to-the-batter turn as part of his deception. His command of his breaking pitch, a cross between a slider and a curve, continues to improve as he matures as a starter. Though his changeup is a very good pitch and keeps hitters off stride, Daal continues to tinker with his grip on it. His 86-87 MPH fastball mainly is used to set up his other pitches.

Defense & Hitting

Daal has a very good move to first base, and he varies it so that he's extremely difficult to read. He gave up just seven stolen bases in 1999, and he ranked fourth in the National League by allowing just a 41 percent success rate. Daal's quickness helps him get off the mound and field as well as anyone in the league. He's also one of the best bunting pitchers in the NL, both for a sacrifice or for a hit. When he swings away, he makes consistent contact and can move the runner over when needed.

2000 Outlook

Daal planned to lighten his winter-ball workload in Venezuela to compensate for his increased role with the Diamondbacks. He's entering the prime of his career without a lot of miles on his arm. But without a dominating out pitch or an above-average fastball, it's unlikely he'll improve much over his 1999 season.

Overall Statistics

	W	L	Pct.	ERA	G	GS	Sv	IP	H	BB	SO	HR	Ratio
1999	16	9	.640	3.65	32	32	0	214.2	188	79	148	21	1.24
Career	36	32	.529	4.02	270	64	1	591.0	567	229	445	57	1.35

How Often He Throws Strikes

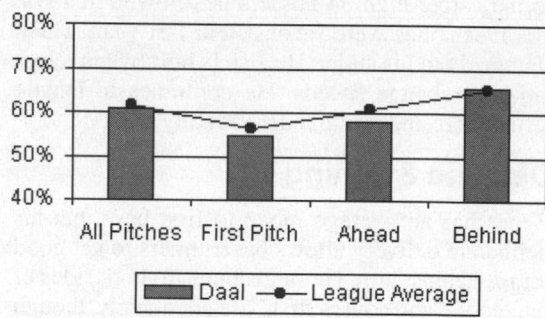

1999 Situational Stats

	W	L	ERA	Sv	IP		AB	H	HR	RBI	Avg
Home	8	5	3.32	0	111.0	LHB	142	29	2	10	.204
Road	8	4	3.99	0	103.2	RHB	656	159	19	74	.242
First Half	8	5	3.47	0	124.2	Sc Pos	174	43	4	63	.247
Scnd Half	8	4	3.90	0	90.0	Clutch	63	12	2	6	.190

1999 Rankings (National League)

- 4th in lowest batting average allowed (.236) and lowest stolen-base percentage allowed (41.2)
- 6th in runners caught stealing (10)
- 7th in pickoff throws (161) and lowest slugging percentage allowed (.378)
- 9th in lowest on-base percentage allowed (.308) and fewest baserunners allowed per nine innings (11.5)
- 10th in ERA, wins and balks (2)
- Led the Diamondbacks in balks (2), GDPs induced (18), highest groundball/flyball ratio allowed (1.3) and lowest stolen-base percentage allowed (41.2)

Erubiel Durazo

Position: 1B
Bats: L **Throws:** L
Ht: 6' 3" **Wt:** 225

Opening Day Age: 26
Born: 1/23/74 in Hermosillo, Mexico
ML Seasons: 1
Pronunciation: ur-ROO-bee-ell dew-RAH-zoh

1999 Season

Purchased from the Mexican League's Monterrey Sultans in December 1998, Erubiel Durazo led the minors with a .404 batting average, becoming the first full-season minor leaguer in 38 years to top the .400 mark. He never stopped hitting after getting called up by the Diamondbacks in late July, quickly taking the first-base job against righthanders. Durazo's .422 on-base percentage and .594 slugging percentage easily would have led the team if he had enough at-bats to qualify.

Hitting

Considering how much power he generates, Durazo has an extremely short stroke. He uses a light bat, which allows him to get it through the strike zone quickly. Most of his home runs go between center and right-center field. He rarely hits a ball to straightaway left field. Durazo struggled with offspeed pitches at first after he was recalled, but improved with experience. He hit lefthanders well in the minors, but surprisingly wasn't given the opportunity in the majors. He had just four hits in 18 at-bats against big league southpaws, but three of those hits were homers and he also drew seven walks.

Baserunning & Defense

Durazo's athleticism doesn't compare to that of Travis Lee, his competitor for Arizona's first-base job. Durazo is much slower, pretty much a station-to-station baserunner who's no threat to steal. He's a very ordinary first baseman. His range and arm are average. His best defensive attribute is his ability to anticipate and handle bunts well.

2000 Outlook

Durazo's success in the Mexican League and in his U.S. pro debut indicate that he's for real. Durazo must continue to produce because the Diamondbacks invested a $10 million bonus in Lee, who is a better all-around player. Lee will begin 2000 in right field, leaving the first-base job for Durazo. Arizona should give him a chance to play against lefthanders because there's no reason yet to think he couldn't handle southpaws.

Overall Statistics

	G	AB	R	H	D	T	HR	RBI	SB	BB	SO	Avg	OBP	Slg
1999	52	155	31	51	4	2	11	30	1	26	43	.329	.422	.594
Career	52	155	31	51	4	2	11	30	1	26	43	.329	.422	.594

Where He Hits the Ball

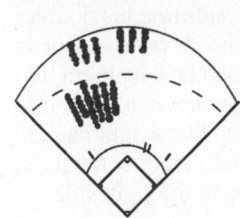
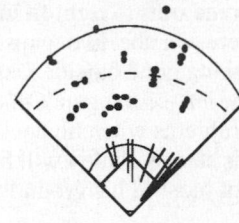

Vs. LHP   **Vs. RHP**

1999 Situational Stats

	AB	H	HR	RBI	Avg		AB	H	HR	RBI	Avg
Home	76	26	4	13	.342	LHP	18	4	3	7	.222
Road	79	25	7	17	.316	RHP	137	47	8	23	.343
First Half	0	0	0	0	-	Sc Pos	30	14	4	23	.467
Scnd Half	155	51	11	30	.329	Clutch	18	5	3	8	.278

1999 Rankings (National League)

- Did not rank near the top or bottom in any category

Steve Finley

Gold Glover

1999 Season

Arizona's biggest position-player signing of the offseason at four years and $21.5 million, Steve Finley rebounded from his 1998 season-long slump. He set career highs in home runs, RBI and walks despite playing with a herniated disk after mid-June. In the National League, only Mark McGwire (nine) had more multi-homer games than Finley (seven). He also won his third Gold Glove and first since 1996.

Hitting

Finley is a streak hitter who can carry his team for a week at a time. He started to focus on hitting for power in 1996, and while he succeeded he also no longer hits for average. Finley pulls most of his home runs to right field while splitting his doubles between the two gaps. He has become adept at taking good outside fastballs and driving them into the left-center gap. Offspeed pitches can cause him problems when he doesn't keep his weight back in his stance. Finley will hit flyballs all over the park, but most of his groundballs go to the right side.

Baserunning & Defense

Finley is well suited to the large center field of Bank One Ballpark. He gets a good jump on flyballs and doesn't shy away from the fence. His range remains above average, though injuries have weakened his arm. Even though runners test him more often, he registered just five assists in 1999. Because of his recent back problems he steals less often than he did earlier in his career. Finley still has good speed on the basepaths and will take the extra base.

2000 Outlook

Finley's back trouble seemed to quiet after a couple of epidural cortisone shots. This type of injury can become chronic and may catch up with him in time. He's becoming fairly one-dimensional as an offensive player and shouldn't be expected to duplicate his 1999 production.

Position: CF
Bats: L **Throws:** L
Ht: 6' 2" **Wt:** 180

Opening Day Age: 35
Born: 3/12/65 in Union City, TN
ML Seasons: 11

Overall Statistics

	G	AB	R	H	D	T	HR	RBI	SB	BB	SO	Avg	OBP	Slg
1999	156	590	100	156	32	10	34	103	8	63	94	.264	.336	.525
Career	1538	5788	905	1586	275	85	153	649	242	469	766	.274	.329	.430

Where He Hits the Ball

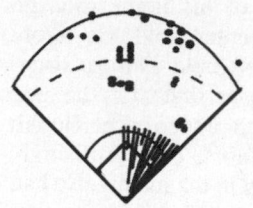
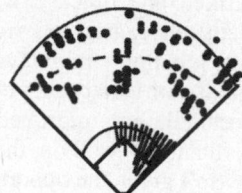

Vs. LHP **Vs. RHP**

1999 Situational Stats

	AB	H	HR	RBI	Avg		AB	H	HR	RBI	Avg
Home	282	74	17	47	.262	LHP	189	49	10	38	.259
Road	308	82	17	56	.266	RHP	401	107	24	65	.267
First Half	331	89	17	63	.269	Sc Pos	146	33	11	66	.226
Scnd Half	259	67	17	40	.259	Clutch	89	20	1	3	.225

1999 Rankings (National League)

- 2nd in fielding percentage in center field (.995)
- 3rd in triples
- 5th in fewest GDPs per GDP situation (3.3%)
- 9th in lowest batting average
- Led the Diamondbacks in fewest GDPs per GDP situation (3.3%) and games played
- Led NL center fielders in fewest GDPs per GDP situation (3.3%), home runs, triples and total bases (310)

Luis Gonzalez

1999 Season

Looking to make payroll room for Gregg Jefferies, the Tigers traded Luis Gonzalez and $500,000 to the Diamondbacks for Karim Garcia last December. Gonzalez started as a platoon player but had a career season, putting together a 30-game hitting streak early in the year that made him a fan favorite. He posted career highs in batting average, homers and RBI, earning a three-year, $12.5 contract extension in August.

Hitting

Gonzalez always has been a line-drive hitter who uses the entire field. He now has the ability to hit a mistake out of the park more often by pulling it, and he also has gap power to the opposite field. His success last season can be traced to making better and harder contact than he had in the past. In 1999, Gonzalez also was able to lay off high fastballs, which had been a weakness. He generates most of his power against righthanders.

Baserunning & Defense

Gonzalez still has slightly above average speed and he uses it to his advantage on the basepaths, though he has become less aggressive during the past couple of seasons. He steals a few bases with his combination of quickness and a decent first step. He's an adequate left fielder who is helped by his experience. He charges groundballs very well, the remants of his early years as a first baseman. His arm is below average but not a major weakness.

2000 Outlook

Gonzalez appeared at home in Arizona almost from the beginning of the season, and that contributed to his success. Like many players, he has discovered power later in his career. He should have another solid year, but it's more likely to be in the neighborhood of .280-20-90 rather than a repeat of .336-26-111.

Position: LF
Bats: L **Throws:** R
Ht: 6' 2" **Wt:** 200

Opening Day Age: 32
Born: 9/2/67 in Tampa, FL
ML Seasons: 10

Overall Statistics

	G	AB	R	H	D	T	HR	RBI	SB	BB	SO	Avg	OBP	Slg
1999	153	614	112	206	45	4	26	111	9	66	63	.336	.403	.549
Career	1275	4478	644	1242	282	42	133	661	98	474	602	.277	.350	.448

Where He Hits the Ball

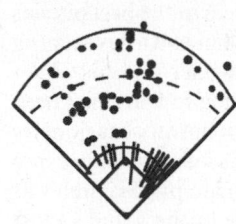

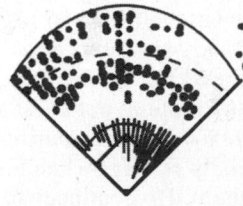

Vs. LHP　　　　**Vs. RHP**

1999 Situational Stats

	AB	H	HR	RBI	Avg		AB	H	HR	RBI	Avg
Home	299	95	10	49	.318	LHP	165	54	3	32	.327
Road	315	111	16	62	.352	RHP	449	152	23	79	.339
First Half	333	120	14	57	.360	Sc Pos	161	54	6	77	.335
Scnd Half	281	86	12	54	.306	Clutch	86	33	6	19	.384

1999 Rankings (National League)

- 1st in hits
- 2nd in batting average and doubles
- 3rd in batting average in the clutch
- Led the Diamondbacks in on-base percentage, batting average in the clutch, batting average vs. righthanded pitchers, slugging percentage vs. righthanded pitchers (.575), on-base percentage vs. righthanded pitchers (.396) and batting average with two strikes (.260)
- Led NL left fielders in slugging percentage, batting average in the clutch, batting average vs. righthanded pitchers, batting average with two strikes (.260), batting average, at-bats, runs scored, hits, singles, doubles, total bases (337), times on base (279) and plate appearances (693)

Arizona

Randy Johnson

1999 Season

Picking Arizona over Anaheim, Los Angeles and Texas, Randy Johnson signed a $52.4 million, four-year contract as a free agent. Any questions as to his health or age were quickly answered, as he had one of the most dominating seasons ever. His strikeout total of 364 ranks fourth in modern history, and he became the first pitcher to lead the National League in strikeouts and ERA since Nolan Ryan in 1987. He lost five wins to blown saves and the Diamondbacks failed to provide adequate run support on numerous occasions, preventing him from winning 20 games. He still got his due as the NL's Cy Young Award winner.

Pitching

Even at 36, Johnson still has two of the best pitches in baseball: a 96-97 MPH fastball and a devastating slider. He rarely sees a lefthander and his slider chews up righthanders, breaking toward the knees and topping out at 89 MPH. Johnson occasionally mixes in a changeup and a two-seam fastball, especially on days when his two main pitches aren't as sharp. He continues to be one of the game's most durable starters, averaging 122 pitches per outing last season.

Defense & Hitting

Johnson gets off the mound well for a man his size and fields bunts and slow grounders equally well. His move to first base is deceptive, though he gave up a major league-high 42 steals last year because opponents believe they need to run to have any chance to score off him. Johnson is an awkward hitter and an inconsistent bunter.

2000 Outlook

Johnson quieted questions about his back trouble last year. He has a strong conditioning program that helps him maintain his remarkable velocity. He got stronger as 1999 wore on and shows no signs of slowing down. Another dominating season is expected from him this year. His long-term value would be enhanced if the Diamondbacks tried to reduce his workload somewhat.

Position: SP
Bats: R **Throws:** L
Ht: 6'10" **Wt:** 230

Opening Day Age: 36
Born: 9/10/63 in Walnut Creek, CA
ML Seasons: 12
Nickname: Big Unit

Overall Statistics

	W	L	Pct.	ERA	G	GS	Sv	IP	H	BB	SO	HR	Ratio
1999	17	9	.654	2.48	35	35	0	271.2	207	70	364	30	1.02
Career	160	88	.645	3.26	331	322	2	2250.0	1730	1013	2693	199	1.22

How Often He Throws Strikes

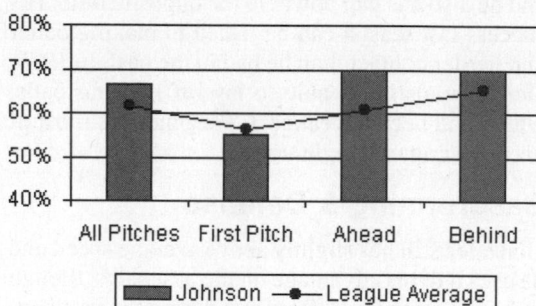

1999 Situational Stats

	W	L	ERA	Sv	IP		AB	H	HR	RBI	Avg
Home	9	6	2.96	0	127.2	LHB	87	9	0	3	.103
Road	8	3	2.06	0	144.0	RHB	906	198	30	74	.219
First Half	9	7	2.95	0	152.2	Sc Pos	197	38	7	48	.193
Scnd Half	8	2	1.89	0	119.0	Clutch	126	31	2	10	.246

1999 Rankings (National League)

- 1st in ERA, complete games (12), innings pitched, batters faced (1,079), strikeouts, pitches thrown (4,206), stolen bases allowed (42), most strikeouts per nine innings (12.1), ERA on the road, lowest batting average allowed with runners in scoring position, games started, runners caught stealing (17) and lowest batting average on an 0-2 count (.000)
- Led the Diamondbacks in ERA, wins, complete games (12), shutouts (2), innings pitched, batters faced (1,079), hit batsmen (9), strikeouts, balks (2), pitches thrown (4,206), stolen bases allowed (42), winning percentage, highest strikeout/walk ratio (5.2), lowest batting average allowed (.208) and lowest slugging percentage allowed (.335)

Travis Lee

1999 Season

Travis Lee may have set the standard for sopho-more slumps. It took him until June to get his average above .250, and then he went 0-for-30 in late July. He lost his job to an Erubiel Durazo-Greg Colbrunn platoon. While working on playing the outfield, Lee suffered a badly sprained ankle that kept him out until mid-September. About the only positive was that Lee walked more than he struck out, an encouraging sign for a young hitter.

Hitting

Lee has the ability to use his quick hands to spray the ball to all fields. Because his stroke is level, he's a classic line-drive hitter. He struggles when he pulls offspeed pitches rather than going with them. When he's hot, Lee can handle all types of pitches. Lee says he sees the ball much better at Bank One Ballpark, where he has hit 67 points higher and with more power than he has on the road. He has yet to prove he can handle major league lefthanders.

Baserunning & Defense

Unlike most first baseman, Lee is above average in terms of both speed and baserunning. His quick first step makes him a dangerous basestealer when he picks his spots. A good athlete, Lee already is an accomplished first baseman. He scoops low throws in the dirt with the best in the National League. He's still unproven as an outfielder, but he has the athleticism to handle right field. His arm should be at least average.

2000 Outlook

The Diamondbacks were in the middle of a pennant race when Lee slumped and the Erubiel Durazo story was born. The darling of the organization when he signed for a then-record $10 million bonus in 1996, Lee was a disappointment last year. Durazo has taken his job, though Arizona will try to keep Lee's bat in the lineup by playing him in right field and moving Tony Womack to shortstop. Lee has the tools to play the outfield, but it's his offense that bears the most watching.

Position: 1B
Bats: L **Throws:** L
Ht: 6' 3" **Wt:** 214

Opening Day Age: 24
Born: 5/26/75 in San Diego, CA
ML Seasons: 2

Overall Statistics

	G	AB	R	H	D	T	HR	RBI	SB	BB	SO	Avg	OBP	Slg
1999	120	375	57	89	16	2	9	50	17	58	50	.237	.337	.363
Career	266	937	128	240	36	4	31	122	25	125	173	.256	.342	.402

Where He Hits the Ball

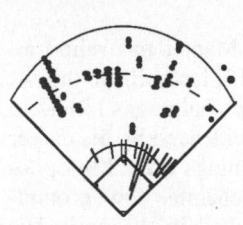
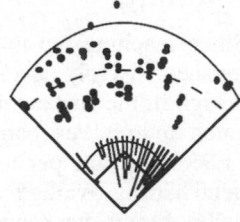

Vs. LHP   **Vs. RHP**

1999 Situational Stats

	AB	H	HR	RBI	Avg		AB	H	HR	RBI	Avg
Home	176	53	7	33	.301	LHP	102	22	3	18	.216
Road	199	36	2	17	.181	RHP	273	67	6	32	.245
First Half	303	78	9	45	.257	Sc Pos	104	23	5	42	.221
Scnd Half	72	11	0	5	.153	Clutch	65	16	2	10	.246

1999 Rankings (National League)
- 1st in fielding percentage at first base (.997)
- 6th in stolen-base percentage (85.0)
- Led the Diamondbacks in stolen-base percentage (85.0) and highest percentage of extra bases taken as a runner (60.0)
- Led NL first basemen in stolen-base percentage (85.0) and batting average with the bases loaded (.500)

Matt Mantei

1999 Season

After a season and a half of closing games for a team that had few save situations, Matt Mantei was rescued from the Marlins in an early July trade. The cost was steep—premium pitching prospects Brad Penny and Vladimir Nunez, plus stud outfielder Abraham Nunez—but the Diamondbacks felt their biggest weakness was a leaky bullpen. Mantei solved the problem, saving 22 games in 25 chances for Arizona. He was even better than during his breakthrough 1998 performance. He did serve up the pitch that ended Arizona's season, a 10th-inning homer by the Mets' Todd Pratt in Game 4 of the Division Series, but the Diamondbacks never regretted the trade.

Pitching

Since reaching the majors, Mantei has relied almost exclusively on a 97-MPH fastball. He throws it high in the strike zone and challenges hitters to catch up to it. Few can, as evidenced by his career 11.99 strikeouts per nine innings and .200 opponent batting average. He generates few ground-balls, though he keeps the ball in the park. His curveball is inconsistent, but when it's sharp it's a solid complement to his fastball. Mantei's latest project is a slider that has been able to help him get righthanders out. He issues too many walks but survives because he's so unhittable.

Defense & Hitting

Mantei is somewhat sluggish in getting off the mound but fields his position adequately. His move to first base is slow and ineffective. Because he believes he can strike out any hitter he faces, his focus always seems to be on the batter and not runners. Mantei bats infrequently and his hitting skills are limited.

2000 Outlook

Mantei's fastball alone makes him a dominating closer. If he becomes more consistent with his curveball and slider, he can move into the elite class of closers. He works best when used in one-inning stints, so a capable setup corps is critical to his success.

Position: RP
Bats: R **Throws:** R
Ht: 6' 1" **Wt:** 190

Opening Day Age: 26
Born: 7/7/73 in Tampa, FL
ML Seasons: 4
Pronunciation: MAN-tie

Overall Statistics

	W	L	Pct.	ERA	G	GS	Sv	IP	H	BB	SO	HR	Ratio
1999	1	3	.250	2.76	65	0	32	65.1	44	44	99	5	1.35
Career	5	8	.385	3.44	133	0	41	151.2	107	101	202	9	1.37

How Often He Throws Strikes

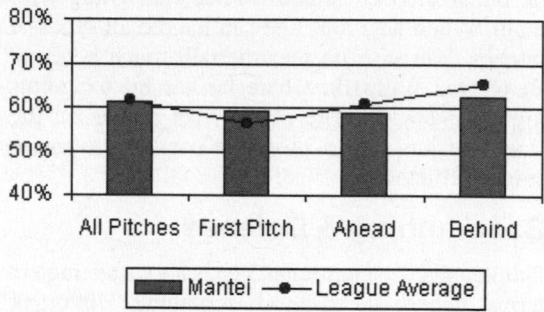

1999 Situational Stats

	W	L	ERA	Sv	IP		AB	H	HR	RBI	Avg
Home	0	1	2.35	10	30.2	LHB	113	18	4	13	.159
Road	1	2	3.12	22	34.2	RHB	120	26	1	8	.217
First Half	1	2	2.65	11	37.1	Sc Pos	64	11	2	16	.172
Scnd Half	0	1	2.89	21	28.0	Clutch	160	33	4	19	.206

1999 Rankings (National League)

- 3rd in most strikeouts per nine innings in relief (13.6)
- 5th in save percentage (86.5) and lowest batting average allowed in relief (.189)
- 6th in games finished (60)
- 8th in saves (32) and lowest batting average allowed in relief with runners on base (.175)
- 9th in save opportunities (37)
- Led the Diamondbacks in saves (22), save opportunities (25) and save percentage (88.0)

Todd Stottlemyre

1999 Season

Todd Stottlemyre signed a four-year, $32 million contract as a free agent last winter. He went 4-1 in his first eight starts before leaving an outing May 17 with tightness in his pitcher shoulder. Tests revealed a slightly torn rotator cuff and he didn't pitch for three months. He returned August 20 and was moderately effective the rest of the way. His final start was his best, a 7-1 win over the Mets in Game 2 of the Division Series.

Pitching

Most of Stottlemyre's velocity came back after he rehabbed, but his slider's sharp break didn't return completely. He needs it because his slider is his out pitch. Greg Swindell taught him a splitter that serves as a changeup at times. Lefthanders continue to be a problem for Stottlemyre because he throws most of his pitches at the same speed. He continues to be inefficient, working deep into the count on many hitters.

Defense & Hitting

Stottlemyre is able to get off the mound quickly for a power pitcher because he finishes his delivery with good balance. He fields both bunts and slow groundballs in front of the plate equally well. Because he's a good athlete, he covers first base better than most pitchers. Stottlemyre's move to first base is average. He's not an automatic out and will make solid contact with mistake pitches.

2000 Outlook

Whether Stottlemyre can continue to pitch without needing surgery remains in doubt. Some pitchers have attempted to come back from a torn rotator cuff without an operation, but eventually have suffered a full tear. Stottlemyre's greatest asset in this battle is his dedication and willingness to spend the time in the weight room. He still is somewhat of a question mark for this season, which doesn't bode well for an Arizona rotation that figures to be without free agent Andy Benes.

Position: SP
Bats: L **Throws:** R
Ht: 6' 3" **Wt:** 200

Opening Day Age: 34
Born: 5/20/65 in Yakima, WA
ML Seasons: 12
Pronunciation: STAH-till-my-er

Overall Statistics

	W	L	Pct.	ERA	G	GS	Sv	IP	H	BB	SO	HR	Ratio
1999	6	3	.667	4.09	17	17	0	101.1	106	40	74	12	1.44
Career	129	113	.533	4.22	349	317	1	2076.0	2076	773	1499	224	1.37

How Often He Throws Strikes

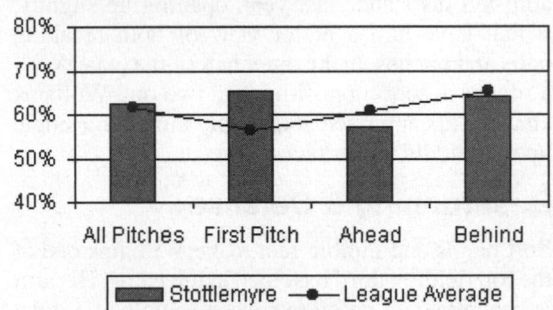

1999 Situational Stats

	W	L	ERA	Sv	IP		AB	H	HR	RBI	Avg
Home	4	1	4.75	0	47.1	LHB	170	53	6	22	.312
Road	2	2	3.50	0	54.0	RHB	226	53	6	26	.235
First Half	4	1	3.59	0	57.2	Sc Pos	96	25	3	33	.260
Scnd Half	2	2	4.74	0	43.2	Clutch	21	5	0	2	.238

1999 Rankings (National League)

- Did not rank near the top or bottom in any category

Matt Williams

1999 Season

Matt Williams signed a five-year, $45 million extension after being traded to Arizona in November 1997, then went out and had a subpar, injury-riddled 1998 season during which he was distracted by family difficulties. With those problems cleared up, he rebounded in 1999 and set career highs in batting average, doubles and RBI. Williams finished second in the National League in RBI and third in the Most Valuable Player race.

Hitting

Williams is at his best when he's aggressive. He often swings at the first pitch and takes advantage of pitchers who try to get ahead in the count. He adjusted his stance last year, opening up slightly, which gave him a better view of both breaking balls and pitches on the outer half of the plate. With a runner in scoring position and two out, Williams changes his approach and simply aims for a single up the middle, often succeeding.

Baserunning & Defense

Soft hands and nimble feet make Williams one of the top fielding third basemen in the game. His arm is accurate, and he knows when to unload or take his time. Williams' footwork and lateral movement improved last season after he put in extra conditioning work. He handles balls toward the line better than ones toward the hole. Williams has lost a step or two on the basepaths because of various foot ailments. He's no threat to steal.

2000 Outlook

Williams should continue to be highly productive at the plate. But a big part of his success was due to the years Tony Womack, Jay Bell and Luis Gonzalez had in front of him, so Williams may not get as many chances to drive in runs. As always, the key for him will be staying healthy. Last season was just the fourth in which he played 150 or more games.

Position: 3B
Bats: R **Throws:** R
Ht: 6' 2" **Wt:** 214

Opening Day Age: 34
Born: 11/28/65 in Bishop, CA
ML Seasons: 13

Overall Statistics

	G	AB	R	H	D	T	HR	RBI	SB	BB	SO	Avg	OBP	Slg
1999	154	627	98	190	37	2	35	142	2	41	93	.303	.344	.536
Career	1560	5872	850	1575	274	31	334	1050	48	390	1175	.268	.316	.496

Where He Hits the Ball

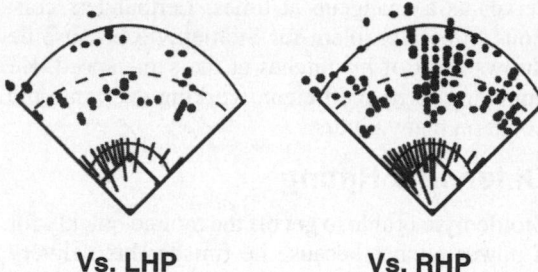

Vs. LHP   **Vs. RHP**

1999 Situational Stats

	AB	H	HR	RBI	Avg		AB	H	HR	RBI	Avg
Home	308	86	17	64	.279	LHP	177	59	12	45	.333
Road	319	104	18	78	.326	RHP	450	131	23	97	.291
First Half	358	114	23	82	.318	Sc Pos	177	60	13	106	.339
Scnd Half	269	76	12	60	.283	Clutch	93	28	9	33	.301

1999 Rankings (National League)

- 1st in fewest pitches seen per plate appearance (3.07)
- 2nd in fielding percentage at third base (.977), RBI and lowest percentage of pitches taken (43.7)
- 4th in batting average with the bases loaded (.588)
- 5th in at-bats
- Led the Diamondbacks in batting average with runners in scoring position, batting average with the bases loaded (.588) and cleanup slugging percentage (.538)
- Led NL third basemen in batting average with runners in scoring position, at-bats, RBI and sacrifice flies (8)

Tony Womack

1999 Season

Initially disappointed by his spring-training trade to Arizona for minor league outfielder Paul Weichard and his resulting position switch from second base to right field, Tony Womack nonetheless adapted well. He became a capable outfielder and became the first player to lead the National League in stolen bases for three straight seasons since Vince Coleman in 1985-90.

Hitting

Womack doesn't have any power, so he slaps the ball in the hole and up the middle, then uses his speed to generate hits. He has been hurt by his inability to draw many walks or develop into anything more than an average bunter. Womack becomes impatient at times and doesn't work counts deep enough. His on-base percentage was a career-high .332 last season, but that mark is still far from acceptable for a leadoff man.

Baserunning & Defense

Womack is one of the fastest players in the game and the majority of his stolen bases are the result of his pure speed. He continues to improve at reading pitchers and getting good jumps. His career 87 percent success rate is the highest among active big leaguers with at least 200 attempts. Womack also can take an extra base as well as anyone. His transition to the outfield wasn't easy at first. He appears more comfortable in right field than during the few games he played in center, where he had problems on balls hit over his head. He uses his athletic ability and speed to compensate for inexperience. Runners take advantage of his weak arm.

2000 Outlook

The Diamondbacks have two first basemen and no clear shortstop, so they'll try to move Travis Lee to right field and shift Womack to short. That may be a stretch, because as a second baseman he had trouble going to his left. His arm also isn't up to shortstop standards. Even if he can't handle another position switch, he'll stay in the lineup somewhere because Arizona needs his speed. The club rewarded him with a four-year, $17 million contract in December, a deal it almost certainly will come to regret.

Position: RF/2B/SS
Bats: L **Throws:** R
Ht: 5' 9" **Wt:** 159

Opening Day Age: 30
Born: 9/25/69 in Danville, VA
ML Seasons: 6

Overall Statistics

	G	AB	R	H	D	T	HR	RBI	SB	BB	SO	Avg	OBP	Slg
1999	144	614	111	170	25	10	4	41	72	52	68	.277	.332	.370
Career	495	1976	301	549	80	27	13	144	194	144	278	.278	.327	.365

Where He Hits the Ball

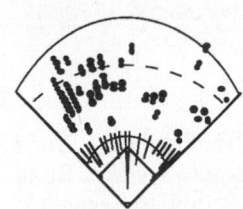
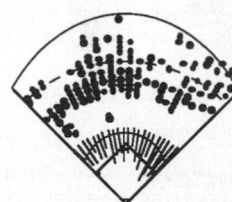

Vs. LHP   **Vs. RHP**

1999 Situational Stats

	AB	H	HR	RBI	Avg		AB	H	HR	RBI	Avg
Home	320	84	1	19	.263	LHP	169	49	2	18	.290
Road	294	86	3	22	.293	RHP	445	121	2	23	.272
First Half	328	88	2	20	.268	Sc Pos	112	25	1	34	.223
Scnd Half	286	82	2	21	.287	Clutch	97	28	2	12	.289

1999 Rankings (National League)

- 1st in stolen bases
- 2nd in fielding percentage in right field (.992)
- 3rd in triples
- 4th in singles and lowest HR frequency (153.5 ABs per HR)
- 5th in bunts in play (21) and steals of third (9)
- Led the Diamondbacks in highest groundball/flyball ratio (1.3), on-base percentage for a leadoff hitter (.333), bunts in play (21) and steals of third (9)
- Led NL right fielders in stolen-base percentage (84.7), bunts in play (21), singles, sacrifice bunts (9), stolen bases and caught stealing (13)

Arizona

Brian Anderson

Position: SP/RP
Bats: B **Throws:** L
Ht: 6' 1" **Wt:** 183

Opening Day Age: 27
Born: 4/26/72 in
Geneva, OH
ML Seasons: 7

Overall Statistics

	W	L	Pct.	ERA	G	GS	Sv	IP	H	BB	SO	HR	Ratio
1999	8	2	.800	4.57	31	19	1	130.0	144	28	75	18	1.32
Career	40	31	.563	4.82	121	104	1	650.0	719	136	309	111	1.32

1999 Situational Stats

	W	L	ERA	Sv	IP		AB	H	HR	RBI	Avg
Home	7	0	2.97	1	88.0	LHB	108	32	1	4	.296
Road	1	2	7.93	0	42.0	RHB	408	112	17	51	.275
First Half	2	1	6.94	1	59.2	Sc Pos	98	34	6	39	.347
Scnd Half	6	1	2.56	0	70.1	Clutch	26	11	2	7	.423

1999 Season

The offseason signings of Randy Johnson, Todd Stottlemyre and Armando Reynoso knocked Brian Anderson from the Arizona rotation. He seemed to be a prime candidate for a trade, but remained with the Diamondbacks. Anderson moved into the rotation when Stottlemyre was injured, pitched very well in the second half and earned a Division Series start over Andy Benes.

Pitching, Defense & Hitting

Anderson works by spotting his 90-91 MPH fastball and above-average changeup on both sides of the plate. He also throws a slider. His career average of 1.88 walks per nine innings ranks sixth among active pitchers with at least 500 innings. After surrendering a National League-high 39 homers (one per 5.3 innings) in 1998, he cut that down to 18 (one per 7.2 innings) last year. Anderson is a very good fielder and has an effective pickoff move. A switch-hitter, he handles the bat well and can run.

2000 Outlook

The confidence from his late surge in 1999, combined with a predetermined role, should allow Anderson to blossom. If he can continue to avoid giving up homers, he has the command to win 15 games.

Greg Colbrunn

Position: 1B
Bats: R **Throws:** R
Ht: 6' 0" **Wt:** 205

Opening Day Age: 30
Born: 7/29/69 in
Fontana, CA
ML Seasons: 8

Overall Statistics

	G	AB	R	H	D	T	HR	RBI	SB	BB	SO	Avg	OBP	Slg
1999	67	135	20	44	5	3	5	24	1	12	23	.326	.392	.519
Career	703	2087	239	594	108	8	66	312	29	100	345	.285	.325	.439

1999 Situational Stats

	AB	H	HR	RBI	Avg		AB	H	HR	RBI	Avg
Home	64	20	2	14	.313	LHP	97	35	5	19	.361
Road	71	24	3	10	.338	RHP	38	9	0	5	.237
First Half	60	19	2	10	.317	Sc Pos	35	12	1	18	.343
Scnd Half	75	25	3	14	.333	Clutch	18	3	0	5	.167

1999 Season

Signed to a two-year, $1.8 million contract as a free agent to strengthen Arizona's bench, Greg Colbrunn did exactly that. After two-thirds of a season as an effective pinch-hitter, he took over as part of a platoon at first base when Travis Lee slumped.

Hitting, Baserunning & Defense

Colbrunn is an aggressive hitter who usually makes solid contact. Though he was much more effective against lefthanders and rarely faced righthanders in 1999, in the past his platoon splits were nearly identical. He has below-average speed and won't steal bases, but he's intelligent and won't make mistakes. Colbrunn had major elbow surgery early in his career, and his arm is below average. He's an adequate first baseman, though he struggles on balls hit to his right. He can serve as an emergency catcher, his original position as a pro.

2000 Outlook

With Erubiel Durazo likely to get a full-time shot at first base, Colbrunn once again will come off the bench. He accepts the reserve role without complaint and has thrived in it.

Andy Fox

Position: SS/3B
Bats: L **Throws:** R
Ht: 6' 4" **Wt:** 202

Opening Day Age: 29
Born: 1/12/71 in Sacramento, CA
ML Seasons: 4

Overall Statistics

	G	AB	R	H	D	T	HR	RBI	SB	BB	SO	Avg	OBP	Slg
1999	99	274	34	70	12	2	6	33	4	33	61	.255	.351	.380
Career	373	996	140	253	38	8	18	91	31	103	195	.254	.340	.362

1999 Situational Stats

	AB	H	HR	RBI	Avg		AB	H	HR	RBI	Avg
Home	128	33	4	16	.258	LHP	46	7	0	5	.152
Road	146	37	2	17	.253	RHP	228	63	6	28	.276
First Half	152	43	5	24	.283	Sc Pos	64	14	1	26	.219
Scnd Half	122	27	1	9	.221	Clutch	54	13	1	5	.241

1999 Season

After Tony Batista was traded to Toronto in June, Andy Fox was Arizona's shortstop against righthanders until he suffered a ribcage injury in late August. A fan favorite for his versatility and all-out play, Fox played far less than he did in 1998 because of an influx of veterans.

Hitting, Baserunning & Defense

Because he can't hit lefthanders, Fox is relegated to strict platoon roles and late-inning defensive assignments. His swing isn't quick enough to pull inside pitches, especially fastballs. He needs to improve on taking outside pitches to the opposite field. Fox steals bases more with his aggressiveness than his slightly above-average speed. He can play second and third base, but shortstop is where he's most comfortable. His range is adequate, as is his arm. He also can handle a corner outfield spot without embarrassing himself.

2000 Outlook

As the Diamondbacks have evolved from an expansion club to a playoff team, Fox' playing time has diminished. Manager Buck Showalter likes his versatility and has confidence in his defense, but Fox never will be more than a role player in Arizona.

Bernard Gilkey

Position: RF/LF
Bats: R **Throws:** R
Ht: 6' 0" **Wt:** 198

Opening Day Age: 33
Born: 9/24/66 in St. Louis, MO
ML Seasons: 10

Overall Statistics

	G	AB	R	H	D	T	HR	RBI	SB	BB	SO	Avg	OBP	Slg
1999	94	204	28	60	16	1	8	39	2	29	42	.294	.379	.500
Career	1096	3791	581	1057	232	23	113	517	115	438	649	.279	.356	.442

1999 Situational Stats

	AB	H	HR	RBI	Avg		AB	H	HR	RBI	Avg
Home	78	26	4	19	.333	LHP	104	35	4	26	.337
Road	126	34	4	20	.270	RHP	100	25	4	13	.250
First Half	111	34	4	14	.306	Sc Pos	58	20	3	32	.345
Scnd Half	93	26	4	25	.280	Clutch	41	14	0	8	.341

1999 Season

A contract technicality allowed Bernard Gilkey to veto a spring-training trade that would have sent him to Pittsburgh. He opted to stay in Arizona despite no promise of regular playing time. He adapted to a pinch-hitting role and by the second half, he was the starting right fielder against lefthanders.

Hitting, Baserunning & Defense

Laser-eye surgery in September 1998 has allowed Gilkey to pick up the spin of the ball better. He hits lefthanders very well, though he struggles against pitches on the outer half from righthanders. He batted .333 last year as a pinch-hitter and seems well suited for the role. Gilkey has above-average speed but rarely attempts to steal anymore. He uses his wheels to his advantage in playing the corner outfield positions, charging balls like an infielder and making accurate throws. That compensates for a barely average arm.

2000 Outlook

Gilkey again could be crowded out of the Arizona outfield, with Steve Finley and Luis Gonzalez signed to long-term deals and $10 million bonus baby Travis Lee slated for right field. With a $5 million salary, Gilkey may be tough to trade.

Damian Miller

Position: C
Bats: R **Throws:** R
Ht: 6' 2" **Wt:** 212

Opening Day Age: 30
Born: 10/13/69 in LaCrosse, WI
ML Seasons: 3

Overall Statistics

	G	AB	R	H	D	T	HR	RBI	SB	BB	SO	Avg	OBP	Slg
1999	86	296	35	80	19	0	11	47	0	19	78	.270	.316	.446
Career	168	530	57	146	34	2	16	74	1	32	133	.275	.318	.438

1999 Situational Stats

	AB	H	HR	RBI	Avg		AB	H	HR	RBI	Avg
Home	156	39	3	21	.250	LHP	103	33	5	17	.320
Road	140	41	8	26	.293	RHP	193	47	6	30	.244
First Half	191	50	5	31	.262	Sc Pos	94	24	4	34	.255
Scnd Half	105	30	6	16	.286	Clutch	47	10	1	5	.213

1999 Season

Given a chance to play more than ever, Damian Miller responded by showing more home-run power than he had in the past. He became Randy Johnson's personal catcher for most of the season, catching 29 of the Cy Young Award winner's 35 starts. Miller's season ended on September 21, when he broke his right hand blocking a pitch in the dirt.

Hitting, Baserunning & Defense

Miller had shown gap power before 1999, then suddenly learned how to drive balls over the fence. He's much more effective against lefthanders and fared best when batting eighth in the lineup last year. Like fellow Diamondbacks catcher Kelly Stinnett, Miller can run hot or cold at the plate for long stretches. With more playing time last year, his catching improved. He has a solid arm, though he needs to improve at blocking balls. He runs well for a catcher.

2000 Outlook

Miller will continue to share Arizona's catching duties with Stinnett, as he has for the past one-and-a-half seasons. Miller has turned out to be a nice find for a second-round expansion-draft pick.

Gregg Olson

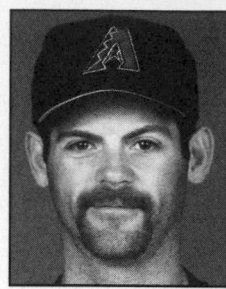

Position: RP
Bats: R **Throws:** R
Ht: 6' 4" **Wt:** 208

Opening Day Age: 33
Born: 10/11/66 in Scribner, NE
ML Seasons: 12

Overall Statistics

	W	L	Pct.	ERA	G	GS	Sv	IP	H	BB	SO	HR	Ratio
1999	9	4	.692	3.71	61	0	14	60.2	54	25	45	9	1.30
Career	40	37	.519	3.23	581	0	217	629.2	551	303	549	38	1.36

1999 Situational Stats

	W	L	ERA	Sv	IP		AB	H	HR	RBI	Avg
Home	5	1	3.19	6	31.0	LHB	90	27	3	13	.300
Road	4	3	4.25	8	29.2	RHB	137	27	6	23	.197
First Half	4	4	4.71	11	28.2	Sc Pos	60	16	4	29	.267
Scnd Half	5	0	2.81	3	32.0	Clutch	148	34	8	28	.230

1999 Season

Gregg Olson began the year as Arizona's closer, a role he handled well in 1998. But with three blown saves in the first week and six in his first 14 save chances, he lost the job. After the arrival of closer Matt Mantei from Florida in July, Olson fared better as Arizona's righthanded setup man.

Pitching, Defense & Hitting

Olson finally has adjusted to compensate for the decline in his great curveball, which is now merely good and no longer an out pitch. He has added a sinking action to his fastball, inducing more groundballs. He also has a solid changeup that tends to run away from righthanders. Olson is an adequate fielder who struggles to hold runners. He's overmatched as a hitter.

2000 Outlook

Olson should be able to continue his career as a middle reliever or setup man. But he probably will not do so for Arizona, after he became a free agent and the club signed Russ Springer for two years and $4 million.

Dan Plesac

Position: RP
Bats: L **Throws:** L
Ht: 6' 5" **Wt:** 217

Opening Day Age: 38
Born: 2/4/62 in Gary, IN
ML Seasons: 14
Pronunciation:
PLEE-sack
Nickname: Sac,
Sac-Man

Overall Statistics

	W	L	Pct.	ERA	G	GS	Sv	IP	H	BB	SO	HR	Ratio
1999	2	4	.333	5.89	64	0	1	44.1	50	17	53	7	1.51
Career	51	61	.455	3.67	822	14	154	917.0	853	323	850	88	1.28

1999 Situational Stats

	W	L	ERA	Sv	IP		AB	H	HR	RBI	Avg
Home	0	1	4.76	0	22.2	LHB	98	20	1	9	.204
Road	2	3	7.06	1	21.2	RHB	78	30	6	25	.385
First Half	0	4	7.28	0	29.2	Sc Pos	56	18	6	33	.321
Scnd Half	2	0	3.07	1	14.2	Clutch	83	25	3	19	.301

1999 Season

Arizona acquired Dan Plesac in June for shortstop Tony Batista and reliever John Frascatore. Though those two went on to have good seasons for Toronto, the Diamondbacks never regretted the move because they needed a lefthanded specialist.

Pitching, Defense & Hitting

Plesac's slider remains his best pitch and makes him tough on lefthanders. The velocity on his fastball decreased last year, rarely reaching 91-92 MPH as it had in the past. Late last season, he adjusted where he sets up on the pitching rubber, allowing him to work away from righties more easily. Plesac comes off the mound hard toward the third base side on his delivery, making it difficult for him to field balls to the right side or to cover first base on a close play. Basestealers rarely test him. He's a terrible hitter.

2000 Outlook

By making 60 appearances in 1999, Plesac guaranteed his $1.5 million contract for this year. Arizona has some lefthanders in the minors, but none that show the promise of soon filling the lefty-on-lefty role that every contender needs and Plesac has proven he can handle.

Armando Reynoso

Position: SP
Bats: R **Throws:** R
Ht: 6' 0" **Wt:** 204

Opening Day Age: 33
Born: 5/1/66 in San
Luis Potosi, Mexico
ML Seasons: 9
Pronunciation:
ray-NOH-so

Overall Statistics

	W	L	Pct.	ERA	G	GS	Sv	IP	H	BB	SO	HR	Ratio
1999	10	6	.625	4.37	31	27	0	167.0	178	67	79	20	1.47
Career	56	44	.560	4.56	156	147	1	860.2	945	310	448	103	1.46

1999 Situational Stats

	W	L	ERA	Sv	IP		AB	H	HR	RBI	Avg
Home	4	3	3.50	0	82.1	LHB	323	85	11	37	.263
Road	6	3	5.21	0	84.2	RHB	322	93	9	44	.289
First Half	5	1	3.46	0	96.1	Sc Pos	159	43	4	61	.270
Scnd Half	5	5	5.60	0	70.2	Clutch	40	6	0	2	.150

1999 Season

The Diamondbacks signed Armando Reynoso to a two-year, $5 million contract as part of their offseason run on free-agent pitchers. Coming off major arm surgery that knocked him out for half of 1998, Reynoso went 10-2, 3.74 through the first five months. But he ran out of gas in September, going 0-4, 8.85, and was left off the postseason roster.

Pitching, Defense & Hitting

Reynoso throws a variety of pitches from a variety of angles. His main pitch is a cut fastball, and he uses a screwball to keep lefthanders off balance. A forkball and curveball round out his arsenal. He lacks a true out pitch, so he needs to mix speeds and locations to be effective. Reynoso's pickoff move may be the best among major league righthanders. He handles all routine plays around the mound and swings the bat well for a pitcher.

2000 Outlook

Now that he has pitched his first full season since his surgery, Reynoso should be stronger in 2000. He's an ideal fifth starter whose turn can be skipped on occasion.

Kelly Stinnett

Position: C
Bats: R **Throws:** R
Ht: 5'11" **Wt:** 225

Opening Day Age: 30
Born: 2/4/70 in Lawton, OK
ML Seasons: 6
Pronunciation: STIH-net

Overall Statistics

	G	AB	R	H	D	T	HR	RBI	SB	BB	SO	Avg	OBP	Slg
1999	88	284	36	66	13	0	14	38	2	24	83	.232	.302	.426
Career	348	966	117	229	45	4	31	107	6	104	270	.237	.324	.388

1999 Situational Stats

	AB	H	HR	RBI	Avg		AB	H	HR	RBI	Avg
Home	115	26	3	9	.226	LHP	66	20	3	10	.303
Road	169	40	11	29	.237	RHP	218	46	11	28	.211
First Half	146	31	7	16	.212	Sc Pos	79	17	1	20	.215
Scnd Half	138	35	7	22	.254	Clutch	44	13	3	9	.295

1999 Season

Despite a deep thigh bruise early in the season and problems with his left hand late in the year, Kelly Stinnett set career bests in home runs and RBI in 1999. His average was as low as .170 on June 2, but he hit .260 from then on. As in 1998, Stinnett split time behind the plate with Damian Miller.

Hitting, Baserunning & Defense

Stinnett is a free swinger with occasional power. He didn't have severe platoon splits before last year, when he hammered lefthanders and was feeble against righthanders. He struggles versus offspeed pitches on the outer half of the plate. A streak hitter, he can stay hot or slump for a month at a time. Stinnett is slow and rarely tries to steal. He's a good receiver who blocks pitches well, and pitchers enjoy throwing to him. His arm is strong but his release is a bit slow.

2000 Outlook

Stinnett will continue as a part-timer because he doesn't hit righthanders enough to play on a regular basis. His tendency to disappear offensively for long stretches also doesn't help his cause.

Greg Swindell

Position: RP
Bats: R **Throws:** L
Ht: 6'3" **Wt:** 230

Opening Day Age: 35
Born: 1/2/65 in Fort Worth, TX
ML Seasons: 14
Pronunciation: swin-DELL

Overall Statistics

	W	L	Pct.	ERA	G	GS	Sv	IP	H	BB	SO	HR	Ratio
1999	4	0	1.000	2.51	63	0	1	64.2	54	21	51	8	1.16
Career	119	108	.524	3.82	502	269	4	2070.2	2153	468	1413	234	1.27

1999 Situational Stats

	W	L	ERA	Sv	IP		AB	H	HR	RBI	Avg
Home	2	0	4.82	1	28.0	LHB	93	20	1	5	.215
Road	2	0	0.74	0	36.2	RHB	142	34	7	18	.239
First Half	1	0	3.82	1	30.2	Sc Pos	55	11	1	13	.200
Scnd Half	3	0	1.32	0	34.0	Clutch	98	22	2	7	.224

1999 Season

A Red Sox free agent, Greg Swindell signed a three-year, $5.7 million contract with Arizona last offseason. His season was interrupted in June by a pulled ribcage muscle that landed him on the disabled list, but he appeared in 30 of the Diamondbacks' final 67 games after returning. He never got comfortable pitching at Bank One Ballpark, posting a 4.82 ERA in Arizona. But he more than made up for it with a microscopic 0.74 ERA on the road.

Pitching, Defense & Hitting

Swindell has an average fastball and finishes hitters off with a splitter. He's almost as effective against righthanders as he is versus lefthanders. He can work a few days in a row and more than an inning at a time. When his release point drops below three-quarters, his fastball tends to hang in the strike zone. Swindell's move to first base is excellent and he handles all of the routine plays in the field. He's a decent hitter for a pitcher.

2000 Outlook

After working in 209 games the past three seasons, Swindell seems primed to continue in a setup role. He hit the wall as a starter with the Astros, but since has become one of the game's better lefthanded relievers.

Other Arizona Diamondbacks

Dan Carlson (Pos: RHP, Age: 30)

	W	L	Pct.	ERA	G	GS	Sv	IP	H	BB	SO	HR	Ratio
1999	0	0	-	9.00	2	0	0	4.0	5	0	3	0	1.25
Career	1	0	1.000	6.70	23	0	0	47.0	63	18	37	10	1.72

For a third straight season Carlson didn't perform well in a brief big league stint. He made two June appearances and found himself back at Triple-A. 2000 Outlook: D

Bobby Chouinard (Pos: RHP, Age: 27)

	W	L	Pct.	ERA	G	GS	Sv	IP	H	BB	SO	HR	Ratio
1999	5	2	.714	2.68	32	0	1	40.1	31	12	23	3	1.07
Career	9	6	.600	4.54	72	13	1	140.2	152	55	82	18	1.47

Chouinard emerged as one of Arizona's better relievers in 1999. He'll be remembered for serving up the game-winning grand slam to Edgardo Alfonzo in Game 1 of the Division Series. 2000 Outlook: B

David Dellucci (Pos: RF/LF, Age: 26, Bats: L)

	G	AB	R	H	D	T	HR	RBI	SB	BB	SO	Avg	OBP	Slg
1999	63	109	27	43	7	1	1	15	2	11	24	.394	.463	.505
Career	204	552	73	157	27	13	7	69	5	48	134	.284	.349	.418

Dellucci lost his starting job when Arizona added Steve Finley, Luis Gonzalez and Tony Womack. Dellucci hit .394 as a reserve before a career-threatening wrist injury sidelined him in July. 2000 Outlook: C

Edwin Diaz (Pos: 2B, Age: 25, Bats: R)

	G	AB	R	H	D	T	HR	RBI	SB	BB	SO	Avg	OBP	Slg
1999	4	5	2	2	2	0	0	1	0	3	1	.400	.625	.800
Career	7	12	2	2	2	0	0	1	0	3	3	.167	.333	.333

Diaz had a decent second season in Triple-A, then signed a minor league deal with Texas. He could start for the Rangers. 2000 Outlook: B

Hanley Frias (Pos: SS, Age: 26, Bats: B)

	G	AB	R	H	D	T	HR	RBI	SB	BB	SO	Avg	OBP	Slg
1999	69	150	27	41	3	2	1	16	4	29	18	.273	.391	.340
Career	98	199	35	49	4	3	2	19	4	30	27	.246	.345	.327

After two trips to Triple-A, Frias stayed with the big club for the second half of 1999. He hit .317 with a .432 OBP in 104 at-bats after the break. 2000 Outlook: C

Lenny Harris (Pos: 2B/RF, Age: 35, Bats: L)

	G	AB	R	H	D	T	HR	RBI	SB	BB	SO	Avg	OBP	Slg
1999	110	187	17	58	13	0	1	20	2	6	7	.310	.330	.396
Career	1309	3059	368	837	129	14	27	279	110	211	249	.274	.322	.351

Acquired from the Rockies at the trade deadline, Harris finished two pinch-hits shy of John Vander Wal's big league record. Harris is a nice role player but not every-day material. 2000 Outlook: B

Darren Holmes (Pos: RHP, Age: 33)

	W	L	Pct.	ERA	G	GS	Sv	IP	H	BB	SO	HR	Ratio
1999	4	3	.571	3.70	44	0	0	48.2	50	25	35	3	1.54
Career	32	28	.533	4.18	436	6	57	564.0	584	224	472	49	1.43

Arizona acquired Holmes from the Yankees in late March. He was dependable before a six-week stint on the disabled list with back troubles in July. 2000 Outlook: B

Danny Klassen (Pos: 2B, Age: 24, Bats: R)

	G	AB	R	H	D	T	HR	RBI	SB	BB	SO	Avg	OBP	Slg
1999	1	1	0	1	0	0	0	0	0	0	0	1.000	1.000	1.000
Career	30	109	12	22	2	1	3	8	1	9	33	.202	.269	.321

The pop in Klassen's bat is tantalizing, but his defensive work at second isn't. It's hard to imagine how he could crack Arizona's lineup. 2000 Outlook: C

Dante Powell (Pos: CF, Age: 26, Bats: R)

	G	AB	R	H	D	T	HR	RBI	SB	BB	SO	Avg	OBP	Slg
1999	22	25	4	4	3	0	0	1	2	2	6	.160	.222	.280
Career	57	68	14	18	4	0	2	5	3	9	17	.265	.351	.412

Powell made the Opening Day roster but he didn't stay long. His performance never has caught up with his tools. He went to the Cardinals in a December trade for Luis Ordaz. 2000 Outlook: C

Rob Ryan (Pos: RF, Age: 26, Bats: L)

	G	AB	R	H	D	T	HR	RBI	SB	BB	SO	Avg	OBP	Slg
1999	20	29	4	7	1	0	2	5	0	1	8	.241	.267	.483
Career	20	29	4	7	1	0	2	5	0	1	8	.241	.267	.483

Ryan has a little juice in his bat, but not enough to play regularly in the majors as a corner outfielder. He was outrighted in November. 2000 Outlook: C

Erik Sabel (Pos: RHP, Age: 25)

	W	L	Pct.	ERA	G	GS	Sv	IP	H	BB	SO	HR	Ratio
1999	0	0	-	6.52	7	0	0	9.2	12	6	6	1	1.86
Career	0	0	-	6.52	7	0	0	9.2	12	6	6	1	1.86

Sabel tasted success at the Triple-A level for the first time in 1999, but he was roughed in the majors during September. He may need more seasoning. 2000 Outlook: C

Ed Vosberg (Pos: LHP, Age: 38)

	W	L	Pct.	ERA	G	GS	Sv	IP	H	BB	SO	HR	Ratio
1999	0	1	.000	8.18	19	0	0	11.0	22	3	8	1	2.27
Career	9	14	.391	4.37	213	3	13	195.2	218	87	145	17	1.56

A late bloomer who was especially effective during a three-year stretch in the mid-1990s, Vosberg is nearing the end of the line. 2000 Outlook: D

Turner Ward (Pos: CF/RF, Age: 34, Bats: B)

	G	AB	R	H	D	T	HR	RBI	SB	BB	SO	Avg	OBP	Slg
1999	59	114	8	27	3	0	2	15	2	15	15	.237	.326	.316
Career	594	1481	204	376	68	11	39	213	32	180	234	.254	.335	.394

The Pirates released Ward in August after he spent two months on the disabled list with a sore knee. He hit .348 with two homers in 23 at-bats for Arizona before the knee sidelined him again. 2000 Outlook: C

Ernie Young (Pos: RF, Age: 30, Bats: R)

	G	AB	R	H	D	T	HR	RBI	SB	BB	SO	Avg	OBP	Slg
1999	6	11	1	2	0	0	0	0	0	3	2	.182	.400	.182
Career	280	781	108	175	33	4	27	90	10	85	206	.224	.307	.380

Young has many tools, but only his speed and defensive prowess are clearly of major league caliber. He doesn't make enough contact at the plate to help much offensively. 2000 Outlook: C

Arizona

Arizona Diamondbacks Minor League Prospects

Organization Overview:

While the Diamondbacks shelled out $118.9 million for free agents last offseason, their subsequent National League West title was not solely the result of aggressive spending. Arizona signed first baseman Erubiel Durazo as an amateur free agent out of the Mexican League. The team also signed power pitchers Vladimir Nunez and Brad Penny, and outfielder Abraham Nunez, who were traded to the Marlins for closer Matt Mantei, who filled the Diamondbacks' biggest hole. Arizona works the international market as well as any club, signing three players (Durazo and pitchers Byung-Hung Kim and Vicente Padilla) who debuted in 1999 and made the majors almost immediately. They also drafted two players last June, third baseman Ryan Owens and righthander Jeremy Ward, who progressed so quickly that they could play in Arizona this year.

Rod Barajas

Position: C   **Opening Day Age:** 24
Bats: R **Throws:** R   **Born:** 9/5/75 in Ontario,
Ht: 6' 2" **Wt:** 220   CA

Recent Statistics

	G	AB	R	H	D	T	HR	RBI	SB	BB	SO	Avg
1999 AA El Paso	127	510	77	162	41	2	14	95	2	24	73	.318
1999 NL Arizona	5	16	3	4	1	0	1	3	0	1	1	.250
1999 MLE	127	482	55	134	34	1	10	68	1	14	78	.278

Barajas wasn't drafted out of Cerritos (Calif.) Junior College in 1996, but he signed as a free agent with the Diamondbacks and since has blossomed into their best catching prospect. He's aggressive at the plate and has batted .300 with gap power in the minor leagues. His biggest flaw offensively is a reluctance to draw walks. Managers rated him the best defensive catcher in the Double-A Texas League last year. He has an average arm, blocks balls in the dirt well and received good reviews for his game-calling skill from Arizona pitchers. Damian Miller and Kelly Stinnett will split the Diamondbacks' catching duties again in 2000, but Barajas could challenge for a major league role the following year.

Nick Bierbrodt

Position: P   **Opening Day Age:** 21
Bats: L **Throws:** L   **Born:** 5/16/78 in
Ht: 6' 5" **Wt:** 190   Tarzana, CA

Recent Statistics

	W	L	ERA	G	GS	Sv	IP	H	R	BB	SO	HR
1998 A High Desert	8	7	3.40	24	23	0	129.2	122	66	64	88	7
1999 AA El Paso	5	6	4.62	14	14	0	76.0	78	45	37	55	3
1999 AAA Tucson	1	4	7.27	11	11	0	43.1	57	42	30	43	9

Arizona used its first-ever draft pick in 1996 to take Bierbrodt, and he became the organization's first draftee to reach the majors, though he didn't get into a big league game after being recalled last summer. Bierbrodt's best

pitch is his changeup, and he also throws a sinker with average velocity and a curveball. Bierbrodt was shelled in Triple-A and needs a full season to refine his command at that level before making a push to join Arizona's rotation. He eventually could become a No. 3 starter.

Jack Cust

Position: OF   **Opening Day Age:** 21
Bats: L **Throws:** R   **Born:** 1/7/79 in
Ht: 6' 1" **Wt:** 205   Flemington, NJ

Recent Statistics

	G	AB	R	H	D	T	HR	RBI	SB	BB	SO	Avg
1998 A South Bend	16	62	5	15	3	0	4	0	0	5	20	.242
1998 R Lethbridge	73	223	75	77	20	2	11	56	15	86	71	.345
1999 A High Desert	125	455	107	152	42	3	32	112	1	96	145	.334

Cust is one of the best young hitters in the minor leagues. At age 20, he led the high Class-A California League in home runs, on-base percentage (.450) and slugging percentage (.651). A 1997 first-round pick, his power took a huge leap forward last year when he learned to turn on inside pitches. He already has tremendous plate discipline, something most hitters take years to develop. Cust's only offensive weakness is a propensity for strikeouts, but the Diamondbacks will gladly accept that as a tradeoff for his production. He doesn't run well and is nothing much at left field or first base, but his bat will carry him. He might require just one more season in the minors before establishing residence in the middle of Arizona's lineup.

Byung-Hyun Kim

Position: P   **Opening Day Age:** 21
Bats: R **Throws:** R   **Born:** 1/21/79 in
Ht: 5'11" **Wt:** 176   Kwangsan-ku, Korea

Recent Statistics

	W	L	ERA	G	GS	Sv	IP	H	R	BB	SO	HR
1999 AA El Paso	2	0	2.11	10	0	0	21.1	6	5	9	32	0
1999 R Diamondbcks	0	0	0.00	1	1	0	2.0	1	0	1	2	0
1999 AAA Tucson	4	0	2.40	11	3	1	30.0	21	9	15	40	2
1999 NL Arizona	1	2	4.61	25	0	1	27.1	20	15	20	31	2

Kim helped pitch Korea to the championship at the 1998 Asian Games, earning a reprieve from mandatory military service. That enabled him to sign a four-year major league deal worth $2.25 million with the Diamondbacks last February, and he shot through the minors, reaching Arizona three months later. He's extremely deceptive, delivering low-90s sinkers and wicked sliders from a sidearm angle. Righthanders have an especially difficult time picking up his pitches. He just needs to trust his stuff and challenge hitters, which he didn't do in the majors. Kim initially was used as a closer before the midseason trade for Matt Mantei. Kim could be a dynamite starter if he picked up a changeup, but the Diamondbacks likely will keep him in relief.

Vicente Padilla

Position: P
Bats: R **Throws:** R
Ht: 6' 2" **Wt:** 200

Opening Day Age: 22
Born: 9/27/77 in
Chinandega, Nicaragua

Recent Statistics

	W	L	ERA	G	GS	Sv	IP	H	R	BB	SO	HR
1999 A High Desert	4	1	3.73	9	9	0	50.2	50	27	17	55	3
1999 AAA Tucson	7	4	3.75	18	14	0	93.2	107	47	24	58	6
1999 NL Arizona	0	1	16.88	5	0	0	2.2	7	5	3	0	1

Signed out of Nicaragua in August 1998, Padilla made his pro debut in April and his major league debut just two months later. He's a sinker-slider pitcher with above-average velocity. Padilla keeps his pitches down and throws strikes. Despite his inexperience, he held up well in the upper minors despite being based in two hitters' parks. Padilla was less successful in the majors, where he was used in relief rather than in his typical starting role. He consistently pitched from behind in the count and got hammered. The Diamondbacks like his upside, but it isn't as high if his age, which has been questioned, is really closer to 26.

John Patterson

Position: P
Bats: R **Throws:** R
Ht: 6' 6" **Wt:** 197

Opening Day Age: 22
Born: 1/30/78 in Orange,
TX

Recent Statistics

	W	L	ERA	G	GS	Sv	IP	H	R	BB	SO	HR
1998 A High Desert	8	7	2.83	25	25	0	127.0	102	54	42	148	12
1999 AA El Paso	8	6	4.77	18	18	0	100.0	98	61	42	117	16
1999 AAA Tucson	1	5	7.04	7	6	0	30.2	43	26	18	29	3

Patterson was drafted fifth overall by the Expos in 1996, but a contract snafu made him a free agent and landed him a $6.075 million bonus from Arizona. Strict pitch counts have restricted his chances to earn victories, and he never has pitched more than 130.2 innings in a season despite perfect health. He has two outstanding pitches, a 95-96 MPH fastball that touches 99 MPH and a hard curveball that was rated the best breaking pitch in the Double-A Texas League. He's still developing a changeup and refining his command, but he has the look of a future No. 1 starter. His mechanics are very smooth, so he should stay injury-free. Patterson could make his big league debut after the All-Star break this year.

Jackie Rexrode

Position: 2B
Bats: L **Throws:** R
Ht: 5' 11" **Wt:** 175

Opening Day Age: 21
Born: 9/16/78 in
Washington, DC

Recent Statistics

	G	AB	R	H	D	T	HR	RBI	SB	BB	SO	Avg
1998 A South Bend	50	175	33	51	7	2	0	7	22	45	31	.291
1998 A High Desert	53	208	51	71	5	4	1	23	19	46	42	.341
1999 AA Birmingham	70	213	39	57	7	5	0	25	14	28	30	.268
1999 AA El Paso	37	144	30	46	7	2	2	11	7	29	16	.319
1999 MLE	107	342	49	88	11	4	1	27	13	36	49	.257

Arizona has good organizational depth at second base, but Rexrode may be the best bet to eventually succeed Jay Bell. He plays the game the way Diamondbacks manager Buck Showalter likes, relentlessly scrapping for any advantage. A 17th-round pick in 1996, Rexrode has batted .303 as a pro. He doesn't have much power, but he excels at making contact and getting on base. He runs well and is an efficient basestealer. Defensively, Rexrode has good range and turns the double play very well. He won't be a frontline player, but he can be a solid contributor on a winning team.

Jeremy Ward

Position: P
Bats: R **Throws:** R
Ht: 6' 3" **Wt:** 220

Opening Day Age: 22
Born: 2/24/78 in Rocky
Mount, NC

Recent Statistics

	W	L	ERA	G	GS	Sv	IP	H	R	BB	SO	HR
1999 A High Desert	0	0	2.08	4	4	0	8.2	5	2	3	12	0
1999 AA El Paso	1	1	2.45	19	0	7	25.2	18	7	9	26	1
1999 AAA Tucson	0	0	0.00	1	0	0	1.2	2	0	2	1	0

Ward has thrived since being converted into a reliever at Long Beach State this spring. Drafted in the second round, he joined Oakland's Barry Zito as the only 1999 draftees to reach Triple-A. Ward is a pure power pitcher, throwing a consistent 93-95 MPH fastball along with a heavy slider. Both pitches are tough to drive, and he allowed just one homer in 36 pro innings. Arizona manager Buck Showalter says that Ward reminds him of Brewers closer Bob Wickman with a harder sinker. Ward's lack of an offspeed pitch doesn't matter in his new role. He could make the Diamondbacks with an impressive performance in spring training.

Others to Watch

A 32nd-round pick in Arizona's initial draft, **Jason Conti** (25) has hit .315 as a pro. He lacks the power to start in left or right field and the speed to play in center, but he'll make a nice fourth outfielder. . . Righthander **Nelson Figueroa** (25) probably will be the first guy the Diamondbacks turn to if they need another starter. His curveball is his lone above-average pitch and his fastball is underwhelming, but he throws strikes and wins, going 51-33 in five years. . . Lefthander **Ben Norris** (22) survived Double-A El Paso, a notorious hitters' park, going 10-6, 4.16 in 20 starts. His best pitch is his changeup, and his fastball is average. . . A seventh-round pick last summer, **Ryan Owens** (22) batted .356 and reached Double-A after signing. He's an athletic third baseman with developing power. . . Outfielder **Luis Terrero** (20) has drawn comparisons to a young Bernie Williams. He's a sound hitter with power potential, speed, center-field range and a nice arm. . . Second baseman **Carlos Urquiola** (19) is a speedster who won the Class-A Midwest League batting title last year with a .362 average. Because he has no power, he'll need to enhance his ability to reach base.

Ted Turner Field

Offense

Turner Field was designed with the Braves' current team in mind. Pitchers love working in Atlanta. The deep gaps, particularly in right field, make the longball difficult to come by and allows righthanded pitchers to challenge lefties more often. The ball carries well down the lines but often dies when hit in the gaps, the result of the large opening in the ballpark beyond the center-field wall. The park forces manager Bobby Cox to run more often at home. The only advantage hitters have is a lack of foul territory.

Defense

The spacious middle garden at Turner Field makes having a fleet-footed, Gold Glove-caliber center fielder a must. While Andruw Jones covers more ground than anyone in the National League, marginal center fielders on other teams surrender numerous bloop singles and extra-base hits in the gaps. A chain-link fence in right field creates softer bounces than the rest of the outfield wall, which can make life tricky for visiting defenders. The plush, well-manicured grass is one of the game's best playing surfaces.

Who It Helps The Most

In Turner Field's first season, 1997, Chipper Jones hit two-thirds of his 21 homers on the road. He has adapted well, developing pull power to the extent that he hit 25 homers in Atlanta last season. Every Braves pitcher prefers pitching at home. Kevin Millwood said Turner Field's dimensions helped him relax during his rookie season.

Who It Hurts The Most

Lefthanded hitters who depend upon homers hate Turner Field, with Ryan Klesko a perfect example. He hit a career-high 34 homers in 1996 but hasn't approached that total since the club changed ballparks.

Rookies & Newcomers

The best chance for a rookie to make the Atlanta roster this year is in the bullpen. Jason Marquis and Luis Rivera are hard-throwing righthanders who could use Turner Field to their advantage.

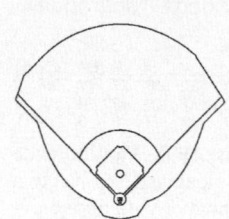

Dimensions: LF-335, LCF-380, CF-401, RCF-390, RF-330

Capacity: 49,714

Elevation: 1050 feet

Surface: Grass

Foul Territory: Small

Park Factors

1999 Season

	Home Games			Away Games			
	Braves	Opp	Total	Braves	Opp	Total	Index
G	72	72	144	72	72	144	—
Avg	.264	.234	.249	.270	.258	.264	94
AB	2358	2461	4819	2581	2457	5038	96
R	366	245	611	388	312	700	87
H	622	576	1198	696	633	1329	90
2B	139	92	231	135	112	247	98
3B	9	8	17	14	6	20	89
HR	78	61	139	101	56	157	93
BB	258	191	449	283	252	535	88
SO	390	555	945	461	518	979	101
E	52	62	114	48	55	103	111
E-Infield	44	50	94	42	45	87	108
LHB-Avg	.252	.226	.238	.281	.265	.273	87
LHB-HR	26	24	50	26	24	50	105
RHB-Avg	.270	.239	.254	.264	.253	.259	98
RHB-HR	52	37	89	75	32	107	87

1997-1999

	Home Games			Away Games			
	Braves	Opp	Total	Braves	Opp	Total	Index
G	220	220	440	217	217	434	—
Avg	.273	.238	.255	.265	.247	.256	100
AB	7234	7514	14748	7624	7197	14821	98
R	1088	768	1856	1123	827	1950	94
H	1976	1788	3764	2024	1775	3799	98
2B	381	306	687	403	305	708	98
3B	42	32	74	38	25	63	118
HR	239	158	397	286	157	443	90
BB	798	631	1429	796	653	1449	99
SO	1383	1672	3055	1469	1601	3070	100
E	157	181	338	128	174	302	110
E-Infield	132	145	277	108	145	253	108
LHB-Avg	.276	.233	.256	.268	.257	.263	97
LHB-HR	96	54	150	104	59	163	90
RHB-Avg	.271	.241	.255	.264	.241	.252	101
RHB-HR	143	104	247	182	98	280	90

1999 Rankings (National League)
- Lowest walk factor
- Lowest LHB batting-average factor
- Second-lowest batting-average factor
- Second-lowest run factor
- Second-lowest hit factor

Bobby Cox

1999 Season

Last year, no manager did a better job of living up to expectations without all of the pieces than Bobby Cox. Despite losing his cleanup hitter and closer before the season started and his All-Star catcher shortly after the break, the Braves piled up a major league-best 103 wins. Not a rah-rah leader, Cox prefers a professional, low-key approach in which everyone knows his role. He goes the extra mile to allow a player to work his way out of a slump. Cox also prefers veterans in crunch time, which is the reason the Braves are active every year at the trading deadline.

Offense

Cox is one of the league's best managers in working with the hand he's dealt. He'll platoon at any position, which is how he got the most out of first base from Ryan Klesko, Brian Hunter and Randall Simon. Cox is conservative. He will hit-and-run on occasion but prefers the station-to-station game. Because of his willingness to platoon, Cox will pinch-hit early in games when a pitching change is made. His goal is to put his players into situations in which they have the best chance for success.

Pitching & Defense

Cox will allow his veteran starters to remain in the game an inning longer than conventional wisdom would dictate, but will pull youngsters shortly after trouble begins. Cox prefers to have one closer, but is willing to try several options in order to find the right one. Defensively, Cox demands good gloves up the middle, which is why he opted for Walt Weiss at shortstop during the postseason. Cox uses double switches almost on a nightly basis.

2000 Outlook

It would be hard to imagine a manager having more security than Cox. The Braves could be much better this year if Andres Galarraga, Kerry Ligtenberg and Javy Lopez return from injuries. Cox' efforts are vastly underrated, and it's not by accident that he has climbed into the top 20 among all-time managerial victories.

Born: 5/21/41 in Tulsa, OK

Playing Experience: 1968-1969, NYY

Managerial Experience: 18 seasons

Manager Statistics

Year	Team, Lg	W	L	Pct	GB	Finish
1999	Atlanta, NL	103	59	.636	—	1st East
18 Seasons		1521	1204	.558	—	—

1999 Starting Pitchers by Days Rest

	<=3	4	5	6+
Braves Starts	5	88	45	18
Braves ERA	0.93	3.31	4.52	4.53
NL Avg Starts	3	81	48	21
NL ERA	4.84	4.53	4.72	4.98

1999 Situational Stats

	Bobby Cox	NL Average
Hit & Run Success %	42.6	33.6
Stolen Base Success %	69.2	70.2
Platoon Pct.	57.6	55.2
Defensive Subs	34	25
High-Pitch Outings	13	13
Quick/Slow Hooks	10/14	16/15
Sacrifice Attempts	89	89

1999 Rankings (National League)
- 1st in hit-and-run percentage (42.6%)
- 2nd in pitchouts (54), pitchouts with a runner moving (13), starts on three days rest (5) and 2+ pitching changes in low-scoring games (33)
- 3rd in defensive substitutions (34)

Atlanta

Bret Boone

1999 Season

The Braves said they had acquired the game's best second baseman after obtaining Bret Boone in a five-player trade with Cincinnati last winter. Noted for both his glove and power, Boone was a mild disappointment in both phases. Hot in April and May, when he put together a career-best 14-game hitting streak, Boone struggled in June and July, and didn't homer in 43 straight games. He didn't get on base enough batting second in Atlanta's lineup.

Hitting

Boone reverted to his old form by showing little patience and overswinging, particularly late in games. While he reached the 20-homer plateau for the second straight season, his power can be his enemy when Boone tries to go deep instead of focusing on making solid contact. He's capable of hitting all types of pitches and showed improvement against lefthanders last season. Boone's disappearance in crunch time was disconcerting. He was hitless in 10 at-bats with the bases loaded and batted just .209 after the sixth inning.

Baserunning & Defense

Boone upgraded the Atlanta defense at second base with his soft hands and steady glove. His range wasn't as good as the Braves expected, but he did an excellent job of turning the double play. Boone has a good arm for his position and can make the spectacular play on occasion. His speed isn't what most teams would like for a No. 2 hitter, but Boone's aggressiveness on the basepaths allows him to reach double digits in stolen bases.

2000 Outlook

Because he was dealt in the middle of a multiyear contract, Boone could have demanded a trade. He didn't, but if he had the Braves would have been hesitant to give him a lucrative contract after watching him struggle with his consistency at the plate. Yet he remains one of the game's better all-around second basemen.

Position: 2B
Bats: R **Throws:** R
Ht: 5'10" **Wt:** 180

Opening Day Age: 30
Born: 4/6/69 in El Cajon, CA
ML Seasons: 8

Overall Statistics

	G	AB	R	H	D	T	HR	RBI	SB	BB	SO	Avg	OBP	Slg
1999	152	608	102	153	38	1	20	63	14	47	112	.252	.310	.416
Career	945	3448	442	880	197	12	106	462	39	257	661	.255	.310	.412

Where He Hits the Ball

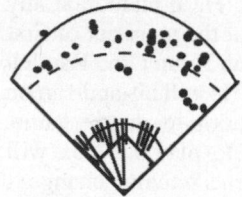 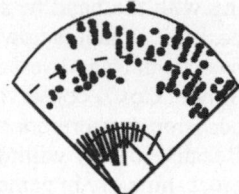

Vs. LHP   **Vs. RHP**

1999 Situational Stats

	AB	H	HR	RBI	Avg		AB	H	HR	RBI	Avg
Home	292	79	9	31	.271	LHP	164	46	5	15	.280
Road	316	74	11	32	.234	RHP	444	107	15	48	.241
First Half	343	87	11	33	.254	Sc Pos	134	35	3	41	.261
Scnd Half	265	66	9	30	.249	Clutch	85	19	4	12	.224

1999 Rankings (National League)

- 1st in lowest stolen-base percentage (60.9%)
- 3rd in lowest batting average with the bases loaded (.000) and lowest batting average vs. righthanded pitchers
- 4th in lowest batting average, lowest on-base percentage vs. righthanded pitchers (.299), lowest batting average on the road and errors at second base (13)
- 5th in lowest on-base percentage
- Led the Braves in at-bats, strikeouts, pitches seen (2,602), most pitches seen per plate appearance (3.88), highest percentage of pitches taken (59.4%), lowest percentage of swings that missed (18.7%) and highest percentage of swings put into play (47.9%)

Tom Glavine

1999 Season

No pitcher suffered more from the revamped strike zone last year than Tom Glavine. Accustomed to getting called strikes off the outside corner, the reigning Cy Young Award winner had a 3-7, 5.00 record in early June. He rebounded to win 11 of his last 15 decisions to reach double digits in victories for the 11th consecutive season. His 164 victories in the 1990s trailed only Greg Maddux' 176.

Pitching

Deprived of his steady diet of called strikes, Glavine often wound up leaving the ball over the plate during the season's first two months, leading to a major-league high 259 hits allowed. He adjusted by throwing two versions of a slider, one for lefthanders and another for righties, while working off his devastating changeup and above-average fastball. His pitch counts continued to increase, and he ranked eighth in the National League with 108 per start. Yet using his solid control, durability and dogged determination, Glavine persevered and was again one of the league's more consistent performers.

Defense & Hitting

Glavine is an excellent fielder whose glove is often overshadowed by that of Maddux. Glavine also does a fine job of holding runners, and has become crafty in the second decade of his career by offering a variety of moves to first base. An above-average hitter, Glavine slumped at the plate last year with a .138 average and just four RBI.

2000 Outlook

Like Maddux, Glavine may be showing some early signs of slippage, but he would have to drop significantly to join the middle of the game's pitching pack. Having made the adjustments to the strike zone, Glavine shouldn't surprise anyone if he wins close to 20 games this season.

Position: SP
Bats: L **Throws:** L
Ht: 6' 0" **Wt:** 185

Opening Day Age: 34
Born: 3/25/66 in Concord, MA
ML Seasons: 13
Pronunciation: GLA-vin

Overall Statistics

	W	L	Pct.	ERA	G	GS	Sv	IP	H	BB	SO	HR	Ratio
1999	14	11	.560	4.12	35	35	0	234.0	259	83	138	18	1.46
Career	187	116	.617	3.38	399	399	0	2659.2	2529	900	1659	178	1.29

How Often He Throws Strikes

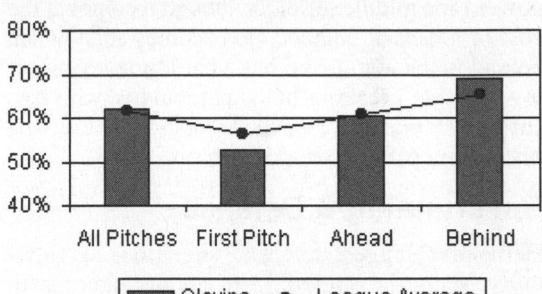

1999 Situational Stats

	W	L	ERA	Sv	IP		AB	H	HR	RBI	Avg
Home	8	4	3.55	0	124.1	LHB	202	54	2	21	.267
Road	6	7	4.76	0	109.2	RHB	702	205	16	87	.292
First Half	7	8	4.14	0	130.1	Sc Pos	215	59	2	81	.274
Scnd Half	7	3	4.08	0	103.2	Clutch	65	17	0	7	.262

1999 Rankings (National League)

- 1st in games started and hits allowed
- 3rd in batters faced (1,023) and pitches thrown (3,772)
- 5th in innings pitched
- 6th in fewest home runs allowed per 9 innings (.69)
- 9th in lowest slugging percentage allowed (.390)
- 10th in GDPs induced (22), highest stolen-base percentage allowed (76.5%) and fewest strikeouts per 9 innings (5.3)
- Led the Braves in losses, games started, innings pitched, hits allowed, batters faced (1,023), walks allowed, hit batsmen (4), pitches thrown (3,772) and GDPs induced (22)

Atlanta

Jose Hernandez

1999 Season

The loss of Javy Lopez in July forced the Braves to add some offense at other positions. Atlanta upgraded at shortstop by acquiring Jose Hernandez along with Terry Mulholland from the Cubs for three minor league pitchers. Hernandez took over the starting duties from Walt Weiss and Ozzie Guillen during the season's last two months before hitting the bench for the playoffs in favor of Weiss' steadier glove.

Hitting

Hernandez is one of the game's better offensive shortstops, and established career highs in hits, walks and stolen bases last year. He has very good power for a middle infielder, though it comes at the cost of a lack of contact. He becomes antsy when behind in the count, and has a hard time laying off low, outside breaking balls, particularly with two strikes. Hernandez also lacks consistency at the plate when playing on a daily basis.

Baserunning & Defense

Hernandez' biggest defensive strength is his flexibility. While he started 43 of his 48 games with Atlanta at short, Hernandez is a capable center fielder and third baseman who also can handle the corner outfield positions and first base in a pinch. Though no threat to win a Gold Glove, he has an above-average arm, relatively soft hands and good range despite possessing only adequate speed. His mediocre wheels and average baserunning skills don't pose a threat when he reaches base.

2000 Outlook

A free agent, Hernandez found an everyday job at third base with the Brewers. He signed a three-year deal worth $10 million. The Braves have shortstop prospect Rafael Furcal on the way, so re-signing Hernandez wasn't a priority.

Position: SS/CF
Bats: R **Throws:** R
Ht: 6' 1" **Wt:** 180

Opening Day Age: 30
Born: 7/14/69 in Vega Alta, Puerto Rico
ML Seasons: 8
Pronunciation: her-NAN-dezz

Overall Statistics

	G	AB	R	H	D	T	HR	RBI	SB	BB	SO	Avg	OBP	Slg
1999	147	508	79	135	20	2	19	62	11	52	145	.266	.339	.425
Career	745	1989	303	499	80	23	73	257	24	154	555	.251	.306	.424

Where He Hits the Ball

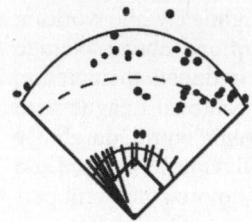
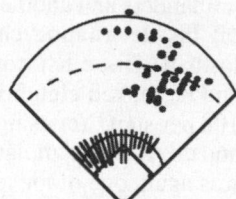

Vs. LHP   **Vs. RHP**

1999 Situational Stats

	AB	H	HR	RBI	Avg		AB	H	HR	RBI	Avg
Home	221	61	6	32	.276	LHP	168	49	8	24	.292
Road	287	74	13	30	.258	RHP	340	86	11	38	.253
First Half	288	77	13	35	.267	Sc Pos	130	36	4	41	.277
Scnd Half	220	58	6	27	.264	Clutch	83	22	2	6	.265

1999 Rankings (National League)

- 3rd in strikeouts
- 6th in errors at shortstop (17) and fielding percentage at shortstop (.969)
- 9th in most pitches seen per plate appearance (4.05) and lowest slugging percentage vs. righthanded pitchers (.388)
- 10th in lowest batting average, highest groundball/flyball ratio (1.5) and lowest batting average vs. righthanded pitchers
- Led the Braves in batting average on a 3-1 count (.714)
- Led NL shortstops in strikeouts and most pitches seen per plate appearance (4.05)

Andruw Jones

1999 Season

Many observers believed that Andruw Jones would enjoy a breakthrough season in 1999, but he merely provided a carbon copy of his 1998 output, including his second straight 20-20 effort. Jones did make major strides in his development, maturing in all phases of the game. He didn't miss a single game, giving the Braves a sure thing every night in center field.

Hitting

Jones was a free swinger during his first two full seasons. While he's effective when taking hacks early in the count, he showed more patience last year and nearly doubled his walk total from 1998. A dead fastball hitter, Jones also laid off the steady diet of benders and offspeed pitches that came his way. He hits righthanders and lefthanders with equal consistency, and thrives late in games.

Baserunning & Defense

There's no better defensive center fielder in the game than Jones, who won his second straight Gold Glove in 1999. No one gets a better jump on balls, and no one made more spectacular plays in the gaps last year. That ability enabled Jones to lead the majors with 492 putouts. He also holsters a cannon on his right shoulder, and led the Braves with a dozen outfield assists. While Jones has the speed to equal the 56 bases he stole at Class-A Macon in 1995, he's more valuable hitting in the middle of the lineup and avoiding the wear and tear. He will take an extra base whenever he gets the chance, doing so more often than any other National Leaguer last season.

2000 Outlook

Considering the subtle improvements Jones made last year, he could blossom into a MVP candidate as soon as this season. He has as much raw ability as anyone in the game and is on the verge of learning how to put his skills to their greatest use. And he has yet to turn 23.

Position: CF
Bats: R **Throws:** R
Ht: 6' 1" **Wt:** 185

Opening Day Age: 22
Born: 4/23/77 in Willemstad, Curacao
ML Seasons: 4

Overall Statistics

	G	AB	R	H	D	T	HR	RBI	SB	BB	SO	Avg	OBP	Slg
1999	162	592	97	163	35	5	26	84	24	76	103	.275	.365	.483
Career	505	1679	257	436	93	15	80	257	74	179	368	.260	.335	.476

Where He Hits the Ball

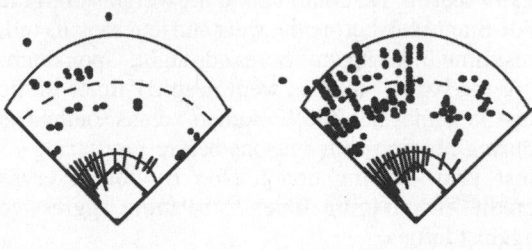

Vs. LHP   **Vs. RHP**

1999 Situational Stats

	AB	H	HR	RBI	Avg		AB	H	HR	RBI	Avg
Home	285	74	10	37	.260	LHP	141	38	6	20	.270
Road	307	89	16	47	.290	RHP	451	125	20	64	.277
First Half	330	89	16	50	.270	Sc Pos	166	45	8	59	.271
Scnd Half	262	74	10	34	.282	Clutch	84	26	3	14	.310

1999 Rankings (National League)

- 1st in errors in center field (10), games played and highest percentage of extra bases taken as a runner (70.2%)
- 7th in lowest stolen-base percentage (66.7%) and fielding percentage in center field (.981)
- 8th in intentional walks (11)
- 10th in caught stealing (12)
- Led the Braves in triples, caught stealing (12), hit by pitch (9), games played and highest percentage of extra bases taken as a runner (70.2%)
- Led NL center fielders in intentional walks (11), games played (162) and highest percentage of extra bases taken as a runner (70.2%)

Chipper Jones

Position: 3B
Bats: B **Throws:** R
Ht: 6' 4" **Wt:** 210

Opening Day Age: 27
Born: 4/24/72 in DeLand, FL
ML Seasons: 6

1999 Season

After a turbulent offseason that included marital problems and fathering a child out of wedlock, Chipper Jones took his game to a higher level and won the National League MVP Award. He became the first major leaguer ever to hit at least .300 with 40 doubles, 40 homers, 100 walks and 20 stolen bases. Jones reached base safely in 39 straight midseason games, and singlehandedly defeated the Mets in September to help the Braves clinch the division title.

Hitting

An intense winter conditioning program paid huge dividends for Jones during the latter half of the 1999 season. He continued to lift weights until the All-Star break before the wear and tear took its toll, resulting in a 21-game homer drought. Upon ditching the barbells, Jones went deep 21 times in the last 55 games. He had 12 homers versus southpaws during his first four seasons before registering 15 last year. Hitting coach Don Baylor deserves credit, encouraging Jones to be more aggressive against lefties.

Baserunning & Defense

Jones is a steady third baseman with a strong arm, soft hands and the ability to barehand slow rollers. He also has good range to his left and does a solid job of defending the bunt. Jones has surprising speed and is one of the game's smarter baserunners. Among his career highs last season were his 25 stolen bases.

2000 Outlook

It's no accident that the Braves have won their division in each of Jones' five major league seasons. He's the quintessential No. 3 hitter and one of the most productive players in the game. He has improved a different part of his game every season. After picking up his option for 2000, Atlanta will have to pay dearly to keep him beyond this season.

Overall Statistics

	G	AB	R	H	D	T	HR	RBI	SB	BB	SO	Avg	OBP	Slg
1999	157	567	116	181	41	1	45	110	25	126	94	.319	.441	.633
Career	779	2890	542	871	166	17	153	524	83	459	463	.301	.394	.529

Where He Hits the Ball

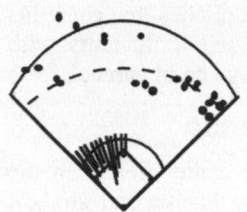

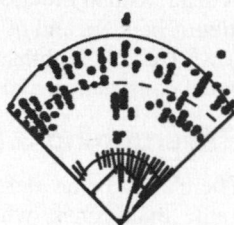

Vs. LHP **Vs. RHP**

1999 Situational Stats

	AB	H	HR	RBI	Avg		AB	H	HR	RBI	Avg
Home	276	101	25	59	.366	LHP	142	50	15	35	.352
Road	291	80	20	51	.275	RHP	425	131	30	75	.308
First Half	326	102	21	57	.313	Sc Pos	133	41	10	70	.308
Scnd Half	241	79	24	53	.328	Clutch	84	35	7	15	.417

1999 Rankings (National League)

- 1st in batting average in the clutch and slugging percentage vs. lefthanded pitchers (.739)
- 2nd in intentional walks (18), times on base (309) and stolen-base percentage (89.3%)
- 3rd in home runs, walks, GDPs (20) and batting average at home
- Led the Braves in batting average, home runs, runs scored, hits, doubles, total bases (359), walks, intentional walks (18), times on base (309), GDPs (20), plate appearances (701), slugging percentage, on-base percentage, HR frequency (12.6 ABs per HR), highest groundball/flyball ratio (1.2), stolen-base percentage (89.3%), batting average in the clutch and batting average vs. lefthanded pitchers

Brian Jordan

1999 Season

Signed to a five-year, $40 million deal as a Cardinals free agent, Brian Jordan was a primary reason the Braves were able to overcome the loss of Andres Galarraga. Jordan carried Atlanta offensively during the first half of the season, earning his first trip to the All-Star Game. His numbers dropped in the second half after he was hit on the right hand by a pitch from Mike Thurman on June 22, yet a late-September cortisone shot helped Jordan pick up his output during the playoffs. He established a career high for RBI while reaching the century mark in runs scored for the second straight season.

Hitting

Jordan is an explosive righthanded hitter who thrives in key situations. An excellent fastball hitter with power to all fields, Jordan led Atlanta with a .317 batting average with runners in scoring position, and batted .500 with 16 RBI with the bases loaded. He dares pitchers to throw inside while he crowds the plate, yet rarely gets tied up. Jordan's production has improved of late because of increased health as well as greater patience. He drew a career-high 51 walks in 1999.

Baserunning & Defense

With Jordan in right field and Andruw Jones manning center, the Braves field two of the game's top flycatchers. Equally capable in center and right, Jordan possesses great instincts that allow him to get to balls that otherwise would be extra-base hits. His arm is a weapon that ranks in the top five in the National League. Aggressive on the basepaths, Jordan is a good basestealer and takes the extra base when needed most.

2000 Outlook

St. Louis, Jordan's previous employer, had concerns about the his durability. If the last two seasons provide an accurate indication, such worries are no longer legitimate. Jordan will be a fixture in the Atlanta outfield for the next several seasons and a key ingredient in the team's success.

Position: RF
Bats: R **Throws:** R
Ht: 6' 1" **Wt:** 205

Opening Day Age: 33
Born: 3/29/67 in Baltimore, MD
ML Seasons: 8

Overall Statistics

	G	AB	R	H	D	T	HR	RBI	SB	BB	SO	Avg	OBP	Slg
1999	153	576	100	163	28	4	23	115	13	51	81	.283	.346	.465
Career	796	2882	446	834	150	28	107	482	99	190	454	.289	.340	.472

Where He Hits the Ball

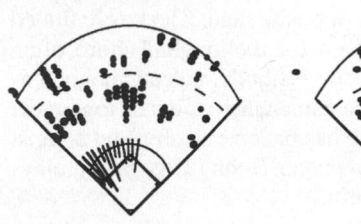

Vs. LHP   **Vs. RHP**

1999 Situational Stats

	AB	H	HR	RBI	Avg		AB	H	HR	RBI	Avg
Home	270	74	11	53	.274	LHP	124	41	6	32	.331
Road	306	89	12	62	.291	RHP	452	122	17	83	.270
First Half	339	100	17	71	.295	Sc Pos	183	58	9	93	.317
Scnd Half	237	63	6	44	.266	Clutch	82	24	3	12	.293

1999 Rankings (National League)

- 2nd in lowest stolen-base percentage (61.9%)
- 3rd in sacrifice flies (9)
- 4th in lowest cleanup slugging percentage (.465) and fielding percentage in right field (.990)
- 8th in errors in right field (3) and bunts in play (3)
- 10th in RBI and batting average with the bases loaded (.500)
- Led the Braves in singles, RBI, sacrifice flies (9), hit by pitch (9), batting average with runners in scoring position, batting average with the bases loaded (.500), batting average on an 0-2 count (.268), cleanup slugging percentage (.465), batting average on the road and bunts in play (3)
- Led NL right fielders in sacrifice flies (9)

Ryan Klesko

1999 Season

Atlanta hoped that the absence of Andres Galarraga would lead to Ryan Klesko's emergence as a big-time run producer. Yet all Klesko could manage was his typical 20-homer, 80-RBI effort. He saw significant activity at first base for the first time in his major league career, but lost playing time to Brian Hunter and Randall Simon in the infield and to Gerald Williams in the outfield as the season progressed.

Hitting

Klesko benefited from hitting coach Don Baylor's advice and wound up producing the second-highest batting average of his career. While he showed a little more patience at the plate and even opted to take pitches to the opposite field, Klesko continued to overswing and go for the longball more often than not. He feasts on fastballs and can hit a ball as far as anyone in the game when a pitch is low in the strike zone. But he has become so abysmal against lefthanders that manager Bobby Cox rarely plays Klesko against them.

Baserunning & Defense

A first baseman in the minors, Klesko was rusty at the position last season and no longer appears to be the long-term answer there once Galarraga retires. He hit 27 points higher when toiling in the outfield compared to first base, and has developed into an average defender in left field. His arm is strong and accurate for left, but his hands looked hard when playing first. Despite his large frame, Klesko has good speed and easily could reach double digits in stolen bases if the opportunity presented itself.

2000 Outlook

Klesko has been mentioned in trade rumors for the past few winters, a trend that will continue. This could be the year Klesko moves on, if the Braves believe that Williams can continue to hit and Galarraga will regain his old form. He'd be best suited for a DH role, probably as part of a platoon.

Position: 1B/LF
Bats: L **Throws:** L
Ht: 6' 3" **Wt:** 220

Opening Day Age: 28
Born: 6/12/71 in Westminster, CA
ML Seasons: 8

Overall Statistics

	G	AB	R	H	D	T	HR	RBI	SB	BB	SO	Avg	OBP	Slg
1999	133	404	55	120	28	2	21	80	5	53	69	.297	.376	.532
Career	792	2431	374	684	140	18	139	450	26	301	523	.281	.361	.525

Where He Hits the Ball

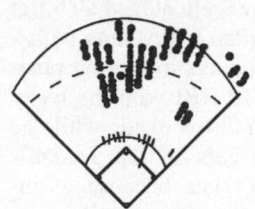
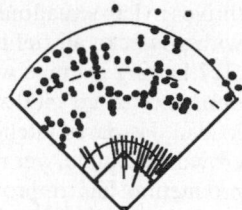

Vs. LHP **Vs. RHP**

1999 Situational Stats

	AB	H	HR	RBI	Avg		AB	H	HR	RBI	Avg
Home	214	57	12	41	.266	LHP	49	5	1	7	.102
Road	190	63	9	39	.332	RHP	355	115	20	73	.324
First Half	228	69	13	49	.303	Sc Pos	100	31	5	53	.310
Scnd Half	176	51	8	31	.290	Clutch	50	9	0	6	.180

1999 Rankings (National League)

- 3rd in lowest batting average on a 3-2 count (.071)
- 10th in slugging percentage vs. righthanded pitchers (.583) and errors at first base (6)
- Led the Braves in batting average vs. righthanded pitchers
- Led NL first basemen in fewest GDPs per GDP situation (7.1%)

Javy Lopez

Position: C
Bats: R **Throws:** R
Ht: 6' 3" **Wt:** 200

Opening Day Age: 29
Born: 11/5/70 in Ponce, Puerto Rico
ML Seasons: 8
Pronunciation: HAH-vee LOE-pezz

1999 Season

A pair of knee injuries limited Javy Lopez to a career-low 65 games last season. He initially visited the disabled list in late June after spraining his right knee. Eleven days after his return in July, Lopez partially tore the anterior cruciate ligament in his right knee, costing him the rest of the campaign. Prior to the ailments, Lopez was one of the Braves' primary offensive forces and a steady influence behind the plate.

Hitting

Lopez is a rare offensive catcher in that he can hit for power and average. While he loves fastballs low in the strike zone, he has learned to lay off pitches in the dirt, thereby increasing his average and lowering his strikeout totals. Through hard work in the weight room and natural maturation, Lopez is one of the strongest players in the game and can hit the ball out of any part of any stadium. Oddly, most of Lopez's power came on the road last season, with 10 of his 11 home runs occurring in visiting ballparks.

Baserunning & Defense

Criticized for his defensive abilities early in his career, Lopez is now one of the top receivers in the game. His footwork is vastly improved and gets better every season. He usually does an excellent job of blocking balls in the dirt, though he can occasionally get lazy late in a season. Despite his strong arm, Lopez had difficulty throwing out basestealers in 1999. His speed was no better than average before his knee injuries.

2000 Outlook

Others may receive more national attention, but Lopez is the best all-around catcher in the Senior Circuit. While the Braves had some major concerns regarding his knee problems, no one will work harder in his rehab than Lopez. More All-Star recognition remains in his future.

Overall Statistics

	G	AB	R	H	D	T	HR	RBI	SB	BB	SO	Avg	OBP	Slg
1999	65	246	34	78	18	1	11	45	0	20	41	.317	.375	.533
Career	656	2280	283	662	109	9	119	378	7	149	413	.290	.338	.503

Where He Hits the Ball

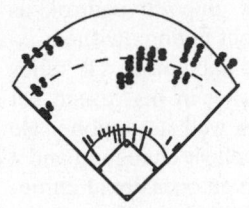

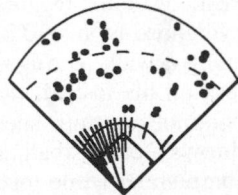

Vs. LHP   **Vs. RHP**

1999 Situational Stats

	AB	H	HR	RBI	Avg		AB	H	HR	RBI	Avg
Home	108	31	1	17	.287	LHP	53	18	5	13	.340
Road	138	47	10	28	.341	RHP	193	60	6	32	.311
First Half	209	67	11	37	.321	Sc Pos	71	21	2	31	.296
Scnd Half	37	11	0	8	.297	Clutch	43	14	3	12	.326

1999 Rankings (National League)
- 5th in lowest batting average on a 3-2 count (.077)

Greg Maddux

1999 Season

Greg Maddux had the Braves concerned two months into the 1999 season. Following a 4-0 start in April, the four-time Cy Young Award winner looked mortal in May. He went 0-3, 6.10 in six starts, and surrendered a career-high eight earned runs versus St. Louis on May 4. Maddux rebounded to go 14-5 in his last 21 starts and recorded 15 or more wins for the 12th consecutive campaign. He concluded the 1990s with a 2.54 ERA, the third-lowest ERA in any decade since the 1910s, behind only Hoyt Wilhelm's 2.16 and Sandy Koufax' 2.36 in the 1960s.

Pitching

After failing to get the outside strike early in the year, Maddux regained his pinpoint control, as evidenced by his 30.2 straight innings without issuing a walk in August and September. He relies less on his fastball than earlier in his career, yet continues to mix speeds as well as anyone. He throws a cut fastball, an excellent changeup and a sharp slider while mixing in an occasional curveball and straight fastball. While his offerings appear hittable, resulting in an average of just 92 pitches per start, Maddux' outstanding movement and pitching knowledge enables him to succeed.

Defense & Hitting

Though Maddux committed four errors in 91 chances last year, he remains one of the best fielding pitchers in the game's history. He won every NL Gold Glove in the 1990s. He also is adept at helping himself with the lumber, pacing Atlanta's pitchers with two homers and 13 sacrifice hits while tying for honors with seven RBI. His biggest weakness is controlling the running game, though he was decent last year.

2000 Outlook

Maddux' days of complete dominance may be past, but he should remain one of the game's elite pitchers for the foreseeable future. While his 3.57 ERA last year was his highest since 1987, his control and knowledge of hitters make him a perennial 20-win candidate.

Position: SP
Bats: R **Throws:** R
Ht: 6' 0" **Wt:** 185

Opening Day Age: 33
Born: 4/14/66 in San Angelo, TX
ML Seasons: 14

Overall Statistics

	W	L	Pct.	ERA	G	GS	Sv	IP	H	BB	SO	HR	Ratio
1999	19	9	.679	3.57	33	33	0	219.1	258	37	136	16	1.34
Career	221	126	.637	2.81	436	432	0	3068.2	2761	691	2160	157	1.12

How Often He Throws Strikes

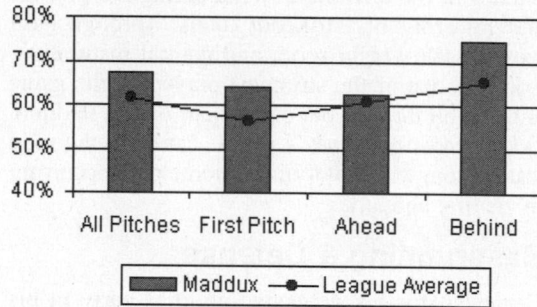

1999 Situational Stats

	W	L	ERA	Sv	IP		AB	H	HR	RBI	Avg
Home	12	4	2.86	0	135.1	LHB	410	123	8	51	.300
Road	7	5	4.71	0	84.0	RHB	469	135	8	46	.288
First Half	10	5	3.40	0	127.0	Sc Pos	216	66	6	82	.306
Scnd Half	9	4	3.80	0	92.1	Clutch	48	9	1	3	.188

1999 Rankings (National League)

- 1st in fewest pitches thrown per batter (3.24)
- 2nd in sacrifice bunts (13), hits allowed, fewest home runs allowed per 9 innings (.66) and walks per 9 innings (1.5)
- 3rd in wins and highest groundball/flyball ratio allowed (2.2)
- 5th in complete games (4) and ERA at home
- Led the Braves in sacrifice bunts (13), wins, complete games (4), hit batsmen (4), pickoff throws (139), stolen bases allowed (21), runners caught stealing (10), highest groundball/flyball ratio allowed (2.2), fewest pitches thrown per batter (3.24), most run support per 9 innings (6.3), fewest home runs allowed per 9 innings (.66) and walks per 9 innings (1.5)

Kevin Millwood

Position: SP
Bats: R **Throws:** R
Ht: 6' 4" **Wt:** 220

Opening Day Age: 25
Born: 12/24/74 in Gastonia, NC
ML Seasons: 3

1999 Season

He doesn't own a Cy Young Award yet, but Kevin Millwood may be the Braves' best starter. In just his second full major league season, he led the majors by limiting opponents to a .202 batting average while ranking second in ERA. He proved to be a workhorse by averaging nearly seven innings per start and earned his first All-Star Game invitation. Against St. Louis on August 28, he became the first Brave since Frank LaCorte in 1976 to pitch 10 scoreless innings in one game.

Pitching

Millwood overpowers hitters with his mid-90s fastball and a hard slider, and took his game to the next level by bettering both his changeup and curveball. He keeps his pitches low in the strike zone and throws a heavy ball. Millwood gets stronger as the game progresses and flirted with no-hitters on three occasions last year. He also discovered success on the road after struggling away from Turner Field in 1998.

Defense & Hitting

Though never a weak fielder, Millwood upgraded his glovework last season. While he made two errors, he did a better job of grabbing balls hit back through the box and showed improved quickness in getting off the mound to field bunts. The lone negative was that 13 of 17 basestealers succeeded with Millwood on the hill. He also enhanced his hitting, recording his first home run in the process.

2000 Outlook

Millwood has won 38 games and recorded a 3.28 ERA since joining the rotation for good on August 30, 1997. It's scary to think that at age 25, he should get better for the next few years. His .690 career winning percentage already is the best among active pitchers with at least 50 decisions.

Overall Statistics

	W	L	Pct.	ERA	G	GS	Sv	IP	H	BB	SO	HR	Ratio
1999	18	7	.720	2.68	33	33	0	228.0	168	59	205	24	1.00
Career	40	18	.690	3.37	76	70	0	453.2	398	136	410	43	1.18

How Often He Throws Strikes

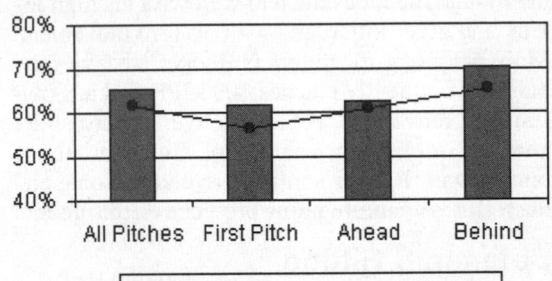

Millwood —●— League Average

1999 Situational Stats

	W	L	ERA	Sv	IP		AB	H	HR	RBI	Avg
Home	11	3	2.70	0	100.0	LHB	413	95	15	41	.230
Road	7	4	2.67	0	128.0	RHB	418	73	9	33	.175
First Half	11	4	3.20	0	118.0	Sc Pos	166	40	2	43	.241
Scnd Half	7	3	2.13	0	110.0	Clutch	69	10	2	4	.145

1999 Rankings (National League)

- 1st in lowest batting average allowed (.202), lowest on-base percentage allowed (.258), fewest baserunners allowed per 9 innings (9.1), fewest GDPs induced per 9 innings (0.2), lowest batting average allowed vs. lefthanded batters and lowest batting average allowed vs. righthanded batters
- 2nd in ERA and ERA on the road
- 3rd in winning percentage and lowest batting average on an 0-2 count (.000)
- Led the Braves in ERA, home runs allowed, hit batsmen (4), strikeouts, winning percentage, lowest batting average allowed (.202), lowest slugging percentage allowed (.337) and lowest on-base percentage allowed (.258)

Atlanta

John Rocker

1999 Season

The season-ending injury to Kerry Ligtenberg and the demise of Mark Wohlers left Atlanta without a closer. The Braves opted to give a shot to second-year pitcher John Rocker, who responded by winning Reliever of the Month honors for May en route to 38 saves, one shy of the franchise record. The hard-throwing lefty got better as the season progressed, with 14 straight scoreless outings in July and early August. He didn't surrended an earned run in 13 postseason innings.

Pitching

A starter for much of his minor league career, Rocker has found his niche as a closer. Active on the mound, he hides the ball well with his high leg kick and gives hitters fits with his arm movement. More troubling for hitters is Rocker's heavy fastball that frequently reaches 100 MPH and has outstanding movement. He also delivers a hard slider and an improving changeup. Combine those pitches with Rocker's mildly psycho persona, and the result is an intimidating presence on the mound.

Defense & Hitting

Rocker is light on his feet for a big man and does a good job of fielding his position. He hasn't committed an error in two major league seasons. For a lefty, his move to first base is average at best, and he has a tendency to forget about runners at second, thereby creating opportunities to swipe third. Rocker has yet to get an at-bat at the game's top level.

2000 Outlook

Manager Bobby Cox feels that Rocker is one of the game's top three closers and only will get better. There's no reason to doubt Cox, for Rocker has the mindset and the tools necessary to dominate. He should shut Atlanta's revolving door at the position for the long haul.

Position: RP
Bats: R **Throws:** L
Ht: 6' 4" **Wt:** 225

Opening Day Age: 25
Born: 10/17/74 in Statesboro, GA
ML Seasons: 2

Overall Statistics

	W	L	Pct.	ERA	G	GS	Sv	IP	H	BB	SO	HR	Ratio
1999	4	5	.444	2.49	74	0	38	72.1	47	37	104	5	1.16
Career	5	8	.385	2.37	121	0	40	110.1	69	59	146	9	1.16

How Often He Throws Strikes

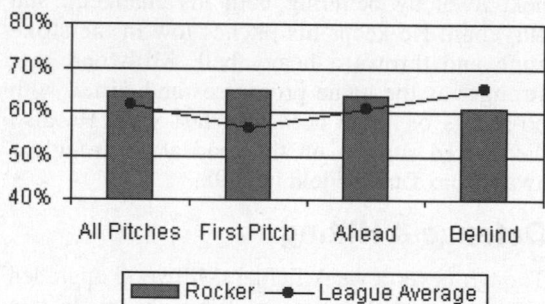

1999 Situational Stats

	W	L	ERA	Sv	IP		AB	H	HR	RBI	Avg
Home	2	1	0.71	19	38.0	LHB	57	8	2	11	.140
Road	2	4	4.46	19	34.1	RHB	204	39	3	21	.191
First Half	2	3	2.93	17	40.0	Sc Pos	78	19	2	29	.244
Scnd Half	2	2	1.95	21	32.1	Clutch	189	34	4	30	.180

1999 Rankings (National League)

- 3rd in save opportunities (45) and first batter efficiency (.145)
- 4th in saves, lowest batting average allowed in relief (.180) and most strikeouts per 9 innings in relief (12.9)
- 5th in games finished (61)
- Led the Braves in games pitched, saves, games finished (61), wild pitches (7), save opportunities (45), save percentage (84.4%), blown saves (7), first batter efficiency (.145), lowest batting average allowed in relief (.180), fewest baserunners allowed per 9 innings in relief (10.6) and most strikeouts per 9 innings in relief (12.9)

John Smoltz

1999 Season

After undergoing elbow surgery prior to the 1998 season and battling tenderness in his arm during the first half of the 1999 campaign, John Smoltz knew something was wrong despite the first 5-0 start of his career. Two stints on the disabled list followed along with a revamped delivery. Smoltz dropped his arm angle to a low three-quarters, giving hitters a different look and enabling him to reach double digits in wins for the 10th time in 11 years while ranking fifth in the National League in ERA.

Pitching

Craig Biggio joined the masses when he said facing Smoltz' low three-quarters delivery was like facing an entirely new hurler. A power pitcher who worked off a hard slider and a mid-90s fastball during the first decade of his career, he started using his slider sparingly while adding a new changeup in August and a beginner's knuckleball in September. Two things that haven't changed are his above-average velocity and his toughness in tight situations.

Defense & Hitting

Smoltz is another Atlanta starter who helps himself in the field. He committed just one error in 40 chances, and allowed just nine stolen bases in 16 tries. He's also the Braves' best hitting pitcher, leading the moundsmen with a .274 batting average and drilling the fifth homer of his career.

2000 Outlook

Because of his spotty health, the past two years have been an emotional roller coaster for Smoltz, a trend the pitcher does not expect to change for the rest of his playing days. His new delivery could extend his career and should enable him to remain among the game's elite pitchers for the next few seasons. There's also some talk among scouts that he could become a dominant closer if his elbow stopped allowing him to remain in the rotation.

Position: SP
Bats: R **Throws:** R
Ht: 6' 3" **Wt:** 220

Opening Day Age: 32
Born: 5/15/67 in Warren, MI
ML Seasons: 12

Overall Statistics

	W	L	Pct.	ERA	G	GS	Sv	IP	H	BB	SO	HR	Ratio
1999	11	8	.579	3.19	29	29	0	186.1	168	40	156	14	1.12
Career	157	113	.581	3.35	356	356	0	2414.1	2092	774	2098	195	1.19

How Often He Throws Strikes

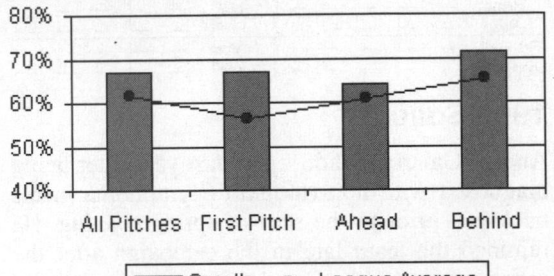

1999 Situational Stats

	W	L	ERA	Sv	IP		AB	H	HR	RBI	Avg
Home	7	3	3.14	0	86.0	LHB	311	82	7	32	.264
Road	4	5	3.23	0	100.1	RHB	376	86	7	34	.229
First Half	8	3	3.49	0	95.1	Sc Pos	147	37	7	56	.252
Scnd Half	3	5	2.87	0	91.0	Clutch	55	13	2	6	.236

1999 Rankings (National League)

- 4th in fewest baserunners allowed per 9 innings (10.2) and fewest home runs allowed per 9 innings (.68)
- 5th in ERA, highest strikeout/walk ratio (3.9), lowest on-base percentage allowed (.288), walks per 9 innings (1.9) and ERA on the road
- 6th in lowest slugging percentage allowed (.374)
- 8th in lowest batting average allowed (.245)
- Led the Braves in hit batsmen (4), highest strikeout/walk ratio (3.9), lowest stolen-base percentage allowed (56.3%) and most GDPs induced per 9 innings (0.9)

Atlanta

Andres Galarraga

Position: 1B
Bats: R **Throws:** R
Ht: 6' 3" **Wt:** 235

Opening Day Age: 38
Born: 6/18/61 in
Caracas, Venezuela
ML Seasons: 14
Pronunciation:
ON-dress
gahl-lah-RAH-guh
Nickname: Big Cat

Overall Statistics

	G	AB	R	H	D	T	HR	RBI	SB	BB	SO	Avg	OBP	Slg
1999						Did Not Play								
Career	1774	6629	1011	1921	364	30	332	1172	121	467	1615	.290	.347	.504

1999 Situational Stats

	AB	H	HR	RBI	Avg		AB	H	HR	RBI	Avg
Home	—	—	—	—	—	LHP	—	—	—	—	—
Road	—	—	—	—	—	RHP	—	—	—	—	—
First Half	—	—	—	—	—	Sc Pos	—	—	—	—	—
Scnd Half	—	—	—	—	—	Clutch	—	—	—	—	—

1999 Season

Andres Galarraga didn't play last year after being diagnosed with non-Hodgkin's lymphoma in his back just prior to the start of spring training. He rejoined the team late in the campaign after the cancer was considered to be in remission, but did not play.

Hitting, Baserunning & Defense

Galarraga was one of the game's premier power hitters during most of the 1990s. It would have been interesting to see what type of numbers he would have produced working with batting coach Don Baylor, whom Galarraga credits for his resurgence at the plate. Galarraga uses the entire field and typically produces a couple of hitting streaks of 10 or more games during a season. His lone weakness is outside sliders, yet he sometimes will turn those into rocket shots. Amazingly agile for a man his size, Galarraga has above-average speed and figures to upgrade Atlanta's infield defense after the Braves used Ryan Klesko, Brian Hunter and Randall Simon at first base during his absence.

2000 Outlook

All indications point to a complete recovery for Galarraga. Though he's 38, he should rejuvenate the Braves' power attack from the cleanup spot.

Kevin McGlinchy

Position: RP
Bats: R **Throws:** R
Ht: 6' 5" **Wt:** 220

Opening Day Age: 22
Born: 6/28/77 in
Malden, MA
ML Seasons: 1

Overall Statistics

	W	L	Pct.	ERA	G	GS	Sv	IP	H	BB	SO	HR	Ratio
1999	7	3	.700	2.82	64	0	0	70.1	66	30	67	6	1.36
Career	7	3	.700	2.82	64	0	0	70.1	66	30	67	6	1.36

1999 Situational Stats

	W	L	ERA	Sv	IP		AB	H	HR	RBI	Avg
Home	4	2	3.12	0	34.2	LHB	96	22	3	9	.229
Road	3	1	2.52	0	35.2	RHB	163	44	3	21	.270
First Half	5	3	3.45	0	44.1	Sc Pos	81	20	0	22	.247
Scnd Half	2	0	1.73	0	26.0	Clutch	105	19	1	8	.181

1999 Season

Kevin McGlinchy was the surprise of spring training for the Braves. Despite having only a month of experience above Class-A, McGlinchy earned a job in Atlanta's bullpen. He didn't allow a run in 13 straight games early in the year, and surrendered just five earned runs in his final 23 appearances.

Pitching, Defense & Hitting

McGlinchy succeeds with a limited repertoire. His best pitch is a mid-90s fastball, which increased by 8 MPH after he moved to the bullpen in 1998. His second offering is a splitter that looks similar to his heater before the bottom falls out. McGlinchy has good command but loses his concentration at times. First batters hit .273 against him last year, a trend the Braves want to see improve. His defense, like McGlinchy's hitting ability, is acceptable. His hard stuff makes him tough to run on.

2000 Outlook

McGlinchy's rapid rise has been compared to John Rocker's. Both pitchers are better suited for short relief than starting, their role in the minors. Provided McGlinchy continues to make the proper adjustments and increases his intensity, he should be a fixture in Atlanta's bullpen.

Terry Mulholland

Position: SP/RP
Bats: R **Throws:** L
Ht: 6' 3" **Wt:** 220

Opening Day Age: 37
Born: 3/9/63 in Uniontown, PA
ML Seasons: 13

Overall Statistics

	W	L	Pct.	ERA	G	GS	Sv	IP	H	BB	SO	HR	Ratio
1999	10	8	.556	4.39	42	24	1	170.1	201	45	83	21	1.44
Career	103	115	.472	4.22	415	287	4	1990.0	2108	514	1046	201	1.32

1999 Situational Stats

	W	L	ERA	Sv	IP		AB	H	HR	RBI	Avg
Home	5	2	4.42	0	71.1	LHB	145	42	4	21	.290
Road	5	6	4.36	1	99.0	RHB	532	159	17	58	.299
First Half	4	5	5.07	0	92.1	Sc Pos	166	48	4	56	.289
Scnd Half	6	3	3.58	1	78.0	Clutch	85	22	4	10	.259

1999 Season

Lacking a veteran fifth starter who also could relieve when needed, the Braves acquired Terry Mulholland from the Cubs for three prospects on July 31. Mulholland split his 16 Atlanta outings between the rotation and bullpen, posting a 2.98 ERA and four wins, including the 100th triumph of his major league career. His efforts were an unheralded reason for the Braves' eighth straight trip to the postseason.

Pitching, Defense & Hitting

Mulholland mixes four pitches well and forces hitters to keep the ball on the ground. Though not known for his stamina, he went at least six innings in seven of eight starts with the Braves. Mulholland's forte is holding runners at bay. Basestealers have gone 8-for-35 against him since 1992. He's not much of a fielder or hitter.

2000 Outlook

With one year remaining on his contract, Mulholland should resume a similar role in Atlanta, particularly with fifth starter Odalis Perez expected to miss four months of the season. Mulholland's experience and versatility make him a treasured commodity for veteran-loving manager Bobby Cox.

Greg Myers

Signed By ORIOLES

Position: C
Bats: L **Throws:** R
Ht: 6' 2" **Wt:** 225

Opening Day Age: 33
Born: 4/14/66 in Riverside, CA
ML Seasons: 12

Overall Statistics

	G	AB	R	H	D	T	HR	RBI	SB	BB	SO	Avg	OBP	Slg
1999	84	200	19	53	6	0	5	24	0	26	30	.265	.348	.370
Career	807	2253	234	574	115	7	52	278	3	173	374	.255	.306	.381

1999 Situational Stats

	AB	H	HR	RBI	Avg		AB	H	HR	RBI	Avg
Home	93	21	3	11	.226	LHP	29	7	0	3	.241
Road	107	32	2	13	.299	RHP	171	46	5	21	.269
First Half	128	37	3	15	.289	Sc Pos	58	13	1	20	.224
Scnd Half	72	16	2	9	.222	Clutch	35	11	1	3	.314

1999 Season

For the second time in three seasons, Greg Myers was acquired by the Braves for the pennant drive. After platooning behind the plate in San Diego, he joined Atlanta on July 26 in exchange for minor league righthander Doug Dent. Myers served as Eddie Perez' primary backup following Javy Lopez' season-ending injury.

Hitting, Baserunning & Defense

Myers was an emergency acquisition whose all-around skills are barely average at a weak major league position. He was hitting a career-best .289 with the Padres before coming back to earth with Atlanta. His strength centers on his occasional power, which is negated by lefthanders, and making contact early in the count. Myers is good at blocking pitches and has a decent arm. His foot speed can be clocked with a sundial.

2000 Outlook

A free agent, Myers signed a two-year contract worth approximately $1 million with the Orioles. He'll back up Charles Johnson.

Atlanta

Eddie Perez

Position: C
Bats: R **Throws:** R
Ht: 6' 1" **Wt:** 185

Opening Day Age: 31
Born: 5/4/68 in Cuidad Ojeda, Venezuela
ML Seasons: 5

Overall Statistics

	G	AB	R	H	D	T	HR	RBI	SB	BB	SO	Avg	OBP	Slg
1999	104	309	30	77	17	0	7	30	0	17	40	.249	.299	.372
Career	313	818	88	212	44	1	24	101	1	50	124	.259	.308	.403

1999 Situational Stats

	AB	H	HR	RBI	Avg		AB	H	HR	RBI	Avg
Home	139	28	0	9	.201	LHP	101	27	1	6	.267
Road	170	49	7	21	.288	RHP	208	50	6	24	.240
First Half	151	35	2	12	.232	Sc Pos	73	15	3	23	.205
Scnd Half	158	42	5	18	.266	Clutch	47	6	0	1	.128

1999 Season

Following nine years in the minors and three as Javy Lopez' backup, Eddie Perez responded well when Lopez was lost for the season in July. Perez handled the pitching staff with aplomb and set career bests in most offensive categories. He batted .500 and earned MVP honors in the National League Championship Series.

Hitting, Baserunning & Defense

Despite decent power, Perez fits toward the bottom of the order because he doesn't hit for much of an average or draw many walks. His strengths are his game-calling ability and his prowess behind the plate. Few catchers are more adept at blocking pitches in the dirt. He also has an above-average arm and nails his share of basestealers. His defensive quickness doesn't equate to speed on the basepaths.

2000 Outlook

Perez could start for many teams but is content with his role in Atlanta. He gives the Braves a solid option should Lopez have problems returning from his knee injury.

Odalis Perez

Position: SP
Bats: L **Throws:** L
Ht: 6' 0" **Wt:** 150

Opening Day Age: 21
Born: 6/7/78 in La Matas de Farfan, Dominican Republic
ML Seasons: 2
Pronunciation: oh-DALL-iss

Overall Statistics

	W	L	Pct.	ERA	G	GS	Sv	IP	H	BB	SO	HR	Ratio
1999	4	6	.400	6.00	18	17	0	93.0	100	53	82	12	1.65
Career	4	7	.364	5.82	28	17	0	103.2	110	57	87	13	1.61

1999 Situational Stats

	W	L	ERA	Sv	IP		AB	H	HR	RBI	Avg
Home	4	3	4.02	0	62.2	LHB	51	17	3	11	.333
Road	0	3	10.09	0	30.1	RHB	312	83	9	40	.266
First Half	4	5	5.28	0	87.0	Sc Pos	93	26	0	32	.280
Scnd Half	0	1	16.50	0	6.0	Clutch	12	5	0	2	.417

1999 Season

The Braves had an opening at fifth starter last spring and watched Odalis Perez take the job from the leading candidate, fellow rookie Bruce Chen. Perez won four of his first six decisions and pitched well through his June 8 victory over Tampa Bay. He struggled with his consistency for the next six weeks before tearing the medial collateral ligament in his pitching elbow in late July.

Pitching, Defense & Hitting

Though slight of build, Perez is an overpowering lefty with a mid-90s fastball. Despite that heat, his best pitch is a sharp-breaking curveball. Perez struggles when he leaves pitches high in the strike zone. He also tends to overemphasize strikeouts rather than outs. Perez is an above-average fielder and a decent hitter for a pitcher. He has a good pickoff move yet is easy to run on.

2000 Outlook

Perez is expected to be sidelined until at least midseason as he recovers from elbow surgery. He likely will work his way back into shape as a reliever before rejoining the rotation, and Chen may establish himself before Perez can return.

Mike Remlinger

Position: RP
Bats: L **Throws:** L
Ht: 6' 1" **Wt:** 210

Opening Day Age: 34
Born: 3/23/66 in
Middletown, NY
ML Seasons: 7
Pronunciation:
REM-lin-jurr

Overall Statistics

	W	L	Pct.	ERA	G	GS	Sv	IP	H	BB	SO	HR	Ratio
1999	10	1	.909	2.37	73	0	1	83.2	66	35	81	9	1.21
Career	29	32	.475	4.25	221	59	3	495.2	454	261	448	62	1.44

1999 Situational Stats

	W	L	ERA	Sv	IP		AB	H	HR	RBI	Avg
Home	5	1	0.92	0	39.0	LHB	83	17	3	10	.205
Road	5	0	3.63	1	44.2	RHB	224	49	6	11	.219
First Half	2	1	1.33	0	40.2	Sc Pos	63	10	1	12	.159
Scnd Half	8	0	3.35	1	43.0	Clutch	152	27	3	7	.178

1999 Season

For the first time in his inconsistent career, Mike Remlinger was used exclusively out of the bullpen. Considered a throw-in during last winter's five-player deal with the Reds for Bret Boone, Remlinger had the best season of the four. He became Atlanta's top lefthanded setup man while posting 10 wins, the most for an Atlanta reliever since Cecil Upshaw's 11 in 1971.

Pitching, Defense & Hitting

Remlinger always has displayed a great arm but never got the ball over the plate consistently. Rarely pitching more than an inning at a time last year, he stayed ahead in the count and kept hitters off balance with a low-90s fastball, a hard slider with late movement and a solid changeup. He's a decent fielder but could hold runners better. He's a poor hitter.

2000 Outlook

After winning eight games in the final two months, Remlinger earned a new two-year contract. Few teams have a more dependable lefty setup man, and he'll be a significant part of Atlanta's bullpen again this season.

Randall Simon

Position: 1B
Bats: L **Throws:** L
Ht: 6' 0" **Wt:** 180

Opening Day Age: 24
Born: 5/26/75 in
Willemstad, Curacao
ML Seasons: 3

Overall Statistics

	G	AB	R	H	D	T	HR	RBI	SB	BB	SO	Avg	OBP	Slg
1999	90	218	26	69	16	0	5	25	2	17	25	.317	.367	.459
Career	110	248	30	78	17	0	5	30	2	18	28	.315	.361	.444

1999 Situational Stats

	AB	H	HR	RBI	Avg		AB	H	HR	RBI	Avg
Home	95	26	2	12	.274	LHP	18	4	1	4	.222
Road	123	43	3	13	.350	RHP	200	65	4	21	.325
First Half	137	42	2	12	.307	Sc Pos	57	9	0	14	.158
Scnd Half	81	27	3	13	.333	Clutch	43	8	0	3	.186

1999 Season

Randall Simon rebounded from a disappointing 1998 season at Triple-A Richmond by making 55 starts at first base for the Braves and placing second on the team with a .317 batting average. While injuries at other positions forced Simon to make 10-day trips to the minors in May and August, the rookie proved he could provide some lefthanded pop at the game's top level.

Hitting, Baserunning & Defense

Simon always has been an effective hitter, though he lacks the pop teams want in an everyday first baseman. He's not afraid to swing the bat—four of his five home runs in 1999 came on the first pitch—but he would benefit by walking more often. Lefthanders give him trouble, and he may never rise above a platoon role. He's capable at first base and left field. His arm and speed are average, and he's no threat to steal.

2000 Outlook

Simon believes he should be the Braves' full-time starter at first base. That won't happen in Atlanta with Andres Galarraga returning.

Walt Weiss

Position: SS
Bats: B **Throws:** R
Ht: 6' 0" **Wt:** 188

Opening Day Age: 36
Born: 11/28/63 in Tuxedo, NY
ML Seasons: 13
Pronunciation: WICE

Overall Statistics

	G	AB	R	H	D	T	HR	RBI	SB	BB	SO	Avg	OBP	Slg
1999	110	279	38	63	13	4	2	29	7	35	48	.226	.315	.323
Career	1415	4494	594	1157	176	29	25	368	95	632	626	.257	.351	.326

1999 Situational Stats

	AB	H	HR	RBI	Avg		AB	H	HR	RBI	Avg
Home	114	28	0	13	.246	LHP	75	15	2	7	.200
Road	165	35	2	16	.212	RHP	204	48	0	22	.235
First Half	182	44	1	20	.242	Sc Pos	64	17	0	25	.266
Scnd Half	97	19	1	9	.196	Clutch	41	11	0	7	.268

1999 Season

For the second time in as many seasons with the Braves, Walt Weiss struggled with a quadriceps injury. He spent most of June on the disabled list, then produced miserably at the plate in July before losing the starting shortstop job to newcomer Jose Hernandez. Even so, Weiss regained the starting nod during the postseason because of his glove.

Hitting, Baserunning & Defense

After handling the leadoff duties for much of 1998, Weiss batted just .193 at the top of the lineup last year. Though he has very little power, he adds to his value by drawing walks. Defense is why he remains in the league. Weiss anticipates plays with the game's best, and helped solidify Atlanta's infield with his consistency. Despite possessing average speed, Weiss is a heady baserunner who makes the most of his opportunities.

2000 Outlook

With one season remaining on his contract, Weiss hopes to be a platoon starter at short. Given his declining production at the plate and his inability to stay healthy, his days as Atlanta's answer at the position are history.

Gerald Williams

Position: LF/RF
Bats: R **Throws:** R
Ht: 6' 2" **Wt:** 187

Opening Day Age: 33
Born: 8/10/66 in New Orleans, LA
ML Seasons: 8

Overall Statistics

	G	AB	R	H	D	T	HR	RBI	SB	BB	SO	Avg	OBP	Slg
1999	143	422	76	116	24	1	17	68	19	33	67	.275	.335	.457
Career	766	1941	308	510	124	14	55	240	72	115	330	.263	.309	.426

1999 Situational Stats

	AB	H	HR	RBI	Avg		AB	H	HR	RBI	Avg
Home	213	62	7	38	.291	LHP	182	52	9	32	.286
Road	209	54	10	30	.258	RHP	240	64	8	36	.267
First Half	168	44	6	30	.262	Sc Pos	114	32	6	55	.281
Scnd Half	254	72	11	38	.283	Clutch	72	14	1	10	.194

1999 Season

After failing to keep starting jobs in the past, Gerald Williams jumpstarted the Braves when he moved into the leadoff spot on Aug. 5. Williams helped Atlanta go 39-14 the rest of the way by putting together his best all-around season. He had a career-best 15-game hitting streak in late July and early August, and reached career highs in runs, homers, RBI and walks.

Hitting, Baserunning & Defense

Williams' success last year centered on his improved ability to hit righthanders. He was more patient and shortened his swing, thanks to the help of hitting coach Don Baylor. He has very good power for a leadoff man, though he has a subpar on-base percentage for the role. Williams is an above-average outfielder with a strong and accurate arm. His outstanding speed can translate into stolen bases, though he gets caught too often.

2000 Outlook

A free agent, Williams signed with Tampa Bay for two years and $5.75 million. He'll compete with Quinton McCracken to start in center field for the Devil Rays.

Other Atlanta Braves

Howard Battle (Pos: 3B, Age: 28, Bats: R)

	G	AB	R	H	D	T	HR	RBI	SB	BB	SO	Avg	OBP	Slg
1999	15	17	2	6	0	0	1	5	0	2	3	.353	.421	.529
Career	29	37	5	9	0	0	1	5	1	6	13	.243	.349	.324

Battle was Toronto's third baseman of the future a few years ago, but his star has faded. He rekindled the dream by hitting .284-24-74 for Triple-A Richmond, yet he wouldn't play much in Atlanta. 2000 Outlook: C

Sean Bergman (Pos: RHP, Age: 29)

	W	L	Pct.	ERA	G	GS	Sv	IP	H	BB	SO	HR	Ratio
1999	5	6	.455	5.21	25	16	0	105.1	135	29	44	9	1.56
Career	35	42	.455	4.84	181	103	0	682.1	801	239	420	81	1.52

Bergman seemed to turn a corner in 1998, but he wasn't able to duplicate his success in '99, when his ERA re-inflated. Atlanta signed him after Houston released him in September. The Twins claimed him on waivers in October. 2000 Outlook: C

Mike Cather (Pos: RHP, Age: 29)

	W	L	Pct.	ERA	G	GS	Sv	IP	H	BB	SO	HR	Ratio
1999	1	0	1.000	10.13	4	0	0	2.2	5	1	0	2	2.25
Career	5	6	.455	3.42	75	0	0	81.2	67	32	62	10	1.21

After two promising seasons in the Atlanta bullpen, Cather closed 1998 by having a rib removed to remedy a compressed artery. He spent most of 1999 at Triple-A Richmond and never got untracked. 2000 Outlook: C

David Cortes (Pos: RHP, Age: 26)

	W	L	Pct.	ERA	G	GS	Sv	IP	H	BB	SO	HR	Ratio
1999	0	0	-	4.91	4	0	0	3.2	3	4	2	0	1.91
Career	0	0	-	4.91	4	0	0	3.2	3	4	2	0	1.91

Cortes successfully closed games for Triple-A Richmond in 1999, recording 22 saves and a 3.35 ERA. He was OK in four late-season appearances with the Braves, and he should get a look in the spring. 2000 Outlook: C

Mark DeRosa (Pos: SS, Age: 25, Bats: R)

	G	AB	R	H	D	T	HR	RBI	SB	BB	SO	Avg	OBP	Slg
1999	7	8	0	0	0	0	0	0	0	0	2	.000	.000	.000
Career	12	11	2	1	0	0	0	0	0	0	3	.091	.091	.091

After a quick four-year climb through the Braves system, DeRosa spent most of June and September in the bigs. He wasn't spectacular at Triple-A Richmond, and he didn't get an opportunity in Atlanta. 2000 Outlook: C

Derrin Ebert (Pos: LHP, Age: 23)

	W	L	Pct.	ERA	G	GS	Sv	IP	H	BB	SO	HR	Ratio
1999	0	1	.000	5.63	5	0	1	8.0	9	5	4	2	1.75
Career	0	1	.000	5.63	5	0	1	8.0	9	5	4	2	1.75

Ebert has been unimpressive for two seasons at Triple-A Richmond, and he allowed runs in four of his five outings with the Braves. Yet he's young and could blossom. 2000 Outlook: C

Jorge Fabregas (Pos: C, Age: 30, Bats: L)

	G	AB	R	H	D	T	HR	RBI	SB	BB	SO	Avg	OBP	Slg
1999	88	231	20	46	10	2	3	21	0	26	27	.199	.280	.299
Career	485	1382	118	340	44	3	15	156	3	95	178	.246	.293	.315

Fabregas hasn't hit above the Mendoza line the last two seasons, and he's played for six teams over the last three years. He may be recycled by a few more clubs, but he isn't likely to ever start again. 2000 Outlook: C

Freddy Garcia (Pos: LF, Age: 27, Bats: R)

	G	AB	R	H	D	T	HR	RBI	SB	BB	SO	Avg	OBP	Slg
1999	57	132	17	31	5	0	7	24	0	5	42	.235	.261	.432
Career	175	401	53	89	18	2	19	56	0	33	121	.222	.283	.419

This Pirates prospect was traded to the Braves in September. His chances of playing third base are just as dim in Atlanta. He has some pop but doesn't make contact. 2000 Outlook: C

Ozzie Guillen (Pos: SS, Age: 36, Bats: L)

	G	AB	R	H	D	T	HR	RBI	SB	BB	SO	Avg	OBP	Slg
1999	92	232	21	56	16	0	1	20	4	15	17	.241	.284	.323
Career	1930	6579	751	1738	271	69	26	607	168	233	504	.264	.288	.338

A reliable veteran off the bench, Guillen was a regular in June when Walt Weiss was out with a quadriceps injury. The Braves needed a dependable infielder, and he also provided an occasional clutch hit. 2000 Outlook: C

Brian Hunter (Pos: 1B, Age: 32, Bats: R)

	G	AB	R	H	D	T	HR	RBI	SB	BB	SO	Avg	OBP	Slg
1999	114	181	28	45	12	1	6	30	0	31	40	.249	.367	.425
Career	612	1415	173	334	85	7	59	236	4	121	296	.236	.296	.431

With Andres Galarraga out battling cancer in 1999, Hunter eased into a platoon role at first base, sharing the job with Ryan Klesko and Randall Simon. A healthy Galarraga limits Hunter's playing time. 2000 Outlook: C

Kerry Ligtenberg (Pos: RHP, Age: 28)

	W	L	Pct.	ERA	G	GS	Sv	IP	H	BB	SO	HR	Ratio
1999						Did Not Play							
Career	4	2	.667	2.76	90	0	31	88.0	63	28	98	10	1.03

A torn elbow ligament discovered in March ended Ligtenberg's season before it began. Whether Atlanta's closer in 1998 comes back with the same velocity won't be known until spring training begins. 2000 Outlook: B

Keith Lockhart (Pos: 2B, Age: 35, Bats: L)

	G	AB	R	H	D	T	HR	RBI	SB	BB	SO	Avg	OBP	Slg
1999	108	161	20	42	3	1	1	21	3	19	21	.261	.337	.311
Career	572	1424	189	392	81	10	31	184	25	110	146	.275	.327	.412

Lockhart produced nine homers and 30 extra-base hits as a part-time player in 1998, but he didn't display the same pop last season. His pinch-hitting wasn't as good, though he batted .309 in the second half. 2000 Outlook: B

Pascual Matos (Pos: C, Age: 25, Bats: R)

	G	AB	R	H	D	T	HR	RBI	SB	BB	SO	Avg	OBP	Slg
1999	6	8	0	1	0	0	0	2	0	0	1	.125	.125	.125
Career	6	8	0	1	0	0	0	2	0	0	1	.125	.125	.125

Matos made four trips to Atlanta in 1999, but he wasn't likely to play much or succeed. He has batted .233 with just 20 walks and 149 strikeouts in the high minors the last two seasons. 2000 Outlook: D

Otis Nixon (Pos: LF, Age: 41, Bats: B)

	G	AB	R	H	D	T	HR	RBI	SB	BB	SO	Avg	OBP	Slg
1999	84	151	31	31	2	1	0	8	26	23	15	.205	.309	.232
Career	1709	5115	878	1379	142	27	11	318	620	585	694	.270	.343	.314

A slow starter in recent years, Nixon's slow start as a part-time player in 1999 lasted the entire first half, when he hit .172. It was an off year for Nixon, who missed a month with a cervical sprain. 2000 Outlook: C

Rudy Seanez (Pos: RHP, Age: 31)

	W	L	Pct.	ERA	G	GS	Sv	IP	H	BB	SO	HR	Ratio
1999	6	1	.857	3.35	56	0	3	53.2	47	21	41	3	1.27
Career	14	7	.667	4.63	181	0	8	188.2	176	102	177	17	1.47

For a second straight season Seanez pitched well out of the Atlanta pen, but then he suffered a stress fracture in his elbow last August. September surgery should have him ready to go in the spring. 2000 Outlook: B

Justin Speier (Pos: RHP, Age: 26)

	W	L	Pct.	ERA	G	GS	Sv	IP	H	BB	SO	HR	Ratio
1999	0	0	-	5.65	19	0	0	28.2	28	13	22	8	1.43
Career	0	3	.000	6.93	38	0	0	49.1	55	26	39	15	1.64

After a rocky 1998 in the majors, Speier seemed to settle down last season after arriving in an April trade with the Marlins. He pitched OK in April and May, but blew up in June. He didn't rebound at Triple-A Richmond, either. 2000 Outlook: C

Russ Springer (Pos: RHP, Age: 31)

	W	L	Pct.	ERA	G	GS	Sv	IP	H	BB	SO	HR	Ratio
1999	2	1	.667	3.42	49	0	1	47.1	31	22	49	5	1.12
Career	17	28	.378	5.00	281	27	7	452.0	462	208	414	61	1.48

Back surgery sidelined Springer the first six weeks of 1999, but he came back to pitch well for a second straight season. He was remarkable after the All-Star break, posting a 1.86 ERA in 29 innings. Arizona signed him to a two-year, $4 million contract as a free agent. 2000 Outlook: A

Everett Stull (Pos: RHP, Age: 28)

	W	L	Pct.	ERA	G	GS	Sv	IP	H	BB	SO	HR	Ratio
1999	0	0	-	13.50	1	0	0	0.2	2	2	0	0	6.00
Career	0	1	.000	15.75	4	0	0	4.0	9	6	2	1	3.75

Stull made his second trip to the bigs with Atlanta in September. He took a line drive in the face sitting on the bench and needed surgery to insert a plate in his head. 2000 Outlook: C

Joe Winkelsas (Pos: RHP, Age: 26)

	W	L	Pct.	ERA	G	GS	Sv	IP	H	BB	SO	HR	Ratio
1999	0	0	-	54.00	1	0	0	0.1	4	1	0	0	15.00
Career	0	0	-	54.00	1	0	0	0.1	4	1	0	0	15.00

Winkelsas retired just one batter in a rough April debut, then went to Double-A Greenville and turned in a so-so season. He's not young, so his window of opportunity won't be open for long. 2000 Outlook: C

Mark Wohlers (Pos: RHP, Age: 30)

	W	L	Pct.	ERA	G	GS	Sv	IP	H	BB	SO	HR	Ratio
1999	0	0	-	27.00	2	0	0	0.2	1	6	0	0	10.50
Career	31	22	.585	3.73	388	0	112	386.1	331	204	437	20	1.38

Wohlers couldn't overcome his Steve Blass Disease with the Braves, who sent him to the Reds for John Hudek in April. Wohlers walked 10 in four minor league innings, spent most of the year on the DL with anxiety disorder, then was released in October. 2000 Outlook: D

Atlanta Braves Minor League Prospects

Organization Overview:

Atlanta continues to churn out talent as well as any organization. Chipper Jones, Ryan Klesko and Javy Lopez arrived in the middle of the decade, followed in the last couple of years by Andruw Jones, Kevin Millwood and John Rocker. There's plenty more where that came from, which is why the Braves found it easy to part with three pitching prospects when they needed role players Jose Hernandez and Terry Mulholland last summer. Atlanta is willing to spend money on player development, a big reason why it often acquires first-round talent with lower-round draft picks and uncovers gems on the international market. Former farm and scouting director Paul Snyder, who retired during the 1999 season, was the unsung hero behind the Braves' unprecedented streak of eight consecutive division titles.

Bruce Chen

Position: P
Bats: B **Throws:** L
Ht: 6' 1" **Wt:** 180

Opening Day Age: 22
Born: 6/19/77 in
Panama City, Panama

Recent Statistics

	W	L	ERA	G	GS	Sv	IP	H	R	BB	SO	HR
1999 AAA Richmond	6	3	3.81	14	14	0	78.0	73	36	26	90	10
1999 NL Atlanta	2	2	5.47	16	7	0	51.0	38	32	27	45	11

Expected to claim the final spot in the Atlanta rotation, Chen struggled in spring training and only surfaced when injuries struck John Smoltz and Odalis Perez. Another example of the Braves' prowess in international scouting, Chen didn't sulk in Triple-A, where International League managers rated him the circuit's best pitching prospect. Often compared to a young Tom Glavine, Chen succeeds with command more than stuff. He paints both sides of the plate with an average fastball, changing speeds and locations as he mixes in curveballs and changeups. He was hit hard during the spring and in Atlanta because he couldn't spot his pitches as well as usual. With Perez sidelined after elbow surgery, the Braves need Chen to step up in 2000.

Rafael Furcal

Position: SS
Bats: B **Throws:** R
Ht: 5' 10" **Wt:** 150

Opening Day Age: 19
Born: 8/24/80 in Loma
de Cabrera, Dom. Rep.

Recent Statistics

	G	AB	R	H	D	T	HR	RBI	SB	BB	SO	Avg
1998 R Danville	66	268	56	88	15	4	0	23	60	36	29	.328
1999 A Macon	83	335	73	113	15	1	1	29	73	41	36	.337
1999 A Myrtle Bch	43	184	32	54	9	3	0	12	23	14	42	.293

Furcal electrified two Class-A leagues last year, leading the minors with 96 stolen bases and winning the South Atlantic League batting title at age 18. Sally League managers certainly noticed him, naming him the league's

outstanding prospect, best hitting prospect, fastest baserunner, best defensive shortstop and best infield arm. The only thing the Dominican won't do is hit for power, but he already has a good working knowledge of the strike zone and projects as the dynamic leadoff man sorely lacking on the Braves. Furcal also will fill the large void at shortstop in Atlanta, perhaps by the end of 2001.

Marcus Giles

Position: 2B
Bats: R **Throws:** R
Ht: 5' 8" **Wt:** 180

Opening Day Age: 21
Born: 5/18/78 in San
Diego, CA

Recent Statistics

	G	AB	R	H	D	T	HR	RBI	SB	BB	SO	Avg
1998 A Macon	135	505	111	166	38	3	37	108	12	85	103	.329
1999 A Myrtle Bch	126	497	80	162	40	7	13	73	9	54	89	.326

While his brother Brian was enjoying a breakthrough season for the Pirates, Marcus was winning his second straight minor league MVP award, this time in the high Class-A Carolina League. A 53rd-round pick in 1996 who signed after a year at Grossmont (Calif.) Junior College, Giles has the same short, stocky build as his older sibling. Possessing impressive bat speed, he won the Carolina League batting title with a .326 average that dropped his career mark to .331. He has gap power and a fine eye at the plate. He's slow afoot and rough defensively, but his arm and hands make him an average second baseman. Giles could push Bret Boone in a couple of years.

Wes Helms

Position: 1B
Bats: R **Throws:** R
Ht: 6' 4" **Wt:** 230

Opening Day Age: 23
Born: 5/12/76 in
Gastonia, NC

Recent Statistics

	G	AB	R	H	D	T	HR	RBI	SB	BB	SO	Avg
1998 AAA Richmond	125	451	56	124	27	1	13	75	6	35	103	.275
1999 R Braves	9	33	1	15	2	0	0	10	0	5	4	.455
1999 AA Greenville	30	113	15	34	6	0	8	26	1	7	34	.301

Helms' steady progress toward Atlanta was interrupted by rotator-cuff surgery on his right shoulder, which was supposed to keep him out for all of 1999. He worked diligently to return ahead of schedule, only to separate his left shoulder in a collision while playing first base. The son of former major leaguer Tommy Helms and a 10th-round pick in 1994, Wes has the raw power and arm strength teams covet in third basemen. His swing is long, he's impatient at the plate and he tries to pull too many pitches, which is why his pop hasn't translated into more home runs. If Chipper Jones becomes too expensive to retain as a free agent after 2000, Helms would be next in line at third base for the Braves.

Atlanta

George Lombard

Position: OF
Bats: L **Throws:** R
Ht: 6' 0" **Wt:** 212

Opening Day Age: 24
Born: 9/14/75 in Atlanta, GA

Recent Statistics

	G	AB	R	H	D	T	HR	RBI	SB	BB	SO	Avg
1999 AAA Richmond	74	233	25	48	11	3	7	29	21	35	98	.206
1999 NL Atlanta	6	6	1	2	0	0	0	0	2	1	2	.333
1999 MLE	74	226	19	41	9	2	5	22	15	27	102	.181

Though a groin injury cost him half a season and severely limited him when he played, Lombard still was named the most exciting player in the Triple-A International League. When healthy, there's little the 1994 second-round pick can't do. He gets from the plate to first base in 4.0 seconds and has refined his basestealing technique. He also offers plenty of power (he led the Arizona Fall League with 11 homers and 37 RBI) and gets on base, though he could make more contact. His arm is his only below-average tool, and once he improves his reads on flyballs he should be a competent left fielder. Lombard could use a full year in Triple-A before starting for Atlanta in 2001.

Jason Marquis

Position: P
Bats: L **Throws:** R
Ht: 6' 1" **Wt:** 185

Opening Day Age: 21
Born: 8/21/78 in Manhasset, NY

Recent Statistics

	W	L	ERA	G	GS	Sv	IP	H	R	BB	SO	HR
1998 A Danville	2	12	4.87	22	22	0	114.2	120	65	41	135	3
1999 A Myrtle Bch	3	0	0.28	6	6	0	32.0	22	2	17	41	0
1999 AA Greenville	3	4	4.58	12	12	0	55.0	52	33	29	35	7

Though Marquis won just two of his 22 starts at high Class-A Danville in 1998, the Braves never doubted him. He returned to the Carolina League and was named the league's top pitching prospect before being promoted to Double-A at age 20. A 1995 first-round pick, he throws 96 MPH with an excellent curveball and two changeups. Hitters have a hard time taking him deep, connecting for just 20 homers in his 366.2 pro innings. Marquis' command wavered in Double-A, where he was bothered by a sore elbow and a strained ribcage muscle. Neither his control nor his health is a long-term concern. He just needs to continue to learn how to pitch, and his Atlanta ETA is probably 2002.

Luis Rivera

Position: P
Bats: R **Throws:** R
Ht: 6' 3" **Wt:** 163

Opening Day Age: 21
Born: 6/21/78 in Chihuahua, Mexico

Recent Statistics

	W	L	ERA	G	GS	Sv	IP	H	R	BB	SO	HR
1998 A Macon	5	5	3.98	20	20	0	92.2	78	53	41	118	8
1999 A Myrtle Bch	0	2	3.11	25	13	0	66.2	45	25	23	81	3

Rivera is yet another product of Atlanta's international scouting efforts. He was signed out of Mexico by Bill Clark, one of the game's top global scouts, who surpris-

ingly was let go by the Braves after Paul Snyder retired. Rivera throws his fastball, rated the best in the high Class-A Carolina League in 1999, as hard as 95 MPH, though it tends to be straight and probably would have more movement with less velocity. His slider and changeup are still developing, though his biggest need is to stay healthy. Back problems in 1998 and blisters last season have limited him to 159.1 innings in two years. If Rivera's secondary pitches don't come around, he has the heat to be a closer.

Scott Sobkowiak

Position: P
Bats: R **Throws:** R
Ht: 6' 5" **Wt:** 230

Opening Day Age: 22
Born: 10/26/77 in Woodstock, IL

Recent Statistics

	W	L	ERA	G	GS	Sv	IP	H	R	BB	SO	HR
1998 A Eugene	3	2	1.55	8	8	0	40.2	25	12	13	55	1
1999 A Myrtle Bch	9	4	2.84	27	26	0	139.1	100	50	63	161	10

A 1998 seventh-round pick out of Northern Iowa, Sobkowiak has dominated hitters since turning pro. In 180 innings, he has posted a 2.55 ERA and allowed just 125 hits while fanning 216 batters. He led the high Class-A Carolina League in opponent average (.199) and strikeouts per nine innings (10.4) last year. His combination of a fastball that reaches 95 MPH and a knee-buckling curveball has proved unhittable thus far. Like most young pitchers, Sobkowiak needs to refine his changeup and control. Once he does that, he'll be on the fast track toward Atlanta.

Others to Watch

Dominican righthander **Winston Abreu** (22) has an average fastball and slider, but his delivery is so deceptive that he allowed just 94 hits and struck out 171 in 138 Class-A innings in 1999. . . Another Dominican, shortstop **Wilson Betemit** (19), batted .320 with power from both sides of the plate at Rookie-level Danville in his first year as a switch-hitter. He has a strong arm, but may outgrow short and move to third base. . . Korean lefthander **Jung Bong** (18) has Bruce Chen's pitching knowledge and better stuff. Bong throws in the low 90s and is fearless. . . **Ryan Langerhans** (20), who signed for $775,000 as a 1998 third-round pick, was named the best defensive outfielder and best outfield arm in the Class-A South Atlantic League last year. He also should hit for power and average. . . Venezuelan **Asdrubal Oropeza** (19) finished second in the New York-Penn League with 14 homers last year despite being three years younger than many of the players in the short-season circuit. He's also an agile third baseman with very good hands. . . Lefthander **Jimmy Osting** (21) led the Sally League with 14 victories after missing all of 1998 following Tommy John surgery. He's deceptive and features an outstanding changeup.

Wrigley Field

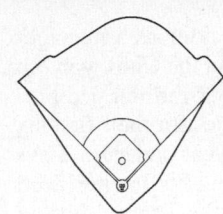

Offense

Wrigley can be a hitter's best friend or worst enemy, depending on the time of year. Early in the season, the cold wind blows in off Lake Michigan, knocking down flyballs and keeping them in the park. Once it warms up, Wrigley boosts batting averages and run production. The gaps are the easiest parts of the park to reach, and players with power to the alleys tend to benefit the most.

Defense

A pitcher's only hope here is to keep the ball on the ground. The thick grass slows bouncers and enables range-deficient infielders to give the appearance of competence. Outfielders must be able to find their way to the wall, especially the corner men, who must deal with the wells near the foul lines where the walls drop back. A misjudgment may result in a collision with the bricks. The bullpen mounds can be a challenge for an unfamiliar fielder tracking a foul.

Who It Helps The Most

Power hitters aren't the only ones who find Wrigley so friendly. Though Sammy Sosa and Henry Rodriguez have enjoyed Wrigley's help, Mickey Morandini has fared well here too. Jeff Reed hit well in Chicago during his limited time with the Cubs, as did Jose Nieves. Glenallen Hill simply was born to hit at Wrigley. Few pitchers can boast of consistent success at Wrigley. Kevin Tapani had been, but he didn't do well there last year.

Who It Hurts The Most

Rodney Myers has been brutally abused at Wrigley, despite pitching decently on the road. Rick Aguilera had terrible problems adjusting to Wrigley last year, as did Scott Sanders.

Rookies & Newcomers

Shane Andrews hit four homers in nine home games after joining the Cubs, and should fare better in Chicago than he did in Montreal. The same is true of Joe Girardi, Ricky Gutierrez and Eric Young, all of whom arrive from pitchers' parks. Wrigley Field won't hurt Damon Buford either. But it might bother Ismael Valdes, whose career ERA is 4.34 away from Dodger Stadium.

Dimensions: LF-355, LCF-368, CF-400, RCF-368, RF-353

Capacity: 38,884

Elevation: 595 feet

Surface: Grass

Foul Territory: Small

Park Factors

1999 Season

	Home Games			Away Games			
	Cubs	Opp	Total	Cubs	Opp	Total	Index
G	72	72	144	75	75	150	—
Avg	.266	.285	.276	.244	.281	.263	105
AB	2410	2604	5014	2561	2523	5084	103
R	352	429	781	320	405	725	112
H	642	741	1383	626	709	1335	108
2B	125	132	257	108	124	232	112
3B	20	12	32	12	25	37	88
HR	88	111	199	85	91	176	115
BB	270	239	509	252	238	490	105
SO	504	471	975	561	426	987	100
E	66	45	111	56	45	101	114
E-Infield	51	38	89	48	37	85	109
LHB-Avg	.273	.304	.287	.252	.277	.263	109
LHB-HR	24	36	60	30	34	64	101
RHB-Avg	.261	.274	.268	.238	.283	.262	102
RHB-HR	64	75	139	55	57	112	121

1997-1999

	Home Games			Away Games			
	Cubs	Opp	Total	Cubs	Opp	Total	Index
G	220	220	440	224	224	448	—
Avg	.272	.267	.270	.247	.274	.260	104
AB	7387	7805	15192	7763	7539	15302	101
R	1087	1122	2209	953	1128	2081	108
H	2011	2087	4098	1916	2068	3984	105
2B	349	388	737	352	416	768	97
3B	54	38	92	44	61	105	88
HR	260	293	553	221	247	468	119
BB	768	775	1543	709	766	1475	105
SO	1477	1592	3069	1637	1400	3037	102
E	158	160	318	161	152	313	103
E-Infield	126	135	261	130	134	264	101
LHB-Avg	.288	.277	.282	.258	.275	.266	106
LHB-HR	79	98	177	82	93	175	105
RHB-Avg	.261	.261	.261	.239	.274	.256	102
RHB-HR	181	195	376	139	154	293	126

1999 Rankings (National League)
- Second-highest batting-average factor
- Second-highest run factor
- Second-highest hit factor
- Second-highest home-run factor
- Second-highest error factor
- Second-highest RHB batting-average factor
- Second-highest RHB home-run factor
- Third-highest double factor
- Third-highest LHB batting-average factor

Chicago (NL)

369

Don Baylor

1999 Season

Several teams pursued Don Baylor as a manager once the 1999 season ended, and the Cubs won out with a four-year deal worth $5.2 million. He previously had managed the Rockies for their first six seasons, and after a disastrous year under Jim Leyland, Colorado management regrets having fired Baylor. He spent the year as the Braves' hitting coach, getting credit for helping Chipper Jones win the National League MVP Award.

Offense

Though Baylor managed six seasons in a hitters' paradise in Colorado, he showed a surprising fondness for one-run strategies like the sacrifice, steal and hit-and-run. He seemed to prefer power over speed in Colorado, though the park's spacious outfield required swift runners and the thin air guaranteed that longballs never would be in short supply. Baylor pinch-hits often and calls for a lot of sacrifices, often surprisingly early in the game.

Pitching & Defense

Baylor's tendencies are extreme in a couple of regards. First, he calls for more pitchouts than almost any other major league manager, and his team catches baserunners in motion a fair amount of the time. Second, he calls for fewer intentional walks than any other manager. He had no qualms about relying heavily upon rookie pitchers in Colorado, though he may have had little choice. The fact that few of them developed probably can be ascribed to the horrors of Coors Field rather than any mishandling by Baylor. He prefers strong defense from his middle infielders.

2000 Outlook

Baylor takes over a club in transition. While it might be a stretch to think of the Cubs as contenders, there's optimism in Chicago after the club acquired Joe Girardi, Ricky Gutierrez, Ismael Valdes and Eric Young without giving up anything significant. In any case, Baylor already has proven he can help build a franchise from nothing. When he took over the Cubs, the situation was only slightly better.

Born: 6/28/49 in Austin, TX

Playing Experience: 1970-1988, Bal, Oak, Ana, NYY, Bos, Min

Managerial Experience: 6 seasons
Nickname: Groove

Manager Statistics

Year Team, Lg	W	L	Pct	GB	Finish
1999	—	—	—	—	—
6 Seasons	440	469	.484	—	—

1999 Starting Pitchers by Days Rest

	<=3	4	5	6+
Cubs Starts	—	—	—	—
Cubs ERA	—	—	—	—
NL Avg Starts	3	81	48	21
NL ERA	4.84	4.53	4.72	4.98

1999 Situational Stats

	Don Baylor	NL Average
Hit & Run Success %	—	33.6
Stolen Base Success %	—	70.2
Platoon Pct.	—	55.2
Defensive Subs	—	25
High-Pitch Outings	—	13
Quick/Slow Hooks	—	16/15
Sacrifice Attempts	—	89

1999 Rankings (National League)
- Did not manage in the majors last year

Terry Adams

Position: RP
Bats: R **Throws:** R
Ht: 6' 3" **Wt:** 205

Opening Day Age: 27
Born: 3/6/73 in Mobile, AL
ML Seasons: 5

1999 Season

After struggling through the second half of 1998, Terry Adams missed the first five weeks of 1999 with a bad elbow. When he returned, he was up to his old tricks. He pitched well at times but never consistently, performing well enough to get a few save opportunities but not well enough to nail down the Cubs' closer job.

Pitching

Adams throws a two-seam fastball in the low 90s with excellent life, plus a good slider. The combination can be tough to hit, especially for lefties, but equally tough to control. With runners on base, he fears bouncing a pitch to the backstop, and becomes tentative and quite hittable. Otherwise Adams is highly effective, producing almost nothing but strikeouts and groundballs. His walk total, which always had been on the high side, improved last year. He gave up an uncharacteristically large number of home runs, however. He was worked heavily earlier in his career, and had a history of second-half fades before coming down with a sore elbow last spring. Thus his health is an ongoing concern.

Defense & Hitting

Adams has neither a strong move to first nor a quick delivery, and basestealers tend to have their way with him. He's nothing special with the glove. He's hitless in 11 major league at-bats, putting the ball in play only four times.

2000 Outlook

The Dodgers wanted to dump salaries, so they traded Ismael Valdes and Eric Young to the Cubs for Adams plus minor league righthanders Chad Ricketts and Brian Stephenson. Adams will be used to set up Jeff Shaw in Los Angeles. The injury he suffered last spring—a sprained elbow ligament—was the same one Kerry Wood had during his rookie season. Wood's sprain later developed into a complete tear, and Adams' might too.

Overall Statistics

	W	L	Pct.	ERA	G	GS	Sv	IP	H	BB	SO	HR	Ratio
1999	6	3	.667	4.02	52	0	13	65.0	60	28	57	9	1.35
Career	19	26	.422	4.03	276	0	37	330.2	329	168	287	25	1.50

How Often He Throws Strikes

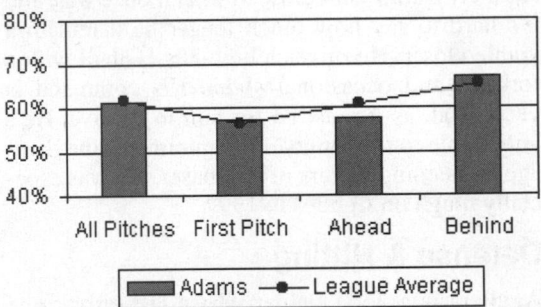

1999 Situational Stats

	W	L	ERA	Sv	IP		AB	H	HR	RBI	Avg
Home	2	0	4.02	5	31.1	LHB	102	19	3	10	.186
Road	4	3	4.01	8	33.2	RHB	143	41	6	26	.287
First Half	2	2	3.08	5	26.1	Sc Pos	68	20	3	29	.294
Scnd Half	4	1	4.66	8	38.2	Clutch	131	28	4	20	.214

1999 Rankings (National League)

- Led the Cubs in saves, games finished (38), save opportunities (18), relief ERA (4.02), relief wins (6), lowest batting average allowed in relief (.245) and fewest baserunners allowed per nine innings in relief (12.2)

Chicago (NL)

Rick Aguilera

1999 Season

Veteran closer Rick Aguilera got off to a good start with Minnesota last year before being traded to the Cubs in late May to replace the injured Rod Beck. Aguilera took a while to adjust to a new league and ballpark, and he pitched horribly for the next month, helping the Cubs fall out of the Central Division race. He missed time in August with a strained calf, then returned to pitch very well in September. Though his overall numbers looked OK, his season will be remembered for the awful stretch he went through at the worst possible time for the Cubs.

Pitching

Aguilera's stuff isn't close to what it once was, and it's hard to say how much longer he'll remain a viable closer. He mixes a high-80s fastball with a forkball and occasional slider. His command is very good, as it must be for him to survive. He's vulnerable to the longball but minimizes the damage by keeping batters off the bases. He was especially tough on righties in 1999.

Defense & Hitting

Aguilera is a good fielder whose last error came four years ago. He's decent at holding runners but slow to the plate. Basestealers didn't hurt him last year but have in the past. Aguilera was a good-hitting pitcher with the Mets but has batted only twice in the last 10 years.

2000 Outlook

In November Aguilera exercised the option he held for the 2000 season. While a rebuilding club like the Cubs may hold little appeal for a veteran with few years left, his option offered a better paycheck than he probably would have secured on the open market. The closer job became his by default when Terry Adams was traded to Los Angeles at the Winter Meetings.

Position: RP
Bats: R **Throws:** R
Ht: 6' 5" **Wt:** 208

Opening Day Age: 38
Born: 12/31/61 in San Gabriel, CA
ML Seasons: 15
Pronunciation: ag-yuh-LAIR-uh
Nickname: Aggie

Overall Statistics

	W	L	Pct.	ERA	G	GS	Sv	IP	H	BB	SO	HR	Ratio
1999	9	4	.692	2.93	61	0	14	67.2	54	12	45	8	0.98
Career	85	79	.518	3.52	678	89	289	1243.2	1186	333	992	127	1.22

How Often He Throws Strikes

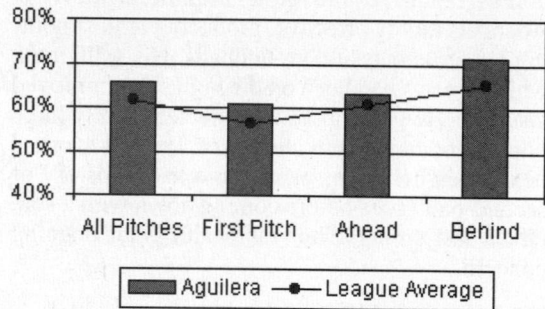

1999 Situational Stats

	W	L	ERA	Sv	IP		AB	H	HR	RBI	Avg
Home	4	3	4.09	7	33.0	LHB	96	28	4	13	.292
Road	5	1	1.82	7	34.2	RHB	151	26	4	17	.172
First Half	6	4	4.05	10	40.0	Sc Pos	59	15	2	22	.254
Scnd Half	3	0	1.30	4	27.2	Clutch	160	42	6	22	.263

1999 Rankings (National League)

- 8th in first batter efficiency (.171)
- Led the Cubs in most GDPs induced per GDP situation (18.8%), first batter efficiency (.171) and relief wins (6)

Mark Grace

Position: 1B
Bats: L **Throws:** L
Ht: 6' 2" **Wt:** 200

Opening Day Age: 35
Born: 6/28/64 in
Winston-Salem, NC
ML Seasons: 12

1999 Season

As is his custom, Mark Grace enjoyed another productive season that was virtually indistinguishable from his previous ones. He missed only one game, hit better than .300 for the fifth straight year and played his usual Gold Glove-caliber defense. An offseason workout regimen kept him strong throughout the entire season. His durability and consistency gained some recognition after he finished with the most base hits of any batter in the 1990s.

Hitting

Grace provides an ongoing clinic on how to hit .300. He works the count in his favor, waiting for his pitch or settling for a walk. When he gets what he's looking for, he uses a short, quick stroke to hit the ball on a line where it's pitched. With this approach, he rarely strikes out and remains dangerous in all situations, even with two strikes or a southpaw on the mound. He has less home-run power than a typical middle-of-the-order hitter, but his singles and doubles bring home a decent number of runs and create more RBI opportunities for the batters after him.

Baserunning & Defense

Grace has earned a reputation as one of the smoothest-fielding first basemen around. With soft hands and quick reflexes, he's able to dig throws out of the dirt and snare hard-hit balls down the line. His arm isn't particularly accurate, but it seldom costs him. Though he has no foot speed whatsoever, he runs with alertness and intelligence, and always knows when to go for an extra base.

2000 Outlook

Grace signed a one-year extension worth $5.3 million last August. He should keep cranking out .300 seasons as long as his body allows. It's clear he's yielded nothing to age so far. Grace is a Cubs icon and probably will remain with the club to the end of his career, though he made noise about possibly joining his hometown Padres after his contract expires.

Overall Statistics

	G	AB	R	H	D	T	HR	RBI	SB	BB	SO	Avg	OBP	Slg
1999	161	593	107	183	44	5	16	91	3	83	44	.309	.390	.481
Career	1767	6646	982	2058	415	42	137	922	66	851	533	.310	.386	.447

Where He Hits the Ball

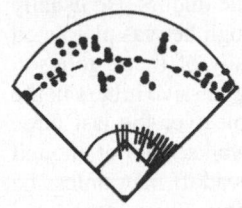

Vs. LHP

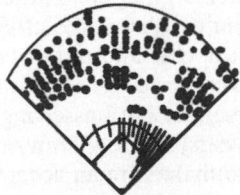

Vs. RHP

1999 Situational Stats

	AB	H	HR	RBI	Avg		AB	H	HR	RBI	Avg
Home	297	98	8	49	.330	LHP	199	61	4	34	.307
Road	296	85	8	42	.287	RHP	394	122	12	57	.310
First Half	310	97	11	53	.313	Sc Pos	140	47	3	71	.336
Scnd Half	283	86	5	38	.304	Clutch	85	29	1	19	.341

1999 Rankings (National League)

- 1st in sacrifice flies (10)
- 2nd in batting average on an 0-2 count (.323)
- Led the Cubs in batting average, hits, singles, doubles, sacrifice flies (10), walks, times on base (268), on-base percentage, batting average with runners in scoring position, batting average in the clutch, batting average with the bases loaded (.417), batting average vs. righthanded pitchers, batting average on an 0-2 count (.323), on-base percentage vs. righthanded pitchers (.402), batting average at home, batting average on the road, batting average with two strikes (.227), highest percentage of pitches taken (55.7%) and highest percentage of extra bases taken as a runner (60.5%)

Chicago (NL)

Lance Johnson

1999 Season

After hitting very well during the second half of 1998, Lance Johnson was expected to be the Cubs' leadoff man and offensive catalyst in '99. Injuries prevented him from being anything of the sort. He got off to a slow start before suffering an abdominal strain in June. The injury was slow to heal, which led to a July confrontation with manager Jim Riggleman. Johnson was activated in August after the Cubs threatened to release him. He played regularly for the rest of the year, but wasn't able to run well and didn't contribute much.

Hitting

Johnson has a history of slow starts and fast finishes. He's a slap hitter and one of the more extreme groundball hitters in the majors. He usually isn't bothered by lefties, though he was platooned last year and didn't face many of them. Johnson used to be one of the more aggressive hitters in the majors, but has changed a bit over the last three years. He now draws more walks, but not enough to make him an acceptable leadoff man unless he keeps his average close to .300.

Baserunning & Defense

Once a premier basestealer, Johnson's persistent physical woes have kept him from running as often as he used to. He hardly ran at all during the second half last year. He remains an excellent percentage basestealer when healthy. His speed is his main asset on defense as well. He covers a lot of ground in center field when he's 100 percent. His arm is weak but he can compensate when he's able to get to balls quickly.

2000 Outlook

Johnson was released by the Cubs two days after the season ended. Though he was quite durable earlier in his career, his age and recent injury history may make it hard for him to land another regular job. A role as a fourth outfielder may be the most he'll find. His replacement in Chicago will be Damon Buford, whom the Cubs acquired in a December trade with the Red Sox for Manny Alexander.

Position: CF
Bats: L **Throws:** L
Ht: 5'11" **Wt:** 165

Opening Day Age: 36
Born: 7/6/63 in Lincoln Heights, OH
ML Seasons: 13

Overall Statistics

	G	AB	R	H	D	T	HR	RBI	SB	BB	SO	Avg	OBP	Slg
1999	95	335	46	87	11	6	1	21	13	37	20	.260	.332	.337
Career	1430	5349	761	1556	174	117	34	484	325	352	377	.291	.334	.386

Where He Hits the Ball

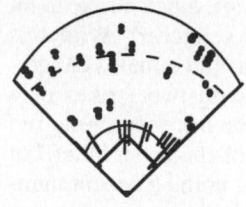

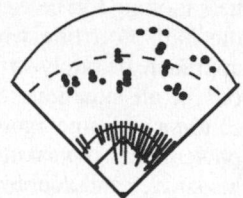

Vs. LHP   **Vs. RHP**

1999 Situational Stats

	AB	H	HR	RBI	Avg		AB	H	HR	RBI	Avg
Home	166	43	1	15	.259	LHP	69	13	0	2	.188
Road	169	44	0	6	.260	RHP	266	74	1	19	.278
First Half	200	52	1	13	.260	Sc Pos	64	15	0	19	.234
Scnd Half	135	35	0	8	.259	Clutch	51	10	0	3	.196

1999 Rankings (National League)

- 5th in lowest on-base percentage for a leadoff hitter (.327)
- 9th in lowest batting average on a 3-1 count (.077)
- Led the Cubs in triples, stolen bases, on-base percentage for a leadoff hitter (.327) and steals of third (3)

Jon Lieber

Position: SP
Bats: L **Throws:** R
Ht: 6' 3" **Wt:** 225

Opening Day Age: 29
Born: 4/2/70 in Council Bluffs, IA
ML Seasons: 6
Pronunciation: LEE-burr

1999 Season

It's hard not to feel for Jon Lieber. After years of pitching decently and getting stuck with poor won-lost records with the hapless Pirates, he was traded last winter to the Cubs, who were fresh off a wild-card season. It looked like he might finally get to pitch for a winning team, but his arrival coincided with the Cubs' return to the cellar. Lieber did a creditable job, enjoying a strong first half before slumping over the season's final months.

Pitching

With a sinking fastball in the low 90s, a good slider and excellent command, Lieber is one of the game's tougher pitchers on righthanders. The problem is that he has no workable game plan against lefties, who routinely light him up. He has a changeup, but it's little more than a decent third pitch. If he ever adds a pitch to throw to lefties, he could make a big leap forward. Last year's second-half fade did nothing to allay concerns about his conditioning. He didn't adjust well to Wrigley Field, where he allowed 18 of his 28 home runs and dropped eight of 12 decisions.

Defense & Hitting

Lieber uses a slide step to keep runners close and allowed just five steals last year. He isn't especially quick off the mound but generally fields his position adequately. He's a very weak hitter but has become an acceptable bunter.

2000 Outlook

In light of the Cubs' rebuilding plan, Lieber's hopes of pitching for a successful team may have to wait. It's a shame, because he has the ability to post a respectable record with a better team behind him. He never has had serious arm problems, so he can be counted upon to take the hill every five days and keep his team in the game. Chicago signed him to a three-year contract worth $15 million in the offseason.

Overall Statistics

	W	L	Pct.	ERA	G	GS	Sv	IP	H	BB	SO	HR	Ratio
1999	10	11	.476	4.07	31	31	0	203.1	226	46	186	28	1.34
Career	48	58	.453	4.30	182	135	2	886.0	976	204	694	112	1.33

How Often He Throws Strikes

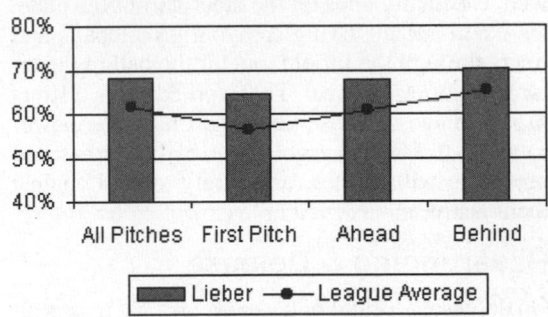

1999 Situational Stats

	W	L	ERA	Sv	IP		AB	H	HR	RBI	Avg
Home	4	8	4.20	0	113.2	LHB	360	120	18	55	.333
Road	6	3	3.91	0	89.2	RHB	450	106	10	40	.236
First Half	8	3	3.26	0	105.0	Sc Pos	151	36	3	59	.238
Scnd Half	2	8	4.94	0	98.1	Clutch	55	12	2	5	.218

1999 Rankings (National League)

- 3rd in most strikeouts per nine innings (8.2) and highest batting average allowed vs. lefthanded batters
- 4th in highest strikeout/walk ratio (4.0)
- 6th in least walks per nine innings (2.0)
- 8th in strikeouts
- 9th in complete games (3)
- 10th in hits allowed, balks (2) and fewest pitches thrown per batter (3.54)
- Led the Cubs in sacrifice bunts (7), ERA, wins, hits allowed, strikeouts, winning percentage, highest strikeout/walk ratio (4.0), lowest batting average allowed (.279), lowest slugging percentage allowed (.432) and lowest on-base percentage allowed (.315)

Chicago (NL)

Mickey Morandini

1999 Season

Mickey Morandini was one of the victims of Chicago's dismal season. He was having a fairly representative year for the first four months, batting around .260 and playing solid defense. In August, when the Cubs were well out of contention, they began to look to the 2000 season. They offered potential free agent Morandini a contract extension, and when he rejected it, he was benched in favor of rookie Chad Meyers. Morandini got few at-bats over the last two months and did little with what he got.

Hitting

Morandini has a quick bat and handles fastballs well, especially ones on the inner half of the plate. He has made his living spraying groundballs and liners through the infield, but hit the ball in the air far more often last year. That worked to his distinct disadvantage, because he doesn't have the power to reach the fences regularly. He always has had problems with lefties, and rarely started against them last year.

Baserunning & Defense

On defense, Morandini lacks pizzazz but makes all the plays. He has good range, an accurate arm and a quick double-play pivot. He committed only five errors last year and had the second-best fielding percentage among National League second basemen. He didn't run often or effectively last year, but might improve with a team that falls behind early less often.

2000 Outlook

Morandini became a free agent and won't return to the Cubs. He'll miss hitting in Wrigley Field, which boosted his average each of the last two seasons. His best years may be behind him, but he remains capable of contributing in the right situation. He hinted that he might be interested in returning to the Phillies, who certainly came out ahead when they traded him for Doug Glanville.

Position: 2B
Bats: L **Throws:** R
Ht: 5'11" **Wt:** 180

Opening Day Age: 33
Born: 4/22/66 in Leechburg, PA
ML Seasons: 10
Pronunciation: mor-an-DEE-nee

Overall Statistics

	G	AB	R	H	D	T	HR	RBI	SB	BB	SO	Avg	OBP	Slg
1999	144	456	60	110	18	5	4	37	6	48	61	.241	.319	.329
Career	1172	4149	556	1117	194	50	32	322	117	401	637	.269	.340	.363

Where He Hits the Ball

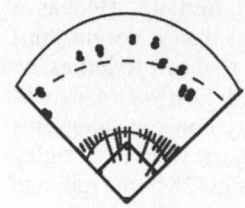 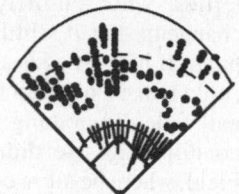

Vs. LHP   **Vs. RHP**

1999 Situational Stats

	AB	H	HR	RBI	Avg		AB	H	HR	RBI	Avg
Home	219	59	3	26	.269	LHP	97	15	0	2	.155
Road	237	51	1	11	.215	RHP	359	95	4	35	.265
First Half	281	73	3	23	.260	Sc Pos	90	24	1	34	.267
Scnd Half	175	37	1	14	.211	Clutch	69	19	0	4	.275

1999 Rankings (National League)

- 2nd in fielding percentage at second base (.991), lowest batting average, lowest slugging percentage and lowest batting average on the road
- 4th in lowest slugging percentage vs. righthanded pitchers (.354)
- 6th in lowest HR frequency (114.0 ABs per HR)
- 7th in lowest on-base percentage
- 8th in lowest batting average on a 3-1 count (.077)
- Led the Cubs in sacrifice bunts (7) and highest groundball/flyball ratio (1.2)

Jose Nieves

1999 Season

When the Cubs gave up on the 1999 season and looked to the future, they decided to give rookie shortstop Jose Nieves a good, long look. Nieves displayed few pluses and plenty of minuses while Chicago played him regularly during the last two months. He showed good tools and plenty of natural ability, but his game was unacceptably raw in almost all areas. In many ways, he resembled a young Manny Alexander: a good athlete who hadn't learned to use his skills.

Hitting

Nieves' approach at the plate was to dig in and start hacking. He did pitchers many favors by chasing bad pitches, and drew only eight walks all season. He showed some pop in the minors but little in the majors, apart from his nine doubles. Nieves showed promise against lefthanders but looked hopelessly weak versus righthanders. This may have been an aberration, because his platoon splits were fairly balanced in the minors.

Baserunning & Defense

Nieves' fielding was the most frustrating aspect of his game. He has quick feet and a strong arm, and he made his share of dazzling plays. He botched many routine ones, though, committing 16 errors in only 52 games—a 50-error pace over a full season. And while he has good speed, he lacks basestealing technique and was thrown out both times he tried to steal.

2000 Outlook

The Cubs clearly wanted Nieves to be their shortstop of the future, but he simply didn't show that he could handle that responsibility. Chicago opted for a stopgap move in December, signing free agent Ricky Gutierrez for two years and $4.5 million. Nieves may need to show some improvement this spring in order to avoid a return trip to Triple-A.

Position: SS
Bats: R **Throws:** R
Ht: 6' 1" **Wt:** 185

Opening Day Age: 24
Born: 6/16/75 in Guacara, Venezuela
ML Seasons: 2
Pronunciation: nee-AY-vuss

Overall Statistics

	G	AB	R	H	D	T	HR	RBI	SB	BB	SO	Avg	OBP	Slg
1999	54	181	16	45	9	1	2	18	0	8	25	.249	.291	.343
Career	56	182	16	45	9	1	2	18	0	8	25	.247	.289	.341

Where He Hits the Ball

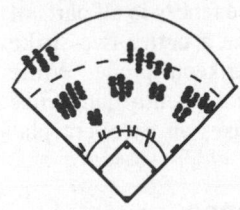 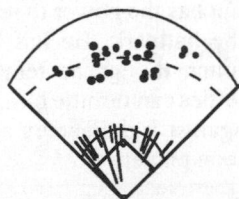

Vs. LHP   **Vs. RHP**

1999 Situational Stats

	AB	H	HR	RBI	Avg			AB	H	HR	RBI	Avg
Home	113	32	2	13	.283	LHP		45	14	1	4	.311
Road	68	13	0	5	.191	RHP		136	31	1	14	.228
First Half	0	0	0	0	-	Sc Pos		46	11	2	17	.239
Scnd Half	181	45	2	18	.249	Clutch		28	8	0	3	.286

1999 Rankings (National League)
- 7th in errors at shortstop (16)

Henry Rodriguez

1999 Season

One player who wasn't affected by the malaise that enveloped the Cubs last year was left fielder Henry Rodriguez. He had a big first half, and despite cooling off over the second half he finished with a career-high .304 average. Though he continued to be platooned, he showed some improvement in his limited at-bats against lefthanders. He was at his best in clutch situations and provided many big hits over the course of the season.

Hitting

Any pitcher who starts Rodriguez with a knee-high fastball is asking for trouble. He's a dead low-ball hitter who isn't afraid to go after the first good pitch he sees. He pulls the ball in the air quite often, but has the power to reach the fences in all parts of the ballpark. He has become a better two-strike hitter, though he remains strikeout-prone. While lefties can throttle him, he's consistently dangerous against righthanders and makes an excellent platoon player.

Baserunning & Defense

Rodriguez' reputation hasn't yet caught up to his defensive performance. When initially tried in left field, he was regarded as a miscast first baseman. That may have been accurate at the time, but Rodriguez has made himself into an acceptable if limited left fielder. His lack of speed is apparent on artificial turf, but he's reliable and fundamentally sound. His arm is strong enough and his throws are generally accurate. On the bases, he moves 90 feet at a time.

2000 Outlook

Going into the last year of his contract, Rodriguez may be shopped by the cost-conscious Cubs. If he remains with them through the start of the season, he may be picked up by a contending team at the trade deadline. His power is no Wrigley Field illusion and he ought to remain productive in any park, as long as his exposure to southpaws is limited.

Position: LF
Bats: L **Throws:** L
Ht: 6' 2" **Wt:** 220

Opening Day Age: 32
Born: 11/8/67 in Santo Domingo, Dominican Republic
ML Seasons: 8

Overall Statistics

	G	AB	R	H	D	T	HR	RBI	SB	BB	SO	Avg	OBP	Slg
1999	130	447	72	136	29	0	26	87	2	56	113	.304	.381	.544
Career	813	2636	341	689	155	8	140	459	9	236	690	.261	.322	.486

Where He Hits the Ball

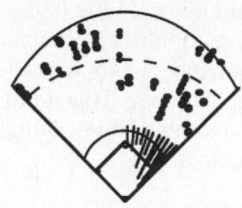
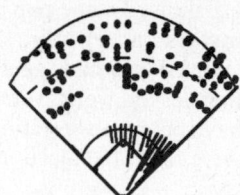

Vs. LHP   **Vs. RHP**

1999 Situational Stats

	AB	H	HR	RBI	Avg		AB	H	HR	RBI	Avg
Home	234	71	14	44	.303	LHP	139	33	8	18	.237
Road	213	65	12	43	.305	RHP	308	103	18	69	.334
First Half	249	84	15	58	.337	Sc Pos	111	37	7	60	.333
Scnd Half	198	52	11	29	.263	Clutch	64	21	6	16	.328

1999 Rankings (National League)

- 6th in errors in left field (6) and lowest fielding percentage in left field (.974)
- Led NL third basemen in batting average with the bases loaded (.412)

Sammy Sosa

Position: RF/CF
Bats: R **Throws:** R
Ht: 6' 0" **Wt:** 210

Opening Day Age: 31
Born: 11/12/68 in San Pedro de Macoris, Dominican Republic
ML Seasons: 11

1999 Season

For the second straight year, Sammy Sosa and Mark McGwire made a run at the home-run record, and once again, Sosa came up a tad short. That certainly was nothing to be ashamed of, as Sosa bashed 63 home runs to approach his total of 66 the year before. He didn't miss a game all year, and the daily grind—combined with the constant media attention—might have worn him down late in the year. It looked like Sosa might have a shot at McGwire's record of 70 when Sosa entered September with 55, but a September slump cost him. McGwire passed him and won the NL home-run crown in the season's final days.

Hitting

Formerly a notorious first-pitch hitter, Sosa has blossomed after learning to take a strike or two. He's an excellent low-ball hitter, with the ability to take a pitch off his shoetops and send it over the fence on a line. He no longer chases many breaking balls down and away, but he can be induced to go for fastballs up and out of the strike zone. He sacrifices little power on two-strike counts.

Baserunning & Defense

Sosa's fatigue was most apparent on the basepaths. He used to be good for around 20 steals a year, but was thrown out on seven of 11 attempts after April last season. He also was somewhat less aggressive in going for the extra base. He has a strong arm and good enough range to cover center, which he did for 25 games last year. His attention sometimes wanders in the field, especially when the Cubs are out of the race.

2000 Outlook

Sosa feeds on emotion and is at his best when the Cubs are in contention. It may be difficult for him to sustain his recent pace if the club endures another hopeless season. No matter what happens, he should remain one of the top sluggers in the game.

Overall Statistics

	G	AB	R	H	D	T	HR	RBI	SB	BB	SO	Avg	OBP	Slg
1999	162	625	114	180	24	2	63	141	7	78	171	.288	.367	.635
Career	1409	5289	841	1413	206	35	336	941	224	428	1369	.267	.324	.510

Where He Hits the Ball

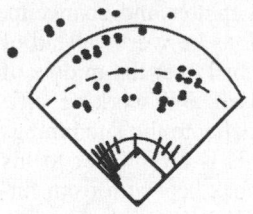
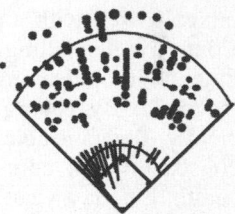

Vs. LHP   **Vs. RHP**

1999 Situational Stats

	AB	H	HR	RBI	Avg		AB	H	HR	RBI	Avg
Home	308	100	33	71	.325	LHP	163	51	18	37	.313
Road	317	80	30	70	.252	RHP	462	129	45	104	.279
First Half	336	96	32	74	.286	Sc Pos	154	46	16	81	.299
Scnd Half	289	84	31	67	.291	Clutch	91	27	7	25	.297

1999 Rankings (National League)

- 1st in total bases (397), strikeouts, cleanup slugging percentage (.695) and games played
- 2nd in home runs, HR frequency (9.9 ABs per HR), slugging percentage vs. lefthanded pitchers (.712), errors in right field (8), bunts in play (8) and lowest fielding percentage in right field (.976)
- 3rd in RBI and slugging percentage
- Led the Cubs in home runs, at-bats, runs scored, total bases (397), RBI, caught stealing (8), intentional walks (8), strikeouts, GDPs (17), pitches seen (2,857), plate appearances (712), slugging percentage, HR frequency (9.9 ABs per HR), most pitches seen per plate appearance (4.01) and batting average vs. lefthanded pitchers

Kevin Tapani

1999 Season

Kevin Tapani seemed to be on track for one of his best seasons in mid-June, when he had a 5-2, 2.51 record. Then Father Time seemed to catch up with him all at once. He suffered injury after injury and began to get hammered repeatedly. Tapani made 12 more starts, but only two were quality starts—both of the six-inning, three-earned run variety. After dropping his last nine decisions, he was shut down in August because of a chronic lower-back condition. All in all, it may have been the *worst* season of his 11-year career.

Pitching

When healthy, Tapani is the prototypical veteran finesse pitcher. His fastball is only average, but he mixes it well with a good splitter and changeup. Control is his calling card, as he works ahead of hitters without leaving the ball over the middle of the plate. By pacing himself and working efficiently, Tapani is able to pitch into the late innings consistently. Of course, this is all subject to his health. Late last year, his back kept him from finishing his pitches, costing him movement on his splitter and leaving him little to fall back on. He also seemed to tire much more easily.

Defense & Hitting

Tapani is ordinarily a fine fielder, but his back problems limited his mobility last year. He's still a sure glove man and hasn't committed an error in three years. Though he lacks a good pickoff move, he checks the running game with a compact stretch delivery. He can bunt when needed, but had a lousy year at the plate after faring rather well the season before.

2000 Outlook

If Tapani's back continues to plague him, it will severely hamper his value, because durability always has been one of his biggest assets. The Cubs will need him to show early on that he's still capable of giving them seven solid innings. If he isn't, it may be a long summer.

Position: SP
Bats: R **Throws:** R
Ht: 6' 1" **Wt:** 195

Opening Day Age: 36
Born: 2/18/64 in Des Moines, IA
ML Seasons: 11
Pronunciation: TAP-uh-nee
Nickname: Tap

Overall Statistics

	W	L	Pct.	ERA	G	GS	Sv	IP	H	BB	SO	HR	Ratio
1999	6	12	.333	4.83	23	23	0	136.0	151	33	73	12	1.35
Career	126	99	.560	4.27	302	295	0	1901.0	2013	467	1183	201	1.30

How Often He Throws Strikes

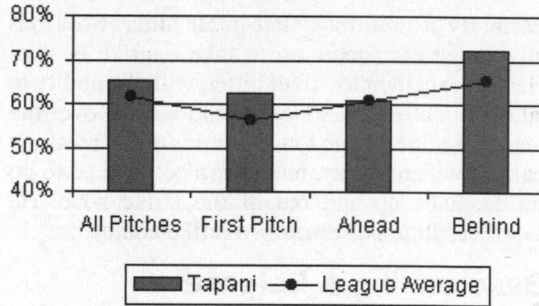

1999 Situational Stats

	W	L	ERA	Sv	IP		AB	H	HR	RBI	Avg
Home	3	6	5.66	0	55.2	LHB	235	62	7	31	.264
Road	3	6	4.26	0	80.1	RHB	304	89	5	46	.293
First Half	6	5	4.04	0	93.2	Sc Pos	143	42	3	63	.294
Scnd Half	0	7	6.59	0	42.1	Clutch	34	13	2	4	.382

1999 Rankings (National League)

- 6th in lowest winning percentage
- 10th in highest batting average allowed vs. righthanded batters
- Led the Cubs in hit batsmen (4) and lowest batting average allowed vs. lefthanded batters

Steve Trachsel

Position: SP
Bats: R **Throws:** R
Ht: 6' 4" **Wt:** 205

Opening Day Age: 29
Born: 10/31/70 in Oxnard, CA
ML Seasons: 7
Pronunciation: TRACK-sil

1999 Season

Steve Trachsel was one of the Cubs' biggest disappointments last year. After signing a one-year deal worth more than $5 million, he posted the worst season of his career, losing a major league-high 18 games. He got off to a fair start, but went through a brutal stretch from late May through early July when he dropped eight straight decisions. The skid was marked by repeated first-inning troubles and many early exits. After the trading deadline, he turned his season around, going 5-4, 3.78.

Pitching

Trachsel doesn't have an out pitch or outstanding stuff, but he has a deep repertoire and knows how to use it. He mixes 90-MPH two-seamers and four-seamers with a split-finger fastball. The splitter has enough drop to produce groundballs and is slow enough to upset hitters' timing. He can't throw the ball by people, so he must have the command to work the corners without leaving pitches out over the plate. When he doesn't have a good feel for his splitter, he'll go to his breaking ball. He often has been more effective against lefthanders, though that wasn't the case last year.

Defense & Hitting

Trachsel lacks a good pickoff move, so he wears runners down by throwing to first incessantly. He isn't especially quick to the plate, though. He's a fine fielder who played errorless ball last year, and he has led Cubs pitchers in total chances during three of the last four seasons. Trachsel had hit decently in the past, but his off year carried over to the batter's box as well.

2000 Outlook

Trachsel became a free agent after the season. His year wasn't as bad as it looked, and the dropoff in his numbers was more the result of bad run support, bad bullpen support and plain bad luck than any decline in his effectiveness. He's quite capable of coming back with a winning year.

Overall Statistics

	W	L	Pct.	ERA	G	GS	Sv	IP	H	BB	SO	HR	Ratio
1999	8	18	.308	5.56	34	34	0	205.2	226	64	149	32	1.41
Career	60	69	.465	4.35	187	186	0	1146.1	1159	412	829	169	1.37

How Often He Throws Strikes

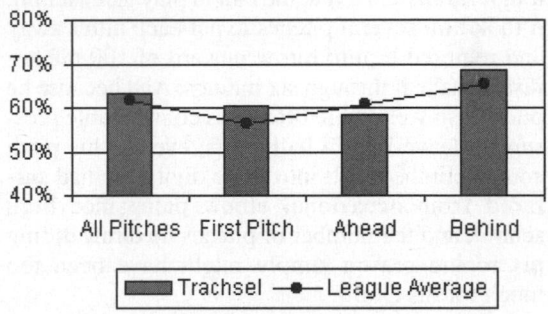

1999 Situational Stats

	W	L	ERA	Sv	IP		AB	H	HR	RBI	Avg
Home	4	8	5.14	0	98.0	LHB	355	101	16	53	.285
Road	4	10	5.93	0	107.2	RHB	452	125	16	63	.277
First Half	3	12	6.53	0	111.2	Sc Pos	179	53	5	82	.296
Scnd Half	5	6	4.40	0	94.0	Clutch	27	6	0	2	.222

1999 Rankings (National League)

- 1st in losses
- 3rd in balks (3) and least run support per nine innings (4.1)
- 4th in lowest winning percentage
- 5th in complete games (4) and highest ERA on the road
- Led the Cubs in sacrifice bunts (7), losses, games started, complete games (4), innings pitched, hits allowed, batters faced (894), home runs allowed, walks allowed, wild pitches (8), balks (3), pitches thrown (3,379), pickoff throws (126), stolen bases allowed (19), runners caught stealing (6), GDPs induced (17) and most GDPs induced per nine innings (0.7)

Kerry Wood

1999 Season

The worst nightmare of Cubs fans was realized last spring when Kerry Wood went down for the season with a torn elbow ligament. He sprained the ligament the previous August, and after just one spring-training start he learned that it was fully torn. The 1998 National League Rookie of the Year underwent a full elbow reconstruction soon thereafter, and later began rehabilitation in hopes of being ready for the 2000 season.

Pitching

Ironically, Wood's tremendous arsenal—an unhittable high-90s fastball, hard curve and slider—may have contributed to his downfall. Because it was so tough for batters to put the ball in play against him, it took him several pitches to put each hitter away and required him to throw upward of 100 pitches just to make it through six innings. And because he pitched so well, there often was considerable pressure to leave him in ballgames, even as his pitch counts climbed well into triple digits. He had suffered from occasional elbow pain since high school, and the number of pitches he threw during his rookie season simply might have been too much for his elbow.

Defense & Hitting

Wood's control of the running game was impressive for a young pitcher. He showed a good pickoff move and never let runners detract from his pitching. His work at the plate was a surprise as well, as he clouted a pair of home runs and made several long outs in 1998. He fielded his position creditably.

2000 Outlook

Wood is expected to pitch for the Cubs this year, though it remains to be seen whether he'll be ready for Opening Day. These days, pitchers are bouncing back from Tommy John surgery stronger than ever. Wood's stuff was so impressive that he won't need to get all of it back to become effective again. The question for now is how much of it he'll have in 2000.

Position: SP
Bats: R **Throws:** R
Ht: 6' 5" **Wt:** 225

Opening Day Age: 22
Born: 6/16/77 in Irving, TX
ML Seasons: 1

Overall Statistics

	W	L	Pct.	ERA	G	GS	Sv	IP	H	BB	SO	HR	Ratio
1999					Did Not Play								
Career	13	6	.684	3.40	26	26	0	166.2	117	85	233	14	1.21

How Often He Throws Strikes (1998)

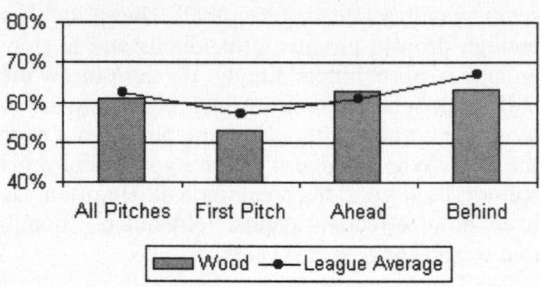

1999 Situational Stats

	W	L	ERA	Sv	IP		AB	H	HR	RBI	Avg
Home	—	—	—	—	—	LHB	—	—	—	—	—
Road	—	—	—	—	—	RHB	—	—	—	—	—
First Half	—	—	—	—	—	Sc Pos	—	—	—	—	—
Scnd Half	—	—	—	—	—	Clutch	—	—	—	—	—

1999 Rankings (National League)

- Did not rank near the top or bottom in any category

Manny Alexander

Position: SS/3B/2B
Bats: R **Throws:** R
Ht: 5'10" **Wt:** 180

Opening Day Age: 29
Born: 3/20/71 in San Pedro de Macoris, Dominican Republic
ML Seasons: 7

Overall Statistics

	G	AB	R	H	D	T	HR	RBI	SB	BB	SO	Avg	OBP	Slg
1999	90	177	17	48	11	2	0	15	4	10	38	.271	.309	.356
Career	440	1004	131	239	42	8	11	89	35	68	218	.238	.290	.329

1999 Situational Stats

	AB	H	HR	RBI	Avg		AB	H	HR	RBI	Avg
Home	89	27	0	6	.303	LHP	93	27	0	10	.290
Road	88	21	0	9	.239	RHP	84	21	0	5	.250
First Half	98	28	0	11	.286	Sc Pos	39	11	0	14	.282
Scnd Half	79	20	0	4	.253	Clutch	40	6	0	3	.150

1999 Season

From Manny Alexander's perspective, the 1999 season was an absolute disaster. When the trade of Jose Hernandez left the Cubs' shortstop job wide open, Alexander—for whom Cal Ripken was once moved to third base—wasn't given even a cursory look. He made more than half of his appearances as a pinch-hitter and did little else beyond providing infield depth.

Hitting, Baserunning & Defense

Alexander is a notoriously impatient hitter who has trouble making contact and constantly falls behind in the count. He simply lacks the ability to recognize a bad pitch and let it pass. For some reason, he's done quite well as a pinch-hitter during each of the last two seasons. Alexander is quick on the bases and almost never gets caught when he tries to steal. He has good range and a very strong arm, and has filled in capably at second, third and short.

2000 Outlook

Alexander has become a bit player rather than a regular-in-waiting. He was traded to the Red Sox for Damon Buford, who will start in center field for the Cubs.

Shane Andrews

Position: 3B/1B
Bats: R **Throws:** R
Ht: 6' 0" **Wt:** 220

Opening Day Age: 28
Born: 8/28/71 in Dallas, TX
ML Seasons: 5
Nickname: Mongo, Caveman

Overall Statistics

	G	AB	R	H	D	T	HR	RBI	SB	BB	SO	Avg	OBP	Slg
1999	117	348	41	68	12	0	16	51	1	50	109	.195	.295	.368
Career	496	1499	169	330	70	4	72	224	6	163	453	.220	.295	.416

1999 Situational Stats

	AB	H	HR	RBI	Avg		AB	H	HR	RBI	Avg
Home	171	29	9	28	.170	LHP	91	21	4	9	.231
Road	177	39	7	23	.220	RHP	257	47	12	42	.183
First Half	145	32	4	17	.221	Sc Pos	106	20	3	36	.189
Scnd Half	203	36	12	34	.177	Clutch	67	17	1	11	.254

1999 Season

After suffering through years of his injury problems, flashes of power and extended slumps, the Expos finally gave up on Shane Andrews last September, releasing him outright. The Cubs signed him, and he hit five home runs in 19 games for Chicago.

Hitting, Baserunning & Defense

Andrews likes the ball up and struggles mightily with breaking pitches or anything down in the strike zone. He always has had trouble making contact and keeping his batting average out of the low .200s, and a bulging disc last year only compounded his problems. Andrews never hit well at Olympic Stadium, so the change of scenery may help. His speed is just average. He was an underrated defensive third baseman with good range and a strong arm, until last year, when his stiff back robbed him of mobility. He can play a decent first base.

2000 Outlook

Signed to a one-year contract, Andrews is the frontrunner for the Cubs' third-base job, though he may be pushed by young Cole Liniak. The condition of his back may determine his future, because he was a borderline talent even when healthy.

Chicago (NL)

Jeff Blauser

Position: 2B/SS/3B
Bats: R **Throws:** R
Ht: 6' 1" **Wt:** 190

Opening Day Age: 34
Born: 11/8/65 in Los Gatos, CA
ML Seasons: 13
Pronunciation: BLAU-zer

Overall Statistics

	G	AB	R	H	D	T	HR	RBI	SB	BB	SO	Avg	OBP	Slg
1999	104	200	41	48	5	2	9	26	2	26	52	.240	.347	.420
Career	1407	4522	691	1187	217	33	122	513	65	569	937	.262	.354	.406

1999 Situational Stats

	AB	H	HR	RBI	Avg		AB	H	HR	RBI	Avg
Home	117	26	7	16	.222	LHP	94	25	4	9	.266
Road	83	22	2	10	.265	RHP	106	23	5	17	.217
First Half	108	30	5	17	.278	Sc Pos	44	10	0	15	.227
Scnd Half	92	18	4	9	.196	Clutch	35	10	3	5	.286

1999 Season

Coming back from elbow surgery, Jeff Blauser failed to recapture a starting job despite his $4.2 million salary. He played second base against lefties, pinch-hit and filled in around the infield.

Hitting, Baserunning & Defense

When healthy, Blauser is a useful hitter who contributes a decent average and some power. The problem is that he's so susceptible to injury that he rarely is able to play an entire season at full strength. His inability to hit at Wrigley Field in a Cubs uniform is a mystery because he hit so well there as a Brave. He never was a top-notch glove man, and his various ailments have left him better suited to a backup role. He has little speed left and rarely runs anymore.

2000 Outlook

It was no surprise when the Cubs declined to pick up Blauser's $7 million option for 2000. His signing by the Cubs can only be described as a colossal and expensive mistake. Teams may be wary, and it will be an upset if anyone entrusts him with a regular job at this point in his career.

Kyle Farnsworth

Position: SP
Bats: R **Throws:** R
Ht: 6' 4" **Wt:** 220

Opening Day Age: 23
Born: 4/14/76 in Wichita, KS
ML Seasons: 1

Overall Statistics

	W	L	Pct.	ERA	G	GS	Sv	IP	H	BB	SO	HR	Ratio
1999	5	9	.357	5.05	27	21	0	130.0	140	52	70	28	1.48
Career	5	9	.357	5.05	27	21	0	130.0	140	52	70	28	1.48

1999 Situational Stats

	W	L	ERA	Sv	IP		AB	H	HR	RBI	Avg
Home	1	5	4.62	0	76.0	LHB	214	59	10	33	.276
Road	4	4	5.67	0	54.0	RHB	302	81	18	44	.268
First Half	2	3	7.58	0	57.0	Sc Pos	133	36	7	48	.271
Scnd Half	3	6	3.08	0	73.0	Clutch	17	4	1	2	.235

1999 Season

The Cubs promoted righthander Kyle Farnsworth from Triple-A in late April after a rash of injuries hit their pitching staff. He won two of his first three starts, but a string of rocky outings cost him his spot in the rotation. He was shipped back to Triple-A and recalled twice. After the final recall, he suddenly got hot, going 3-2, 2.63 in his last six starts.

Pitching, Defense & Hitting

Farnsworth throws in the mid-90s, but it wasn't until he picked up a two-seam fastball late in the year that he was able to find any success. His slider hadn't been cutting it as a second pitch, but was useful as a third pitch once he added the two-seamer. Farnsworth needs work on other aspects of the game. He was easy to run on, made four errors and batted .086.

2000 Outlook

Farnsworth's late-season turnaround gives the Cubs reason for optimism. There almost certainly will be some more bumps in the road ahead, but it seems a safe bet that Farnsworth will be able to improve on last year's numbers.

Felix Heredia

Position: RP
Bats: L **Throws:** L
Ht: 6' 0" **Wt:** 180

Opening Day Age: 23
Born: 6/18/76 in
Barahona, Dominican
Republic
ML Seasons: 4
Pronunciation:
her-RAY-dee-uh

Overall Statistics

	W	L	Pct.	ERA	G	GS	Sv	IP	H	BB	SO	HR	Ratio
1999	3	1	.750	4.85	69	0	1	52.0	56	25	50	7	1.56
Career	12	8	.600	4.70	217	2	3	184.0	187	103	168	13	1.58

1999 Situational Stats

	W	L	ERA	Sv	IP		AB	H	HR	RBI	Avg
Home	1	0	5.70	1	23.2	LHB	93	23	3	19	.247
Road	2	1	4.13	0	28.1	RHB	113	33	4	22	.292
First Half	3	0	4.91	1	33.0	Sc Pos	74	19	3	35	.257
Scnd Half	0	1	4.74	0	19.0	Clutch	76	16	3	14	.211

1999 Season

The Cubs tried Felix Heredia as a setup man last year, but the experiment failed. After getting off to a good start, Heredia wore down in June and lost his command. He subsequently was returned to his old role as a lefthanded specialist, but Heredia didn't stifle lefties as he had in the past.

Pitching, Defense & Hitting

Heredia features a 90-MPH fastball and a wide, sweeping slider that can be tough to control. Until he comes up with a way to combat righthanders, he may not be useful as anything but a one-batter lefty. It was especially worrisome that lefthanders began to catch on to him last year. His delivery makes him tough to run on, but leaves him in poor position to field. Though he has virtually no experience at the plate, he did notch a couple of hits last year and is 3-for-9 lifetime.

2000 Outlook

Heredia is still very young, so there's hope that he'll mature into a more useful pitcher. But if he can't expand his repertoire, he may be stuck in his limited role.

Glenallen Hill

Position: LF/RF
Bats: R **Throws:** R
Ht: 6' 2" **Wt:** 230

Opening Day Age: 35
Born: 3/22/65 in Santa
Cruz, CA
ML Seasons: 11

Overall Statistics

	G	AB	R	H	D	T	HR	RBI	SB	BB	SO	Avg	OBP	Slg
1999	99	253	43	76	9	1	20	55	5	22	61	.300	.353	.581
Career	1042	3349	479	908	178	20	158	526	96	251	749	.271	.323	.478

1999 Situational Stats

	AB	H	HR	RBI	Avg		AB	H	HR	RBI	Avg
Home	105	30	11	27	.286	LHP	106	38	4	16	.358
Road	148	46	9	28	.311	RHP	147	38	16	39	.259
First Half	146	51	15	36	.349	Sc Pos	84	24	4	37	.286
Scnd Half	107	25	5	19	.234	Clutch	58	13	2	12	.224

1999 Season

Glenallen Hill served as the Cubs' left fielder against lefthanders and fourth outfielder, the role in which he'd performed so well over the second half of 1998. He got off to a sizzling start, missed most of May with a strained hamstring, then picked up where he'd left off in June. He cooled in the second half, but still finished with good numbers.

Hitting, Baserunning & Defense

Tremendously strong, Hill always swings for the fences and can drive the ball out to any part of the park. He kills fastballs but chases bad pitches after falling behind in the count. He was the Cubs' top hitter off the bench, slamming four pinch-homers. Though he's not a terrible outfielder, Hill often staggers unsteadily under flyballs. He does have a strong arm and fairly good speed, and he stole five bases in 1999 after running infrequently the last few years.

2000 Outlook

Hill signed a one-year extension in September and will be back this year in the same capacity. Expect him to keep hitting as long as the sun shines at Wrigley Field.

Chicago (NL)

385

Chad Meyers

Position: 2B/CF
Bats: R **Throws:** R
Ht: 6' 0" **Wt:** 185

Opening Day Age: 24
Born: 8/8/75 in Omaha, NE
ML Seasons: 1

Overall Statistics

	G	AB	R	H	D	T	HR	RBI	SB	BB	SO	Avg	OBP	Slg
1999	43	142	17	33	9	0	0	4	4	9	27	.232	.292	.296
Career	43	142	17	33	9	0	0	4	4	9	27	.232	.292	.296

1999 Situational Stats

	AB	H	HR	RBI	Avg		AB	H	HR	RBI	Avg
Home	69	18	0	1	.261	LHP	42	6	0	0	.143
Road	73	15	0	3	.205	RHP	100	27	0	4	.270
First Half	0	0	0	0	-	Sc Pos	22	4	0	4	.182
Scnd Half	142	33	0	4	.232	Clutch	15	0	0	0	.000

1999 Season

Chad Meyers was one half of the rookie double-play duo installed by the Cubs late last year. Like shortstop Jose Nieves, Meyers did little to impress. After hitting for a good average and stealing a lot of bases in the minors, he did neither in his 43-game stint with Chicago.

Hitting, Baserunning & Defense

Meyers is a pure slap hitter who aims for nothing more than singles and a few leg doubles. He has good speed, and thus has been able to make the approach work in the minors. Meyers probably could hit .270 in the majors once he adjusts. It's a mystery why he didn't steal a single base during September and October despite playing regularly. He's a limited second baseman with a weak arm and unimpressive range. He played some center field, as he had done in the minors, and held his own there.

2000 Outlook

The Cubs hope that Meyers will develop into a long-term solution at second base, but he has a ways to go. It will take a strong showing this spring for him to break camp with Chicago after it traded for Damon Buford and Eric Young during the off-season.

Jeff Reed

Position: C
Bats: L **Throws:** R
Ht: 6' 2" **Wt:** 202

Opening Day Age: 37
Born: 11/12/62 in Joliet, IL
ML Seasons: 16

Overall Statistics

	G	AB	R	H	D	T	HR	RBI	SB	BB	SO	Avg	OBP	Slg
1999	103	256	29	66	16	2	3	28	1	45	58	.258	.373	.371
Career	1144	2872	285	725	134	10	57	298	7	347	498	.252	.333	.366

1999 Situational Stats

	AB	H	HR	RBI	Avg		AB	H	HR	RBI	Avg
Home	133	33	0	14	.248	LHP	37	6	1	7	.162
Road	123	33	3	14	.268	RHP	219	60	2	21	.274
First Half	114	29	2	13	.254	Sc Pos	61	14	0	19	.230
Scnd Half	142	37	1	15	.261	Clutch	50	12	2	6	.240

1999 Season

Veteran backstop Jeff Reed got caught in a numbers game in Colorado last year. He lost playing time to Kirt Manwaring and rookie Henry Blanco, and didn't hit as he had in the past, so he was released in July. The Cubs signed him a few days later and platooned him with Benito Santiago in the second half.

Hitting, Baserunning & Defense

Reed's biggest asset is his lefthanded bat. He won't hit for great power or average outside of Coors Field, but he contributes a fair share for a backup catcher. Platooned for years, he hasn't hit lefties well when he's faced them. He can be dangerous when he extends his arms and is able to pull fastballs on the outer half of the plate. He isn't particularly mobile behind the plate and his throwing arm is just average. He has no speed.

2000 Outlook

The Cubs exercised their option to bring Reed back for 2000. He'll share time behind the plate with free-agent signee Joe Girardi, who got a three-year, $5.5 million contract.

Scott Sanders

Position: RP
Bats: R **Throws:** R
Ht: 6' 4" **Wt:** 220

Opening Day Age: 31
Born: 3/25/69 in
Hannibal, MO
ML Seasons: 7

Overall Statistics

	W	L	Pct.	ERA	G	GS	Sv	IP	H	BB	SO	HR	Ratio
1999	4	7	.364	5.52	67	6	2	104.1	112	53	89	19	1.58
Career	34	45	.430	4.86	235	88	5	681.2	674	276	632	93	1.39

1999 Situational Stats

	W	L	ERA	Sv	IP		AB	H	HR	RBI	Avg
Home	3	4	5.19	0	60.2	LHB	137	41	7	19	.299
Road	1	3	5.98	2	43.2	RHB	268	71	12	47	.265
First Half	2	4	5.31	2	62.2	Sc Pos	102	27	3	40	.265
Scnd Half	2	3	5.83	0	41.2	Clutch	87	25	1	12	.287

1999 Season

Signed as a free agent after San Diego released him, Scott Sanders began last year in Chicago's rotation. Six starts later, he was exiled to the bull-pen. He pitched decently in middle relief at first, but hit the skids in mid-June and took two months to recover. By September, he'd been relegated to mopup work.

Pitching, Defense & Hitting

Sanders throws a low-90s fastball and hard slider. When he has command of his slider he can be quite effective. Most of the time he struggles to get the slider over, allowing hitters to sit on his fastball. He has nothing else to fall back on, and never has had an out pitch for lefthanders. He works up in the zone and is vulnerable to the longball. Sanders doesn't hold runners particularly well. He had a poor year in the field, but has fielded decently in the past. He's a decent hitter and capable bunter.

2000 Outlook

The Cubs decided against bringing Sanders back for 2000, declining to tender him a contract in December. After trying for three years to recapture his 1996 form, he may be running out of chances.

Benito Santiago

Position: C
Bats: R **Throws:** R
Ht: 6' 1" **Wt:** 195

Opening Day Age: 35
Born: 3/9/65 in Ponce,
Puerto Rico
ML Seasons: 14
Pronunciation:
sahn-tee-AH-go

Overall Statistics

	G	AB	R	H	D	T	HR	RBI	SB	BB	SO	Avg	OBP	Slg
1999	109	350	28	87	18	3	7	36	1	32	71	.249	.313	.377
Career	1467	5145	569	1340	231	28	170	677	79	324	970	.260	.305	.415

1999 Situational Stats

	AB	H	HR	RBI	Avg		AB	H	HR	RBI	Avg
Home	168	42	2	14	.250	LHP	132	33	5	21	.250
Road	182	45	5	22	.247	RHP	218	54	2	15	.248
First Half	249	56	5	26	.225	Sc Pos	94	24	3	31	.255
Scnd Half	101	31	2	10	.307	Clutch	50	11	1	4	.220

1999 Season

Benito Santiago returned to action last year after a serious automobile accident cost him almost all of the 1998 season. Needing a catcher, the Cubs signed him as a free agent. He caught regularly over the first half, but his inadequate hitting led to the signing of Jeff Reed in July. Afterward, Santiago was reduced to a platoon role.

Hitting, Baserunning & Defense

After more than a decade in the majors, the book on Santiago hasn't changed. He has straightaway power on fastballs but pulls off breaking balls. His impatience is his Achilles heel, and he'll often get himself out if the pitcher feeds him junk. Santiago still has a cannon of an arm, though he had trouble blocking balls, which may be a lingering effect of the leg injuries he suffered in the car wreck. Those injuries sapped most of what remained of his speed.

2000 Outlook

The Cubs declined to pick up their option on Santiago, making him a free agent. It's clear that age and injuries have taken their toll, and he may have seen his last full-time job in the majors.

Other Chicago Cubs

Bobby Ayala (Pos: RHP, Age: 30)

	W	L	Pct.	ERA	G	GS	Sv	IP	H	BB	SO	HR	Ratio
1999	1	7	.125	3.51	66	0	0	82.0	71	39	79	10	1.34
Career	37	44	.457	4.78	406	14	59	576.0	581	245	541	71	1.43

Seattle traded Ayala to Montreal in the opening days of the season, and the Expos released him in August. Chicago signed him on September 3. He actually pitched OK for both the Expos and Cubs, but he's a free agent all over again. 2000 Outlook: B

Richie Barker (Pos: RHP, Age: 27)

	W	L	Pct.	ERA	G	GS	Sv	IP	H	BB	SO	HR	Ratio
1999	0	0	-	7.20	5	0	0	5.0	6	4	3	0	2.00
Career	0	0	-	7.20	5	0	0	5.0	6	4	3	0	2.00

Barker took Kevin Tapani's spot on the roster in late April, when Tapani was disabled with shoulder tightness. Barker didn't pitch well enough to stay, and he wasn't especially effective at Triple-A Iowa. 2000 Outlook: C

Roosevelt Brown (Pos: LF, Age: 24, Bats: L)

	G	AB	R	H	D	T	HR	RBI	SB	BB	SO	Avg	OBP	Slg
1999	33	64	6	14	6	1	1	10	1	2	14	.219	.239	.391
Career	33	64	6	14	6	1	1	10	1	2	14	.219	.239	.391

Brown's power blossomed in 1999, as he hit .358-22-78 with 25 doubles in just 268 at-bats at Triple-A Iowa. This minor league Rule 5 pickup from the Marlins is young and has a chance to contribute in the majors. 2000 Outlook: B

Doug Creek (Pos: LHP, Age: 31)

	W	L	Pct.	ERA	G	GS	Sv	IP	H	BB	SO	HR	Ratio
1999	0	0	-	10.50	3	0	0	6.0	6	8	6	1	2.33
Career	1	4	.200	6.30	75	3	0	74.1	65	57	68	13	1.64

Creek returned to starting in the minors, and he had a respectable 1999 season in Triple-A. The Cubs promoted him briefly in June, and he gave up runs in each of his three relief appearances. 2000 Outlook: C

Gary Gaetti (Pos: 3B, Age: 41, Bats: R)

	G	AB	R	H	D	T	HR	RBI	SB	BB	SO	Avg	OBP	Slg
1999	113	280	22	57	9	1	9	46	0	21	51	.204	.260	.339
Career	2502	8941	1130	2280	443	39	360	1340	96	634	1599	.255	.308	.434

A hitting surge by Gaetti after the Cubs inked him on his 40th birthday in 1998 produced a contract for '99. But Gaetti played like a 41-year-old man in '99, earning his release. 2000 Outlook: C

Jeremi Gonzalez (Pos: RHP, Age: 25)

	W	L	Pct.	ERA	G	GS	Sv	IP	H	BB	SO	HR	Ratio
1999						Did Not Play							
Career	18	16	.529	4.71	43	43	0	254.0	250	110	163	29	1.42

Gonzalez endured reconstructive elbow surgery in July, so he won't pitch before the All-Star break in 2000. The Cubs hope he'll eventually regain his 1997 form, when he went 11-9, 4.25 as a rookie. 2000 Outlook: C

Mark Guthrie (Pos: LHP, Age: 34)

	W	L	Pct.	ERA	G	GS	Sv	IP	H	BB	SO	HR	Ratio
1999	1	3	.250	5.37	57	0	2	58.2	57	24	45	10	1.38
Career	35	40	.467	4.13	502	43	12	764.1	795	283	595	77	1.41

After signing with Boston last offseason, Guthrie spent three weeks on the disabled list with an Achilles injury before being traded to the Cubs for Rod Beck on August 31. 2000 Outlook: B

Robin Jennings (Pos: 3B, Age: 27, Bats: L)

	G	AB	R	H	D	T	HR	RBI	SB	BB	SO	Avg	OBP	Slg
1999	5	5	0	1	0	0	0	0	0	0	2	.200	.200	.200
Career	45	81	8	17	6	0	0	6	1	3	13	.210	.244	.284

Jennings does a lot of things well but doesn't excel at any of them. A crowded outfield picture and his recent injury woes have kept him from sticking with the Cubs. Minnesota signed him as a free agent in November. 2000 Outlook: C

Matt Karchner (Pos: RHP, Age: 32)

	W	L	Pct.	ERA	G	GS	Sv	IP	H	BB	SO	HR	Ratio
1999	1	0	1.000	2.50	16	0	0	18.0	16	9	9	3	1.39
Career	20	12	.625	4.09	210	0	27	226.2	223	121	161	27	1.52

The Cubs parted with former first-round pick Jon Garland to acquire Karchner during their wild-card run in 1998. Karchner hasn't done much to justify the deal, and his 1999 season was compromised by a groin injury. 2000 Outlook: B

Ray King (Pos: LHP, Age: 26)

	W	L	Pct.	ERA	G	GS	Sv	IP	H	BB	SO	HR	Ratio
1999	0	0	-	5.91	10	0	0	10.2	11	10	5	2	1.97
Career	0	0	-	5.91	10	0	0	10.2	11	10	5	2	1.97

King has been solid in his second season at each level of the high minors. He posted a 1.88 ERA at Triple-A Iowa after a 5.01 mark there in '98. Can he turn his 5.91 ERA with the Cubs into a thing of beauty? 2000 Outlook: C

Andrew Lorraine (Pos: LHP, Age: 27)

	W	L	Pct.	ERA	G	GS	Sv	IP	H	BB	SO	HR	Ratio
1999	2	5	.286	5.55	11	11	0	61.2	71	22	40	9	1.51
Career	5	8	.385	6.29	36	20	0	121.2	152	54	73	18	1.69

Lorraine had a respectable season at Triple-A Iowa in 1999, but he wasn't as successful in 11 starts with the Cubs. He debuted with a three-hit shutout of Houston, but he had just three quality starts. 2000 Outlook: C

Sandy Martinez (Pos: C, Age: 27, Bats: L)

	G	AB	R	H	D	T	HR	RBI	SB	BB	SO	Avg	OBP	Slg
1999	17	30	1	5	0	0	1	1	0	0	11	.167	.167	.267
Career	203	539	38	126	30	4	6	51	1	37	136	.234	.289	.338

A decent receiver behind the plate, Martinez hasn't hit much in the minors or majors. Even with the Cubs hurting for catching, he signed with Florida in November. Martinez is third-catcher material. 2000 Outlook: C

Brian McNichol (Pos: LHP, **Age**: 25)

	W	L	Pct.	ERA	G	GS	Sv	IP	H	BB	SO	HR	Ratio
1999	0	2	.000	6.75	4	2	0	10.2	15	7	12	4	2.06
Career	0	2	.000	6.75	4	2	0	10.2	15	7	12	4	2.06

McNichol was solid in his second season in Double-A in 1998, but he wasn't as effective in Triple-A in '99 before debuting with the Cubs in September. More Triple-A seasoning is required. 2000 Outlook: C

Kurt Miller (Pos: RHP, **Age**: 27)

	W	L	Pct.	ERA	G	GS	Sv	IP	H	BB	SO	HR	Ratio
1999	0	0	-	18.00	4	0	0	3.0	6	3	1	1	3.00
Career	2	7	.222	7.48	44	9	0	80.2	104	50	55	11	1.91

A former first-round pick, Miller had an excellent Triple-A season in 1998, but a strained ribcage muscle disabled him twice and cost him most of April and May in 1999. He wasn't the same last year. 2000 Outlook: C

Jose Molina (Pos: C, **Age**: 24, **Bats**: R)

	G	AB	R	H	D	T	HR	RBI	SB	BB	SO	Avg	OBP	Slg
1999	10	19	3	5	1	0	0	1	0	2	4	.263	.333	.316
Career	10	19	3	5	1	0	0	1	0	2	4	.263	.333	.316

The Cubs recalled Molina because they needed catching help, not because they needed his bat. He impressed Chicago with his strong arm and his work with pitchers. 2000 Outlook: C

Rodney Myers (Pos: RHP, **Age**: 30)

	W	L	Pct.	ERA	G	GS	Sv	IP	H	BB	SO	HR	Ratio
1999	3	1	.750	4.38	46	0	0	63.2	71	25	41	10	1.51
Career	5	2	.714	4.90	108	1	0	158.0	170	76	112	20	1.56

Myers has mostly relieved the last two seasons, and that's what he did in the first inning on August 31, when he tossed 6.2 innings of three-hit ball. That was enough to make the Cubs think about starting him. 2000 Outlook: C

Bo Porter (Pos: LF, **Age**: 27, **Bats**: R)

	G	AB	R	H	D	T	HR	RBI	SB	BB	SO	Avg	OBP	Slg
1999	24	26	2	5	1	0	0	0	0	2	13	.192	.250	.231
Career	24	26	2	5	1	0	0	0	0	2	13	.192	.250	.231

Porter stroked 24 doubles and a career-high 27 homers in his first full season in Triple-A last year. He also draws walks and steals bases, but he's no longer a prospect. Might succeed as a bench player. 2000 Outlook: C

Steve Rain (Pos: RHP, **Age**: 24)

	W	L	Pct.	ERA	G	GS	Sv	IP	H	BB	SO	HR	Ratio
1999	0	1	.000	9.20	16	0	0	14.2	28	7	12	1	2.39
Career	0	1	.000	9.20	16	0	0	14.2	28	7	12	1	2.39

Rain had his best season in the high minors in 1999, with 24 saves and a 1.59 ERA in Double-A and a 2.00 ERA with two saves in Triple-A. He might be ready for Chicago now. 2000 Outlook: B

Dan Serafini (Pos: LHP, **Age**: 26)

	W	L	Pct.	ERA	G	GS	Sv	IP	H	BB	SO	HR	Ratio
1999	3	2	.600	6.93	42	4	1	62.1	86	32	17	9	1.89
Career	12	8	.600	6.27	77	18	1	168.0	215	74	79	21	1.72

Serafini has pitched reasonably well in Triple-A the last two summers, but he has been very hittable when promoted to the majors. More chances will come. 2000 Outlook: C

Brad Woodall (Pos: LHP, **Age**: 30)

	W	L	Pct.	ERA	G	GS	Sv	IP	H	BB	SO	HR	Ratio
1999	0	1	.000	5.63	6	3	0	16.0	17	6	7	5	1.44
Career	10	14	.417	5.31	55	27	0	190.0	208	67	119	37	1.45

A lefty who needs pinpoint control to succeed, Woodall hasn't had a very good season since 1996, when he went 9-7, 3.38 at Triple-A Richmond. He's still looking for a breakthrough season in the big leagues. 2000 Outlook: C

Chicago Cubs Minor League Prospects

Organization Overview:

The Cubs' wild-card run in 1998 ultimately may prove detrimental to the organization. Convinced it could contend again last year, Chicago kept an old team intact and collapsed, falling to last place. They gave opportunities to young infielders Chad Meyers and Jose Nieves in the last two months, but their shortcomings only highlighted the dearth of talent in the upper levels of the farm system. The Cubs don't have the young talent to rebuild quickly, even if Kerry Wood's arm comes back to life. What they do have is Corey Patterson, whose upside is as good as any hitter's in the minors. Patterson headlined a talent-laden Class-A Lansing team that should help rejuvenate the major league club. . . but not for another two or three years.

Micah Bowie

Position: P   **Opening Day Age:** 25
Bats: L **Throws:** L   **Born:** 11/10/74 in
Ht: 6' 4" **Wt:** 185   Humble, TX

Recent Statistics

	W	L	ERA	G	GS	Sv	IP	H	R	BB	SO	HR
1999 AAA Richmond	4	4	2.96	13	13	0	73.0	65	24	14	82	4
1999 NL Atlanta	0	1	13.50	3	0	0	4.0	8	6	4	2	1
1999 NL Chicago	2	6	9.96	11	11	0	47.0	73	54	30	39	8

When the Cubs realized their 1999 season was becoming a disaster, they traded veterans Jose Hernandez and Terry Mulholland to the Braves for three young pitchers: Bowie, Joey Nation and Ruben Quevedo. Though Bowie immediately replaced Mulholland in Chicago's rotation, he doesn't have as high a ceiling as Nation and Quevedo. He projects more as a fourth or fifth starter. A 1993 eighth-round pick, Bowie throws an 89-91 MPH fastball, a curveball and a changeup. He lacks an out pitch, so he must throw strikes and keep his pitches down. He didn't do that during his first taste of the majors, getting pounded for a 10.24 ERA and a .363 batting average. The Cubs need starters, however, so he'll get another chance.

Hee Seop Choi

Position: 1B   **Opening Day Age:** 21
Bats: L **Throws:** L   **Born:** 3/16/79 in Chon
Ht: 6' 5" **Wt:** 240   Nam, Korea

Recent Statistics

	G	AB	R	H	D	T	HR	RBI	SB	BB	SO	Avg
1999 A Lansing	79	290	71	93	18	6	18	70	2	50	68	.321

Corey Patterson grabbed most of the notoriety at Class-A Lansing, but Choi actually had a slightly more productive season once he finally got started. Signed out of Korean University, Choi had visa problems that delayed his pro debut. The Cubs were intrigued by his raw power, and he didn't disappoint, hitting several tape-measure shots. He's more than just a slugger, however. Choi hit for average, showed plenty of patience and exhibited decent speed. He did all that at age 20 while adjusting to both pro ball and life in the United States. Mark Grace hasn't shown any signs of slowing down in Chicago, but Choi could push him as early as 2002.

Scott Downs

Position: P   **Opening Day Age:** 24
Bats: L **Throws:** L   **Born:** 3/17/76 in
Ht: 6' 2" **Wt:** 180   Louisville, KY

Recent Statistics

	W	L	ERA	G	GS	Sv	IP	H	R	BB	SO	HR
1998 A Daytona	8	9	3.90	27	27	0	161.2	179	83	55	117	12
1999 AA New Britain	0	0	8.69	6	3	0	19.2	33	21	10	22	5
1999 A Fort Myers	0	1	0.00	2	2	0	9.2	7	3	6	9	0
1999 A Daytona	5	0	1.88	7	7	0	48.0	41	12	11	41	2
1999 AA West Tenn	8	1	1.35	13	12	0	80.0	56	13	28	101	2

Believing that they could contend and that they desperately needed a closer, the Cubs surrendered pitching prospects Kyle Lohse and Jason Ryan to the Twins last May so they could acquire Rick Aguilera. Both Aguilera and Chicago's season were disappointments, but at least the club salvaged Downs as part of the trade. A 1997 third-round pick out of the University of Kentucky, Downs had been sent to Minnesota after the 1998 season as the player to be named in the Mike Morgan trade. His curveball is his best pitch, and he also has an effective changeup to go with an average fastball. Like Micah Bowie, Downs projects as an end-of-the-rotation starter, but he needs some time in Triple-A.

Cole Liniak

Position: 3B   **Opening Day Age:** 23
Bats: R **Throws:** R   **Born:** 8/23/76 in
Ht: 6' 1" **Wt:** 181   Encinitas, CA

Recent Statistics

	G	AB	R	H	D	T	HR	RBI	SB	BB	SO	Avg
1999 AAA Pawtucket	95	348	55	92	25	0	12	42	0	40	57	.264
1999 NL Chicago	12	29	3	7	2	0	0	2	0	1	4	.241
1999 MLE	95	338	43	82	24	0	9	32	0	31	59	.243

When the Red Sox needed some bullpen reinforcements for the stretch drive last year, they traded Liniak and Mark Guthrie to the Cubs for Rod Beck in August. Once considered Boston's third baseman of the future, Liniak was surpassed by Wilton Veras in 1999, making him expendable. A 1995 seventh-round pick, Liniak stalled as a hitter in two seasons at Triple-A. He batted .261 and .264 while failing to develop the power teams want at the hot corner. He's more of a contact, line-drive guy who uses the entire field. Defensively, he plays a steady if unspectacular third base. Ultimately, Liniak's value depends on whether he can learn to hit home runs. Shane Andrews, another late-season Cubs acquisition, was more impressive last September and is the frontrunner to start 2000 at third for Chicago.

Mike Meyers

Position: P
Bats: R **Throws:** R
Ht: 6' 2" **Wt:** 210

Opening Day Age: 22
Born: 10/18/77 in London, Canada

Recent Statistics

	W	L	ERA	G	GS	Sv	IP	H	R	BB	SO	HR
1998 A Rockford	7	5	3.36	17	16	0	85.2	75	37	32	86	3
1999 A Daytona	10	3	1.93	19	17	0	107.1	68	30	40	122	9
1999 AA West Tenn	4	0	1.09	5	5	0	33.0	21	5	10	51	1

Meyers led all minor league pitchers with a 1.73 ERA, lowering his career mark to a 2.18. All his career totals are dazzling, as he has gone 24-9 with 201 hits, 96 walks and 306 strikeouts in 268.1 innings. Not bad for a Black Hawk (Ill.) Junior College product who lasted until the 26th round in the 1997 draft. Meyers' stuff isn't as overwhelming as his statistics. His ceiling is probably as a No. 3 starter. He has an average fastball that he works inside on hitters. His curveball is his top pitch, and his changeup could develop into a second above-average offering. A member of Canada's 1999 Pan American Games team, Meyers will start 2000 in Double-A.

Phillip Norton

Position: P
Bats: R **Throws:** L
Ht: 6' 1" **Wt:** 185

Opening Day Age: 24
Born: 2/1/76 in Texarkana, TX

Recent Statistics

	W	L	ERA	G	GS	Sv	IP	H	R	BB	SO	HR
1998 A Daytona	4	3	3.27	10	10	0	66.0	57	30	26	54	4
1998 AA West Tenn	6	6	3.52	19	19	0	120.1	118	60	50	119	11
1999 AA West Tenn	7	4	2.39	14	13	0	86.2	72	32	42	81	5
1999 AAA Iowa	5	6	6.67	14	14	0	79.2	98	63	33	61	20

Norton's 1999 performance can be evaluated in two ways. On one hand, he was named the Double-A Southern League's top pitching prospect in a midseason survey of managers. At that point, his record stood at 37-22, 2.95 since the Cubs drafted him in the 10th round out of Texarkana (Texas) Junior College in 1996. On the other hand, Norton struggled mightily in Triple-A, getting hammered for a 6.67 ERA and 20 homers in 79.2 innings. He has a solid average fastball, and his curve was rated the best breaking ball in the Southern League. He'll need to improve his location within the strike zone and bolster his changeup before he's ready for Chicago.

Corey Patterson

Position: OF
Bats: L **Throws:** R
Ht: 5' 10" **Wt:** 175

Opening Day Age: 20
Born: 8/13/79 in Atlanta, GA

Recent Statistics

	G	AB	R	H	D	THR	RBI	SB	BB	SO	Avg
1999 A Lansing	112	475	94	152	35	17	20	79	33	25	85	.320

The third overall pick in the 1998 draft, Patterson is making his then-record $3.7 million bonus look like a bargain. He debuted last year by leading the Midwest League in slugging percentage and earning the Class-A circuit's prospect of the year award. The only flaw in his game right now is that he doesn't draw walks, partly because he has the ability to drive almost any pitch, even those off the plate. He'll hit for power and average, and his top-of-the-line speed makes him that much more dangerous offensively. Managers named him the Midwest League's most exciting player and best defensive outfielder, as he plays a flashy center field and has an above-average arm. The Cubs have a gaping hole in center field, and there already is some talk that Patterson may fill it sometime in the second half of 2000.

Ruben Quevedo

Position: P
Bats: R **Throws:** R
Ht: 6' 1" **Wt:** 180

Opening Day Age: 21
Born: 1/5/79 in Valencia, Venezuela

Recent Statistics

	W	L	ERA	G	GS	Sv	IP	H	R	BB	SO	HR
1998 A Macon	11	3	3.13	25	15	0	112.0	114	50	31	117	13
1998 A Danville	0	2	3.58	6	6	0	32.2	28	22	13	35	2
1999 AAA Richmond	6	5	5.37	21	21	0	105.2	112	65	34	98	26
1999 AAA Iowa	3	1	3.45	7	7	0	44.1	34	18	21	50	1

For the Cubs, Quevedo was the key to the Jose Hernandez-Terry Mulholland trade with Atlanta. Quevedo skipped Double-A, and at age 20 was the youngest pitcher to begin the 1999 season in Triple-A. His results were mixed while with Richmond, but he was quite impressive with Chicago's Iowa affiliate. Most important, his fastball maintained the gains it had made the year before, when it jumped from 86-90 to 88-94 MPH. His textbook mechanics make his fastball look even quicker. Quevedo's curveball gives him another above-average pitch at times but is inconsistent. He also has a fine changeup. The Cubs won't contend in 2000, so there's no need to rush him, but Quevedo could surface in the second half.

Others to Watch

Jeff Goldbach (20) is the Cubs' top prospect at catcher, a position sorely lacking on the big league club. He's developing both offensively and defensively, with power potential his best tool. . . Chicago has been searching for a third baseman since the departure of Ron Santo, and has three candidates in the lower minors in **Ryan Gripp** (21), **Eric Hinske** (22) and **David Kelton** (20). For now, Hinske is the best hitter and Gripp has the most power, but Kelton has the sweetest swing and the best arm. . . Lefthander **Joey Nation** (21) joined Chicago in the Jose Hernandez-Terry Mulholland trade with Atlanta. His changeup is his best pitch, and his fastball and curveball are solid. He has 311 strikeouts in 306 pro innings, and he permitted just eight homers in 136.2 Class-A innings last year. . . Righthander **Carlos Zambrano** (18) has the best arm in the system, capable of throwing 94-95 MPH deep into games. He's still learning how to pitch. . . First baseman **Julio Zuleta** (25) hit .295 with 21 homers in Double-A. Unfortunately for him, he's trapped between Mark Grace and Hee Seop Choi.

Cinergy Field

Offense

Last March, Hamilton County commissioners finalized a plan to build a new grass stadium for the Reds, which will be open to the Ohio River and debut in 2003. Until then, the Reds will continue to play in Cinergy Field, a cookie-cutter park with artificial turf. The surface aids Cincinnati's speed game, as groundballs shoot through the brick-hard infield. The park is fairly neutral, though balls usually carry well, leading to an increase in doubles and homers.

Defense

Middle infielders Barry Larkin and Pokey Reese are perfectly suited to play on artificial turf because they have the exceptional range needed to reach balls in the hole. At the same time, Mike Cameron was made to order to play in the deep center-field gaps. Outfielders always have to guard against balls bouncing over their heads, and catching balls down the lines always is complicated by the location of the bullpens.

Who It Helps Most

Larkin has hit 39 points higher at home than on the road over the last five seasons, and he batted .320 at Cinergy Field in 1999. In his first season with the Reds, Cameron hit 62 points better in Cincinnati than elsewhere. Young relievers Dennys Reyes and Scott Williamson have been far more effective at home, as has starter Brett Tomko.

Who It Hurts Most

Eddie Taubensee hit .358 on the road and .255 at home in 1999, though his splits were fairly even in his first five years with the Reds. Departed outfielders Jeffrey Hammonds and Greg Vaughn won't miss Cinergy Field. Ron Villone's ERA was 2.99 on the road, compared to 5.61 in Cincinnati.

Rookies & Newcomers

Park adjustments to translate Dante Bichette's Coors Field stats into Cinergy Field numbers indicate that he would have lost 37 points of average, seven homers and 33 RBI had he been traded to the Reds for 1999. Cincinnati's artificial turf also will take a toll on his aching knees.

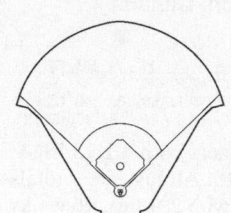

Dimensions: LF-330, LCF-375, CF-404, RCF-375, RF-330

Capacity: 52,953

Elevation: 550 feet

Surface: Turf

Foul Territory: Small

Park Factors

1999 Season

	Home Games			Away Games			
	Reds	Opp	Total	Reds	Opp	Total	Index
G	76	76	152	72	72	144	—
Avg	.264	.239	.252	.276	.238	.258	98
AB	2531	2588	5119	2586	2315	4901	99
R	373	341	714	398	291	689	98
H	669	619	1288	713	551	1264	97
2B	132	149	281	148	121	269	100
3B	15	9	24	21	12	33	70
HR	92	103	195	99	67	166	112
BB	274	297	571	235	271	506	108
SO	493	519	1012	528	460	988	98
E	51	44	95	42	71	113	80
E-Infield	40	39	79	36	57	93	80
LHB-Avg	.276	.246	.259	.314	.252	.282	92
LHB-HR	31	31	62	34	26	60	101
RHB-Avg	.259	.235	.248	.257	.230	.245	101
RHB-HR	61	72	133	65	41	106	119

1997-1999

	Home Games			Away Games			
	Reds	Opp	Total	Reds	Opp	Total	Index
G	221	221	442	223	223	446	—
Avg	.261	.244	.252	.261	.257	.259	97
AB	7300	7563	14863	7845	7344	15189	99
R	1026	1037	2063	1031	1003	2034	102
H	1905	1844	3749	2047	1884	3931	96
2B	395	440	835	402	386	788	108
3B	37	41	78	49	41	90	89
HR	220	256	476	230	225	455	107
BB	819	837	1656	731	779	1510	112
SO	1443	1578	3021	1644	1451	3095	100
E	151	138	289	159	185	344	85
E-Infield	122	112	234	125	149	274	86
LHB-Avg	.263	.261	.262	.279	.260	.270	97
LHB-HR	85	86	171	88	70	158	113
RHB-Avg	.260	.233	.246	.249	.254	.252	98
RHB-HR	135	170	305	142	155	297	103

1999 Rankings (National League)

- Second-highest walk factor
- Third-highest home-run factor
- Third-highest RHB home-run factor
- Second-lowest error factor
- Third-lowest infield-error factor
- Third-lowest LHB batting-average factor

Jack McKeon

1999 Season

There was little argument when Jack McKeon was named National League Manager of the Year. The third-oldest manager in big league history, he took an unheralded, low-budget club to within a victory of a wild-card berth. The Reds played hard from Opening Day, establishing themselves as contenders with midseason road sweeps in Arizona and Houston. Their success away from home earned them the nickname Big Road Machine.

Offense

Cincinnati upped its power production from 1998 by 71 home runs but remained an aggressive club on the bases. They ranked among National League leaders in stolen bases and stolen-base percentage. McKeon didn't hesitate to sit slumping regulars or ride hot hands. Aaron Boone was sent to the minors in May, and the demotion turned around Boone's season. Meanwhile, Dmitri Young sat for much of the first half but returned to everyday action when he got hot later in the summer.

Pitching & Defense

Without question, the key to McKeon's success last year was his use of the bullpen. Saddled for much of the year by a rotation that didn't eat enough innings, McKeon leaned heavily on his relievers. He shunned the modern practice of reserving his closer for one inning's work. Instead, McKeon used a different group of pitchers to close games each day. He didn't hesitate to use a reliever for two or three innings at a time, counting on his depth to keep the bullpen effective the next day. He was well above average utilyzing defensive subs.

2000 Outlook

McKeon and the Reds sparred for weeks over a new contract until he finally signed for another season. At 69, McKeon obviously isn't a long-term managerial option, and speculation is that bench coach Ken Griffey Sr. will replace him in 2001. McKeon has assembled an outstanding coaching staff to which he gives much authority, and his role is largely confined to setting the club's mood and dealing with the media. He's excellent in both aspects.

Born: 11/23/30 in South Amboy, NJ

Playing Experience: No major league experience

Managerial Experience: 11 seasons

Nickname: Trader Jack

Manager Statistics

Year	Team, Lg	W	L	Pct	GB	Finish
1999	Cincinnati, NL	96	67	.589	1.5	2nd Central
11 Seasons		686	658	.510	—	—

1999 Starting Pitchers by Days Rest

	<=3	4	5	6+
Reds Starts	0	96	43	16
Reds ERA	0.00	4.50	4.14	3.12
NL Avg Starts	3	81	48	21
NL ERA	4.84	4.53	4.72	4.98

1999 Situational Stats

	Jack McKeon	NL Average
Hit & Run Success %	28.6	33.6
Stolen Base Success %	75.2	70.2
Platoon Pct.	50.5	55.2
Defensive Subs	38	25
High-Pitch Outings	9	13
Quick/Slow Hooks	25/9	16/15
Sacrifice Attempts	88	89

1999 Rankings (National League)

- 1st in intentional walks (43) and saves with over 1 inning pitched (28)
- 2nd in steals of second base (136), defensive substitutions (38) and quick hooks (25)
- 3rd in stolen-base percentage (75.2%) and steals of third base (28)

Aaron Boone

1999 Season

Following a promotion from Triple-A in late May, Aaron Boone finally established himself as a legitimate major league third baseman. A September slump prevented him from batting .300, though he still ended up among the Reds' RBI leaders. Boone showed consistent power for the first time in his career and even provided Cincinnati with another basestealing option. Boone's defense became more consistent as he settled in as a regular.

Hitting

Boone has added strength over the last two years. Though he may never be the huge homer threat ideally desired in a third baseman, at least now he's capable of approaching 20 home runs. Boone is an excellent fastball hitter but still is vulnerable to offspeed pitches. Though he hits righthanded, his career-long struggles with southpaws show no signs of abating. Boone needs to develop better patience at the plate, though he makes respectable contact. He likes to swing at fastballs early in the count.

Baserunning & Defense

Boone has better-than-average speed, and he has made himself into a solid basestealer by developing a quick first step and studying the moves of pitchers. Only speedsters Pokey Reese, Barry Larkin and Mike Cameron had more stolen bases last year for Cincinnati. Boone's range at third base isn't exceptional, but he has very soft hands and a strong, accurate arm. He's very dependable at the hot corner.

2000 Outlook

Cincinnati would like to get more power from its third baseman and has explored trade options toward that goal. The pool of quality third basemen, however, is slim. The Reds were very pleased with Boone's development last season, and they view him as good enough to be a third baseman on a playoff team.

Position: 3B
Bats: R **Throws:** R
Ht: 6' 2" **Wt:** 200

Opening Day Age: 27
Born: 3/9/73 in La Mesa, CA
ML Seasons: 3

Overall Statistics

	G	AB	R	H	D	T	HR	RBI	SB	BB	SO	Avg	OBP	Slg
1999	139	472	56	132	26	5	14	72	17	30	79	.280	.330	.445
Career	213	702	85	195	40	7	16	105	24	47	120	.278	.332	.423

Where He Hits the Ball

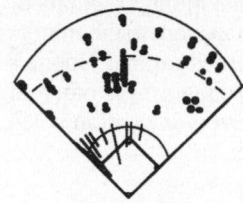
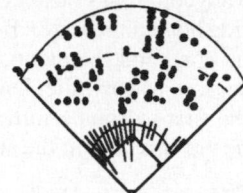

Vs. LHP   **Vs. RHP**

1999 Situational Stats

	AB	H	HR	RBI	Avg		AB	H	HR	RBI	Avg
Home	236	64	7	42	.271	LHP	105	23	2	8	.219
Road	236	68	7	30	.288	RHP	367	109	12	64	.297
First Half	190	55	4	24	.289	Sc Pos	131	37	7	63	.282
Scnd Half	282	77	10	48	.273	Clutch	68	23	2	8	.338

1999 Rankings (National League)

- 6th in errors at third base (15) and lowest fielding percentage at third base (.958)
- 7th in batting average on a 3-1 count (.667)
- 8th in fewest pitches seen per plate appearance (3.34) and lowest percentage of pitches taken (47.8)
- 9th in batting average with the bases loaded (.500)
- 10th in lowest on-base percentage
- Led the Reds in batting average in the clutch, batting average with the bases loaded (.500), batting average on a 3-1 count (.667), batting average on an 0-2 count (.286), batting average on a 3-2 count (.308), batting average with two strikes (.217) and sacrifice flies (5)

Mike Cameron

1999 Season

After the Reds traded slugging prospect Paul Konerko to the White Sox to get him, Mike Cameron showed flashes of playing up to his exceptional ability in his first National League season. Though he continued to be plagued by inconsistency and strikeouts, he set career highs in most major offensive categories and played an outstanding center field. Hampered late in the year by hamstring problems, Cameron batted .187 during the final five weeks.

Hitting

Cameron has a quick bat and can turn around fastballs for power. To his credit, Cameron has worked on improving his patience at the plate, and last year he improved his on-base percentage by 73 points. Cameron set a Reds record for strikeouts because he still gives away too many at-bats by chasing pitches, especially offspeed stuff, out of the strike zone. His career batting average against righthanders is just .238, so if he doesn't improve he could get slotted as a platoon player.

Baserunning & Defense

As he continues to learn better discipline at the plate, Cameron should grow into a top basestealer. He has improved his ability to get jumps and worked hard last year at learning NL pitchers. Cameron is among the game's fastest players and constantly looks for chances to take the extra base. He also is one of baseball's best center fielders, especially in terms of range. Cameron still makes too many mistakes with his strong but sometimes wild arm.

2000 Outlook

Cameron's tools are better than most players', and his center-field skills make him a valuable part of the Reds' immediate future. If he can mature offensively, Cameron has a chance to be an all-around star with a ceiling of 30 homers and 50 steals.

Position: CF
Bats: R **Throws:** R
Ht: 6' 2" **Wt:** 190

Opening Day Age: 27
Born: 1/8/73 in LaGrange, GA
ML Seasons: 5

Overall Statistics

	G	AB	R	H	D	T	HR	RBI	SB	BB	SO	Avg	OBP	Slg
1999	146	542	93	139	34	9	21	66	38	80	145	.256	.357	.469
Career	442	1366	214	328	70	17	44	166	88	176	369	.240	.332	.413

Where He Hits the Ball

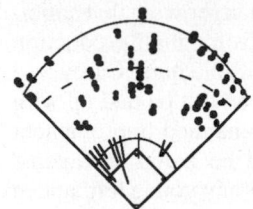 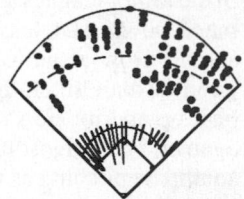

Vs. LHP   **Vs. RHP**

1999 Situational Stats

	AB	H	HR	RBI	Avg		AB	H	HR	RBI	Avg
Home	275	79	12	33	.287	LHP	120	35	7	15	.292
Road	267	60	9	33	.225	RHP	422	104	14	51	.246
First Half	300	81	10	39	.270	Sc Pos	137	28	5	46	.204
Scnd Half	242	58	11	27	.240	Clutch	80	19	1	9	.238

1999 Rankings (National League)

- 2nd in errors in center field (8)
- 3rd in strikeouts and lowest batting average on the road
- 4th in lowest fielding percentage in center field (.979)
- 5th in triples and stolen bases
- Led the Reds in most pitches seen per plate appearance (4.04), fewest GDPs per GDP situation (4.5%), on-base percentage for a leadoff hitter (.366), slugging percentage vs. lefthanded pitchers (.575), on-base percentage vs. lefthanded pitchers (.418), bunts in play (18), triples, stolen bases, caught stealing (12) and strikeouts
- Led NL center fielders in most pitches seen per plate appearance (4.04), walks and strikeouts

Sean Casey

1999 Season

Sean Casey built on the progress he made in the second half of his rookie 1998 season, blossoming into one of the game's rising young stars last year. He led the National League in batting for half the season and earned his first All-Star Game berth. Though he hit 85 points lower in the second half, Casey continued to produce RBI and looked right at home as the No. 3 hitter in the Cincinnati lineup. His infectious personality quickly made him a fan favorite.

Hitting

Many scouts view Casey as a special player who has the potential to win a batting title and produce more than 30 home runs and 100 RBI. He hit .346 in the minor leagues and began showing that anticipated power last season. His longball production should grow as he learns NL pitchers. Casey is a good fastball hitter, though he can be tied up with heat up and in. He shows continued improvement against breaking stuff, and he hangs in against southpaw pitching as well as any young lefthanded hitter in recent years.

Baserunning & Defense

Speed isn't among Casey's physical gifts, and he didn't steal a base last year. Still, he runs the bases intelligently and can take an extra base at times. He made impressive improvement as a first baseman last year, bettering his range and his ability to dig low throws out of the dirt. The Reds think he'll be a quality first sacker when he gains more experience.

2000 Outlook

Years from now, Cincinnati's trade of pitcher Dave Burba for Casey may be viewed in the same way as Houston's acquisition of Jeff Bagwell for reliever Larry Andersen. In Casey, the Reds have a piece of their foundation for the next decade. With his great ability and work ethic, he's destined for stardom.

Position: 1B
Bats: L **Throws:** R
Ht: 6' 4" **Wt:** 215

Opening Day Age: 25
Born: 7/2/74 in Willingboro, NJ
ML Seasons: 3

Overall Statistics

	G	AB	R	H	D	T	HR	RBI	SB	BB	SO	Avg	OBP	Slg
1999	151	594	103	197	42	3	25	99	0	61	88	.332	.399	.539
Career	253	906	148	281	63	4	32	152	1	105	135	.310	.387	.494

Where He Hits the Ball

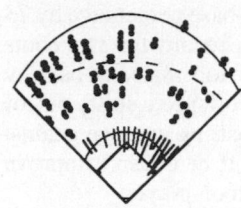

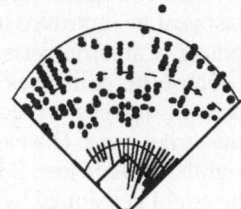

Vs. LHP   **Vs. RHP**

1999 Situational Stats

	AB	H	HR	RBI	Avg		AB	H	HR	RBI	Avg
Home	298	96	11	40	.322	LHP	170	46	8	29	.271
Road	296	101	14	59	.341	RHP	424	151	17	70	.356
First Half	318	118	17	57	.371	Sc Pos	139	47	4	63	.338
Scnd Half	276	79	8	42	.286	Clutch	90	23	5	12	.256

1999 Rankings (National League)

- 1st in batting average vs. righthanded pitchers
- 3rd in fielding percentage at first base (.995)
- 4th in batting average and hits
- 5th in intentional walks (13)
- Led the Reds in slugging percentage, on-base percentage, highest groundball/flyball ratio (1.8), batting average with runners in scoring position, batting average vs. righthanded pitchers, slugging percentage vs. righthanded pitchers (.568), on-base percentage vs. righthanded pitchers (.415), batting average, at-bats, hits, singles, doubles, total bases (320), sacrifice flies (5), intentional walks (13), hit by pitch (9), times on base (267), GDPs (15) and batting average at home

Juan Guzman

1999 Season

Cincinnati got what it hoped for when it sent pitching prospects B.J. Ryan and Jacobo Sequea to Baltimore for Juan Guzman at the trade deadline. Guzman went 6-3 in his 12 starts for the Reds. He worked at least seven innings in eight of those outings, and nine of his 12 games were quality starts. Guzman's overall 3.74 ERA was his lowest since he led the American League in that category in 1996.

Pitching

There always have been questions about Guzman's durability, but he looked like a perfectly healthy pitcher for Cincinnati. His fastball consistently was locked in at 92-94 MPH, and he had command of a slider and splitter that rank among the best in the game. Guzman will give up his share of home runs when he gets his fastball up in the strike zone, but he showed much more consistent control after joining the Reds. He also showed the ability to maintain his stuff past the 100-pitch mark.

Defense & Hitting

Guzman is subpar at holding runners. National League basestealers succeeded in 13 of 15 attempts, quickly learning to take advantage of his slow delivery to the plate. He also doesn't get himself into good fielding position and is prone to hurrying throws, particularly on bunt plays. Guzman never batted much before last season and is no threat at the plate.

2000 Outlook

The free-agent crop of pitchers was increasingly thin, making Guzman one of the most attractive arms available. The Reds would love to keep him after what they saw in 1999, so they offered him arbitration to maintain their negotiating rights. Don't be surprised if he lands a three-year contract in the neighborhood of $18 million.

Position: SP
Bats: R **Throws:** R
Ht: 5'11" **Wt:** 195

Opening Day Age: 33
Born: 10/28/66 in Santo Domingo, Dominican Republic
ML Seasons: 9
Pronunciation: GOOZ-mahn

Overall Statistics

	W	L	Pct.	ERA	G	GS	Sv	IP	H	BB	SO	HR	Ratio
1999	11	12	.478	3.74	33	33	0	200.0	194	86	155	28	1.40
Career	91	78	.538	4.03	239	239	0	1481.2	1353	665	1240	147	1.36

How Often He Throws Strikes

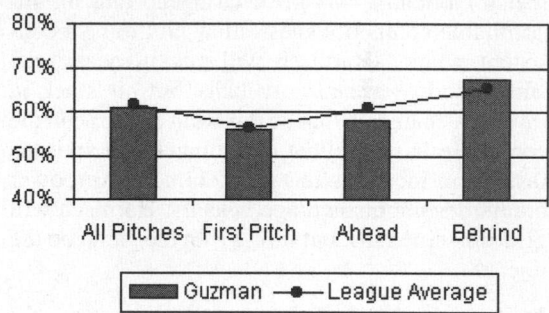

1999 Situational Stats

	W	L	ERA	Sv	IP		AB	H	HR	RBI	Avg
Home	5	7	3.66	0	105.2	LHB	371	96	8	46	.259
Road	6	5	3.82	0	94.1	RHB	391	98	20	42	.251
First Half	4	7	4.31	0	102.1	Sc Pos	194	45	6	60	.232
Scnd Half	7	5	3.13	0	97.2	Clutch	37	10	1	3	.270

1999 Rankings (National League)

- Did not rank near the top or bottom in any category

Pete Harnisch

1999 Season

There were few more courageous pitching performances than what Pete Harnisch provided for the Reds in 1999. Laboring with an injured shoulder all season and still adjusting to medication needed for his depression, Harnisch was the rock of the Cincinnati rotation. He missed only one start despite the shoulder pain, leading the Reds in wins and innings, and finishing his season with two clutch victories in the final week to keep the Reds in the playoff hunt.

Pitching

Harnisch rarely throws his fastball harder than 90 MPH, especially with his shoulder ailing. Yet his feel for pitching, his great changeup and his indomitable competitiveness allow him to be a consistent winner. Harnisch will mix in occasional sliders and overhand curveballs, but his stock in trade is a changeup that he throws at any time in the count. He has excellent control and will spot his fastball in locations that allow him to overpower hitters despite his average velocity. Harnisch will give up home runs, but rarely with the game on the line.

Defense & Hitting

Harnisch's stocky build belies his excellent agility. He gets himself into good fielding position and is quick coming off the mound to field bunts. His slow delivery makes him fairly easy to steal upon, but Harnisch helps himself by holding runners with throws to first, and with slide steps and varied deliveries to home. He can help himself with either a bunt or occasional power. Last year, he had four doubles and a homer among his 10 hits.

2000 Outlook

Rather than have surgery, Harnisch underwent an extensive offseason conditioning program for his shoulder. He expects to be completely healthy in time for spring training. As long as he can take his regular turn in the rotation, he'll remain a leader of the Reds' staff. He's a reliable starter who can be depended upon for 14-16 wins every year.

Position: SP
Bats: R **Throws:** R
Ht: 6' 0" **Wt:** 228

Opening Day Age: 33
Born: 9/23/66 in Commack, NY
ML Seasons: 12
Pronunciation: HARN-ish

Overall Statistics

	W	L	Pct.	ERA	G	GS	Sv	IP	H	BB	SO	HR	Ratio
1999	16	10	.615	3.68	33	33	0	198.1	190	57	120	25	1.25
Career	102	94	.520	3.78	292	289	0	1792.2	1641	653	1280	191	1.28

How Often He Throws Strikes

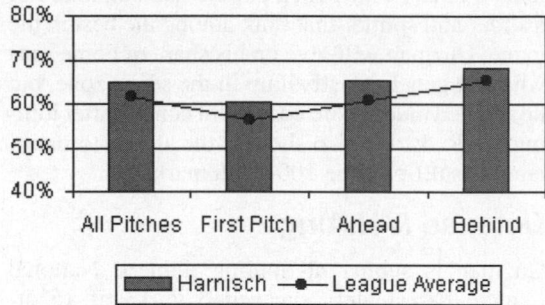

1999 Situational Stats

	W	L	ERA	Sv	IP		AB	H	HR	RBI	Avg
Home	5	5	3.29	0	79.1	LHB	336	86	14	39	.256
Road	11	5	3.93	0	119.0	RHB	418	104	11	42	.249
First Half	9	6	3.42	0	108.0	Sc Pos	163	46	5	59	.282
Scnd Half	7	4	3.99	0	90.1	Clutch	32	8	3	3	.250

1999 Rankings (National League)

- 2nd in shutouts (2)
- 3rd in lowest groundball/flyball ratio allowed (0.8)
- 5th in highest stolen-base percentage allowed (81.3)
- Led the Reds in ERA, wins, losses, complete games (2), shutouts (2), innings pitched, hits allowed, batters faced (833), pitches thrown (2,953), lowest batting average allowed (.252), lowest slugging percentage allowed (.420), lowest on-base percentage allowed (.307), lowest stolen-base percentage allowed (81.3), fewest pitches thrown per batter (3.55), fewest baserunners allowed per nine innings (11.4) and most run support per nine innings (5.8)

Barry Larkin

1999 Season

Barry Larkin worried Cincinnati fans when he was beneath the Mendoza Line nearly two months into the season, but he started hitting in late May and didn't stop. He batted .310 during the final four months en route to a typical Barry Larkin season. He reached 100 runs for the second time in his career and also ranked among team leaders in RBI. Thanks to a year-round workout program, Larkin is in the best condition of his career despite being in his mid-30s. He played in 161 games, a career high.

Hitting

Each season Larkin seems to have one month-long slump that starts when he begins chasing balls out of the strike zone. Once he escapes his swoon, which he always does, Larkin becomes one of the game's most solid all-around hitters. He's a Tony Gwynn-like hit machine with gap power, consistent RBI production and a high on-base percentage. The Reds used him in both the second and fifth spots in their lineup last season, and he has the skills to adapt to any spot in the batting order.

Baserunning & Defense

Larkin won't add to his collection of three Gold Gloves as long as Rey Ordonez is in the National League, but his defensive skills remain brilliant in all areas. He has a strong arm and quick release, and he gets to balls most other shortstops can't. Larkin is one of the most efficient baserunners in the game, taking extra bases and swiping bags at a high percentage.

2000 Outlook

Larkin has spent several recent offseasons anticipating that the Reds would trim payroll by dealing him away to a well-heeled contender. With last year's dramatic run for the playoffs and construction finally underway for a new ballpark, Cincinnati could be on the verge of reawakening its proud baseball tradition. Larkin should stay put and enjoy another strong season, though he'll be eligible for free agency after 2000.

Position: SS
Bats: R **Throws:** R
Ht: 6' 0" **Wt:** 185

Opening Day Age: 35
Born: 4/28/64 in Cincinnati, OH
ML Seasons: 14

Overall Statistics

	G	AB	R	H	D	T	HR	RBI	SB	BB	SO	Avg	OBP	Slg
1999	161	583	108	171	30	4	12	75	30	93	57	.293	.390	.420
Career	1707	6291	1063	1884	335	65	168	793	345	764	633	.299	.376	.454

Where He Hits the Ball

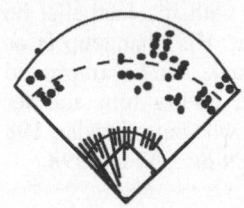

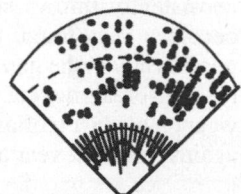

Vs. LHP **Vs. RHP**

1999 Situational Stats

	AB	H	HR	RBI	Avg		AB	H	HR	RBI	Avg
Home	281	90	7	39	.320	LHP	147	38	5	19	.259
Road	302	81	5	36	.268	RHP	436	133	7	56	.305
First Half	311	97	9	52	.312	Sc Pos	151	46	3	62	.305
Scnd Half	272	74	3	23	.272	Clutch	82	21	1	8	.256

1999 Rankings (National League)

- 4th in fielding percentage at shortstop (.978)
- 5th in steals of third (9) and games played
- 7th in highest percentage of pitches taken (61.5)
- 8th in errors at shortstop (14) and walks
- 9th in singles
- 10th in highest percentage of extra bases taken as a runner (60.9)
- Led the Reds in highest percentage of pitches taken (61.5), steals of third (9), runs scored, walks, pitches seen (2,649), plate appearances (687) and games played
- Led NL shortstops in on-base percentage, batting average vs. righthanded pitchers, on-base percentage vs. righthanded pitchers (.404), runs scored, caught stealing (8) and walks

Denny Neagle

1999 Season

The Reds acquired Denny Neagle, Michael Tucker and top pitching prospect Rob Bell in the offseason from the Braves, in exchange for Bret Boone and Mike Remlinger. From the opening of spring training, shoulder troubles shadowed Neagle. He answered many questions, however, when he returned at midseason to help carry the Cincinnati rotation down the stretch. Neagle kept the Reds in all but two of his 19 starts and won nine times.

Pitching

Once he regained his strength and feel for pitching, Neagle resembled the 20-game winner he was for Atlanta in 1997. He had both his sinking fastball and his cutter close to 90 MPH again. When Neagle consistently throws strikes with his fastballs, he becomes very tough to beat. His changeup is as good as any in the game. Neagle also has improved his big-breaking curveball, giving him another weapon against lefthanders, who batted under .198 against him last year after hitting .257 in 1998.

Defense & Hitting

Neagle learned his lessons well in Atlanta. Like the other great Braves starters, he helps his own cause. Neagle is a reliable fielder who doesn't get rattled on defensive plays and is rarely out of fielding position. Baserunners rarely test him, and when they do they don't have much success. He also can handle the bat. He has three career homers and can lay a bunt down when needed.

2000 Outlook

When Cincinnati acquired Neagle, it was assumed he never would last the season with the Reds. He looked more like a short-term rental who would be traded away for prospects. After his strong rebound from shoulder problems and the Reds' uplifting season, it seems the club is committed to keeping Neagle as a part of the club's nucleus. If not a bona fide No. 1 starter, he's at worst a very good top-of-the-rotation pitcher who should win 15-17 games a year.

Position: SP
Bats: L **Throws:** L
Ht: 6' 3" **Wt:** 225

Opening Day Age: 31
Born: 9/13/68 in Gambrills, MD
ML Seasons: 9
Pronunciation: NAY-gull

Overall Statistics

	W	L	Pct.	ERA	G	GS	Sv	IP	H	BB	SO	HR	Ratio
1999	9	5	.643	4.27	20	19	0	111.2	95	40	76	23	1.21
Career	90	60	.600	3.82	286	188	3	1311.0	1268	378	998	152	1.26

How Often He Throws Strikes

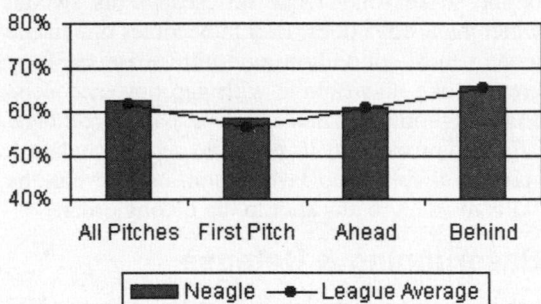

Neagle —■— League Average —●—

1999 Situational Stats

	W	L	ERA	Sv	IP		AB	H	HR	RBI	Avg
Home	6	3	4.41	0	67.1	LHB	81	16	4	10	.198
Road	3	2	4.06	0	44.1	RHB	334	79	19	40	.237
First Half	0	3	8.17	0	25.1	Sc Pos	88	18	3	23	.205
Scnd Half	9	2	3.13	0	86.1	Clutch	11	2	0	0	.182

1999 Rankings (National League)

- Did not rank near the top or bottom in any category

Pokey Reese

1999 Season

Pokey Reese entered 1999 with a .228 career average, but he won Cincinnati's second-base job in spring training and blossomed into one of the game's most exciting middle infielders. Primarily a shortstop for most of his career, Reese adapted so well defensively that he won a Gold Glove. More surprising, he had a solid offensive season that combined his speed with some new pop and consistency.

Hitting

The book on Reese used to be that you could knock the bat out of his hands with an average major league fastball. Working with Reds batting coach Denis Menke, Reese shortened his stroke and made much more consistent contact. He also has added some bulk to his slight frame, and the result was unexpected gap power. The biggest drawback was that he was less patient than ever, so his on-base percentage was .330, far from acceptable for a player who spent much of 1999 as a leadoff hitter.

Baserunning & Defense

With his blinding speed, quick first step and good judgment, Reese easily can become a high-percentage, 50-steal man. He aggressively looks to take the extra base. In the field, Reese has Roberto Alomaresque range at second base. He also has a strong arm and soft hands, and by midseason last year he was turning double plays like a veteran. He's considered the heir apparent to Barry Larkin at short, and some scouts already think that Reese would be an upgrade defensively over the perennial All-Star.

2000 Outlook

Cincinnati knew what it was doing when it traded Bret Boone to acquire Denny Neagle and open up second base for Reese, though he'll need to show that 1999 was no fluke after tailing off in the second half. In December, the Reds broke off talks with the Mariners to acquire Ken Griffey Jr. because of Seattle's insistence on Reese. A year earlier, no one would have imagined that Reese would be the key to a trade for arguably the game's best player.

Position: 2B/SS
Bats: R **Throws:** R
Ht: 5'11" **Wt:** 180

Opening Day Age: 26
Born: 6/10/73 in Columbia, SC
ML Seasons: 3

Overall Statistics

	G	AB	R	H	D	T	HR	RBI	SB	BB	SO	Avg	OBP	Slg
1999	149	585	85	167	37	5	10	52	38	35	81	.285	.330	.417
Career	336	1115	153	288	54	7	15	94	66	80	191	.258	.312	.360

Where He Hits the Ball

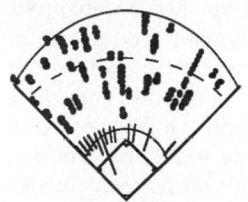
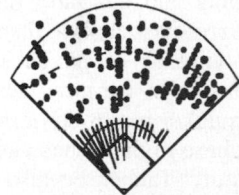

Vs. LHP   **Vs. RHP**

1999 Situational Stats

	AB	H	HR	RBI	Avg		AB	H	HR	RBI	Avg
Home	273	72	5	23	.264	LHP	146	43	3	13	.295
Road	312	95	5	29	.304	RHP	439	124	7	39	.282
First Half	332	99	5	29	.298	Sc Pos	126	32	2	42	.254
Scnd Half	253	68	5	23	.269	Clutch	88	19	2	10	.216

1999 Rankings (National League)

- 3rd in fielding percentage at second base (.991)
- 4th in lowest on-base percentage for a leadoff hitter (.316)
- 5th in highest percentage of extra bases taken as a runner (67.5) and stolen bases
- 7th in steals of third (8)
- 8th in stolen-base percentage (84.4)
- 9th in lowest on-base percentage
- 10th in lowest on-base percentage vs. righthanded pitchers (.323)
- Led the Reds in stolen-base percentage (84.4), highest percentage of extra bases taken as a runner (67.5), sacrifice flies (5) and stolen bases

Eddie Taubensee

1999 Season

Whenever a team comes out of nowhere like Cincinnati did last year, it usually has a number of players who enjoy career years. None of the Reds exceeded his normal performance more than Eddie Taubensee. Previously a career .267 hitter, Taubensee was the first Cincinnati catcher to hit better than .300 in 43 years. After hitting just 64 homers in his previous eight seasons, Taubensee last year became the first Reds catcher to hit more than 20 since 1980.

Hitting

Long considered a platoon player, Taubensee has made himself into a tough out against both lefthanders and righthanders. He usually puts the ball into play and has built himself up into a dangerous extra-base threat. Teams still make the mistake of trying to get in on Taubensee with early-count fastballs. He now clears his front side and has a quicker bat to drive inside heat a long way. He'll chase high pitches and can be fooled by offspeed stuff. Taubensee also doesn't work many walks because he usually is hacking early in the count.

Baserunning & Defense

On a club that has excellent speed throughout the lineup, Taubensee's slowness is not a problem. More of a concern is his defensive mediocrity. He threw out 13 percent of basestealers in 1999, the worst rate in the major leagues. The year before, he ranked last in the National League at 19 percent. Taubensee also isn't adept at blocking pitches. He has worked with pitching coach Don Gullett to improve his ability to call games and handle pitchers. Taubensee has improved his framing of pitches as well.

2000 Outlook

Taubensee never is going to be Johnny Bench behind the plate. Yet he has become an important source of power and run production in the Cincinnati lineup. The Reds can more than live with his defensive shortcomings.

Position: C
Bats: L **Throws:** R
Ht: 6' 3" **Wt:** 230

Opening Day Age: 31
Born: 10/31/68 in Beeville, TX
ML Seasons: 9
Pronunciation: TAW-ben-see

Overall Statistics

	G	AB	R	H	D	T	HR	RBI	SB	BB	SO	Avg	OBP	Slg
1999	126	424	58	132	22	2	21	87	0	30	67	.311	.354	.521
Career	842	2492	306	684	137	8	85	384	11	224	511	.274	.332	.438

Where He Hits the Ball

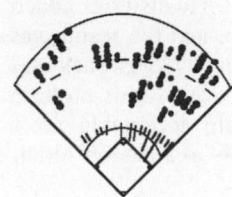 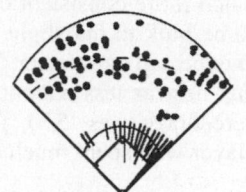

Vs. LHP   **Vs. RHP**

1999 Situational Stats

	AB	H	HR	RBI	Avg		AB	H	HR	RBI	Avg
Home	192	49	8	36	.255	LHP	60	20	2	11	.333
Road	232	83	13	51	.358	RHP	364	112	19	76	.308
First Half	226	70	9	41	.310	Sc Pos	121	40	5	65	.331
Scnd Half	198	62	12	46	.313	Clutch	68	17	5	14	.250

1999 Rankings (National League)

- 1st in lowest percentage of runners caught stealing as a catcher (13.4)
- 3rd in errors at catcher (9)
- Led the Reds in sacrifice flies (5)
- Led NL catchers in batting average with runners in scoring position, batting average vs. righthanded pitchers and on-base percentage vs. righthanded pitchers (.354)

Brett Tomko

1999 Season

Once considered a potential ace, Brett Tomko slipped completely out of Cincinnati's rotation by the end of the year. He was demoted to the minors after five shaky early-season starts. He won just five of his 26 starts and spent September in long relief. The Reds had expected three times as many victories.

Pitching

The quality of Tomko's stuff is a given. He throws both his sinker and his cut fastball in the low 90s. He also has a very underrated straight change and has improved the consistency of his curveball. Yet Tomko's development has stalled. He chronically struggles to maintain command of the strike zone. Manager Jack McKeon has questioned Tomko's toughness in public, and the pitcher has sparred with McKeon and pitching coach Don Gullett over how often he needs to pitch inside. Too often, Tomko nibbles with offspeed stuff or pitches off the plate. He gives up too many homers, most often when he either falls behind in the count or hangs a curveball.

Defense & Hitting

Tomko hasn't done enough to improve his ability to hold runners. He has a slow delivery home and hasn't felt comfortable using a slide step to help keep runners close. That makes him very easy to steal on. He's an average fielder and can help himself at the plate. He hit .213 last season and also put down eight sacrifices.

2000 Outlook

When the Reds briefly banished Tomko to the minors at the end of April, it was a signal that their patience had grown thin. After his return, he showed only flashes of his promise. As a result, the Reds listened to trade offers for him and made it clear that Tomko would have to earn his way back into their future plans. If they make a major deal during the offseason, he's almost certain to be included.

Position: SP
Bats: R **Throws:** R
Ht: 6' 4" **Wt:** 215

Opening Day Age: 26
Born: 4/7/73 in Cleveland, OH
ML Seasons: 3

Overall Statistics

	W	L	Pct.	ERA	G	GS	Sv	IP	H	BB	SO	HR	Ratio
1999	5	7	.417	4.92	33	26	0	172.0	175	60	132	31	1.37
Career	29	26	.527	4.35	89	79	0	508.2	479	171	389	67	1.28

How Often He Throws Strikes

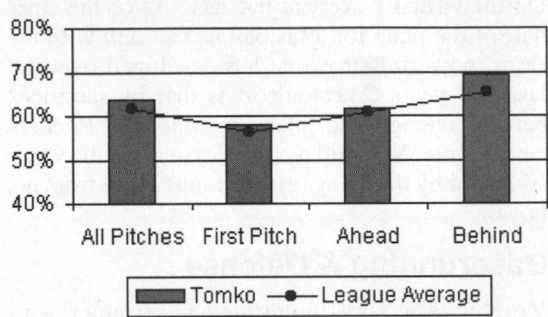

1999 Situational Stats

	W	L	ERA	Sv	IP		AB	H	HR	RBI	Avg
Home	2	4	4.35	0	91.0	LHB	320	80	12	35	.250
Road	3	3	5.56	0	81.0	RHB	346	95	19	58	.275
First Half	3	5	5.42	0	94.2	Sc Pos	152	45	8	69	.296
Scnd Half	2	2	4.31	0	77.1	Clutch	50	11	2	2	.220

1999 Rankings (National League)

- 2nd in highest stolen-base percentage allowed (85.7) and most home runs allowed per nine innings (1.62)
- 5th in lowest batting average allowed vs. lefthanded batters and highest slugging percentage allowed (.488)
- 8th in highest ERA on the road
- 9th in home runs allowed
- 10th in highest batting average allowed with runners in scoring position
- Led the Reds in home runs allowed, strikeouts, stolen bases allowed (18), highest strikeout/walk ratio (2.2), most strikeouts per nine innings (6.9), ERA at home, lowest batting average allowed vs. lefthanded batters and sacrifice bunts (8)

Cincinnati

Greg Vaughn

1999 Season

Greg Vaughn showed that his 50-homer season in 1998 was no fluke, hammering 45 homers after the Padres traded him and Mark Sweeney to the Reds in February for Reggie Sanders, Damian Jackson and minor league pitcher Josh Harris. Unlike his big year with San Diego, when he did his best hitting in May, June and July, Vaughn started slowly in 1999 before closing with a flurry. As Cincinnati made a push for the postseason, he provided 16 homers and 37 RBI in September and October.

Hitting

There are few better fastball hitters than Vaughn. During virtually every at-bat, he looks on the inner half of the plate for a fastball he can pull with the short, powerful stroke he has developed over the last two years. The tradeoff is that he sacrifices batting average and piles up strikeouts. Pitchers can handle Vaughn by employing an effective sinker, or by throwing offspeed stuff away from his power.

Baserunning & Defense

Vaughn is a very underrated baserunner who knows how to pick his spots when trying to steal bases. Last year, he swiped 15 in 17 attempts. He doesn't have exceptional outfield skills, possessing below-average range for a left fielder. He does work hard to get the most out of his ability. Runners challenge Vaughn's weak arm, and he responded last year with eight assists.

2000 Outlook

The Reds have a medium-sized budget and quickly determined that they couldn't afford Vaughn when he became a free agent. They didn't even offer him arbitration for fear that he would accept, and he signed with the Devil Rays for a four-year, $34 million contract. Tropicana Field is a poor home-run park for righthanded hitters, so Vaughn may be hard-pressed to reach 40 longballs this season. Anticipating Vaughn's departure, Cincinnati traded Jeffrey Hammonds and Stan Belinda to Colorado for Dante Bichette in October. How well Bichette will do without Coors Field remains to be seen.

Position: LF
Bats: R **Throws:** R
Ht: 6' 0" **Wt:** 202

Opening Day Age: 34
Born: 7/3/65 in Sacramento, CA
ML Seasons: 11

Overall Statistics

	G	AB	R	H	D	T	HR	RBI	SB	BB	SO	Avg	OBP	Slg
1999	153	550	104	135	20	2	45	118	15	85	137	.245	.347	.535
Career	1377	4869	824	1197	219	20	292	882	99	665	1160	.246	.337	.479

Where He Hits the Ball

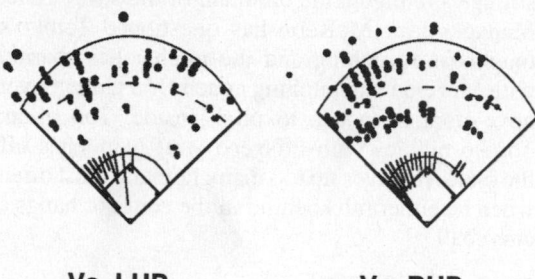

Vs. LHP   **Vs. RHP**

1999 Situational Stats

	AB	H	HR	RBI	Avg			AB	H	HR	RBI	Avg
Home	270	61	20	50	.226		LHP	141	37	11	32	.262
Road	280	74	25	68	.264		RHP	409	98	34	86	.240
First Half	288	67	20	54	.233		Sc Pos	149	46	14	73	.309
Scnd Half	262	68	25	64	.260		Clutch	79	15	5	10	.190

1999 Rankings (National League)

- 2nd in lowest batting average vs. righthanded pitchers and lowest batting average at home
- 3rd in home runs and lowest batting average
- 4th in HR frequency (12.2 ABs per HR) and fielding percentage in left field (.986)
- 7th in strikeouts
- 9th in RBI and lowest on-base percentage vs. righthanded pitchers (.323)
- 10th in errors in left field (4)
- Led the Reds in HR frequency (12.2 ABs per HR), cleanup slugging percentage (.543), home runs, RBI and sacrifice flies (5)
- Led NL left fielders in HR frequency (12.2 ABs per HR), home runs and games played (153)

Dmitri Young

Position: RF/LF
Bats: B **Throws:** R
Ht: 6' 2" **Wt:** 235

Opening Day Age: 26
Born: 10/11/73 in Vicksburg, MS
ML Seasons: 4

1999 Season

For the first three months of the season, Dmitri Young was a major disappointment. He was hitting just .234 with 11 RBI at the All-Star break, and he couldn't stay in the Cincinnati lineup on a regular basis. Young found his stroke and heated up the rest of the way, batting .339 in the second half and driving in 37 runs in his final 200 at-bats.

Hitting

The switch-hitting Young remains more effective from the left side. He has better plate coverage and more power, and he chases fewer pitches than when he bats righthanded. He's an excellent fastball hitter and showed improvement late last season in handling offspeed stuff. Young likes to do damage early in the count, so he doesn't walk much. He gets more anxious when he falls behind in the count. Those shortcomings haven't prevented him from posting consecutive seasons at .300 or better. He also has developed into an excellent pinch-hitter.

Baserunning & Defense

Cincinnati would like to see Young in better physical condition because he has become a subpar baserunner and outfielder. His speed is below average and he's not a threat to steal. He does look to take the extra base, however, and he has 78 doubles in the last two years. In 1999 Young played mostly right field, where his mediocre range and throwing arm are less than ideal. He'd be better off in left, or in the American League as a DH.

2000 Outlook

Youthful .300 hitters are hard to find, which is why Young continues to have value. Until he improves his power and run production and shows better awareness in the field, however, Cincinnati probably will view him as merely part of the outfield mix and not as a bona fide everyday player.

Overall Statistics

	G	AB	R	H	D	T	HR	RBI	SB	BB	SO	Avg	OBP	Slg
1999	127	373	63	112	30	2	14	56	3	30	71	.300	.352	.504
Career	397	1271	185	371	92	6	33	175	11	119	233	.292	.353	.452

Where He Hits the Ball

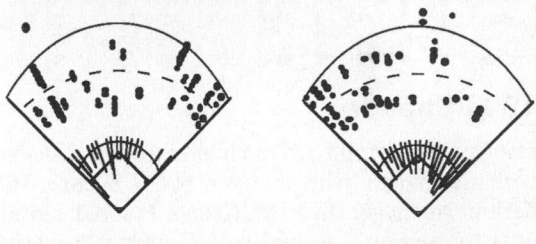

Vs. LHP   **Vs. RHP**

1999 Situational Stats

	AB	H	HR	RBI	Avg		AB	H	HR	RBI	Avg
Home	191	58	9	30	.304	LHP	109	29	3	13	.266
Road	182	54	5	26	.297	RHP	264	83	11	43	.314
First Half	137	32	3	11	.234	Sc Pos	107	28	4	43	.262
Scnd Half	236	80	11	45	.339	Clutch	62	19	0	8	.306

1999 Rankings (National League)
- 8th in errors in right field (3)

Danny Graves

Position: RP
Bats: R **Throws:** R
Ht: 5'11" **Wt:** 185

Opening Day Age: 26
Born: 8/7/73 in Saigon, Vietnam
ML Seasons: 4

Overall Statistics

	W	L	Pct.	ERA	G	GS	Sv	IP	H	BB	SO	HR	Ratio
1999	8	7	.533	3.08	75	0	27	111.0	90	49	69	10	1.25
Career	12	8	.600	3.59	167	0	35	248.0	236	107	146	20	1.38

1999 Situational Stats

	W	L	ERA	Sv	IP			AB	H	HR	RBI	Avg
Home	4	6	3.93	15	55.0	LHB		173	38	4	16	.220
Road	4	1	2.25	12	56.0	RHB		223	52	6	28	.233
First Half	6	3	3.54	12	61.0	Sc Pos		105	17	0	29	.162
Scnd Half	2	4	2.52	15	50.0	Clutch		233	55	7	32	.236

1999 Season

Danny Graves followed his impressive 1998 debut with Cincinnati with an even better encore. He became manager Jack McKeon's favored closer over the season's second half. Graves is a workhorse, ranking second to teammate Scott Sullivan in relief innings among National Leaguers.

Pitching, Defense & Hitting

Graves goes right after hitters with a two-seam fastball in the low 90s, and he mixes in a solid changeup that also sinks. He's equally effective against lefthanders and righthanders. He can be hittable when he leaves the ball up in the strike zone or falls behind in the count. Graves fields adequately, though like most relievers, he doesn't hold runners well. He's no threat as a hitter.

2000 Outlook

Teammate Scott Williamson has better pure stuff, but Graves enters 2000 as the Reds' prime closer. Don't be surprised, however, if Williamson wrests a greater share of the team's saves from him. In any case, Graves will continue to be a key element of Cincinnati's bullpen, the club's biggest strength.

Jeffrey Hammonds

Traded To ROCKIES

Position: RF/LF/CF
Bats: R **Throws:** R
Ht: 6'0" **Wt:** 195

Opening Day Age: 29
Born: 3/5/71 in Scotch Plains, NJ
ML Seasons: 7

Overall Statistics

	G	AB	R	H	D	T	HR	RBI	SB	BB	SO	Avg	OBP	Slg
1999	123	262	43	73	13	0	17	41	3	27	64	.279	.347	.523
Career	559	1697	275	455	93	9	68	235	42	149	331	.268	.329	.454

1999 Situational Stats

	AB	H	HR	RBI	Avg			AB	H	HR	RBI	Avg
Home	105	26	5	12	.248	LHP		140	42	8	17	.300
Road	157	47	12	29	.299	RHP		122	31	9	24	.254
First Half	141	33	7	22	.234	Sc Pos		66	14	1	20	.212
Scnd Half	121	40	10	19	.331	Clutch		43	12	3	6	.279

1999 Season

Once again Jeffrey Hammonds showed only glimpses of living up to his potential and couldn't prove he was worthy of playing every day. Hammonds played well in spots for Cincinnati as a part-time outfielder, batting .331 in the second half.

Hitting, Baserunning & Defense

Always a good fastball hitter, Hammonds has yet to show the ability to adjust to offspeed stuff or to consistently work counts in his favor. He gets himself out by trying to pull too many pitches. He was considered a five-tool prospect, but he lacks aggressiveness on the bases and his speed has eroded due to frequent leg problems. He's a dependable outfielder with just an average arm.

2000 Outlook

Hammonds couldn't earn an everyday job for the Reds, who traded him and Stan Belinda to the Rockies for Dante Bichette in October. Scheduled to make $3.1 million in the final season of a three-year contract, Hammonds will get a huge boost from Coors Field, where he hit three homers last May 19. He's the leading candidate to start in left field for Colorado.

Brian Johnson

Signed By ROYALS

Position: C
Bats: R **Throws:** R
Ht: 6' 2" **Wt:** 210

Opening Day Age: 32
Born: 1/8/68 in Oakland, CA
ML Seasons: 6

Overall Statistics

	G	AB	R	H	D	T	HR	RBI	SB	BB	SO	Avg	OBP	Slg
1999	45	117	12	27	7	0	5	18	0	9	31	.231	.286	.419
Career	431	1286	123	324	54	6	45	177	1	76	239	.252	.297	.408

1999 Situational Stats

	AB	H	HR	RBI	Avg		AB	H	HR	RBI	Avg
Home	68	16	3	12	.235	LHP	60	16	3	10	.267
Road	49	11	2	6	.224	RHP	57	11	2	8	.193
First Half	80	22	4	15	.275	Sc Pos	35	10	1	14	.286
Scnd Half	37	5	1	3	.135	Clutch	21	2	0	1	.095

1999 Season

A knee injury and Eddie Taubensee's breakout season limited Brian Johnson to only 26 starts with Cincinnati after he signed as a free agent for one year and $750,000. Johnson did little after returning from knee surgery in August, managing just five hits the rest of the year in brief action.

Hitting, Baserunning & Defense

Johnson has the strength to hit 15-20 homers if he plays regularly. He always has been streaky and injury-prone, so he never has done more than share time. He has solid power to the opposite field but has difficulty hitting good breaking stuff. What speed he had has been compromised by injuries, and he's no threat on the bases. Johnson is a solid receiver with an above-average arm.

2000 Outlook

Enamored of rookie catcher Jason LaRue, the Reds released Johnson in October. He signed two months later with the Royals, who gave him $550,000 for one season, with an additional $1 million if he catches 125 games. He could start for Kansas City.

Steve Parris

Position: SP
Bats: R **Throws:** R
Ht: 6' 0" **Wt:** 195

Opening Day Age: 32
Born: 12/17/67 in Joliet, IL
ML Seasons: 4

Overall Statistics

	W	L	Pct.	ERA	G	GS	Sv	IP	H	BB	SO	HR	Ratio
1999	11	4	.733	3.50	22	21	0	128.2	124	52	86	16	1.37
Career	23	18	.561	4.31	63	56	0	336.0	337	128	251	41	1.38

1999 Situational Stats

	W	L	ERA	Sv	IP		AB	H	HR	RBI	Avg
Home	6	2	4.22	0	64.0	LHB	209	63	6	23	.301
Road	5	2	2.78	0	64.2	RHB	268	61	10	29	.228
First Half	5	1	3.86	0	72.1	Sc Pos	110	23	6	36	.209
Scnd Half	6	3	3.04	0	56.1	Clutch	17	3	0	0	.176

1999 Season

Cincinnati sent Steve Parris to Triple-A to open the season, but upon his return in early May, he became one of the Reds' most important pitchers. He won seven of his first eight decisions before a strained tricep sidelined him for a month. Parris got the ball for the wild-card playoff game against the Mets, but lasted just 2.2 innings in a 5-0 loss to the Mets.

Pitching, Defense & Hitting

With average velocity, Parris doesn't overpower anyone. He succeeds thanks to his excellent feel for pitching. He mixes speeds well, keeps his two-seam fastball down in the strike zone and won't give in to hitters. Parris is far more effective versus righthanders, against whom his sinker tails away. He holds runners fairly well, is a solid fielder and can help himself with the bat.

2000 Outlook

After years of battling to keep his job, Parris has gone 17-9 in the last two seasons for the Reds. He has developed into a late bloomer who could be a double-digit winner for the next few years.

Cincinnati

Dennys Reyes

Position: RP
Bats: R **Throws:** L
Ht: 6' 3" **Wt:** 246

Opening Day Age: 22
Born: 4/19/77 in
Higuera de Zaragoza,
Mexico
ML Seasons: 3
Pronunciation:
RAY-ess

Overall Statistics

	W	L	Pct.	ERA	G	GS	Sv	IP	H	BB	SO	HR	Ratio
1999	2	2	.500	3.79	65	1	2	61.2	53	39	72	5	1.49
Career	7	10	.412	4.09	98	16	2	176.0	166	104	185	12	1.53

1999 Situational Stats

	W	L	ERA	Sv	IP		AB	H	HR	RBI	Avg
Home	1	1	1.82	2	34.2	LHB	95	23	2	14	.242
Road	1	1	6.33	0	27.0	RHB	133	30	3	19	.226
First Half	2	1	1.72	1	36.2	Sc Pos	69	18	1	29	.261
Scnd Half	0	1	6.84	1	25.0	Clutch	63	15	1	8	.238

1999 Season

Acquired in mid-1998 as part of the Jeff Shaw trade with the Dodgers, Dennys Reyes settled into Cincinnati's busy bullpen last year as an effective lefthanded middle reliever. Reyes never had made more than nine relief outings in a season, and he wore down en route to 64 appearances. His second-half ERA was 6.84, and he posted a 9.00 mark when called upon 14 times in the final month.

Pitching, Defense & Hitting

Reyes relies on a cut fastball, which he uses with equal success against lefthanders and righthanders. He'll change speeds with the cutter and spot a big overhand curve, which he often uses as a strikeout pitch. Reyes isn't in very good shape, which hurts him in several areas. He's error-prone as a fielder, vulnerable to basestealers and a very poor hitter.

2000 Outlook

Cincinnati quickly soured on Reyes as a starter. They hope his conditioning improves so he can sustain a role as a utility lefthander.

Scott Sullivan (Rubber Arm)

Position: RP
Bats: R **Throws:** R
Ht: 6' 3" **Wt:** 210

Opening Day Age: 29
Born: 3/13/71 in
Carrollton, AL
ML Seasons: 5

Overall Statistics

	W	L	Pct.	ERA	G	GS	Sv	IP	H	BB	SO	HR	Ratio
1999	5	4	.556	3.01	79	0	3	113.2	88	47	78	10	1.19
Career	15	12	.556	3.77	215	0	5	324.2	276	120	265	36	1.22

1999 Situational Stats

	W	L	ERA	Sv	IP		AB	H	HR	RBI	Avg
Home	3	2	3.33	0	51.1	LHB	153	37	3	15	.242
Road	2	2	2.74	3	62.1	RHB	253	51	7	27	.202
First Half	3	0	2.48	1	65.1	Sc Pos	92	18	2	30	.196
Scnd Half	2	4	3.72	2	48.1	Clutch	93	27	2	13	.290

1999 Season

In an age when pitchers are pampered more than ever, Scott Sullivan is a throwback. He has logged more than 100 relief innings in each of his two first season, last year becoming the first man to lead the National League in that category in two consecutive seasons since Kent Tekulve in 1978-79. Sullivan bounced back from a subpar 1998, lowering his ERA by 2.20 runs.

Pitching, Defense & Hitting

Sullivan's sidearm delivery and low-90s MPH fastball make him tough on righthanders. With an improved slider and more consistent running action of his fastball, he also handled lefties well last year. Sullivan had been a very easy mark for basestealers until 1999, when nine of 13 were caught on his watch. He's a shaky fielder and rarely makes contact as a hitter.

2000 Outlook

Sullivan's ability to take the ball nearly every day makes him a key member of the Reds' relief corps. He's a tough competitor who can be used as a closer, setup man or long reliever.

Michael Tucker

Position: RF/CF
Bats: L **Throws:** R
Ht: 6' 2" **Wt:** 185

Opening Day Age: 28
Born: 6/25/71 in South Boston, VA
ML Seasons: 5

Overall Statistics

	G	AB	R	H	D	T	HR	RBI	SB	BB	SO	Avg	OBP	Slg
1999	133	296	55	75	8	5	11	44	11	37	81	.253	.338	.426
Career	571	1725	267	451	88	19	54	216	43	188	429	.261	.339	.428

1999 Situational Stats

	AB	H	HR	RBI	Avg		AB	H	HR	RBI	Avg
Home	131	31	5	23	.237	LHP	39	6	2	7	.154
Road	165	44	6	21	.267	RHP	257	69	9	37	.268
First Half	186	49	6	31	.263	Sc Pos	89	26	2	33	.292
Scnd Half	110	26	5	13	.236	Clutch	43	14	2	6	.326

1999 Season

Acquired from Atlanta in the Denny Neagle-for-Bret Boone trade, Michael Tucker saw frequent action as a platoon outfielder. He struggled with the bat, especially in the second half, when he hit just .236 and endured a 1-for-29 slump.

Hitting, Baserunning & Defense

Once considered a top prospect, Tucker has become a part-time player because of his inability to hit lefthanders. He never has made adjustments at the plate, so he still overswings and tries to pull too many pitches. He hit .417 in his first month in the National League, but he's batted just .251 since. Tucker is very quick but isn't a particularly prolific basestealer. He's a solid outfielder with good range and an average arm, and he can play all three outfield positions.

2000 Outlook

Tucker still has too many flaws to be a productive everyday player. His skills make him a useful part-timer, though. Tucker's playing time could be reduced in 2000 if Dmitri Young grabs the right-field job all to himself.

Ron Villone

Position: SP
Bats: L **Throws:** L
Ht: 6' 3" **Wt:** 237

Opening Day Age: 30
Born: 1/16/70 in Englewood, NJ
ML Seasons: 5
Pronunciation: VA-lone

Overall Statistics

	W	L	Pct.	ERA	G	GS	Sv	IP	H	BB	SO	HR	Ratio
1999	9	7	.563	4.23	29	22	2	142.2	114	73	97	8	1.31
Career	13	11	.542	4.32	186	22	5	310.1	273	190	253	32	1.49

1999 Situational Stats

	W	L	ERA	Sv	IP		AB	H	HR	RBI	Avg
Home	4	4	5.61	0	67.1	LHB	87	22	2	13	.253
Road	5	3	2.99	2	75.1	RHB	433	92	6	47	.212
First Half	4	2	3.42	1	50.0	Sc Pos	136	35	2	48	.257
Scnd Half	5	5	4.66	1	92.2	Clutch	29	6	0	0	.207

1999 Season

Released by the Indians at the end of spring training, Ron Villone signed with the Reds and spent six weeks in Triple-A before being promoted in mid-May. Though he hadn't started a professional game since 1994, Villone moved into the rotation a month later and was a pleasant surprise. He won eight of 22 starts. At times he was overpowering, allowing just one hit in four different starts.

Pitching, Defense & Hitting

Control has kept Villone from breaking through, and he still walks too many hitters. To his credit, he has made his delivery more compact, which has helped him find the strike zone without sacrificing his low-90s velocity. He has developed a good curve and improved his changeup. Villone is an erratic fielder with a very good pickoff move, but his slow delivery allows basestealers to get good jumps. He's a feeble hitter.

2000 Outlook

With a full spring to train as a starter, Villone can become a solid part of the Cincinnati rotation. He has the stuff to win 12-15 games if he can maintain decent command.

Cincinnati

Gabe White

Position: RP
Bats: L **Throws:** L
Ht: 6' 2" **Wt:** 200

Opening Day Age: 28
Born: 11/20/71 in
Sebring, FL
ML Seasons: 5

Overall Statistics

	W	L	Pct.	ERA	G	GS	Sv	IP	H	BB	SO	HR	Ratio
1999	1	2	.333	4.43	50	0	0	61.0	68	14	61	13	1.34
Career	10	12	.455	4.68	157	15	11	250.0	243	69	211	47	1.25

1999 Situational Stats

	W	L	ERA	Sv	IP			AB	H	HR	RBI	Avg
Home	0	1	3.48	0	33.2	LHB		74	27	2	14	.365
Road	1	1	5.60	0	27.1	RHB		168	41	11	27	.244
First Half	1	2	4.05	0	40.0	Sc Pos		65	19	6	34	.292
Scnd Half	0	1	5.14	0	21.0	Clutch		69	19	4	16	.275

1999 Season

Gabe White shared Cincinnati's closing duties in 1998 after Jeff Shaw was traded, and was expected to open last season in the same role. But the emergence of eventual Rookie of the Year Scott Williamson relegated him to middle relief. White was ineffective at times, partly because he went long stretches without being used, but he did retire 22 straight batters at one point in June.

Pitching, Defense & Hitting

White throws an average fastball, a sinker and a changeup. With no real out pitch, he must hit his spots with his sinker or changeup to be effective. Lefthanders batted .365 against him last year, and he surrendered 11 homers to righties because he lacks the velocity to overpower them inside. White has yet to make a major league error and has a good pickoff move. He can't hit, though he can bunt.

2000 Outlook

White remains a serviceable lefthander who can pitch well in middle-inning roles. He's too hittable, however, to be viewed as an important part of the Cincinnati bullpen.

Scott Williamson

Position: RP
Bats: R **Throws:** R
Ht: 6' 0" **Wt:** 185

Opening Day Age: 24
Born: 2/17/76 in Ft.
Polk, LA
ML Seasons: 1

Overall Statistics

	W	L	Pct.	ERA	G	GS	Sv	IP	H	BB	SO	HR	Ratio
1999	12	7	.632	2.41	62	0	19	93.1	54	43	107	8	1.04
Career	12	7	.632	2.41	62	0	19	93.1	54	43	107	8	1.04

1999 Situational Stats

	W	L	ERA	Sv	IP			AB	H	HR	RBI	Avg
Home	8	1	1.72	8	52.1	LHB		146	25	5	12	.171
Road	4	6	3.29	11	41.0	RHB		169	29	3	17	.172
First Half	7	4	1.66	11	59.2	Sc Pos		77	12	2	19	.156
Scnd Half	5	3	3.74	8	33.2	Clutch		205	36	8	24	.176

1999 Season

A ninth-round pick in 1997, Scott Williamson never had made a pro relief appearance before making the Reds in spring training. He burst into the National League with a Rookie of the Year season that could have been even better if not for a finger injury and shoulder tendinitis late in the season. As it was, he led all NL rookies in wins, saves and relief innings.

Pitching, Defense & Hitting

Williamson has electric stuff, including a riding fastball that routinely is clocked in the upper 90s. He also throws a hard slider and is learning a changeup. He dominated both lefthanders and righthanders in 1999, as opponents batted just .171 against him. An average fielder, Williamson is easy pickings for basestealers, who went 13-for-13 with him on the mound. At the plate, he went hitless and fanned six times in seven at-bats.

2000 Outlook

After May, Williamson's ERA rose in each of the last four months, so he may not be able to duplicate his overpowering season. Yet he has special ability and should be a major force in the Cincy bullpen for years to come.

Other Cincinnati Reds

Steve Avery (Pos: LHP, Age: 29)

	W	L	Pct.	ERA	G	GS	Sv	IP	H	BB.	SO	HR	Ratio
1999	6	7	.462	5.16	19	19	0	96.0	75	78	51	11	1.59
Career	94	83	.531	4.17	278	261	0	1538.2	1510	562	974	143	1.35

Avery's control problems were as bad as ever before a torn labrum ended his season in late July. He's a free agent after declining an option with the Reds. 2000 Outlook: C

Stan Belinda (Pos: RHP, Age: 33)

	W	L	Pct.	ERA	G	GS	Sv	IP	H	BB	SO	HR	Ratio
1999	3	1	.750	5.27	29	0	2	42.2	42	18	40	11	1.41
Career	40	34	.541	3.89	529	0	78	638.2	535	263	571	71	1.25

Belinda missed the first half of 1999 with bicep tendinitis, and an acute case of gopheritis plagued him upon returning. The balls may fly out in 2000 as well, as he went to Colorado in an offseason trade. 2000 Outlook: B

Rick Greene (Pos: RHP, Age: 29)

	W	L	Pct.	ERA	G	GS	Sv	IP	H	BB	SO	HR	Ratio
1999	0	0	-	4.76	1	0	0	5.2	7	1	3	2	1.41
Career	0	0	-	4.76	1	0	0	5.2	7	1	3	2	1.41

While he doesn't strike out many hitters, Greene has been a solid Triple-A reliever the last three seasons. He was manhandled in his only Reds outing in 1999, allowing two homers in a Milwaukee romp in June. 2000 Outlook: C

Mark Lewis (Pos: 3B, Age: 30, Bats: R)

	G	AB	R	H	D	T	HR	RBI	SB	BB	SO	Avg	OBP	Slg
1999	88	173	18	44	16	0	6	28	0	7	24	.254	.280	.451
Career	814	2600	299	689	137	13	46	282	22	183	473	.265	.314	.381

With the emergence of both Pokey Reese and Aaron Boone, Lewis didn't play or produce much with the Reds in 1999. Still, he re-signed with the club for one year and $600,000. 2000 Outlook: B

Hal Morris (Pos: 1B, Age: 34, Bats: L)

	G	AB	R	H	D	T	HR	RBI	SB	BB	SO	Avg	OBP	Slg
1999	80	102	10	29	9	0	0	16	0	10	21	.284	.348	.373
Career	1147	3829	511	1169	237	20	73	499	45	325	522	.305	.360	.435

Even in a part-time role, Morris hit for average in his return to the Reds after one season in Kansas City. He broke a wrist in August, but he will stay in Cincinnati after signing a one-year, $500,000 contract in November. 2000 Outlook: B

Kerry Robinson (Pos: LF, Age: 26, Bats: L)

	G	AB	R	H	D	T	HR	RBI	SB	BB	SO	Avg	OBP	Slg
1999	9	1	4	0	0	0	0	0	0	0	1	.000	.000	.000
Career	11	4	4	0	0	0	0	0	0	0	2	.000	.000	.000

Robinson, a speedster who has hit for average in the high minors, was traded from Seattle to the Reds in July. He was used primarily as a pinch-runner the final month. 2000 Outlook: C

Chris Stynes (Pos: 2B, Age: 27, Bats: R)

	G	AB	R	H	D	T	HR	RBI	SB	BB	SO	Avg	OBP	Slg
1999	73	113	18	27	1	0	2	14	5	12	13	.239	.310	.301
Career	303	785	116	217	25	2	14	77	36	61	70	.276	.334	.367

Stynes hasn't come close to duplicating his 1997 performance—.348-6-28 in 198 at-bats—and he hit more than 100 points lower than that in '99. Yet he batted .348 in 46 at-bats from August on. 2000 Outlook: B

Mark Sweeney (Pos: 1B, Age: 30, Bats: L)

	G	AB	R	H	D	T	HR	RBI	SB	BB	SO	Avg	OBP	Slg
1999	37	31	6	11	3	0	2	7	0	4	9	.355	.429	.645
Career	409	634	76	168	29	3	11	80	7	93	122	.265	.358	.372

Sweeney was 5-for-14 with two homers and five RBI as a pinch-hitter before a numbers squeeze forced his demotion to the minors in mid-May. He came back in September and delivered more clutch hits. 2000 Outlook: B

Cincinnati Reds Minor League Prospects

Organization Overview:

The Reds' rejuvenation extended past their return to playoff contention in 1999. Their farm system was extremely productive after suffering from years of neglect until Marge Schott was exiled. Scott Williamson, a ninth-round pick in 1997, developed much more quickly than expected and won the National League Rookie of the Year Award. Aaron Boone grew into the third-base job. Even more indicative of the strides made by Cincinnati in player development was the fact that it actually had young, homegrown players that Seattle was willing to take in exchange for Ken Griffey Jr. Among the names mentioned were Pokey Reese, Brett Tomko, Williamson, minor league shortstop Travis Dawkins and 1999 first-round pick Ty Howington.

Rob Bell

Position: P **Opening Day Age:** 23
Bats: R **Throws:** R **Born:** 1/17/77 in
Ht: 6' 5" **Wt:** 225 Newburgh, NY

Recent Statistics

	W	L	ERA	G	GS	Sv	IP	H	R	BB	SO	HR
1998 A Danville	7	9	3.28	28	28	0	178.1	169	79	46	197	8
1999 R Reds	0	0	1.13	2	2	0	8.0	3	1	0	11	0
1999 AA Chattanooga	3	6	3.13	12	12	0	72.0	75	30	17	68	7

For the Reds, Rob Bell was the key to the Denny Neagle-Bret Boone trade with the Braves in November 1998. Cincinnati GM Jim Bowden immediately likened Bell to a cross between John Smoltz and Darryl Kile, who may be the two National League pitchers with the best pure stuff. A 1995 third-round pick, Bell scared the Reds when he strained his elbow in mid-April, but he didn't require surgery and returned strong in the second half. Easily the best pitching prospect in the system, he throws a sharp curveball and a 92-95 MPH fastball with fine command. Bell still needs a changeup, and he'll work on refining one this year in Triple-A.

Ben Broussard

Position: OF **Opening Day Age:** 23
Bats: L **Throws:** L **Born:** 9/24/76 in
Ht: 6' 2" **Wt:** 220 Beaumont, TX

Recent Statistics

	G	AB	R	H	D	T	HR	RBI	SB	BB	SO	Avg
1999 R Billings	38	145	39	59	11	2	14	48	1	34	30	.407
1999 A Clinton	5	20	8	11	4	1	2	6	0	3	4	.550
1999 AA Chattanooga	35	127	26	27	5	0	8	21	1	11	41	.213

Broussard has been the biggest surprise to come out of the 1999 draft, with the Reds or any organization. He went from an obscure senior at McNeese State to a second-round pick, then absolutely assaulted pro pitching. He batted .332-24-75 in 78 games, including 35 games at Double-A, then went to the California Fall League and topped all players with nine homers and 34 RBI while finishing second in hitting at .387. Broussard seemingly is limitless as a hitter. He has power, uses the entire field and walks a ton. He has good speed and made a decent conversion from first base to left field. Broussard is definitely in Dante Bichette's rear-view mirror.

Travis Dawkins

Position: SS **Opening Day Age:** 20
Bats: R **Throws:** R **Born:** 5/12/79 in
Ht: 6' 1" **Wt:** 180 Newberry, SC

Recent Statistics

	G	AB	R	H	D	T	HR	RBI	SB	BB	SO	Avg
1999 A Rockford	76	305	56	83	10	6	8	32	38	35	38	.272
1999 AA Chattanooga	32	129	24	47	7	0	2	13	15	14	17	.364
1999 NL Cincinnati	7	7	1	1	0	0	0	0	0	0	4	.143

Since being drafted in 1997's second round, Travis Dawkins has been compared to Pokey Reese. Both were high draft choices out of South Carolina high schools, and both initially excelled at shortstop while struggling at the plate. While Reese had a breakthrough season in the majors last year, Dawkins did the same in the minors. He backed up his stunning selection as the starting short-stop on the U.S. Pan American Games team by leading the Americans to a silver-medal finish that qualified them for the 2000 Olympics. He spent half the season in the Class-A Midwest League, where he was named the best baserunner, fastest baserunner and best defensive shortstop, before hitting .364 in 32 games in Double-A. Dawkins improved his power, patience and basestealing ability. He may need just a half-season in Triple-A before being ready for Cincinnati, but for now he's blocked by Barry Larkin and Reese.

Alejandro Diaz

Position: OF **Opening Day Age:** 21
Bats: R **Throws:** R **Born:** 7/9/78 in San
Ht: 5' 9" **Wt:** 175 Pedro de Macoris, D.R.

Recent Statistics

	G	AB	R	H	D	T	HR	RBI	SB	BB	SO	Avg
1999 A Clinton	55	221	39	63	14	3	6	41	28	12	35	.285
1999 AA Chattanooga	55	220	27	58	9	8	7	35	6	8	31	.264
1999 MLE	55	211	20	49	8	5	5	26	4	5	33	.232

After Alfonso Soriano "retired" from the Hiroshima Toyo Carp and signed with the Yankees for $3.1 million, the Japanese and U.S. major leagues entered an agreement that would allow Japanese clubs to sell their players directly to U.S. teams. The only player to go through the process in the first year afterward has been Diaz, whose rights were won by the Reds in a silent auction. They gave him a bonus of $1.175 million and their total cost reportedly approached $2 million. He already is a gifted center fielder with lots of speed and a strong arm. Diaz is more raw as a hitter, though he does have bat speed and power potential. If Mike Cameron falters, Diaz could challenge for his job after a season in Triple-A.

Adam Dunn

Position: OF   **Opening Day Age:** 20
Bats: L **Throws:** R   **Born:** 11/9/79 in
Ht: 6' 5"   **Wt:** 240   Houston, TX

Recent Statistics

	G	AB	R	H	D	T	HR	RBI	SB	BB	SO	Avg.
1998 R Billings	34	125	26	36	3	1	4	13	4	22	23	.288
1999 A Rockford	93	313	62	96	16	2	11	44	21	46	64	.307

Dunn is a prime example of Cincinnati's new emphasis on athletes. The Reds drafted him in the second round in 1998, gave him a $772,000 bonus and allowed him to play quarterback for the University of Texas. Dunn has held his own despite being one of the youngest players in his league in each of his two pro seasons, and there are few superior athletes in the game. He has prodigious power, is very fast for his size and even can throw in the low 90s. Despite splitting his efforts between two sports, he's a very advanced hitter. Dunn has decided to focus on baseball full-time, so the Reds won't have to worry about losing him to the gridiron and can develop him more quickly. His big league ETA is 2002.

Austin Kearns

Position: OF   **Opening Day Age:** 19
Bats: R **Throws:** R   **Born:** 5/20/80 in
Ht: 6' 4"   **Wt:** 210   Lexington, KY

Recent Statistics

	G	AB	R	H	D	T	HR	RBI	SB	BB	SO	Avg.
1998 R Billings	30	108	17	34	9	0	1	14	1	23	22	.315
1999 A Rockford	124	426	72	110	36	5	13	48	21	50	120	.258

Ryan Klesko was a highly regarded pitching prospect before injuring his arm in high school, but he recovered to have a successful big league career as a left fielder. Kearns may follow the same path. He threw 93-94 MPH as a high school junior before his fastball mysteriously plunged into the low 80s as a senior. Undaunted, the Reds made him the seventh overall pick in 1998 as an outfielder. He's an advanced hitter who should produce for both power and average. Kearns also has decent speed and an above-average arm. He's six months younger than Adam Dunn and has been pushed at the same rapid pace.

Brandon Larson

Position: 3B   **Opening Day Age:** 23
Bats: R **Throws:** R   **Born:** 5/24/76 in San
Ht: 6' 0"   **Wt:** 205   Angelo, TX

Recent Statistics

	G	AB	R	H	D	T	HR	RBI	SB	BB	SO	Avg.
1998 A Burlington	18	68	5	15	3	0	2	9	2	4	16	.221
1999 A Rockford	69	250	38	75	18	1	13	52	12	25	67	.300
1999 AA Chattanooga	43	172	28	49	10	0	12	42	4	10	51	.285

Larson's career had been a disaster since he was named College World Series MVP in June 1997, when he led Louisiana State to the national title. He sprained an ankle shortly after signing, then tore the anterior cruciate ligament in his left knee early in 1998. But after playing just 29 games in his first two pro seasons, he was healthy for most of 1999. He showed the power that got him drafted in the first round, driving balls out to all fields. Larson will hit for a better average if he can fine-tune his plate discipline. A college shortstop, he has made a nice transition to third base, where he shows a strong arm. If Larson can turn in a similar season in the upper minors this year, he could challenge Aaron Boone in 2001.

Jason LaRue

Position: C   **Opening Day Age:** 26
Bats: R **Throws:** R   **Born:** 3/19/74 in
Ht: 5' 11"   **Wt:** 200   Houston, TX

Recent Statistics

	G	AB	R	H	D	T	HR	RBI	SB	BB	SO	Avg.
1999 AAA Indianapolis	70	263	42	66	12	2	12	37	0	15	52	.251
1999 NL Cincinnati	36	90	12	19	7	0	3	10	4	11	32	.211
1999 MLE	70	252	30	55	10	1	8	27	0	11	54	.218

LaRue entered last season known primarily as an offensive player, having led Class-A hitters with 50 doubles in 1997 and Double-A players with a .365 batting average in 1998. In 1999, he made a huge impression as a defender. International League managers rated him the best defensive catcher in the Triple-A circuit, and he wowed the Reds with his work behind the plate when he was recalled last June. A 1995 fifth-round pick from Dallas Baptist, LaRue threw out 38 percent of basestealers who tested him in the majors, and his receiving skills improved significantly. He regressed at the plate, however, lengthening his swing and becoming less selective. LaRue will back up Eddie Taubensee in 2000.

Others to Watch

A converted catcher and the cousin of Hall of Famer Juan Marichal, righthander **Jose Acevedo** (22) has a fastball that fluctuates from 88 to 95 MPH. He struck out 136 in 133.2 Class-A innings last year. . . Outfielder **Brady Clark** (26) was the Southern League's MVP after leading the Double-A circuit in hitting at .326. He also has gap power, a good eye and an arm that was rated the best among Southern League outfielders. Though he's a bit old, the Reds love his makeup and will give him a chance. . . Outfielder **Mike Frank** (25) reached Cincinnati barely a year after signing as a 1997 seventh-round pick, but he was pretty much a forgotten man in 1999. He tried to add power and cost himself average, hitting .296—54 points below his minor league career mark entering the year. . . Lefthander **Ty Howington** (19), the Reds' 1999 first-round pick, signed late for $1.75 million and will make his pro debut in 2000. He throws a 93-96 MPH fastball and a hard curveball. . . Shortstop **Antonio Perez** (18) contributes to the organization's impressive middle-infield depth. He has blazing speed as well as surprising pop for a 5-foot-11, 175-pounder. . . Righthander **John Riedling** (24) could make the Reds as a middle reliever in the near future. He challenges hitters with a 90-95 MPH fastball and throws three other pitches.

Cincinnati

Coors Field

Offense

Combine the altitude, the dry air and the vast outfield, and Coors Field embellishes offensive numbers like no other ballpark in the history of the game. Scientists claim the ball carries 11 percent farther because of the elements. Breaking pitches break less. Outfielders must play deeper, allowing more hits to fall in. Many pitchers become timid in Colorado, walking hitters rather than challenging them, which sets the stage for big innings.

Defense

Coors Field places a premium on speed in the outfield because of its spacious dimensions. The Rockies plan to grow the infield grass taller this year to slow down grounders and give the pitchers one element in their favor. The grass has been so short and the ground so hard that the infield has played like artificial turf.

Who It Helps The Most

In 1999, the Rockies hit 77 points higher and drilled 144 of their 223 homers at Coors Field. The park has turned Larry Walker into a two-time batting champion, and Dante Bichette into an All-Star. It also has inflated the statistics of youngsters Todd Helton and Neifi Perez. Jerry Dipoto has survived Colorado better than any pitcher, posting a lower ERA at home (3.97) than on the road (4.53) in three years as a Rockie.

Who It Hurts The Most

Name a pitcher, any pitcher. Last year, the Rockies' ERA was 2.27 runs higher and they gave up 159 of their opponents' 237 homers at home. Nobody felt the impact more than Darryl Kile, whose 7.44 home ERA last season was worst in baseball.

Rookies & Newcomers

The Rockies have made several changes in the offseason, and it's easy to determine how the new players will be affected. Hitters Jeff Cirillo, Tom Goodwin, Jeffrey Hammonds, Aaron Ledesma, Brent Mayne, Ben Petrick and Scott Servais will enjoy Coors Field. Pitchers Rolando Arrojo, Manny Aybar, Stan Belinda, Rick Croushore, Jose Jimenez, Scott Karl, Mike Myers and Julian Tavarez won't.

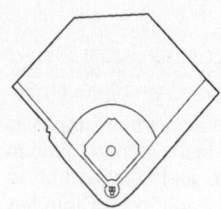

Dimensions: LF-347, LCF-390, CF-415, RCF-375, RF-350

Capacity: 50,381

Elevation: 5280 feet

Surface: Grass

Foul Territory: Small

Park Factors

1999 Season

	Home Games			Away Games			
	Rockies	Opp	Total	Rockies	Opp	Total	Index
G	75	75	150	75	75	150	—
Avg	.328	.329	.329	.249	.271	.259	127
AB	2731	2790	5521	2575	2451	5026	110
R	532	581	1113	310	373	683	163
H	895	919	1814	641	663	1304	139
2B	163	170	333	122	135	257	118
3B	26	22	48	11	15	26	168
HR	135	145	280	74	66	140	182
BB	247	356	603	221	324	545	101
SO	360	484	844	448	467	915	84
E	56	59	115	58	55	113	102
E-Infield	42	50	92	48	51	99	93
LHB-Avg	.356	.329	.343	.268	.296	.281	122
LHB-HR	58	50	108	31	23	54	187
RHB-Avg	.308	.330	.319	.235	.255	.245	130
RHB-HR	77	95	172	43	43	86	179

1997-1999

	Home Games			Away Games			
	Rockies	Opp	Total	Rockies	Opp	Total	Index
G	223	223	446	223	223	446	—
Avg	.325	.316	.320	.253	.273	.262	122
AB	7926	8180	16106	7625	7273	14898	108
R	1503	1500	3003	932	1050	1982	152
H	2572	2581	5153	1926	1982	3908	132
2B	466	475	941	362	403	765	114
3B	66	66	132	40	49	89	137
HR	347	351	698	247	199	446	145
BB	756	842	1598	665	865	1530	97
SO	1148	1302	2450	1479	1298	2777	82
E	152	190	342	157	155	312	110
E-Infield	111	156	267	134	131	265	101
LHB-Avg	.344	.323	.333	.271	.289	.280	119
LHB-HR	126	139	265	100	86	186	130
RHB-Avg	.312	.310	.311	.241	.260	.250	124
RHB-HR	221	212	433	147	113	260	156

1999 Rankings (National League)

- Highest batting-average factor
- Highest run factor
- Highest hit factor
- Highest home-run factor
- Highest LHB batting-average factor
- Highest LHB home-run factor
- Highest RHB batting-average factor
- Highest RHB home-run factor
- Second-highest double factor
- Second-highest triple factor
- Lowest strikeout factor

Buddy Bell

1999 Season

Fired by Detroit in September 1998, Buddy Bell spent last year as Cincinnati's farm director. He also managed the U.S. Pan American Games team to a silver medal, qualifying the United States for the 2000 Olympics. His strong feelings for the potential of new Rockies general manager Dan O'Dowd led him to accept the Colorado job for three years and $2.25 million. He replaced Jim Leyland, who resigned after just one season. Bell had other alternatives. He was considered the heir apparent to Jack McKeon in Cincinnati, where he grew up and still lived, and also was on the short lists in Baltimore and Cleveland.

Offense

Bell understands a hitters' park, having spent nearly three seasons managing Detroit. Now he gets to spend 81 games in the ultimate offensive hotbed, Coors Field. Bell likes to keep his team in motion by aggressively employing the steal and the hit-and-run. That was a key to the success the Rockies enjoyed under Don Baylor, but a missing element during Leyland's disappointing reign.

Pitching & Defense

Bell will rely heavily on Marcel Lachemann to handle the mound corps. One of the most respected pitching coaches in the game, Lachemann will have the challenge of refining raw potential that others haven't been able to refine, particularly with Manny Aybar, Jose Jimenez and Jamey Wright. Bell is a big believer in fundamentals, which he mastered as a Gold Glove third baseman. He's a stickler for not giving away outs or allowing baserunners to take extra bases.

2000 Outlook

Bell faces a year of regrouping for the Rockies, who are coming off the first last-place finish in franchise history and an offseason of roster re-vamping. The expectations won't be as high as they had been after the Rockies surprised baseball by claiming the National League wild card in 1995. Bell helped young players develop in Detroit, and Colorado hopes he can do the same with Todd Helton, Neifi Perez and Ben Petrick.

Born: 8/27/51 in Pittsburgh, PA

Playing Experience: 1972-1989, Cle, Tex, Cin, Hou

Managerial Experience: 3 seasons

Manager Statistics

Year	Team, Lg	W	L	Pct	GB	Finish
1999		—	—	—	—	—
3 Seasons		184	277	.399	—	—

1999 Starting Pitchers by Days Rest

	<=3	4	5	6+
Rockies Starts	—	—	—	—
Rockies ERA	—	—	—	—
NL Avg Starts	3	81	48	21
NL ERA	4.84	4.53	4.72	4.98

1999 Situational Stats

	Buddy Bell	NL Average
Hit & Run Success %	—	33.6
Stolen Base Success %	—	70.2
Platoon Pct.	—	55.2
Defensive Subs	—	25
High-Pitch Outings	—	13
Quick/Slow Hooks	—	16/15
Sacrifice Attempts	—	89

1999 Rankings (National League)

- Did not manage in the majors last year

Pedro Astacio

1999 Season

Pedro Astacio enjoyed a breakthrough season for Colorado. He equaled a franchise record with 17 wins, and set Rockies marks for complete games, innings and strikeouts. He learned to ignore the high-scoring games that are a given at Coors Field, and didn't change his approach. Astacio ranked second in the National League with 12 road wins, compiling a 3.60 ERA away from Colorado.

Pitching

The key for Astacio is mixing his four pitches and keeping hitters off balance. His success starts with challenging hitters with a lively 92-93 MPH fastball. When he gets ahead in the count, he can toy with a hard slider and a big-breaking curve. He battles lefthanders with a changeup. When Astacio has the confidence he showed last year, he doesn't lock onto his fastball when he's in trouble. He can get groundballs when he needs them in a jam.

Defense & Hitting

Astacio is agile on the mound, though he makes needless errors when his concentration wanders. He has a quick release to the plate, which allows catchers a chance to throw out basestealers. Astacio got serious about his hitting last year and set a Rockies record for pitchers with 20 hits. He also can lay down a bunt when he puts his mind to it.

2000 Outlook

Now that he knows he can be a big winner, Astacio can take the next step. He realizes that victories, not ERA, get people's attention, especially when he's trying to survive at Coors Field. Given his confidence and the guidance of new pitching coach Marcel Lachemann, look for Astacio to build off 1999. He has a shot at becoming the first 20-game winner in franchise history.

Position: SP
Bats: R **Throws:** R
Ht: 6' 2" **Wt:** 210

Opening Day Age: 30
Born: 11/28/69 in Hato Mayor, Dominican Republic
ML Seasons: 8
Pronunciation: uh-STAH-see-oh

Overall Statistics

	W	L	Pct.	ERA	G	GS	Sv	IP	H	BB	SO	HR	Ratio
1999	17	11	.607	5.04	34	34	0	232.0	258	75	210	38	1.44
Career	83	73	.532	4.32	250	207	0	1376.2	1400	441	1029	164	1.34

How Often He Throws Strikes

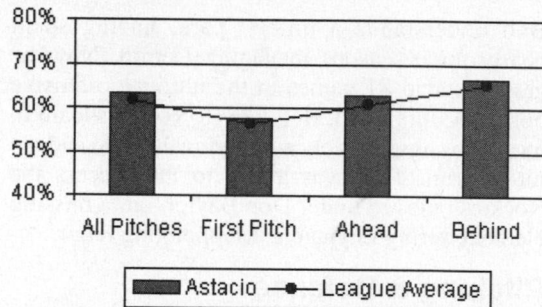

1999 Situational Stats

	W	L	ERA	Sv	IP		AB	H	HR	RBI	Avg
Home	5	5	7.16	0	94.1	LHB	409	125	13	54	.306
Road	12	6	3.60	0	137.2	RHB	497	133	25	74	.268
First Half	8	8	5.67	0	125.1	Sc Pos	224	66	7	90	.295
Scnd Half	9	3	4.30	0	106.2	Clutch	81	20	1	6	.247

1999 Rankings (National League)

- 1st in home runs allowed
- 2nd in hits allowed
- 3rd in complete games (7), strikeouts, runners caught stealing (14) and highest ERA at home
- Led the Rockies in ERA, wins, complete games (7), innings pitched, hits allowed, batters faced (1,008), home runs allowed, strikeouts, pitches thrown (3,649), winning percentage, highest strikeout/walk ratio (2.8), lowest batting average allowed (.285), lowest slugging percentage allowed (.479), lowest on-base percentage allowed (.343), lowest stolen-base percentage allowed (63.2), fewest pitches thrown per batter (3.62), fewest baserunners allowed per nine innings (13.3)

Dante Bichette

Position: LF
Bats: R **Throws:** R
Ht: 6' 3" **Wt:** 238

Opening Day Age: 36
Born: 11/18/63 in West Palm Beach, FL
ML Seasons: 12
Pronunciation: DON-tay bih-SHET

Colorado

1999 Season

Another year, another 30-plus home runs and 120-plus RBI for Dante Bichette. The only thing missing was another .300 season, as a late-season fade left him two points shy. His left-field play became a growing concern, and it cost Bichette some at-bats when he was pulled for late-inning defensive replacements.

Hitting

Bichette is a legitimate run producer. He'll make the adjustments if he gets behind in the count or the game is on the line, spreading out his stance and looking to the opposite field. He has bulked up so much in recent years that he has to cheat to have a chance on inside fastballs. Bichette guesses on every pitch and is one of the game's best at staying on breaking pitches when he correctly predicts that they're coming. He actually showed some discipline last year but tends to throw away at-bats early in the game, which can take the team out of big innings.

Baserunning & Defense

Bichette thought reconstructive knee surgery after the 1996 season would be a cure-all, but he lost a couple of steps. He now has below-average speed and also has become a stiff player. He's poor on a straight steal but has some success at reading pitchers and working a delayed steal. Bichette doesn't read balls well off the bat, misses cutoff men consistently and floats throws to the infield. His 13 errors led major league left fielders in 1999. So did his 17 assists, the result of the fact that every runner challenges him.

2000 Outlook

Looking to remake the Rockies, new GM Dan O'Dowd traded Bichette to the Reds for Jeffrey Hammonds and Stan Belinda in October. The only salvation for Bichette is that outside of Coors Field, he hits better at Cinergy Field than anywhere else. But project his road stats for the last five years over a full season, and he'd hit .273-17-84, not much for a left fielder who will make $7 million in each of the next two seasons.

Overall Statistics

	G	AB	R	H	D	T	HR	RBI	SB	BB	SO	Avg	OBP	Slg
1999	151	593	104	177	38	2	34	133	6	54	84	.298	.354	.541
Career	1442	5415	809	1625	339	24	239	1002	145	286	911	.300	.335	.504

Where He Hits the Ball

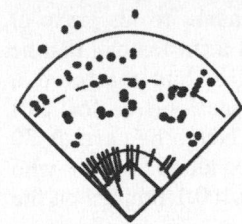

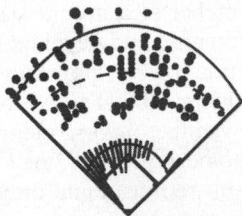

Vs. LHP   **Vs. RHP**

1999 Situational Stats

	AB	H	HR	RBI	Avg		AB	H	HR	RBI	Avg
Home	318	98	20	82	.308	LHP	166	52	8	33	.313
Road	275	79	14	51	.287	RHP	427	125	26	100	.293
First Half	331	92	18	70	.278	Sc Pos	181	62	6	91	.343
Scnd Half	262	85	16	63	.324	Clutch	96	32	4	17	.333

1999 Rankings (National League)

- 1st in errors in left field (13), sacrifice flies (10) and lowest fielding percentage in left field (.952)
- 4th in RBI
- 8th in lowest percentage of extra bases taken as a runner (37.9)
- 10th in total bases (321)
- Led the Rockies in cleanup slugging percentage (.544), RBI, sacrifice flies (10), caught stealing (6), strikeouts and GDPs (15)
- Led NL left fielders in cleanup slugging percentage (.544), RBI and sacrifice flies (10)

Brian Bohanon

1999 Season

After signing a three-year, $9 million contract as a free agent, Brian Bohanon showed his toughness. He refused to come out of the rotation despite five bone chips in his left elbow, which required post-season surgery. On days when the chips didn't bother him, he displayed a feel for pitching that allowed him to notch 12 wins despite a 6.20 ERA. Though he struggled at Coors Field as all Rockies pitchers do, he didn't let it bother him as much as most.

Pitching

Bohanon's stuff is mediocre at best. His fastball is usually in the mid-80s, though he can touch 90 MPH on a good day. He has gone from a borderline pitcher to a decent starter, thanks to his grasp of pitching and development of a cut fastball that he runs in on righthanders. He has mastered a changeup that allows him to sneak his fastball past even the biggest swingers. Though he gave up 30 homers in 1999, he's a groundball pitcher who allowed just eight dingers in 100.1 innings on the road.

Defense & Hitting

Bohanon's bulky body costs him mobility. He can field his position but is slow to cover first base. He doesn't have a particularly good move to first, and his reliance makes him vulnerable to basestealers. Bohanon can handle the bat, bunting well and putting the ball in play.

2000 Outlook

Bohanon has had a year to adjust to Coors Field and a winter to recover from arthroscopic elbow surgery. He's a sleeper for a 15-win season because he's mentally tough. He knows he'll get pounded in Colorado and realize the key to success there isn't overpowering hitters but simply outpitching his opponent. Bohanon's statistics won't be pretty, but he'll get the job done.

Position: SP
Bats: L **Throws:** L
Ht: 6' 2"   **Wt:** 240

Opening Day Age: 31
Born: 8/1/68 in Denton, TX
ML Seasons: 10
Pronunciation: boe-HAN-un

Overall Statistics

	W	L	Pct.	ERA	G	GS	Sv	IP	H	BB	SO	HR	Ratio
1999	12	12	.500	6.20	33	33	0	197.1	236	92	120	30	1.66
Career	37	42	.468	5.07	250	112	2	842.0	921	363	526	98	1.52

How Often He Throws Strikes

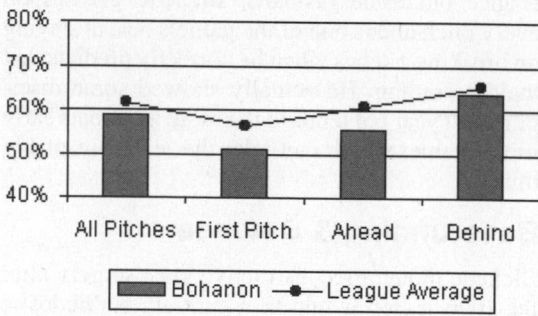

1999 Situational Stats

	W	L	ERA	Sv	IP		AB	H	HR	RBI	Avg
Home	6	5	7.42	0	97.0	LHB	147	47	7	23	.320
Road	6	7	5.02	0	100.1	RHB	628	189	23	112	.301
First Half	9	7	6.62	0	103.1	Sc Pos	220	72	8	100	.327
Scnd Half	3	5	5.74	0	94.0	Clutch	28	9	3	6	.321

1999 Rankings (National League)

- 2nd in hit batsmen (14), highest ERA, highest batting average allowed (.305), highest on-base percentage allowed (.387), most baserunners allowed per nine innings (15.6), highest ERA at home and highest batting average allowed with runners in scoring position
- 4th in highest slugging percentage allowed (.498)
- 5th in stolen bases allowed (25)
- Led the Rockies in hit batsmen (14), stolen bases allowed (25) and fewest home runs allowed per nine innings (1.37)

Vinny Castilla

1999 Season

The expectations that Vinny Castilla has created are underscored by the fact that his 1999 performance was a disappointment. Coming off a career .319-46-144 season, he fell short of 40 homers and 110 RBI for the first time since the shortened 1995 season. He also failed to hit .300 for the first time in the five years he has been a regular, never making a serious challenge at the mark. Castilla was bothered by some back soreness that affected his agility.

Hitting

The harder the fastball, the more Castilla likes it. He's particularly explosive if a pitcher hasn't learned to never throw a first-pitch fastball to Mexico's all-time home-run leader. When Castilla is locked in he'll drive the ball to the center of the field, and during those stretches he can hit anything and anyone. He has the power to hit the ball out to the biggest part of any park in the major leagues. When he goes into a funk, though, he becomes pull-conscious and chases bad breaking pitches.

Baserunning & Defense

Castilla is slow. He doesn't steal bases and he's a station-to-station runner. He'll only run in hit-and-run situations. A solid third baseman, Castilla lacks the first-step quickness to get the Gold Glove consideration he craves. He has an extremely powerful and accurate arm, which allows him to cheat toward the bag. He charges the ball extremely well and will get off a strong throw even if he's off balance, making it difficult for the opposition to bunt.

2000 Outlook

Castilla was shipped to Tampa Bay in a four-team deal that netted the Rockies his replacement, Jeff Cirillo, plus starters Rolando Arrojo and Scott Karl. Castilla skipped winter ball for the first time in his career this year to make sure his back is healthy for 2000. His pride was hurt by a season that didn't meet expectations, and he has something to prove. He'll miss Coors Field, though he'll make a run at 30 homers.

Position: 3B
Bats: R **Throws:** R
Ht: 6' 1"   **Wt:** 205

Opening Day Age: 32
Born: 7/4/67 in Oaxaca, Mexico
ML Seasons: 9
Pronunciation: cas-TEE-yah

Colorado

Overall Statistics

	G	AB	R	H	D	T	HR	RBI	SB	BB	SO	Avg	OBP	Slg
1999	158	615	83	169	24	1	33	102	2	53	75	.275	.331	.478
Career	956	3516	518	1049	166	17	203	611	22	223	521	.298	.342	.528

Where He Hits the Ball

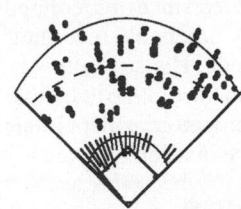

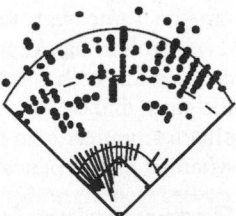

Vs. LHP   **Vs. RHP**

1999 Situational Stats

	AB	H	HR	RBI	Avg		AB	H	HR	RBI	Avg
Home	307	86	20	56	.280	LHP	169	38	8	19	.225
Road	308	83	13	46	.269	RHP	446	131	25	83	.294
First Half	329	92	19	57	.280	Sc Pos	172	43	6	63	.250
Scnd Half	286	77	14	45	.269	Clutch	89	23	5	19	.258

1999 Rankings (National League)

- 3rd in errors at third base (19)
- 5th in fewest pitches seen per plate appearance (3.27), lowest fielding percentage at third base (.954) and lowest percentage of pitches taken (46.2)
- 6th in lowest batting average vs. lefthanded pitchers
- 8th in at-bats and lowest on-base percentage vs. lefthanded pitchers (.307)
- Led the Rockies in GDPs (15)
- Led NL third basemen in highest groundball/fly-ball ratio (1.2)

Todd Helton

Position: 1B
Bats: L **Throws:** L
Ht: 6' 2" **Wt:** 206

Opening Day Age: 26
Born: 8/20/73 in Knoxville, TN
ML Seasons: 3

1999 Season

Todd Helton, the 1998 runner-up for National League Rookie of the Year, successfully avoided the sophomore jinx. His batting average was just .262 on June 11, but by the end of the season he had surpassed his first-year numbers. He did have problems against lefthanders and on the road, however.

Hitting

In two full big league seasons, Helton already has done more than what scouts projected when he came out of the University of Tennessee as a first-round pick. He now turns on pitches and drives them out of the park. He can be overpowered by high fastballs, but pitchers pay if they try to get him out the same way twice. Ever since his college days, Helton has kept a daily notebook, recording every pitch he has been thrown. His strength is in the gaps, and he has the mental discipline to handle clutch situations. He becomes a more patient hitter when he has a chance to drive in a run.

Baserunning & Defense

It's obvious that the Volunteers didn't run the option when Helton was their quarterback. He generally takes one base at a time, though he'll take advantage if an outfielder gets lackadaisical. Helton is a solid defensive first baseman with a chance to get better. He doesn't move exceptionally well, but he has the soft hands to pick throws out of the dirt. He also has a strong and accurate arm, and isn't afraid to look for the force at second or third.

2000 Outlook

This year Helton figures to take another step toward becoming one of the game's more productive hitters. To be accepted as such, he'll need to improve on the road, where he has batted .262-26-77 in 580 at-bats. Helton should move into the No. 5 slot in the batting order, giving him more RBI opportunities.

Overall Statistics

	G	AB	R	H	D	T	HR	RBI	SB	BB	SO	Avg	OBP	Slg
1999	159	578	114	185	39	5	35	113	7	68	77	.320	.395	.587
Career	346	1201	205	378	78	7	65	221	10	129	142	.315	.384	.554

Where He Hits the Ball

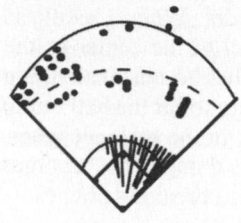 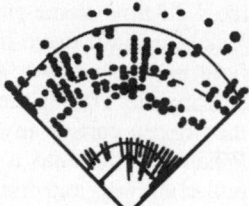

Vs. LHP   **Vs. RHP**

1999 Situational Stats

	AB	H	HR	RBI	Avg		AB	H	HR	RBI	Avg
Home	296	114	23	75	.385	LHP	163	40	4	28	.245
Road	282	71	12	38	.252	RHP	415	145	31	85	.349
First Half	300	89	16	56	.297	Sc Pos	156	49	13	82	.314
Scnd Half	278	96	19	57	.345	Clutch	79	19	5	21	.241

1999 Rankings (National League)

- 2nd in batting average vs. righthanded pitchers, slugging percentage vs. righthanded pitchers (.670) and batting average at home
- 4th in errors at first base (9)
- 5th in total bases (339) and lowest fielding percentage at first base (.993)
- Led the Rockies in most pitches seen per plate appearance (3.79), batting average vs. righthanded pitchers, slugging percentage vs. righthanded pitchers (.670), on-base percentage vs. righthanded pitchers (.424), highest percentage of pitches taken (56.7), runs scored, doubles, total bases (339), caught stealing (6), walks, times on base (259), pitches seen (2,492) and games played

Darryl Kile

Position: SP
Bats: R **Throws:** R
Ht: 6' 5" **Wt:** 212

Opening Day Age: 31
Born: 12/2/68 in
Garden Grove, CA
ML Seasons: 9

1999 Season

After two years, even Darryl Kile had to admit that Coors Field won the battle. He had the highest home ERA (7.44) of any big league starter last year. His struggles carried over to the road, where he went 3-10 and the Rockies lost 14 of his 17 starts. Kile's control disappeared and he never won consecutive starts before a sore shoulder ended his season in late September.

Pitching

Kile has one of the game's premier curveballs and can change speeds with it. He also has a solid average fastball, but that's the pitch that betrayed him at Coors Field. He throws a two-seamer and four-seamer, but has a tendency to fall in love with the latter, which comes on the same plane as his curve and gets hammered. Kile was so tentative last year that he couldn't throw his fastball for strikes, allowing hitters to ignore his curve. Trying to figure out a way to catch hitters off guard, he has developed a decent slider and will throw a splitter when he has the count in his favor.

Defense & Hitting

Kile has to work at everything he does because he's not a natural athlete. He has become a decent fielder, but rushes and makes sloppy mistakes on bunts. He'll use a slide step to give catchers a chance to throw out basestealers. Kile prides himself on being able to handle the bat, but last year even that was a challenge.

2000 Outlook

Rather than pay him $8 million for 2000, the Rockies traded Kile, Luther Hackman and Dave Veres to St. Louis in November for Manny Aybar, Rick Croushore, Jose Jimenez and minor league shortstop Brent Butler. Kile has reason to be excited after escaping Coors Field, where his problems were exaggerated last year by the lack of an experienced pitching coach who could help get his mechanics back in order. With guidance from Cardinals pitching guru Dave Duncan, who specializes in fixing broken veteran pitchers, Kile could have a big season.

Overall Statistics

	W	L	Pct.	ERA	G	GS	Sv	IP	H	BB	SO	HR	Ratio
1999	8	13	.381	6.61	32	32	0	190.2	225	109	116	33	1.75
Career	92	95	.492	4.32	277	249	0	1621.0	1610	767	1247	150	1.47

How Often He Throws Strikes

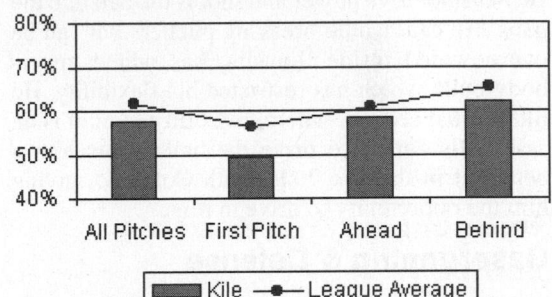

1999 Situational Stats

	W	L	ERA	Sv	IP		AB	H	HR	RBI	Avg
Home	5	3	7.44	0	88.1	LHB	359	114	16	79	.318
Road	3	10	5.89	0	102.1	RHB	395	111	17	55	.281
First Half	5	7	5.93	0	112.1	Sc Pos	216	68	8	99	.315
Scnd Half	3	6	7.58	0	78.1	Clutch	45	17	3	8	.378

1999 Rankings (National League)

- 1st in highest ERA, lowest strikeout/walk ratio (1.1), highest on-base percentage allowed (.387), most baserunners allowed per nine innings (16.0) and highest ERA at home
- 2nd in GDPs induced (28) and most walks per nine innings (5.1)
- 3rd in walks allowed, wild pitches (13) and highest slugging percentage allowed (.504)
- 4th in highest batting average allowed with runners in scoring position and most home runs allowed per nine innings (1.56)
- 5th in home runs allowed
- Led the Rockies in losses, walks allowed, wild pitches (13), GDPs induced (28) and highest groundball/flyball ratio allowed (1.3)

Mike Lansing

1999 Season

Nothing has gone right for Mike Lansing in the two years since he got his long-desired trade to the Rockies, allowing him to play near his home in Wyoming. Slowed by back problems in 1998, Lansing underwent an extensive offseason conditioning program and even had laser eye surgery in an effort to ensure a strong rebound last year. It didn't work, and by early May his back problems flared up again. Lansing needed major back surgery, just like he did a decade earlier after his junior year at Wichita State.

Hitting

Lansing has a short stroke made for Coors Field. He has line-drive power and shoots the ball into the gaps. He can handle breaking pitchers but can be overpowered inside. Lansing has added upper-body bulk, which has restricted his flexibility. He likes to bat second, where his ability to bunt is an asset. His ability to drive the ball makes him a better fit in the No. 7 slot with Colorado, giving him the opportunity to drive in runs.

Baserunning & Defense

Lansing's speed has begun to disappear and his surgery doesn't figure to help. No longer much of a threat to steal, he's smart enough to make pitchers pay if they ignore him. He's an aggressive baserunner and will take the extra base. Lansing isn't a fluid second baseman, but he's not afraid to get dirty and gets the job done. He's tough enough to hang in on the double play, though his back problems have made it difficult for him to move well around the bag. They've also restricted his range, and he dives for balls other second baseman can reach much more easily.

2000 Outlook

Lansing's future is a crapshoot. Players don't come back quickly from back surgery, and he may need two years to return to form. Lansing, however, has been through all this before. He was slightly ahead of schedule in his rehab and has a desire to prove he belongs in Colorado.

Position: 2B
Bats: R **Throws:** R
Ht: 6' 0" **Wt:** 195

Opening Day Age: 31
Born: 4/3/68 in Rawlins, WY
ML Seasons: 7
Nickname: Laser

Overall Statistics

	G	AB	R	H	D	T	HR	RBI	SB	BB	SO	Avg	OBP	Slg
1999	35	145	24	45	9	0	4	15	2	7	22	.310	.344	.455
Career	865	3294	437	915	213	11	65	346	108	239	445	.278	.332	.408

Where He Hits the Ball

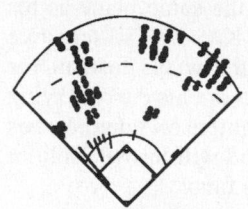
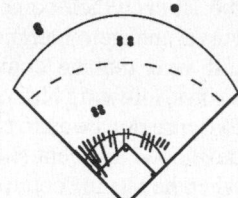

Vs. LHP   **Vs. RHP**

1999 Situational Stats

	AB	H	HR	RBI	Avg		AB	H	HR	RBI	Avg
Home	58	18	2	6	.310	LHP	53	18	1	5	.340
Road	87	27	2	9	.310	RHP	92	27	3	10	.293
First Half	145	45	4	15	.310	Sc Pos	33	9	0	10	.273
Scnd Half	0	0	0	0	-	Clutch	16	6	1	3	.375

1999 Rankings (National League)

- Did not rank near the top or bottom in any category

Neifi Perez

Position: SS
Bats: B **Throws:** R
Ht: 6' 0" **Wt:** 175

Opening Day Age: 25
Born: 2/2/75 in Villa Mella, Dominican Republic
ML Seasons: 4
Pronunciation: NAY-fee

Colorado

1999 Season

Neifi Perez was thrown into the uncomfortable role of hitting leadoff last season. It wasn't an ideal situation for a player who entered the year with a career .313 on-base percentage, and he prefers to bat second, but that didn't prevent Perez from putting together a solid second full year in the big leagues. He reached double figures in doubles, triples and homers, and he continued to look at ease at shortstop.

Hitting

Perez taught himself to switch-hit in his first year of pro ball. He has more power from his natural right side, but he's a better hitter lefthanded. He's helped tremendously by Coors Field, away from which he's about as productive as Rey Ordonez. Perez is one of the game's best bunters, though he got away from that part of his game in 1999. He likes fastballs and has the bat speed to drive them. He remains susceptible to breaking pitches and will chase sliders in the dirt. Perez has yet to learn the patience to force pitchers to challenge him. If he learns to swing only at strikes, he'll be special.

Baserunning & Defense

Perez is an above-average runner, but lacks the first-step explosiveness needed to become a basestealing threat. His speed, however, does show up when he hits balls in the gap. He loves running out triples. His athleticism—the Rockies discovered him playing for a junior national basketball team in his native Dominican Republic—is apparent with his play at shortstop. He has soft hands and a strong arm. He'll hang in on double plays, but often commits errors on ill-advised throws.

2000 Outlook

Aided by Coors Field, Perez could claim a place among the game's elite shortstops. With two full big league seasons to his credit and the return of hitting coach Clint Hurdle, who has a special rapport with him, Perez should finally reach the .300 level. He figures to drop down in the lineup, either to second or seventh, which will give him a chance to drive in more runs.

Overall Statistics

	G	AB	R	H	D	T	HR	RBI	SB	BB	SO	Avg	OBP	Slg
1999	157	690	108	193	27	11	12	70	13	28	54	.280	.307	.403
Career	419	1695	238	468	67	30	26	163	24	87	175	.276	.311	.397

Where He Hits the Ball

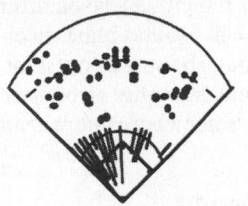 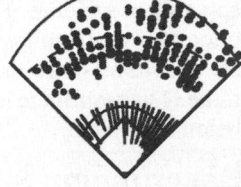

Vs. LHP   **Vs. RHP**

1999 Situational Stats

	AB	H	HR	RBI	Avg		AB	H	HR	RBI	Avg
Home	356	109	8	46	.306	LHP	209	48	6	22	.230
Road	334	84	4	24	.251	RHP	481	145	6	48	.301
First Half	345	100	7	41	.290	Sc Pos	148	39	4	52	.264
Scnd Half	345	93	5	29	.270	Clutch	94	24	1	11	.255

1999 Rankings (National League)

- 1st in at-bats, triples, lowest on-base percentage for a leadoff hitter (.297) and lowest on-base percentage vs. lefthanded pitchers (.257)
- 2nd in fielding percentage at shortstop (.981) and plate appearances (732)
- 3rd in bunts in play (29), singles, lowest on-base percentage and fewest pitches seen per plate appearance (3.18)
- Led the Rockies in fewest GDPs per GDP situation (3.3%), batting average with the bases loaded (.455), highest percentage of extra bases taken as a runner (66.7), bunts in play (29), at-bats, hits, singles, triples, sacrifice bunts (9) and plate appearances (732)

Ben Petrick

1999 Season

A second-round draft pick in 1995, Ben Petrick finally had the breakthrough offensive year the Rockies had anticipated. After opening the season at Double-A for the second year in a row, he earned the starting job for the U.S. team in the Futures Game at Fenway Park. Petrick made his major league debut in September and quickly took a liking to Coors Field. He homered four times in 12 home games.

Hitting

Petrick has a quick bat and the strength to drive the ball. With the spaciousness of Coors Field and his line-drive ability, he should hit plenty of doubles. He already has the power to reach double figures in homers, and could hit 20 or more in a season after he gains experience. Petrick has sound plate discipline for a young player, though he strikes out a lot. He should hit more than enough to play elsewhere if the Rockies decide he fits somewhere better than behind the plate.

Baserunning & Defense

A former Oregon high school football player of the year as a quarterback/defensive back, Petrick is very athletic for a catcher, resembling Craig Biggio when he broke in with the Astros. Petrick has the speed and instincts to be a basestealer and take extra bases. The question is whether he can translate his physical gifts into success behind the plate. He needs to clean up mechanical problems that have hindered his throwing for two season, though the arm strength is there. He's agile enough to become a solid receiver.

2000 Outlook

New manager Buddy Bell is convinced that with the season-long tutelage of coach Fred Kendall, Petrick can blossom at the big league level. The Rockies will give him a chance to be their primary catcher, though they added insurance by signing two Giants free agents. Brent Mayne got a two-year deal worth $4.15 million, while Scott Servais inked a one-year pact for $625,000.

Position: C
Bats: R **Throws:** R
Ht: 6' 0" **Wt:** 199

Opening Day Age: 22
Born: 4/7/77 in Salem, OR
ML Seasons: 1
Pronunciation: PEET-trick

Overall Statistics

	G	AB	R	H	D	T	HR	RBI	SB	BB	SO	Avg	OBP	Slg
1999	19	62	13	20	3	0	4	12	1	10	13	.323	.417	.565
Career	19	62	13	20	3	0	4	12	1	10	13	.323	.417	.565

Where He Hits the Ball

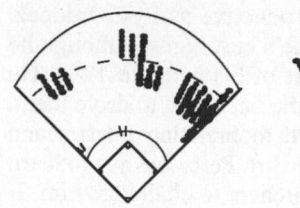

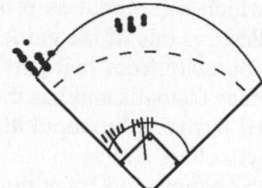

Vs. LHP   **Vs. RHP**

1999 Situational Stats

	AB	H	HR	RBI	Avg		AB	H	HR	RBI	Avg
Home	40	14	4	12	.350	LHP	12	4	0	0	.333
Road	22	6	0	0	.273	RHP	50	16	4	12	.320
First Half	0	0	0	0	-	Sc Pos	17	7	0	7	.412
Scnd Half	62	20	4	12	.323	Clutch	5	0	0	0	.000

1999 Rankings (National League)

• Did not rank near the top or bottom in any category

Dave Veres

Position: RP
Bats: R **Throws:** R
Ht: 6' 2" **Wt:** 220

Opening Day Age: 33
Born: 10/19/66 in Montgomery, AL
ML Seasons: 6
Pronunciation: VEERZ

1999 Season

The Rockies' surprise choice as their closer during spring training, Dave Veres warmed to the role quickly. He had his bad days at Coors Field, allowing three or more runs in six separate innings, but generally handled the job well. Not only did he convert 20 of 21 save opportunities outside of Colorado, but he never allowed more than one run in any of his 35 appearances on the road.

Pitching

Veres has as good a split-finger fastball as any pitcher in the majors, and it's the nasty out pitch that a closer has to have. He learned the splitter from former big leaguer Brent Strom while at Triple-A in the Astros organization. What makes Veres' splitter so effective is his 92-MPH fastball and his ability to get ahead in the count. He also throws a hard slider. Veres needs to have confidence that his catcher can block splitters in the dirt, and that was the case with Henry Blanco last year.

Defense & Hitting

Veres is an excellent athlete. He fields his position well, getting off the mound quickly on bunts and making strong, accurate throws to the bases. He has a minimal motion that allows for a quick delivery, which keeps basestealers in check. When he's ahead in the count, though, runners can take advantage because they know how difficult his splitter is for a catcher to handle. Though he rarely bats, he's a career .300 hitter.

2000 Outlook

Veres moved to St. Louis in the Darryl Kile trade in November, and the change of scenery only can help him. Away from Coors Field, he has a career ERA of 2.99 and has permitted just 24 homers in 337.2 innings. Ricky Bottalico had a disappointing 1999 season, and Veres should supplant him as the Cardinals' closer. Colorado will give Jerry Dipoto the first shot to replace Veres.

Overall Statistics

	W	L	Pct.	ERA	G	GS	Sv	IP	H	BB	SO	HR	Ratio
1999	4	8	.333	5.14	73	0	31	77.0	88	37	71	14	1.62
Career	23	19	.548	3.40	361	0	46	437.1	436	160	395	44	1.36

How Often He Throws Strikes

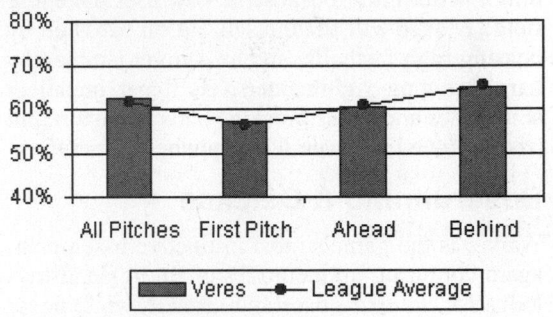

1999 Situational Stats

	W	L	ERA	Sv	IP		AB	H	HR	RBI	Avg
Home	4	6	7.40	11	41.1	LHB	128	42	6	19	.328
Road	0	2	2.52	20	35.2	RHB	175	46	8	27	.263
First Half	2	2	3.77	14	43.0	Sc Pos	93	26	2	32	.280
Scnd Half	2	6	6.88	17	34.0	Clutch	187	62	10	37	.332

1999 Rankings (National League)
- 1st in relief losses (8)
- 2nd in games finished (63)
- 5th in blown saves (8)
- 6th in highest batting average allowed in relief (.290)
- 7th in save opportunities (39), lowest save percentage (79.5) and highest relief ERA (5.14)
- 8th in games pitched
- 9th in saves
- Led the Rockies in games pitched, saves, games finished (63), save opportunities (39), save percentage (79.5), blown saves (8), first batter efficiency (.197), relief losses (8) and most strikeouts per nine innings in relief (8.3)

Larry Walker

1999 Season

Larry Walker complained of an aching left knee all season and had arthroscopic surgery to correct the problem late in the season. Even on a bad leg, though, he became the first player since George Brett in 1980 to lead a major league in average, on-base percentage and slugging percentage. Walker also won his fifth Gold Glove and even stole 11 bases.

Hitting

Walker is in charge when he's at the plate. After signing with the Rockies in 1995, he quickly learned that he could drive the ball out of Coors Field the opposite way. That knowledge has made him a better hitter because he now uses the entire field. Walker will get himself out on occasion by chasing high fastballs, and he can get jammed by hard-throwing righthanders. He'll get impatient sometimes and chase breaking balls in the dirt, but has improved his overall discipline.

Baserunning & Defense

Walker is the game's most instinctive baserunner, again conjuring up memories of Brett. He always looks for the extra base and takes it, while never making a mistake. As a right fielder, Walker is at the top of the class. He doesn't have the flash of others, but he has plus arm strength, always makes his throws on a line so they can be cut off, and never throws to the wrong base. He takes pride in deking runners into thinking he can catch balls, and plays caroms off the wall perfectly.

2000 Outlook

Walker is primed for another big year. His six-year, $75 million contract extension kicks in this season. His knee no longer should bother him. And the Rockies made it clear that this is Walker's team when they dealt away Dante Bichette, eliminating the ongoing ego battle between the two that has been a clubhouse distraction.

Position: RF
Bats: L **Throws:** R
Ht: 6' 3" **Wt:** 237

Opening Day Age: 33
Born: 12/1/66 in Maple Ridge, Canada
ML Seasons: 11

Overall Statistics

	G	AB	R	H	D	T	HR	RBI	SB	BB	SO	Avg	OBP	Slg
1999	127	438	108	166	26	4	37	115	11	57	52	.379	.458	.710
Career	1298	4592	886	1431	314	36	262	855	190	532	807	.312	.389	.567

Where He Hits the Ball

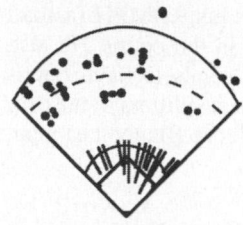

Vs. LHP

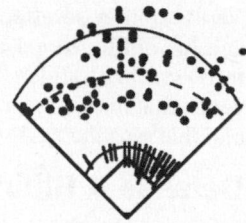

Vs. RHP

1999 Situational Stats

	AB	H	HR	RBI	Avg		AB	H	HR	RBI	Avg
Home	232	107	26	70	.461	LHP	142	49	9	37	.345
Road	206	59	11	45	.286	RHP	296	117	28	78	.395
First Half	275	105	25	77	.382	Sc Pos	112	47	10	77	.420
Scnd Half	163	61	12	38	.374	Clutch	68	24	8	20	.353

1999 Rankings (National League)

- 1st in slugging percentage, on-base percentage, batting average with runners in scoring position, batting average and batting average at home
- 2nd in batting average with two strikes (.288)
- 3rd in HR frequency (11.8 ABs per HR)
- Led the Rockies in slugging percentage, on-base percentage, HR frequency (11.8 ABs per HR), highest groundball/flyball ratio (1.4), batting average with runners in scoring position, batting average vs. lefthanded pitchers, batting average on an 0-2 count (.300), slugging percentage vs. lefthanded pitchers (.620), on-base percentage vs. lefthanded pitchers (.424), batting average with two strikes (.288), batting average, home runs, intentional walks (8) and hit by pitch (12)

Jamey Wright

1999 Season

Jamey Wright was given an early-season wakeup call when he was banished to Triple-A for three months. Colorado Springs pitching coach Jim Wright (no relation) worked with him on his mental approach. Once he returned to Colorado, Wright did a solid job in the final two months. The Rockies won eight of his last nine starts, during which he went 4-1, 4.21.

Pitching

Wright has a 92-94 MPH two-seam fastball that scouts compare to the out pitches of Kevin Brown and Darren Dreifort. But Wright has yet to master the offspeed and breaking pitches that will allow him to survive when his sinker is at less than its best. Wright has had a tendency to fall victim to big innings. After his trip to the minors last year, he did a much better job of not letting one mistake turn into a nightmarish rally.

Defense & Hitting

Wright has one of the better pickoff moves among big league righthanders. He has quick feet and can catch runners napping at first or second base. He hurts himself by falling awkwardly off the mound in his follow-through, which allows too many balls to go through the middle for base hits. He has to learn that handling the bat is critical if he wants to work deep into games. He gives away too many at-bats and doesn't get down bunts with regularity.

2000 Outlook

Rather than wait for a breakthrough season from Wright, the Rockies sent him to Milwaukee in a four-team deal in December. The depleted Brewers likely will keep him in their rotation all season. The key for Wright is to believe in his ability as much as others do. Not many hitters can handle his hard sinker if he throws it for strikes. He just may surprise now that he has escaped from Coors Field.

Position: SP
Bats: R **Throws:** R
Ht: 6' 5" **Wt:** 221

Opening Day Age: 25
Born: 12/24/74 in Oklahoma City, OK
ML Seasons: 4

Overall Statistics

	W	L	Pct.	ERA	G	GS	Sv	IP	H	BB	SO	HR	Ratio
1999	4	3	.571	4.87	16	16	0	94.1	110	54	49	10	1.74
Career	25	33	.431	5.57	92	91	0	541.2	648	261	239	61	1.68

How Often He Throws Strikes

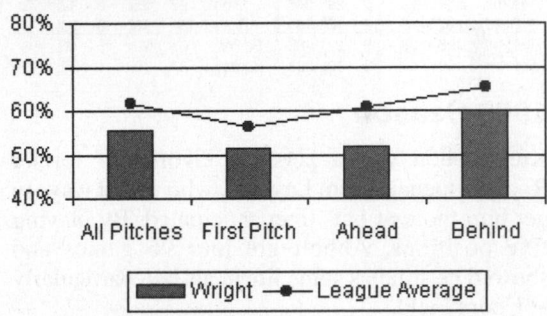

Legend: Wright — League Average

1999 Situational Stats

	W	L	ERA	Sv	IP		AB	H	HR	RBI	Avg
Home	2	1	6.81	0	39.2	LHB	152	50	3	20	.329
Road	2	2	3.46	0	54.2	RHB	205	60	7	29	.293
First Half	0	1	7.58	0	19.0	Sc Pos	92	25	3	35	.272
Scnd Half	4	2	4.18	0	75.1	Clutch	14	4	0	0	.286

1999 Rankings (National League)

- Led the Rockies in pickoff throws (104)

Kurt Abbott

Position: 2B
Bats: R **Throws:** R
Ht: 6' 0" **Wt:** 198

Opening Day Age: 30
Born: 6/2/69 in
Zanesville, OH
ML Seasons: 7

Overall Statistics

	G	AB	R	H	D	T	HR	RBI	SB	BB	SO	Avg	OBP	Slg
1999	96	286	41	78	17	2	8	41	3	16	69	.273	.310	.430
Career	617	1878	251	487	102	22	56	230	20	119	517	.259	.307	.427

1999 Situational Stats

	AB	H	HR	RBI	Avg		AB	H	HR	RBI	Avg
Home	159	55	6	29	.346	LHP	92	25	2	12	.272
Road	127	23	2	12	.181	RHP	194	53	6	29	.273
First Half	126	36	5	22	.286	Sc Pos	67	29	5	36	.433
Scnd Half	160	42	3	19	.263	Clutch	37	10	1	2	.270

1999 Season

Kurt Abbott was a personal favorite of former Rockies manager Jim Leyland, who found ways to get him more at-bats than anticipated. By playing five positions, Abbott got into 96 games and showed he still has some life in his bat, particularly at Coors Field.

Hitting, Baserunning & Defense

Abbott doesn't get cheated. He goes up to the plate swinging, though he misses too often and rarely takes a walk. He'll turn on fastballs but is susceptible to pitches up and out of the strike zone. Abbott runs decently and can take the extra base, but he isn't going to steal very often. Though he came to the big leagues as a shortstop, his best position is second base. His range and arm are unspectacular. Abbott also can play third base and the outfield, but it's his bat that gets him into a lineup.

2000 Outlook

Abbott declared free agency and won't return to the Rockies, who acquired Aaron Ledesma to be their utilityman. Abbott wants to be an everyday player again, but that's not likely to happen.

Jeff Barry

Position: CF/RF/LF
Bats: B **Throws:** R
Ht: 6' 1" **Wt:** 205

Opening Day Age: 31
Born: 9/22/68 in
Medford, OR
ML Seasons: 3

Overall Statistics

	G	AB	R	H	D	T	HR	RBI	SB	BB	SO	Avg	OBP	Slg
1999	74	168	19	45	16	0	5	26	0	19	29	.268	.344	.452
Career	104	217	25	53	18	0	5	28	0	22	48	.244	.314	.396

1999 Situational Stats

	AB	H	HR	RBI	Avg		AB	H	HR	RBI	Avg
Home	91	23	4	16	.253	LHP	40	13	2	12	.325
Road	77	22	1	10	.286	RHP	128	32	3	14	.250
First Half	22	5	1	3	.227	Sc Pos	38	9	1	18	.237
Scnd Half	146	40	4	23	.274	Clutch	34	11	1	9	.324

1999 Season

Jeff Barry had just 30 major league games to show for 10 seasons as a pro when he was promoted to Colorado in late June. In his first extended opportunity at the big league level, he did a solid job as part of the revolving door in center field.

Hitting, Baserunning & Defense

A natural righthanded hitter, the switch-hitting Barry is more of a threat from that side. He does have gap power but can be overpowered when batting lefthanded. He's vulnerable to breaking pitchers once he falls behind in the count. When he started, the Rockies usually batted him sixth or seventh. Barry is a fundamentally sound outfielder who makes good reads and has an accurate arm. However, he's a tad short in every area, which is why he never has played regularly in the majors.

2000 Outlook

Barry is a fifth outfielder in the big leagues. He'll get some chances to play because he doesn't make mistakes, but never will be able to claim a full-time job.

Henry Blanco

Traded To BREWERS

Position: C
Bats: R **Throws:** R
Ht: 5'11" **Wt:** 170

Opening Day Age: 28
Born: 8/29/71 in Caracas, Venezuela
ML Seasons: 2

Overall Statistics

	G	AB	R	H	D	T	HR	RBI	SB	BB	SO	Avg	OBP	Slg
1999	88	263	30	61	12	3	6	28	1	34	38	.232	.320	.369
Career	91	268	31	63	12	3	7	29	1	34	39	.235	.321	.381

1999 Situational Stats

	AB	H	HR	RBI	Avg		AB	H	HR	RBI	Avg
Home	136	39	3	21	.287	LHP	99	22	3	13	.222
Road	127	22	3	7	.173	RHP	164	39	3	15	.238
First Half	133	38	2	17	.286	Sc Pos	69	14	2	21	.203
Scnd Half	130	23	4	11	.177	Clutch	37	7	2	6	.189

1999 Season

Signed as a minor league free agent and called up in May when Kirt Manwaring dislocated a finger, Henry Blanco emerged as the best catcher in Rockies history. He had surprising success at the plate until spraining his left ankle in a home-plate collision in Milwaukee on August 10. He continued to play, but lost his ability to push off at the plate and his average fell from .271 to .232.

Hitting, Baserunning & Defense

Blanco's best offensive tool is a dose of power. Though he can be overpowered, he does hang in fairly well against breaking pitches. Blanco might be the slowest runner this side of Kirt Manwaring. Where he stands out is behind the plate. Blanco led all National League catchers by gunning down 39 percent of basestealers in 1999. He moves well behind the plate, giving hurlers the confidence to bounce pitches in the dirt.

2000 Outlook

Blanco proved last year that he belongs in the big leagues. He'll start for the Brewers, who acquired him in a four-team deal at the Winter Meetings. His lack of offensive potential better suits him to be a backup.

Edgard Clemente

Position: CF
Bats: R **Throws:** R
Ht: 5'11" **Wt:** 188

Opening Day Age: 24
Born: 12/15/75 in Santurce, Puerto Rico
ML Seasons: 2

Overall Statistics

	G	AB	R	H	D	T	HR	RBI	SB	BB	SO	Avg	OBP	Slg
1999	57	162	24	41	10	2	8	25	0	7	46	.253	.282	.488
Career	68	179	26	47	10	3	8	27	0	9	54	.263	.296	.486

1999 Situational Stats

	AB	H	HR	RBI	Avg		AB	H	HR	RBI	Avg
Home	105	30	7	20	.286	LHP	52	17	3	7	.327
Road	57	11	1	5	.193	RHP	110	24	5	18	.218
First Half	22	6	1	2	.273	Sc Pos	36	9	0	13	.250
Scnd Half	140	35	7	23	.250	Clutch	21	7	0	1	.333

1999 Season

The nephew of Hall of Famer Roberto Clemente, Edgard Clemente has spent most of the last three seasons in Triple-A. Promoted by the Rockies last August with the announced intention to play him every day in center field, Clemente instead found himself sharing time with Terry Shumpert and Jeff Barry.

Hitting, Baserunning & Defense

Clemente has five-tool potential but still needs to develop. His plus power is hampered by his willingness to chase pitches out of the strike zone. He's a step above average as a runner, but doesn't have the aggressiveness to be a basestealer. Clemente shouldn't be a center fielder, particularly not in the wide-open spaces of Coors Field. He does have a strong arm and plays both corner positions well.

2000 Outlook

Clemente is out of options and has too much ability to risk exposing him to waivers. He'll stick with the Rockies this year, probably as the fourth outfielder. It's possible he could compete with Jeffrey Hammonds for the left-field job.

Colorado

Jerry Dipoto

Position: RP
Bats: R **Throws:** R
Ht: 6' 2" **Wt:** 205

Opening Day Age: 31
Born: 5/24/68 in Jersey City, NJ
ML Seasons: 7
Pronunciation: dih-POE-toe

Overall Statistics

	W	L	Pct.	ERA	G	GS	Sv	IP	H	BB	SO	HR	Ratio
1999	4	5	.444	4.26	63	0	1	86.2	91	44	69	10	1.56
Career	27	24	.529	4.05	373	0	49	481.2	511	216	343	32	1.51

1999 Situational Stats

	W	L	ERA	Sv	IP		AB	H	HR	RBI	Avg
Home	2	3	4.97	1	50.2	LHB	148	42	2	18	.284
Road	2	2	3.25	0	36.0	RHB	178	49	8	23	.275
First Half	3	2	5.09	1	46.0	Sc Pos	97	20	1	28	.206
Scnd Half	1	3	3.32	0	40.2	Clutch	110	30	4	16	.273

1999 Season

Displaced in spring training as Colorado's closer, Jerry Dipoto bounced back to put together a consistent and durable season as the setup man for Dave Veres. He led National League relievers by allowing just 12.5 percent of his inherited runners to score. Dipoto is the rare Rockies pitcher who actually has posted lower ERAs at Coors Field than on the road, though that was not the case in 1999.

Pitching, Defense & Hitting

Dipoto lives with hard stuff, a nasty slider and a two-seam fastball that consistently reaches the low to mid-90s. Two years ago, he added a four-seamer that isn't as hard but surprises hitters by riding high in the strike zone. Dipoto is a good athlete with quick moves to first and the plate. He's 1-for-21 as a big league hitter.

2000 Outlook

With the November trade of Veres to St. Louis, Dipoto figures to regain his past role as closer. Shortly before the deal, he re-signed with Colorado for two years and $4.9 million. No matter what role he's used in, Dipoto should put up solid numbers, taking into consideration that he pitches at Coors Field.

Angel Echevarria

Position: RF/LF/1B
Bats: R **Throws:** R
Ht: 6' 3" **Wt:** 226

Opening Day Age: 28
Born: 5/25/71 in Bridgeport, CT
ML Seasons: 4

Overall Statistics

	G	AB	R	H	D	T	HR	RBI	SB	BB	SO	Avg	OBP	Slg
1999	102	191	28	56	7	0	11	35	1	17	34	.293	.360	.503
Career	162	261	41	78	12	0	12	50	1	23	47	.299	.366	.483

1999 Situational Stats

	AB	H	HR	RBI	Avg		AB	H	HR	RBI	Avg
Home	85	33	5	21	.388	LHP	98	28	7	19	.286
Road	106	23	6	14	.217	RHP	93	28	4	16	.301
First Half	89	24	6	15	.270	Sc Pos	38	13	2	22	.342
Scnd Half	102	32	5	20	.314	Clutch	43	15	3	15	.349

1999 Season

Angel Echevarria refused to give up on himself after he was drafted in the 17th round in 1992 and later spent most of three years stuck in Triple-A. His commitment finally paid off last year, his first full season in the majors. He was a capable backup at first base and in the outfield, and batted .319 with four homers as a pinch-hitter.

Hitting, Baserunning & Defense

Echevarria never gives away an at-bat. He has an idea of what he needs to do each time he goes up, and will work the pitcher for the situation he wants. His swing is a tad long, making it tough for him to catch up to top-flight fastballs, but he jumps on pitchers with average stuff. Echevarria is a station-to-station baserunner and has to be careful not to try to do too much. He's acceptable in the outfield but raw at first base. His arm is average.

2000 Outlook

Echevarria is strictly reserve material. His playing time will be limited by the Rockies' set lineup, but he'll get the bulk of the pinch-hitting opportunities for a righthander because of his power.

Bobby Jones

Position: SP/RP
Bats: R **Throws:** L
Ht: 6' 0" **Wt:** 178

Opening Day Age: 27
Born: 4/11/72 in
Orange, NJ
ML Seasons: 3

Overall Statistics

	W	L	Pct.	ERA	G	GS	Sv	IP	H	BB	SO	HR	Ratio
1999	6	10	.375	6.33	30	20	0	112.1	132	77	74	24	1.86
Career	14	19	.424	5.90	69	44	0	273.0	315	155	188	38	1.72

1999 Situational Stats

	W	L	ERA	Sv	IP		AB	H	HR	RBI	Avg
Home	3	5	6.94	0	59.2	LHB	90	22	6	14	.244
Road	3	5	5.64	0	52.2	RHB	362	110	18	70	.304
First Half	4	7	5.83	0	78.2	Sc Pos	130	37	6	58	.285
Scnd Half	2	3	7.49	0	33.2	Clutch	2	1	1	1	.500

1999 Season

Bobby Jones found himself splitting time between the rotation and bullpen for the second consecutive year. He prefers to start, but once again failed to show the stamina to claim a full-time spot in the rotation.

Pitching, Defense & Hitting

Jones has the stuff but not the command to be a quality lefthander. He has a low-90s fastball and a hard-breaking slider. He uses the latter to get righthanders out. Jones' delivery is complicated and easily falls out of sync, leading to control problems. Though he's athletic, Jones doesn't field or hold runners well. He hits decently for a pitcher.

2000 Outlook

Jones will be used as a mid-game lefty out of the bullpen. He'll be the latest challenge for new pitching coach Marcel Lachemann, who will try to find a way to get Jones to maintain his focus. During the offseason, Jones adopted a shoulder-strengthening program prescribed by Dr. James Andrews during the offseason and made the commitment to come to Denver to work under the direction of club officials.

Curtis Leskanic

Traded To
BREWERS

Position: RP
Bats: R **Throws:** R
Ht: 6' 0" **Wt:** 186

Opening Day Age: 31
Born: 4/2/68 in
Homestead, PA
ML Seasons: 7
Pronunciation:
les-CAN-ik

Overall Statistics

	W	L	Pct.	ERA	G	GS	Sv	IP	H	BB	SO	HR	Ratio
1999	6	2	.750	5.08	63	0	0	85.0	87	49	77	7	1.60
Career	31	20	.608	4.92	356	11	20	470.0	472	221	415	52	1.47

1999 Situational Stats

	W	L	ERA	Sv	IP		AB	H	HR	RBI	Avg
Home	2	1	5.61	0	51.1	LHB	110	33	3	25	.300
Road	4	1	4.28	0	33.2	RHB	210	54	4	32	.257
First Half	3	1	4.73	0	51.1	Sc Pos	116	30	2	47	.259
Scnd Half	3	1	5.61	0	33.2	Clutch	94	20	0	15	.213

1999 Season

As usual, Curtis Leskanic was resilient and turned in a decent year in middle relief. He won six of eight decisions and contributed eight holds, with his biggest drawback being inconsistent control.

Pitching, Defense & Hitting

Leskanic has a legitimate 90-plus-MPH fastball and a hard slider. He continues to toy with a cut fastball that, against lefthanders in particular, causes him nothing but trouble. Leskanic is athletic and has a good move to first, but concentration lapses cost him in fielding and shutting down the running game. He went 2-for-4 with a homer in 1999, raising his career average to .194.

2000 Outlook

Leskanic has a live arm, but he hasn't improved since the day he came to the big leagues in 1993. That was endlessly frustrating for the Rockies, who traded him to the Brewers in mid-November for lefty specialist Mike Myers. Leskanic knows he needs to be more aggressive and he has the stuff to challenge hitters. If he ever does, he could make an impact.

Colorado

431

Kirt Manwaring

Position: C
Bats: R **Throws:** R
Ht: 5'11" **Wt:** 198

Opening Day Age: 34
Born: 7/15/65 in Elmira, NY
ML Seasons: 13
Pronunciation: MAN-ware-ing

Overall Statistics

	G	AB	R	H	D	T	HR	RBI	SB	BB	SO	Avg	OBP	Slg
1999	48	137	17	41	7	1	2	14	0	12	23	.299	.374	.409
Career	1008	2982	248	733	111	20	21	278	10	243	505	.246	.311	.318

1999 Situational Stats

	AB	H	HR	RBI	Avg		AB	H	HR	RBI	Avg
Home	77	25	1	9	.325	LHP	38	12	1	7	.316
Road	60	16	1	5	.267	RHP	99	29	1	7	.293
First Half	70	24	0	7	.343	Sc Pos	32	11	0	11	.344
Scnd Half	67	17	2	7	.254	Clutch	11	1	0	1	.091

1999 Season

Kirt Manwaring served the Rockies well in a backup role, though a dislocated right thumb sidelined him in May. He hit for a surprising average, but a lot of that had to do with his limited usage.

Hitting, Baserunning & Defense

Manwaring is a throwback. He's a hard-nosed receiver, willing to sacrifice his body to block the plate or keep pitches from getting past him. He has an accurate arm and a decent release, but has lost the zip on his throws. His strength is calling a game. Manwaring's weakness is hitting, though he closed his stance last year and was able to stay on pitches better. He's a singles hitter with no speed.

2000 Outlook

A free agent, Manwaring won't return to the Rockies after they didn't offer him arbitration. He has accepted the fact that he no longer has the skills to be a starting catcher. He's willing to work with the pitchers even when he's not catching and is anxious to teach young catchers. Manwaring will give his new team a solid effort but can't catch for extended periods.

Terry Shumpert

Position: 2B/3B
Bats: R **Throws:** R
Ht: 6' 0" **Wt:** 195

Opening Day Age: 33
Born: 8/16/66 in Paducah, KY
ML Seasons: 10

Overall Statistics

	G	AB	R	H	D	T	HR	RBI	SB	BB	SO	Avg	OBP	Slg
1999	92	262	58	91	26	3	10	37	14	31	41	.347	.413	.584
Career	460	1146	162	288	67	11	28	131	58	92	227	.251	.309	.402

1999 Situational Stats

	AB	H	HR	RBI	Avg		AB	H	HR	RBI	Avg
Home	150	61	8	29	.407	LHP	86	34	3	8	.395
Road	112	30	2	8	.268	RHP	176	57	7	29	.324
First Half	66	23	5	14	.348	Sc Pos	61	17	2	26	.279
Scnd Half	196	68	5	23	.347	Clutch	43	17	2	7	.395

1999 Season

After spending time with five organizations in the previous five years, Shumpert re-signed with the Rockies as a minor league free agent. When Mike Lansing's back flared up, Shumpert got an opportunity and proved to be a valuable utility player. He played six positions and was in the lineup regularly during the last four months.

Hitting, Baserunning & Defense

Shumpert finally began to go with pitches instead of pulling everything, and the new approach paid off. He knows how to steal a base, leading the Rockies with 14 in as many attempts last year. Once considered the heir apparent to Frank White in Kansas City, Shumpert has the speed and arm to do at least a passable job anywhere except for pitcher and catcher. Second base remains his best position.

2000 Outlook

Shumpert became a free agent, but the Rockies re-signed him for one year and $750,000. Lansing's return from back surgery is far from certain, so Shumpert could start at second base. Don't expect him to match his 1999 numbers.

Other Colorado Rockies

Rigo Beltran (Pos: LHP, **Age**: 30)

	W	L	Pct.	ERA	G	GS	Sv	IP	H	BB	SO	HR	Ratio
1999	1	1	.500	4.50	33	0	0	42.0	50	19	50	7	1.64
Career	2	3	.400	3.88	75	4	1	104.1	103	40	105	11	1.37

Beltran bounced between Triple-A Norfolk and the Mets and pitched well at both locales. Dealt to Colorado in the Darryl Hamilton trade on July 31, he struggled after the deal. 2000 Outlook: B

Mark Brownson (Pos: RHP, **Age**: 24)

	W	L	Pct.	ERA	G	GS	Sv	IP	H	BB	SO	HR	Ratio
1999	0	2	.000	7.89	7	7	0	29.2	42	8	21	8	1.69
Career	1	2	.333	6.91	9	9	0	43.0	58	10	29	10	1.58

Colorado wasn't a desirable locale for Brownson, who didn't pitch well at Triple-A Colorado Springs or in Denver the last two seasons. Luckily for him, the Phillies claimed him off waivers in November. 2000 Outlook: C

John Cangelosi (Pos: LF, **Age**: 37, **Bats**: B)

	G	AB	R	H	D	T	HR	RBI	SB	BB	SO	Avg	OBP	Slg
1999	7	6	0	1	1	0	0	0	0	0	4	.167	.167	.333
Career	1038	2004	328	501	73	15	12	134	154	358	322	.250	.370	.319

After 13 seasons in which he surpassed 200 at-bats just three times, Cangelosi retired with 100 extra-base hits and 154 steals. The Cubs have hired him as an outfield instructor. 2000 Outlook: D

Mike DeJean (Pos: RHP, **Age**: 29)

	W	L	Pct.	ERA	G	GS	Sv	IP	H	BB	SO	HR	Ratio
1999	2	4	.333	8.41	56	0	0	61.0	83	32	31	13	1.89
Career	10	5	.667	4.97	170	1	4	203.0	235	80	96	21	1.55

DeJean showed some promise in Denver in 1998, but nothing worked for him last summer. Elbow problems late in the season led to surgery to have bone chips removed in December. 2000 Outlook: B

Mike Kelly (Pos: RF, **Age**: 29, **Bats**: R)

	G	AB	R	H	D	T	HR	RBI	SB	BB	SO	Avg	OBP	Slg
1999	2	2	0	1	0	0	0	0	0	0	0	.500	.500	1.000
Career	327	684	111	165	45	6	22	86	30	54	187	.241	.300	.421

A bad spring led to Kelly's release by Tampa Bay at the end of spring training. The Rockies signed him, but Kelly didn't cash in on the altitude at Triple-A Colorado Springs. He has signed with the Mets. 2000 Outlook: C

David Lee (Pos: RHP, **Age**: 27)

	W	L	Pct.	ERA	G	GS	Sv	IP	H	BB	SO	HR	Ratio
1999	3	2	.600	3.67	36	0	0	49.0	43	29	38	4	1.47
Career	3	2	.600	3.67	36	0	0	49.0	43	29	38	4	1.47

Lee gave up a big three-run homer to Jay Bell in his major league debut on May 22, ˙ut from August 1 until the end of the season, Lee allowed just one homer and posted a 2.01 ERA in 22.1 innings. 2000 Outlook: B

Chris Petersen (Pos: 2B, **Age**: 29, **Bats**: R)

	G	AB	R	H	D	T	HR	RBI	SB	BB	SO	Avg	OBP	Slg
1999	7	13	1	2	0	0	0	2	0	2	3	.154	.267	.154
Career	7	13	1	2	0	0	0	2	0	2	3	.154	.267	.154

Petersen hasn't shown much offensively in four Triple-A seasons, but he was steady defensively in the middle infield during a couple stints with the Rockies. He signed a minor league deal with the Cubs in November. 2000 Outlook: C

J.R. Phillips (Pos: RF, **Age**: 29, **Bats**: L)

	G	AB	R	H	D	T	HR	RBI	SB	BB	SO	Avg	OBP	Slg
1999	25	39	5	9	4	0	2	4	0	0	13	.231	.250	.487
Career	242	501	52	94	19	1	23	67	2	38	180	.188	.247	.367

Phillips, who now has 150 Triple-A homers, stroked a career-best 41 longballs at Triple-A Colorado Springs in '99 and showed pop in Denver. He's a free agent again. 2000 Outlook: C

Mike Porzio (Pos: LHP, **Age**: 27)

	W	L	Pct.	ERA	G	GS	Sv	IP	H	BB	SO	HR	Ratio
1999	0	0	-	8.59	16	0	0	14.2	21	10	10	5	2.11
Career	0	0	-	8.59	16	0	0	14.2	21	10	10	5	2.11

Allowing five homers in just 14.2 innings suggests Porzio was in over his head, but it's worth noting that all five longballs came in just two of his 16 games. Eleven outings were scoreless efforts. 2000 Outlook: C

Roberto Ramirez (Pos: LHP, **Age**: 27)

	W	L	Pct.	ERA	G	GS	Sv	IP	H	BB	SO	HR	Ratio
1999	1	5	.167	8.26	32	4	1	40.1	68	22	32	8	2.23
Career	2	5	.286	7.69	53	4	1	55.0	80	34	49	12	2.07

For a second straight season Ramirez pitched well in the Pacific Coast League, but major league hitters played home-run derby with him both years. Ramirez was sold to Japan's Hanshin Tigers in November. 2000 Outlook: D

Chris Sexton (Pos: 2B, **Age**: 28, **Bats**: R)

	G	AB	R	H	D	T	HR	RBI	SB	BB	SO	Avg	OBP	Slg
1999	35	59	9	14	0	1	1	7	4	11	10	.237	.357	.322
Career	35	59	9	14	0	1	1	7	4	11	10	.237	.357	.322

Sexton hasn't shown much pop, not even in the Colorado air, but he has drawn 472 walks in the minors while fanning just 364 times. He has signed with the Reds. 2000 Outlook: B

Juan Sosa (Pos: CF, **Age**: 24, **Bats**: R)

	G	AB	R	H	D	T	HR	RBI	SB	BB	SO	Avg	OBP	Slg
1999	11	9	3	2	0	0	0	0	0	2	2	.222	.364	.222
Career	11	9	3	2	0	0	0	0	0	2	2	.222	.364	.222

Sosa is young, but he hasn't demonstrated power or patience as a minor league hitter. He picked up some innings in the infield and the outfield, so versatility eventually may work in his favor. 2000 Outlook: C

John Thomson (Pos: RHP, Age: 26)

	W	L	Pct.	ERA	G	GS	Sv	IP	H	BB	SO	HR	Ratio
1999	1	10	.091	8.04	14	13	0	62.2	85	36	34	11	1.93
Career	16	30	.348	5.28	67	66	0	390.0	452	136	246	47	1.51

Thomson always looked like a gem of a prospect, even pitching well at Triple-A Colorado Springs in 1997. Succeeding in Denver, though, has been a difficult proposition. 2000 Outlook: C

Dave Wainhouse (Pos: RHP, Age: 32)

	W	L	Pct.	ERA	G	GS	Sv	IP	H	BB	SO	HR	Ratio
1999	0	0	-	6.91	19	0	0	28.2	37	16	18	6	1.85
Career	2	2	.500	7.19	76	0	0	96.1	117	57	61	13	1.81

Wainhouse has been effective at the Triple-A level for much of the 1990s, but hasn't had the same success in the majors. He's now a free agent. 2000 Outlook: C

Pat Watkins (Pos: RF, Age: 27, Bats: R)

	G	AB	R	H	D	T	HR	RBI	SB	BB	SO	Avg	OBP	Slg
1999	16	19	2	1	0	0	0	0	0	2	5	.053	.143	.053
Career	116	195	15	46	10	1	2	15	2	10	36	.236	.271	.328

The Marlins traded Watkins to Colorado at the end of spring training, but he found himself in the minors after going 1-for-19 in May. He signed with the Reds, his original team, in the offseason. 2000 Outlook: C

Colorado Rockies Minor League Prospects

Organization Overview:

The Rockies knew from the day they were granted a franchise that the rare air of Colorado would lead to high-scoring games. Figuring it would be easier to lure hitters than pitchers, they decided to focus on developing arms. They've had 40 picks in the first five rounds of the draft, and they've selected 28 pitchers. That sounds like a good plan, they just haven't executed it well. After seven major league seasons, their leading winner among homegrown hurlers is Jamey Wright, with a mere 25 victories. With Wright now a Brewer, they may not have a Rockies-developed pitcher in their rotation this year, and their best mound prospects spent 1999 at Class-A or below. And while Colorado has received credit for signing Todd Helton and Neifi Perez, consider that both have played the equivalent of little more than a full season's worth of road games in the majors. In those contests, Helton has hit .262-26-77 and Perez .242-9-57, below-average production for their positions. Both have promise, but have been pumped up greatly by Coors Field.

Brent Butler

Position: SS   **Opening Day Age:** 22
Bats: R **Throws:** R   **Born:** 2/11/78 in
Ht: 6' 0" **Wt:** 180   Laurinburg, NC

Recent Statistics

	G	AB	R	H	D	T	HR	RBI	SB	BB	SO	Avg
1998 A Pr William	126	475	63	136	27	2	11	76	3	39	74	.286
1999 AA Arkansas	139	528	68	142	21	1	13	54	0	26	47	.269
1999 MLE	139	513	57	127	19	0	10	45	0	18	49	.248

Acquired in the trade that sent Darryl Kile to St. Louis in November, Butler has been one of the best-hitting short-stops in the minors since signing as a 1996 third-round pick. However, his star is beginning to fade, as his batting average, on-base percentage and slugging percentage have declined each year. He makes good contact and still has plenty of pop for a middle infielder, but his walk totals are rapidly shrinking, which will restrict his ability to hit for average. Because he has thick legs and lacks first-step quickness, Butler's ability to play short-stop has been questioned. Neifi Perez is a supremely better defender, so Butler's future in Colorado is probably at second base. He'll play in Triple-A this year.

Choo Freeman

Position: OF   **Opening Day Age:** 20
Bats: R **Throws:** R   **Born:** 10/20/79 in Pine
Ht: 6' 2" **Wt:** 200   Bluff, AR

Recent Statistics

	G	AB	R	H	D	T	HR	RBI	SB	BB	SO	Avg
1998 R Rockies	40	147	35	47	3	6	1	24	14	15	25	.320
1999 A Asheville	131	485	82	133	22	4	14	66	16	39	132	.274

Freeman was expected to go in the top 10 picks of the 1998 draft, but apparently his scholarship to play wide receiver for Texas A&M scared clubs off, so the Rockies got him with the 36th overall selection. A five-tool athlete, he signed for $1.4 million and almost immediately became the organization's top prospect. He's a bit raw and still learning to play baseball, but last year he had a decent season for a 19-year-old in a Class-A league. Once Freeman learns the strike zone, Colorado is convinced he'll be a 30-30 center fielder. He's probably three years away from joining the Rockies.

Jody Gerut

Position: OF   **Opening Day Age:** 22
Bats: L **Throws:** L   **Born:** 9/18/77 in
Ht: 6' 0" **Wt:** 190   Elmhurst, IL

Recent Statistics

	G	AB	R	H	D	T	HR	RBI	SB	BB	SO	Avg
1999 A Salem	133	499	80	144	33	11	11	63	25	61	65	.289

Gerut was a 1998 second-round pick out of Stanford, a compensation pick from the Braves for the signing of free agent Walt Weiss. Consider that a trade that the Rockies are glad to have made. Gerut made his pro debut last year, showing a nice set of offensive skills. He can hit for average, has gap power, walks nearly as much as he strikes out and steals bases. He's a borderline center fielder, but he'll probably move to a corner with Choo Freeman and Juan Pierre coming up behind him. Gerut will start 2000 in Double-A and could reach Colorado by the second half of the next season.

Derrick Gibson

Position: OF   **Opening Day Age:** 25
Bats: R **Throws:** R   **Born:** 2/5/75 in Winter
Ht: 6' 2" **Wt:** 238   Haven, FL

Recent Statistics

	G	AB	R	H	D	T	HR	RBI	SB	BB	SO	Avg
1999 AAA Colo Spngs	110	385	68	106	19	6	17	67	12	30	82	.275
1999 NL Colorado	10	28	2	5	1	0	2	6	0	0	7	.179
1999 MLE	110	384	52	105	18	5	17	51	8	23	80	.273

Considered the Rockies' best prospect two years ago, Gibson was bypassed this winter when the club acquired Jeffrey Hammonds and Tom Goodwin. Though he's as strong as anyone in the game, Gibson has hit a total of just 31 homers in two seasons at Colorado Springs, one of the best launching pads in Triple-A. A 13th-round pick in 1993, he's a very good athlete for his size—Auburn recruited him to play linebacker—but he just hasn't developed. He doesn't work the strike zone well or have enough loft in his swing. His basestealing has dropped off as well, and he won't be more than an average left fielder. Colorado has several outfield prospect on the rise, and Gibson's time appears to have passed. He may make Colorado as a reserve this season.

Colorado

Jason Jennings

Position: P **Opening Day Age:** 21
Bats: R **Throws:** R **Born:** 7/17/78 in Dallas,
Ht: 6' 2" **Wt:** 230 TX

Recent Statistics

	W	L	ERA	G	GS	Sv	IP	H	R	BB	SO	HR
1999 A Portland	1	0	1.00	2	2	0	9.0	5	1	2	11	0
1999 A Asheville	2	2	3.70	12	12	0	58.1	55	27	8	69	3

Jennings entered the 1999 season as a projected third- or fourth-round pick, then rose to the 16th overall selection after winning *Baseball America's* College Player of the Year Award. Jennings was a two-way star at Baylor, but the Rockies will keep him on the mound after signing him for $1.675 million. He throws two- and four-seam fastballs to both sides of the plate, and he can maintain his 94-MPH velocity on the four-seamer into the late innings. He also has a curveball and an above-average changeup. Jennings enhances his repertoire with impeccable command and he's very durable. Jennings could begin this year in Double-A, and the pitching-starved Rockies could move him quickly.

Josh Kalinowski

Position: P **Opening Day Age:** 23
Bats: L **Throws:** L **Born:** 12/12/76 in Pasco,
Ht: 6' 2" **Wt:** 190 WA

Recent Statistics

	W	L	ERA	G	GS	Sv	IP	H	R	BB	SO	HR
1998 A Asheville	12	10	3.92	28	28	0	172.1	159	93	65	215	15
1999 A Salem	11	6	2.11	27	27	0	162.1	119	47	71	176	3

The Rockies liked Kalinowski so much that they drafted him twice, in the 37th round out of high school in 1996 and in the 33rd round out of Indian Hills (Iowa) Community College a year later, before signing him in 1998 as a draft-and-follow. He has led his league in strikeouts in both of his two full pro seasons, and last year also topped the Carolina League in ERA while being named the high Class-A circuit's pitcher of the year. Kalinowski has devastated hitters with his curveball, and he also throws a solid fastball. He still needs to fine-tune his changeup and his control. Double-A is a proving ground for breaking-ball pitchers, and he'll be put to the test in 2000.

Juan Pierre

Position: OF **Opening Day Age:** 22
Bats: L **Throws:** L **Born:** 8/14/77 in Mobile,
Ht: 6' 0" **Wt:** 170 AL

Recent Statistics

	G	AB	R	H	D	T	HR	RBI	SB	BB	SO	Avg
1998 A Portland	64	264	55	93	9	2	0	30	38	19	11	.352
1999 A Asheville	140	585	93	187	28	5	1	55	66	38	37	.320

Pierre has been a revelation since signing as a 13th-round pick from the University of South Alabama in 1998. He led the short-season Northwest League in hitting and stolen bases in his debut, and last year he led the minors with 187 hits while batting .320 with 66 steals. He also struck out just once in ever 17.5 plate appearances, the best rate among Class-A players. The encore convinced the Rockies that he's for real, so they'll accelerate his development. Pierre could stand to get stronger and more patient. His speed and center-field defense are positives. If Colorado decides to keep both Pierre and Choo Freeman in center this season, they might skip Pierre up a level to Double-A.

Juan Uribe

Position: SS **Opening Day Age:** 19
Bats: R **Throws:** R **Born:** 7/22/80 in Bani,
Ht: 5' 11" **Wt:** 173 Dominican Republic

Recent Statistics

	G	AB	R	H	D	T	HR	RBI	SB	BB	SO	Avg
1998 R Rockies	40	148	25	41	5	3	0	17	8	12	25	.277
1999 A Asheville	125	430	57	115	28	3	9	46	11	20	79	.267

Uribe's shortstop tools are so impressive that Rockies incumbent Neifi Perez says that Uribe eventually will force him to second base. He has the arm, hands and range to contend for Gold Gloves once he reaches the major leagues. Offensively, he still has a long way to go. His .267 average last year wasn't bad for an 18-year-old in a full-season Class-A league, and he does have the ability to sting the ball in the gaps on occasion. But he'll need to develop much more discipline and make better contact at the plate. He has some speed but won't pile up significant stolen-base totals. It's unlikely that Uribe will play regularly in Colorado until 2003.

Others to Watch

Matt Holliday (20) was one of the top high school quarterbacks in the nation and had a scholarship to play for Oklahoma State before signing with the Rockies in 1998. His power and his arm are his two best tools, and he does everything well but run. . . Converted to relief, righthander **Craig House** (22) saw his sinking fastball zoom from 92 MPH to 95-98 while he struck out 58 and didn't allow a homer in 34.2 innings at short-season Portland. He also has a mid-80s slider, but his funky delivery could lead to an arm injury. . . Righthander **Ryan Kibler** (19), Colorado's 1999 second-round pick, throws an 88-91 MPH sinker, a curveball and a changeup. His fastball projects to get quicker, and he made the all-star team in the Rookie-level Gulf Coast League. . . The Rockies intend to become major players in the international market, and they made their first big splash by signing righthander **Tsao Chin-Hui** (18) for $2.2 million. He's a four-pitch pitcher with a 92-93 MPH fastball that touches 96, and he'll make his pro debut this season at Class-A Asheville. . . Righthander **Jermaine Van Buren** (19) won the pitching triple crown in the Rookie-level Arizona League in 1998, then made the jump to Class-A last year and struck out 133 in 143 innings. He has a 91-94 MPH fastball and a sharp curveball. . . Second baseman **Juan Ventura** (19) won the Arizona League batting title with a .399 average last year. He also has speed and plenty of range.

Pro Player Stadium

Offense

Home attendance dropped again in 1999, and Pro Player Stadium's roomy dimensions were held at least partly accountable. Scoring was 12 percent higher when the Marlins were on the road, and home runs were 45 percent more plentiful away from the land of teal. New owner John W. Henry mused aloud several times about bringing in the fences, especially in the "Bermuda Triangle" in deep left-center, which regularly turns what elsewhere would be homers into doubles and triples.

Defense

The biggest challenge is the Teal Tower, a 28-foot high scoreboard in left-center field that seems to attract horsehide. Odd caroms often flummox Marlins and opponent outfielders alike. Pro Player has the highest error and infield-error factors in the National League, but that's a reflection of poor lighting and erratic scorekeeping.

Who It Helps the Most

Pitchers, especially flyball pitchers. Brian Meadows' ERA was 2.61 runs lower at home than on the road last year. Ryan Dempster allowed just five of his 21 home runs at home and had a 2.57 ERA disparity. Closer Antonio Alfonseca, though a marked groundball pitcher, had a 1.98 ERA at home, compared with a whopping 5.53 mark on the road.

Who It Hurts the Most

Hitters, especially power hitters. Just eight of Preston Wilson's 26 home runs last year came at Pro Player, while just four of Derrek Lee's 22 home runs in two seasons have been at home. Batting averages also suffer. Cliff Floyd (136 points lower) felt the biggest drain in 1999, but Mike Redmond (75) and Alex Gonzalez (37) were penalized as well.

Rookies & Newcomers

Outfielder Brant Brown's so-so power will be blunted by Pro Player Stadium, but Three Rivers Stadium didn't do much for him anyway. Catcher Ramon Castro went just 1-for-13 at home in a September callup. Righthander A.J. Burnett allowed no homers in a pair of home starts.

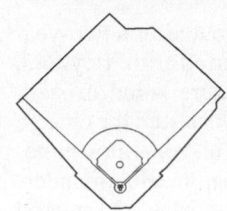

Dimensions: LF-330, LCF-385, CF-404, RCF-385, RF-345

Capacity: 35,521

Elevation: 10 feet

Surface: Grass

Foul Territory: Large

Park Factors

1999 Season

| | Home Games | | | Away Games | | | |
	Marlins	Opp	Total	Marlins	Opp	Total	Index
G	71	71	142	73	73	146	—
Avg	.260	.266	.263	.258	.297	.277	95
AB	2443	2501	4944	2496	2417	4913	103
R	287	336	623	294	426	720	89
H	634	665	1299	645	717	1362	98
2B	117	128	245	114	133	247	99
3B	24	22	46	15	14	29	158
HR	43	66	109	72	86	158	69
BB	235	288	523	189	309	498	104
SO	465	473	938	567	358	925	101
E	59	54	113	54	36	90	129
E-Infield	49	45	94	40	27	67	144
LHB-Avg	.248	.272	.262	.259	.305	.286	91
LHB-HR	10	30	40	13	47	60	63
RHB-Avg	.265	.261	.263	.258	.290	.272	97
RHB-HR	33	36	69	59	39	98	72

1997-1999

| | Home Games | | | Away Games | | | |
	Marlins	Opp	Total	Marlins	Opp	Total	Index
G	219	219	438	218	218	436	—
Avg	.256	.258	.257	.256	.290	.273	94
AB	7316	7600	14916	7562	7285	14847	100
R	909	1029	1938	940	1202	2142	90
H	1875	1962	3837	1933	2116	4049	94
2B	349	365	714	376	389	765	93
3B	57	62	119	42	57	99	120
HR	146	212	358	199	229	428	83
BB	829	902	1731	687	908	1595	108
SO	1432	1513	2945	1602	1289	2891	101
E	170	163	333	177	139	316	105
E-Infield	145	138	283	144	111	255	110
LHB-Avg	.256	.267	.261	.258	.303	.280	93
LHB-HR	44	80	124	58	91	149	80
RHB-Avg	.257	.253	.255	.254	.282	.268	95
RHB-HR	102	132	234	141	138	279	85

1999 Rankings (National League)

- Highest error factor
- Highest infield-error factor
- Second-lowest home-run factor
- Second-lowest LHB batting-average factor
- Second-lowest LHB home-run factor
- Second-lowest RHB home-run factor
- Third-lowest run factor

John Boles

1999 Season

John Boles returned to the dugout after a two-year absence, replacing the departed Jim Leyland. Boles' unflaggingly upbeat nature stood in stark contrast to Leyland's mood swings, and the change seemed to help several young players, most notably second baseman Luis Castillo. Boles underwent major back surgery in late May and missed just two games. He later suffered a setback and missed a week, but never complained. He was less tolerant of loafing or tardiness by his players, yanking Castillo, Cliff Floyd and Alex Gonzalez from the lineup at various times during the season.

Offense

Boles didn't experiment much with his lineup and was careful to keep free-swinging rookie Preston Wilson out of the cleanup spot. Castillo was given the green light to steal at midseason, but just one other Marlin (Wilson) managed double figures in stolen bases. Though only the Twins hit fewer home runs than the Marlins, Boles steadfastly refused to play small ball. Boles doesn't like to platoon or use pinch-runners.

Pitching & Defense

Boles had one of the quicker hooks in the league, rarely letting his young pitchers or the rehabilitating Alex Fernandez pile up high pitch counts. Fernandez was limited to a 100-pitch maximum all season, which put added strain on an overmatched bullpen. Boles takes a back seat to no one when it comes to the double switch. He wasn't afraid to ignore lefty-righty matchups if, for instance, he needed a groundball or a strikeout. When protecting a lead in the late innings, Boles likes to guard the lines and move his outfielders a few steps back.

2000 Outlook

Having produced a 10-game improvement in the first season of his second Marlins tenure, Boles no doubt will eye an even bigger leap forward this time around. His contract runs through 2001, about the time the front office anticipates its young players will be ready to contend for the wild-card. Patience and a positive attitude are perhaps Boles' two strongest traits, so he seems ideally suited for the long road back.

Born: 8/19/48 in Chicago, Illinois

Playing Experience: No major league experience

Managerial Experience: 2 seasons

Manager Statistics

Year	Team, Lg	W	L	Pct	GB	Finish
1999	Florida, NL	64	98	.395	39.0	5th East
2 Seasons		104	133	.439	—	—

1999 Starting Pitchers by Days Rest

	<=3	4	5	6+
Marlins Starts	1	78	49	23
Marlins ERA	4.05	4.92	4.63	4.86
NL Avg Starts	3	81	48	21
NL ERA	4.84	4.53	4.72	4.98

1999 Situational Stats

	John Boles	NL Average
Hit & Run Success %	27.4	33.6
Stolen Base Success %	66.7	70.2
Platoon Pct.	49.3	55.2
Defensive Subs	14	25
High-Pitch Outings	16	13
Quick/Slow Hooks	22/13	16/15
Sacrifice Attempts	67	89

1999 Rankings (National League)

- 1st in fewest caught stealings of third base (1)
- 2nd in relief appearances (453), mid-inning pitching changes (194) and one-batter pitcher appearances (45)
- 3rd in intentional walks (39), quick hooks (22) and 2+ pitching changes in low-scoring games (25)

Antonio Alfonseca

1999 Season

Previously known as the perpetually silly Dominican with six fingers and toes on each hand and foot, Antonio Alfonseca transformed himself and his reputation. He dropped 35 pounds from a lumpy frame and provided capable setup work over the first three months of the season. When Matt Mantei was traded to Arizona just before the All-Star break, Alfonseca quickly seized the opportunity and shut down the Marlins' plans for a bullpen-by-committee. He blew just two of 23 save chances after the Mantei trade. Those who knew Alfonseca best marveled at his newfound seriousness.

Pitching

Alfonseca is blessed with tremendous movement on all his pitches, particularly a fastball he throws at 95-97 MPH with hard boring action. His slider was much improved and his changeup became a reliable weapon against lefties. His strikeout numbers weren't those of a prototypical closer, but solid contact was rare against his nasty stuff. He attacked lefties and righties with similar success, producing tons of groundballs with his downward movement. He allowed just four home runs all year, and only one after June 1. Strangely, Alfonseca's struggles on the road can't be blamed on artificial turf. His turf numbers were better than those on grass.

Defense & Hitting

Like all closers, Alfonseca gets tested by the better basestealers. He managed to thwart them with a quick motion and a reliance on hard stuff. He rarely bats and is awkward in the field.

2000 Outlook

Alfonseca will open the year as the undisputed closer for the first time in his career. Even with Braden Looper on hand, Alfonseca will be given every opportunity to prove his second-half performance was no fluke. He could be eligible for salary arbitration next winter, which will make his follow-up showing all the more important.

Position: RP
Bats: R **Throws:** R
Ht: 6' 5" **Wt:** 235

Opening Day Age: 27
Born: 4/16/72 in La Romana, Dom. Rep.
ML Seasons: 3
Pronunciation: AL-fonn-say-kuh
Nickname: Pulpo, Dragonslayer

Overall Statistics

	W	L	Pct.	ERA	G	GS	Sv	IP	H	BB	SO	HR	Ratio
1999	4	5	.444	3.24	73	0	21	77.2	79	29	46	4	1.39
Career	9	14	.391	3.83	148	0	29	174.0	190	72	111	17	1.51

How Often He Throws Strikes

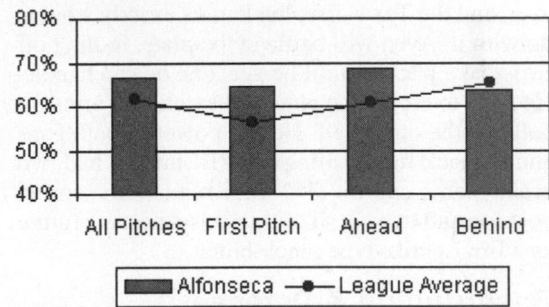

1999 Situational Stats

	W	L	ERA	Sv	IP		AB	H	HR	RBI	Avg
Home	3	1	1.98	10	50.0	LHB	126	34	1	11	.270
Road	1	4	5.53	11	27.2	RHB	162	45	3	18	.278
First Half	4	5	3.63	1	44.?	Sc Pos	78	20	0	23	.256
Scnd Half	0	0	2.73	20	33.0	Clutch	148	38	0	18	.257

1999 Rankings (National League)
- 3rd in fewest strikeouts per 9 innings in relief (5.3)
- 7th in save percentage (84.0%) and most GDPs induced per GDP situation (19.4%)
- 8th in games pitched
- Led the Marlins in games pitched, saves, games finished (49), save opportunities (25), save percentage (84.0%), most GDPs induced per GDP situation (19.4%), first batter efficiency (.200), relief ERA (3.24), lowest batting average allowed in relief (.274) and fewest baserunners allowed per 9 innings in relief (13.0)

Bruce Aven

1999 Season

Bruce Aven was one of the surprise stories in all of baseball. Claimed off waivers from the Indians, he came to spring training as a nonroster invitee, eight months removed from ligament-transplant surgery on his throwing elbow. At first known for his penchant for alligator wrestling, Aven quickly earned respect for his bat. The rookie's role steadily expanded, from opportunistic pinch-hitter to occasional starter to consistent run producer.

Hitting

Opponents gradually figured Aven out, feeding him sliders and changeups off the plate that he was too willing to chase. He slumped noticeably in the second half. Give him a fastball in the zone, however, and the Texas fireplug knows exactly what to do with it. Aven will battle at the plate, fouling off two-strike pitches until he gets one he can handle. He likes to crowd the plate and extend his arms for balls on the outer half. He has power to both gaps and a knack for smelling the RBI hit. He had two grand slams and hit .361 with runners in scoring position and two out. If nothing else, he has a future as a Jim Leyritz-type pinch-hitter.

Baserunning & Defense

Aven has average speed, offsetting his short stride with extreme effort. He doesn't steal bases but doesn't run himself into outs either. His arm remains below average following surgery, but he's adequate in left field, even throwing out a handful of runners thanks to solid footwork. He played 24 games in right, and his deficiencies really showed up in his brief exposure to center.

2000 Outlook

A former 30th-round pick, Aven was buried in the Indians system for years. After finding success with the Marlins, he was traded to the Pirates for Brant Brown in December. Both players will open 2000 as fourth outfielders with their new clubs. Aven is valued highly for his attitude and pinch-hitting prowess.

Position: LF/RF
Bats: R **Throws:** R
Ht: 5' 9" **Wt:** 180

Opening Day Age: 28
Born: 3/4/72 in Orange, TX
ML Seasons: 2
Pronunciation: AY-ven
Nickname: Gator

Overall Statistics

	G	AB	R	H	D	T	HR	RBI	SB	BB	SO	Avg	OBP	Slg
1999	137	381	57	110	19	2	12	70	3	44	82	.289	.370	.444
Career	150	400	61	114	20	2	12	72	3	45	87	.285	.365	.435

Where He Hits the Ball

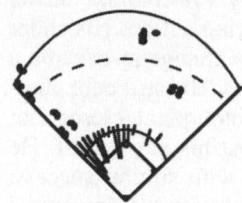 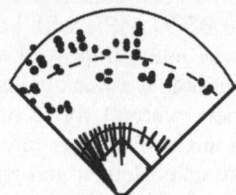

Vs. LHP **Vs. RHP**

1999 Situational Stats

	AB	H	HR	RBI	Avg		AB	H	HR	RBI	Avg
Home	170	50	3	28	.294	LHP	105	29	4	19	.276
Road	211	60	9	42	.284	RHP	276	81	8	51	.293
First Half	187	61	7	47	.326	Sc Pos	104	33	6	57	.317
Scnd Half	194	49	5	23	.253	Clutch	79	27	1	12	.342

1999 Rankings (National League)

- Led the Marlins in batting average in the clutch

Luis Castillo

1999 Season

Luis Castillo won a spring-training duel with incumbent Craig Counsell for the starting second-base job, then had a dream season. Playing with renewed confidence for a manager who knew which buttons to push, Castillo flashed the four-tool ability previously known only by his minor league teams. He tied a club record with a 22-game hitting streak and set another mark with 16 consecutive stolen bases. He was benched for loafing in late July, but quickly shook off the one-game penalty.

Hitting

For years Castillo battled a weak lefthanded swing, and he gave up switch-hitting numerous times before something finally clicked in the spring. He hit .300 or better from both sides of the plate, and actually began driving the ball from the left side, though solely down the line to the opposite field. He has learned to lay off high fastballs but still chases breaking balls that run out of the zone. Castillo led the majors in bunts put in play and proved a difficult strikeout victim. He warmed to his natural role as leadoff man, fouling off pitches and working walks. He hit nearly five groundballs for every flyball, the most pronounced ratio in the majors and exactly what someone with his speed should do.

Baserunning & Defense

Castillo finally got the green light to steal just before the All-Star break, and he ran wild thereafter. Manager John Boles fully expects Castillo to challenge for the stolen-base title on an annual basis. His raw speed finally was complemented by better instincts and pitch selection. Castillo has one of the strongest arms among second basemen. His concentration improved in the field as well, and he made routine plays more consistently while continuing to make spectacular ones on occasion.

2000 Outlook

Castillo had surgery on his left shoulder, which has given him trouble for years. He was expected to report for spring training at full strength. He is the club's unquestioned second baseman.

Position: 2B
Bats: B **Throws:** R
Ht: 5'11" **Wt:** 175

Opening Day Age: 24
Born: 9/12/75 in San Pedro de Macoris, Dominican Republic
ML Seasons: 4
Pronunciation: cas-TEE-oh

Overall Statistics

	G	AB	R	H	D	T	HR	RBI	SB	BB	SO	Avg	OBP	Slg
1999	128	487	76	147	23	4	0	28	50	67	85	.302	.384	.366
Career	288	1067	150	284	36	7	2	54	86	130	217	.266	.346	.319

Where He Hits the Ball

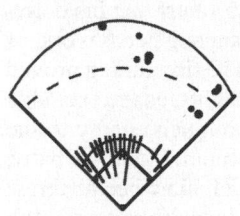 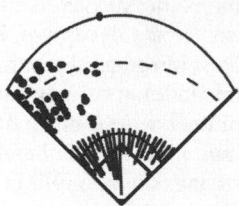

Vs. LHP   **Vs. RHP**

1999 Situational Stats

	AB	H	HR	RBI	Avg		AB	H	HR	RBI	Avg
Home	262	77	0	12	.294	LHP	100	31	0	8	.310
Road	225	70	0	16	.311	RHP	387	116	0	20	.300
First Half	291	82	0	13	.282	Sc Pos	89	22	0	27	.247
Scnd Half	196	65	0	15	.332	Clutch	73	24	0	8	.329

1999 Rankings (National League)

- 1st in lowest HR frequency (974.0 ABs per HR) and highest groundball/flyball ratio (4.9)
- 2nd in caught stealing (17), errors at second base (15) and lowest fielding percentage at second base (.976)
- Led the Marlins in batting average, singles, stolen bases, caught stealing (17), walks, times on base (214), pitches seen (2,264), on-base percentage, highest groundball/flyball ratio (4.9), stolen-base percentage (74.6%), most pitches seen per plate appearance (4.02), fewest GDPs per GDP situation (5.3%), batting average vs. righthanded pitchers, on-base percentage for a leadoff hitter (.385) and on-base percentage vs. righthanded pitchers (.381)

Ryan Dempster

1999 Season

Given an opportunity to make the Marlins out of spring training, Ryan Dempster had a miserable audition before going to Triple-A Calgary and righting himself. He returned on May 7 and remained in the rotation the rest of the year. A brutal July threatened to wipe out his progress, but the agreeable Canadian managed to keep pushing forward. Dempster finished with eight shutout innings against the Braves on the final day of the season.

Pitching

Dempster relies on a 92-94 MPH fastball with late sink, and a ferocious slider that he'll throw to both righties and lefties. The Marlins believe Dempster's slider to be the equal of almost any in the National League. It doesn't hurt that his delivery is very deceptive. His changeup needs work, as does his general command. The first inning proved his undoing on a number of nights, as the excitable pitcher would bring a tad too much energy to the mound. At times his release point could go batty, such as on the night in Philadelphia when he threw 10 straight balls before finishing with a career-high 10 strikeouts. His ERA on the road was almost twice as high as it was at home, and he allowed three times as many home runs on the road.

Defense & Hitting

Dempster does a good job against the running game. He's quick to the plate and holds runners well. His fielding is spotty at times, and he's a much worse hitter than he should be, considering his athletic ability. His bunting needs plenty of work as well.

2000 Outlook

After making 36 starts in the majors over the last two years, Dempster is penciled into the No. 2 or 3 slot in Florida's rotation this spring. His confidence and polish seem to increase with each outing, and club officials believe the former third-round pick's ceiling is very high.

Position: SP
Bats: R **Throws:** R
Ht: 6' 1" **Wt:** 201

Opening Day Age: 22
Born: 5/3/77 in Sachelt, Canada
ML Seasons: 2

Overall Statistics

	W	L	Pct.	ERA	G	GS	Sv	IP	H	BB	SO	HR	Ratio
1999	7	8	.467	4.71	25	25	0	147.0	146	93	126	21	1.63
Career	8	13	.381	5.36	39	36	0	201.2	218	131	161	27	1.73

How Often He Throws Strikes

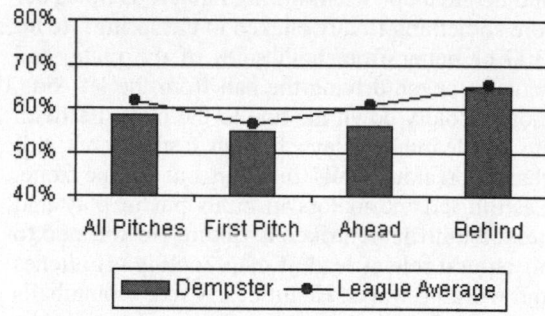

1999 Situational Stats

	W	L	ERA	Sv	IP		AB	H	HR	RBI	Avg
Home	4	2	3.33	0	67.2	LHB	262	74	12	33	.282
Road	3	6	5.90	0	79.1	RHB	296	72	9	31	.243
First Half	4	5	5.09	0	58.1	Sc Pos	126	27	2	35	.214
Scnd Half	3	3	4.47	0	88.2	Clutch	34	8	0	1	.235

1999 Rankings (National League)

- 6th in walks allowed
- 7th in lowest batting average allowed with runners in scoring position
- Led the Marlins in walks allowed, strikeouts, wild pitches (8), winning percentage and lowest batting average allowed vs. righthanded batters

Alex Fernandez

1999 Season

Alex Fernandez achieved success with his first pitch of the year. Nearly 19 months passed between starts for Fernandez, who blew out his rotator cuff during the 1997 National League Championship Series. His comeback from reconstructive shoulder surgery inspired teammates and opponents alike. He endured two stints on the disabled list and received two cortisone shots before shutting it down for the year in early September. He made 17 of his 24 starts at home, including 10 day games, as the club carefully protected his shoulder. He operated on a 100-pitch limit all year.

Pitching

Even Fernandez was amazed at how quickly his command returned. Though his fastball lacked its pre-surgery velocity, usually topping out in the high 80s, Fernandez showed he still could locate any of his four pitches at any time. He stayed away from lefthanders, keeping them off balance with curves and changeups. He ate up righties with hard sliders and well-placed fastballs. He got by on guile and guts. Fernandez would have ranked sixth in the National League in ERA had he pitched enough innings to qualify.

Defense & Hitting

Basestealers were unusually successful against Fernandez, whose run-stopping fundamentals are otherwise strong. Perhaps it was a result of his increased reliance on offspeed pitches. Despite regaining much of the weight he lost during rehab, Fernandez remains an excellent fielder. His .233 batting average topped Marlins starters and his three homers equaled the combined output of Luis Castillo, Todd Dunwoody and Mike Redmond.

2000 Outlook

With another offseason to recuperate, Fernandez hopes his velocity will return to the 91-93 MPH range. If it does, the Marlins expect to have a 200-inning, 15-win horse at the top of their rotation. His $7 million annual salary ate up 41 percent of Florida's year-end payroll, and he has two years remaining on a five-year, $35 million deal. A trade remains possible, but only to one of seven cities Fernandez approves in advance.

Position: SP
Bats: R **Throws:** R
Ht: 6' 1" **Wt:** 225

Opening Day Age: 30
Born: 8/13/69 in Miami Beach, FL
ML Seasons: 9

Overall Statistics

	W	L	Pct.	ERA	G	GS	Sv	IP	H	BB	SO	HR	Ratio
1999	7	8	.467	3.38	24	24	0	141.0	135	41	91	10	1.25
Career	103	83	.554	3.73	255	253	0	1708.0	1634	536	1225	183	1.27

How Often He Throws Strikes

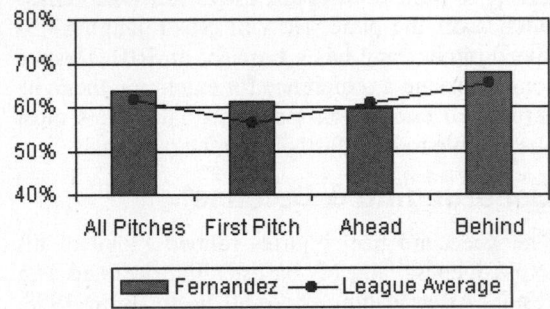

1999 Situational Stats

	W	L	ERA	Sv	IP		AB	H	HR	RBI	Avg
Home	5	4	2.92	0	95.2	LHB	283	78	7	35	.276
Road	2	4	4.37	0	45.1	RHB	253	57	3	23	.225
First Half	4	5	3.06	0	79.1	Sc Pos	127	25	2	46	.197
Scnd Half	3	3	3.79	0	61.2	Clutch	10	2	0	0	.200

1999 Rankings (National League)

- 2nd in lowest batting average allowed with runners in scoring position
- 6th in ERA at home
- Led the Marlins in winning percentage, ERA at home, lowest batting average allowed vs. lefthanded batters and lowest batting average allowed with runners in scoring position

Cliff Floyd

1999 Season

Handed a four-year, $19 million contract over the winter, Cliff Floyd proceeded to validate those who derisively call him "Glass" for his fragile body. He hurt his left knee in spring training and missed the season's first three weeks following arthroscopic surgery. Just as he was rounding into form, he went back on the disabled list in mid-June with a torn right Achilles. He didn't return until early September, and the Marlins clearly suffered in his absence.

Hitting

In less than half a season, Floyd showed he still retains his basic gifts at the plate: tremendous power to all fields, a discerning batting eye and the ability to punish mistakes. Floyd refuses to chase pitches off the plate. He will crush hanging off-speed pitches and has a nose for an RBI. Despite long arms and a preference for extending them, he turns well enough on inside fastballs. He's most susceptible to high fastballs on the outer half.

Baserunning & Defense

The knee and heel injuries robbed Floyd of his explosiveness, and his basestealing declined as a result. After leading the club in steals in 1998, Floyd failed in more than half his attempts. It was sad to watch him hobble around first and struggle to leg out what used to be easy doubles. His arm is below average and runners frequently took advantage of his diminished speed. He's only an average outfielder even when 100 percent.

2000 Outlook

Floyd's future is cloudy again. When healthy, he provides the Marlins a legitimate middle-of-the-order presence and their only true lefthanded power. Problem is, he's rarely healthy. Another problem? He's a future DH stuck in the wrong league. A return to first base is out of the question because that's where he was playing when he shattered his left wrist in a freak collision in 1995. Floyd remains Florida's left fielder for now.

Position: LF
Bats: L **Throws:** R
Ht: 6' 4" **Wt:** 235

Opening Day Age: 27
Born: 12/5/72 in Chicago, IL
ML Seasons: 7

Overall Statistics

	G	AB	R	H	D	T	HR	RBI	SB	BB	SO	Avg	OBP	Slg
1999	69	251	37	76	19	1	11	49	5	30	47	.303	.379	.518
Career	539	1637	226	439	108	13	51	235	58	162	338	.268	.338	.443

Where He Hits the Ball

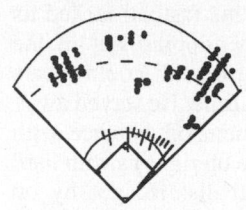

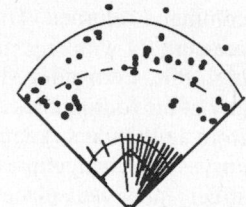

Vs. LHP   **Vs. RHP**

1999 Situational Stats

	AB	H	HR	RBI	Avg		AB	H	HR	RBI	Avg
Home	124	29	4	21	.234	LHP	59	18	4	9	.305
Road	127	47	7	28	.370	RHP	192	58	7	40	.302
First Half	171	47	7	33	.275	Sc Pos	68	22	1	33	.324
Scnd Half	80	29	4	16	.363	Clutch	50	11	2	11	.220

1999 Rankings (National League)

- 6th in errors in left field (6)

Alex Gonzalez

1999 Season

Handed the starting shortstop job after Edgar Renteria was traded, Alex Gonzalez endured a strangely mixed rookie season. He was benched twice for failing to run out groundballs, once in April and again in September. In between, he became the first National League rookie shortstop ever to play in the All-Star Game. He drew raves for his defense and power in the first half, then experienced notable declines in both areas after the break. Another doghouse stint came after he rushed back from a knee injury in early August.

Hitting

Gonzalez is not an ideal No. 2 hitter. He's far too free a swinger—virtually impossible to walk—and grounds into too many double plays. Incredibly, he laid down just a single sacrifice bunt last year. He made the same mistakes all season, chasing high fastballs and breaking balls in the dirt, falling off balance and lofting easy popups. His aggressiveness and quick wrists make him an extra-base threat when he does make contact. He likes to crowd the plate and led the team in hit by pitches.

Baserunning & Defense

Gonzalez made several highlight-quality plays in the first half but struggled making routine plays down the stretch. A winter-ball warrior in his native Venezuela, Gonzalez seemed to wear down after the break. He has a strong arm and slightly better range to his right, and he makes the pivot quickly and easily. His speed is just average and he's no threat to steal, though triples have always come for him.

2000 Outlook

More walks, fewer strikeouts, higher average, more smiles. Those are points of emphasis for Gonzalez, who sulked openly by the end of his rookie season. This is a key year for him. The Marlins need to find out if Gonzalez can be their shortstop for the next decade or if he's merely keeping the spot warm for prospect Pablo Ozuna.

Position: SS
Bats: R **Throws:** R
Ht: 6' 0" **Wt:** 170

Opening Day Age: 23
Born: 2/15/77 in Cagua, Venezuela
ML Seasons: 2

Florida

Overall Statistics

	G	AB	R	H	D	T	HR	RBI	SB	BB	SO	Avg	OBP	Slg
1999	136	560	81	155	28	8	14	59	3	15	113	.277	.308	.430
Career	161	646	92	168	30	8	17	66	3	24	143	.260	.299	.410

Where He Hits the Ball

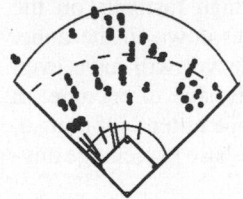 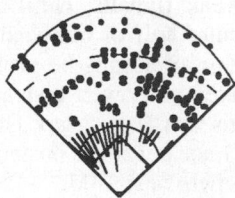

Vs. LHP   **Vs. RHP**

1999 Situational Stats

	AB	H	HR	RBI	Avg		AB	H	HR	RBI	Avg
Home	286	74	7	31	.259	LHP	114	29	3	13	.254
Road	274	81	7	28	.296	RHP	446	126	11	46	.283
First Half	340	99	9	39	.291	Sc Pos	140	39	5	45	.279
Scnd Half	220	56	5	20	.255	Clutch	74	23	1	10	.311

1999 Rankings (National League)

- 2nd in errors at shortstop (27) and lowest fielding percentage at shortstop (.955)
- 3rd in lowest percentage of pitches taken (43.7%)
- 4th in hit by pitch (12) and lowest on-base percentage
- 7th in triples and lowest on-base percentage vs. righthanded pitchers (.318)
- 9th in lowest batting average with the bases loaded (.091)
- 10th in lowest batting average at home
- Led the Marlins in at-bats, runs scored, hits, doubles, hit by pitch (12) and plate appearances (591)
- Led NL shortstops in hit by pitch (12)

Mark Kotsay

1999 Season

Mark Kotsay entered his second full season entrenched as the starting right fielder and hoping to build on the gains of a solid rookie year. Instead he experienced declines in all major categories and raised doubts about his long-term role in the Marlins' rebuilding project. Frustration set in early, especially during a .196 May.

Hitting

Kotsay hit 20 home runs in his only full minor league season, but he has just 19 after two years with the Marlins. He rarely pulls pitches, preferring to shoot line drives to left-center. Impatience became a problem as Kotsay increasingly swung at the first pitch with poor results, often producing weak flyballs. He'll chase high fastballs on the outer half or offspeed pitches down in the zone. Kotsay admits he probably never will have even average power. Instead, he'll have to become, in his words, a "Mark Grace-type hitter." Of course, Grace never has posted an on-base percentage anywhere near .306.

Baserunning & Defense

For the second straight year Kotsay led the majors in outfield assists. What he lacks in pure arm strength he more than offsets through accuracy, positioning and footwork. Kotsay has great defensive instincts, takes impeccable routes and several times affected a game's outcome with his defense. He also saw action in 19 games (12 starts) at first base, where he adapted well enough but was not as adventurous as he was in the outfield. Kotsay is an intelligent baserunner with average speed, but he's not a basestealing threat. He was slowed by a nagging case of shin splints.

2000 Outlook

Kotsay's attitude remains exemplary, his makeup beyond question. No one works harder, but his production must improve to ensure he doesn't get lost in the club's increasingly crowded outfield picture. Kotsay will enter the year as the starting right fielder, but there are no guarantees he'll stay there all season, especially if prized prospect Julio Ramirez eventually pushes Preston Wilson to right.

Position: RF/1B
Bats: L **Throws:** L
Ht: 6' 0" **Wt:** 190

Opening Day Age: 24
Born: 12/2/75 in Whittier, CA
ML Seasons: 3

Overall Statistics

	G	AB	R	H	D	T	HR	RBI	SB	BB	SO	Avg	OBP	Slg
1999	148	495	57	134	23	9	8	50	7	29	50	.271	.306	.402
Career	316	1125	134	305	49	17	19	122	20	67	118	.271	.310	.396

Where He Hits the Ball

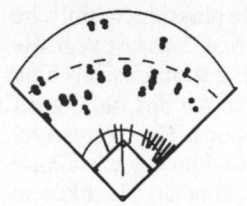
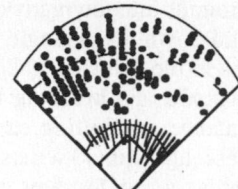

Vs. LHP **Vs. RHP**

1999 Situational Stats

	AB	H	HR	RBI	Avg		AB	H	HR	RBI	Avg
Home	245	69	5	28	.282	LHP	81	22	1	11	.272
Road	250	65	3	22	.260	RHP	414	112	7	39	.271
First Half	276	71	6	27	.257	Sc Pos	120	24	1	36	.200
Scnd Half	219	63	2	23	.288	Clutch	80	21	3	8	.263

1999 Rankings (National League)

- 1st in lowest on-base percentage
- 3rd in sacrifice flies (9) and lowest fielding percentage in right field (.982)
- 4th in errors in right field (5) and bunts in play (5)
- 5th in triples and lowest on-base percentage vs. righthanded pitchers (.304)
- Led the Marlins in triples, sacrifice flies (9), batting average with the bases loaded (.556), batting average on an 0-2 count (.308), bunts in play (5) and highest percentage of swings put into play (52.9%)
- Led NL right fielders in sacrifice flies (9), batting average on an 0-2 count (.308), lowest percentage of swings that missed (12.2%) and highest percentage of swings put into play (52.9%)

Mike Lowell

1999 Season

After finally being liberated from the Yankees organization for three pitching prospects in the offseason, Mike Lowell was eager to make a big league splash in his hometown. A stunning diagnosis of testicular cancer on the eve of spring training altered those plans. Lowell endured several minor league rehab assignments, and it took him until August before he seemed to regain anything close to full strength. His timing was off much of the year, but he showed enough flashes to excite the Marlins.

Hitting

Lowell was acquired because of his legitimate 30-homer potential, something the Marlins lacked throughout their system. Lowell seems all too aware of his reputation, however, trying to pull everything and struggling with breaking balls on the outer half. He does have the ability to turn on inside fastballs, and his power began to show itself more frequently as he regained his strength. He has a natural lift to his swing, which produces few groundballs. A streaky hitter, Lowell carried the club at times from the No. 7 spot in the batting order. He figures to move up a spot or three once he proves he's all the way back.

Baserunning & Defense

Even before his health problems, Lowell was slower than slow. He's absolutely no threat to steal and doubles must be obvious for him to chance advancing. His arm and range are average, and he has a tendency to get lazy with his feet. He rarely makes a highlight play and struggles with balls to his right. Last year he was very steady with the balls he could reach, making just four errors.

2000 Outlook

Lowell is the Marlins' third baseman of the present and future. He showed enough flashes down the stretch to convince Florida to trade Kevin Orie to the Dodgers. Lowell's actions are expected to become more explosive, both at the plate and in the field, as he puts more distance between himself and his surgery.

Position: 3B
Bats: R **Throws:** R
Ht: 6' 4" **Wt:** 205

Opening Day Age: 26
Born: 2/24/74 in San Juan, Puerto Rico
ML Seasons: 2

Overall Statistics

	G	AB	R	H	D	T	HR	RBI	SB	BB	SO	Avg	OBP	Slg
1999	97	308	32	78	15	0	12	47	0	26	69	.253	.317	.419
Career	105	323	33	82	15	0	12	47	0	26	70	.254	.315	.412

Where He Hits the Ball

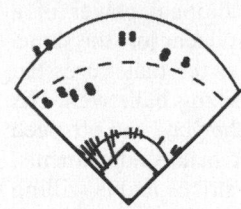 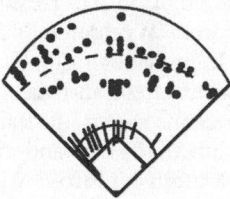

Vs. LHP   **Vs. RHP**

1999 Situational Stats

	AB	H	HR	RBI	Avg		AB	H	HR	RBI	Avg
Home	143	41	7	28	.287	LHP	72	18	6	14	.250
Road	165	37	5	19	.224	RHP	236	60	6	33	.254
First Half	95	24	2	13	.253	Sc Pos	71	19	4	35	.268
Scnd Half	213	54	10	34	.254	Clutch	53	15	5	15	.283

1999 Rankings (National League)

- 3rd in batting average on a 3-1 count (.750)
- Led the Marlins in batting average on a 3-1 count (.750)

Kevin Millar

1999 Season

Kevin Millar spent the first six weeks of the season in Triple-A, where he caused a messy flap when a Calgary reporter quoted him challenging the big-league Marlins to a seven-game series, with the winners staying in the majors. Millar quickly apologized and got his first real chance in mid-May, when he switched places with struggling first baseman Derrek Lee. Millar wasted no time seizing his opportunity, hitting a game-winning, inside-the-park home run at Wrigley Field in his first week on the job. Millar slipped neatly into the cleanup spot, while Lee didn't return until September.

Hitting

Though Millar lacks the traditional power of a corner infielder, he's a run producer just the same. He punishes fastballs out over the plate, uses the whole field and stays on breaking balls well. His weaknesses are fastballs off the plate and offspeed stuff that's low and away. He makes adjustments, shortens his stroke with two strikes and is willing to work a walk. Like Bruce Aven, his former Lamar University teammate, Millar excels in RBI situations. He slumped badly in the final two months as opponents learned his tendencies.

Baserunning & Defense

No one will mistake Millar for J.T. Snow at first base. That just happens to be the position where he does the least damage. Millar's hands are decent, but his range is extremely limited and his throwing could best be classified as careful. He has below-average speed and is basically a station-to-station runner.

2000 Outlook

Millar went undrafted out of high school, undrafted out of college, then had to be rescued from the independent Northern League. Still, he has hit at every level and will come to spring training on even footing with Lee, a former first-round pick the club desperately wants to see succeed. At the very least Millar has earned a reserve role.

Position: 1B
Bats: R **Throws:** R
Ht: 6' 0" **Wt:** 185

Opening Day Age: 28
Born: 9/24/71 in Los Angeles, CA
ML Seasons: 2

Overall Statistics

	G	AB	R	H	D	T	HR	RBI	SB	BB	SO	Avg	OBP	Slg
1999	105	351	48	100	17	4	9	67	1	40	64	.285	.362	.433
Career	107	353	49	101	17	4	9	67	1	41	64	.286	.364	.433

Where He Hits the Ball

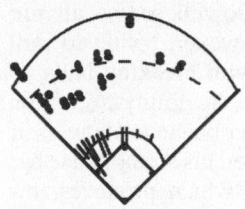 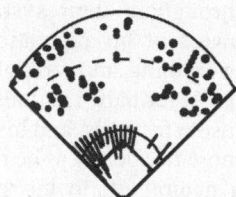

Vs. LHP **Vs. RHP**

1999 Situational Stats

	AB	H	HR	RBI	Avg		AB	H	HR	RBI	Avg
Home	183	52	3	29	.284	LHP	93	27	3	19	.290
Road	168	48	6	38	.286	RHP	258	73	6	48	.283
First Half	143	49	4	34	.343	Sc Pos	109	40	1	53	.367
Scnd Half	208	51	5	33	.245	Clutch	46	8	2	8	.174

1999 Rankings (National League)

- 3rd in lowest cleanup slugging percentage (.432)
- 5th in batting average with runners in scoring position
- 7th in batting average with two strikes (.262)
- 8th in sacrifice flies (8)
- 9th in lowest batting average in the clutch
- Led the Marlins in batting average with runners in scoring position, cleanup slugging percentage (.432) and batting average with two strikes (.262)
- Led NL first basemen in batting average with runners in scoring position and batting average with two strikes (.262)

Vladimir Nunez

1999 Season

Vladimir Nunez opened the year at Triple-A Tucson, then was called up to Arizona and given a chance to close for the Diamondbacks. When Nunez struggled in the role, blowing two of three save chances, he was shipped to the Marlins with prospect Brady Penny on July 9 in exchange for Matt Mantei. Florida later received stud outfield prospect Abraham Nunez (no relation) as a player to be named. After making five relief outings for the Marlins, Vladimir moved into the rotation and stayed there the rest of the year. His pitch limit gradually was extended, and Nunez lasted into the seventh inning or beyond in five of his final eight starts.

Pitching

Nunez was outspoken in his distaste for relief pitching. He prefers to use his full four-pitch arsenal and tight end's frame to wear down hitters as the innings tick past. His 92-94 MPH fastball has good movement and heavy sink, and Nunez complements it with a plus slider, developing changeup and nasty splitter. The latter proved so unhittable that lefties learned to lay off the pitch and take walks instead. Nunez, like fellow Cuban Rolando Arrojo, will change arm angles and throw from a three-quarters slot without warning. The Marlins would like him to keep a consistent arm slot and rely more on his overwhelming stuff.

Defense & Hitting

Nunez had trouble stopping the running game as he attempted to shed bad habits acquired in relief. His pickoff move needs work, and he could be quicker to the plate. He's an excellent fielder but a poor hitter and bunter. As a Diamondbacks reliever, he rarely took batting practice. Nunez appears a good enough athlete to improve in these areas with time.

2000 Outlook

Nunez will open the year in the Marlins' rotation, possibly as high as the No. 2 starter behind Alex Fernandez. His development alone has made the organization feel good about the Mantei trade. What's more, Nunez appears a significant upgrade in the Cuban-defector department over Livan Hernandez.

Position: RP/SP
Bats: R **Throws:** R
Ht: 6' 4" **Wt:** 224

Opening Day Age: 25
Born: 3/15/75 in Mariano, Cuba
ML Seasons: 2
Pronunciation: NOON-yez

Florida

Overall Statistics

	W	L	Pct.	ERA	G	GS	Sv	IP	H	BB	SO	HR	Ratio
1999	7	10	.412	4.06	44	12	1	108.2	95	54	86	11	1.37
Career	7	10	.412	4.34	48	12	1	114.0	102	56	88	11	1.39

How Often He Throws Strikes

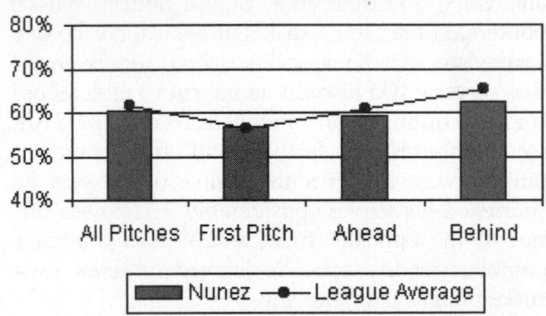

1999 Situational Stats

	W	L	ERA	Sv	IP		AB	H	HR	RBI	Avg
Home	3	6	4.36	1	53.2	LHB	153	41	6	21	.268
Road	4	4	3.76	0	55.0	RHB	239	54	5	26	.226
First Half	3	2	2.83	1	35.0	Sc Pos	103	26	5	39	.252
Scnd Half	4	8	4.64	0	73.2	Clutch	55	16	1	9	.291

1999 Rankings (National League)

- Did not rank near the top or bottom in any category

Preston Wilson

1999 Season

Preston Wilson began the year as Florida's starting left fielder, filling in for the injured Cliff Floyd. When Wilson failed to take advantage of the opportunity, barely hitting .200 over the first six weeks, he nearly was shipped back to Triple-A. Todd Dunwoody was sent down instead. Granted a reprieve, Wilson blossomed in late May, claimed center field as his own and finished second in National League Rookie of the Year balloting.

Hitting

Few young hitters can match Wilson's raw power. His quick wrists and strong forearms generate some mammoth blasts, and the likes of Eric Davis and Gary Sheffield took public notice. Wilson obliterated the club's strikeout record, but no one seemed to care because his overall improvement was so great. He also set an unofficial club record for extra hitting hours, and the hard work paid off. He still chases high fastballs and offspeed pitches tailing away, but over the course of the year he shortened his stroke considerably. His power carries to the opposite field, and Wilson's average climbed steadily once he learned to shoot two-strike pitches the other way.

Baserunning & Defense

Wilson isn't a natural basestealer, but he showed improvement in that area by season's end. He has plus speed and good instincts on the basepaths. His defense was spotty early in the year but his routes improved markedly through extra work. He still makes things interesting but he can outrun balls, especially those hit over his head. Though he managed to record his share of assists, his arm is just average.

2000 Outlook

Having finally harnessed his vast set of tools after six years in the minors, Wilson's star is on the rise. He enters the spring as the unquestioned starter in center field, and there's talk of 40-homer potential. He might even get a crack at the cleanup spot, a role the Marlins shielded him from in his breakthrough year.

Position: CF/LF/RF
Bats: R **Throws:** R
Ht: 6' 2" **Wt:** 193

Opening Day Age: 25
Born: 7/19/74 in Bamberg, SC
ML Seasons: 2

Overall Statistics

	G	AB	R	H	D	T	HR	RBI	SB	BB	SO	Avg	OBP	Slg
1999	149	482	67	135	21	4	26	71	11	46	156	.280	.350	.502
Career	171	533	74	143	23	4	27	74	12	52	177	.268	.341	.478

Where He Hits the Ball

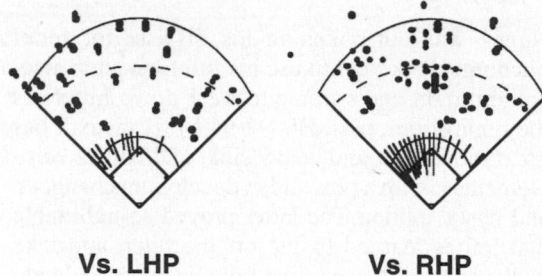

Vs. LHP   **Vs. RHP**

1999 Situational Stats

	AB	H	HR	RBI	Avg		AB	H	HR	RBI	Avg
Home	233	59	8	31	.253	LHP	123	35	9	23	.285
Road	249	76	18	40	.305	RHP	359	100	17	48	.279
First Half	253	66	17	41	.261	Sc Pos	121	30	5	46	.248
Scnd Half	229	69	9	30	.301	Clutch	76	24	5	10	.316

1999 Rankings (National League)

- 2nd in strikeouts and lowest fielding percentage in center field (.975)
- 3rd in lowest percentage of swings put into play (32.2%)
- Led the Marlins in home runs, total bases (242), RBI, strikeouts, GDPs (15), slugging percentage, HR frequency (18.5 ABs per HR), batting average vs. lefthanded pitchers, slugging percentage vs. lefthanded pitchers (.585), slugging percentage vs. righthanded pitchers (.474), on-base percentage vs. lefthanded pitchers (.366) and games played
- Led NL center fielders in strikeouts, GDPs (15) and slugging percentage vs. lefthanded pitchers (.585)

Danny Bautista

Position: RF/LF/CF
Bats: R **Throws:** R
Ht: 5'11" **Wt:** 170

Opening Day Age: 27
Born: 5/24/72 in Santo Domingo, Dominican Republic
ML Seasons: 7
Pronunciation: bah-TEESE-tah

Overall Statistics

	G	AB	R	H	D	T	HR	RBI	SB	BB	SO	Avg	OBP	Slg
1999	70	205	32	59	10	1	5	24	3	4	30	.288	.303	.420
Career	395	967	122	236	42	4	25	110	15	43	191	.244	.277	.373

1999 Situational Stats

	AB	H	HR	RBI	Avg			AB	H	HR	RBI	Avg
Home	91	28	2	13	.308	LHP		65	18	1	6	.277
Road	114	31	3	11	.272	RHP		140	41	4	18	.293
First Half	75	20	3	9	.267	Sc Pos		45	11	0	16	.244
Scnd Half	130	39	2	15	.300	Clutch		40	12	0	4	.300

1999 Season

Released by the Braves at the end of spring training, Danny Bautista hooked on with the Marlins and spent the first two months at Triple-A Calgary. Called up on June 11, he worked into a four-man outfield rotation when injuries felled left fielder Cliff Floyd for more than two months.

Hitting, Baserunning & Defense

Bautista has limited power but can drive mistakes into the gaps. He uses the whole field, showing good pop to right-center. He struggles with sliders and changeups down and away. He thrived as a pinch-hitter in 1999, but showed no inclination to take a walk. Though Bautista has average speed and good baserunning instincts, he's no threat to steal. In the outfield, he looked lost at times early in the year before improving greatly through extra daily work. He has enough arm to play right field, where he seemed most comfortable.

2000 Outlook

Marlins manager John Boles admitted Bautista grew on him. The Marlins loved his attitude and instincts, and they were intrigued by his tools and experience. He'll come to spring training battling Brant Brown and Mark Kotsay for outfield time.

Dave Berg

Position: SS/2B/3B
Bats: R **Throws:** R
Ht: 5'11" **Wt:** 185

Opening Day Age: 29
Born: 9/3/70 in Roseville, CA
ML Seasons: 2

Overall Statistics

	G	AB	R	H	D	T	HR	RBI	SB	BB	SO	Avg	OBP	Slg
1999	109	304	42	87	18	1	3	25	2	27	59	.286	.348	.382
Career	190	486	60	144	29	1	5	46	5	53	105	.296	.366	.391

1999 Situational Stats

	AB	H	HR	RBI	Avg			AB	H	HR	RBI	Avg
Home	129	44	1	15	.341	LHP		83	20	0	3	.241
Road	175	43	2	10	.246	RHP		221	67	3	22	.303
First Half	122	35	1	9	.287	Sc Pos		68	18	0	20	.265
Scnd Half	182	52	2	16	.286	Clutch		64	19	0	9	.297

1999 Season

Utilityman Dave Berg turned in another solid season off the bench. His versatility and attitude earned his manager's constant praise. There was talk at one point of a Dave Berg Day, when he would play all nine positions, but the idea eventually was squelched.

Hitting, Baserunning & Defense

Berg can make solid contact with a Randy Johnson fastball, slap the ball the other way and adjust to any situation. Next to Mark Kotsay, he's probably the Marlins' best hit-and-run batter. Berg tends to chase breaking balls down and away, and fastballs that ride in on his hands. A natural second baseman, he worked hard to improve his hands and range on the left side of the infield. He saw the bulk of his time at shortstop in relief of mercurial rookie Alex Gonzalez. Berg has an average arm and compensates with positioning and a quick release. He's a smart baserunner with average speed.

2000 Outlook

Berg enters his third season entrenched as the Marlins' Mr. Fix-It. He doesn't have a flashy nickname like Super Joe McEwing, but the Marlins consider him perhaps the best role player in the National League.

Todd Dunwoody

Traded To
ROYALS

Position: CF
Bats: L **Throws:** L
Ht: 6' 1" **Wt:** 195

Opening Day Age: 24
Born: 4/11/75 in Lafayette, IN
ML Seasons: 3

Overall Statistics

	G	AB	R	H	D	T	HR	RBI	SB	BB	SO	Avg	OBP	Slg
1999	64	186	20	41	6	3	2	20	3	12	41	.220	.270	.317
Career	199	670	80	163	35	12	9	55	10	40	175	.243	.291	.372

1999 Situational Stats

	AB	H	HR	RBI	Avg		AB	H	HR	RBI	Avg
Home	102	21	1	12	.206	LHP	27	6	0	4	.222
Road	84	20	1	8	.238	RHP	159	35	2	16	.220
First Half	126	27	1	12	.214	Sc Pos	49	12	0	17	.245
Scnd Half	60	14	1	8	.233	Clutch	32	9	1	8	.281

1999 Season

Todd Dunwoody entered his second full season in the majors as the Marlins' starting center fielder. He spent the offseason bulking up in hopes of increasing his power and taking his game to another level. Instead, by May 20 he was on his way to Triple-A Calgary.

Hitting, Baserunning & Defense

Spending his rookie season in the leadoff spot did nothing to help Dunwoody's strike-zone judgment. Issuing him a walk again seemed next to impossible as he chased high fastballs and all sorts of offspeed stuff. The home-run power he showed in the minors hasn't translated to the majors, though he does have decent gap power. Dunwoody has plus speed, the kind that results in triples but not stolen bases. He has a plus arm and the aggressiveness to play center field, but his bat remains the big question.

2000 Outlook

The Marlins traded Dunwoody to the Royals in December for third baseman Sean McNally, who had a big Double-A season in 1999 but is 27. Dunwoody might be able to tap into his tools in another environment. He enters the 2000 season as a reserve.

Derrek Lee

Position: 1B
Bats: R **Throws:** R
Ht: 6' 5" **Wt:** 225

Opening Day Age: 24
Born: 9/6/75 in Sacramento, CA
ML Seasons: 3

Overall Statistics

	G	AB	R	H	D	T	HR	RBI	SB	BB	SO	Avg	OBP	Slg
1999	70	218	21	45	9	1	5	20	2	17	70	.206	.263	.326
Career	233	726	92	165	41	2	23	98	7	73	214	.227	.305	.384

1999 Situational Stats

	AB	H	HR	RBI	Avg		AB	H	HR	RBI	Avg
Home	115	25	0	8	.217	LHP	47	11	1	5	.234
Road	103	20	5	12	.194	RHP	171	34	4	15	.199
First Half	158	30	3	14	.190	Sc Pos	55	10	2	14	.182
Scnd Half	60	15	2	6	.250	Clutch	39	8	0	4	.205

1999 Season

Much to Derrek Lee's horror, a nightmarish rookie September carried over to his sophomore campaign. The big first baseman was hitting just .190 when the Marlins mercifully shipped him to Triple-A Calgary at the end of May. He remained in the minors until the end of the Pacific Coast League season.

Hitting, Baserunning & Defense

The book on Lee remains the same. Pound him inside with fastballs, make him climb the ladder and feed him sliders in the dirt. Lee's long arms help him generate tremendous power when he connects. Problem is, his long swing makes him an easy mark for strikeouts. He worked with club official Tony Perez in September to shorten his swing, with mixed results. Lee has below-average speed and is a poor baserunner. His soft hands, large wingspan and accurate arm make him a potential Gold Glove first baseman.

2000 Outlook

While plenty of other teams would have pulled the plug on Lee by now, the Marlins vow to remain patient. His raw power and intelligence merit at least another look. He'll duel Kevin Millar in spring training for the first-base job.

Braden Looper

Position: RP
Bats: R **Throws:** R
Ht: 6' 5" **Wt:** 225

Opening Day Age: 25
Born: 10/28/74 in
Weatherford, OK
ML Seasons: 2

Brian Meadows

Traded To
PADRES

Position: SP
Bats: R **Throws:** R
Ht: 6' 4" **Wt:** 200

Opening Day Age: 24
Born: 11/21/75 in
Montgomery, AL
ML Seasons: 2

Overall Statistics

	W	L	Pct.	ERA	G	GS	Sv	IP	H	BB	SO	HR	Ratio
1999	3	3	.500	3.80	72	0	0	83.0	96	31	50	7	1.53
Career	3	4	.429	3.86	76	0	0	86.1	101	32	54	8	1.54

1999 Situational Stats

	W	L	ERA	Sv	IP		AB	H	HR	RBI	Avg
Home	1	0	3.25	0	44.1	LHB	137	47	4	25	.343
Road	2	3	4.42	0	38.2	RHB	191	49	3	33	.257
First Half	1	1	3.81	0	49.2	Sc Pos	115	33	2	49	.287
Scnd Half	2	2	3.78	0	33.1	Clutch	100	35	3	20	.350

Overall Statistics

	W	L	Pct.	ERA	G	GS	Sv	IP	H	BB	SO	HR	Ratio
1999	11	15	.423	5.60	31	31	0	178.1	214	57	72	31	1.52
Career	22	28	.440	5.41	62	62	0	352.2	436	103	160	51	1.53

1999 Situational Stats

	W	L	ERA	Sv	IP		AB	H	HR	RBI	Avg
Home	5	7	4.26	0	86.2	LHB	351	110	18	57	.313
Road	6	8	6.87	0	91.2	RHB	358	104	13	43	.291
First Half	6	10	5.59	0	104.2	Sc Pos	167	46	7	69	.275
Scnd Half	5	5	5.62	0	73.2	Clutch	20	9	2	6	.450

1999 Season

Acquired from St. Louis in the Edgar Renteria trade, Braden Looper entered the year as the Marlins' closer-in-waiting. He struggled with his command, proved surprisingly hittable and watched as Antonio Alfonseca assumed the closer duties after Matt Mantei was traded to Arizona.

Pitching, Defense & Hitting

Looper's velocity tends to fluctuate. He reportedly hit 100 MPH in the Arizona Fall League, but his fastball stayed in the 93-94 MPH range early in the year. He topped out at 98 MPH late in the season, showing a heavy two-seamer that produces nearly two groundouts for every flyball. He's still learning a four-seamer and trying to refine a slider and changeup. He changed the grip on his slider three times during the season, finally settling on one used by veteran reliever Archie Corbin. Looper didn't bat in 1999 and proved easy to run on.

2000 Outlook

When he was drafted out of Wichita State with the No. 3 overall pick in 1996, Looper was considered a prototypical closer. That may have been overly optimistic, considering his progression to this point. He likely will set up Alfonseca for another year.

1999 Season

For the second straight year, Brian Meadows led the Marlins in victories but little else. He regressed from his rookie season, again proving eminently hittable and repeatedly running out of gas in the middle innings.

Pitching, Defense & Hitting

Meadows lacks a dominating pitch, so he must be especially fine with his 87-90 MPH fastball and offspeed stuff. He has a plus slider at times and an average curveball. His changeup has a nagging habit of fading back over the plate when he throws it to lefties. Meadows struggles with command and location, leaving far too many pitches up in the zone. A below-average fielder, Meadows is slow to the plate, has a poor pickoff move and is fairly easy to run against. He led the club in sacrifice bunts but needs work in that area as well.

2000 Outlook

Meadows wasn't guaranteed a rotation spot by the Marlins, who traded him to San Diego in November for setup man Dan Miceli. The Padres had a need for starters after dealing ace Andy Ashby to Philadelphia. At this point, Meadows has Paul Byrd's arsenal without the same results.

Florida

Kevin Orie

Traded To DODGERS

Position: 3B
Bats: R **Throws:** R
Ht: 6' 4" **Wt:** 215

Opening Day Age: 27
Born: 9/1/72 in West Chester, PA
ML Seasons: 3
Pronunciation: OHR-ee

Overall Statistics

	G	AB	R	H	D	T	HR	RBI	SB	BB	SO	Avg	OBP	Slg
1999	77	240	26	61	16	0	6	29	1	22	43	.254	.322	.396
Career	303	983	113	244	61	6	22	111	5	93	159	.248	.320	.390

1999 Situational Stats

	AB	H	HR	RBI	Avg		AB	H	HR	RBI	Avg
Home	122	32	1	11	.262	LHP	57	15	1	3	.263
Road	118	29	5	18	.246	RHP	183	46	5	26	.251
First Half	192	51	5	25	.266	Sc Pos	47	15	1	21	.319
Scnd Half	48	10	1	4	.208	Clutch	50	9	0	2	.180

1999 Season

Kevin Orie opened the year as the Marlins' starting third baseman, thanks in part to rival Mike Lowell's testicular cancer. Orie started fast, batting .324 in the opening month. But then a pulled groin landed him on the disabled list in late May, and he was slowed by quadriceps and wrist injuries the rest of the summer.

Hitting, Baserunning & Defense

When he's on, Orie has gap power. On the downside, he gets jammed far too easily and chases balls just off the plate. He has a sweeping swing that leaves him susceptible to offspeed pitches. Scouts ripped Orie for his poor instincts on the bases and at third base, and cited a general sluggishness in his play. Orie made a number of routine errors and failed to turn in the surprise plays he had in a two-month audition the previous year. His speed is below average.

2000 Outlook

Lowell won Florida's third-base job, so the Marlins traded Orie to the Dodgers in November for a player to be named. Los Angeles may lose Adrian Beltre to free agency, in which case Orie would be a stopgap starter.

Mike Redmond

Position: C
Bats: R **Throws:** R
Ht: 6' 1" **Wt:** 185

Opening Day Age: 28
Born: 5/5/71 in Seattle, WA
ML Seasons: 2

Overall Statistics

	G	AB	R	H	D	T	HR	RBI	SB	BB	SO	Avg	OBP	Slg
1999	84	242	22	73	9	0	1	27	0	26	34	.302	.381	.351
Career	121	360	32	112	18	0	3	39	0	31	50	.311	.377	.386

1999 Situational Stats

	AB	H	HR	RBI	Avg		AB	H	HR	RBI	Avg
Home	121	32	0	10	.264	LHP	92	28	1	11	.304
Road	121	41	1	17	.339	RHP	150	45	0	16	.300
First Half	118	34	0	15	.288	Sc Pos	64	23	1	26	.359
Scnd Half	124	39	1	12	.315	Clutch	30	8	0	1	.267

1999 Season

Mike Redmond entered his second season in a loose platoon with the more established Jorge Fabregas. With each passing week, it became more apparent Redmond was the better catcher. What he lacks in pedigree and tools, Redmond more than offsets with desire, hustle and intelligence.

Hitting, Baserunning & Defense

Redmond has absolutely no power or speed, but he knows his limitations and is content to slap soft line drives to the opposite field. With two strikes he shortens up even more, and he has made a habit of drawing 10-pitch walks. Redmond is especially good with runners in scoring position. He has trouble with splitters and inside fastballs. He's a good bunter and a determined, if glacial, baserunner. Defensively, Redmond calls a first-rate game, sacrifices his body to block balls and ranked among National League leaders in throwing out basestealers.

2000 Outlook

Redmond's projected role is to serve as caddie to former first-round pick Ramon Castro. But Castro struggled mightily at the plate in a September audition, and it would be no surprise if Redmond assumed an even greater role.

Jesus Sanchez

Position: RP/SP
Bats: L **Throws:** L
Ht: 5'10" **Wt:** 155

Opening Day Age: 25
Born: 10/11/74 in Bani,
Dominican Republic
ML Seasons: 2

Dennis Springer   (Knuckleballer)

Position: SP
Bats: R **Throws:** R
Ht: 5'10" **Wt:** 185

Opening Day Age: 35
Born: 2/12/65 in
Fresno, CA
ML Seasons: 5

Overall Statistics

	W	L	Pct.	ERA	G	GS	Sv	IP	H	BB	SO	HR	Ratio
1999	5	7	.417	6.01	59	10	0	76.1	84	60	62	16	1.89
Career	12	16	.429	4.95	94	39	0	249.1	262	151	199	34	1.66

1999 Situational Stats

	W	L	ERA	Sv	IP		AB	H	HR	RBI	Avg
Home	4	4	6.14	0	36.2	LHB	90	23	3	17	.256
Road	1	3	5.90	0	39.2	RHB	199	61	13	48	.307
First Half	1	4	5.81	0	57.1	Sc Pos	92	26	2	45	.283
Scnd Half	4	3	6.63	0	19.0	Clutch	67	20	4	20	.299

Overall Statistics

	W	L	Pct.	ERA	G	GS	Sv	IP	H	BB	SO	HR	Ratio
1999	6	16	.273	4.86	38	29	1	196.1	231	64	83	23	1.50
Career	23	45	.338	5.17	123	93	1	623.2	662	249	283	103	1.46

1999 Situational Stats

	W	L	ERA	Sv	IP		AB	H	HR	RBI	Avg
Home	2	7	4.11	0	100.2	LHB	317	104	12	55	.328
Road	4	9	5.64	1	95.2	RHB	445	127	11	63	.285
First Half	3	10	4.50	0	100.0	Sc Pos	197	61	5	94	.310
Scnd Half	3	6	5.23	1	96.1	Clutch	65	18	7	14	.277

1999 Season

Jesus Sanchez opened the year in the Florida rotation but was exiled to the bullpen after 10 unimpressive starts. He thrived initially in a situational relief role, but lost velocity in the second half. By the end of the year Sanchez had become one of the most vilified players in the Marlins' short history.

Pitching, Defense & Hitting

Another heavy winter of pitching in his native Dominican Republic seemed to take a toll on Sanchez. His fastball, which had topped out at 93 MPH in his rookie season, dropped to 88-90 MPH. He struggled terribly with command of his fastball, piling up nearly as many walks as strikeouts. A big-breaking curve is his best pitch and neutralizes lefthanders. His changeup is inconsistent, leaving righties to feast on his fastball. His pickoff move remains the best on the team and he's quick to the plate, but he's just an average fielder and a particularly bad hitter.

2000 Outlook

Poor mental preparation and limited endurance likely will relegate Sanchez to a bullpen role for the foreseeable future. The Marlins have no plans to use him as a starter.

1999 Season

Brought to spring training as a nonroster invitee after he was released by the Devil Rays, Dennis Springer made the club and resurrected his career. Springer proved a valuable find, leading the club in innings, complete games (three) and shutouts (two).

Pitching, Defense & Hitting

Following the release of Tom Candiotti, Springer was one of just three knuckleballers left in the majors (joining Steve Sparks and Tim Wakefield). As always, Springer was at the mercy of wind patterns and the quirks of his trick pitch. He generally threw 70 percent knucklers, mixing in enough 78-MPH fastballs and below-average sliders to keep hitters honest. Springer is a poor hitter and a subpar fielder. Basestealers tested him more than twice as often as any other Marlins pitcher, but succeeded just half the time. He varies his delivery and has a good pickoff move.

2000 Outlook

Springer refused an assignment to Triple-A and was granted free agency at season's end. The Marlins thanked him for his contributions but had no interest in a return engagement. Springer likely will hold a similar swing role with another lower-tier club.

Other Florida Marlins

Armando Almanza (Pos: LHP, Age: 27)

	W	L	Pct.	ERA	G	GS	Sv	IP	H	BB	SO	HR	Ratio
1999	0	1	.000	1.72	14	0	0	15.2	8	9	20	1	1.09
Career	0	1	.000	1.72	14	0	0	15.2	8	9	20	1	1.09

Almanza struggled in April at Triple-A, earning a demotion to Double-A. By the start of August, though, he was ready to make an impressive debut with Florida. 2000 Outlook: B

Brent Billingsley (Pos: LHP, Age: 24)

	W	L	Pct.	ERA	G	GS	Sv	IP	H	BB	SO	HR	Ratio
1999	0	0	-	16.43	8	0	0	7.2	11	10	3	3	2.74
Career	0	0	-	16.43	8	0	0	7.2	11	10	3	3	2.74

After three impressive seasons in the minors, Billingsley hit the wall at Triple-A in 1999. That didn't stop the Marlins from giving him a look, and he was roughed up in September. Montreal claimed him on waivers two months later. 2000 Outlook: C

Chris Clapinski (Pos: 3B, Age: 28, Bats: B)

	G	AB	R	H	D	T	HR	RBI	SB	BB	SO	Avg	OBP	Slg
1999	36	56	6	13	1	2	0	2	1	9	12	.232	.348	.321
Career	36	56	6	13	1	2	0	2	1	9	12	.232	.348	.321

Clapinski's minor league numbers aren't remarkable, though he recorded three hits in his third big league start. He's versatile, but not likely to be a regular. 2000 Outlook: C

Archie Corbin (Pos: RHP, Age: 32)

	W	L	Pct.	ERA	G	GS	Sv	IP	H	BB	SO	HR	Ratio
1999	0	1	.000	7.29	17	0	0	21.0	25	15	30	2	1.90
Career	2	1	.667	4.44	37	0	0	50.2	50	39	51	4	1.76

In April Corbin made his first big league appearance since 1996. In May he went on the disabled list with a sore elbow, and he was sidelined again in June. He's a free agent. 2000 Outlook: D

Reid Cornelius (Pos: RHP, Age: 29)

	W	L	Pct.	ERA	G	GS	Sv	IP	H	BB	SO	HR	Ratio
1999	1	0	1.000	3.26	5	2	0	19.1	16	5	12	0	1.09
Career	4	7	.364	5.02	23	12	0	86.0	91	35	51	11	1.47

Cornelius' sixth Triple-A season was one of his best as a starter, and he pitched respectably during a September callup. The best thing going for him is the Florida staff's inexperience and lack of depth. 2000 Outlook: C

Vic Darensbourg (Pos: LHP, Age: 29)

	W	L	Pct.	ERA	G	GS	Sv	IP	H	BB	SO	HR	Ratio
1999	0	1	.000	8.83	56	0	0	34.2	50	21	16	3	2.05
Career	0	8	.000	5.37	115	0	1	105.2	102	51	90	8	1.45

Darensbourg made an impressive debut in 1998, fanning 74 in 71 innings while allowing just 82 baserunners. This late bloomer had trouble finding the plate in '99, however. 2000 Outlook: B

Brian Edmondson (Pos: RHP, Age: 27)

	W	L	Pct.	ERA	G	GS	Sv	IP	H	BB	SO	HR	Ratio
1999	5	8	.385	5.84	68	0	1	94.0	106	44	58	11	1.60
Career	9	12	.429	4.98	121	0	1	170.0	182	81	98	21	1.55

Edmondson has established himself in the Florida bullpen, but he wasn't as effective in 1999. While he was solid with runners on base in '98, batters hit .325 against him with runners on last year. 2000 Outlook: B

Guillermo Garcia (Pos: C, Age: 27, Bats: R)

	G	AB	R	H	D	T	HR	RBI	SB	BB	SO	Avg	OBP	Slg
1999	4	4	0	1	0	0	0	0	0	0	2	.250	.250	.250
Career	16	40	3	8	2	0	2	4	0	2	15	.200	.238	.400

Traded last offseason by the Reds to the Marlins for Manny Barrios, Garcia was sold back to Cincinnati in April. He has a little power, but he's mainly an emergency replacement. 2000 Outlook: C

Tim Hyers (Pos: 1B/LF, Age: 28, Bats: L)

	G	AB	R	H	D	T	HR	RBI	SB	BB	SO	Avg	OBP	Slg
1999	58	81	8	18	4	1	2	12	0	14	11	.222	.333	.370
Career	133	230	22	50	8	1	2	19	3	27	32	.217	.298	.287

Hyers bounced between Triple-A and Florida in 1999, and he wasn't particularly productive in either locale. He doesn't hit for power, draw walks or steal bases. He doesn't have a ticket to the bigs. 2000 Outlook: D

Rafael Medina (Pos: RHP, Age: 25)

	W	L	Pct.	ERA	G	GS	Sv	IP	H	BB	SO	HR	Ratio
1999	1	1	.500	5.79	20	0	0	23.1	20	20	16	3	1.71
Career	3	7	.300	5.96	32	12	0	90.2	96	72	65	11	1.85

Control continues to be Medina's biggest hurdle. One of three players the Marlins received for Kevin Brown, Medina was waived in December and claimed by the Braves. 2000 Outlook: C

Kirt Ojala (Pos: LHP, Age: 31)

	W	L	Pct.	ERA	G	GS	Sv	IP	H	BB	SO	HR	Ratio
1999	0	1	.000	14.34	8	1	0	10.2	21	6	5	1	2.53
Career	3	10	.231	4.71	56	19	0	164.1	177	83	99	19	1.58

After making the team in spring training, Ojala earned a one-way ticket to Triple-A Calgary in May. He wasn't successful against lefties in 1998 or '99, and that's his ticket to a major league career. 2000 Outlook: C

John Roskos (Pos: C, Age: 25, Bats: R)

	G	AB	R	H	D	T	HR	RBI	SB	BB	SO	Avg	OBP	Slg
1999	13	12	0	2	2	0	0	1	0	1	7	.167	.231	.333
Career	23	22	1	3	2	0	0	1	0	1	12	.136	.174	.227

Roskos hit 24 homers in his second season at Double-A Portland (1997) and Triple-A Calgary (1999). He added 44 doubles at Calgary and batted .320. He signed a minor league deal with San Diego in November. 2000 Outlook: B

Florida Marlins Minor League Prospects

Organization Overview:

At what point do the Marlins stop rebuilding? Florida has lost 206 games in the two seasons since their 1997 World Series championship, with no end in sight. While GM Dave Dombrowski has done an admirable job of converting veterans into prospects, even when the teams he's dealing with know he has to slice payroll, there are no cornerstones in place at the major league level. The Marlins landed four quality arms and outfielder Abraham Nunez in exchange for Livan Hernandez and Matt Mantei last summer, but it also sent a message that they're still not committed to winning. And with the inevitable fading of some of their prospects, it now appears that they'll get nothing out of the deals that cost them Moises Alou, Kevin Brown and Robb Nen.

A.J. Burnett

Position: P
Bats: R **Throws:** R
Ht: 6' 5" **Wt:** 205
Opening Day Age: 23
Born: 1/3/77 in North Little Rock, AR

Recent Statistics

	W	L	ERA	G	GS	Sv	IP	H	R	BB	SO	HR
1999 AA Portland	6	12	5.52	26	23	0	120.2	132	91	71	121	15
1999 NL Florida	4	2	3.48	7	7	0	41.1	37	23	25	33	3

It's hard to say which is more eye-catching: Burnett's nipple rings or his lively mid-90s fastball. He was a 1995 eighth-round pick by the Mets, who sent him to Florida in a six-player trade for Al Leiter in February 1998. Burnett nearly made the Marlins out of spring training last year, which would have represented jumping four levels from Class-A ball, then had a lackluster year in Double-A. His spike curveball, previously an above-average pitch, repeatedly flattened out. His changeup is developing. Burnett was dynamite in seven late-season starts for Florida, allowing opponents to bat just .242 with three homers in 41.1 innings. It will be an upset if he doesn't open 2000 in the big league rotation.

Ramon Castro

Position: C
Bats: R **Throws:** R
Ht: 6' 3" **Wt:** 225
Opening Day Age: 24
Born: 3/1/76 in Vega Baja, Puerto Rico

Recent Statistics

	G	AB	R	H	D	T	HR	RBI	SB	BB	SO	Avg
1999 AAA Calgary	97	349	43	90	22	0	15	61	0	24	64	.258
1999 NL Florida	24	67	4	12	4	0	2	4	0	10	14	.179
1999 MLE	97	331	30	72	17	0	10	43	0	17	67	.218

The Astros made Castro the first Puerto Rican ever drafted in the first round when they took him 17th overall, then traded him to the Marlins to get Jay Powell in July 1998. Castro's two best tools are his powerful bat and arm. He has the juice to hit 20 homers per season, though the tradeoffs will be a batting average around .250 and lots of strikeouts. He generates his pop with

strength more than with a long swing, so there's hope he could become a hitter with more experience. While he batted just .179 in a late-season trial with Florida, he did impress by throwing out eight of 19 basestealers. Castro should make the Marlins this year and eventually will start in front of Mike Redmond.

Jason Grilli

Position: P
Bats: R **Throws:** R
Ht: 6' 4" **Wt:** 185
Opening Day Age: 23
Born: 11/11/76 in Royal Oak, MI

Recent Statistics

	W	L	ERA	G	GS	Sv	IP	H	R	BB	SO	HR
1998 AA Shreveport	7	10	3.79	21	21	0	123.1	113	60	37	100	11
1998 AAA Fresno	2	3	5.14	8	8	0	42.0	49	30	18	37	7
1999 AAA Fresno	7	5	5.54	19	19	0	100.2	124	69	39	76	22
1999 AAA Calgary	1	5	7.68	8	8	0	41.0	56	48	23	27	7

Though his numbers don't reflect it, Grilli was the key player for the Marlins in the Livan Hernandez trade with the Giants last July. The son of former major league pitcher Steve Grilli, Jason was the fourth overall pick in the 1997 draft. His stuff is excellent, led by a 92-94 MPH fastball and a promising changeup. However, his curveball has slipped since he left Seton Hall. Grilli made his pro debut at Double-A and hasn't pitched well since reaching Triple-A late in 1998. He has relied too much on his fastball and left his pitches up in the strike zone. As soon as he corrects those flaws, he'll get the call to Florida.

Abraham Nunez

Position: OF
Bats: B **Throws:** R
Ht: 6' 2" **Wt:** 165
Opening Day Age: 20
Born: 2/5/80 in Haina, Dominican Republic

Recent Statistics

	G	AB	R	H	D	T	HR	RBI	SB	BB	SO	Avg
1998 A South Bend	110	364	44	93	14	2	9	47	12	67	81	.255
1999 A High Desert	130	488	106	133	29	6	22	93	40	86	122	.273

Nunez had the best all-around tools in the Arizona system and is on the fast track, playing a full season in the high Class-A California League at age 19. He was a nice bonus for the Marlins, who got him as the player to be named in the Matt Mantei trade that earlier netted them power pitchers Vladimir Nunez and Brad Penny. Arizona was disputing Florida's claim to Abraham, and may get him back. He had a solid year and was voted the league's most exciting player and best outfield arm by the managers. He's a switch-hitter with power, basestealing ability and a good knowledge of the strike zone. Nunez covers a lot of ground in right field. He needs to gain experience more than address any specific flaw in his game, though he raised some questions about his maturity when he taunted opponents after homers last year. Nunez should be ready for the majors in 2002.

Pablo Ozuna

Position: SS
Bats: R **Throws:** R
Ht: 6' 0" **Wt:** 160

Opening Day Age: 21
Born: 8/25/78 in Santo Domingo, Dom. Rep.

Recent Statistics

	G	AB	R	H	D	T	HR	RBI	SB	BB	SO	Avg
1998 A Peoria	133	538	122	192	27	10	9	62	62	29	56	.357
1999 AA Portland	117	502	62	141	25	7	7	46	31	13	50	.281
1999 MLE	117	484	51	123	22	5	5	38	23	9	53	.254

Perhaps the Marlins' best fire-sale trade came in December 1998, when they decided Alex Gonzalez was ready to take over at shortstop. That made Edgar Renteria expendable, and he netted Ozuna and pitchers Armando Almanza and Braden Looper from the Cardinals. With his short stroke and speed, Florida envisions Ozuna becoming a .300 hitter with 50-steal potential. To do that, he'll need to be more selective. Ozuna has been decent at shortstop, though he's expected to move to second base after Gonzalez was an All-Star as a rookie. Center field is also a long-term possibility. Though he'll repeat Double-A this year, Ozuna still is on the fast track.

Brad Penny

Position: P
Bats: R **Throws:** R
Ht: 6' 4" **Wt:** 200

Opening Day Age: 21
Born: 5/24/78 in Blackwell, OK

Recent Statistics

	W	L	ERA	G	GS	Sv	IP	H	R	BB	SO	HR
1998 A High Desert	14	5	2.96	28	28	0	164.0	138	65	35	207	15
1999 AA El Paso	2	7	4.80	17	17	0	90.0	109	56	25	100	9
1999 AA Portland	1	0	3.90	6	6	0	32.1	28	15	14	35	1

A 1996 fifth-round pick, Penny was considered by many to be the best righthanded pitching prospect in the game entering last season. But the Diamondbacks coveted Matt Mantei, so they included Penny in the three-prospect package that landed them the closer. He throws a consistent 92-94 MPH sinker, a hard curveball and a good changeup. His mechanics aren't the smoothest, but he has had no arm problems. After dominating the Arizona Fall League, Penny could make the Marlins with a big spring training, but he's more likely to spend a half-season in Triple-A.

Julio Ramirez

Position: OF
Bats: R **Throws:** R
Ht: 5' 11" **Wt:** 170

Opening Day Age: 22
Born: 8/10/77 in San Juan de la Maguana, D.R.

Recent Statistics

	G	AB	R	H	D	T	HR	RBI	SB	BB	SO	Avg
1999 AA Portland	138	568	87	148	30	10	13	64	64	39	150	.261
1999 NL Florida	15	21	3	3	1	0	0	2	0	1	6	.143
1999 MLE	138	549	71	129	26	8	10	52	46	27	160	.235

The Marlins have had more success finding talent on the international market than via the draft, signing such players as Luis Castillo, Alex Gonzalez, Livan Hernandez and Edgar Renteria. Their next foreign gem could be Ramirez, a five-tool player. Eastern League managers rated him the fastest baserunner and best outfield arm in the Double-A circuit, and one Florida official says the only center fielder with more range than Ramirez is Andruw Jones. The question, and it's a big one, is whether Ramirez will learn to hit. He negates his physical gifts, which also include impressive strength, with an inability to get on base or make consistent contact. Nevertheless, he did lead the EL with 64 steals in 78 attempts last season. Time is still on Ramirez' side at age 22, and he'll move up to Triple-A in 2000.

Michael Tejera

Position: P
Bats: L **Throws:** L
Ht: 5' 9" **Wt:** 175

Opening Day Age: 23
Born: 10/18/76 in Havana, Cuba

Recent Statistics

	W	L	ERA	G	GS	Sv	IP	H	R	BB	SO	HR
1999 AAA Calgary	0	2	12.00	2	2	0	9.0	19	14	4	5	2
1999 AA Portland	13	4	2.62	25	25	0	154.2	137	55	45	152	13
1999 NL Florida	0	0	11.37	3	1	0	6.1	10	8	5	7	1

Tejera defected from the Cuban junior national team in 1994, jumping the club while at the Miami International Airport. He stayed in the city, graduating from high school and getting drafted in the sixth round by the Marlins a year later. It took him three years to make it out of short-season ball, but he has moved quickly since then, going 22-9 in Double-A the last two seasons. Tejera's best pitch is his changeup, which he sets up with impeccable command of an 87-90 MPH fastball. His curveball is an effective third pitch. Florida doesn't have another lefthanded starting candidate, so he should surface in the rotation sometime this year.

Others to Watch

Righthander **Hector Almonte** (24) seems certain to make Florida's bullpen after impressing in 15 big league appearances. He has heavy sink on his fastball, which he throws in the low 90s. . . Former Texas A&M quarterback recruit **Chip Ambres** (20) was rated the top prospect in the Rookie-level Gulf Coast League in 1999. He has all five tools, including a very quick bat, and already has a sound knowledge of hitting. . . Righthander **Wes Anderson** (20) has a fastball that already touches 97 MPH and an above-average slider. He struck out 134 in 137.1 innings at Class A Kane County and could reach Florida in two years. . . Righthander **Josh Beckett** (19) guaranteed his timetable would be accelerated when he signed a $7 million big league deal after being selected second overall in the 1999 draft. Yet to make his pro debut, he has a fastball that has reached 99 MPH and a power curve. . . Righthander **Nate Bump** (23) arrived from San Francisco last summer in the Livan Hernandez trade. With a 90-92 MPH fastball and an above-average curve, he projects as high as a No. 3 starter. . . Second baseman **Amaury Garcia** (24) had the best offensive year of his career in 1999, batting .317-17-53 in Triple-A, and also improved his defense. But he'll have a tough time contending with Luis Castillo and Pablo Ozuna.

Enron Field

Offense

The Astrodome held down offensive performance, even when the dimensions were made more hitter-friendly in recent years. Life will change for the Astros when Enron Field opens in 2000. Though it will be 435 feet to dead center, the power alleys and foul lines will be inviting targets. There's a 21-foot mini-Green Monster in left field, but the right-field fence is only seven feet high. As in most new parks, the distance between the plate and the stands is minimal, another offensive advantage.

Defense

The effects of Enron Field's retractable roof remain to be seen in a city that hasn't hosted outdoor baseball since 1964. Hot, humid weather is conducive to scoring, but the sweltering, hot and wet Houston weather likely will mean the roof is frequently closed. The most important defensive consideration will be having a fleet and savvy center fielder to cover both the expanses and the unusual bounces off the walls.

Who It Helps The Most

The Astros' two healthy power sources—Jeff Bagwell and Craig Biggio—are pull hitters who should benefit from the short lines and alleys, and Biggio may pad his already sky-high doubles totals with the left-field wall. All but one of the projected starting pitchers rely on a sinker. Playing on grass instead of turf should help the team's aging infield get to more groundballs.

Who It Hurts The Most

Jose Lima has allowed 64 homers the past two seasons despite pitching in the Astrodome, and he'll be more prone to surrendering longballs in Enron Field. Moises Alou and Derek Bell tend to hit balls up the middle and may see their power numbers affected.

Rookies & Newcomers

Lance Berkman and Daryle Ward probably are salivating at the thought of hitting at Enron Field, as is Mitch Meluskey. When looking for a shortstop this offseason, the Astros won't have to emphasize quickness as much as if they still played on artificial turf.

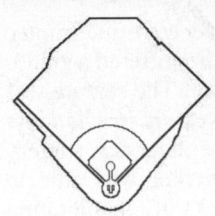

Dimensions: LF-315, LCF-362, CF-435, RCF-373, RF-326

Capacity: 42,000

Elevation: 22 feet

Surface: Grass

Foul Territory: Small

Park Factors

1999 Season (Astrodome)

| | Home Games | | | Away Games | | | |
	Astros	Opp	Total	Astros	Opp	Total	Index
G	76	76	152	71	71	142	—
Avg	.265	.256	.260	.266	.277	.271	96
AB	2493	2623	5116	2468	2431	4899	98
R	381	296	677	364	317	681	93
H	661	671	1332	656	674	1330	94
2B	150	126	276	119	122	241	110
3B	12	20	32	8	11	19	161
HR	61	49	110	90	67	157	67
BB	338	220	558	325	221	546	98
SO	534	627	1161	508	462	970	115
E	51	71	122	45	55	100	114
E-Infield	39	65	104	40	47	87	112
LHB-Avg	.281	.273	.276	.285	.276	.280	99
LHB-HR	22	22	44	31	28	59	71
RHB-Avg	.258	.245	.252	.258	.278	.267	94
RHB-HR	39	27	66	59	39	98	65

1997-1999 (Astrodome)

| | Home Games | | | Away Games | | | |
	Astros	Opp	Total	Astros	Opp	Total	Index
G	221	221	442	221	221	442	—
Avg	.270	.248	.259	.266	.267	.267	97
AB	7353	7680	15033	7785	7490	15275	98
R	1112	829	1941	1132	953	2085	93
H	1982	1905	3887	2074	2003	4077	95
2B	448	383	831	413	347	760	111
3B	46	43	89	36	33	69	131
HR	187	165	352	234	210	444	81
BB	908	612	1520	910	723	1633	95
SO	1504	1827	3331	1575	1415	2990	113
E	146	181	327	175	180	355	92
E-Infield	116	158	274	150	150	300	91
LHB-Avg	.271	.255	.261	.276	.269	.272	96
LHB-HR	40	65	105	54	79	133	78
RHB-Avg	.269	.244	.257	.263	.266	.265	97
RHB-HR	147	100	247	180	131	311	82

1999 Rankings (National League/Astrodome)

- Third-highest triple factor
- Third-highest strikeout factor
- Third-highest error factor
- Third-highest infield-error factor
- Lowest home-run factor
- Lowest RHB home-run factor
- Third-lowest LHB home-run factor

Houston

Larry Dierker

1999 Season

Larry Dierker's season and life were interrupted dramatically on June 13, when he suffered a grand-mal seizure in the Astros dugout. The seizure was caused by a tangle of blood vessels in Dierker's brain, which was repaired in emergency surgery two days later. Incredibly, Dierker was able to return to the team after six weeks of rehabilitation with no lasting side effects. Houston went on to reach the postseason for the third consecutive time in Dierker's three years as manager.

Offense

Dierker prefers to go with a set lineup but was unable to do so in 1999 because of Houston's injury problems. He was forced to start whomever was available, especially during the second half, when he played infielders Craig Biggio and Bill Spiers in the outfield. Dierker preaches patience at the plate and aggressiveness on the bases. Despite an aging and sometimes dysfunctional lineup, the Astros led the National League in walks and steals. Not coincidentally, Houston pitchers walked fewer hitters than any other National League staff and allowed the second-fewest number of steals.

Pitching & Defense

Dierker's trademark is letting his starters take the ball for as long as possible. His three lead starters (Shane Reynolds, Mike Hampton and Jose Lima) each pitched more than 230 innings. Dierker prefers to spread out the bullpen responsibilities but was handicapped by uneven performance, injuries and Scott Elarton's move to the rotation. Dierker doesn't invest in one-out strategies either offensively or defensively, and was one of only four managers who did not have a lefthanded reliever with more games than innings pitched.

2000 Outlook

If anything, Dierker's near-tragic health problems have solidified his icon status in Houston. If that's to continue, though, he'll have to lead the Astros past the first round of the playoffs or risk a Mike Hargrove-type situation. One thing he must do in 2000 is keep Jeff Bagwell and Craig Biggio out of the lineup more frequently so they're more rested for late September and October.

Born: 9/22/46 in Hollywood, CA

Playing Experience: 1964-1977, Hou, StL

Managerial Experience: 3 seasons
Pronunciation: DEER-ker

Manager Statistics

Year	Team, Lg	W	L	Pct	GB	Finish
1999	Houston, NL	97	65	.599	—	1st Central
3 Seasons		283	203	.582	—	—

1999 Starting Pitchers by Days Rest

	<=3	4	5	6+
Astros Starts	5	100	35	15
Astros ERA	1.80	3.81	4.36	2.99
NL Avg Starts	3	81	48	21
NL ERA	4.84	4.53	4.72	4.98

1999 Situational Stats

	Larry Dierker	NL Average
Hit & Run Success %	35.5	33.6
Stolen Base Success %	68.9	70.2
Platoon Pct.	52.9	55.2
Defensive Subs	22	25
High-Pitch Outings	10	13
Quick/Slow Hooks	5/12	16/15
Sacrifice Attempts	106	89

1999 Rankings (National League)

- 1st in stolen base attempts (241)
- 2nd in steals of third base (32) and starts on three days rest (5)
- 3rd in steals of second base (133), double steals (11), sacrifice bunt attempts (106) and saves with over 1 inning pitched (13)

Moises Alou

1999 Season

Moises Alou didn't have a 1999 season, at least in the sense that he put on a uniform. He injured his knee during an offseason treadmill workout in the Dominican Republic and had surgery. When Alou's rehab was ahead of schedule and the club was contemplating activating him for the pennant drive in September, Alou fell off a bike while playing with his kids at home and tweaked the knee again. The second injury didn't require additional surgery, but was enough of a setback to sideline him for the rest of the season. The Astros were strangely quiet about Alou's status after the second injury, and there could be some hard feelings about his carelessness and its cost to the team.

Hitting

Alou was coming off his career year in 1998, and for the first time in his career had shown above-average home-run power. Late in 1998, Alou began pulling off the ball and losing the power from his hips, which left him homerless after September 1. He has become a more patient hitter with experience, and had improved his overall numbers for three straight seasons before his injury.

Baserunning & Defense

Before his knee problems, Alou was a close to average runner on the bases and had good range and a strong arm for a left fielder. At his age Alou normally would be expected to start slowing down, and his surgery and subsequent troubles may hasten that process. Left field in Enron Field will be far less spacious than in the Astrodome, and losing a step won't hurt Alou at home. Neither will playing all his home games on a grass field.

2000 Outlook

Alou's return is complicated by the Astros' incredible glut of outfielders. The most likely scenario is for Houston to work Alou back slowly into the left-field job, perhaps as part of a platoon with youngsters Lance Berkman and Daryle Ward. Alou has two years left on a lucrative contract.

Position: LF
Bats: R **Throws:** R
Ht: 6' 3" **Wt:** 195

Opening Day Age: 33
Born: 7/3/66 in Atlanta, GA
ML Seasons: 8
Pronunciation: MOY-sezz ah-LOO

Overall Statistics

	G	AB	R	H	D	T	HR	RBI	SB	BB	SO	Avg	OBP	Slg
1999					Did Not Play									
Career	919	3271	535	966	201	26	145	612	73	337	476	.295	.362	.506

Where He Hits the Ball (1998)

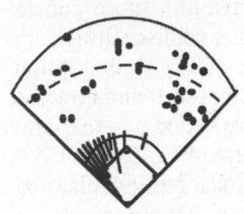
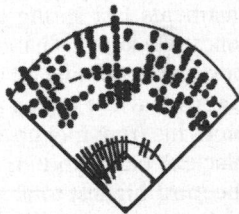

Vs. LHP   **Vs. RHP**

1999 Situational Stats

	AB	H	HR	RBI	Avg		AB	H	HR	RBI	Avg
Home	—	—	—	—	—	LHB	—	—	—	—	—
Road	—	—	—	—	—	RHB	—	—	—	—	—
First Half	—	—	—	—	—	Sc Pos	—	—	—	—	—
Scbd Half	—	—	—	—	—	Clutch	—	—	—	—	—

1999 Rankings (National League)

- Did not play

Jeff Bagwell

1999 Season

Jeff Bagwell just missed adding another MVP trophy to the award he collected in 1994. At 31, he established career highs in runs scored and walks, bashed 42 homers and became a 30-30 player for the second time in three years. The problem with Bagwell's season was a fade that contributed to the Astros' third straight quick exit from the playoffs. Bagwell is now a career .121 postseason hitter with no extra-base hits.

Hitting

No other hitter in baseball has the hand strength and quickness to hit like Bagwell does. While he always has had one of the most unorthodox stances and swings in baseball, he made some simple adjustments last spring that gave him more consistency. He kept his hands higher while waiting for a pitch and eliminated much of his timing hitch. Bagwell also lessened his weight shift and now just picks his front foot up and puts in down in the same place. A patient hitter, he drew 149 walks in 1999, the third-highest total in National League history.

Baserunning & Defense

Bagwell may be the slowest runner ever to steal 30 bases in a season. He makes up for his lack of speed with a quick first step, uncanny instincts and a peerless grasp of game situations. His ability to take the extra base during a play is just as outstanding. Bagwell's defense isn't likely to garner him a Gold Glove, but he ranks among the top half of defensive first basemen. He's aggressive to a fault on groundballs and bunts.

2000 Outlook

Enron Field may not provide Bagwell the boost it will to other Astros hitters, because before 1999 he always had hit well in the Astrodome. One of the game's elite hitters, he should be good for another .300-40-125 season with 125 walks and 25 steals.

Position: 1B
Bats: R **Throws:** R
Ht: 6' 0" **Wt:** 195

Opening Day Age: 31
Born: 5/27/68 in Boston, MA
ML Seasons: 9

Overall Statistics

	G	AB	R	H	D	T	HR	RBI	SB	BB	SO	Avg	OBP	Slg
1999	162	562	143	171	35	0	42	126	30	149	127	.304	.454	.591
Career	1317	4759	921	1447	314	21	263	961	158	885	906	.304	.416	.545

Where He Hits the Ball

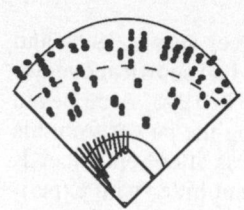
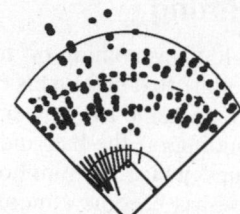

Vs. LHP   **Vs. RHP**

1999 Situational Stats

	AB	H	HR	RBI	Avg		AB	H	HR	RBI	Avg
Home	277	75	12	47	.271	LHP	130	46	9	26	.354
Road	285	96	30	79	.337	RHP	432	125	33	100	.289
First Half	305	96	28	78	.315	Sc Pos	148	49	17	92	.331
Scnd Half	257	75	14	48	.292	Clutch	76	24	7	20	.316

1999 Rankings (National League)

- 1st in runs scored, walks, times on base (331) and games played
- 2nd in pitches seen (2,962), on-base percentage and on-base percentage vs. righthanded pitchers (.448)
- 3rd in intentional walks (16), plate appearances (729), lowest groundball/flyball ratio (0.8) and on-base percentage vs. lefthanded pitchers (.476)
- Led the Astros in home runs, runs scored, total bases (332), RBI, stolen bases, walks, intentional walks (16), hit by pitch (11), times on base (331), pitches seen (2,962), slugging percentage, on-base percentage, HR frequency (13.4 ABs per HR), most pitches seen per plate appearance (4.06) and batting average vs. lefthanded pitchers

Derek Bell

1999 Season

Derek Bell may have been the most ineffective offensive player in baseball in 1999, given his background and role with the Astros. While he never has been a consistent hitter, Bell didn't even mix in a hot streak into his 1999 season. With Astros outfielders dropping with injuries left and right, Bell joined them with groin and rib problems, forcing the team to start infielders at the corner outfield positions. Part of Bell's struggles have been attributed to his close friend and hitting guru, coach Tommy McCraw, missing much of the season with prostate surgery.

Hitting

Bell has excellent bat speed and many have predicted that he'll mature into a 30-homer hitter. That has yet to take place. Bell never has been a patient hitter, and he was easy prey in 1999 for any righthander who could throw a slider off the outside corner. Bell handled lefthanders who brought the ball into his quick hands much better. Perhaps the Astros should have Bell's eyes checked after he hit .175 during day games.

Baserunning & Defense

Though he has lost a step to age, Bell remains a threat on the bases and a solid defender in right field. His arm strength is well above average and runners rarely try to take liberties against him. Bell also has toned down the careless and overaggressive mistakes he used to make. He's still adept at making sliding catches on balls near the foul line.

2000 Outlook

The three-year contract Bell signed before the 1997 season automatically vested its option year for 2000, leaving the Astros with a $5 million outfielder they really don't want and can't find a taker for. Youngsters Lance Berkman, Richard Hidalgo and Daryle Ward need to play. How Bell reacts to a potential part-time role will be one of the touchiest situations manager Larry Dierker handles this spring.

Position: RF
Bats: R **Throws:** R
Ht: 6' 2" **Wt:** 215

Opening Day Age: 31
Born: 12/11/68 in Tampa, FL
ML Seasons: 9

Overall Statistics

	G	AB	R	H	D	T	HR	RBI	SB	BB	SO	Avg	OBP	Slg
1999	128	509	61	120	22	0	12	66	18	50	129	.236	.306	.350
Career	1020	3876	541	1090	198	14	111	586	162	287	792	.281	.336	.425

Where He Hits the Ball

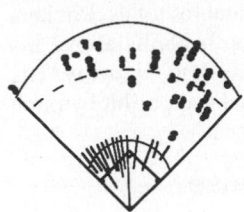 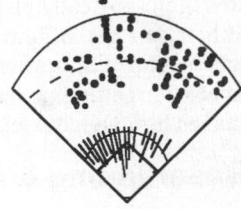

Vs. LHP   **Vs. RHP**

1999 Situational Stats

	AB	H	HR	RBI	Avg		AB	H	HR	RBI	Avg
Home	232	52	5	30	.224	LHP	122	37	5	23	.303
Road	277	68	7	36	.245	RHP	387	83	7	43	.214
First Half	358	87	10	48	.243	Sc Pos	152	32	2	51	.211
Scnd Half	151	33	2	18	.219	Clutch	73	19	3	16	.260

1999 Rankings (National League)
- 1st in lowest batting average, lowest batting average vs. righthanded pitchers, lowest cleanup slugging percentage (.302), lowest slugging percentage vs. righthanded pitchers (.310) and lowest batting average at home
- 2nd in lowest on-base percentage and lowest on-base percentage vs. righthanded pitchers (.288)
- 3rd in GDPs (20) and lowest slugging percentage
- 4th in highest groundball/flyball ratio (1.8)
- Led the Astros in strikeouts, GDPs (20), highest groundball/flyball ratio (1.8) and bunts in play (3)
- Led NL right fielders in GDPs (20)

Craig Biggio

1999 Season

Though Craig Biggio didn't match his career year of 1998, he quietly put together another All-Star campaign. Biggio led the National League in doubles for the second straight season, this time with a career-high 56, the sixth-highest total in league history. His 123 runs scored tied for third in the NL, and he has averaged 126 per season from 1995-99.

Hitting

Biggio still is extremely quick to the ball and stings line drives to all parts of the field. His home runs tend to come on balls that he can pull down the left-field line. Playing in Houston's new Enron Field, which features a Fenwayesque 21-foot left-field wall 315 feet from the plate, should be a boost to Biggio's already historic doubles totals. Pitchers still try to get Biggio out on fastballs above his hands, especially after setting him up away. His knack for getting on base via a walk or hit by pitch makes him an ideal leadoff man.

Baserunning & Defense

There are signs that the 34-year-old Biggio is slowing down, though he's still one of the most durable players in the game. In 1999 he was only 28-for-42 in steals and didn't hit a triple for the first time in his career. Biggio was surehanded defensively at second base but lost a step of range, especially up the middle. During their outfield injury epidemic in August, the Astros even played Biggio in left field for six games and he looked very comfortable at that position.

2000 Outlook

Biggio played with a torn left labrum the second half of last season, which was surgically repaired during the offseason. Entering the last year of his contract in 2000, his 13th season in an Astros uniform, Biggio skipped an opportunity to go on the open market by signing a three-year, $28 million extension in December. Manager Larry Dierker will rest him more often, as Biggio's late-season and postseason performances have been poor the past three years.

Position: 2B
Bats: R **Throws:** R
Ht: 5'11" **Wt:** 180

Opening Day Age: 34
Born: 12/14/65 in Smithtown, NY
ML Seasons: 12
Pronunciation: BIDG-jee-oh

Overall Statistics

	G	AB	R	H	D	T	HR	RBI	SB	BB	SO	Avg	OBP	Slg
1999	160	639	123	188	56	0	16	73	28	88	107	.294	.386	.457
Career	1699	6389	1120	1868	389	38	152	706	346	786	973	.292	.380	.437

Where He Hits the Ball

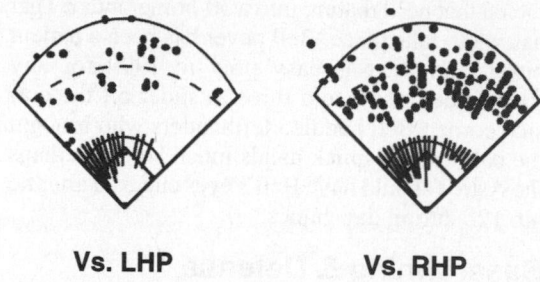

Vs. LHP   **Vs. RHP**

1999 Situational Stats

	AB	H	HR	RBI	Avg		AB	H	HR	RBI	Avg
Home	324	92	10	37	.284	LHP	150	46	4	18	.307
Road	315	96	6	36	.305	RHP	489	142	12	55	.290
First Half	356	104	8	44	.292	Sc Pos	137	43	1	56	.314
Scnd Half	283	84	8	29	.297	Clutch	99	34	3	13	.343

1999 Rankings (National League)

- 1st in doubles and plate appearances (749)
- 2nd in at-bats
- 3rd in runs scored and on-base percentage for a leadoff hitter (.386)
- 4th in fielding percentage at second base (.985)
- 5th in caught stealing (14) and times on base (287)
- Led the Astros in at-bats, hits, singles, doubles, caught stealing (14), hit by pitch (11), plate appearances (749), batting average in the clutch, batting average on a 3-1 count (.667), on-base percentage for a leadoff hitter (.386), steals of third (7) and highest percentage of extra bases taken as a runner (60.9%)

Ken Caminiti

Position: 3B
Bats: B **Throws:** R
Ht: 6' 0" **Wt:** 200

Opening Day Age: 36
Born: 4/21/63 in Hanford, CA
ML Seasons: 13
Pronunciation: kam-un-NET-ee
Nickname: The Gun

1999 Season

Ken Caminiti's 36-year-old body, which had kept him from playing more than 146 games in a season since 1991, finally blew a major gasket during the 1999 season. His pulled calf muscle limited him to 273 at-bats, mostly at the beginning and end of the season. Though Caminiti's hitting didn't seem to be affected by his injury, his range and defense suffered. The Astros knew all this might happen when they brought Caminiti back to Houston last winter. They got much of what they wanted: leadership and a number of big, big hits in September and October.

Hitting

Always a strong righthanded hitter, Caminiti has evolved into an increasingly dangerous hitter from the left side. He likes the ball up and over the plate from both sides. As he has grown older and lost some bat speed, he has become increasingly selective.

Baserunning & Defense

Caminiti's leg injuries have cost him the explosive step and dive that were the root of so many of his spectacular defensive plays. While his arm strength remains above average, it too has slipped a grade and he's more error-prone on throws. On the bases, Caminiti remains a savvy and aggressive runner. He never has had good straight-ahead running speed, but always has been able to get a good jump and take the extra base when there's an opportunity.

2000 Outlook

It would be unrealistic to expect Caminiti to put together a 400 at-bat season in 2000. The best arrangement might be a semi-platoon situation with the similarly fragile Bill Spiers or with youngster Russ Johnson, which could enable Caminiti to get to September and October unscathed. That's when the Astros really want him in peak form, anyway.

Houston

Overall Statistics

	G	AB	R	H	D	T	HR	RBI	SB	BB	SO	Avg	OBP	Slg
1999	78	273	45	78	11	1	13	56	6	46	58	.286	.386	.476
Career	1583	5724	816	1566	318	16	209	897	85	642	1041	.274	.346	.444

Where He Hits the Ball

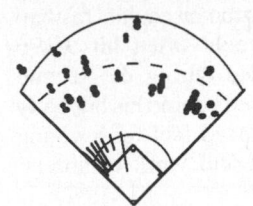

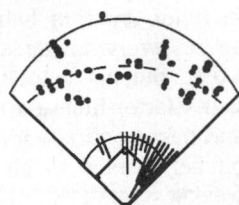

Vs. LHP   **Vs. RHP**

1999 Situational Stats

	AB	H	HR	RBI	Avg		AB	H	HR	RBI	Avg
Home	146	43	4	25	.295	LHP	68	23	1	7	.338
Road	127	35	9	31	.276	RHP	205	55	12	49	.268
First Half	130	38	2	17	.292	Sc Pos	86	19	4	44	.221
Scnd Half	143	40	11	39	.280	Clutch	44	10	4	14	.227

1999 Rankings (National League)

- 6th in lowest cleanup slugging percentage (.521)
- 8th in errors at third base (14)

Scott Elarton

1999 Season

The Astros might have landed Roger Clemens had they been willing to include Scott Elarton in a trade with the Blue Jays. Elarton stayed in Houston and was the best setup man in the National League before the All-Star break. Manager Larry Dierker finally made the long-awaited move of putting Elarton in the starting rotation on July 3, though he was kept on a strict pitch limit. Elarton performed well in the role before coming down with a sore shoulder in September.

Pitching

Elarton has three quality pitches, a sinking fastball that he throws in the low 90s, a sharp curveball and a changeup that has good sinking action. Pitching in relief the first half, Elarton used his fastball aggressively inside and would often hit 95-96 MPH, but his velocity faded during the second half. Elarton hides the ball well behind his big body and has shown a very advanced feel for a young pitcher in how to hit spots and work to hitters' weaknesses.

Defense & Hitting

Despite his 6-foot-7 frame, Elarton is an above-average hitter and defensive player. He hit .192 with seven sacrifice bunts in 1999. Elarton allowed only four stolen bases last season, thanks to a quick slide step that keeps runners from getting good jumps. Though he doesn't have good speed, Elarton is fundamentally sound at fielding bunts and covering first base.

2000 Outlook

The Astros were dismayed when Elarton was diagnosed with a partial tear of his rotator cuff, which will require offseason surgery. Though he should make a full recovery, he may not be ready to pitch until May. He has the potential to become Houston's No. 1 starter in the near future, passing Shane Reynolds and 20-game winners Mike Hampton and Jose Lima.

Position: RP/SP
Bats: R **Throws:** R
Ht: 6' 7" **Wt:** 240

Opening Day Age: 24
Born: 2/23/76 in Lamar, CO
ML Seasons: 2

Overall Statistics

	W	L	Pct.	ERA	G	GS	Sv	IP	H	BB	SO	HR	Ratio
1999	9	5	.643	3.48	42	15	1	124.0	111	43	121	8	1.24
Career	11	6	.647	3.43	70	17	3	181.0	151	63	177	13	1.18

How Often He Throws Strikes

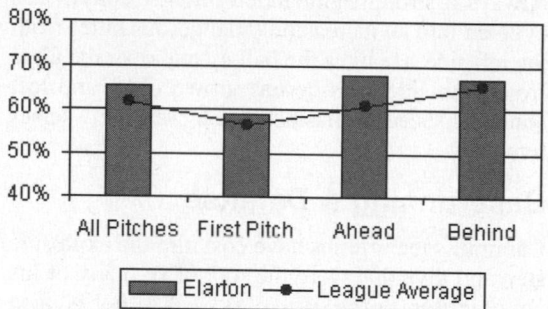

1999 Situational Stats

	W	L	ERA	Sv	IP		AB	H	HR	RBI	Avg
Home	4	3	3.43	0	57.2	LHB	215	54	4	22	.251
Road	5	2	3.53	1	66.1	RHB	251	57	4	33	.227
First Half	5	3	3.23	1	47.1	Sc Pos	128	27	2	44	.211
Scnd Half	4	2	3.64	0	76.2	Clutch	86	15	2	11	.174

1999 Rankings (National League)

- 5th in lowest batting average allowed with runners in scoring position
- 6th in lowest batting average allowed vs. lefthanded batters
- Led the Astros in blown saves (3), lowest batting average allowed vs. lefthanded batters, lowest batting average allowed with runners in scoring position and relief wins (5)

Carl Everett

Traded To
RED SOX

1999 Season

While Jeff Bagwell almost won the NL Most Valuable Player Award, a strong case could be made for Carl Everett being the team MVP for the Astros. Not only did the switch-hitter rack up career highs in every major offensive category, he timed his best games and biggest hits for when the Astros needed them the most. Everett was especially potent just after coming off the disabled list in the second half following groin and hamstring pulls.

Hitting

Everett stands on top of the plate batting lefthanded and dares pitchers to try to throw inside to him. When they do, he unleashes a cobra-quick bat to pull the ball to right field. Though he'll occasionally get impatient, pitchers can't pitch him away because Everett will take balls the other way. He's a high-average hitter batting righthanded but doesn't have the same type of power. Against changeup and sinkerball southpaws like Steve Avery and Tom Glavine, Everett will sometimes bat lefthanded. He hit a two-run homer off Avery batting lefthanded last summer.

Baserunning & Defense

An ineffective and tentative baserunner in 1998 despite above-average speed, Everett blossomed on the bases last year. He stole 27 bases in 34 attempts despite batting cleanup much of the year and suffering from various leg muscle problems. Defensively, Everett has above-average arm strength and will be well-suited to range Fenway Park's spacious center field.

2000 Outlook

Everett will enter this season with a guaranteed starting job for the first time in his career—with the Red Sox. Houston freed up some cash and alleviated a logjam in its outfield by trading Everett for a top shortstop prospect, Adam Everett, and minor league lefthander Greg Miller. The Boston-bound Everett should fare well spraying the ball around Fenway Park, and the Red Sox hope to lock him up with a long-term contract.

Position: CF/RF
Bats: B **Throws:** R
Ht: 6' 0" **Wt:** 190

Opening Day Age: 29
Born: 6/3/70 in Tampa, FL
ML Seasons: 7

Overall Statistics

	G	AB	R	H	D	T	HR	RBI	SB	BB	SO	Avg	OBP	Slg
1999	123	464	86	151	33	3	25	108	27	50	94	.325	.398	.571
Career	605	1925	300	533	117	12	69	317	71	190	442	.277	.348	.458

Where He Hits the Ball

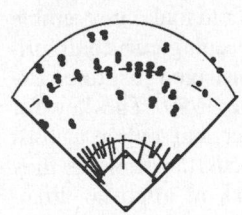 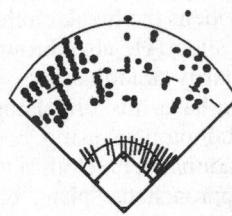

Vs. LHP   **Vs. RHP**

1999 Situational Stats

	AB	H	HR	RBI	Avg		AB	H	HR	RBI	Avg
Home	226	72	11	52	.319	LHP	117	38	4	20	.325
Road	238	79	14	56	.332	RHP	347	113	21	88	.326
First Half	309	97	11	65	.314	Sc Pos	138	48	6	82	.348
Scnd Half	155	54	14	43	.348	Clutch	82	28	6	20	.341

1999 Rankings (National League)

- 3rd in cleanup slugging percentage (.587)
- 5th in lowest fielding percentage in center field (.980)
- Led the Astros in batting average, sacrifice flies (8), hit by pitch (11), stolen-base percentage (79.4%), fewest GDPs per GDP situation (4.2%), batting average with runners in scoring position, batting average with the bases loaded (.467), batting average vs. righthanded pitchers, cleanup slugging percentage (.587), slugging percentage vs. righthanded pitchers (.608) and batting average at home
- Led NL center fielders in batting average, sacrifice flies (8), hit by pitch (11) and batting average with runners in scoring position

Houston

467

Mike Hampton

1999 Season

Mike Hampton posted career bests in wins, innings, strikeouts and ERA. He improved dramatically against lefthanders, allowing a .149 batting average to them after they hit .277 off him in 1998. Incredibly, the Astros were 29-5 in Hampton's starts, including a National League Central-clinching win on the final day of the regular season.

Pitching

Hampton has mastered the art of changing speeds, movement and location, and he does it with power stuff. He throws three types of fastballs: a 92-94 MPH hard rider, an 88-90 MPH heavy sinker and a cut fastball at about the same speed. Hampton will let up on the sinker to use it as a changeup, and widens the break on the cutter to make it resemble a slider. He also throws a sweeping curveball, primarily to lefthanders, who managed just three extra-base hits off Hampton in 1999. The key for Hampton is using his sinker and cutter against righthanders. Both pitches look the same as they approach the plate, but break in opposite directions.

Defense & Hitting

Hampton is probably the best athlete among major league pitchers. He's cat quick on the mound fielding groundballs and covering first base. He permitted just eight stolen bases in 239 innings last summer. Hampton won the 1999 Silver Slugger for hitting excellence among NL pitchers, batting .311 and using his above-average speed to collect three triples, the first pitcher to do so since Bob Forsch in 1975.

2000 Outlook

Since making a commitment to changing speeds at midseason in 1997, Hampton has gone 44-14. He's just entering his prime and should be an annual Cy Young Award candidate beginning in 2000. Entering the final year of his contract, Hampton told the Astros he'll test the free-agent market next winter. Houston could trade him beforehand.

Position: SP
Bats: R **Throws:** L
Ht: 5'10" **Wt:** 180

Opening Day Age: 27
Born: 9/9/72 in Brooksville, FL
ML Seasons: 7

Overall Statistics

	W	L	Pct.	ERA	G	GS	Sv	IP	H	BB	SO	HR	Ratio
1999	22	4	.846	2.90	34	34	0	239.0	206	101	177	12	1.28
Career	70	43	.619	3.50	208	154	1	1043.0	1040	390	701	78	1.37

How Often He Throws Strikes

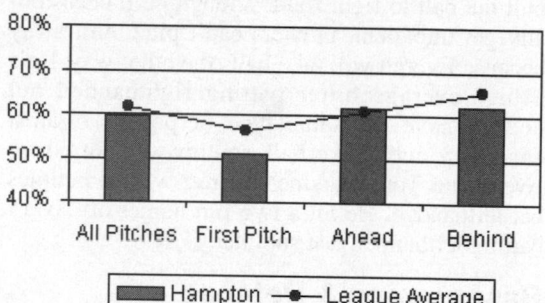

1999 Situational Stats

	W	L	ERA	Sv	IP		AB	H	HR	RBI	Avg
Home	13	2	2.49	0	141.0	LHB	141	21	2	9	.149
Road	9	2	3.49	0	98.0	RHB	713	185	10	66	.259
First Half	11	3	3.02	0	125.1	Sc Pos	186	45	3	63	.242
Scnd Half	11	1	2.77	0	113.2	Clutch	68	19	1	7	.279

1999 Rankings (National League)

- 1st in wins, GDPs induced (38), winning percentage, lowest slugging percentage allowed (.324), highest groundball/flyball ratio allowed (2.6), fewest home runs allowed per 9 innings (.45) and most GDPs induced per 9 innings (1.4)
- 2nd in shutouts (2) and most run support per 9 innings (6.8)
- 3rd in ERA and ERA at home
- 4th in innings pitched and walks allowed
- Led the Astros in ERA, wins, shutouts (2), walks allowed, wild pitches (9), pitches thrown (3,640), GDPs induced (38), winning percentage, lowest batting average allowed (.241), lowest slugging percentage allowed (.324) and highest groundball/flyball ratio allowed (2.6)

Richard Hidalgo

1999 Season

Richard Hidalgo entered the season with high hopes, even without a clear opening for him. The season ended up a wash for the young Venezuelan, though, because of a genetic malformation in his kneecap that hobbled him from the start of the season and finally forced him to have surgery in August. The biggest effect his knee had on his game was to limit his ability to plant his foot and get torque in his swing, causing his average to drop from .303 in 1998 to .227 in 1999.

Hitting

Hidalgo has very good bat speed and has the strength to be a first-class power hitter. However, he's at a crossroads that many young hitters reach. When he stays within himself and concentrates on solid contact, he's a .300 hitter. Last year, many in the Astros organization felt Hidalgo became too homer-conscious trying to replace Moises Alou in the lineup. What had been line-drive base hits to center and right field in 1998 became harmless popups and groundballs in 1999.

Baserunning & Defense

Despite playing a new position, left field, for the first time and battling a painful knee, Hidalgo was leading the National League in assists with 15 when he went on the disabled list. His arm is well above average both in strength and accuracy. Hidalgo gets excellent jumps in the outfield, which more than make up for his average speed, and he's fearless around the outfield wall. Hidalgo isn't a good baserunner. He doesn't get good jumps on steals nor runs sharp routes around the bases.

2000 Outlook

Hidalgo will enter this season with a new lease on life after the Astros traded away Carl Everett to Boston. It looked as though Everett's impressive 1999 season and Moises Alou's return from injury would limit Hidalgo's opportunities. Now he's certain to be the Opening Day center fielder. The gifted Hidalgo should be healthy and ready.

Position: LF/CF
Bats: R **Throws:** R
Ht: 6' 3" **Wt:** 190

Opening Day Age: 24
Born: 7/2/75 in Caracas, Venezuela
ML Seasons: 3

Overall Statistics

	G	AB	R	H	D	T	HR	RBI	SB	BB	SO	Avg	OBP	Slg
1999	108	383	49	87	25	2	15	56	8	56	73	.227	.328	.420
Career	201	656	88	170	45	2	24	97	12	77	128	.259	.339	.444

Where He Hits the Ball

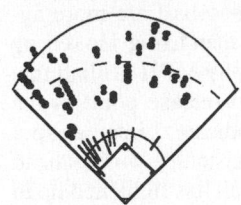
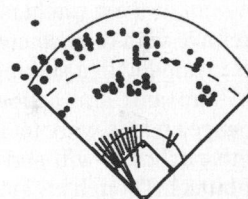

Vs. LHP   **Vs. RHP**

1999 Situational Stats

	AB	H	HR	RBI	Avg		AB	H	HR	RBI	Avg
Home	183	39	5	26	.213	LHP	98	22	3	17	.224
Road	200	48	10	30	.240	RHP	285	65	12	39	.228
First Half	305	75	14	51	.246	Sc Pos	111	23	3	39	.207
Scnd Half	78	12	1	5	.154	Clutch	47	8	1	7	.170

1999 Rankings (National League)

- 8th in lowest batting average in the clutch
- Led NL left fielders in fewest GDPs per GDP situation (5.2%)

Houston

Jose Lima

Position: SP
Bats: R **Throws:** R
Ht: 6' 2" **Wt:** 205

Opening Day Age: 27
Born: 9/30/72 in Santiago, Dominican Republic
ML Seasons: 6
Pronunciation: LEE-muh

1999 Season

Jose Lima's ascension from mopup reliever in 1997 to 21-game winner and Cy Young candidate last season has been amazing. No one seems more pleased with it than Lima himself. His emotional nature, crazy antics and willingness to dance and shout at every opportunity draw amused glances from his teammates and not-so-amused stares from opponents. Lima's 246.1 innings ranked third in the National League, but there was some concern he tired in September, when he finished 2-3, 6.21 ERA.

Pitching

Lima's bread-and-butter pitch is a devastating sinking changeup that he'll throw to any batter in any count. Few pitchers in baseball are more aggressive with their changeup than Lima. He sets up his change with a sinking 88-89 MPH fastball that has the same arm action and release point as the change. As his walk totals indicate, Lima can spot both pitches at will and consistently works ahead of hitters. Though his curveball has tightened up in the past two years, it's definitely a secondary pitch. Lima gets in trouble when he gets overly emotional on the mound and starts throwing 91-92 MPH. His fastball then straightens out and is easy to handle. There also is talk among scouts that Lima tips his pitches on occasion.

Defense & Hitting

Lima is an active and agile fielder who helps himself defensively when he's under control. He holds runners well. At the plate, Lima is an ineffective hitter when swinging away but is a confident and accomplished bunter.

2000 Outlook

Lima's age is listed as 27, which means he'd be entering his prime, but that age has been openly questioned in the baseball world. Lima's pitching style and lack of heavy use until the past two years points to a long career, though.

Overall Statistics

	W	L	Pct.	ERA	G	GS	Sv	IP	H	BB	SO	HR	Ratio
1999	21	10	.677	3.58	35	35	0	246.1	256	44	187	30	1.22
Career	46	40	.535	4.37	177	89	5	707.2	747	135	522	98	1.25

How Often He Throws Strikes

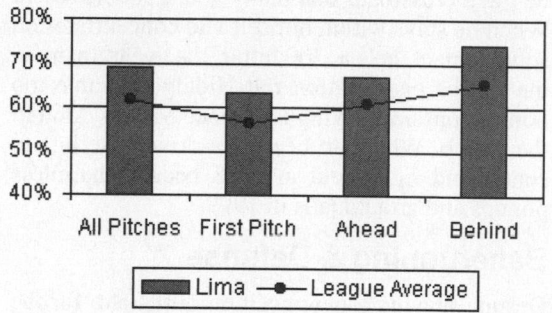

1999 Situational Stats

	W	L	ERA	Sv	IP		AB	H	HR	RBI	Avg
Home	9	5	2.31	0	113.0	LHB	421	121	14	48	.287
Road	12	5	4.66	0	133.1	RHB	545	135	16	54	.248
First Half	13	4	3.23	0	139.1	Sc Pos	195	52	6	73	.267
Scnd Half	8	6	4.04	0	107.0	Clutch	93	23	1	12	.247

1999 Rankings (National League)

- 1st in games started
- 2nd in sacrifice bunts (13), wins, batters faced (1,024) and ERA at home
- 3rd in innings pitched, highest strikeout/walk ratio (4.3), fewest GDPs induced per 9 innings (0.3) and fewest walks per 9 innings (1.6)
- 4th in hits allowed
- Led the Astros in games started, innings pitched, hits allowed, batters faced (1,024), home runs allowed, lowest on-base percentage allowed (.296), fewest baserunners allowed per 9 innings (11.0), ERA at home and lowest batting average allowed vs. righthanded batters

Shane Reynolds

Position: SP
Bats: R **Throws:** R
Ht: 6' 3" **Wt:** 210

Opening Day Age: 32
Born: 3/26/68 in
Bastrop, LA
ML Seasons: 8

1999 Season

Overshadowed by 20-game winners Mike Hampton and Jose Lima, Shane Reynolds seemed like the forgotten man of the Astros rotation, but he's still the acknowledged leader of the staff. Reynolds reached 16 wins, 230 innings and 190 strikeouts for the third time in the last four seasons. The only time he fell short of those levels was in 1997, when knee surgery caused him to miss five starts.

Pitching

Reynolds' pitching style is highly predictable but highly refined. He tries to get ahead early in the count by throwing 87-90 MPH sinking or cut fastballs low in the strike zone, then finishes hitters off with devastating split-finger pitches. Reynolds went more to his slider than his curveball in 1999, but both pitches are thrown mostly for show purposes. Reynolds makes hitters beat him as well as any pitcher in baseball. In addition to only allowing 1.44 walks per nine innings last year, he didn't commit a balk and only hit one batter.

Defense & Hitting

Though Hampton received more attention for his hitting, Reynolds was arguably more effective. He led all National League pitchers with 14 RBI on 11 hits, which included two doubles and a home run. Reynolds also led all NL hittters by putting down 17 sacrifice bunts. Defensively, Reynolds is above average fielding comebackers, but basestealers can run on his split-finger fastball.

2000 Outlook

Reynolds is a fanatical worker, a perfectionist and one of the most well-prepared athletes in baseball. It's unlikely that the attention given to his fellow starters will harm Reynolds' ego either. With a little more run support from his teammates, he just might have his first 20-win season in 2000.

Overall Statistics

	W	L	Pct.	ERA	G	GS	Sv	IP	H	BB	SO	HR	Ratio
1999	16	14	.533	3.85	35	35	0	231.2	250	37	197	23	1.24
Career	79	61	.564	3.70	211	185	0	1234.2	1300	251	1067	114	1.26

How Often He Throws Strikes

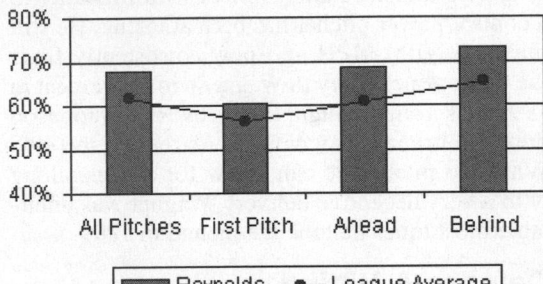

1999 Situational Stats

	W	L	ERA	Sv	IP		AB	H	HR	RBI	Avg
Home	10	6	3.90	0	120.0	LHB	418	118	10	39	.282
Road	6	8	3.79	0	111.2	RHB	491	132	13	57	.269
First Half	11	6	3.62	0	129.1	Sc Pos	187	53	5	69	.283
Scnd Half	5	8	4.13	0	102.1	Clutch	56	19	2	5	.339

1999 Rankings (National League)

- 1st in sacrifice bunts (17), games started, highest strikeout/walk ratio (5.3) and fewest walks per 9 innings (1.4)
- 2nd in shutouts (2)
- 4th in losses and GDPs induced (26)
- 5th in complete games (4), hits allowed and strikeouts
- Led the Astros in sacrifice bunts (17), losses, games started, complete games (4), shutouts (2), strikeouts, highest strikeout/walk ratio (5.3), fewest pitches thrown per batter (3.49), most strikeouts per 9 innings (7.7) and fewest walks per 9 innings (1.4)

Houston

Billy Wagner

1999 Season

The only thing that compares to Billy Wagner's dominance during the 1999 season, when he gained recognition as perhaps the best closer in the game, is his dominance in 1997 and 1998. He struck out a record 14.9 hitters per nine innings last year, breaking the records he had set in each of the previous two years. Righthanded hitters struck out an incredible 111 times in 211 at-bats. Without an inexplicable five-batter, five-run outing against Arizona early in the season, Wagner's ERA would have been 0.96. He allowed runs in just seven of 66 games, and only once after July 31.

Pitching

Wagner's transformation from a wild fireballer to a control/power pitcher has been amazing. He still throws 97-100 MPH and now consistently finds the strike zone. A key to Wagner's improvement in 1999 was a slider taught to him by Randy Johnson during Johnson's stay with the Astros late in 1998. With two pitches he can throw for strikes, along with a very deceptive delivery, Wagner was unhittable most times he took the mound in 1999.

Defense & Hitting

Wagner rarely gets a chance to either hit or do much in the field. What few baserunners reach against Wagner tend to take liberties, stealing six bases in as many attempts last year.

2000 Outlook

Wagner ended the year with a strained elbow and wasn't able to pitch in the deciding game of the Astros' playoff loss to Atlanta. The injury is believed to be minor. Assuming Wagner is healthy, he could break through the 40-save barrier for the first time in his career.

Position: RP
Bats: L **Throws:** L
Ht: 5'11" **Wt:** 180

Opening Day Age: 28
Born: 7/25/71 in Tannersville, VA
ML Seasons: 5

Overall Statistics

	W	L	Pct.	ERA	G	GS	Sv	IP	H	BB	SO	HR	Ratio
1999	4	1	.800	1.57	66	0	39	74.2	35	23	124	5	0.78
Career	17	14	.548	2.35	224	0	101	253.0	158	108	394	22	1.05

How Often He Throws Strikes

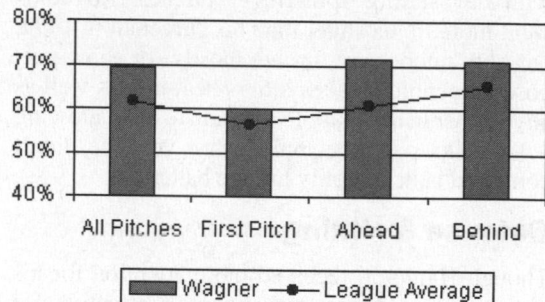

Wagner — League Average

1999 Situational Stats

	W	L	ERA	Sv	IP		AB	H	HR	RBI	Avg
Home	2	1	2.00	20	36.0	LHB	48	8	1	5	.167
Road	2	0	1.16	19	38.2	RHB	211	27	4	10	.128
First Half	1	1	2.20	23	41.0	Sc Pos	61	9	1	11	.148
Scnd Half	3	0	0.80	16	33.2	Clutch	193	23	4	14	.119

1999 Rankings (National League)

- 1st in fewest GDPs induced per GDP situation (0.0%), relief ERA (1.57), lowest batting average allowed in relief (.135), fewest baserunners allowed per 9 innings in relief (7.1) and most strikeouts per 9 innings in relief (14.9)
- 2nd in save percentage (92.9%) and lowest batting average allowed in relief with runners on base (.151)
- 3rd in saves
- 4th in first batter efficiency (.145)
- Led the Astros in saves, games finished (55), save opportunities (42), save percentage (92.9%), blown saves (3), first batter efficiency (.145) and lowest batting average allowed in relief with runners on base (.151)

Tim Bogar

Position: SS/3B
Bats: R **Throws:** R
Ht: 6' 2" **Wt:** 198

Opening Day Age: 33
Born: 10/28/66 in Indianapolis, IN
ML Seasons: 7

Overall Statistics

	G	AB	R	H	D	T	HR	RBI	SB	BB	SO	Avg	OBP	Slg
1999	106	309	44	74	16	2	4	31	3	38	52	.239	.328	.343
Career	579	1197	144	277	58	7	15	126	12	106	215	.231	.298	.329

1999 Situational Stats

	AB	H	HR	RBI	Avg		AB	H	HR	RBI	Avg
Home	144	37	2	19	.257	LHP	101	22	2	12	.218
Road	165	37	2	12	.224	RHP	208	52	2	19	.250
First Half	183	45	3	22	.246	Sc Pos	85	17	0	26	.200
Scnd Half	126	29	1	9	.230	Clutch	53	11	0	6	.208

1999 Season

Injuries to fellow shortstop Ricky Gutierrez and Tim Bogar's usual steady defense enabled the 33-year-old utilityman to set career highs in most offensive categories, including games and at-bats. His defense was especially valued by a sinker-oriented pitching staff.

Hitting, Baserunning & Defense

Bogar has evolved into the Astros' steadiest defensive infielder. He positions himself excellently and has range that far surpasses his speed, plus a strong and accurate arm. Bogar has a slow bat and limited power, so his offensive contributions are limited to moving runners along. Bogar isn't a threat on the bases either.

2000 Outlook

Gutierrez signed with the Cubs as a free agent and the Astros don't have a shortstop prospect ready to step in at the big league level, so Bogar becomes their stopgap starter this year. He's really better suited to be a utilityman.

Tony Eusebio

Position: C
Bats: R **Throws:** R
Ht: 6' 2" **Wt:** 210

Opening Day Age: 32
Born: 4/27/67 in San Jose de los Llanos, Dominican Republic
ML Seasons: 7
Pronunciation: you-SAY-bee-oh

Overall Statistics

	G	AB	R	H	D	T	HR	RBI	SB	BB	SO	Avg	OBP	Slg
1999	103	323	31	88	15	0	4	33	0	40	67	.272	.353	.356
Career	465	1367	139	379	61	5	18	194	1	140	245	.277	.345	.369

1999 Situational Stats

	AB	H	HR	RBI	Avg		AB	H	HR	RBI	Avg
Home	157	43	2	19	.274	LHP	117	39	4	16	.333
Road	166	45	2	14	.271	RHP	206	49	0	17	.238
First Half	182	46	2	12	.253	Sc Pos	99	22	0	24	.222
Scnd Half	141	42	2	21	.298	Clutch	48	13	1	5	.271

1999 Season

Tony Eusebio enjoyed a solid if unspectacular season while splitting catching duties with Paul Bako. His playing time increased after Brad Ausmus was traded to Detroit and Mitch Meluskey had season-ending shoulder surgery. Eusebio's fragile knees were up to the task and he didn't miss any time due to injury. The Astros played a loose platoon, but Eusebio also served as Shane Reynolds' regular catcher for much of the year.

Hitting, Baserunning & Defense

Eusebio is a patient hitter with a quick inside-out swing that makes him an excellent hit-and-run candidate. Eusebio was particularly effective against lefthanders, batting .333. Because of his approach, he rarely drives the ball with much extra-base power. Eusebio's defense has matured over the years, especially in managing a game, and he has a strong, accurate arm. He's one of the slowest runners in baseball.

2000 Outlook

Wanting insurance in case Meluskey can't bounce back, the Astros re-signed Eusebio as a free agent for two years and $2.4 million. Eusebio's playing time probably will decrease slightly.

Ricky Gutierrez

Position: SS
Bats: R **Throws:** R
Ht: 6' 1" **Wt:** 175

Opening Day Age: 29
Born: 5/23/70 in Miami, FL
ML Seasons: 7
Pronunciation: goo-tee-AIR-ez

Overall Statistics

	G	AB	R	H	D	T	HR	RBI	SB	BB	SO	Avg	OBP	Slg
1999	85	268	33	70	7	5	1	25	2	37	45	.261	.354	.336
Career	692	2149	274	558	80	20	13	186	37	227	405	.260	.335	.334

1999 Situational Stats

	AB	H	HR	RBI	Avg		AB	H	HR	RBI	Avg
Home	142	43	1	16	.303	LHP	66	25	0	8	.379
Road	126	27	0	9	.214	RHP	202	45	1	17	.223
First Half	135	36	1	12	.267	Sc Pos	80	18	0	23	.225
Scnd Half	133	34	0	13	.256	Clutch	38	12	0	3	.316

1999 Season

Coming off a strong 1998 season, Ricky Gutierrez was expected to hold down the Astros' regular shortstop role in 1999. A broken hand sidelined him for two months, though, and Gutierrez spent the rest of the season in a loose platoon role with Tim Bogar. While Gutierrez' offensive game prospered in the arrangement and he hit .379 against lefthanders, he didn't appear as comfortable in the field.

Hitting, Baserunning & Defense

Gutierrez has evolved into one of the most pronounced groundball hitters in baseball and gave up any pretense of trying to drive the ball the second half, perhaps the result of his hand injury. He has above-average arm strength and is capable of making highlight-reel plays, especially on groundballs up the middle. He does have heavy legs, however, and his range is now below average. The same is true of his speed, and his baserunning instincts are only fair.

2000 Outlook

A free agent, Gutierrez signed with the Cubs for two years and $4.5 milion, a contract Houston couldn't afford. The Astros will give Tim Bogar his job in 2000.

Chris Holt

Position: SP
Bats: R **Throws:** R
Ht: 6' 4" **Wt:** 205

Opening Day Age: 28
Born: 9/18/71 in Dallas, TX
ML Seasons: 3

Overall Statistics

	W	L	Pct.	ERA	G	GS	Sv	IP	H	BB	SO	HR	Ratio
1999	5	13	.278	4.66	32	26	1	164.0	193	57	115	12	1.52
Career	13	26	.333	4.04	69	58	1	378.1	409	121	210	29	1.40

1999 Situational Stats

	W	L	ERA	Sv	IP		AB	H	HR	RBI	Avg
Home	4	8	3.72	0	109.0	LHB	309	95	4	31	.307
Road	1	5	6.55	1	55.0	RHB	329	98	8	44	.298
First Half	1	9	5.23	0	82.2	Sc Pos	160	41	3	59	.256
Scnd Half	4	4	4.09	0	81.1	Clutch	35	15	0	5	.429

1999 Season

After missing 1998 following shoulder surgery, Chris Holt was a question mark. He earned a starting job in spring training and pitched better than his 5-13 record would indicate. Holt's 4.27 runs per game of support was the worst mark among Astros starters and more than two runs less than 22-game winner Mike Hampton received. His 4.66 ERA matched the league average for starting pitchers, a strong statement for a team's No. 5 starter.

Pitching, Defense & Hitting

Holt's velocity rebounded and he threw 92-93 MPH most of the year before tailing off in September. Holt relies on his heavy sinker to get hitters to bounce balls into the ground. While his changeup is a solid second pitch, Holt still needs to improve his curveball to take the next step as a pitcher. He's a poor hitter and a below-average bunter. He holds runners well and saw a club-high nine runners caught stealing while he was on the mound.

2000 Outlook

Holt should remain Houston's fifth starter as long as he's healthy. He can give the club a consistent six innings per start and 170-190 innings over the course of a season. Salary pressures and the lack of a top prospect in Triple-A to take his place give him job security.

Stan Javier

Position: LF/RF/CF
Bats: B **Throws:** R
Ht: 6' 0" **Wt:** 202

Opening Day Age: 36
Born: 1/9/64 in San Francisco de Macoris, Dominican Republic
ML Seasons: 15
Pronunciation: HAH-vee-air

Overall Statistics

	G	AB	R	H	D	T	HR	RBI	SB	BB	SO	Avg	OBP	Slg
1999	132	397	61	113	19	2	3	34	16	38	63	.285	.347	.365
Career	1569	4424	676	1182	193	34	48	430	231	500	728	.267	.342	.359

1999 Situational Stats

	AB	H	HR	RBI	Avg		AB	H	HR	RBI	Avg
Home	182	49	2	19	.269	LHP	109	35	3	11	.321
Road	215	64	1	15	.298	RHP	288	78	0	23	.271
First Half	258	74	3	25	.287	Sc Pos	92	24	0	30	.261
Scnd Half	139	39	0	9	.281	Clutch	71	18	1	6	.254

1999 Season

Acquired from the Giants in late August for minor league pitcher Joe Messman, Stan Javier filled a spot in the Astros' injury-decimated outfield. With San Francisco, Javier had filled in at both corners for the frequently injured Barry Bonds and Ellis Burks. Javier was especially effective against lefthanded pitchers, hitting .321.

Hitting, Baserunning & Defense

Javier is a consummate professional in all areas of the game. He makes solid line-drive contact at the plate, will work counts for walks and hits behind the runner. Though his arm strength is short for right field and his range less than ideal for center, he can play all three outfield positions. Formerly one of the highest-percentage basestealers in the game, Javier has lost a step on the bases but is still a threat.

2000 Outlook

With diminishing speed and limited power, the switch-hitting Javier's ideal role is as a backup outfielder capable of playing all three outfield positions. Seattle will use him in just that manner after signing him for one year and $1.8 million.

Russ Johnson

Position: 3B/2B
Bats: R **Throws:** R
Ht: 5'10" **Wt:** 180

Opening Day Age: 27
Born: 2/22/73 in Baton Rouge, LA
ML Seasons: 3

Overall Statistics

	G	AB	R	H	D	T	HR	RBI	SB	BB	SO	Avg	OBP	Slg
1999	83	156	24	44	10	0	5	23	2	20	31	.282	.358	.442
Career	112	229	33	65	12	0	7	32	4	27	50	.284	.358	.428

1999 Situational Stats

	AB	H	HR	RBI	Avg		AB	H	HR	RBI	Avg
Home	65	17	2	6	.262	LHP	60	17	2	11	.283
Road	91	27	3	17	.297	RHP	96	27	3	12	.281
First Half	54	12	1	6	.222	Sc Pos	37	11	1	18	.297
Scnd Half	102	32	4	17	.314	Clutch	29	4	1	3	.138

1999 Season

Russ Johnson appeared headed for a third full season at Triple-A New Orleans before Ken Caminiti went down with a serious calf problem. Recalled to platoon with Bill Spiers at third base, Johnson showed surprising power. He hit five home runs in 156 at-bats after hitting only seven in a full Triple-A season in 1998.

Hitting, Baserunning & Defense

Johnson's strongest suits are his fundamentals and desire. He's a line-drive hitter with excellent plate discipline, which makes him valuable as a No. 2 hitter or pinch-hitter. Johnson's defense at third base was solid and he showed enough range and quickness around the bag to spell Craig Biggio at second base next season. Johnson's speed is below average but he rarely makes mental mistakes on the bases.

2000 Outlook

Johnson's offensive performance and versatility make him a strong candidate to stick with the club in a utility role. He likely isn't the answer for an everyday job should Caminiti's health problems continue, but Johnson has the hard-nosed attitude and all-around skills that managers like to have available on the bench. A former shortstop, he's a longshot to factor into the mix at that position.

Houston

Mitch Meluskey

Position: C
Bats: B **Throws:** R
Ht: 6' 0" **Wt:** 185

Opening Day Age: 26
Born: 9/18/73 in
Yakima, WA
ML Seasons: 2
Pronunciation:
muh-LUSK-ee

Overall Statistics

	G	AB	R	H	D	T	HR	RBI	SB	BB	SO	Avg	OBP	Slg
1999	10	33	4	7	1	0	1	3	1	5	6	.212	.316	.333
Career	18	41	5	9	2	0	1	3	1	6	10	.220	.319	.341

1999 Situational Stats

	AB	H	HR	RBI	Avg		AB	H	HR	RBI	Avg
Home	15	3	0	1	.200	LHP	6	2	0	1	.333
Road	18	4	1	2	.222	RHP	27	5	1	2	.185
First Half	33	7	1	3	.212	Sc Pos	8	1	0	2	.125
Scnd Half	0	0	0	0	.-	Clutch	6	0	0	0	.000

1999 Season

Coming off a 1998 minor league season that estab-lished him as one of the better catching prospects in baseball, Mitch Meluskey was expected to chal-lenge for at least a platoon role with Houston. Then he injured his shoulder late in spring training and had season-ending surgery after playing in just 10 games.

Hitting, Baserunning & Defense

Meluskey's forte is his hitting ability. A switch-hit-ter with above-average bat speed and exacting pa-tience from both sides of the plate, he has the strength to hit 15-20 home runs in the big leagues. Meluskey has average receiving and throwing skills, but he's still raw in terms of calling games. He's a below-average runner but doesn't clog the bases.

2000 Outlook

Meluskey was back to regular baseball activities by October and, barring any setbacks, should be fully healthy for spring training. He should be able to seize the starting job, and expect strong offen-sive numbers if he does so.

Jay Powell

Position: RP
Bats: R **Throws:** R
Ht: 6' 4" **Wt:** 225

Opening Day Age: 28
Born: 1/9/72 in
Meridian, MS
ML Seasons: 5

Overall Statistics

	W	L	Pct.	ERA	G	GS	Sv	IP	H	BB	SO	HR	Ratio
1999	5	4	.556	4.32	67	0	4	75.0	82	40	77	3	1.63
Career	23	16	.590	3.78	279	0	15	304.2	289	149	260	17	1.44

1999 Situational Stats

	W	L	ERA	Sv	IP		AB	H	HR	RBI	Avg
Home	2	2	5.00	0	36.0	LHB	125	38	3	20	.304
Road	3	2	3.69	4	39.0	RHB	166	44	0	20	.265
First Half	4	1	3.72	2	38.2	Sc Pos	104	28	0	35	.269
Scnd Half	1	3	4.95	2	36.1	Clutch	155	46	1	22	.297

1999 Season

Jay Powell entered last year counted on to be one of closer Billy Wagner's leading setup men. While Powell led the club with 67 appearances and 75 relief innings, he was inconsistent from game to game and couldn't pick up the slack when Scott Elarton moved to the starting rotation in July.

Pitching, Defense & Hitting

Powell has excellent arm strength and regularly throws his heavy, sinking fastball at 93-95 MPH. He complements his heat with a good, late-break-ing slider. The problem last year was that his sinker was up in the zone too much and he couldn't throw his slider for strikes when behind in the count. Lefthanders had an especially easy time against Powell's stuff. Powell is a big, slow man who's easy to steal on and he's not quick off the mound. He has two hits in 10 career at-bats.

2000 Outlook

Now entering the second year of a three-year con-tract, Powell will be looked on to improve upon his 1999 performance. It isn't a matter of raw stuff, as Powell has been projected as a future closer. It's more a matter of having the confidence and me-chanics to throw his fastball to the lower half of the plate.

Bill Spiers

Position: 3B/LF/SS
Bats: L **Throws:** R
Ht: 6' 2" **Wt:** 190

Opening Day Age: 33
Born: 6/5/66 in Orangeburg, SC
ML Seasons: 11
Pronunciation: SPY-ers

Overall Statistics

	G	AB	R	H	D	T	HR	RBI	SB	BB	SO	Avg	OBP	Slg
1999	127	393	56	113	18	5	4	39	10	47	45	.288	.363	.389
Career	1124	3050	436	814	141	32	34	345	90	305	458	.267	.335	.368

1999 Situational Stats

	AB	H	HR	RBI	Avg		AB	H	HR	RBI	Avg
Home	196	51	1	13	.260	LHP	40	15	0	10	.375
Road	197	62	3	26	.315	RHP	353	98	4	29	.278
First Half	205	60	3	26	.293	Sc Pos	102	28	0	34	.275
Scnd Half	188	53	1	13	.282	Clutch	63	18	1	7	.286

1999 Season

Bill Spiers went from a sound platoon third baseman and dependable pinch-hitter to one of the most versatile players in baseball in 1999. He and St. Louis' David Howard were the only two big leaguers to play seven positions during the season, and Spiers started everywhere except first base and catcher. Because of the Astros' injury epidemic, Spiers got 393 at-bats, his most in eight years.

Hitting, Baserunning & Defense

Spiers is a strong fundamental player who is adept at working pitchers into fastball counts, where he's a much stronger hitter. With increased playing time he had a rare opportunity to face lefthanders, and responded by hitting .375, an aberration. Spiers' best defensive position is third base, but his average speed and strong throwing arm enable him to play the outfield well. The Astros would love to play him at shortstop, but he lacks first-step quickness.

2000 Outlook

With the left side of the Houston infield either wide open (shortstop) or injury-prone (Ken Caminiti), Spiers will continue to be a valuable player for the Astros. He periodically has suffered from back problems, but playing on natural turf at new Enron Field should help him.

Brian Williams

Position: RP
Bats: R **Throws:** R
Ht: 6' 2" **Wt:** 225

Opening Day Age: 31
Born: 2/15/69 in Fort Lawn, SC
ML Seasons: 8

Overall Statistics

	W	L	Pct.	ERA	G	GS	Sv	IP	H	BB	SO	HR	Ratio
1999	2	1	.667	4.41	50	0	0	67.1	69	35	53	4	1.54
Career	25	37	.403	5.22	227	59	5	553.0	604	301	377	56	1.64

1999 Situational Stats

	W	L	ERA	Sv	IP		AB	H	HR	RBI	Avg
Home	1	0	4.55	0	29.2	LHB	111	36	1	21	.324
Road	1	1	4.30	0	37.2	RHB	143	33	3	24	.231
First Half	0	1	4.78	0	37.2	Sc Pos	86	24	0	38	.279
Scnd Half	2	0	3.94	0	29.2	Clutch	20	5	0	4	.250

1999 Season

Brian Williams returned from a one-year purgatory in Japan to prove that he still could pitch in the big leagues. He made the club as the long man in the bullpen and pitched respectably. Manager Larry Dierker hesitated to use him in pressure situations.

Pitching, Defense & Hitting

Williams still has the solid stuff that made him a top prospect with the Astros in the early 1990s. He complements a 91-93 MPH fastball with a slider, curveball and effective straight change. The problems with Williams are command and approach. He gets behind hitters and then grooves pitches over the middle of the plate. Though he has gained weight since his prospect days, Williams is an outstanding athlete who once played the outfield for the U.S. national team. He's a quick fielder, controls the running game and is a career .169 hitter.

2000 Outlook

A free agent, Williams may be able to claim a No. 5 starter's job somewhere. He unquestionably has the pitches and physical ability to do so, but never has applied himself mentally or physically to the task. He could be a surprise in 2000, or find himself pitching overseas again.

Houston

Other Houston Astros

Paul Bako (Pos: C, Age: 27, Bats: L)

	G	AB	R	H	D	T	HR	RBI	SB	BB	SO	Avg	OBP	Slg
1999	73	215	16	55	14	1	2	17	1	26	57	.256	.332	.358
Career	169	520	39	138	26	2	5	47	2	49	139	.265	.325	.352

Bako is a solid defensive catcher who will perform better as a part-time player. He won't hurt the team with his bat, so he should remain a valuable commodity as long as he isn't playing every day. 2000 Outlook: B

Glen Barker (Pos: CF, Age: 28, Bats: B)

	G	AB	R	H	D	T	HR	RBI	SB	BB	SO	Avg	OBP	Slg
1999	81	73	23	21	2	0	1	11	17	11	19	.288	.384	.356
Career	81	73	23	21	2	0	1	11	17	11	19	.288	.384	.356

In spot duty Barker hit .288 in 73 at-bats as a rookie, and his .384 OBP provided some extra chances to steal. He won't start, but he'll be running and serve as a defensive replacement. 2000 Outlook: C

Jose Cabrera (Pos: RHP, Age: 28)

	W	L	Pct.	ERA	G	GS	Sv	IP	H	BB	SO	HR	Ratio
1999	4	0	1.000	2.15	26	0	0	29.1	21	9	28	3	1.02
Career	4	0	1.000	2.39	41	0	0	49.0	34	16	47	4	1.02

Cabrera earned some serious frequent-flyer miles between Houston and Triple-A New Orleans in 1999, and he pitched very well at both destinations. 2000 Outlook: B

Alex Diaz (Pos: LF, Age: 31, Bats: B)

	G	AB	R	H	D	T	HR	RBI	SB	BB	SO	Avg	OBP	Slg
1999	30	50	3	11	2	0	1	7	2	3	13	.220	.264	.320
Career	366	816	102	195	31	7	8	75	41	33	107	.239	.271	.324

Diaz made the Opening Day roster, but a shoulder injury sidelined him in June. He was released upon being activated on August 31. The end is near. 2000 Outlook: D

Doug Henry (Pos: RHP, Age: 36)

	W	L	Pct.	ERA	G	GS	Sv	IP	H	BB	SO	HR	Ratio
1999	2	3	.400	4.65	35	0	2	40.2	45	24	36	8	1.70
Career	28	36	.438	3.98	457	0	81	511.2	479	247	422	57	1.42

Henry wasn't as effective as he was in 1998, when he won eight games and allowed just 55 hits in 71 innings. Time may be creeping up on him. 2000 Outlook: B

Carlos Hernandez (Pos: 2B, Age: 24, Bats: R)

	G	AB	R	H	D	T	HR	RBI	SB	BB	SO	Avg	OBP	Slg
1999	16	14	4	2	0	0	0	1	3	0	0	.143	.143	.143
Career	16	14	4	2	0	0	0	1	3	0	0	.143	.143	.143

Hernandez might have had a shot at the vacant shortstop job, but his play in Triple-A convinced the Astros he's a second baseman. A utility role is in his future. 2000 Outlook: C

Jack Howell (Pos: 1B, Age: 38, Bats: L)

	G	AB	R	H	D	T	HR	RBI	SB	BB	SO	Avg	OBP	Slg
1999	37	33	2	7	2	0	1	0	8	9	.212	.366	.364
Career	941	2639	345	632	129	16	108	337	14	300	626	.239	.318	.423

Over the last four seasons, Howell has hit 24 homers in 330 at-bats against righthanders, but he has missed most of the last two campaigns with injuries. Now 38, Howell is the ultimate injury risk. 2000 Outlook: C

Randy Knorr (Pos: C, Age: 31, Bats: R)

	G	AB	R	H	D	T	HR	RBI	SB	BB	SO	Avg	OBP	Slg
1999	13	30	2	5	1	0	0	0	0	1	8	.167	.194	.200
Career	204	551	64	123	23	3	19	76	0	39	136	.223	.276	.379

With rookie catcher Mitch Meluskey going down for the season in April, Knorr was recalled a couple of times in 1999. He didn't hit, and signed with Pittsburgh in December. 2000 Outlook: C

Jeff McCurry (Pos: RHP, Age: 30)

	W	L	Pct.	ERA	G	GS	Sv	IP	H	BB	SO	HR	Ratio
1999	0	1	.000	15.75	5	0	0	4.0	11	2	3	1	3.25
Career	3	12	.200	5.89	111	0	1	128.1	169	63	60	24	1.81

McCurry has put some time in the majors in each of the last five seasons, but neither his major league work nor his Triple-A numbers suggest he's likely to grab a big league job and keep it. 2000 Outlook: D

Matt Mieske (Pos: LF/RF, Age: 32, Bats: R)

	G	AB	R	H	D	T	HR	RBI	SB	BB	SO	Avg	OBP	Slg
1999	78	150	24	46	5	0	9	29	0	8	31	.307	.338	.520
Career	590	1458	215	390	77	8	54	219	7	116	295	.267	.323	.442

Mieske is a platoon player, but he's made a career out of pounding lefthanded pitching. Mieske hit .354 and slugged .622 against southpaws in 1999, stroking four doubles and six homers in 82 at-bats. 2000 Outlook: B

Trever Miller (Pos: LHP, Age: 26)

	W	L	Pct.	ERA	G	GS	Sv	IP	H	BB	SO	HR	Ratio
1999	3	2	.600	5.07	47	0	1	49.2	58	29	37	6	1.75
Career	5	6	.455	4.74	89	5	2	119.2	143	58	75	13	1.68

Miller's 1998 season was encouraging, but his '99 performance suffered because he didn't have the command to make his average stuff work. He retired lefties successfully, but righties hit him hard. 2000 Outlook: B

Joe Slusarski (Pos: RHP, Age: 33)

	W	L	Pct.	ERA	G	GS	Sv	IP	H	BB	SO	HR	Ratio
1999	0	0	-	0.00	3	0	0	3.2	1	3	3	0	1.09
Career	11	13	.458	5.25	52	34	0	212.2	237	99	108	33	1.58

Slusarski made three July appearances for Houston after a four-year absence from the majors. A week after his arrival he went on the disabled list with a strained groin muscle. He may never be back. 2000 Outlook: D

Ryan Thompson (Pos: CF, Age: 32, Bats: R)

	G	AB	R	H	D	T	HR	RBI	SB	BB	SO	Avg	OBP	Slg
1999	12	20	2	4	1	0	1	5	0	2	7	.200	.273	.400
Career	303	1039	131	249	54	4	41	136	8	77	289	.240	.300	.418

A highly regarded prospect in the early 1990s, Thompson never has managed to stick in the majors after a stint with the Mets. A free agent, he might resurface as a bench player if the right situation arises. 2000 Outlook: C

Houston Astros Minor League Prospects

Organization Overview:

The Astros have some intriguing sluggers and pitchers rising through their system, and unlike the prospects who came before them, these guys may find a home in Houston. The Astros have eight straight .500-or-better seasons and three consecutive National League Central titles, all without a huge payroll or an influx of homegrown players. Most of their best players were either drafted in the 1980s (Craig Biggio, Shane Reynolds) or acquired in trades (Jeff Bagwell, Mike Hampton, Jose Lima). The biggest breakthroughs by Houston signees last year came in Seattle, where Freddy Garcia and John Halama flourished after arriving in a 1998 deal for Randy Johnson. In 2000, Scott Elarton and Richard Hidalgo will be ready for expanded roles, Mitch Meluskey may take over at catcher a year later than expected, and Lance Berkman and Daryle Ward will be pressing for playing time.

Lance Berkman

Position: OF   **Opening Day Age:** 24
Bats: B **Throws:** L   **Born:** 2/10/76 in Waco,
Ht: 6' 1" **Wt:** 205   TX

Recent Statistics

	G	AB	R	H	D	T	HR	RBI	SB	BB	SO	Avg
1999 AAA New Orleans	64	226	42	73	20	0	8	49	7	39	47	.323
1999 NL Houston	34	93	10	22	2	0	4	15	5	12	21	.237
1999 MLE	64	213	30	60	18	0	4	35	4	27	53	.282

Though Jeff Bagwell is entrenched as the Astros' first baseman, they couldn't pass on Berkman, a product of crosstown Rice, in the first round of the 1997 draft. In 256 minor league games, Berkman has batted .305 with 50 homers and 186 RBI while walking nearly as often as he has struck out. Because of Bagwell's presence, Berkman has been converted to left field. He's a better athlete than he appears at first glance, and he's an adequate outfielder with an average arm. Daryle Ward's numbers were gaudier than Berkman's last year, but Ward has three times as much experience and isn't really an outfielder. Berkman is the club's left fielder of the future, though he may see some time in Triple-A this season.

Adam Everett

Position: SS   **Opening Day Age:** 23
Bats: R **Throws:** R   **Born:** 2/6/77 in Austell,
Ht: 6' 1" **Wt:** 167   GA

Recent Statistics

	G	AB	R	H	D	T	HR	RBI	SB	BB	SO	Avg
1998 A Lowell	21	71	11	21	6	2	0	9	2	11	13	.296
1999 AA Trenton	98	338	56	89	11	0	10	44	21	41	64	.263
1999 MLE	98	330	46	81	10	0	8	36	13	28	68	.245

Everett came to the Astros from the Red Sox in December, along with lefthander Greg Miller, when Houston traded Carl Everett (no relation) in a cost-cutting move.

Adam was drafted in 1997's first round out of South Carolina on the basis of his strong defense. Boston considered him a better shortstop than Nomar Garciaparra, though Everett's bat isn't in the same class. He didn't homer in his first 271 pro at-bats, though he went deep 10 times in his final 138 at-bats last year. Because he can bunt, handle the bat and steal 25-30 bases a year, Everett probably will be a No. 2 hitter in a major league lineup. He'll still need to get stronger because pitchers can jam him with fastballs. He's very similar to Julio Lugo, and it will be interesting to see who gets playing time in Triple-A this year and wins the major league job in 2001.

Eric Ireland

Position: P   **Opening Day Age:** 23
Bats: R **Throws:** R   **Born:** 3/11/77 in
Ht: 6' 1" **Wt:** 170   Granada Hills, CA

Recent Statistics

	W	L	ERA	G	GS	Sv	IP	H	R	BB	SO	HR
1998 A Quad City	14	9	2.88	29	28	0	206.0	172	80	71	191	15
1999 AA Jackson	0	1	4.30	3	3	0	14.2	19	9	2	15	1
1999 A Kissimmee	10	7	2.06	24	24	0	170.1	145	59	30	133	12

Ireland tossed the high Class-A Florida State League's first perfect game in 24 years last August. Managers voted him the FSL pitcher with the best breaking ball and the best control, and that's his approach in a nutshell. A 1995 second-round pick, he'll pitch inside fearlessly with an 86-88 MPH fastball, then use his curve to get strikeouts. He also uses a changeup. Since hitting full-season ball in 1998, Ireland has gone 24-17, 2.58, though his 391 innings over those two seasons are a cause for concern. He'll open 2000 in Double-A and projects as a starter in the back half of a big league rotation.

Julio Lugo

Position: SS   **Opening Day Age:** 24
Bats: R **Throws:** R   **Born:** 11/16/75 in
Ht: 6' 0" **Wt:** 165   Barahona, Dom. Rep.

Recent Statistics

	G	AB	R	H	D	T	HR	RBI	SB	BB	SO	Avg
1998 A Kissimmee	128	509	81	154	20	14	7	62	51	49	72	.303
1999 AA Jackson	116	445	77	142	24	5	10	42	25	44	53	.319
1999 MLE	116	424	60	121	22	3	7	32	17	28	59	.285

The Astros work the draft-and-follow process as well as any major league organization, and Lugo is one of their finds. They took him in the 43rd round in 1994 out of Connors State (Okla.) Junior College, retained his rights and signed him the following year. Lugo could fit as a No. 2 hitter because he has plenty of speed, surprising pop and reasonable patience. He has excellent range and a strong arm, and he was named the best defensive shortstop and most exciting player in the Double-A Texas League last year. Lugo will compete with newcomer Adam Everett for Triple-A playing time in 2000 and a big league job the following year.

Houston

479

Tony McKnight

Position: P
Bats: L **Throws:** R
Ht: 6' 5" **Wt:** 205

Opening Day Age: 22
Born: 6/29/77 in Texarkana, AR

Recent Statistics

	W	L	ERA	G	GS	Sv	IP	H	R	BB	SO	HR
1998 A Kissimmee	11	13	4.67	28	28	0	154.1	191	101	50	104	12
1999 AA Jackson	9	9	2.75	24	24	0	160.1	134	60	44	118	15

When the Astros selected McKnight with the 22nd overall pick in 1995 and signed him for $500,000, the lowest bonus in the first round, there were whispers that he was drafted more for signability than ability. After scuffling for four years in the minors, McKnight broke through in 1999. His 2.75 ERA in Double-A was 2.05 better than his previous career mark, and he was named the best control pitcher in the Texas League. McKnight throws his above-average fastball to both sides of the plate while mixing in a power curveball and a developing changeup. He's a future No. 3 starter who will get a shot at Houston after spending a season in Triple-A.

Wade Miller

Position: P
Bats: R **Throws:** R
Ht: 6' 2" **Wt:** 185

Opening Day Age: 23
Born: 9/13/76 in Reading, PA

Recent Statistics

	W	L	ERA	G	GS	Sv	IP	H	R	BB	SO	HR
1999 AAA New Orleans	11	9	4.38	26	26	0	162.1	156	85	64	135	16
1999 NL Houston	0	1	9.58	5	1	0	10.1	17	11	5	8	4

Miller was a real find for the Astros, who drafted him in the 20th round in 1996 after he dropped out of tiny Alvernia (Pa.) College. He reached Double-A in just two years, but lost most of the 1998 season to problems with a tendon in the middle finger on his pitching hand. Houston promoted him to Triple-A upon his return last year, where he was a bit over his head. He has true power stuff, a mid-90s fastball and a hard slider, though his breaking ball is inconsistent. Miller needs to improve his changeup and will get another season in Triple-A to do so. He and Tony McKnight could be battling for the last spot in Houston's rotation in 2001.

Wilfredo Rodriguez

Position: P
Bats: L **Throws:** L
Ht: 6' 3" **Wt:** 180

Opening Day Age: 21
Born: 3/20/79 in Bolivar, Venezuela

Recent Statistics

	W	L	ERA	G	GS	Sv	IP	H	R	BB	SO	HR
1998 A Quad City	11	5	3.05	28	27	0	165.0	122	70	62	170	7
1999 A Kissimmee	15	7	2.88	25	24	0	153.1	108	55	62	148	8

While Houston's renowned Venezuelan academy has produced 11 big leaguers, it has yet to reap any pitching benefits for the Astros. That should change with Rodriguez, who has the biggest upside of all the arms in the Houston organization. After a fine season in the Class-A Midwest League in 1998, he added velocity and now throws a consistent 93-95 MPH fastball with late sink. His curve is an out pitch and he also has a changeup. At age 20, Rodriguez led the Florida State League in wins, strikeouts and opponent batting average (.199). Ticketed for Double-A in 2000, he possibly could arrive in Houston the following year if his rapid development continues.

Daryle Ward

Position: 1B
Bats: L **Throws:** L
Ht: 6' 2" **Wt:** 230

Opening Day Age: 24
Born: 6/27/75 in Lynwood, CA

Recent Statistics

	G	AB	R	H	D	T	HR	RBI	SB	BB	SO	Avg
1999 AAA New Orleans	61	241	56	85	15	1	28	65	1	23	43	.353
1999 NL Houston	64	150	11	41	6	0	8	30	0	9	31	.273
1999 MLE	61	224	40	68	13	0	18	47	0	16	47	.304

Ward's prowess at the plate is creating a dilemma for the Astros, who acquired him in a nine-player trade with the Tigers in December 1996. A 1994 15th-round pick out of Rancho Santiago (Calif.) Junior College and the son of former All-Star Gary Ward, Daryle may be a better hitter than his father. He slammed 36 homers in 391 at-bats between Triple-A and Houston last year, slugging .657 along the way. The problem is finding a place for him to play. He's a poor left fielder, and Moises Alou and Lance Berkman will be competing for playing time there anyway. Ward is really a first baseman, but Jeff Bagwell is signed through 2001. Ward probably will stick in Houston as a reserve this season.

Others to Watch

First baseman **Aaron McNeal** (21), who resembles Cecil Fielder, was named Class-A Midwest League MVP and best power prospect after leading the league with 38 homers and 131 RBI. . . Righthander **Mike Nannini** (19) was a bit overwhelmed as a teenager in the Midwest League, but posted a 1.90 ERA and 86-17 strikeout-walk ratio after going to short-season Auburn. He throws 91-94 MPH, though his secondary pitches need work. . . Righthander **Roy Oswalt** (22) was a costly draft-and-follow, signing for $500,000 in 1997. He gets his share of strikeouts with a 93-95 MPH fastball, but also gets hit when he leaves it up in the strike zone. . . Righthander **Tim Redding** (22), a converted center fielder, flourished after moving from the rotation to the bullpen at Class-A Michigan. Owner of a 96-97 MPH fastball with good movement, he has 239 strikeouts and just 133 hits allowed in 178.2 pro innings. . . Lefthander **Jeriome Robertson** (23) led the Double-A Texas League with 15 victories and 191 innings last year. He's a potential No. 5 starter whose best pitch is his changeup. . . Third baseman **Chris Truby** (26) has totaled 59 homers in the last two seasons. A sound defender, he's the organization's best candidate to eventually replace Ken Caminiti.

Dodger Stadium

Offense

Since its debut in the early 1960s, Dodger Stadium has been one of the friendliest parks to pitchers in the major leagues. It was a little less amiable last season, as home runs were up 11 percent compared to road games, and should become even less so this year. In order to squeeze out more revenue, the Fox Group is adding more field-level seats, which will drastically reduce the vast foul territory behind home plate. The park is symmetrical with deep gaps. With an ocean breeze usually blowing from left to right, lefthanded pull hitters get some help, but flyballs get knocked down by the heavy air during night games.

Defense

No matter how much the groundskeepers hose down the infield, the dirt becomes harder as the dry season goes along, resulting in many tough hops. During day games, the sun can be downright brutal on the right side. The outfield walls have no odd angles or niches, but the corner guys must fight with fans for flyballs hit right down the lines.

Who It Helps The Most

Pitchers are greatly aided by the stadium, especially flyball pitchers such as the departed Ismael Valdes. Hitters who pound the ball sharply on the ground get on base more because of the hard infield. In his first full season with the Dodgers, Mark Grudzielanek hit 64 points higher at home.

Who It Hurts The Most

Despite the power surge in 1999, Dodgers Stadium usually decreases home runs. Gary Sheffield has hit 30 of his 50 homers with the Dodgers on the road. Adrian Beltre hit 38 points higher away from Los Angeles in his first full year in the majors.

Rookies & Newcomers

SkyDome actually has reduced homers more than Dodger Stadium has over the past three seasons, so Shawn Green's production shouldn't be curtailed too much. Orel Hershiser has done some of his best pitching in Los Angeles. Angel Pena, a dead-pull power hitter, won't be helped by the park, but young pitchers Eric Gagne, Mike Judd and Jeff Williams will.

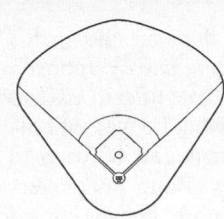

Dimensions: LF-330, LCF-385, CF-395, RCF-385, RF-330

Capacity: 56,000

Elevation: 340 feet

Surface: Grass

Foul Territory: Large

Park Factors

1999 Season

	Home Games			Away Games			
	Dodgers	Opp	Total	Dodgers	Opp	Total	Index
G	72	72	144	75	75	150	—
Avg	.266	.252	.259	.260	.266	.263	98
AB	2389	2502	4891	2650	2548	5198	98
R	323	354	677	383	366	749	94
H	636	631	1267	690	678	1368	96
2B	99	114	213	129	139	268	84
3B	8	7	15	13	19	32	50
HR	82	95	177	87	82	169	111
BB	252	254	506	289	290	579	93
SO	413	470	883	526	499	1025	92
E	68	53	121	58	66	124	102
E-Infield	58	41	99	49	56	105	98
LHB-Avg	.263	.256	.259	.227	.296	.270	96
LHB-HR	21	38	59	22	37	59	107
RHB-Avg	.267	.250	.259	.271	.243	.259	100
RHB-HR	61	57	118	65	45	110	114

1997-1999

	Home Games			Away Games			
	Dodgers	Opp	Total	Dodgers	Opp	Total	Index
G	221	221	442	221	221	442	—
Avg	.262	.237	.249	.259	.261	.260	96
AB	7259	7555	14814	7766	7428	15194	97
R	936	875	1811	1033	1045	2078	87
H	1904	1788	3692	2008	1939	3947	94
2B	289	319	608	342	391	733	85
3B	32	17	49	44	60	104	48
HR	226	222	448	242	223	465	99
BB	679	741	1420	729	831	1560	93
SO	1330	1579	2909	1555	1590	3145	95
E	176	164	340	176	191	367	93
E-Infield	155	133	288	147	148	295	98
LHB-Avg	.249	.249	.249	.242	.278	.264	94
LHB-HR	37	96	133	40	97	137	99
RHB-Avg	.267	.227	.249	.264	.248	.258	97
RHB-HR	189	126	315	202	126	328	99

1999 Rankings (National League)

- Lowest triple factor
- Second-lowest double factor
- Third-lowest walk factor

Davey Johnson

1999 Season

Having never finished lower than second in his first 10 full years as a manager, Davey Johnson took over the Dodgers fully expecting to extend that string. Little did he know what he was inheriting. Regarded as a player's manager, he tried to protect his veteran ballclub by giving his players occasional days off. In appreciation, he was cursed and castigated by paranoid guys who thought they were being blamed for the team's troubles.

Offense

Despite sporting a lineup not known for its speed, the Dodgers finished second in the National League in stolen bases while maintaining a 71 percent success rate. Recognizing early on that his club would have trouble scoring runs, Johnson put guys in motion and used the sacrifice more than he has in the past. Feeling handcuffed by the dearth of lefthanded hitters at his disposal, he used Todd Hollandsworth as a wild card, moving him from position to position to break up the string of righties in the middle of the lineup.

Pitching & Defense

Johnson kept ace Kevin Brown on a schedule of four days' rest whenever possible, skipping other pitchers' starts when necessary. Johnson is very aware of pitch counts and seldom let anyone top 120. He maintained fairly strict roles in his bullpen, almost never bringing closer Jeff Shaw in unless it was a save situation. Johnson clearly looks for offense over defense. He doesn't like to put runners on base via the intentional walk.

2000 Outlook

With a roster full of overpriced players on long-term contracts, the Dodgers will have to get creative to retool. Johnson has made it clear that he would prefer a team of interchangeable parts rather than the set lineup that he inherited, and GM Kevin Malone seemed to be on the same page by season's end. Acquiring Shawn Green was a nice first step.

Born: 1/30/43 in Orlando, FL

Playing Experience: 1965-1978, Bal, Atl, Phi, ChC

Managerial Experience: 13 seasons

Manager Statistics

Year	Team, Lg	W	L	Pct	GB	Finish
1999	Los Angeles, NL	77	85	.475	23.0	3rd West
13 Seasons		1062	812	.566	—	—

1999 Starting Pitchers by Days Rest

	<=3	4	5	6+
Dodgers Starts	2	93	38	19
Dodgers ERA	3.75	4.33	4.62	6.04
NL Avg Starts	3	81	48	21
NL ERA	4.84	4.53	4.72	4.98

1999 Situational Stats

	Davey Johnson	NL Average
Hit & Run Success %	35.9	33.6
Stolen Base Success %	71.1	70.2
Platoon Pct.	50.8	55.2
Defensive Subs	9	25
High-Pitch Outings	8	13
Quick/Slow Hooks	16/16	16/15
Sacrifice Attempts	89	89

1999 Rankings (National League)

- 1st in steals of third base (37) and double steals (18)
- 2nd in steals of home plate (2) and sacrifice-bunt percentage (87.6%)
- 3rd in stolen base attempts (235), hit-and-run attempts (103) and first-batter platoon percentage (66.4%)

Adrian Beltre

1999 Season

Despite being overmatched in his 1998 debut, Adrian Beltre entered last season knowing that he was going to be an everyday third baseman. He hit .301 for the first two months, only struggling when manager Davey Johnson moved him up in the lineup. Though the National League caught up with Beltre, he never went into an extended slump.

Hitting

Beltre is rather undisciplined at the plate, which should come as no surprise because he played only two full seasons in the minors. He should become more patient. For now, he's a sucker for breaking balls down and away, and also will chase hard stuff upstairs. When he connects he has power to all fields, and a lot of his current doubles will clear the wall as he gets older and stronger. He seldom looked overmatched last season, even versus the strongest pitchers.

Baserunning & Defense

Beltre has good speed and makes solid decisions on the basepaths. He has the tools to steal 25-30 bases per season. He's still learning in the field, as evidenced by his major league-leading 29 errors at third base. Beltre has trouble on choppers hit straight at him, allowing the ball to play him rather than attacking it. He's terrific on soft toppers and bunts, though he'll sometimes throw the ball away. He ranges well to both sides, especially to his left, with a lightning-quick first step and soft hands.

2000 Outlook

The Dodgers learned in October that Beltre was 15, not the required 16, when he was signed by the previous front office. They reported the discrepancy to the Commissioner's Office, which ruled that the statute of limitations had expired. Nevertheless, the Dodgers were fined an undisclosed amount and banned from scouting in or signing anyone from the Dominican Republic for one year. The Major League Baseball Players Association planned to appeal the decision in hopes of getting Beltre declared a free agent. He looks like a future superstar and his loss would devastate Los Angeles. The Dodgers acquired Kevin Orie from Florida in November for a player to be named.

Position: 3B
Bats: R **Throws:** R
Ht: 5'11" **Wt:** 165

Opening Day Age: 21
Born: 4/7/78 in Santo Domingo, Dominican Republic
ML Seasons: 2
Pronunciation: BELL-tray

Overall Statistics

	G	AB	R	H	D	T	HR	RBI	SB	BB	SO	Avg	OBP	Slg
1999	152	538	84	148	27	5	15	67	18	61	105	.275	.352	.428
Career	229	733	102	190	36	5	22	89	21	75	142	.259	.333	.412

Where He Hits the Ball

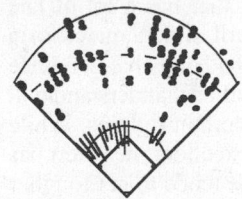 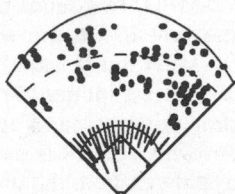

Vs. LHP　　　　**Vs. RHP**

1999 Situational Stats

	AB	H	HR	RBI	Avg		AB	H	HR	RBI	Avg
Home	266	68	6	28	.256	LHP	135	31	1	15	.230
Road	272	80	9	39	.294	RHP	403	117	14	52	.290
First Half	282	83	9	36	.294	Sc Pos	135	32	3	49	.237
Scnd Half	256	65	6	31	.254	Clutch	91	18	1	7	.198

1999 Rankings (National League)

- 1st in errors at third base (29)
- 2nd in lowest fielding percentage at third base (.931)
- 3rd in lowest slugging percentage vs. lefthanded pitchers (.319)
- 4th in lowest batting average with the bases loaded (.063)
- 5th in highest percentage of extra bases taken as a runner (67.5%)
- 6th in intentional walks (12)
- 8th in fewest GDPs per GDP situation (3.8%) and lowest batting average vs. lefthanded pitchers
- 9th in lowest batting average at home
- Led the Dodgers in triples and intentional walks (12)

Kevin Brown

1999 Season

Needless to say, Kevin Brown entered the 1999 season with a lot expected of him after signing a record seven-year, $105 million contract. By season's end, he was one of the few Dodgers who earned his money. Dodger Stadium helped him quite a bit, as his ERA was 1.99 runs better than on the road. He had some rough outings in the first couple of months, then really turned it on after the break.

Pitching

Brown is intensity personified when he's on the mound. He stands so far to the first-base side of the rubber that the Braves argue that he defies the rulebook. His stuff is just nasty, starting with a 92-MPH, two-seam fastball that has a lot of late movement. He throws a hard slider, mixes in a 94-MPH four-seamer, curveball and changeup. He also uses a splitter to finish off lefthanders and will drop down sidearm against certain righties. While Brown's control is usually excellent, he often has trouble early in the game. He tends to get tougher as he goes through a lineup a second and third time because he expands his repertoire to keep hitters guessing.

Defense & Hitting

Brown finishes his delivery with a Frankenstein-like stalk down the front of the mound, leaving him in decent shape to handle comebackers. He gets after bunts and covers first base pretty well. Most of Brown's major league-high six errors came on errant pickoff throws, and he doesn't deter the running game. He's anemic at the plate.

2000 Outlook

Brown isn't known as the most supportive teammate. He grouses a lot on the bench and glares when he believes the effort he puts out isn't matched by a player in the field. One wonders how long he'll accept playing on an underachieving ballclub. That said, he's a warrior who has pitched 200-plus innings in seven of the last eight non-strike years. He should continue to be one of the top handful of pitchers in the game.

Position: SP
Bats: R **Throws:** R
Ht: 6' 4" **Wt:** 200

Opening Day Age: 35
Born: 3/14/65 in McIntyre, GA
ML Seasons: 13

Overall Statistics

	W	L	Pct.	ERA	G	GS	Sv	IP	H	BB	SO	HR	Ratio
1999	18	9	.667	3.00	35	35	0	252.1	210	59	221	19	1.07
Career	157	108	.592	3.27	349	347	0	2430.2	2313	683	1701	140	1.23

How Often He Throws Strikes

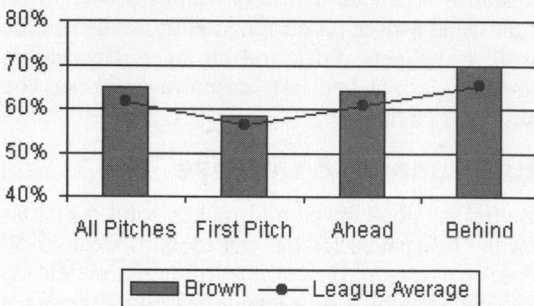

1999 Situational Stats

	W	L	ERA	Sv	IP		AB	H	HR	RBI	Avg
Home	9	3	1.95	0	120.0	LHB	478	122	7	51	.255
Road	9	6	3.94	0	132.1	RHB	466	88	12	40	.189
First Half	9	6	3.53	0	132.2	Sc Pos	210	47	5	69	.224
Scnd Half	9	3	2.41	0	119.2	Clutch	95	20	0	9	.211

1999 Rankings (National League)

- 1st in games started, ERA at home and errors at pitcher (6)
- 2nd in sacrifice bunts (13), innings pitched, strikeouts, pitches thrown (3,790) and lowest batting average allowed vs. righthanded batters
- 3rd in lowest batting average allowed (.222), lowest slugging percentage allowed (.336), lowest on-base percentage allowed (.273) and fewest baserunners allowed per 9 innings (9.8)
- Led the Dodgers in sacrifice bunts (13), ERA, wins, games started, complete games (5), innings pitched, batters faced (1,018), strikeouts, pitches thrown (3,790), GDPs induced (19), winning percentage, highest strikeout/walk ratio (3.7) and lowest batting average allowed (.222)

Darren Dreifort

1999 Season

No Dodger was affected more by the trading of Charles Johnson than his former U.S. Olympic teammate, Darren Dreifort. Once Dreifort was able to ignore Todd Hundley's throwing woes and just pitch, he performed better. That is, until September arrived and he had to be shut down with a sore shoulder for the second year in a row. Of Dreifort's 474.1 major league innings, just 43 have come in the final month of the season.

Pitching

Dreifort has a sinker-slider combination quite similar to Kevin Brown's. Both pitches are nasty, with the fastball boring down and in on righthanders at 92-93 MPH and the slider breaking wickedly in the opposite direction. His changeup is coming along. What he lacks are command and composure. While Dreifort doesn't walk too many hitters, he leaves too many of his offerings out over the plate, especially when he falls behind in the count. Opponents hit 60 points higher with runners on base than with the bags empty last season, continuing a career-long trend. His pitches lose some movement when he pitches from the stretch position.

Defense & Hitting

Dreifort's follow-through leaves him in a vulnerable position, so he has trouble with comebackers. His pickoff move is only fair. Combine that with a fairly slow delivery to the plate, and it's understandable why he missed Johnson. Dreifort was a DH in college and has a career .213 average in the majors.

2000 Outlook

A reliever in college and for his first three years in the majors, Dreifort is adamant about remaining a starter. There are questions about the ability of his arm to hold up under the duress of bullpen work, but his consecutive late-season collapses also raise warning flags. He tires during his individual starts as well, as opponents hit .400 from the seventh inning on last year. Though much is said of his potential, he could be traded if the right deal came along.

Position: SP
Bats: R **Throws:** R
Ht: 6' 2" **Wt:** 211

Opening Day Age: 27
Born: 5/3/72 in Wichita, KS
ML Seasons: 5
Pronunciation: DRY-fort

Overall Statistics

	W	L	Pct.	ERA	G	GS	Sv	IP	H	BB	SO	HR	Ratio
1999	13	13	.500	4.79	30	29	0	178.2	177	76	140	20	1.42
Career	27	36	.429	4.33	156	55	10	474.1	461	194	417	37	1.38

How Often He Throws Strikes

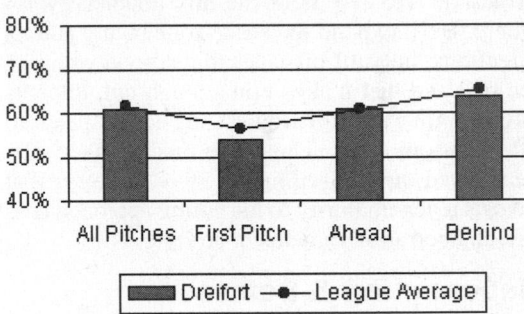

Legend: Dreifort — League Average

1999 Situational Stats

	W	L	ERA	Sv	IP		AB	H	HR	RBI	Avg
Home	7	6	4.79	0	97.2	LHB	308	84	11	48	.273
Road	6	7	4.78	0	81.0	RHB	372	93	9	42	.250
First Half	7	8	5.77	0	98.1	Sc Pos	160	42	3	59	.263
Scnd Half	6	5	3.59	0	80.1	Clutch	21	11	1	4	.524

1999 Rankings (National League)

- 1st in balks (4)
- 8th in most run support per 9 innings (6.3)
- 9th in highest groundball/flyball ratio allowed (1.8)
- 10th in losses
- Led the Dodgers in balks (4), fewest pitches thrown per batter (3.63), most run support per 9 innings (6.3) and most GDPs induced per 9 innings (0.8)

Mark Grudzielanek

1999 Season

After winning the everyday shortstop job over Jose Vizcaino in spring training, Mark Grudzielanek came out of the gate trying too hard to impress and batted a soft .284 through the first couple of months. When he finally found something he could hit, it was a concrete wall. A fractured right hand put him on the disabled list for almost all of June. Upon his return, he caught fire and hit .348 during the last three months.

Hitting

Grudzielanek is a very aggressive hitter. He's a slashing hitter who sprays line drives from foul line to foul line. While his home-run power is almost exclusively to left field, he hits doubles everywhere. He'll expand the strike zone in any and all directions, but still manages to get good wood on the ball and that makes him a tough out. Pitchers have to move the ball around and change speeds to offset his quick bat. Though he disdains the walk, he showed more discipline in 1999. Whether that reveals a new maturity to his hitting approach or is just an aberration remains to be seen.

Baserunning & Defense

After hearing about his lousy defense in an arbitration session before last season, Mark Grudzielanek vowed to improve and attended Bucky Dent's camp in Florida. The difference was dramatic. No longer off balance when making the transition from fielder to thrower, he made strong, true throws across the infield. He still doesn't get good jumps on grounders, but his routes are fine and his hands aren't bad. Though he has above-average speed, he wasn't asked to steal nearly as often as in the past. He sometimes makes silly mistakes on the bases.

2000 Outlook

Despite Los Angeles' glitzy reputation, the fans appreciate Grudzielanek's blue-collar approach. There has been talk of moving him to second base after the trade of Eric Young, but there was really nothing wrong with Grudzielanek's defense at shortstop and his bat spoke for itself.

Position: SS
Bats: R **Throws:** R
Ht: 6' 1" **Wt:** 185

Opening Day Age: 29
Born: 6/30/70 in Milwaukee, WI
ML Seasons: 5
Pronunciation: gruzz-ell-AH-neck

Overall Statistics

	G	AB	R	H	D	T	HR	RBI	SB	BB	SO	Avg	OBP	Slg
1999	123	488	72	159	23	5	7	46	6	31	65	.326	.376	.436
Career	666	2652	336	763	144	15	28	228	90	120	344	.288	.328	.385

Where He Hits the Ball

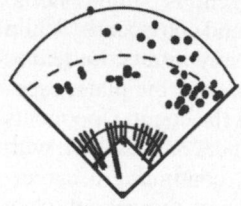 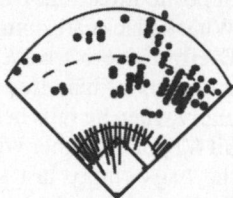

Vs. LHP   **Vs. RHP**

1999 Situational Stats

	AB	H	HR	RBI	Avg		AB	H	HR	RBI	Avg
Home	219	79	4	22	.361	LHP	144	56	2	14	.389
Road	269	80	3	24	.297	RHP	344	103	5	32	.299
First Half	190	57	3	19	.300	Sc Pos	130	33	3	41	.254
Scnd Half	298	102	4	27	.342	Clutch	75	19	0	5	.253

1999 Rankings (National League)

- 1st in batting average vs. lefthanded pitchers
- 5th in on-base percentage vs. lefthanded pitchers (.451) and fielding percentage at shortstop (.974)
- 6th in batting average
- 8th in highest groundball/flyball ratio (1.7)
- 9th in lowest HR frequency (69.7 ABs per HR) and highest percentage of extra bases taken as a runner (64.3%)
- 10th in singles
- Led the Dodgers in batting average, singles, triples, highest groundball/flyball ratio (1.7), batting average vs. lefthanded pitchers, batting average on an 0-2 count (.250) and on-base percentage vs. lefthanded pitchers (.451)

Eric Karros

1999 Season

Every year Eric Karros is mentioned in numerous trade rumors, and every year he ends up staying with the Dodgers, supplying power and driving in runs in the middle of the lineup. After a rather slow start last year, he went on a characteristic hot streak around midseason, coincidentally or not right before the trading deadline. He set career highs in batting average, doubles, home runs and RBI.

Hitting

Karros is very smart and adjusts with every at-bat, so opposing pitchers know that they can't get him out the same way repeatedly. He likes balls up and away where he can gets his arms extended, but also will golf low and inside pitches down the left-field line. He has the power to drive a ball out of any part of the park and when he's in a groove, Karros will take outside pitches up the middle and to right-center. During a slump, he'll ground those pitches to shortstop.

Baserunning & Defense

Karros has a creaky left knee that's never completely pain-free. Though he's not quick, he picks up an occasional steal by remaining alert and picking his spots. While he has improved with the glove, he's still a below-average first baseman. He has little range and his hands are poor. Hard throws tend to handcuff him even when they're not in the dirt, and on bounced throws he's virtually helpless. To his credit, he does a good job when he has to make the throw to second, a tough play for any righthander.

2000 Outlook

Karros is one of the more consistent hitters in baseball. Whether his .280-30-100 numbers continue to come with the Dodgers is up for grabs. Acquiring lefthanded-hitting Shawn Green for righty-swinging Raul Mondesi lends more balance to the lineup, so Karros is likely to finish the final year of his contract in Los Angeles.

Position: 1B
Bats: R **Throws:** R
Ht: 6' 4" **Wt:** 226

Opening Day Age: 32
Born: 11/4/67 in Hackensack, NJ
ML Seasons: 9
Pronunciation: CARE-ose

Overall Statistics

	G	AB	R	H	D	T	HR	RBI	SB	BB	SO	Avg	OBP	Slg
1999	153	578	74	176	40	0	34	112	8	53	119	.304	.362	.550
Career	1183	4456	574	1217	225	9	211	734	46	376	808	.273	.329	.470

Where He Hits the Ball

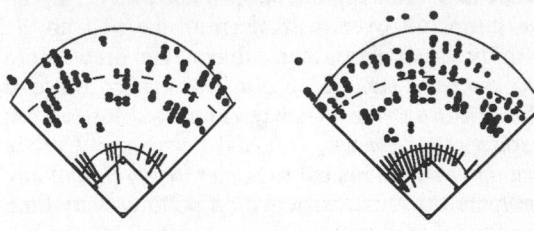

Vs. LHP   **Vs. RHP**

1999 Situational Stats

	AB	H	HR	RBI	Avg		AB	H	HR	RBI	Avg
Home	269	80	17	55	.297	LHP	146	45	11	34	.308
Road	309	96	17	57	.311	RHP	432	131	23	78	.303
First Half	306	90	17	49	.294	Sc Pos	161	45	10	80	.280
Scnd Half	272	86	17	63	.316	Clutch	103	27	5	21	.262

1999 Rankings (National League)

- 2nd in errors at first base (13)
- 3rd in lowest fielding percentage at first base (.991)
- 5th in GDPs (18)
- 8th in cleanup slugging percentage (.555)
- 10th in doubles
- Led the Dodgers in home runs, hits, doubles, total bases (318), RBI, GDPs (18), slugging percentage, batting average in the clutch, batting average vs. righthanded pitchers, cleanup slugging percentage (.555), slugging percentage vs. lefthanded pitchers (.582), slugging percentage vs. righthanded pitchers (.539) and batting average on the road

Raul Mondesi

1999 Season

Early last season, when he was being uncharacter-istically selective at the plate, there was talk of a new Raul Mondesi. Despite walking a career-high 71 times and establishing other personal bests in home runs, RBI and stolen bases, the new version was clearly not an improvement. His disappointing season was punctuated by a profanity-laced tirade Mondesi directed at manager Davey Johnson and GM Kevin Malone.

Position: RF
Bats: R **Throws:** R
Ht: 5'11" **Wt:** 215

Opening Day Age: 29
Born: 3/12/71 in San Cristobal, Dominican Republic
ML Seasons: 7
Pronunciation: MAHN-de-see

Hitting

Mondesi's obsession with hitting home runs has made him much more pull-conscious. That makes him even more vulnerable to what was already a weakness, breaking pitches low and away. Though he jumps all over fastballs from the belt up, he simply can't recognize sliders. He drew more walks last season because many pitchers refuse to throw him a strike. When he connects, Mondesi has prodigious power to left and left-center. He has enough juice in his bat to homer to any part of any ballpark, but his insistence on pulling everything results in a lot of harmless groundballs to the left side. His batting average and doubles totals have dropped precipitously.

Overall Statistics

	G	AB	R	H	D	T	HR	RBI	SB	BB	SO	Avg	OBP	Slg
1999	159	601	98	152	29	5	33	99	36	71	134	.253	.332	.483
Career	916	3487	543	1004	190	37	163	518	140	230	663	.288	.334	.504

Where He Hits the Ball

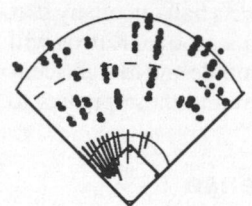
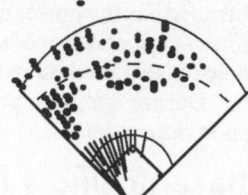

Vs. LHP   **Vs. RHP**

Baserunning & Defense

Mondesi is a joy to watch on the basepaths. When he gets up a head of steam, he resembles a tailback hitting the hole. Though he can be a fine basestealer, his head and heart have to be into it. A great right fielder, he gets excellent jumps and chews up turf in a hurry. Though his arm is still a cannon, his throws haven't been as accurate as they were in the past. He seems more interested in showing his arm off than in gunning down runners.

1999 Situational Stats

	AB	H	HR	RBI	Avg		AB	H	HR	RBI	Avg
Home	286	76	18	47	.266	LHP	139	38	6	20	.273
Road	315	76	15	52	.241	RHP	462	114	27	79	.247
First Half	324	82	19	54	.253	Sc Pos	162	41	9	64	.253
Scnd Half	277	70	14	45	.253	Clutch	94	24	9	16	.255

2000 Outlook

The Dodgers were elated when the cost-conscious Blue Jays gave them Shawn Green and second-base prospect Jorge Nunez for Mondesi and Pedro Borbon. Mondesi has plenty of talent, but he hasn't improved his game and his attitude often leaves something to be desired. Moving to a new club could be the best thing for him, and it certainly was for the Dodgers.

1999 Rankings (National League)

- 1st in lowest batting average with the bases loaded (.000)
- 2nd in fewest GDPs per GDP situation (2.1%)
- 3rd in errors in right field (6), bunts in play (6) and highest percentage of extra bases taken as a runner (70.0%)
- 4th in lowest fielding percentage in right field (.982) and steals of third (10)
- 5th in lowest batting average
- Led the Dodgers in at-bats, triples, strikeouts, plate appearances (680), stolen-base percentage (80.0%), fewest GDPs per GDP situation (2.1%), bunts in play (6), games played and highest percentage of extra bases taken as a runner (70.0%)

Chan Ho Park

1999 Season

In the offseason, Chan Ho Park helped the Korean national team win the Asian Games, earning an exemption from his homeland's mandatory military service. Little went right after that. He gave up two grand slams in one inning to Fernando Tatis on April 23, and earned a seven-game suspension after a June 5 Kung Fu-fighting exhibition with Tim Belcher. Ongoing contract negotiations were also a distraction to Park, who didn't pitch like he had in the past until late in the year, when he won seven of his last nine starts.

Pitching

All of Park's pitches were off last season. He normally starts with a fastball in the low to mid-90s, but his velocity was down a few ticks and his heater had little movement. His curveball wasn't nearly as sharp as it had been and his slider always has been flat. He's making slow progress on his changeup, a pitch that eventually will come in handy versus lefthanders, who pounded him last year. Park always has struggled to find both his command and control, and last season he walked 100 batters while surrendering a career-high 31 longballs.

Defense & Hitting

Park is a very good fielder, with quickness off the mound and good reactions. His move to first base is just fair, but he keeps the running game in check by getting rid of the ball rather quickly. He goes up to the plate hacking and he can put a charge into the ball when he makes contact. He gets upset when he can't get a bunt down, which sometimes happens when he tries to be too fine with his placement.

2000 Outlook

While Park cost himself some money by pitching so poorly going into his arbitration years, he remains as untouchable as any Dodger. He's emotional and admittedly became mentally tired while battling through 1999. The good news is that his arm has shown no signs of strain. He certainly has the physical ability to succeed in the big leagues.

Position: SP
Bats: R **Throws:** R
Ht: 6' 2" **Wt:** 204

Opening Day Age: 26
Born: 6/30/73 in Kong Ju City, Korea
ML Seasons: 6

Overall Statistics

	W	L	Pct.	ERA	G	GS	Sv	IP	H	BB	SO	HR	Ratio
1999	13	11	.542	5.23	33	33	0	194.1	208	100	174	31	1.58
Career	47	33	.588	4.07	151	107	0	723.2	645	345	663	80	1.37

How Often He Throws Strikes

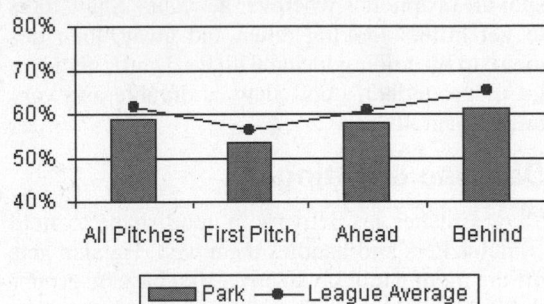

1999 Situational Stats

	W	L	ERA	Sv	IP		AB	H	HR	RBI	Avg
Home	3	6	5.46	0	90.2	LHB	344	123	18	58	.358
Road	10	5	5.04	0	103.2	RHB	410	85	13	50	.207
First Half	5	7	6.52	0	96.2	Sc Pos	205	49	6	76	.239
Scnd Half	8	4	3.96	0	97.2	Clutch	42	14	2	7	.333

1999 Rankings (National League)

- 1st in highest batting average allowed vs. lefthanded batters
- 2nd in hit batsmen (14)
- 3rd in runners caught stealing (14), most baserunners allowed per 9 innings (14.9) and lowest batting average allowed vs. righthanded batters
- 4th in highest on-base percentage allowed (.369) and highest walks per 9 innings (4.6)
- 5th in walks allowed and fewest GDPs induced per 9 innings (0.4)
- Led the Dodgers in walks allowed, hit batsmen (14), wild pitches (11), runners caught stealing (14), lowest stolen-base percentage allowed (53.3%) and most strikeouts per 9 innings (8.1)

Jeff Shaw

1999 Season

By convincing Jeff Shaw to sign a lucrative three-year deal before last season, the Dodgers avoided the embarrassment of losing their newfound closer just a few months after giving up two prospects to get him. Except for a rough stretch at the end of July, Shaw was extremely reliable.

Pitching

Though Shaw can't just blow the ball by hitters, he has some giddyup on his fastball. It gets up there in the low 90s with some good tailing action. He uses a slider as his second pitch against righthanders and a splitter versus lefties. His impeccable control is one of the main reasons for his success. He can spot all his pitches wherever he wants. Shaw likes to get hitters looking down and away, then ties them up by coming inside with hard stuff, getting a lot of groundball outs. Shaw is durable and very tough mentally.

Defense & Hitting

Shaw finishes his delivery in good shape to field comebackers and handles them well. He also gets off the mound quickly to cover first base on grounders to the right side. Though he throws over to first a lot, his pickoff move is nothing special and basestealers have an easy time against him. He rarely bats and is ineffective when he does.

2000 Outlook

While Shaw may not be a prototypical closer, he gets the job done. As the Dodgers try to turn their shipwreck around, the back of their bullpen is already in good shape. But should they get off to another rough start, it's not inconceivable that they'd be willing to field offers for Shaw. Despite his occasional bouts with minor shoulder trouble, he should be able to pitch at his current level for another few years.

Position: RP
Bats: R **Throws:** R
Ht: 6' 2" **Wt:** 200

Opening Day Age: 33
Born: 7/7/66 in Washington Courthouse, OH
ML Seasons: 10

Overall Statistics

	W	L	Pct.	ERA	G	GS	Sv	IP	H	BB	SO	HR	Ratio
1999	2	4	.333	2.78	64	0	34	68.0	64	15	43	6	1.16
Career	28	45	.384	3.48	496	19	133	716.0	697	200	448	74	1.25

How Often He Throws Strikes

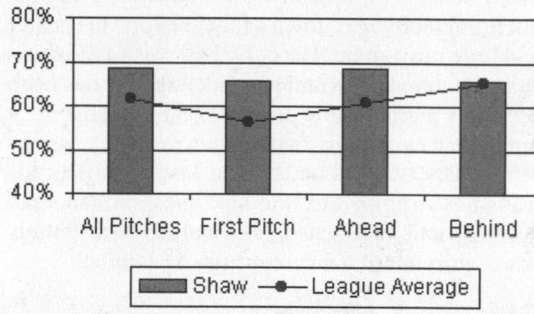

1999 Situational Stats

	W	L	ERA	Sv	IP		AB	H	HR	RBI	Avg
Home	2	3	3.57	15	35.1	LHB	134	27	3	12	.201
Road	0	1	1.93	19	32.2	RHB	131	37	3	16	.282
First Half	2	2	2.37	19	38.0	Sc Pos	59	17	1	21	.288
Scnd Half	0	2	3.30	15	30.0	Clutch	185	46	2	21	.249

1999 Rankings (National League)

- 4th in save percentage (87.2%)
- 7th in saves and save opportunities (39)
- 8th in games finished (56) and fewest strikeouts per 9 innings in relief (5.7)
- 9th in fewest baserunners allowed per 9 innings in relief (10.6)
- Led the Dodgers in saves, games finished (56), save opportunities (39), save percentage (87.2%), blown saves (5), first batter efficiency (.210), relief ERA (2.78) and fewest baserunners allowed per 9 innings in relief (10.6)

Gary Sheffield

1999 Season

If ever there were a season in which Gary Sheffield would have had an excuse to frequently beg out of the lineup, 1999 would have been it. His two pals from Florida, Charles Johnson and Bobby Bonilla, were traded during the winter and the season was an unmitigated disaster. Instead, the moody left fielder became a team leader. Not only did he collect 500 at-bats for just the third time in his career, but he also became the second Dodger ever and first since Duke Snider in 1955 to hit .300 with 100 or more runs, RBI and walks.

Hitting

Disciplined and willing to take a walk, Sheffield is a rarity on a team full of free swingers. He's always aware of the game situation and tailors his hitting style accordingly, and almost never will swing bad balls. If he chases a pitch out of the strike zone, it's usually a high fastball. Sheffield has one of the quickest bats in the game and can adjust when he recognizes a breaking ball. Some teams use an infield shift against him, but he has the bat control to just poke the ball through the right side. Opponents would rather see that than a bomb, as Sheffield has big-time power to left and center.

Baserunning & Defense

Because he's rather fragile physically, Sheffield picks his spots to hustle and toss his body around. Despite getting some late jumps on flyballs and often looking a bit awkward, Sheffield usually makes the play and has a strong and accurate arm. He has good instincts on the basepaths and is an effective if not prolific basestealer.

2000 Outlook

Perhaps he has matured or maybe he's just mellowing with age, but Sheffield's reputation as an injury-prone malcontent no longer seems valid. As long as he can stay in the lineup, he should continue to be one of the toughest outs in the game. His combination of patience and power is a rare and potent mix.

Position: LF
Bats: R **Throws:** R
Ht: 5'11" **Wt:** 205

Opening Day Age: 31
Born: 11/18/68 in Tampa, FL
ML Seasons: 12

Overall Statistics

	G	AB	R	H	D	T	HR	RBI	SB	BB	SO	Avg	OBP	Slg
1999	152	549	103	165	20	0	34	101	11	101	64	.301	.407	.523
Career	1308	4645	779	1345	241	16	236	807	156	757	550	.290	.392	.501

Where He Hits the Ball

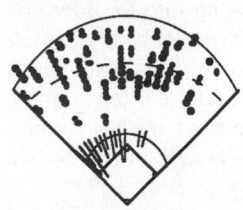
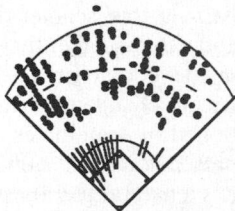

Vs. LHP   **Vs. RHP**

1999 Situational Stats

	AB	H	HR	RBI	Avg		AB	H	HR	RBI	Avg
Home	265	78	15	42	.294	LHP	146	49	8	33	.336
Road	284	87	19	59	.306	RHP	403	116	26	68	.288
First Half	297	88	16	47	.296	Sc Pos	140	38	9	67	.271
Scnd Half	252	77	18	54	.306	Clutch	84	17	4	9	.202

1999 Rankings (National League)

- 3rd in sacrifice flies (9) and errors in left field (7)
- 4th in lowest fielding percentage in left field (.972) and lowest percentage of extra bases taken as a runner (32.8%)
- Led the Dodgers in home runs, runs scored, sacrifice flies (9), walks, times on base (270), pitches seen (2,619), on-base percentage, HR frequency (16.1 ABs per HR), most pitches seen per plate appearance (3.95) and on-base percentage vs. righthanded pitchers (.398)
- Led NL left fielders in walks and pitches seen (2,619)

Ismael Valdes

Position: SP
Bats: R **Throws:** R
Ht: 6' 3" **Wt:** 215

Opening Day Age: 26
Born: 8/21/73 in Victoria, Mexico
ML Seasons: 6
Pronunciation: ISH-mail val-DEZZ

1999 Season

For a good part of last season, Ismael Valdes was the most consistent starter on the Los Angeles staff, even if his record didn't reflect it. Though new skipper Davey Johnson did his best to stretch him out, Valdes continued to show an inability to pitch deep into games. Normally stronger as the season progresses and the weather heats up, he completely ran out of gas in September.

Pitching

Valdes has command of four different pitches. His best pitch is a curveball that he'll throw at any point in the count. He might rely on it too much, as quite a few of the career-high 32 homers he allowed last year came on hanging curves. He throws two fastballs, a four-seamer that gets up into the low 90s and a two-seamer that he likes to tail back over the inside corner on lefthanders. Valdes also has a decent changeup. While his courage often is questioned by teammates, no one can deny the mound presence he has shown since arriving in 1994. He has a natural feel for pitching.

Defense & Hitting

As with everything else, Valdes is methodical with his fielding. What he lacks in style, he makes up for with consistency. He has a poor pickoff move and a slow delivery, so basestealers can run at will. Though he's clueless with a bat in his hands, he usually can get a sacrifice down.

2000 Outlook

Valdes wasn't liked by his teammates, with many believing he was more concerned with his personal statistics than with the club winning. The Dodgers were willing to give Valdes to anyone who would take Eric Young's contract, and the Cubs jumped at the opportunity, giving up Terry Adams and minor league righthanders Chad Ricketts and Brian Stephenson. Valdes may have touble in Wrigley Field. His career road ERA is 4.34, 1.84 runs higher than at home. He could be replaced in the Dodgers rotation by free agent Orel Hershiser, who signed for one year and $2 million.

Overall Statistics

	W	L	Pct.	ERA	G	GS	Sv	IP	H	BB	SO	HR	Ratio
1999	9	14	.391	3.98	32	32	0	203.1	213	58	143	32	1.33
Career	61	54	.530	3.38	176	150	1	1025.0	963	286	756	104	1.22

How Often He Throws Strikes

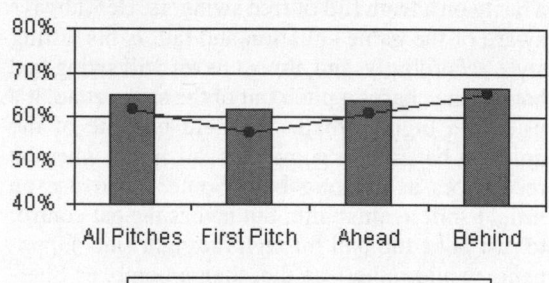

1999 Situational Stats

	W	L	ERA	Sv	IP		AB	H	HR	RBI	Avg
Home	6	8	2.99	0	120.1	LHB	336	91	14	39	.271
Road	3	6	5.42	0	83.0	RHB	454	122	18	51	.269
First Half	7	7	3.36	0	118.0	Sc Pos	175	40	6	60	.229
Scnd Half	2	7	4.85	0	85.1	Clutch	46	15	4	8	.326

1999 Rankings (National League)

- 1st in pickoff throws (208)
- 3rd in stolen bases allowed (26)
- 4th in losses
- 7th in home runs allowed
- 9th in ERA at home and highest ERA on the road
- 10th in lowest groundball/flyball ratio allowed (0.9) and most home runs allowed per 9 innings (1.42)
- Led the Dodgers in losses, hits allowed, home runs allowed, pickoff throws (208) and stolen bases allowed (26)

Devon White

Position: CF
Bats: B **Throws:** R
Ht: 6' 2" **Wt:** 190

Opening Day Age: 37
Born: 12/29/62 in Kingston, Jamaica
ML Seasons: 15
Nickname: Devo

1999 Season

Signed to a three-year deal worth $12.4 million as a Diamondbacks free agent, Devon White performed about as well as the Dodgers should have expected. He suffered from minor aches and pains all season long, and manager Davey Johnson rested him at least once per week to try to keep him fresh. White hit .382 in July, just when it became apparent the Dodgers were going nowhere.

Hitting

Originally a righthanded hitter, White's natural ability has resurfaced and made him a better hitter from that side in the last few years. He seems to see the ball better versus lefthanders, drawing more walks and making better contact. He has a quick bat from both sides of the plate and pitchers need to change speeds to keep him off balance. From the left side, White has a lot of trouble laying off breaking balls down and in, and he also will chase fastballs up and away. He gets into the habit of swinging for the fences at times, especially from the left side, but doesn't have much power and just hits lazy fly balls.

Baserunning & Defense

White's distinctive loping gait makes it look like he's not running very fast. While he certainly has lost a step, he still gets around the bases quickly and steals as well as ever. The owner of seven Gold Gloves, White won't add another. He still goes to his left and right very well, but often gets bad breaks on balls hit over his head. He must play extremely deep to compensate, so a lot of singles drop in front of him. His arm is below average.

2000 Outlook

When they signed White, the Dodgers were staring at the numbers he had compiled in a free-agent year in a hitter-friendly environment. He has the irritating knack of turning his game up a notch when it doesn't mean anything. His signing, along with the trade for Todd Hundley, are the moves that detractors of GM Kevin Malone point to first.

Overall Statistics

	G	AB	R	H	D	T	HR	RBI	SB	BB	SO	Avg	OBP	Slg
1999	134	474	60	127	20	2	14	68	19	39	88	.268	.337	.407
Career	1768	6796	1047	1784	348	68	190	786	325	504	1401	.263	.318	.418

Where He Hits the Ball

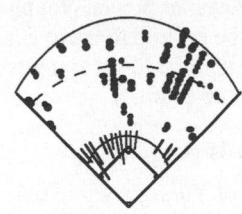 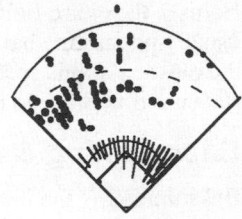

Vs. LHP **Vs. RHP**

1999 Situational Stats

	AB	H	HR	RBI	Avg		AB	H	HR	RBI	Avg
Home	227	69	8	41	.304	LHP	139	40	5	22	.288
Road	247	58	6	27	.235	RHP	335	87	9	46	.260
First Half	247	66	7	36	.267	Sc Pos	140	34	5	55	.243
Scnd Half	227	61	7	32	.269	Clutch	72	13	0	2	.181

1999 Rankings (National League)

- 5th in lowest batting average on the road
- 6th in fielding percentage in center field (.986)
- 8th in hit by pitch (11)
- 10th in errors in center field (4)
- Led the Dodgers in hit by pitch (11), batting average with the bases loaded (.417) and batting average at home
- Led NL center fielders in hit by pitch (11) and batting average on a 3-2 count (.366)

Eric Young

1999 Season

Eric Young's 1999 season started to unravel on May 16, when Eric Davis slid into him, severely bruising Young's left ankle. Young insisted he was hurt, but the Dodgers wanted to trade him so they kept playing him. A few days before the trading deadline, they finally relented and put him on the disabled list. After a few weeks of recuperation, Young returned with a vengeance and played well during the final two months.

Hitting

Even after leaving Coors Field for Dodger Stadium, Young has maintained a healthy on-base percentage. He makes contact and was one of the few Dodgers who recognizes the value of a walk. He uses the entire field and has gap power. Young usually pounds the ball into the ground to try to get the most out of his speed. He could add several hits per year if he were to bunt more often.

Baserunning & Defense

Baserunning is the one area of Young's game that is above average. He gets good jumps, which is becoming more important as he loses a step or two to age. In fact, he has suffered from various nagging leg injuries in each of the past few years. His glovework leaves a lot to be desired. Though he can range pretty far in both directions, he has bad hands and often can't come up with balls. He's very slow in making the pivot on the double play and has a weak throwing arm to boot.

2000 Outlook

Young's years in Colorado established unrealistic expectations based on the numbers he put up in the thin air. That and his inability to play solid defense put him in manager Davey Johnson's doghouse. The Dodgers were desperate to dump the two years and $9 million remaining on Young's contract. They gave him and Ismael Valdes to the Cubs for Terry Adams and two minor leaguers. Young will fill Chicago's gaping holes at second base and in the leadoff spot. Either Mark Grudzielanek or Jose Vizcaino will play at second for Los Angeles.

Position: 2B
Bats: R **Throws:** R
Ht: 5' 9" **Wt:** 170

Opening Day Age: 32
Born: 5/18/67 in New Brunswick, NJ
ML Seasons: 8
Nickname: E.Y.

Overall Statistics

	G	AB	R	H	D	T	HR	RBI	SB	BB	SO	Avg	OBP	Slg
1999	119	456	73	128	24	2	2	41	51	63	26	.281	.371	.355
Career	935	3314	566	959	155	33	43	338	292	384	239	.289	.369	.395

Where He Hits the Ball

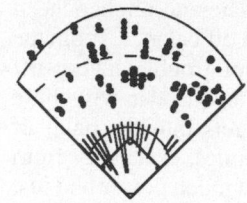 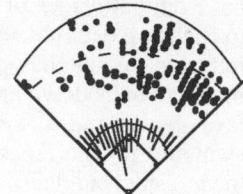

Vs. LHP   **Vs. RHP**

1999 Situational Stats

	AB	H	HR	RBI	Avg		AB	H	HR	RBI	Avg
Home	217	59	2	18	.272	LHP	132	39	1	11	.295
Road	239	69	0	23	.289	RHP	324	89	1	30	.275
First Half	287	77	2	24	.268	Sc Pos	100	30	0	37	.300
Scnd Half	169	51	0	17	.302	Clutch	68	16	1	9	.235

1999 Rankings (National League)

- 1st in caught stealing (22) and highest percentage of swings put into play (62.9%)
- 2nd in steals of third (14)
- 3rd in stolen bases, lowest HR frequency (228.0 ABs per HR), most GDPs per GDP situation (18.8%) and highest percentage of pitches taken (63.5%)
- Led the Dodgers in stolen bases, caught stealing (22), batting average with runners in scoring position, on-base percentage for a leadoff hitter (.382), highest percentage of pitches taken (63.5%), lowest percentage of swings that missed (9.4%), highest percentage of swings put into play (62.9%), steals of third (14) and highest percentage of pitches taken (63.5%)

Pedro Borbon

Traded To BLUE JAYS

Position: RP
Bats: L **Throws:** L
Ht: 6' 1" **Wt:** 205

Opening Day Age: 32
Born: 11/15/67 in Mao, Dominican Republic
ML Seasons: 5

Overall Statistics

	W	L	Pct.	ERA	G	GS	Sv	IP	H	BB	SO	HR	Ratio
1999	4	3	.571	4.09	70	0	1	50.2	39	29	33	5	1.34
Career	9	6	.600	3.70	159	0	4	121.2	99	57	100	8	1.28

1999 Situational Stats

	W	L	ERA	Sv	IP		AB	H	HR	RBI	Avg
Home	2	2	3.22	0	22.1	LHB	90	14	2	8	.156
Road	2	1	4.76	1	28.1	RHB	97	25	3	16	.258
First Half	2	1	1.64	0	33.0	Sc Pos	42	9	0	15	.214
Scnd Half	2	2	8.66	1	17.2	Clutch	89	20	2	10	.225

1999 Season

Pedro Borbon hadn't pitched in the big leagues since reconstructive elbow surgery in 1996 when the Dodgers signed him last offseason. Used mainly as a situational lefthander, he was very effective in the first half, then faded terribly after the All-Star break.

Pitching, Defense & Hitting

Borbon is extremely tough on lefthanders, who hit just .156 against him. Though his fastball tops out around 87 MPH, it has a good deal of movement. His other pitch is a big, flat curveball that lefties tend to give up on too soon. With such mediocre stuff, he tends to nibble. Just being a lefty helps him keep runners close, though his move is nothing special. He gets the job done defensively and can bunt when needed.

2000 Outlook

Borbon could improve as he gets more comfortable with his post-operative arm. His strikeout-walk ratio was much better before his surgery and may rebound. Included in the Shawn Green-Raul Mondesi trade with Toronto, Borbon will continue to be used as a lefty specialist by the Blue Jays.

Craig Counsell

Position: 2B
Bats: L **Throws:** R
Ht: 6' 0" **Wt:** 175

Opening Day Age: 29
Born: 8/21/70 in South Bend, IN
ML Seasons: 4

Overall Statistics

	G	AB	R	H	D	T	HR	RBI	SB	BB	SO	Avg	OBP	Slg
1999	87	174	24	38	7	0	0	11	1	14	24	.218	.274	.259
Career	249	674	87	171	35	7	5	67	5	84	88	.254	.341	.349

1999 Situational Stats

	AB	H	HR	RBI	Avg		AB	H	HR	RBI	Avg
Home	90	17	0	7	.189	LHP	24	6	0	4	.250
Road	84	21	0	4	.250	RHP	150	32	0	7	.213
First Half	89	16	0	4	.180	Sc Pos	29	6	0	11	.207
Scnd Half	85	22	0	7	.259	Clutch	26	7	0	4	.269

1999 Season

Buried in Florida, Craig Counsell joined the Dodgers in a mid-June trade for a player to be named. Acquired as second-base insurance for Eric Young, he didn't get much more playing time in Los Angeles, where he was used mostly as a defensive replacement.

Hitting, Baserunning & Defense

Though he's just a little guy with little power, Counsell tries to pull everything and generates a lot of groundball outs. He has a good eye and will battle for a walk, but he's overmatched by hard throwers. To his credit, he holds his own against lefties. He has just average speed but is a heady baserunner. On defense, he ranges well in both directions, has soft hands and turns the double play quickly.

2000 Outlook

The Dodgers have an opening at second base after trading Eric Young, but Counsell probably won't contend for a starting spot. His chances to stick in the big leagues are enhanced by his attitude and lefthanded bat, while they're hampered by his lackluster skills and ability to play just one position.

Los Angeles

Todd Hollandsworth

Position: CF/LF/1B
Bats: L **Throws:** L
Ht: 6' 2" **Wt:** 215

Opening Day Age: 26
Born: 4/20/73 in Dayton, OH
ML Seasons: 5

Overall Statistics

	G	AB	R	H	D	T	HR	RBI	SB	BB	SO	Avg	OBP	Slg
1999	92	261	39	74	12	2	9	32	5	24	61	.284	.345	.448
Career	443	1313	181	357	66	12	33	155	37	101	285	.272	.325	.416

1999 Situational Stats

	AB	H	HR	RBI	Avg		AB	H	HR	RBI	Avg
Home	134	37	5	18	.276	LHP	29	9	2	6	.310
Road	127	37	4	14	.291	RHP	232	65	7	26	.280
First Half	93	26	2	10	.280	Sc Pos	66	14	2	22	.212
Scnd Half	168	48	7	22	.286	Clutch	44	14	2	5	.318

1999 Season

While Todd Hollandsworth continued to prove his worth as a role player, he also added to his reputation of being injury-prone. He had two stints on the disabled list last season, for a pulled hamstring and a strained oblique muscle, adding to the thumb, hand, elbow and shoulder problems he has had in five major league seasons.

Hitting, Baserunning & Defense

Hollandsworth is a free-swinging gap hitter who occasionally can yank a pitch over the right-field wall. He has trouble laying off hard breaking balls down and in, and also will chase fastballs above and outside of the strike zone. He's an aggressive player on the bases as well and has above-average speed. Though Hollandsworth can handle any of the outfield spots, his arm is best suited for left field. He also can play first base.

2000 Outlook

Because of the lack of balance in the Los Angeles lineup, manager Davey Johnson tried to use Hollandsworth's lefthanded bat whenever possible. The arrival of Shawn Green reduces that need somewhat, though Hollandsworth should continue to be a decent part-time player.

Todd Hundley

Position: C
Bats: L **Throws:** R
Ht: 5'11" **Wt:** 199

Opening Day Age: 30
Born: 5/27/69 in Martinsville, VA
ML Seasons: 10

Overall Statistics

	G	AB	R	H	D	T	HR	RBI	SB	BB	SO	Avg	OBP	Slg
1999	114	376	49	78	14	0	24	55	3	44	113	.207	.295	.436
Career	943	2925	389	690	132	7	148	452	14	343	737	.236	.319	.438

1999 Situational Stats

	AB	H	HR	RBI	Avg		AB	H	HR	RBI	Avg
Home	162	36	10	19	.222	LHP	57	6	0	5	.105
Road	214	42	14	36	.196	RHP	319	72	24	50	.226
First Half	205	47	12	30	.229	Sc Pos	104	17	4	30	.163
Scnd Half	171	31	12	25	.181	Clutch	66	14	6	12	.212

1999 Season

The trade for Todd Hundley at the cost of Roger Cedeno and Charles Johnson was one of the main reasons for the Dodgers' lack of success last season. Not only did Hundley flirt with the Mendoza Line, but his physical problems had more to do with the club's ineffective pitching than can be quantified.

Hitting, Baserunning & Defense

Though Hundley has good power to all fields, he has become too pull-conscious. He just looks for fastballs on the inner half and tries to yank them out. He expands his strike zone upward and can be completely fooled by anything offspeed. After lowering his lifetime average to .200 versus southpaws, he finally gave up switch-hitting in early August. Hundley gunned down just 23 of 130 runners trying to steal, showing a slow release and bouncing several throws. He's strictly a station-to-station runner.

2000 Outlook

Hundley was throwing better later in the year, and if he could hit for power and be even average defensively, he would help the Dodgers immensely. Now that he only bats lefthanded, he probably will be platooned with either Paul LoDuca or Angel Pena.

Mike Maddux

Position: RP
Bats: L **Throws:** R
Ht: 6' 2" **Wt:** 185

Opening Day Age: 38
Born: 8/27/61 in
Dayton, OH
ML Seasons: 14

Overall Statistics

	W	L	Pct.	ERA	G	GS	Sv	IP	H	BB	SO	HR	Ratio
1999	1	1	.500	3.77	53	0	0	59.2	63	22	45	6	1.42
Career	37	35	.514	3.98	451	48	20	834.1	842	272	547	61	1.34

1999 Situational Stats

	W	L	ERA	Sv	IP		AB	H	HR	RBI	Avg
Home	0	0	2.21	0	36.2	LHB	100	27	2	9	.270
Road	1	1	6.26	0	23.0	RHB	129	36	4	22	.279
First Half	0	1	3.38	0	29.1	Sc Pos	57	14	2	24	.246
Scnd Half	1	0	4.15	0	30.1	Clutch	79	22	1	9	.278

1999 Season

Declaring his free agency after the Expos tried to send him to Triple-A, Mike Maddux signed with the bullpen-challenged Dodgers in late April. After a few weeks tuning up in the minors, he was brought up to the big league club. Aside from closer Jeff Shaw, Maddux was the most consistent reliever on the team.

Pitching, Defense & Hitting

While he may not have the best stuff in the world, Maddux, like his younger brother Greg, sure knows how to pitch. He moves the ball around, in and out, up and down, always keeping hitters off balance with his funky delivery. He starts them off with a tight slider, then he'll throw another one and yet another, occasionally mixing in a sinking fastball in the upper 80s. Defensively, Maddux is fundamentally sound, keeps an eye on baserunners and gets rid of the ball quickly. He's ineffective at the plate.

2000 Outlook

Maddux has pitched for six different clubs in the last six years, and he's a free agent once again. A true professional, he'll set a good example and serve as a second pitching coach wherever he winds up.

Onan Masaoka

Position: RP
Bats: R **Throws:** L
Ht: 6' 0" **Wt:** 188

Opening Day Age: 22
Born: 10/27/77 in Hilo, HI
ML Seasons: 1
Pronunciation:
OH-nen
mass-ay-OH-kuh

Overall Statistics

	W	L	Pct.	ERA	G	GS	Sv	IP	H	BB	SO	HR	Ratio
1999	2	4	.333	4.32	54	0	1	66.2	55	47	61	8	1.53
Career	2	4	.333	4.32	54	0	1	66.2	55	47	61	8	1.53

1999 Situational Stats

	W	L	ERA	Sv	IP		AB	H	HR	RBI	Avg
Home	2	1	4.24	1	34.0	LHB	92	20	2	11	.217
Road	0	3	4.41	0	32.2	RHB	156	35	6	22	.224
First Half	1	1	2.97	1	39.1	Sc Pos	66	15	2	23	.227
Scnd Half	1	3	6.26	0	27.1	Clutch	33	8	1	7	.242

1999 Season

Despite coming into the spring with 373 professional innings under his belt, most of them as a starter, Onan Masaoka won a job in the Los Angeles bullpen. Used as a long reliever and situational southpaw, he proved difficult to hit.

Pitching, Defense & Hitting

Masaoka has a live 91-94 MPH fastball. He complements it with a flat curveball that nevertheless freezes lefthanders because of his three-quarter delivery. His mechanics are inconsistent, however, and he needs to work to create better balance on the mound. Though his release leaves him a bit vulnerable defensively, he makes up for it with his athleticism. His move to first is pretty good and he's unproven as a hitter.

2000 Outlook

Masaoka would prefer to become a starter again. To succeed in that role, he'll need better command and a reliable offspeed pitch. The trade of Pedro Borbon to the Blue Jays makes it more likely that the Dodgers will keep Masaoka in the bullpen.

Alan Mills

Position: RP
Bats: B **Throws:** R
Ht: 6' 1" **Wt:** 195

Opening Day Age: 33
Born: 10/18/66 in Lakeland, FL
ML Seasons: 10

Overall Statistics

	W	L	Pct.	ERA	G	GS	Sv	IP	H	BB	SO	HR	Ratio
1999	3	4	.429	3.73	68	0	0	72.1	70	43	49	10	1.56
Career	34	30	.531	3.88	418	5	13	572.2	501	349	411	68	1.48

1999 Situational Stats

	W	L	ERA	Sv	IP		AB	H	HR	RBI	Avg
Home	1	2	3.08	0	26.1	LHB	103	32	3	12	.311
Road	2	2	4.11	0	46.0	RHB	165	38	7	29	.230
First Half	2	1	3.08	0	38.0	Sc Pos	89	16	3	29	.180
Scnd Half	1	3	4.46	0	34.1	Clutch	160	43	7	29	.269

1999 Season

Familiar to both GM Kevin Malone and Davey Johnson from their years together in Baltimore, Alan Mills was one of the new regime's first free-agent signings. The 10-year veteran became the main righthanded setup man, ranking among the National League leaders in holds.

Pitching, Defense & Hitting

Though Mills has a fastball in the low 90s, it's rather straight. He complements it with a hard slider and a splitter. He struggles with both his command and his control, so he tends to go deep into counts and walks almost as many batters as he strikes out. When he can't throw his splitter for strikes, lefthanders pound him. Mills is slow to the plate and his move to first is nothing special, so basestealers have their way with him. He's also not a particularly strong fielder and went hitless when he made his first two career plate appearances last season.

2000 Outlook

Mills has neither the stuff nor the control to be a closer and hasn't started a game since 1992. Signed through 2001, he remains a valuable and rather durable component in the Dodger bullpen.

Angel Pena

Position: C
Bats: R **Throws:** R
Ht: 5'10" **Wt:** 228

Opening Day Age: 25
Born: 2/16/75 in San Pedro de Macoris, Dominican Republic
ML Seasons: 2
Pronunciation: PAIN-yuh

Overall Statistics

	G	AB	R	H	D	T	HR	RBI	SB	BB	SO	Avg	OBP	Slg
1999	43	120	14	25	6	0	4	21	0	12	24	.208	.276	.358
Career	49	133	15	28	6	0	4	21	0	12	30	.211	.272	.346

1999 Situational Stats

	AB	H	HR	RBI	Avg		AB	H	HR	RBI	Avg
Home	80	17	2	10	.213	LHP	52	12	4	15	.231
Road	40	8	2	11	.200	RHP	68	13	0	6	.191
First Half	84	18	2	10	.214	Sc Pos	34	10	2	18	.294
Scnd Half	36	7	2	11	.194	Clutch	24	3	0	1	.125

1999 Season

Angel Pena began the season at Triple-A Albuquerque as arguably the best catching prospect in the minors. Recalled when Todd Hundley and Paul LoDuca struggled coming out of the gate, Pena wasn't ready offensively or defensively. He sulked when he was sent back down, hurt his elbow in August and was suspended for insubordination at the tail end of the season.

Hitting, Baserunning & Defense

Though Pena has good power, it comes from a wild swing that's easily exposed by offspeed stuff. Last year he tried to pull everything, so pitchers kept working him away with breaking balls. He had been more patient in the minors. Though no basestealer, he runs pretty well for a short, stocky guy. He let his offensive struggles affect his defense, which dissatisfied the Dodgers the most. He has a good arm, though he still needs work on his accuracy.

2000 Outlook

While Pena has considerable talent, he hasn't shown the attitude necessary to improve his game. He could platoon with Todd Hundley or even win the starting job in 2000, but only if he grows up and shapes up.

Carlos Perez

Pivotal Season

Position: SP
Bats: L **Throws:** L
Ht: 6' 3" **Wt:** 210

Opening Day Age: 29
Born: 1/14/71 in Nigua, Dominican Republic
ML Seasons: 4

Overall Statistics

	W	L	Pct.	ERA	G	GS	Sv	IP	H	BB	SO	HR	Ratio
1999	2	10	.167	7.43	17	16	0	89.2	116	39	40	23	1.73
Career	35	45	.438	4.20	112	105	0	678.2	708	178	384	83	1.31

1999 Situational Stats

	W	L	ERA	Sv	IP		AB	H	HR	RBI	Avg
Home	0	7	8.00	0	45.0	LHB	96	32	8	18	.333
Road	2	3	6.85	0	44.2	RHB	270	84	15	52	.311
First Half	2	9	6.95	0	77.2	Sc Pos	91	34	4	44	.374
Scnd Half	0	1	10.50	0	12.0	Clutch	16	7	2	7	.438

1999 Season

Signed to a three-year, $15 million contract in spring training, Carlos Perez had a total meltdown. Already off to a slow start, he suffered a mysterious thigh bruise in Montreal, then was sent to the bullpen and eventually to Triple-A Albuquerque. The nightmare was ended by a hard liner off his knee that shut him down before he could be promoted.

Pitching, Defense & Hitting

While Perez never has been a hard thrower, his fastball was down to the low 80s last year. He mixes in a sloppy curveball and a changeup that he turns over like a screwball. His deceptive motion was the key to his past success, but he couldn't win with a mediocre fastball. Perez comes out of his delivery ready to field. His move to first is just average, but he keeps runners close with repeated pickoff throws. He batted .296 last season and is a career .174 hitter.

2000 Outlook

Mechanical alterations had Perez throwing close to 90 MPH by season's end, so there's hope for a comeback. The Dodgers seem set on trading one or more starters and may have an opening for him.

Jose Vizcaino

Position: SS/2B
Bats: B **Throws:** R
Ht: 6' 1" **Wt:** 180

Opening Day Age: 32
Born: 3/26/68 in San Cristobal, Dominican Republic
ML Seasons: 11
Pronunciation: vis-kye-EE-noh

Overall Statistics

	G	AB	R	H	D	T	HR	RBI	SB	BB	SO	Avg	OBP	Slg
1999	94	266	27	67	9	0	1	29	2	20	23	.252	.304	.297
Career	1068	3574	428	968	123	32	21	325	59	257	498	.271	.319	.341

1999 Situational Stats

	AB	H	HR	RBI	Avg		AB	H	HR	RBI	Avg
Home	140	33	1	10	.236	LHP	70	23	0	9	.329
Road	126	34	0	19	.270	RHP	196	44	1	20	.224
First Half	180	43	1	19	.239	Sc Pos	62	19	0	26	.306
Scnd Half	86	24	0	10	.279	Clutch	48	10	0	3	.208

1999 Season

Jose Vizcaino is a useful player to have on a ballclub, but the fact that he makes $3.5 million dollars per year changes the equation a bit. Expected to compete for the starting shortstop job, he only got a chance to play every day when Mark Grudzielanek cracked his hand on a dugout wall.

Hitting, Baserunning & Defense

A switch-hitter, Vizcaino has had a lot of trouble making contact from the left side lately, batting .227 against righthanders the past two seasons. As a righty, his stroke is level and he hits line drives all over the field. Pitchers like to pound him down and away with hard stuff, and he has trouble laying off breaking pitches down and in when batting lefty. While Vizcaino can play third and short, his arm is best suited for second base, where he turns the pivot well. He has average speed yet is a good baserunner.

2000 Outlook

Clearly on the downside of his career, Vizcaino hasn't looked the same since severely spraining his ankle in 1998. If heatlhy, he could return to the starting lineup at either second or short in the wake of the Eric Young trade.

Los Angeles

Other Los Angeles Dodgers

Jamie Arnold (**Pos**: RHP, **Age**: 26)

	W	L	Pct.	ERA	G	GS	Sv	IP	H	BB	SO	HR	Ratio
1999	2	4	.333	5.48	36	3	1	69.0	81	34	26	6	1.67
Career	2	4	.333	5.48	36	3	1	69.0	81	34	26	6	1.67

The Dodgers weathered a tough rookie season from Arnold, who hadn't experienced success during three seasons in the high minors. 2000 Outlook: C

Doug Bochtler (**Pos**: RHP, **Age**: 29)

	W	L	Pct.	ERA	G	GS	Sv	IP	H	BB	SO	HR	Ratio
1999	0	0	-	5.54	12	0	0	13.0	11	6	7	3	1.31
Career	9	16	.360	4.51	214	0	6	251.2	218	156	211	34	1.49

After two good seasons with the Padres in 1995 and '96, Bochtler's control deserted him. The Royals signed him to a minor league contract in November. 2000 Outlook: C

Juan Castro (**Pos**: 2B, **Age**: 27, **Bats**: R)

	G	AB	R	H	D	T	HR	RBI	SB	BB	SO	Avg	OBP	Slg
1999	2	1	0	0	0	0	0	0	0	0	1	.000	.000	.000
Career	212	432	44	81	15	4	2	23	1	33	86	.188	.244	.255

After spending much of 1998 with Los Angeles, the good-fielding Castro failed to make the team last spring. He may never hit much. 2000 Outlook: C

Robinson Checo (**Pos**: RHP, **Age**: 28)

	W	L	Pct.	ERA	G	GS	Sv	IP	H	BB	SO	HR	Ratio
1999	2	2	.500	10.34	9	2	0	15.2	24	13	11	5	2.36
Career	3	5	.375	7.61	16	6	0	36.2	47	21	30	8	1.85

While Checo impressed in his Boston debut in 1997, his major league work hasn't been very good since then. 2000 Outlook: C

Brent Cookson (**Pos**: LF, **Age**: 30, **Bats**: R)

	G	AB	R	H	D	T	HR	RBI	SB	BB	SO	Avg	OBP	Slg
1999	3	5	0	1	0	0	0	0	0	0	1	.200	.200	.200
Career	25	40	2	6	1	0	0	5	1	2	8	.150	.190	.175

Cookson batted .360 at Triple-A Tucson in 1998 and .321-28-70 in 277 at-bats at Triple-A Albuquerque in '99. That kind of hitting should earn him a bench job, but it hasn't. 2000 Outlook: C

Tripp Cromer (**Pos**: 2B, **Age**: 32, **Bats**: R)

	G	AB	R	H	D	T	HR	RBI	SB	BB	SO	Avg	OBP	Slg
1999	33	52	5	10	0	0	2	8	0	5	10	.192	.263	.308
Career	184	512	52	116	22	0	12	47	0	26	100	.227	.266	.340

Cromer's familiarity with the disabled list continued in 1999, as he was diagnosed with an irregular heartbeat. 2000 Outlook: C

Dave Hansen (**Pos**: 1B/3B, **Age**: 31, **Bats**: L)

	G	AB	R	H	D	T	HR	RBI	SB	BB	SO	Avg	OBP	Slg
1999	100	107	14	27	8	1	2	17	0	26	20	.252	.404	.402
Career	684	1096	108	291	48	3	17	121	2	158	184	.266	.359	.361

Hansen wasn't as successful as a bench player last season after a strong performance with the Cubs in 1998. He may rebound. 2000 Outlook: B

Matt Herges (**Pos**: RHP, **Age**: 29)

	W	L	Pct.	ERA	G	GS	Sv	IP	H	BB	SO	HR	Ratio
1999	0	2	.000	4.07	17	0	0	24.1	24	8	18	5	1.32
Career	0	2	.000	4.07	17	0	0	24.1	24	8	18	5	1.32

A career minor leaguer, Herges made the jump from the Triple-A rotation to the Dodgers bullpen, pitching respectably in 24 games. He may stick. 2000 Outlook: C

Trenidad Hubbard (**Pos**: LF/CF, **Age**: 33, **Bats**: R)

	G	AB	R	H	D	T	HR	RBI	SB	BB	SO	Avg	OBP	Slg
1999	82	105	23	33	5	0	1	13	4	13	24	.314	.387	.390
Career	280	497	86	142	25	4	14	57	19	54	110	.286	.358	.437

Hubbard has hit better than .300 in Triple-A for eight straight years, and he hit .314 in Los Angeles in 1999. 2000 Outlook: B

Jeff Kubenka (**Pos**: LHP, **Age**: 25)

	W	L	Pct.	ERA	G	GS	Sv	IP	H	BB	SO	HR	Ratio
1999	0	1	.000	11.74	6	0	0	7.2	13	4	2	1	2.22
Career	1	1	.500	5.82	12	0	0	17.0	17	12	12	1	1.71

Kubenka has been stellar in Triple-A the last two seasons, but the soft-tossing lefty struggled in Los Angeles in 1999. The Dodgers waived him in September and the Diamondbacks picked him up. 2000 Outlook: C

Paul LoDuca (**Pos**: C, **Age**: 27, **Bats**: R)

	G	AB	R	H	D	T	HR	RBI	SB	BB	SO	Avg	OBP	Slg
1999	36	95	11	22	1	0	3	11	1	10	9	.232	.312	.337
Career	42	109	13	26	2	0	3	12	1	10	10	.239	.309	.339

For a fourth straight season LoDuca hit better than .300 with little power in the minors, but he didn't fare as well with the Dodgers. 2000 Outlook: B

Antonio Osuna (**Pos**: RHP, **Age**: 26)

	W	L	Pct.	ERA	G	GS	Sv	IP	H	BB	SO	HR	Ratio
1999	0	0	-	7.71	5	0	0	4.2	4	3	5	0	1.50
Career	21	15	.583	3.15	219	0	10	259.2	204	106	276	25	1.19

Osuna had offseason elbow surgery a year ago, needed a bone spur removed from the elbow in May, then butted heads with the Dodgers over Tommy John surgery. He relented in September and will miss this year. 2000 Outlook: D

Chance Sanford (**Pos**: 2B, **Age**: 27, **Bats**: L)

	G	AB	R	H	D	T	HR	RBI	SB	BB	SO	Avg	OBP	Slg
1999	5	8	1	2	0	0	0	2	0	0	1	.250	.250	.250
Career	19	36	4	6	1	1	0	5	0	1	7	.167	.189	.250

Sanford was recalled when Mark Grudzielanek broke his hand in early June. Sanford was gone in a week and may not be back. 2000 Outlook: D

Rick Wilkins (**Pos**: C, **Age**: 32, **Bats**: L)

	G	AB	R	H	D	T	HR	RBI	SB	BB	SO	Avg	OBP	Slg
1999	3	4	0	0	0	0	0	0	0	0	2	.000	.000	.000
Career	704	2081	274	508	94	7	80	266	9	274	561	.244	.333	.411

Wilkins made the Opening Day roster with Todd Hundley's health in question, but was sent to Triple-A on April 26. 2000 Outlook: D

Los Angeles Dodgers Minor League Prospects

Organization Overview:

When Kevin Malone took over as Dodgers GM following the 1998 season, he cleaned house with the minor league and scouting departments. It was hard to blame him. Los Angeles drafted poorly throughout the 1990s, finding virtually all of its talent on the foreign market. Just two of the Dodgers' first-round picks during the decade reached the majors, and three of their better draft picks—Peter Bergeron, Paul Konerko and Ted Lilly—were traded during the ill-fated GM tenure of Tom Lasorda. The new regime is trying to emphasize athleticism and focused on shortstops and center fielders in its first draft. The biggest strides the organization made in 1999 came in Taiwan, where they landed Chin-Feng Chen and Hong-Chih Kuo.

Luke Allen

Position: 3B
Bats: L **Throws:** R
Ht: 6' 2" **Wt:** 208
Opening Day Age: 21
Born: 8/4/78 in Covington, GA

Recent Statistics

	G	AB	R	H	D	T	HR	RBI	SB	BB	SO	Avg
1998 A San Berndno	105	399	51	119	25	6	4	46	18	30	93	.298
1998 AA San Antonio	23	78	9	26	3	1	3	10	1	6	16	.333
1999 AA San Antonio	137	533	90	150	16	12	14	82	14	44	102	.281
1999 MLE	137	501	65	118	12	6	9	59	9	26	108	.236

Los Angeles' best U.S. prospect didn't even come from the draft, as Allen was signed as a nondrafted free agent in 1996. He has the tools to become an offensive force, especially with his above-average power. To do so, he'll have to be more selective at the plate and start using the entire field. He runs well, has good range and a cannon that was rated the best infield arm in the Double-A Texas League. Though he led the minors with 53 errors last year, the Dodgers aren't concerned. If Adrian Beltre is declared a free agent, at least they have Allen to fall back on. He'll start 2000 back in Double-A.

Hiram Bocachica

Position: 2B
Bats: R **Throws:** R
Ht: 5' 11" **Wt:** 165
Opening Day Age: 24
Born: 3/4/76 in Ponce, Puerto Rico

Recent Statistics

	G	AB	R	H	D	T	HR	RBI	SB	BB	SO	Avg
1998 AA Harrisburg	80	296	39	78	18	4	4	27	20	21	61	.264
1998 AAA Ottawa	12	41	5	8	3	1	0	5	2	6	14	.195
1998 AAA Albuquerque	26	101	16	24	7	1	4	16	5	13	24	.238
1999 AA San Antonio	123	477	84	139	22	10	11	60	30	60	71	.291
1999 MLE	123	447	60	109	17	5	7	43	19	36	75	.244

Bocachica joined the Dodgers in 1998 in the regrettable Mark Grudzielanek-Carlos Perez trade with Montreal, a deal that cost Los Angeles four players, including Peter Bergeron and Ted Lilly. A 1994 first-round pick as a shortstop, he since has moved to center field and second base. Bocachica has nice raw tools but hasn't made the most of them yet. If he can maintain the patience he showed last year, that and his speed might make him an effective top-of-the-order hitter. He also has gap power, and Texas League managers rated him the best defensive second baseman in the Double-A circuit. The trade of Eric Young clears a path for Bocachica to start in Los Angeles in 2001.

Chin-Feng Chen

Position: OF
Bats: R **Throws:** R
Ht: 6' 1" **Wt:** 189
Opening Day Age: 22
Born: 10/28/77 in Tainan City, Taiwan

Recent Statistics

	G	AB	R	H	D	T	HR	RBI	SB	BB	SO	Avg
1999 A San Berndno	131	510	98	161	22	10	31	123	31	75	129	.316

The first Taiwanese player in the U.S. minor leagues since 1975, Chen signed with the Dodgers for $680,000 shortly after last winter's Asian Games, where he homered off Chan Ho Park. That bonus looks like a bargain after Chen destroyed the high Class-A California League. He recorded the first 30-30 season in league history, winning MVP honors and being named the circuit's top prospect. He even showed more speed than Los Angeles expected, and the only drawback is an arm that will keep him in left field. Corner outfielders Shawn Green and Gary Sheffield are under contract through 2005 and 2003, respectively, but Chen should be ready before then. It's an interesting dilemma for the Dodgers.

Alex Cora

Position: SS
Bats: L **Throws:** R
Ht: 6' 0" **Wt:** 180
Opening Day Age: 24
Born: 10/18/75 in Caguas, Puerto Rico

Recent Statistics

	G	AB	R	H	D	T	HR	RBI	SB	BB	SO	Avg
1999 AAA Albuquerque	80	302	51	93	11	7	4	37	9	12	37	.308
1999 NL Los Angeles	11	30	2	5	1	0	0	3	0	0	4	.167
1999 MLE	80	280	35	71	8	3	2	25	6	8	38	.254

The Dodgers don't have a better defensive shortstop than Cora, but he's blocked by questions about his bat and the expensive contracts of Mark Grudzielanek and Jose Vizcaino. The younger brother of former major league second baseman Joey Cora, Alex was a 1996 first-round pick out of the University of Miami. He made some strides at the plate in his second half-season in Triple-A, though he's still too impatient and has very little power. An average runner, he lacks a basestealer's mentality, so he has only minimal offensive potential. Unless Los Angeles can dump Vizcaino, Cora will spend most of 2000 in Triple-A.

Randey Dorame

Position: P
Bats: L **Throws:** L
Ht: 6' 2" **Wt:** 205
Opening Day Age: 21
Born: 1/23/79 in Huatabampo, Mexico

Recent Statistics

	W	L	ERA	G	GS	Sv	IP	H	R	BB	SO	HR
1999 A Vero Beach	0	2	5.73	3	2	0	11.0	15	9	1	5	2
1999 A San Berndno	14	3	2.51	24	24	0	154.1	130	52	37	159	9

Chin-Feng Chen wasn't the only Dodger to light up the high Class-A California League in his first season in the U.S. minors last year. Dorame, who spent 1997 in the Dominican Summer League and 1998 in the Mexican League, was named Cal League pitcher of the year after leading the circuit in wins and ERA. His curveball is his best pitch, followed by an average fastball and a changeup. He succeeds because of his control, which was rated the best in the California League. Unless Carlos Perez suddenly turns his career around, Los Angeles won't have a lefty starter until Dorame is ready in two years.

Eric Gagne

Position: P
Bats: R **Throws:** R
Ht: 6' 2" **Wt:** 195
Opening Day Age: 24
Born: 1/7/76 in Montreal, Canada

Recent Statistics

	W	L	ERA	G	GS	Sv	IP	H	R	BB	SO	HR
1999 AA San Antonio	12	4	2.63	26	26	0	167.2	122	55	64	185	17
1999 NL Los Angeles	1	1	2.10	5	5	0	30.0	18	8	15	30	3

While Randy Dorame was winning pitcher-of-the-year honors in the California League, Gagne was doing the same one level up in the Double-A Texas League. He led the league in ERA, strikeouts and opponent batting average (.201) just two years after missing the entire 1997 season following reconstructive elbow surgery. Gagne throws an extremely lively 92-93 MPH fastball and an outstanding changeup. His curveball is a good third pitch when it's on. Gagne carried his success to the majors during a September callup, throwing six shutout innings in his debut and limiting hitters to a .175 average. He's the favorite to fill the one opening in Los Angeles' rotation.

Mike Judd

Position: P
Bats: R **Throws:** R
Ht: 6' 1" **Wt:** 217
Opening Day Age: 24
Born: 6/30/75 in San Diego, CA

Recent Statistics

	W	L	ERA	G	GS	Sv	IP	H	R	BB	SO	HR
1999 AAA Albuquerque	8	7	6.67	21	21	0	110.2	132	90	47	122	22
1999 NL Los Angeles	3	1	5.46	7	4	0	28.0	30	17	12	22	4

Acquiring Judd from the Yankees for Billy Brewer in 1996 initially looked like a steal for the Dodgers, but Judd has stalled since reaching Triple-A two years later. A 1995 ninth-round pick out of Grossmont (Calif.) Junior College, he has a 6.04 ERA above Double-A. He led the Pacific Coast League with 9.92 strikeouts per nine innings last year, but still got shelled. Rather than trust a fastball that can reach the mid-90s, he got too cute with cut fastballs and couldn't drive his pitches down in the strike zone. There's an outside chance he could start for Los Angeles if Eric Gagne falters in spring training, but it's more likely that Judd will make the team as a middle reliever.

Jeff Williams

Position: P
Bats: R **Throws:** L
Ht: 6' 0" **Wt:** 185
Opening Day Age: 27
Born: 6/6/72 in Canberra, Australia

Recent Statistics

	W	L	ERA	G	GS	Sv	IP	H	R	BB	SO	HR
1999 AAA Albuquerque	9	7	5.01	42	14	4	125.2	151	77	47	86	14
1999 NL Los Angeles	2	0	4.08	5	3	0	17.2	12	10	9	7	2

Williams worked so much for Southeastern Louisiana and the Australian Olympic team in 1996 that at times he struggled to throw harder than 80 MPH. Since signing with the Dodgers as a nondrafted free agent, he has improved his velocity so much that he now averages 91 MPH. He also throws a curveball and a changeup. Williams won the last game ever played at 3Com Park and generally impressed Los Angeles during a September callup. The trade of Pedro Borbon enhances Williams' chances of making the Dodgers as a reliever, and he could get a brief look as a starter if needed.

Others to Watch

Steve Colyer (21) got one of the highest bonuses ever given a draft-and-follow, signing for $650,000 a year after the Dodgers took him in the second round in 1997. He throws 93-94 MPH, very good velocity for a lefthander, and also has a hard curve. . . The Dodgers hope Taiwanese righthander **Hong-Chi Kuo** (18) turns out as well as Chin-Feng Chen after signing Kuo for $1.25 million in July. Kuo, who has yet to debut in the minors, averages 94-95 MPH with his fastball and also has a promising curveball. . . Outfielder **Tony Mota** (22), the son of longtime Dodgers player and coach Manny Mota, was enjoying a breakthrough season in Double-A before tearing a ligament in his left thumb. He's a switch-hitter with some power and speed. . . Second baseman **Jorge Nunez** (22) was a nice bonus in the Shawn Green trade with Toronto. Nunez has plenty of speed and arm strength, and he may move back to shortstop. . . Righthander **Luke Prokopec** (22), a converted outfielder, got hammered in Double-A last year. But he still has potential with an average fastball and a tough knuckle-curve. . . Shortstop **Jason Repko** (19), the Dodgers' 199 first-round pick, has exceptional speed and could develop into a five-tool player. He slugged .551 in his debut at Rookie-level Great Falls.

County Stadium

Offense

County Stadium is a tough place to figure. Though it's been a pitchers' park for most of its history, in recent years it has become more of a hitters' park. And while the most famous teams that have played there have hit a lot of homers, the one thing the park certainly doesn't do is favor the longball. The weather often dictates the park's effect on a given day or in a given season. Early in the year, it favors the pitcher. After it warms up in late May, the advantage shifts to the batter.

Defense

County Stadium has fairly typical dimensions and doesn't put unusual demands on any particular defensive position. The infield is quick, so turning the double play can take on added significance. The Brewers have a history of finding excellent pivot men, from Jim Gantner to Fernando Vina.

Who It Helps The Most

Batters who put the ball in play tend to derive the most benefit. Ron Belliard and Mark Loretta are helped the most. Likewise, pitchers who keep the ball out of play tend to do well. Hideo Nomo was Milwaukee's only real strikeout pitcher last year, and he pitched fairly well at County Stadium.

Who It Hurts The Most

Power hitters are hurt because County Stadium contains many long drives that would leave other yards. Dave Nilsson has seen his home-run power muted, as has Jose Valentin. Even players with mid-range home-run power like Marquis Grissom are hurt. Pitchers who put the ball in play, such as Bob Wickman and Steve Woodard, have had markedly better records on the road.

Rookies & Newcomers

Jose Hernandez might lose a couple of homers to County Stadium. Rookie first baseman Kevin Barker is a power hitter, and he fared better away from Milwaukee after his promotion last year. Righthanders Curtis Leskanic and Jamey Wright will be happy just to have escaped Coors Field. The park shouldn't affect Juan Acevedo or Jimmy Haynes very much.

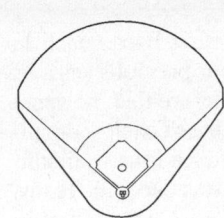

Dimensions: LF-315, LCF-376, CF-402, RCF-376, RF-315

Capacity: 53,192

Elevation: 635 feet

Surface: Grass

Foul Territory: Large

Park Factors

1999 Season

	Home Games			Away Games			
	Brewers	Opp	Total	Brewers	Opp	Total	Index
G	72	72	144	75	75	150	—
Avg	.266	.286	.276	.274	.279	.277	100
AB	2405	2578	4983	2659	2592	5251	99
R	325	418	743	404	390	794	97
H	640	737	1377	729	723	1452	99
2B	124	118	242	154	142	296	86
3B	9	13	22	16	19	35	66
HR	64	99	163	79	96	175	98
BB	287	272	559	308	300	608	97
SO	408	445	853	558	453	1011	89
E	46	43	89	64	52	116	80
E-Infield	37	32	69	51	41	92	78
LHB-Avg	.256	.281	.268	.277	.280	.278	96
LHB-HR	37	34	71	48	26	74	103
RHB-Avg	.273	.289	.281	.272	.278	.275	102
RHB-HR	27	65	92	31	70	101	95

1997-1999

	Home Games			Away Games			
	Brewers	Opp	Total	Brewers	Opp	Total	Index
G	221	221	442	220	220	440	—
Avg	.266	.276	.271	.261	.270	.266	102
AB	7374	7848	15222	7700	7357	15057	101
R	983	1151	2134	1012	1087	2099	101
H	1959	2164	4123	2012	1990	4002	103
2B	391	397	788	393	392	785	99
3B	33	35	68	34	49	83	81
HR	182	273	455	228	264	492	91
BB	799	767	1566	732	797	1529	101
SO	1254	1412	2666	1541	1378	2919	90
E	157	146	303	159	145	304	99
E-Infield	123	116	239	129	118	247	96
LHB-Avg	.262	.270	.266	.263	.274	.268	99
LHB-HR	104	90	194	127	91	218	89
RHB-Avg	.268	.280	.274	.260	.268	.264	104
RHB-HR	78	183	261	101	173	274	93

1999 Rankings (National League)
- Lowest infield-error factor
- Second-lowest strikeout factor
- Third-lowest double factor
- Third-lowest triple factor
- Third-lowest error factor

Milwaukee

Davey Lopes

1999 Season

Davey Lopes was the Padres' first base coach in 1999, as he had been for the four previous seasons under manager Bruce Bochy. Before that, he spent three years as the Orioles' first-base coach for manager Johnny Oates. That followed a four-year stint as Bobby Valentine's first-base coach in Texas. Lopes has no previous managerial experience in the majors or minors, though he did pilot Arizona Fall League teams in 1993 and 1996.

Offense

As a player, Lopes was a terrific basestealer who rarely was thrown out. He may be able to impart his technique to youngster Ronnie Belliard, a good basestealer in the minors who hasn't learned to steal in the majors. Lopes also had large platoon splits and spent three years at the end of his career as an effective platoon player. Thus he may be more willing to experiment with platoon arrangements, perhaps at first base and behind the plate.

Pitching & Defense

Lopes was a converted outfielder, as was his long-time double-play partner, Bill Russell. Having made a successful position switch himself, he may be more willing to try players at new positions. Jose Valentin would be a prime candidate. He has been error-prone at shortstop but may have the athleticism to make a switch to the outfield. Lopes' Dodgers teams were known more for their power and pitching than their defense, but the Brewers don't appear to have enough power or pitching to overcome subpar fielding.

2000 Outlook

Lopes played most of his big league career under Tommy Lasorda and is one of a handful of managers who played or coached for Lasorda. Overall, Lasorda's disciples have had mixed results. Dusty Baker and Valentine have been successful, as have Oates and, to a lesser extent, Jim Lefebvre. Russell, on the other hand, was an abject failure. The Brewers hope that Lopes' long apprenticeship at the hands of Oates and Bochy will pay off.

Born: 5/03/45 in East Providence, RI

Playing Experience: 1972-1987, LA, Oak, ChC, Hou

Managerial Experience: 0 seasons

Pronunciation: LOAPS

Manager Statistics

Year	Team, Lg	W	L	Pct	GB	Finish
1999		—	—	—	—	—
0 Seasons		—	—	—	—	—

1999 Starting Pitchers by Days Rest

	<=3	4	5	6+
Brewers Starts	—	—	—	—
Brewers ERA	—	—	—	—
NL Avg Starts	3	81	48	21
NL ERA	4.84	4.53	4.72	4.98

1999 Situational Stats

	Davey Lopes	NL Average
Hit & Run Success %	—	28.1
Stolen Base Success %	—	71.1
Platoon Pct.	—	58.1
Defensive Subs	—	15
High-Pitch Outings	—	6
Quick/Slow Hooks	—	18/17
Sacrifice Attempts	—	111

1999 Rankings (National League)

- Did not manage in the majors last year

Ron Belliard

1999 Season

Ron Belliard had a fine debut for the Brewers, batting .295 while playing solid defense. He would have had a good shot at National League Rookie of the Year honors in most other seasons. Fernando Vina's early-season injury opened the door for Belliard, who was called up in May and played regularly for the rest of the year. He showed the potential to be a top-of-the-order hitter for years to come.

Hitting

Belliard displayed uncommon patience and maturity at the plate, the kind that's especially valuable in a leadoff or No. 2 hitter. He rarely swings at the first pitch and likes to look over a few pitches before going after one. He often batted lower in the order last year, but it's clear that his future is as a tablesetter. He hits liners to all fields against all types of pitching, and remains tough even with two strikes. He has good pop for a middle infielder, and he's a far superior hitter to his cousin, former major league shortstop Rafael Belliard.

Baserunning & Defense

Despite having speed and a good track record as a basestealer in the minors, Belliard ran tentatively last year. He may need to refine his basestealing technique in order to become a legitimate threat at the major league level. He made some rookie mistakes on the bases but generally has good instincts. Belliard has quick feet, which translate into good range and a strong double-play pivot on defense. His arm is strong for a second baseman.

2000 Outlook

Belliard appears to have a bright career ahead of him. Milwaukee found a way to keep him in the lineup by trading Vina to St. Louis. Belliard clearly is the Brewers' second baseman of the future.

Position: 2B
Bats: R **Throws:** R
Ht: 5' 8" **Wt:** 180

Opening Day Age: 24
Born: 4/7/75 in Bronx, NY
ML Seasons: 2

Overall Statistics

	G	AB	R	H	D	T	HR	RBI	SB	BB	SO	Avg	OBP	Slg
1999	124	457	60	135	29	4	8	58	4	64	59	.295	.379	.429
Career	132	462	61	136	29	4	8	58	4	64	59	.294	.377	.426

Where He Hits the Ball

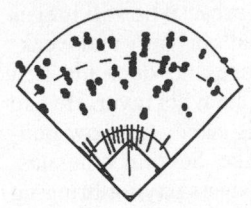
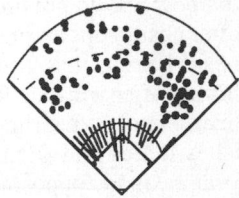

Vs. LHP　　　　**Vs. RHP**

1999 Situational Stats

	AB	H	HR	RBI	Avg		AB	H	HR	RBI	Avg
Home	221	70	5	30	.317	LHP	121	33	4	17	.273
Road	236	65	3	28	.275	RHP	336	102	4	41	.304
First Half	187	60	4	22	.321	Sc Pos	113	38	2	49	.336
Scnd Half	270	75	4	36	.278	Clutch	68	25	1	16	.368

1999 Rankings (National League)

- 3rd in lowest fielding percentage at second base (.978)
- 4th in errors at second base (13)
- 5th in batting average in the clutch
- Led the Brewers in GDPs (16), highest ground-ball/flyball ratio (1.4), batting average in the clutch and highest percentage of pitches taken (58.9)
- Led NL second basemen in batting average with runners in scoring position, GDPs (16) and batting average at home

Jeromy Burnitz

1999 Season

Jeromy Burnitz had another big year for the Brewers in 1999 despite missing more than a month with a broken bone in his right hand. An errant Jose Rosado pitch put him on the shelf from mid-July to late August, but upon his return Burnitz showed no ill effects and quickly resumed driving in runs. His strong season cemented his standing as one of the National League's best lefthanded power hitters.

Hitting

Burnitz is a deadly fastball hitter, especially on pitches up and in. He has great bat speed and is nearly impossible to tie up inside. With a pronounced uppercut, he hits most balls in the air and grounds into few double plays. Changing speeds is the best way to get him out because he still lunges after changeups at times. That's his only real weakness. Burnitz has a good eye and does his best hitting after working the count in his favor. He had been platooned earlier in his career but now punishes lefties and righties alike. Several times last year, he made opposing managers pay for bringing in a lefthanded specialist to face him.

Baserunning & Defense

Burnitz has good speed and is capable of stealing a base, though he doesn't run as often as he used to. He's a good right fielder with a strong, accurate arm, and probably could cover center field if needed. Cutting off balls in the corner is the only thing he doesn't do well.

2000 Outlook

The Brewers have Burnitz tied up for the next two years and will look to build their lineup around his big lefthanded bat. He should be a perennial All-Star candidate for Milwaukee. Expect him to continue batting cleanup and driving in lots of runs.

Position: RF
Bats: L **Throws:** R
Ht: 6' 0" **Wt:** 205

Opening Day Age: 30
Born: 4/15/69 in Westminster, CA
ML Seasons: 7
Pronunciation: burr-NITZ

Overall Statistics

	G	AB	R	H	D	T	HR	RBI	SB	BB	SO	Avg	OBP	Slg
1999	130	467	87	126	33	2	33	103	7	91	124	.270	.402	.561
Career	678	2183	381	580	127	17	123	406	42	330	551	.266	.367	.508

Where He Hits the Ball

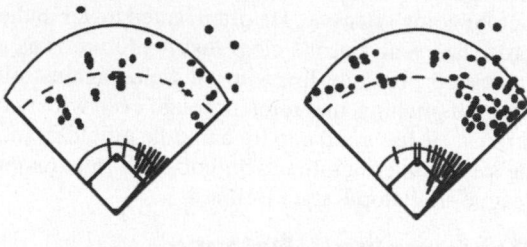

Vs. LHP   Vs. RHP

1999 Situational Stats

	AB	H	HR	RBI	Avg		AB	H	HR	RBI	Avg
Home	210	59	12	51	.281	LHP	162	40	11	41	.247
Road	257	67	21	52	.261	RHP	305	86	22	62	.282
First Half	317	89	26	73	.281	Sc Pos	136	34	8	67	.250
Scnd Half	150	37	7	30	.247	Clutch	68	15	4	12	.221

1999 Rankings (National League)

- 2nd in hit by pitch (16)
- 4th in most pitches seen per plate appearance (4.26) and errors in right field (5)
- 5th in lowest groundball/flyball ratio (0.8) and lowest fielding percentage in right field (.982)
- 6th in cleanup slugging percentage (.565)
- 9th in HR frequency (14.2 ABs per HR) and walks
- Led the Brewers in home runs, RBI, walks, intentional walks (7), hit by pitch (16), strikeouts, slugging percentage, on-base percentage, HR frequency (14.2 ABs per HR), most pitches seen per plate appearance (4.26), cleanup slugging percentage (.565) and steals of third (4)
- Led NL right fielders in hit by pitch (16)

Jeff Cirillo

Position: 3B
Bats: R **Throws:** R
Ht: 6' 1" **Wt:** 195

Opening Day Age: 30
Born: 9/23/69 in
Pasadena, CA
ML Seasons: 6
Pronunciation:
suh-RILL-o

1999 Season

In 1999, Jeff Cirillo gave the Brewers everything they've come to expect from him: consistent line-drive hitting and top-notch defense at third base. Once again, it was virtually impossible to get him out of the lineup, as he played 157 games. Since becoming a regular in 1996, he has averaged 156 games per season.

Hitting

Cirillo has quick hands and is able to cover the entire plate. He's especially adept at shooting inside pitches into right field, and he's one of the better two-strike hitters in the National League. The best way to negate his gap power is to keep the ball down. With his ability to hit for average and his sound batting eye, he makes a good No. 2 hitter. As a singles and doubles machine, he's adequate but not especially well suited to the third spot in the order, where he batted last year.

Baserunning & Defense

Cirillo is one of the best and most underrated glove men in the game. He has superior hands and reflexes, and a strong, accurate arm. He annually participates in more double plays than almost all other major league third basemen. Charging bunts is another one of his strengths. He has good lateral range, though he didn't seem to get to as many balls last year as he had in the past. Cirillo isn't fast, but he's a heady baserunner who rarely gets thrown out.

2000 Outlook

The Brewers decided to trade Cirillo, who's scheduled to make $8.15 million over the next two years, rather than rebuild around him. In a four-team trade at the Winter Meetings, Milwaukee sent Cirillo and Scott Karl to Colorado. The Brewers received Henry Blanco and Jamey Wright from the Rockies, plus Jimmy Haynes from the Athletics. With Coors Field pumping up his statistics even further, Cirillo finally should get the recognition he deserves. Milwaukee gave free agent Jose Hernandez a three-year, $10 million contract to take over at third base.

Overall Statistics

	G	AB	R	H	D	T	HR	RBI	SB	BB	SO	Avg	OBP	Slg
1999	157	607	98	198	35	1	15	88	7	75	83	.326	.401	.461
Career	789	2811	444	864	186	13	66	372	32	330	372	.307	.384	.453

Where He Hits the Ball

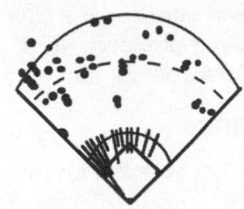 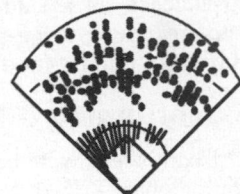

Vs. LHP   **Vs. RHP**

1999 Situational Stats

	AB	H	HR	RBI	Avg		AB	H	HR	RBI	Avg
Home	294	104	6	53	.354	LHP	158	51	9	33	.323
Road	313	94	9	35	.300	RHP	449	147	6	55	.327
First Half	334	107	8	52	.320	Sc Pos	184	55	4	74	.299
Scnd Half	273	91	7	36	.333	Clutch	91	21	0	11	.231

1999 Rankings (National League)

- 2nd in singles
- 3rd in fielding percentage at third base (.966) and hits
- Led the Brewers in batting average, at-bats, runs scored, hits, singles, total bases (280), sacrifice flies (7), times on base (278), pitches seen (2,660), plate appearances (697), batting average vs. lefthanded pitchers, batting average vs. righthanded pitchers, slugging percentage vs. lefthanded pitchers (.557), on-base percentage vs. lefthanded pitchers (.422), on-base percentage vs. righthanded pitchers (.393), batting average at home, batting average on the road, games played (157) and highest percentage of extra bases taken as a runner (60.0)

Milwaukee

Marquis Grissom

1999 Season

Marquis Grissom rebounded from an injury-plagued 1998 season to play the way the Brewers had expected when they traded for him two years ago. No longer slowed by leg problems, he began to steal bases and flash his strong defense again. He even returned to the leadoff spot late in the year.

Hitting

Grissom is an aggressive line-drive hitter who hits the ball to all fields. He always has had respectable power against lefties. Pitchers are better off keeping the ball down against him. When he was in his prime and able to keep his average close to .300, Grissom was a useful leadoff man, but those days are behind him. He no longer gets on base enough to succeed as a leadoff man and doesn't have enough power to be a true run producer, so it's difficult to find a good offensive role for him.

Baserunning & Defense

Grissom's legs were healthy last year and his running game returned. He doesn't run as often as he used to, but picks his spots and is a good percentage basestealer. He ran more aggressively after returning to the leadoff spot late in the year, showing that he still might be capable of stealing 40 bases if used in the top spot. His range also returned in center field. Grissom glides to the ball and covers a lot of ground. His arm is accurate but not nearly as strong as it once was.

2000 Outlook

Though Grissom had a decent year, he's still of questionable value to the Brewers because they're rebuilding and have a lot of money tied up in him. He's at the point where he's going to have to work hard to prevent his skills from eroding. There's little competition from within the organization, however, and it might be difficult for Milwaukee to unload his contract, so the center-field job should be his for at least another year.

Position: CF
Bats: R **Throws:** R
Ht: 5'11" **Wt:** 188
Opening Day Age: 32
Born: 4/17/67 in Atlanta, GA
ML Seasons: 11
Pronunciation: mar-KEESE
Nickname: Grip

Overall Statistics

	G	AB	R	H	D	T	HR	RBI	SB	BB	SO	Avg	OBP	Slg
1999	154	603	92	161	27	1	20	83	24	49	109	.267	.320	.415
Career	1435	5603	839	1550	267	44	131	601	382	412	783	.277	.327	.410

Where He Hits the Ball

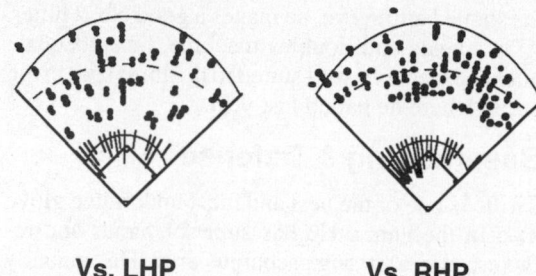

Vs. LHP   **Vs. RHP**

1999 Situational Stats

	AB	H	HR	RBI	Avg		AB	H	HR	RBI	Avg
Home	295	72	9	33	.244	LHP	171	55	4	20	.322
Road	308	89	11	50	.289	RHP	432	106	16	63	.245
First Half	311	87	9	44	.280	Sc Pos	152	40	6	63	.263
Scnd Half	292	74	11	39	.253	Clutch	86	25	2	17	.291

1999 Rankings (National League)

- 3rd in lowest on-base percentage for a leadoff hitter (.316) and lowest on-base percentage vs. righthanded pitchers (.293)
- 4th in fielding percentage in center field (.987)
- 5th in lowest batting average vs. righthanded pitchers and lowest batting average at home
- 8th in errors in center field (5) and lowest on-base percentage
- Led the Brewers in stolen bases, caught stealing (6) and stolen-base percentage (80.0)
- Led NL center fielders in GDPs (12)

Geoff Jenkins

Position: LF
Bats: L **Throws:** R
Ht: 6' 1" **Wt:** 204

Opening Day Age: 25
Born: 7/21/74 in Olympia, WA
ML Seasons: 2

1999 Season

For the first time in his pro career, Geoff Jenkins began to make good on his offensive potential, and he did it in a big way. He began the year as the Brewers' left fielder against righthanders. For the first few months of the season, he didn't see many lefthanders and didn't do much against the few he saw. But the more he was allowed to face southpaws, the better he fared, and by the end of the season he was playing every day.

Hitting

Jenkins always has had terrific bat speed, and a spring adjustment tightened his stroke even further. It's hard to get a fastball by him. He can stay back on a breaking ball or two-strike pitch and still hit it on a line. He covers the plate well and his power extends to all parts of the ballpark. Jenkins' improvement against lefties during the second half last year showed that he'll be more than a mere platoon player.

Baserunning & Defense

Jenkins runs decently and stole five bases in six attempts last year. He probably never will be much of a stolen-base threat, however. His defense was a pleasant surprise. After years of shoulder problems, his throwing improved markedly last year. He gunned down 14 baserunners, one of the top figures in the National League. His range is adequate for left field.

2000 Outlook

Last year marked a giant leap forward for Jenkins, but it was no fluke. A return to health and a mechanical adjustment at the plate was all that was needed to help him become the kind of feared hitter he'd been at the University of Southern California. The Brewers are counting on him to be one of the keys to their rebuilding effort. This year will be the first where he'll play regularly right from the start.

Overall Statistics

	G	AB	R	H	D	T	HR	RBI	SB	BB	SO	Avg	OBP	Slg
1999	135	447	70	140	43	3	21	82	5	35	87	.313	.371	.564
Career	219	709	103	200	55	4	30	110	6	55	148	.282	.341	.498

Where He Hits the Ball

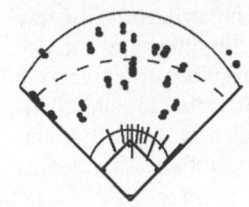

Vs. LHP

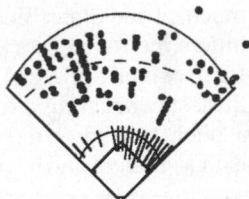

Vs. RHP

1999 Situational Stats

	AB	H	HR	RBI	Avg		AB	H	HR	RBI	Avg
Home	220	71	10	40	.323	LHP	85	22	2	15	.259
Road	227	69	11	42	.304	RHP	362	118	19	67	.326
First Half	229	70	14	43	.306	Sc Pos	124	43	5	59	.347
Scnd Half	218	70	7	39	.321	Clutch	61	17	3	14	.279

1999 Rankings (National League)

- 3rd in errors in left field (7)
- 4th in lowest percentage of pitches taken (44.2)
- 5th in doubles and lowest fielding percentage in left field (.974)
- Led the Brewers in doubles, intentional walks (7), batting average with runners in scoring position, batting average on a 3-1 count (.625) and slugging percentage vs. righthanded pitchers (.602)
- Led NL left fielders in batting average with runners in scoring position and slugging percentage vs. righthanded pitchers (.602)

Scott Karl

1999 Season

Once again, Milwaukee lefthander Scott Karl enjoyed an up-and-down year but finished with virtually the same numbers that he always does. Though he allowed more hits and struck out fewer batters than he had in the past, he logged a .500 record on a losing club and pitched fairly well over the last two months.

Pitching

Karl is the prototypical nibbler. His arsenal—a low-80s fastball, a slider and a palmball—isn't impressive, so he must work the corners to get by. He has good enough command to do that, but gives up a decent number of walks as a result. He often gets burned when he allows a pitch to catch too much of the plate. Because he strikes out so few hitters, he relies heavily on the quality of the defense behind him. Karl became more effective over the last two months after resurrecting his curveball, a pitch he hadn't thrown since college. Stamina isn't a strength and he must be kept on a short leash.

Defense & Hitting

Karl is a very good fielder and his excellent pickoff move makes him tough to run against, though he occasionally throws the ball away. He has improved markedly as a hitter and rarely gets himself out swinging at bad pitches. He notched 11 hits last year, including two doubles and a pair of homers. He's also a good bunter and laid down a team-high 12 sacrifice bunts, which ranked sixth in the National League.

2000 Outlook

The Brewers dumped Karl's $3.3 million salary in the trade that also sent Jeff Cirillo to Colorado. He should be in for a rude awakening in Coors Field.

Position: SP
Bats: L **Throws:** L
Ht: 6' 2" **Wt:** 209

Opening Day Age: 28
Born: 8/9/71 in Riverside, CA
ML Seasons: 5

Overall Statistics

	W	L	Pct.	ERA	G	GS	Sv	IP	H	BB	SO	HR	Ratio
1999	11	11	.500	4.78	33	33	0	197.2	246	69	74	21	1.59
Career	50	51	.495	4.57	155	148	0	914.2	1038	324	475	104	1.49

How Often He Throws Strikes

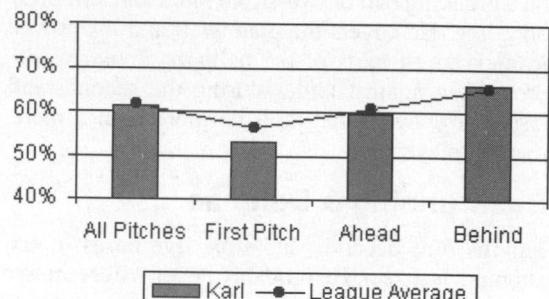

1999 Situational Stats

	W	L	ERA	Sv	IP		AB	H	HR	RBI	Avg
Home	2	7	6.16	0	92.0	LHB	130	37	2	11	.285
Road	9	4	3.58	0	105.2	RHB	659	209	19	94	.317
First Half	7	7	4.84	0	109.2	Sc Pos	210	58	5	80	.276
Scnd Half	4	4	4.70	0	88.0	Clutch	41	19	3	10	.463

1999 Rankings (National League)

- 1st in highest batting average allowed (.312), fewest strikeouts per nine innings (3.4) and highest batting average allowed vs. righthanded batters
- 2nd in lowest strikeout/walk ratio (1.1)
- 3rd in highest on-base percentage allowed (.370)
- Led the Brewers in sacrifice bunts (12), losses, games started, innings pitched, hits allowed, batters faced (885), hit batsmen (8), balks (2), pitches thrown (3,214), GDPs induced (26), lowest stolen-base percentage allowed (64.3), fewest home runs allowed per nine innings (.96), most GDPs induced per nine innings (1.2) and ERA on the road

Mark Loretta

1999 Season

For the third straight year, Mark Loretta began the season trying to wrest the Brewers' shortstop job from Jose Valentin. This time, Valentin obliged by getting injured in April. Loretta took over and performed admirably until Valentin returned at mid-season. Loretta was shifted to first base, but won back the shortstop job—possibly for good—late in the year.

Hitting

Loretta is an excellent contact hitter with few weaknesses at the plate. He sprays line drives to all fields against all types of pitching. His excellent bat control makes him one of the National League's toughest hitters to strike out. With strong wrists and a quick bat, Loretta can get wood on most two-strike pitches. Breaking balls don't bother him and he always has hit well against both lefties and righties. He batted leadoff most often in 1999 and displayed more patience in that role, posting a fine .392 on-base percentage.

Baserunning & Defense

Loretta is one of the most fundamentally sound players around. Though his range at short isn't exceptional, he has terrific hands and an accurate arm. He committed only four errors in 74 games at short last year, and just seven miscues in 130 contests there during the last two years. Loretta also is a good first baseman, with first baseman's hands and a shortstop's range. He can hold his own at second and third base as well. He isn't fast and doesn't steal many bases, but he runs intelligently.

2000 Outlook

For the first time in his career, Loretta may go into spring training with an inside track on the shortstop job. As always, Valentin's health and production may determine where and how often Loretta will play. But his chance to be the regular shortstop is better than it ever has been, and in the long run it seems all but inevitable that he'll inherit the position. When he does, he'll be one of the most quietly efficient shortstops in the game.

Position: SS/1B/2B/3B
Bats: R **Throws:** R
Ht: 6' 0" **Wt:** 180

Opening Day Age: 28
Born: 8/14/71 in Santa Monica, CA
ML Seasons: 5

Overall Statistics

	G	AB	R	H	D	T	HR	RBI	SB	BB	SO	Avg	OBP	Slg
1999	153	587	93	170	34	5	5	67	4	52	59	.290	.354	.390
Career	517	1643	237	483	86	10	18	184	21	159	188	.294	.359	.391

Where He Hits the Ball

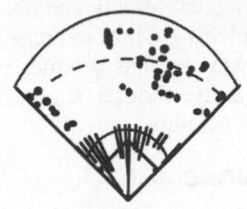

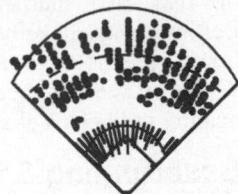

Vs. LHP **Vs. RHP**

1999 Situational Stats

	AB	H	HR	RBI	Avg		AB	H	HR	RBI	Avg
Home	278	89	2	31	.320	LHP	160	48	0	17	.300
Road	309	81	3	36	.262	RHP	427	122	5	50	.286
First Half	322	95	3	44	.295	Sc Pos	141	42	0	56	.298
Scnd Half	265	75	2	23	.283	Clutch	88	24	1	12	.273

1999 Rankings (National League)

- 2nd in on-base percentage for a leadoff hitter (.392)
- 5th in lowest HR frequency (117.4 ABs per HR)
- 8th in singles and lowest slugging percentage
- Led the Brewers in triples, batting average with the bases loaded (.462), on-base percentage for a leadoff hitter (.392) and bunts in play (15)
- Led NL shortstops in on-base percentage for a leadoff hitter (.392)

Milwaukee

Dave Nilsson

1999 Season

After spending three years at first base and in the outfield, Dave Nilsson moved back behind the plate and had the best year of his career. Many doubted the brittle Australian would be able to hold up under the strain of catching, but he surprised them all. Nilsson caught every day, hit as well as ever and made the All-Star team before a broken thumb ended his season in August.

Hitting

Nilsson is a line-drive hitter who drives the ball hard to all fields. He doesn't loft the ball enough to be a true home-run hitter, but he produces many long drives into the gaps. He makes good contact for someone who's able to put such a charge into the ball. He's murder on pitches down and in. Lefties always have been able to get him to chase breaking balls down and away. He has produced whenever he has been healthy, though staying healthy has been a challenge for him.

Baserunning & Defense

Nilsson has a slow release and a scattershot arm, and opposing baserunners took full advantage of it last year. His mechanics behind the plate are acceptable. He can fill in at first base but is stretched to cover left or right field. On the bases, he's strictly a station-to-station man.

2000 Outlook

A free agent, Nilsson has discussed taking the 2000 season off to play in the Olympics being held in his native Australia. The only certainty seems to be that he won't be back with Milwaukee. Having proven he still can get by behind the plate, he should be a sought-after commodity. Even as a first baseman or DH, his skills would be helpful for many clubs. In a more favorable home-run park, he could come through with a surprising number of longballs. Henry Blanco, acquired in a four-team trade in December, will be Milwaukee's regular catcher in 2000.

Position: C
Bats: L **Throws:** R
Ht: 6' 3" **Wt:** 229

Opening Day Age: 30
Born: 12/14/69 in Brisbane, Australia
ML Seasons: 8
Pronunciation: NILL-son
Nickname: Thunder

Overall Statistics

	G	AB	R	H	D	T	HR	RBI	SB	BB	SO	Avg	OBP	Slg
1999	115	343	56	106	19	1	21	62	1	53	64	.309	.400	.554
Career	837	2779	389	789	157	10	105	470	15	320	424	.284	.356	.461

Where He Hits the Ball

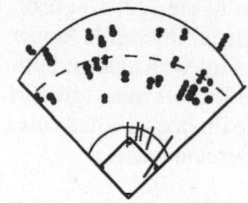 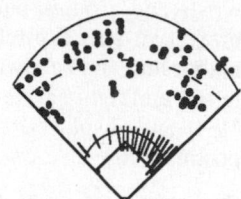

Vs. LHP   **Vs. RHP**

1999 Situational Stats

	AB	H	HR	RBI	Avg		AB	H	HR	RBI	Avg
Home	157	43	9	25	.274	LHP	91	23	5	15	.253
Road	186	63	12	37	.339	RHP	252	83	16	47	.329
First Half	251	78	19	52	.311	Sc Pos	97	31	4	41	.320
Scnd Half	92	28	2	10	.304	Clutch	55	18	4	11	.327

1999 Rankings (National League)

- 2nd in lowest percentage of runners caught stealing as a catcher (15.4)
- 5th in batting average with two strikes (.272)
- Led the Brewers in batting average on an 0-2 count (.250) and batting average with two strikes (.272)
- Led NL catchers in batting average in the clutch, batting average with two strikes (.272) and walks

Hideo Nomo

1999 Season

After being virtually left for dead last spring, Hideo Nomo resurrected his career in Milwaukee. He had elbow surgery during the offseason, then was hit hard during spring training and was released by the Mets a week before the season began. Nomo signed a deal with the Cubs that called for his promotion or release after three minor league starts, and Chicago opted to release him. A tryout with the Indians brought little interest. Finally, the Brewers came through with a one-year deal. Nomo accepted it, made one Double-A start and was promoted in May. Against all odds, he got off to a hot start and remained one of Milwaukee's most effective starters for the rest of the year.

Pitching

Nomo still makes his living by getting batters to confuse his heavy forkball with a high fastball. This approach began to fail after his velocity dropped off in 1998, but his fastball returned to the 90-MPH range last year and that was good enough. His command, which often deserted him in 1998, came back last year as well. He gives up a ton of flyballs, mostly on high fastballs. Nomo began to wear down late in the year after a run of taxing outings, and it has been a while since he has had the stamina to consistently work late into games.

Defense & Hitting

Nomo's long, twisting delivery leaves him especially vulnerable to the running game. He gave up 41 stolen bases last year, the second-highest total in the majors. He doesn't field many balls, but he's reliable. Generally a below-average hitter, Nomo had a good year at the plate, batting .214.

2000 Outlook

The Brewers offered Nomo a two-year, $8.5 million contract that could have escalated to $14.5 million over three seasons, but he turned it down. They released him and he was claimed on waivers by the Phillies, but he opted for free agency. He seems to be over his physical problems and should remain effective wherever he lands.

Position: SP
Bats: R **Throws:** R
Ht: 6' 2" **Wt:** 220

Opening Day Age: 31
Born: 8/31/68 in Osaka, Japan
ML Seasons: 5
Pronunciation: hih-DAY-oh NO-mo

Overall Statistics

	W	L	Pct.	ERA	G	GS	Sv	IP	H	BB	SO	HR	Ratio
1999	12	8	.600	4.54	28	28	0	176.1	173	78	161	27	1.42
Career	61	49	.555	3.82	151	150	0	960.2	800	427	1031	106	1.28

How Often He Throws Strikes

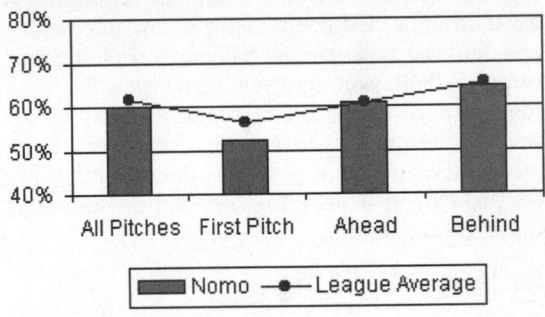

1999 Situational Stats

	W	L	ERA	Sv	IP		AB	H	HR	RBI	Avg
Home	5	6	4.20	0	90.0	LHB	319	89	11	40	.279
Road	7	2	4.90	0	86.1	RHB	357	84	16	49	.235
First Half	7	2	3.95	0	82.0	Sc Pos	179	38	8	62	.212
Scnd Half	5	6	5.06	0	94.1	Clutch	45	14	2	5	.311

1999 Rankings (National League)

- 2nd in stolen bases allowed (41) and lowest groundball/flyball ratio allowed (0.8)
- Led the Brewers in wins, home runs allowed, walks allowed, strikeouts, wild pitches (10), stolen bases allowed (41), runners caught stealing (9), winning percentage, lowest batting average allowed (.256), lowest slugging percentage allowed (.441), most run support per nine innings (6.3), most strikeouts per nine innings (8.2), ERA at home, lowest batting average allowed vs. righthanded batters and lowest batting average allowed with runners in scoring position

Milwaukee

Kyle Peterson

1999 Season

As Milwaukee's starting rotation struggled during the first half of the season, the club resisted the urge to promote 1997 first-round pick Kyle Peterson from Triple-A. But by the middle of July they could wait no longer. He pitched decently at first, though a lack of run support ruined his won-lost record. A September slump and concerns about his workload landed him in the bullpen late in the year. Peterson had a quietly impressive year, posting a 4.24 ERA as a starter, the best figure on the club.

Pitching

Peterson isn't overpowering but knows how to pitch. He throws both two-seam and four-seam fastballs as well as a slider, and his out pitch is a good straight changeup. Using a low-three-quarters delivery, he keeps the ball down, yielding tons of groundballs and very few home runs. He has a long, clunky delivery that includes an odd hesitation in mid-motion. Scouts say it may lead to an arm injury, but he has been very durable thus far in his pro career. If anything, the odd motion helps throw off the hitters.

Defense & Hitting

Peterson's unique delivery makes him very easy to run on. He surrendered 11 steals in 13 attempts last year. He's athletic for a man his size and gets off the mound fairly well, but he hasn't thrown well to the bases so far. As a hitter, he has had little pro experience and it shows.

2000 Outlook

The Brewers aren't expecting the world from Peterson, but he may surprise. He was able to adjust quickly to the demands of major league pitching last year, succeeding more than his numbers might suggest. Peterson is quite intelligent and can be counted on to make the necessary adjustments as he continues to develop. He'll start the year in the rotation and should be one of the Brewers' better starters.

Position: SP
Bats: L **Throws:** R
Ht: 6' 3" **Wt:** 215

Opening Day Age: 23
Born: 4/9/76 in Elkhorn, NE
ML Seasons: 1

Overall Statistics

	W	L	Pct.	ERA	G	GS	Sv	IP	H	BB	SO	HR	Ratio
1999	4	7	.364	4.56	17	12	0	77.0	87	25	34	3	1.45
Career	4	7	.364	4.56	17	12	0	77.0	87	25	34	3	1.45

How Often He Throws Strikes

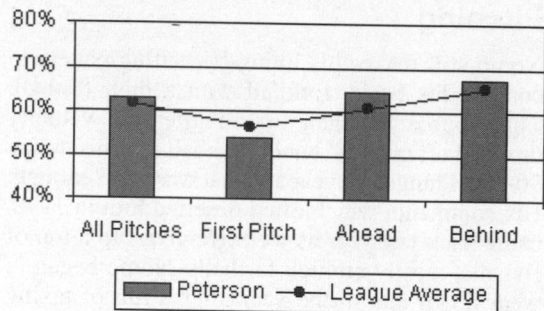

1999 Situational Stats

	W	L	ERA	Sv	IP		AB	H	HR	RBI	Avg
Home	3	3	5.17	0	47.0	LHB	136	41	2	16	.301
Road	1	4	3.60	0	30.0	RHB	169	46	1	22	.272
First Half	0	0	-	0	0.0	Sc Pos	82	25	1	33	.305
Scnd Half	4	7	4.56	0	77.0	Clutch	30	7	0	5	.233

1999 Rankings (National League)

- Did not rank near the top or bottom in any category

Bob Wickman

1999 Season

In his first full season as Milwaukee's closer, Bob Wickman performed capably, erasing any doubts raised by his second-half swoon the year before. The Brewers gave him virtually every save opportunity that was available, and he converted a respectable percentage, finishing with 37 saves in 45 tries.

Pitching

Wickman's stuff is nothing like that of a typical closer, as he relies on movement rather than velocity. He lost the tip of his right index finger in a childhood accident, and as a result his pitches have tremendous life. His sinking two-seam fastball and slider produce tons of groundballs. He isn't that tough to hit, but it's difficult to get good loft on his pitches and he seldom gives up the longball. He keeps the ball down so well and his pitches move so much that he gives up a high number of walks. All in all, he may put a couple of people on base, but he usually manages to close things out without giving up a back-breaking hit. His resilient arm responds well to work on consecutive days.

Defense & Hitting

Wickman always has been easy to run on, permitting 50 steals in 57 attempts during the last five years. Normally a fine fielder, he had an uncharacteristically poor year with the glove, committing four errors. Though he's stocky, he has good reflexes and is mobile enough to cover first when necessary. He got his second professional at-bat last year and still is looking for his first hit.

2000 Outlook

In the middle of a multiyear deal, Wickman has a firm grip on the closer's job in Milwaukee. He's one of the most reliable pitchers in baseball, at least from a health standpoint. He never has been on the disabled list in his pro career, something few closers can boast.

Position: RP
Bats: R **Throws:** R
Ht: 6' 1" **Wt:** 227

Opening Day Age: 31
Born: 2/6/69 in Green Bay, WI
ML Seasons: 8

Overall Statistics

	W	L	Pct.	ERA	G	GS	Sv	IP	H	BB	SO	HR	Ratio
1999	3	8	.273	3.39	71	0	37	74.1	75	38	60	6	1.52
Career	50	37	.575	3.83	452	28	74	688.1	687	311	482	53	1.45

How Often He Throws Strikes

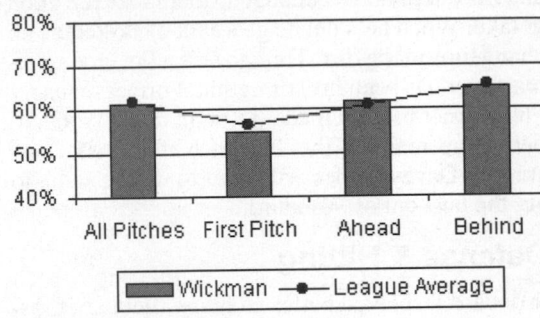

1999 Situational Stats

	W	L	ERA	Sv	IP		AB	H	HR	RBI	Avg
Home	1	2	3.68	15	29.1	LHB	127	25	2	13	.197
Road	2	6	3.20	22	45.0	RHB	159	50	4	19	.314
First Half	2	4	3.10	18	40.2	Sc Pos	82	19	1	25	.232
Scnd Half	1	4	3.74	19	33.2	Clutch	200	52	5	27	.260

1999 Rankings (National League)

- 1st in relief losses (8)
- 2nd in games finished (63)
- 3rd in save opportunities (45)
- 5th in saves and blown saves (8)
- 6th in errors at pitcher (4)
- 8th in save percentage (82.2)
- Led the Brewers in games pitched, saves, games finished (63), save opportunities (45), save percentage (82.2), blown saves (8), first batter efficiency (.230), relief ERA (3.39) and relief losses (8)

Steve Woodard

1999 Season

Steve Woodard came to camp in excellent shape last year and was in the midst of a fine season when he cracked a bone in his left wrist during a home-plate collision in late July. He continued to pitch with the injury but soon was forced onto the disabled list. Woodard returned in September, sooner than expected, but pitched poorly over the final month of the season. He ended up with a respectable record, but it could have been much better. He didn't win a single game after the wrist injury.

Pitching

Woodard's control is among the best in the game. He works the corners with a fastball and curveball, and his out pitch is a changeup that looks too good to take. When he's on, he gets a lot of strikeouts on changeups in the dirt. Though he's a big guy, stamina never has been his strong suit. Former manager Phil Garner usually made it a point to lift Woodard before he reached the 100-pitch mark, and new skipper Davey Lopes will need to do the same to get the best out of Woodard.

Defense & Hitting

Woodard displayed better mobility afield after losing a considerable amount of weight over the winter. He holds runners close with a decent pickoff move, but is somewhat slow to the plate and most runners can get a good jump against him. Woodard remains a weak hitter, though he has learned to bunt and to wait out a walk against a wild pitcher.

2000 Outlook

The slimmed-down Woodard was on target for the best year of his career before hurting his wrist, and he ought to resume his winning ways this year. He has the ability to take a big step forward and possibly win 15-18 games. With the departure of Hideo Nomo, the Brewers are counting on Woodard as their No. 1 starter.

Position: SP
Bats: L **Throws:** R
Ht: 6' 4" **Wt:** 217

Opening Day Age: 24
Born: 5/15/75 in Hartselle, AL
ML Seasons: 3

Overall Statistics

	W	L	Pct.	ERA	G	GS	Sv	IP	H	BB	SO	HR	Ratio
1999	11	8	.579	4.52	31	29	0	185.0	219	36	119	23	1.38
Career	24	23	.511	4.44	72	62	0	387.1	428	75	286	47	1.30

How Often He Throws Strikes

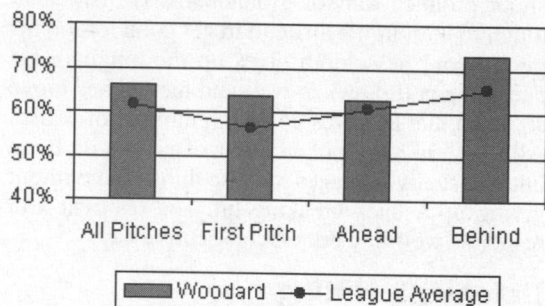

Legend: Woodard — League Average

1999 Situational Stats

	W	L	ERA	Sv	IP		AB	H	HR	RBI	Avg
Home	5	5	4.40	0	90.0	LHB	330	92	9	39	.279
Road	6	3	4.64	0	95.0	RHB	416	127	14	53	.305
First Half	10	5	4.37	0	123.2	Sc Pos	172	55	4	65	.320
Scnd Half	1	3	4.84	0	61.1	Clutch	34	12	0	2	.353

1999 Rankings (National League)

- 1st in highest stolen-base percentage allowed (88.2)
- 2nd in fewest pitches thrown per batter (3.24)
- 3rd in highest batting average allowed with runners in scoring position
- Led the Brewers in ERA, complete games (2), highest strikeout/walk ratio (3.3), lowest on-base percentage allowed (.330), highest ground-ball/flyball ratio allowed (1.3), fewest pitches thrown per batter (3.24), fewest baserunners allowed per nine innings (12.7), least walks per nine innings (1.8), most GDPs induced per GDP situation (14.4%) and lowest batting average allowed vs. lefthanded batters

Brian Banks

Position: 1B/C
Bats: B **Throws:** R
Ht: 6' 3" **Wt:** 208

Opening Day Age: 29
Born: 9/28/70 in Mesa, AZ
ML Seasons: 4

Overall Statistics

	G	AB	R	H	D	T	HR	RBI	SB	BB	SO	Avg	OBP	Slg
1999	105	219	34	53	7	1	5	22	6	25	59	.242	.317	.352
Career	161	318	48	78	12	1	8	37	6	36	85	.245	.319	.365

1999 Situational Stats

	AB	H	HR	RBI	Avg		AB	H	HR	RBI	Avg
Home	117	25	4	11	.214	LHP	54	12	1	5	.222
Road	102	28	1	11	.275	RHP	165	41	4	17	.248
First Half	115	31	3	9	.270	Sc Pos	58	12	1	16	.207
Scnd Half	104	22	2	13	.212	Clutch	56	14	1	4	.250

1999 Season

Brian Banks' versatility enabled him to spend the entire 1999 season on the Brewers' major league roster. As a switch-hitter with the ability to catch and play first base and the outfield, he proved to be fairly useful.

Hitting, Baserunning & Defense

Banks is a decent hitter with a little pop. He has shown more power from the right side in the minors but hasn't yet shown much of a platoon differential in the majors. Banks sometimes has trouble making contact and is especially vulnerable with two strikes. He's rough behind the plate and basestealers took full advantage of his inexperience last year, swiping 27 bases in 28 attempts. He has enough mobility to get by at either corner outfield spot and didn't embarrass himself at first base. His speed is average.

2000 Outlook

Banks may need to improve his work behind the plate in order to retain his spot on Milwaukee's bench. If the Brewers can't use him as a catcher, there isn't much that sets him apart from other reserve candidates.

Sean Berry

Position: 1B
Bats: R **Throws:** R
Ht: 5'11" **Wt:** 200

Opening Day Age: 34
Born: 3/22/66 in Santa Monica, CA
ML Seasons: 10

Overall Statistics

	G	AB	R	H	D	T	HR	RBI	SB	BB	SO	Avg	OBP	Slg
1999	106	259	26	59	11	1	2	23	0	17	50	.228	.281	.301
Career	827	2363	309	650	151	10	80	367	47	202	423	.275	.337	.449

1999 Situational Stats

	AB	H	HR	RBI	Avg		AB	H	HR	RBI	Avg
Home	118	27	0	6	.229	LHP	80	14	0	7	.175
Road	141	32	2	17	.227	RHP	179	45	2	16	.251
First Half	201	48	2	20	.239	Sc Pos	78	15	1	22	.192
Scnd Half	58	11	0	3	.190	Clutch	48	14	0	4	.292

1999 Season

Franklin Stubbs is finally off the hook. Sean Berry officially has replaced him as the Brewers' most disastrous free-agent signing ever. Signed to a two-year, $3.6 million contract, Berry was expected to play first base and provide some offensive punch. Instead, he was a complete washout and was buried on the bench after June.

Hitting, Baserunning & Defense

Berry, who has battled shoulder problems for several years, seemed to have lost all the power from his swing last year. He also was overly tentative and watched many hittable pitches go by. He never had been a burner, and hamstring problems reduced him to half-speed for much of the year. After spending his entire career at third base, Berry struggled with the transition across the diamond. He can catch the ball but must work on learning the position.

2000 Outlook

Always prone to early-season slumps, Berry might have found his groove if the Brewers had shown more patience. But the way he was hitting gave little reason for optimism. Rookie Kevin Barker will be given the first-base job, and the best Berry can hope for is a platoon role.

Milwaukee

Cal Eldred

Position: SP
Bats: R **Throws:** R
Ht: 6' 4" **Wt:** 237

Opening Day Age: 32
Born: 11/24/67 in
Cedar Rapids, IA
ML Seasons: 9

Overall Statistics

	W	L	Pct.	ERA	G	GS	Sv	IP	H	BB	SO	HR	Ratio
1999	2	8	.200	7.79	20	15	0	82.0	101	46	60	19	1.79
Career	64	65	.496	4.51	174	169	0	1078.2	1057	448	686	137	1.40

1999 Situational Stats

	W	L	ERA	Sv	IP		AB	H	HR	RBI	Avg
Home	0	6	12.44	0	29.2	LHB	157	56	5	31	.357
Road	2	2	5.16	0	52.1	RHB	183	45	14	35	.246
First Half	1	5	8.29	0	51.0	Sc Pos	100	28	2	41	.280
Scnd Half	1	3	6.97	0	31.0	Clutch	0	0	0	0	-

1999 Season

Cal Eldred missed the first few weeks of the 1999 season with the elbow problem that had shut him down the year before. When he finally did return, his command was sorely lacking. He lost his spot in the rotation in June and later missed a month with a recurrence of elbow troubles.

Pitching, Defense & Hitting

Eldred throws a straight four-seam fastball, an overhand curve and a changeup. His arm problems have affected his command more than his velocity, and he doesn't have the stuff to get by with laying one over the plate once he falls behind. When he can't get his curve over, he has little to fall back on. Many of his high fastballs end up in the seats. He's a poor hitter but a good athlete and a fine fielder. He has an acceptable pickoff move but remains vulnerable to the running game because of his high leg kick.

2000 Outlook

With each successive season, Eldred's multimillion dollar contract looks like more of a disaster for the Brewers. He has been unable to stay healthy, and when he has pitched he hasn't shown much. Milwaukee acquired starters Juan Acevedo, Jimmy Haynes and Jamey Wright during the offseason, so Eldred probably won't make the rotation.

Bobby Hughes

Position: C
Bats: R **Throws:** R
Ht: 6' 4" **Wt:** 229

Opening Day Age: 28
Born: 4/10/71 in
Burbank, CA
ML Seasons: 2

Overall Statistics

	G	AB	R	H	D	T	HR	RBI	SB	BB	SO	Avg	OBP	Slg
1999	48	101	10	26	2	0	3	8	0	5	28	.257	.292	.366
Career	133	319	38	76	9	2	12	37	1	21	82	.238	.287	.392

1999 Situational Stats

	AB	H	HR	RBI	Avg		AB	H	HR	RBI	Avg
Home	53	14	0	1	.264	LHP	49	11	2	6	.224
Road	48	12	3	7	.250	RHP	52	15	1	2	.288
First Half	87	23	3	8	.264	Sc Pos	23	4	0	5	.174
Scnd Half	14	3	0	0	.214	Clutch	15	4	0	0	.267

1999 Season

After sharing the Brewers' catching chores during his rookie season of 1998, Bobby Hughes took a big step backward last year. With Dave Nilsson returning behind the plate, Hughes was relegated to backup duty. Elbow problems hampered him all year and ultimately ended his season in August.

Hitting, Baserunning & Defense

Hughes is an aggressive hitter with decent pop. He can put a charge into the ball but has a major problem making consistent contact. On the bases, he's as slow as they come and is no threat to run any farther than he has to. His best defensive tool is his strong throwing arm, but elbow inflammation negated it last year. His receiving skills are just adequate and his pitch calling isn't a strength.

2000 Outlook

Hughes probably will back up Henry Blanco in 2000. It says a lot about the Brewers' opinion of Hughes that they saw no solutions to the catching problem within the organization.

Alex Ochoa

Position: LF/RF
Bats: R **Throws:** R
Ht: 6' 0" **Wt:** 195

Opening Day Age: 28
Born: 3/29/72 in Miami Lakes, FL
ML Seasons: 5
Pronunciation: oh-CHO-uh

Overall Statistics

	G	AB	R	H	D	T	HR	RBI	SB	BB	SO	Avg	OBP	Slg
1999	119	277	47	83	16	3	8	40	6	45	43	.300	.404	.466
Career	419	1083	157	299	64	9	17	120	20	92	150	.276	.336	.399

1999 Situational Stats

	AB	H	HR	RBI	Avg		AB	H	HR	RBI	Avg
Home	148	44	8	21	.297	LHP	138	44	5	25	.319
Road	129	39	0	19	.302	RHP	139	39	3	15	.281
First Half	108	37	3	17	.343	Sc Pos	74	24	2	34	.324
Scnd Half	169	46	5	23	.272	Clutch	53	15	1	7	.283

1999 Season

The ultimate illustration of how far Alex Ochoa's star had fallen was the offseason deal in which the Twins shipped him to the Brewers for a player to be named later. With Milwaukee, a bulked-up Ochoa gradually re-established himself. He began the year as the Brewers' left fielder against lefthanders, and took over as the regular right fielder while Jeromy Burnitz was out for a month.

Hitting, Baserunning & Defense

Not only did Ochoa begin to drive the ball in the air more often, but he also became a markedly more patient hitter. His 45 walks nearly equaled his previous career total. It remains to be seen whether his improvement against righthanders was a fluke. Ochoa is fast but doesn't have the technique to steal many bases. He's a strong defender at all three outfield positions, and his arm is among the game's strongest.

2000 Outlook

Ochoa has put himself in position to land a full-time job should any of the Brewers' three outfield positions open up. At the very least, he'll begin the year as their fourth outfielder.

Eric Plunk

Position: RP
Bats: R **Throws:** R
Ht: 6' 6" **Wt:** 220

Opening Day Age: 36
Born: 9/3/63 in Wilmington, CA
ML Seasons: 14

Overall Statistics

	W	L	Pct.	ERA	G	GS	Sv	IP	H	BB	SO	HR	Ratio
1999	4	4	.500	5.02	68	0	0	75.1	71	43	63	15	1.51
Career	72	58	.554	3.82	714	41	35	1151.0	1009	647	1081	122	1.44

1999 Situational Stats

	W	L	ERA	Sv	IP		AB	H	HR	RBI	Avg
Home	3	2	5.45	0	39.2	LHB	91	24	4	15	.264
Road	1	2	4.54	0	35.2	RHB	192	47	11	32	.245
First Half	0	1	3.14	0	43.0	Sc Pos	95	18	1	29	.189
Scnd Half	4	3	7.52	0	32.1	Clutch	121	22	3	16	.182

1999 Season

Eric Plunk was having a decent year as a middle reliever and setup man before completely melting down late in the season. His ERA was a lofty 7.52 in 32.1 innings after the All-Star break.

Pitching, Defense & Hitting

Once a very hard thrower, Plunk still cracks 90 MPH but has come to rely more heavily on his wide-breaking slider. He works up in the strike zone and is vulnerable to the longball. His durability and ability to work two innings at a time are pluses, but his inability to work on consecutive days somewhat limits his use. As a fielder, Plunk has limited mobility and hasn't recorded a putout in two years. His high leg kick makes him very easy to run on. He has fanned in both of his big league at-bats.

2000 Outlook

The Brewers decided not to pick up Plunk's $1.8 million option for 2000, and his late-season troubles may make it difficult for him to find work elsewhere. If he does manage to catch on with another club, expect him to put up similar numbers.

Bill Pulsipher

Position: SP
Bats: L **Throws:** L
Ht: 6' 3" **Wt:** 200

Opening Day Age: 26
Born: 10/9/73 in Fort Benning, GA
ML Seasons: 3
Pronunciation: PUL-sih-fir
Nickname: Pulse

Overall Statistics

	W	L	Pct.	ERA	G	GS	Sv	IP	H	BB	SO	HR	Ratio
1999	5	6	.455	5.98	19	16	0	87.1	100	36	42	19	1.56
Career	13	17	.433	4.87	62	44	0	286.1	308	112	174	38	1.47

1999 Situational Stats

	W	L	ERA	Sv	IP		AB	H	HR	RBI	Avg
Home	2	3	6.20	0	45.0	LHB	76	25	5	15	.329
Road	3	3	5.74	0	42.1	RHB	273	75	14	40	.275
First Half	2	1	5.14	0	14.0	Sc Pos	83	21	3	34	.253
Scnd Half	3	5	6.14	0	73.1	Clutch	6	2	0	0	.333

1999 Season

Bill Pulsipher endured another lost year. Hoping to get his career on track after coming back from reconstructive elbow surgery the previous season, Pulsipher missed most of the first half of 1999 with lower-back problems. He rejoined Milwaukee's rotation in the second half but pitched woefully.

Pitching, Defense & Hitting

Pulsipher's approach is predictable. He works 90-MPH two-seam fastballs and sliders in on righthanders' fists. He must throw his fastball for strikes to get batters to chase his slider, but he gets beat too often on first-pitch fastballs. He needs to develop a reliable offspeed pitch. Pulsipher repeatedly had trouble getting out of the first inning last year. He has yet to commit his first major league error, though he's prone to occasional mental lapses in the field. He has a decent move to first but hasn't shown much at the plate.

2000 Outlook

Pulsipher's second-half troubles were especially worrisome because health problems no longer provided him an excuse. With a new regime taking over in Milwaukee, he may need to show something soon in order to remain in the club's plans.

Jose Valentin

Position: SS
Bats: B **Throws:** R
Ht: 5'10" **Wt:** 173

Opening Day Age: 30
Born: 10/12/69 in Manati, Puerto Rico
ML Seasons: 8
Pronunciation: VAL-en-teen

Overall Statistics

	G	AB	R	H	D	T	HR	RBI	SB	BB	SO	Avg	OBP	Slg
1999	89	256	45	58	9	5	10	38	3	48	52	.227	.347	.418
Career	762	2409	378	577	132	18	90	343	78	298	585	.240	.323	.421

1999 Situational Stats

	AB	H	HR	RBI	Avg		AB	H	HR	RBI	Avg
Home	119	26	3	16	.218	LHP	75	19	1	11	.253
Road	137	32	7	22	.234	RHP	181	39	9	27	.215
First Half	87	25	5	12	.287	Sc Pos	50	13	3	26	.260
Scnd Half	169	33	5	26	.195	Clutch	52	11	2	11	.212

1999 Season

Coming off his worst season since becoming a regular, Jose Valentin went through an even more trying year in 1999. He tore a thumb ligament in April, costing him two months before a second-half batting and fielding slump landed him on the bench.

Hitting, Baserunning & Defense

A switch-hitter, Valentin has been notoriously poor from the right side. He has begun to make better contact as a righty, but still doesn't display any of the considerable power he flashes from the left side. He takes a power hitter's approach, taking a lot of pitches, swinging and missing a lot, and hitting a lot of balls in the air. Valentin is Milwaukee's best baserunner, with good speed and even better acceleration and instincts. At shortstop, he can be both thrilling and frustrating. While he has terrific range and a gun for an arm, he still makes far too many bobbles and errant throws.

2000 Outlook

It remains to be seen how Valentin will be utilized by new manager Davey Lopes. The possibility of a conversion to center field even has been discussed. The Brewers renegotiated his contract, saving themselves nearly $2 million.

Fernando Vina

Position: 2B
Bats: L **Throws:** R
Ht: 5' 9" **Wt:** 170

Opening Day Age: 30
Born: 4/16/69 in Sacramento, CA
ML Seasons: 7
Pronunciation: VEEN-yah

Overall Statistics

	G	AB	R	H	D	T	HR	RBI	SB	BB	SO	Avg	OBP	Slg
1999	37	154	17	41	7	0	1	16	5	14	6	.266	.339	.331
Career	631	2126	320	600	92	26	22	172	66	156	152	.282	.350	.381

1999 Situational Stats

	AB	H	HR	RBI	Avg		AB	H	HR	RBI	Avg
Home	74	17	0	8	.230	LHP	44	15	0	6	.341
Road	80	24	1	8	.300	RHP	110	26	1	10	.236
First Half	154	41	1	16	.266	Sc Pos	31	9	0	14	.290
Scnd Half	0	0	0	0	-	Clutch	24	7	1	4	.292

1999 Season

It was a lost season for Fernando Vina. In early May, he collided with right fielder Jeromy Burnitz while chasing a pop fly and suffered a bruise above his left knee. The injury didn't seem serious at the time, but it ultimately sidelined Vina for virtually the remainder of the year.

Hitting, Baserunning & Defense

Vina is an excellent contact hitter who tries to get on top of the ball and pull it into right field. Lefthanders don't bother him a bit, and he has worked on improving his patience at the plate. Though he has decent speed, he's overaggressive and is thrown out as often as anyone in the game. At second base, he's a Gold Glove candidate and the best pivot man in the majors. He has terrific range and a good arm.

2000 Outlook

A strong showing by Ron Belliard prompted Milwaukee to trade Fernando Vina to St. Louis in December for Juan Acevedo and two minor leaguers to be named. Vina will start for the Cardinals, while Acevedo could make the Brewers rotation.

Dave Weathers

Position: RP
Bats: R **Throws:** R
Ht: 6' 3" **Wt:** 231

Opening Day Age: 30
Born: 9/25/69 in Lawrenceburg, TN
ML Seasons: 9

Overall Statistics

	W	L	Pct.	ERA	G	GS	Sv	IP	H	BB	SO	HR	Ratio
1999	7	4	.636	4.65	63	0	2	93.0	102	38	74	14	1.51
Career	31	36	.463	5.37	251	67	2	606.1	725	279	421	57	1.66

1999 Situational Stats

	W	L	ERA	Sv	IP		AB	H	HR	RBI	Avg
Home	2	2	5.81	0	48.0	LHB	124	36	7	21	.290
Road	5	2	3.40	2	45.0	RHB	242	66	7	32	.273
First Half	6	3	4.09	2	55.0	Sc Pos	99	29	2	36	.293
Scnd Half	1	1	5.45	0	38.0	Clutch	141	39	7	22	.277

1999 Season

After pitching for five major league teams, David Weathers finally found his niche in 1998 as a long man out of the Milwaukee bullpen. He continued in that role last year and remained effective, often coming in after a starter was knocked out early and contributing several decent innings. Though he hit the wall in the season's final months, Weathers was one of the Brewers' more useful relievers.

Pitching, Defense & Hitting

Weathers is a fastball-slider pitcher who's tough on righthanders but needs to come up with an out pitch for lefties. He throws a four-seam fastball and a sinking two-seamer. His slow delivery makes him easy to run on. Though he's big, he's a decent fielder with fair mobility. At the plate, he swings hard and strikes out most of the time.

2000 Outlook

Weathers is a useful man to have on a staff, as long as he isn't asked to fill a critical role. He became a free agent before re-signing with Milwaukee for a two-year deal worth $1.85 million.

Milwaukee

Other Milwaukee Brewers

Jim Abbott (Pos: LHP, Age: 32)

	W	L	Pct.	ERA	G	GS	Sv	IP	H	BB	SO	HR	Ratio
1999	2	8	.200	6.91	20	15	0	82.0	110	42	37	14	1.85
Career	87	108	.446	4.25	263	254	0	1674.0	1779	620	888	154	1.43

It may be the end of the line for Abbott, who was released by the Brewers on July 22. He has been an inspirational athlete to so many of us. 2000 Outlook: D

Jason Bere (Pos: RHP, Age: 28)

	W	L	Pct.	ERA	G	GS	Sv	IP	H	BB	SO	HR	Ratio
1999	5	0	1.000	6.08	17	14	0	66.2	79	50	47	9	1.94
Career	47	34	.580	5.23	130	122	0	661.1	641	430	537	83	1.62

A promising kid who could throw high fastballs by everyone before elbow troubles in 1996, Bere is trying to make the transition to finesse pitcher. The Reds cut him in August and Milwaukee picked him up, then re-signed him in November for $800,000. 2000 Outlook: C

Robinson Cancel (Pos: C, Age: 23, Bats: R)

	G	AB	R	H	D	T	HR	RBI	SB	BB	SO	Avg	OBP	Slg
1999	15	44	5	8	2	0	0	5	0	2	12	.182	.234	.227
Career	15	44	5	8	2	0	0	5	0	2	12	.182	.234	.227

Cancel turned red-hot after a promotion from Double-A to Triple-A, batting .368-5-28 in 117 at-bats. That earned him a first taste of the majors in September. 2000 Outlook: C

Lou Collier (Pos: SS, Age: 26, Bats: R)

	G	AB	R	H	D	T	HR	RBI	SB	BB	SO	Avg	OBP	Slg
1999	74	135	18	35	9	0	2	21	3	14	32	.259	.325	.370
Career	202	506	51	122	22	6	4	58	6	46	113	.241	.308	.332

Collier bounced between the majors and Triple-A, where he batted .385 with a .472 OBP in 27 games. He didn't fare as well with the Brewers, but played several positions in a utility role. 2000 Outlook: B

Rocky Coppinger (Pos: RHP, Age: 26)

	W	L	Pct.	ERA	G	GS	Sv	IP	H	BB	SO	HR	Ratio
1999	5	4	.556	5.40	40	2	0	58.1	60	42	56	13	1.75
Career	16	11	.593	5.34	74	29	0	219.0	223	125	195	43	1.59

Coppinger was traded by Baltimore to the Brewers in July after a disagreement about a demotion to Triple-A. Once the Orioles' top prospect, he may be useful as a reliever. 2000 Outlook: B

Jeff D'Amico (Pos: RHP, Age: 24)

	W	L	Pct.	ERA	G	GS	Sv	IP	H	BB	SO	HR	Ratio
1999	0	0	-	0.00	1	0	0	1.0	1	0	1	0	1.00
Career	15	13	.536	4.97	41	40	0	222.2	228	74	148	46	1.36

D'Amico, a former first-round pick, has seen his career dramatically compromised by shoulder surgery. He returned to pitch one inning in October, but the real test begins in March. 2000 Outlook: C

Carl Dale (Pos: RHP, Age: 27)

	W	L	Pct.	ERA	G	GS	Sv	IP	H	BB	SO	HR	Ratio
1999	0	1	.000	20.25	4	0	0	4.0	8	6	4	2	3.50
Career	0	1	.000	20.25	4	0	0	4.0	8	6	4	2	3.50

In August, the Brewers acquired Dale from Oakland for Rich Becker. Dale was pitching respectably in Triple-A at the time, but he wasn't as good after switching organizations. 2000 Outlook: C

Valerio de los Santos (Pos: LHP, Age: 24)

	W	L	Pct.	ERA	G	GS	Sv	IP	H	BB	SO	HR	Ratio
1999	0	1	.000	6.48	7	0	0	8.1	12	7	5	1	2.28
Career	0	1	.000	3.90	20	0	0	30.0	23	9	23	5	1.07

The Brewers view the hard-throwing de los Santos as their closer of the future, but his progress was slowed by a lower-back ailment that sidelined him for most of the year. 2000 Outlook: B

Horacio Estrada (Pos: LHP, Age: 24)

	W	L	Pct.	ERA	G	GS	Sv	IP	H	BB	SO	HR	Ratio
1999	0	0	-	7.36	4	0	0	7.1	10	4	5	4	1.91
Career	0	0	-	7.36	4	0	0	7.1	10	4	5	4	1.91

Estrada struggled after arthroscopic shoulder surgery in 1998. His future may be in middle relief, though he has been a starter in the minors. 2000 Outlook: C

Steve Falteisek (Pos: RHP, Age: 28)

	W	L	Pct.	ERA	G	GS	Sv	IP	H	BB	SO	HR	Ratio
1999	0	0	-	7.50	10	0	0	12.0	18	3	5	3	1.75
Career	0	0	-	5.85	15	0	0	20.0	26	6	7	3	1.60

Falteisek put together a solid season at Double-A in 1995, but hasn't been able to duplicate it at Triple-A or the majors. He has a 5.90 ERA in 238 Triple-A innings during the last two seasons. 2000 Outlook: D

Chad Fox (Pos: RHP, Age: 29)

	W	L	Pct.	ERA	G	GS	Sv	IP	H	BB	SO	HR	Ratio
1999	0	0	-	10.80	6	0	0	6.2	11	4	12	1	2.25
Career	1	5	.167	4.25	85	0	0	91.0	91	40	104	9	1.44

Fox looked like a candidate to step in if Bob Wickman faltered as the closer, but elbow troubles sidelined him for the season in late April. His elbow was rebuilt in 1996, so the jury's out. 2000 Outlook: B

Charlie Greene (Pos: C, Age: 29, Bats: R)

	G	AB	R	H	D	T	HR	RBI	SB	BB	SO	Avg	OBP	Slg
1999	32	42	4	8	1	0	0	1	0	5	11	.190	.271	.214
Career	52	66	5	12	2	0	0	2	0	5	20	.182	.236	.212

For a fourth year in a row Greene was promoted to the majors, but he hit .190 in his longest audition yet. He hasn't hit better than .212 in three Triple-A seasons, so there's little hope for success. Toronto signed him to a minor league contract. 2000 Outlook: D

Reggie Harris (Pos: RHP, Age: 31)

	W	L	Pct.	ERA	G	GS	Sv	IP	H	BB	SO	HR	Ratio
1999	0	0	-	3.00	8	0	0	12.0	8	7	11	1	1.25
Career	2	3	.400	4.91	86	1	0	121.0	106	81	95	10	1.55

Harris spent time in the majors when the Brewers recalled him in July. He pitched better than he had in his three previous trips, but not good enough to stay. 2000 Outlook: C

Lyle Mouton (Pos: LF, Age: 30, Bats: R)

	G	AB	R	H	D	T	HR	RBI	SB	BB	SO	Avg	OBP	Slg
1999	14	17	2	3	1	0	1	3	0	2	3	.176	.263	.412
Career	265	691	81	197	36	1	20	99	8	61	173	.285	.344	.427

Mouton was a valuable part-time player with the White Sox, but wasn't given much of a chance the last two seasons. Maybe he'll get a shot after hitting .357-19-77 in 305 Triple-A at-bats. 2000 Outlook: C

Mike Myers (Pos: LHP, Age: 30)

	W	L	Pct.	ERA	G	GS	Sv	IP	H	BB	SO	HR	Ratio
1999	2	1	.667	5.23	71	0	0	41.1	46	13	35	7	1.43
Career	6	12	.333	4.79	325	0	9	218.0	229	101	198	31	1.51

Myers led the National League with 23 holds in 1998, but he wasn't quite as effective last year. Milwaukee traded him to Colorado for Curtis Leskanic in November. 2000 Outlook: B

Jim Pittsley (Pos: RHP, Age: 25)

	W	L	Pct.	ERA	G	GS	Sv	IP	H	BB	SO	HR	Ratio
1999	1	3	.250	6.00	20	5	0	42.0	53	25	20	5	1.86
Career	7	12	.368	6.02	81	29	0	225.2	268	117	116	36	1.71

A former Royals first-round pick, Pittsley once had the hard stuff and the potential to anchor a major league rotation. After arm problems, he now is looking to secure a niche in a major league bullpen. 2000 Outlook: B

Hector Ramirez (Pos: RHP, Age: 28)

	W	L	Pct.	ERA	G	GS	Sv	IP	H	BB	SO	HR	Ratio
1999	1	2	.333	3.43	15	0	0	21.0	19	11	9	1	1.43
Career	1	2	.333	3.43	15	0	0	21.0	19	11	9	1	1.43

In his third go-round, Ramirez turned in his best season at the Triple-A level in 1999, working out of the bullpen. He certainly wasn't dominating, but he may have earned a long look in spring training. 2000 Outlook: C

Rafael Roque (Pos: LHP, Age: 26)

	W	L	Pct.	ERA	G	GS	Sv	IP	H	BB	SO	HR	Ratio
1999	1	6	.143	5.34	43	9	1	84.1	96	42	66	16	1.64
Career	5	8	.385	5.17	52	18	1	132.1	138	66	100	25	1.54

Roque is a soft-tossing southpaw who fared well his first time through the National League in 1998. He hasn't been able to counter the adjustments that major league hitters have made to his average stuff. 2000 Outlook: C

Eddie Zosky (Pos: 3B, Age: 32, Bats: R)

	G	AB	R	H	D	T	HR	RBI	SB	BB	SO	Avg	OBP	Slg
1999	8	7	1	1	0	0	0	0	0	1	2	.143	.250	.143
Career	40	46	4	8	1	2	0	3	0	1	12	.174	.188	.283

The once-heralded shortstop prospect made his fourth trip to the majors and first since 1995. He wasn't able to push his career average above the Mendoza Line with the Brewers. 2000 Outlook: D

Milwaukee Brewers Minor League Prospects

Organization Overview:

The Brewers overhauled their organization, starting with the firings of manager Phil Garner and GM Sal Bando in August, followed by the cleaning out of their scouting and player-development personnel once new GM Dean Taylor took over. The team was in need of a massive facelift. Milwaukee hasn't contended for a postseason berth since 1992 and won't anytime soon. While the farm system has produced Ron Belliard, Geoff Jenkins and Steve Woodward in the past two seasons, there's very little left. The Brewers have positioned themselves as the poster children for small-revenue teams, and years of neglecting foreign talent and refusing to pay market value for draft picks have caught up to them. They have one high-ceiling prospect who hasn't exhibited a major flaw, and that guy, Ben Sheets, has pitched just 35.2 innings as a pro.

Kevin Barker

Position: 1B
Bats: L **Throws:** L
Ht: 6' 3" **Wt:** 205
Opening Day Age: 24
Born: 7/26/75 in Bristol, VA

Recent Statistics

	G	AB	R	H	D	T	HR	RBI	SB	BB	SO	Avg
1999 AAA Louisville	121	442	89	123	27	5	23	87	2	59	94	.278
1999 NL Milwaukee	38	117	13	33	3	0	3	23	1	9	19	.282
1999 MLE	121	423	67	104	23	3	16	66	1	45	96	.246

Barker is the lone position player in the system who will make his presence felt in Milwaukee in the next couple of years. A 1996 third-round pick out of Virginia Tech, he has had at least 100 RBI in each of his three full pro seasons. Sean Berry flopped so badly last year that Barker was promoted in August, ahead of schedule, and he should keep the first-base job in 2000. His best tool is his power, though his home-run totals were enhanced by a short right-field porch in Triple-A Louisville. He may have average pop at best for a first baseman. Barker will need to shorten his swing and display more patience, and he has yet to prove he can hit lefthanders. Barker is unexceptional as a runner or defender, so his bat will have to carry him.

J.M. Gold

Position: P
Bats: R **Throws:** R
Ht: 6' 5" **Wt:** 225
Opening Day Age: 19
Born: 4/10/80 in Belleville, NJ

Recent Statistics

	W	L	ERA	G	GS	Sv	IP	H	R	BB	SO	HR
1998 R Ogden	1	0	2.61	5	5	0	20.2	21	13	7	15	1
1999 A Beloit	6	10	5.40	21	21	0	111.2	120	82	54	93	16

Gold was the consensus top high school pitching prospect in the 1998 draft, when the Brewers took him 13th overall and signed him for $1.675 million. Though he has a 92-94 MPH fastball and a hard curveball, he strug-gled in his first full pro season. He was pitching at age 19 in a full-season Class-A league, so that's a bit understandable. He needs to develop a changeup and better command, and must learn to pitch in the strike zone. Gold isn't in the best of shape and throws across his body, leading to health concerns. He had shoulder surgery in 1996 and was shut down briefly last year with a sore elbow. While he has a high ceiling, he's very raw and at least three years away from contributing in Milwaukee.

Chad Green

Position: OF
Bats: B **Throws:** R
Ht: 5' 10" **Wt:** 180
Opening Day Age: 24
Born: 6/28/75 in Dunkirk, NY

Recent Statistics

	G	AB	R	H	D	T	HR	RBI	SB	BB	SO	Avg
1998 A Stockton	40	151	30	52	13	2	0	17	22	12	22	.344
1998 AA El Paso	7	6	0	0	0	0	0	0	0	1	3	.000
1999 AA Huntsville	116	422	56	104	22	3	10	46	28	46	109	.246
1999 MLE	116	407	42	89	19	2	6	34	19	29	112	.219

Rather than pay the going rate for a first-round pick in 1996, the Brewers made a prearranged deal with Chad Green worth $1 million and took him eighth overall out of the University of Kentucky. He's one of the fastest players in the minors, which gives him great basestealing ability and terrific range in center field. But even after hitting .267 in four seasons as a pro, he still doesn't understand that he should stop trying to hit home runs and play a little man's game. He hits too many flyballs and doesn't draw nearly enough walks. But because they have no other options, the Brewers consider Green their eventual replacement for Marquis Grissom.

Scott Kirby

Position: 3B
Bats: R **Throws:** R
Ht: 6' 2" **Wt:** 190
Opening Day Age: 22
Born: 7/18/77 in Lakeland, FL

Recent Statistics

	G	AB	R	H	D	T	HR	RBI	SB	BB	SO	Avg
1998 A Beloit	107	359	51	73	19	2	8	40	5	47	109	.203
1999 A Beloit	68	247	54	75	14	1	17	47	3	47	59	.304
1999 A Stockton	60	202	35	58	15	3	10	36	3	25	59	.287

Kirby's career may have been on the line entering 1999, as he had batted just .222 and hadn't advanced past Class-A ball in three pro seasons. A 30th-round draft-and-follow in 1995 who signed after a year at Polk (Fla.) Community College, he broke through last season by hitting .296 with 27 homers. He also showed improved plate discipline and held his own in the high Class-A California League. He's improving as a third baseman. Kirby is probably two full seasons away from Milwaukee.

Allen Levrault

Position: P
Bats: R **Throws:** R
Ht: 6' 3" **Wt:** 238

Opening Day Age: 22
Born: 8/15/77 in Fall River, MA

Recent Statistics

	W	L	ERA	G	GS	Sv	IP	H	R	BB	SO	HR
1998 A Stockton	9	3	2.87	16	15	0	97.1	76	33	27	86	8
1998 AA El Paso	1	5	5.89	11	11	0	62.2	77	51	17	46	7
1999 AA Huntsville	9	2	3.43	16	16	0	99.2	77	44	33	82	11
1999 AAA Louisville	1	3	8.65	9	5	0	34.1	48	37	16	33	9

Levrault was enjoying a fine Double-A season before his nose was broken by a batting-practice smash at midseason. He didn't pitch well after coming off the disabled list, but still it was a year of progress. A 13th-round pick from the Community College of Rhode Island in 1996, he has a low-90s fastball and an exceptional changeup. He sometimes struggles to throw his curveball for strikes, which leads him to rely too much on his fastball. If he can't develop an effective third pitch, he could become a setup man or closer, and some Brewers officials believe that the bullpen is his best bet. In 2000, he'll stay in the rotation in Triple-A to gain more experience.

Nick Neugebauer

Position: P
Bats: R **Throws:** R
Ht: 6' 3" **Wt:** 225

Opening Day Age: 19
Born: 7/15/80 in Riverside, CA

Recent Statistics

	W	L	ERA	G	GS	Sv	IP	H	R	BB	SO	HR
1999 A Beloit	7	5	3.90	18	18	0	80.2	50	41	80	125	4

If anyone wanted to make a sequel to "Bull Durham," Neugebauer would make a perfect Nuke LaLoosh. After being surprised to get J.M. Gold with the 13th pick in the 1998 draft, the Brewers were delighted to find Neugebauer available in the second round. He signed for $1 million, a club record for a non-first-rounder, and didn't make his pro debut until 1999. Neugebauer led all minor league starters in both strikeouts per nine innings (13.9) and opponent batting average (.178), but he also had 80 walks in 80.2 innings. He has the best raw stuff in the organization, featuring a high-90s fastball and an electric slider. He's just a thrower for now, and he must discover a third pitch and consistent mechanics, which would enhance his control. The Brewers will be patient with Neugebauer, starting him in high Class-A in 2000.

Santiago Perez

Position: SS
Bats: B **Throws:** R
Ht: 6' 2" **Wt:** 150

Opening Day Age: 24
Born: 12/30/75 in Santo Domingo, Dom. Rep.

Recent Statistics

	G	AB	R	H	D	T	HR	RBI	SB	BB	SO	Avg
1998 AA El Paso	107	454	73	139	20	13	11	64	21	28	70	.306
1998 AAA Louisville	36	133	18	36	4	3	3	14	6	6	31	.271
1999 AAA Louisville	108	407	57	107	23	8	7	38	21	31	94	.263
1999 MLE	108	392	43	92	20	5	4	28	15	23	95	.235

A throw-in in the Bryce Florie-Mike Myers trade with Detroit in November 1997, Perez excited the Brewers in 1998 by showing surprising power and a strong glove in Double-A. He faded on both fronts last year in Triple-A, and it appears his pop was an illusion created by an extreme hitters' park in El Paso. In 1999, Perez was too homer-conscious, resulting in too many harmless flyballs and strikeouts and not enough walks or stolen bases. He has the speed, hands and arm to be a good shortstop, but he was too lackadaisical last year, committing 30 errors. Perez hasn't been written off, but he'll be asked to repeat Triple-A rather than push for a job in Milwaukee in 2000.

Ben Sheets

Position: P
Bats: R **Throws:** R
Ht: 6' 1" **Wt:** 195

Opening Day Age: 21
Born: 7/18/78 in Baton Rouge, LA

Recent Statistics

	W	L	ERA	G	GS	Sv	IP	H	R	BB	SO	HR
1999 R Ogden	0	1	5.63	2	2	0	8.0	8	5	2	12	2
1999 A Stockton	1	0	3.58	5	5	0	27.2	23	11	14	28	1

Sheets was projected to go fourth overall in the 1999 draft, but when the Diamondbacks overdrafted high school third baseman Corey Myers, Sheets slid until the Brewers took him with the 10th pick. Signed for a club-record $2.45 million bonus, he first emerged as a prospect during the summer of 1998 in the Cape Cod League, then went 14-1 as a junior at Northeast Louisiana. *Baseball America* rated both his fastball and his curveball the best among college draft prospects. Sheets throws a 93-94 MPH fastball, a hard curveball and a decent changeup. The Brewers will start him in Double-A this year and rush him to the majors as soon as possible.

Others to Watch

Righthander **Jose Garcia** (21) missed all of 1999 with an elbow injury, a huge blow to an organization short on pitching prospects. When healthy, he throws a low-90s fastball and a sharp curveball. . . The cousin of Expos Vladimir and Wilton Guerrero, **Cristian Guerrero** (18) is a five-tool outfielder who batted .310 in the Rookie-level Pioneer League in his pro debut last year. He also stole 26 bases in 28 attempts. . . The Brewers have another tools outfielder in **Derry Hammond** (20), but he's not nearly as polished as Guerrero despite being two years older. Hammond batted .229 with 17 homers at Class-A Beloit in 1999. . . Righthander **Jose Mieses** (20) was eight strikeouts shy of winning the Pioneer League's pitching triple crown in his pro debut last year. His best pitch is his palmball, and his 87-89 MPH fastball has room for growth. . . Righthander **Jeff Robinson** (22), a seventh-round pick last June, had 65 strikeouts and allowed just 49 hits in 61.2 Pioneer League innings. He keeps the ball down and his 89-91 MPH fastball is very projectable. . . **Chris Rowan** (21) may be the best shortstop in the system, even after hitting .237 at high Class-A Stockton. He has a strong arm and very good pop for a middle infielder.

Olympic Stadium

Offense

Olympic Stadium is a symmetrical park with artificial turf and a lot of foul territory. It usually favors pitchers, though it boosted scoring last season after the roof was covered. Among National League parks over the past three years, only the Astrodome and Pro Player Stadium have cut down on homers more than the Big O. It's especially tough on lefthanded power hitters. The hard turf creates an above-average number of doubles and triples.

Defense

The park's ancient carpet is notorious for its unevenness and resulting bad hops, particularly on the infield. Hard shots down the line can be especially challenging for the corner infielders. Speed is at a premium in the outfield, where hard-hit liners can skid to the wall. Basestealers can run well on the hard turf, so it's important to have a catcher with a strong arm.

Who It Helps The Most

For some reason, Chris Widger hits for better power and average at Olympic Stadium. Vladimir Guerrero's home-run total isn't hurt and his average is boosted. Rookie Jeremy Powell was markedly more effective in Montreal in 1999, as Carl Pavano has been over each of the last two years.

Who It Hurts The Most

Both Brad Fullmer and Rondell White lose home runs to the park. Wilton Guerrero hasn't hit well in Montreal during his time with the Expos. Dustin Hermanson hasn't pitched well at Olympic Stadium, and Mike Thurman has been hurt badly by the park.

Rookies & Newcomers

Outfield prospects Peter Bergeron and Milton Bradley have the line-drive stroke and speed suited to Olympic Stadium. Fernando Seguignol has batted .333 with power in his brief exposure to the Big O, but he hasn't hit well enough on the road to stick in the majors. The Big O should benefit potential starters Tony Armas Jr. and Ted Lilly, as well as free-agent reliever Graeme Lloyd, by keeping some of their mistakes in the park.

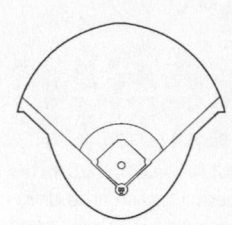

Dimensions: LF-325, LCF-375, CF-404, RCF-375, RF-325

Capacity: 46,500

Elevation: 90 feet

Surface: Turf

Foul Territory: Large

Park Factors

1999 Season

	Home Games			Away Games			
	Expos	Opp	Total	Expos	Opp	Total	Index
G	72	72	144	72	72	144	—
Avg	.269	.275	.272	.262	.270	.266	102
AB	2424	2551	4975	2536	2435	4971	100
R	334	409	743	310	369	679	109
H	651	702	1353	664	658	1322	102
2B	161	154	315	125	133	258	122
3B	20	15	35	23	11	34	103
HR	74	62	136	74	75	149	91
BB	203	256	459	186	257	443	104
SO	374	477	851	452	462	914	93
E	79	59	138	69	58	127	109
E-Infield	54	50	104	55	48	103	101
LHB-Avg	.293	.293	.293	.251	.271	.263	111
LHB-HR	13	21	34	23	31	54	63
RHB-Avg	.259	.262	.260	.266	.269	.268	97
RHB-HR	61	41	102	51	44	95	108

1997-1999

	Home Games			Away Games			
	Expos	Opp	Total	Expos	Opp	Total	Index
G	220	220	440	217	217	434	—
Avg	.259	.260	.260	.257	.265	.261	100
AB	7328	7703	15031	7542	7159	14701	101
R	935	1065	2000	924	1103	2027	97
H	1898	2006	3904	1935	1899	3834	100
2B	443	396	839	400	359	759	108
3B	53	47	100	51	40	91	107
HR	207	183	390	229	229	458	83
BB	616	742	1358	555	783	1338	99
SO	1353	1477	2830	1422	1398	2820	98
E	213	163	376	188	150	338	110
E-Infield	161	133	294	150	127	277	105
LHB-Avg	.263	.266	.265	.247	.265	.257	103
LHB-HR	58	67	125	77	90	167	72
RHB-Avg	.257	.256	.256	.262	.265	.263	97
RHB-HR	149	116	265	152	139	291	90

1999 Rankings (National League)

- Highest double factor
- Second-highest LHB batting-average factor
- Third-highest batting-average factor
- Third-highest run factor
- Third-highest hit factor
- Lowest LHB home-run factor

Felipe Alou

1999 Season

It was another trying season for Felipe Alou's Expos. They got off to a terrible start and finished with the third-worst record in the National League at 68-94. There were some hopeful signs, however. Several young players made progress, and the club played nearly .500 ball during the last two months. If Montreal's goal was to build for the future rather than to win ballgames, the 1999 season was a moderate success.

Offense

Alou refuses to give his baserunners the green light until they've proven to him that they've mastered the technique of reading pitchers' deliveries. He isn't nearly as emphatic about making his hitters learn to work the count. He's willing to experiment with players in various offensive roles, and always gives a player a fair shot before deeming the trial a failure or success. Alou is patient with youngsters whose hitting lags behind their fielding, but always keeps a few veteran pinch-hitters on the bench for key situations.

Pitching & Defense

Alou is one of the best in the game at bringing along young pitchers. He never pushes them too hard and is willing to let them work through the inevitable rough stretches. Few managers are less concerned with batter-pitcher matchups. In making pitching changes, Alou is more worried about allowing a quality pitcher to remain on the mound as long as he's effective, while being careful to lift him a batter too soon rather than a batter too late. He's willing to experiment on defense and isn't afraid to try a player at an unfamiliar position.

2000 Outlook

The sale of the Expos to art dealer Jeffrey Loria has created new optimism in Montreal. The team will stay put and look to trade for a veteran or two after years of jettisoning its best players for salary reasons. The Expos will continue to develop youngsters with an eye toward contending in the near future. Alou remains the perfect manager to oversee the process.

Born: 5/12/35 in Haina, Dominican Republic

Playing Experience: 1958-1974, SF, Atl, Oak, NYY, Mon, Mil

Managerial Experience: 8 seasons
Pronunciation: fuh-LEEP-ay ah-LOO

Manager Statistics

Year	Team, Lg	W	L	Pct	GB	Finish
1999	Montreal, NL	68	94	.420	35.0	4th East
8 Seasons		603	590	.505	—	—

1999 Starting Pitchers by Days Rest

	<=3	4	5	6+
Expos Starts	1	77	57	16
Expos ERA	4.50	4.87	4.39	5.55
NL Avg Starts	3	81	48	21
NL ERA	4.84	4.53	4.72	4.98

1999 Situational Stats

	Felipe Alou	NL Average
Hit & Run Success %	30.9	33.6
Stolen Base Success %	57.9	70.2
Platoon Pct.	49.1	55.2
Defensive Subs	55	25
High-Pitch Outings	5	13
Quick/Slow Hooks	20/15	16/15
Sacrifice Attempts	84	89

1999 Rankings (National League)

- 1st in defensive substitutions (55) and starting lineups used (143)
- 2nd in fewest caught stealings of third base (2)

Michael Barrett

Position: 3B/C
Bats: R **Throws:** R
Ht: 6' 2" **Wt:** 195

Opening Day Age: 23
Born: 10/22/76 in
Atlanta, GA
ML Seasons: 2

1999 Season

Former first-round pick Michael Barrett had a very encouraging rookie season for the Expos. Drafted as a shortstop and quickly converted to catcher in the minors, Barrett showed his versatility by dividing his time between catcher and third base. He got off to a hot start, was temporarily derailed by a home-plate collision in June, then rebounded strongly over the last two months. Despite taking a pounding behind the plate and being shifted continually between positions, he kept his average close to .300 all year and was one of the league's top rookies.

Hitting

Barrett is a terrific contact hitter, and has proven to be one of the toughest strikeouts and best two-strike hitters in the game. He has an uncomplicated approach, hitting the first good pitch he sees wherever it's thrown. He may develop double-digit home-run power before long. He has hit lefthanders and righthanders equally well in each of the last two years. For now, he's a line-drive hitter with good doubles power who uses the whole field.

Baserunning & Defense

Barrett drew raves for his work behind the plate, where he showed good mobility and a strong, accurate arm. He has the tools to be a good defensive third baseman, but his inexperience at the hot corner was evident. He showed poor anticipation and substandard range. It's assumed he'll develop into a top defender wherever the Expos ultimately decide to put him. Several years of receiving have robbed him of his speed, and he's no factor on the bases.

2000 Outlook

Barrett hopes to improve his power numbers this year after pumping iron over the winter. The Expos want to see him grow into a middle-of-the-order hitter, and he'll have a better chance to develop offensively at third base than at catcher. The club is expected to make a decision on his position this spring.

Overall Statistics

	G	AB	R	H	D	T	HR	RBI	SB	BB	SO	Avg	OBP	Slg
1999	126	433	53	127	32	3	8	52	0	32	39	.293	.345	.436
Career	134	456	56	134	34	3	9	54	0	35	45	.294	.349	.441

Where He Hits the Ball

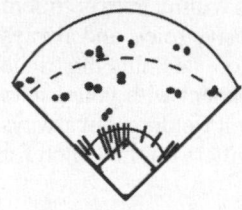 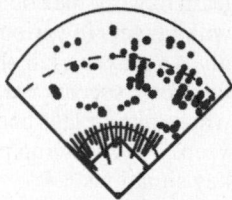

Vs. LHP   **Vs. RHP**

1999 Situational Stats

	AB	H	HR	RBI	Avg		AB	H	HR	RBI	Avg
Home	214	66	5	31	.308	LHP	116	31	2	14	.267
Road	219	61	3	21	.279	RHP	317	96	6	38	.303
First Half	212	58	3	27	.274	Sc Pos	112	33	3	40	.295
Scnd Half	221	69	5	25	.312	Clutch	72	27	3	14	.375

1999 Rankings (National League)

- 1st in most GDPs per GDP situation (21.7%)
- 3rd in batting average on an 0-2 count (.323)
- 4th in batting average in the clutch and batting average with two strikes (.281)
- 5th in GDPs (18)
- Led the Expos in batting average in the clutch, batting average on an 0-2 count (.323), batting average with two strikes (.281) and GDPs (18)
- Led NL third basemen in batting average on an 0-2 count (.323) and batting average with two strikes (.281)

Orlando Cabrera

1999 Season

Shortstop Orlando Cabrera enjoyed a decent if unremarkable season that ended in August with a severely sprained left ankle. Though inconsistent at the plate, he played strong defense and showed the potential to develop further. It wasn't easy to find an offensive role for him, but his glove was valued on a team with many young pitchers and few other quality defenders.

Hitting

Like several other of the Expos' young hitters, Cabrera is aggressive, impatient and raw. He's at his best when he uses the whole field and tries to keep the ball on the ground. He makes good contact, collects doubles on liners into the gaps, and sends an occasional cripple pitch over the fence. He gets himself in trouble when he starts pulling the ball in the air. Cabrera sometimes batted leadoff last year, where his inability to work a walk was a conspicuous weakness. He hit over his head as a rookie in 1998 and it wasn't a complete surprise when his average dropped off a bit last year.

Baserunning & Defense

Cabrera was a very good basestealer in the minors and has the speed to be one in the majors. He has yet to earn the green light, however, and may not until he begins to display better judgment on the basepaths. Cabrera has good range and a very strong arm. He may win recognition as one of the National League's better-fielding shortstops before long.

2000 Outlook

Cabrera may never be an outstanding batter, but he still has time to mature. Even if he never grows into a top-of-the-order hitter, his glove should be enough to keep him in the lineup. He'll begin 2000 as Montreal's regular shortstop. He always had been a durable player until last year's injury and can be expected to be in the lineup every day.

Position: SS
Bats: R **Throws:** R
Ht: 5'10" **Wt:** 175

Opening Day Age: 25
Born: 11/2/74 in Cartagena, Colombia
ML Seasons: 3

Overall Statistics

	G	AB	R	H	D	T	HR	RBI	SB	BB	SO	Avg	OBP	Slg
1999	104	382	48	97	23	5	8	39	2	18	38	.254	.293	.403
Career	199	661	96	174	39	10	11	63	9	37	68	.263	.305	.402

Where He Hits the Ball

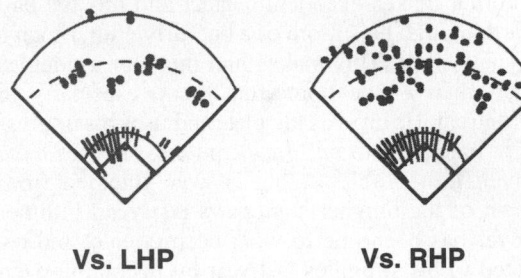

Vs. LHP   **Vs. RHP**

1999 Situational Stats

	AB	H	HR	RBI	Avg		AB	H	HR	RBI	Avg
Home	206	52	6	27	.252	LHP	93	31	1	8	.333
Road	176	45	2	12	.256	RHP	289	66	7	31	.228
First Half	313	82	5	28	.262	Sc Pos	94	22	3	31	.234
Scnd Half	69	15	3	11	.217	Clutch	58	20	3	12	.345

1999 Rankings (National League)

- 3rd in fielding percentage at shortstop (.979)
- 9th in batting average in the clutch and most GDPs per GDP situation (16.7%)

Brad Fullmer

1999 Season

Brad Fullmer got off to a brutal start in 1999, landing in manager Felipe Alou's doghouse when he refused to alter his approach at the plate. The result was a surprising demotion to Triple-A Ottawa in May. Recalled in late June and sent back down three days later, Fullmer initially refused to play in Triple-A because he insisted he had a knee injury. Doctors didn't find anything, and he further infuriated the Expos when he suggested they trade him. Once he decided to play again in the minors, he soon got his swing back and began pounding the ball. Fullmer continued to hit well after his July recall before slumping in September.

Hitting

Fullmer makes excellent contact and hits the ball hard, though he's more of a line-drive hitter than a flyball hitter. This makes him more of a doubles man than a true home-run threat, especially in Montreal. He crowds the plate and uses his impressive bat speed to pull inside pitches. Lefties have given him problems, but he was shielded from most of the tougher southpaws last year. Fullmer never has been one to work deep counts, and reacted to his struggles last year by becoming even more aggressive. Though he's sometimes criticized for his lack of home-run power, his extra-base pop is rather remarkable for a hitter who strikes out so infrequently. That trait bodes well for his future.

Baserunning & Defense

Fullmer has had relatively little experience at first base and still hasn't mastered the basics of the position. The footwork doesn't come naturally to him, and he hasn't thrown well since having rotator-cuff surgery following his first pro season. He's adequate on pure reaction plays. On the basepaths, Fullmer has below-average speed and poor instincts.

2000 Outlook

Fullmer quite possibly salvaged his future in Montreal with his sizzling two-month stretch in July and August. He has a bright future ahead of him, but a trade would not come as a complete surprise.

Position: 1B
Bats: L **Throws:** R
Ht: 6' 1" **Wt:** 220

Opening Day Age: 25
Born: 1/17/75 in Chatsworth, CA
ML Seasons: 3

Overall Statistics

	G	AB	R	H	D	T	HR	RBI	SB	BB	SO	Avg	OBP	Slg
1999	100	347	38	96	34	2	9	47	2	22	35	.277	.321	.464
Career	259	892	100	246	80	4	25	128	8	63	112	.276	.326	.459

Where He Hits the Ball

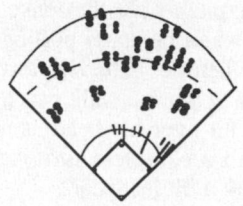
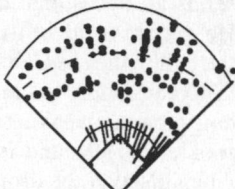

Vs. LHP   **Vs. RHP**

1999 Situational Stats

	AB	H	HR	RBI	Avg		AB	H	HR	RBI	Avg
Home	177	50	4	20	.282	LHP	50	12	2	13	.240
Road	170	46	5	27	.271	RHP	297	84	7	34	.283
First Half	105	23	3	11	.219	Sc Pos	93	24	1	34	.258
Scnd Half	242	73	6	36	.302	Clutch	41	12	1	5	.293

1999 Rankings (National League)
- 2nd in most GDPs per GDP situation (20.3%)
- 8th in errors at first base (7)

Vladimir Guerrero

Future MVP

1999 Season

Few players in history have achieved such a high level of play before the age of 24 as Vladimir Guerrero. After a breakout season in 1998, he took another small step forward last year despite encountering growing pains along the way. He committed errors in bunches early in the year and frequently exasperated manager Felipe Alou with his overaggressiveness at the plate. Yet Guerrero still managed to improve his power numbers while maintaining his batting average, drawing more walks and striking out less frequently.

Hitting

Guerrero lives for first-pitch fastballs and rarely holds back when he sees one. Though many equally impatient hitters can be exploited by savvy pitchers, Guerrero is able to maintain his productivity even with runners on base and no strong hitters behind him, situations where pitchers are certain to work off the plate. His aggressiveness may make him frustrating to watch, but his ability to make hard contact more than compensates. He pounds lefties and righties alike, and is especially deadly against pitchers who work up in the zone. Guerrero's power is tremendous and extends to all fields.

Baserunning & Defense

Guerrero remains raw in the outfield. He'll make a spectacular over-the-fence grab or unleash a cannon throw to cut down a runner, then come right back and drop an easy flyball or misplay a carom off the wall. He committed a major league-high 19 outfield errors in 1999, 10 of them coming in his first 34 games. He always has had more than enough speed to steal bases, and has developed enough technique to swipe an occasional bag against a righthander.

2000 Outlook

It must terrify National League pitchers to think that Guerrero likely has several more years of improvement ahead. Based on last year's drop in strikeouts, he may be ready to take another big step forward this year. There's every reason to think he'll be one of baseball's very best hitters over the next decade.

Position: RF
Bats: R **Throws:** R
Ht: 6' 3" **Wt:** 205

Opening Day Age: 24
Born: 2/9/76 in Nizao Bani, Dominican Republic
ML Seasons: 4
Nickname: Miqueas

Overall Statistics

	G	AB	R	H	D	T	HR	RBI	SB	BB	SO	Avg	OBP	Slg
1999	160	610	102	193	37	5	42	131	14	55	62	.316	.378	.600
Career	418	1585	256	498	96	14	92	281	28	116	199	.314	.367	.567

Where He Hits the Ball

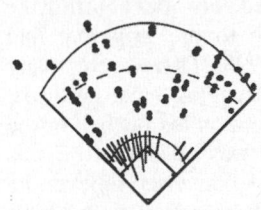 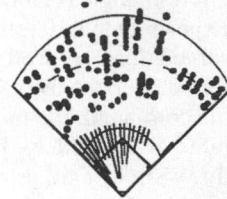

Vs. LHP   **Vs. RHP**

1999 Situational Stats

	AB	H	HR	RBI	Avg		AB	H	HR	RBI	Avg
Home	314	104	23	75	.331	LHP	129	37	12	27	.287
Road	296	89	19	56	.301	RHP	481	156	30	104	.324
First Half	317	93	18	65	.293	Sc Pos	167	63	11	91	.377
Scnd Half	293	100	24	66	.341	Clutch	91	29	4	17	.319

1999 Rankings (National League)

- 1st in errors in right field (19), lowest fielding percentage in right field (.948) and lowest percentage of pitches taken (42.3)
- Led the Expos in slugging percentage, on-base percentage, HR frequency (14.5 ABs per HR), batting average with runners in scoring position, batting average with the bases loaded (.182), batting average vs. righthanded pitchers, cleanup slugging percentage (.593), slugging percentage vs. righthanded pitchers (.597), on-base percentage vs. righthanded pitchers (.383), batting average on a 3-2 count (.346), batting average, home runs, at-bats, runs scored, hits, total bases (366), RBI, caught stealing (7), walks, intentional walks (14), times on base (255) and GDPs (18)

531

Dustin Hermanson

1999 Season

With Carlos Perez traded to Los Angeles in late 1998, Dustin Hermanson entered the 1999 season as the Expos' ace for the first time. He came to camp in great shape and seemed up to the challenge. But after getting off to a decent start, he fell into a three-month skid that saw him drop 10 of 11 decisions at one point. Shoulder woes were rumored to be the problem. Hermanson turned things around in August and went 6-4, 2.37 over the final two months.

Pitching

Hermanson is a power pitcher with a mid-90s fastball, a hard slider and a changeup. Some of his struggles resulted in part from trying to perfect a circle change. He rebounded only after aborting the experiment and returning to the grip that had served him so well in 1998. There were many theories about his early struggles—that he'd lost his command, the movement on his fastball or the bite on his slider—but it was clear that he was throwing as hard as ever. A converted reliever, he has been brought along slowly and still hasn't built up the stamina to last much beyond the 100-pitch mark.

Defense & Hitting

Hermanson is a good athlete and fielder who rarely hurts himself with the glove. His slump last year detracted from his attention to the running game, which he'd controlled well in the past. He still has a good pickoff move and nabbed three runners last year. After contributing a homer and 10 walks in 1998, Hermanson had an abysmal year at the plate in 1999. He did improve his bunting, the only competent aspect of his hitting.

2000 Outlook

After a season of consolidation, Hermanson may now be ready to resume his climb up the ranks of major league starters. His late-season rebound proved that there's nothing wrong with his arm. As the ace of a young club that's expected to improve, he should make gains as well. This could be his best season yet.

Position: SP
Bats: R **Throws:** R
Ht: 6' 3" **Wt:** 205

Opening Day Age: 27
Born: 12/21/72 in Springfield, OH
ML Seasons: 5

Overall Statistics

	W	L	Pct.	ERA	G	GS	Sv	IP	H	BB	SO	HR	Ratio
1999	9	14	.391	4.20	34	34	0	216.1	225	69	145	20	1.36
Career	35	34	.507	3.97	132	92	0	607.0	575	217	465	67	1.30

How Often He Throws Strikes

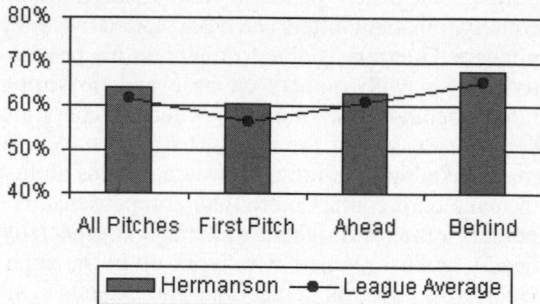

1999 Situational Stats

	W	L	ERA	Sv	IP		AB	H	HR	RBI	Avg
Home	2	9	5.49	0	100.0	LHB	378	103	10	45	.272
Road	7	5	3.09	0	116.1	RHB	451	122	10	55	.271
First Half	3	7	5.48	0	106.2	Sc Pos	216	60	6	82	.278
Scnd Half	6	7	2.95	0	109.2	Clutch	27	6	1	2	.222

1999 Rankings (National League)

- 1st in least run support per nine innings (3.9)
- 3rd in highest stolen-base percentage allowed (83.3)
- Led the Expos in ERA, wins, losses, innings pitched, hits allowed, batters faced (928), home runs allowed, walks allowed, strikeouts, pitches thrown (3,326), pickoff throws (122), highest strikeout/walk ratio (2.1), lowest batting average allowed (.271), lowest slugging percentage allowed (.419), lowest on-base percentage allowed (.330), highest groundball/flyball ratio allowed (0.9), lowest stolen-base percentage allowed (83.3), fewest pitches thrown per batter (3.58), fewest baserunners allowed per nine innings (12.5) and most strikeouts per nine innings (6.0)

Carl Pavano

1999 Season

Expectations have always been high for Carl Pavano, the principal player acquired from the Red Sox in the Pedro Martinez trade two years ago. The Expos hoped Pavano would take a step forward after finishing the 1998 season strongly, but he got off to a brutal start in 1999 and never fully recovered. He missed almost the entire second half with elbow tendinitis, which was particularly worrisome because he also had missed a chunk of the previous season with shoulder problems.

Pitching

Despite all his problems, Pavano looked good at times last year. When he's on, he mixes a low-90s fastball, a slider and a changeup, and works ahead of the hitters. Lefthanders fare no better against him than righthanders. Though his ERA was quite ugly, poor defense behind him was partly to blame. He had problems from the stretch last year despite pitching well from the full windup, suggesting that he may have been tipping his pitches. Pavano was a workhorse in the minors but hasn't been pushed hard by the Expos because of his recent arm troubles.

Defense & Hitting

Pavano is a good fielder who makes more than his share of plays. He has improved his move to first base and no longer is an easy mark for basestealers. He's a poor hitter but a fair bunter.

2000 Outlook

Pavano's elbow didn't require surgery and he's expected to be ready for spring training. There's good reason for caution, however. He threw a lot of innings while in the Red Sox system, and his recent arm problems suggest that some permanent damage may have been done. He remains capable of pitching well if healthy, but his durability is in question.

Position: SP
Bats: R **Throws:** R
Ht: 6' 5" **Wt:** 225

Opening Day Age: 24
Born: 1/8/76 in New Britain, CT
ML Seasons: 2

Overall Statistics

	W	L	Pct.	ERA	G	GS	Sv	IP	H	BB	SO	HR	Ratio
1999	6	8	.429	5.63	19	18	0	104.0	117	35	70	8	1.46
Career	12	17	.414	4.83	43	41	0	238.2	247	78	153	26	1.36

How Often He Throws Strikes

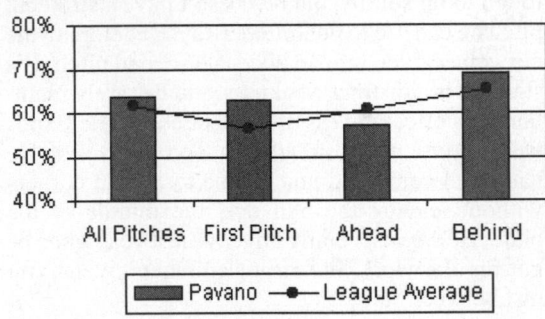

1999 Situational Stats

	W	L	ERA	Sv	IP		AB	H	HR	RBI	Avg
Home	4	3	4.24	0	68.0	LHB	207	60	5	24	.290
Road	2	5	8.25	0	36.0	RHB	204	57	3	29	.279
First Half	6	8	5.59	0	103.0	Sc Pos	102	32	4	43	.314
Scnd Half	0	0	9.00	0	1.0	Clutch	27	6	1	1	.222

1999 Rankings (National League)

- 3rd in balks (3)
- Led the Expos in balks (3)

Montreal

Mike Thurman

1999 Season

Mike Thurman underwent knee surgery before the 1999 season and struggled badly over the first two months. He suddenly turned it around in June, though, and became one of the team's most effective starters over the remainder of the season. After the end of May, he started 20 games and compiled a fine 3.20 ERA. He pitched surprisingly well overall, though bad luck, poor run support and shoddy defense behind him hurt his record.

Pitching

Thurman relies primarily on a 90-MPH two-seam fastball and mixes in a curveball and changeup. The two-seamer has good sinking movement and is tough to hit solidly, but he doesn't have a strikeout pitch he can use to put hitters away. Developing the curve has given him an adequate second pitch. His stamina is a distinct weakness, and he rarely maintains his effectiveness after 90 pitches. The Expos were careful not to stretch him too far last year. He has good command and is able to hit the corners without leaving the ball over the middle of the plate. He was especially effective last year when he got regular work, but struggled when given extra rest between starts.

Defense & Hitting

Thurman's fielding is competent. However, he lacks a good move to first and has had trouble stopping the running game. Thurman is perhaps the most inept hitter in the majors. He has 49 strikeouts and two hits in 65 major league at-bats.

2000 Outlook

With Thurman expected to start 2000 at full strength, the Expos will count on him to pitch all season the way he did during the second half of 1999. His improvement the last couple of years has been real, and he's quite capable of being a solid middle-of-the-rotation starter.

Position: SP
Bats: R **Throws:** R
Ht: 6' 5" **Wt:** 210

Opening Day Age: 26
Born: 7/22/73 in Corvallis, OR
ML Seasons: 3

Overall Statistics

	W	L	Pct.	ERA	G	GS	Sv	IP	H	BB	SO	HR	Ratio
1999	7	11	.389	4.05	29	27	0	146.2	140	52	85	17	1.31
Career	12	16	.429	4.31	48	42	0	225.1	208	82	125	27	1.29

How Often He Throws Strikes

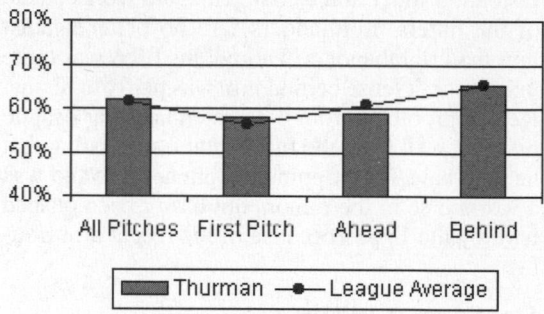

1999 Situational Stats

	W	L	ERA	Sv	IP		AB	H	HR	RBI	Avg
Home	3	6	5.21	0	67.1	LHB	263	75	6	22	.285
Road	4	5	3.06	0	79.1	RHB	294	65	11	41	.221
First Half	3	5	4.52	0	73.2	Scd Pos	126	33	6	47	.262
Scnd Half	4	6	3.58	0	73.0	Clutch	28	11	1	4	.393

1999 Rankings (National League)

- 5th in stolen bases allowed (25)
- 6th in lowest batting average allowed vs. righthanded batters
- 10th in lowest winning percentage
- Led the Expos in stolen bases allowed (25) and lowest batting average allowed vs. righthanded batters

Ugueth Urbina

Position: RP
Bats: R **Throws:** R
Ht: 6' 2" **Wt:** 205

Opening Day Age: 26
Born: 2/15/74 in Caracas, Venezuela
ML Seasons: 5
Pronunciation: ooo-GET ur-BEE-nuh
Nickname: Oogy

1999 Season

Though his ERA jumped by 2.39 runs last year, Ugueth Urbina posted another remarkable season. He led the National League with 41 saves despite pitching for a club that won only 68 games. The scarcity of late-inning leads often left him idle for several days in a row, but he never lost his rhythm. A few poor outings inflated his ERA, which didn't accurately reflect the overall quality of his work.

Pitching

Urbina has the classic closer's arsenal: a high-90s fastball and a sharp, hard slider. The two pitches are so difficult to distinguish out of his hand that he's virtually unhittable once he gets ahead in the count. He'll work in a changeup, though he rarely feels the need to. Lefthanders used to give him big problems, but he has learned to shut them down over the last two years. He has no problem working on consecutive days or for more than an inning at a time. He threw more than one inning on 15 occasions last year, something modern closers rarely are asked to do.

Defense & Hitting

Urbina gives up very few comebackers and makes little effort to finish his delivery in good fielding position. He's generally reliable afield when the need arises. He concentrates on the hitter so completely that he's one of the easiest pitchers to run on in the majors. Basestealers went 20-for-21 against him last year and are 58-for-64 during his career. His efforts at the plate are futile and he hasn't had a hit in three years.

2000 Outlook

Urbina remains one of the premier closers in the game. He hasn't been overworked and ought to have several more prime years ahead of him. An upswing in the Expos' fortunes might enable him to post even better numbers and finally win the recognition he deserves.

Overall Statistics

	W	L	Pct.	ERA	G	GS	Sv	IP	H	BB	SO	HR	Ratio
1999	6	6	.500	3.69	71	0	41	75.2	59	36	100	6	1.26
Career	29	24	.547	3.40	238	21	102	346.2	276	156	401	41	1.25

How Often He Throws Strikes

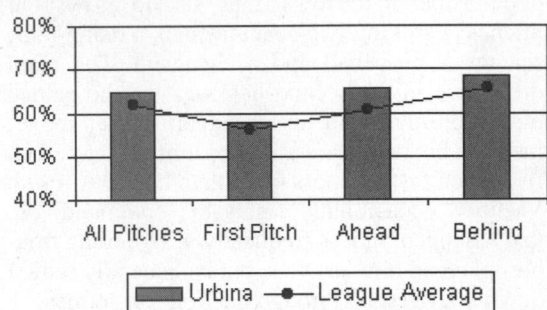

1999 Situational Stats

	W	L	ERA	Sv	IP		AB	H	HR	RBI	Avg
Home	3	4	3.82	18	35.1	LHB	121	24	3	19	.198
Road	3	2	3.57	23	40.1	RHB	163	35	3	20	.215
First Half	5	4	4.23	19	44.2	Sc Pos	102	22	1	32	.216
Scnd Half	1	2	2.90	22	31.0	Clutch	216	44	4	30	.204

1999 Rankings (National League)

- 1st in saves, save opportunities (50) and blown saves (9)
- 4th in games finished (62)
- 5th in most strikeouts per nine innings in relief (11.9)
- 9th in lowest save percentage (82.0)
- 10th in relief losses (6) and lowest batting average allowed in relief (.208)
- Led the Expos in saves, games finished (62), wild pitches (6), save opportunities (50), save percentage (82.0), blown saves (9), first batter efficiency (.194), relief losses (6), lowest batting average allowed in relief (.208), fewest baserunners allowed per nine innings in relief (11.3) and most strikeouts per nine innings in relief (11.9)

Montreal

Javier Vazquez

1999 Season

It was clear that the Expos were force-feeding young righthander Javier Vazquez when he posted a 5-15 record as a 21-year-old rookie in 1998. His struggles intensified last year, and he was sent to Triple-A Ottawa in June with a fat 6.63 ERA. Rejoining Montreal after the All-Star break, Vazquez put it all together and became one of the Expos' best starters, winning seven of 11 decisions to finish with a winning record. The Expos always knew he had potential, but hadn't expected him to turn the corner so dramatically.

Pitching

Vazquez isn't a pure power pitcher, but he has a good fastball in the low to mid-90s. He throws four pitches: a sinking two-seam fastball, a rising four-seamer, a curveball and a changeup. The main difference in the second half was that he gained more confidence in his changeup. Better movement on his two-seamer helped him get burned on first-pitch fastballs less often than he had in 1998. Vazquez occasionally fights his command, but that's happening less frequently. First-inning troubles plagued him last year, but he generally settled down after getting through the first few frames.

Defense & Hitting

Vazquez is a good athlete and helps himself both in the field and at the plate. He's quick off the mound and has yet to commit his first major league error. He also has a good pickoff move and checks the running game fairly well. Only two pitchers topped his .286 batting average last year. Vazquez strikes out less frequently than many regular hitters and is an adept bunter as well.

2000 Outlook

Vazquez undoubtedly will hit some more bumps in the road before reaching his full potential. He made significant progress last year, however, and the Expos expect him to be an important part of their rotation for years to come. He may be surprisingly competent this year.

Position: SP
Bats: R **Throws:** R
Ht: 6' 2" **Wt:** 190

Opening Day Age: 23
Born: 7/25/76 in Ponce, Puerto Rico
ML Seasons: 2

Overall Statistics

	W	L	Pct.	ERA	G	GS	Sv	IP	H	BB	SO	HR	Ratio
1999	9	8	.529	5.00	26	26	0	154.2	154	52	113	20	1.33
Career	14	23	.378	5.56	59	58	0	327.0	350	120	252	51	1.44

How Often He Throws Strikes

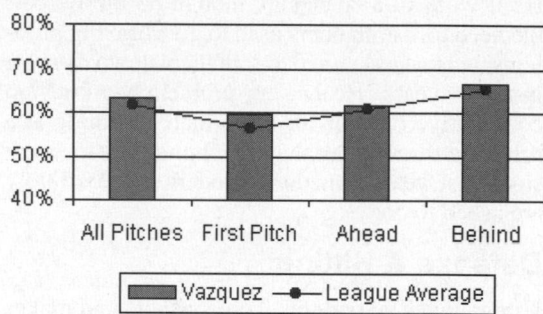

1999 Situational Stats

	W	L	ERA	Sv	IP		AB	H	HR	RBI	Avg
Home	4	4	4.22	0	85.1	LHB	274	64	8	40	.234
Road	5	4	5.97	0	69.1	RHB	331	90	12	43	.272
First Half	2	4	6.63	0	57.0	Sc Pos	140	40	6	59	.286
Scnd Half	7	4	4.05	0	97.2	Clutch	26	3	0	1	.115

1999 Rankings (National League)

- 2nd in lowest batting average allowed vs. lefthanded batters
- 9th in complete games (3)
- Led the Expos in wins, complete games (3), home runs allowed, GDPs induced (13), ERA at home and lowest batting average allowed vs. lefthanded batters

Jose Vidro

1999 Season

Jose Vidro was the Expos' most pleasant surprise last year. After showing newfound power in winter ball, he got off to a hot start at the plate. He began the year splitting time at second base with Wilton Guerrero, but soon nailed down the full-time job. Though his defense was adequate at best, Vidro established himself as a key offensive performer. Fatigue and injuries dragged him down in September, but he still finished with fine numbers.

Hitting

Though he's a switch-hitter, Vidro does most of his damage from the left side of the plate. The main difference last year was that he developed confidence in his ability to drive the ball and looked to do so whenever he got ahead in the count. He's aggressive and rarely walks, but makes good contact and hits liners to all fields. Vidro often batted third or fifth last year, but didn't drive in many runs in either spot. He performed best when batting second despite his aversion to the base on balls.

Baserunning & Defense

Vidro may not be cut out to be a second baseman. His range and double-play pivot are subpar. They may remain below standard because he lacks the quick feet of a middle infielder. His arm is more than strong enough for third base, which is where his future may be. Vidro's speed is unimpressive and he was gunned down on all four of his steal attempts last year.

2000 Outlook

Vidro may regress a bit at the plate in 2000, but he should remain an above-average run producer for a second baseman. He's still young and can be expected to develop further in the years ahead. A shift to third base may be a possibility, especially if the Expos decide to put Michael Barrett behind the plate on a full-time basis.

Position: 2B/1B
Bats: B **Throws:** R
Ht: 5'11" **Wt:** 190

Opening Day Age: 25
Born: 8/27/74 in Mayaguez, Puerto Rico
ML Seasons: 3
Pronunciation: VEE-droh

Overall Statistics

	G	AB	R	H	D	T	HR	RBI	SB	BB	SO	Avg	OBP	Slg
1999	140	494	67	150	45	2	12	59	0	29	51	.304	.346	.476
Career	290	868	110	237	69	3	14	94	3	67	104	.273	.329	.408

Where He Hits the Ball

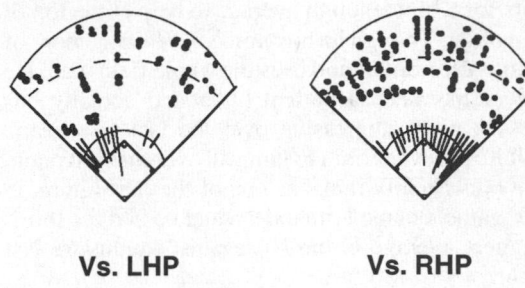

Vs. LHP   **Vs. RHP**

1999 Situational Stats

	AB	H	HR	RBI	Avg		AB	H	HR	RBI	Avg
Home	247	79	5	31	.320	LHP	100	26	1	10	.260
Road	247	71	7	28	.287	RHP	394	124	11	49	.315
First Half	238	75	8	30	.315	Sc Pos	114	28	4	44	.246
Scnd Half	256	75	4	29	.293	Clutch	72	13	1	8	.181

1999 Rankings (National League)
- 2nd in doubles
- 6th in fewest pitches seen per plate appearance (3.30)
- 7th in fielding percentage at second base (.982)
- Led the Expos in doubles
- Led NL second basemen in batting average vs. righthanded pitchers and doubles

Montreal

537

Rondell White

1999 Season

Rondell White's sore knee forced the Expos to move him to left field at the beginning of last season, and it may have been a blessing in disguise. With less ground to cover, he was able to stay relatively healthy and enjoyed one of the best seasons of his career. He did spend two stints on the disabled list with a strained right hamstring at midseason. White returned to center field in the second half.

Hitting

White began the year hitting third and later returned to the leadoff spot, where he had batted earlier in his career. He has enough power to bat third, and while he doesn't draw many walks, he hits for a high enough average to help at the top of the order. Though he hits homers, White is more of a line-drive hitter and uses the whole field well. He never has been a patient hitter and actually has grown more aggressive over the last few years. White is never afraid to jump all over the first pitch. He consistently ranks as one of the best hitters in the game against lefthanders, and he had the third-highest average in the NL against southpaws last year.

Baserunning & Defense

White's knee and hamstring troubles have taken their toll on the basepaths and in the outfield. While his speed is still well above average, he was a non-factor as a basestealer last year. He was over-qualified for left field but didn't cover center quite as skillfully as he used to. His range remains above average, though. His weak throwing arm is his only liability.

2000 Outlook

On several occasions, White has chafed under the leadership of manager Felipe Alou. With several outfield prospects in the pipeline, the Expos may try to peddle White. He always has hit better on the road and almost certainly would hold up better away from Olympic Stadium's unforgiving artificial turf. Getting out of Montreal may be the best thing for him.

Position: LF/CF
Bats: R **Throws:** R
Ht: 6' 0" **Wt:** 210

Opening Day Age: 28
Born: 2/23/72 in Milledgeville, GA
ML Seasons: 7

Overall Statistics

	G	AB	R	H	D	T	HR	RBI	SB	BB	SO	Avg	OBP	Slg
1999	138	539	83	168	26	6	22	64	10	32	85	.312	.359	.505
Career	667	2466	368	719	141	23	90	330	83	172	427	.292	.345	.477

Where He Hits the Ball

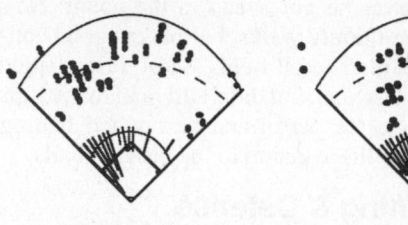

Vs. LHP   **Vs. RHP**

1999 Situational Stats

	AB	H	HR	RBI	Avg		AB	H	HR	RBI	Avg
Home	271	79	10	28	.292	LHP	123	46	8	22	.374
Road	268	89	12	36	.332	RHP	416	122	14	42	.293
First Half	236	76	10	30	.322	Sc Pos	118	30	3	40	.254
Scnd Half	303	92	12	34	.304	Clutch	80	15	1	6	.188

1999 Rankings (National League)

- 3rd in batting average vs. lefthanded pitchers, errors in left field (7) and lowest fielding percentage in left field (.956)
- 4th in most GDPs per GDP situation (17.9%)
- Led the Expos in highest groundball/flyball ratio (1.5), most pitches seen per plate appearance (3.41), batting average vs. lefthanded pitchers, on-base percentage for a leadoff hitter (.371), slugging percentage vs. lefthanded pitchers (.659), on-base percentage vs. lefthanded pitchers (.415), singles, sacrifice flies (6) and hit by pitch (11)
- Led NL left fielders in highest groundball/flyball ratio (1.5), batting average vs. lefthanded pitchers, hit by pitch (11) and GDPs (17)

Chris Widger

1999 Season

Chris Widger had his best season last year, thanks in part to the presence of Michael Barrett. Widger is plagued endlessly by nagging ailments, beyond the usual punishment a catcher absorbs. Barrett's ability to catch enabled Widger to get the frequent rest he needs to stay sharp. Though he still wore down in September, he finished with a career-high .264 average and provided decent production from the bottom third of the order.

Hitting

Widger is downright dangerous against lefthanders, batting .350 and slugging .580 against them last season. He remains an easy mark for righthanders, though, and often pulls off their breaking balls. He has decent power but does his best hitting when he uses the whole field. He always has hit best early in the year, before he has been worn down by months of catching. Widger doesn't read pitches well and often will chase ones he has no chance of hitting. Pitchers can expand the zone on him quite easily after getting ahead in the count.

Baserunning & Defense

Widger's throwing accuracy has improved with better footwork, though his caught-stealing percentage was down last year because a sprained left knee slowed his release. He's slow even by catchers' standards and advances only as far as he has to.

2000 Outlook

Widger is a useful receiver, though he's somewhat limited by his fragility. If the Expos opt to make Barrett the full-time catcher, Widger probably will be dealt. He might have been traded to Milwaukee for Jeff Cirillo, but Montreal didn't want to take Scott Karl's contract in the deal. If Barrett moves back to third base, Widger almost certainly will remain the Expos' primary backstop. He ought to remain productive as long as the club carries a secondary receiver to share a good chunk of the load. Arthroscopic surgery in October corrected his knee problem.

Position: C
Bats: R **Throws:** R
Ht: 6' 3" **Wt:** 215

Opening Day Age: 28
Born: 5/21/71 in Wilmington, DE
ML Seasons: 5

Overall Statistics

	G	AB	R	H	D	T	HR	RBI	SB	BB	SO	Avg	OBP	Slg
1999	124	383	42	101	24	1	14	56	1	28	86	.264	.325	.441
Career	371	1134	111	274	62	5	37	148	9	82	246	.242	.297	.403

Where He Hits the Ball

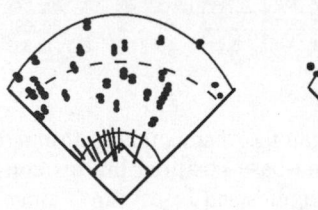
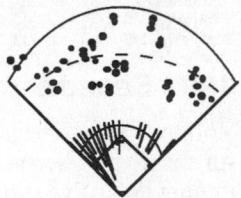

Vs. LHP   **Vs. RHP**

1999 Situational Stats

	AB	H	HR	RBI	Avg		AB	H	HR	RBI	Avg
Home	204	60	11	34	.294	LHP	100	35	5	19	.350
Road	179	41	3	22	.229	RHP	283	66	9	37	.233
First Half	207	61	9	34	.295	Sc Pos	118	24	1	34	.203
Scnd Half	176	40	5	22	.227	Clutch	66	15	2	8	.227

1999 Rankings (National League)

- 4th in lowest percentage of runners caught stealing as a catcher (20.5)
- 8th in errors at catcher (6)
- 9th in lowest batting average with runners in scoring position
- Led the Expos in fewest GDPs per GDP situation (6.9%) and highest percentage of pitches taken (51.3)
- Led NL catchers in caught stealing (4)

Wilton Guerrero

Position: 2B/LF
Bats: B **Throws:** R
Ht: 6' 0" **Wt:** 175

Opening Day Age: 25
Born: 10/24/74 in Don Gregorio, Dominican Republic
ML Seasons: 4

Overall Statistics

	G	AB	R	H	D	T	HR	RBI	SB	BB	SO	Avg	OBP	Slg
1999	132	315	42	92	15	7	2	31	7	13	38	.292	.324	.403
Career	364	1076	132	310	39	25	8	90	21	35	155	.288	.311	.393

1999 Situational Stats

	AB	H	HR	RBI	Avg		AB	H	HR	RBI	Avg
Home	144	37	0	14	.257	LHP	97	32	1	11	.330
Road	171	55	2	17	.322	RHP	218	60	1	20	.275
First Half	166	46	0	13	.277	Sc Pos	64	25	1	27	.391
Scnd Half	149	46	2	18	.309	Clutch	68	24	0	11	.353

1999 Season

Wilton Guerrero began the year as the frontrunner for the Expos' second-base position, but his continuing defensive struggles and Jose Vidro's emergence bumped Guerrero to the bench. He excelled as a pinch-hitter and didn't play much until September, when he was tried in left field with mixed results.

Hitting, Baserunning & Defense

Guerrero is a pure slap hitter from either side of the plate. He's stronger from the right side, and manager Felipe Alou has suggested he scrap switch-hitting altogether. Guerrero is extremely impatient and produces almost nothing but groundballs to the opposite field. At second base, his double-play pivot is inadequate and may prevent him from ever playing regularly there again. His inexperience and his weak arm were apparent in the outfield, though he has good range. He still hasn't learned to put his speed to work as a basestealer.

2000 Outlook

Even if the Expos give Guerrero a chance to start in left field, he may not hold the job because he lacks the power normally expected from the position. Though it may be hard for him to accept, his best role may be as a utilityman.

Steve Kline

Position: RP
Bats: B **Throws:** L
Ht: 6' 0" **Wt:** 210

Opening Day Age: 27
Born: 8/22/72 in Sunbury, PA
ML Seasons: 3

Overall Statistics

	W	L	Pct.	ERA	G	GS	Sv	IP	H	BB	SO	HR	Ratio
1999	7	4	.636	3.75	82	0	0	69.2	56	33	69	8	1.28
Career	14	14	.500	3.99	206	1	1	194.0	191	97	182	22	1.48

1999 Situational Stats

	W	L	ERA	Sv	IP		AB	H	HR	RBI	Avg
Home	5	3	3.51	0	41.0	LHB	93	18	1	9	.194
Road	2	1	4.08	0	28.2	RHB	164	38	7	17	.232
First Half	3	2	4.17	0	36.2	Sc Pos	58	12	1	16	.207
Scnd Half	4	2	3.27	0	33.0	Clutch	118	24	2	13	.203

1999 Season

Lefthander Steve Kline was the most valuable member of the Montreal bullpen last year after closer Ugueth Urbina. He performed admirably and led the majors with 82 appearances.

Pitching, Defense & Hitting

Kline gets groundballs with a sinking two-seam fastball and a hard slider. He continued to destroy lefthanders last year, holding them to a sub-.200 average for the second year in a row. He's tough on righties too, and needn't be lifted when one comes off the bench. Kline is a good athlete and an active fielder, especially for a lefty. He's fairly easy to run on, and basestealers succeeded in seven of eight tries against him in 1999. He has no hits in six major league at-bats but has successfully laid down a couple of sacrifice bunts.

2000 Outlook

As long as Kline stays healthy, he ought to remain one of the most effective and least heralded members of the Expos pen. Surprisingly, Montreal spent $9 million over three seasons to sign another lefty reliever, free agent Graeme Lloyd, in December.

Manny Martinez

Position: CF
Bats: R **Throws:** R
Ht: 6' 2" **Wt:** 185

Opening Day Age: 29
Born: 10/3/70 in San Pedro de Macoris, Dominican Republic
ML Seasons: 3

Overall Statistics

	G	AB	R	H	D	T	HR	RBI	SB	BB	SO	Avg	OBP	Slg
1999	137	331	48	81	12	7	2	26	19	17	51	.245	.279	.341
Career	232	564	74	138	25	12	8	53	23	30	111	.245	.284	.374

1999 Situational Stats

	AB	H	HR	RBI	Avg		AB	H	HR	RBI	Avg
Home	152	42	1	13	.276	LHP	106	29	0	8	.274
Road	179	39	1	13	.218	RHP	225	52	2	18	.231
First Half	227	63	2	20	.278	Sc Pos	65	15	0	21	.231
Scnd Half	104	18	0	6	.173	Clutch	42	9	1	8	.214

1999 Season

The Expos picked up Manny Martinez, who'd been released by the Pirates, and started him in center field when Rondell White's balky knee relegated him to left. Martinez played good defense and got off to a decent start at the plate, carrying a .280 batting average as late as August. But he then hit a brutal slump, one that cost him his job and relegated him to a late-inning defensive replacement.

Hitting, Baserunning & Defense

Martinez isn't selective enough to be a productive hitter. He was tried as a leadoff hitter, but his inability to reach base doomed that experiment. He has very little power. What he does have is excellent speed on the bases and in the outfield. He swiped 19 bases in 25 attempts and was the club's best defensive outfielder last year. His throwing arm is better than average.

2000 Outlook

Martinez' extended trial last year proved that he's best suited for a smaller role. Manager Felipe Alou seems to be fond of him, so the Expos may keep him around as a reserve.

Ryan McGuire

Position: 1B/LF
Bats: L **Throws:** L
Ht: 6' 1" **Wt:** 215

Opening Day Age: 28
Born: 11/23/71 in Bellflower, CA
ML Seasons: 3

Overall Statistics

	G	AB	R	H	D	T	HR	RBI	SB	BB	SO	Avg	OBP	Slg
1999	88	140	17	31	7	2	2	18	1	27	33	.221	.347	.343
Career	302	549	56	121	31	4	6	45	2	78	122	.220	.316	.324

1999 Situational Stats

	AB	H	HR	RBI	Avg		AB	H	HR	RBI	Avg
Home	81	22	1	12	.272	LHP	18	5	0	2	.278
Road	59	9	1	6	.153	RHP	122	26	2	16	.213
First Half	112	26	2	15	.232	Sc Pos	40	11	1	16	.275
Scnd Half	28	5	0	3	.179	Clutch	30	6	1	5	.200

1999 Season

The Expos finally gave up on Ryan McGuire last year. He got a handful of starts at first base in May and June but failed to take advantage. After Brad Fullmer was recalled in July, McGuire all but disappeared and rarely was used for anything more than late-inning defense.

Hitting, Baserunning & Defense

McGuire's bat has been a distinct disappointment. His smooth lefthanded stroke produced good batting averages in the minors but simply hasn't yielded results in the majors. Though he's patient, his power is limited to liners that reach the gaps. McGuire is a very good defensive first baseman, and he can hold his own in left or right field despite his lack of speed. His strong throwing arm is an asset.

2000 Outlook

Outrighted off Montreal's 40-man roster in November, McGuire refused his assignment to Triple-A and became a free agent. He signed a minor league contract with the Mets, with whom his role is unclear. There aren't many first basemen who manage to stick in the majors on the strength of their defense alone.

Montreal

Orlando Merced

Position: LF
Bats: L **Throws:** R
Ht: 6' 1" **Wt:** 195

Opening Day Age: 33
Born: 11/2/66 in San Juan, Puerto Rico
ML Seasons: 10
Pronunciation: mer-SED

Overall Statistics

	G	AB	R	H	D	T	HR	RBI	SB	BB	SO	Avg	OBP	Slg
1999	93	194	25	52	12	1	8	26	2	26	27	.268	.353	.464
Career	1051	3398	490	951	193	22	88	500	45	432	546	.280	.361	.427

1999 Situational Stats

	AB	H	HR	RBI	Avg		AB	H	HR	RBI	Avg
Home	96	30	3	15	.313	LHP	10	3	0	1	.300
Road	98	22	5	11	.224	RHP	184	49	8	25	.266
First Half	122	34	7	16	.279	Sc Pos	44	11	1	17	.250
Scnd Half	72	18	1	10	.250	Clutch	33	8	1	5	.242

1999 Season

Veteran Orlando Merced was signed to a minor league deal by Montreal over the winter and made the club out of spring training. He served as one of the team's top pinch-hitters and sometimes played left field against righthanders. He hit fairly well, though he didn't get as much playing time as he had in previous years.

Hitting, Baserunning & Defense

Merced is a line-drive hitter with power from alley to alley. He hits for moderate power and is tough to strike out. A former switch-hitter who now bats exclusively lefthanded, he always has been bothered by southpaws. His production against righthanders makes him useful in a platoon role or off the bench. His best position is first base, but he can get by in left or right field. His arm is strong enough for right field. Merced's speed is average and he's not a threat to steal, but he runs the bases aggressively when healthy.

2000 Outlook

Merced became a free agent after the season. He underwent arthroscopic surgery on both knees but is expected to be ready for the start of the season.

Mike Mordecai

Position: 2B/SS/3B
Bats: R **Throws:** R
Ht: 5'11" **Wt:** 180

Opening Day Age: 32
Born: 12/13/67 in Birmingham, AL
ML Seasons: 6

Overall Statistics

	G	AB	R	H	D	T	HR	RBI	SB	BB	SO	Avg	OBP	Slg
1999	109	226	29	53	10	2	5	25	2	20	31	.235	.297	.363
Career	382	613	72	139	27	5	14	60	4	54	107	.227	.288	.356

1999 Situational Stats

	AB	H	HR	RBI	Avg		AB	H	HR	RBI	Avg
Home	122	26	4	14	.213	LHP	67	17	2	7	.254
Road	104	27	1	11	.260	RHP	159	36	3	18	.226
First Half	109	27	4	16	.248	Sc Pos	58	14	0	15	.241
Scnd Half	117	26	1	9	.222	Clutch	44	11	0	6	.250

1999 Season

The Expos got another useful season out of utility-man Mike Mordecai last year. Though he didn't hit much, he played all over the infield and provided solid glovework, something the team often lacked. Injuries and instability in the infield allowed him to get more playing time than ever before.

Hitting, Baserunning & Defense

Mordecai is a No. 8 hitter if there ever was one. He hits for a poor average and rarely flashes any power. Both lefthanders and righthanders can retire him with relative ease. Mordecai's strong defensive play at second, third and shortstop has kept him in the majors. Though his range isn't exceptional, he possesses soft hands and a strong, accurate arm. His pivot work at second is first-rate. He runs the bases with intelligence, but his speed is only average and he's no basestealer.

2000 Outlook

Mordecai is signed for 2000 with an option for 2001, so he'll continue to caddy for Montreal's young infielders as they gain experience. It doesn't hurt that his contract is close to the bottom of the scale.

Guillermo Mota

Position: RP
Bats: R **Throws:** R
Ht: 6' 6" **Wt:** 200

Opening Day Age: 26
Born: 7/25/73 in San Pedro de Macoris, Dominican Republic
ML Seasons: 1

Overall Statistics

	W	L	Pct.	ERA	G	GS	Sv	IP	H	BB	SO	HR	Ratio
1999	2	4	.333	2.93	51	0	0	55.1	54	25	27	5	1.43
Career	2	4	.333	2.93	51	0	0	55.1	54	25	27	5	1.43

1999 Situational Stats

	W	L	ERA	Sv	IP		AB	H	HR	RBI	Avg
Home	2	1	3.73	0	31.1	LHB	88	22	3	9	.250
Road	0	3	1.88	0	24.0	RHB	122	32	2	15	.262
First Half	1	3	1.69	0	26.2	Sc Pos	68	11	0	16	.162
Scnd Half	1	1	4.08	0	28.2	Clutch	66	18	2	10	.273

1999 Season

In only his third season on the mound, converted infielder Guillermo Mota was promoted in May and kept his ERA under 2.00 before an August slump. He wasn't as effective as his ERA would suggest, but he was a useful middle reliever and setup man.

Pitching, Defense & Hitting

Mota pitched all year with a bone spur in his elbow, and it was obvious he wasn't 100 percent. His fastball, in the high 90s in the minors, was about 5 MPH slower in the majors. His control was uncharacteristically poor after he'd shown fine command in the minors. Mota's cranky elbow often prevented him from working on consecutive days. He certainly hasn't forgotten how to hit or field. He defended his position well and showed a decent pickoff move, though his delivery gives runners a decent jump. He slammed a home run in his first major league at-bat.

2000 Outlook

Mota had the bone spur removed after the close of the season and is expected to be in good health this spring. He was able to contribute last year despite his physical problems, so he may do much more when healthy.

Jeremy Powell

Position: SP
Bats: R **Throws:** R
Ht: 6' 6" **Wt:** 225

Opening Day Age: 23
Born: 6/18/76 in La Miranda, CA
ML Seasons: 2

Overall Statistics

	W	L	Pct.	ERA	G	GS	Sv	IP	H	BB	SO	HR	Ratio
1999	4	8	.333	4.73	17	17	0	97.0	113	44	44	14	1.62
Career	5	13	.278	5.39	24	23	0	122.0	140	55	58	19	1.60

1999 Situational Stats

	W	L	ERA	Sv	IP		AB	H	HR	RBI	Avg
Home	2	2	2.72	0	39.2	LHB	164	41	4	14	.250
Road	2	6	6.12	0	57.1	RHB	210	72	10	38	.343
First Half	0	1	3.75	0	12.0	Sc Pos	86	23	2	32	.267
Scnd Half	4	7	4.87	0	85.0	Clutch	6	1	0	0	.167

1999 Season

Rookie righthander Jeremy Powell had a promising year before running out of gas in September. After being called up in July, he posted a 3.34 ERA in his first 12 starts, only to have his numbers ruined by a severe slump over the last four weeks of the season. He threw a total of 188 innings between Triple-A Ottawa and Montreal, 29.1 more than he ever had in a season, so his fatigue was understandable.

Pitching, Defense & Hitting

Powell's finesse approach belies his size. He throws a 90-MPH sinker, a curveball, a changeup and a splitter. Oddly, he held his own against lefthanders but was hit hard by righties in the majors, a problem he'd never had in the minors. His stamina is unproven. Powell is competent afield and does an especially good job controlling the running game with his compact stretch delivery. He's not much of a hitter, though.

2000 Outlook

Powell has a good chance to make the Expos rotation out of spring training, though his numbers from last year certainly won't guarantee him a spot. He may need more seasoning.

Dan Smith

Position: SP
Bats: R **Throws:** R
Ht: 6' 3" **Wt:** 210

Opening Day Age: 24
Born: 9/15/75 in
Flemington, NJ
ML Seasons: 1

Overall Statistics

	W	L	Pct.	ERA	G	GS	Sv	IP	H	BB	SO	HR	Ratio
1999	4	9	.308	6.02	20	17	0	89.2	104	39	72	12	1.59
Career	4	9	.308	6.02	20	17	0	89.2	104	39	72	12	1.59

1999 Situational Stats

	W	L	ERA	Sv	IP		AB	H	HR	RBI	Avg
Home	2	6	6.36	0	52.1	LHB	146	47	8	26	.322
Road	2	3	5.54	0	37.1	RHB	209	57	4	32	.273
First Half	1	3	4.94	0	31.0	Sc Pos	94	31	3	46	.330
Scnd Half	3	6	6.60	0	58.2	Clutch	18	2	1	3	.111

1999 Season

Claimed on waivers from the Rangers in the offseason, righthander Dan Smith wasn't expected to see the majors in 1999. After pitching decently in Triple-A for the first two months, he was summoned to Montreal and immediately inserted into the rotation. He had a sterling major league debut, striking out nine Red Sox to tie an Expos rookie record. It was all downhill from there, however.

Pitching, Defense & Hitting

Smith is a sinker-slider pitcher who doesn't throw especially hard. He must have precise command to get by, but doesn't always have it. He mixes in an occasional changeup. He struggled mightily against lefthanders last year, though he hadn't had that problem in the minors. Smith has a good pick-off move and is tough to run on. He can't hit a lick, though, and is an unremarkable fielder.

2000 Outlook

Smith had shoulder surgery during the last week of the season, which may partially explain his late-season struggles. He's expected to be ready for spring training, but needs to find a new club after the Expos non-tendered him in December.

Anthony Telford Rubber Arm

Position: RP
Bats: R **Throws:** R
Ht: 6' 0" **Wt:** 195

Opening Day Age: 34
Born: 3/6/66 in San
Jose, CA
ML Seasons: 6

Overall Statistics

	W	L	Pct.	ERA	G	GS	Sv	IP	H	BB	SO	HR	Ratio
1999	5	4	.556	3.94	79	0	2	96.0	112	38	69	3	1.56
Career	15	19	.441	3.98	241	9	4	346.1	355	133	239	33	1.41

1999 Situational Stats

	W	L	ERA	Sv	IP		AB	H	HR	RBI	Avg
Home	3	3	3.65	1	44.1	LHB	171	56	1	26	.327
Road	2	1	4.18	1	51.2	RHB	209	56	2	32	.268
First Half	2	2	3.06	1	53.0	Sc Pos	130	38	2	53	.292
Scnd Half	3	2	5.02	1	43.0	Clutch	133	40	1	21	.301

1999 Season

For the third straight year, Anthony Telford was the Expos' most heavily used middle reliever and setup man. His 79 appearances and 96 relief innings each ranked among the top three in the National League. Though his numbers were close to what they'd been in recent years, he gave up more key hits and wasn't quite as effective as he'd been in 1997 and 1998.

Pitching, Defense & Hitting

Telford gets groundballs with an average fastball, a slider and a curve. In the past he got lefthanders out with a cutter, but they gave him trouble last year. His biggest asset is his ability to thrive under heavy work. He had been an active and competent fielder before committing four errors in 1999, and he has problems holding runners. Telford has very little professional experience at the plate, but he has fared decently in his limited opportunities.

2000 Outlook

Telford has been a valuable and economical contributor for the past three years. He's now eligible for arbitration, so the Expos may opt to deal him before his salary becomes an issue.

Other Montreal Expos

Miguel Batista (Pos: RHP, **Age**: 29)

	W	L	Pct.	ERA	G	GS	Sv	IP	H	BB	SO	HR	Ratio
1999	8	7	.533	4.88	39	17	1	134.2	146	58	95	10	1.51
Career	11	17	.393	4.57	116	36	1	319.1	336	157	221	27	1.54

Batista looked good in winning his first two starts, but he had an erratic year and floated between the rotation and the pen. 2000 Outlook: B

Shayne Bennett (Pos: RHP, **Age**: 27)

	W	L	Pct.	ERA	G	GS	Sv	IP	H	BB	SO	HR	Ratio
1999	0	1	.000	14.29	5	1	0	11.1	24	3	4	4	2.38
Career	5	7	.417	5.87	83	1	1	125.2	142	57	71	14	1.58

Bennett didn't pitch well at Triple-A Ottawa or in Montreal, so he'll be fighting for a job in the spring. 2000 Outlook: C

Geoff Blum (Pos: SS, **Age**: 26, **Bats**: B)

	G	AB	R	H	D	T	HR	RBI	SB	BB	SO	Avg	OBP	Slg
1999	45	133	21	32	7	2	8	18	1	17	25	.241	.327	.504
Career	45	133	21	32	7	2	8	18	1	17	25	.241	.327	.504

Blum came up in August when Orlando Cabrera was hurt. Blum debuted with a six-game hit streak, including a two-homer game in Colorado. 2000 Outlook: B

Trace Coquillette (Pos: 3B, **Age**: 25, **Bats**: R)

	G	AB	R	H	D	T	HR	RBI	SB	BB	SO	Avg	OBP	Slg
1999	17	49	2	13	3	0	0	4	1	4	7	.265	.333	.327
Career	17	49	2	13	3	0	0	4	1	4	7	.265	.333	.327

Coquillette keeps hitting as he climbs the ladder. He batted .326 in Triple-A last year and performed decently after a September callup. 2000 Outlook: B

Darron Cox (Pos: C, **Age**: 32, **Bats**: R)

	G	AB	R	H	D	T	HR	RBI	SB	BB	SO	Avg	OBP	Slg
1999	15	25	2	6	1	0	1	2	0	0	5	.240	.296	.400
Career	15	25	2	6	1	0	1	2	0	0	5	.240	.296	.400

After a career-best year as a minor league hitter in 1998 (.302-9-35 in 278 AB), Cox made the Expos last spring. He hurt his left knee running on an AstroTurf seam in June and was lost for the season, then became a free agent. 2000 Outlook: C

Rick DeHart (Pos: LHP, **Age**: 30)

	W	L	Pct.	ERA	G	GS	Sv	IP	H	BB	SO	HR	Ratio
1999	0	0	-	21.60	3	0	0	1.2	6	3	1	2	5.40
Career	2	1	.667	5.64	52	0	1	59.0	73	30	44	12	1.75

DeHart wasn't particularly effective in Triple-A last year, and he was even less successful in Montreal. 2000 Outlook: C

Jose Fernandez (Pos: 3B, **Age**: 25, **Bats**: R)

	G	AB	R	H	D	T	HR	RBI	SB	BB	SO	Avg	OBP	Slg
1999	8	24	0	5	2	0	0	1	0	1	7	.208	.240	.292
Career	8	24	0	5	2	0	0	1	0	1	7	.208	.240	.292

Fernandez has a little power but no patience and a weak glove. Montreal released him in December. 2000 Outlook: C

Mike Johnson (Pos: RHP, **Age**: 24)

	W	L	Pct.	ERA	G	GS	Sv	IP	H	BB	SO	HR	Ratio
1999	0	0	-	8.64	3	1	0	8.1	12	7	6	2	2.28
Career	2	8	.200	7.52	30	19	2	105.1	134	46	67	26	1.71

Johnson hasn't pitched very well since reaching the high minors in 1998. He still has time to turn the corner. 2000 Outlook: C

Terry Jones (Pos: CF, **Age**: 29, **Bats**: B)

	G	AB	R	H	D	T	HR	RBI	SB	BB	SO	Avg	OBP	Slg
1999	17	63	4	17	1	1	0	3	1	3	14	.270	.303	.317
Career	89	285	40	66	8	3	1	19	17	24	63	.232	.290	.291

Jones has averaged 32 stolen bases a year in Triple-A, but he doesn't show enough pop or patience. He signed a minor league deal with the Dodgers. 2000 Outlook: C

Robert Machado (Pos: C, **Age**: 26, **Bats**: R)

	G	AB	R	H	D	T	HR	RBI	SB	BB	SO	Avg	OBP	Slg
1999	17	22	3	4	1	0	0	0	0	2	6	.182	.250	.227
Career	65	154	19	34	8	1	3	19	0	10	34	.221	.268	.344

In May the White Sox released Machado, a defensive specialist, and he hooked up with the Expos. The Mariners signed him after the season. 2000 Outlook: C

James Mouton (Pos: LF/CF/RF, **Age**: 31, **Bats**: R)

	G	AB	R	H	D	T	HR	RBI	SB	BB	SO	Avg	OBP	Slg
1999	95	122	18	32	5	1	2	13	6	18	31	.262	.364	.369
Career	561	1273	175	315	60	6	14	120	89	133	255	.247	.323	.337

Mouton had one of his better seasons in the majors, then signed a minor league deal with the Brewers. His speed remains his biggest asset. 2000 Outlook: B

Mel Rojas (Pos: RHP, **Age**: 33)

	W	L	Pct.	ERA	G	GS	Sv	IP	H	BB	SO	HR	Ratio
1999	0	0	-	18.00	13	0	0	14.0	22	9	10	6	2.21
Career	34	31	.523	3.82	525	0	126	667.0	591	254	562	65	1.27

Less than three years after signing a big contract to close games for the Cubs, Rojas was released by both the Tigers and Expos during the 1999 season. He has hit rock bottom and he can't get up. 2000 Outlook: D

J.D. Smart (Pos: RHP, **Age**: 26)

	W	L	Pct.	ERA	G	GS	Sv	IP	H	BB	SO	HR	Ratio
1999	0	1	.000	5.02	29	0	0	52.0	56	17	21	4	1.40
Career	0	1	.000	5.02	29	0	0	52.0	56	17	21	4	1.40

Smart was solid in Triple-A, but didn't do as well in Montreal. He may come around. 2000 Outlook: C

Chris Stowers (Pos: CF, **Age**: 25, **Bats**: L)

	G	AB	R	H	D	T	HR	RBI	SB	BB	SO	Avg	OBP	Slg
1999	4	2	0	0	0	0	0	0	0	0	0	.000	.000	.000
Career	4	2	0	0	0	0	0	0	0	0	0	.000	.000	.000

Stowers' average dropped to .237 and his power disappeared in his first Triple-A season in 1999. He's a fringe prospect at best. 2000 Outlook: C

Montreal

Montreal Expos Minor League Prospects

Organization Overview:

Christmas came 25 days early for Expos fans, when Major League Baseball approved the sale of controlling interest in the club to New York art dealer Jeffrey Loria for $75 million. Loria immediately insisted that Montreal no longer would be a farm system for other teams, dealing away Pedro Martinezes and Larry Walkers to win Cy Young Awards and batting titles elsewhere. The planned opening of new Labatt Park in 2002 also should pump revenue into a moribund franchise. The Expos introduced a purely homegrown infield of Brad Fullmer, Jose Vidro, Orlando Cabrera and Michael Barrett last season, but their development efforts have slowed down after a few years of worrying more about signability than ability. Most of their current top upper-level prospects came via trades.

Tony Armas Jr.

Position: P
Bats: R **Throws:** R
Ht: 6' 4" **Wt:** 175

Opening Day Age: 21
Born: 4/29/78 in Puerto Piritu, Venezuela

Recent Statistics

	W	L	ERA	G	GS	Sv	IP	H	R	BB	SO	HR
1999 AA Harrisburg	9	7	2.89	24	24	0	149.2	123	62	55	106	10
1999 NL Montreal	0	1	1.50	1	1	0	6.0	8	4	2	2	0

As much as it pained the Expos to trade Pedro Martinez in November 1997, they have to be pleased that they got Carl Pavano and Armas from the Red Sox. The son of former home-run champion Tony Armas, Tony Jr. was rated the Double-A Eastern League's best pitching prospect last season. He has a repertoire that includes a 93-94 MPH fastball, a wicked slider and a nice changeup. He has an effortless delivery that allows him to throw all of his pitches for strikes. Armas is ready for the majors, but the Expos may give him some Triple-A time.

Peter Bergeron

Position: OF
Bats: L **Throws:** R
Ht: 6' 2" **Wt:** 185

Opening Day Age: 22
Born: 11/9/77 in Greenfield, MA

Recent Statistics

	G	AB	R	H	D	T	HR	RBI	SB	BB	SO	Avg
1999 AA Harrisburg	42	162	29	53	14	2	4	18	9	24	29	.327
1999 AAA Ottawa	58	194	36	61	12	3	3	20	14	23	40	.314
1999 NL Montreal	16	45	12	11	2	0	0	1	0	9	5	.244
1999 MLE	100	343	52	101	24	3	5	30	16	34	73	.294

Tom Lasorda's brief reign as Dodgers GM resulted in one of the most favorably one-sided trades in Expos history. Los Angeles got three overrated players (Hiram Bocachica, Mark Grudzielanek, Carlos Perez), while Montreal received four youngsters, including their lead-off man of the future (Bergeron) and the top lefthander in their system (Ted Lilly). A 1996 fourth-round pick, Bergeron reminds scouts of a young Steve Finley. He hits line drives, has gap power, draws walks, makes contact and has excellent bunting ability. He has the above-average speed to play center field, though his arm is a question after he had offseason surgery to repair a labrum tear. Bergeron is the favorite to fill voids in the leadoff spot and left field for Montreal in 2000.

Milton Bradley

Position: OF
Bats: B **Throws:** R
Ht: 6' 0" **Wt:** 170

Opening Day Age: 21
Born: 4/15/78 in Harbor City, FL

Recent Statistics

	G	AB	R	H	D	T	HR	RBI	SB	BB	SO	Avg
1998 A Cape Fear	75	281	54	85	21	4	6	50	13	23	57	.302
1998 A Jupiter	67	261	55	75	14	1	5	34	17	30	42	.287
1999 AA Harrisburg	87	346	62	114	22	5	12	50	14	33	61	.329
1999 MLE	87	332	50	100	21	4	8	40	10	22	65	.301

For the second straight year, Bradley's exciting tools were overshadowed by an altercation with an umpire. He punched a Maryland Fall League ump in 1998, then spit gum at an arbiter last summer. When he wasn't battling a shoulder injury or joining Peter Bergeron on the silver medal-winning U.S. Pan American Games team, Bradley did have an excellent Double-A season. His two-out, bottom-of-the-ninth grand slam won the Eastern League playoffs. He's still raw, but he has fine hitting ability from both sides of the plate and could grow into a 30-30 player. He's also a spectacular center fielder with a powerful arm. If Bradley can control his anger and continue to develop in Triple-A, he could make Rondell White expendable after 2000.

Ted Lilly

Position: P
Bats: L **Throws:** L
Ht: 6' 1" **Wt:** 177

Opening Day Age: 24
Born: 1/4/76 in Lemeta, CA

Recent Statistics

	W	L	ERA	G	GS	Sv	IP	H	R	BB	SO	HR
1999 AAA Ottawa	8	5	3.84	16	16	0	89.0	81	40	23	78	12
1999 NL Montreal	0	1	7.61	9	3	0	23.2	30	20	9	28	7

The Dodgers made a tremendous draft pick when they took Lilly out of Fresno (Calif.) City College in the 23rd round in 1996, then gave him away in their ill-fated trade for Hiram Bocachica, Mark Grudzielanek and Carlos Perez. Lilly has very good stuff for a lefthander, led by a curveball that was rated the best breaking pitch in the Triple-A International League. It always has been a strikeout pitch for him, and he fanned 28 in 23.2 big league innings last year. He also throws a four-seam fastball that can reach the low 90s, and his changeup is solid. Lilly got hammered with the Expos because he pitched up in the strike zone, so he may need to pick up a two-seamer. After offseason surgery to remove bone chips from his elbow, he should contend for a spot in Montreal's rotation this spring.

Fernando Seguignol

Position: 1B
Bats: B **Throws:** R
Ht: 6' 5" **Wt:** 179

Opening Day Age: 25
Born: 1/19/75 in Bocas del Toro, Panama

Recent Statistics

	G	AB	R	H	D	T	HR	RBI	SB	BB	SO	Avg
1999 AAA Ottawa	87	312	54	89	17	3	23	74	3	40	96	.285
1999 NL Montreal	35	105	14	27	9	0	5	10	0	5	33	.257
1999 MLE	87	301	44	78	16	2	16	60	2	32	100	.259

When the 1994 strike was settled and the Expos began dumping salaries, they traded star closer John Wetteland to the Yankees for Seguignol and $1 million. Seguignol was a candidate for Montreal's left-field job in spring training and got a look at first base at midseason, but both times he failed to win over manager Felipe Alou. Seguignol's strong suit is power from both sides of the plate. His lack of plate discipline cuts into his batting average, and though he's a decent athlete for a man his size, he's not going to win a big league job with his skills as a basestealer or defender. The development of Peter Bergeron, Milton Bradley and Brad Fullmer is cutting off Seguignol's chances of playing regularly for the Expos.

T.J. Tucker

Position: P
Bats: R **Throws:** R
Ht: 6' 3" **Wt:** 245

Opening Day Age: 21
Born: 8/20/78 in Clearwater, FL

Recent Statistics

	W	L	ERA	G	GS	Sv	IP	H	R	BB	SO	HR
1998 R Expos	1	0	0.75	7	7	0	36.0	23	5	5	40	1
1998 A Vermont	3	1	2.18	6	6	0	33.0	24	9	15	34	0
1998 A Jupiter	1	1	1.00	2	1	0	9.0	5	1	0	10	0
1999 A Jupiter	5	1	1.23	7	7	0	44.0	24	7	16	35	2
1999 AA Harrisburg	8	5	4.10	19	19	0	116.1	110	55	38	85	12

A 1997 supplemental first-round pick, Tucker needed two years before he was ready for full-season ball. He blossomed quickly last year, reaching Double-A and improving his career record to 19-8, 2.67. He has two solid pitches, a 90-94 MPH fastball and a tight curveball, and his changeup is an effective third option. He throws strikes, works both sides of the plate and comes after hitters. After shutting him down late last year with a tired arm, the Expos would like to see him become stronger. They'll send him back to Double-A in 2000 and hope to see him reach the majors sometime the following year.

Jake Westbrook

Position: P
Bats: R **Throws:** R
Ht: 6' 3" **Wt:** 180

Opening Day Age: 22
Born: 9/29/77 in Athens, GA

Recent Statistics

	W	L	ERA	G	GS	Sv	IP	H	R	BB	SO	HR
1998 A Jupiter	11	6	3.26	27	27	0	171.0	169	70	60	79	11
1999 AA Harrisburg	11	5	3.92	27	27	0	174.2	180	88	63	90	14

Westbrook is a product of yet another trade, arriving with two other minor leaguers when Mike Lansing was dealt to Colorado in November 1997. A 1996 first-round pick, Westbrook throws an 89-92 MPH sinker and is still trying to master his secondary pitches, which is why he hasn't posted dominant strikeout-walk or hit-inning ratios. Westbrook got a rough introduction to Double-A last year, going 2-4, 6.18 in his first 12 starts. But he recovered, going 9-1, 2.35 in his final 15 outings. He'll pitch in Triple-A in 2000 and must expand his arsenal before getting a call to Montreal.

Brad Wilkerson

Position: OF
Bats: L **Throws:** L
Ht: 6' 0" **Wt:** 190

Opening Day Age: 22
Born: 6/1/77 in Daviess, KY

Recent Statistics

	G	AB	R	H	D	T	HR	RBI	SB	BB	SO	Avg
1999 AA Harrisburg	138	422	66	99	21	3	8	49	3	88	100	.235
1999 MLE	138	411	53	88	19	2	6	39	2	60	107	.214

Baseball America rated Wilkerson as the best junior (16- to 18-year-old) player from the United States in the 1990s, and he had a banner two-way career at the University of Florida before the Expos made him a supplemental first-round pick in 1998. Montreal will use him strictly as a hitter, and they thought enough of him to let him start his pro career in Double-A last season. Wilkerson was over his head, though his quick bat and power potential remained evident. He was very patient at the plate, perhaps too patient. He's an average runner with the arm to be a top right fielder. His lackluster year didn't worry the Expos, though he won't displace Vladimir Guerrero and will have to contend with other outfield prospects when he's ready for the majors in 2001.

Others to Watch

With the exception of T.J. Tucker, righthander **Donnie Bridges** (21) is the most promising of Montreal's eight 1997 first-round picks. He throws his fastball in the low to mid-90s and also has a hard curveball. . . Lefthander **Josh Girdley** (19), a 1999 first-rounder, signed for a club-record $1.7 million despite being a signability pick. His best pitch is his curveball, and he can touch 93 MPH with his fastball. . . Righthander **Mark Mangum** (21), a Rockies' first-rounder in 1997, was traded to the Expos a year later in a deal for Dave Veres. He's a three-pitch pitcher whose fastball peaks at 92 MPH. . . Catcher **Brian Schneider** (23) had 14 homers in four pro seasons before slamming 17 last year in Double-A. He's mobile behind the plate and has an accurate arm, though it's not particularly strong. . . In his first full pro season, righthander **Jim Serrano** (23) posted a 2.13 ERA with 59 hits allowed and 118 strikeouts in 93 high Class-A innings, then tied for the Arizona Fall League lead with five victories. Though he's just 5-foot-8, he has an outstanding curve and a 90-92 MPH fastball. . . Righthander **Scott Strickland's** (23) ERA kept sinking as he moved up the ladder in 1999, going from 3.51 in high Class-A to 2.48 in Double-A to 1.63 in Triple-A. After showing a 93-94 MPH fastball and a potential plus slider in the AFL, he has a good chance to make the Expos.

Montreal

Shea Stadium

Offense

Shea Stadium continues to be one of the best pitchers' parks in the National League. The ball doesn't carry well, especially to left field, and the lighting is among the worst in the majors. Batting averages suffer here too, so there's no obvious way to build an offense that can exploit the park. Lefthanded power hitters are hurt the least, and most successful Mets clubs have had lefthanded power hitters.

Defense

Shea has a grass surface and symmetrical outfield walls, and makes no unique demands upon defenders. The grass surface has helped the current club to succeed with a groundball staff and strong defensive infield. The park doesn't dictate such a strategy, however, and the Mets of the mid- to late 1980s won with several below-average glove men on the infield.

Who It Helps The Most

Few hitters derive any actual benefit from Shea. The current Met who has been hurt the least by it is Robin Ventura. Benny Agbayani hit better in New York, but his entire season was a fluke and that aspect was no different. Most pitchers are more effective here, especially Al Leiter and Rick Reed. Rookie Octavio Dotel pitched much better at Shea than on the road last year.

Who It Hurts The Most

Righthanded hitters, especially those with power, lose both extra-base hits and points on their batting average. Edgardo Alfonzo and Mike Piazza both fare better on the road. Roger Cedeno and Rickey Henderson both hit better on the road than they did at Shea in 1999. Orel Hershiser derived no advantage from pitching in New York last year, and John Franco never has.

Rookies & Newcomers

Shea will continue to assist Dotel's development. Todd Zeile, who was signed to replace John Olerud, won't get any help, however.

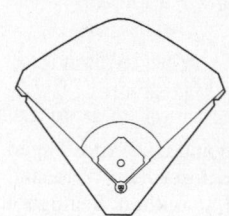

Dimensions: LF-338, LCF-378, CF-410, RCF-378, RF-338

Capacity: 55,777

Elevation: 20 feet

Surface: Grass

Foul Territory: Large

Park Factors

1999 Season

| | Home Games | | | Away Games | | | |
	Mets	Opp	Total	Mets	Opp	Total	Index
G	72	72	144	73	73	146	—
Avg	.262	.253	.257	.293	.249	.272	95
AB	2363	2441	4804	2580	2384	4964	98
R	342	315	657	415	323	738	90
H	619	617	1236	757	594	1351	93
2B	104	136	240	163	132	295	84
3B	3	24	27	9	28	37	75
HR	70	64	134	91	80	171	81
BB	289	289	578	347	251	598	100
SO	419	567	986	466	495	961	106
E	30	52	82	28	46	74	112
E-Infield	24	43	67	25	38	63	108
LHB-Avg	.286	.256	.272	.291	.268	.281	97
LHB-HR	30	15	45	35	30	65	72
RHB-Avg	.244	.251	.248	.295	.239	.267	93
RHB-HR	40	49	89	56	50	106	86

1997-1999

| | Home Games | | | Away Games | | | |
	Mets	Opp	Total	Mets	Opp	Total	Index
G	220	220	440	218	218	436	—
Avg	.265	.251	.258	.269	.260	.265	97
AB	7276	7568	14844	7653	7230	14883	99
R	1038	904	1942	1066	943	2009	96
H	1927	1899	3826	2059	1883	3942	96
2B	369	396	765	409	399	808	95
3B	27	55	82	31	53	84	98
HR	196	190	386	223	219	442	88
BB	823	739	1562	838	728	1566	100
SO	1300	1582	2882	1462	1379	2841	102
E	134	151	285	126	138	264	107
E-Infield	107	123	230	100	112	212	108
LHB-Avg	.289	.259	.275	.270	.272	.271	101
LHB-HR	101	65	166	94	82	176	95
RHB-Avg	.246	.246	.246	.268	.253	.260	94
RHB-HR	95	125	220	129	137	266	83

1999 Rankings (National League)

- Lowest double factor
- Second-lowest RHB batting-average factor
- Third-lowest batting-average factor
- Third-lowest hit factor
- Third-lowest home-run factor

Bobby Valentine

1999 Season

Few managers ever have enjoyed a season as tumultuous as Bobby Valentine's 1999. When the Mets got off to a sluggish start and several of the coaches closest to him were fired in June, Valentine publicly proclaimed that he ought to be fired if the club failed to make the playoffs. That same month, he was suspended for two games and fined $5,000 for returning to the dugout in disguise after being ejected from a game. New York surged during the middle months of the season, then collapsed in the final days. Valentine rallied the troops, who rebounded and caught the Reds at the wire. A victory in a one-game playoff put them in the postseason, where they lost in heroic fashion to the Braves in the National League Championship Series.

Offense

Valentine has come to value on-base ability above all else. When Rickey Henderson was signed last winter, that was one of his few skills that remained in evidence. Valentine has had little patience for players who won't take a walk, such as Carl Everett and Butch Huskey. The ability to pinch-hit in the late innings is especially important to Valentine, and he tries to keep his bench stocked with bats. He generally employs the sacrifice and the hit-and-run more than most managers, but didn't bunt much last season.

Pitching & Defense

Valentine won by building a staff of finesse and groundball pitchers and putting an outstanding defensive infield behind them. He's attuned to each starter's limitations and takes care not to overwork them. This requires him to make extensive use of the bullpen, so he's especially fond of relievers who can work often without breaking down, such as Dennis Cook and Turk Wendell. As Valentine demonstrated in the playoffs, he'll call for the intentional pass more frequently than most managers.

2000 Outlook

Valentine's outspokenness has won him few friends. Therefore the Mets must continue to win in order for his job to remain secure. A poor start could put him on the hot seat.

Born: 5/13/50 in Stamford, CT

Playing Experience: 1969-1979, LA, Ana, SD, NYM, Sea

Managerial Experience: 12 seasons

Manager Statistics

Year	Team, Lg	W	L	Pct	GB	Finish
1999	New York, NL	97	66	.595	6.5	2nd East
12 Seasons		866	838	.508	—	—

1999 Starting Pitchers by Days Rest

	<=3	4	5	6+
Mets Starts	3	53	75	24
Mets ERA	1.96	4.53	4.42	5.30
NL Avg Starts	3	81	48	21
NL ERA	4.84	4.53	4.72	4.98

1999 Situational Stats

	Bobby Valentine	NL Average
Hit & Run Success %	37.0	33.6
Stolen Base Success %	71.1	70.2
Platoon Pct.	55.3	55.2
Defensive Subs	26	25
High-Pitch Outings	13	13
Quick/Slow Hooks	16/12	16/15
Sacrifice Attempts	72	89

1999 Rankings (National League)

- 1st in sacrifice-bunt percentage (94.4%), hit-and-run attempts (119), pinch-hitters used (323) and 2+ pitching changes in low-scoring games (35)
- 3rd in pitchouts (51)

Edgardo Alfonzo

1999 Season

Shifted back to second base last season after New York signed Robin Ventura to play third base, Edgardo Alfonzo blossomed into a superstar. He led National League second basemen with a .304 batting average, and finished second in home runs and RBI to Arizona's Jay Bell. Batting second in the lineup, Alfonzo logged 41 doubles and 85 walks, putting himself on base for the Mets' middle-of-the-order hitters.

Hitting

Alfonzo continues to use the opposite field far more often than most power hitters, though he has learned to turn on the ball when he gets a pitch to drive. During the last two years, he has become more patient and gotten better loft on the ball. Alfonzo tends to take the first strike, but becomes more aggressive afterward. He's still a singles hitter at heart, and knows how to shorten up and protect the plate with two strikes. He has a very quick bat and can adjust to a pitch's movement as well as any hitter in the game.

Baserunning & Defense

Alfonzo proved that he hadn't forgotten how to play the keystone and could make a case for the Gold Glove that went to Cincinnati's Pokey Reese. Alfonzo committed just five errors all year, one of the lowest totals in history for a second baseman. He also turned 98 double plays, more than all but two NL second sackers. Not only does he have all the physical tools—good range, soft hands, accurate arm—but he also has great instincts and fundamentals. Alfonzo doesn't have great speed, though he reads righthanders' moves well enough to steal a handful of bases each season without getting caught very often.

2000 Outlook

With John Olerud heading to Seattle as a free agent, Alfonzo probably will move into the No. 3 spot in the lineup. After one season, he's probably the best all-around second baseman in the NL, and even better years may lie ahead.

Position: 2B
Bats: R **Throws:** R
Ht: 5'11" **Wt:** 187

Opening Day Age: 26
Born: 11/8/73 in St. Teresa, Venezuela
ML Seasons: 5

Overall Statistics

	G	AB	R	H	D	T	HR	RBI	SB	BB	SO	Avg	OBP	Slg
1999	158	628	123	191	41	1	27	108	9	85	85	.304	.385	.502
Career	677	2406	363	698	124	12	62	339	31	250	311	.290	.356	.429

Where He Hits the Ball

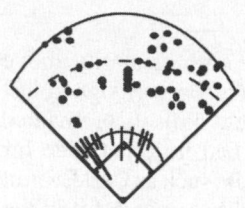

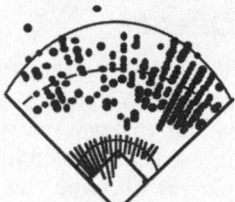

Vs. LHP **Vs. RHP**

1999 Situational Stats

	AB	H	HR	RBI	Avg		AB	H	HR	RBI	Avg
Home	303	85	11	42	.281	LHP	138	37	6	20	.268
Road	325	106	16	66	.326	RHP	490	154	21	88	.314
First Half	348	103	12	55	.296	Sc Pos	157	48	6	77	.306
Scnd Half	280	88	15	53	.314	Clutch	86	25	4	12	.291

1999 Rankings (National League)

- 1st in fielding percentage at second base (.993)
- 2nd in lowest groundball/flyball ratio (0.7)
- 3rd in at-bats, runs scored, sacrifice flies (9) and pitches seen (2,951)
- 4th in plate appearances (726)
- 7th in most pitches seen per plate appearance (4.06), hits, doubles and times on base (279)
- 8th in lowest batting average with the bases loaded (.091)
- Led the Mets in batting average on an 0-2 count (.270), at-bats, runs scored, hits, singles, doubles, total bases (315), sacrifice flies (9), pitches seen (2,951) and plate appearances (726)

Armando Benitez

Position: RP
Bats: R **Throws:** R
Ht: 6' 4" **Wt:** 229

Opening Day Age: 27
Born: 11/3/72 in Ramon Santana, Dominican Republic
ML Seasons: 6
Pronunciation: buh-NEE-tezz

1999 Season

Armando Benitez finally matured, both as a pitcher and a person, after the Orioles sent him to New York in a three-way trade that also netted the Mets Roger Cedeno and cost them Todd Hundley and minor league pitcher Arnold Gooch. Benitez excelled over the first half as a setup man, and stepped up as the closer after John Franco went down in July. Benitez notched 19 saves over the last three months and remained the closer even after Franco returned in September. Furthermore, Benitez handled the pressure of the role admirably and pitched effectively in the postseason despite an injured ankle. His 14.77 strikeouts per nine innings were the second-highest total in major league history, trailing only Billy Wagner's 14.95 last year.

Pitching

Benitez has an upper-90s fastball that's among the fastest in the game. He turned the corner last year after improving his split-finger fastball. The splitter gave him a reliable second pitch, enabling him to spot his less reliable slider. The variation in speed and movement between his splitter and four-seam fastball made him more unhittable than ever. He held hitters to a .148 batting average, the second-lowest mark in the majors. He still works up in the strike zone but no longer is plagued by the longball, allowing just four last season.

Defense & Hitting

Benitez induces fewer groundballs than any pitcher in baseball, so he rarely gets the chance to participate in the field. He's adequate with the glove and hasn't made an error in three years. He pays absolutely no attention to baserunners and is easy to steal against. Benitez got his first five professional at-bats last year and still is looking for his first hit.

2000 Outlook

Benitez grabbed the closer's job last year and may hold it for years to come. Even a completely recovered John Franco probably won't be able to bump him back to middle relief. There's every reason to think Benitez will be one of the major leagues' best finishers over the next few seasons.

Overall Statistics

	W	L	Pct.	ERA	G	GS	Sv	IP	H	BB	SO	HR	Ratio
1999	4	3	.571	1.85	77	0	22	78.0	40	41	128	4	1.04
Career	15	19	.441	3.15	284	0	59	291.2	189	170	411	31	1.23

How Often He Throws Strikes

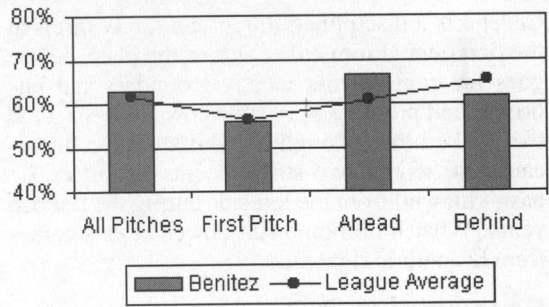

1999 Situational Stats

	W	L	ERA	Sv	IP		AB	H	HR	RBI	Avg
Home	3	1	1.54	12	41.0	LHB	113	20	2	10	.177
Road	1	2	2.19	10	37.0	RHB	158	20	2	11	.127
First Half	0	2	1.39	6	45.1	Sc Pos	85	12	1	17	.141
Scnd Half	4	1	2.48	16	32.2	Clutch	177	30	4	18	.169

1999 Rankings (National League)

- 2nd in relief ERA (1.85), lowest batting average allowed in relief (.148) and most strikeouts per nine innings in relief (14.8)
- 3rd in lowest batting average allowed in relief with runners on base (.156) and fewest baserunners allowed per nine innings in relief (9.3)
- Led the Mets in saves, games finished (42), save opportunities (28), blown saves (6), first batter efficiency (.148), lowest batting average allowed in relief with runners on base (.156), lowest percentage of inherited runners scored (20.0), relief ERA (1.85), lowest batting average allowed in relief (.148), fewest baserunners allowed per nine innings in relief (9.3) and most strikeouts per nine innings in relief (14.8)

Roger Cedeno

1999 Season

Of all of the Mets' offseason acquisitions last year, the biggest steal was Roger Cedeno, who came over from the Dodgers in a three-way trade and ended up nearly leading the National League in steals himself. All New York had to give up to get Cedeno and Armando Benitez was Todd Hundley and minor leaguer Arnold Gooch. Cedeno became New York's regular non-regular, often starting in right field against righthanders. He also started in left and center, pinch-hit and served as a defensive replacement. He batted leadoff whenever Rickey Henderson was out, batted .313 and did a fine job all around.

Hitting

Cedeno is a disciplined hitter who rarely offers at the first pitch. From either side of the plate, he just goes for contact, hits mostly grounders and line drives, and provides very little power. He's a good two-strike hitter, though he whiffs quite a bit because he works two-strike counts so often. He hasn't hit well from the left side during the last two years. What little home-run power he has comes from his natural right side.

Baserunning & Defense

Though Cedeno was a good basestealer when given the opportunity in Los Angeles, his 66-for-83 performance last year still was a pleasant surprise. He proved that he was able to steal even in big situations when opposing teams were keying on him. He always has been very quick, both on the bases and in the outfield. Cedeno's range is good in center field and well above average at the corners. His arm is a little weak for right field, but he gets to the ball quickly and throws accurately.

2000 Outlook

Cedeno's walks and steals fell off in the second half last year, so he may regress a bit in 2000 as opponents pay more attention to him at the plate and on the bases. He's still very young and looks to have a fine future as a leadoff man.

Position: RF/CF/LF
Bats: B **Throws:** R
Ht: 6' 1" **Wt:** 205

Opening Day Age: 25
Born: 8/16/74 in Valencia Edo. Carabobo, Venezuela
ML Seasons: 5
Pronunciation: suh-DAYN-yoh

Overall Statistics

	G	AB	R	H	D	T	HR	RBI	SB	BB	SO	Avg	OBP	Slg
1999	155	453	90	142	23	4	4	36	66	60	100	.313	.396	.408
Career	466	1140	184	315	57	8	11	91	89	139	258	.276	.357	.369

Where He Hits the Ball

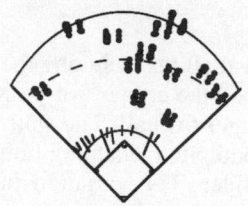 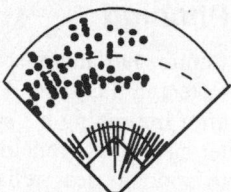

Vs. LHP   **Vs. RHP**

1999 Situational Stats

	AB	H	HR	RBI	Avg		AB	H	HR	RBI	Avg
Home	229	64	4	14	.279	LHP	67	13	3	8	.194
Road	224	78	0	22	.348	RHP	386	129	1	28	.334
First Half	241	80	2	20	.332	Sc Pos	109	31	1	33	.284
Scnd Half	212	62	2	16	.292	Clutch	56	15	0	6	.268

1999 Rankings (National League)

- 1st in steals of third (16)
- 2nd in highest groundball/flyball ratio (2.2), stolen bases and caught stealing (17)
- Led the Mets in highest groundball/flyball ratio (2.2), stolen-base percentage (79.5), fewest GDPs per GDP situation (6.0%), batting average vs. righthanded pitchers, bunts in play (19), steals of third (16), triples, stolen bases and caught stealing (17)
- Led NL right fielders in highest groundball/fly-ball ratio (2.2), on-base percentage for a leadoff hitter (.371), steals of third (16), sacrifice bunts (7), stolen bases and caught stealing (17)

John Franco

Position: RP
Bats: L **Throws:** L
Ht: 5'10" **Wt:** 185

Opening Day Age: 39
Born: 9/17/60 in Brooklyn, NY
ML Seasons: 16

1999 Season

In his 16th year in the majors, John Franco finally made it to the postseason. The road there was far from smooth, however. He was proceeding as usual in his accustomed role as the Mets' closer when he tore a tendon in his left middle finger in June. By the time he returned in August, young Armando Benitez had taken over as the closer. Franco was spotted carefully in September, though he returned to pitch well in the playoffs. He needed six cortisone shots in his sore left shoulder along the way just to make it there.

Pitching

Franco pitches more like a veteran starter than a closer. His sinking fastball is nothing special. He succeeds by throwing sliders and changeups that look like strikes for the first 50 feet. He's great at getting groundballs and keeping the ball in the park. Lefthanders can hit him, but not hard. No lefty has homered off him in the last six years. In light of his age and various physical woes last year, he may not be capable of pitching on consecutive days as often as he once was.

Defense & Hitting

Basestealers went 10-for-10 against Franco last year, though that had more to do with the abilities of the Mets' catchers than his inattention. Before 1999, he'd allowed only seven steals during the previous five years. He's a reliable fielder whose last error came in 1991. As a closer, he rarely gets the chance to hit.

2000 Outlook

Franco's days as the Mets' full-time closer may be behind him. Benitez grew into the role last year, and Franco may have to be content to contribute in a less glamorous capacity. His soft stuff provides an excellent contrast to Benitez' sheer heat, so Franco may do well in a setup role while picking up the odd save when matchups dictate that he pitch the ninth.

Overall Statistics

	W	L	Pct.	ERA	G	GS	Sv	IP	H	BB	SO	HR	Ratio
1999	0	2	.000	2.88	46	0	19	40.2	40	19	41	1	1.45
Career	77	70	.524	2.64	878	0	416	1041.1	961	404	801	56	1.31

How Often He Throws Strikes

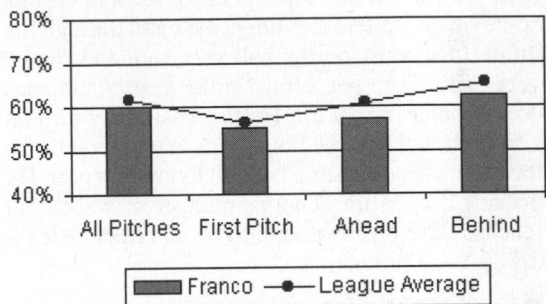

1999 Situational Stats

	W	L	ERA	Sv	IP			AB	H	HR	RBI	Avg
Home	0	2	3.05	10	20.2	LHB		30	9	0	3	.300
Road	0	0	2.70	9	20.0	RHB		127	31	1	12	.244
First Half	0	2	3.45	19	31.1	Sc Pos		39	11	1	15	.282
Scnd Half	0	0	0.96	0	9.1	Clutch		89	29	0	12	.326

1999 Rankings (National League)

- 3rd in save percentage (90.5)
- Led the Mets in save percentage (90.5)

Darryl Hamilton

1999 Season

The Mets obtained Darryl Hamilton and Chuck McElroy from the Rockies at the trade deadline for Brian McRae and Rigo Beltran. Hamilton gave them what McRae couldn't: a center fielder capable of making a decent offensive contribution. Hamilton played with a sore left knee all year and was bothered at times by a sore left Achilles tendon. Both ailments affected him on the bases and, to a lesser extent, in the field. It didn't bother him at the plate, as he posted a career-high .315 average.

Hitting

Hamilton is a pure singles hitter, using his wrists to flick the ball wherever it's pitched. Most of his hits come on grounders and liners over and through the infield. He waits on the ball very well and can be very difficult to get a third strike past. Southpaws don't bother him at all. He'll occasionally turn on a fastball, but his five home runs in two months for the Mets are something he isn't likely to repeat. He doesn't draw a tremendous number of walks, but reaches base often enough to be an effective leadoff or No. 2 hitter.

Baserunning & Defense

Hamilton's basestealing totals have been in decline for several years, but last year's 6-for-14 performance was by far his worst. Offseason surgery may fix his knee, but he no longer has the quickness to be much of a basestealer even when healthy. Hamilton still has the range to cover center field, though. Even with a bum knee, he got good jumps and ran down his share of flyballs, and he didn't commit a single error all year. His throwing arm is weak, but his throws are accurate.

2000 Outlook

Hamilton has two years remaining on a three-season, $10.5 million contract he signed with Colorado as a free agent. Because he was traded in the midst of a multiyear deal, he had the right to demand a trade, which he exercised. If the Mets don't comply or reach agreement with him on a new contract by March 15, he'll become a free agent. Offseason surgery on his knee and toe may help him have a better year in 2000.

Position: CF
Bats: L **Throws:** R
Ht: 6' 1" **Wt:** 192

Opening Day Age: 35
Born: 12/3/64 in Baton Rouge, LA
ML Seasons: 11
Nickname: Hambone

Overall Statistics

	G	AB	R	H	D	T	HR	RBI	SB	BB	SO	Avg	OBP	Slg
1999	146	505	82	159	19	4	9	45	6	57	39	.315	.386	.422
Career	1233	4346	672	1277	193	35	49	443	158	460	454	.294	.361	.388

Where He Hits the Ball

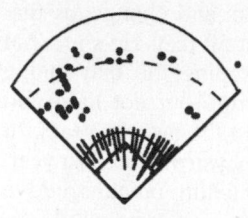 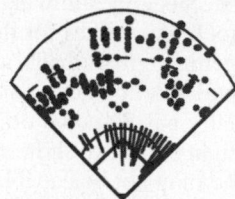

Vs. LHP   **Vs. RHP**

1999 Situational Stats

	AB	H	HR	RBI	Avg		AB	H	HR	RBI	Avg
Home	235	85	5	24	.362	LHP	147	42	2	9	.286
Road	270	74	4	21	.274	RHP	358	117	7	36	.327
First Half	297	92	3	21	.310	Sc Pos	114	32	2	36	.281
Scnd Half	208	67	6	24	.322	Clutch	76	22	1	7	.289

1999 Rankings (National League)

- 1st in batting average on an 0-2 count (.333)
- 4th in batting average at home (.362)
- 6th in singles (127)
- 8th in batting average vs. righthanded pitchers (.327)
- 10th in on-base percentage for a leadoff hitter (.367) and lowest slugging percentage vs. lefthanded pitchers (.347)
- Led NL center fielders in highest groundball/flyball ratio (1.5), batting average on an 0-2 count (.333), batting average with two strikes (.253) and batting average at home (.362)

Rickey Henderson

Position: LF
Bats: R **Throws:** L
Ht: 5'10" **Wt:** 190

Opening Day Age: 41
Born: 12/25/58 in Chicago, IL
ML Seasons: 21

1999 Season

The Mets signed ancient Rickey Henderson to a one-year, $1.8 million contract as a free agent, hoping he had one more decent year left in him. He exceeded all expectations, raising his average 79 points over his 1998 mark while providing the spark for one of the most potent lineups in the game. Though knee and hamstring problems sidelined him early on, he was a big contributor over the last four months of the season as the Mets attained the National League wild-card berth.

Hitting

Henderson's batting average had trailed off in recent years, but the return to New York seemed to rejuvenate him. He showed more power than he had in years, especially away from Shea Stadium, where he didn't hit all that well. His biggest asset remains his ability to work a walk. His crouch gives him a small strike zone, and he has a quick enough bat to stay alive with two strikes. His ability to reach base is the reason he remains one of the game's best leadoff men. He's a hot-weather hitter and tends to do his best work in the midsummer months.

Baserunning & Defense

Though most players his age have given up basestealing altogether, Henderson remains one of the most effective thieves in the game. He's still quick and reads pitchers as well as anyone. He was regularly removed for late-inning defense last year, but that was as much to save his legs as anything. He's a decent left fielder with enough speed to overcome his sometimes uncertain jumps. His throwing arm is his only real weakness, and he didn't register a single assist last year during the regular season.

2000 Outlook

Henderson's contract option for 2000 automatically kicked in with his 500th plate appearance in 1999. Despite his strong numbers, he caused friction with teammates and manager Bobby Valentine, so the Mets may shop him. Regardless of where he plays, Henderson ought to remain an effective leadoff man.

Overall Statistics

	G	AB	R	H	D	T	HR	RBI	SB	BB	SO	Avg	OBP	Slg
1999	121	438	89	138	30	0	12	42	37	82	82	.315	.423	.466
Career	2733	9911	2103	2816	472	60	278	1020	1334	1972	1472	.284	.405	.428

Where He Hits the Ball

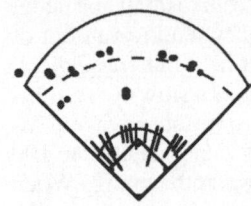

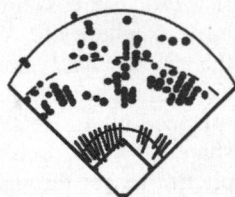

Vs. LHP   **Vs. RHP**

1999 Situational Stats

	AB	H	HR	RBI	Avg		AB	H	HR	RBI	Avg
Home	200	54	1	14	.270	LHP	105	36	6	9	.343
Road	238	84	11	28	.353	RHP	333	102	6	33	.306
First Half	200	60	6	19	.300	Sc Pos	79	17	1	30	.215
Scnd Half	238	78	6	23	.328	Clutch	53	17	1	7	.321

1999 Rankings (National League)

- 1st in on-base percentage for a leadoff hitter (.417), on-base percentage vs. lefthanded pitchers (.481) and highest percentage of pitches taken (65.0)
- Led the Mets in most pitches seen per plate appearance (4.27), batting average in the clutch, batting average vs. lefthanded pitchers, on-base percentage for a leadoff hitter (.417), slugging percentage vs. lefthanded pitchers (.581), on-base percentage vs. lefthanded pitchers (.481), batting average with two strikes (.258), highest percentage of extra bases taken as a runner (64.3), highest percentage of pitches taken (65.0) and batting average

Al Leiter

1999 Season

Though he did his best to gut it out, it's clear that Al Leiter was greatly hampered by the knee problem that plagued him last year. The patellar tendinitis in his left knee originally developed in the second half of 1998. He aggravated the injury in late April and struggled mightily for the next month. He righted himself in June and pitched well for the rest of the year—but not quite as well as a fully healthy Leiter might have. He rose to the occasion in the wild-card playoff game with the Reds, tossing a two-hit shutout.

Pitching

After learning to use the outside corner more in 1998, Leiter went back to pounding hitters in on the fists last year. His hard two-seam fastball and cutter have excellent life. While they tend to run out of the strike zone, batters can't help but chase them. Leiter mixes in a slider and uses a slow curve as his offspeed pitch. He's tough to hit but gives up his share of walks, and usually takes well over 100 pitches to get through the seventh inning. When he's on his game, he'll allow few well-hit balls. Stamina has been a strength of his until last year, when he often tired after 80 or 90 pitches.

Defense & Hitting

Leiter normally combats the running game fairly well, though he wasn't able to prevent runners from challenging the Mets' catchers last year. He's normally reliable in the field but committed four errors in 1999. His delivery makes it hard for him to get over to cover first base, and his knee further hampered his mobility last year. Though his hitting remains weak, he's become an adept bunter.

2000 Outlook

Leiter got his knee repaired after the close of the season. He was pitching the best ball of his life before the condition cropped up in mid-1998. If his knee is sound, he's a good bet to make a strong comeback.

Position: SP
Bats: L **Throws:** L
Ht: 6' 3" **Wt:** 220

Opening Day Age: 34
Born: 10/23/65 in Toms River, NJ
ML Seasons: 13
Pronunciation: LITE-er

Overall Statistics

	W	L	Pct.	ERA	G	GS	Sv	IP	H	BB	SO	HR	Ratio
1999	13	12	.520	4.23	32	32	0	213.0	209	93	162	19	1.42
Career	90	71	.559	3.82	233	203	2	1294.2	1136	683	1107	94	1.40

How Often He Throws Strikes

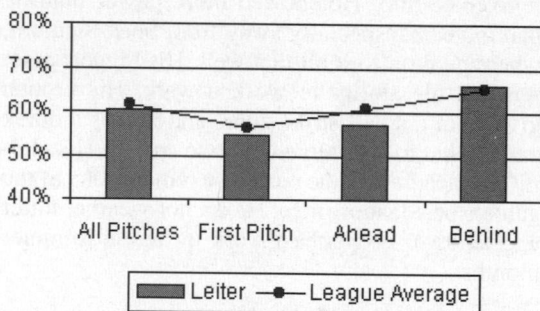

Leiter — League Average

1999 Situational Stats

	W	L	ERA	Sv	IP		AB	H	HR	RBI	Avg
Home	8	5	4.18	0	112.0	LHB	123	32	2	17	.260
Road	5	7	4.28	0	101.0	RHB	675	177	17	83	.262
First Half	8	6	4.81	0	110.1	Sc Pos	211	56	6	81	.265
Scnd Half	5	6	3.59	0	102.2	Clutch	56	20	5	13	.357

1999 Rankings (National League)

- 3rd in stolen bases allowed (26)
- 5th in most pitches thrown per batter (3.89)
- Led the Mets in ERA, wins, losses, innings pitched, hits allowed, batters faced (923), walks allowed, strikeouts, pitches thrown (3,587), pick-off throws (102), stolen bases allowed (26), GDPs induced (24), most strikeouts per nine innings (6.8), ERA at home, lowest batting average allowed with runners in scoring position, sacrifice bunts (11), games started and runners caught stealing (8)

John Olerud

1999 Season

The middle of the Mets' batting order was one of the most potent in baseball last year, and John Olerud deserves a lot of credit. Batting third in the lineup, he both drove in close to 100 runs and got on base for the run producers behind him. He didn't miss a single game and played his usual flawless defense. Olerud's demeanor and style of play may not attract attention, but he managed to grab the spotlight in spite of himself when he came through with several big hits in the postseason.

Hitting

Olerud uses his textbook swing to send liners to all fields. He's especially dangerous on pitches down and in. He hits lefthanders well, though his average against them was down last year. He takes southpaws' breaking balls to left field. Most of his power comes against righthanders when he's able to pull the ball. He's strongest on inside pitches and covers the entire plate well. With a terrific eye and amazing bat control, he's one of the toughest two-strike hitters around.

Baserunning & Defense

Olerud has been among the best-fielding first basemen for years, and only now is beginning to get his due. He committed nine errors last year, his highest total in six years, but was properly recognized for helping to form baseball's best defensive infield. Olerud went 26-4 as a pitcher at Washington State and has one of the best arms of any major league first baseman. On the bases, he's a plodder who knows his limits.

2000 Outlook

Olerud declared free agency and ultimately was torn between returning to New York or heading home to Seattle. Both the Mets and Mariners made similar offers, and Olerud signed with Seattle for three years and $20 million. His relationship with Mariners GM Pat Gillick, who orchestrated Olerud's original signing with Toronto, may have been the difference. Few players are better bets to remain consistent and productive. After his departure, the Mets quickly signed Todd Zeile to replace him, at the cost of three years and $18 million.

Position: 1B
Bats: L **Throws:** L
Ht: 6' 5" **Wt:** 220

Opening Day Age: 31
Born: 8/5/68 in Seattle, WA
ML Seasons: 11
Pronunciation: OAL-uh-rude

Overall Statistics

	G	AB	R	H	D	T	HR	RBI	SB	BB	SO	Avg	OBP	Slg
1999	162	581	107	173	39	0	19	96	3	125	66	.298	.427	.463
Career	1396	4765	752	1434	322	11	172	762	8	820	636	.301	.406	.481

Where He Hits the Ball

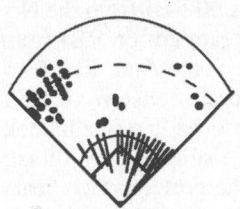 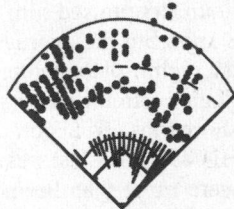

Vs. LHP   **Vs. RHP**

1999 Situational Stats

	AB	H	HR	RBI	Avg		AB	H	HR	RBI	Avg
Home	283	84	11	53	.297	LHP	166	41	2	20	.247
Road	298	89	8	43	.299	RHP	415	132	17	76	.318
First Half	304	94	13	52	.309	Sc Pos	160	48	6	72	.300
Scnd Half	277	79	6	44	.285	Clutch	86	23	4	19	.267

1999 Rankings (National League)

- 1st in games played
- 2nd in highest percentage of pitches taken (64.7), times on base (309) and GDPs (22)
- 3rd in on-base percentage vs. righthanded pitchers (.447)
- 4th in errors at first base (9) and walks
- 5th in on-base percentage, plate appearances (723) and lowest slugging percentage vs. lefthanded pitchers (.325)
- Led the Mets in on-base percentage, on-base percentage vs. righthanded pitchers (.447), walks, hit by pitch (11), times on base (309) and games played

Rey Ordonez

1999 Season

Rey Ordonez had his finest season last year. At shortstop, he was the centerpiece of what was hailed as the greatest defensive infield of all time. His hitting was better than ever—though still a liability—and he took his already stellar defense to another level.

Hitting

Ordonez is the worst-hitting regular in the majors. His batting average is adequate, but represents the sum total of his offensive contributions. He's far too aggressive, rarely walks and has virtually no power. His on-base plus slugging percentage was the lowest in the National League last year, as it was in 1998. In the postseason, television announcers praised him for his 60 RBI from the No. 8 spot, but the average NL team got 66 RBI from its eighth-place hitters last year. And 13 of 15 Senior Circuit clubs got more offense from their shortstops. To his credit, Ordonez is a fine bunter. His 49 walks last year, while still too low a total, were more than he had in the previous two years combined.

Baserunning & Defense

Ordonez' defensive contributions are so great that his inability to hit never has come close to costing him his job. He no longer is merely spectacular, but reliable as well. Ordonez made just four errors last year, the second-lowest total in history for a regular shortstop. Meanwhile, he continued to make the jaw-dropping stops and off-balance throws that have become his trademark. Winner of three consecutive Gold Gloves, Ordonez is one of the most creative defenders of his generation, making plays in ways that never have been seen before. He had better success on the bases last year, but his baserunning still can't be called an asset.

2000 Outlook

It would be foolish to expect Ordonez to duplicate last year's nearly flawless season afield, but it's now clear that his defensive reputation rests on more than flash and style. He may never hit, and the Mets may never care.

Position: SS
Bats: R **Throws:** R
Ht: 5' 9" **Wt:** 159

Opening Day Age: 27
Born: 11/11/72 in Havana, Cuba
ML Seasons: 4
Pronunciation: RAY or-DOAN-yez

Overall Statistics

	G	AB	R	H	D	T	HR	RBI	SB	BB	SO	Avg	OBP	Slg
1999	154	520	49	134	24	2	1	60	8	49	59	.258	.319	.317
Career	578	1883	181	464	61	11	4	165	23	112	208	.246	.288	.297

Where He Hits the Ball

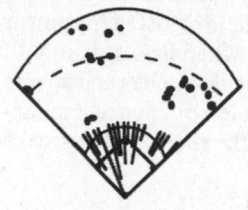
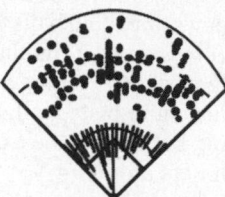

Vs. LHP **Vs. RHP**

1999 Situational Stats

	AB	H	HR	RBI	Avg		AB	H	HR	RBI	Avg
Home	253	59	1	24	.233	LHP	130	30	0	14	.231
Road	267	75	0	36	.281	RHP	390	104	1	46	.267
First Half	264	73	0	30	.277	Sc Pos	160	42	1	60	.263
Scnd Half	256	61	1	30	.238	Clutch	67	9	0	6	.134

1999 Rankings (National League)

- 1st in fielding percentage at shortstop (.994), lowest slugging percentage and lowest slugging percentage vs. lefthanded pitchers (.269)
- 2nd in lowest HR frequency (520.0 ABs per HR) and lowest slugging percentage vs. righthanded pitchers (.333)
- 3rd in lowest batting average at home
- 4th in fewest pitches seen per plate appearance (3.23) and lowest batting average in the clutch
- 5th in highest groundball/flyball ratio (1.8) and lowest on-base percentage vs. lefthanded pitchers (.295)
- Led the Mets in sacrifice bunts (11) and intentional walks (12)

Mike Piazza

1999 Season

In his first full season with the Mets, Mike Piazza had another fine year at the plate. Batting cleanup, he matched his career highs with 40 homers and 124 RBI in just 141 games. The downside was that he was unable to produce when the Mets needed him most. By the time New York had made it to the playoffs, a series of foul tips and home-plate collisions had left Piazza battered and bruised. His poor hitting and throwing contributed to the Mets' National League Championship Series defeat, and left some wondering if they might be better off shifting their best hitter to a less hazardous position.

Hitting

Piazza is one of the most powerful hitters in the game and can clear the fences in any part of the ballpark. His strong wrists and hands not only give him explosive power but also impressive bat control. He remains dangerous even with two strikes. In the past, pitchers tried to survive by keeping the ball down and trying to make him hit it on the ground, but he did a better job of getting the ball in the air last year. He sometimes will press in clutch situations and chase fastballs up and out of the zone.

Baserunning & Defense

Piazza is a poor defensive catcher. His weak, erratic throwing arm is his greatest liability. Opponents stole an NL-high 115 bases against him last year, and he nailed just 30 basestealers. Piazza isn't very mobile or adept at blocking balls in the dirt. He has no speed at all and runs the bases conservatively.

2000 Outlook

Piazza caught the third-most innings in the majors last year, and the workload obviously took its toll. He may resist the move, but the Mets may need to shift him to first base within the next season or two, simply to keep his bat in the lineup. The free-agent defection of John Olerud may open the door for such a shift. As a first baseman, Piazza conceivably could reach greater offensive heights.

Position: C
Bats: R **Throws:** R
Ht: 6' 3" **Wt:** 215

Opening Day Age: 31
Born: 9/4/68 in Norristown, PA
ML Seasons: 8
Pronunciation: pee-AH-zuh

Overall Statistics

	G	AB	R	H	D	T	HR	RBI	SB	BB	SO	Avg	OBP	Slg
1999	141	534	100	162	25	0	40	124	2	51	70	.303	.361	.575
Career	981	3653	611	1200	173	4	240	768	13	381	563	.328	.391	.575

Where He Hits the Ball

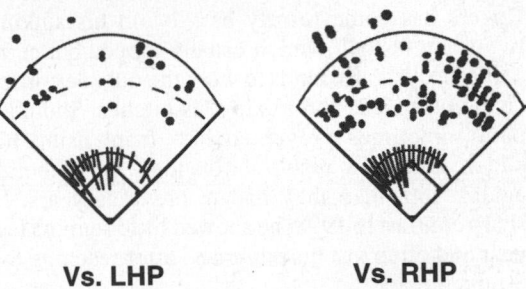

Vs. LHP   Vs. RHP

1999 Situational Stats

	AB	H	HR	RBI	Avg		AB	H	HR	RBI	Avg
Home	252	71	18	56	.282	LHP	131	39	11	27	.298
Road	282	91	22	68	.323	RHP	403	123	29	97	.305
First Half	271	86	19	57	.317	Sc Pos	167	49	8	77	.293
Scnd Half	263	76	21	67	.289	Clutch	69	15	5	14	.217

1999 Rankings (National League)

- 1st in GDPs (27)
- 2nd in errors at catcher (11)
- 4th in cleanup slugging percentage (.577) and lowest fielding percentage at catcher (.989)
- 6th in most GDPs per GDP situation (17.1%)
- 7th in HR frequency (13.4 ABs per HR), home runs and RBI
- 8th in intentional walks (11)
- 9th in slugging percentage
- Led the Mets in slugging percentage, HR frequency (13.4 ABs per HR), cleanup slugging percentage (.577), slugging percentage vs. righthanded pitchers (.573), batting average on a 3-2 count (.348), home runs, RBI and GDPs (27)

Kenny Rogers

1999 Season

It was an unsatisfying season for Kenny Rogers, who was plagued by persistent physical ailments and rarely was at his best. Coming off one of his best years, he began the season in Oakland but made it clear that he wanted out. Back, shoulder and hamstring problems affected his performance, even after he was shipped to the Mets in July for minor leaguers Terrence Long and Leo Vazquez. Though he posted a decent won-lost record, Rogers rarely pitched into the late innings and had an atrocious postseason. With weaker teams behind him, his numbers would have been more reflective of the mediocre season he had.

Pitching

Rogers has come to rely heavily on his sinking two-seam fastball, which usually topped out at 90 MPH last year. He tends to work the outside corner, changing speeds and mixing his pitches. Shoulder pain sometimes prevented him from using his slider, and as a result, lefthanders fared better against him than they had in previous years. In sharp contrast to 1998, he showed little stamina last year and often lost his command after reaching the 80-pitch mark.

Defense & Hitting

Rogers' pickoff move is one of the best in the business and completely negates the running game. It's simply impossible to get a good jump against him. He's a good fielder, scooping up many of the groundballs he induces. After having spent his entire career in the American League, he showed nothing at the plate during his first go-round in the National League.

2000 Outlook

The Mets wanted to offer Rogers arbitration, but a clause in his contract might have precluded that and he threatened to file a grievance if they did. He'll attract plenty of interest as a free agent, but teams may be understandably wary of his spotty health record. He could be in line for a much better year if he's 100 percent, but banking on Rogers to be 100 percent is always a gamble.

Position: SP
Bats: L **Throws:** L
Ht: 6' 1" **Wt:** 217

Opening Day Age: 35
Born: 11/10/64 in Savannah, GA
ML Seasons: 11

Overall Statistics

	W	L	Pct.	ERA	G	GS	Sv	IP	H	BB	SO	HR	Ratio
1999	10	4	.714	4.19	31	31	0	195.1	206	69	126	16	1.41
Career	114	78	.594	4.05	502	217	28	1701.1	1686	651	1114	166	1.37

How Often He Throws Strikes

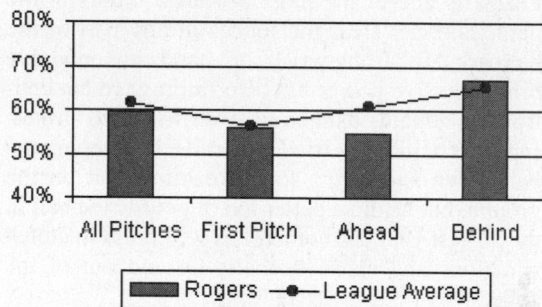

1999 Situational Stats

	W	L	ERA	Sv	IP		AB	H	HR	RBI	Avg
Home	6	0	3.93	0	103.0	LHB	157	43	6	23	.274
Road	4	4	4.48	0	92.1	RHB	592	163	10	64	.275
First Half	4	3	4.02	0	107.1	Sc Pos	159	44	3	69	.277
Scnd Half	6	1	4.40	0	88.0	Clutch	39	16	0	7	.410

1999 Rankings (National League)
- Led the Mets in complete games (2)

Robin Ventura

1999 Season

Robin Ventura turned out to be one of last year's best free-agent signings. After having spent his entire career with the White Sox, he came to the Mets for four years and $32 million. He responded with his best season ever, posting personal highs with a .301 average and 120 RBI, and did his part to make the Mets' infield the best defensive unit in baseball. Ventura was hobbled by torn cartilage in his left knee during the stretch run and postseason, but gutted it out and missed only one game all year.

Hitting

Ventura was a line-drive hitter when he first came up, but over the last few years has become more of a true home-run hitter, lofting more high flyballs. He's a straight pull hitter whose power extends from the right-field gap to the line. He hangs in well against lefthanders' breaking balls, and some of the pitchers he hits best are the southpaw specialists often brought in to face him. His performance last year dispelled any notions that he'd lost some bat speed.

Baserunning & Defense

Ventura won a Gold Glove in his first National League season after winning five with the White Sox. Though he lacks speed, he has good reactions and first-step quickness. With soft hands and a strong, accurate arm, he makes the tough plays look easy. Ventura hasn't lost much speed, despite a severe ankle injury in 1996. He didn't have much to lose, though. He has remained aggressive on the bases, though it doesn't always pay off for him. He knows better than to try to steal bases.

2000 Outlook

Ventura had successful knee surgery after the season and should be 100 percent for spring training, He appears to have several prime years left. The Mets hope he'll remain a fixture in the middle of their batting order for many years to come. If last season was any indication, the National League and Shea Stadium seem to suit Ventura just fine.

Position: 3B
Bats: L **Throws:** R
Ht: 6' 1" **Wt:** 198

Opening Day Age: 32
Born: 7/14/67 in Santa Maria, CA
ML Seasons: 11

Overall Statistics

	G	AB	R	H	D	T	HR	RBI	SB	BB	SO	Avg	OBP	Slg
1999	161	588	88	177	38	0	32	120	1	74	109	.301	.379	.529
Career	1415	5130	746	1421	257	12	203	861	16	742	768	.277	.366	.450

Where He Hits the Ball

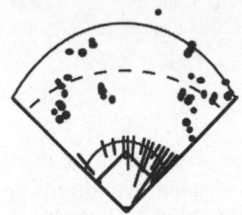

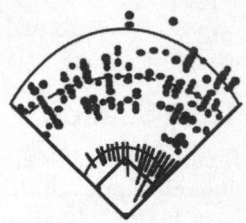

Vs. LHP   **Vs. RHP**

1999 Situational Stats

	AB	H	HR	RBI	Avg		AB	H	HR	RBI	Avg
Home	282	87	13	56	.309	LHP	181	49	9	39	.271
Road	306	90	19	64	.294	RHP	407	128	23	81	.314
First Half	315	89	15	66	.283	Sc Pos	160	54	7	86	.338
Scnd Half	273	88	17	54	.322	Clutch	84	21	3	10	.250

1999 Rankings (National League)

- 1st in fielding percentage at third base (.980)
- 5th in games played
- 8th in batting average with the bases loaded (.529) and RBI
- 9th in lowest groundball/flyball ratio (0.8)
- 10th in intentional walks (10)
- Led the Mets in batting average with runners in scoring position, batting average with the bases loaded (.529), strikeouts and batting average at home
- Led NL third basemen in games played (161)

Benny Agbayani

Position: LF/RF
Bats: R **Throws:** R
Ht: 6' 0" **Wt:** 225

Opening Day Age: 28
Born: 12/28/71 in Honolulu, HI
ML Seasons: 2
Nickname: The Hawaiian Punch
Pronunciation: ag-by-YAWN-ee

Overall Statistics

	G	AB	R	H	D	T	HR	RBI	SB	BB	SO	Avg	OBP	Slg
1999	101	276	42	79	18	3	14	42	6	32	60	.286	.363	.525
Career	112	291	43	81	18	3	14	42	6	33	65	.278	.355	.505

1999 Situational Stats

	AB	H	HR	RBI	Avg		AB	H	HR	RBI	Avg
Home	139	40	10	24	.288	LHP	104	31	5	11	.298
Road	137	39	4	18	.285	RHP	172	48	9	31	.279
First Half	132	40	11	21	.303	Sc Pos	84	25	2	29	.298
Scnd Half	144	39	3	21	.271	Clutch	38	6	1	4	.158

1999 Season

Benny Agbayani's emergence was one of the most unlikely stories of the Mets' season. Called up on May 11, the 27-year-old rookie hit like Babe Ruth incarnate for the rest of the month, batting .442 with six homers. Though he batted .237 over the remainder of the season, he shared time in left and right field and remained an important contributor.

Hitting, Baserunning & Defense

Agbayani is a pull hitter with decent power. He never hit more than 11 home runs in any minor league season, so he probably won't repeat last year's slugging exhibition. Despite an unathletic build, he has decent speed. He's proficient in both left and right field, though his throwing arm isn't much. He tried to surprise people with a few stolen-base attempts but didn't succeed often enough to help.

2000 Outlook

Like Shane Spencer with the Yankees in 1998, Agbayani is a veteran minor leaguer who came up and played over his head for a few weeks. He may remain useful as a role player, but just as easily could slip back to the minors.

Dennis Cook

Position: RP
Bats: L **Throws:** L
Ht: 6' 3" **Wt:** 190

Opening Day Age: 37
Born: 10/4/62 in Lamarque, TX
ML Seasons: 12

Overall Statistics

	W	L	Pct.	ERA	G	GS	Sv	IP	H	BB	SO	HR	Ratio
1999	10	5	.667	3.86	71	0	3	63.0	50	27	68	11	1.22
Career	56	41	.577	3.80	498	71	7	883.0	823	335	635	112	1.31

1999 Situational Stats

	W	L	ERA	Sv	IP		AB	H	HR	RBI	Avg
Home	6	3	4.41	1	32.2	LHB	71	15	0	6	.211
Road	4	2	3.26	2	30.1	RHB	160	35	11	28	.219
First Half	7	2	2.61	1	41.1	Sc Pos	66	8	3	21	.121
Scnd Half	3	3	6.23	2	21.2	Clutch	116	21	4	15	.181

1999 Season

Dennis Cook was the Mets' best setup man over the first half of 1999. All the work took its toll however, and he completely collapsed in the second half. He was scaled back to one-out situations but never regained his effectiveness until the postseason, when he pitched scoreless ball.

Pitching, Defense & Hitting

Cook tries to get batters to chase his fastball up and out of the strike zone, and to fish for forkballs and sliders in the dirt. He won't come in with a strike until he has to. He began to have problems with righthanders last year for the first time in his career, but continued to shut down lefties. He always had thrived on heavy use before finding his limit last year. Cook's move to first is fairly good and he fields his position adequately. A two-way star in college, Cook is perhaps the best-hitting pitcher in the game but rarely gets a chance to show it.

2000 Outlook

The Mets hope Cook's second-half collapse was nothing more than a case of fatigue. If his arm bounces back, he ought to resume his place as one of their key short relievers.

Shawon Dunston

Position: CF/LF
Bats: R **Throws:** R
Ht: 6' 1" **Wt:** 180

Opening Day Age: 37
Born: 3/21/63 in
Brooklyn, NY
ML Seasons: 15
Pronunciation: SHAWN

Overall Statistics

	G	AB	R	H	D	T	HR	RBI	SB	BB	SO	Avg	OBP	Slg
1999	104	243	35	78	11	3	5	41	10	2	39	.321	.337	.453
Career	1556	5378	675	1457	266	57	128	591	205	192	888	.271	.298	.413

1999 Situational Stats

	AB	H	HR	RBI	Avg		AB	H	HR	RBI	Avg
Home	122	42	4	22	.344	LHP	94	32	1	14	.340
Road	121	36	1	19	.298	RHP	149	46	4	27	.309
First Half	125	44	5	24	.352	Sc Pos	59	27	2	37	.458
Scnd Half	118	34	0	17	.288	Clutch	44	12	1	5	.273

1999 Season

In 1999, Shawon Dunston played for his fifth and sixth teams of the last three years and finally landed with a winner. He began the year with St. Louis, where he served as a virtual one-man bench, playing all over the diamond. He was dealt to the Mets for Craig Paquette at the trade deadline, and served New York as a part-time outfielder.

Hitting, Baserunning & Defense

Dunston's bat came back to life, as he raised his average 99 points from the year before. Aggressive to the point of absurdity, he swings at everything yet makes decent contact. He shows occasional pop and bunts expertly. He still runs well and can swipe a bag when needed. Originally a shortstop, Dunston has played every position but pitcher and catcher during the last two years. At this point, he's more comfortable in the outfield, though he has the speed, arm and athleticism to get by wherever he plays.

2000 Outlook

Dunston's contract ran out at the end of the season. He enjoyed playing for the Mets and might return after the club surprisingly offered him arbitration.

Orel Hershiser

New York (NL)

Position: SP
Bats: R **Throws:** R
Ht: 6' 3" **Wt:** 195

Opening Day Age: 41
Born: 9/16/58 in
Buffalo, NY
ML Seasons: 17
Pronunciation:
HURR-shy-zer
Nickname: Bulldog

Overall Statistics

	W	L	Pct.	ERA	G	GS	Sv	IP	H	BB	SO	HR	Ratio
1999	13	12	.520	4.58	32	32	0	179.0	175	77	89	14	1.41
Career	203	145	.583	3.41	500	460	5	3105.2	2897	993	2001	230	1.25

1999 Situational Stats

	W	L	ERA	Sv	IP		AB	H	HR	RBI	Avg
Home	6	6	4.88	0	83.0	LHB	291	82	9	39	.282
Road	7	6	4.31	0	96.0	RHB	383	93	5	37	.243
First Half	9	6	5.06	0	96.0	Sc Pos	155	42	2	60	.271
Scnd Half	4	6	4.01	0	83.0	Clutch	14	4	0	1	.286

1999 Season

The Mets signed free agent Orel Hershiser to a one-year, $2 million deal in March. They wanted some veteran stability for their rotation, and that's exactly what he provided. While the team's other starters ran hot and cold and fought through injuries, Hershiser quietly contributed six solid innings every fifth day.

Pitching, Defense & Hitting

Hershiser's sinker always has been his money pitch, but he rarely hits 90 MPH with it these days. He doesn't rely on it as heavily as he used to. Last year, he made more extensive use of his curveball and changeup, offering curves at varying speeds. Lefthanders give him trouble. He's a master at keeping the ball down and getting groundballs. Hershiser remains a first-rate fielder, though his aggressiveness occasionally leads to errors. He's quick to the plate and basestealers rarely test him. Usually a decent hitter and bunter, he had an off year at the plate last season.

2000 Outlook

Hershiser became a free agent again and signed a one-year deal with the Dodgers for $2 million. Though he's 41, he has proven that he still can get by with a good infield behind him. That won't necessarily be the case in Los Angeles.

Bobby Jones

Position: SP
Bats: R **Throws:** R
Ht: 6' 4" **Wt:** 225

Opening Day Age: 30
Born: 2/10/70 in
Fresno, CA
ML Seasons: 7

Overall Statistics

	W	L	Pct.	ERA	G	GS	Sv	IP	H	BB	SO	HR	Ratio
1999	3	3	.500	5.61	12	9	0	59.1	69	11	31	3	1.35
Career	63	50	.558	4.00	166	163	0	1061.0	1084	304	629	112	1.31

1999 Situational Stats

	W	L	ERA	Sv	IP		AB	H	HR	RBI	Avg
Home	2	2	5.92	0	38.0	LHB	91	30	3	17	.330
Road	1	1	5.06	0	21.1	RHB	143	39	0	18	.273
First Half	3	3	5.81	0	52.2	Sc Pos	58	22	1	30	.379
Scnd Half	0	0	4.05	0	6.2	Clutch	6	0	0	0	.000

1999 Season

Bobby Jones won his first three starts in 1999, but soon began to slide. After getting bombed in three straight outings, he went on the disabled list in late May with a sore shoulder. The injury never was diagnosed conclusively. He returned to make three forgettable relief appearances in September.

Pitching, Defense & Hitting

When healthy, Jones is a limited but useful starter. At 85 MPH his fastball is misnomered, but he gets by with a deep repertoire and good command. By mixing pitches, changing speeds and staying away from the heart of the plate, he can throw seven solid innings before tiring. His cutter moves away from lefthanders and helps him keep them in check. Jones aids his own cause with his glove and bat. He doesn't have a good move to first but compensates with a speedy stretch delivery.

2000 Outlook

Jones will make $5.25 million in 2000, the final year on his three-year contract, so the Mets will give him every chance to rebound. His ability to do so depends entirely upon the condition of his shoulder.

Todd Pratt

Position: C
Bats: R **Throws:** R
Ht: 6' 3" **Wt:** 230

Opening Day Age: 33
Born: 2/9/67 in
Bellevue, NE
ML Seasons: 7

Overall Statistics

	G	AB	R	H	D	T	HR	RBI	SB	BB	SO	Avg	OBP	Slg
1999	71	140	18	41	4	0	3	21	2	15	32	.293	.369	.386
Career	253	610	66	156	34	2	16	94	2	57	165	.256	.323	.397

1999 Situational Stats

	AB	H	HR	RBI	Avg		AB	H	HR	RBI	Avg
Home	73	19	1	9	.260	LHP	43	12	2	8	.279
Road	67	22	2	12	.328	RHP	97	29	1	13	.299
First Half	99	29	3	17	.293	Sc Pos	37	9	0	14	.243
Scnd Half	41	12	0	4	.293	Clutch	24	7	0	4	.292

1999 Season

After playing for six organizations and spending a year out of the game, Todd Pratt hooked on with the Mets for the entire 1999 season and became an unlikely postseason hero. He served as Mike Piazza's backup and performed admirably early in the year when Piazza was hurt. Pratt's Division Series-winning home run against the Diamondbacks was one of the highlights of the Mets' season.

Hitting, Baserunning & Defense

Pratt is a strong righthanded hitter who can do some damage against lefthanders. As he proved in October, he can hit a high fastball, though he tends to struggle against righthanders' breaking stuff. Pratt has a strong throwing arm, but is a somewhat crude receiver who has trouble blocking balls in the dirt. He can play first base if needed. Pratt's speed is minimal.

2000 Outlook

Pratt is amply qualified for a backup role, and his play last season gives him some job security for the first time in his career. He won't push Piazza aside but should continue to help the Mets, who re-signed him for two years and $1.1 million.

Rick Reed

Position: SP
Bats: R **Throws:** R
Ht: 6' 1" **Wt:** 195

Opening Day Age: 34
Born: 8/16/65 in
Huntington, WV
ML Seasons: 11

Overall Statistics

	W	L	Pct.	ERA	G	GS	Sv	IP	H	BB	SO	HR	Ratio
1999	11	5	.688	4.58	26	26	0	149.1	163	47	104	23	1.41
Career	49	40	.551	3.90	151	130	1	836.1	851	165	515	104	1.21

1999 Situational Stats

	W	L	ERA	Sv	IP		AB	H	HR	RBI	Avg
Home	3	2	3.86	0	65.1	LHB	250	74	13	34	.296
Road	8	3	5.14	0	84.0	RHB	330	89	10	39	.270
First Half	6	3	4.79	0	92.0	Sc Pos	123	34	7	47	.276
Scnd Half	5	2	4.24	0	57.1	Clutch	16	3	0	1	.188

1999 Season

A torn calf muscle set Rick Reed back early in the year, and his normally impeccable control was off when he returned. Later in the summer, a sprained finger put him on the shelf for three weeks. He never found his groove and was able to post an 11-5 record only with the help of unusually good run support.

Pitching, Defense & Hitting

When he's right, Reed is one of the most precise control pitchers in the game. His fastball doesn't crack 90 MPH, but he's able to cut it and run it in and out, shooting the corners like Greg Maddux. Reed also throws a curveball and a changeup. He never has had much stamina and tired more easily than ever last year, often struggling to get through the fifth inning. Reed helps himself in the field and cuts off the running game quite well. He's an adept hitter and bunter.

2000 Outlook

Reed's luck has to turn sometime. If he's able to avoid the injuries that plagued him last year, there's no reason why he can't return to top form.

Billy Taylor

Position: RP
Bats: R **Throws:** R
Ht: 6' 8" **Wt:** 235

Opening Day Age: 38
Born: 10/16/61 in
Monticello, FL
ML Seasons: 5

Overall Statistics

	W	L	Pct.	ERA	G	GS	Sv	IP	H	BB	SO	HR	Ratio
1999	1	6	.143	4.95	61	0	26	56.1	68	23	52	5	1.62
Career	15	25	.375	4.02	299	0	100	309.0	299	124	291	24	1.37

1999 Situational Stats

	W	L	ERA	Sv	IP		AB	H	HR	RBI	Avg
Home	1	2	5.60	15	27.1	LHB	98	38	1	14	.388
Road	0	4	4.34	11	29.0	RHB	127	30	4	17	.236
First Half	1	4	2.41	22	37.1	Sc Pos	71	19	1	26	.268
Scnd Half	0	2	9.95	4	19.0	Clutch	133	38	4	25	.286

1999 Season

Billy Taylor got off to a fine start as the Athletics' closer last year, converting 23 of his first 27 save chances through mid-July. A line drive to the forehead precipitated a major slump. Dealt to the Mets for Jason Isringhausen and Greg McMichael, his struggles continued in the National League. He rarely appeared in an important situation during the last seven weeks of the season.

Pitching, Defense & Hitting

Taylor is a sidearming righthander with a sinking fastball in the high 80s, a changeup and a wide-breaking slider. He's very tough on righthanders, but lefties have given him tremendous trouble throughout his career. The lanky veteran has a slow delivery and no move to first, and basestealers routinely take liberties with him. Taylor is slow off the mound, but is surehanded and throws accurately. He never has batted in the majors.

2000 Outlook

Taylor underwent offseason surgery to repair torn cartilage in his left knee, which may permit a return to effectiveness. He became a free agent when the Mets non-tendered him in December.

Turk Wendell [Rubber Arm]

Position: RP
Bats: L **Throws:** R
Ht: 6' 2" **Wt:** 205

Opening Day Age: 32
Born: 5/19/67 in Pittsfield, MA
ML Seasons: 7
Pronunciation: WENN-dull

Overall Statistics

	W	L	Pct.	ERA	G	GS	Sv	IP	H	BB	SO	HR	Ratio
1999	5	4	.556	3.05	80	0	3	85.2	80	37	77	9	1.37
Career	21	19	.525	3.88	337	6	30	415.1	385	209	348	42	1.43

1999 Situational Stats

	W	L	ERA	Sv	IP		AB	H	HR	RBI	Avg
Home	3	3	2.45	3	44.0	LHB	127	34	2	11	.268
Road	2	1	3.67	0	41.2	RHB	200	46	7	23	.230
First Half	2	1	3.06	2	53.0	Sc Pos	92	15	5	29	.163
Scnd Half	3	3	3.03	1	32.2	Clutch	168	35	4	11	.208

1999 Season

Turk Wendell had a good season as the Mets' primary righthanded setup man. He made 80 relief appearances, the most in the majors by a righty, and thrived on the frequent work. He was worked especially hard over the first half but never showed any signs of wearing down.

Pitching, Defense & Hitting

Batters come to the plate knowing they'll see Wendell's slider. What they can't know for sure is whether he'll try to start it up and drop it into the strike zone, or start it in the middle of the plate and make it break into the dirt. He throws a hard, sharp-breaking slider and a softer one with more sink. He'll mix in an average fastball and changeup only as often as he has to. Righthanders have an especially hard time against him. Wendell has a decent move to first and generally helps himself in the field. He can't hit or even bunt.

2000 Outlook

Wendell seems to have found his niche as an eighth-inning pitcher. His arm is extremely resilient and durable, so he should continue to get the job done.

Masato Yoshii

Position: SP
Bats: R **Throws:** R
Ht: 6' 2" **Wt:** 210

Opening Day Age: 34
Born: 4/20/65 in Osaka, Japan
ML Seasons: 2
Pronunciation: muh-SAH-toh YOH-shee

Overall Statistics

	W	L	Pct.	ERA	G	GS	Sv	IP	H	BB	SO	HR	Ratio
1999	12	8	.600	4.40	31	29	0	174.0	168	58	105	25	1.30
Career	18	16	.529	4.17	60	58	0	345.2	334	111	222	47	1.29

1999 Situational Stats

	W	L	ERA	Sv	IP		AB	H	HR	RBI	Avg
Home	3	4	4.82	0	84.0	LHB	292	79	11	31	.271
Road	9	4	4.00	0	90.0	RHB	354	89	14	49	.251
First Half	6	7	5.02	0	95.0	Sc Pos	134	41	7	58	.306
Scnd Half	6	1	3.65	0	79.0	Clutch	19	6	0	0	.316

1999 Season

It was a season of extremes for Masato Yoshii. He pitched so poorly during spring training that he nearly drew his release, and he continued to get clobbered through the first month of the season. He rebounded in May and June, but crashed again in July after tendinitis cropped up in his right knee. He even lost his spot in the rotation for a spell, but became the Mets' best starter down the stretch.

Pitching, Defense & Hitting

Yoshii has a deep repertoire, but turned his season around after concentrating on using his two-seam fastball and forkball. He works best on long rest, which he was accustomed to getting in Japan. He doesn't have much stamina and tends to start getting the ball up after about 90 pitches. Yoshii has a mediocre pickoff move and isn't quick to the plate, so basestealers can take advantage. He showed improvement both in the field and at the plate last year.

2000 Outlook

Yoshii should remain useful if the Mets continue to handle him with care. His numbers from his first two seasons were similar, and expect more of the same in 2000.

Other New York Mets

Jermaine Allensworth (Pos: RF/CF, Age: 28, Bats: R)

	G	AB	R	H	D	T	HR	RBI	SB	BB	SO	Avg	OBP	Slg
1999	40	73	14	16	2	0	3	9	2	9	23	.219	.310	.370
Career	342	1031	155	268	49	8	15	114	42	104	228	.260	.339	.367

Allensworth bounced between Triple-A and New York in 1999. After his disappointing season, the Mets traded him to Boston for Jon Nunnally. 2000 Outlook: B

Bobby Bonilla (Pos: RF, Age: 37, Bats: B)

	G	AB	R	H	D	T	HR	RBI	SB	BB	SO	Avg	OBP	Slg
1999	60	119	12	19	5	0	4	18	0	19	16	.160	.277	.303
Career	1906	6800	1044	1912	388	58	277	1124	44	852	1100	.281	.359	.478

Two trips to the disabled list cost Bonilla nearly half the season. He hasn't been productive when healthy, and the Mets can't trade his hefty contract. 2000 Outlook: C

Matt Franco (Pos: 1B/3B/LF, Age: 30, Bats: L)

	G	AB	R	H	D	T	HR	RBI	SB	BB	SO	Avg	OBP	Slg
1999	122	132	18	31	5	0	4	21	0	28	21	.235	.366	.364
Career	367	504	65	131	19	2	11	58	1	65	79	.260	.345	.371

Franco has been a valuable pinch-hitter and part-time player for the Mets, and even pitched a couple of times last year. 2000 Outlook: B

Shane Halter (Pos: SS, Age: 30, Bats: R)

	G	AB	R	H	D	T	HR	RBI	SB	BB	SO	Avg	OBP	Slg
1999	7	0	0	0	0	0	0	0	0	0	0	-	-	-
Career	167	327	33	79	17	1	4	23	6	22	66	.242	.294	.336

After going to camp with the Royals, Halter was traded to the Mets last March. He spent most of 1999 in Triple-A. 2000 Outlook: C

Mike Kinkade (Pos: LF, Age: 26, Bats: R)

	G	AB	R	H	D	T	HR	RBI	SB	BB	SO	Avg	OBP	Slg
1999	28	46	3	9	2	1	2	6	1	3	9	.196	.275	.413
Career	31	48	5	9	2	1	2	6	1	3	9	.188	.264	.396

Kinkade won the final roster spot in the spring by playing five positions, including shortstop and catcher. He didn't get an at-bat after May. 2000 Outlook: C

Luis Lopez (Pos: SS/2B, Age: 29, Bats: B)

	G	AB	R	H	D	T	HR	RBI	SB	BB	SO	Avg	OBP	Slg
1999	68	104	11	22	4	0	2	13	1	12	33	.212	.308	.308
Career	420	965	107	232	49	4	9	86	8	68	217	.240	.299	.327

Lopez is a versatile infielder who provides defensive help up the middle. His average bounces up and down from season to season, and he battled the Mendoza Line last summer. 2000 Outlook: B

Pat Mahomes (Pos: RHP, Age: 29)

	W	L	Pct.	ERA	G	GS	Sv	IP	H	BB	SO	HR	Ratio
1999	8	0	1.000	3.68	39	0	0	63.2	44	37	51	7	1.27
Career	29	28	.509	5.57	174	51	5	452.2	472	242	279	79	1.58

Mahomes turned in his best big league season in 1999, pitching especially well in midsummer. He faded late in the year but had a fine postseason. 2000 Outlook: B

Josias Manzanillo (Pos: RHP, Age: 32)

	W	L	Pct.	ERA	G	GS	Sv	IP	H	BB	SO	HR	Ratio
1999	0	0	-	5.79	12	0	0	18.2	19	4	25	5	1.23
Career	5	6	.455	4.81	105	1	3	147.2	141	71	138	18	1.44

For two seasons now, Manzanillo has posted ERAs higher than 5.00. Sent down in May, now he's a free agent. 2000 Outlook: C

Chuck McElroy (Pos: LHP, Age: 32)

	W	L	Pct.	ERA	G	GS	Sv	IP	H	BB	SO	HR	Ratio
1999	3	1	.750	5.50	50	0	0	54.0	60	36	44	9	1.78
Career	33	27	.550	3.64	562	0	17	601.0	577	282	507	46	1.43

After a career year in 1998 with the Rockies, McElroy wasn't nearly as effective last year. He went to the Mets in a trade-deadline deal on July 31 and was sent to the Orioles for Jesse Orosco in December. 2000 Outlook: B

Melvin Mora (Pos: LF/CF, Age: 28, Bats: R)

	G	AB	R	H	D	T	HR	RBI	SB	BB	SO	Avg	OBP	Slg
1999	66	31	6	5	0	0	0	1	2	4	7	.161	.278	.161
Career	66	31	6	5	0	0	0	1	2	4	7	.161	.278	.161

In his fourth Triple-A season, Mora did his best hitting ever in the high minors. He was recalled when Rey Ordonez missed time with a sore knee in May, and he had an impressive postseason. 2000 Outlook: B

Glendon Rusch (Pos: LHP, Age: 25)

	W	L	Pct.	ERA	G	GS	Sv	IP	H	BB	SO	HR	Ratio
1999	0	1	.000	12.60	4	0	0	5.0	8	3	4	1	2.20
Career	12	25	.324	5.78	63	51	1	330.0	405	105	214	51	1.55

Rusch struggled at the big league level with Kansas City in 1997 and '98, and he spent most of 1999 in Triple-A. He was traded to the Mets in September. 2000 Outlook: C

Jeff Tam (Pos: RHP, Age: 29)

	W	L	Pct.	ERA	G	GS	Sv	IP	H	BB	SO	HR	Ratio
1999	0	0	-	5.40	10	0	0	11.2	8	4	8	3	1.03
Career	1	1	.500	5.88	25	0	0	26.0	21	8	16	5	1.12

Tam's 1999 season was sidetracked by elbow surgery that kept him out until May. Cleveland claimed him off waivers in June, and the Mets reclaimed him in August. Oakland signed him in November. 2000 Outlook: C

Vance Wilson (Pos: C, Age: 27, Bats: R)

	G	AB	R	H	D	T	HR	RBI	SB	BB	SO	Avg	OBP	Slg
1999	1	0	0	0	0	0	0	0	0	0	0	-	-	-
Career	1	0	0	0	0	0	0	0	0	0	0	-	-	-

Wilson has come up the last two seasons, but getting a chance to prove his worth has been difficult because of injuries. 2000 Outook: C

New York Mets Minor League Prospects

Organization Overview:

Unlike their crosstown rivals, the Mets haven't been able to balance winning with developing talent. Their nucleus features just two homegrown players, Edgardo Alfonzo and Rey Ordonez. New York has sacrificed its farm system in trades for veterans, giving up prospects such as A.J. Burnett, Cesar Crespo, Preston Wilson and Ed Yarnall in deals for Al Leiter and Mike Piazza. The club's win-now philosophy shows no sign of changing, either. The Mets' two best Triple-A prospects last year were Octavio Dotel and Terrence Long. They sent Long to Oakland in a July trade for Kenny Rogers, who blew up in the postseason before becoming a free agent. And if Ken Griffey Jr. had approved a tentative December deal, Dotel would have been one of three players exchanged for the Seattle slugger.

Lesli Brea

Position: P
Bats: R **Throws:** R
Ht: 5' 11" **Wt:** 170

Opening Day Age: 21
Born: 10/12/78 in San Pedro de Macoris, D.R.

Recent Statistics

	W	L	ERA	G	GS	Sv	IP	H	R	BB	SO	HR
1998 A Wisconsin	3	4	2.76	49	0	12	58.2	47	26	40	86	1
1999 A St. Lucie	1	7	3.73	32	18	3	120.2	95	64	68	136	4

If there's an organziation that has traded away more prospects than the Mets, it's the Mariners, who sent Brea to New York in a December 1998 trade for veteran Butch Huskey. Brea is one of the better strikeout pitchers in the lower minors, having more whiffs than innings in each of his four pro seasons and averaging 11.4 per nine innings for his pro career. Hitters haven't been able to touch his combination of a 94-96 MPH fastball and a mid-80s slider. Though he started in 1999, that was just to give him more innings to work on his shaky command, and he returned to the bullpen in the California Fall League. A potential closer if he can throw more strikes, Brea is two years away from New York.

Eric Cammack

Position: P
Bats: R **Throws:** R
Ht: 6' 1" **Wt:** 175

Opening Day Age: 24
Born: 8/14/75 in Nederland, TX

Recent Statistics

	W	L	ERA	G	GS	Sv	IP	H	R	BB	SO	HR
1998 A Capital Cty	4	0	2.81	25	0	8	32.0	17	13	13	49	2
1998 A St. Lucie	3	2	2.02	29	0	11	35.2	22	12	14	53	2
1999 AA Binghamton	4	2	2.38	45	0	15	56.2	28	17	38	83	2
1999 AAA Norfolk	0	0	3.12	9	0	4	8.2	7	3	1	17	1

Cammack has been more untouchable than Lesli Brea and reached Triple-A in his second full season after signing as a 13th-round pick in 1997 out of Lamar. Last year he led minor league relievers with 13.8 strikeouts per nine innings and Double-A relievers with 4.4 hits per nine innings, running his career averages to 12.8 and 4.5, respectively. His lifetime 2.14 ERA isn't too shabby, either. Cammack isn't overpowering, relying instead on four pitches and guts. He works his 88-91 MPH fastball inside and uses a curveball against lefthanders and a slider against righthanders. He should be able to help the New York bullpen this year.

Octavio Dotel

Position: P
Bats: R **Throws:** R
Ht: 6' 0" **Wt:** 160

Opening Day Age: 24
Born: 11/25/75 in Santo Domingo, Dom. Rep.

Recent Statistics

	W	L	ERA	G	GS	Sv	IP	H	R	BB	SO	HR
1999 AAA Norfolk	5	2	3.84	13	13	0	70.1	52	33	34	90	9
1999 NL New York	8	3	5.38	19	14	0	85.1	69	52	49	85	12

Dotel is the Mets' best prospect and one of the best young pitchers in the game, but they were willing to include him in a trade that also would have sent Armando Benitez and Roger Cedeno to Seattle for Ken Griffey Jr. Dotel showed flashes of brilliance in his major league debut last year, striking out nearly a batter per inning and limiting hitters to a .226 average. He won eight of 11 decisions, though he struggled with walks and home runs. His 92-94 MPH fastball was rated the best in the Triple-A International League in 1999, and his hard curveball gives him two overpowering pitches. Dotel could use an offspeed pitch, and has a double-jointed pitching shoulder that could lead to an injury at some point. After winning Game 5 of the National League Championship Series in relief last October, he'll pitch in New York's rotation this year. Barring a trade, that is.

Alex Escobar

Position: OF
Bats: R **Throws:** R
Ht: 6' 1" **Wt:** 185

Opening Day Age: 21
Born: 9/6/78 in Valencia, Venezuela

Recent Statistics

	G	AB	R	H	D	THR	HR	RBI	SB	BB	SO	Avg
1998 A Capital Cty	112	416	90	129	23	5	27	91	49	54	133	.310
1999 R Mets	2	8	1	3	2	0	0	1	0	1	2	.375
1999 A St. Lucie	1	3	1	2	0	0	1	3	1	1	1	.667

Escobar had a breakthrough 1998 season that prompted comparisons to Vladimir Guerrero, but last year was a complete washout. He missed the first half with a stress fracture in his lower back, then tore the labrum in his left shoulder while hitting a home run in the first game after his return. Escobar is a five-tool center fielder who knows how to use his skills. He hits for power and average, steals bases and is a solid defensive player. Despite the lost season, he'll enter 2000 as the organization's top minor league prospect. He'll probably begin the year in high Class-A and could move quickly.

Jay Payton

Position: OF
Bats: R **Throws:** R
Ht: 5' 10" **Wt:** 185

Opening Day Age: 27
Born: 11/22/72 in
Zanesville, OH

Recent Statistics

	G	AB	R	H	D	T	HR	RBI	SB	BB	SO	Avg
1999 A St. Lucie	7	26	3	9	1	1	0	3	0	4	5	.346
1999 AAA Norfolk	38	144	27	56	13	2	8	35	2	12	13	.389
1999 NL New York	13	8	1	2	1	0	0	1	1	0	2	.250

The Mets have had more than their share of prospects ravaged by injuries, and Payton is the poster boy for the epidemic. A 1994 supplemental first-round pick out of Georgia Tech, he won batting titles and MVP awards in his first two pro seasons. Since then, however, he has had three surgeries on his right elbow and another on his left shoulder, and last year he was slowed by a ribcage injury. Payton could hit .300 with 20 homers per season in the majors if he were able to stay healthy. He also runs well, though his throwing arm has been ravaged by the elbow operations. His best fit might be as a DH if New York trades him to an American League team.

Grant Roberts

Position: P
Bats: R **Throws:** R
Ht: 6' 3" **Wt:** 205

Opening Day Age: 22
Born: 9/13/77 in El
Cajon, CA

Recent Statistics

	W	L	ERA	G	GS	Sv	IP	H	R	BB	SO	HR
1998 A St. Lucie	4	5	4.23	17	17	0	72.1	72	37	37	70	11
1999 AA Binghamton	7	6	4.87	23	23	0	131.1	135	81	49	94	9
1999 AAA Norfolk	2	1	4.50	5	5	0	28.0	32	15	11	30	1

Roberts was the Mets' best prospect in 1997, when he dominated the Class-A South Atlantic League, but hasn't been quite the same pitcher since minor elbow surgery after that season. Before the operation, he went 22-5, 2.25 with 9.4 strikeouts per nine innings. Since then, he has gone 13-12, 4.62 with 7.5 whiffs per nine innings, though he has reached Triple-A. An 11th-round pick in 1995, Roberts has gotten his stuff back. He throws a 93-94 MPH fastball, an above-average slider and a curveball. His arm is as good as Dotel's, and Roberts may be able to contribute in New York after the All-Star break this year.

Jorge Toca

Position: 1B-OF
Bats: R **Throws:** R
Ht: 6' 3" **Wt:** 220

Opening Day Age: 29
Born: 1/7/71 in
Remedios, Cuba

Recent Statistics

	G	AB	R	H	D	T	HR	RBI	SB	BB	SO	Avg
1999 AA Binghamton	75	279	60	86	15	1	20	67	5	32	43	.308
1999 AAA Norfolk	49	176	25	59	12	1	5	29	0	6	23	.335
1999 NL New York	4	3	0	1	0	0	0	0	0	0	2	.333
1999 MLE	124	431	66	121	22	0	17	74	3	25	70	.281

Toca defected from Cuba in 1998 and signed with the Mets for $1.4 million. Though he batted .326 with 25 homers in the upper minors during his pro debut last year, the organization was disappointed to learn that he's 29, not 25 as previously thought. Toca is solely a hitter, capable of producing for average as well as power if he continues to loft the ball. His speed and arm are below average, and though he played left field last year, he's much better suited for first base. It's revealing that in the wake of John Olerud's defection to Seattle, New York moved quickly to sign Todd Zeile rather than give Toca a shot at the first-base job.

Jason Tyner

Position: OF
Bats: L **Throws:** L
Ht: 6' 1" **Wt:** 170

Opening Day Age: 22
Born: 4/23/77 in
Bedford, TX

Recent Statistics

	G	AB	R	H	D	T	HR	RBI	SB	BB	SO	Avg
1998 A St. Lucie	50	201	30	61	2	3	0	16	15	17	20	.303
1999 AA Binghamton	129	518	91	162	19	5	0	33	49	62	46	.313
1999 AAA Norfolk	3	8	0	0	0	0	0	0	0	0	5	.000
1999 MLE	132	504	71	140	16	3	0	26	32	41	54	.278

A 1998 first-round pick out of Texas A&M, Tyner has batted .307 as a pro and reached Triple-A in his first full pro season. He does everything a leadoff man should do: hit for average, draw walks, make contact, steal bases. In 1999, he was the toughest batter in the Double-A Eastern League to strike out and swiped 49 bases in 64 attempts. He also is a fine bunter with exceptional speed. That said, Tyner won't make much of an impact in the majors unless he gets stronger. He hasn't homered since high school and his pro slugging percentage is .358, just 51 points higher than his batting average. Tyner's best-case scenario is to become a Brett Butler.

Others to Watch

Outfielder **Brian Cole** (21) was *Baseball America's* 1998 Junior College Player of the Year at Navarro (Texas) JC. He batted .316 with 41 doubles, 18 homers and 50 steals at Class-A Capital City in 1999, his first full season as a pro. . . Shortstop **Enrique Cruz** (18) hit game-winning homers in both games of the Rookie-level Gulf Coast League playoffs last year. He hit .306 in the GCL in his pro debut, and has power potential and a strong arm. . . One of the best control pitchers in the minors, righthander **Dicky Gonzalez** (21) has a 459-86 strikeout-walk ratio in 499 pro innings. His status has risen after his fastball improved from 88-89 MPH to 90-91 MPH last year. . . In his first full season last year, **Pat Strange** (19) also showed impressive command, striking out 113 and walking just 29 in 154 Class-A innings. He has better stuff than Gonzalez, highlighted by an 89-94 MPH fastball. . . 1996 first-round pick **Bobby Stratton** (22) hit 21 homers in 95 games at Capital City. He's had problems staying healthy, however, and missed time with a hand injury last year. . . Lefthander **Rene Vega** (23) was the toughest starter to hit (.192) in the Class-A South Atlantic League and had 148 strikeouts in 146 innings. But his stuff is marginal, and he'll have to dominate at higher levels before the Mets get excited.

Veterans Stadium

Offense

Veterans Stadium is an ugly, cookie-cutter ballpark with no distinguishing characteristics whatsoever. Hitters pick the ball up well out of the pitcher's hand, especially during night games. The artificial turf is one of the hardest and most unforgiving surfaces in the game, and it assures batters above-average numbers of doubles and triples. All in all, the Vet is one of the better hitters' parks in the National League.

Defense

While the rock-hard turf affords infielders true hops, it places significant physical demands on the Phillies' everyday players. They've attempted to man their infield spots with young, rangy players with strong throwing arms. Franchise cornerstone Scott Rolen has been outspoken in his criticism of the turf, and many attribute his back injury in part to the constant pounding. Without a new ballpark or at least a new surface in the Vet, key Phillies such as Bobby Abreu and Rolen may go elsewhere when they become free agents.

Who It Helps The Most

Slashing gap hitters such as Abreu and Marlon Anderson are helped most by the Vet. Most Phillies pitchers do better on the road, but Robert Person and Randy Wolf were far more successful at home in 1999.

Who It Hurts The Most

Veterans Stadium actually slightly increases homers, but don't tell Mike Lieberthal or Rolen, the club's top two home-run hitters in 1999. Lieberthal hit 21 of his 31 homers away from Philadelphia, and Rolen had 17 of his 26 longballs come on the road.

Rookies & Newcomers

Qualcomm Stadium is the best pitchers' park in the National League, so Andy Ashby may give up a few more runs after coming from San Diego via a trade. Mike Jackson shouldn't notice any significant differences from his former home, Jacobs Field. Rookie Pat Burrell, one of the top offensive prospects in the minors, shouldn't have any problems fitting in.

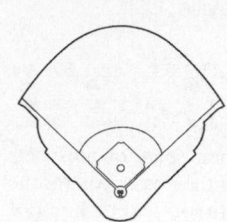

Dimensions: LF-330, LCF-371, CF-408, RCF-371, RF-330

Capacity: 62,363

Elevation: 20 feet

Surface: Turf

Foul Territory: Large

Park Factors

1999 Season

| | Home Games | | | Away Games | | | |
	Phillies	Opp	Total	Phillies	Opp	Total	Index
G	72	72	144	72	72	144	—
Avg	.280	.256	.268	.264	.282	.273	98
AB	2471	2508	4979	2488	2404	4892	102
R	392	365	757	331	389	720	105
H	693	641	1334	658	679	1337	100
2B	140	129	269	114	135	249	106
3B	21	9	30	17	15	32	92
HR	70	100	170	70	90	160	104
BB	300	304	604	254	251	505	118
SO	495	533	1028	467	399	866	117
E	33	46	79	57	47	104	76
E-Infield	31	36	67	48	36	84	80
LHB-Avg	.309	.267	.287	.250	.295	.273	105
LHB-HR	31	43	74	22	28	50	143
RHB-Avg	.263	.248	.256	.273	.274	.273	94
RHB-HR	39	57	96	48	62	110	87

1997-1999

| | Home Games | | | Away Games | | | |
	Phillies	Opp	Total	Phillies	Opp	Total	Index
G	220	220	440	217	217	434	—
Avg	.273	.260	.266	.253	.269	.261	102
AB	7402	7706	15108	7528	7210	14738	101
R	1072	1113	2185	902	1122	2024	106
H	2018	2002	4020	1908	1941	3849	103
2B	415	463	878	354	400	754	114
3B	57	46	103	43	48	91	110
HR	194	261	455	165	256	421	105
BB	809	801	1610	687	793	1480	106
SO	1432	1694	3126	1450	1393	2843	107
E	125	160	285	166	155	321	88
E-Infield	107	119	226	140	124	264	84
LHB-Avg	.288	.267	.277	.255	.284	.269	103
LHB-HR	80	99	179	60	98	158	112
RHB-Avg	.262	.255	.258	.252	.258	.255	101
RHB-HR	114	162	276	105	158	263	101

1999 Rankings (National League)

- Highest walk factor
- Second-highest strikeout factor
- Second-highest LHB home-run factor
- Lowest error factor
- Second-lowest infield-error factor
- Third-lowest RHB batting-average factor

Terry Francona

1999 Season

It was a season of peaks and valleys for the Phillies and their manager, Terry Francona. Philadelphia surprisingly contended through the first two-thirds of the season, standing 13 games over .500 in the first week of August. Then the pitching staff imploded, and the Phils finished eight games below .500 by season's end.

Offense

Throughout his tenure with the Phillies, Francona has adjusted his style to the club's personnel. Last year's team possessed more speed than its immediate predecessors, so he emphasized the stolen base to a greater extent. The Phillies also utilized the hit-and-run quite often. Francona energized the lineup by moving Bobby Abreu from sixth to third in the order. Reluctant to trade an out for a base, Francona isn't a big fan of the sacrifice bunt. He prefers a set lineup.

Pitching & Defense

Francona would love to let his starting pitchers finish games, though that rarely happened after Curt Schilling went down. Francona isn't a strict adherent to pitch counts, and will let a pitcher go deep into a game if he likes the way he's throwing. He likes to utilize a single closer. Francona hasn't had the luxury of possessing more than one lefty in the bullpen at a time, and thus hasn't had the opportunity to fully manipulate situational matchups. He places a high premium on defensive ability when selecting his starters and doesn't make many late-inning substitutions. He doesn't like to issue intentional walks.

2000 Outlook

Francona signed a two-year extension through 2001 during the club's late-season slump. The expectations haven't been high thus far in Francona's career, but Philadelphia is expected to contend in 2000. He has been criticized for sacrificing the urgency to win a particular day's game for a more long-term view, and some have speculated that his laid-back approach has rubbed off a little too much on his players. Expect a little more fire from Francona and the Phillies in 2000 as the stakes increase.

Born: 4/22/59 in Aberdeen, SD

Playing Experience: 1981-1990, Mon, ChC, Cin, Cle, Mil

Managerial Experience: 3 seasons

Manager Statistics

Year	Team, Lg	W	L	Pct	GB	Finish
1999	Philadelphia, NL	77	85	.475	26.0	3rd East
3 Seasons		220	266	.453	—	—

1999 Starting Pitchers by Days Rest

	<=3	4	5	6+
Phillies Starts	1	94	32	23
Phillies ERA	33.75	4.66	5.33	6.18
NL Avg Starts	3	81	48	21
NL ERA	4.84	4.53	4.72	4.98

1999 Situational Stats

	Terry Francona	NL Average
Hit & Run Success %	34.3	33.6
Stolen Base Success %	78.1	70.2
Platoon Pct.	50.6	55.2
Defensive Subs	31	25
High-Pitch Outings	16	13
Quick/Slow Hooks	18/20	16/15
Sacrifice Attempts	81	89

1999 Rankings (National League)

- 1st in stolen-base percentage (78.1%)
- 2nd in fewest caught stealings of second base (32), fewest caught stealings of third base (2) and slow hooks (20)
- 3rd in pitchouts with a runner moving (9)

Bobby Abreu

1999 Season

Bobby Abreu established himself as a legitimate star with a brilliant 1999 campaign. He ranked third in the National League in batting average, showed big-time power against righthanders and drew plenty of walks while settling for a bunch of singles against lefties. His early-season success prompted the Phillies to promote him from sixth to third in the batting order.

Hitting

Abreu possesses one of the most picturesque swings in the game. He's very patient for a young-ster, often working himself into fastball counts. He doesn't try to hit home runs but can drive a fastball out of the park to any field. He keeps his hands back on breaking pitches and only rarely expands his strike zone. He still swings through a number of pitches and strikes out a lot. Abreu applies a very conservative approach against lefties, sacrificing power for contact. It has worked well for him, as he has batted .320 and .298 against southpaws in the last two seasons, respectively, though he's still looking for his first big league homer against them. He'll become an elite hitter if he can add power against lefties.

Baserunning & Defense

Abreu is an exciting, instinctive baserunner who has developed into an outstanding basestealer. He has a graceful stride and needs only a few steps to accelerate to peak speed. Defensively, he has solid range for a right fielder and takes direct routes to flyballs. His above-average throwing arm earned the respect of NL baserunners when he racked up 17 assists in 1998. They tested him less often last year.

2000 Outlook

The sky is the limit for Abreu, who could win batting titles and blossom into a 30-homer guy. Expect him to continue to develop all facets of his game in 2000 as the Phillies' everyday right fielder and No. 3 hitter. The club will try to lock him up with a lucrative long-term contract offer.

Position: RF
Bats: L **Throws:** R
Ht: 6' 0" **Wt:** 186

Opening Day Age: 26
Born: 3/11/74 in Aragua, Venezuela
ML Seasons: 4
Pronunciation: uh-BRAY-oo

Overall Statistics

	G	AB	R	H	D	T	HR	RBI	SB	BB	SO	Avg	OBP	Slg
1999	152	546	118	183	35	11	20	93	27	109	113	.335	.446	.549
Career	377	1253	209	390	75	19	40	194	53	216	297	.311	.412	.497

Where He Hits the Ball

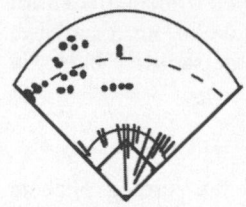 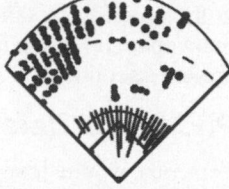

Vs. LHP   **Vs. RHP**

1999 Situational Stats

	AB	H	HR	RBI	Avg		AB	H	HR	RBI	Avg
Home	275	94	13	57	.342	LHP	141	42	0	20	.298
Road	271	89	7	36	.328	RHP	405	141	20	73	.348
First Half	279	90	13	45	.323	Sc Pos	136	47	7	74	.346
Scnd Half	267	93	7	48	.348	Clutch	75	18	0	11	.240

1999 Rankings (National League)

- 1st in triples and on-base percentage vs. righthanded pitchers (.453)
- 2nd in most pitches seen per plate appearance (4.31)
- 3rd in batting average, on-base percentage and batting average vs. righthanded pitchers
- Led the Phillies in batting average, runs scored, triples, total bases (300), caught stealing (9), walks, intentional walks (8), times on base (295), pitches seen (2,854), on-base percentage, highest groundball/flyball ratio (1.5), most pitches seen per plate appearance (4.31), batting average with runners in scoring position, batting average with the bases loaded (.455), batting average vs. righthanded pitchers and steals of third (4)

Marlon Anderson

1999 Season

Handed the Phillies' everyday second-base job in spring training, Marlon Anderson endured an uneven rookie campaign that left doubts as to whether he can be a long-term starter. He failed in the No. 2 spot in the order at the start of the season and was moved down to seventh. He showed above-average speed, but was impatient at the plate and erratic in the field.

Hitting

Anderson has a compact, line-drive swing that is capable of smoking the ball to the gaps. But his overaggressiveness at the plate often drops him behind in the count and limits the number of fastballs he sees. He's not a particularly effective situational hitter. For example, he often will swing early in the count after the pitcher has walked a batter. Despite his fundamental flaws, Anderson has acquitted himself well against lefthanders. He still hasn't fully incorporated his speed into his offensive game. A slight uppercut in his swing produces too many lazy flyballs, and he's not a particularly effective bunter.

Baserunning & Defense

Anderson has solid raw speed, which allowed him to steal 13 bases in 15 tries as a rookie. Yet he hasn't established himself as a quality baserunner. He takes unwise chances and appears oblivious to game situations. Defensively, Anderson has a quick first step and above-average range at second base, but his footwork and ability to make the routine play remain inconsistent. His throwing arm is adequate.

2000 Outlook

The Phillies point to Anderson's youth when rationalizing his lack of success in 1999, but he was in fact a little older than most rookies. It will be interesting to see if Philadelphia keeps him in the lineup if they're contending but he's struggling. They don't appear to have a viable alternative at this point.

Position: 2B
Bats: L **Throws:** R
Ht: 5'11" **Wt:** 200

Opening Day Age: 26
Born: 1/6/74 in Montgomery, AL
ML Seasons: 2

Overall Statistics

	G	AB	R	H	D	T	HR	RBI	SB	BB	SO	Avg	OBP	Slg
1999	129	452	48	114	26	4	5	54	13	24	61	.252	.292	.361
Career	146	495	52	128	29	4	6	58	15	25	67	.259	.295	.370

Where He Hits the Ball

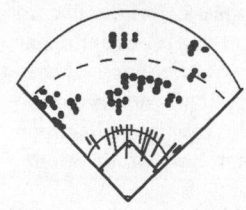 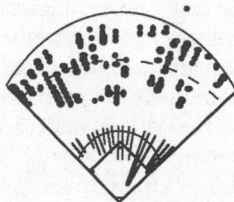

Vs. LHP   **Vs. RHP**

1999 Situational Stats

	AB	H	HR	RBI	Avg		AB	H	HR	RBI	Avg
Home	234	70	4	29	.299	LHP	64	19	0	10	.297
Road	218	44	1	25	.202	RHP	388	95	5	44	.245
First Half	258	64	4	37	.248	Sc Pos	115	37	2	48	.322
Scnd Half	194	50	1	17	.258	Clutch	53	13	0	8	.245

1999 Rankings (National League)

- 1st in lowest on-base percentage vs. righthanded pitchers (.286)
- 3rd in lowest slugging percentage vs. righthanded pitchers (.353)
- 4th in lowest batting average vs. righthanded pitchers and lowest fielding percentage at second base (.979)
- 9th in errors at second base (11)

Rico Brogna

1999 Season

Rico Brogna's 24 homers and team-leading 102 RBI might seem to indicate he had a pretty solid season. But considering that National League first basemen had a .370 on-base percentage and .489 slugging percentage as a whole, Brogna's corresponding marks of .336 and .454 don't look so hot. Brogna did take part in 157 games despite arthritic knees and played his usual splendid defense.

Hitting

In Brogna's early major league seasons, two glaring weaknesses held him back: an inability to hit lefthanders and a lack of plate discipline. He gradually has addressed the first weakness, raising his average to a nearly respectable level and showing decent power against southpaws. While his 54 walks in 1999 were a career high, Brogna has shown no signs of enhancing his patience. He remains an easy mark for high fastballs and breaking pitches off the plate. He handles low fastballs much better, especially on the outer half of the plate, driving them to all fields.

Baserunning & Defense

What Brogna lacks in raw offensive talent, he compensates for in other areas. He doesn't possess raw speed but is a very intelligent baserunner who has averaged nine steals per year for the Phillies. Defensively, he's one of baseball's best-kept secrets. He has an exceptionally quick first step and well above-average range, and he scoops everything out of the dirt. No NL first baseman initiates the 3-6-3 double play better than Brogna.

2000 Outlook

The Phillies again extended Brogna's contract by a season, giving him $4.2 million for 2000. In an additional vote of confidence, they moved top prospect Pat Burrell from first base to left field. Brogna underwent arthroscopic shoulder surgery following the season, but was expected to be fine by spring training. He'll continue to knock in scads of runs as long as he bats directly behind Bobby Abreu and Scott Rolen, though he offers mediocre production for a first baseman.

Position: 1B
Bats: L **Throws:** L
Ht: 6' 2" **Wt:** 205

Opening Day Age: 29
Born: 4/18/70 in Turners Falls, MA
ML Seasons: 7
Pronunciation: BRONE-yuh

Overall Statistics

	G	AB	R	H	D	T	HR	RBI	SB	BB	SO	Avg	OBP	Slg
1999	157	619	90	172	29	4	24	102	8	54	132	.278	.336	.454
Career	695	2567	344	701	150	13	101	416	28	203	568	.273	.325	.460

Where He Hits the Ball

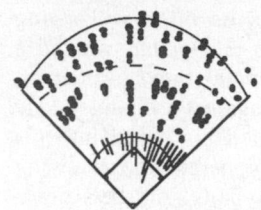 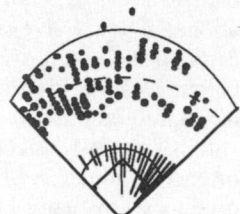

Vs. LHP   **Vs. RHP**

1999 Situational Stats

	AB	H	HR	RBI	Avg		AB	H	HR	RBI	Avg
Home	297	90	14	55	.303	LHP	186	49	9	33	.263
Road	322	82	10	47	.255	RHP	433	123	15	69	.284
First Half	329	86	11	44	.261	Sc Pos	181	50	7	76	.276
Scnd Half	290	86	13	58	.297	Clutch	90	20	3	12	.222

1999 Rankings (National League)

- 2nd in lowest cleanup slugging percentage (.419)
- 5th in GDPs (18) and fielding percentage at first base (.995)
- 7th in at-bats
- 8th in errors at first base (7)
- 9th in strikeouts
- Led the Phillies in RBI, strikeouts, GDPs (18) and games played
- Led NL first basemen in at-bats

Paul Byrd

1999 Season

It was a tale of two distinctly different half-seasons for Paul Byrd. In the first half, he battled for the major league lead in wins and became one of the unlikeliest All-Star Game participants in recent memory. Following the break, Byrd hit the wall physically and often was dispatched by the fifth inning. All in all, the Phillies couldn't be disappointed by Byrd's performance. The late-1998 waiver pickup gave them 199.2 competent big league innings.

Pitching

Byrd's stuff isn't overly impressive. He possesses a mid-80s fastball that is effective only when he changes speeds and locations. He mixes in sliders, curveballs and a steady diet of changeups, and must quickly claim the inside part of the plate to experience success. If Byrd can keep hitters from digging in, his propensity to leave the ball up in the strike zone won't necessarily be fatal. When he's not hitting his spots, he gets into trouble, as evidenced by the 34 homers he surrendered in 1999.

Defense & Hitting

Byrd is a gritty sort who isn't afraid to throw his body around defensively to make plays. He sometimes tries too hard, which is why he led major league pitchers with six errors in 1999. Last season, he didn't control the running game as well as he had in the past. He's not much of a threat when he's swinging away, but he's a solid bunter who led the club in sacrifices.

2000 Outlook

Byrd isn't a true No. 2 starter, and the Phillies know it. That's why they traded for Andy Ashby during the offseason, and Byrd will be slotted into a more appropriate spot further back in the rotation. He won't win 15 games again, but he could be more consistent if he adds some strength and gets better bullpen support.

Position: SP
Bats: R **Throws:** R
Ht: 6' 1" **Wt:** 185

Opening Day Age: 29
Born: 12/3/70 in Louisville, KY
ML Seasons: 5

Overall Statistics

	W	L	Pct.	ERA	G	GS	Sv	IP	H	BB	SO	HR	Ratio
1999	15	11	.577	4.60	32	32	0	199.2	205	70	106	34	1.38
Career	27	19	.587	4.21	127	44	0	378.1	363	144	239	54	1.34

How Often He Throws Strikes

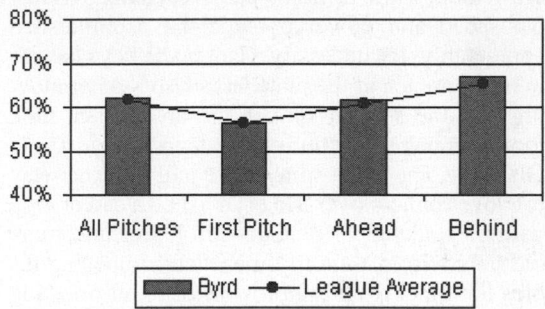

1999 Situational Stats

	W	L	ERA	Sv	IP		AB	H	HR	RBI	Avg
Home	8	7	4.92	0	100.2	LHB	365	111	17	57	.304
Road	7	4	4.27	0	99.0	RHB	409	94	17	48	.230
First Half	11	5	3.94	0	121.0	Sc Pos	176	47	8	73	.267
Scnd Half	4	6	5.61	0	78.2	Clutch	46	11	2	9	.239

1999 Rankings (National League)

- 1st in hit batsmen (17), most run support per nine innings (7.1), errors at pitcher (6) and lowest fielding percentage at pitcher (.854)
- 3rd in home runs allowed and balks (3)
- Led the Phillies in sacrifice bunts (11), wins, games started, innings pitched, hits allowed, batters faced (872), walks allowed, hit batsmen (17), wild pitches (11), balks (3), pitches thrown (3,118), pickoff throws (52), runners caught stealing (7), GDPs induced (18), fewest pitches thrown per batter (3.58), most run support per nine innings (7.1) and most GDPs induced per nine innings (0.8)

Ron Gant

Position: LF
Bats: R **Throws:** R
Ht: 6' 0" **Wt:** 200

Opening Day Age: 35
Born: 3/2/65 in Victoria, TX
ML Seasons: 12

1999 Season

At worst, the Phillies believed they simply had swapped problems with the Cardinals in November 1998. They acquired Ron Gant, $5 million to pay off half of Gant's remaining two-year deal, Jeff Brantley and Cliff Politte for Ricky Bottalico and Garrett Stephenson. Surprisingly, they found Gant to be a stabilizing presence in the clubhouse and a steady offensive and defensive performer. He responded surprisingly well when shifted into the No. 2 spot in the lineup early in the season.

Hitting

Gant's approach was pretty simple early in his major league career. He'd look for fastballs and crush them while trying to pull everything. His raw bat speed and power potential have diminished appreciably. By necessity, Gant made key changes in his approach at the plate last season. After moving into the second spot in the order, Gant took more pitches to accommodate leadoff man Doug Glanville, and often sprayed the ball the other way to move runners over. He established a career high with 85 walks in 1999. Gant still lapses into some old habits from time to time, such as opening his hips too quickly and pulling his head off breaking pitches. Thus he's vulnerable to extended slumps.

Baserunning & Defense

Though not the speed demon he was before breaking his right leg in a 1994 minibike accident, Gant retains above-average speed and solid baserunning instincts. He bludgeons middle infielders when breaking up the double play. He doesn't steal as often as he used to, but his success rate has increased. Defensively, Gant worked extremely hard to make himself a better left fielder on the Phils' difficult home turf. His arm is just average, but Gant accumulates decent assist totals because runners challenge him.

2000 Outlook

Gant's future as a starter in Philadelphia depends on prospect Pat Burrell's development. Gant is under contract through 2000 and is a solid bet to open the season in left field. The Phillies hope he'll open strong and establish some trade value before they hand the job to Burrell.

Overall Statistics

	G	AB	R	H	D	T	HR	RBI	SB	BB	SO	Avg	OBP	Slg
1999	138	516	107	134	27	5	17	77	13	85	112	.260	.364	.430
Career	1497	5422	903	1393	256	43	266	856	228	641	1172	.257	.336	.467

Where He Hits the Ball

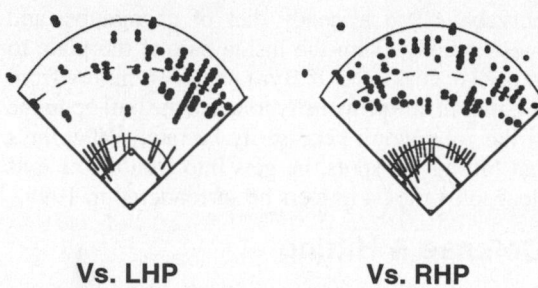

Vs. LHP   **Vs. RHP**

1999 Situational Stats

	AB	H	HR	RBI	Avg		AB	H	HR	RBI	Avg
Home	235	60	6	33	.255	LHP	130	39	5	22	.300
Road	281	74	11	44	.263	RHP	386	95	12	55	.246
First Half	281	73	9	38	.260	Sc Pos	122	38	4	60	.311
Scnd Half	235	61	8	39	.260	Clutch	68	18	2	11	.265

1999 Rankings (National League)

- 1st in fielding percentage in left field (.993)
- 6th in most pitches seen per plate appearance (4.10) and lowest batting average vs. righthanded pitchers
- 8th in lowest batting average and lowest batting average at home
- Led the Phillies in fewest GDPs per GDP situation (6.0%)

Doug Glanville

1999 Season

Last year, Doug Glanville continued to evolve into one of the better all-around center fielders in the game. After getting off to a brilliant start before tiring late in 1998, Glanville stayed strong for the duration of 1999, finishing second in the National League in hits. He hit the ball with more authority and was more aggressive on the bases. He reverted to his wild-swinging ways after a patient first two months, however, finishing the season with just 48 walks.

Hitting

Glanville has improved his physical strength and now drives the ball to all fields. He looks for fastballs to drill early in the count, or he can slap breaking balls the other way for singles. If he continues to develop, he could become a 20-homer guy. The two areas that Glanville needs to improve in are hitting lefthanders and drawing walks. For a leadoff man with a .325 batting average, a .376 on-base percentage is disappointing.

Baserunning & Defense

An excellent basestealer, Glanville has remarkable speed, studies pitchers and consistently gets good jumps. He generally makes good decisions on the basepaths. Defensively, he's a fluid, exciting center fielder who is as good as anyone in the majors not named Andruw Jones. He reads balls very well off the bat, takes charge on drives to the gaps and is exceptional at catching balls hit over his head. His arm strength is above average, and his aim and judgment are usually true.

2000 Outlook

Glanville is an intelligent player who has worked hard to advance his game. Look for his average to stay near .300 and his power and speed numbers to continue to rise. If his walks edge into the 65-75 range, he'll be a true star.

Position: CF
Bats: R **Throws:** R
Ht: 6' 2" **Wt:** 180

Opening Day Age: 29
Born: 8/25/70 in Hackensack, NJ
ML Seasons: 4

Overall Statistics

	G	AB	R	H	D	T	HR	RBI	SB	BB	SO	Avg	OBP	Slg
1999	150	628	101	204	38	6	11	73	34	48	82	.325	.376	.457
Career	503	1863	296	555	93	19	24	167	78	117	228	.298	.342	.407

Where He Hits the Ball

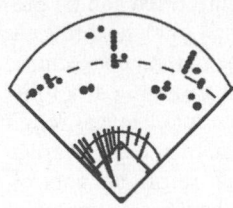 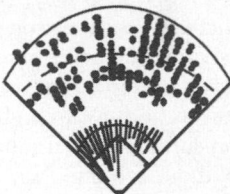

Vs. LHP   **Vs. RHP**

1999 Situational Stats

	AB	H	HR	RBI	Avg		AB	H	HR	RBI	Avg
Home	304	87	5	39	.286	LHP	140	35	2	11	.250
Road	324	117	6	34	.361	RHP	488	169	9	62	.346
First Half	343	110	6	48	.321	Sc Pos	130	44	4	62	.338
Scnd Half	285	94	5	25	.330	Clutch	79	25	1	7	.316

1999 Rankings (National League)

- 1st in singles, stolen-base percentage (94.4) and batting average on the road
- 2nd in hits and errors in center field (8)
- 3rd in at-bats
- 4th in batting average vs. righthanded pitchers
- Led the Phillies in at-bats, hits, singles, doubles, stolen bases, plate appearances (692), stolen-base percentage (94.4), on-base percentage for a leadoff hitter (.376), batting average on the road and batting average with two strikes (.250)
- Led NL center fielders in at-bats, hits, singles, doubles, plate appearances (692), stolen-base percentage (94.4), batting average vs. righthanded pitchers, batting average on the road and steals of third (4)

Wayne Gomes

1999 Season

Wayne Gomes assumed Philadelphia's closer role after Jeff Brantley blew out his shoulder in late April. Gomes was solid through most of the first half, getting ahead of hitters and finishing them off with his curveball. His control evaporated down the stretch, and by the end of the season the Phillies were doling out save opportunities to the likes of Scott Aldred and Steve Montgomery.

Pitching

Gomes has two pitches, a low-90s fastball and a nasty, sinking curveball. His curveball is his out pitch, but he throws it for strikes less than half the time, making it a necessity that he get his fastball over the plate early in the count. He's a streaky pitcher whose success or failure often can be predicted by the location of the first pitch he throws in an outing. Gomes can take the ball on consecutive days and often for more than an inning at a time, unless he runs up high pitch counts. He was tough on lefthanders, limiting them to a .254 average without a home run. If he can refine his control, Gomes has the raw ability to become a successful closer.

Defense & Hitting

Though he has improved his conditioning since his rookie season, Gomes still isn't in the best of shape. He doesn't field his position that well, as his delivery often leaves him out of position. He's also not particularly adept at controlling the running game with his slow delivery and mediocre pickoff move. Gomes has fanned in four of his five major league at-bats.

2000 Outlook

The Phillies plan to contend in 2000 and they didn't have enough faith to trust Gomes as their closer. In December, they signed reliever Mike Jackson to an incentive-laden deal that guarantees him $3 million for this year and could be worth as much as $15 million over three seasons. Jackson has a history of elbow, knee and shoulder problems, however, so Gomes may get another shot. He'd help himself by reporting to camp in peak condition.

Position: RP
Bats: R **Throws:** R
Ht: 6' 2" **Wt:** 215

Opening Day Age: 27
Born: 1/15/73 in Hampton, VA
ML Seasons: 3
Pronunciation: GOAMZ

Overall Statistics

	W	L	Pct.	ERA	G	GS	Sv	IP	H	BB	SO	HR	Ratio
1999	5	5	.500	4.26	73	0	19	74.0	70	56	58	5	1.70
Career	19	12	.613	4.46	181	0	20	210.0	209	115	168	18	1.54

How Often He Throws Strikes

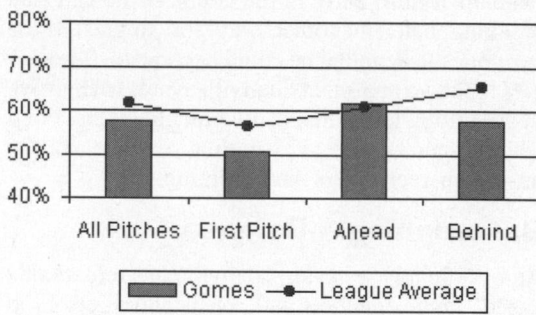

Legend: Gomes — League Average

1999 Situational Stats

	W	L	ERA	Sv	IP		AB	H	HR	RBI	Avg
Home	4	3	3.86	10	39.2	LHB	114	29	0	11	.254
Road	1	2	4.72	9	34.1	RHB	161	41	5	22	.255
First Half	2	1	3.63	12	39.2	Sc Pos	87	17	1	27	.195
Scnd Half	3	4	4.98	7	34.1	Clutch	157	44	1	20	.280

1999 Rankings (National League)

- 3rd in lowest percentage of inherited runners scored (16.7)
- 5th in most baserunners allowed per nine innings in relief (15.6)
- 6th in lowest save percentage (79.2)
- 7th in games finished (58)
- 8th in games pitched
- Led the Phillies in games pitched, saves, games finished (58), save opportunities (24), save percentage (79.2), blown saves (5), first batter efficiency (.259), lowest percentage of inherited runners scored (16.7), relief wins (5) and relief innings (74.0)

Mike Liberthal

1999 Season

Mike Liberthal blossomed into one of the best all-around catchers in the game in 1999, leading the Phillies in homers and ranking second in RBI while earning his first Gold Glove. He had a brilliant first half, ranking among National League batting leaders as late as July. By the end of the season, his heavy workload took its toll and his offense became more sporadic.

Hitting

Liberthal has come a long way since being drafted in the first round in 1990 as a scrawny defensive specialist. He has a wiry strong build and has developed longball power to all fields. He's a deadly fastball hitter who can turn on and crush any heaters on the inside half of the plate. He holds his own against breaking stuff, often spraying outside pitches the other way for singles. Liberthal still goes into extended slumps in which he attempts to pull everything, and he gets himself out too often on high fastballs. This isn't a major concern to the Phils. He bats low in the order, where walks are of lesser value.

Baserunning & Defense

For a catcher, Liberthal runs well. Though he didn't attempt to steal a base in 1999, he's a smart baserunner who can take the extra base. Even if his offensive development slows, Liberthal is assured of an extravagant salary because of his prowess behind the plate. His presence alone deters most baserunners, and he threw out 29 percent of those who tested him last season. He excels at calling a game. Only Pudge Rodriguez logged more innings at catcher in 1999.

2000 Outlook

The Phillies locked Liberthal into a long-term deal near the end of last season. He'll get $19 million over the next three seasons, with a club option for 2003 at $7.25 million. It would be unfair to expect him to duplicate his career-high 1999 offensive numbers, but Liberthal should continue to rank among the best all-around catchers in the game. Look for the Phils to reduce his workload.

Position: C
Bats: R **Throws:** R
Ht: 6' 0" **Wt:** 185

Opening Day Age: 28
Born: 1/18/72 in Glendale, CA
ML Seasons: 6
Pronunciation: LEE-ber-thal

Philadelphia

Overall Statistics

	G	AB	R	H	D	T	HR	RBI	SB	BB	SO	Avg	OBP	Slg
1999	145	510	84	153	33	1	31	96	0	44	86	.300	.363	.551
Career	455	1570	210	420	88	6	67	250	5	123	246	.268	.326	.459

Where He Hits the Ball

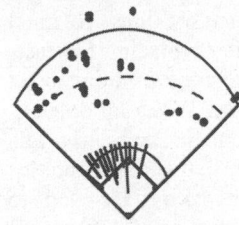 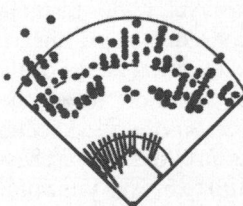

Vs. LHP   **Vs. RHP**

1999 Situational Stats

	AB	H	HR	RBI	Avg		AB	H	HR	RBI	Avg
Home	245	67	10	36	.273	LHP	122	46	10	29	.377
Road	265	86	21	60	.325	RHP	388	107	21	67	.276
First Half	273	84	18	61	.308	Sc Pos	141	45	9	69	.319
Scnd Half	237	69	13	35	.291	Clutch	76	17	3	13	.224

1999 Rankings (National League)

- 1st in fielding percentage at catcher (.997)
- 2nd in batting average vs. lefthanded pitchers
- 4th in slugging percentage vs. lefthanded pitchers (.697)
- Led the Phillies in home runs, sacrifice flies (8), hit by pitch (11), slugging percentage, HR frequency (16.5 ABs per HR), batting average vs. lefthanded pitchers, batting average on a 3-1 count (.667), batting average on an 0-2 count (.302), slugging percentage vs. lefthanded pitchers (.697) and on-base percentage vs. lefthanded pitchers (.443)
- Led NL catchers in doubles, sacrifice flies (8), on-base percentage, most pitches seen per plate appearance (3.68) and games played (143)

Robert Person

Position: SP/RP
Bats: R **Throws:** R
Ht: 6' 0" **Wt:** 190

Opening Day Age: 30
Born: 10/6/69 in St. Louis, MO
ML Seasons: 5

1999 Season

Robert Person opened the season on Toronto's disabled list with a pulled right hamstring, then got off to a horrible start as the Jays' closer because of poor control. Traded to Philadelphia on May 5 for Paul Spoljaric, Person was an extremely pleasant surprise as a starter. His command still was problematic at times, contributing to high pitch counts that usually rendered him little more than a six-inning pitcher.

Pitching

Logic would dictate that a pitcher with Person's repertoire would thrive out of the bullpen and struggle as a starter, but that hasn't been the case. Person throws nothing but hard stuff, combining a heavy, low-90s fastball with a nasty slider. He must consistently get ahead of hitters, placing his fastball on the edges of the strike zone in order to set up his slider to put them away. When he doesn't, Person often is knocked out of the box early. His control is spotty at best, but his stuff often enables him to escape jams of his own making. He needs to be used in a consistent manner to be effective.

Defense & Hitting

Person is a solid athlete, but his powerful motion often leaves him out of position on balls hit back through the middle. He's rather slow getting the ball to home plate and doesn't have much of a pickoff move. Person has little clue at the plate.

2000 Outlook

Person exceeded expectations with the Phillies, but he's no lock for the rotation. Curt Schilling, Andy Ashby and Paul Byrd are guaranteed spots, and Randy Wolf can earn one with a strong spring. It's likely Person will be slotted in at the back end of the rotation in April, and he could move to the bullpen if he struggles early.

Overall Statistics

	W	L	Pct.	ERA	G	GS	Sv	IP	H	BB	SO	HR	Ratio
1999	10	7	.588	4.68	42	22	2	148.0	139	85	139	24	1.51
Career	23	23	.500	5.04	122	58	8	416.1	400	204	355	69	1.45

How Often He Throws Strikes

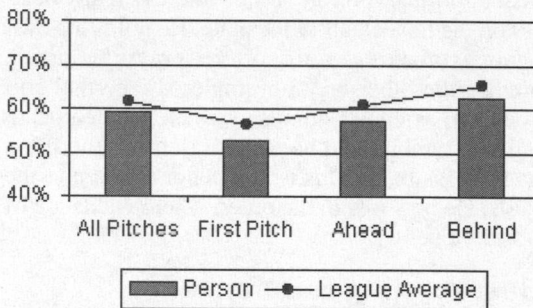

1999 Situational Stats

	W	L	ERA	Sv	IP		AB	H	HR	RBI	Avg
Home	5	1	3.90	2	67.0	LHB	249	68	12	42	.273
Road	5	6	5.33	0	81.0	RHB	306	71	12	38	.232
First Half	2	4	6.35	2	51.0	Sc Pos	141	34	7	58	.241
Scnd Half	8	3	3.80	0	97.0	Clutch	34	6	2	6	.176

1999 Rankings (National League)

- Led the Phillies in walks allowed (70)

Scott Rolen

1999 Season

After crushing the ball during spring training, Scott Rolen appeared poised for a massive year. While hitting .268-26-77 in 421 at-bats would be a solid year for most, it didn't measure up to the lofty standards that Rolen has set for himself. One reason for Rolen's struggles was a sore back that cost him the last month of the season. Perhaps an even bigger reason was his noticeable focus on driving the ball for distance.

Hitting

Rolen is a gifted physical specimen with exceptional strength, quickness and hand-eye coordination. As he rose through the minors, he focused on working deep counts, getting fastballs and then driving them where they were pitched. His power came naturally. He got away from that approach in 1999, concentrating on pulling the ball for distance and getting much more aggressive early in the count. His doubles and walk totals suffered, and Bobby Abreu surpassed him as the Phillies' best offensive player.

Baserunning & Defense

Blessed with above-average speed, Rolen is a wild man on the bases. Usually, he plays with inspired aggressiveness, which works out well for the club. Occasionally, however, he'll make a glaring faux pas on the bases. He can steal a base and often is used on the front end of hit-and-run plays. Rolen is truly amazing at the hot corner. He has a cat-quick first step to either side, and has led National League third basemen in range factor by a wide margin during the last two seasons. He also has a powerful throwing arm. Essentially, he has shortstop skills at third base.

2000 Outlook

Rolen's back is expected to heal with rest during the offseason. When he's healthy, his physical skills are complemented by uncommon maturity and intelligence. Even after his subpar 1999 campaign, he still compares favorably to a young Mike Schmidt at a similar stage in development. Rolen could hit .300 with 40 home runs in 2000.

Position: 3B
Bats: R **Throws:** R
Ht: 6' 4" **Wt:** 225

Opening Day Age: 24
Born: 4/4/75 in Jasper, IN
ML Seasons: 4
Pronunciation: ROH-len

Overall Statistics

	G	AB	R	H	D	T	HR	RBI	SB	BB	SO	Avg	OBP	Slg
1999	112	421	74	113	28	1	26	77	12	67	114	.268	.368	.525
Career	465	1713	297	479	115	8	82	297	42	249	420	.280	.376	.500

Where He Hits the Ball

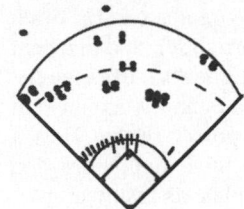
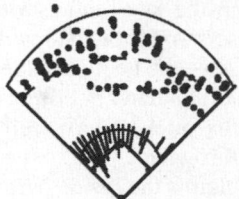

Vs. LHP **Vs. RHP**

1999 Situational Stats

	AB	H	HR	RBI	Avg		AB	H	HR	RBI	Avg
Home	203	54	9	39	.266	LHP	91	30	9	22	.330
Road	218	59	17	38	.271	RHP	330	83	17	55	.252
First Half	314	82	19	54	.261	Sc Pos	133	33	5	51	.248
Scnd Half	107	31	7	23	.290	Clutch	60	15	5	12	.250

1999 Rankings (National League)

- 4th in fielding percentage at third base (.960)
- 5th in cleanup slugging percentage (.569)
- 8th in errors at third base (14)
- 9th in lowest batting average vs. righthanded pitchers
- Led the Phillies in cleanup slugging percentage (.569)
- Led NL third basemen in cleanup slugging percentage (.569)

Curt Schilling

1999 Season

The Phillies got a glimpse of the best and worst of Curt Schilling in 1999. For much of the first half of the season, Schilling ranked with Pedro Martinez and Randy Johnson as the game's best starting pitchers, lasting well more than seven innings per start while combining raw power with pinpoint control. During the second half, Schilling was sidelined with inflammation in his right shoulder. He made just two starts in the final eight weeks.

Pitching

Schilling is a power pitcher in every respect. He relies heavily on a mid-90s fastball with exceptional movement. His velocity holds up remarkably well as games progress, and actually increases in the late innings when he's really on. He often sets up his fastball with a sharp slider, and in recent seasons he has added a splitter to use against lefthanders. Schilling is a craftsman who can spot his pitches very well for a power hurler. He's a throwback who expects to finish ballgames and claims the inside part of the plate as his own.

Defense & Hitting

A perfectionist who takes all facets of the game seriously, Schilling is a very good athlete who fields his position well. He holds runners on base extremely well for a power pitcher. He gets the ball to the plate quickly and has a fine move to first base. Only four basestealers tested Schilling in 1999, and just two were successful. Though traditionally a difficult out at the plate, Schilling had a poor offensive season in 1999, batting .100 with 28 strikeouts in 50 at-bats. He's a solid bunter who dropped nine successful sacrifices in 1999.

2000 Outlook

Philadelphia's playoff aspirations took a huge hit in December, when Schilling learned that he needed shoulder surgery. He'll miss at least six weeks of the regular season and may not return until the All-Star break. Schilling is the rock of the pitching staff, and the Phillies need his 17-20 wins and 200-plus innings to make a realistic run at the postseason.

Position: SP
Bats: R **Throws:** R
Ht: 6' 4" **Wt:** 230

Opening Day Age: 33
Born: 11/14/66 in Anchorage, AK
ML Seasons: 12
Pronunciation: SHILL-ing

Overall Statistics

	W	L	Pct.	ERA	G	GS	Sv	IP	H	BB	SO	HR	Ratio
1999	15	6	.714	3.54	24	24	0	180.1	159	44	152	25	1.13
Career	99	83	.544	3.38	326	215	13	1691.2	1483	454	1571	153	1.15

How Often He Throws Strikes

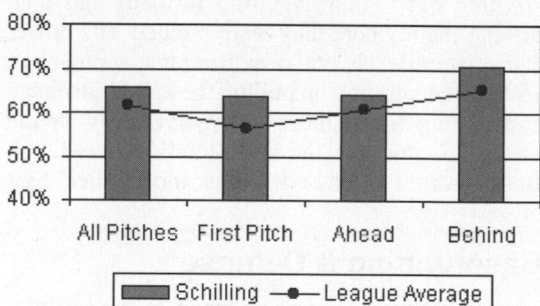

1999 Situational Stats

	W	L	ERA	Sv	IP		AB	H	HR	RBI	Avg
Home	7	4	4.10	0	98.2	LHB	334	83	12	37	.249
Road	8	2	2.87	0	81.2	RHB	338	76	13	34	.225
First Half	13	4	3.13	0	149.2	Sc Pos	122	25	5	41	.205
Scnd Half	2	2	5.58	0	30.2	Clutch	79	22	1	16	.278

1999 Rankings (National League)

- 2nd in complete games (8)
- 3rd in ERA on the road
- Led the Phillies in ERA, wins, complete games (8), strikeouts, winning percentage, highest strikeout/walk ratio (3.5), lowest batting average allowed (.237), lowest slugging percentage allowed (.396), lowest on-base percentage allowed (.287), highest groundball/flyball ratio allowed (1.2), lowest stolen-base percentage allowed (50.0), fewest baserunners allowed per nine innings (10.4), fewest home runs allowed per nine innings (1.25), most strikeouts per nine innings (7.6), least walks per nine innings (2.2), ERA at home, ERA on the road and lowest batting average allowed vs. lefthanded batters

Randy Wolf

1999 Season

Randy Wolf split time between Triple-A and the majors in 1999, faring the same at both levels. He got off to strong starts, including winning his first five decisions after being promoted to the majors on June 11. He struggled thereafter in both cases because he couldn't throw his breaking pitches for strikes early in the count. Wolf was overmatched for virtually all of his final 15 starts in the majors, and his confidence gradually waned.

Pitching

Wolf isn't overpowering but he can pick hitters apart by hitting his spots. He combines a darting 90-MPH fastball with a solid changeup and a passable curveball. He needs to have all three pitches working to be effective. Despite his lack of raw velocity, he struck out nearly a batter per inning in his rookie season because he set up hitters effectively. His control of his curve is spotty, however, and it became quite clear that he can't get by on his fastball alone. Hitters did a lot of damage when he threw high fastballs, and he's prone to huge first innings. Despite his overall struggles, Wolf was very effective against lefties. He's a battler who often ground out five or six passable innings on nights when he didn't have his best stuff.

Defense & Hitting

Wolf is an exceptional athlete who does all of the little things well. He has excellent reflexes and fields his position expertly. He delivers the ball quickly to the plate and has a deft move to first base, neutralizing the running game. Only one baserunner tried to steal against Wolf last season, and he was unsuccessful. Wolf is an excellent hitter for a pitcher.

2000 Outlook

Despite his at-times promising debut, Wolf isn't guaranteed a rotation spot for 2000. He needs more command to succeed, and if he doesn't show it during spring training then he could be headed for some more time in Triple-A. Even if that happens, his future looks bright.

Position: SP
Bats: L **Throws:** L
Ht: 6' 0" **Wt:** 198

Opening Day Age: 23
Born: 8/22/76 in Canoga Park, CA
ML Seasons: 1

Overall Statistics

	W	L	Pct.	ERA	G	GS	Sv	IP	H	BB	SO	HR	Ratio
1999	6	9	.400	5.55	22	21	0	121.2	126	67	116	20	1.59
Career	6	9	.400	5.55	22	21	0	121.2	126	67	116	20	1.59

How Often He Throws Strikes

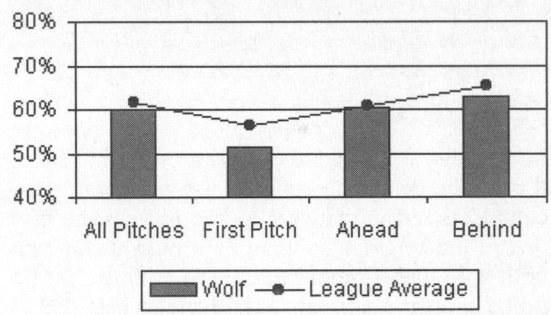

1999 Situational Stats

	W	L	ERA	Sv	IP		AB	H	HR	RBI	Avg
Home	3	4	4.98	0	65.0	LHB	86	18	4	11	.209
Road	3	5	6.19	0	56.2	RHB	388	108	16	62	.278
First Half	4	0	3.49	0	38.2	Sc Pos	117	30	4	46	.256
Scnd Half	2	9	6.51	0	83.0	Clutch	14	2	0	0	.143

1999 Rankings (National League)

- Did not rank near the top or bottom in any category

Scott Aldred

Position: RP
Bats: L **Throws:** L
Ht: 6' 4" **Wt:** 215

Opening Day Age: 31
Born: 6/12/68 in Flint, MI
ML Seasons: 8

Overall Statistics

	W	L	Pct.	ERA	G	GS	Sv	IP	H	BB	SO	HR	Ratio
1999	4	3	.571	4.45	66	0	1	56.2	59	29	41	2	1.55
Career	19	36	.345	6.03	206	67	1	479.1	558	220	291	75	1.62

1999 Situational Stats

	W	L	ERA	Sv	IP		AB	H	HR	RBI	Avg
Home	2	0	2.00	1	27.0	LHB	84	26	1	20	.310
Road	2	3	6.67	0	29.2	RHB	130	33	1	20	.254
First Half	3	2	5.25	0	24.0	Sc Pos	77	23	0	34	.299
Scnd Half	1	1	3.86	1	32.2	Clutch	60	17	0	13	.283

1999 Season

Scott Aldred started the season with the Devil Rays, who designated him for assignment in mid-July. Claimed on waivers by the Phillies, he was one of the brighter lights in their hideous bullpen until a couple of poor late-season outings. Yet he failed at his primary job, as lefthanders batted .310 against him.

Pitching, Defense & Hitting

Aldred is still in the major leagues because he's lefthanded and can touch 90 MPH with his fastball. It hasn't mattered that his fastball is pretty straight, his control is spotty at best and he never has developed a consistent breaking pitch. His career ERA is 6.03, an indication of his lack of effectiveness. Aldred is an ordinary fielder who holds runners poorly for a lefty. He fanned in his only major league at-bat.

2000 Outlook

Aldred is squarely on the major league fringe. He'll compete for a job as the Phillies' situational lefty, but he's no lock to make the club as it looks to upgrade its bullpen.

Alex Arias

Position: SS
Bats: R **Throws:** R
Ht: 6' 3" **Wt:** 197

Opening Day Age: 32
Born: 11/20/67 in New York, NY
ML Seasons: 8
Pronunciation: AIR-ee-us

Overall Statistics

	G	AB	R	H	D	T	HR	RBI	SB	BB	SO	Avg	OBP	Slg
1999	118	347	43	105	20	1	4	48	2	36	31	.303	.373	.401
Career	629	1474	167	410	66	6	14	169	8	147	159	.278	.349	.360

1999 Situational Stats

	AB	H	HR	RBI	Avg		AB	H	HR	RBI	Avg
Home	178	45	4	33	.253	LHP	95	24	0	9	.253
Road	169	60	0	15	.355	RHP	252	81	4	39	.321
First Half	144	45	2	20	.313	Sc Pos	102	35	2	44	.343
Scnd Half	203	60	2	28	.296	Clutch	64	23	3	13	.359

1999 Season

The Phillies signed Alex Arias to a two-year, $1 million deal prior to the 1999 season to be an all-purpose infield backup. He became an everyday shortstop last June, when Desi Relaford went on the disabled list for almost three months with a wrist injury. Arias performed admirably and was a steadying veteran presence in the Phils' youthful clubhouse.

Hitting, Baserunning & Defense

Arias is a spray hitter who has evolved into a difficult out. He always has made consistent contact and has learned to work favorable counts much more frequently. He hits the ball where it's pitched, with occasional power to the gaps. Power and speed are noticeably missing from Arias' offensive repertoire, however. Arias is a heady baserunner who looks to take the extra base on occasion. Defensively, his range is mediocre, but he turns everything he reaches into outs. He offers credible defense at second base, shortstop and third base.

2000 Outlook

Arias once again will provide insurance for the still-unproven Relaford. It's unlikely Arias will get 347 at-bats or bat .300 again, but he'll continue to give the Phillies peace of mind.

Rob Ducey

Position: LF/RF
Bats: L **Throws:** R
Ht: 6' 2" **Wt:** 180

Opening Day Age: 34
Born: 5/24/65 in Toronto, Canada
ML Seasons: 11
Pronunciation: DOO-see

Overall Statistics

	G	AB	R	H	D	T	HR	RBI	SB	BB	SO	Avg	OBP	Slg
1999	104	188	29	49	10	2	8	33	2	38	57	.261	.383	.463
Career	529	1041	154	260	70	12	22	108	21	119	272	.250	.329	.403

1999 Situational Stats

	AB	H	HR	RBI	Avg		AB	H	HR	RBI	Avg
Home	97	27	3	21	.278	LHP	7	1	0	2	.143
Road	91	22	5	12	.242	RHP	181	48	8	31	.265
First Half	78	20	5	18	.256	Sc Pos	42	15	4	28	.357
Scnd Half	110	29	3	15	.264	Clutch	30	5	2	4	.167

1999 Season

After spending parts of 10 seasons as a spare out-fielder in the American League, Rob Ducey brought his act to the National League for the first time in 1999. Signed as a free agent, he had his best offensive campaign to date. He was the Phillies' best lefthanded bench bat and one of their best situational hitters.

Hitting, Baserunning & Defense

Ducey is a deadly fastball hitter who had been plagued by poor plate discipline throughout his AL tenure. In 1999, he showed more willingness to take breaking pitches off the plate and work deep counts, which produced more fastballs and career-best power totals. Ducey is a fine athlete who runs well, though he isn't particularly aggressive on the bases. He plays competent defense at all three outfield positions, though his lack of outstanding speed or arm strength makes him best suited for left field.

2000 Outlook

The Phillies acknowledged Ducey's 1999 contributions by inking him to a two-year, $1 million deal. He could get more playing time this year, though it's unlikely he'll be as productive on a per-at-bat basis.

Bobby Estalella

Traded To GIANTS

Position: C
Bats: R **Throws:** R
Ht: 6' 1" **Wt:** 205

Opening Day Age: 25
Born: 8/23/74 in Hialeah, FL
ML Seasons: 4
Pronunciation: ess-tah-LAY-yah

Overall Statistics

	G	AB	R	H	D	T	HR	RBI	SB	BB	SO	Avg	OBP	Slg
1999	9	18	2	3	0	0	0	1	0	4	7	.167	.318	.167
Career	76	229	32	50	7	1	14	34	1	25	69	.218	.295	.441

1999 Situational Stats

	AB	H	HR	RBI	Avg		AB	H	HR	RBI	Avg
Home	9	1	0	1	.111	LHP	3	1	0	0	.333
Road	9	2	0	0	.222	RHP	15	2	0	1	.133
First Half	0	0	0	0	-	Sc Pos	7	1	0	1	.143
Scnd Half	18	3	0	1	.167	Clutch	4	1	0	1	.250

1999 Season

Bobby Estalella began the season on the disabled list rehabbing a torn rotator cuff, then suffered through a subpar offensive year in Triple-A. Once considered the Phillies' catcher of the future, his injuries and inconsistency have caused his stock to drop sharply.

Hitting, Baserunning & Defense

A strapping physical specimen, Estalella can clout a mistake a long way. But except during a strong 1998 Triple-A campaign, he has been unable to work his way into fastball counts in recent seasons. He gets into big trouble when he attempts to pull outside breaking pitches, resulting in strikeouts or weak grounders to the left side of the infield. Estalella is a slow, station-to-station baserunner. Defensively, he has a very strong throwing arm but only an average release. His mechanics can be inconsistent at times, making him slow to spring into throwing position.

2000 Outlook

Estalella was traded to San Francisco in December for righthander Chris Brock, a candidate for the Philadelphia rotation. It was a good move for Estalella, who was blocked by Mike Lieberthal on the Phillies but should start for the Giants.

Philadelphia

Kevin Jordan

Position: 3B/2B/1B
Bats: R **Throws:** R
Ht: 6' 1" **Wt:** 206

Opening Day Age: 30
Born: 10/9/69 in San Francisco, CA
ML Seasons: 5

Overall Statistics

	G	AB	R	H	D	T	HR	RBI	SB	BB	SO	Avg	OBP	Slg
1999	120	347	36	99	17	3	4	51	0	24	34	.285	.339	.386
Career	383	959	99	262	49	3	17	126	2	42	119	.273	.308	.384

1999 Situational Stats

	AB	H	HR	RBI	Avg		AB	H	HR	RBI	Avg
Home	174	51	2	25	.293	LHP	123	37	2	19	.301
Road	173	48	2	26	.277	RHP	224	62	2	32	.277
First Half	115	33	1	8	.287	Sc Pos	105	31	1	44	.295
Scnd Half	232	66	3	43	.284	Clutch	55	14	0	5	.255

1999 Season

Every year, the Phillies expect Kevin Jordan to play no more than a supporting role. Every year, Jordan winds up playing much more than expected. In 1999, he got plenty of starts at second base against lefties, spelling rookie Marlon Anderson, and played third base every day down the stretch after Scott Rolen hurt his back.

Hitting, Baserunning & Defense

Jordan is an aggressive contact hitter who hits line drives to all fields. Though he rarely walks, Jordan also is very difficult to strike out. He can foul off breaking pitches at will, often frustrating pitchers into throwing a fastball he can handle. A broken leg and knee surgery made Jordan a below-average runner years ago. Defensively, he's surehanded within his limited range and is competent at second base, shortstop and third base.

2000 Outlook

The Phillies love Jordan's flexibility and enthusiasm. His lack of patience and power-speed capability are exposed when he's in the starting lineup for long stretches, but in short bursts he can spell an injured regular with little dropoff.

Carlton Loewer

Traded To PADRES

Position: SP
Bats: R **Throws:** R
Ht: 6' 6" **Wt:** 200

Opening Day Age: 26
Born: 9/24/73 in Lafayette, LA
ML Seasons: 2
Pronunciation: LOW-er

Overall Statistics

	W	L	Pct.	ERA	G	GS	Sv	IP	H	BB	SO	HR	Ratio
1999	2	6	.250	5.12	20	13	0	89.2	100	26	48	9	1.41
Career	9	14	.391	5.68	41	34	0	212.1	254	65	106	27	1.50

1999 Situational Stats

	W	L	ERA	Sv	IP		AB	H	HR	RBI	Avg
Home	2	2	4.25	0	53.0	LHB	156	47	4	22	.301
Road	0	4	6.38	0	36.2	RHB	192	53	5	28	.276
First Half	2	5	5.31	0	78.0	Sc Pos	69	25	3	39	.362
Scnd Half	0	1	3.86	0	11.2	Clutch	24	7	1	1	.292

1999 Season

Former first-round pick Carlton Loewer opened the 1999 season in Philadelphia's rotation, but was shut down in early June with a stress fracture in his pitching arm. Loewer rehabbed frantically and was reinstated to the major league roster in early September, though he was used sparingly in mopup relief the rest of the way.

Pitching, Defense & Hitting

Loewer has a prototypical pitcher's body and a four-pitch repertoire, featuring a 90-MPH fastball, curveball, slider and changeup. None of his pitches possess exceptional movement and he rarely makes hitters miss. Loewer has averaged only 4.5 strikeouts per nine innings during his major league career, ridiculously low for a pitcher with his stuff. He needs to tweak his mechanics and find that extra movement or velocity that could make a significant difference. Loewer is a solid fielder who holds runners on base. He's a decent hitter.

2000 Outlook

Loewer, Steve Montgomery and prospect Adam Eaton were traded to San Diego in November for Andy Ashby. Healthy again, Loewer probably will serve as the Padres' No. 4 starter. He's a strikeout pitch away from being a successful major league starter.

Steve Montgomery

Position: RP
Bats: R **Throws:** R
Ht: 6' 4" **Wt:** 200

Opening Day Age: 29
Born: 12/25/70 in Westminster, CA
ML Seasons: 3

Overall Statistics

	W	L	Pct.	ERA	G	GS	Sv	IP	H	BB	SO	HR	Ratio
1999	1	5	.167	3.34	53	0	3	64.2	54	31	55	10	1.31
Career	2	6	.250	4.78	65	0	3	84.2	82	52	64	17	1.58

1999 Situational Stats

	W	L	ERA	Sv	IP		AB	H	HR	RBI	Avg
Home	1	3	3.24	3	41.2	LHB	90	18	4	7	.200
Road	0	2	3.52	0	23.0	RHB	146	36	6	16	.247
First Half	0	3	3.23	0	30.2	Sc Pos	48	8	1	11	.167
Scnd Half	1	2	3.44	3	34.0	Clutch	122	27	4	9	.221

1999 Season

Signed to a minor league contract during the off-season, journeyman Steve Montgomery was the most effective pitcher in the minefield that was Philadelphia's bullpen. He performed well as the club's primary setup man and was called upon to close games late in the season. He stranded 19 of 21 inherited baserunners.

Pitching, Defense & Hitting

Montgomery relies on a heavy, high-80s fastball that moves sharply. He also throws a hard slider that at times is effective as an out pitch against lefties. Getting ahead of hitters and spotting the ball within the strike zone are keys for Montgomery. He nibbled around the edges of the plate in two previous big league trials and was hammered both times. When he misses, he tends to miss high and becomes vulnerable to home runs. Montgomery fields his position and holds runners well. He singled in his only major league at-bat.

2000 Outlook

Montgomery was included with Adam Eaton and Carlton Loewer in the November trade that brought Andy Ashby from the Padres. In San Diego, Montgomery will assist Donne Wall in setting up closer Trevor Hoffman.

Chad Ogea

Position: SP
Bats: R **Throws:** R
Ht: 6' 2" **Wt:** 220

Opening Day Age: 29
Born: 11/9/70 in Lake Charles, LA
ML Seasons: 6
Pronunciation: OH-jay

Overall Statistics

	W	L	Pct.	ERA	G	GS	Sv	IP	H	BB	SO	HR	Ratio
1999	6	12	.333	5.63	36	28	0	168.0	192	61	77	36	1.51
Career	37	35	.514	4.88	129	94	0	632.2	672	214	369	93	1.40

1999 Situational Stats

	W	L	ERA	Sv	IP		AB	H	HR	RBI	Avg
Home	1	7	5.02	0	80.2	LHB	281	90	16	54	.320
Road	5	5	6.18	0	87.1	RHB	386	102	20	49	.264
First Half	4	9	5.43	0	104.1	Sc Pos	181	48	10	71	.265
Scnd Half	2	3	5.94	0	63.2	Clutch	26	2	1	1	.077

1999 Season

Chad Ogea was an unmitigated disaster as the Phillies' No. 3 starter. Obtained from the Indians in November 1998 for reliever Jerry Spradlin, Ogea arguably was the most hittable National League starter last season. Despite appearing only sparingly in mopup roles down the stretch, he held onto the league lead in homers allowed until the season's last week and allowed 89 extra-base hits in 168 innings.

Pitching, Defense & Hitting

Ogea enjoyed spurts of major league success with the Indians, especially when he was able to set up his changeup with a darting, high-80s fastball that he kept low in the zone. Success didn't follow him to Philadelphia. His fastball rarely reached 85 MPH and he left his pitches up in the strike zone too often. Ogea is an average fielder but doesn't hold runners well. He can't hit, either.

2000 Outlook

The Phillies removed Ogea from their 40-man roster three days after the season ended, and he opted for free agency. He signed a minor league contract with the Tigers in November, then was taken by the Devil Rays in the major league Rule 5 draft in December. He figures to make Tampa Bay's wide-open rotation.

Desi Relaford

Position: SS
Bats: B **Throws:** R
Ht: 5' 9" **Wt:** 175

Opening Day Age: 26
Born: 9/16/73 in
Valdosta, GA
ML Seasons: 4

Overall Statistics

	G	AB	R	H	D	T	HR	RBI	SB	BB	SO	Avg	OBP	Slg
1999	65	211	31	51	11	2	1	26	4	19	34	.242	.322	.327
Career	237	783	81	186	39	7	6	74	17	60	136	.238	.297	.328

1999 Situational Stats

	AB	H	HR	RBI	Avg		AB	H	HR	RBI	Avg
Home	102	25	0	15	.245	LHP	44	11	0	7	.250
Road	109	26	1	11	.239	RHP	167	40	1	19	.240
First Half	169	44	1	26	.260	Sc Pos	59	18	0	24	.305
Scnd Half	42	7	0	0	.167	Clutch	28	6	1	1	.214

1999 Season

Desi Relaford was expected to stake his claim to the Phillies' starting shortstop position in 1999. It didn't work out that way, due in large part to a torn ligament in his throwing wrist, which limited him to 65 games.

Hitting, Baserunning & Defense

Though he lacks size, Relaford is a strong man capable of lashing the ball to the gaps. His swing retains too much of an uppercut, however, and he doesn't have the power to be a home-run hitter. He has expanded his strike zone dramatically since reaching the majors. Relaford has well above-average speed and decent basestealing technique, but doesn't get a chance to show it often while batting eighth. Defensively, he has the quick first step and cannon arm to be an exceptional turf shortstop. Yet he has a tendency to boot routine plays.

2000 Outlook

Relaford will enter the season as Philadelphia's everyday shortstop, but he needs to perform to remain in the club's master plan. Alex Arias has proven himself to be more than capable as a fill-in over extended periods of time, and prospect Jimmy Rollins is almost ready.

Kevin Sefcik

Position: LF/CF/RF/2B
Bats: R **Throws:** R
Ht: 5'10" **Wt:** 180

Opening Day Age: 29
Born: 2/10/71 in Oak
Lawn, IL
ML Seasons: 5
Pronunciation: SEF-sik

Overall Statistics

	G	AB	R	H	D	T	HR	RBI	SB	BB	SO	Avg	OBP	Slg
1999	111	209	28	58	15	3	1	11	9	29	24	.278	.368	.392
Career	325	617	77	176	30	8	6	46	17	67	83	.285	.364	.389

1999 Situational Stats

	AB	H	HR	RBI	Avg		AB	H	HR	RBI	Avg
Home	99	34	1	7	.343	LHP	91	31	1	6	.341
Road	110	24	0	4	.218	RHP	118	27	0	5	.229
First Half	102	29	1	9	.284	Sc Pos	52	10	0	7	.192
Scnd Half	107	29	0	2	.271	Clutch	36	11	0	1	.306

1999 Season

Kevin Sefcik was an integral part of a productive Phillies bench, spelling all three outfield starters and filling in at second base. Once physically overmatched by quality major league fastballs, Sefcik consistently provided quality at-bats last season.

Hitting, Baserunning & Defense

Sefcik has a precise, disciplined approach at the plate. He works deep counts, slaps the ball to all fields and is a solid bunter. He also has developed a touch of gap power in recent seasons. Sefcik's speed is a shade above average. He's an aggressive baserunner who is unafraid to take the extra base when appropriate, and his on-base ability and baserunning instincts make him a natural for the first or second spots in the batting order when he gets a spot start. Defensively, he can play any infield or outfield position in a pinch, and he complements his average range and arm strength with superior positioning.

2000 Outlook

Sefcik's playing time is dictated by the health and productivity of the outfield and second-base starters. He's perfectly suited for the 150-200 at-bat role he has assumed in the last two seasons.

Other Philadelphia Phillies

Gary Bennett (Pos: C, Age: 27, Bats: R)

	G	AB	R	H	D	T	HR	RBI	SB	BB	SO	Avg	OBP	Slg
1999	36	88	7	24	4	0	1	21	0	4	11	.273	.298	.352
Career	52	136	11	37	4	0	1	25	0	11	23	.272	.320	.324

Bennett spent the entire 1999 season in the majors as a backup to Mike Lieberthal. Apparently manager Terry Francona knows how to use Bennett, as he hit better than his .239 career average in the minors. 2000 Outlook: C

Joel Bennett (Pos: RHP, Age: 30)

	W	L	Pct.	ERA	G	GS	Sv	IP	H	BB	SO	HR	Ratio
1999	2	1	.667	9.00	5	3	0	17.0	26	7	13	10	1.94
Career	2	1	.667	8.53	7	3	0	19.0	28	10	13	10	2.00

Bennett has had some Triple-A success the last two seasons, but he gave up a whopping 10 homers in 17 innings when the Phils called in May. He's a free agent looking for another opportunity. 2000 Outlook: C

Jeff Brantley (Pos: RHP, Age: 36)

	W	L	Pct.	ERA	G	GS	Sv	IP	H	BB	SO	HR	Ratio
1999	1	2	.333	5.19	10	0	5	8.2	5	8	11	0	1.50
Career	41	38	.519	3.17	542	18	149	783.0	664	328	660	88	1.27

In May Brantley had surgery for a torn labrum, a shoulder injury he says he had in 1998 that never was diagnosed because he didn't have an MRI. Angry when the Phillies signed closer Mike Jackson, Brantley still signed a one-year deal with $250,000 in base salary. 2000 Outlook: C

Billy Brewer (Pos: LHP, Age: 31)

	W	L	Pct.	ERA	G	GS	Sv	IP	H	BB	SO	HR	Ratio
1999	1	1	.500	7.01	25	0	2	25.2	30	14	28	4	1.71
Career	11	11	.500	4.79	203	0	5	178.2	172	93	137	26	1.48

After a decent first half with Triple-A Scranton, Brewer had a chance to re-establish himself as a major league middle reliever in the second half. A handful of brutal outings with the Phils changed that. 2000 Outlook: C

Domingo Cedeno (Pos: SS, Age: 31, Bats: B)

	G	AB	R	H	D	T	HR	RBI	SB	BB	SO	Avg	OBP	Slg
1999	53	108	9	19	6	0	3	13	1	10	31	.176	.252	.315
Career	429	1219	160	306	54	13	15	121	14	83	280	.251	.300	.354

It wasn't a good year for Cedeno, who started 1999 with the Mariners but was sent down in May. On June 7, he was traded to the Phils, but he batted .152 with Philly and was released in mid-September. 2000 Outlook: C

David Doster (Pos: 2B, Age: 29, Bats: R)

	G	AB	R	H	D	T	HR	RBI	SB	BB	SO	Avg	OBP	Slg
1999	99	97	9	19	2	0	3	10	1	12	23	.196	.282	.309
Career	138	202	23	47	10	0	4	18	1	19	44	.233	.297	.342

After hitting for decent average with a little bit of power at Triple-A Scranton for two seasons, Doster spent all of 1999 with the big club. He slumped in the second half, going 9-for-54 (.167). 2000 Outlook: C

Mike Grace (Pos: RHP, Age: 29)

	W	L	Pct.	ERA	G	GS	Sv	IP	H	BB	SO	HR	Ratio
1999	1	4	.200	7.69	27	5	0	55.0	80	30	28	5	2.00
Career	16	16	.500	4.96	68	40	0	275.2	310	90	156	27	1.45

Grace had promising stints with the Phils in 1996 and '97, but injuries shortened those seasons. He hasn't been effective in Triple-A or Philadelphia since then, and now he's a free agent. 2000 Outlook: C

Joe Grahe (Pos: RHP, Age: 32)

	W	L	Pct.	ERA	G	GS	Sv	IP	H	BB	SO	HR	Ratio
1999	1	4	.200	3.86	13	5	0	32.2	40	17	16	1	1.74
Career	22	30	.423	4.41	187	39	45	400.1	451	182	204	27	1.58

The Angels' closer in the early 1990s, Grahe made his first big league appearance last summer since 1995. His recent Triple-A stats haven't been bad, but it's hard to be encouraged about Grahe's chances. 2000 Outlook: C

Torey Lovullo (Pos: 1B, Age: 34, Bats: B)

	G	AB	R	H	D	T	HR	RBI	SB	BB	SO	Avg	OBP	Slg
1999	17	38	3	8	0	0	2	5	0	3	11	.211	.268	.368
Career	303	737	80	165	35	1	15	60	9	80	121	.224	.301	.335

Lovullo has been a late-season callup for two straight seasons, and he has batted .211 both years in a limited role. He became a free agent in October. 2000 Outlook: C

Wendell Magee (Pos: CF, Age: 27, Bats: R)

	G	AB	R	H	D	T	HR	RBI	SB	BB	SO	Avg	OBP	Slg
1999	12	14	4	5	1	0	2	5	0	1	4	.357	.400	.857
Career	108	346	29	79	18	1	6	39	1	26	68	.228	.281	.338

Magee nearly duplicated his 1998 season at Triple-A Scranton by batting .283-20-79 in '99, and he hit well with the Phils in September. He had his chance a few years ago. Now there may not be room for him. 2000 Outlook: C

Yorkis Perez (Pos: LHP, Age: 32)

	W	L	Pct.	ERA	G	GS	Sv	IP	H	BB	SO	HR	Ratio
1999	3	1	.750	3.94	35	0	0	32.0	29	15	26	4	1.38
Career	12	14	.462	4.50	281	0	1	232.0	205	119	213	21	1.40

After a rough stretch in the mid-1990s, Perez has been effective with the Phils the last two seasons. Elbow inflammation sidelined him in July and he never returned. Now he's a free agent. 2000 Outlook: B

Cliff Politte (Pos: RHP, Age: 26)

	W	L	Pct.	ERA	G	GS	Sv	IP	H	BB	SO	HR	Ratio
1999	1	0	1.000	7.13	13	0	0	17.2	19	15	15	2	1.92
Career	3	3	.500	6.59	21	8	0	54.2	64	33	37	8	1.77

Politte was effective in a swing role in Double-A in 1999, but he wasn't effective in the Philly bullpen in September. Acquired from the Cards a year ago, he'll get another look this spring. 2000 Outlook: C

Tom Prince (Pos: C, **Age**: 35, **Bats**: R)

	G	AB	R	H	D	T	HR	RBI	SB	BB	SO	Avg	OBP	Slg
1999	4	6	1	1	0	0	0	0	0	1	1	.167	.286	.167
Career	326	699	61	138	44	2	9	79	3	61	149	.197	.273	.305

Prince tore two wrist ligaments while checking a swing during a spring training game, and he didn't play until September. That wasn't enough time to catch the elusive Bob Uecker (.200) in career average. 2000 Outlook: C

Ken Ryan (Pos: RHP, **Age**: 31)

	W	L	Pct.	ERA	G	GS	Sv	IP	H	BB	SO	HR	Ratio
1999	1	2	.333	6.32	15	0	0	15.2	16	11	9	2	1.72
Career	14	16	.467	3.91	240	1	30	285.2	266	164	225	21	1.51

Injuries have sidetracked Ryan's career as a closer, but last summer he threw more than 50 innings for the first time since 1996. Pittsburgh signed him after Philadelphia released him in August, and Kansas City picked him up as a minor league free agent during the offseason. 2000 Outlook: C

Steve Schrenk (Pos: RHP, **Age**: 31)

	W	L	Pct.	ERA	G	GS	Sv	IP	H	BB	SO	HR	Ratio
1999	1	3	.250	4.29	32	2	1	50.1	41	14	36	6	1.09
Career	1	3	.250	4.29	32	2	1	50.1	41	14	36	6	1.09

After an 11-year stint as a minor league starter, Schrenk has been impressive in the pen for two straight Triple-A campaigns. He arrived in June and provided some decent relief work for the Phils. 2000 Outlook: B

Anthony Shumaker (Pos: LHP, **Age**: 26)

	W	L	Pct.	ERA	G	GS	Sv	IP	H	BB	SO	HR	Ratio
1999	0	3	.000	5.96	8	4	0	22.2	23	14	17	3	1.63
Career	0	3	.000	5.96	8	4	0	22.2	23	14	17	3	1.63

Shumaker pitched very well in Double-A in 1999, but couldn't match that success in Triple-A or Philadelphia. His familiarity with the roads between Scranton and Philly may serve him well. 2000 Outlook: C

Amaury Telemaco (Pos: RHP, **Age**: 26)

	W	L	Pct.	ERA	G	GS	Sv	IP	H	BB	SO	HR	Ratio
1999	4	0	1.000	5.77	49	0	0	53.0	52	26	43	10	1.47
Career	16	20	.444	4.91	125	40	0	337.0	357	114	214	52	1.40

After a solid 1998 campaign in which Telemaco seemed ready to blossom as a major leaguer, he sat out April with shoulder tendinitis and didn't pitch well. He was picked up on waivers from Arizona in June. 2000 Outlook: B

Philadelphia Phillies Minor League Prospects

Organization Overview:

It took the Phillies six years, but they finally contended for a playoff spot again in 1999 before an ugly late-season fade. They did so without any major forays into the free-agent market. All of their best players are either homegrown (Mike Lieberthal, Scott Rolen) or were acquired through markedly one-sided trades (Bobby Abreu for Kevin Stocker, Doug Glanville for Mickey Morandini, Curt Schilling for Jason Grimsley). Philadelphia dealt for Andy Ashby in November, though the cost was three pitchers, including former first-round picks Adam Eaton and Carlton Loewer. The Phillies were able to part with arms because they have several mound prospects in the lower levels of their system. The organization jewel is Pat Burrell, who has as much offensive promise as any player in the minors.

Brad Baisley

Position: P   **Opening Day Age:** 20
Bats: R **Throws:** R   **Born:** 8/24/79 in Dade
Ht: 6' 9" **Wt:** 200   City, FL

Recent Statistics

	W	L	ERA	G	GS	Sv	IP	H	R	BB	SO	HR
1998 R Martinsvlle	3	2	3.58	7	7	0	27.2	27	12	4	14	2
1999 A Piedmont	10	7	2.26	23	23	0	147.2	116	56	55	110	5

With the departure of Adam Eaton to San Diego in the Andy Ashby trade, Baisley becomes the top pitching prospect in the system. He easily handled full-season Class-A ball as a teenager, as he threw a no-hitter and had his curveball rated the best breaking ball in the South Atlantic League. His fastball was a so-so 88-90 MPH when he signed as a 1998 second-round pick, but he was considered very projectable at 6-foot-9 and 205 pounds. Baisley added 2 MPH last year and should pick up more velocity in the future. His changeup is coming along, and he just needs some more experience and strength. He's two to three years away from Philadelphia.

Jason Brester

Position: P   **Opening Day Age:** 23
Bats: L **Throws:** L   **Born:** 12/7/76 in Lincoln,
Ht: 6' 3" **Wt:** 190   NE

Recent Statistics

	W	L	ERA	G	GS	Sv	IP	H	R	BB	SO	HR
1998 AA Shreveport	2	8	3.82	19	19	0	113.0	117	58	44	79	11
1998 AA New Haven	2	0	1.59	5	4	0	22.2	22	7	7	15	0
1999 AA Carolina	2	6	5.76	11	11	0	59.1	71	45	26	44	8
1999 AA Reading	7	5	3.76	16	16	0	105.1	105	48	26	87	8

Drafted in the second round in 1995 by the Giants, Brester went to the Rockies in the Ellis Burks trade in 1998 and was claimed on waivers by the Phillies when Colorado needed to clear roster space last summer. He's not a high-ceiling guy—one Philadelphia official likened him to Matt Beech—but he's a lefthanded starter with decent stuff, a fairly rare commodity. His fastball is a borderline average pitch, but his curveball is above average when it's on. He also has a changeup. Brester needs at least a year in Triple-A to improve, but he's also Philadelphia's most viable starting option in the upper minors.

Pat Burrell

Position: 1B   **Opening Day Age:** 23
Bats: R **Throws:** R   **Born:** 10/10/76 in
Ht: 6' 4" **Wt:** 230   Eureka Springs, AR

Recent Statistics

	G	AB	R	H	D	T	HR	RBI	SB	BB	SO	Avg
1998 A Clearwater	37	132	29	40	7	1	7	30	2	27	22	.303
1999 AA Reading	117	417	84	139	28	6	28	90	3	79	103	.333
1999 AAA Scranton-WB	10	33	4	5	0	0	1	4	0	4	8	.152
1999 MLE	127	436	73	130	27	4	23	78	2	60	120	.298

No minor league hitter combines power and average like Burrell, who has justified his No. 1 overall selection in the 1998 draft. In 164 pro games, most in the upper minors, he has hit .316-36-124 with 110 walks. He has raw strength, bat speed, plate discipline and the intelligence to make adjustments. In short, he has no offensive weakness. A third baseman at the University of Miami, he wasn't going to take that position from Scott Rolen. Burrell initially played first base as a pro, then moved to left field last summer. Though he's not quick, he is a solid defender with an average arm. The only question is how soon the Phillies will call him up, and whether they'll use him at first or in left. He's ready now.

Josue Perez

Position: OF   **Opening Day Age:** 22
Bats: B **Throws:** R   **Born:** 8/12/77 in
Ht: 6' 0" **Wt:** 180   Havana, Cuba

Recent Statistics

	G	AB	R	H	D	T	HR	RBI	SB	BB	SO	Avg
1999 A Vero Beach	62	201	24	56	14	1	2	22	14	21	29	.279
1999 A Clearwater	23	93	15	23	2	0	0	6	6	7	17	.247

First baseman Juan Diaz and Perez, fellow Cuban defectors and Dodgers farmhands, were declared free agents last June when the commissioner's office ruled that Los Angeles had signed them illegally. The Dodgers broke baseball rules by holding tryouts for the players in Cuba, for which the club also was fined $200,000 and banned from re-signing them. Diaz was still entertaining bids from teams in late December, while Perez signed quickly with the Phillies for $850,000. He's a true center fielder who has the speed to bat leadoff. He'll need to improve offensively, but Philadelphia thinks he has the chance to hit from both sides of the plate. His body is reminiscent of a young Rickey Henderson's. Perez has played just one season in the U.S. minors and still is raw, so he's at least two years away from the majors.

Jimmy Rollins

Position: SS   **Opening Day Age:** 21
Bats: B **Throws:** R   **Born:** 11/27/78 in
Ht: 5' 8" **Wt:** 160   Oakland, CA

Recent Statistics

	G	AB	R	H	D	T	HR	RBI	SB	BB	SO	Avg
1998 A Clearwater	119	495	72	121	18	9	6	35	23	41	62	.244
1999 AA Reading	133	532	81	145	21	8	11	56	24	51	47	.273
1999 AAA Scranton-WB	4	13	0	1	1	0	0	0	1	1	1	.077
1999 MLE	137	530	67	131	21	6	9	46	17	37	53	.247

After sharing the Phillies' minor league hitter of the year award in 1997, Rollins lost his luster with a mediocre 1998 season. Still, he was promoted to Double-A at age 20 and got back on track. A 1996 second-round pick who's the cousin of big league outfielder Tony Tarasco, Rollins is a switch-hitter with a little juice in his bat and plenty of speed. It's still uncertain how much he'll hit, but he did walk more than he struck out in 1999. He has the range and arm needed to play shortstop. Desi Relaford leaves a lot to be desired, so Rollins could challenge for his job late this year.

Carlos Silva

Position: P   **Opening Day Age:** 20
Bats: R **Throws:** R   **Born:** 4/23/79 in Puerto
Ht: 6' 4" **Wt:** 198   Ordaz, Venezuela

Recent Statistics

	W	L	ERA	G	GS	Sv	IP	H	R	BB	SO	HR
1998 R Martinsvlle	1	4	5.05	7	7	0	41.0	48	24	4	21	2
1998 A Batavia	2	3	6.35	9	7	0	45.1	61	37	9	27	4
1999 A Piedmont	11	8	3.12	26	26	0	164.1	176	79	41	99	6

Silva has a tremendous yet raw arm and is still learning to use it. Signed out of Venezuela at age 16, he made his U.S. debut at 17 and spent three years in short-season ball. He throws a very heavy fastball that can reach 95-96 MPH, and Class-A hitters found it nearly impossible to knock out of the park. His statistics were so-so because he's still putting together the rest of his repertoire. He must develop his curveball and changeup so he can keep batters off balance. If he can't, the bullpen could become his destination.

Reggie Taylor

Position: OF   **Opening Day Age:** 23
Bats: L **Throws:** R   **Born:** 1/12/77 in
Ht: 6' 1" **Wt:** 175   Newberry, SC

Recent Statistics

	G	AB	R	H	D	T	HR	RBI	SB	BB	SO	Avg
1998 AA Reading	79	337	49	92	14	6	5	22	22	12	73	.273
1999 AA Reading	127	526	75	140	17	10	15	61	38	18	79	.266
1999 MLE	127	513	62	127	16	8	12	51	28	13	86	.248

Taylor went 14th overall in the 1995 draft because of his considerable athleticism, but he's been slow to translate his physical gifts into baseball skills. He had his best pro season yet in 1999, though he was repeating Double-A. While he hit .266 with a career-high 15 homers, there still were plenty of holes in his offensive game. His 79-18 strikeout-walk ratio was just plain horrid, his on-base

(.293) and slugging (.422) percentages were substandard, and he led the Eastern League with 20 caught stealings, negating the value of his 38 steals. His defense is further along, as he was rated the EL's best defensive outfielder. He has Gold Glove potential in center field, with wide range and a strong arm. Still, it's hard to see Taylor cracking the Phillies' future outfield of Eric Valent, Doug Glanville and Bobby Abreu.

Eric Valent

Position: OF   **Opening Day Age:** 22
Bats: L **Throws:** L   **Born:** 4/4/77 in La
Ht: 6' 0" **Wt:** 191   Mirada, CA

Recent Statistics

	G	AB	R	H	D	T	HR	RBI	SB	BB	SO	Avg
1998 A Piedmont	22	89	24	38	12	0	8	28	0	14	19	.427
1998 A Clearwater	34	125	24	33	8	1	5	25	1	16	29	.264
1999 A Clearwater	134	520	91	150	31	9	20	106	5	58	110	.288

When the Phillies weren't able to sign 1997 first-round pick J.D. Drew, their consolation prize was a supplemental first-round choice a year later. They turned that into Valent, who broke former UCLA teammate Troy Glaus' Pacific-10 Conference home-run record. In his first full pro season, Valent led the Class-A Florida State League with 106 RBI while showing all-around hitting skills. He'll hit for average with power both to the gaps and over the fence. His intensity makes him a more effective runner than his speed would alone, and he's a solid right fielder in terms of both range and arm. Valent's presence means that fellow 1998 draftee Pat Burrell's ultimate big league position likely will be first base.

Others to Watch

Greg Kubes (23) joins Brad Baisley and Carlos Silva as legitimate prospects who pitched in Class-A Piedmont's 1999 rotation. Kubes is a finesse lefthander whose strong suits are his curveball and command. . . **Jason Michaels** (23) could make a nice fourth outfielder. He has average tools across the board, though he does nothing exceptionally well. . . The 12th overall pick in the 1999 draft, righthander **Brett Myers** (19) signed for $2.05 million. He completely overmatched the Rookie-level Gulf Coast League with a 92-94 MPH fastball and a hard curve. . . Acquired from the Angels in a 1998 trade, righthander **Doug Nickle** (25) could make that a very one-sided deal for the Phillies. Converted to a closer last year, he saw his fastball jump from the high 80s to 92-96 MPH with more life. . . Originally signed by the Dodgers, **Franklin Nunez** (23) never made it to the U.S. minors and spent two years out of the game before signing with the Phillies in 1998. Last year at Piedmont, he showed a 95-96 MPH fastball and posted an 88-25 strikeout-walk ratio in 77 innings. . . Lefthander **Kris Stevens** (22) reached Double-A at age 20 before missing the entire 1999 season after tearing an anterior cruciate ligament in his knee during a spring-training drill. He has good life on his fastball and a nice changeup.

Three Rivers Stadium

Offense

Three Rivers Stadium is a neutral park with symmetrical dimensions. Doubles, triples and homers usually increase in Pittsburgh, though triples were down in 1999. The ball carries better into the gaps than down the lines. Balls also take high hops off the artificial turf, adding a few more extra-base hits. The springy turf puts a premium on players who can leg out doubles and triples.

Defense

Three Rivers has few quirks but the corner outfield positions can be difficult to play. Fences in front of the bullpen down the lines can create tricky bounces with balls shooting in various directions. Left field is also difficult to play in night games because the lights bounce off the glass windows of the Allegheny Club on the first-base side and into the left fielder's eyes. Some right fielders also have trouble in night games because of the way some of the lights on the third-base side are banked.

Who It Helps The Most

The Pirates' three best hitters all enjoyed Three Rivers last year. Center fielder Brian Giles hit .336-24-71 in 265 Pittsburgh at-bats. Catcher Jason Kendall hit .360 at home before dislocating his right ankle July 4. First baseman Kevin Young hit .324 with 16 of his 26 homers at Three Rivers. As for the pitchers, closer Mike Williams' ERA was more than three runs better at home (3.52 versus 6.83).

Who It Hurts The Most

Kris Benson didn't pitch well in Pittsburgh during his rookie season, posting a 4.76 ERA at home compared to 3.33 on the road. Pat Meares, who spent most of the season on the disabled list after hand surgery, hit .152 at home and .397 on the road.

Rookies & Newcomers

Offseason acquisitions Bruce Aven and Wil Cordero should get a power boost in Pittsburgh. Rookie Chad Hermansen figures to get first crack at center field this season, and Three Rivers Stadium should be a good fit for him. Third baseman Aramis Ramirez has hit better in Three Rivers than on the road in his limited major league time.

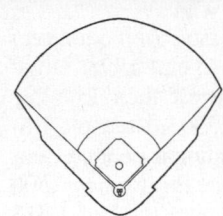

Dimensions: LF-335, LCF-375, CF-400, RCF-375, RF-335

Capacity: 48,044

Elevation: 730 feet

Surface: Turf

Foul Territory: Large

Park Factors

1999 Season

	Home Games			Away Games			
	Pirates	Opp	Total	Pirates	Opp	Total	Index
G	75	75	150	71	71	142	—
Avg	.261	.250	.256	.249	.269	.259	99
AB	2456	2559	5015	2469	2401	4870	97
R	360	342	702	316	355	671	99
H	642	640	1282	616	646	1262	96
2B	142	138	280	109	140	249	109
3B	21	11	32	17	18	35	89
HR	78	75	153	68	66	134	111
BB	270	276	546	255	302	557	95
SO	547	535	1082	555	448	1003	105
E	62	56	118	68	51	119	94
E-Infield	52	49	101	56	40	96	100
LHB-Avg	.276	.256	.267	.256	.282	.268	99
LHB-HR	48	33	81	41	27	68	115
RHB-Avg	.250	.247	.248	.244	.262	.253	98
RHB-HR	30	42	72	27	39	66	107

1997-1999

	Home Games			Away Games			
	Pirates	Opp	Total	Pirates	Opp	Total	Index
G	220	220	440	223	223	446	—
Avg	.263	.257	.260	.251	.269	.260	100
AB	7242	7587	14829	7731	7479	15210	99
R	1021	1003	2024	933	1043	1976	104
H	1908	1953	3861	1939	2009	3948	99
2B	409	416	825	357	395	752	113
3B	70	37	107	48	46	94	117
HR	194	206	400	171	202	373	110
BB	684	753	1437	658	842	1500	98
SO	1545	1559	3104	1641	1413	3054	104
E	183	185	368	197	163	360	104
E-Infield	156	164	320	164	136	300	108
LHB-Avg	.268	.262	.265	.252	.294	.274	97
LHB-HR	83	91	174	69	87	156	116
RHB-Avg	.260	.254	.257	.250	.251	.251	103
RHB-HR	111	115	226	102	115	217	106

1999 Rankings (National League)

- Did not rank near the top or bottom of any category

Gene Lamont

1999 Season

Gene Lamont came into the season on the hot seat after the Pirates lost 25 of 30 to end 1998. However, the Pirates took the heat off their low-key manager by hovering around .500 all season, finishing 78-83 and third in the National League Central. Lamont did well to keep the Pirates near .500 considering that 21 players spent a total of 1,313 days on the disabled list.

Offense

The Pirates hit more homers in 1999 than in any season in club history. As a result, Lamont toned down his usual aggressive style a bit. A big believer in starting runners and employing the hit-and-run, he didn't rank near the top of NL managers in those categories. Lamont usually goes by the book when it comes to platooning. One statistic Lamont disregards is on-base percentage. He dropped Jason Kendall from the leadoff spot last April and replaced him with Al Martin, who never walks.

Pitching & Defense

There was a distinct change in Lamont's philosophy of handling pitchers last season. He began giving starters a chance to go deeper into games. Lamont's rationale is the Pirates are at a point in their rebuilding program where they need to know what starters can be counted on to get important outs in the late innings. Lamont also showed decisive action in removing Rich Loiselle as the closer after a bad spring training and replacing him with journeyman Mike Williams, who recorded 23 saves. Lamont is a big believer in good defense and the fact the Pirates finished 15th among 16 NL teams in fielding percentage galled him.

2000 Outlook

Lamont enters the final year of his contract, which will put a certain amount of pressure on him. The Pirates will be in the fourth year of a five-year rebuilding plan and owner Kevin McClatchy expects his club to break the .500 barrier for the first time since 1992. If the Pirates don't have a winning season, they very well could have a new manager for the unveiling of PNC Park in 2001.

Born: 12/25/46 in Rockford, IL

Playing Experience: 1970-1975, Det

Managerial Experience: 7 seasons

Manager Statistics

Year	Team, Lg	W	L	Pct	GB	Finish
1999	Pittsburgh, NL	78	83	.484	18.5	3rd Central
7 Seasons		484	469	.508	—	—

1999 Starting Pitchers by Days Rest

	<=3	4	5	6+
Pirates Starts	0	75	52	26
Pirates ERA	0.00	4.78	4.95	3.21
NL Avg Starts	3	81	48	21
NL ERA	4.84	4.53	4.72	4.98

1999 Situational Stats

	Gene Lamont	NL Average
Hit & Run Success %	26.3	33.6
Stolen Base Success %	71.8	70.2
Platoon Pct.	59.4	55.2
Defensive Subs	24	25
High-Pitch Outings	16	13
Quick/Slow Hooks	19/13	16/15
Sacrifice Attempts	107	89

1999 Rankings (National League)
- 1st in squeeze plays (14)
- 2nd in sacrifice bunt attempts (107) and intentional walks (40)

Kris Benson

1999 Season

The No. 1 overall pick in the 1996 amateur draft, Kris Benson came to spring training as a longshot to make the club after going 8-10, 5.37 at Triple-A Nashville in 1998. Benson had a phenomenal exhibition season, posting a 0.75 ERA in 24 innings to make the starting rotation. Benson went on to lead all National League rookie starters in ERA, innings and strikeouts.

Pitching

Benson has four pitches he can throw for strikes at any time in the count, a rarity for a young pitcher. He has a fastball that reaches 95 MPH and explodes out of his hand from a nice, easy motion. He also has a knee-buckling curveball that's his second-best pitch. Last season Benson gained command of his slider, a pitch that acts more like a cut fastball at this point. He also can throw a changeup for strikes, though he doesn't need to rely on it much with three other plus pitches. An intelligent sort, Benson has a good feel for pitching and how to attack hitters.

Defense & Hitting

Benson struggles somewhat defensively. He can be slow in charging bunts and covering first base. He also tends to forget about baserunners and needs to improve his pickoff move. Benson has worked hard on his hitting and drove in seven runs in 1999. He also is a reliable bunter.

2000 Outlook

Benson should improve on last season's victory total of 11 now that he has a year of major league experience. Highly touted ever since being the first overall draft pick, he justified the expectations last season. There are very few No. 1 starters in the major leagues, and Benson has a good chance to join that elite group in the not-so-distant future.

Position: SP
Bats: R **Throws:** R
Ht: 6' 4" **Wt:** 190

Opening Day Age: 25
Born: 11/7/74 in Superior, WI
ML Seasons: 1

Overall Statistics

	W	L	Pct.	ERA	G	GS	Sv	IP	H	BB	SO	HR	Ratio
1999	11	14	.440	4.07	31	31	0	196.2	184	83	139	16	1.36
Career	11	14	.440	4.07	31	31	0	196.2	184	83	139	16	1.36

How Often He Throws Strikes

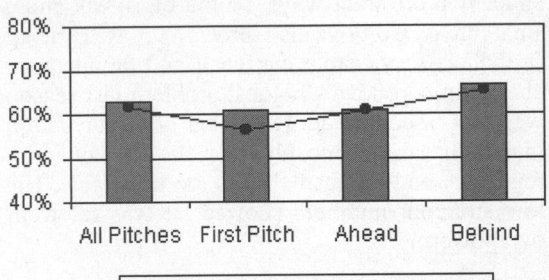

1999 Situational Stats

	W	L	ERA	Sv	IP		AB	H	HR	RBI	Avg
Home	6	8	4.76	0	102.0	LHB	339	94	7	40	.277
Road	5	6	3.33	0	94.2	RHB	399	90	9	50	.226
First Half	6	7	4.86	0	100.0	Sc Pos	165	44	6	75	.267
Scnd Half	5	7	3.26	0	96.2	Clutch	48	11	1	5	.229

1999 Rankings (National League)

- 4th in losses and pickoff throws (169)
- 5th in lowest slugging percentage allowed (.367)
- 6th in ERA on the road
- 8th in fewest home runs allowed per 9 innings (.73)
- 9th in lowest batting average allowed (.249) and lowest batting average allowed vs. righthanded batters
- 10th in GDPs induced (22) and least run support per 9 innings (4.8)
- Led the Pirates in losses, complete games (2), hit batsmen (6), pickoff throws (169), stolen bases allowed (17), runners caught stealing (7), lowest batting average allowed (.249) and lowest slugging percentage allowed (.367)

Francisco Cordova

1999 Season

The Pirates gave Francisco Cordova the ball on Opening Day for a second straight year, but he never pitched like a No. 1 starter. He went on the disabled list with a sore shoulder after two starts and missed a month. He didn't miss a start after being activated, but he never looked like the Cordova of old as he posted the highest ERA of his career. Cordova also appeared 15-20 pounds heavier than in past seasons.

Pitching

Cordova has a good sinker-slider combination. His sinker has outstanding movement, tops out at 90 MPH and will break many bats. He can throw his slider two different ways, with a big break and a small break. Cordova also throws a 93-MPH rising fastball, a serviceable curveball and an adequate changeup. Cordova's biggest problem last season was lack of command. His sinker often stayed too high in the strike zone, his slider flattened out with regularity and his fastball was too unreliable. His low strikeout numbers showed he was far from overpowering.

Defense & Hitting

Slow off the mound, Cordova doesn't field his position well. He holds runners close and has a very good pickoff move. Cordova has come a long way as a hitter from the days when he would be bailing out on every pitch. He now makes consistent contact and usually can be counted on to lay down a bunt.

2000 Outlook

The Pirates have asked Cordova to be something he's not, a No. 1 starter. Cordova's slide last season worried the Pirates and there's speculation that he's older than his listed age of 27. It quietly became known around baseball last season that Cordova could be had in the right trade, a sign he's losing stature in Pittsburgh.

Position: SP
Bats: R **Throws:** R
Ht: 6' 1" **Wt:** 191

Opening Day Age: 27
Born: 4/26/72 in Veracruz, Mexico
ML Seasons: 4
Pronunciation: core-DOE-vuh

Overall Statistics

	W	L	Pct.	ERA	G	GS	Sv	IP	H	BB	SO	HR	Ratio
1999	8	10	.444	4.43	27	27	0	160.2	166	59	98	16	1.40
Career	36	39	.480	3.78	148	95	12	658.2	648	197	471	63	1.28

How Often He Throws Strikes

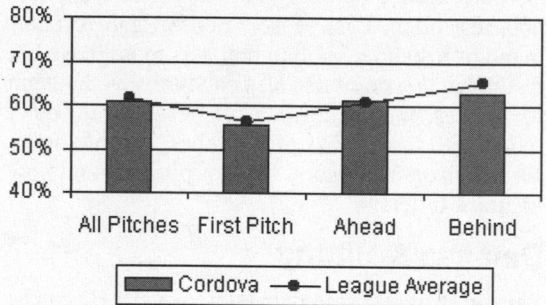

1999 Situational Stats

	W	L	ERA	Sv	IP		AB	H	HR	RBI	Avg
Home	5	4	4.24	0	74.1	LHB	285	80	7	29	.281
Road	3	6	4.59	0	86.1	RHB	323	86	9	43	.266
First Half	4	4	4.81	0	67.1	Sc Pos	144	43	9	61	.299
Scnd Half	4	6	4.15	0	93.1	Clutch	40	10	0	1	.250

1999 Rankings (National League)

- 8th in highest batting average allowed with runners in scoring position
- Led the Pirates in complete games (2)

Brian Giles

1999 Season

Acquired from Cleveland in an offseason trade for Ricardo Rincon, Brian Giles got his first chance to play every day and quickly established himself as a rising star. Giles probably would have become only the third Pirate to hit 40 homers, joining Hall of Famers Ralph Kiner and Willie Stargell, had he not broken his right middle finger with 11 games left in the season. Giles began the season in left field, moved to right in mid-April when Jose Guillen was sent to the minors, then shifted to center in mid-May when Brant Brown was benched.

Hitting

Giles has the rare combination of being able to hit the ball with authority while staying extremely patient at the plate. That leads to high slugging and on-base percentages, making him an outstanding offensive player. Giles is an excellent low-ball hitter who can drive the ball out to any field. He also is a smart hitter who doesn't try to hit home runs. Instead, Giles just looks to make contact and drive balls into the gaps. His natural power takes balls over the fence.

Baserunning & Defense

Though he takes short, choppy steps, Giles motors pretty well. He isn't a big basestealing threat, but he runs the bases well and can take the extra base when needed. Giles is better than advertised in center field, especially at going back on balls. He's able to play shallow because of his range. Giles has a below-average arm, though, which makes him better suited for left field.

2000 Outlook

Giles' challenge this season will be to prove last season wasn't a fluke. There's no reason to think Giles can't duplicate his 1999 numbers, as he's just reaching his prime. Giles is an emerging superstar who could be an MVP someday if the Pirates ever return to playoff contention.

Position: CF/RF
Bats: L **Throws:** L
Ht: 5'10" **Wt:** 200

Opening Day Age: 29
Born: 1/20/71 in El Cajon, CA
ML Seasons: 5
Pronunciation: JYLES

Overall Statistics

	G	AB	R	H	D	T	HR	RBI	SB	BB	SO	Avg	OBP	Slg
1999	141	521	109	164	33	3	39	115	6	95	80	.315	.418	.614
Career	440	1378	259	407	81	7	78	272	32	250	219	.295	.401	.534

Where He Hits the Ball

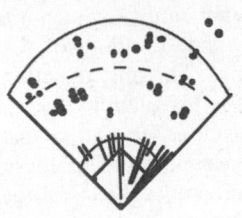
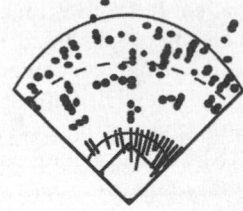

Vs. LHP	Vs. RHP

1999 Situational Stats

	AB	H	HR	RBI	Avg		AB	H	HR	RBI	Avg
Home	265	89	24	71	.336	LHP	177	53	9	28	.299
Road	256	75	15	44	.293	RHP	344	111	30	87	.323
First Half	300	94	18	57	.313	Sc Pos	140	43	11	79	.307
Scnd Half	221	70	21	58	.317	Clutch	74	19	2	14	.257

1999 Rankings (National League)

- 3rd in slugging percentage vs. righthanded pitchers (.663) and fielding percentage in center field (.992)
- 5th in slugging percentage and on-base percentage vs. righthanded pitchers (.430)
- Led the Pirates in batting average, home runs, runs scored, total bases (320), RBI, sacrifice flies (8), walks, intentional walks (7), times on base (262), GDPs (14), slugging percentage, on-base percentage, HR frequency (13.4 ABs per HR), batting average with runners in scoring position, batting average vs. righthanded pitchers, batting average on a 3-1 count (.643), batting average on an 0-2 count (.308) and slugging percentage vs. righthanded pitchers (.663)

Pittsburgh

Jason Kendall

1999 Season

Jason Kendall began the season as a novelty and ended it as a question mark. He started off as a leadoff-hitting catcher, though that experiment ended in late April when he was hitting only .274. Kendall moved to the No. 5 hole and was having another fine year when he dislocated his right ankle July 4 while trying to beat out a bunt. He missed the rest of the season.

Hitting

Kendall is a professional hitter who battles in every at-bat and sprays line drives to all fields. His power is beginning to emerge from beyond the gaps and there are scouts who believe Kendall eventually can hit 18-20 homers a year. Kendall is also a very patient hitter. He'll take a walk, rarely swings at a bad pitch and has a better understanding of the strike zone than some umpires. The only question about Kendall batting fifth is his inability to hit with runners in scoring position. He batted just .181 in those situations last year, and his .262 mark with runners in scoring position over the last three seasons is 54 points lower than his overall average.

Baserunning & Defense

Kendall was easily the best running catcher in baseball before his ankle injury, stealing a club-high 22 bases last season despite missing the second half of the year. He figures to lose some speed because of the injury, though how much remains to be seen. Kendall is a good defensive catcher who takes charge behind the plate. He handles pitchers well and sets a good target. Kendall is an average thrower. He has good arm strength but his release is slow.

2000 Outlook

No one knows for sure what to expect from Kendall this season. He should be fully recovered from his ankle injury by the time spring training opens, but his speed is a question mark. If his ability to squat is affected, then the Pirates would be forced to move Kendall to another position, probably third base or the outfield. At a position other than catcher, Kendall wouldn't be as valuable offensively.

Position: C
Bats: R **Throws:** R
Ht: 6' 0" **Wt:** 193

Opening Day Age: 25
Born: 6/26/74 in San Diego, CA
ML Seasons: 4

Overall Statistics

	G	AB	R	H	D	T	HR	RBI	SB	BB	SO	Avg	OBP	Slg
1999	78	280	61	93	20	3	8	41	22	38	32	.332	.428	.511
Career	501	1715	281	535	115	15	31	207	71	173	166	.312	.399	.451

Where He Hits the Ball

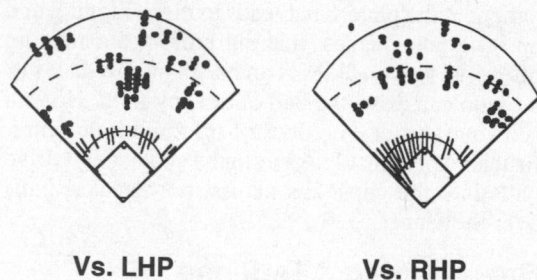

Vs. LHP   Vs. RHP

1999 Situational Stats

	AB	H	HR	RBI	Avg		AB	H	HR	RBI	Avg
Home	136	49	5	24	.360	LHP	59	16	4	9	.271
Road	144	44	3	17	.306	RHP	221	77	4	32	.348
First Half	280	93	8	41	.332	Sc Pos	83	15	2	29	.181
Scnd Half	0	0	0	0	-	Clutch	45	12	0	6	.267

1999 Rankings (National League)

- 3rd in stolen-base percentage (88.0%)
- 4th in hit by pitch (12), lowest batting average with runners in scoring position and errors at catcher (7)
- 6th in batting average with two strikes (.271)
- Led the Pirates in stolen bases, stolen-base percentage (88.0%), batting average with the bases loaded (.400) and batting average with two strikes (.271)
- Led NL catchers in triples, stolen bases, hit by pitch (12), stolen-base percentage (88.0%) and batting average with the bases loaded (.400)

Al Martin

Position: LF
Bats: L **Throws:** L
Ht: 6' 2" **Wt:** 214

Opening Day Age: 32
Born: 11/24/67 in West Covina, CA
ML Seasons: 8

1999 Season

Al Martin rose from the dead to have a fine season for the Pirates. He nearly was traded to Arizona in the early days of spring training, but Diamondbacks outfielder Bernard Gilkey nixed the deal when he refused to rework minor contract language. Martin started the season on the bench after six years as the Pittsburgh's starting left fielder but regained his spot in the lineup two weeks into the season and set a career high with 24 homers.

Hitting

Two factors changed Martin as a hitter last season. He had LASIK refractive surgery on his eyes and opened his batting stance. Martin's improved vision enabled him to recognize breaking and off-speed pitches, and his new stance gave him extra time to wait on them. Martin is still a fastball hitter first and foremost, but he is no longer an automatic out against breaking offspeed stuff. Martin has good pop, though his lack of plate discipline makes him ill-suited for the leadoff spot.

Baserunning & Defense

Martin runs well and has learned when to steal as he has gotten older. He's now a high-percentage basestealer while remaining a threat to take the extra base on singles and doubles. Martin's defense also improved thanks to the eye surgery, as he's now able to track flyballs better. However, Martin still has a very weak arm and rarely throws out anyone.

2000 Outlook

Still steamed that he was benched by manager Gene Lamont to begin 1999, Martin reportedly asked to be traded at season's end. He'll face a challenge for the left-field job from free-agent signee Wil Cordero, who landed a three-year, $9 million contract. Eye surgery has made Martin a better player, capable of repeating his 1999 numbers.

Overall Statistics

	G	AB	R	H	D	T	HR	RBI	SB	BB	SO	Avg	OBP	Slg
1999	143	541	97	150	36	8	24	63	20	49	119	.277	.337	.506
Career	897	3241	523	907	178	34	107	381	152	300	684	.280	.342	.455

Where He Hits the Ball

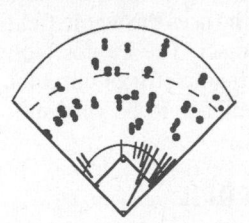

Vs. LHP

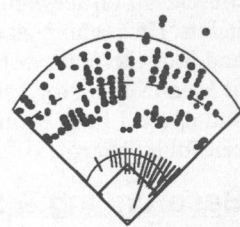

Vs. RHP

1999 Situational Stats

	AB	H	HR	RBI	Avg		AB	H	HR	RBI	Avg
Home	275	81	12	30	.295	LHP	120	29	2	9	.242
Road	266	69	12	33	.259	RHP	421	121	22	54	.287
First Half	294	90	11	37	.306	Sc Pos	106	26	3	36	.245
Scnd Half	247	60	13	26	.243	Clutch	87	20	1	5	.230

1999 Rankings (National League)

- 2nd in errors in left field (10) and lowest fielding percentage in left field (.952)
- 4th in stolen-base percentage (87.0%)
- 5th in lowest batting average with the bases loaded (.077)
- 6th in lowest on-base percentage for a leadoff hitter (.327)
- 7th in triples and lowest on-base percentage vs. lefthanded pitchers (.305)
- Led the Pirates in triples and on-base percentage for a leadoff hitter (.327)
- Led NL left fielders in triples and stolen-base percentage (87.0%)

Pat Meares

1999 Season

Released by Minnesota on December 20, 1998, Pat Meares had a trying offseason. He had to wait until spring training before signing a one-year contract with the Pirates. He agreed to a four-year, $15 million extension on April 30, but then damaged a tendon in his left hand shortly thereafter. Meares had surgery and didn't return until late September, playing in a total of just 21 games.

Hitting

Meares has a little bit of pop and hits for a decent average. He has bulked up in recent years and the Pirates believe he could hit 12-15 homers per season. Meares, though, occasionally tries too hard to muscle up on the ball, which leads him into bad habits. He's at his best when he uses the whole field and looks to make solid contact. The Pirates look at Meares as a No. 2 hitter but he strikes out a lot and doesn't have enough patience to be very successful in that role.

Baserunning & Defense

Meares has adequate speed and will steal an occasional base when the defense is napping. Now that he has switched from the American League to the National League, he likely will be asked to run more in an aggressive Pittsburgh offense. Meares is a solid defensive shortstop. He has decent range, particularly to his left, and a good arm. He is steady and makes the routine play with consistency.

2000 Outlook

The Pirates have made a long-term commitment to Meares despite having shortstop prospect Abraham Nunez in the organization. The Pirates expect Meares to be the same steady player he was in Minnesota.

Position: SS
Bats: R **Throws:** R
Ht: 6' 0"   **Wt:** 187

Opening Day Age: 31
Born: 9/6/68 in Salina, KS
ML Seasons: 7
Pronunciation: MEERS

Overall Statistics

	G	AB	R	H	D	T	HR	RBI	SB	BB	SO	Avg	OBP	Slg
1999	21	91	15	28	4	0	0	7	0	9	20	.308	.382	.352
Career	763	2555	319	681	124	21	41	310	42	104	452	.267	.304	.380

Where He Hits the Ball

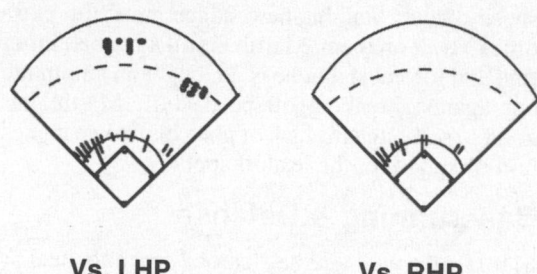

Vs. LHP   **Vs. RHP**

1999 Situational Stats

	AB	H	HR	RBI	Avg		AB	H	HR	RBI	Avg
Home	33	5	0	0	.152	LHP	44	15	0	3	.341
Road	58	23	0	7	.397	RHP	47	13	0	4	.277
First Half	74	22	0	5	.297	Sc Pos	20	5	0	7	.250
Scnd Half	17	6	0	2	.353	Clutch	16	8	0	2	.500

1999 Rankings (National League)

- Did not rank near the top or bottom in any category

Warren Morris

1999 Season

Despite never having played in the major leagues, Warren Morris was handed the Pirates' second-base job in the early days of spring training when two-time National League stolen-base champion Tony Womack was traded to Arizona. Morris seized the opportunity by having one of the best rookie seasons in the NL. The only damper on Morris' season was that he hit .200 in his last 25 games.

Hitting

Morris has a nice, short line-drive stroke from the left side, making him a rarity among middle infielders. He has good gap power with enough strength to eventually hit 20 home runs a season. Morris has a good understanding of hitting and knows how to use the whole field, a big reason why no one pitching pattern seems to get him out. Morris also controls the strike zone well, staying patient at the plate while rarely chasing a bad pitch.

Baserunning & Defense

Morris is a bit slow and not much of a basestealing threat. However, he will go from first to third or second to home on a single if the outfielder doesn't pay attention to him. The knock on Morris always has been that he's a below-average defender. He went a long way toward dispelling that notion last season. Morris doesn't have great range but does a good job of positioning himself. He also has soft hands, a good arm and has a knack turning the double play.

2000 Outlook

Morris had a good rookie season last year and only should get better. He has the look of a perennial .300 hitter who will offer lefthanded power. There are some All-Star Game visits in Morris' future.

Position: 2B
Bats: L **Throws:** R
Ht: 5'11" **Wt:** 185

Opening Day Age: 26
Born: 1/11/74 in Alexandria, LA
ML Seasons: 1

Overall Statistics

	G	AB	R	H	D	T	HR	RBI	SB	BB	SO	Avg	OBP	Slg
1999	147	511	65	147	20	3	15	73	3	59	88	.288	.360	.427
Career	147	511	65	147	20	3	15	73	3	59	88	.288	.360	.427

Where He Hits the Ball

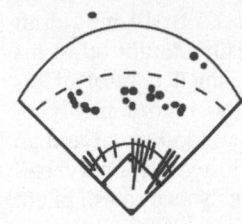

Vs. LHP

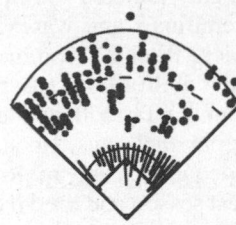

Vs. RHP

1999 Situational Stats

	AB	H	HR	RBI	Avg		AB	H	HR	RBI	Avg
Home	251	73	9	36	.291	LHP	110	37	2	17	.336
Road	260	74	6	37	.285	RHP	401	110	13	56	.274
First Half	282	85	9	47	.301	Sc Pos	139	39	6	62	.281
Scnd Half	229	62	6	26	.271	Clutch	91	25	1	10	.275

1999 Rankings (National League)

- 3rd in errors at second base (14)
- 5th in lowest fielding percentage at second base (.979)
- 6th in lowest percentage of extra bases taken as a runner (34.9%)
- Led the Pirates in singles, highest groundball/flyball ratio (1.2) and batting average in the clutch

Todd Ritchie

Position: SP
Bats: R **Throws:** R
Ht: 6' 3" **Wt:** 215

Opening Day Age: 28
Born: 11/7/71 in Portsmouth, VA
ML Seasons: 3

1999 Season

Todd Ritchie failed to make the Pittsburgh bullpen as a nonroster invitee in spring training and began the season in Triple-A Nashville's starting rotation. The Pirates called him up to make a spot start during the second weekend of the season, and he never went back to the minors. The club's first 15-game winner since Doug Drabek in 1992, Ritchie was particularly effective after the All-Star break. He went 6-3, 2.95 in 11 starts as his confidence grew.

Pitching

Ritchie always has had a great arm, dating back to his days as a schoolboy in 1990, when he outdueled highly touted Todd Van Poppel in the Texas state semifinals and was Minnesota's first-round draft pick. Ritchie's command finally caught up to his raw ability last season. He gained control of his sinking fastball and used it to record plenty of groundball outs. He also has a good slider and an adequate changeup. Ritchie dusted off a curveball last season and used it effectively as a fourth pitch. Considering he spent the 1997 and 1998 seasons as a reliever with the Twins before being outrighted, Ritchie shows good stamina as a starter. He had some rough first innings in the early going last year, but overcame that problem by altering his warmup routine.

Defense & Hitting

A good athlete, Ritchie is quick off the mound and an excellent fielder. He also has an extremely quick pickoff move for a righthander and picked off five runners last season. Ritchie enjoys hitting and handles the bat well. He's a reliable bunter.

2000 Outlook

Was Ritchie a flash in the pan or is he a late bloomer? Ritchie has a lot of ability, and now he has the control and confidence to go with it. There's no reason to think he won't duplicate last season's performance again.

Overall Statistics

	W	L	Pct.	ERA	G	GS	Sv	IP	H	BB	SO	HR	Ratio
1999	15	9	.625	3.50	28	26	0	172.1	169	54	107	17	1.29
Career	17	12	.586	3.99	85	26	0	271.0	286	91	172	29	1.39

How Often He Throws Strikes

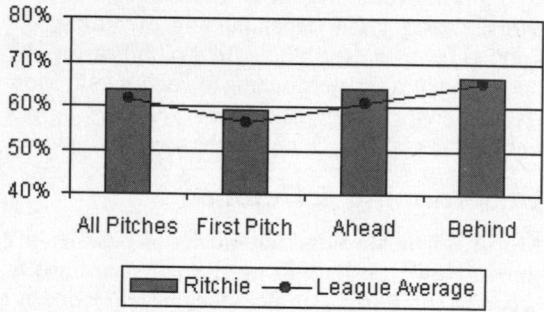

Legend: Ritchie — League Average

1999 Situational Stats

	W	L	ERA	Sv	IP		AB	H	HR	RBI	Avg
Home	9	3	3.13	0	86.1	LHB	275	77	8	34	.280
Road	6	6	3.87	0	86.0	RHB	377	92	9	35	.244
First Half	9	6	3.94	0	96.0	Sc Pos	132	37	4	51	.280
Scnd Half	6	3	2.95	0	76.1	Clutch	60	16	1	5	.267

1999 Rankings (National League)

- 3rd in most GDPs induced per GDP situation (21.2%)
- 4th in most GDPs induced per 9 innings (1.3)
- Led the Pirates in ERA, wins, complete games (2), wild pitches (7), GDPs induced (25), winning percentage, highest strikeout/walk ratio (2.0), lowest on-base percentage allowed (.319), highest groundball/flyball ratio allowed (1.8), fewest pitches thrown per batter (3.49), fewest baserunners allowed per 9 innings (11.9), most run support per 9 innings (6.2), most GDPs induced per 9 innings (1.3), fewest walks per 9 innings (2.8), most GDPs induced per GDP situation (21.2%) and ERA at home

Jason Schmidt

1999 Season

Jason Schmidt had a consistent season, never winning more than two decisions in a row or losing more than two straight. When it was over, he had established a career high with 13 wins.

Pitching

A power pitcher, Schmidt throws a 95-MPH fastball and a sharp slider. Schmidt can dominate with his fastball but his main problem is a lack of command of his heater. He leaves too many fastballs over the heart of the plate. His slider is a plus pitch when he stays on top of it. Schmidt falls in love with his changeup at times, though, and gets away from a power game. One big negative about Schmidt is he tends to lose concentration on the mound and lets adversity get to him. In short, he can be rattled, though he has become better with runners on base as he's gained experience.

Defense & Hitting

Schmidt's delivery causes him to fall to the first-base side of the mound, leaving him out of position to field balls hit back through the box. He's also slow off the mound and shaky covering bunts. Schmidt is relatively quick to the plate and holds runners very well. He usually can get down a bunt but isn't much of a threat with the bat.

2000 Outlook

The Pirates have held out hope Schmidt could become a No. 1 starter since acquiring him in the 1996 Denny Neagle trade with Atlanta. That hasn't happened, and time is running out for Schmidt. He has more the look of a middle-of-the-rotation starter who can win 12-14 games than that of an ace. He also doesn't seem to want the responsibility of being a No. 1 guy.

Position: SP
Bats: R **Throws:** R
Ht: 6' 5" **Wt:** 211

Opening Day Age: 27
Born: 1/29/73 in Lewiston, ID
ML Seasons: 5

Overall Statistics

	W	L	Pct.	ERA	G	GS	Sv	IP	H	BB	SO	HR	Ratio
1999	13	11	.542	4.19	33	33	0	212.2	219	85	148	24	1.43
Career	41	42	.494	4.51	126	117	0	736.0	775	303	535	76	1.46

How Often He Throws Strikes

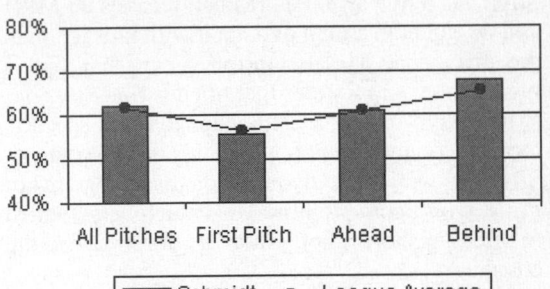

Schmidt —●— League Average

1999 Situational Stats

	W	L	ERA	Sv	IP		AB	H	HR	RBI	Avg
Home	9	4	3.36	0	99.0	LHB	379	109	17	58	.288
Road	4	7	4.91	0	113.2	RHB	456	110	7	37	.241
First Half	8	6	4.30	0	113.0	Sc Pos	226	45	3	69	.199
Scnd Half	5	5	4.06	0	99.2	Clutch	51	15	1	3	.294

1999 Rankings (National League)

- 1st in balks (4)
- 3rd in lowest batting average allowed with runners in scoring position
- 6th in sacrifice bunts (12)
- 7th in most pitches thrown per batter (3.82)
- 9th in batters faced (937) and pitches thrown (3,583)
- 10th in games started
- Led the Pirates in games started, complete games (2), innings pitched, hits allowed, batters faced (937), home runs allowed, walks allowed, strikeouts, balks (4), pitches thrown (3,583), runners caught stealing (7), lowest stolen-base percentage allowed (63.2%) and lowest batting average allowed with runners in scoring position

Jose Silva

1999 Season

Jose Silva began the season on the disabled list after being struck in the face by a one-hopper while pitching in a minor league exhibition game in spring training. Silva returned in late April and went 1-8, 7.62 in 12 starts. He was outstanding after being moved to the bullpen, though, compiling a 1.95 ERA in 22 relief appearances. Silva even got a shot at the closer's role in September, though that experiment was aborted when biceps tendinitis forced him to miss the final two-and-a-half weeks of the season. Silva converted four of his five save opportunities.

Pitching

Silva has a live arm. His fastball reaches 95 MPH and he can both sink it and cut it with late action in the strike zone. He also throws a curveball that is inconsistent and a slider that often is flat. Silva has struggled to master a changeup. His arm speed is too slow on the change, which tips it off to batters. Silva has worked many hours on the changeup but it just won't come to him. He's much better suited to pitching short relief, where he doesn't need the changeup.

Defense & Hitting

Moving fairly well around the mound, Silva is an adequate fielder for a big man. He pays close attention to baserunners, has a decent pickoff move and is relatively quick to the plate. Silva is a poor hitter and unreliable in sacrifice situations.

2000 Outlook

The Pirates are divided on what to do with Silva. Some in the organization think he can be a top-of-the-rotation starter. Others believe he could become a top-flight closer. Silva has the mental makeup to be a closer and could flourish in that role with his dominating fastball. He'll be held back, though, by offseason surgery to repair a small tear in his shoulder. Pittsburgh doesn't expect him to be ready until mid-May.

Position: RP/SP
Bats: R **Throws:** R
Ht: 6' 5" **Wt:** 227

Opening Day Age: 26
Born: 12/19/73 in Tijuana, Mexico
ML Seasons: 4

Overall Statistics

	W	L	Pct.	ERA	G	GS	Sv	IP	H	BB	SO	HR	Ratio
1999	2	8	.200	5.73	34	12	4	97.1	108	39	77	10	1.51
Career	10	16	.385	5.26	65	34	4	236.0	269	85	171	22	1.50

How Often He Throws Strikes

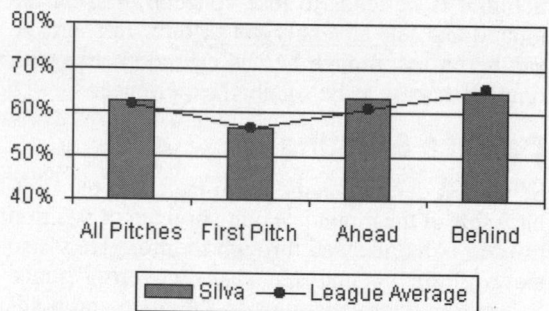

1999 Situational Stats

	W	L	ERA	Sv	IP		AB	H	HR	RBI	Avg
Home	2	3	5.51	2	47.1	LHB	161	37	5	22	.230
Road	0	5	5.94	2	50.0	RHB	224	71	5	42	.317
First Half	2	7	6.72	0	68.1	Sc Pos	107	37	2	53	.346
Scnd Half	0	1	3.41	4	29.0	Clutch	55	13	2	4	.236

1999 Rankings (National League)

- 3rd in balks (3)

Ed Sprague

1999 Season

Signed to a one-year, $1 million contract as a free agent from Oakland following the 1998 season, Ed Sprague looked like a steal through the first half of 1999. He was the Pirates' lone representative at the All-Star Game as he hit .300 with 16 homers and 53 RBI before the break. Following his career pattern, Sprague struggled after the break, hitting just .220-6-28 in 56 games before breaking his left hand with two weeks left in the season.

Hitting

Sprague has good power with the ability to hit the ball out to the deepest part of the park. He likes to pull the ball but is also strong enough to hit it far the other way. Sprague showed good plate discipline in the first half last season, then became a free swinger in the second half and his production dropped sharply. He can crush a ball over the middle of the plate but can be jammed by good fastballs and made to chase outside breaking pitches.

Baserunning & Defense

Though Sprague has little speed, the Pirates inexplicably had him attempt nine stolen bases last season. He's smart enough to play it safe and usually goes one base at a time. Sprague is shaky at third base, as his 29 errors in 1999 attest. He has little range and his hands aren't exceptionally soft. Sprague had shoulder surgery in 1997 and his arm is still scattershot.

2000 Outlook

Sprague reportedly turned down a two-year, $6 million contract extension from the Pirates right after last year's All-Star break. He may regret that. Sprague became a free agent at the end of the season and it's doubtful many—if any—clubs will offer a multiyear deal after his poor second half. Pittsburgh is likely to hand its third-base job to top prospect Aramis Ramirez, while Sprague will get a chance elsewhere. He doesn't look capable of duplicating his 1999 numbers.

Position: 3B
Bats: R **Throws:** R
Ht: 6' 2" **Wt:** 205

Opening Day Age: 32
Born: 7/25/67 in Castro Valley, CA
ML Seasons: 9
Pronunciation: SPRAYG

Overall Statistics

	G	AB	R	H	D	T	HR	RBI	SB	BB	SO	Avg	OBP	Slg
1999	137	490	71	131	27	2	22	81	3	50	93	.267	.352	.465
Career	1052	3733	467	917	202	12	138	506	6	322	757	.246	.318	.417

Where He Hits the Ball

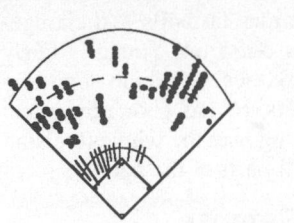

Vs. LHP

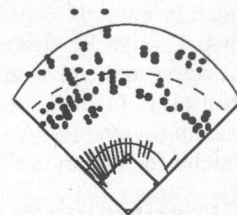

Vs. RHP

1999 Situational Stats

	AB	H	HR	RBI	Avg		AB	H	HR	RBI	Avg
Home	252	66	10	42	.262	LHP	137	29	6	23	.212
Road	238	65	12	39	.273	RHP	353	102	16	58	.289
First Half	290	87	16	53	.300	Sc Pos	135	41	6	59	.304
Scnd Half	200	44	6	28	.220	Clutch	82	22	3	9	.268

1999 Rankings (National League)

- 1st in hit by pitch (17), errors at third base (29) and lowest fielding percentage at third base (.919)
- 4th in lowest batting average vs. lefthanded pitchers
- 9th in lowest on-base percentage vs. lefthanded pitchers (.311) and lowest percentage of extra bases taken as a runner (38.3%)
- Led the Pirates in hit by pitch (17)
- Led NL third basemen in hit by pitch (17)

Kevin Young

1999 Season

Kevin Young signed the richest deal in club history in spring training, a four-year, $24 million contract extension that keeps him under the Pirates' control until 2003. He then went out and justified the contract by joining Jeff Bagwell and Rafael Palmeiro as the only first basemen in baseball history to have 100 runs, 40 doubles, 20 homers and 20 steals in a season. Young turned on the power after the All-Star break, hitting 16 of his 26 homers in the second half.

Hitting

With an unorthodox swing that can get very long, Young has trouble against good breaking pitches. However, Young is able to get his bat around quickly enough to hammer fastballs and change-ups. Though he strikes out a lot, Young is fairly selective at the plate and does a good job of putting himself in fastball counts. He has good power and can hit for average. Young uses the whole field and can hit the ball out to all parts of the park.

Baserunning & Defense

Young has decent speed and is very aggressive on the basepaths. He looks to force the issue by stealing a base or by going from first to third or second to home on singles. Young made an uncharacteristic 23 errors last season, many on forced throws in which he had no chance to make a play. Young needs to rein in his aggressiveness. He does have outstanding range and soft hands, the qualities of a good defensive first baseman.

2000 Outlook

Young again will be the Pirates' cleanup hitter. He has put together three good seasons in a row and now is the type of player who can be counted on to hit .280-.300 with 25-30 homers and 100 RBI on a yearly basis.

Position: 1B
Bats: R **Throws:** R
Ht: 6' 3" **Wt:** 224

Opening Day Age: 30
Born: 6/16/69 in Alpena, MI
ML Seasons: 8

Overall Statistics

	G	AB	R	H	D	T	HR	RBI	SB	BB	SO	Avg	OBP	Slg
1999	156	584	103	174	41	6	26	106	22	75	124	.298	.387	.522
Career	733	2400	338	643	145	16	92	395	55	200	541	.268	.330	.457

Where He Hits the Ball

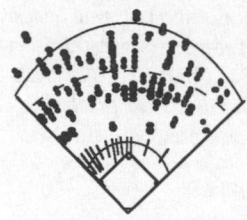

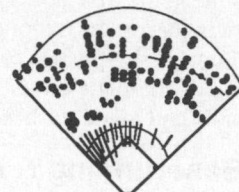

Vs. LHP   **Vs. RHP**

1999 Situational Stats

	AB	H	HR	RBI	Avg		AB	H	HR	RBI	Avg
Home	287	93	16	61	.324	LHP	159	49	5	25	.308
Road	297	81	10	45	.273	RHP	425	125	21	81	.294
First Half	321	100	10	49	.312	Sc Pos	171	52	6	76	.304
Scnd Half	263	74	16	57	.281	Clutch	98	26	4	19	.265

1999 Rankings (National League)

- 1st in errors at first base (23) and lowest fielding percentage at first base (.985)
- 4th in hit by pitch (12)
- 7th in doubles, pitches seen (2,708) and lowest cleanup slugging percentage (.524)
- 8th in lowest percentage of swings put into play (34.6%)
- 9th in lowest stolen-base percentage (68.8%)
- Led the Pirates in at-bats, hits, doubles, stolen bases, caught stealing (10), strikeouts, pitches seen (2,708), plate appearances (675), most pitches seen per plate appearance (4.01), batting average vs. lefthanded pitchers, cleanup slugging percentage (.524), slugging percentage vs. lefthanded pitchers (.535) and games played

Mike Benjamin

Position: SS/2B
Bats: R **Throws:** R
Ht: 6' 0" **Wt:** 169

Opening Day Age: 34
Born: 11/22/65 in Euclid, OH
ML Seasons: 11

Overall Statistics

	G	AB	R	H	D	T	HR	RBI	SB	BB	SO	Avg	OBP	Slg
1999	110	368	42	91	26	7	1	37	10	20	90	.247	.288	.364
Career	617	1573	192	361	89	12	22	147	39	87	353	.229	.278	.343

1999 Situational Stats

	AB	H	HR	RBI	Avg		AB	H	HR	RBI	Avg
Home	185	47	1	18	.254	LHP	142	37	0	16	.261
Road	183	44	0	19	.240	RHP	226	54	1	21	.239
First Half	220	48	1	27	.218	Sc Pos	91	24	0	34	.264
Scnd Half	148	43	0	10	.291	Clutch	64	17	0	6	.266

1999 Season

Mike Benjamin figured to be the Pirates' utility infielder after signing a two-year contract as a free agent from Boston in the offseason. However, he wound up starting the majority of games at shortstop when Pat Meares was limited to 21 games because of hand surgery.

Hitting, Baserunning & Defense

Once challenged to hit .200, Benjamin has improved his offense as he has gotten older. He has developed some mild gap power but has little patience for someone with almost no pop. Benjamin is a decent No. 2 hitter because he can bunt and execute the hit-and-run play. Benjamin has adequate speed and knows when to pick his spots to steal a base. He's very reliable in the field, with soft hands that serve him well at shortstop and second base, and a strong enough arm to play third.

2000 Outlook

Assuming Meares is healthy, Benjamin will settle back into a bench role this season. Benjamin is no longer an automatic out and his increased competency with the bat, coupled with solid defense, makes him a good backup middle infielder.

Adrian Brown

Position: RF/CF
Bats: B **Throws:** R
Ht: 6' 0" **Wt:** 185

Opening Day Age: 26
Born: 2/7/74 in McComb, MS
ML Seasons: 3

Overall Statistics

	G	AB	R	H	D	T	HR	RBI	SB	BB	SO	Avg	OBP	Slg
1999	116	226	34	61	5	2	4	17	5	33	39	.270	.364	.363
Career	205	525	71	132	15	3	5	32	17	55	75	.251	.327	.320

1999 Situational Stats

	AB	H	HR	RBI	Avg		AB	H	HR	RBI	Avg
Home	103	31	2	8	.301	LHP	112	28	2	8	.250
Road	123	30	2	9	.244	RHP	114	33	2	9	.289
First Half	83	21	2	9	.253	Sc Pos	40	6	0	12	.150
Scnd Half	143	40	2	8	.280	Clutch	51	11	1	6	.216

1999 Season

Adrian Brown surprisingly made the Pirates out of spring training, was sent to the minors for three weeks in late May and early June, then came back and was Pittsburgh's most reliable player on a weak bench for the final four months. He easily set career highs in nearly every offensive category.

Hitting, Baserunning & Defense

Brown has little extra-base power but knows how to take advantage of his offensive strengths. He's a very patient hitter who works counts and draws walks. He also knows how to use his above-average speed. Brown is an excellent drag bunter and hits the ball on the ground consistently. A switch-hitter, he used to be weak from the right side but has improved. Brown can steal a base when called upon. Brown also is a good defensive outfielder who can cover a lot of ground at all three spots, though center field is his natural position. He has average arm strength and makes accurate throws.

2000 Outlook

Though Brown isn't quite good enough to be a starting outfielder, he does enough things well to be a fine bench player. He figures to stick with the Pirates as a fifth outfielder, getting an occasional start against lefthanders.

Brant Brown

Traded To MARLINS

Position: RF/CF
Bats: L **Throws:** L
Ht: 6' 3" **Wt:** 205

Opening Day Age: 28
Born: 6/22/71 in Porterville, CA
ML Seasons: 4

Overall Statistics

	G	AB	R	H	D	T	HR	RBI	SB	BB	SO	Avg	OBP	Slg
1999	130	341	49	79	20	3	16	58	3	22	114	.232	.283	.449
Career	329	894	131	233	45	11	40	130	12	61	254	.261	.312	.470

1999 Situational Stats

	AB	H	HR	RBI	Avg		AB	H	HR	RBI	Avg
Home	163	34	4	25	.209	LHP	47	10	0	1	.213
Road	178	45	12	33	.253	RHP	294	69	16	57	.235
First Half	197	47	7	30	.239	Sc Pos	99	24	5	42	.242
Scnd Half	144	32	9	28	.222	Clutch	49	7	1	4	.143

1999 Season

Brant Brown entered the season as Pittsburgh's starting center fielder after arriving from the Cubs in an offseason trade for Jon Lieber. With a bad start offensively and looking very shaky defensively, Brown lost his job in mid-May. With the exile of Jose Guillen to Tampa Bay, Brown started more games in right field than any other Pirate.

Hitting, Baserunning & Defense

Despite his subpar 1999, Brown has some offensive skills. He has decent pop and could hit 20-25 home runs if he received 500 at-bats in a season, though his lack of success against lefties likely would preclude that much playing time. Brown has hit for a high average throughout much of his professional career, though that changed last season when he lost all concept of the strike zone. Brown has decent speed but doesn't steal bases. He's not a good defensive outfielder, as he plays too deep and has a below-average arm. Brown is solid at first base, his natural position.

2000 Outlook

Brown didn't fit in with the Pirates, who traded him to the Marlins for Bruce Aven in December. Aven will assume the fourth-outfielder role in which Pittsburgh found Brown lacking. Florida will play Brown in the outfield and first base.

Jason Christiansen

Position: RP
Bats: R **Throws:** L
Ht: 6' 5" **Wt:** 242

Opening Day Age: 30
Born: 9/21/69 in Omaha, NE
ML Seasons: 5

Overall Statistics

	W	L	Pct.	ERA	G	GS	Sv	IP	H	BB	SO	HR	Ratio
1999	2	3	.400	4.06	39	0	3	37.2	26	22	35	2	1.27
Career	12	12	.500	3.99	234	0	9	236.2	219	119	234	18	1.43

1999 Situational Stats

	W	L	ERA	Sv	IP		AB	H	HR	RBI	Avg
Home	1	0	2.25	0	20.0	LHB	44	9	0	3	.205
Road	1	3	6.00	3	18.0	RHB	88	17	2	10	.193
First Half	2	2	2.81	3	32.0	Sc Pos	37	6	0	10	.162
Scnd Half	0	1	10.50	0	6.0	Clutch	74	17	1	8	.230

1999 Season

Jason Christiansen's season continually was interrupted by injury. He was forced to the disabled list three times because of stiffness in his neck. Christiansen had a pretty decent year when healthy, taking over for the traded Ricardo Rincon as the Pirates' primary lefthanded setup reliever.

Pitching, Defense & Hitting

Christiansen is a power lefty whose fastball reaches 94 MPH when he's healthy. He didn't always throw that hard last year, when he had a hard time extending his arm because of his neck problems. Christiansen complements the heater with a slider that has a quick, late break that is lethal on lefthanders. He also throws a curveball and changeup, mainly for show. Christiansen is a decent defensive pitcher for a big man and he does a good job of holding runners on, which is rare for a short reliever. He's not much of a hitter.

2000 Outlook

A healthy Christiansen will be a key member of the Pittsburgh bullpen. He's a first-rate lefty setup man with enough stuff to get an occasional save when the situation arises. With the Pirates' bullpen situation so unsettled, it wouldn't be out of the question to see Christiansen emerge as a potential co-closer with Jose Silva or Mike Williams.

Abraham Nunez

Position: SS/2B
Bats: B **Throws:** R
Ht: 5'11" **Wt:** 175

Opening Day Age: 24
Born: 3/16/76 in Santo Domingo, Dominican Republic
ML Seasons: 3
Pronunciation: NOON-yez

Overall Statistics

	G	AB	R	H	D	T	HR	RBI	SB	BB	SO	Avg	OBP	Slg
1999	90	259	25	57	8	0	0	17	9	28	54	.220	.299	.251
Career	133	351	34	76	12	2	1	25	14	43	78	.217	.305	.271

1999 Situational Stats

	AB	H	HR	RBI	Avg		AB	H	HR	RBI	Avg
Home	131	25	0	7	.191	LHP	81	19	0	4	.235
Road	128	32	0	10	.250	RHP	178	38	0	13	.213
First Half	103	22	0	9	.214	Sc Pos	57	10	0	15	.175
Scnd Half	156	35	0	8	.224	Clutch	40	6	0	0	.150

1999 Season

Abraham Nunez was supposed to spend 1999 as Triple-A Nashville's shortstop. Instead, he spent all but three weeks with the Pirates as starting shortstop Pat Meares was sidelined for most of the season by hand surgery. Nunez wound up starting 58 games at shortstop, sharing time with Mike Benjamin, and 14 more at second base.

Hitting, Baserunning & Defense

The switch-hitting Nunez is overmatched by major league pitching from both sides of the plate. To his credit, Nunez understands his limitations. He slaps the ball on the ground and is also a good bunter. He realizes he must take advantage of his speed to become an offensive weapon. Nunez is a good baserunner, though he's still somewhat timid and doesn't run as much as he should. He's a slick-fielding shortstop with outstanding range and a good arm. He also plays second base well.

2000 Outlook

With Meares expected to be 100 percent and Benjamin returning as his backup, the Pirates will have no room on the major league roster for Nunez. Curiously, Pittsburgh also has given Meares a long-term contract extension. The club would like Nunez to spend a full season in Triple-A, though it also could trade him in the right deal.

Keith Osik

Position: C
Bats: R **Throws:** R
Ht: 6' 0" **Wt:** 198

Opening Day Age: 31
Born: 10/22/68 in Port Jefferson, NY
ML Seasons: 4
Pronunciation: OH-sick

Overall Statistics

	G	AB	R	H	D	T	HR	RBI	SB	BB	SO	Avg	OBP	Slg
1999	66	167	12	31	3	1	2	13	0	11	30	.186	.239	.251
Career	202	510	48	120	30	3	3	41	2	47	89	.235	.305	.324

1999 Situational Stats

	AB	H	HR	RBI	Avg		AB	H	HR	RBI	Avg
Home	81	15	1	7	.185	LHP	61	13	0	6	.213
Road	86	16	1	6	.186	RHP	106	18	2	7	.170
First Half	67	14	1	6	.209	Sc Pos	41	7	0	11	.171
Scnd Half	100	17	1	7	.170	Clutch	39	9	0	3	.231

1999 Season

Thanks to starting catcher Jason Kendall's season-ending dislocated ankle, Keith Osik was pressed into the most action of his four-year career. Osik went on the disabled list himself three weeks after Kendall with a strained hamstring. While Osik was sidelined, the Pirates acquired veteran catcher Joe Oliver from Tampa Bay. Osik and Oliver split time after that.

Hitting, Baserunning & Defense

Osik came to the major leagues after hitting .336 for Triple-A Calgary in 1995. That average proved to be an aberration, as he has hit .214 and .186, respectively, in the last two seasons. Osik is overmatched by hard stuff and can be fooled by good breaking pitches. Like most catchers, he doesn't run well. Defensively, Osik throws well and is mobile behind the plate.

2000 Outlook

The Pirates used to say Osik was the best backup catcher in the National League. Then he was exposed with more playing time in 1999. Osik is signed through 2000, the final year of a three-year contract. He will be back but the Pirates may look to add another backup catcher as insurance while Kendall tries to come back from his injury.

Scott Sauerbeck

Position: RP
Bats: R **Throws:** L
Ht: 6' 3" **Wt:** 190

Opening Day Age: 28
Born: 11/9/71 in
Cincinnati, OH
ML Seasons: 1

Overall Statistics

	W	L	Pct.	ERA	G	GS	Sv	IP	H	BB	SO	HR	Ratio
1999	4	1	.800	2.00	65	0	2	67.2	53	38	55	6	1.34
Career	4	1	.800	2.00	65	0	2	67.2	53	38	55	6	1.34

1999 Situational Stats

	W	L	ERA	Sv	IP		AB	H	HR	RBI	Avg
Home	2	0	2.21	1	36.2	LHB	90	15	5	20	.167
Road	2	1	1.74	1	31.0	RHB	151	38	1	8	.252
First Half	1	0	1.83	0	39.1	Sc Pos	76	13	2	21	.171
Scnd Half	3	1	2.22	2	28.1	Clutch	68	19	2	12	.279

1999 Season

Scott Sauerbeck was an unknown when he was selected from the Mets in the major league Rule 5 Draft. He proved to be a steal for the Pirates as he became one of the top lefthanded relievers in the National League. He allowed only two earned runs in his last 22 outings and finished third in the league in relief ERA.

Pitching, Defense & Hitting

A starter for most of his five seasons in the Mets system, Sauerbeck made a seamless transition to relief. His best pitch is a big-breaking curveball that is almost impossible for lefthanders to hit. Sauerbeck sinks his average fastball and runs it away from righthanded hitters. He also throws an occasional changeup. Sauerbeck is quick off the mound and does an outstanding job of holding runners with a good pickoff move. Sauerbeck doesn't bat much as a short reliever, but knows how to handle the stick from his days as a starter.

2000 Outlook

Will the league catch up to Sauerbeck in his second season? Perhaps, but he showed the ability to make adjustments last season. Sauerbeck has a nice future as a lefthanded specialist.

Pete Schourek

Position: SP/RP
Bats: L **Throws:** L
Ht: 6' 5" **Wt:** 215

Opening Day Age: 30
Born: 5/10/69 in Austin, TX
ML Seasons: 9
Pronunciation: SHUR-ek

Overall Statistics

	W	L	Pct.	ERA	G	GS	Sv	IP	H	BB	SO	HR	Ratio
1999	4	7	.364	5.34	30	17	0	113.0	128	49	94	20	1.57
Career	62	62	.500	4.54	234	155	2	1011.1	1047	367	730	119	1.40

1999 Situational Stats

	W	L	ERA	Sv	IP		AB	H	HR	RBI	Avg
Home	2	4	5.33	0	74.1	LHB	80	22	4	15	.275
Road	2	3	5.35	0	38.2	RHB	366	106	16	53	.290
First Half	2	5	5.06	0	69.1	Sc Pos	101	29	5	48	.287
Scnd Half	2	2	5.77	0	43.2	Clutch	18	9	0	3	.500

1999 Season

The Pirates signed Pete Schourek to a two-year contract as a free agent from Boston, hoping he would fill a void in the middle of the starting rotation. However, he didn't work out as planned, twice getting removed from the starting rotation before finishing the season in long relief.

Pitching, Defense & Hitting

Schourek is strictly a finesse pitcher after three arm operations. His fastball is barely average and he needs to spot it in the strike zone while mixing it with his curveball, slider and changeup in order to be effective. Schourek's location was poor last season and he paid the price. He also lacks stamina and often is hit hard after reaching the 60-pitch mark. Schourek doesn't hold runners well, is an ordinary fielder and went 0-for-25 at the plate last season.

2000 Outlook

Though Schourek doesn't look like he can be an effective starter anymore, the Pirates were impressed by his bullpen work last September. They owe him $2 million in 2000 and will give him a chance to win a starting job in spring training because of the financial commitment.

Jeff Wallace

Position: RP
Bats: L **Throws:** L
Ht: 6' 2" **Wt:** 228

Opening Day Age: 23
Born: 4/12/76 in
Wheeling, WV
ML Seasons: 2

Overall Statistics

	W	L	Pct.	ERA	G	GS	Sv	IP	H	BB	SO	HR	Ratio
1999	1	0	1.000	3.69	41	0	0	39.0	26	38	41	2	1.64
Career	1	0	1.000	3.00	52	0	0	51.0	34	46	55	2	1.57

1999 Situational Stats

	W	L	ERA	Sv	IP		AB	H	HR	RBI	Avg
Home	0	0	3.05	0	20.2	LHB	46	12	1	10	.261
Road	1	0	4.42	0	18.1	RHB	87	14	1	3	.161
First Half	1	0	3.69	0	31.2	Sc Pos	42	6	0	10	.143
Scnd Half	0	0	3.68	0	7.1	Clutch	39	6	0	5	.154

1999 Season

After missing all of 1998 following reconstructive elbow surgery, Jeff Wallace bounced back to have a decent rookie season. He was bothered by a stiff shoulder that forced him to miss six weeks after the All-Star break, but his elbow never bothered him.

Pitching, Defense & Hitting

Wallace is a rare power lefthanded reliever. His fastball reached 98 MPH before his operation. Though he topped out at 94 MPH last year, doctors believe he'll eventually get back to where he was. Wallace's biggest problem at this early stage of his career is command. He has a hard time finding the strike zone and part of that can be attributed to sitting out a whole year and having to relearn his mechanics. Wallace is an adequate fielder and does a decent job holding runners. He has yet to bat in his major league career.

2000 Outlook

Wallace should only get better. He has the raw ability to become a closer some day, but his lack of command leaves him better suited for non-pressurized situations for now. Wallace was fast-tracked to the major leagues and could use a little more time in the minors.

Mike Williams

Position: RP
Bats: R **Throws:** R
Ht: 6' 2" **Wt:** 209

Opening Day Age: 31
Born: 7/29/68 in
Radford, VA
ML Seasons: 8

Overall Statistics

	W	L	Pct.	ERA	G	GS	Sv	IP	H	BB	SO	HR	Ratio
1999	3	4	.429	5.09	58	0	23	58.1	63	37	76	9	1.71
Career	20	33	.377	4.64	204	55	24	508.0	528	206	372	61	1.44

1999 Situational Stats

	W	L	ERA	Sv	IP		AB	H	HR	RBI	Avg
Home	1	1	3.52	13	30.2	LHB	79	20	3	11	.253
Road	2	3	6.83	10	27.2	RHB	149	43	6	30	.289
First Half	1	2	2.67	13	33.2	Sc Pos	84	25	2	32	.298
Scnd Half	2	2	8.39	10	24.2	Clutch	126	29	2	22	.230

1999 Season

After Rich Loiselle faltered in spring training and in his first outing of the regular season, Mike Williams took over as Pittsburgh's closer in early April. He was outstanding for four-and-a-half months, then fell apart. He was on the disabled list with biceps tendinitis from June 24 to July 9, and his arm weakened by the end of August. Williams' ERA after August 30 was 24.00 and he lost the closer's role early in September.

Pitching, Defense & Hitting

Williams' best pitch is a late-breaking slider. When he has control of it, the pitch is almost unhittable. Williams becomes a very ordinary pitcher when his slider isn't working because his fastball and changeup are only average pitches at best. Williams has a quick pickoff move but he occasionally gets hurt by throwing wildly to first. Williams isn't much of a hitter but that doesn't matter since he works in short relief.

2000 Outlook

Williams will have to win his closer's job back in spring training after a hideous finish to 1999. He really isn't the overpowering kind of pitcher a team looks for in a closer and is better suited to pitch in a setup role.

Other Pittsburgh Pirates

Jason Boyd (**Pos**: RHP, **Age**: 27)

	W	L	Pct.	ERA	G	GS	Sv	IP	H	BB	SO	HR	Ratio
1999	0	0	-	3.38	4	0	0	5.1	5	2	4	0	1.31
Career	0	0	-	3.38	4	0	0	5.1	5	2	4	0	1.31

After a solid showing in Triple-A for Arizona, Boyd was sent to Pittsburgh to complete the Tony Womack deal. He was OK in four September outings and will compete for work in the pen. 2000 Outlook: B

Emil Brown (**Pos**: LF, **Age**: 25, **Bats**: R)

	G	AB	R	H	D	T	HR	RBI	SB	BB	SO	Avg	OBP	Slg
1999	6	14	0	2	1	0	0	0	0	0	3	.143	.143	.214
Career	85	148	18	29	4	1	2	9	5	11	46	.196	.287	.277

Brown has hit .330 and .304 in the high minors the last two seasons, and will get a chance to make the Pirates as a spare outfielder. He has more upside than Adrian Brown, no relation. 2000 Outlook: B

Brad Clontz (**Pos**: RHP, **Age**: 28)

	W	L	Pct.	ERA	G	GS	Sv	IP	H	BB	SO	HR	Ratio
1999	1	3	.250	2.74	56	0	2	49.1	49	24	40	6	1.48
Career	22	8	.733	4.32	267	0	8	270.2	269	109	202	29	1.40

After pitching admirably for the Braves in 1997, Clontz struggled between Triple-A and two major league stops. He got it together again 1999, then was traded to Arizona in December for minor league righthander Roberto Manzueta. 2000 Outlook: A

Ivan Cruz (**Pos**: 1B, **Age**: 31, **Bats**: L)

	G	AB	R	H	D	T	HR	RBI	SB	BB	SO	Avg	OBP	Slg
1999	5	10	3	4	0	0	1	2	0	0	2	.400	.400	.700
Career	16	30	3	9	1	0	1	5	0	2	6	.300	.344	.433

A perennial power threat at Triple-A, Cruz earned his second trip to the majors in his 11th pro season when the injury bug hit the Bucs in June. But a strained oblique muscle began an unending cycle of rehab. 2000 Outlook: C

Jim Dougherty (**Pos**: RHP, **Age**: 32)

	W	L	Pct.	ERA	G	GS	Sv	IP	H	BB	SO	HR	Ratio
1999	0	0	-	9.00	2	0	0	2.0	3	3	1	0	3.00
Career	8	8	.500	5.99	79	0	0	94.2	110	46	59	11	1.65

The sidearmer stuck with Houston in 1995, but wasn't able to build on his rookie season. His Triple-A numbers since have been steady, but he hasn't succeeded when big league teams have called. 2000 Outlook: D

Mike Garcia (**Pos**: RHP, **Age**: 31)

	W	L	Pct.	ERA	G	GS	Sv	IP	H	BB	SO	HR	Ratio
1999	1	0	1.000	1.29	7	0	0	7.0	2	3	9	1	0.71
Career	1	0	1.000	1.29	7	0	0	7.0	2	3	9	1	0.71

After five seasons in Mexico and Taiwan, Garcia pitched effectively in Triple-A in 1999, striking out 35 in 27.1 innings. He was just as good in a September callup, earning a chance at a bullpen job this year. 2000 Outlook: B

Yamid Haad (**Pos**: C, **Age**: 22, **Bats**: R)

	G	AB	R	H	D	T	HR	RBI	SB	BB	SO	Avg	OBP	Slg
1999	1	1	0	0	0	0	0	0	0	0	0	.000	.000	.000
Career	1	1	0	0	0	0	0	0	0	0	0	.000	.000	.000

Haad secured his first major league at-bat the day after Jason Kendall went down in July, but he hasn't shown that he will be much at the plate. Haad is destined for the minors in 2000. 2000 Outlook: D

Greg Hansell (**Pos**: RHP, **Age**: 29)

	W	L	Pct.	ERA	G	GS	Sv	IP	H	BB	SO	HR	Ratio
1999	3	3	.250	3.89	33	0	0	39.1	42	11	34	5	1.35
Career	4	4	.500	5.56	106	0	3	137.2	159	49	98	25	1.51

After shining in 22 Triple-A appearances, Hansell was recalled in June and produced his best big league season. He was sold to Japan's Hanshin Tigers in December. 2000 Outlook: B

Tim Laker (**Pos**: C, **Age**: 30, **Bats**: R)

	G	AB	R	H	D	T	HR	RBI	SB	BB	SO	Avg	OBP	Slg
1999	6	9	0	3	0	0	0	0	0	0	2	.333	.333	.333
Career	165	325	31	73	14	2	4	34	3	22	83	.225	.275	.317

Despite Jason Kendall's injury, Laker spent most of the year in Triple-A. The time has passed for this one-time prospect who blew out his elbow in 1996, though the Pirates did re-sign him. 2000 Outlook: C

Rich Loiselle (**Pos**: RHP, **Age**: 28)

	W	L	Pct.	ERA	G	GS	Sv	IP	H	BB	SO	HR	Ratio
1999	3	2	.600	5.28	13	0	0	15.1	16	9	14	2	1.63
Career	7	14	.333	3.41	144	3	48	163.2	170	77	137	14	1.51

Pittsburgh's closer in 1997, Loiselle underwent reconstructive elbow surgery in July. It will be a long road back, as he never has been as effective as he was when he saved 29 games in '97. 2000 Outlook: C

Joe Oliver (**Pos**: C, **Age**: 34, **Bats**: R)

	G	AB	R	H	D	T	HR	RBI	SB	BB	SO	Avg	OBP	Slg
1999	45	134	10	27	8	0	1	13	2	10	33	.201	.253	.284
Career	990	3119	283	766	159	2	91	438	11	232	584	.246	.298	.385

The Pirates acquired Oliver from Tampa Bay as a stopgap measure after Jason Kendall went down in July. Oliver hasn't hit for two years, so he's doubtful to play much wherever he ends up. 2000 Outlook: C

Chris Peters (**Pos**: LHP, **Age**: 28)

	W	L	Pct.	ERA	G	GS	Sv	IP	H	BB	SO	HR	Ratio
1999	5	4	.556	6.59	19	11	0	71.0	98	27	46	17	1.76
Career	17	20	.459	4.72	105	43	1	320.1	350	128	194	45	1.49

After establishing himself in the Pittsburgh rotation in 1998, Peters missed half of '99 with shoulder inflammation. He turned in just three quality starts and must show he's healthy and ready. 2000 Outlook: B

Jason Phillips (Pos: RHP, Age: 26)

	W	L	Pct.	ERA	G	GS	Sv	IP	H	BB	SO	HR	Ratio
1999	0	0	-	11.57	6	0	0	7.0	11	6	7	2	2.43
Career	0	0	-	11.57	6	0	0	7.0	11	6	7	2	2.43

Phillips debuted with the Pirates in April and struggled. In May he went on the disabled list in Triple-A with shoulder troubles. He never returned and was dropped from the 40-man roster in October. 2000 Outlook: C

Dale Sveum (Pos: 3B, Age: 36, Bats: B)

	G	AB	R	H	D	T	HR	RBI	SB	BB	SO	Avg	OBP	Slg
1999	49	71	7	15	5	1	3	13	0	7	28	.211	.278	.437
Career	862	2526	305	597	125	13	69	340	10	227	656	.236	.298	.378

Two years ago Sveum hit 12 homers for the Pirates. It was an aberration. He hasn't had that many extra-base hits since then, and he has batted .186 in 129 at-bats the last two seasons. 2000 Outlook: D

Chris Tremie (Pos: C, Age: 30, Bats: R)

	G	AB	R	H	D	T	HR	RBI	SB	BB	SO	Avg	OBP	Slg
1999	9	14	1	1	0	0	0	1	0	2	4	.071	.188	.071
Career	21	41	3	6	1	0	0	1	0	4	7	.146	.222	.171

Tremie got a brief look right after Jason Kendall fractured his ankle in July. As expected, Tremie didn't hit. He signed a minor league deal with Florida. 2000 Outlook: C

John Wehner (Pos: LF, Age: 32, Bats: R)

	G	AB	R	H	D	T	HR	RBI	SB	BB	SO	Avg	OBP	Slg
1999	39	65	6	12	2	0	1	4	1	7	12	.185	.264	.262
Career	397	703	86	175	29	4	3	43	13	59	118	.249	.307	.314

The utilityman resurfaced in Pittsburgh, but he didn't hit enough to assure his return in 2000. While Wehner lacks pop and speed, he was able to fill in at six positions last season. 2000 Outlook: C

Marc Wilkins (Pos: RHP, Age: 29)

	W	L	Pct.	ERA	G	GS	Sv	IP	H	BB	SO	HR	Ratio
1999	2	3	.400	4.24	46	0	0	51.0	49	26	44	3	1.47
Career	15	11	.577	3.86	179	2	3	217.0	202	104	170	17	1.41

Wilkins got his career back on track after groin and shoulder troubles. With so many righties in Pittsburgh's pen, he hurt himself by following a solid August (1.35 ERA) with a dismal September (6.00). 2000 Outlook: B

Pittsburgh Pirates Minor League Prospects

Organization Overview:

The Pirates haven't reached .500 since winning their third consecutive National League East title in 1992, mainly because they didn't have the budget to keep their stars or sign new ones. They finally decided to spend some money on talent last season, but invested in re-treads such as Mike Benjamin, Pat Meares, Pete Schourek and Ed Sprague. Still, there were some positives. Brian Giles looked like a star after being plucked from the Indians in a deal for Ricky Rincon, and former No. 1 overall draft pick Kris Benson pitched up to his billing as a rookie. The ever-resourceful Pirates found two more keepers for the pitching staff via minor league free agency (Todd Ritchie) and the major league Rule 5 draft (Scott Sauerbeck). They also did well in the draft, picking up polished high school righthander Bobby Bradley with the eighth overall pick and offensively gifted catcher J.R. House in the fifth round.

Jimmy Anderson

Position: P **Opening Day Age:** 24
Bats: L **Throws:** L **Born:** 1/22/76 in
Ht: 6' 1" **Wt:** 190 Portsmouth, VA

Recent Statistics

	W	L	ERA	G	GS	Sv	IP	H	R	BB	SO	HR
1999 AAA Nashville	11	2	3.84	21	21	0	133.2	153	67	41	93	5
1999 NL Pittsburgh	2	1	3.99	13	4	0	29.1	25	15	16	13	2

Entering 1999, Anderson seemed like he would be just another finesse pitcher who hit the wall in Triple-A. A 1994 ninth-round pick, he had gone 25-15, 2.44 before reaching the Pacific Coast League at age 21. But in two stints in Triple-A, he went 16-16, 5.32 and headed back there last season. For the first time, however, he believed in his stuff and the results showed. Rather than nibble at the corners of the plate, Anderson went after hitters with an average fastball that has plenty of life, a slider and a changeup. Pittsburgh should have at least one opening in its rotation for 2000, and Anderson will compete for the job in spring training.

Bronson Arroyo

Position: P **Opening Day Age:** 23
Bats: R **Throws:** R **Born:** 2/24/77 in Key
Ht: 6' 5" **Wt:** 180 West, FL

Recent Statistics

	W	L	ERA	G	GS	Sv	IP	H	R	BB	SO	HR
1998 AA Carolina	9	8	5.46	23	22	0	127.0	158	91	51	90	18
1999 AA Altoona	15	4	3.65	25	25	0	153.0	167	73	58	100	15
1999 AAA Nashville	0	2	10.38	3	3	0	13.0	22	15	10	11	1

Arroyo was a projection when the Pirates took him in the third round of the 1995 draft. Tall and skinny, he offered the promise of an exceptional fastball as he filled out. That hasn't happened yet and his fastball is still an average 88-92 MPH, yet Arroyo reached Double-A at age 21 and has yet to post a losing season. After struggling with minor back and ankle injuries in 1998, he bounced back to lead the Eastern League in victories last season. There's still hope that he'll get stronger, but for now he succeeds with a four-pitch repertoire that also includes a hard slider, a curveball and a changeup. Arroyo needs a full year in Triple-A, where he got crushed in three late-season starts in 1999, before he's ready.

Kevin Haverbusch

Position: 3B **Opening Day Age:** 23
Bats: R **Throws:** R **Born:** 6/16/76 in
Ht: 6' 3" **Wt:** 197 Rockville Centre, NY

Recent Statistics

	G	AB	R	H	D	T	HR	RBI	SB	BB	SO	Avg
1998 A Lynchburg	49	181	35	60	12	1	8	39	4	9	33	.331
1998 AA Carolina	46	168	28	63	10	0	3	29	1	13	20	.375
1999 AA Altoona	93	332	57	95	22	2	14	61	6	12	60	.286
1999 MLE	93	318	42	81	20	1	10	45	4	7	64	.255

Haverbusch has hit .318 as a pro but has yet to play more than 95 games in a season. He had back problems in 1998 and suffered through a series of abdominal, back, groin and hip strains last year. A 20th-round pick in 1997 from the University of Maryland, he's an aggressive hitter with power potential. He must learn to take a walk, as he was hit by more pitches (19) than he drew free passes in 1999. A converted shortstop, he has the arm to play a solid third base. Moreso than his health, Haverbusch's biggest problem is the presence of Aramis Ramirez in the system.

Chad Hermansen

Position: OF **Opening Day Age:** 22
Bats: R **Throws:** R **Born:** 9/10/77 in Salt
Ht: 6' 2" **Wt:** 185 Lake City, UT

Recent Statistics

	G	AB	R	H	D	T	HR	RBI	SB	BB	SO	Avg
1999 AAA Nashville	125	496	89	134	27	3	32	97	19	35	119	.270
1999 NL Pittsburgh	19	60	5	14	3	0	1	1	2	7	19	.233
1999 MLE	125	473	62	111	24	2	22	68	13	24	124	.235

One of the best young power hitters in the minors, Hermansen should play regularly for the Pirates at age 22 after hitting 60 homers in Triple-A the last two seasons. A 1994 first-round pick as a shortstop, he moved to second base before settling in center field in 1997. He can play all three outfield positions, and probably will shift to a corner at some point. His ticket, obviously, is his bat. In his second year in Triple-A, Hermansen boosted his batting average 12 points while making much better contact. He'll need to recapture the discipline he showed before 1999, when he took just 35 walks after previously averaging 62 per full season.

Alex Hernandez

Position: OF
Bats: L **Throws:** L
Ht: 6' 4" **Wt:** 186
Opening Day Age: 22
Born: 5/28/77 in San Juan, Puerto Rico

Recent Statistics

	G	AB	R	H	D	T	HR	RBI	SB	BB	SO	Avg
1998 AA Carolina	115	452	62	117	22	7	8	48	11	41	81	.259
1999 AA Altoona	126	475	76	122	26	3	15	63	11	54	110	.257
1999 MLE	126	457	56	104	23	2	11	47	7	34	117	.228

Hernandez may have the best tools of any of Pittsburgh's several outfield prospects, but his athleticism, raw speed and power potential haven't translated into success at the Double-A level. A 1995 fourth-round pick, he hasn't batted .260 or stolen 12 bases in either of the last two years. He has made the most progress with his power, nearly doubling his home-run total from eight to 15. Hernandez needs to make better contact but has developed a better eye at the plate. Defensively, he has center-field range and a right-field arm. He probably needs a third shot at Double-A.

Aramis Ramirez

Position: 3B
Bats: R **Throws:** R
Ht: 6' 1" **Wt:** 215
Opening Day Age: 21
Born: 6/25/78 in Santo Domingo, Dom. Rep.

Recent Statistics

	G	AB	R	H	D	T	HR	RBI	SB	BB	SO	Avg
1999 AAA Nashville	131	460	92	151	35	1	21	74	5	73	56	.328
1999 NL Pittsburgh	18	56	2	10	2	1	0	7	0	6	9	.179
1999 MLE	131	434	64	125	31	0	14	52	3	51	58	.288

Ramirez spent half of 1998 in Pittsburgh, becoming the first teenager to play for the Pirates since Miguel Dilone in 1974. When the Bucs lost 25 of their final 30 games, management decided to sign some veterans, and the arrival of Ed Sprague relegated Ramirez to Triple-A last season. Ramirez improved in all facets of his game: hitting a career-high .328 while also establishing personal bests in on-base (.425) and slugging (.546) percentage. He also has an unbelievable arm at third base, though he sometimes gets caught flat-footed and relies on his cannon too much, which led to a Pacific Coast League-high 42 errors. Sprague has left Pittsburgh as a free agent, leaving the third-base job for Ramirez.

Rico Washington

Position: C
Bats: L **Throws:** R
Ht: 5' 10" **Wt:** 179
Opening Day Age: 21
Born: 5/30/78 in Milledgeville, GA

Recent Statistics

	G	AB	R	H	D	T	HR	RBI	SB	BB	SO	Avg
1998 R Pirates	1	3	0	0	0	0	0	0	0	0	2	.000
1998 A Erie	51	197	31	65	14	2	6	31	1	17	33	.330
1998 A Augusta	12	50	12	15	2	1	2	12	2	7	9	.300
1999 A Hickory	76	287	70	102	15	1	13	50	5	48	45	.355
1999 A Lynchburg	57	205	31	58	7	0	7	32	4	30	45	.283

Washington is the best pure hitter in the system. A career .314 hitter as a pro, he really blossomed in 1999, batting a combined .325 with 20 homers for two Class-A teams. His smooth swing produces more line drives than loft, so the Pirates aren't sure how much power he'll have as he moves up the system. He commands the strike zone very well, so Washington should continue to hit for average. Drafted as a third baseman in the 10th round in 1997, he converted to catcher last season. He fared decently behind the plate, showing a quick release. Pittsburgh will play Washington at catcher, third and second base, and he'll spend 2000 in Double-A.

Craig Wilson

Position: DH
Bats: R **Throws:** R
Ht: 6' 2" **Wt:** 220
Opening Day Age: 23
Born: 11/30/76 in Fountain Valley, CA

Recent Statistics

	G	AB	R	H	D	T	HR	RBI	SB	BB	SO	Avg
1998 A Lynchburg	61	219	26	59	12	2	12	45	2	22	53	.269
1998 AA Carolina	45	148	20	49	11	0	5	21	4	14	32	.331
1999 AA Altoona	111	362	57	97	21	3	20	69	1	40	104	.268
1999 MLE	111	348	42	83	19	2	14	51	0	25	111	.239

Soon after Pittsburgh acquired six players from Toronto in November 1996 for Carlos Garcia, Orlando Merced and Dan Plesac, it looked like the Pirates had won a one-sided deal. While none of the three veterans did much for the Blue Jays, only Jose Silva has panned out for the Pirates. Their last hope is to get something out of Wilson, a 1995 second-round pick. He has the chance to be a rare offensive performer for a catcher because he has plenty of power. The question is how much he'll bounce back from reconstructive elbow surgery in 1998 that limited him to just 34 games behind the plate last year. Wilson had an average arm before his operation. He has enough bat to play another position, and also tried first base and left field in 1999.

Others to Watch

Righthander **Bobby Bradley** (19), Pittsburgh's 1999 first-round pick, had the best breaking ball and command and was the closest to being ready for the majors among the draft's high school prospects, according to *Baseball America*. He also has an 88-92 MPH fastball that has touched 94. . . Catcher **Humberto Cota** (21) joined the Pirates in the midseason Jose Guillen-Joe Oliver trade with the Devil Rays. He's a good receiver with quick feet and a solid arm, and he can hit for some power and average. . . Coming back from elbow surgery, **J.J. Davis** (21) slammed 19 homers in 86 games for Class-A Hickory. If his arm bounces back, he'll have four average tools to go with his considerable power. . . Lefthander **John Grabow** (21) had 164 strikeouts and just 32 walks in 156.1 innings at Hickory. His curveball is his top pitch. . . Pittsburgh initially envisioned lefthander **Clint Johnston** (22), but he may become a starter after adding a nifty changeup to go with his fastball and slider. His heater, which had been clocked as high as 94 MPH before 1999, was merely average last year but the Pirates aren't concerned. . . Righthander **Luis Torres** (19) dominated the Rookie-level Gulf Coast League with a fastball that touches 98 MPH and a nasty slider.

Busch Stadium

Offense

This isn't the ballpark Whitey Herzog used to love. The new Busch Stadium is Big Mac Land, the home of some of baseball's most epic home runs. It more closely resembles an old-time American League ballpark. The ball now carries well to left and right field. At the same time, speed is less of an asset in St. Louis than it once was. The grass surface has slowed down grounders that used to scoot into the gaps for doubles.

Defense

St. Louis needs sinkerball pitchers to take advantage of the grass infield and to limit the increasing home-run damage that can be done. Range in both the infield and outfield is not as vital as it was when Busch had artificial turf. However, the infield is usually very hard and sure-handed infielders are needed more than ever. The outfield gaps still require a better-than-average center fielder.

Who It Helps The Most

Since joining the Cardinals, Mark McGwire has hit 88 of his 159 homers in St. Louis. Ricky Bottalico, who joined the Cardinals last year, had a 2.29 ERA at home and a 7.34 mark on the road.

Who It Hurts The Most

In his first full season in St. Louis, Fernando Tatis hit 45 points higher and slugged 130 points better on the road. Young pitchers Manny Aybar and Jose Jimenez, since traded to Colorado, were torched at Busch.

Rookies & Newcomers

Darryl Kile and Dave Veres will have improved pitching numbers just from escaping Coors Field. Likewise, Pat Hentgen will benefit from leaving SkyDome, where he had a 6.83 ERA in 1999. New leadoff man Fernando Vina, acquired from Milwaukee for Juan Acevedo and two minor leaguers to be named, shouldn't be affected by the change in teams. Rookie lefthander Rick Ankiel fared fine in his brief exposure to Busch last year.

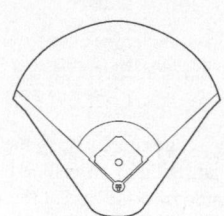

Dimensions: LF-330, LCF-372, CF-402, RCF-372, RF-330

Capacity: 49,676

Elevation: 535 feet

Surface: Grass

Foul Territory: Large

Park Factors

1999 Season

	Home Games Cardinals	Opp	Total	Away Games Cardinals	Opp	Total	Index
G	71	71	142	75	75	150	
Avg	.258	.274	.266	.257	.275	.266	100
AB	2385	2529	4914	2620	2491	5111	102
R	341	385	726	380	362	742	103
H	615	692	1307	673	685	1358	102
2B	101	143	244	144	135	279	91
3B	11	9	20	16	21	37	56
HR	91	70	161	83	73	156	107
BB	284	307	591	284	299	583	105
SO	489	459	948	610	469	1079	91
E	71	50	121	51	69	120	107
E-Infield	60	42	102	43	51	94	115
LHB-Avg	.265	.269	.267	.246	.276	.262	102
LHB-HR	18	27	45	20	22	42	116
RHB-Avg	.255	.276	.265	.262	.274	.267	99
RHB-HR	73	43	116	63	51	114	104

1997-1999

	Home Games Cardinals	Opp	Total	Away Games Cardinals	Opp	Total	Index
G	220,	220	440	223	223	446	—
Avg	.262	.258	.260	.253	.275	.264	99
AB	7434	7791	15225	7759	7421	15180	102
R	1075	1041	2116	1042	1052	2094	102
H	1949	2011	3960	1962	2039	4001	100
2B	378	373	751	388	385	773	97
3B	42	29	71	48	53	101	70
HR	261	203	464	256	182	438	106
BB	890	813	1703	802	813	1615	105
SO	1531	1461	2992	1774	1384	3158	94
E	201	136	337	163	158	321	106
E-Infield	165	109	274	132	123	255	109
LHB-Avg	.274	.255	.264	.263	.275	.270	98
LHB-HR	77	80	157	81	58	139	114
RHB-Avg	.255	.260	.258	.247	.274	.260	99
RHB-HR	184	123	307	175	124	299	102

1999 Rankings (National League)
- Second-highest infield-error factor
- Third-highest walk factor
- Third-highest LHB home-run factor
- Second-lowest triple factor

Tony La Russa

1999 Season

Another St. Louis season was killed by injuries and ineffective pitching. The Cardinals never had a stable rotation or bullpen and were disappointed by Eric Davis, J.D. Drew, Ray Lankford and Eli Marrero, who all posted poor seasons. For the first time in St. Louis, manager Tony La Russa was the object of criticism. The Cards failed to contend for three straight seasons, and despite the Mark McGwire sideshow and booming attendance, their great baseball fans had started complaining about La Russa by the end of last summer.

Offense

La Russa has lacked the luxury of a true leadoff hitter, which has forced him to juggle personnel to get production from the top of the lineup. Though La Russa has the reputation for being a manager who likes to put his runners in motion with steals and hit-and-run plays, he doesn't have much speed to work with. As a result, the St. Louis attack ends up waiting for someone to hit a home run or move runners along station to station.

Pitching & Defense

La Russa saw Alan Benes and Matt Morris, his top two young pitchers, sustain career-threatening injuries in 1998. As a result, he never has had an ace on his staff. La Russa also has run through an array of closers, and he has demonstrated his impatience by moving a number of pitchers in and out of different roles looking for an effective bullpen. His teams always are well prepared and fundamentally sound in the field.

2000 Outlook

It wasn't until well after the season that La Russa officially signed a contract extension to remain in St. Louis. The delay reflected not only his own indecision but also some restlessness among Cardinals fans. Still, the club's ownership seems committed to La Russa. If St. Louis finally can enjoy some pitching stability, the Cards are good enough to contend. His intense style becomes a big plus when it's injected into a pennant race. The acquisitions of Pat Hentgen and Darryl Kile should solidify the rotation and make La Russa's job much easier.

Born: 10/04/44 in Tampa, FL

Playing Experience: 1963-1973, Oak, Atl, ChC

Managerial Experience: 21 seasons

Manager Statistics

Year	Team, Lg	W	L	Pct	GB	Finish
1999	St. Louis, NL	75	86	.466	21.5	4th Central
21 Seasons		1639	1511	.520	—	—

1999 Starting Pitchers by Days Rest

	<=3	4	5	6+
Cardinals Starts	2	82	44	20
Cardinals ERA	5.73	4.79	4.52	4.87
NL Avg Starts	3	81	48	21
NL ERA	4.84	4.53	4.72	4.98

1999 Situational Stats

	Tony La Russa	NL Average
Hit & Run Success %	39.3	33.6
Stolen Base Success %	73.6	70.2
Platoon Pct.	47.3	55.2
Defensive Subs	28	25
High-Pitch Outings	13	13
Quick/Slow Hooks	26/14	16/15
Sacrifice Attempts	103	89

1999 Rankings (National League)

- 1st in quick hooks (26), relief appearances (454) and mid-inning pitching changes (199)
- 2nd in hit-and-run attempts (117), hit-and-run percentage (39.3%), starting lineups used (138) and saves with over 1 inning pitched (14)
- 3rd in pitchouts with a runner moving (9) and one-batter pitcher appearances (38)

Rick Ankiel

1999 Season

Few young pitchers have arrived with a bigger buildup than Rick Ankiel. In his second professional season, Ankiel rolled through two minor league levels and reached the majors in August. Among his nine appearances with St. Louis were five starts, and though Ankiel still is looking for his first major league win, he definitely wasn't overmatched by National League hitters. He struck out 39 in 33 innings and allowed opponents a mere .215 batting average. He also was named Minor League Player of the Year by *Baseball America*.

Pitching

For such an inexperienced pitcher, Ankiel already brings a very complete package to the mound. He throws a moving fastball in the mid-90s and isn't afraid to come inside with it. Ankiel also has a big-breaking curve, a pitch he throws at varying speeds. Over the course of last season he significantly improved his straight changeup. Ankiel has started learning a slider, which will make him even harder to hit. He has excellent control and remarkable maturity. His biggest need probably is just to fine-tune his command within the strike zone.

Defense & Hitting

Ankiel is a good athlete who doesn't get rattled defensively. He has the makings of a good pickoff move and pays attention to baserunners. He had only one hit in 10 at-bats, but St. Louis thinks he'll develop into a very serviceable hitting pitcher as he gains more experience.

2000 Outlook

The sky is the limit for Ankiel, whom St. Louis signed for $2.5 million as a 1997 second-round pick. He has the stuff and the makeup to develop into an ace. In the short term, the Cardinals think that Ankiel can win 12-15 games this year. He'll face less pressure after the Cardinals traded for Pat Hentgen and Darryl Kile.

Position: SP
Bats: L **Throws:** L
Ht: 6' 1"   **Wt:** 210

Opening Day Age: 20
Born: 7/19/79 in Fort Pierce, FL
ML Seasons: 1
Pronunciation: ANN-keel

Overall Statistics

	W	L	Pct.	ERA	G	GS	Sv	IP	H	BB	SO	HR	Ratio
1999	0	1	.000	3.27	9	5	1	33.0	26	14	39	2	1.21
Career	0	1	.000	3.27	9	5	1	33.0	26	14	39	2	1.21

How Often He Throws Strikes

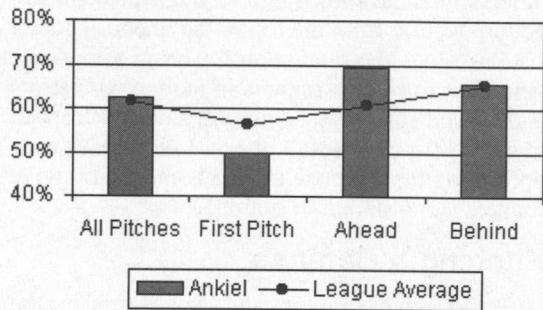

1999 Situational Stats

	W	L	ERA	Sv	IP		AB	H	HR	RBI	Avg
Home	0	0	1.80	1	15.0	LHB	17	4	0	0	.235
Road	0	1	4.50	0	18.0	RHB	104	22	2	11	.212
First Half	0	0	-	0	0.0	Sc Pos	33	6	0	9	.182
Scnd Half	0	1	3.27	1	33.0	Clutch	10	2	0	0	.200

1999 Rankings (National League)

- Did not rank near the top or bottom in any category

Ricky Bottalico

1999 Season

The Cardinals hoped they finally had solidified their bullpen when they traded Ron Gant, Jeff Brantley, Cliff Politte and $5 million to the Phillies for Ricky Bottalico and Garrett Stephenson in November 1998. But Bottalico wasn't the answer. In fact, he was one of St. Louis' major disappointments. He blew eight of his 28 save opportunities, and lost seven games while compiling the second-worst ERA of his career.

Pitching

After elbow surgery in 1998, Bottalico was close to regaining his velocity, routinely clocked in the low- to mid-90s. At times, Bottalico can use either a curve or a changeup to get outs. His lack of control, though, has become a major problem. He gets behind far too many batters, thus being forced to throw fastballs. He continues to struggle to get lefthanders out, a problem that's getting worse as his career progresses. Bottalico has labored to maintain his composure as well. When he hits a wild streak, his tendency to lose his temper just aggravates the situation.

Defense & Hitting

By varying his delivery and using a decent pickoff move, Bottalico is a rare closer who doesn't allow easy stolen bases. He has permitted just two in the past two seasons. Bottalico is prone to mistakes in the field, largely because of his tendency to fall off the mound toward third base and his lapses in temper. He rarely gets a chance to hit.

2000 Outlook

Once an All-Star closer, Bottalico has reached a crossroads in his career. Disappointed in his performance, St. Louis traded for Dave Veres and would have signed Mike Jackson had Jackson passed a physical. Bottalico now is headed for a setup and middle-inning role, with his days as a closer gone unless he regains his command.

Position: RP
Bats: L **Throws:** R
Ht: 6' 1" **Wt:** 217

Opening Day Age: 30
Born: 8/26/69 in New Britain, CT
ML Seasons: 6
Pronunciation: buh-TAL-ih-co

Overall Statistics

	W	L	Pct.	ERA	G	GS	Sv	IP	H	BB	SO	HR	Ratio
1999	3	7	.300	4.91	68	0	20	73.1	83	49	66	8	1.80
Career	15	25	.375	3.84	302	0	95	349.0	305	182	346	35	1.40

How Often He Throws Strikes

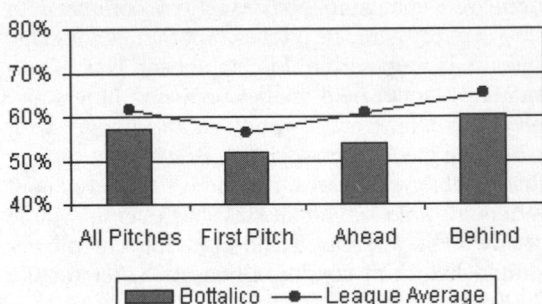

1999 Situational Stats

	W	L	ERA	Sv	IP		AB	H	HR	RBI	Avg
Home	2	1	2.29	10	35.1	LHB	113	35	3	18	.310
Road	1	6	7.34	10	38.0	RHB	179	48	5	28	.268
First Half	1	5	3.99	12	47.1	Sc Pos	93	27	2	36	.290
Scnd Half	2	2	6.58	8	26.0	Clutch	177	50	5	32	.282

1999 Rankings (National League)

- 2nd in lowest save percentage (71.4), worst first batter efficiency (.339) and most baserunners allowed per nine innings in relief (16.6)
- 5th in blown saves (8) and relief losses (7)
- 9th in highest batting average allowed in relief (.284)
- Led the Cardinals in games pitched, saves, games finished (40), save opportunities (28), save percentage (71.4), blown saves (8) and relief losses (7)

Kent Bottenfield

1999 Season

Kent Bottenfield was the Cardinals' most pleasant surprise. For the first time in his career, he got the chance to spend a full season in the rotation. And Bottenfield made the most of the opportunity, earning an All-Star berth and leading the National League in victories for much of the season before a late-season slump cost him a chance to be a 20-game winner. He posted career highs in innings, wins and strikeouts.

Pitching

Bottenfield is proof that a pitcher doesn't need overpowering stuff to be a major league winner. He combines a good sinking fastball, a slider and an improved changeup with excellent command to stay in every game he pitches. Another factor in his success is preparation. Pitching coach Dave Duncan says Bottenfield studies opposing hitters and plans his attack as diligently as any pitcher with whom he has been associated. Bottenfield can get into trouble with walks, and there's concern about him being able to maintain his stuff over the whole season. His year as a full-time starting pitcher should help him condition himself better for the 2000 campaign.

Defense

With a decent slide step and his constant attention to the running game, Bottenfield limits the damage done by basestealers. He's an average fielder who doesn't have great agility because of his large frame. He's capable of getting bunts down and can drive in an occasional run.

2000 Outlook

With St. Louis trading for Pat Hentgen and Darryl Kile, Bottenfield should be well served as a No. 3 starter. He's a solid competitor who, with run support and bullpen help, can be expected to win 14-16 games.

Position: SP
Bats: R **Throws:** R
Ht: 6' 3" **Wt:** 240

Opening Day Age: 31
Born: 11/14/68 in Portland, OR
ML Seasons: 7

Overall Statistics

	W	L	Pct.	ERA	G	GS	Sv	IP	H	BB	SO	HR	Ratio
1999	18	7	.720	3.97	31	31	0	190.1	197	89	124	21	1.50
Career	36	34	.514	4.19	250	78	8	688.0	704	292	421	77	1.45

How Often He Throws Strikes

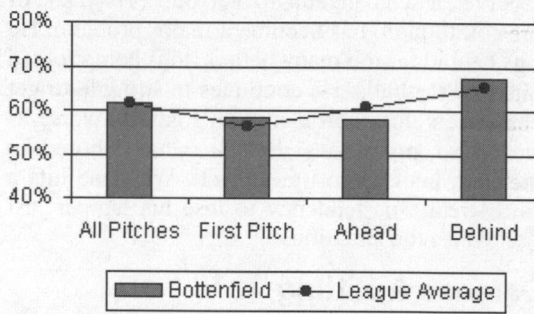

1999 Situational Stats

	W	L	ERA	Sv	IP		AB	H	HR	RBI	Avg
Home	9	3	4.21	0	92.0	LHB	322	79	7	34	.245
Road	9	4	3.75	0	98.1	RHB	407	118	14	51	.290
First Half	14	3	3.78	0	112.0	Sc Pos	173	39	2	52	.225
Scnd Half	4	4	4.25	0	78.1	Clutch	42	13	0	5	.310

1999 Rankings (National League)

- 3rd in winning percentage and lowest batting average allowed vs. lefthanded batters
- 4th in wins
- 6th in lowest groundball/flyball ratio allowed (0.9), fewest GDPs induced per nine innings (0.4) and most walks per nine innings (4.2)
- 9th in walks allowed and lowest batting average allowed with runners in scoring position
- 10th in lowest strikeout/walk ratio (1.4) and most pitches thrown per batter (3.79)
- Led the Cardinals in ERA, wins, hits allowed, batters faced (843), home runs allowed, walks allowed, strikeouts, pitches thrown (3,195), winning percentage, most run support per nine innings (6.1), ERA at home and ERA on the road

Eric Davis

1999 Season

The Cardinals had hoped Eric Davis would supply some outfield pop when they gave him a two-year, $8 million contract prior to the 1999 season. But the 16-year veteran never approached the big numbers he put up for Baltimore in 1998. Davis was plagued by shoulder troubles that eventually ended his season on June 29 after only 191 at-bats.

Hitting

Since arriving in Cincinnati 16 years ago, Davis has had some of the best bat speed in baseball. And even now after his many injuries and a bout with colon cancer, Davis still can turn on the best fastballs. When he's healthy and swinging the bat well, Davis is a tough hitter to defense. He can drive breaking balls or fastballs away for power to the right-center gap, and he also can turn on inside pitches with considerable power to left. Davis chases pitches at times and will pile up his share of strikeouts. He can look bad for three at-bats and then do damage late in the same game during his final trip to the plate.

Baserunning & Defense

His days as a big-time basestealer are long gone, but Davis still can pick his spots and occasionally run with success. He also is an intelligent baserunner who rarely tries for the extra base and fails. His injuries have robbed him of what once were outstanding defensive skills. His throwing arm has deteriorated to below average and his range isn't exceptional anymore.

2000 Outlook

St. Louis knew there was risk in making a two-year investment in the aging and injury-prone Davis, and it didn't get much of a return last season. The Cardinals think he'll rebound this season after he recovers from his shoulder troubles. Whether Davis can remain an effective everyday player is a concern, but with a year remaining on his contract and the Cards lacking an option in right field, he's likely to start. If he can avoid physical problems, Davis has the potential for 20 homers and 80 RBI.

Position: RF
Bats: R **Throws:** R
Ht: 6' 3" **Wt:** 200

Opening Day Age: 37
Born: 5/29/62 in Los Angeles, CA
ML Seasons: 15

Overall Statistics

	G	AB	R	H	D	T	HR	RBI	SB	BB	SO	Avg	OBP	Slg
1999	58	191	27	49	9	2	5	30	5	30	49	.257	.359	.403
Career	1460	4911	883	1321	218	23	272	872	347	691	1300	.269	.360	.489

Where He Hits the Ball

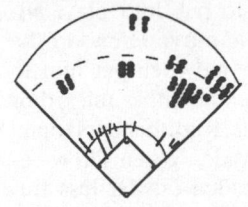

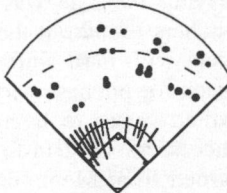

Vs. LHP **Vs. RHP**

1999 Situational Stats

	AB	H	HR	RBI	Avg		AB	H	HR	RBI	Avg
Home	87	20	2	11	.230	LHP	49	14	2	8	.286
Road	104	29	3	19	.279	RHP	142	35	3	22	.246
First Half	191	49	5	30	.257	Sc Pos	50	17	1	24	.340
Scnd Half	0	0	0	0	-	Clutch	28	9	0	4	.321

1999 Rankings (National League)

- Did not rank near the top or bottom in any category

J.D. Drew

1999 Season

Before the season even started, many experts already had made J.D. Drew the National League Rookie of the Year. Then the controversial, much-heralded Drew laid an egg in his first full major league season. He began the year as the Cardinals' center fielder, but when he struggled as a hitter and suffered through a quadriceps injury, Drew was sent to Triple-A Memphis in mid-May. Returning six weeks later, Drew started showing his long-awaited power. His 13 homers were the fourth-best total on the club.

Hitting

Before his trip to the minors, Drew was striking out in roughly 30 percent of his at-bats and rarely driving balls he was able to put into play. NL pitchers found out they could move Drew off the plate with hard stuff inside and then get him to reach for pitches away, which he either missed or pulled weakly to the right side. Righthanders found success running fastballs inside. When Drew returned from Memphis, he bailed out far less frequently and worked more favorable counts. As a result, he started making better contact and looked more like the prospect everybody expected to see. Drew also showed improved patience in the second half.

Baserunning & Defense

Drew is a legitimate five-tool prospect. His speed is outstanding and he has excellent basestealing skills for a young player. In 1999, he stole 19 bases in 22 attempts. Drew has outstanding range but doesn't always get good jumps on the ball, something that should improve with experience. He has a strong arm but sometimes makes throws to show it off, rather than making the correct toss to the proper base.

2000 Outlook

Many baseball people, especially those all-knowing Philadelphia types, were gloating early last season when Drew was overmatched by big league pitching. He survived a year of growing pains, and no one should be surprised if Drew begins his rise as one of the next decade's stars with a 30-30 season.

Position: CF
Bats: L **Throws:** R
Ht: 6' 1" **Wt:** 195

Opening Day Age: 24
Born: 11/20/75 in Valdosta, GA
ML Seasons: 2

Overall Statistics

	G	AB	R	H	D	T	HR	RBI	SB	BB	SO	Avg	OBP	Slg
1999	104	368	72	89	16	6	13	39	19	50	77	.242	.340	.424
Career	118	404	81	104	19	7	18	52	19	54	87	.257	.350	.473

Where He Hits the Ball

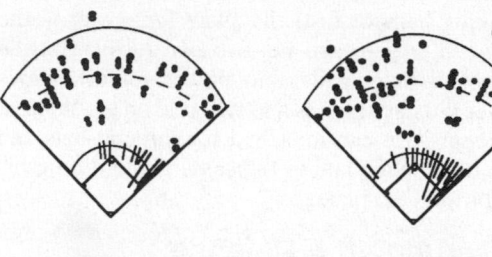

Vs. LHP   **Vs. RHP**

1999 Situational Stats

	AB	H	HR	RBI	Avg		AB	H	HR	RBI	Avg
Home	190	48	5	19	.253	LHP	106	28	5	12	.264
Road	178	41	8	20	.230	RHP	262	61	8	27	.233
First Half	116	26	5	15	.224	Sc Pos	73	22	4	25	.301
Scnd Half	252	63	8	24	.250	Clutch	56	8	0	1	.143

1999 Rankings (National League)

- 2nd in batting average on a 3-1 count (.750)
- 5th in stolen-base percentage (86.4) and lowest batting average in the clutch
- 6th in errors in center field (7)
- 9th in lowest batting average on a 3-2 count (.116)
- Led the Cardinals in stolen-base percentage (86.4), batting average on a 3-1 count (.750), batting average on an 0-2 count (.227) and triples
- Led NL center fielders in batting average on a 3-1 count (.750)

Jose Jimenez

Position: SP
Bats: R **Throws:** R
Ht: 6' 3" **Wt:** 190

Opening Day Age: 26
Born: 7/7/73 in San
Pedro de Macoris,
Dominican Republic
ML Seasons: 2
Pronunciation:
HIM-enn-ezz

1999 Season

Freeze-frame two starts against Arizona just prior to the All-Star break, and rookie Jose Jimenez could have been one of the season's biggest stories. Unfortunately, Jimenez started 26 games in addition to his no-hitter and complete-game shutout against the Diamondbacks. He ended up among the National League leaders with 14 defeats, and his .263 winning percentage was the worst in the circuit. Even with those two shutouts, Jimenez' ERA was close to six.

Pitching

Jimenez' two brilliant starts weren't entire flukes. When he keeps his delivery together and throws strike after strike with his heavy sinker, Jimenez is as tough as anyone to hit. He can't consistently maintain his proper release point, though, and he can unravel in a hurry. Then his sinker either will stay up or dive into the dirt, which is why he had 10 wild pitches in 1999. Jimenez then gets frustrated and abandons his sinker to throw an inconsistent cutter or slider, which too often sits over the plate. He needs a pitch to combat lefthanders after they hit .304 against him last year.

Defense & Hitting

Jimenez is fairly quick to the plate, making him tough to run on. He has good athletic skills and can become a good fielder with more work. Jimenez isn't afraid to take his cuts at the plate, but they rarely produce hits. He's a very poor bunter as well.

2000 Outlook

If the key that can unlock Jimenez' full potential ever is found, he could be a big winner. But he's not a kid anymore. He took seven years to reach the majors and remains wildly inconsistent. All of which is why the Cardinals were willing to include him in the trade that sent Manny Aybar, Rick Croushore and shortstop prospect Brent Butler to Colorado and brought Darryl Kile, Dave Veres and pitching prospect Luther Hackman to St. Louis in November.

Overall Statistics

	W	L	Pct.	ERA	G	GS	Sv	IP	H	BB	SO	HR	Ratio
1999	5	14	.263	5.85	29	28	0	163.0	173	71	113	16	1.50
Career	8	14	.364	5.52	33	31	0	184.1	195	79	125	16	1.49

How Often He Throws Strikes

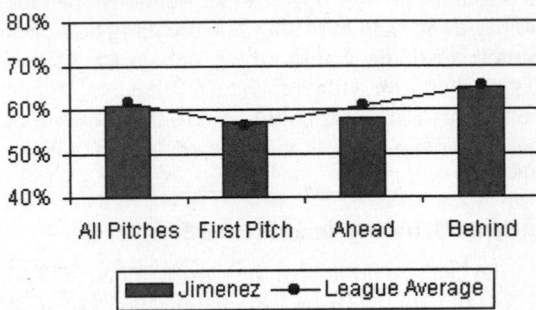

Jimenez ●—League Average

1999 Situational Stats

	W	L	ERA	Sv	IP		AB	H	HR	RBI	Avg
Home	2	6	7.22	0	72.1	LHB	296	90	11	57	.304
Road	3	8	4.76	0	90.2	RHB	333	83	5	35	.249
First Half	5	9	5.73	0	110.0	Sc Pos	154	45	4	68	.292
Scnd Half	0	5	6.11	0	53.0	Clutch	55	12	1	4	.218

1999 Rankings (National League)

- 1st in lowest winning percentage
- 2nd in shutouts (2) and highest groundball/flyball ratio allowed (2.5)
- 3rd in highest ERA
- 4th in losses, hit batsmen (11) and least run support per nine innings (4.3)
- 5th in lowest stolen-base percentage allowed (41.2)
- Led the Cardinals in losses, complete games (2), shutouts (2), hit batsmen (11), wild pitches (10), highest groundball/flyball ratio allowed (2.5), lowest stolen-base percentage allowed (41.2), fewest pitches thrown per batter (3.67), most strikeouts per nine innings (6.2) and lowest batting average allowed vs. righthanded batters

St. Louis

Ray Lankford

1999 Season

Another year passed without Ray Lankford rising into the game's top echelon. Knee surgery during the 1998-99 offseason kept him from being 100 percent the entire season, and that irked the club because it never authorized the operation. Lankford missed 40 games and never was a factor until the Cardinals long since had fallen out of the race.

Hitting

Even at his best, Lankford doesn't hit enough home runs to justify his whopping strikeout totals. After 10 years, he still can't be convinced to cut down his swing or work more counts into his favor. When he isn't being overly aggressive at the plate, Lankford is a tough out with power to all fields. He has the ability to hit both hard stuff and breaking balls, but prefers fastballs. Lankford's penchant for bailing out makes him vulnerable to lefthanders. When he's in his groove, though, Lankford is capable of being an extra-base hit machine against all types of pitching.

Baserunning & Defense

By the last two months of the season, Lankford had recovered enough from his knee problems to steal 10 bases. Still, his stolen-base abilities have declined sharply because of his physical problems. His speed is no longer top notch, just very good, and his judgment on the bases is erratic. The arrival of J.D. Drew means Lankford's future is in left field, where he should continue to be an asset. His chronic knee problems have compromised the range that made him an excellent center fielder. Lankford's weak but accurate throwing arm is better suited for left also.

2000 Outlook

By giving Lankford a contract extension two years ago, the Cardinals in effect chose to keep him long term instead of Brian Jordan. The decision doesn't look great right now. In the right lineup, however, a healthy Lankford is capable of decent power and speed numbers, though he may never be the superstar St. Louis expected him to be. He spent the offseason rehabilitating his knees to avoid more surgery.

Position: LF
Bats: L **Throws:** L
Ht: 5'11" **Wt:** 200

Opening Day Age: 32
Born: 6/5/67 in
Modesto, CA
ML Seasons: 10

Overall Statistics

	G	AB	R	H	D	T	HR	RBI	SB	BB	SO	Avg	OBP	Slg
1999	122	422	77	129	32	1	15	63	14	49	110	.306	.380	.493
Career	1269	4561	781	1267	291	45	181	703	239	637	1141	.278	.367	.480

Where He Hits the Ball

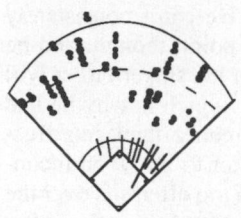

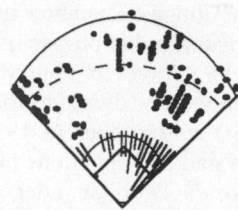

Vs. LHP   **Vs. RHP**

1999 Situational Stats

	AB	H	HR	RBI	Avg		AB	H	HR	RBI	Avg
Home	210	64	8	28	.305	LHP	114	27	2	16	.237
Road	212	65	7	35	.307	RHP	308	102	13	47	.331
First Half	206	66	12	37	.320	Sc Pos	115	35	0	41	.304
Scnd Half	216	63	3	26	.292	Clutch	86	26	3	14	.302

1999 Rankings (National League)

- 3rd in fielding percentage in left field (.986)
- 8th in lowest cleanup slugging percentage (.538)

Eli Marrero

1999 Season

Rarely does a player's stock fall faster than Eli Marrero's did over the past year. He showed admirable courage by battling back from cancer, and the Cardinals entered the 1999 season believing that Marrero had developed into their everyday catcher. But by August, Marrero had fallen out of favor with manager Tony La Russa because of his months-long slump.

Hitting

Once Marrero started slumping, his problems snowballed. He pressed at the plate, often getting himself out by swinging early in the count. Being anxious often led to falling behind pitchers or making a weak out. He went fishing for low and outside breaking balls more frequently as the season progressed, which contributed to his woes. Marrero still has a quick stroke and can pull fastballs with power. But by the end of the season, he was showing a total lack of confidence in his ability, feeling for the ball too often instead of attacking pitches.

Baserunning & Defense

All the physical tools are in place for Marrero to be a solid major league player. He runs better than most catchers, stealing 11 bases in 13 attempts in 1999. He also goes from first base to third very well. Marrero has solid all-around catching skills. His strong arm and quick release allowed him to throw out 37 percent of opposing basestealers last season. Marrero has soft hands, frames pitches well and calls a good game.

2000 Outlook

One of St. Louis' key organizational decisions revolves around Marrero. His collapse was a jarring development after it seemed Marrero was a lock as the Cardinals' starting catcher. There's a real question in St. Louis whether Marrero will ever recover from last season. He needs to show improvement from the first day of spring training or face being passed over. One thing working in his favor is that he faces little competition. The Cardinals traded Alberto Castillo and failed to sign Joe Girardi, instead settling for the weak stick of Mike Matheny.

Position: C/1B
Bats: R **Throws:** R
Ht: 6' 1" **Wt:** 180

Opening Day Age: 26
Born: 11/17/73 in Havana, Cuba
ML Seasons: 3
Pronunciation: muh-RARE-oh

Overall Statistics

	G	AB	R	H	D	T	HR	RBI	SB	BB	SO	Avg	OBP	Slg
1999	114	317	32	61	13	1	6	34	11	18	56	.192	.236	.297
Career	214	616	64	134	33	2	12	61	21	48	111	.218	.273	.336

Where He Hits the Ball

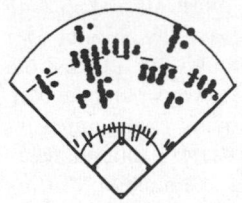 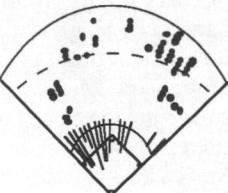

Vs. LHP   **Vs. RHP**

1999 Situational Stats

	AB	H	HR	RBI	Avg		AB	H	HR	RBI	Avg
Home	158	26	3	17	.165	LHP	74	15	1	7	.203
Road	159	35	3	17	.220	RHP	243	46	5	27	.189
First Half	235	48	6	23	.204	Sc Pos	94	18	0	24	.191
Scnd Half	82	13	0	11	.159	Clutch	57	12	2	10	.211

1999 Rankings (National League)

- 2nd in lowest fielding percentage at catcher (.987)
- 4th in errors at catcher (7)
- 5th in most GDPs per GDP situation (17.3%)
- 6th in lowest batting average with runners in scoring position and lowest batting average with two strikes (.122)

Mark McGwire

1999 Season

What to do for an encore? Though accompanied by far less fanfare and drama, Mark McGwire in many ways had just as remarkable a season as his 70-homer 1998 epic. McGwire hit 65 homers, giving him an amazing 245 longballs in his last four seasons. McGwire drove in 147 runs and walked 133 times, further demonstrating his impressive ability to get on base and bring baserunners home.

Hitting

The frustration of playing again for a non-contender seemed to affect McGwire's hitting at times last year. Usually a very disciplined hitter, he chased waste pitches out of the strike zone more frequently and his average suffered for it. Most pitchers try to go after McGwire up and in with hard stuff. However, if they leave the ball out over the plate or don't get it up enough, he'll take it out of the park. McGwire almost always pulls the ball, and teams have begun employing exaggerated infield shifts on him. Shifts are useless, though, when McGwire is getting his arms extended and lifting majestic 500-foot moonshots. He had less success versus lefthanders last season than in previous years.

Baserunning & Defense

McGwire finally ending his record triple drought of 4,618 at-bats last season, but speed obviously isn't his game. He lumbers on the bases, yet he's an intelligent runner who usually doesn't make errors in judgment. McGwire is an underrated defensive first baseman with soft hands and decent range. He handles bunts and slow rollers to first with average ability. His erratic throws around first base are his main weakness.

2000 Outlook

The only man to hit his 400th and 500th home runs in successive seasons, McGwire could challenge Hank Aaron's career home-run record. In addition to staying healthy, a key for McGwire will be the caliber of the club around him. He was anxious at the plate for much of last year, and at this stage of his career he needs to play for a contender to be at his best.

Position: 1B
Bats: R **Throws:** R
Ht: 6' 5" **Wt:** 250

Opening Day Age: 36
Born: 10/1/63 in Pomona, CA
ML Seasons: 14
Nickname: Sack, Big Mac

Overall Statistics

	G	AB	R	H	D	T	HR	RBI	SB	BB	SO	Avg	OBP	Slg
1999	153	521	118	145	21	1	65	147	0	133	141	.278	.424	.697
Career	1688	5652	1059	1498	240	6	522	1277	11	1185	1400	.265	.394	.587

Where He Hits the Ball

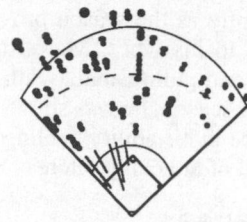

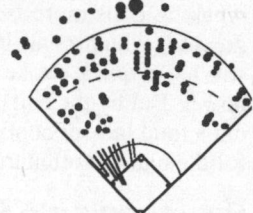

Vs. LHP   **Vs. RHP**

1999 Situational Stats

	AB	H	HR	RBI	Avg		AB	H	HR	RBI	Avg
Home	260	74	37	89	.285	LHP	122	31	16	30	.254
Road	261	71	28	58	.272	RHP	399	114	49	117	.286
First Half	289	77	28	72	.266	Sc Pos	135	48	19	87	.356
Scnd Half	232	68	37	75	.293	Clutch	81	19	5	14	.235

1999 Rankings (National League)

- 1st in HR frequency (8.0 ABs per HR), slugging percentage vs. righthanded pitchers (.694), home runs, RBI, intentional walks (21), lowest groundball/flyball ratio (0.6) and lowest percentage of extra bases taken as a runner (13.4)
- Led the Cardinals in slugging percentage, on-base percentage, HR frequency (8.0 ABs per HR), batting average with runners in scoring position, slugging percentage vs. lefthanded pitchers (.705), slugging percentage vs. righthanded pitchers (.694), on-base percentage vs. lefthanded pitchers (.425), on-base percentage vs. righthanded pitchers (.423), home runs, runs scored, total bases (363), RBI, walks, intentional walks (21), times on base (280) and strikeouts

Darren Oliver

1999 Season

Often plagued by poor support, Darren Oliver had a better year than his 9-9 record would suggest. He led the Cardinals in innings pitched and posted a 3.35 ERA after the All-Star break. Oliver has been remarkably consistent since coming to St. Louis in July 1998. He has gone 13-13 with the Cardinals and has had identical 4.26 ERAs in both of his National League seasons.

Pitching

When Oliver stays aggressive with his stuff, he can be a solid lefthander. His velocity doesn't get much past 90 MPH, but he has been trying to develop movement with both his two-seam fastball and a cutter. Oliver always has had a good changeup, which he has begun turning over to get downward movement. At times, he can become tentative and will nibble his way into too many deep counts. He also fell in love with his cutter at times last season, one of the reasons why lefthanders hit him so well. Since coming to St. Louis, Oliver has improved his stamina and usually can be counted on to get into the seventh inning.

Defense & Hitting

Oliver has worked hard to improve his ability to hold runners. His pickoff move can be deceptive and he's fairly quick to the plate, which usually allows his catcher a chance to throw out basestealers. While he isn't considered a great athlete, he gets to all the balls he is expected to retrieve and isn't a detriment to his team in the field. Oliver also has become one of the better-hitting pitchers, batting .274 with 20 hits last year.

2000 Outlook

Lefthanders are always in demand and Oliver, a free agent in an offseason with a weak crop of pitchers, received a lot of interest. He's entering what should be the prime of his career. With a little more movement on his pitches, he has a chance to be a solid double-figure winner over the next several years.

Position: SP
Bats: R **Throws:** L
Ht: 6' 2" **Wt:** 210

Opening Day Age: 29
Born: 10/6/70 in Kansas City, MO
ML Seasons: 7

Overall Statistics

	W	L	Pct.	ERA	G	GS	Sv	IP	H	BB	SO	HR	Ratio
1999	9	9	.500	4.26	30	30	0	196.1	197	74	119	16	1.38
Career	54	40	.574	4.55	183	128	2	834.0	893	366	515	91	1.51

How Often He Throws Strikes

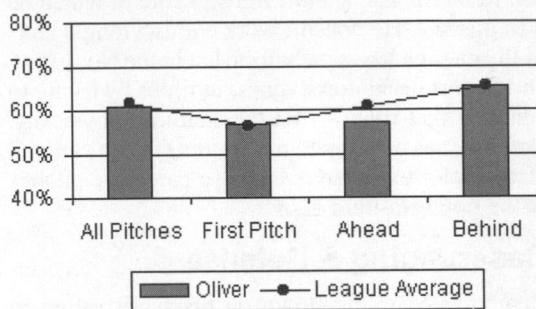

1999 Situational Stats

	W	L	ERA	Sv	IP		AB	H	HR	RBI	Avg
Home	4	5	4.23	0	95.2	LHB	126	41	2	15	.325
Road	5	4	4.29	0	100.2	RHB	616	156	14	68	.253
First Half	4	6	5.10	0	102.1	Sc Pos	184	44	3	63	.239
Scnd Half	5	3	3.35	0	94.0	Clutch	58	15	4	9	.259

1999 Rankings (National League)

- 4th in hit batsmen (11)
- 5th in runners caught stealing (11)
- Led the Cardinals in complete games (2), innings pitched, hits allowed, hit batsmen (11), balks (2), pickoff throws (140), stolen bases allowed (13), GDPs induced (22), highest strikeout/walk ratio (1.6), lowest batting average allowed (.266), lowest slugging percentage allowed (.396), lowest on-base percentage allowed (.339), fewest baserunners allowed per nine innings (12.9), fewest walks per nine innings (3.4), runners caught stealing (11) and fewest home runs allowed per nine innings (.73).

Edgar Renteria

1999 Season

In need of a quality shortstop, the Cardinals packaged top prospects Armando Almanza, Braden Looper and Pablo Ozuna to pry Edgar Renteria from the Marlins in December 1998. A sore right knee hampered Renteria in April, when he hit just .254 with one steal, but after that he was the player St. Louis thought it was getting. His 11 homers nearly equaled the total of 12 he hit in his first three seasons, and he also improved markedly as a basestealer. The only disappointment was his inconsistent play in the field.

Hitting

For much of the 1999 season, it was necessary to use Renteria as a leadoff hitter, a role in which he was miscast. He doesn't work enough long counts or log enough bases on balls to bat in the No. 1 spot, and he lost his aggressiveness at times by trying to adapt to that role. As he has matured physically, Renteria has developed more strength. He can pull fastballs for extra bases and also can drive pitches to the opposite-field gaps.

Baserunning & Defense

Renteria's knee cut down on his basestealing in April, but he ran wild afterward. He's a solid thief with the ability and judgment to approach 50 steals a season. He has very good instincts on the bases and rarely makes an error in judgment when going for the extra base. Renteria has all the physical skills to be an outstanding shortstop. Still, he tends to be too casual with his throws and his concentration will waver on routine plays, a reason why he had 26 errors last year. Renteria also has room to improve his range.

2000 Outlook

With Renteria, the best should be yet to come. He should be healthy coming into spring training and he's at an age where he could blossom into a top all-around shortstop. St. Louis is counting on that happening. He won't have to bat leadoff after the Cardinals traded for Fernando Vina.

Position: SS
Bats: R **Throws:** R
Ht: 6' 1" **Wt:** 180

Opening Day Age: 24
Born: 8/7/75 in Barranquilla, Colombia
ML Seasons: 4
Pronunciation: ren-ter-REE-uh

Overall Statistics

	G	AB	R	H	D	T	HR	RBI	SB	BB	SO	Avg	OBP	Slg
1999	154	585	92	161	36	2	11	63	37	53	82	.275	.334	.400
Career	547	2150	329	611	93	10	23	177	126	179	336	.284	.340	.369

Where He Hits the Ball

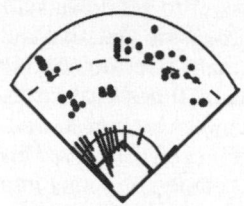

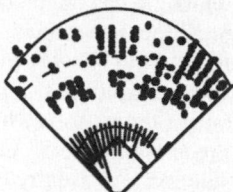

Vs. LHP   **Vs. RHP**

1999 Situational Stats

	AB	H	HR	RBI	Avg		AB	H	HR	RBI	Avg
Home	297	79	6	22	.266	LHP	140	35	2	16	.250
Road	288	82	5	41	.285	RHP	445	126	9	47	.283
First Half	307	92	5	40	.300	Sc Pos	138	42	1	51	.304
Scnd Half	278	69	6	23	.248	Clutch	106	28	0	11	.264

1999 Rankings (National League)

- 3rd in errors at shortstop (26)
- 4th in lowest fielding percentage at shortstop (.959)
- 7th in stolen bases
- 10th in stolen-base percentage (82.2), batting average on a 3-2 count (.378), lowest slugging percentage and lowest on-base percentage for a leadoff hitter (.352)
- Led the Cardinals in on-base percentage for a leadoff hitter (.352), steals of third (6), at-bats, hits, singles, doubles, sacrifice flies (7), stolen bases, GDPs (16) and games played
- Led NL shortstops in stolen-base percentage (82.2), doubles, sacrifice flies (7), stolen bases, caught stealing (8) and GDPs (16)

Fernando Tatis

1999 Season

It was a breakthrough year for young third baseman Fernando Tatis. He emerged as one of the league's up-and-coming stars, smashing 34 home runs and collecting 107 RBI in just his second full year in the majors. On April 23 he made baseball history by being the first player ever to hit two grand slams in the same inning—both off Chan Ho Park in Dodger Stadium. Tatis was the first Cardinals infielder ever to hit at least 20 homers and steal at least 20 bases in the same season.

Hitting

Tatis' emerging power didn't surprise the Cardinals. What was even more impressive, though, was that he also hit nearly .300. An aggressive swinger who will strike out frequently, Tatis has learned to cut down his swing with two strikes. He has big-time power when he pulls, but Tatis also has the strength and plate coverage to hit balls out to all fields. Labeled by many scouts as a first-pitch, fastball hitter, Tatis has significantly improved his ability to hit breaking balls. He remains too anxious against offspeed stuff, and his bad habit of overswinging occasionally resurfaces. He's becoming a more disciplined hitter, which should help him avoid the lengthy droughts he experienced at times last year.

Baserunning & Defense

While he may be guilty at times of trying too hard to make things happen on the bases, Tatis emerged as a dangerous basestealer with his above-average speed. Tatis has all the tools to be an outstanding third baseman, as he has an extremely strong arm, good range and very soft hands. Most of his errors come on wild throws from behind the bag.

2000 Outlook

St. Louis has had mixed results with recent acquisitions, but the July trade-deadline deal in 1998 for Tatis could prove to be a steal. He has just started to refine his many skills and his big numbers of last year were no mirage. Tatis could become a perennial All-Star.

Position: 3B
Bats: R **Throws:** R
Ht: 5'10" **Wt:** 170

Opening Day Age: 25
Born: 1/1/75 in San Pedro de Macoris, Dominican Republic
ML Seasons: 3
Pronunciation: tah-TEESE

Overall Statistics

	G	AB	R	H	D	T	HR	RBI	SB	BB	SO	Avg	OBP	Slg
1999	149	537	104	160	31	2	34	107	21	82	128	.298	.404	.553
Career	359	1292	202	364	73	6	53	194	37	132	293	.282	.357	.471

Where He Hits the Ball

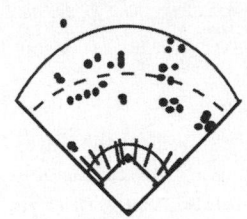

Vs. LHP   **Vs. RHP**

1999 Situational Stats

	AB	H	HR	RBI	Avg		AB	H	HR	RBI	Avg
Home	272	75	16	43	.276	LHP	138	40	10	29	.290
Road	265	85	18	64	.321	RHP	399	120	24	78	.301
First Half	287	83	18	59	.289	Sc Pos	148	49	9	75	.331
Scnd Half	250	77	16	48	.308	Clutch	106	34	4	16	.321

1999 Rankings (National League)

- 1st in batting average with the bases loaded (.692)
- 2nd in hit by pitch (16)
- 5th in most pitches seen per plate appearance (4.10) and errors at third base (16)
- Led the Cardinals in most pitches seen per plate appearance (4.10), batting average in the clutch, batting average with the bases loaded (.692), batting average vs. righthanded pitchers, cleanup slugging percentage (.546), highest percentage of extra bases taken as a runner (57.8), highest percentage of pitches taken (58.6), batting average, caught stealing (9), hit by pitch (16) and pitches seen (2,621)

St. Louis

Manny Aybar

Position: RP
Bats: R **Throws:** R
Ht: 6' 1" **Wt:** 177

Opening Day Age: 25
Born: 10/5/74 in Bani, Dominican Republic
ML Seasons: 3
Pronunciation: EYE-bar

Overall Statistics

	W	L	Pct.	ERA	G	GS	Sv	IP	H	BB	SO	HR	Ratio
1999	4	5	.444	5.47	65	1	3	97.0	104	36	74	13	1.44
Career	12	15	.444	5.30	97	27	3	246.1	260	107	172	27	1.49

1999 Situational Stats

	W	L	ERA	Sv	IP		AB	H	HR	RBI	Avg
Home	1	3	6.71	0	51.0	LHB	141	43	4	23	.305
Road	3	2	4.11	3	46.0	RHB	242	61	9	43	.252
First Half	4	3	3.34	2	67.1	Sc Pos	115	38	5	54	.330
Scnd Half	0	2	10.31	1	29.2	Clutch	138	36	4	22	.261

1999 Season

Once considered a prospect destined for the Cardinals' rotation, Manny Aybar was shifted to long- and middle-relief roles with mixed results in 1999. He posted ERAs of 3.00 and 2.86 in April and June respectively, but otherwise struggled with gopheritis and control problems. Aybar managed four wins and three saves in relief.

Pitching, Defense & Hitting

Because Aybar's command still is lacking at times, his consistency suffers. His fastball is in the low 90s but lacks much life. While he has a good hard slider with late movement, Aybar's offspeed stuff isn't refined. Lefthanders gave him problems all season long in 1999. He makes the routine plays around the mound, but doesn't excel in the field. His pickoff move is average at best and his focus on baserunners is lacking at times when he gets into jams. He's aggressive at the plate but rarely generates a base hit.

2000 Outlook

In their effort to get more proven pitching, the Cardinals packaged Aybar in the offseason deal with Colorado that brought them Darryl Kile and Dave Veres. Pitching in Coors Field won't help his home-run troubles, but Aybar is young and talented enough to develop into a useful pitcher.

Alan Benes

Position: RP
Bats: R **Throws:** R
Ht: 6' 5" **Wt:** 215

Opening Day Age: 28
Born: 1/21/72 in Evansville, IN
ML Seasons: 4
Pronunciation: BENN-ess

Overall Statistics

	W	L	Pct.	ERA	G	GS	Sv	IP	H	BB	SO	HR	Ratio
1999	0	0	-	0.00	2	0	0	2.0	2	0	2	0	1.00
Career	23	21	.523	4.15	62	58	0	370.2	346	159	313	42	1.36

1999 Situational Stats

	W	L	ERA	Sv	IP		AB	H	HR	RBI	Avg
Home	0	0	0.00	0	2.0	LHB	2	0	0	0	.000
Road	—	—	—	—	—	RHB	—	—	—	—	—
First Half	0	0	-	0	0.0	Sc Pos	1	0	0	0	.000
Scnd Half	0	0	0.00	0	2.0	Clutch	0	0	0	0	-

1999 Season

The long road to recovery for Alan Benes finally may be complete. After missing nearly two full seasons following shoulder surgery, Benes was able to make it back to the majors, making two token relief appearances in September.

Pitching, Defense & Hitting

St. Louis must wait until spring to see what Benes can do. Prior to his shoulder troubles, he had a rising fastball in the mid-90s, a hard cutter and a power curveball. His pitching knowledge and control always have been assets. Benes hasn't excelled at hitting or fielding in his brief major league career, but he does a good job of holding runners.

2000 Outlook

With their offseason moves and a core of young pitching prospects on the way, the Cardinals don't have to count on Benes. Yet he could become a major bonus if he returns anywhere close to his previous ability, when he seemed to be an ace in the making. The Cardinals plan on bringing him along slowly this season, preferably working him out of the bullpen as he regains his arm strength and sheds the rust.

Darren Bragg

Position: CF/RF/LF
Bats: L **Throws:** R
Ht: 5' 9" **Wt:** 180

Opening Day Age: 30
Born: 9/7/69 in
Waterbury, CT
ML Seasons: 6

Overall Statistics

	G	AB	R	H	D	T	HR	RBI	SB	BB	SO	Avg	OBP	Slg
1999	93	273	38	71	12	1	6	26	3	44	67	.260	.369	.377
Career	562	1776	252	463	108	9	36	201	41	236	384	.261	.351	.392

1999 Situational Stats

	AB	H	HR	RBI	Avg			AB	H	HR	RBI	Avg
Home	124	32	4	9	.258	LHP		61	14	1	4	.230
Road	149	39	2	17	.262	RHP		212	57	5	22	.269
First Half	236	65	4	22	.275	Sc Pos		65	19	2	21	.292
Scnd Half	37	6	2	4	.162	Clutch		47	9	1	3	.191

1999 Season

St. Louis signed Darren Bragg as a free agent, hoping he could combine with Eric Davis to produce solid numbers in right field. Like Davis, however, Bragg had his year cut short by injury. A torn anterior cruciate ligament in his right knee ended his season in August. Before getting hurt, Bragg had seen action at all three outfield spots, providing occasional offensive spark.

Hitting, Baserunning & Defense

Bragg is best when he's spotted against righthanders. He's a good fastball hitter with surprising power to left-center and occasionally can pull a pitch for power. He always has struggled against lefthanders and breaking balls. Though an aggressive player, Bragg doesn't have the speed to be a stolen-base threat. His arm is too weak to make him a regular right fielder, but he has the range to play any outfield spot without hurting his team. His throws are accurate, especially from left field.

2000 Outlook

As a bit player on a good club, Bragg has value. As St. Louis discovered, Bragg doesn't produce enough to play every day. In December the Cardinals designated him for assignment to make room on the 40-man roster for free-agent catcher Mike Matheny.

Alberto Castillo

Traded To
BLUE JAYS

Position: C
Bats: R **Throws:** R
Ht: 6' 0" **Wt:** 185

Opening Day Age: 30
Born: 2/10/70 in San Juan de la Maguana, Dominican Republic
ML Seasons: 5
Pronunciation: cas-TEE-oh

Overall Statistics

	G	AB	R	H	D	T	HR	RBI	SB	BB	SO	Avg	OBP	Slg
1999	93	255	21	67	8	0	4	31	0	24	48	.263	.326	.341
Career	185	437	40	103	13	0	6	45	1	45	94	.236	.310	.307

1999 Situational Stats

	AB	H	HR	RBI	Avg			AB	H	HR	RBI	Avg
Home	122	32	2	14	.262	LHP		86	15	0	1	.174
Road	133	35	2	17	.263	RHP		169	52	4	30	.308
First Half	118	27	1	9	.229	Sc Pos		82	22	2	29	.268
Scnd Half	137	40	3	22	.292	Clutch		35	4	1	6	.114

1999 Season

A major league Rule 5 draft pickup, Alberto Castillo became the Cardinals' everyday catcher when Eli Marrero couldn't recover from a massive slump. Castillo held his own offensively and had the distinction of catching Jose Jimenez' no-hitter. He set career highs in most categories and got stronger as the season progressed.

Hitting, Baserunning & Defense

Castillo never has been considered much of an offensive threat. He has occasional power when he gets a hanging breaking ball to pull. He still can be overmatched by hard stuff inside and will chase offspeed stuff off the plate. Though he bats righthanded, he struggled against lefthanders while making very good contact versus righties in 1999. Castillo is an excellent receiver who handles pitchers well, possesses a strong arm and an exceptionally quick release. He's a very slow runner.

2000 Outlook

Castillo, Lance Painter and minor league righthander Matt DeWitt were traded to Toronto in November for Pat Hentgen and Paul Spoljaric. With the Blue Jays, Castillo will back up Darrin Fletcher. St. Louis signed free agent Mike Matheny for one year and $800,000. He'll handle reserve duties behind the plate.

St. Louis

Rick Croushore

Traded To ROCKIES

Position: RP
Bats: R **Throws:** R
Ht: 6' 4" **Wt:** 210

Opening Day Age: 29
Born: 8/7/70 in Lakehurst, NJ
ML Seasons: 2
Pronunciation: KRAU-shore

Overall Statistics

	W	L	Pct.	ERA	G	GS	Sv	IP	H	BB	SO	HR	Ratio
1999	3	7	.300	4.14	59	0	3	71.2	68	43	88	9	1.55
Career	3	10	.231	4.50	100	0	11	126.0	112	72	135	15	1.46

1999 Situational Stats

	W	L	ERA	Sv	IP		AB	H	HR	RBI	Avg
Home	2	4	2.06	2	39.1	LHB	121	25	2	20	.207
Road	1	3	6.68	1	32.1	RHB	154	43	7	31	.279
First Half	2	2	2.52	0	39.1	Sc Pos	116	30	8	49	.259
Scnd Half	1	5	6.12	3	32.1	Clutch	152	38	7	31	.250

1999 Season

For the second straight year, Rick Croushore didn't capitalize on an opportunity to be the Cardinals' closer. He suffered seven defeats and blew seven of his 10 save opportunities, and ended up doing most of his work in middle relief and mopup situations. He was terrific in those roles before wearing down in the second half.

Pitching, Defense & Hitting

Croushore can blow away hitters with his heavy sinker and mid-90s four-seam fastball. However, he always has had trouble maintaining a consistent release point. When he can't, his pitches flatten out and he gets hit hard. He has yet to develop a useable offspeed pitch. With his slow delivery home, Croushore is an easy target for basestealers, who are 18-for-22 against him in the last two years.

2000 Outlook

Croushore gets a fresh start in Colorado after being sent to the Rockies in the Darryl Kile deal during the offseason. He has failed to take advantage of an open closer's job the past two years, so his role is uncertain entering spring training. Still, Croushore's hard sinker will come in handy in the thin air of Coors Field. He very well may end up finishing games for Colorado.

Thomas Howard

Position: RF
Bats: B **Throws:** R
Ht: 6' 2" **Wt:** 205

Opening Day Age: 35
Born: 12/11/64 in Middletown, OH
ML Seasons: 10

Overall Statistics

	G	AB	R	H	D	T	HR	RBI	SB	BB	SO	Avg	OBP	Slg
1999	98	195	16	57	10	0	6	28	1	17	26	.292	.353	.436
Career	929	2350	284	627	119	21	38	236	65	158	398	.267	.314	.384

1999 Situational Stats

	AB	H	HR	RBI	Avg		AB	H	HR	RBI	Avg
Home	101	30	3	12	.297	LHP	37	13	1	7	.351
Road	94	27	3	16	.287	RHP	158	44	5	21	.278
First Half	84	21	2	9	.250	Sc Pos	65	19	2	22	.292
Scnd Half	111	36	4	19	.324	Clutch	59	18	2	12	.305

1999 Season

After inking a minor league deal before the 1999 season, veteran outfielder Thomas Howard did a decent job in his customary role as part-time player. Getting most of his playing time in right field and as a pinch-hitter, the switch-hitter batted .351 from the right side.

Hitting, Baserunning & Defense

Howard is clearly best suited to be a spot player. He can drive the occasional early-count fastball for power but he always has chased breaking balls out of the strike zone. He clearly was more comfortable against lefthanders in 1999, though he provided five of his six homers against righties. Howard is just an average outfielder. While his arm is now slightly below average, it still remains fairly accurate. Once a solid basestealer, Howard rarely tries to run anymore.

2000 Outlook

Howard became a free agent at the end of the 1999 season. A classic journeyman, Howard usually ends up sticking somewhere because he can provide workmanlike effort off the bench. He also has developed into a decent pinch-hitter who can help a contender.

Joe McEwing

Position: 2B/LF/CF/RF
Bats: R **Throws:** R
Ht: 5'11" **Wt:** 170

Opening Day Age: 27
Born: 10/19/72 in Bristol, PA
ML Seasons: 2
Nickname: Super Joe

Overall Statistics

	G	AB	R	H	D	T	HR	RBI	SB	BB	SO	Avg	OBP	Slg
1999	152	513	65	141	28	4	9	44	7	41	87	.275	.333	.398
Career	162	533	70	145	29	4	9	45	7	42	90	.272	.330	.392

1999 Situational Stats

	AB	H	HR	RBI	Avg		AB	H	HR	RBI	Avg
Home	239	65	5	15	.272	LHP	154	45	2	11	.292
Road	274	76	4	29	.277	RHP	359	96	7	33	.267
First Half	325	99	4	30	.305	Sc Pos	121	32	0	33	.264
Scnd Half	188	42	5	14	.223	Clutch	86	24	3	8	.279

1999 Season

For the first three months of the season, Super Joe McEwing was one of baseball's best stories, hustling his way to a spot among the National League's batting leaders. However, his average dropped 82 points in the second half. He lost his everyday second-base job, though he still got plenty of playing time at a variety of positions.

Hitting, Baserunning & Defense

McEwing is a good fastball hitter who can hang in against the hardest throwers. Teams started having success against him by avoiding fastball counts and feeding McEwing a steady diet of offspeed pitches and breaking balls. He has surprising extra-base power for his size. An intelligent baserunner, he has average speed but is aggressive on the bases. Second base probably is his best position, but he can adequately play all three outfield positions as well as first and third base.

2000 Outlook

McEwing's tools are likely too limited for him to be a full-time major league player. Good teams always need a player like him, however, and manager Tony La Russa has the utmost confidence in him. He can play anywhere and pinch-hit, and he gives 100 percent at whatever he's asked to do.

Matt Morris

Position: SP
Bats: R **Throws:** R
Ht: 6'5" **Wt:** 210

Opening Day Age: 25
Born: 8/9/74 in Middletown, NY
ML Seasons: 2

Overall Statistics

	W	L	Pct.	ERA	G	GS	Sv	IP	H	BB	SO	HR	Ratio
1999					Did Not Play								
Career	19	14	.576	2.97	50	50	0	330.2	309	111	228	20	1.27

1999 Situational Stats

	W	L	ERA	Sv	IP		AB	H	HR	RBI	Avg
Home	—	—	—	—	—	LHB	—	—	—	—	—
Road	—	—	—	—	—	RHB	—	—	—	—	—
First Half	—	—	—	—	—	Sc Pos	—	—	—	—	—
Scnd Half	—	—	—	—	—	Clutch	—	—	—	—	—

1999 Season

Nothing was more devastating for St. Louis last season than losing Matt Morris. The impressive young pitcher went down with a season-ending elbow injury in late March and had Tommy John surgery the first week in April. He began long toss early in October and spent the winter in Florida rehabilitating his right elbow.

Pitching, Defense & Hitting

Before being injured, Morris had it all: a 95-MPH four-seam fastball, a lively two-seamer, a big-breaking overhand curve and an improving straight changeup. He threw strikes with all of his pitches, and had exceptional command and poise for young pitcher. Morris had a fairly slow delivery home, and runners took advantage. He was an average fielder and a passable hitter.

2000 Outlook

Morris will need a full 18 months to recover from his elbow surgery. The Cardinals don't expect him to pitch in a game until midseason, and he's not likely to pitch in St. Louis until late in the year, if at all. The good news is that many pitchers are coming back from Tommy John surgery these days stronger than they were before.

St. Louis

Donovan Osborne

Position: SP
Bats: L **Throws:** L
Ht: 6' 2" **Wt:** 210

Opening Day Age: 30
Born: 6/21/69 in
Roseville, CA
ML Seasons: 7

Overall Statistics

	W	L	Pct.	ERA	G	GS	Sv	IP	H	BB	SO	HR	Ratio
1999	1	3	.250	5.52	6	6	0	29.1	34	10	21	4	1.50
Career	47	45	.511	3.92	143	138	0	840.0	851	231	535	96	1.29

1999 Situational Stats

	W	L	ERA	Sv	IP			AB	H	HR	RBI	Avg
Home	0	2	6.57	0	12.1	LHB		9	2	0	2	.222
Road	1	1	4.76	0	17.0	RHB		105	32	4	14	.305
First Half	1	3	5.52	0	29.1	Sc Pos		35	12	1	13	.343
Scnd Half	0	0	-	0	0.0	Clutch		0	0	0	0	-

1999 Season

Injuries resulted in Donovan Osborne being the Cardinals' Opening Day pitcher. It was all downhill from there, though, as Osborne ended up making only six ineffective starts before having his season shut down by shoulder problems. In late May he had arthroscopic surgery to relieve arthritic pain in the joint.

Pitching & Defense

If he ever could stay healthy, Osborne has the stuff to be a big winner. He moves his low-90s fastball around the strike zone and has an excellent changeup, which he can turn over and sink away from righthanders. He also throws a slider, which he tends to hang, and he's prone to nibbling and running long counts. Osborne has an excellent pickoff move to first and can swing the bat.

2000 Outlook

Osborne isn't expected to pitch until late spring. And because he has worked a total of just 193.1 innings the past three seasons, he's a high-risk investment for any team. The Cardinals kept hoping for a return to his 1996 form, but they finally gave up on him. They won't re-sign him as a free agent.

Placido Polanco

Position: 2B
Bats: R **Throws:** R
Ht: 5'10" **Wt:** 168

Opening Day Age: 24
Born: 10/10/75 in Santo Domingo, Dominican Republic
ML Seasons: 2
Pronunciation:
PLAH-see-doh
poh-LAHNK-oh

Overall Statistics

	G	AB	R	H	D	T	HR	RBI	SB	BB	SO	Avg	OBP	Slg
1999	88	220	24	61	9	3	1	19	1	15	24	.277	.321	.359
Career	133	334	34	90	12	5	2	30	3	20	33	.269	.311	.353

1999 Situational Stats

	AB	H	HR	RBI	Avg		AB	H	HR	RBI	Avg
Home	114	29	0	10	.254	LHP	81	28	1	7	.346
Road	106	32	1	9	.302	RHP	139	33	0	12	.237
First Half	157	43	0	15	.274	Sc Pos	57	16	0	18	.281
Scnd Half	63	18	1	4	.286	Clutch	38	12	0	6	.316

1999 Season

Placido Polanco is one of several players with whom the Cardinals have attempted to plug their second-base hole. Polanco played much of the second half, especially against lefthanders, whom he hit .346 against. While his batting average appeared solid, it was a very unproductive .277.

Hitting, Baserunning & Defense

Polanco has a fairly quick bat and can do damage against fastballs. He has little extra-base pop but usually can be counted on to put the ball into play. Polanco has average speed and doesn't have good basestealing instincts, making poor decisions at times. He can play any infield position, though most of his experience is at second. He covers more ground going to his right, but erratic throws have hurt his effectiveness at times.

2000 Outlook

Though Polanco has some offensive potential, he hasn't shown much of it. He had hoped to win the Cards' second-base job this spring, but the December trade for Fernando Vina removed that possibility. Unless he makes progress soon, Polanco will be a utilityman for the rest of his career.

Other St. Louis Cardinals

Juan Acevedo (Pos: RHP, Age: 29)

	W	L	Pct.	ERA	G	GS	Sv	IP	H	BB	SO	HR	Ratio
1999	6	8	.429	5.89	50	12	4	102.1	115	48	52	17	1.59
Career	21	18	.538	4.61	142	34	19	314.0	332	119	181	45	1.44

Acevedo started 1999 as the St. Louis closer, but after a couple of beatings while blowing saves in early May, he was moved to the rotation. He was traded to the Brewers for Fernando Vina in December. 2000 Outlook: B

Mike Busby (Pos: RHP, Age: 27)

	W	L	Pct.	ERA	G	GS	Sv	IP	H	BB	SO	HR	Ratio
1999	0	1	.000	7.13	15	0	0	17.2	21	14	7	2	1.98
Career	5	6	.455	6.48	45	6	0	82.0	99	37	50	11	1.66

Busby made the Opening Day roster, bounced back and forth between Triple-A and St. Louis, but by the All-Star break he was solidly lodged in the minors. Milwaukee has signed him to a minor league deal. 2000 Outlook: C

Rick Heiserman (Pos: RHP, Age: 27)

	W	L	Pct.	ERA	G	GS	Sv	IP	H	BB	SO	HR	Ratio
1999	0	0	-	8.31	3	0	0	4.1	8	4	4	2	2.77
Career	0	0	-	8.31	3	0	0	4.1	8	4	4	2	2.77

Heiserman has been a closer in the minors, though a hittable one. He had 20 saves and a 5.11 ERA in Triple-A in 1999, and his taste of the bigs included a beating in a 17-1 Giants win on May 25. 2000 Outlook: C

David Howard (Pos: SS, Age: 33, Bats: B)

	G	AB	R	H	D	T	HR	RBI	SB	BB	SO	Avg	OBP	Slg
1999	52	82	3	17	4	0	1	6	0	7	27	.207	.286	.293
Career	645	1583	169	362	57	14	11	148	23	137	311	.229	.291	.303

Howard missed nearly half the season with right groin and left hamstring ailments. He wasn't offered arbitration, and the man who played seven positions in 1999 became a free agent. 2000 Outlook: C

Marcus Jensen (Pos: C, Age: 27, Bats: B)

	G	AB	R	H	D	T	HR	RBI	SB	BB	SO	Avg	OBP	Slg
1999	16	34	5	8	5	0	1	1	0	6	12	.235	.350	.471
Career	65	140	15	25	8	0	2	9	0	22	49	.179	.290	.279

A solid defender, Jensen belatedly posted his best average (.291) and slugging percentage (.519) of his career in Triple-A last year. He had just eight homers and 44 RBI, but got a September look in St. Louis. The highlight of his summer came when he was a hero for Team USA at the Pan American Games. 2000 Outlook: C

Curtis King (Pos: RHP, Age: 29)

	W	L	Pct.	ERA	G	GS	Sv	IP	H	BB	SO	HR	Ratio
1999	0	0	-	18.00	2	0	0	1.0	3	0	1	0	3.00
Career	6	2	.750	3.43	68	0	2	81.1	91	31	42	5	1.50

King has posted Triple-A ERAs under three for three straight seasons. He went on the disabled list with a bad shoulder a few days after his June recall and never made it back. 2000 Outlook: B

Larry Luebbers (Pos: RHP, Age: 30)

	W	L	Pct.	ERA	G	GS	Sv	IP	H	BB	SO	HR	Ratio
1999	3	3	.500	5.12	8	8	0	45.2	46	16	16	8	1.36
Career	5	8	.385	4.76	22	22	0	123.0	120	54	54	15	1.41

Luebbers had his winningest season in 1999, going 13-4, 4.03 in Triple-A. But he was barely average in his first big league shot since '93. He has signed with the Reds. 2000 Outlook: C

Willie McGee (Pos: RF/LF/CF, Age: 41, Bats: B)

	G	AB	R	H	D	T	HR	RBI	SB	BB	SO	Avg	OBP	Slg
1999	132	271	25	68	7	0	0	20	7	17	60	.251	.293	.277
Career	2201	7649	1010	2254	350	94	79	856	352	448	1238	.295	.333	.396

McGee retired following the 1999 campaign, closing a career that included a World Series championship in 1982, an MVP Award in 1985 and two National League batting titles. 2000 Outlook: D

Mike Mohler (Pos: LHP, Age: 31)

	W	L	Pct.	ERA	G	GS	Sv	IP	H	BB	SO	HR	Ratio
1999	1	1	.500	4.38	48	0	1	49.1	47	23	31	3	1.42
Career	13	25	.342	4.70	310	20	10	383.1	387	208	264	40	1.55

Mohler struggled in the first half, but replaced an injured Scott Radinsky in July. Mohler had a 2.60 ERA in the second half and pitched very effectively against lefties. 2000 Outlook: B

Luis Ordaz (Pos: SS, Age: 24, Bats: R)

	G	AB	R	H	D	T	HR	RBI	SB	BB	SO	Avg	OBP	Slg
1999	10	9	3	1	0	0	0	2	1	1	2	.111	.200	.111
Career	79	184	15	38	6	0	0	11	6	14	22	.207	.263	.239

Ordaz was with the Cards for parts of April and September, but spent the rest of 1999 in Triple-A. While he hit .285, Ordaz showed little pop or plate patience there. His glove is his ticket, and he was traded to the shortstop-needy Diamondbacks for Dante Powell in December. 2000 Outlook: C

Lance Painter (Pos: LHP, Age: 32)

	W	L	Pct.	ERA	G	GS	Sv	IP	H	BB	SO	HR	Ratio
1999	4	5	.444	4.83	56	4	1	63.1	63	25	56	6	1.39
Career	22	16	.579	5.22	227	26	3	336.1	372	131	247	47	1.50

Painter once again was the primary southpaw reliever in the St. Louis pen, holding lefty hitters to a .222 average in 1999. He joins the Toronto staff after changing teams in the Pat Hentgen trade. 2000 Outlook: B

Craig Paquette (Pos: RF, Age: 31, Bats: R)

	G	AB	R	H	D	T	HR	RBI	SB	BB	SO	Avg	OBP	Slg
1999	48	157	21	45	6	0	10	37	1	6	38	.287	.309	.516
Career	474	1582	188	376	73	7	65	232	19	65	412	.238	.268	.416

While Paquette won't get the at-bats to hit the 22 homers he delivered for the Royals in 1996, he can be a useful bench player with pop. 2000 Outlook: B

St. Louis

Eduardo Perez (**Pos**: LF, **Age**: 30, **Bats**: R)

	G	AB	R	H	D	T	HR	RBI	SB	BB	SO	Avg	OBP	Slg
1999	21	32	6	11	2	0	1	9	0	7	6	.344	.462	.500
Career	348	917	113	219	41	3	34	149	13	95	213	.239	.314	.401

After batting .320-18-82 in Triple-A , Perez continued to hit well after a September callup. Mark McGwire is standing in his way at first base, so Perez played in left field in September. 2000 Outlook: C

Scott Radinsky (**Pos**: LHP, **Age**: 32)

	W	L	Pct.	ERA	G	GS	Sv	IP	H	BB	SO	HR	Ratio
1999	2	1	.667	4.88	43	0	3	27.2	27	18	17	2	1.63
Career	42	25	.627	3.34	554	0	52	479.2	457	205	355	31	1.38

After posting sub-3.00 ERAs for three straight seasons, Radinsky had an off year in 1999. In July he was sidelined with an elbow ailment that led to surgery to remove bone spurs. 2000 Outlook: B

Heathcliff Slocumb (**Pos**: RHP, **Age**: 33)

	W	L	Pct.	ERA	G	GS	Sv	IP	H	BB	SO	HR	Ratio
1999	3	2	.600	3.77	50	0	2	62.0	64	39	60	5	1.66
Career	26	33	.441	3.97	483	0	97	562.1	567	321	467	29	1.58

In 1999, Slocumb rebounded from two bad seasons in which he collectively went 2-14, 5.24. He's not likely to close games again, but the Cards re-signed him to a two-year, $3.45 million contract in November. 2000 Outlook: B

Clint Sodowsky (**Pos**: RHP, **Age**: 27)

	W	L	Pct.	ERA	G	GS	Sv	IP	H	BB	SO	HR	Ratio
1999	0	1	.000	15.63	3	1	0	6.1	15	6	2	1	3.32
Career	8	14	.364	6.17	106	20	0	183.2	214	117	118	21	1.80

Sodowsky's 1997 stint with Pittsburgh (3.63 ERA with five holds in 45 games) was his best in the majors. He has done little since then to establish himself as a big leaguer. 2000 Outlook: C

Garrett Stephenson (**Pos**: RHP, **Age**: 28)

	W	L	Pct.	ERA	G	GS	Sv	IP	H	BB	SO	HR	Ratio
1999	6	3	.667	4.22	18	12	0	85.1	90	29	59	11	1.39
Career	14	12	.538	4.39	47	36	0	231.2	238	89	160	26	1.41

Acquired in the 1998 deal that sent Ron Gant to the Phils, Stephenson pitched well in the minors and made 12 starts for the Cards. He was stellar in August but slumped in September. 2000 Outlook: B

Mark Thompson (**Pos**: RHP, **Age**: 28)

	W	L	Pct.	ERA	G	GS	Sv	IP	H	BB	SO	HR	Ratio
1999	1	3	.250	2.76	5	5	0	29.1	26	17	22	1	1.47
Career	17	23	.425	5.80	74	52	0	312.0	380	146	179	51	1.69

After shoulder trouble in 1998, Thompson struggled early on and was released by Cincinnati. He signed with the Cards, posting ERAs of 2.94 in Triple-A and 2.76 in St. Louis. He was a bit lucky stranding runners. 2000 Outlook: B

St. Louis Cardinals Minor League Prospects

Organization Overview:

The Cardinals have very little left in the farm system, though their player-development efforts undoubtedly have bolstered the major league club. In December 1998, they traded three of their best minor leaguers (Armando Almanza, Braden Looper, Pablo Ozuna) to get Edgar Renteria. J.D. Drew and Rick Ankiel entered 1999 as the game's best hitting and pitching prospects, respectively, and were fast-tracked to St. Louis. After the season, the Cardinals included young arms Manny Aybar and Jose Jimenez plus minor league shortstop Brent Butler in a trade with Colorado for Darryl Kile and Dave Veres. They also gave up so-so pitching prospect Matt DeWitt in a deal for Toronto's Pat Hentgen. St. Louis' minor league winning percentage was .442 last year, the worst in baseball, and could dip lower in 2000. But if the big league club can stop underachieving, the ravaging of the system will have been worth it.

Justin Brunette

Position: P   **Opening Day Age:** 24
Bats: L **Throws:** L   **Born:** 10/7/75 in Los
Ht: 6' 1" **Wt:** 200   Alamitos, CA

Recent Statistics

	W	L	ERA	G	GS	Sv	IP	H	R	BB	SO	HR
1999 A Peoria	3	1	1.81	38	0	2	44.2	34	9	16	44	2
1999 AA Arkansas	1	2	1.96	18	0	0	18.1	21	12	7	23	3

Brunette's pro career began rather inauspiciously in 1997. A 20th-round pick out of San Diego State, he posted a 7.94 ERA in the short-season New York-Penn League before having Tommy John surgery that fall. After missing all of 1998, he returned last year and discovered that his velocity had increased. While his fastball peaked at 87 MPH in college, Brunette regularly exceeded that in 1999 and threw as hard as 93 MPH. He also throws a good slider, though it's not a power pitch. It's too early to label him as a potential closer, but the Cardinals believe Brunette at worst will be a good situation lefthanded reliever.

Chris Haas

Position: 3B   **Opening Day Age:** 23
Bats: L **Throws:** R   **Born:** 10/15/76 in
Ht: 6' 2" **Wt:** 210   Paducah, KY

Recent Statistics

	G	AB	R	H	D	T	HR	RBI	SB	BB	SO	Avg
1998 AA Arkansas	132	445	75	122	27	4	20	83	1	73	129	.274
1999 AAA Memphis	114	397	63	91	19	2	18	73	4	66	155	.229
1999 MLE	114	387	52	81	17	1	15	61	2	55	161	.209

Haas is symptomatic of the lack of depth in the Cardinals system. The organization features several players with an outstanding tool or tools, but they haven't shown an aptitude for playing the game. In Haas' case, he has tremendous raw power that's easily the best among St.

Louis minor leaguers. That's about the extent of his contributions. He hasn't had a big homer season because he doesn't make consistent contact. A 1995 supplemental first-round pick, Haas also has a strong arm. He would have had a brighter future if a conversion to catcher had worked out, but it didn't. He doesn't have the speed to play even left field, and that leaves him playing either first or third base, where he's blocked by Mark McGwire and Fernando Tatis, respectively.

Luther Hackman

Position: P   **Opening Day Age:** 25
Bats: R **Throws:** R   **Born:** 10/10/74 in
Ht: 6' 4" **Wt:** 195   Lawndale, MS

Recent Statistics

	W	L	ERA	G	GS	Sv	IP	H	R	BB	SO	HR
1999 AA Carolina	4	3	4.04	11	10	0	62.1	53	33	28	50	4
1999 AAA ColoSprngs	7	6	3.74	15	15	0	101.0	106	49	44	88	7
1999 NL Colorado	1	2	10.69	5	3	0	16.0	26	19	12	10	5

The least-known player in the trade that sent Manny Aybar, Rick Croushore, Jose Jimenez and minor league shortstop Brent Butler to Colorado in November for Darryl Kile and Dave Veres, Hackman could be a sleeper. He allowed just seven homers in 101 innings for Triple-A Colorado Springs, where the ball jumps out of the park like it does at nearby Coors Field. A 1994 sixth-round pick, he throws a low-90s fastball, a hard slider and a changeup. His size and stuff remind scouts of Jim Bibby. Hackman's control has been spotty, and though he finally enjoyed success as a starter in 1999, his long-term future may be as a reliever.

Chad Hutchinson

Position: P   **Opening Day Age:** 23
Bats: R **Throws:** R   **Born:** 2/21/77 in Del
Ht: 6' 5" **Wt:** 220   Mar, CA

Recent Statistics

	W	L	ERA	G	GS	Sv	IP	H	R	BB	SO	HR
1998 A New Jersey	0	1	3.52	3	3	0	15.1	15	7	4	20	0
1998 A Pr William	2	0	2.79	5	5	0	29.0	20	12	11	31	4
1999 AA Arkansas	7	11	4.72	25	25	0	141.0	127	79	85	150	12
1999 AAA Memphis	2	0	2.19	2	2	0	12.1	4	3	8	16	2

Hutchinson is easily the best Cardinals prospect who will start 2000 in the minors. Drafted in 1995's first-round by the Braves, he instead opted to play football and baseball for Stanford, where he was named MVP of the 1996 Sun Bowl. Signability questions let Hutchinson slide until the second round of the 1998 draft, but the Cardinals didn't have any trouble getting him to agree to a $3.4 million major league contract. He's a pure power pitcher, featuring a mid-90s fastball and an unhittable slider. Hutchinson is still learning how to pitch, and he needs better command of his fastball and an improved changeup. He'll work on those goals in Triple-A this year and will reach St. Louis as soon as he achieves them.

Adam Kennedy

Position: 2B
Bats: L **Throws:** R
Ht: 6' 1" **Wt:** 180

Opening Day Age: 24
Born: 1/10/76 in
Riverside, CA

Recent Statistics

	G	AB	R	H	D	T	HR	RBI	SB	BB	SO	Avg
1999 AAA Memphis	91	367	69	120	22	4	10	63	20	29	36	.327
1999 NL St. Louis	33	102	12	26	10	1	1	16	0	3	8	.255
1999 MLE	91	354	57	107	20	2	8	52	15	24	37	.302

Last year Kennedy was the only player to participate in the Futures Game, the Triple-A All-Star Game and the Pan American Games. At the Pan Am Games, he led Team USA with a .367 average and helped it qualify for the 2000 Olympics. A 1997 first-round pick out of Cal State Northridge, Kennedy has hit .309 in the minors. He has a quick bat and surprising pop, and he uses the entire field. He's an aggressive runner and was named the Triple-A Pacific Coast League's best defensive second baseman last year. The Fernando Vina deal probably means that Kennedy will get more time in Triple-A.

Jose Leon

Position: 3B
Bats: R **Throws:** R
Ht: 6' 0" **Wt:** 160

Opening Day Age: 23
Born: 12/8/76 in
Caguas, Puerto Rico

Recent Statistics

	G	AB	R	H	D	T	HR	RBI	SB	BB	SO	Avg
1998 A Pr William	124	436	77	127	31	3	21	74	5	53	137	.291
1999 AA Arkansas	112	335	37	78	17	0	18	54	3	25	114	.233
1999 MLE	112	327	31	70	15	0	15	45	2	17	120	.214

Leon is another St. Louis prospect whose tools have been far more impressive than his performance. In his first taste of Double-A last year, he batted .233 and had a 114-25 strikeout-walk ratio, a disappointing encore to all-star seasons in Class-A leagues in 1997 and 1998. A 22nd-round pick in 1994, Leon has power but won't fully tap it until he makes adjustments at the plate. Similarly, he has a tremendous throwing arm but needs to work to overcome poor footwork and lackluster range at third base. The Cardinals may try him in the outfield, considerig that they're set at third with Fernando Tatis.

Luis Saturria

Position: OF
Bats: R **Throws:** R
Ht: 6' 2" **Wt:** 165

Opening Day Age: 23
Born: 7/21/76 in San
Pedro de Macoris, D.R.

Recent Statistics

	G	AB	R	H	D	T	HR	RBI	SB	BB	SO	Avg
1998 A Pr William	129	462	70	136	25	9	12	73	26	28	104	.294
1999 AA Arkansas	139	484	66	118	30	4	16	61	16	35	134	.244
1999 MLE	139	471	55	105	27	2	13	51	11	24	142	.223

Saturria may have the best all-around tools in the system, but he struggled mightily in his first Double-A season. In some respects, the Cardinals were just happy to have him after temporarily losing him to the Blue Jays in the 1997 major league Rule 5 draft. He has the quick bat to hit for average and at least gap power, though he won't do either unless he's more selective at the plate. He's very fast but

needs to improve his reads and jumps to become an effective basestealer. His speed and arm are an asset in the outfield, where he could fit in either center or right. Saturria probably will repeat Double-A to start this year.

Jason Woolf

Position: SS
Bats: B **Throws:** R
Ht: 6' 1" **Wt:** 170

Opening Day Age: 22
Born: 6/6/77 in Miami, FL

Recent Statistics

	G	AB	R	H	D	T	HR	RBI	SB	BB	SO	Avg
1998 AA Arkansas	76	294	63	78	22	5	4	16	28	34	84	.265
1999 AA Arkansas	86	320	46	87	18	4	8	15	11	28	86	.272
1999 MLE	86	310	38	77	16	2	6	12	7	19	90	.248

Jason Woolf has been hailed as the fastest Cardinal since Vince Coleman, but since signing as a 1995 second-round pick, he has been more brittle than Steve Ontiveros. Woolf's litany of physical ailments includes injuries to his shoulder, hamstrings, quadriceps and groin, as well as migraine headaches. And that doesn't include 1999, when a sore elbow sidelined him in spring training and he later missed time with hamstring problems and the second broken finger of his career. He has played just 371 games in five pro seasons and just hasn't gotten the experience he needs to improve. Woolf was rated the fastest baserunner in the Double-A Texas League last year and is a huge stolen-base threat—when he's fully healthy. He has fine range and a strong arm at shortstop, though he needs to hone his offensive skills if he's to bat at the top of a lineup. Ticketed for Triple-A in 2000, Woolf is blocked by Edgar Renteria in St. Louis.

Others to Watch

Righthander **John Ambrose** (25), acquired from the White Sox for Sean Lowe in a preseason trade, has a 93-96 MPH fastball and a good curveball. The Cardinals think he'll have more success in the bullpen, where he moved in the second half last year. . . Righthander **Chance Caple** (21), St. Louis' first-round pick last June, has wildly inconsistent stuff. His fastball fluctuated from 86-96 MPH at Texas A&M, and his curveball is probably his best pitch. . . **Ben Johnson** (18) might have been a steal as a 1999 fourth-rounder. He's a five-tool right fielder who hit .330 with 10 homers and 14 steals in 57 games in the Rookie-level Appalachian League. . . Lefthander **Bud Smith** (20) isn't physically imposing, but he throws three pitches for strikes, including a quality changeup. He had a 2.92 ERA in 157.1 Class-A innings last year, notching more strikeouts (152) than he allowed hits (144). . . Righthander **Nick Stocks** (21), a 1999 supplemental first-rounder, has made a successful recovery from Tommy John surgery. He throws a 90-92 MPH fastball and a hard curveball. . . After winning the Appy League batting title in his first pro season in 1998, shortstop **Jack Wilson** (22) hit .319 in Class-A last year. He doesn't have much in the way of tools, but he runs aggressively and makes the plays at short.

Qualcomm Stadium

Offense

No National League park suppresses scoring to the extent that Qualcomm Stadium does. Though batters reach the fences with regularity, a ball that stays in the park is more likely to be turned into an out there than in any other stadium. The park is at sea level, which should help make it more favorable for pitchers, but that effect is usually seen in the suppression of home runs. Instead, Qualcomm cuts down all types of hits *except* home runs. Perhaps the park's tendencies are the result of a poor hitter's background or subpar lighting.

Defense

Qualcomm is known for its fast infield, with the grass playing almost like artificial turf. Infielders must have soft hands to stop some of the shots that skid across the grass, and Chris Gomez is perfectly suited to the park in this regard. The wedges of foul territory near the poles can create challenges for the corner outfielders, who can lose sight of much of the field while chasing balls in there.

Who It Helps The Most

The majority of Padres pitchers derive an immense benefit from Qualcomm. Donne Wall is the most extreme case, allowing just nine earned runs in 74 innings there the last two years. Among the starters, Sterling Hitchcock has been the most Qualcomm-aided. The type of hitter that seems to do well there are true power hitters, like Gary Sheffield and Barry Bonds.

Who It Hurts The Most

Almost all hitters, including mid-range power hitters, tend to feel the park's effect. Steve Finley, who had pretty fair home-run power, lost a good chunk of offense to the park in his days with the Padres. Among the current Padres, Ruben Rivera is hurt the most.

Rookies & Newcomers

The Padres don't figure to have many rookies who'll make an impact this season. The park will continue to work against Ben Davis' offensive development, while providing a forgiving home for young hurlers Matt Clement, Carlton Loewer and Brian Meadows.

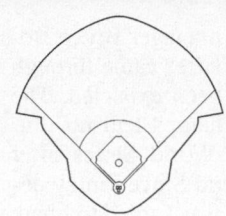

Dimensions: LF-327, LCF-370, CF-405, RCF-370, RF-330

Capacity: 46,510

Elevation: 20 feet

Surface: Grass

Foul Territory: Large

Park Factors

1999 Season

	Home Games			Away Games			
	Padres	Opp	Total	Padres	Opp	Total	Index
G	71	71	142	76	76	152	—
Avg	.270	.252	.261	.239	.286	.262	99
AB	2344	2431	4775	2566	2535	5101	100
R	336	311	647	329	425	754	92
H	632	612	1244	614	725	1339	99
2B	106	114	220	127	120	247	95
3B	16	10	26	5	18	23	121
HR	65	78	143	81	100	181	84
BB	288	212	500	271	264	535	100
SO	503	500	1003	550	469	1019	105
E	54	56	110	65	52	117	101
E-Infield	48	46	94	54	43	97	104
LHB-Avg	.293	.256	.275	.255	.309	.282	97
LHB-HR	18	22	40	19	38	57	72
RHB-Avg	.252	.249	.251	.229	.271	.250	100
RHB-HR	47	56	103	62	62	124	92

1997-1999

	Home Games			Away Games			
	Padres	Opp	Total	Padres	Opp	Total	Index
G	217	217	434	225	225	450	—
Avg	.256	.249	.252	.258	.284	.271	93
AB	7185	7514	14699	7783	7609	15392	99
R	956	917	1873	1076	1177	2253	86
H	1839	1871	3710	2010	2160	4170	92
2B	326	315	641	404	403	807	83
3B	29	31	60	35	54	89	71
HR	207	218	425	228	233	461	97
BB	824	634	1458	841	799	1640	93
SO	1520	1621	3141	1555	1430	2985	110
E	151	160	311	179	153	332	97
E-Infield	130	134	264	149	126	275	100
LHB-Avg	.274	.254	.264	.280	.293	.286	92
LHB-HR	82	77	159	101	84	185	91
RHB-Avg	.241	.246	.243	.239	.277	.259	94
RHB-HR	125	141	266	127	149	276	100

1999 Rankings (National League)
- Did not rank at the top or bottom of any category

San Diego

Bruce Bochy

1999 Season

Last season was undoubtedly manager Bruce Bochy's toughest year, and the Padres came through it as smoothly as could have been expected. The defending National League champs had no illusions about returning to the World Series after Kevin Brown, Ken Caminiti and Steve Finley departed via free agency. Bochy was forced to break in untested rookies at several positions simultaneously. The club also suffered debilitating injuries to regulars Tony Gwynn, Carlos Hernandez and Wally Joyner. Despite all the adversity, Bochy was able to keep morale from sinking through the floor.

Offense

Last season revealed little about Bochy's offensive tendencies. Between the injuries and the overall lack of talent, he had very few options. Generally, he favors a set lineup and prefers to use his extra bench spots for pinch-hitters rather than platoon players. He's patient and gives a player a fair chance to succeed before making a change. When Bochy makes a major adjustment, he does so decisively, such as when he pulled the plug on third baseman George Arias last year and installed Phil Nevin there instead.

Pitching & Defense

Bochy always has had a preference for veteran pitchers, and has a flair for getting good performances out of rather nondescript veterans like Brian Boehringer and Carlos Reyes. He keeps his pitchers within their physical limits, and they have an excellent record of staying healthy for him. Bochy puts a premium on sound defensive play, and his teams almost always have excellent glove men up the middle. Last year, he gave considerable playing time to Ruben Rivera and Damian Jackson, each of whom played good defense but contributed almost nothing at the plate.

2000 Outlook

The Padres aren't close to getting back into contention, so the focus is on the development of their young players. It will be a challenge for Bochy to keep the club on the rise when many of his players are on the decline.

Born: 4/16/55 in Landes de Bussac, France

Playing Experience: 1978-1987, Hou, NYM, SD

Managerial Experience: 5 seasons
Pronunciation: BOE-chee

Manager Statistics

Year	Team, Lg	W	L	Pct	GB	Finish
1999	San Diego, NL	74	88	.457	26.0	4th West
5 Seasons		409	383	.516	—	—

1999 Starting Pitchers by Days Rest

	<=3	4	5	6+
Padres Starts	0	80	60	14
Padres ERA	0.00	4.81	3.97	4.01
NL Avg Starts	3	81	48	21
NL ERA	4.84	4.53	4.72	4.98

1999 Situational Stats

	Bruce Bochy	NL Average
Hit & Run Success %	39.1	33.6
Stolen Base Success %	72.2	70.2
Platoon Pct.	60.2	55.2
Defensive Subs	21	25
High-Pitch Outings	4	13
Quick/Slow Hooks	19/12	16/15
Sacrifice Attempts	60	89

1999 Rankings (National League)

- 1st in stolen base attempts (241), steals of second base (141) and steals of home plate (5)
- 2nd in double steals (15)
- 3rd in steals of third base (28), hit-and-run percentage (39.1%), intentional walks (39), starting lineups used (137) and pinch-hitters used (298)

Andy Ashby

Traded To

PHILLIES

Position: SP
Bats: R **Throws:** R
Ht: 6' 5" **Wt:** 202

Opening Day Age: 32
Born: 7/11/67 in Kansas City, MO
ML Seasons: 9

1999 Season

The offseason departure of Kevin Brown left Andy Ashby to assume the mantle as the ace of the San Diego staff. For the second straight year, Ashby had a strong first half only to wear down in the season's last two months. It was a fine campaign nonetheless, as Ashby went 14-10 for a team that finished 14 games under .500. He missed a few starts with a disc problem but was otherwise durable.

Pitching

Ashby's bread-and-butter pitch is a hard, two-seam fastball that rides in on righthanders' fists. He gets plenty of jam shots and weak grounders with it, and mixes it well with a four-seamer, a splitter and a slider. Because his pitches have excellent life, he can afford to go right at hitters. It's tough to get much loft on the ball against him, as he works down in the strike zone to begin with and his two-seamer produces mostly groundballs. He's so efficient that he has no problem pitching into the seventh inning on a consistent basis.

Defense & Hitting

Ashby expects to be an active participant in the infield defense and does a good job of getting to grounders back up the middle. He annually places among the leaders in total chances at his position. Though he sometimes hurries his throws, he makes few errors and isn't afraid to go for the out at second base. He has a fair pickoff move and isn't a particularly easy target for basestealers. Ashby can bunt but is a poor hitter.

2000 Outlook

San Diego is looking to reduce payroll, and because Ashby is one of the club's most marketable and expensive players, he was traded to the Phillies for righthanders Adam Eaton, Carlton Loewer and Steve Montgomery. Pitching behind Curt Schilling, Ashby should give the Phillies one of the best No. 2 starters in baseball. He'll head the Philadelphia rotation until Schilling returns from shoulder surgery.

Overall Statistics

	W	L	Pct.	ERA	G	GS	Sv	IP	H	BB	SO	HR	Ratio
1999	14	10	.583	3.80	31	31	0	206.0	204	54	132	26	1.25
Career	72	74	.493	3.98	223	210	1	1343.0	1357	396	910	146	1.31

How Often He Throws Strikes

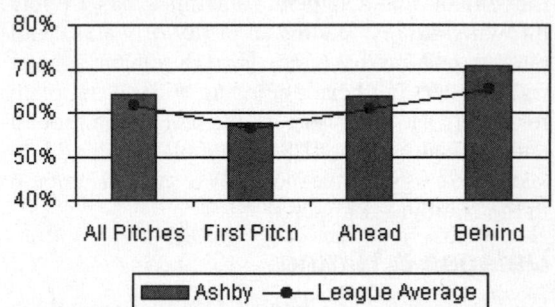

Ashby ——●—— League Average

1999 Situational Stats

	W	L	ERA	Sv	IP		AB	H	HR	RBI	Avg
Home	5	6	4.20	0	100.2	LHB	356	100	9	35	.281
Road	9	4	3.42	0	105.1	RHB	434	104	17	50	.240
First Half	8	4	3.19	0	104.1	Sc Pos	179	46	5	56	.257
Scnd Half	6	6	4.43	0	101.2	Clutch	69	27	3	11	.391

1999 Rankings (National League)

- 1st in shutouts (3)
- 5th in complete games (4)
- Led the Padres in sacrifice bunts (7), ERA, wins, complete games (4), shutouts (3), stolen bases allowed (23), winning percentage, lowest slugging percentage allowed (.406), lowest on-base percentage allowed (.311), highest groundball/flyball ratio allowed (2.0), fewest pitches thrown per batter (3.54), fewest baserunners allowed per 9 innings (11.6), walks per 9 innings (2.4) and ERA on the road

San Diego

Matt Clement

1999 Season

Heralded rookie pitcher Matt Clement got off to a terrible start and carried a dismal 6-12 record as late as September. He closed with a rush, however, winning his last four decisions to finish with a decent record and an ERA below the National League average. For a first-year pitcher on a weak club, his season was fairly encouraging.

Pitching

Clement's pitches have so much life that his arsenal has been compared to Kevin Brown's. Clement throws a sinking two-seam fastball that runs down and in to righthanders, a slurve with good drop, and a change. The two-seamer and slurve have so much movement that Clement sometimes has trouble throwing strikes, leading to plenty of walks, wild pitches and hit batsmen. He's dominant against righthanders but hasn't come up with an out pitch for lefties. He always keeps the ball on the ground and the Padres turned 28 double plays behind him last year, a figure exceeded only by Mike Hampton in the National League.

Defense & Hitting

For a young pitcher, Clement does an excellent job of combating the running game. He has a decent move to first and is quick to the plate. Only 11 baserunners tried to run on him last year, and five of them were cut down. He's a decent fielder but a truly awful hitter, contributing nothing beyond an occasional bunt.

2000 Outlook

All signs point to continuing improvement from Clement. He's young, has excellent stuff and hasn't been overworked. If he's able to harness his stuff and come up with a way to keep lefthanders in check, there's no reason he can't become one of the NL's elite pitchers.

Position: SP
Bats: R **Throws:** R
Ht: 6' 3" **Wt:** 195

Opening Day Age: 25
Born: 8/12/74 in McCandless Township, PA
ML Seasons: 2

Overall Statistics

	W	L	Pct.	ERA	G	GS	Sv	IP	H	BB	SO	HR	Ratio
1999	10	12	.455	4.48	31	31	0	180.2	190	86	135	18	1.53
Career	12	12	.500	4.49	35	33	0	194.1	205	93	148	18	1.53

How Often He Throws Strikes

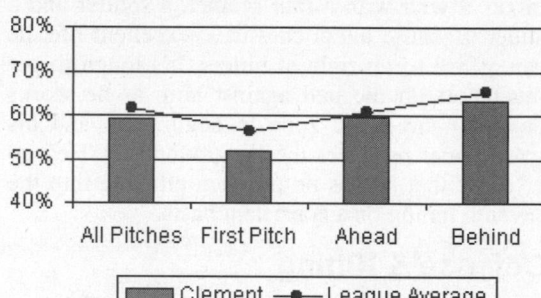

1999 Situational Stats

	W	L	ERA	Sv	IP		AB	H	HR	RBI	Avg
Home	8	5	3.66	0	110.2	LHB	320	102	11	57	.319
Road	2	7	5.79	0	70.0	RHB	375	88	7	31	.235
First Half	5	8	4.78	0	96.0	Sc Pos	183	49	4	67	.268
Scnd Half	5	4	4.15	0	84.2	Clutch	33	7	0	0	.212

1999 Rankings (National League)

- 2nd in GDPs induced (28) and most GDPs induced per 9 innings (1.4)
- 5th in highest walks per 9 innings (4.3)
- 6th in wild pitches (11), most baserunners allowed per 9 innings (14.2) and highest batting average allowed vs. lefthanded batters
- 8th in highest on-base percentage allowed (.358) and highest groundball/flyball ratio allowed (1.9)
- 9th in hit batsmen (9)
- 10th in walks allowed and lowest stolen-base percentage allowed (54.5%)
- Led the Padres in walks allowed, hit batsmen (9), GDPs induced (28), fewest home runs allowed per 9 innings (.90) and most GDPs induced per 9 innings (1.4)

Ben Davis

1999 Season

The second overall pick in the 1995 draft, Ben Davis was called up by the Padres in June and immediately became their regular catcher at age 22. He started hot but fell into a protracted slump late in the year. His defense was an asset all year. While Davis didn't tear up the National League, it's a credit to him that his play wasn't regarded as a disappointment. After all, very few major league catchers are able to make major contributions with both the bat and the glove—especially at Davis' age.

Hitting

Davis is a natural switch-hitter, performing equally well from either side of the plate. His power potential is evident when he lines balls into the gaps, though he's still working on being more selective and making better contact. He may hit better with a little more rest. He wore down late last year and batted .187 over the season's final two months.

Baserunning & Defense

Though Davis' footwork is a little raw, his defense is more advanced than his bat at this point. He has one of the strongest and most accurate throwing arms in the league, and may soon be in Ivan Rodriguez' and Charles Johnson's league as a basestealing deterrent. That would be a major help to the Padres, keeping the double play in order for a staff that features several groundball pitchers. It's safe to say that Davis runs like a catcher—an old catcher, to be specific.

2000 Outlook

Davis may not make the All-Star team this season or even the next, but the Padres unquestionably see him as one of the cornerstones of their rebuilding effort. Many project him as a true two-way player once he matures. For now, he'll help them behind the plate while honing his batting stroke.

Position: C
Bats: B **Throws:** R
Ht: 6' 4" **Wt:** 215

Opening Day Age: 23
Born: 3/10/77 in Chester, PA
ML Seasons: 2

Overall Statistics

	G	AB	R	H	D	T	HR	RBI	SB	BB	SO	Avg	OBP	Slg
1999	76	266	29	65	14	1	5	30	2	25	70	.244	.307	.361
Career	77	267	29	65	14	1	5	30	2	25	70	.243	.306	.360

Where He Hits the Ball

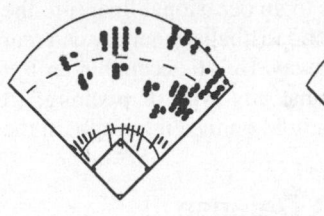
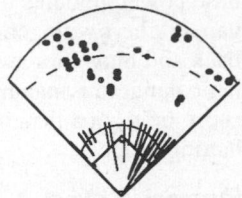

Vs. LHP   **Vs. RHP**

1999 Situational Stats

	AB	H	HR	RBI	Avg		AB	H	HR	RBI	Avg
Home	133	39	1	13	.293	LHP	67	16	1	11	.239
Road	133	26	4	17	.195	RHP	199	49	4	19	.246
First Half	63	18	0	8	.286	Sc Pos	70	14	1	23	.200
Scnd Half	203	47	5	22	.232	Clutch	44	10	0	3	.227

1999 Rankings (National League)
- 1st in lowest batting average with the bases loaded (0.000)
- 4th in errors at catcher (7)

San Diego

Chris Gomez

Position: SS
Bats: R **Throws:** R
Ht: 6' 1" **Wt:** 195

Opening Day Age: 28
Born: 6/16/71 in Los Angeles, CA
ML Seasons: 7

1999 Season

The first year of Chris Gomez' $7.8 million, three-year contract was hardly encouraging. Plagued by pain in both knees from the start of spring training, Gomez saw his range decline and batting average plummet. He finally submitted to surgery in June and returned to action two months later. His hitting subsequently recovered a bit, but his knees weren't up to everyday play.

Hitting

Even when fully healthy, Gomez is little more than a singles hitter without any real offensive strengths. He's reasonably patient, and thus is able to make his on-base percentage halfway respectable as long as he keeps his average up. His extra-base power amounts to an occasional liner into the gap. Pitchers with good fastballs generally can rear back and blow him away. He's a decent bunter but isn't dangerous against any type of pitching. In short, he's got a firm hold on the eighth spot in the batting order.

Baserunning & Defense

Gomez never had great speed and his knee problems have slowed him further. His infrequent attempts at basestealing have grown increasingly futile, as he has been gunned down on 13 of 20 attempts over the last three years. It's his fielding that's kept him in the majors. While neither flashy nor the possessor of great range, Gomez is a fundamentally sound shortstop with soft hands and a quick release. To continue to justify his presence in the lineup, however, he may need to recover the range he lost last year.

2000 Outlook

Having locked Gomez into an expensive long-term deal, there's little the Padres can do but hope he returns to form. There's no guarantee that this will happen, as his knees may remain an ongoing concern. In light of the San Diego's rebuilding effort, Damian Jackson's presence may pose a threat to Gomez' playing time.

Overall Statistics

	G	AB	R	H	D	T	HR	RBI	SB	BB	SO	Avg	OBP	Slg
1999	76	234	20	59	8	1	1	15	1	27	49	.252	.331	.308
Career	761	2516	282	632	126	10	33	267	21	271	511	.251	.328	.349

Where He Hits the Ball

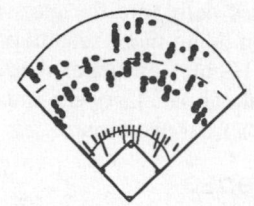

Vs. LHP

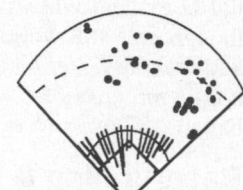

Vs. RHP

1999 Situational Stats

	AB	H	HR	RBI	Avg		AB	H	HR	RBI	Avg
Home	119	34	1	8	.286	LHP	68	20	0	7	.294
Road	115	25	0	7	.217	RHP	166	39	1	8	.235
First Half	108	24	0	3	.222	Sc Pos	38	12	0	14	.316
Scnd Half	126	35	1	12	.278	Clutch	34	6	0	4	.176

1999 Rankings (National League)

- Did not rank near the top or bottom in any category

Tony Gwynn

1999 Season

Leg woes seem to cut into Tony Gwynn's playing time more and more each season, but he just keeps on hitting. Last year, a strained left calf sidelined him from late May until late July, except for an aborted one-week trial in June. When he was in the lineup, he batted .338 to fall only one point short of his career average. That mark would have placed second in the National League had he accumulated enough plate appearances to qualify for the batting championship.

Hitting

No hitter is better at making contact or protecting the plate with two strikes. Gwynn is known for shooting line drives through the left side of the infield. He'll sit on a particular pitch on the first pitch or when he's ahead in the count, and if he gets what he's looking for he can drive the ball from gap to gap. He goes after the first good pitch he sees and almost always gets it, so pitchers have a hard time setting him up.

Baserunning & Defense

Gwynn's persistent leg woes have robbed him of speed and made him tentative in the outfield and on the bases. In 1999, he ranked next to last in putouts per game among major league outfielders for the second straight year. He's a surehanded fielder, though, and throws with decent strength and good accuracy.

2000 Outlook

Now going on age 40, how much longer can Gwynn hold up? Chances are, like John Kruk, his body will wear out before his batting eye will. Another 500 at-bat season may be too much to ask. Over the next couple of years, Gwynn may be eased into a fourth outfielder/pinch-hitter role, the way Willie McGee was late in his career. That said, Gwynn's bat is as healthy as ever and his career is far from over.

Position: RF
Bats: L **Throws:** L
Ht: 5'11" **Wt:** 220

Opening Day Age: 39
Born: 5/9/60 in Los Angeles, CA
ML Seasons: 18

Overall Statistics

	G	AB	R	H	D	T	HR	RBI	SB	BB	SO	Avg	OBP	Slg
1999	111	411	59	139	27	0	10	62	7	29	14	.338	.381	.477
Career	2333	9059	1361	3067	522	84	133	1104	318	771	421	.339	.389	.459

Where He Hits the Ball

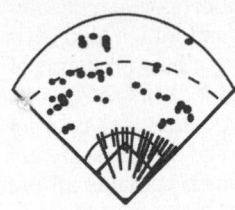 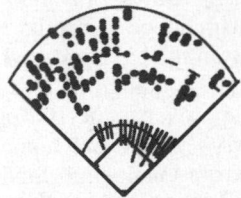

Vs. LHP   **Vs. RHP**

1999 Situational Stats

	AB	H	HR	RBI	Avg		AB	H	HR	RBI	Avg
Home	203	69	5	31	.340	LHP	139	45	6	26	.324
Road	208	70	5	31	.337	RHP	272	94	4	36	.346
First Half	160	54	3	20	.338	Sc Pos	97	40	7	55	.412
Scnd Half	251	85	7	42	.339	Clutch	62	19	2	17	.306

1999 Rankings (National League)

- 1st in batting average on a 3-2 count (.500), batting average with two strikes (.296) and fielding percentage in right field (.993)
- 2nd in batting average with runners in scoring position
- Led the Padres in hits, singles, doubles, GDPs (15), batting average with runners in scoring position, batting average in the clutch, batting average vs. lefthanded pitchers, batting average on a 3-2 count (.500) and batting average with two strikes (.296)
- Led NL right fielders in batting average on a 3-2 count (.500) and batting average with two strikes (.296)

San Diego

Sterling Hitchcock

1999 Season

Following a rocky start, Sterling Hitchcock rebounded to post one of his better seasons. He pitched a career-high 205.2 innings, allaying fears that his elbow woes would return after his extra postseason work in 1998. He also proved that his fine work in 1998 was no fluke. When he's healthy and has his full arsenal, Hitchcock is one of the better lefthanders in the National League.

Pitching

Though he throws five pitches, it's the combination of Hitchcock's four-seam fastball and splitter that make him effective. His curve, slider and straight change give hitters something else to think about, but it's the diving splitter that gets them to lunge. The splitter runs in to righthanders, which enables Hitchcock to handle righties and lefties alike. His stamina has improved since his elbow problems of 1997, though he still tends to lose his stuff as he approaches the 100-pitch mark. He gives up a lot of flyballs and home runs, and benefits greatly from Qualcomm Stadium, which contains all but the hardest-hit balls.

Defense & Hitting

Hitchcock's high leg kick gives basestealers a leg up, so to speak. He has a good pickoff move, but he doesn't employ a slide step and can be victimized once he commits to the plate. His fielding is acceptable, but his hitting is downright awful. To his credit, he has learned to bunt acceptably.

2000 Outlook

Hitchcock's 12-14 record was more attributable to the dire state of the Padres than the quality of his pitching. If the team gets back on the right side of .500, Hitchcock could get 15-17 victories. That may not happen this year, but he can be counted upon to continue to post quality innings.

Position: SP
Bats: L **Throws:** L
Ht: 6' 0" **Wt:** 205

Opening Day Age: 28
Born: 4/29/71 in
Fayetteville, NC
ML Seasons: 8

Overall Statistics

	W	L	Pct.	ERA	G	GS	Sv	IP	H	BB	SO	HR	Ratio
1999	12	14	.462	4.11	33	33	0	205.2	202	76	194	29	1.35
Career	60	56	.517	4.67	198	164	3	1001.1	1046	369	780	140	1.41

How Often He Throws Strikes

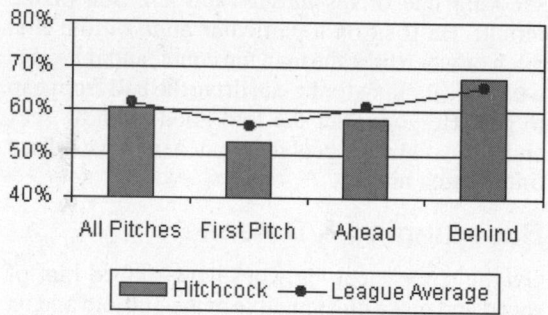

| Hitchcock | League Average |

1999 Situational Stats

	W	L	ERA	Sv	IP		AB	H	HR	RBI	Avg
Home	7	6	3.16	0	108.1	LHB	158	40	7	18	.253
Road	5	8	5.18	0	97.1	RHB	638	162	22	72	.254
First Half	8	6	4.15	0	110.2	Sc Pos	162	37	7	60	.228
Scnd Half	4	8	4.07	0	95.0	Clutch	23	7	0	1	.304

1999 Rankings (National League)

- 1st in wild pitches (15)
- 2nd in fewest GDPs induced per 9 innings (0.3) and most strikeouts per 9 innings (8.5)
- 3rd in most pitches thrown per batter (3.91)
- 4th in losses
- Led the Padres in sacrifice bunts (7), losses, games started, batters faced (892), strikeouts, wild pitches (15), balks (2), pitches thrown (3,487), pickoff throws (87), highest strikeout/walk ratio (2.6), lowest batting average allowed (.254), most run support per 9 innings (5.0), most strikeouts per 9 innings (8.5), ERA at home and lowest batting average allowed with runners in scoring position

Trevor Hoffman

Position: RP
Bats: R **Throws:** R
Ht: 6' 0" **Wt:** 215

Opening Day Age: 32
Born: 10/13/67 in
Bellflower, CA
ML Seasons: 7

1999 Season

After finishing second in the 1998 National League Cy Young Award balloting, Trevor Hoffman got off to a somewhat shaky start in 1999. There were whispers that he'd lost something off his fastball, but he put any concerns to rest with a spectacular four-month run. From June 3 through the end of the season, he converted 31 straight save opportunities and compiled a microscopic 0.96 ERA. Pitching on a club where opportunities were relatively scarce, he finished second in the league with 40 saves and led the majors in save percentage for the second straight season.

Pitching

When hitters face Hoffman, they know what's coming and they still can't touch him. He starts them with 95-MPH fastballs and finishes them off with one of the best straight changeups in the game. He mixes in a slider for good measure. Hoffman's delivery makes his pitches very tough to pick up, which helps make the fastball-changeup combination so devastating. He's a tireless worker and can pitch more than one inning at a time or several days in a row as needed.

Defense & Hitting

A former shortstop, Hoffman now has little occasion to serve as a fielder but does the job when necessary. As a hitter, he swings hard and occasionally hits the ball hard. He notched a two-run double in one of his three at-bats last year. Worrying about baserunners isn't something he needs to do often. His ability to pump high fastballs past hitters serves as enough of a deterrent for potential basestealers.

2000 Outlook

An improvement in the Padres' fortunes may provide more save opportunities for Hoffman and possibly enable him to return to Cy Young consideration. Last year's lighter workload might even help him to get off to a stronger start in 2000. As he proved last year, he still has the stuff to be the best reliever in baseball.

Overall Statistics

	W	L	Pct.	ERA	G	GS	Sv	IP	H	BB	SO	HR	Ratio
1999	2	3	.400	2.14	64	0	40	67.1	48	15	73	5	0.94
Career	36	28	.563	2.69	439	0	228	509.0	365	164	580	46	1.04

How Often He Throws Strikes

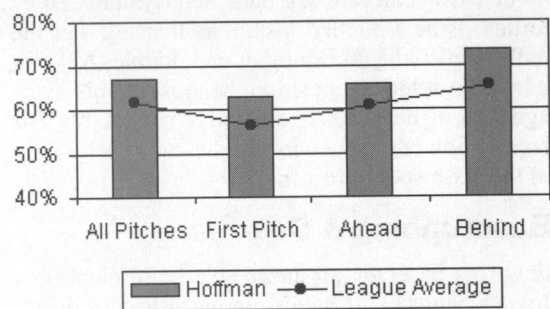

1999 Situational Stats

	W	L	ERA	Sv	IP		AB	H	HR	RBI	Avg
Home	1	1	1.67	24	37.2	LHB	107	23	1	12	.215
Road	1	2	2.73	16	29.2	RHB	137	25	4	11	.182
First Half	0	3	3.08	21	38.0	Sc Pos	63	10	1	18	.159
Scnd Half	2	0	0.92	19	29.1	Clutch	177	32	4	19	.181

1999 Rankings (National League)

- 1st in save percentage (93.0%)
- 2nd in saves and fewest baserunners allowed per 9 innings in relief (8.4)
- 4th in relief ERA (2.14)
- 5th in save opportunities (43)
- Led the Padres in saves, games finished (54), save opportunities (43), save percentage (93.0%), lowest batting average allowed in relief with runners on base (.180), lowest batting average allowed in relief with runners in scoring position (.159), relief ERA (2.14), lowest batting average allowed in relief (.197), fewest baserunners allowed per 9 innings in relief (8.4) and most strikeouts per 9 innings in relief (9.8)

San Diego

Wally Joyner

1999 Season

After signing a two-year, $6.7 million contract extension over the winter, Wally Joyner went out and had the worst year of his career. A basepath collision in April contributed to his slow start, and he played another month before a fracture in his left shoulder joint was discovered. He returned in late June and began to hit before bicep tendinitis bothered him in the second half.

Hitting

Joyner's smooth, controlled stroke produces line drives to all fields. Last year, his shoulder problems prevented him from getting enough lift to send balls into the gaps. He's a low-ball hitter who feasts on breaking balls and isn't particularly bothered by lefties. If he's pitched inside, he'll inside-out the ball to left field. As a singles and doubles hitter at a home run hitter's position, he must get his average back up near .300 in order to be productive. His lack of power or speed means that he's useful only in the sixth spot or lower.

Baserunning & Defense

Few first basemen are more quietly efficient than Joyner, whose soft hands dig out difficult throws with ease. His physical maladies sometimes affected his throwing last year, though he has an accurate arm when healthy. He has very little speed and runs the bases very conservatively. He rarely runs into outs but can clog the basepaths at times.

2000 Outlook

The Padres have a lot of money invested in Joyner, practically ensuring that he'll have every opportunity to get back on track this year. He needs to prove that he can stay healthy and get his average back up to his normal range. In light of his contract and recent injury history, it may be hard for San Diego to trade him unless he's able to stage a full recovery. He has a history of fast starts at the plate, so that might help.

Position: 1B
Bats: L **Throws:** L
Ht: 6' 2" **Wt:** 200

Opening Day Age: 37
Born: 6/16/62 in Atlanta, GA
ML Seasons: 14

Overall Statistics

	G	AB	R	H	D	T	HR	RBI	SB	BB	SO	Avg	OBP	Slg
1999	110	323	34	80	14	2	5	43	0	58	54	.248	.363	.350
Career	1861	6755	935	1961	392	25	196	1060	59	789	776	.290	.363	.443

Where He Hits the Ball

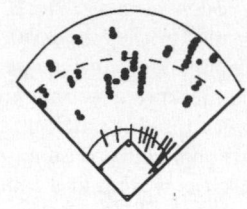
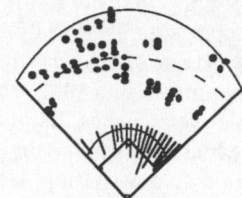

Vs. LHP   **Vs. RHP**

1999 Situational Stats

	AB	H	HR	RBI	Avg		AB	H	HR	RBI	Avg
Home	169	50	2	25	.296	LHP	81	20	3	16	.247
Road	154	30	3	18	.195	RHP	242	60	2	27	.248
First Half	155	39	3	27	.252	Sc Pos	87	22	0	35	.253
Scnd Half	168	41	2	16	.244	Clutch	52	12	2	5	.231

1999 Rankings (National League)

- 4th in fielding percentage at first base (.995)
- Led the Padres in intentional walks (6)

Phil Nevin

Position: 3B/C/1B
Bats: R **Throws:** R
Ht: 6' 2" **Wt:** 231

Opening Day Age: 29
Born: 1/19/71 in Fullerton, CA
ML Seasons: 5

1999 Season

The most pleasant surprise on the 1999 Padres was Phil Nevin, who didn't land a regular job until August but still led the club with 85 RBI. He was acquired over the winter to be a backup catcher and utilityman, and got a shot at third base only after George Arias and others were found wanting. Nevin took the job and ran with it, driving in almost 50 runs over the last two months and establishing himself as the club's third sacker and cleanup hitter. The team rewarded him with a multiyear contract extension late in the season.

Hitting

Nevin always has hit well against lefties, but it wasn't until last season that he became dangerous against righthanders as well. The key was becoming more disciplined and laying off pitches out of the strike zone. He has a quick, powerful stroke with power to all fields. Mainly a flyball hitter, he remains dangerous with two strikes. He lacked real home-run power when he first came up with the Astros, but after going back to the minors, he has resurfaced with the kind of power he showed in college.

Baserunning & Defense

Nevin doesn't have much speed, but always runs hard and breaks up double plays with the best of them. As a third baseman, he has fair range and a strong, accurate arm. He's learned to become a competent, if rough, catcher, but probably won't need to don shinguards much from now on.

2000 Outlook

For the first time in his major league career, the No. 1 overall pick in the 1992 draft will go into a season with a job all locked up. Nevin's power hitting last year was a revelation. He may not be able to keep up the pace over a full season, but he should remain productive enough to continue to hit cleanup in the Padres' lackluster attack.

Overall Statistics

	G	AB	R	H	D	T	HR	RBI	SB	BB	SO	Avg	OBP	Slg
1999	128	383	52	103	27	0	24	85	1	51	82	.269	.352	.527
Career	381	1147	139	279	60	3	51	179	3	119	296	.243	.319	.434

Where He Hits the Ball

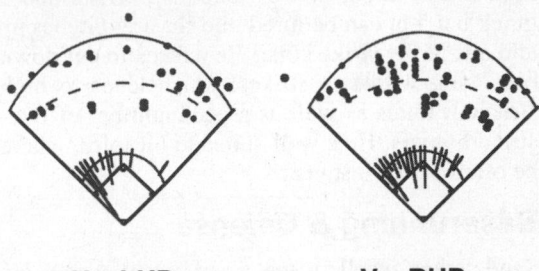

Vs. LHP   **Vs. RHP**

1999 Situational Stats

	AB	H	HR	RBI	Avg		AB	H	HR	RBI	Avg
Home	184	54	12	48	.293	LHP	137	37	11	38	.270
Road	199	49	12	37	.246	RHP	246	66	13	47	.268
First Half	137	35	11	34	.255	Sc Pos	119	36	10	63	.303
Scnd Half	246	68	13	51	.276	Clutch	73	20	3	17	.274

1999 Rankings (National League)

- 3rd in batting average with the bases loaded (.600)
- 7th in cleanup slugging percentage (.563)
- Led the Padres in doubles, RBI, batting average with the bases loaded (.600), cleanup slugging percentage (.563) and slugging percentage vs. lefthanded pitchers (.569)

San Diego

Reggie Sanders

1999 Season

Reggie Sanders came to the Padres in a blockbuster February trade with the Reds for slugger Greg Vaughn. Though he didn't fully replace Vaughn's 50 home runs and 119 RBI, Sanders stayed relatively healthy and finished with his best all-around numbers since 1995. He took a .300 average into September before a late slump dragged his average down to .285. After coming to town with a reputation as a fragile player, he held up for 133 games.

Hitting

Born and raised in South Carolina, Sanders is a hot-weather hitter. He's prone to slow starts and finishes, and almost always is at his best during the midsummer months. He has strong wrists and a quick bat, but can be lured into chasing pitches up and out of the strike zone. He refuses to cut down his swing with two strikes, which leads to high strikeout totals as well as a good number of two-strike homers. He's well-suited to hit third, where he often batted last year.

Baserunning & Defense

Sanders has excellent speed and uses it wisely. He reads pitchers' moves well and is capable of stealing in any situation. The move from artificial turf to grass seemed to rejuvenate him, as he ran more aggressively last year. He has the tools to play all three outfield positions. He spent most of last year in left, where he sometimes looked uncomfortable, after having spent most of his career in center or right. He has a strong, accurate arm.

2000 Outlook

The Padres picked up Sanders' option for 2000, and he'll be a fixture in their lineup as long as his health permits. He was hampered by his usual share of aches and pains last year, but wasn't sidelined for any extended periods. The Padres will be satisfied to get as much out of him this year as they did in '99.

Position: LF/RF/CF
Bats: R **Throws:** R
Ht: 6' 1" **Wt:** 185

Opening Day Age: 32
Born: 12/1/67 in Florence, SC
ML Seasons: 9

Overall Statistics

	G	AB	R	H	D	T	HR	RBI	SB	BB	SO	Avg	OBP	Slg
1999	133	478	92	136	24	7	26	72	36	65	108	.285	.376	.527
Career	938	3363	591	917	176	40	151	503	194	411	885	.273	.356	.483

Where He Hits the Ball

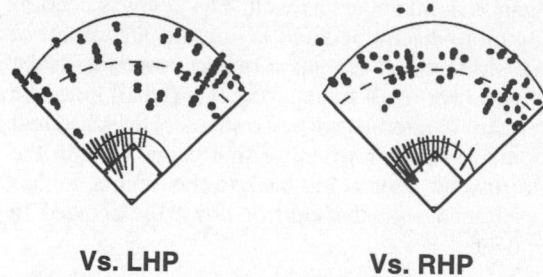

Vs. LHP   **Vs. RHP**

1999 Situational Stats

	AB	H	HR	RBI	Avg		AB	H	HR	RBI	Avg
Home	217	64	11	37	.295	LHP	142	43	8	16	.303
Road	261	72	15	35	.276	RHP	336	93	18	56	.277
First Half	233	73	15	37	.313	Sc Pos	116	28	5	41	.241
Scnd Half	245	63	11	35	.257	Clutch	66	12	1	11	.182

1999 Rankings (National League)

- 8th in caught stealing (13) and errors in left field (5)
- 9th in triples and stolen bases
- Led the Padres in batting average, home runs, at-bats, triples, total bases (252), stolen bases, walks, hit by pitch (6), times on base (207), plate appearances (550), slugging percentage, on-base percentage, HR frequency (18.4 ABs per HR), batting average on a 3-1 count (.556), slugging percentage vs. righthanded pitchers (.518), on-base percentage vs. lefthanded pitchers (.396), on-base percentage vs. righthanded pitchers (.368), batting average at home and batting average on the road

Quilvio Veras

1999 Season

Quilvio Veras is nothing if not consistent. Each year he plays good defense, steals bases, hits for a decent average, scores runs and loses considerable time to leg injuries. Last season was no different. He set personal highs with a .280 average and 95 runs scored, but started only 119 games. Offseason shoulder surgery threatened to sideline him for the start of the season, but Veras made it back in time for the opener. Still, assorted hamstring, knee and quadricep injuries bothered him throughout the year. His basestealing was affected but he had a fine year otherwise.

Hitting

Veras is an especially patient hitter. While this helps him work a good number of walks, it also puts him behind in the count quite often. With his slap-hitting approach, Veras always hits like he already has two strikes. The results are usually groundballs or line drives to the opposite field. He's an outstanding bunter and a threat to lay one down at any time.

Baserunning & Defense

When his legs are healthy, Veras is an excellent basestealer with good speed and first-step quickness. He's at his best in situations where a base has to be stolen, such as the late innings of close games. He was thrown out quite a bit in the first half last year, but improved his percentage as his hamstrings healed over the second half. He's a good defensive second baseman with above-average range and an excellent double-play pivot. His arm is accurate enough.

2000 Outlook

As always, the one thing the Padres would like Veras to do is improve his durability. Strengthening his legs might be the key, but it remains to be seen whether Veras will put in the necessary offseason work. Even if he doesn't, he'll remain a valuable leadoff man and second baseman whenever he's in the lineup.

Position: 2B
Bats: B **Throws:** R
Ht: 5'10" **Wt:** 183

Opening Day Age: 28
Born: 4/3/71 in Santo Domingo, Dominican Republic
ML Seasons: 5
Pronunciation: KILL-vee-oh VARE-ess

Overall Statistics

	G	AB	R	H	D	T	HR	RBI	SB	BB	SO	Avg	OBP	Slg
1999	132	475	95	133	25	2	6	41	30	65	88	.280	.368	.379
Career	612	2224	374	593	100	13	24	177	151	352	360	.267	.371	.356

Where He Hits the Ball

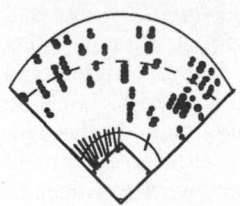 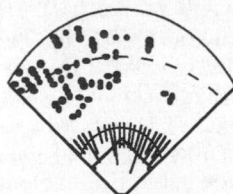

Vs. LHP   **Vs. RHP**

1999 Situational Stats

	AB	H	HR	RBI	Avg		AB	H	HR	RBI	Avg
Home	263	73	4	30	.278	LHP	132	38	2	12	.288
Road	212	60	2	11	.283	RHP	343	95	4	29	.277
First Half	269	74	3	26	.275	Sc Pos	90	23	1	34	.256
Scnd Half	206	59	3	15	.286	Clutch	73	16	0	6	.219

1999 Rankings (National League)

- 2nd in caught stealing (17)
- 3rd in highest groundball/flyball ratio (2.1)
- 4th in lowest stolen-base percentage (63.8%)
- Led the Padres in runs scored, caught stealing (17), walks, pitches seen (2,141), highest groundball/flyball ratio (2.1), most pitches seen per plate appearance (3.93), batting average vs. righthanded pitchers, on-base percentage for a leadoff hitter (.377), highest percentage of pitches taken (61.5%) and highest percentage of extra bases taken as a runner (59.3%)

San Diego

Woody Williams

1999 Season

Coming into 1999, Woody Williams was very much a question mark. His second-half collapse the year before convinced the Blue Jays to ship him to San Diego as part of a package for Joey Hamilton. Williams pitched decently before hitting a rough six-week stretch from early July until mid-August. He rebounded strongly, though, winning seven of his last eight decisions to finish with a career-high 12 victories. He made the trade look good from the Padres' point of view, as Hamilton suffered a complete meltdown for the Blue Jays.

Pitching

A flyball pitcher, Williams found spacious Qualcomm Stadium very much to his liking. He added a cut fastball, relying less on his slider and changeup than he had in the past. He now offers mostly 90-MPH four-seam fastballs, cutters and curves. The cutter gives him a better weapon against lefties, who gave him trouble in the past. Williams tries to expand the strike zone up and down, but is hittable when he catches too much of the plate.

Defense & Hitting

Williams made great strides at holding runners last year, as 10 of 16 basestealers against him were thrown out. The year before, 17 of 22 were successful. After spending his entire career in the American League, Williams proved surprisingly competent at the plate. He drove in six runs with 13 hits, including four doubles. He isn't much of a bunter, though. He doesn't hurt himself with the glove.

2000 Outlook

If the Padres are hoping that Williams' late-season turnaround is a sign of better things to come, they may be disappointed. One thing the Blue Jays eventually learned is that he simply runs hot and cold. At season's end, though, he normally ends up with decent numbers for a pitcher in the back end of the rotation. He'll likely do the same again as long as he doesn't exhaust the Padres' patience.

Position: SP
Bats: R **Throws:** R
Ht: 6' 0" **Wt:** 195

Opening Day Age: 33
Born: 8/19/66 in Houston, TX
ML Seasons: 7

Overall Statistics

	W	L	Pct.	ERA	G	GS	Sv	IP	H	BB	SO	HR	Ratio
1999	12	12	.500	4.41	33	33	0	208.1	213	73	137	33	1.37
Career	40	46	.465	4.33	199	109	0	821.2	802	324	576	121	1.37

How Often He Throws Strikes

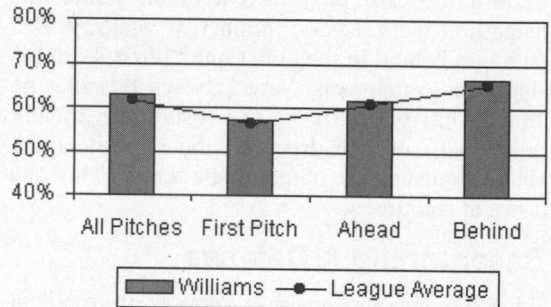

1999 Situational Stats

	W	L	ERA	Sv	IP		AB	H	HR	RBI	Avg
Home	6	3	3.63	0	89.1	LHB	356	92	10	41	.258
Road	6	9	4.99	0	119.0	RHB	438	121	23	60	.276
First Half	4	7	4.50	0	112.0	Sc Pos	171	42	7	70	.246
Scnd Half	8	5	4.30	0	96.1	Clutch	42	8	0	3	.190

1999 Rankings (National League)

- 3rd in lowest stolen-base percentage allowed (37.5%)
- 4th in lowest groundball/flyball ratio allowed (0.9)
- 5th in home runs allowed
- Led the Padres in games started, innings pitched, hits allowed, home runs allowed, runners caught stealing (10), lowest stolen-base percentage allowed (37.5%) and lowest batting average allowed vs. lefthanded batters

Brian Boehringer

Position: RP/SP
Bats: B **Throws:** R
Ht: 6' 2" **Wt:** 190

Opening Day Age: 30
Born: 1/8/70 in St. Louis, MO
ML Seasons: 5
Pronunciation: BOH-ring-irr

Overall Statistics

	W	L	Pct.	ERA	G	GS	Sv	IP	H	BB	SO	HR	Ratio
1999	6	5	.545	3.24	33	11	0	94.1	97	35	64	10	1.40
Career	16	16	.500	4.46	145	18	0	282.2	281	155	231	35	1.54

1999 Situational Stats

	W	L	ERA	Sv	IP		AB	H	HR	RBI	Avg
Home	5	3	3.91	0	50.2	LHB	148	33	3	12	.223
Road	1	2	2.47	0	43.2	RHB	215	64	7	26	.298
First Half	5	2	2.98	0	60.1	Sc Pos	91	21	2	28	.231
Scnd Half	1	3	3.71	0	34.0	Clutch	40	12	2	11	.300

1999 Season

What began as a potential breakthrough year for Brian Boehringer ended on a surgeon's table in August. The career middle reliever moved into the San Diego rotation in June and reeled off a string of quality starts. Shoulder problems cropped up, however, and he needed arthroscopic surgery to repair a partially torn rotator cuff.

Pitching, Defense & Hitting

When healthy, Boehringer mixes a low-90s fastball with a slider and curveball. For some reason, he consistently shuts down lefthanded hitters, a rare trait for a righthander. It remains to be seen if his velocity will be affected by his surgery. He tended to hit the wall rather quickly as a starter, but this was after having pitched out of the bullpen for several seasons. He has a decent move to first and defends his position adequately. He has very limited experience at the plate and is an especially weak hitter.

2000 Outlook

Boehringer is expected to contend for a spot in San Diego's rotation as soon as his recovery is complete. It isn't clear whether that will be during spring training or sometime after the start of the regular season.

Damian Jackson

Position: SS/2B
Bats: R **Throws:** R
Ht: 5'11" **Wt:** 185

Opening Day Age: 26
Born: 8/16/73 in Los Angeles, CA
ML Seasons: 4

Overall Statistics

	G	AB	R	H	D	T	HR	RBI	SB	BB	SO	Avg	OBP	Slg
1999	133	388	56	87	20	2	9	39	34	53	105	.224	.320	.356
Career	171	472	70	109	29	3	10	49	38	64	121	.231	.325	.369

1999 Situational Stats

	AB	H	HR	RBI	Avg		AB	H	HR	RBI	Avg
Home	177	45	6	17	.254	LHP	117	22	2	6	.188
Road	211	42	3	22	.199	RHP	271	65	7	33	.240
First Half	240	61	6	26	.254	Sc Pos	94	20	1	27	.213
Scnd Half	148	26	3	13	.176	Clutch	67	12	1	6	.179

1999 Season

Acquired in the Reggie Sanders-Greg Vaughn swap with the Reds, rookie Damian Jackson was pressed into action when Chris Gomez went down with an injury in May. Jackson performed decently for six weeks or so, but slumped severely and returned to the bench when Gomez returned in August.

Hitting, Baserunning & Defense

Jackson has electrifying speed and could steal a ton of bases if he ever learns to reach base consistently. He already steals almost at will, on speed alone. The problem is that he takes a power hitter's approach with a big, lofting swing instead of simply trying to make contact. He's often spectacular at short, but just as often bobbles a routine grounder or throws one away. He played an acceptable second base in limited action.

2000 Outlook

With so much of the Padres' money tied up in Gomez, it doesn't look like Jackson will be starting at shortstop any time soon. He could use some time to smooth over the rough spots in his game and may be useful off the bench.

San Diego

Dave Magadan

Position: 3B/1B
Bats: L **Throws:** R
Ht: 6' 4" **Wt:** 215

Opening Day Age: 37
Born: 9/30/62 in Tampa, FL
ML Seasons: 14

Overall Statistics

	G	AB	R	H	D	T	HR	RBI	SB	BB	SO	Avg	OBP	Slg
1999	116	248	20	68	12	1	2	30	1	45	36	.274	.377	.355
Career	1396	3899	491	1129	204	13	39	462	11	674	503	.290	.392	.379

1999 Situational Stats

	AB	H	HR	RBI	Avg		AB	H	HR	RBI	Avg
Home	117	37	1	18	.316	LHP	38	8	0	3	.211
Road	131	31	1	12	.237	RHP	210	60	2	27	.286
First Half	183	54	2	25	.295	Sc Pos	74	13	1	27	.176
Scnd Half	65	14	0	5	.215	Clutch	56	15	0	7	.268

1999 Season

Dave Magadan got more playing time than he expected over the first half of last year, but after the All-Star break his role all but disappeared. He began the year platooning at third base with George Arias and gradually took a greater share of the job as Arias faltered. Magadan performed decently, as he normally does, before Phil Nevin took the third-base job all for himself.

Hitting, Baserunning & Defense

Reaching base is Magadan's forte. He's a patient hitter who strokes line drives to the opposite field with ease. His weaknesses are a lack of power and a lack of speed. He always had performed well as a pinch-hitter before 1999. Magadan is a passable third baseman, with sure hands and a decent arm but very little range. He's more adept at first base. In short, he has the skills to be a useful reserve but not a starter.

2000 Outlook

Magadan goes into the final year of his contract looking at a cut in playing time. The emergence of Nevin and the expected return to health of Wally Joyner leaves little apparent playing time for Magadan.

Dan Miceli

Traded To MARLINS

Position: RP
Bats: R **Throws:** R
Ht: 6' 0" **Wt:** 216

Opening Day Age: 29
Born: 9/9/70 in Newark, NJ
ML Seasons: 7
Pronunciation: muh-SELL-ee

Overall Statistics

	W	L	Pct.	ERA	G	GS	Sv	IP	H	BB	SO	HR	Ratio
1999	4	5	.444	4.46	66	0	2	68.2	67	36	59	7	1.50
Career	25	27	.481	4.77	343	9	31	400.1	402	188	361	53	1.47

1999 Situational Stats

	W	L	ERA	Sv	IP		AB	H	HR	RBI	Avg
Home	3	2	2.65	0	37.1	LHB	93	25	2	13	.269
Road	1	3	6.61	2	31.1	RHB	159	42	5	21	.264
First Half	3	2	3.75	1	36.0	Sc Pos	70	21	2	27	.300
Scnd Half	1	3	5.23	1	32.2	Clutch	116	35	3	14	.302

1999 Season

Dan Miceli was another Padre who was rewarded with a new contract in 1998 and didn't perform up to expectations in 1999. He came to camp 35 pounds lighter, but that cost him his customary zip on his fastball. So did occasional bouts of arm stiffness.

Pitching, Defense & Hitting

Miceli throws a four-seam fastball in the low 90s as well as a sinking two-seamer. He used the latter pitch to induce 13 double-play grounders last year, one of the best totals in the National League among relievers. He also throws a slider, change and split-finger fastball. Miceli got hurt on first-pitch fastballs quite a bit last year. He's ordinary at fielding and controlling the running game, and poor at hitting.

2000 Outlook

In November, San Diego traded Miceli to Florida for starter Brian Meadows. Miceli worked a lot of ballgames to help the Padres win the pennant in 1998, and the Marlins hope that last year's struggles were only a temporary result of his long season the year before.

Eric Owens

Position: LF/CF/RF/1B
Bats: R **Throws:** R
Ht: 6' 0" **Wt:** 198

Opening Day Age: 29
Born: 2/3/71 in
Danville, VA
ML Seasons: 5

Overall Statistics

	G	AB	R	H	D	T	HR	RBI	SB	BB	SO	Avg	OBP	Slg
1999	149	440	55	117	22	3	9	61	33	38	50	.266	.327	.391
Career	300	744	94	180	30	3	10	78	52	67	105	.242	.306	.331

1999 Situational Stats

	AB	H	HR	RBI	Avg		AB	H	HR	RBI	Avg
Home	202	54	2	22	.267	LHP	130	30	4	21	.231
Road	238	63	7	39	.265	RHP	310	87	5	40	.281
First Half	242	70	6	40	.289	Sc Pos	116	35	2	50	.302
Scnd Half	198	47	3	21	.237	Clutch	83	21	0	16	.253

1999 Season

Eric Owens was one of the Padres' more pleasant surprises over the first four months of the season, going into August with a .296 batting average. Playing all three outfield positions as well as some first base, he became a regular of sorts. He slumped over the last two months, but still played in a team-high 149 games.

Hitting, Baserunning & Defense

Owens runs well and makes good contact, but he's a very mediocre offensive player overall. He doesn't hit for a high average, pile up extra-base hits or get on base often enough to score many runs. He hustles and makes the most of his basestealing opportunities. Owens' greatest asset is his versatility. He can get by at all three outfield spots, as well as any infield position except for shortstop. His arm is a little short for right field, but he throws with accuracy.

2000 Outlook

Owens could make a fine utilityman, but when he leads the team in games played it's a sure sign that the club is in trouble. If anything goes right at all for the Padres this year, he'll get far fewer at-bats.

Carlos Reyes

Position: RP
Bats: B **Throws:** R
Ht: 6' 0" **Wt:** 190

Opening Day Age: 30
Born: 4/4/69 in Miami,
FL
ML Seasons: 6
Pronunciation:
RAY-ess

Overall Statistics

	W	L	Pct.	ERA	G	GS	Sv	IP	H	BB	SO	HR	Ratio
1999	2	4	.333	3.72	65	0	1	77.1	76	24	57	11	1.29
Career	19	30	.388	4.56	261	26	3	490.0	511	202	330	69	1.46

1999 Situational Stats

	W	L	ERA	Sv	IP		AB	H	HR	RBI	Avg
Home	1	2	4.08	0	35.1	LHB	128	37	4	24	.289
Road	1	2	3.43	1	42.0	RHB	171	39	7	26	.228
First Half	2	1	2.96	1	45.2	Sc Pos	92	21	4	42	.228
Scnd Half	0	3	4.83	0	31.2	Clutch	54	16	2	9	.296

1999 Season

Carlos Reyes returned to the Padres over the winter of 1998, signing a minor league deal. For much of the season, he was one of their most effective relievers, but a September slump hurt his numbers.

Pitching, Defense & Hitting

For someone who rarely makes it past the mid-80s on the radar gun, Reyes is about as effective as a pitcher can be. This is both a strength and a weakness. Every organization he has been with has found him to be less impressive in person than he is on the stats sheet. He mixes his sinker and slider, painting the corners with precision. When he keeps the ball down and gets groundballs, he survives. He doesn't have much of a move to first but controls the running game with a quick stretch delivery. He struck out in his first major league at-bat last year.

2000 Outlook

The Phillies claimed Reyes off waivers soon after the 1999 season ended. Like the Padres and Red Sox before them, they may get decent work out of Reyes but then ultimately deem him expendable.

San Diego

Ruben Rivera

Position: CF
Bats: R **Throws:** R
Ht: 6' 3" **Wt:** 208

Opening Day Age: 26
Born: 11/14/73 in La Chorrera, Panama
ML Seasons: 5

Overall Statistics

	G	AB	R	H	D	T	HR	RBI	SB	BB	SO	Avg	OBP	Slg
1999	147	411	65	80	16	1	23	48	18	55	143	.195	.295	.406
Career	310	692	115	146	30	4	31	94	31	98	231	.211	.314	.400

1999 Situational Stats

	AB	H	HR	RBI	Avg		AB	H	HR	RBI	Avg
Home	197	35	10	16	.178	LHP	140	28	8	18	.200
Road	214	45	13	32	.210	RHP	271	52	15	30	.192
First Half	227	51	16	33	.225	Sc Pos	107	17	2	24	.159
Scnd Half	184	29	7	15	.158	Clutch	82	18	6	11	.220

1999 Season

The Padres turned over center field to Ruben Rivera and waited for him to begin to make good on his considerable potential. They're still waiting. Rivera displayed the same deficiencies last year that he always had. Even more alarming, he was unable to make adjustments as the season progressed.

Hitting, Baserunning & Defense

Rivera has good power but swings from the heels on every pitch, regardless of the count or situation. Breaking balls and offspeed pitches continue to mystify him. His inability to make contact will doom him unless he changes his approach. In the outfield, he covers lots of ground and unleashes strong, accurate throws. His speed enables him to steal a few bases, but his technique and ability to read pitchers is lacking.

2000 Outlook

The Padres, understandably, have been very patient with Rivera. The question is whether Rivera will make any progress before San Diego exhausts its patience. He has gotten this far on natural ability alone, but he simply must learn how the game is to be played.

John Vander Wal

Position: LF/1B
Bats: L **Throws:** L
Ht: 6' 2" **Wt:** 197

Opening Day Age: 33
Born: 4/29/66 in Grand Rapids, MI
ML Seasons: 9

Overall Statistics

	G	AB	R	H	D	T	HR	RBI	SB	BB	SO	Avg	OBP	Slg
1999	132	246	26	67	18	0	6	41	2	37	59	.272	.368	.419
Career	849	1318	160	333	69	12	37	197	17	172	302	.253	.338	.407

1999 Situational Stats

	AB	H	HR	RBI	Avg		AB	H	HR	RBI	Avg
Home	139	42	2	24	.302	LHP	18	2	0	2	.111
Road	107	25	4	17	.234	RHP	228	65	6	39	.285
First Half	153	47	5	34	.307	Sc Pos	76	22	2	33	.289
Scnd Half	93	20	1	7	.215	Clutch	43	7	0	4	.163

1999 Season

Last year John Vander Wal got the opportunity to expand on his traditional pinch-hitting role. Injuries to Wally Joyner and Tony Gwynn gave Vander Wal some starts at first base and left field. He hit well, batting .307 over the first half, but Joyner and Gwynn's return to the lineup sent Vander Wal back to the bench after the All-Star break. He remained one of the club's top pinch-hitters all year long.

Hitting, Baserunning & Defense

Vander Wal's biggest asset is his ability bring his lefthanded bat off the bench. He's a good fastball hitter who can be made to expand his strike zone with two strikes. He has little speed and negligible defensive value. His weak arm is a hindrance in the outfield, but he can get by at first base.

2000 Outlook

With another year left on his contract, Vander Wal may be another veteran the Padres will try to unload. He can help a club off the bench, but for a young, rebuilding team like San Diego, his presence isn't nearly as critical.

Donne Wall

Position: RP
Bats: R **Throws:** R
Ht: 6' 1" **Wt:** 205

Opening Day Age: 32
Born: 7/11/67 in Potosi, MO
ML Seasons: 5
Pronunciation: DONN-ee

Overall Statistics

	W	L	Pct.	ERA	G	GS	Sv	IP	H	BB	SO	HR	Ratio
1999	7	4	.636	3.07	55	0	0	70.1	58	23	53	11	1.15
Career	26	22	.542	4.11	141	37	1	356.2	364	110	249	47	1.33

1999 Situational Stats

	W	L	ERA	Sv	IP		AB	H	HR	RBI	Avg
Home	6	0	1.66	0	38.0	LHB	108	20	3	9	.185
Road	1	4	4.73	0	32.1	RHB	157	38	8	26	.242
First Half	6	1	2.79	0	38.2	Sc Pos	55	18	3	27	.327
Scnd Half	1	3	3.41	0	31.2	Clutch	137	33	8	24	.241

1999 Season

Donne Wall, who came out of nowhere to have a great season out of the bullpen in 1998, proved it was no fluke by continuing to excel as a setup man and middle reliever. A sore elbow bothered him at times, but he didn't let it sideline him for more than a few days at a time.

Pitching, Defense & Hitting

Wall's 90-MPH fastball is straight and quite hittable, but he spots it well. He makes his living by changing speeds and working the corners, throwing sliders, changeups and splitters with excellent command. He throws a good overhand curve to lefties and handles them exceptionally well for a righthander. He's quick to the plate and few basestealers try to run on him. He also fields his position well. He hit well in the minors, though he rarely gets the chance in the big leagues.

2000 Outlook

It's comforting to the Padres to know that Wall will be there to help bridge the gap between their starters and closer Trevor Hoffman. As long as his arm holds up, he'll continue to be one of their bullpen's unsung heroes.

Matt Whisenant

Position: RP
Bats: R **Throws:** L
Ht: 6' 3" **Wt:** 215

Opening Day Age: 28
Born: 6/8/71 in Los Angeles, CA
ML Seasons: 3

Overall Statistics

	W	L	Pct.	ERA	G	GS	Sv	IP	H	BB	SO	HR	Ratio
1999	4	5	.444	5.63	67	0	1	54.1	50	36	37	4	1.58
Career	7	6	.538	5.14	165	0	3	136.2	130	87	102	7	1.59

1999 Situational Stats

	W	L	ERA	Sv	IP		AB	H	HR	RBI	Avg
Home	2	1	5.86	0	27.2	LHB	82	18	2	14	.220
Road	2	4	5.40	1	26.2	RHB	118	32	2	20	.271
First Half	4	3	5.54	1	26.0	Sc Pos	67	18	1	29	.269
Scnd Half	0	2	5.72	0	28.1	Clutch	73	25	0	19	.342

1999 Season

Lefthander Matt Whisenant was signed by the Padres in August after the Royals released him. He worked as a lefty specialist and middle reliever for San Diego, with mixed results. Though he was tough to hit, he continued to display control problems.

Pitching, Defense & Hitting

The Padres took a chance on Whisenant because he's a rare lefty with a power arm. He has a low-90s heater and a sharp slider, but his command always has been his undoing. Though he's often wide of the plate, he rarely leaves pitches up and can be very difficult to take deep. Lefties have a tough time against him, but righthanders can take him apart. He shuts down the running game, having allowed just five stolen bases in his three major league seasons. He's a good athlete and a competent fielder, but he's completely unproven at the plate.

2000 Outlook

If Whisenant manages to stick with San Diego, he'll have to start in middle relief and work his way up. His presence in the majors is due more to his stuff than his record.

San Diego

Other San Diego Padres

Carlos Almanzar (Pos: RHP, Age: 26)

	W	L	Pct.	ERA	G	GS	Sv	IP	H	BB	SO	HR	Ratio
1999	0	0	-	7.47	28	0	0	37.1	48	15	30	6	1.69
Career	2	3	.400	6.36	57	0	0	69.1	83	24	54	11	1.54

Almanzar was great at Triple-A Syracuse in 1998 before the Padres got him in the Woody Williams-Joey Hamilton deal. He was brutal afterward. 2000 Outlook: C

George Arias (Pos: 3B, Age: 28, Bats: R)

	G	AB	R	H	D	T	HR	RBI	SB	BB	SO	Avg	OBP	Slg
1999	55	164	20	40	8	0	7	20	0	6	54	.244	.271	.421
Career	173	480	46	114	10	2	14	55	2	25	121	.238	.278	.371

Expected to excel as a power-hitting third baseman, Arias hasn't made enough contact in the majors. His chances may be drying up. 2000 Outlook: C

Will Cunnane (Pos: RHP, Age: 25)

	W	L	Pct.	ERA	G	GS	Sv	IP	H	BB	SO	HR	Ratio
1999	2	1	.667	5.23	24	0	0	31.0	34	12	22	8	1.48
Career	8	4	.667	5.67	81	8	0	125.1	152	62	102	20	1.71

After spending 1997 in the majors as a major league Rule 5 pickup, Cunnane hasn't been able to stick since. His success in Triple-A last year (0.98 ERA, 54 K in 36.2 IP) didn't follow him to San Diego. 2000 Outlook: C

Carlos Garcia (Pos: 3B, Age: 32, Bats: R)

	G	AB	R	H	D	T	HR	RBI	SB	BB	SO	Avg	OBP	Slg
1999	6	11	1	2	0	0	0	0	0	1	3	.182	.250	.182
Career	610	2178	274	580	102	17	33	197	73	115	340	.266	.307	.374

Garcia started the season in a third-base platoon and made two costly errors in three games, then was demoted on April 16. He may never come back. 2000 Outlook: D

Ed Giovanola (Pos: 3B/2B, Age: 31, Bats: L)

	G	AB	R	H	D	T	HR	RBI	SB	BB	SO	Avg	OBP	Slg
1999	56	58	10	11	0	1	0	3	2	9	8	.190	.294	.224
Career	218	301	41	65	5	4	1	19	4	44	49	.216	.316	.269

Giovanola bounced between Triple-A and San Diego in 1999. His bat never will provide much help, but his versatility may keep him around. 2000 Outlook: C

Domingo Guzman (Pos: RHP, Age: 24)

	W	L	Pct.	ERA	G	GS	Sv	IP	H	BB	SO	HR	Ratio
1999	0	1	.000	21.60	7	0	0	5.0	13	3	4	1	3.20
Career	0	1	.000	21.60	7	0	0	5.0	13	3	4	1	3.20

Guzman can throw 97 MPH, but he was slapped around during a September callup. His command needs a lot of work yet, as Guzman wasn't dominating at Double-A in 1999. More seasoning required. 2000 Outlook: C

Carlos Hernandez (Pos: C, Age: 32, Bats: R)

	G	AB	R	H	D	T	HR	RBI	SB	BB	SO	Avg	OBP	Slg
1999						Did Not Play								
Career	413	1002	79	253	36	1	21	106	3	42	161	.252	.291	.353

After earning his first starting nod in 1999 and signing a three-year deal during the offseason, Hernandez ruptured his left Achilles tendon during a spring training at-bat and missed the season. 2000 Outlook: B

Heath Murray (Pos: LHP, Age: 26)

	W	L	Pct.	ERA	G	GS	Sv	IP	H	BB	SO	HR	Ratio
1999	0	4	.000	5.76	22	8	0	50.0	60	26	25	7	1.72
Career	1	6	.143	6.16	39	11	0	83.1	110	47	41	10	1.88

A soft tosser, Murray started strong at Triple-A Las Vegas in 1999 but hit a wall in San Diego. He needed two seasons to succeed in Double-A and Triple-A ball, so he needs more time. The Reds claimed him on waivers. 2000 Outlook: C

Randy Myers (Pos: LHP, Age: 37)

	W	L	Pct.	ERA	G	GS	Sv	IP	H	BB	SO	HR	Ratio
1999					Did Not Play								
Career	44	63	.411	3.19	728	12	347	884.2	758	396	884	69	1.30

His rotator cuff forced Myers to make his first-ever trip to the disabled list in April, and surgery in June wiped out his season. Age and injury make him a risk. 2000 Outlook: C

David Newhan (Pos: 2B, Age: 26, Bats: L)

	G	AB	R	H	D	T	HR	RBI	SB	BB	SO	Avg	OBP	Slg
1999	32	43	7	6	1	0	2	6	2	1	11	.140	.159	.302
Career	32	43	7	6	1	0	2	6	2	1	11	.140	.159	.302

Newhan has some pop for a second baseman, but he endured an 0-for-23 stretch with the Padres before homering off Dustin Hermanson on September 12. The middle-infield picture is crowded in San Diego. 2000 Outlook: B

Roberto Rivera (Pos: LHP, Age: 31)

	W	L	Pct.	ERA	G	GS	Sv	IP	H	BB	SO	HR	Ratio
1999	1	2	.333	3.86	12	0	0	7.0	6	3	3	1	1.29
Career	1	2	.333	4.50	19	0	0	12.0	14	5	5	2	1.58

After a solid Triple-A season in 1998, Rivera made the Opening Day roster and pitched OK before a demotion to Triple-A Las Vegas in May. Then the wheels came off. 2000 Outlook: C

Stan Spencer (Pos: RHP, Age: 30)

	W	L	Pct.	ERA	G	GS	Sv	IP	H	BB	SO	HR	Ratio
1999	0	7	.000	9.16	9	8	0	38.1	56	11	36	11	1.75
Career	1	7	.125	7.17	15	13	0	69.0	85	15	67	16	1.45

Spencer excited the Padres with just four walks and 31 strikeouts in 30.2 major league innings in 1998, but he wasn't effective at Triple-A Las Vegas or San Diego in '99. His average stuff requires pinpoint control. He became a free agent. 2000 Outlook: C

Matt Whiteside (Pos: RHP, Age: 32)

	W	L	Pct.	ERA	G	GS	Sv	IP	H	BB	SO	HR	Ratio
1999	1	0	1.000	13.91	10	0	0	11.0	9	5	9	1	2.18
Career	16	11	.593	5.11	243	1	9	349.0	394	128	217	38	1.50

Whiteside had a couple of decent seasons for Texas in the early 1990s, but hasn't been able to pitch well enough at the Triple-A level or in the majors the last two years to nail down a big league job. He's looking for work as a free agent. 2000 Outlook: C

San Diego Padres Minor League Prospects

Organization Overview:

Though San Diego's farm system doesn't have much to show for the 1990s, its hope is that it struck it rich in the final draft of the decade. Because of the free-agent defections of Kevin Brown, Ken Caminiti and Steve Finley, the Padres had six of the first 51 selections in the 1999 draft. They signed all six, including athletic center fielder Vince Faison and four high-ceiling pitchers, for nearly $6 million. Righthander Matt Clement and Ben Davis, perhaps San Diego's top two prospects of the 1990s, both grabbed regular roles with the big club in 1999. That wasn't enough to save the job of farm director Jim Skaalen, who was replaced by Ted Simmons.

Sean Burroughs

Position: 3B
Bats: L **Throws:** R
Ht: 6' 1" **Wt:** 195

Opening Day Age: 19
Born: 9/12/80 in Atlanta, GA

Recent Statistics

	G	AB	R	H	D	THR	RBI	SB	BB	SO	Avg
1999 A Fort Wayne	122	426	65	153	30	3	5	80	17	74	59	.359
1999 A Rancho Cuca	6	23	3	10	3	0	1	5	0	3	3	.435

The ninth overall selection in the 1998 draft, Burroughs held out all summer before finally signing for $2.1 million. His pro debut was worth the wait, as he dominated the Class-A Midwest League at age 18. The star of two Little League World Series championship teams coached by his father, former American League MVP Jeff Burroughs, Sean hit .363 in his first season and led the Midwest League with a .464 on-base percentage. He has plenty of raw power, so expect him to quintuple his 1999 homer output as he matures. Managers rated his arm as the best among Midwest League infielders, and Burroughs has the soft hands and quick feet to be an asset at third base. He'll move quickly through the minors and could be starting in San Diego by 2002.

Buddy Carlyle

Position: P
Bats: L **Throws:** R
Ht: 6' 3" **Wt:** 175

Opening Day Age: 22
Born: 12/21/77 in Omaha, NE

Recent Statistics

	W	L	ERA	G	GS	Sv	IP	H	R	BB	SO	HR
1999 AAA Las Vegas	11	8	4.89	25	25	0	160.0	180	99	42	138	25
1999 NL San Diego	1	3	5.97	7	7	0	37.2	36	28	17	29	7

Rarely have two more dissimilar pitchers been traded for one another then when the Reds shipped Carlyle to the Padres for Marc Kroon in April 1998. Kroon is a hard-throwing righthander whose electric stuff never has translated into success, while Carlyle is a finesse lefthander who knows how to pitch. A 1996 second-round pick, he throws his fastball, curveball and changeup for strikes. His changeup is his best pitch, though San Diego was enthused when his usually average fastball was clocked at 93-94 MPH in his final start of 1999. Carlyle was knocked around in seven major league starts last year, but should fare better once he keeps his pitches down to avoid the longball.

Mike Darr

Position: OF
Bats: L **Throws:** R
Ht: 6' 3" **Wt:** 205

Opening Day Age: 24
Born: 3/21/76 in Corona, CA

Recent Statistics

	G	AB	R	H	D	THR	RBI	SB	BB	SO	Avg
1999 AAA Las Vegas	100	383	57	114	34	0	10	62	10	50	103	.298
1999 NL San Diego	25	48	6	13	1	0	2	3	2	5	18	.271
1999 MLE	100	358	38	89	26	0	6	42	6	33	109	.249

A 1994 second-round pick of the Tigers, Darr was stolen by the Padres in a trade three years later for a washed-up Jody Reed. Darr, the son of the former major leaguer of the same name, now enters 2000 as a potential starter for San Diego. He has blossomed into a five-tool outfielder who drives the ball to all fields. He'll show more home-run power as he becomes more pull-conscious. Darr is a defensive standout, with the best outfield arm in the organization and the range to play center field when needed. He has passed Gary Matthews Jr. on the organization depth chart, and Darr could step in whenever the Padres tire of Ruben Rivera.

Adam Eaton

Position: P
Bats: R **Throws:** R
Ht: 6' 2" **Wt:** 190

Opening Day Age: 22
Born: 11/23/77 in Seattle, WA

Recent Statistics

	W	L	ERA	G	GS	Sv	IP	H	R	BB	SO	HR
1998 A Clearwater	9	8	4.44	24	23	0	131.2	152	68	47	89	9
1999 A Clearwater	5	5	3.91	13	13	0	69.0	81	39	24	50	2
1999 AA Reading	5	4	2.92	12	12	0	77.0	60	30	28	67	9
1999 AAA Scranton-WB	1	1	3.00	3	3	0	21.0	17	10	6	10	1

Eaton was the key to the deal for the Padres when they sent Andy Ashby to Philadelphia for three young pitchers. The 11th overall pick in the 1996 draft, Eaton made huge strides once promoted to Double-A at midseason last year. He threw a no-hitter in his first Double-A outing, though he took a 1-0 loss, and finished with three strong starts in Triple-A. His velocity had been inconsistent in the past, but he threw 93-94 MPH regularly in 1999 and reached as high as 97 MPH. His curveball and changeup give him two other potential above-average pitches. Eaton will begin in 2000 in Triple-A but could reach San Diego in short order.

San Diego

Wiki Gonzalez

Position: C
Bats: R **Throws:** R
Ht: 5' 11" **Wt:** 175

Opening Day Age: 25
Born: 5/17/74 in Aragua, Venezuela

Recent Statistics

	G	AB	R	H	D	T	HR	RBI	SB	BB	SO	Avg
1999 AA Mobile	61	225	38	76	16	2	10	49	0	29	28	.338
1999 AAA Las Vegas	24	92	13	25	6	0	6	12	0	5	10	.272
1999 NL San Diego	30	83	7	21	2	1	3	12	0	1	8	.253
1999 MLE	85	297	34	81	16	1	11	41	0	19	40	.273

Though Ben Davis is one of the best catching prospects in years, the Padres may have another keeper behind the plate in Gonzalez. He came much cheaper, via the Double-A Rule 5 draft in 1996, and was re-signed as a six-year minor league free agent after the 1998 season. Gonzalez blossomed in 1999, when he started using the entire field and had his best year ever at the plate. Named the best defensive catcher in the Double-A Southern League, Gonzalez possesses a strong arm. He'd make a nice complement to Davis in San Diego this year, but may spend most of the year in Triple-A because the Padres foolishly gave Carlos Hernandez a three-year contract that doesn't expire until 2001.

Gary Matthews Jr.

Position: OF
Bats: B **Throws:** R
Ht: 6' 3" **Wt:** 200

Opening Day Age: 25
Born: 8/25/74 in San Francisco, CA

Recent Statistics

	G	AB	R	H	D	T	HR	RBI	SB	BB	SO	Avg
1999 AAA Las Vegas	121	422	57	108	22	3	9	52	17	58	104	.256
1999 NL San Diego	23	36	4	8	0	0	0	7	2	9	9	.222
1999 MLE	121	399	38	85	16	1	6	35	10	38	111	.213

While Matthews finally stayed healthy enough to play 100 games for the first time in three years, he had a disappointing season. He regressed at the plate, batting just .256 with little power in one of the best hitters' parks in Triple-A. Signed as a 13th-round draft-and-follow out of Los Angeles Mission Junior College in 1993, Matthews has the speed to steal bases and play center field, and he also has a strong arm. It appears that Matthews won't have the power his father Gary Sr. had, so he probably won't be able to play an outfield corner. Mike Darr has passed Matthews, who may have to wait until Tony Gwynn retires to play regularly in the majors.

Kevin Nicholson

Position: SS
Bats: B **Throws:** R
Ht: 5' 10" **Wt:** 190

Opening Day Age: 24
Born: 3/29/76 in Vancouver, Canada

Recent Statistics

	G	AB	R	H	D	T	HR	RBI	SB	BB	SO	Avg
1998 AA Mobile	132	488	64	105	27	3	5	52	9	47	114	.215
1999 AA Mobile	127	489	84	141	38	3	13	81	16	46	92	.288
1999 MLE	127	460	58	112	28	1	9	56	10	26	100	.243

No Canadian ever had been drafted in the first round until the Padres took Nicholson out of Stetson with the 27th overall pick in 1997. He broke the hamate bone in his right wrist that summer, which continued to sap his hand of strength for much of 1998, when he hit just .215. Nicholson's bat is his best tool, and he showed why when he rebounded last season. He also runs well and has a solid arm. Managers rated him the best defensive shortstop in the Double-A Southern League. Nicholson is a much better offensive threat than either of San Diego's shortstop options, Chris Gomez and Damian Jackson, and could push for a promotion in the second half of 2000.

Wascar Serrano

Position: P
Bats: R **Throws:** R
Ht: 6' 2" **Wt:** 178

Opening Day Age: 21
Born: 7/2/78 in Santo Domingo, Dom. Rep.

Recent Statistics

	W	L	ERA	G	GS	Sv	IP	H	R	BB	SO	HR
1998 A Clinton	9	7	3.22	26	26	0	156.2	150	74	54	143	6
1999 A Rancho Cuca	9	8	3.33	21	21	0	132.1	110	58	43	129	10
1999 AA Mobile	2	3	5.53	7	7	0	42.1	48	27	17	29	5

With Matt Clement graduating to the major leagues, Serrano is now the Padres' best pitchng prospect. His combination of a low-90s fastball that can reach 95 MPH, a sweeping slurve and a changeup has been very tough to hit. Serrano has permitted just 27 homers in 416.1 pro innings and led the high Class-A California League last year by limiting opponents to 7.48 hits per nine innings. He mixes his pitches well and throws strikes. Once Serrano establishes himself at the other levels, he'll be ready for San Diego, probably in late 2001.

Others to Watch

Righthander **Gerik Baxter** (20), the first pitcher drafted by San Diego last year, is a power pitcher who can reach 97 MPH. He fanned 74 and allowed just 48 hits in 60.1 Rookie-level innings . . . Lefthander **Mike Bynum** (22), another 1999 first-rounder, didn't allow a run in his first 29 pro innings. His slider is so good that it has been compared to Hall of Famer Steve Carlton's, and he has an 89-92 MPH fastball. . . Outfielder **Vince Faison** (19) turned down a University of Georgia football scholarship after the Padres took him with their top 1999 pick and offered him $1.415 million. *Baseball America* rated him the fastest high school prospect in the draft and the best prospect in the Rookie-level Arizona League. Faison is similar to fellow Peach State product Corey Patterson of the Cubs, though he's less refined and doesn't have the same power. . . Righthander **Junior Herndon** (21) survived in Double-A at age 20. He throws 91-93 MPH and has a good changeup. . . Righthander **Omar Ortiz** (22), yet another 1999 first-rounder, is a fastball-slider pitcher who can throw as hard as 95 MPH. . . Righthander **Jacob Peavy** (18) is another product of the 1999 draft, though the Padres found him in the 15th round. The winner of the pitching triple crown in the Rookie-level Arizona League, he has a very projectable fastball.

Pacific Bell Park

Offense

3Com Park always was a difficult place to hit, cutting down on batting average and runs more than most National League parks. Set to open in 2000, Pacific Bell Park is located in a much sunnier and less windswept part of San Francisco. It's less cavernous and the right-field line stands just 307 feet away from the plate. The distance between home plate and the first row of stands has been reduced from 74 feet to just 48 feet, which also will help hitters. The only factor in the new park that works against the offense is the deep right-center field power alley, which stretches to 420 feet.

Defense

The wind and cold at 3Com were a hindrance to infielders and outfielders alike. Pac Bell should bring more predictable defensive baseball to the Bay Area. With the deep power alley in right-center, the Giants will need a center fielder with above-average range. They presently don't have one.

Who It Helps The Most

Lefthanded pull hitters would appear to have the biggest advantage. As power hitters age, they tend to pull the ball more, so Barry Bonds may benefit the most. On the Giants' homer-prone pitching staff, the extra space in right-center should help righthanders such as Mark Gardner, Livan Hernandez and Joe Nathan.

Who It Hurts The Most

Most of Ellis Burks' power is to right-center field, so he could have some problems. Likewise, J.T. Snow is primarily a gap-to-gap hitter who will have a harder time reaching the fence unless he pulls the ball down the line. Marvin Benard's less-than-stellar range in center field will become more obvious.

Rookies & Newcomers

New catcher Bobby Estalella has power and should be able to reach the 365-foot power alley in left-center. As his power develops, Armando Rios might find the short right-field porch to his liking.

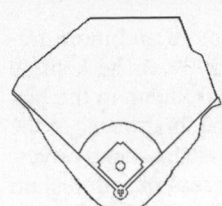

Dimensions: LF-335, LCF-365, CF-404, RCF-420, RF-307

Capacity: 40,800

Elevation: 0 feet

Surface: Grass

Foul Territory: Small

Park Factors

1999 Season (3Com Park)

	Home Games			Away Games			Index
	Giants	Opp	Total	Giants	Opp	Total	
G	75	75	150	72	72	144	—
Avg	.263	.252	.257	.277	.280	.279	92
AB	2473	2626	5099	2560	2468	5028	97
R	360	340	700	424	411	835	80
H	651	661	1312	709	692	1401	90
2B	126	113	239	142	128	270	87
3B	8	7	15	9	11	20	74
HR	82	94	176	93	87	180	96
BB	313	288	601	319	300	619	96
SO	498	561	1059	456	422	878	119
E	46	61	107	51	60	111	93
E-Infield	39	55	94	45	48	93	97
LHB-Avg	.274	.257	.266	.283	.287	.285	94
LHB-HR	37	37	74	41	25	66	105
RHB-Avg	.253	.249	.251	.272	.277	.274	91
RHB-HR	45	57	102	52	62	114	91

1997-1999 (3Com Park)

	Home Games			Away Games			Index
	Giants	Opp	Total	Giants	Opp	Total	
G	221	221	442	222	222	444	—
Avg	.265	.254	.259	.269	.274	.271	96
AB	7255	7679	14934	7883	7546	15429	97
R	1088	975	2063	1175	1160	2335	89
H	1923	1950	3873	2119	2068	4187	93
2B	362	334	696	411	386	797	90
3B	36	34	70	41	43	84	86
HR	230	238	468	238	236	474	102
BB	937	781	1718	909	834	1743	102
SO	1460	1590	3050	1458	1341	2799	113
E	157	172	329	147	161	308	107
E-Infield	126	151	277	129	128	257	108
LHB-Avg	.279	.263	.272	.276	.274	.275	99
LHB-HR	111	87	198	112	70	182	112
RHB-Avg	.250	.249	.249	.261	.274	.268	93
RHB-HR	119	151	270	126	166	292	96

1999 Rankings (National League/3Com Park)

- Highest strikeout factor
- Lowest batting-average factor
- Lowest run factor
- Lowest hit factor
- Lowest RHB batting-average factor

San Francisco

Dusty Baker

1999 Season

The word "magic" was used more and more frequently with Dusty Baker in 1999, as he kept an old, slow and frequently injured lineup in the National League West race until the final weeks of the season. While managers' roles are frequently overemphasized in their teams' success or failures, no one can overrate Baker, a two-time NL Manager of the Year, for his skill in keeping his team focused and competitive.

Offense

The Giants' veteran players are ideal for Baker's offensive philosophy, which emphasizes getting on base and using one-base strategies to combat an overall lack of team speed. Baker had his players bunt more than any team in the game, and he also likes to use the hit-and-run. Despite injuries to their top three sluggers—Barry Bonds, Ellis Burks and Jeff Kent—and a less-than-advantageous home park, the Giants finished third in the NL in runs scored. Injuries to Scott Servais and Charlie Hayes kept Baker from platooning as much as he otherwise would have.

Pitching & Defense

Baker went with a 12-man pitching staff and a seven-man bullpen all season, but none of his hurlers can complain about a lack of opportunity. Baker frequently will switch pitchers in mid-inning to maintain a platoon advantage and almost always will double-switch or pinch-hit to keep a reliever from having to come to the plate. Three members of his bullpen had fewer innings than appearances. Baker generally favors offense over defense and rarely makes defensive substitutions.

2000 Outlook

Baker's current contract expires at the end of 2000. If he doesn't get an extension before the end of the season, the bidding for his services will be as intense as that for any player. Baker is all but irreplaceable to the Giants, who operate on a thin margin of talent and have to maximize every advantage they can get on the field and in the clubhouse. Baker is a master at doing so in both areas.

Born: 6/15/49 in Riverside, CA

Playing Experience: 1968-1986, Atl, LA, SF, Oak

Managerial Experience: 7 seasons

Manager Statistics

Year	Team, Lg	W	L	Pct	GB	Finish
1999	San Francisco, NL	86	76	.531	14.0	2nd West
7 Seasons		558	512	.521	—	—

1999 Starting Pitchers by Days Rest

	<=3	4	5	6+
Giants Starts	1	73	61	21
Giants ERA	4.50	5.23	4.50	5.43
NL Avg Starts	3	81	48	21
NL ERA	4.84	4.53	4.72	4.98

1999 Situational Stats

	Dusty Baker	NL Average
Hit & Run Success %	27.7	33.6
Stolen Base Success %	66.1	70.2
Platoon Pct.	62.3	55.2
Defensive Subs	16	25
High-Pitch Outings	27	13
Quick/Slow Hooks	11/18	16/15
Sacrifice Attempts	113	89

1999 Rankings (National League)

- 1st in sacrifice bunt attempts (113), starts with over 120 pitches (27), starts with over 140 pitches (2), first-batter platoon percentage (69.6%) and one-batter pitcher appearances (47)
- 3rd in relief appearances (450) and 2+ pitching changes in low-scoring games (25)

Rich Aurilia

1999 Season

Rich Aurilla blossomed as an offensive player in 1999, shattering his previous career highs in most categories. He led all National League shortstops in home runs with 22 and finished second to Reds All-Star Barry Larkin with 80 RBI. Aurilia mainly batted seventh and eighth, and was one of the most dangerous lower-in-the-order hitters in the league. Though he faded in August, he rebounded to enjoy his best month of the season in September. He backslid defensively, however, committing 28 errors.

Hitting

Aurilla is a sound fundamental hitter who has developed the ability to drive balls left over the plate. He has well above-average hand-eye coordination and good balance at the plate, which means he can make contact with just about any pitch. If pitchers work him low and on the corners, Aurilla doesn't have the pure strength and bat speed to drive the ball hard through the infield.

Baserunning & Defense

The Giants would like to look at Aurilla's season in the field as an aberration. His formerly soft hands deserted him at times and his arm became erratic when he tried to make off-balance plays. Because Aurilla's range is only average and his arm strength unexceptional, it's imperative that he make the routine plays. Aurilla runs the bases intelligently but has below-average speed and isn't a threat to steal or regularly take an extra base.

2000 Outlook

The NL isn't overly blessed with solid everyday shortstops. If Aurilla regains his defensive consistency, he could establish himself as one of the league's best. As a low-round draft choice and a self-made player, it wouldn't be surprising to see Aurilla bounce back and improve. He has one year remaining on a two-year, $2 million contract he signed before the 1999 season.

Position: SS
Bats: R **Throws:** R
Ht: 6' 1" **Wt:** 185

Opening Day Age: 28
Born: 9/2/71 in Brooklyn, NY
ML Seasons: 5
Pronunciation: ah-REEL-yuh
Nickname: Dickie

Overall Statistics

	G	AB	R	H	D	T	HR	RBI	SB	BB	SO	Avg	OBP	Slg
1999	152	558	68	157	23	1	22	80	2	43	71	.281	.336	.444
Career	434	1410	169	380	68	4	41	178	11	108	202	.270	.322	.411

Where He Hits the Ball

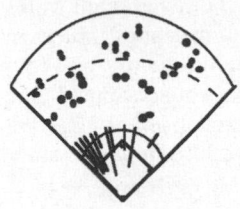 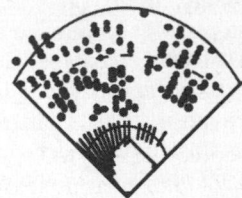

Vs. LHP   Vs. RHP

1999 Situational Stats

	AB	H	HR	RBI	Avg		AB	H	HR	RBI	Avg
Home	275	75	9	26	.273	LHP	142	42	5	22	.296
Road	283	82	13	54	.290	RHP	416	115	17	58	.276
First Half	303	91	13	44	.300	Sc Pos	151	43	5	57	.285
Scnd Half	255	66	9	36	.259	Clutch	85	22	3	10	.259

1999 Rankings (National League)

- 1st in errors at shortstop (28)
- 2nd in lowest percentage of extra bases taken as a runner (29.2%)
- 3rd in lowest fielding percentage at shortstop (.957)
- Led the Giants in singles and GDPs (16)
- Led NL shortstops in home runs, RBI, GDPs (16), slugging percentage, HR frequency (25.4 ABs per HR), batting average with the bases loaded (.471) and slugging percentage vs. righthanded pitchers (.447)

San Francisco

Marvin Benard

1999 Season

After batting .322 in part-time duty in 1998, Marvin Benard showed that was no fluke, proving he was a solid big league leadoff hitter in 1999. He was the only Giants outfielder to remain healthy all season and led the club in batting average, runs scored and stolen bases. His previous career high in home runs as a professional had been seven in 1995, but he more than doubled that with 16 last year.

Hitting

Previously a guy who slapped the ball up the middle or went the other way, Benard learned to turn on the ball when he got an inside pitch in 1999. He has an appreciation for the strike zone like most Giants hitters, but still doesn't draw enough walks to put him among the top half of leadoff hitters in on-base percentage. He more frequently will foul off a borderline pitch than take a chance on it being called a strike. Benard was much more effective against righthanders in 1999, hitting .297 with a .369 on-base percentage.

Baserunning & Defense

Benard has above-average speed on the bases but isn't an accomplished basestealer. His defense in center field is adequate when both Barry Bonds and Ellis Burks have healthy knees and can run, but Benard's lack of true center-field range becomes evident when those two are hobbling. His arm is below average in strength, though he does a good job of hitting his cutoff men.

2000 Outlook

The Giants platooned Benard on a limited basis with F.P. Santangelo last season, and may continue to sit Benard some against southpaws again in 2000, especially if 1999 Pacific Coast League MVP Calvin Murray proves he can hit big league pitching. It may be too much to expect for Benard to build on or even match his 1999 power numbers, but a season with 10-12 home runs and 25-30 stolen bases certainly is possible.

Position: CF/RF
Bats: L **Throws:** L
Ht: 5' 9" **Wt:** 185

Opening Day Age: 30
Born: 1/20/70 in Bluefields, Nicaragua
ML Seasons: 5
Pronunciation: buh-NARD

Overall Statistics

	G	AB	R	H	D	T	HR	RBI	SB	BB	SO	Avg	OBP	Slg
1999	149	562	100	163	36	5	16	64	27	55	97	.290	.359	.457
Career	502	1484	248	415	80	10	26	144	67	162	256	.280	.355	.400

Where He Hits the Ball

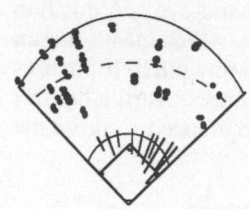

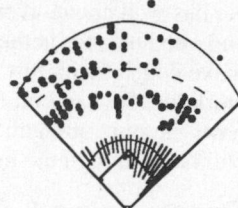

Vs. LHP   **Vs. RHP**

1999 Situational Stats

	AB	H	HR	RBI	Avg		AB	H	HR	RBI	Avg
Home	272	80	9	32	.294	LHP	114	30	3	11	.263
Road	290	83	7	32	.286	RHP	448	133	13	53	.297
First Half	301	89	7	33	.296	Sc Pos	140	42	4	47	.300
Scnd Half	261	74	9	31	.284	Clutch	85	17	1	5	.200

1999 Rankings (National League)

- 1st in highest percentage of extra bases taken as a runner (70.2%)
- 5th in caught stealing (14), lowest stolen-base percentage (65.9%) and fielding percentage in center field (.987)
- 10th in errors in center field (4)
- Led the Giants in batting average, runs scored, hits, triples, stolen bases, caught stealing (14), highest groundball/flyball ratio (1.3), stolen-base percentage (65.9%), batting average vs. righthanded pitchers, batting average on a 3-1 count (.579), on-base percentage for a leadoff hitter (.362), batting average at home and highest percentage of extra bases taken as a runner (70.2%)

Barry Bonds

1999 Season

Though Barry Bonds had been nicked up before, 1999 was the first year that the future Hall of Famer ever had missed significant time with injuries. Surgery for bone spurs and tendon damage in his right wrist cost him nearly two months in the middle of the season, and a balky right knee that required surgery at the end of the season caused him to limp to the finish. Between injuries, he was vintage Bonds on the field.

Hitting

One of the top offensive performers in the game, Bonds was able to fight through his wrist injury in an incredibly short amount of time, thanks to his trademarks as a hitter. He uses a very light bat and is exceptionally short and quick to the ball, which minimizes wrist strain. And Bonds is such a patient hitter that he swings and misses on very few pitches, especially out of the strike zone, which also helped him avoid placing stress on his wrist. Disregard Bonds' low batting average. He batted .202 in September, usually his hottest month, as he was trying to help the Giants' playoff chances when he should have been on the disabled list.

Baserunning & Defense

While Bonds is still a high-percentage basestealer, his 15 swipes were his lowest total ever in the majors. With his knee problems, his days as a threat on the bases are fading. Bonds has won eight Gold Gloves playing left field, a position that doesn't usually produce fielding honorees, but he probably won't win another. His declining speed is beginning to sap his formally outstanding range, and his arm is below average.

2000 Outlook

Bonds' speed numbers won't rebound, but he's hitting with more power than ever. If the Giants' new ballpark proves friendly and he stays healthy, Bonds easily could threaten his personal bests of 46 home runs and 129 RBI. At this stage of his career, though, his health is a legitimate concern.

Position: LF
Bats: L **Throws:** L
Ht: 6' 2" **Wt:** 210

Opening Day Age: 35
Born: 7/24/64 in Riverside, CA
ML Seasons: 14
Nickname: BB

Overall Statistics

	G	AB	R	H	D	T	HR	RBI	SB	BB	SO	Avg	OBP	Slg
1999	102	355	91	93	20	2	34	83	15	73	62	.262	.389	.617
Career	2000	6976	1455	2010	423	65	445	1299	460	1430	1112	.288	.409	.559

Where He Hits the Ball

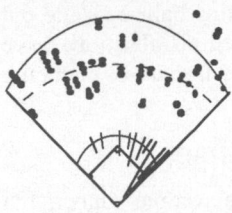 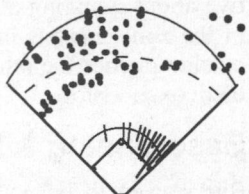

Vs. LHP   **Vs. RHP**

1999 Situational Stats

	AB	H	HR	RBI	Avg		AB	H	HR	RBI	Avg
Home	174	43	16	43	.247	LHP	128	34	12	25	.266
Road	181	50	18	40	.276	RHP	227	59	22	58	.260
First Half	115	31	9	27	.270	Sc Pos	84	21	4	40	.250
Scnd Half	240	62	25	56	.258	Clutch	43	11	1	9	.256

1999 Rankings (National League)
- Led the Giants in home runs, intentional walks (9), fewest GDPs per GDP situation (5.2%) and batting average on an 0-2 count (.250)
- Led NL left fielders in intentional walks (9)

San Francisco

Ellis Burks

1999 Season

Ellis Burks was an extremely effective and productive player when he was able to take the field in 1999. Continuing problems with his knees, both of which underwent surgery before the season, limited Burks to 120 games and restricted him to right field. On a per at-bat basis, Burks was just as productive as Barry Bonds, even to the point of drawing a career-high 69 walks.

Hitting

Burks has matured as a hitter and adapted well to life away from Coors Field. He still loves to turn his bat speed loose against fastballs on the inner half, and he tends to dominate southpaws who come inside on him. Burks has become more selective about swinging at breaking balls low and out of the zone. He has improved his ability to drive outside pitches the other way instead of bouncing them to shortstop.

Baserunning & Defense

Burks used to be an above-average runner, but those days are long gone. His 35-year-old knees don't have him hobbling a la Andre Dawson, but he's headed in that direction. He's strictly a base-to-base runner now, except when his instincts overcome the pain. Burks was an adequate right fielder. He takes good routes on flyballs and has an accurate if not especially strong throwing arm. He'll have problems with the much more spacious and unevenly configured right field at the Giants' new stadium.

2000 Outlook

It would be ideal if the Giants could use Burks as a DH or had enough outfield depth to rest him against tough righthanders. Neither is the case, however. This offseason will be very important as a litmus test for the rest of Burks' career. If he comes to spring training healthy and feeling young, he could enjoy a full and productive 2000 season. If he struggles physically through the offseason, getting 400 at-bats this year would be a major accomplishment.

Position: RF
Bats: R **Throws:** R
Ht: 6' 2" **Wt:** 205

Opening Day Age: 35
Born: 9/11/64 in Vicksburg, MS
ML Seasons: 13

Overall Statistics

	G	AB	R	H	D	T	HR	RBI	SB	BB	SO	Avg	OBP	Slg
1999	120	390	73	110	19	0	31	96	7	69	86	.282	.394	.569
Career	1550	5651	971	1635	313	56	261	916	166	601	1044	.289	.360	.503

Where He Hits the Ball

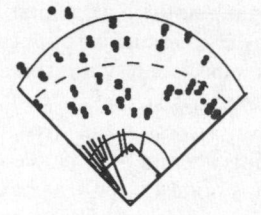

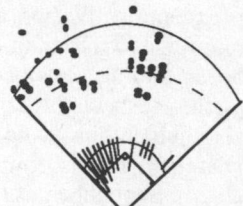

Vs. LHP   **Vs. RHP**

1999 Situational Stats

	AB	H	HR	RBI	Avg			AB	H	HR	RBI	Avg
Home	192	48	16	51	.250		LHP	116	40	9	30	.345
Road	198	62	15	45	.313		RHP	274	70	22	66	.255
First Half	206	56	14	45	.272		Sc Pos	98	37	13	69	.378
Scnd Half	184	54	17	51	.293		Clutch	52	6	2	10	.115

1999 Rankings (National League)

- 2nd in lowest batting average in the clutch and highest batting average with the bases loaded (.625)
- 3rd in batting average with runners in scoring position and fielding percentage in right field (.991)
- Led the Giants in batting average with runners in scoring position, batting average with the bases loaded (.625), batting average vs. lefthanded pitchers, slugging percentage vs. lefthanded pitchers (.612), on-base percentage vs. lefthanded pitchers (.465) and bunts in play (2)
- Led NL right fielders in batting average with the bases loaded (.625) and on-base percentage vs. lefthanded pitchers (.465)

Shawn Estes

1999 Season

While he didn't rebound to the 1997 form that made him one of the top lefthanded starters in the game, Shawn Estes put his career back on track with a solid and healthy 1999 season. He established a career high in innings pitched with 203 and didn't miss a start all season. He still struggled with his control and finished second to teammate Russ Ortiz among big league pitchers in walks. Estes' command problems contributed to the wide swings in his performance during the year.

Pitching

Estes' raw stuff is among the best in baseball. He throws a heavy sinking fastball at 91-94 MPH. The pitch breaks bats when he can hit the inside corner. His curveball is his best pitch, thrown hard with excellent two-plane break. It's effective against both lefthanders and righthanders. Estes' changeup also is an effective pitch. Scouts say that he tries to be too precise with his pitches instead of just trusting his raw stuff and throwing to the middle of the plate. He went through an eight-game stretch starting in July and August when he averaged just 2.28 walks per start, but he reverted back to his usual wild self down the stretch.

Defense & Hitting

For a pitcher, Estes is a very good athlete who helps himself both at the plate and in the field. He hit .164 in 1999, with four doubles and 10 sacrifice bunts. Estes' pickoff move is above average and he's quick off the mound to field groundballs.

2000 Outlook

With more confidence in his ability and more strikes early in the count, Estes could again be the pitcher who went 19-5 three years ago. He showed flashes of that last season, something he didn't do at all in 1998. Estes' problems appear to be mostly mental, not mechanical or physical, and those problems are often the hardest to predict or correct.

Position: SP
Bats: R **Throws:** L
Ht: 6' 2" **Wt:** 195

Opening Day Age: 27
Born: 2/18/73 in San Bernardino, CA
ML Seasons: 5
Pronunciation: EST-us
Nickname: Buck

Overall Statistics

	W	L	Pct.	ERA	G	GS	Sv	IP	H	BB	SO	HR	Ratio
1999	11	11	.500	4.92	32	32	0	203.0	209	112	159	21	1.58
Career	40	36	.526	4.31	103	103	0	640.2	600	336	550	52	1.46

How Often He Throws Strikes

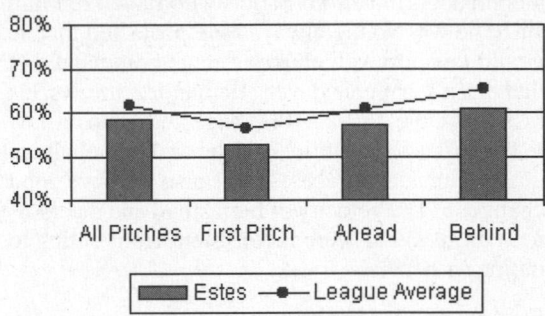

1999 Situational Stats

	W	L	ERA	Sv	IP		AB	H	HR	RBI	Avg
Home	7	5	3.72	0	111.1	LHB	122	33	4	12	.270
Road	4	6	6.38	0	91.2	RHB	658	176	17	90	.267
First Half	6	5	4.87	0	101.2	Sc Pos	199	54	5	82	.271
Scnd Half	5	6	4.97	0	101.1	Clutch	42	11	0	3	.262

1999 Rankings (National League)

- 1st in wild pitches (15)
- 2nd in walks allowed and highest ERA on the road
- 3rd in highest walks per 9 innings (5.0)
- 5th in most baserunners allowed per 9 innings (14.5)
- Led the Giants in sacrifice bunts (10), losses, wild pitches (15), runners caught stealing (10), highest groundball/flyball ratio allowed (1.5), fewest pitches thrown per batter (3.83) and fewest home runs allowed per 9 innings (.93)

Livan Hernandez

1999 Season

The Giants acquired 1997 World Series MVP Livan Hernandez in late July in exchange for two of their top minor league pitching prospects, righthanders Jason Grilli and Nate Bump. While the price was high, San Francisco hoped to both boost its 1999 pennant chances and improve its starting rotation for 2000 and beyond. Hernandez' season almost ended prematurely with a pulled ribcage muscle in September. His overall performance didn't differ much from his somewhat disappointing 1998 campaign.

Pitching

Hernandez has a very balanced, easy delivery and a compact arm action. Scouts who have seen him since he was young always have projected that he would develop well above-average command, but that hasn't happened yet. Hernandez throws his fastball in the 88-92 MPH range and keeps it low in the strike zone. Both his slider and curveball are quality breaking pitches, and he also throws a good changeup. The velocity of his fastball and the tightness of his slider were inconsistent from outing to outing in 1999.

Defense & Hitting

One of the top hitting pitchers in baseball, Hernandez batted .270 with two home runs and eight RBI in 1999. He now has a .223 career average. Despite his size, Hernandez has a quick move to both first base and home plate. He's less mobile on fielding comebackers and covering first base.

2000 Outlook

Removed from the temptations of his adopted hometown of Miami, Hernandez should be more focused in 2000. While he has proven very durable in his two full seasons as a starter, Hernandez still gives up too many hits and walks too many hitters to be the top-of-the-rotation starter many think he can become. If Hernandez remains healthy in his first full season on the West Coast, having a veteran team around him could move him to the next level in 2000.

Position: SP
Bats: R **Throws:** R
Ht: 6' 2" **Wt:** 225

Opening Day Age: 25
Born: 2/20/75 in Villa Clara, Cuba
ML Seasons: 4
Pronunciation: LEE-vahn her-NAN-dezz

Overall Statistics

	W	L	Pct.	ERA	G	GS	Sv	IP	H	BB	SO	HR	Ratio
1999	8	12	.400	4.64	30	30	0	199.2	227	76	144	23	1.52
Career	27	27	.500	4.39	81	80	0	533.1	576	220	380	65	1.49

How Often He Throws Strikes

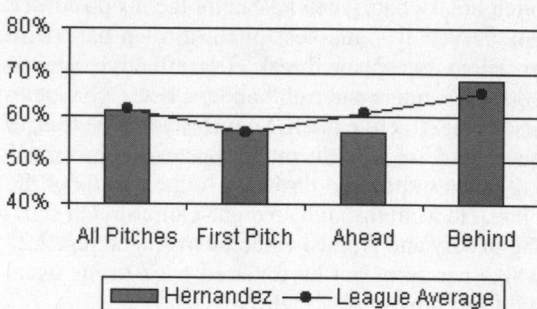

1999 Situational Stats

	W	L	ERA	Sv	IP		AB	H	HR	RBI	Avg
Home	5	7	4.94	0	98.1	LHB	384	112	12	44	.292
Road	3	5	4.35	0	101.1	RHB	411	115	11	52	.280
First Half	5	8	4.51	0	123.2	Sc Pos	181	47	5	71	.260
Scnd Half	3	4	4.86	0	76.0	Clutch	55	16	0	8	.291

1999 Rankings (National League)

- 6th in pickoff throws (164)
- 8th in most pitches thrown per batter (3.82) and fewest GDPs induced per 9 innings (0.5)
- 9th in hits allowed (227) and highest ERA at home (4.94)
- 10th in balks (2)

Jeff Kent

1999 Season

Jeff Kent was hobbled by an aching left foot from June on, and he had Barry Bonds hitting ahead of him for only part of the year. Still, Kent managed to drive in more than 100 runs for the third straight season. In the field, he made just 10 errors and turned more double plays per game than all but three National League second basemen. It was another banner season from one of the most underrated second baseman in the game.

Hitting

Kent continues to rank among the top pure fastball hitters in baseball. It's virtually impossible to blow heaters past him. He also remains a better hitter against righthanders than lefthanders. He uses the entire field against righties and will drive balls away hard to right-center field. Against southpaws, he's more pull-conscious and has trouble lofting the ball as frequently. Overall, he consistently has one of the highest flyball-groundball ratios in the game, as does fellow Giants slugger Barry Bonds.

Baserunning & Defense

His doubles and steals totals while playing with a painful foot injury are a tribute to Kent's intelligence and hustle on the bases. He has excellent instincts about taking an extra base when the opportunity exists. Defensively, Kent's range was affected by his balky foot, but he compensated with his sure hands and his strong double-play pivot. At 32, Kent realistically is looking at a continuing decline in his overall defensive performance, but is locked out of first base by J.T. Snow's contract. Kent has expressed no interest in playing third base.

2000 Outlook

Kent has played more than 140 games just once, in 1997, but his per-game production remains high. He's signed through 2001 with a team option for 2002. As long as he remains relatively healthy, Kent should continue to produce 25 homers and 100 RBI per season.

Position: 2B
Bats: R **Throws:** R
Ht: 6' 1" **Wt:** 205

Opening Day Age: 32
Born: 3/7/68 in Bellflower, CA
ML Seasons: 8

Overall Statistics

	G	AB	R	H	D	T	HR	RBI	SB	BB	SO	Avg	OBP	Slg
1999	138	511	86	148	40	2	23	101	13	61	112	.290	.366	.511
Career	1032	3742	566	1032	233	18	161	668	49	297	770	.276	.335	.477

Where He Hits the Ball

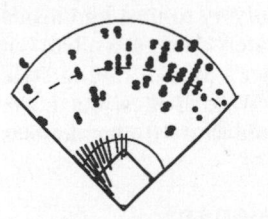

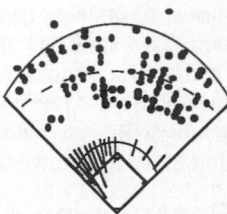

Vs. LHP   **Vs. RHP**

1999 Situational Stats

	AB	H	HR	RBI	Avg		AB	H	HR	RBI	Avg
Home	252	62	11	39	.246	LHP	132	36	7	30	.273
Road	259	86	12	62	.332	RHP	379	112	16	71	.296
First Half	323	96	13	60	.297	Sc Pos	151	49	8	80	.325
Scnd Half	188	52	10	41	.277	Clutch	74	19	2	10	.257

1999 Rankings (National League)

- 4th in lowest groundball/flyball ratio (0.8)
- 5th in lowest cleanup slugging percentage (.518) and highest fielding percentage at second base (.984)
- 6th in lowest batting average at home
- 7th in batting average on the road
- 8th in sacrifice flies (8)
- 10th in doubles and errors at second base (10)
- Led the Giants in doubles, total bases (261), RBI, sacrifice flies (8), slugging percentage, HR frequency (22.2 ABs per HR), cleanup slugging percentage (.518), slugging percentage vs. righthanded pitchers (.501), batting average on the road and steals of third (5)

San Francisco

669

Bill Mueller

1999 Season

Bill Mueller's season started with a limp, literally. He broke his left big toe with a foul ball on Opening Day and missed the rest of April. When he returned, Mueller showed the same on-base ability he had established in 1997, but he failed to develop his power potential. Mueller's tradeoff was a drop from 83 to 52 strikeouts, though 22 of those whiffs came after August 31, as the injury-plagued Giants struggled down the stretch.

Hitting

Mueller is evolving more and more into strictly a slap hitter. He'll wait patiently for a pitch out over the plate and try to line it to the opposite field. He rarely will try to turn on a ball and drive it for extra bases, so pitchers frequently try to bust him inside with hard stuff. He also rarely swings at a ball out of the strike zone. Mueller's overall hitting style resembles a 41-year-old Wade Boggs, but not a younger Boggs, who would slug 40-plus doubles and hit in the mid-.300s.

Baserunning & Defense

While Mueller's on-base ability is ideal for the top of the order, he lacks the raw running speed to be a factor once he reaches base. He scored only 61 runs while reaching base 185 times via walk or hit, the second-worst ratio among Giants regulars, despite hitting in front of the heart of the order. Mueller's fielding continued to be solid once he recovered his range after his toe injury. He has sure hands and good first-step quickness on groundballs.

2000 Outlook

Mueller's lack of power at the third-base position is somewhat offset by Jeff Kent's production at second base, but Mueller's production was disappointing in 1999. He either has to jump his batting average solidly into the .300-plus range or return to the 30-double, 10-homer potential he showed in 1998. Anything less will leave his starting position open to challenge from prospects in 2000, or when his contract expires at the end of the year.

Position: 3B
Bats: B **Throws:** R
Ht: 5'10" **Wt:** 180

Opening Day Age: 29
Born: 3/17/71 in Maryland Heights, MO
ML Seasons: 4
Pronunciation: MIL-ler
Nickname: Ferris, Muley

Overall Statistics

	G	AB	R	H	D	T	HR	RBI	SB	BB	SO	Avg	OBP	Slg
1999	116	414	61	120	24	0	2	36	4	65	52	.290	.388	.362
Career	444	1538	236	457	92	4	18	158	11	216	232	.297	.383	.397

Where He Hits the Ball

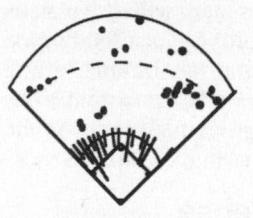 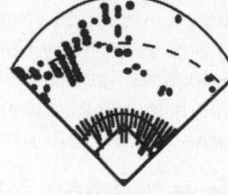

Vs. LHP **Vs. RHP**

1999 Situational Stats

	AB	H	HR	RBI	Avg		AB	H	HR	RBI	Avg
Home	196	57	1	18	.291	LHP	113	28	2	14	.248
Road	218	63	1	18	.289	RHP	301	92	0	22	.306
First Half	175	51	1	19	.291	Sc Pos	102	29	1	32	.284
Scnd Half	239	69	1	17	.289	Clutch	59	17	0	7	.288

1999 Rankings (National League)

- 5th in fielding percentage at third base (.958) and lowest percentage of swings that missed (9.6%)
- 9th in lowest slugging percentage vs. lefthanded pitchers (.336)
- Led the Giants in batting average in the clutch, batting average with two strikes (.242), highest percentage of pitches taken (59.4%), lowest percentage of swings that missed (9.6%) and highest percentage of swings put into play (49.4%)
- Led NL third basemen in sacrifice bunts (8) and lowest percentage of swings that missed (9.6%)

Robb Nen

Position: RP
Bats: R **Throws:** R
Ht: 6' 5" **Wt:** 215

Opening Day Age: 30
Born: 11/28/69 in San Pedro, CA
ML Seasons: 7

1999 Season

Robb Nen clearly was a shadow of himself through much of the 1999 campaign. He underwent elbow surgery during the final week of the season to repair tendon damage and bone spurs that had bothered him since at least the All-Star break, and probably affected him as far back as spring training. Nen allowed more hits than innings, something a closer with a high-90s fastball never should do. He blew nine saves while recording his worst ERA since his rookie season.

Pitching

With a fastball in the upper 90s, Nen fits the classic closer mold. The problem in 1999 was that his elbow kept him from throwing either his slider or his splitter consistently enough to keep hitters off his sometimes-straight fastball. Lefthanders showed no fear against him and were able to sit on his heater, hitting him at a .354 clip. Scouts worry that Nen's violent delivery will keep him from ever having consistent command of his stuff within the strike zone.

Defense & Hitting

Nen's defense and hitting are substandard, even for a reliever. A clumsy fielder, he made two errors in 1999. Nen didn't have a plate appearance, which kept his 0-for-12 career hitting mark intact. Last season was not without its highlights, however. A baserunner was caught stealing with Nen on the mound—for the first time since 1996.

2000 Outlook

The status of Nen's elbow will be uncertain until spring training, and it's possible that his rehab won't be complete by the start of the season. For a pitcher with his natural stuff, Nen always has operated on a thin line, either being dominant or hittable and rarely in between. The Giants have to be concerned about what they will see next spring.

Overall Statistics

	W	L	Pct.	ERA	G	GS	Sv	IP	H	BB	SO	HR	Ratio
1999	3	8	.273	3.98	72	0	37	72.1	79	27	77	8	1.47
Career	31	32	.492	3.29	428	4	185	497.2	448	199	527	39	1.30

How Often He Throws Strikes

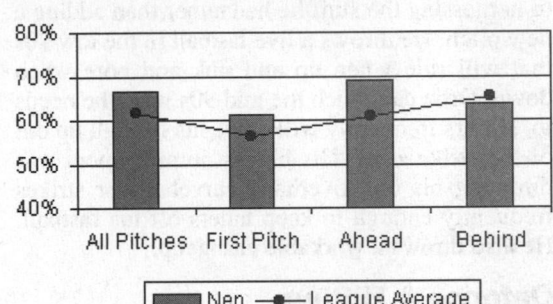

1999 Situational Stats

	W	L	ERA	Sv	IP		AB	H	HR	RBI	Avg
Home	1	4	3.21	23	42.0	LHB	130	46	5	23	.354
Road	2	4	5.04	14	30.1	RHB	157	33	3	17	.210
First Half	3	2	3.59	21	42.2	Sc Pos	90	21	3	33	.233
Scnd Half	0	6	4.55	16	29.2	Clutch	214	57	6	35	.266

1999 Rankings (National League)

- 1st in games finished (64), blown saves (9) and relief losses (8)
- 2nd in save opportunities (46)
- 5th in saves
- 8th in lowest save percentage (80.4%) and worst first batter efficiency (.323)
- Led the Giants in games pitched, saves, games finished (64), save opportunities (46), save percentage (80.4%), blown saves (9), relief losses (8), relief innings (72.1) and most strikeouts per 9 innings in relief (9.6)

San Francisco

Russ Ortiz

Position: SP
Bats: R **Throws:** R
Ht: 6' 1" **Wt:** 210

Opening Day Age: 25
Born: 6/5/74 in Encino, CA
ML Seasons: 2
Pronunciation: or-TEEZ

1999 Season

Russ Ortiz blossomed into one of the top young starters in baseball during 1999, winning 18 games and anchoring the San Francisco staff all season. Incredibly, Ortiz had just 16 victories in his four previous professional seasons combined. There were some negatives in 1999, though. Ortiz led all big league pitchers with 125 walks, plus he mixed in 13 wild pitches and hit six batters. He also allowed 21 unearned runs, the highest total in baseball, despite playing for the league's fourth-best defense.

Pitching

Ortiz' improvement as a pitcher can be attributed to harnessing the stuff he had rather than adding a new pitch. He throws a live fastball in the low 90s that will ride when up and sink and bore when down. Ortiz can touch the mid-90s when he needs to. Hitters frequently will chase his fastball up out of the strike zone. His biggest improvement was throwing his big, overhand curveball for strikes frequently enough to keep hitters off his fastball. He also throws a workable changeup.

Defense & Hitting

Ortiz is a very good hitting pitcher with surprising power. He hit .197 last season with a home run and eight RBI, and slammed a homer as a rookie in 1998 as well. Baserunners had free rein against Ortiz, stealing 25 bases, the fifth-highest total allowed by any pitcher in the National League. Ortiz' athleticism does help him on comebackers and covering first base.

2000 Outlook

Ortiz is likely to come down from his 18 wins and 3.81 ERA of a year ago. He had 66 walks and 64 strikeouts in the second half, an indication that the NL adjusted to him. He had never thrown more than 142 innings in a season before working 207 in 1999, and twice he threw 140 pitches in a game during the latter part of the season. It wouldn't be surprising at all if he struggled with the life in his arm in 2000.

Overall Statistics

	W	L	Pct.	ERA	G	GS	Sv	IP	H	BB	SO	HR	Ratio
1999	18	9	.667	3.81	33	33	0	207.2	189	125	164	24	1.51
Career	22	13	.629	4.17	55	46	0	296.0	279	171	239	35	1.52

How Often He Throws Strikes

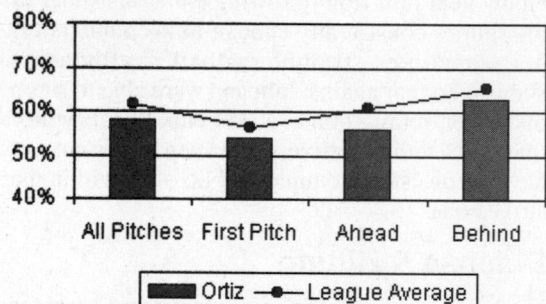

1999 Situational Stats

	W	L	ERA	Sv	IP		AB	H	HR	RBI	Avg
Home	11	3	3.04	0	112.1	LHB	361	91	10	35	.252
Road	7	6	4.72	0	95.1	RHB	413	98	14	61	.237
First Half	11	5	3.32	0	119.1	Sc Pos	185	39	3	62	.211
Scnd Half	7	4	4.48	0	88.1	Clutch	63	21	5	12	.333

1999 Rankings (National League)

- 1st in walks allowed, most pitches thrown per batter (4.04) and highest walks per 9 innings (5.4)
- 3rd in wild pitches (13)
- Led the Giants in ERA, wins, games started, complete games (3), innings pitched, batters faced (922), walks allowed, strikeouts, pitches thrown (3,724), pickoff throws (117), stolen bases allowed (25), winning percentage, lowest batting average allowed (.244), lowest slugging percentage allowed (.388), most strikeouts per 9 innings (7.1), ERA at home, ERA on the road, lowest batting average allowed vs. lefthanded batters and lowest batting average allowed vs. righthanded batters

Kirk Rueter

1999 Season

On the surface, Kirk Rueter's 1999 looks like a continuation of his 13-6 and 16-9 seasons of the previous two years. That isn't the case, though. Rueter's ERA has risen from 3.45 in 1997 to 5.41 last year, while all his other ratios have regressed. Righthanders hammered Rueter for a .520 slugging percentage last year, a major factor in his struggles. The Giants supported Rueter with a team-high 6.6 runs per nine innings and especially bailed him out during his first five starts in April, when Rueter lasted a combined 18 innings but escaped with a 1-1 record.

Pitching

Rueter has little margin for error, depending on location and changing speeds to get hitters out. His fastball reaches just the mid-80s and can be very straight. He'll use his changeup at any time in the count, especially against righthanders. In response to being pounded by righties, Rueter added a cut fastball to work in on their fists, but the cutter proved only marginally effective. His slow curveball is still a good pitch against lefthanders.

Defense & Hitting

Next to impossible to run on, Rueter allowed only four stolen bases in 12 attempts last year. He surrendered just five steals the previous year. He also is a quick and agile fielder. Rueter is a decent hitter and one of the best contact hitters among the pitching fraternity. He struck out just six times in 58 at-bats in 1999 while driving in five runs. He's a good bunter as well.

2000 Outlook

Rueter has stayed healthy despite previous elbow woes, establishing himself as a dependable starter who can work 185 innings a year. The bad news is that he must reverse his decline of the past two years if he wishes to remain in that role. Moving into a more hitter-friendly environment at Pacific Bell Park won't help him, either. Most important, he needs to find a way to get righthanders out.

Position: SP
Bats: L **Throws:** L
Ht: 6' 2" **Wt:** 205

Opening Day Age: 29
Born: 12/1/70 in Centralia, IL
ML Seasons: 7
Pronunciation: REE-ter
Nickname: Woody

Overall Statistics

	W	L	Pct.	ERA	G	GS	Sv	IP	H	BB	SO	HR	Ratio
1999	15	10	.600	5.41	33	33	0	184.2	219	55	94	28	1.48
Career	70	39	.642	4.21	161	160	0	890.1	944	240	466	103	1.33

How Often He Throws Strikes

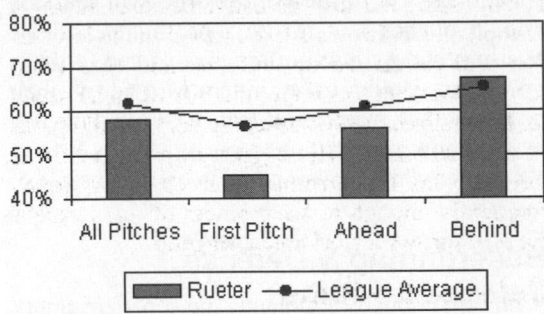

1999 Situational Stats

	W	L	ERA	Sv	IP		AB	H	HR	RBI	Avg
Home	7	5	4.56	0	92.2	LHB	148	35	1	10	.236
Road	8	5	6.26	0	92.0	RHB	589	184	27	99	.312
First Half	7	4	5.36	0	97.1	Sc Pos	148	49	6	74	.331
Scnd Half	8	6	5.46	0	87.1	Clutch	26	6	0	3	.231

1999 Rankings (National League)

- 1st in highest batting average allowed with runners in scoring position
- 2nd in lowest stolen-base percentage allowed (33.3%), most pitches thrown per batter (3.98) and highest batting average allowed vs. righthanded batters
- 3rd in most run support per 9 innings (6.6) and highest ERA on the road
- Led the Giants in games started, hits allowed, home runs allowed, GDPs induced (17), highest strikeout/walk ratio (1.7), lowest on-base percentage allowed (.346), lowest stolen-base percentage allowed (33.3%), fewest baserunners allowed per 9 innings (13.5) and most run support per 9 innings (6.6)

San Francisco

J.T. Snow

Position: 1B
Bats: L **Throws:** L
Ht: 6' 2" **Wt:** 202

Opening Day Age: 32
Born: 2/26/68 in Long Beach, CA
ML Seasons: 8
Nickname: Snowball

1999 Season

J.T. Snow continued to produce in odd-numbered years, hitting 24 homers and driving in 98 runs. In the three odd-numbered years after he broke into the majors in 1993, he has averaged 25 home runs and 101 RBI. In the three even-numbered years, those averages drop to 13 home runs and 59 RBI. Still, 1999 was a disappointing year for Snow in one sense. He gave up switch-hitting late in 1998 after years of struggling as a righthanded hitter, but fared little better swinging lefthanded against southpaws.

Hitting

Snow has a smooth lefthanded swing and is very patient. He's a mistake hitter who will feast on cripple pitches low in the zone, but he can be overmatched by good offspeed stuff and fastballs up and in. Unlike many hitters who add to their power as they mature and learn to turn on the ball better, Snow appears to be more of a Wally Joyner-type hitter whose power peaks in his 20s instead of his 30s.

Baserunning & Defense

With exceptionally soft hands and superb instincts, Snow is one of the top defensive first basemen in baseball. He won his fifth Gold Glove in 1999 for fielding excellence. He's especially adept at the 3-6-3 double play and has a very accurate arm. Snow is one step removed from being a clogger on the basepaths. He lacks good speed getting underway and was caught on all four of his stolen-base attempts last year.

2000 Outlook

Snow signed a four-year, $24 million contract extension in July, which binds him to the Giants through the 2003 season. Hitting behind Barry Bonds and Jeff Kent will give him plenty of RBI opportunities, though Snow must show that he can put consecutive strong seasons together. His inability to be more than a platoon-type player will continue to drag down his production and the Giants' offensive effectiveness.

Overall Statistics

	G	AB	R	H	D	T	HR	RBI	SB	BB	SO	Avg	OBP	Slg
1999	161	570	93	156	25	2	24	98	0	86	121	.274	.370	.451
Career	951	3311	471	870	155	8	132	539	13	427	657	.263	.347	.434

Where He Hits the Ball

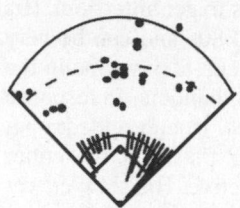

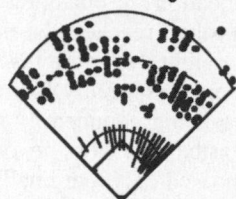

Vs. LHP **Vs. RHP**

1999 Situational Stats

	AB	H	HR	RBI	Avg		AB	H	HR	RBI	Avg
Home	273	66	7	37	.242	LHP	169	39	3	23	.231
Road	297	90	17	61	.303	RHP	401	117	21	75	.292
First Half	315	88	10	55	.279	Sc Pos	158	39	4	69	.247
Scnd Half	255	68	14	43	.267	Clutch	84	22	3	14	.262

1999 Rankings (National League)

- 2nd in fielding percentage at first base (.996)
- 4th in lowest batting average at home
- 5th in games played
- Led the Giants in at-bats, walks, times on base (247), strikeouts, GDPs (16), pitches seen (2,671), plate appearances (668), on-base percentage, most pitches seen per plate appearance (4.00), on-base percentage vs. righthanded pitchers (.394) and games played
- Led NL first basemen in batting average on a 3-1 count (.500)

Alan Embree

Position: RP
Bats: L **Throws:** L
Ht: 6' 2" **Wt:** 190

Opening Day Age: 30
Born: 1/23/70 in Vancouver, WA
ML Seasons: 6
Pronunciation: EMM-bree

Overall Statistics

	W	L	Pct.	ERA	G	GS	Sv	IP	H	BB	SO	HR	Ratio
1999	3	2	.600	3.38	68	0	0	58.2	42	26	53	6	1.16
Career	14	10	.583	4.27	240	4	2	232.0	206	114	209	29	1.38

1999 Situational Stats

	W	L	ERA	Sv	IP		AB	H	HR	RBI	Avg
Home	2	0	2.27	0	31.2	LHB	90	18	4	17	.200
Road	1	2	4.67	0	27.0	RHB	120	24	2	9	.200
First Half	3	0	2.76	0	32.2	Sc Pos	52	12	0	18	.231
Scnd Half	0	2	4.15	0	26.0	Clutch	113	20	2	12	.177

1999 Season

The Giants acquired the well-traveled Alan Embree from Arizona in November 1998, in exchange for underachieving outfield prospect Dante Powell. Embree proved to be a solid acquisition, appearing in 68 games, second on the staff to closer Robb Nen, while allowing barely more than a baserunner per inning.

Pitching, Defense & Hitting

Embree's bread-and-butter pitch is a hard, riding fastball that can touch the mid-90s. He tends to throw high in the strike zone and overpower hitters into harmless flyballs, while mixing in a slurvy-type slider. Embree's maximum-effort delivery also makes the ball hard for hitters to pick up. Baserunners evidently picked up a flaw in his move in 1999, as the number of steals he allowed jumped from just one in 1998 to 11. He hasn't made a major league error since 1992. Embree has a walk and a strikeout in two career plate appearances.

2000 Outlook

Typecast as a situational lefty, Embree appears ready for an expanded role in the San Francisco bullpen. He has learned how to retire righthanders, who hit .200 off him last season.

Mark Gardner

Position: SP
Bats: R **Throws:** R
Ht: 6' 1" **Wt:** 220

Opening Day Age: 38
Born: 3/1/62 in Los Angeles, CA
ML Seasons: 11
Nickname: Gardy

Overall Statistics

	W	L	Pct.	ERA	G	GS	Sv	IP	H	BB	SO	HR	Ratio
1999	5	11	.313	6.47	29	21	0	139.0	142	57	86	27	1.43
Career	83	81	.506	4.56	292	240	1	1524.0	1504	552	1111	204	1.35

1999 Situational Stats

	W	L	ERA	Sv	IP		AB	H	HR	RBI	Avg
Home	2	4	5.55	0	60.0	LHB	226	63	11	31	.279
Road	3	7	7.18	0	79.0	RHB	306	79	16	63	.258
First Half	3	7	6.67	0	86.1	Sc Pos	116	37	10	66	.319
Scnd Half	2	4	6.15	0	52.2	Clutch	18	8	1	4	.444

1999 Season

After matching or exceed his career high in wins for three straight seasons, Mark Gardner went the other direction last season, getting hit hard consistently and finishing the season deep in the San Francisco bullpen. He allowed 27 home runs, the most on the Giants, and was prone to big innings. Gardner underwent surgery after the season to repair damage to his labrum.

Pitching, Defense & Hitting

While Gardner continues to rely on a sharp curveball to get hitters out, his curve spent too much time up in the strike zone in 1999. His mid-80s fastball must be spotted at the edges of or outside the strike zone. Gardner hit his first big league home run last season and has developed into an effective hitter. He hasn't made an error since 1995 and holds runners well.

2000 Outlook

It's rare for a pitcher of Gardner's age to rebound after surgery and such a drastic drop in productivity. His most realistic role appears to be as a long reliever, though he has been a starter for most of his career.

San Francisco

Charlie Hayes

Position: 3B/1B
Bats: R **Throws:** R
Ht: 6' 0" **Wt:** 215

Opening Day Age: 34
Born: 5/29/65 in Hattiesburg, MS
ML Seasons: 12

Overall Statistics

	G	AB	R	H	D	T	HR	RBI	SB	BB	SO	Avg	OBP	Slg
1999	95	264	33	54	9	1	6	48	3	33	41	.205	.292	.314
Career	1395	4842	530	1276	232	16	135	690	46	356	818	.264	.314	.402

1999 Situational Stats

	AB	H	HR	RBI	Avg			AB	H	HR	RBI	Avg
Home	119	24	2	19	.202	LHP		117	23	4	23	.197
Road	145	30	4	29	.207	RHP		147	31	2	25	.211
First Half	175	32	2	31	.183	Sc Pos		99	26	3	41	.263
Scnd Half	89	22	4	17	.247	Clutch		46	8	2	11	.174

1999 Season

Charlie Hayes arguably was the least productive semi-regular in the National League in 1999. He even stopped hitting lefthanded pitchers, a staple for him in the past. Part of the blame has to be laid on Hayes' left wrist, which started bothering him in spring training and finally required surgery in July.

Hitting, Baserunning & Defense

Unable to drive the ball at all, Hayes was an easy out last year for any pitcher who could throw hard. Whether his lack of bat speed and strength were a result of his wrist or declining skills is open to question, but Hayes did hit four of his six home runs in August after the surgery. He's not much of a runner, and his range afield has deteriorated.

2000 Outlook

Based on his performance, Hayes may have to settle for a minor league deal with a spring-training invitation after becoming a free agent. He has an old body and hasn't been diligent in his conditioning. How he approaches this offseason could determine whether he has much of a future as a player.

John Johnstone

Position: RP
Bats: R **Throws:** R
Ht: 6' 3" **Wt:** 210

Opening Day Age: 31
Born: 11/25/68 in Liverpool, NY
ML Seasons: 7
Nickname: JJ, Stoney

Overall Statistics

	W	L	Pct.	ERA	G	GS	Sv	IP	H	BB	SO	HR	Ratio
1999	4	6	.400	2.60	62	0	3	65.2	48	20	56	8	1.04
Career	12	15	.444	3.51	187	0	3	228.1	205	102	197	27	1.34

1999 Situational Stats

	W	L	ERA	Sv	IP			AB	H	HR	RBI	Avg
Home	3	2	2.27	2	35.2	LHB		88	17	4	8	.193
Road	1	4	3.00	1	30.0	RHB		149	31	4	12	.208
First Half	4	4	1.94	2	41.2	Sc Pos		61	8	1	11	.131
Scnd Half	0	2	3.75	1	24.0	Clutch		168	33	6	15	.196

1999 Season

John Johnstone was establishing himself as one of the top setup men in baseball before a car accident in late August left him with a back injury that eventually ended his season. His totals of hits and walks per inning were far superior to closer Robb Nen's, and Johnstone earned the first three saves of his big league career in 1999. He also led the National League with 28 holds.

Pitching, Defense & Hitting

Johnstone is a classic fastball-slider pitcher, mixing in an occasional splitter. He uses his 92-94 MPH fastball up in the zone and inside. He spots the slider on the corners of the plate. Johnstone's control was impeccable at times in 1999, especially against lefthanders. Typical of Giants relievers, Johnstone does a poor job of holding runners. He has yet to collect a big league error or hit.

2000 Outlook

Two consecutive stellar years have taken Johnstone a long way from being released by three teams in less than 12 months before the Giants signed him. If his back heals as expected, he could enter 2000 as San Francisco's temporary closer until Nen proves he's recovered from his elbow surgery.

Brent Mayne

Position: C
Bats: L **Throws:** R
Ht: 6' 1" **Wt:** 192

Opening Day Age: 31
Born: 4/19/68 in Loma Linda, CA
ML Seasons: 10
Nickname: Mayner

Overall Statistics

	G	AB	R	H	D	T	HR	RBI	SB	BB	SO	Avg	OBP	Slg
1999	117	322	39	97	32	0	2	39	2	43	65	.301	.389	.419
Career	765	2065	207	547	115	3	20	218	11	204	337	.265	.333	.353

1999 Situational Stats

	AB	H	HR	RBI	Avg		AB	H	HR	RBI	Avg
Home	163	52	1	19	.319	LHP	56	16	0	8	.286
Road	159	45	1	20	.283	RHP	266	81	2	31	.305
First Half	194	59	1	27	.304	Sc Pos	82	25	0	34	.305
Scnd Half	128	38	1	12	.297	Clutch	55	14	0	7	.255

1999 Season

A 10-year big league veteran, Brent Mayne quietly enjoyed a career year at the plate in 1999, establishing several career highs. Among major league catchers, his .389 on-base percentage ranked second and his 32 doubles ranked third. He also was the Giants' best pinch-hitter, going 7-for-18 with five walks.

Hitting, Baserunning & Defense

Mayne makes up for his lack of physical ability with a fine understanding of his own talents and limitations. He isn't especially strong in the upper body and doesn't have more than average bat speed, but he recognizes pitches well and has a level line-drive stroke. Mayne's speed is adequate for a catcher and he can leg out doubles. His defense is similarly solid but unspectacular. He throws out runners at a league-average rate and worked well with the Giants' young pitchers.

2000 Outlook

Both of San Francisco's regular catchers, Mayne and Scott Servais, became free agents and signed with the Rockies. Mayne, who landed a two-year, $4.15 million deal, will provide veteran support for rookie Ben Petrick. The Giants traded Chris Brock to the Phillies for Bobby Estalella, who's San Francisco's new starting backstop.

Joe Nathan

Position: SP
Bats: R **Throws:** R
Ht: 6' 4" **Wt:** 195

Opening Day Age: 25
Born: 11/22/74 in Houston, TX
ML Seasons: 1

Overall Statistics

	W	L	Pct.	ERA	G	GS	Sv	IP	H	BB	SO	HR	Ratio
1999	7	4	.636	4.18	19	14	1	90.1	84	46	54	17	1.44
Career	7	4	.636	4.18	19	14	1	90.1	84	46	54	17	1.44

1999 Situational Stats

	W	L	ERA	Sv	IP		AB	H	HR	RBI	Avg
Home	4	3	3.89	0	44.0	LHB	130	30	8	19	.231
Road	3	1	4.47	1	46.1	RHB	216	54	9	23	.250
First Half	2	1	3.00	1	30.0	Sc Pos	87	15	2	20	.172
Scnd Half	5	3	4.77	0	60.1	Clutch	21	3	1	3	.143

1999 Season

Joe Nathan had just 199.1 innings of pro pitching experience entering 1999, and at times it showed. The former shortstop was brilliant when everything was clicking for him, as when he threw seven shutout innings in his big league debut on April 21. He was sent to the minors three times during the year, finally settling in San Francisco for good in mid-August.

Pitching, Defense & Hitting

With a long-limbed, 6-foot-4 frame and a mid-90s fastball, Nathan is an intimidating presence on the mound. He complements his fastball with a slurve-type breaking ball, and he mixes in a changeup and cut fastball as well. Lefties touched him for plenty of walks and homers last year, a sure sign he hasn't learned to throw his slurve for strikes against them. As a former position player, Nathan is an agile fielder and a good hitter. He's so-so at holding runners.

2000 Outlook

Nathan is still a work in progress, but he quickly could become a quality big league starter. His ceiling is as high as any pitcher in the organization, including Shawn Estes and Russ Ortiz.

San Francisco

Armando Rios

Position: RF/LF
Bats: L **Throws:** L
Ht: 5' 9" **Wt:** 185

Opening Day Age: 28
Born: 9/13/71 in Santurce, Puerto Rico
ML Seasons: 2

Overall Statistics

	G	AB	R	H	D	T	HR	RBI	SB	BB	SO	Avg	OBP	Slg
1999	72	150	32	49	9	0	7	29	7	24	35	.327	.420	.527
Career	84	157	35	53	9	0	9	32	7	27	37	.338	.435	.567

1999 Situational Stats

	AB	H	HR	RBI	Avg		AB	H	HR	RBI	Avg
Home	70	25	4	17	.357	LHP	26	7	2	8	.269
Road	80	24	3	12	.300	RHP	124	42	5	21	.339
First Half	98	30	4	20	.306	Sc Pos	43	13	1	20	.302
Scnd Half	52	19	3	9	.365	Clutch	28	10	2	6	.357

1999 Season

While most players were competing for jobs in spring training, Armando Rios was with his seriously ill wife. Shortly after being called up in May, Rios dove for a ball in the outfield and tore his left rotator cuff, requiring arthroscopic surgery. He survived both hardships to excel in September, when injuries struck down Barry Bonds and Ellis Burks.

Hitting, Baserunning & Defense

Rios has surprising power for a player his size. He's an extremely patient hitter, and he has learned to recognize the pitches he can drive and those he can't handle. Rios is an average runner who can steal a base, but he doesn't have the ideal range to play center field. His arm strength is good.

2000 Outlook

As long as Bonds and Burks are healthy there's no regular job for Rios, but those two mid-30s sluggers have enough health worries to give Rios plenty of at-bats. With Burks a free agent after 2000, Rios is the in-house favorite to assume the right-field job.

Felix Rodriguez

Position: RP
Bats: R **Throws:** R
Ht: 6' 1" **Wt:** 190

Opening Day Age: 27
Born: 12/5/72 in Montecristi, Dominican Republic
ML Seasons: 4

Overall Statistics

	W	L	Pct.	ERA	G	GS	Sv	IP	H	BB	SO	HR	Ratio
1999	2	3	.400	3.80	47	0	0	66.1	67	29	55	6	1.45
Career	3	6	.333	4.47	127	1	5	167.0	170	91	130	15	1.56

1999 Situational Stats

	W	L	ERA	Sv	IP		AB	H	HR	RBI	Avg
Home	2	1	4.33	0	27.0	LHB	103	23	1	14	.223
Road	0	2	3.43	0	39.1	RHB	153	44	5	30	.288
First Half	1	2	3.65	0	37.0	Sc Pos	88	26	2	40	.295
Scnd Half	1	1	3.99	0	29.1	Clutch	62	12	0	7	.194

1999 Season

Felix Rodriguez was the closest thing to a long man in Giants manager Dusty Baker's seven-man bullpen, throwing 66.1 innings, second among the club's relievers behind closer Robb Nen's 72.1. Rodriguez demonstrated better control in that role than he had as a closer for the Diamondbacks, who traded him to San Francisco in December 1998 for minor leaguers Troy Brohawn and Chris Van Rossum.

Pitching, Defense & Hitting

Rodriguez has a well above-average fastball that can hit 96-97 MPH and consistently reaches 93-94 MPH. His troubles begin when the pitch straightens out and sits in the middle of the plate. Rodriguez' slider has shown improvement but still isn't consistent. Originally a catching prospect in the Dodgers organization, he knows how to handle himself at the plate. He was 2-for-6 with a double and a home run in 1999. Rodriguez' quick release to the plate deters basestealers, and he never has made an error in the majors.

2000 Outlook

The shine that made the Diamondbacks think that Rodriguez could be their closer in 1998 has worn off, but he's making progress towards becoming a steady big league reliever.

F.P. Santangelo

Position: CF/LF/2B
Bats: B **Throws:** R
Ht: 5'10" **Wt:** 180

Opening Day Age: 32
Born: 10/24/67 in
Livonia, MI
ML Seasons: 5
Pronunciation:
san-TAN-jel-oh

Overall Statistics

	G	AB	R	H	D	T	HR	RBI	SB	BB	SO	Avg	OBP	Slg
1999	113	254	49	66	17	3	3	26	12	53	54	.260	.406	.386
Career	552	1478	223	373	79	14	20	145	33	208	269	.252	.369	.365

1999 Situational Stats

	AB	H	HR	RBI	Avg		AB	H	HR	RBI	Avg
Home	112	25	2	15	.223	LHP	132	37	2	12	.280
Road	142	41	1	11	.289	RHP	122	29	1	14	.238
First Half	134	38	2	15	.284	Sc Pos	67	18	1	23	.269
Scnd Half	120	28	1	11	.233	Clutch	39	9	0	2	.231

1999 Season

Signed as a free agent after the Expos non-tendered
him, F.P. Santangelo rebounded from an injury-
plagued 1998 to re-establish himself as one of the
game's more versatile and effective utilitymen. He
played every position but first base and catcher,
platooning mostly against lefthanders, and also
pinch-hit a team-high 29 times. His .406 on-base
percentage led all Giants with 300 plate appearances.

Hitting, Baserunning & Defense

Average speed and arm strength are about the only
notable physical tools that Santangelo can claim.
The rest he has to make up through hard work and
scrappy effort. He kept his swing shorter last year
than in 1998, when he became overly pull-conscious. While Santangelo played mostly outfield
for the Giants in 1999, he's equally adept as a
middle infielder.

2000 Outlook

Santangelo became a free agent after getting non-
tendered in December. His versatility and ability to
reach base should land him a job elsewhere.

Scott Servais

Position: C
Bats: R **Throws:** R
Ht: 6' 2" **Wt:** 210

Opening Day Age: 32
Born: 6/4/67 in
LaCrosse, WI
ML Seasons: 9
Pronunciation:
SURR-viss

Overall Statistics

	G	AB	R	H	D	T	HR	RBI	SB	BB	SO	Avg	OBP	Slg
1999	69	198	21	54	10	0	5	21	0	13	31	.273	.327	.399
Career	769	2368	235	581	126	2	62	306	3	172	387	.245	.306	.379

1999 Situational Stats

	AB	H	HR	RBI	Avg		AB	H	HR	RBI	Avg
Home	80	23	0	6	.288	LHP	89	27	3	9	.303
Road	118	31	5	15	.263	RHP	109	27	2	12	.248
First Half	112	28	4	14	.250	Sc Pos	54	15	0	15	.278
Scnd Half	86	26	1	7	.302	Clutch	28	8	1	4	.286

1999 Season

Scott Servais was headed towards a typical Scott
Servais season, 10 home runs and 40 RBI, when he
dislocated his right thumb on a foul tip in early
June and went on the disabled list. Playing mostly
against lefthanders, against whom he hit .303, Servais batted a career-high .273.

Hitting, Baserunning & Defense

Servais' offensive game is limited and predictable.
He has a long, level swing, which produces lots of
groundballs and prevents him from using his natural strength to loft the ball out of the park. He's
aggressive early in the count. Pitchers like to jam
him with fastballs inside. Servais is one of the
slower runners in baseball. Defensively, he's a
sound handler of pitchers and has no fear of blocking pitches or baserunners. With only adequate arm
strength and a slow release, Servais isn't a threat to
shut down the running game.

2000 Outlook

The Giants let Servais walk as a free agent. He
signed a minor league contract worth $625,000
with Colorado, where he's third on the depth chart.

San Francisco

Other San Francisco Giants

Chris Brock (Pos: RHP, Age: 30)

	W	L	Pct.	ERA	G	GS	Sv	IP	H	BB	SO	HR	Ratio
1999	6	8	.429	5.48	19	19	0	106.2	124	41	76	18	1.55
Career	6	8	.429	5.24	39	25	0	165.0	189	67	111	23	1.55

After strong seasons at Triple-A Richmond and Fresno in 1997 and '98, Brock looked good in April. He struggled after a few good starts, then was lost to reconstructive knee surgery. He was traded to the Phillies in December for catcher Bobby Estalella, who becomes San Francisco's top catcher. 2000 Outlook: C

Jay Canizaro (Pos: 2B, Age: 26, Bats: R)

	G	AB	R	H	D	T	HR	RBI	SB	BB	SO	Avg	OBP	Slg
1999	12	18	5	8	2	0	1	9	1	1	2	.444	.474	.722
Career	55	138	16	32	6	1	3	17	1	10	40	.232	.287	.355

Canizaro looked like the successor to Robby Thompson in the mid-1990s, but he hit the wall in Triple-A. He may have rekindled hope by hitting .280-26-78 at Triple-A Fresno last year. 2000 Outlook: C

Miguel del Toro (Pos: RHP, Age: 27)

	W	L	Pct.	ERA	G	GS	Sv	IP	H	BB	SO	HR	Ratio
1999	0	0	-	4.18	14	0	0	23.2	24	11	20	5	1.48
Career	0	0	-	4.18	14	0	0	23.2	24	11	20	5	1.48

Other than being a bit homer-prone in the Pacific Coast League, del Toro pitched very well in Triple-A in 1999. He struggled with the Giants in April, but pitched better upon returning in September. 2000 Outlook: B

Wilson Delgado (Pos: SS/2B, Age: 24, Bats: B)

	G	AB	R	H	D	T	HR	RBI	SB	BB	SO	Avg	OBP	Slg
1999	35	71	7	18	2	1	0	3	1	5	9	.254	.312	.310
Career	59	112	12	29	4	1	0	6	2	7	19	.259	.320	.313

Rich Aurilia's emergence has killed Delgado's chances of becoming a big league regular, but he's a decent middle infielder who would make an inexpensive utility-man. 2000 Outlook: B

Edwards Guzman (Pos: 3B, Age: 23, Bats: L)

	G	AB	R	H	D	T	HR	RBI	SB	BB	SO	Avg	OBP	Slg
1999	14	15	0	0	0	0	0	0	0	0	4	.000	.000	.000
Career	14	15	0	0	0	0	0	0	0	0	4	.000	.000	.000

Guzman, a contact hitter, hit for even less power in his second year at Triple-A Fresno in 1999. He didn't reach base in his first trip to the bigs, but he needs to because his glove won't earn him a job. 2000 Outlook: C

Ramon Martinez (Pos: 2B/3B/SS, Age: 27, Bats: R)

	G	AB	R	H	D	T	HR	RBI	SB	BB	SO	Avg	OBP	Slg
1999	61	144	21	38	6	0	5	19	1	14	17	.264	.327	.410
Career	80	163	25	44	7	0	5	19	1	18	19	.270	.341	.405

Martinez reached double-digit homers for the first time in the Pacific Coast League last season. He's good defensively, and his bat and glove should earn him a utility role. 2000 Outlook: B

Doug Mirabelli (Pos: C, Age: 29, Bats: R)

	G	AB	R	H	D	T	HR	RBI	SB	BB	SO	Avg	OBP	Slg
1999	33	87	10	22	6	0	1	10	0	9	25	.253	.327	.356
Career	58	129	14	31	9	0	2	15	0	15	38	.240	.322	.357

Mirabelli turned in his best Triple-A season in 1999, batting .313-14-51 with a .402 OBP in 320 at-bats. He'll at least platoon for the Giants this year. 2000 Outlook: B

Bronswell Patrick (Pos: RHP, Age: 29)

	W	L	Pct.	ERA	G	GS	Sv	IP	H	BB	SO	HR	Ratio
1999	1	0	1.000	10.13	6	0	1	5.1	9	3	6	1	2.25
Career	5	1	.833	5.04	38	3	1	84.0	92	32	55	10	1.48

Patrick's numbers at Triple-A Fresno were respectable for the Pacific Coast League, but he couldn't provide much help when he was recalled in September. He was taken off the 40-man roster and became a free agent a month later. 2000 Outlook: C

Rich Rodriguez (Pos: LHP, Age: 37)

	W	L	Pct.	ERA	G	GS	Sv	IP	H	BB	SO	HR	Ratio
1999	3	0	1.000	5.24	62	0	0	56.2	60	28	44	8	1.55
Career	26	17	.605	3.47	485	2	7	544.1	524	217	332	52	1.36

For most of the 1990s Rodriguez has been an effective southpaw specialist, but his numbers have declined steadily since his solid 1997 season. He struggled against lefties last year. 2000 Outlook: B

Jerry Spradlin (Pos: RHP, Age: 32)

	W	L	Pct.	ERA	G	GS	Sv	IP	H	BB	SO	HR	Ratio
1999	3	1	.750	4.87	63	0	0	61.0	65	32	54	5	1.59
Career	13	14	.481	4.35	252	0	4	281.2	270	90	225	29	1.28

After a career year in 1998 with the Phils, Spradlin inked a two-year deal with Cleveland last winter. But the Tribe traded him to the Giants in late April, and he was more run of the mill. They traded him to the Royals in December for a player to be named. 2000 Outlook: B

Julian Tavarez (Pos: RHP, Age: 26)

	W	L	Pct.	ERA	G	GS	Sv	IP	H	BB	SO	HR	Ratio
1999	2	0	1.000	5.93	47	0	0	54.2	65	25	33	7	1.65
Career	29	19	.604	4.41	313	12	1	432.2	488	152	256	42	1.48

Tavarez looked like he might be a budding closer with Cleveland in 1995, but he hasn't been very effective since then. The Rockies claimed him on waivers in November and signed him to a one-year deal worth $1.2 million. 2000 Outlook: C

San Francisco Giants Minor League Prospects

Organization Overview:

The Giants have the worst farm setup in baseball, with no Rookie-level or low Class-A club, leaving only a short-season team below high Class-A. That makes it difficult to develop younger players, so San Francisco focuses on college players while dabbling in high schoolers and mostly ignoring the foreign market. Though the bulk of their big league nucleus came from trading pitching prospects, the Giants have managed to hold onto most of their better arms. They're still much deeper in pitchers than hitters, and Russ Ortiz and Joe Nathan established themselves in the majors in 1999. The only other key players in San Francisco who are homegrown players are Marvin Benard and Bill Mueller, and neither has star potential.

Kurt Ainsworth

Position: P **Opening Day Age:** 21
Bats: R **Throws:** R **Born:** 9/9/78 in Baton
Ht: 6' 3" **Wt:** 185 Rouge, LA

Recent Statistics

	W	L	ERA	G	GS	Sv	IP	H	R	BB	SO	HR
1999 A Salem-Keizr	3	3	1.61	10	10	0	44.2	34	18	18	64	1

The words "Tommy John surgery" once were fatal when mentioned in conjunction with a pitcher's career, but these days many hurlers come back stronger than they ever were. A prime example is Ainsworth, who signed for $1.3 million as the Giants' 1999 first-round pick. After having the surgery at Louisiana State, he returned throwing harder than ever. He now throws a consistent 92-93 MPH, and his curveball and slider are both above-average. His knowledge of pitching allowed him to dominate the short-season Northwest League in his pro debut. Ainsworth could start 2000 as high as Double-A, and San Francisco expects him to move rapidly.

Giuseppe Chiaramonte

Position: C **Opening Day Age:** 24
Bats: R **Throws:** R **Born:** 2/19/76 in Santa
Ht: 6' 0" **Wt:** 200 Cruz, CA

Recent Statistics

	G	AB	R	H	D	T	HR	RBI	SB	BB	SO	Avg
1998 A San Jose	129	502	87	137	33	3	22	87	5	47	139	.273
1999 AA Shreveport	114	400	54	98	20	2	19	74	4	40	88	.245
1999 MLE	114	392	50	90	18	1	17	69	3	32	96	.230

The Giants haven't had a catcher hit more than 20 homers in a season since Dick Dietz in 1971, and they think Chiaramonte may be the guy to end that drought. A 1997 fifth-round pick out of Fresno State, he has drilled 53 longballs in two-and-a-half pro seasons. He lacks plate discipline, and unless he develops it, he'll continue to be an all-or-nothing hitter who produces mediocre batting averages. His biggest strengths as a catcher are his durability and gift for getting the most out of a pitching staff. Chiaramonte's arm strength is average. After a season in Triple-A, he'll compete for at least a platoon role in San Francisco in 2001.

Jake Esteves

Position: P **Opening Day Age:** 24
Bats: R **Throws:** R **Born:** 7/31/75 in Auburn,
Ht: 6' 1" **Wt:** 200 CA

Recent Statistics

	W	L	ERA	G	GS	Sv	IP	H	R	BB	SO	HR
1998 A Salem-Keizr	0	0	2.25	1	1	0	4.0	1	1	0	5	1
1998 A Bakersfield	0	2	4.29	14	6	1	35.2	43	30	12	24	7
1999 A San Jose	6	1	2.01	12	11	1	71.2	59	21	17	56	1
1999 AA Shreveport	8	2	3.63	15	14	0	91.2	76	40	23	53	7

The Giants may have another Russ Ortiz in Esteves. Like Ortiz, Esteves was a two-pitch reliever for a College World Series champion. Unlike Ortiz, Esteves is showing signs of blossoming into a quality starter early in his pro career. A 1998 sixth-round pick, he can reach 95-96 MPH and picks up strikeouts with his slider. He keeps the ball down in the zone and gets plenty of groundballs. In his first full pro season he went 14-3, 2.92, reaching Double-A at the midway point. If Esteves can develop a changeup, he'll be a big league starter. If not, he has closer potential.

Ryan Jensen

Position: P **Opening Day Age:** 24
Bats: R **Throws:** R **Born:** 9/17/75 in Salt
Ht: 6' 0" **Wt:** 205 Lake City, UT

Recent Statistics

	W	L	ERA	G	GS	Sv	IP	H	R	BB	SO	HR
1998 A Bakersfield	11	12	3.37	29	27	0	168.1	162	89	61	164	14
1998 AAA Fresno	0	0	4.76	2	1	0	5.2	4	5	4	6	2
1999 AAA Fresno	11	10	5.12	27	27	0	156.1	160	96	68	150	17

Southern Utah is one of the biggest doormats among NCAA Division I baseball programs, but it has produced a legitimate prospect in Jensen, a 1996 eighth-round pick. He has two good power pitches, a low-90s fastball and a slider, and also throws a curveball or changeup. He needed two years to get out of short-season ball, then reached Triple-A at the end of the next year. Jensen has averaged nearly a strikeout per inning in full-season leagues, but he hasn't been overpowering. He might have benefited from pitching in Double-A in 1999, and he'll probably return to Triple-A in 2000. He's a full year away from San Francisco.

San Francisco

Scott Linebrink

Position: P
Bats: R **Throws:** R
Ht: 6' 3" **Wt:** 185
Opening Day Age: 23
Born: 8/4/76 in Austin, TX

Recent Statistics

	W	L	ERA	G	GS	Sv	IP	H	R	BB	SO	HR
1998 AA Shreveport	10	8	5.02	21	21	0	113.0	101	66	58	128	12
1999 AA Shreveport	1	8	6.44	10	10	0	43.1	48	31	14	33	7

Though he has a 5.41 ERA in two seasons in Double-A and was limited to just 43.1 innings last year after offseason shoulder surgery, Linebrink might have the best pure arm in the system. A 1997 second-round pick from Southwest Texas State, he had his fastball close to its usual 94-95 MPH in the Arizona Fall League, and his slider is nearing the point where it will give him a second overpowering pitch. He's at least one year away from contending for a job with the Giants, who will move him to the bullpen in 2000 to reduce the stress on his arm.

Calvin Murray

Position: OF
Bats: R **Throws:** R
Ht: 5' 11" **Wt:** 185
Opening Day Age: 28
Born: 7/30/71 in Dallas, TX

Recent Statistics

	G	AB	R	H	D	T	HR	RBI	SB	BB	SO	Avg
1999 AAA Fresno	130	548	122	183	31	7	23	73	42	49	88	.334
1999 NL San Francisco	15	19	1	5	2	0	0	5	1	2	4	.263
1999 MLE	130	515	91	150	25	4	16	54	29	37	94	.291

Murray's career has come full circle, from prospect to suspect to complete failure to, surprisingly enough, prospect again. A 1992 first-round pick out of the University of Texas, Murray had batted .238 with 10 homers in 134 Triple-A games before last season. Then he hit .334 with 23 longballs, winning Pacific Coast League MVP honors while leading the circuit in runs, hits, total bases (297) and steals. It must be noted, however, that Fresno is a hitters' ballpark, and Murray batted 47 points higher and bashed 17 of his homers at home. While his offensive performance may have been a fluke, he has blazing speed. He's a terror on the bases and covers plenty of ground as a center fielder, a quality the Giants sorely need as they move to Pacific Bell Park. He'll open 2000 platooning with Marvin Benard in San Francisco.

Jeff Urban

Position: P
Bats: R **Throws:** L
Ht: 6' 8" **Wt:** 215
Opening Day Age: 23
Born: 1/25/77 in Anderson, IN

Recent Statistics

	W	L	ERA	G	GS	Sv	IP	H	R	BB	SO	HR
1998 A Salem-Keizr	1	2	4.98	5	3	0	21.2	21	14	8	22	1
1998 A San Jose	4	0	3.52	4	4	0	23.0	27	13	5	23	2
1999 AA Shreveport	2	7	5.81	14	14	0	69.2	100	54	19	54	8
1999 A San Jose	8	5	3.76	15	13	0	81.1	78	41	18	89	7

The fifth of five Giants first-round picks in 1998, Urban opened a lot of eyes in the Arizona Instructional League following last season. His lively fastball repeatedly hit 94 MPH, and looked even faster because of his effortless delivery. The Ball State product also has an excellent changeup, a hard slider and a so-so curveball. Few lefthanders can match his stuff. He throws strikes but gets hit because he lacks command within the strike zone. He'll work on that this year in Double-A.

Ryan Vogelsong

Position: P
Bats: R **Throws:** R
Ht: 6' 3" **Wt:** 195
Opening Day Age: 22
Born: 7/22/77 in Charlotte, NC

Recent Statistics

	W	L	ERA	G	GS	Sv	IP	H	R	BB	SO	HR
1998 A San Jose	0	0	7.58	4	4	0	19.0	23	16	4	26	3
1998 A Salem-Keizr	6	1	1.77	10	10	0	56.0	37	15	16	66	5
1999 A San Jose	4	4	2.45	13	13	0	69.2	37	26	27	86	3
1999 AA Shreveport	0	2	7.31	6	6	0	28.1	40	25	15	23	7

The Giants landed four premium pitching prospects in the 1998 draft, getting Nate Bump (since sent to the Marlins in the Livan Hernandez trade) and Jeff Urban in the first round, followed by Vogelsong and Jake Esteves in the fifth and sixth, respectively. Though he came from tiny Kutztown (Pa.) University, Vogelsong completely dominated the high Class-A California League in his first full season, then took his lumps in Double-A, where he was shut down with a tender arm. When he was completely healthy, he flashed a 97-MPH fastball. His curveball, slider and changeup are all potentially above-average pitches. Given Vogelsong's small-college background and abbreviated 1999, San Francisco will bring him along slower than its other top arms.

Others to Watch

Outfielder **Doug Clark** (24) has batted .321 since turning pro in 1998, and the Giants compare him to a young Larry Walker. Clark will need to develop a little more power to play as a corner outfielder. . . Pushed to Double-A in his first full pro season, hard-nosed outfielder **Chris Magruder** (22) batted .256 with little power in 1999. San Francisco still likes the switch-hitter's offensive potential, especially if he can stay in center field. . . Shortstop **Cody Ransom** (24) is an athletic defender with nice pop for a middle infielder. He'll be more of an offensive threat, however, once he sheds his homer-hitter's mentality. . . Catcher **Sammy Serrano** (23) is a promising hitter with power to the opposite field. He's still developing behind the plate, with his receiving skills the highlight of his defense. . . 1998 first-round pick **Tony Torcato** (20) hit .291 that season in the Northwest League, nearly becoming the first teenager to bat .300 in the short-season circuit since Ken Griffey Jr. in 1987. The third baseman duplicated his .291 average in the high Class-A California League as a teenager last year, and the Giants believe his power will come. . . Righthander **Jerome Williams** (18) was the second of two first-round picks for the Giants last June. He more than held his own at age 17 in the Northwest League, with a 93-MPH fastball highlighting his four-pitch arsenal.

1999 American League Leaders

Batters

Batting Average
minimum 502 PA

Nomar Garciaparra	**.357**
Derek Jeter	.349
Bernie Williams	.342

Home Runs

Ken Griffey Jr.	**48**
Rafael Palmeiro	47
2 players tied with	44

Runs Batted In

Manny Ramirez	**165**
Rafael Palmeiro	148
2 players tied with	134

Games Played

B.J. Surhoff	**162**
Albert Belle	161
2 players tied with	160

At-Bats

B.J. Surhoff	**673**
Carlos Beltran	663
2 players tied with	631

Runs Scored

Roberto Alomar	**138**
Shawn Green	134
Derek Jeter	134

Hits

Derek Jeter	**219**
B.J. Surhoff	207
Bernie Williams	202

Singles

Randy Velarde	**152**
Derek Jeter	149
Omar Vizquel	146

Doubles

Shawn Green	**45**
Jermaine Dye	44
Mike Sweeney	44

Triples

Jose Offerman	**11**
3 players tied with	9

Stolen Bases

Brian Hunter	**44**
Omar Vizquel	42
Tom Goodwin	39

Caught Stealing

Mike Caruso	**14**
Shannon Stewart	**14**
3 players tied with	12

Walks

Jim Thome	**127**
Jason Giambi	105
2 players tied with	101

Intentional Walks

Ken Griffey Jr.	**17**
Bernie Williams	**17**
Albert Belle	15

Hit by Pitch

Brady Anderson	**24**
Chuck Knoblauch	21
Damion Easley	19

Strikeouts

Jim Thome	**171**
Dean Palmer	153
Troy Glaus	143

GDP

Ivan Rodriguez	**31**
Mike Bordick	25
2 players tied with	24

Sacrifice Hits

Omar Vizquel	**17**
Deivi Cruz	14
Darren Lewis	14

Sacrifice Flies

Roberto Alomar	**13**
Juan Gonzalez	12
4 players tied with	10

Plate Appearances

Derek Jeter	**739**
B.J. Surhoff	727
Carlos Beltran	723

Times on Base

Derek Jeter	**322**
Bernie Williams	303
Jason Giambi	293

Total Bases

Shawn Green	**361**
Rafael Palmeiro	356
Ken Griffey Jr.	349

Slugging Percentage
minimum 502 PA

Manny Ramirez	**.663**
Rafael Palmeiro	.630
Nomar Garciaparra	.603

Slugging vs. LHP
minimum 125 PA

Albert Belle	**.776**
Nomar Garciaparra	.764
Edgar Martinez	.725

Slugging vs. RHP
minimum 377 PA

Rafael Palmeiro	**.656**
Manny Ramirez	.656
Ken Griffey Jr.	.640

Cleanup Slugging
minimum 150 PA

Manny Ramirez	**.667**
Alex Rodriguez	.614
Nomar Garciaparra	.608

On-Base Percentage
minimum 502 PA

Edgar Martinez	**.447**
Manny Ramirez	.442
Derek Jeter	.438

OBP vs. LHP
minimum 125 PA

Albert Belle	**.508**
Manny Ramirez	.493
Edgar Martinez	.478

OBP vs. RHP
minimum 377 PA

Derek Jeter	**.455**
Bernie Williams	.451
Jim Thome	.448

Leadoff Hitters OBP
minimum 150 PA

Brady Anderson	**.408**
Jose Offerman	.406
Kenny Lofton	.404

AB per HR
minimum 502 PA

Manny Ramirez	**11.9**
Alex Rodriguez	12.0
Rafael Palmeiro	12.0

Ground/Fly Ratio
minimum 502 PA

Carlos Febles	**2.54**
Rey Sanchez	2.34
Homer Bush	2.19

% Extra Bases Taken
minimum 40 Opp to Advance

Royce Clayton	**78.6**
Ray Durham	71.9
Todd Walker	70.7

% Runs/Time on Base
minimum 502 PA

Alex Rodriguez	**53.9**
Ivan Rodriguez	51.8
Shawn Green	50.2

SB Success %
minimum 20 SB Attempts

Matt Lawton	**86.7**
Roberto Alomar	86.0
Johnny Damon	85.7

Steals of Third

Omar Vizquel	**13**
Brian Hunter	11
2 players tied with	6

AVG Scoring Position
minimum 100 PA

Tony Fernandez	**.399**
Roberto Alomar	.392
Manny Ramirez	.386

AVG Late & Close
minimum 50 PA

Rafael Palmeiro	**.413**
Omar Vizquel	.397
Nomar Garciaparra	.385

AVG Bases Loaded
minimum 10 PA

Bernie Williams	**.583**
Todd Zeile	.542
Brady Anderson	.526

GDP/GDP Opp
minimum 50 PA

Bob Higginson	**0.02**
Ricky Ledee	0.03
Karim Garcia	0.04

AVG vs. LHP
minimum 125 PA

Mike Bordick	**.402**
Nomar Garciaparra	.400
Manny Ramirez	.383

AVG vs. RHP
minimum 377 PA

Derek Jeter	**.366**
Bernie Williams	.359
Nomar Garciaparra	.346

AVG at Home
minimum 251 PA

Nomar Garciaparra	**.378**
Edgar Martinez	.360
Omar Vizquel	.359

AVG on the Road
minimum 251 PA

Derek Jeter	**.369**
Manny Ramirez	.354
Bernie Williams	.346

AVG on 3-1 Count
minimum 10 PA

Homer Bush	**.833**
Tom Goodwin	.778
Chad Curtis	.667

AVG with Two Strikes
minimum 150 PA

Nomar Garciaparra	**.298**
Bernie Williams	.298
Mike Sweeney	.284

AVG on 0-2 Count
minimum 20 PA

Derek Jeter	**.368**
Orlando Palmeiro	.368
Mark McLemore	.360

AVG on Full Count
minimum 40 PA

Nomar Garciaparra	**.389**
Chuck Knoblauch	.377
Tony Fernandez	.361

Pitches Seen

Roberto Alomar	**2946**
Ray Durham	2827
Jason Giambi	2818

Pitches per PA
minimum 502 PA

John Jaha	**4.38**
Edgar Martinez	4.30
Jim Thome	4.29

% Pitches Taken
minimum 1500 Pitches Seen

John Jaha	**67.1**
Mark McLemore	64.9
Edgar Martinez	64.8

% Swings that Missed
minimum 1500 Pitches Seen

Omar Vizquel	**7.0**
Chuck Knoblauch	7.2
Orlando Palmeiro	7.2

% Swings Put in Play
minimum 1500 Pitches Seen

Mike Caruso	**56.6**
Darren Lewis	56.4
Mark McLemore	55.6

Bunts in Play

Mike Caruso	**47**
Omar Vizquel	45
Cristian Guzman	42

Pitchers

Earned Run Average
minimum 162 IP

Pedro Martinez	**2.07**
David Cone	3.44
Mike Mussina	3.50

Wins

Pedro Martinez	**23**
3 pitchers tied with	18

Losses

Brian Moehler	**16**
Jim Parque	15
Bobby Witt	15

Win-Loss Percentage
minimum 15 decisions

Pedro Martinez	**.852**
Bartolo Colon	.783
Mike Mussina	.720

Games

Buddy Groom	**76**
Bob Wells	**76**
Mike Trombley	75

Games Started

Rick Helling	**35**
6 pitchers tied with	34

Complete Games

David Wells	**7**
Scott Erickson	6
Sidney Ponson	6

Shutouts

Scott Erickson	**3**
4 pitchers tied with	2

Games Finished

Roberto Hernandez	**66**
Mike Jackson	65
Mariano Rivera	63

Innings Pitched

David Wells	**231.2**
Scott Erickson	230.1
Jamie Moyer	228.0

Hits Allowed

David Wells	**246**
Scott Erickson	244
Aaron Sele	244

Batters Faced

Scott Erickson	**995**
David Wells	987
Jamie Moyer	945

Runs Allowed

LaTroy Hawkins	**136**
Jeff Fassero	135
David Wells	132

Earned Runs Allowed

LaTroy Hawkins	**129**
Jeff Fassero	125
David Wells	124

Home Runs Allowed

Rick Helling	**41**
Jeff Fassero	35
Sidney Ponson	35

Walks Allowed

Scott Erickson	**99**
Dave Burba	96
Bobby Witt	96

Hit Batsmen

Jeff Weaver	**17**
Rolando Arrojo	14
3 pitchers tied with	12

Strikeouts

Pedro Martinez	**313**
Chuck Finley	200
Aaron Sele	186

Wild Pitches

Chuck Finley	**15**
Dave Burba	13
Tom Candiotti	13

Balks

Freddy Garcia	**3**
C.J. Nitkowski	**3**
10 pitchers tied with	2

Run Support per 9 IP
minimum 162 IP

Hideki Irabu	**8.19**
Bartolo Colon	7.51
Aaron Sele	7.46

Baserunners per 9 IP
minimum 162 IP

Pedro Martinez	**8.69**
Eric Milton	11.17
Mike Mussina	11.51

Opposition AVG
minimum 162 IP

Pedro Martinez	**.205**
David Cone	.229
Orlando Hernandez	.233

Opposition SLG
minimum 162 IP

Pedro Martinez	**.288**
David Cone	.375
Chuck Finley	.386

Opposition OBP
minimum 162 IP

Pedro Martinez	**.248**
Eric Milton	.299
Jamie Moyer	.311

Home Runs per 9 IP
minimum 162 IP

Pedro Martinez	**0.38**
Mike Mussina	0.71
Freddy Garcia	0.80

Strikeouts per 9 IP
minimum 162 IP

Pedro Martinez	**13.20**
Chuck Finley	8.44
David Cone	8.24

Walks per 9 IP
minimum 162 IP

Gil Heredia	**1.5**
Pedro Martinez	1.6
Brad Radke	1.8

K/BB Ratio
minimum 162 IP

Pedro Martinez	**8.46**
Gil Heredia	3.44
Mike Mussina	3.31

Steals Allowed

David Wells	**37**
Tim Wakefield	35
2 pitchers tied with	27

Caught Stealing Off

Rick Helling	**14**
Sidney Ponson	14
Chuck Finley	13

SB % Allowed
minimum 162 IP

Mike Mussina	**44.4**
Jose Rosado	**44.4**
Sidney Ponson	46.2

GDP Induced

Scott Erickson	**41**
Omar Olivares	31
Andy Pettitte	28

GDP per 9 IP
minimum 162 IP

Scott Erickson	**1.6**
Omar Olivares	1.4
Bobby Witt	1.3

GDP/GDP Opp
minimum 30 GDP BFP

Mike Munoz	**0.24**
Scott Erickson	0.21
Mike Morgan	0.19

Ground/Fly Ratio Off
minimum 162 IP

Scott Erickson	**2.8**
Andy Pettitte	2.1
Aaron Sele	1.9

AVG Allowed Sc Pos
minimum 125 BFP

Tim Hudson	**.181**
Bob Wells	.198
David Cone	.199

Pitches Thrown

Rick Helling	**3814**
Scott Erickson	3716
Chuck Finley	3613

Pitches per Batter		Relief Losses		Relief Runners/9 IP		Errors by Second Base	
minimum 162 IP				minimum 50 relief IP			
Gil Heredia	**3.40**	**Jose Paniagua**	**11**	**Jeff Zimmerman**	**7.7**	**Chuck Knoblauch**	**26**
Charles Nagy	3.49	Mike Timlin	9	Keith Foulke	8.2	Ray Durham	19
Brad Radke	3.53	Mike Trombley	8	Mariano Rivera	8.3	David Bell	17

Pickoff Throws		Saves		Relief Strikeouts/9 IP		Errors by Third Base	
				minimum 50 relief IP			
Andy Pettitte	**213**	**Mariano Rivera**	**45**	**Paul Shuey**	**11.4**	**Greg Norton**	**25**
Jim Parque	200	Roberto Hernandez	43	Bob Howry	10.6	Todd Zeile	25
Steve Sparks	183	John Wetteland	43	Keith Foulke	10.5	Joe Randa	22

ERA at Home		Blown Saves		% Inh Runners Scored		Errors by Shortstop	
minimum 81 IP				minimum 30 inh runners			
David Cone	**1.90**	**Jose Paniagua**	**9**	**Ricky Rincon**	**11.9**	**Royce Clayton**	**25**
Pedro Martinez	2.22	**Mike Timlin**	**9**	Travis Miller	17.5	Mike Caruso	24
Roy Halladay	3.00	Troy Percival	8	Masao Kida	18.9	Cristian Guzman	24

ERA on the Road		Save Opportunities		1st Batter AVG		Errors by Left Field	
minimum 81 IP				minimum 40 relief first BFP			
Pedro Martinez	**1.88**	**John Wetteland**	**50**	**Mariano Rivera**	**.048**	**Ricky Ledee**	**8**
Pat Hentgen	3.13	Mariano Rivera	49	Bob Howry	.121	Chad Allen	7
Brad Radke	3.27	Roberto Hernandez	47	Arthur Rhodes	.132	Juan Encarnacion	7

AVG vs. LHB		Save Percentage		Fielding	Errors by Center Field	
minimum 125 BFP		minimum 20 SvOp				
Mariano Rivera	**.143**	**Mariano Rivera**	**91.8**		**Carlos Beltran**	**12**
Jeff Zimmerman	.158	Roberto Hernandez	91.5	**Errors by Pitcher**	Ken Griffey Jr.	9
Paul Abbott	.159	Mike Jackson	90.7		Ryan Christenson	7

Errors by Pitcher:
Jimmy Haynes **5**
3 pitchers tied with 4

AVG vs. RHB		Holds		Errors by Catcher		Errors by Right Field	
minimum 225 BFP							
Pedro Martinez	**.186**	**Buddy Groom**	**27**	**Jason Varitek**	**11**	**Paul O'Neill**	**8**
Orlando Hernandez	.187	Jeff Zimmerman	24	Einar Diaz	10	3 players tied with	7
Derek Lowe	.188	Doug Brocail	23	2 players tied with	8		

Relief ERA		Relief Innings		Errors by First Base		% CS by Catchers	
minimum 50 relief IP						minimum 70 SB Attempts	
Mariano Rivera	**1.83**	**Derek Lowe**	**109.1**	**Carlos Delgado**	**14**	**Ivan Rodriguez**	**52.8**
Keith Foulke	2.22	Rick White	105.2	Fred McGriff	13	John Flaherty	38.6
Jeff Zimmerman	2.36	Keith Foulke	105.1	Mike Sweeney	12	Charles Johnson	36.7

Relief Wins		Relief AVG Allowed	
		minimum 50 relief IP	
Mark Petkovsek	**10**	**Jeff Zimmerman**	**.166**
T.J. Mathews	9	Mariano Rivera	.176
Jeff Zimmerman	9	Troy Percival	.186

1999 National League Leaders

Batters

Batting Average
minimum 502 PA
Larry Walker	**.379**
Luis Gonzalez	.336
Bobby Abreu	.335

Home Runs
Mark McGwire	**65**
Sammy Sosa	63
2 players tied with	45

Runs Batted In
Mark McGwire	**147**
Matt Williams	142
Sammy Sosa	141

Games Played
Jeff Bagwell	**162**
Andruw Jones	**162**
John Olerud	**162**
Sammy Sosa	**162**

At-Bats
Neifi Perez	**690**
Craig Biggio	639
2 players tied with	628

Runs Scored
Jeff Bagwell	**143**
Jay Bell	132
2 players tied with	123

Hits
Luis Gonzalez	**206**
Doug Glanville	204
Jeff Cirillo	198

Singles
Doug Glanville	**149**
Jeff Cirillo	147
Neifi Perez	143

Doubles
Craig Biggio	**56**
Luis Gonzalez	45
Jose Vidro	45

Triples
Bobby Abreu	**11**
Neifi Perez	**11**
2 players tied with	10

Stolen Bases
Tony Womack	**72**
Roger Cedeno	66
Eric Young	51

Caught Stealing
Eric Young	**22**
3 players tied with	17

Walks

Jeff Bagwell	149
Mark McGwire	133
Chipper Jones	126

Intentional Walks

Mark McGwire	21
Chipper Jones	18
Jeff Bagwell	16

Hit by Pitch

Ed Sprague	17
Jeromy Burnitz	16
Fernando Tatis	16

Strikeouts

Sammy Sosa	171
Preston Wilson	156
2 players tied with	145

GDP

Mike Piazza	27
John Olerud	22
2 players tied with	20

Sacrifice Hits

| Shane Reynolds | 17 |
| 4 players tied with | 13 |

Sacrifice Flies

Dante Bichette	10
Mark Grace	10
5 players tied with	9

Plate Appearances

Craig Biggio	749
Neifi Perez	732
Jeff Bagwell	729

Times on Base

Jeff Bagwell	331
Chipper Jones	309
John Olerud	309

Total Bases

Sammy Sosa	397
Vladimir Guerrero	366
Mark McGwire	363

Slugging Percentage
minimum 502 PA

Larry Walker	.710
Mark McGwire	.697
Sammy Sosa	.635

Slugging vs. LHP
minimum 125 PA

Chipper Jones	.739
Sammy Sosa	.712
Mark McGwire	.705

Slugging vs. RHP
minimum 377 PA

Mark McGwire	.694
Todd Helton	.670
Brian Giles	.663

Cleanup Slugging
minimum 150 PA

Sammy Sosa	.695
Vladimir Guerrero	.593
Carl Everett	.587

On-Base Percentage
minimum 502 PA

Larry Walker	.458
Jeff Bagwell	.454
Bobby Abreu	.446

OBP vs. LHP
minimum 125 PA

Rickey Henderson	.481
Jay Bell	.479
Jeff Bagwell	.476

OBP vs. RHP
minimum 377 PA

Bobby Abreu	.453
Jeff Bagwell	.448
John Olerud	.447

Leadoff Hitters OBP
minimum 150 PA

Rickey Henderson	.417
Mark Loretta	.392
Craig Biggio	.386

AB per HR
minimum 502 PA

Mark McGwire	8.0
Sammy Sosa	9.9
Larry Walker	11.8

Ground/Fly Ratio
minimum 502 PA

Luis Castillo	4.88
Roger Cedeno	2.23
Quilvio Veras	2.05

% Extra Bases Taken
minimum 40 Opp to Advance

Marvin Benard	70.2
Andruw Jones	70.2
Raul Mondesi	70.0

% Runs/Time on Base
minimum 502 PA

Jay Bell	51.6
Bret Boone	49.8
Tony Womack	49.6

SB Success %
minimum 20 SB Attempts

Doug Glanville	94.4
Chipper Jones	89.3
Jason Kendall	88.0

Steals of Third

Roger Cedeno	16
Eric Young	14
Damian Jackson	13

AVG Scoring Position
minimum 100 PA

Larry Walker	.420
Tony Gwynn	.412
Ellis Burks	.378

AVG Late & Close
minimum 50 PA

Chipper Jones	.417
Terry Shumpert	.395
Luis Gonzalez	.384

AVG Bases Loaded
minimum 10 PA

Fernando Tatis	.692
Ellis Burks	.625
Phil Nevin	.600

GDP/GDP Opp
minimum 50 PA

Walt Weiss	0.02
Raul Mondesi	0.02
Damian Jackson	0.02

AVG vs. LHP
minimum 125 PA

Mark Grudzielanek	.389
Mike Lieberthal	.377
Rondell White	.374

AVG vs. RHP
minimum 377 PA

Sean Casey	.356
Todd Helton	.349
Bobby Abreu	.348

AVG at Home
minimum 251 PA

Larry Walker	.461
Todd Helton	.385
Chipper Jones	.366

AVG on the Road
minimum 251 PA

Doug Glanville	.361
Rickey Henderson	.353
Luis Gonzalez	.352

AVG on 3-1 Count
minimum 10 PA

| Dave Hansen | .800 |
| 3 players tied with | .750 |

AVG with Two Strikes
minimum 150 PA

Larry Walker	.288
Michael Barrett	.281
Dave Nilsson	.271

AVG on 0-2 Count
minimum 20 PA

Darryl Hamilton	.333
Mark Grace	.323
Michael Barrett	.323

AVG on Full Count
minimum 40 PA

Jeff Reed	.414
Tim Bogar	.400
Edgar Renteria	.378

Pitches Seen

Jay Bell	3023
Jeff Bagwell	2962
Edgardo Alfonzo	2951

Pitches per PA
minimum 502 PA

Jay Bell	4.39
Bobby Abreu	4.31
Rickey Henderson	4.27

% Pitches Taken
minimum 1500 Pitches Seen

Rickey Henderson	65.0
John Olerud	64.7
Eric Young	63.5

% Swings that Missed
minimum 1500 Pitches Seen

Alex Arias	7.0
Darryl Hamilton	8.5
Mark Loretta	8.8

% Swings Put in Play
minimum 1500 Pitches Seen

Eric Young	62.9
Alex Arias	55.6
Rey Ordonez	55.3

Bunts in Play

Marvin Benard	33
Luis Castillo	31
Neifi Perez	29

Pitchers

Earned Run Average
minimum 162 IP

Randy Johnson	2.48
Kevin Millwood	2.68
Mike Hampton	2.90

Wins

Mike Hampton	22
Jose Lima	21
Greg Maddux	19

Losses

Steve Trachsel	18
Dennis Springer	16
Brian Meadows	15

Win-Loss Percentage
minimum 15 decisions

Mike Hampton	.846
Steve Parris	.733
2 pitchers tied with	.720

Games

Steve Kline	82
Turk Wendell	80
2 pitchers tied with	79

Games Started

Kevin Brown	35
Tom Glavine	35
Randy Johnson	35
Jose Lima	35
Shane Reynolds	35

Complete Games

Randy Johnson	12
Curt Schilling	8
Pedro Astacio	7

Shutouts

Andy Ashby	3
6 pitchers tied with	2

Games Finished

Robb Nen	64
Dave Veres	63
Bob Wickman	63

Innings Pitched

Randy Johnson	271.2
Kevin Brown	252.1
Jose Lima	246.1

Hits Allowed

Tom Glavine	259
Pedro Astacio	258
Greg Maddux	258

Batters Faced

Randy Johnson	1079
Jose Lima	1024
Tom Glavine	1023

Runs Allowed

Darryl Kile	150
Brian Bohanon	146
Pedro Astacio	140

Earned Runs Allowed

Darryl Kile	140
Brian Bohanon	136
Pedro Astacio	130

Home Runs Allowed

Pedro Astacio	38
Chad Ogea	36
2 pitchers tied with	34

Walks Allowed

Russ Ortiz	125
Shawn Estes	112
Darryl Kile	109

Hit Batsmen

Paul Byrd	17
Brian Bohanon	14
Chan Ho Park	14

Strikeouts

Randy Johnson	364
Kevin Brown	221
Pedro Astacio	210

Wild Pitches

Shawn Estes	15
Sterling Hitchcock	15
3 pitchers tied with	13

Balks

Darren Dreifort	4
Jason Schmidt	4
7 pitchers tied with	3

Run Support per 9 IP
minimum 162 IP

Paul Byrd	7.08
Mike Hampton	6.78
Kirk Rueter	6.63

Baserunners per 9 IP
minimum 162 IP

Kevin Millwood	9.12
Randy Johnson	9.47
Kevin Brown	9.84

Opposition AVG
minimum 162 IP

Kevin Millwood	.202
Randy Johnson	.208
Kevin Brown	.222

Opposition SLG
minimum 162 IP

Mike Hampton	.324
Randy Johnson	.335
Kevin Brown	.336

Opposition OBP
minimum 162 IP

Kevin Millwood	.258
Randy Johnson	.266
Kevin Brown	.273

Home Runs per 9 IP
minimum 162 IP

Mike Hampton	0.45
Greg Maddux	0.66
Chris Holt	0.66

Strikeouts per 9 IP
minimum 162 IP

Randy Johnson	12.06
Sterling Hitchcock	8.49
Jon Lieber	8.23

Walks per 9 IP
minimum 162 IP

Shane Reynolds	1.4
Greg Maddux	1.5
Jose Lima	1.6

K/BB Ratio
minimum 162 IP

Shane Reynolds	5.32
Randy Johnson	5.20
Jose Lima	4.25

Steals Allowed

Randy Johnson	42
Hideo Nomo	41
2 pitchers tied with	26

Caught Stealing Off

Randy Johnson	17
Dennis Springer	17
2 pitchers tied with	14

SB % Allowed
minimum 162 IP

Terry Mulholland	20.0
Kirk Rueter	33.3
Woody Williams	37.5

GDP Induced

Mike Hampton	38
Matt Clement	28
Darryl Kile	28

GDP per 9 IP
minimum 162 IP

Mike Hampton	1.4
Matt Clement	1.4
Darryl Kile	1.3

GDP/GDP Opp
minimum 30 BFP

Jamie Arnold	0.24
Dan Miceli	0.22
Todd Ritchie	0.21

Ground/Fly Ratio Off
minimum 162 IP

Mike Hampton	2.56
Jose Jimenez	2.50
Greg Maddux	2.22

AVG Allowed Sc Pos
minimum 125 BFP

Danny Graves	.162
Eric Plunk	.189
Randy Johnson	.193

Pitches Thrown

Randy Johnson	4206
Kevin Brown	3790
Tom Glavine	3772

Pitches per Batter
minimum 162 IP

Greg Maddux	3.24
Steve Woodard	3.24
Terry Mulholland	3.38

Pickoff Throws

Ismael Valdes	208
Armando Reynoso	200
Dennis Springer	172

ERA at Home
minimum 81 IP

Kevin Brown	1.95
Jose Lima	2.31
Mike Hampton	2.49

ERA on the Road
minimum 81 IP

Randy Johnson	2.06
Kevin Millwood	2.67
Curt Schilling	2.87

AVG vs. LHB
minimum 125 BFP

Mike Hampton	.149
Matt Mantei	.159
Scott Williamson	.171

AVG vs. RHB
minimum 225 BFP

Billy Wagner	.128
Kevin Millwood	.175
Kevin Brown	.189

Relief ERA
minimum 50 relief IP

Billy Wagner	1.57
Armando Benitez	1.85
Scott Sauerbeck	2.00

Relief Wins

Scott Williamson	12
Dennis Cook	10
Mike Remlinger	10

Relief Losses

Brian Edmondson	8
Robb Nen	8
Dave Veres	8
Bob Wickman	8

Saves

Ugueth Urbina	41
Trevor Hoffman	40
Billy Wagner	39

Blown Saves

Danny Graves	9
Robb Nen	9
Gregg Olson	9
Ugueth Urbina	9

Save Opportunities

Ugueth Urbina	50
Robb Nen	46
2 pitchers tied with	45

Save Percentage
minimum 20 SvOp

Trevor Hoffman	93.0
Billy Wagner	92.9
John Franco	90.5

Holds

John Johnstone	28
Alan Embree	22
2 pitchers tied with	21

Relief Innings

Scott Sullivan	113.2
Danny Graves	111.0
Anthony Telford	96.0

Relief AVG Allowed
minimum 50 relief IP

Billy Wagner	**.135**
Armando Benitez	.148
Scott Williamson	.171

Relief Runners/9 IP
minimum 50 relief IP

Billy Wagner	**7.1**
Trevor Hoffman	8.4
Armando Benitez	9.3

Relief Strikeouts/9 IP
minimum 50 relief IP

Billy Wagner	**14.9**
Armando Benitez	14.8
Matt Mantei	13.6

% Inh Runners Scored
minimum 30 inh runners

Jerry Dipoto	**12.5**
Mike Myers	15.4
Wayne Gomes	16.7

1st Batter AVG
minimum 40 relief first BFP

Scott Sullivan	**.136**
Lance Painter	.140
John Rocker	.145

Fielding

Errors by Pitcher

Kevin Brown	**6**
Paul Byrd	**6**
Ron Villone	**6**

Errors by Catcher

Todd Hundley	**16**
Mike Piazza	11
Eddie Taubensee	9

Errors by First Base

Kevin Young	**23**
Eric Karros	13
Mark McGwire	13

Errors by Second Base

Jay Bell	**22**
Luis Castillo	15
Warren Morris	14

Errors by Third Base

Adrian Beltre	**29**
Ed Sprague	**29**
Vinny Castilla	19

Errors by Shortstop

Rich Aurilia	**28**
Alex Gonzalez	27
Edgar Renteria	26

Errors by Left Field

Dante Bichette	**13**
Al Martin	10
3 players tied with	7

Errors by Center Field

Andruw Jones	**10**
4 players tied with	8

Errors by Right Field

Vladimir Guerrero	**19**
Sammy Sosa	8
Raul Mondesi	6

% CS by Catchers
minimum 70 SB Attempts

Henry Blanco	**38.5**
Mike Redmond	35.2
Damian Miller	30.2

Stars, Bums and Sleepers: Who's Who in 2000

Who will follow in the footsteps of American League Rookie of the Year Carlos Beltran, one of our sleeper picks for 1999? It will be most of a year before we know for sure, but we present our choices and more in this section of the book.

Some of our sleepers for 1999 were Adrian Beltre, Sean Casey, Freddy Garcia, Brian Giles, John Halama, Geoff Jenkins, Paul Konerko, Warren Morris, John Rocker and Richie Sexson. The system we use to project a future brighter than a player's past performance is the creation of Bill James, who introduced his forecasting methods in *The Bill James Baseball Abstract*. Over the years, Bill and STATS CEO John Dewan have refined the system, combining advice from our scouts and staff experts.

The system is used to project more than just sleepers. The following pages also are dedicated to predicting players in decline and those we can expect consistent performance from in 2000. There are some general truths that go into these projections. Younger players are inclined to improve and older guys tend to decline. Age 27 is when we can expect peak performance and career years from major league hitters. Players who enjoy an unexpectedly good year commonly fail to repeat their success, while those who experience a dropoff in their numbers often rebound.

Each player position in this section is broken into four groups: Expect a Better Year, Look for Consistency, Production Will Drop and Sleepers. Players are placed into these groups based on 1998 performance only.

We take a different approach with Sleepers. The statistics we show here combine major and minor league totals, and we factored in projected playing time for 2000 when we made our decisions late in 1999. Not all of our picks will demonstrate the budding promise of Beltran or Casey, but a number of them will emerge this season.

Major leaguers are considered at their most common position in 1999, with a few adjustments for anticipated positional changes. Then we look at their career trends. Using the complex formula refined by Bill and John, forecasts are generated based on complete careers. That way an unusually good or bad 1999 season isn't the primary determinant of a projection.

When appropriate, minor league numbers also are factored into the system. Bill found that minor league performance, when properly adjusted, is just as reliable as major league performance in making big league projections.

Of course, there are factors outside of our control. While we evaluate teams' positional battles in estimating playing time, spring-training results and injuries will alter the picture for many players. We also concede that pitchers are full of surprises. For every five hitters who perform consistently, there may be just one pitcher who's as reliable.

Catcher

Expect A Better Year

	1999 Statistics			
	Avg	HR	RBI	SB
Jason Kendall	.332	8	41	22
Javy Lopez	.317	11	45	0
Jorge Posada	.245	12	57	1
Dan Wilson	.266	7	38	5
Kelly Stinnett	.232	14	38	2
Mark Johnson	.227	4	16	3
Eli Marrero	.192	6	34	11
Sandy Alomar Jr.	.307	6	25	0
Scott Hatteberg	.275	1	11	0
Carlos Hernandez	DNP—Injured			
Matt Walbeck	.240	3	22	2
Joe Girardi	.239	2	27	3
Javier Valentin	.248	5	28	0
Scott Servais	.273	5	21	0
Mike Matheny	.215	3	17	0

Production Will Drop

	1999 Statistics			
	Avg	HR	RBI	SB
Ivan Rodriguez	.332	35	113	25
Mike Lieberthal	.300	31	96	0
Dave Nilsson	.309	21	62	1
Eddie Taubensee	.311	21	87	0
Brad Ausmus	.275	9	54	12
Darrin Fletcher	.291	18	80	0
John Flaherty	.278	14	71	0
Mike DiFelice	.307	6	27	0
Einar Diaz	.281	3	32	11
Brent Mayne	.301	2	39	2
Brook Fordyce	.297	9	49	2
Tony Eusebio	.272	4	33	0
Benito Santiago	.249	7	36	1
Henry Blanco	.232	6	28	1
Tom Lampkin	.291	9	34	1

Look for Consistency

	1999 Statistics			
	Avg	HR	RBI	SB
Mike Piazza	.303	40	124	2
Jason Varitek	.269	20	76	1
Charles Johnson	.251	16	54	0
Chris Widger	.264	14	56	1
Todd Hundley	.207	24	55	3
Damian Miller	.270	11	47	0
Chad Kreuter	.225	5	35	0
Eddie Perez	.249	7	30	0
Jeff Reed	.258	3	28	1
Mike Redmond	.302	1	27	0
Greg Myers	.265	5	24	0

Sleepers

	1999 Statistics (includes minor leagues)			
	Avg	HR	RBI	SB
Ben Petrick	.313	27	98	13
Ben Davis	.272	12	74	6
Ramon Hernandez	.267	16	76	2
Mitch Meluskey	.212	1	3	1
Sal Fasano	.268	26	65	4
A.J. Hinch	.252	9	31	7
Ramon Castro	.245	17	65	0
Bobby Hughes	.241	4	10	0
Jason LaRue	.241	15	47	4
Paul LoDuca	.292	4	19	2
Angel Pena	.251	5	45	3

First Base

Expect A Better Year

	1999 Statistics			
	Avg	HR	RBI	SB
Jim Thome	.277	33	108	0
Mo Vaughn	.281	33	108	0
Tony Clark	.280	31	99	2
Andres Galarraga	DNP—Injured			
Darin Erstad	.253	13	53	13
Travis Lee	.237	9	50	17
Will Clark	.303	10	29	2
Wally Joyner	.248	5	43	0

Production Will Drop

	1999 Statistics			
	Avg	HR	RBI	SB
Mark McGwire	.278	65	147	0
Rafael Palmeiro	.324	47	148	2
Jason Giambi	.315	33	123	1
Kevin Young	.298	26	106	22
Richie Sexson	.255	31	116	3
Rico Brogna	.278	24	102	8
Mike Sweeney	.322	22	102	6
Fred McGriff	.310	32	104	1
J.T. Snow	.274	24	98	0
Lee Stevens	.282	24	81	2
Mike Stanley	.281	19	72	0
Brian Daubach	.294	21	73	0
Jeff Conine	.291	13	75	0
Ron Coomer	.263	16	65	2

Look for Consistency

	1999 Statistics			
	Avg	HR	RBI	SB
Jeff Bagwell	.304	42	126	30
Todd Helton	.320	35	113	7
Sean Casey	.332	25	99	0
Carlos Delgado	.272	44	134	1
John Olerud	.298	19	96	3
Mark Grace	.309	16	91	3
Eric Karros	.304	34	112	8
Tino Martinez	.263	28	105	3
Paul Konerko	.294	24	81	1
Ryan Klesko	.297	21	80	5
David Segui	.298	14	52	1
Kevin Millar	.285	9	67	1
Doug Mientkiewicz	.229	2	32	1

Sleepers

	1999 Statistics (includes minor leagues)			
	Avg	HR	RBI	SB
Erubiel Durazo	.381	35	113	4
Brad Fullmer	.288	20	79	4
Kevin Barker	.279	26	110	3
Derrek Lee	.253	24	93	5
Fernando Seguignol	.278	28	84	3

Second Base

Expect A Better Year

| | 1999 Statistics | | | |
	Avg	HR	RBI	SB
Carlos Febles	.256	10	53	20
Todd Walker	.279	6	46	18
Fernando Vina	.266	1	16	5
Delino DeShields	.264	6	34	11
Mike Lansing	.310	4	15	2
Carlos Guillen	.158	1	3	0
Mickey Morandini	.241	4	37	6
Marlon Anderson	.252	5	54	13
Craig Counsell	.218	0	11	1

Look for Consistency

| | 1999 Statistics | | | |
	Avg	HR	RBI	SB
Craig Biggio	.294	16	73	28
Warren Morris	.288	15	73	3
Ray Durham	.296	13	60	34
Chuck Knoblauch	.292	18	68	28
Jeff Kent	.290	23	101	13
Damion Easley	.266	20	65	11
Bret Boone	.252	20	63	14
Jose Offerman	.294	8	69	18
Quilvio Veras	.280	6	41	30
Eric Young	.281	2	41	51
Ron Belliard	.295	8	58	4
Frank Catalanotto	.276	11	35	3
Scott Spiezio	.243	8	33	0
Jeff Blauser	.240	9	26	2
Wilton Guerrero	.292	2	31	7
Miguel Cairo	.295	3	36	22
Kurt Abbott	.273	8	41	3

Production Will Drop

| | 1999 Statistics | | | |
	Avg	HR	RBI	SB
Edgardo Alfonzo	.304	27	108	9
Roberto Alomar	.323	24	120	37
Jay Bell	.289	38	112	7
Randy Velarde	.317	16	76	24
Pokey Reese	.285	10	52	38
David Bell	.268	21	78	7
Luis Castillo	.302	0	28	50
Homer Bush	.320	5	55	32
Mark McLemore	.274	6	45	16
Jose Vidro	.304	12	59	0
Joe McEwing	.275	9	44	7
Terry Shumpert	.347	10	37	14
Tony Phillips	.244	15	49	11

Sleepers

| | 1999 Statistics (includes minor leagues) | | | |
	Avg	HR	RBI	SB
Jerry Hairston Jr.	.284	11	65	28
Adam Kennedy	.311	11	79	20
Chad Meyers	.295	3	49	43
Justin Baughman	DNP—Injured			
Placido Polanco	.276	1	29	3
Ramon Martinez	.291	7	36	3

Third Base

Expect A Better Year

| | 1999 Statistics | | | |
	Avg	HR	RBI	SB
Scott Rolen	.268	26	77	12
Troy Glaus	.240	29	79	5
Travis Fryman	.255	10	48	2
Eric Chavez	.247	13	50	1
Adrian Beltre	.275	15	67	18
John Valentin	.253	12	70	0
Ken Caminiti	.286	13	56	6
Bill Mueller	.290	2	36	4
Shane Andrews	.195	16	51	1
Kevin Orie	.254	6	29	1
Brent Gates	.255	3	38	1
Enrique Wilson	.262	2	24	5
Herbert Perry	.254	6	32	0

Look for Consistency

| | 1999 Statistics | | | |
	Avg	HR	RBI	SB
Vinny Castilla	.275	33	102	2
Dean Palmer	.262	38	100	3
Jeff Cirillo	.326	15	88	7
Scott Brosius	.247	17	71	9
Corey Koskie	.310	11	58	4
Greg Norton	.255	16	50	4
Russ Davis	.245	21	59	3
Olmedo Saenz	.275	11	41	1

Production Will Drop

| | 1999 Statistics | | | |
	Avg	HR	RBI	SB
Chipper Jones	.319	45	110	25
Fernando Tatis	.298	34	107	21
Robin Ventura	.301	32	120	1
Matt Williams	.303	35	142	2
Todd Zeile	.293	24	98	1
Joe Randa	.314	16	84	5
Phil Nevin	.269	24	85	1
Ed Sprague	.267	22	81	3
Cal Ripken Jr.	.340	18	57	0
Aaron Boone	.280	14	72	17
Tony Fernandez	.328	6	75	6
Bill Spiers	.288	4	39	10
Kevin Jordan	.285	4	51	0

Sleepers

| | 1999 Statistics (includes minor leagues) | | | |
	Avg	HR	RBI	SB
Pat Burrell	.320	29	94	3
Mike Lowell	.266	14	56	0
Michael Barrett	.295	8	54	0
Aramis Ramirez	.312	21	81	5
Cole Liniak	.263	12	44	0
Wilton Veras	.282	13	88	7
Bobby Smith	.262	17	66	17
Willis Otanez	.237	7	24	0
Russ Johnson	.282	5	23	2

Shortstop

Expect A Better Year

	1999 Statistics			
	Avg	HR	RBI	SB
Orlando Cabrera	.254	8	39	2
Mike Caruso	.250	2	35	12
Pat Meares	.308	0	7	0
Jose Valentin	.227	10	38	3
Alex Gonzalez (Tor)	.292	2	12	4
Gary DiSarcina	.229	1	29	2
Andy Fox	.255	6	33	4
Cristian Guzman	.226	1	26	9
Ricky Gutierrez	.261	1	25	2
Chris Gomez	.252	1	15	1
Walt Weiss	.226	2	29	7

Look for Consistency

	1999 Statistics			
	Avg	HR	RBI	SB
Nomar Garciaparra	.357	27	104	14
Alex Rodriguez	.285	42	111	21
Neifi Perez	.280	12	70	13
Tony Batista	.277	31	100	4
Miguel Tejada	.251	21	84	8
Barry Larkin	.293	12	75	30
Edgar Renteria	.275	11	63	37
Rich Aurilia	.281	22	80	2
Royce Clayton	.288	14	52	8
Deivi Cruz	.284	13	58	1
Alex Gonzalez (Fla)	.277	14	59	3
Mark Loretta	.290	5	67	4

Look for Consistency (continued)

Damian Jackson	.224	9	39	34
Dave Berg	.286	3	25	2
Jose Vizcaino	.252	1	29	2
Kevin Stocker	.299	1	27	9

Production Will Drop

	1999 Statistics			
	Avg	HR	RBI	SB
Derek Jeter	.349	24	102	19
Omar Vizquel	.333	5	66	42
Mike Bordick	.277	10	77	14
Jose Hernandez	.266	19	62	11
Mark Grudzielanek	.326	7	46	6
Rey Sanchez	.294	2	56	11
Rey Ordonez	.258	1	60	8
Denny Hocking	.267	7	41	11
Mike Benjamin	.247	1	37	10
Tim Bogar	.239	4	31	3
Alex Arias	.303	4	48	2

Sleepers

	1999 Statistics (includes minor leagues)			
	Avg	HR	RBI	SB
Jose Nieves	.262	13	77	11
Aaron Ledesma	.257	0	30	1
Desi Relaford	.243	1	27	4
Lou Collier	.310	6	32	9
Andy Sheets	.211	3	33	1

Left Field

Expect A Better Year

	1999 Statistics			
	Avg	HR	RBI	SB
Barry Bonds	.262	34	83	15
Ben Grieve	.265	28	86	4
Ray Lankford	.306	15	63	14
Moises Alou	DNP—Injured			
Carlos Lee	.293	16	84	4
Cliff Floyd	.303	11	49	5
Juan Encarnacion	.255	19	74	33
Brian Hunter	.232	4	34	44
Bubba Trammell	.290	14	39	0
Wil Cordero	.299	8	32	2
Ricky Ledee	.276	9	40	4
Raul Ibanez	.258	9	27	5
Orlando Merced	.268	8	26	2
Kevin Sefcik	.278	1	11	9

Look for Consistency

	1999 Statistics			
	Avg	HR	RBI	SB
Rusty Greer	.300	20	101	2
Shannon Stewart	.304	11	67	37
Troy O'Leary	.280	28	103	1
David Justice	.287	21	88	1
Johnny Damon	.307	14	77	36
Ron Gant	.260	17	77	13
Garret Anderson	.303	21	80	3
Chad Allen	.277	10	46	14
Richard Hidalgo	.227	15	56	8
Paul Sorrento	.235	11	42	1
Stan Javier	.285	3	34	16
Chad Curtis	.262	5	24	8

Production Will Drop

	1999 Statistics			
	Avg	HR	RBI	SB
Gary Sheffield	.301	34	101	11
Dante Bichette	.298	34	133	6
Greg Vaughn	.245	45	118	15
Luis Gonzalez	.336	26	111	9
B.J. Surhoff	.308	28	107	5
Geoff Jenkins	.313	21	82	5
Reggie Sanders	.285	26	72	36
Henry Rodriguez	.304	26	87	2
Al Martin	.277	24	63	20
Rickey Henderson	.315	12	42	37
Bruce Aven	.289	12	70	3
Eric Owens	.266	9	61	33
Gerald Williams	.275	17	68	19
Glenallen Hill	.300	20	55	5
Alex Ochoa	.300	8	40	6

Sleepers

	1999 Statistics (includes minor leagues)			
	Avg	HR	RBI	SB
Mark Quinn	.357	31	102	8
Daryle Ward	.322	36	95	1
Lance Berkman	.298	12	64	12
Peter Bergeron	.312	7	39	23
Shane Spencer	.259	10	30	0
Jeff Abbott	.290	11	43	3
Jeff Liefer	.303	9	48	4

Center Field

Expect A Better Year

	1999 Statistics			
	Avg	HR	RBI	SB
J.D. Drew	.242	13	39	19
Andruw Jones	.275	26	84	24
Jim Edmonds	.250	5	23	5
Jeffrey Hammonds	.279	17	41	3
Jose Cruz	.241	14	45	14
Quinton McCracken	.250	1	18	6
Brian McRae	.218	12	48	2
Lance Johnson	.260	1	21	13

Look for Consistency

	1999 Statistics			
	Avg	HR	RBI	SB
Ken Griffey Jr.	.285	48	134	24
Bernie Williams	.342	25	115	9
Carlos Beltran	.293	22	108	27
Preston Wilson	.280	26	71	11
Rondell White	.312	22	64	10
Kenny Lofton	.301	7	39	25
Mike Cameron	.256	21	66	38
Darren Lewis	.240	2	40	16
Tom Goodwin	.259	3	33	39
Torii Hunter	.255	9	35	10
F.P. Santangelo	.260	3	26	12
Todd Hollandsworth	.284	9	32	5
Rich Becker	.258	6	26	8
Damon Buford	.242	6	38	9
Randy Winn	.267	2	24	9
Manny Martinez	.245	2	26	19

Production Will Drop

	1999 Statistics			
	Avg	HR	RBI	SB
Brian Giles	.315	39	115	6
Steve Finley	.264	34	103	8
Brady Anderson	.282	24	81	36
Doug Glanville	.325	11	73	34
Carl Everett	.325	25	108	27
Marvin Benard	.290	16	64	27
Marquis Grissom	.267	20	83	24
Darryl Hamilton	.315	9	45	6
Chris Singleton	.300	17	72	20
Devon White	.268	14	68	19
Ruben Rivera	.195	23	48	18

Sleepers

	1999 Statistics (includes minor leagues)			
	Avg	HR	RBI	SB
Ruben Mateo	.304	23	80	9
Jacque Jones	.292	13	70	12
Chad Hermansen	.266	33	98	21
Edgard Clemente	.285	25	85	5
Vernon Wells	.323	19	89	25
Ryan Christenson	.253	5	40	14
Jason McDonald	.256	7	26	14
Adrian Brown	.280	4	21	11
Terrell Lowery	.304	17	74	10
Todd Dunwoody	.250	11	56	10

Right Field

Expect A Better Year

	1999 Statistics			
	Avg	HR	RBI	SB
Tim Salmon	.266	17	69	4
Bob Higginson	.239	12	46	4
Mark Kotsay	.271	8	50	7
Matt Lawton	.259	7	54	26
Dmitri Young	.300	14	56	3
Derek Bell	.236	12	66	18
Jay Buhner	.222	14	38	0
Brant Brown	.232	16	58	3
Jose Guillen	.253	3	31	1
Karim Garcia	.240	14	32	2
Eric Davis	.257	5	30	5

Look for Consistency

	1999 Statistics			
	Avg	HR	RBI	SB
Albert Belle	.297	37	117	17
Larry Walker	.379	37	115	11
Vladimir Guerrero	.316	42	131	14
Juan Gonzalez	.326	39	128	3
Raul Mondesi	.253	33	99	36
Matt Stairs	.258	38	102	2
Jeromy Burnitz	.270	33	103	7
Ellis Burks	.282	31	96	7
Trot Nixon	.270	15	52	3
Tony Gwynn	.338	10	62	7
Angel Echevarria	.293	11	35	1
Armando Rios	.327	7	29	7
Michael Tucker	.253	11	44	11
John Mabry	.244	9	33	2
Darren Bragg	.260	6	26	3
Roberto Kelly	.300	8	37	6

Production Will Drop

	1999 Statistics			
	Avg	HR	RBI	SB
Manny Ramirez	.333	44	165	2
Sammy Sosa	.288	63	141	7
Shawn Green	.309	42	123	20
Bobby Abreu	.335	20	93	27
Magglio Ordonez	.301	30	117	13
Brian Jordan	.283	23	115	13
Paul O'Neill	.285	19	110	11
Jermaine Dye	.294	27	119	2
Tony Womack	.277	4	41	72
Roger Cedeno	.313	4	36	66
Dave Martinez	.284	6	66	13
Benny Agbayani	.286	14	42	6
Bernard Gilkey	.294	8	39	2

Sleepers

	1999 Statistics (includes minor leagues)			
	Avg	HR	RBI	SB
Gabe Kapler	.253	21	63	11
Mike Darr	.295	12	65	12
Gary Matthews Jr.	.253	9	59	19
Alex Ramirez	.303	15	68	6
Jacob Cruz	.290	10	48	4

Designated Hitter

Expect A Better Year

	1999 Statistics			
	Avg	HR	RBI	SB
Frank Thomas	.305	15	77	3
Willie Greene	.204	12	41	0
Reggie Jefferson	.277	5	17	0
Darryl Strawberry	.327	3	6	2
Mike Simms	.500	0	0	0
Gregg Jefferies	.200	6	18	3

Look for Consistency

	1999 Statistics			
	Avg	HR	RBI	SB

Production Will Drop

	1999 Statistics			
	Avg	HR	RBI	SB
Edgar Martinez	.337	24	86	7
Jose Canseco	.279	34	95	3
John Jaha	.276	35	111	2
Harold Baines	.312	25	103	1
Marty Cordova	.285	14	70	13
Butch Huskey	.282	22	77	3
Luis Polonia	.324	10	32	17

Sleepers

	1999 Statistics (includes minor leagues)			
	Avg	HR	RBI	SB
Robert Fick	.275	5	20	4
Jeremy Giambi	.304	15	62	1
Todd Greene	.243	19	56	1
Jon Nunnally	.268	23	77	26

Starting Pitchers

Expect A Better Year

	1999 Statistics			
	W	L	ERA	Sv	Ratio
Greg Maddux	19	9	3.57	0	1.34
Denny Neagle	9	5	4.27	0	1.21
Tom Glavine	14	11	4.12	0	1.46
John Smoltz	11	8	3.19	0	1.12
Orlando Hernandez	17	9	4.12	0	1.28
Roger Clemens	14	10	4.60	0	1.47
Al Leiter	13	12	4.23	0	1.42
Rick Reed	11	5	4.58	0	1.41
Todd Stottlemyre	6	3	4.09	0	1.44
Andy Pettitte	14	11	4.70	0	1.59
Carl Pavano	6	8	5.63	0	1.46
Jim Parque	9	15	5.13	0	1.66
Brett Tomko	5	7	4.92	0	1.37
Eric Milton	7	11	4.49	0	1.23
Jeff Weaver	9	12	5.55	0	1.42
Jaret Wright	8	10	6.06	0	1.65
Steve Trachsel	8	18	5.56	0	1.41
Gil Meche	8	4	4.73	0	1.52
Octavio Dotel	8	3	5.38	0	1.38
Justin Thompson	9	11	5.11	0	1.48
Chan Ho Park	13	11	5.23	0	1.58
Kerry Wood	DNP—Injured				
Matt Morris	DNP—Injured				
Alan Benes	0	0	0.00	0	1.00
Kyle Farnsworth	5	9	5.05	0	1.48
Carlton Loewer	2	6	5.12	0	1.41
Rolando Arrojo	7	12	5.18	0	1.58
Jeremy Powell	4	8	4.73	0	1.62
Tim Wakefield	6	11	5.08	15	1.56
Pete Schourek	4	7	5.34	0	1.57
Randy Wolf	6	9	5.55	0	1.59
Odalis Perez	4	6	6.00	0	1.65
Jamey Wright	4	3	4.87	0	1.74
Donovan Osborne	1	3	5.52	0	1.50
Steve Sparks	5	11	5.42	0	1.67
Joey Hamilton	7	8	6.52	0	1.60
Tim Belcher	6	8	6.73	0	1.62
Darryl Kile	8	13	6.61	0	1.75
Ramon Martinez	2	1	3.05	0	1.06
Bobby Jones (NYM)	3	3	5.61	0	1.35
Mark Gardner	5	11	6.47	0	1.43
Dwight Gooden	3	4	6.26	0	1.69
Carlos Perez	2	10	7.43	0	1.73

Expect A Better Year (continued)

Cal Eldred	2	8	7.79	0	1.79
Mark Clark	3	7	8.60	0	1.84
John Thomson	1	10	8.04	0	1.93
Chris Peters	5	4	6.59	0	1.76
Glendon Rusch	0	1	12.60	0	2.20
Jeff Fassero	5	14	7.20	0	1.86

Look for Consistency

	1999 Statistics			
	W	L	ERA	Sv	Ratio
Pedro Martinez	23	4	2.07	0	0.92
Randy Johnson	17	9	2.48	0	1.02
Kevin Brown	18	9	3.00	0	1.07
Curt Schilling	15	6	3.54	0	1.13
Mike Mussina	18	7	3.50	0	1.27
Kevin Millwood	18	7	2.68	0	1.00
Pete Harnisch	16	10	3.68	0	1.25
Shane Reynolds	16	14	3.85	0	1.24
Andy Ashby	14	10	3.80	0	1.25
Omar Daal	16	9	3.65	0	1.24
Jamie Moyer	14	8	3.87	0	1.24
David Cone	12	9	3.44	0	1.31
Brad Radke	12	14	3.75	0	1.29
Tim Hudson	11	2	3.23	0	1.34
Alex Fernandez	7	8	3.38	0	1.25
Steve Parris	11	4	3.50	0	1.37
Jose Rosado	10	14	3.85	0	1.29
Russ Ortiz	18	9	3.81	0	1.51
Juan Guzman	11	12	3.73	0	1.40
Freddy Garcia	17	8	4.07	0	1.47
Dave Burba	15	9	4.25	0	1.40
Sterling Hitchcock	12	14	4.11	0	1.35
Masato Yoshii	12	8	4.40	0	1.30
Kris Benson	11	14	4.07	0	1.36
Ismael Valdes	9	14	3.98	0	1.33
Jon Lieber	10	11	4.07	0	1.34
David Wells	17	10	4.82	0	1.33
Mike Sirotka	11	13	4.00	0	1.40
Jason Schmidt	13	11	4.19	0	1.43
Chuck Finley	12	11	4.43	0	1.36
Woody Williams	12	12	4.41	0	1.37
Dustin Hermanson	9	14	4.20	0	1.36
Gil Heredia	13	8	4.81	0	1.31
Jason Johnson	8	7	5.46	0	1.52

Look for Consistency (continued)

	W	L	ERA	Sv	Ratio
Kenny Rogers	10	4	4.19	0	1.41
Jeff Suppan	10	12	4.53	0	1.36
Darren Oliver	9	9	4.26	0	1.38
Orel Hershiser	13	12	4.58	0	1.41
Steve Woodard	11	8	4.52	0	1.38
Hideo Nomo	12	8	4.54	0	1.42
Dave Mlicki	14	13	4.61	0	1.46
Terry Mulholland	10	8	4.39	1	1.44
Pedro Astacio	17	11	5.04	0	1.44
Hideki Irabu	11	7	4.84	0	1.33
Aaron Sele	18	9	4.79	0	1.53
Charles Nagy	17	11	4.95	0	1.47
Joe Nathan	7	4	4.18	1	1.44
Ryan Rupe	8	9	4.55	0	1.36
Francisco Cordova	8	10	4.43	0	1.40
Darren Dreifort	13	13	4.79	0	1.42
Garrett Stephenson	6	3	4.22	0	1.39
Armando Reynoso	10	6	4.37	0	1.47
Rick Helling	13	11	4.84	0	1.43
Scott Elarton	9	5	3.48	1	1.24
Esteban Loaiza	9	5	4.56	0	1.40
Wilson Alvarez	9	9	4.22	0	1.49
Scott Erickson	15	12	4.81	0	1.49
Sidney Ponson	12	12	4.71	0	1.46
Pat Rapp	6	7	4.12	0	1.48
Javier Vazquez	9	8	5.00	0	1.33
Chris Carpenter	9	8	4.38	0	1.50
Pat Hentgen	11	12	4.79	0	1.46
Andy Benes	13	12	4.81	0	1.50
Robert Person	10	7	4.68	2	1.51
Kevin Appier	16	14	5.17	0	1.50
Matt Clement	10	12	4.48	0	1.53
Kirk Rueter	15	10	5.41	0	1.48
Brian Moehler	10	16	5.04	0	1.47
James Baldwin	12	13	5.10	0	1.51
Livan Hernandez	8	12	4.64	0	1.52
Scott Karl	11	11	4.78	0	1.59
Shawn Estes	11	11	4.92	0	1.58
Chris Holt	5	13	4.66	1	1.52
Kent Mercker	8	5	4.80	0	1.64
Brian Meadows	11	15	5.60	0	1.52
Mark Portugal	7	12	5.51	0	1.46
Mike Oquist	9	10	5.37	0	1.58
Kelvim Escobar	14	11	5.69	0	1.63
Kevin Tapani	6	12	4.83	0	1.35
Steve Avery	6	7	5.16	0	1.59
Brian Boehringer	6	5	3.24	0	1.40
Paul Abbott	6	2	3.10	0	1.13
Joe Mays	6	11	4.37	0	1.44
Sean Bergman	5	6	5.21	0	1.56
John Burkett	9	8	5.62	0	1.56
Chad Ogea	6	12	5.63	0	1.51
Jose Jimenez	5	14	5.85	0	1.50
Mike Morgan	13	10	6.24	0	1.66
Brian Bohanon	12	12	6.20	0	1.66
Bill Pulsipher	5	6	5.98	0	1.56
Bobby Witt	7	15	5.84	0	1.71
Jaime Navarro	8	13	6.09	0	1.73
Ken Hill	4	11	4.77	0	1.60
Jimmy Haynes	7	12	6.34	0	1.68
John Snyder	9	12	6.68	0	1.67
LaTroy Hawkins	10	14	6.66	0	1.71
Bobby Jones (Col)	6	10	6.33	0	1.86
Jason Bere	5	0	6.07	0	1.93
Benj Sampson	3	2	8.11	0	1.99
Stan Spencer	0	7	9.16	0	1.75

Production Will Drop

	1999 Statistics				
	W	L	ERA	Sv	Ratio
Mike Hampton	22	4	2.90	0	1.28
Jose Lima	21	10	3.58	0	1.22
Bret Saberhagen	10	6	2.95	0	1.12

Production Will Drop (continued)

	W	L	ERA	Sv	Ratio
Todd Ritchie	15	9	3.50	0	1.29
Bartolo Colon	18	5	3.95	0	1.27
Paul Byrd	15	11	4.60	0	1.38
Kent Bottenfield	18	7	3.97	0	1.50
Ron Villone	9	7	4.23	2	1.31
Omar Olivares	15	11	4.16	0	1.45
Mark Thompson	1	3	2.76	0	1.47
Mike Thurman	7	11	4.05	0	1.31
John Halama	11	10	4.22	0	1.39
Brian Anderson	8	2	4.57	1	1.32
Roy Halladay	8	7	3.92	1	1.57
Brian Rose	7	6	4.87	0	1.44
Dennis Springer	6	16	4.86	1	1.50
Ryan Dempster	7	8	4.71	0	1.63
Vladimir Nunez	7	10	4.06	1	1.37
Chris Brock	6	8	5.48	0	1.55
Dave Eiland	4	8	5.60	0	1.56
Jay Witasick	9	12	5.57	0	1.73

Sleepers

	1999 Statistics (includes minor leagues)				
	W	L	ERA	Sv	Ratio
Rick Ankiel	13	4	2.53	1	1.17
Bruce Chen	8	5	4.47	0	1.27
Eric Gagne	13	5	2.55	0	1.11
Kip Wells	17	9	3.43	0	1.25
Danys Baez			DNP		
Tony Armas Jr.	9	8	2.83	0	1.21
Kyle Peterson	11	13	3.97	0	1.31
Mark Mulder	6	7	4.06	0	1.42
Aaron Myette	12	9	3.89	0	1.36
Jarrod Washburn	5	10	5.00	0	1.28
Mike Judd	11	8	6.43	0	1.59
Dan Wheeler	10	9	4.53	0	1.40
Tomokazu Ohka	16	2	2.64	0	1.21
Juan Pena	6	3	3.64	0	1.17
Ted Lilly	8	6	4.63	0	1.27
Wade Miller	11	10	4.69	0	1.40
Peter Munro	6	3	4.39	0	1.57
Matt Perisho	15	7	4.48	0	1.49
Jason Rakers	7	8	4.92	0	1.38
Chris Fussell	10	8	5.11	2	1.46
Cliff Politte	10	8	4.12	5	1.41
Larry Luebbers	16	7	4.31	0	1.31
Blake Stein	5	4	4.29	0	1.36
Brian Cooper	13	7	3.57	0	1.18
Jason Ryan	12	12	4.11	0	1.37
Buddy Carlyle	12	11	5.10	0	1.39
Dan Smith	9	13	4.99	0	1.44
Doug Linton	8	9	4.42	0	1.36
Dave Borkowski	8	14	4.49	0	1.42
Ramon Ortiz	16	10	4.02	0	1.32
A.J. Burnett	10	14	5.00	0	1.64
Ed Yarnall	14	4	3.49	0	1.36
Jimmy Anderson	13	3	3.87	0	1.44
Jim Brower	14	12	4.70	0	1.40
Mark Redman	10	9	5.35	0	1.48
Bronswell Patrick	15	11	5.05	1	1.46
Michael Tejera	13	6	3.44	0	1.29
Mike Romano	12	8	4.36	0	1.43
Brent Billingsley	2	9	6.23	0	1.62
Vicente Padilla	11	9	3.98	0	1.41
Corey Lee	11	6	4.17	0	1.34
Doug Davis	11	4	3.25	0	1.35
Rob Ramsay	10	9	4.61	0	1.30
Jin Ho Cho	11	6	4.05	0	1.21
Brett Laxton	13	9	3.68	0	1.32
Pat Daneker	10	12	4.26	0	1.36
Ryan Glynn	8	6	4.84	0	1.54
Mickey Callaway	9	4	4.80	0	1.58
Dan Reichert	11	4	5.04	0	1.50
Matt Riley	13	8	3.30	0	1.24
Micah Bowie	6	11	5.95	0	1.56
Luther Hackman	12	11	4.47	0	1.50

Relief Pitchers

Expect A Better Year

	1999 Statistics			
	W	L	ERA	Sv	Ratio
Derek Lowe	6	3	2.63	15	1.00
Paul Shuey	8	5	3.53	6	1.32
Dave Veres	4	8	5.14	31	1.62
Matt Karchner	1	0	2.50	0	1.39
Jason Christiansen	2	3	4.06	3	1.27
Billy Taylor	1	6	4.95	26	1.62
Gabe White	1	2	4.43	0	1.34
Steve Reed	3	2	4.23	0	1.44
Ricky Bottalico	3	7	4.91	20	1.80
Jason Isringhausen	1	4	4.73	9	1.52
Mike Stanton	2	2	4.33	0	1.43
Dan Miceli	4	5	4.46	2	1.50
Marc Wilkins	2	3	4.24	0	1.47
Jay Powell	5	4	4.32	4	1.63
Doug Henry	2	4	4.63	2	1.69
Greg McMichael	1	1	4.50	0	1.63
Jerry Dipoto	4	5	4.26	1	1.56
Shig. Hasegawa	4	6	4.91	2	1.48
Mike Cather	3	7	6.91	1	1.58
Tom Davey	2	1	4.71	1	1.57
Jerry Spradlin	3	1	4.87	0	1.59
Scott Radinsky	2	1	4.88	3	1.63
Rich Rodriguez	3	0	5.24	0	1.55
Rod Beck	2	5	5.93	10	1.55
Danny Patterson	2	0	5.67	0	1.59
Julian Tavarez	2	0	5.93	0	1.65
Jesse Orosco	0	2	5.34	1	1.50
Carlos Castillo	2	2	5.71	0	1.44
Juan Acevedo	6	8	5.89	4	1.59
Arthur Rhodes	3	4	5.43	3	1.66
Dan Plesac	2	4	5.89	1	1.51
Rafael Roque	1	6	5.34	1	1.64
Chuck McElroy	3	1	5.50	0	1.78
Matt Anderson	2	1	5.68	0	1.79
Willie Blair	3	11	6.85	0	1.59
Mike Fetters	1	0	5.81	0	1.84
Jose Silva	2	8	5.73	4	1.51
Jesus Sanchez	5	7	6.01	0	1.89
Antonio Osuna	0	0	7.71	0	1.50
Mike Holtz	2	3	8.06	0	1.84
Jim Poole	2	1	4.71	1	1.87
Mike DeJean	2	4	8.41	0	1.89
Tom Martin	0	1	8.68	0	1.71
Esteban Yan	3	4	5.90	0	1.79
Paul Spoljaric	2	5	6.26	0	1.69
Val. de los Santos	0	1	6.48	0	2.28
Eric Gunderson	0	0	7.20	0	2.20
Paul Assenmacher	2	1	8.18	0	2.03
Rich DeLucia	0	1	6.75	0	2.36
Carlos Almanzar	0	0	7.47	0	1.69
Vic Darensbourg	0	1	8.83	0	2.05
Ed Vosberg	0	1	8.18	0	2.27
John Hudek	0	2	8.44	0	2.25
Chad Fox	0	0	10.80	0	2.25
Jeff Kubenka	0	1	11.74	0	2.22

Look for Consistency

	1999 Statistics			
	W	L	ERA	Sv	Ratio
Mariano Rivera	4	3	1.83	45	0.88
Trevor Hoffman	2	3	2.14	40	0.94
John Rocker	4	5	2.49	38	1.16
Jeff Shaw	2	4	2.78	34	1.16
Roberto Hernandez	2	3	3.07	43	1.38
John Wetteland	4	4	3.68	43	1.30
Jeff Zimmerman	9	3	2.36	3	0.83
Matt Mantei	1	3	2.76	32	1.35
Bob Wickman	3	8	3.39	37	1.52

Look for Consistency (continued)

	W	L	ERA	Sv	Ratio
Robb Nen	3	8	3.98	37	1.47
Ugueth Urbina	6	6	3.69	41	1.26
Troy Percival	4	6	3.79	31	1.05
Scott Williamson	12	7	2.41	19	1.04
Bob Howry	5	3	3.59	28	1.42
Doug Brocail	4	4	2.52	2	1.04
John Franco	0	2	2.88	19	1.45
Terry Adams	6	3	4.02	13	1.35
Doug Jones	5	5	3.55	10	1.25
Russ Springer	2	1	3.42	1	1.12
Brad Clontz	1	3	2.74	2	1.48
Jose Mesa	3	6	4.98	33	1.81
Rick Aguilera	9	4	2.93	14	0.98
Mike Jackson	3	4	4.06	39	1.25
Mike Timlin	3	9	3.57	27	1.17
Billy Koch	0	5	3.39	31	1.34
Todd Jones	4	4	3.80	30	1.49
T.J. Mathews	9	5	3.81	3	1.12
Dennis Cook	10	5	3.86	3	1.22
Bobby Ayala	1	7	3.51	0	1.34
Bill Simas	6	3	3.75	2	1.46
Paul Quantrill	3	2	3.33	0	1.44
Greg Swindell	4	0	2.51	1	1.16
Mike Trombley	2	8	4.33	24	1.39
Turk Wendell	5	4	3.05	3	1.37
Alan Embree	3	2	3.38	0	1.16
Mike Venafro	3	2	3.29	0	1.24
Sean Runyan	0	1	3.38	0	1.13
Al Levine	1	1	3.39	0	1.24
Jim Mecir	0	1	2.61	0	1.40
Jason Grimsley	7	2	3.60	1	1.41
Mike Magnante	5	2	3.38	0	1.40
Ramiro Mendoza	9	9	4.29	3	1.36
Carlos Reyes	2	4	3.72	1	1.29
Sean DePaula	0	0	4.63	0	0.94
Wayne Gomes	5	5	4.26	19	1.70
Doug Johns	6	4	4.47	0	1.22
Pedro Borbon	4	3	4.09	1	1.34
C.J. Nitkowski	4	5	4.30	0	1.32
David Lee	3	2	3.67	0	1.47
Mike Maddux	1	1	3.77	0	1.42
Anthony Telford	5	4	3.94	2	1.56
Darren Holmes	4	3	3.70	0	1.54
Alan Mills	3	4	3.73	0	1.56
Al Reyes	4	3	4.52	0	1.39
Lance Painter	4	5	4.83	1	1.39
Rich Croushore	3	7	4.14	3	1.55
Albie Lopez	3	2	4.64	1	1.41
Heathcliff Slocumb	3	2	3.77	2	1.66
Jeff Nelson	2	1	4.15	1	1.62
Jim Corsi	1	3	4.34	0	1.61
Eddie Guardado	2	5	4.50	2	1.29
Rick White	5	3	4.08	0	1.57
Mike Mohler	1	1	4.38	1	1.42
Tim Worrell	2	2	4.15	0	1.49
Mike Fyhrie	0	4	5.05	0	1.59
Mark Langston	1	2	5.25	0	1.59
Hector Carrasco	2	3	4.96	1	1.35
Ricky Rincon	2	3	4.43	0	1.46
Manny Aybar	4	5	5.47	3	1.44
Jeff Wallace	1	0	3.69	0	1.64
Onan Masaoka	2	4	4.32	1	1.53
Miguel del Toro	0	0	4.18	0	1.48
Terry Mathews	2	1	4.38	1	1.56
Brian Williams	2	1	4.41	0	1.54
Stan Belinda	3	1	5.27	2	1.41
Buddy Groom	3	2	5.09	0	1.43
Chris Haney	0	2	4.69	0	1.46
Bryce Florie	4	1	4.65	0	1.59
J.D. Smart	0	1	5.02	0	1.40
Mark Guthrie	1	3	5.37	2	1.38

Look for Consistency (continued)

Felix Heredia	3	1	4.85	1	1.56
Eric Plunk	4	4	5.02	0	1.51
Doug Bochtler	0	0	5.54	0	1.31
Mike Myers	2	1	5.23	0	1.43
Curtis Leskanic	6	2	5.08	0	1.60
Will Cunnane	2	1	5.23	0	1.48
Norm Charlton	2	3	4.44	0	1.68
Brad Rigby	4	6	5.06	0	1.59
Jeff Brantley	1	2	5.19	5	1.50
Amaury Telemaco	4	0	5.77	0	1.47
Scott Sanders	4	7	5.52	2	1.58
Matt Whisenant	4	5	5.63	1	1.58
Brian Edmondson	5	8	5.84	1	1.60
Rich Loiselle	3	2	5.28	0	1.63
Trever Miller	3	2	5.07	1	1.75
Jamie Arnold	2	4	5.48	1	1.67
Frank Rodriguez	2	4	5.65	3	1.69
Bryan Rekar	6	6	5.80	0	1.71
Masao Kida	1	0	6.26	1	1.59
Rafael Medina	1	1	5.79	0	1.71
Ricky Bones	0	3	5.98	0	1.79
Makoto Suzuki	2	5	6.79	0	1.71

Production Will Drop

1999 Statistics

	W	L	ERA	Sv	Ratio
Billy Wagner	4	1	1.57	39	0.78
Armando Benitez	4	3	1.85	22	1.04
Ron Mahay	2	0	1.86	1	0.57
Keith Foulke	3	3	2.22	9	0.88
Danny Graves	8	7	3.08	27	1.25
Rich Garces	5	1	1.55	2	1.06
Jose Cabrera	4	0	2.15	0	1.02
John Johnstone	4	6	2.60	3	1.04
Mike Remlinger	10	1	2.37	1	1.21
Armando Almanza	0	1	1.72	0	1.09
Antonio Alfonseca	4	5	3.24	21	1.39
Bobby Chouinard	5	2	2.68	1	1.07
Gregg Olson	9	4	3.71	14	1.30
Scott Sullivan	5	4	3.01	3	1.19
Donne Wall	7	4	3.07	0	1.15
Steve Karsay	10	2	2.97	1	1.28
Mark Petkovsek	10	4	3.47	1	1.28
John Wasdin	8	3	4.12	2	1.13
Bob Wells	8	3	3.81	1	1.23
Rudy Seanez	6	1	3.35	3	1.27
Kevin McGlinchy	7	3	2.82	0	1.36
Graeme Lloyd	5	3	3.63	3	1.26
Pat Mahomes	8	0	3.68	0	1.27
Jose Santiago	3	4	3.42	2	1.27
John Frascatore	8	5	3.73	1	1.34
Steve Kline	7	4	3.75	0	1.28
Steve Montgomery	1	5	3.34	3	1.31
Travis Miller	2	2	2.72	0	1.43
Allen Watson	6	3	3.51	1	1.39

Production Will Drop (continued)

Tim Crabtree	5	1	3.46	0	1.37
Rheal Cormier	2	0	3.69	0	1.25
Roberto Rivera	1	2	3.86	0	1.29
Sean Lowe	4	1	3.67	0	1.42
Yorkis Perez	3	1	3.94	0	1.38
Greg Hansell	1	3	3.89	0	1.35
Eddie Guardado	2	5	4.50	2	1.29
Mike Williams	3	4	5.09	23	1.71
Felix Rodriguez	2	3	3.80	0	1.45
Dennys Reyes	2	2	3.79	2	1.49
Braden Looper	3	3	3.80	0	1.53
Mike Munoz	2	1	3.93	1	1.33
Jose Paniagua	6	11	4.06	3	1.64
Dave Weathers	7	4	4.65	2	1.51
Miguel Batista	8	7	4.88	1	1.51
Rodney Myers	3	1	4.38	0	1.51
Scott Aldred	4	3	4.45	1	1.55
Alvin Morman	2	4	4.05	1	1.67
Scott Sauerbeck	4	1	2.00	2	1.34
Scott Service	5	5	6.09	8	1.71

Sleepers

1999 Statistics (includes minor leagues)

	W	L	ERA	Sv	Ratio
Orber Moreno	3	1	2.86	4	0.89
Chad Harville	3	2	3.03	18	1.36
Hector Almonte	1	6	3.19	23	1.58
J.C. Romero	8	5	3.39	8	1.58
Kazuhiro Sasaki			DNP		
Jay Tessmer	3	3	4.56	28	1.33
Marino Santana	2	3	4.12	1	1.28
Jordan Zimmerman	1	4	3.12	2	1.69
Mike Porzio	5	1	4.71	0	1.83
Jim Morris	3	2	4.96	1	1.59
Aaron Scheffer	4	3	2.99	9	1.30
Mike Garcia	1	2	3.41	2	1.14
Lou Pote	8	10	4.12	3	1.38
B.J. Ryan	4	1	2.85	7	1.17
Guillermo Mota	4	4	2.66	5	1.35
Byung-Hyun Kim	7	2	3.01	2	1.15
Danny Kolb	8	6	4.30	0	1.58
Francisco Cordero	6	3	1.89	27	1.32
Gabe Molina	3	4	4.15	18	1.32
David Riske	4	1	2.76	18	0.99
John Bale	2	5	4.03	1	1.26
Curtis King	2	2	3.09	7	1.06
Carl Dale	4	5	4.83	5	1.44
Chad Bradford	9	3	2.77	5	1.18
Eric Ludwick	11	6	4.25	14	1.79
Sean Spencer	2	1	4.06	7	1.41

Jim Callis' Top 50 Prospects

Former *Baseball America* managing editor Jim Callis ranks the top 50 prospects in baseball below. Only players who haven't exceeded major league rookie limits of 130 at-bats and 50 innings pitched were considered. Ages are as of Opening Day (March 29, 2000).

Hitters	Pos	Age	1999 Levels	G	Avg	HR	RBI	SB	OBP	SLG
2. Corey Patterson, ChC	OF	20	A	112	.320	20	79	33	.358	.592
3. Ruben Mateo, Tex	OF	22	Majors/AAA	95	.304	23	80	9	.348	.549
4. Vernon Wells, Tor	OF	21	Majors/AAA/AA/A+	153	.323	19	89	25	.377	.497
5. Pat Burrell, Phi	OF	23	AAA/AA	127	.320	29	94	3	.425	.602
6. Nick Johnson, NYY	1B	21	AA	132	.345	14	87	8	.525	.548
8. Sean Burroughs, SD	3B	19	A+/A	128	.363	6	85	17	.467	.490
9. Josh Hamilton, TB	OF	18	A-/R+	72	.312	10	55	19	.365	.510
13. Jack Cust, Ari	OF	21	A+	125	.334	32	112	1	.450	.651
14. Travis Dawkins, Cin	SS	20	Majors/AA/A	115	.297	10	45	53	.368	.431
15. Rafael Furcal, Atl	SS	19	A+/A	126	.322	1	41	96	.392	.389
16. Chin-Feng Chen, LA	OF	22	A+	131	.316	31	123	31	.404	.580
17. Michael Cuddyer, Min	3B	21	A+	130	.298	16	82	14	.403	.470
21. Drew Henson, NYY	3B	20	A+	69	.280	13	37	3	.345	.480
23. D'Angelo Jimenez, NYY	SS	22	Majors/AAA	133	.330	15	92	26	.395	.493
24. Alfonso Soriano, NYY	SS	22	Majors/AAA/AA/R	123	.279	19	85	25	.334	.474
25. Eric Munson, Det	1B	22	A+/A	69	.267	14	45	3	.379	.500
26. Dee Brown, KC	OF	22	Majors/AA/A+	138	.318	25	102	30	.422	.545
27. Chad Hermansen, Pit	OF	22	Majors/AAA	144	.266	33	98	21	.321	.509
28. Ben Petrick, Col	C	22	Majors/AAA/AA	123	.313	27	98	13	.402	.597
29. Dernell Stenson, Bos	1B	21	AAA/R	127	.268	20	89	2	.353	.467
34. Lance Berkman, Hou	OF	24	Majors/AAA	98	.298	12	64	12	.391	.480
37. Abraham Nunez, Fla	OF	20	A+	130	.273	22	93	40	.378	.492
39. Peter Bergeron, Mon	OF	22	Majors/AAA/AA	116	.312	7	39	23	.393	.459
40. Milton Bradley, Mon	OF	22	AA	87	.329	12	50	14	.391	.526
41. George Lombard, Atl	OF	24	Majors/AAA	80	.209	7	29	23	.320	.368
42. Matthew LeCroy, Min	C	24	AAA/A+	118	.285	30	99	0	.356	.546
43. Jayson Werth, Bal	C	20	AA/A+	101	.294	4	41	23	.390	.381
44. Adam Piatt, Oak	3B	24	AAA/AA	135	.340	39	138	7	.450	.688
45. Mike Lamb, Tex	3B	24	AAA/AA	139	.324	21	100	4	.388	.557
46. Hee Seop Choi, ChC	1B	21	A	79	.321	18	70	2	.422	.610
47. Jackson Melian, NYY	OF	20	A+	128	.283	6	61	11	.358	.413
48. Adam Dunn, Cin	OF	20	A	93	.307	11	44	21	.409	.476
50. Alex Escobar, NYM	OF	21	A+/R	3	.455	1	4	1	.500	.909

Pitchers	Pos	Age	1999 Levels	W	L	ERA	IP	H	BB	SO
1. Rick Ankiel, StL	LHSP	20	Majors/AAA/AA	13	4	2.53	170.2	124	76	233
7. Matt Riley, Bal	LHSP	20	Majors/AA/A+	13	8	3.30	188.1	164	69	195
10. Mark Mulder, Oak	LHSP	22	AAA	6	7	4.06	128.2	152	31	81
11. Brad Penny, Fla	RHSP	22	AA	3	7	4.56	122.1	137	39	135
12. A.J. Burnett, Fla	RHSP	23	Majors/AA	10	14	5.00	162.0	169	96	154
18. Ryan Anderson, Sea	LHSP	20	AA	9	13	4.50	134.0	131	86	162
19. Ramon Ortiz, Ana	RHSP	23	Majors/AAA/AA	16	10	4.02	203.2	184	84	194
20. Kip Wells, CWS	RHSP	22	Majors/AA/A+	17	9	3.43	191.2	160	80	168
22. Wilfredo Rodriguez, Hou	LHSP	21	A+	15	7	2.88	153.1	108	62	148
30. Jon Garland, CWS	RHSP	20	AA/A+	8	8	3.59	158.0	148	57	111
31. John Patterson, Ari	RHSP	22	AAA/AA	9	11	5.30	130.2	141	60	146
32. Josh Beckett, Fla	RHSP	19	Did Not Play—Signed 2000 Contract							
33. Tony Armas Jr., Mon	RHSP	21	Majors/AA	9	8	2.83	155.2	131	57	108
35. Francisco Cordero, Tex	RHRP	22	Majors/AA	6	3	1.89	71.1	54	40	77
36. Eric Gagne, LA	RHSP	24	Majors/AA	13	5	2.55	197.2	140	79	215
38. Ed Yarnall, NYY	LHSP	24	Majors/AAA	14	4	3.49	162.1	153	67	159
49. Danys Baez, Cle	RHSP	22	Did Not Play—Signed 2000 Contract							

About STATS, Inc.

STATS, Inc. is the nation's leading independent sports information and statistical analysis company, providing detailed sports services for a wide array of commercial clients.

As one of the fastest growing companies in sports, STATS provides the most up-to-the-minute sports information to professional teams, print and broadcast media, software developers and interactive service providers around the country. STATS was recently recognized as "One of Chicago's 100 most influential technology players" by *Crain's Chicago Business* and has been one of 16 finalists for KPMG/Peat Marwick's Illinois High Tech Award for three consecutive years. Some of our major clients are ESPN, the Associated Press, America Online, *The Sporting News*, Fox Sports, Electronic Arts, MSNBC, SONY and Topps. Much of the information we provide is available to the public via STATS On-Line. With a computer and a modem, you can follow action in the four major professional sports, as well as NCAA football and basketball and other professional and college sports. . . as it happens!

STATS Publishing, a division of STATS, Inc., produces 12 annual books, including the *Major League Handbook*, *The Scouting Notebook*, the *Pro Football Handbook*, the *Pro Basketball Handbook* and the *Hockey Handbook*. In 1998, we introduced two baseball encyclopedias, *The All-Time Major League Handbook* and *The All-Time Baseball Sourcebook*. Together they combine for more than 5,000 pages of baseball history. We also published *Ballpark Sourcebook: Diamond Diagrams*, an authoritative look at major and minor league ballparks of today and yesterday. Also available is *From Abba Dabba to Zorro: The World of Baseball Nicknames*, a wacky look at monikers and their origins. A new football title was launched in 1999, the *Pro Football Scoreboard*. These publications deliver STATS' expertise to fans, scouts, general managers and media around the country.

In addition, STATS offers the most innovative—and fun—fantasy sports games around, from Bill James Fantasy Baseball and Bill James Classic Baseball to STATS Fantasy Football and our newest game, Diamond Legends Internet Baseball. Check out our immensely popular Fantasy Portfolios and our great new web-based product, STATS Fantasy Advantage.

Information technology has grown by leaps and bounds in the last decade, and STATS will continue to be at the forefront as both a vendor and supplier of the most up-to-date, in-depth sports information available. For those of you on the information superhighway, you can always catch STATS in our area on America Online or at our Internet site.

For more information on our products, or on joining our reporter network, contact us on:

America Online — (Keyword: STATS)

Internet — www.stats.com

Toll Free in the USA at 1-800-63-STATS (1-800-637-8287)

Outside the USA at 1-847-470-8798

Or write to:

STATS, Inc.
8130 Lehigh Ave.
Morton Grove, IL 60053

Index

Fox, Chad	522	Glynn, Ryan	298
Franco, John	553	Gold, J.M.	524
Franco, Julio	274	Goldbach, Jeff	391
Franco, Matt	567	Gomes, Wayne	578
Francona, Terry	571	Gomez, Chris	644
Frank, Mike	413	Gomez, Richard	142
Franklin, Ryan	251	Gonzalez, Alex (Fla)	445
Frascatore, John	315	Gonzalez, Alex (Tor)	315
Freeman, Choo	435	Gonzalez, Dicky	569
Fregosi, Jim	301	Gonzalez, Jeremi	388
Frias, Hanley	343	Gonzalez, Juan	281
Frye, Jeff	72	Gonzalez, Luis	331
Fryman, Travis	103	Gonzalez, Wiki	660
Fuentes, Brian	253	Gooden, Dwight	117
Fullmer, Brad	530	Goodwin, Curtis	319
Furcal, Rafael	367	Goodwin, Tom	294
Fussell, Chris	157	Gordon, Tom	72
Fyhrie, Mike	27	Grabow, John	615

G

Gaetti, Gary	388	Grabowski, Jason	299
Gagne, Eric	502	Grace, Mark	373
Gaillard, Eddie	274	Grace, Mike	589
Galarraga, Andres	360	Graffanino, Tony	269
Gallagher, Shawn	299	Grahe, Joe	589
Gant, Ron	576	Graman, Alex	209
Garbe, B.J.	187	Graterol, Beiker	140
Garces, Rich	68	Graves, Danny	406
Garcia, Amaury	458	Grebeck, Craig	319
Garcia, Carlos	658	Green, Chad	524
Garcia, Freddy (Atl)	365	Green, Scarborough	297
Garcia, Freddy (Sea)	237	Green, Shawn	308
Garcia, Guillermo	456	Green, Steve	30
Garcia, Jesse	50	Greene, Charlie	522
Garcia, Jose	525	Greene, Rick	411
Garcia, Karim	137	Greene, Todd	22
Garcia, Luis	140	Greene, Willie	316
Garcia, Mike	612	Greer, Rusty	282
Garciaparra, Nomar	56	Greisinger, Seth	140
Gardner, Mark	675	Grieve, Ben	215
Garland, Jon	96	Griffey Jr., Ken	238
Garner, Phil	122	Grilli, Jason	457
Gates, Brent	180	Grimsley, Jason	207
George, Chris	165	Gripp, Ryan	391
German, Esteban	231	Grissom, Marquis	508
Gerut, Jody	435	Groom, Buddy	229
Giambi, Jason	214	Gross, Kip	72
Giambi, Jeremy	149	Grudzielanek, Mark	486
Gibson, Derrick	435	Guardado, Eddie	181
Giles, Brian	597	Gubanich, Creighton	72
Giles, Marcus	367	Guerrero, Cristian	525
Gilkey, Bernard	339	Guerrero, Junior	165
Ginter, Matt	97	Guerrero, Vladimir	531
Giovanola, Ed	658	Guerrero, Wilton	540
Gipson, Charles	251	Guevara, Giomar	251
Girardi, Joe	202	Guillen, Carlos	247
Girdley, Josh	547	Guillen, Jose	262
Glanville, Doug	577	Guillen, Ozzie	365
Glaus, Troy	16	Gunderson, Eric	297
Glavine, Tom	349	Guthrie, Mark	388
Glover, Gary	321	Gutierrez, Ricky	474
		Guzman, Cristian	170
		Guzman, Domingo	658

Guzman, Edwards	680
Guzman, Elpidio	30
Guzman, Juan (Bal)	52
Guzman, Juan (Cin)	397
Gwynn, Tony	645

H

Haad, Yamid	612
Haas, Chris	637
Hacker, Steve	197
Hackman, Luther	637
Hairston Jr., Jerry	46
Halama, John	239
Hall, Toby	277
Halladay, Roy	316
Halter, Shane	567
Hamilton, Darryl	554
Hamilton, Joey	317
Hamilton, Josh	276
Hammond, Derry	525
Hammonds, Jeffrey	406
Hampton, Mike	468
Haney, Chris	117
Hansell, Greg	612
Hansen, Dave	500
Hansen, Jed	162
Hargrove, Mike	32
Harikkala, Tim	72
Harnisch, Pete	398
Harper, Travis	277
Harris, Lenny	343
Harris, Reggie	523
Hart, Jason	231
Harvey, Ken	165
Harville, Chad	230
Hasegawa, Shigetoshi	22
Haselman, Bill	137
Hatteberg, Scott	68
Haverbusch, Kevin	614
Hawkins, LaTroy	171
Hayes, Charlie	676
Haynes, Jimmy	229
Haynes, Nathan	30
Heiserman, Rick	635
Helling, Rick	283
Helms, Wes	367
Helton, Todd	420
Hemphill, Bret	27
Henderson, Rickey	555
Henry, Butch	251
Henry, Doug	478
Henson, Drew	208
Hentgen, Pat	309
Heredia, Felix	385
Heredia, Gil	216
Herges, Matt	500
Hermansen, Chad	614
Hermanson, Dustin	532
Hernandez, Alex	615
Hernandez, Carlos (Hou)	478
Hernandez, Carlos (SD)	658

Hernandez, Jose	350
Hernandez, Livan	668
Hernandez, Orlando	193
Hernandez, Ramon	217
Hernandez, Roberto	263
Herndon, Junior	660
Hershiser, Orel	563
Hidalgo, Richard	469
Higginson, Bob	128
Hiljus, Erik	140
Hill, Glenallen	385
Hill, Ken	17
Hinch, A.J.	225
Hinchliffe, Brett	251
Hinske, Eric	391
Hitchcock, Sterling	646
Hocking, Denny	181
Hoffman, Trevor	647
Holbert, Ray	162
Hollandsworth, Todd	496
Holliday, Matt	436
Hollins, Dave	319
Holmes, Darren	343
Holt, Chris	474
Holtz, Mike	27
Hoover, Paul	277
House, Craig	436
Houston, Tyler	117
Howard, David	635
Howard, Thomas	632
Howe, Art	211
Howell, Jack	478
Howington, Ty	413
Howry, Bob	81
Hubbard, Trenidad	500
Hudek, John	319
Hudson, Tim	218
Huff, Aubrey	276
Hughes, Bobby	518
Hughes, Travis	299
Hundley, Todd	496
Hunter, Brian (Atl)	365
Hunter, Brian (Sea)	240
Hunter, Torii	172
Huskey, Butch	69
Huson, Jeff	23
Hutchins, Norm	30
Hutchinson, Chad	637
Hyers, Tim	456

I

Ibanez, Raul	248
Inge, Brandon	141
Irabu, Hideki	203
Ireland, Eric	479
Isringhausen, Jason	225
Izturis, Cesar	322

J

Jackson, Damian	653
Jackson, Darrin	95
Jackson, Mike	114

Name	Page	Name	Page	Name	Page	Name	Page
Jackson, Ryan	251	Kelton, David	391	Leiter, Mark	251	Maddux, Greg	356
Jacobs Field	98	Kendall, Jason	598	Leius, Scott	162	Maddux, Mike	497
Jaha, John	219	Kennedy, Adam	638	Lennon, Patrick	320	Magadan, Dave	654
Jarvis, Kevin	229	Kent, Jeff	669	Leon, Donny	209	Magee, Wendell	589
Javier, Stan	475	Kibler, Ryan	436	Leon, Jose	638	Magnante, Mike	27
Jefferies, Gregg	138	Kida, Masao	139	Leskanic, Curtis	431	Magruder, Chris	682
Jefferson, Reggie	72	Kielty, Bobby	187	Levine, Al	23	Mahay, Ron	229
Jenkins, Geoff	509	Kile, Darryl	421	Levis, Jesse	117	Mahomes, Pat	567
Jennings, Jason	436	Kim, Byung-Hyun	344	Levrault, Allen	525	Mangum, Mark	547
Jennings, Robin	388	Kim, Sun	74	Lewis, Darren	57	Mantei, Matt	334
Jensen, Marcus	635	King, Curtis	635	Lewis, Mark	411	Manto, Jeff	207
Jensen, Ryan	681	King, Jeff	162	Leyritz, Jim	204	Manuel, Charlie	99
Jeter, Derek	194	King, Ray	388	Lidle, Cory	274	Manuel, Jerry	77
Jimenez, D'Angelo	208	Kingsale, Eugene	52	Lieber, Jon	375	Manwaring, Kirt	432
Jimenez, Jose	623	Kinkade, Mike	567	Lieberthal, Mike	579	Manzanillo, Josias	567
Johns, Doug	47	Kinney, Matt	187	Liefer, Jeff	92	Maroth, Mike	142
Johnson, Ben	638	Kirby, Scott	524	Ligtenberg, Kerry	365	Marquis, Jason	368
Johnson, Brian	407	Klassen, Danny	343	Lilly, Ted	546	Marrero, Eli	625
Johnson, Charles	39	Klesko, Ryan	354	Lima, Jose	470	Marte, Damaso	251
Johnson, Davey	482	Kline, Steve	540	Lincoln, Mike	182	Martin, Al	599
Johnson, Jason	47	Knoblauch, Chuck	195	Linebrink, Scott	682	Martin, Norberto	320
Johnson, Jonathan	297	Knorr, Randy	478	Liniak, Cole	390	Martin, Tom	117
Johnson, Lance	374	Koch, Billy	310	Linton, Doug	50	Martinez, Dave	264
Johnson, Mark	91	Kolb, Danny	299	Lira, Felipe	140	Martinez, Edgar	241
Johnson, Mike	545	Konerko, Paul	82	Lloyd, Graeme	317	Martinez, Felix	162
Johnson, Nick	208	Koskie, Corey	174	Loaiza, Esteban	295	Martinez, Manny	541
Johnson, Randy	332	Kotsay, Mark	446	Lockhart, Keith	365	Martinez, Pedro	58
Johnson, Russ	475	Kreuter, Chad	150	LoDuca, Paul	500	Martinez, Ramon (Bos)	70
Johnston, Clint	615	Kubenka, Jeff	500	Loewer, Carlton	586	Martinez, Ramon (SF)	680
Johnstone, John	676	Kubes, Greg	592	Lofton, Kenny	105	Martinez, Sandy	388
Jones, Andruw	351	Kubinski, Tim	229	Lohse, Kyle	186	Martinez, Tino	196
Jones, Bobby (Col)	431	Kuo Hong-Chi	502	Loiselle, Rich	612	Masaoka, Onan	497
Jones, Bobby (NYM)	564			Lomasney, Steve	74	Mateo, Ruben	284
Jones, Chipper	352	**L**		Lombard, George	368	Matheny, Mike	320
Jones, Doug	226	Laker, Tim	612	Long, Terrence	230	Mathews, T.J.	226
Jones, Jacque	173	Lamb, David	274	Looper, Braden	453	Mathews, Terry	162
Jones, Terry	545	Lamb, Mike	299	Lopes, Davey	504	Matos, Luis	52
Jones, Todd	138	Lamont, Gene	594	Lopez, Albie	274	Matos, Pascual	366
Jordan, Brian	353	Lampkin, Tom	248	Lopez, Felipe	322	Matthews Jr., Gary	660
Jordan, Kevin	586	Langerhans, Ryan	368	Lopez, Javy	355	May, Derrick	50
Joyner, Wally	648	Langston, Mark	117	Lopez, Luis	567	Mayne, Brent	677
Judd, Mike	502	Lankford, Ray	624	Lopez, Mendy	162	Mays, Joe	176
Juden, Jeff	207	Lansing, Mike	422	Loretta, Mark	511	McCracken, Quinton	265
Justice, David	104	Larkin, Barry	399	Lorraine, Andrew	388	McCurry, Jeff	478
		Larson, Brandon	413	Lovullo, Torey	589	McDonald, Darnell	52
K		LaRue, Jason	413	Lowe, Derek	69	McDonald, Donzell	209
Kalinowski, Josh	436	La Russa, Tony	617	Lowe, Sean	92	McDonald, Jason	227
Kamieniecki, Scott	50	Latham, Chris	185	Lowell, Mike	447	McDonald, John	120
Kapler, Gabe	129	Lawrence, Joe	321	Lowery, Terrell	275	McDowell, Jack	27
Karchner, Matt	388	Lawton, Matt	175	Ludwick, Eric	320	McElroy, Chuck	567
Karl, Scott	510	Laxton, Brett	230	Luebbers, Larry	635	McEwing, Joe	633
Karros, Eric	487	LeCroy, Matthew	186	Lugo, Julio	479	McGee, Willie	635
Karsay, Steve	114	Ledee, Ricky	203	Luke, Matt	27	McGlinchy, Kevin	360
Kauffman Stadium	143	Ledesma, Aaron	270	Lundquist, David	95	McGriff, Fred	266
Kearns, Austin	413	Ledezma, Wilfredo	75			McGuire, Ryan	541
Keller, Kris	142	Lee, Carlos	83	**M**		McGwire, Mark	626
Kelly, Kenny	277	Lee, Corey	299	Mabry, John	249	McKeon, Jack	303
Kelly, Mike	433	Lee, David	433	MacDougal, Mike	165	McKnight, Tony	480
Kelly, Pat	319	Lee, Derrek	452	Macfarlane, Mike	229	McLemore, Mark	285
Kelly, Roberto	294	Lee, Travis	333	Machado, Robert	545	McMichael, Greg	229
Kelly, Tom	167	Leiter, Al	556	Macias, Jose	140	McNeal, Aaron	480

Name	#	Name	#	Name	#	Name	#
McNichol, Brian	389	Moyer, Jamie	243	O'Leary, Troy	61	Perez, Eddie	362
McRae, Brian	318	Mueller, Bill	670	Olerud, John	557	Perez, Eduardo	636
Meadows, Brian	453	Mulder, Mark	231	Olivares, Omar	220	Perez, Josue	591
Meares, Pat	600	Mulholland, Terry	361	Oliver, Darren	627	Perez, Neifi	423
Mears, Chris	254	Munoz, Mike	295	Oliver, Joe	612	Perez, Odalis	362
Meche, Gil	249	Munro, Peter	322	Olivo, Miguel	231	Perez, Santiago	525
Mecir, Jim	275	Munson, Eric	142	Olson, Gregg	340	Perez, Yorkis	589
Medina, Rafael	456	Murray, Calvin	682	Olympic Stadium	526	Perisho, Matt	299
Melian, Jackson	209	Murray, Dan	162	O'Neill, Paul	197	Perkins, Dan	185
Meluskey, Mitch	476	Murray, Heath	658	Oquist, Mike	229	Perry, Herbert	275
Mendoza, Ramiro	204	Muser, Tony	144	Ordaz, Luis	635	Person, Robert	580
Menechino, Frank	229	Mussina, Mike	40	Ordonez, Magglio	85	Peterman, Tommy	187
Merced, Orlando	542	Myers, Brett	592	Ordonez, Rey	558	Peters, Chris	612
Mercker, Kent	70	Myers, Greg	361	Orie, Kevin	454	Petersen, Chris	433
Merloni, Lou	72	Myers, Mike	523	Oropeza, Asdrubal	368	Peterson, Kyle	514
Mesa, Jose	242	Myers, Randy	658	Orosco, Jesse	48	Petkovsek, Mark	24
Metrodome	166	Myers, Rodney	389	Ortiz, David	183	Petrick, Ben	424
Meyers, Chad	386	Myette, Aaron	97	Ortiz, Jose	231	Pettitte, Andy	198
Meyers, Mike	391			Ortiz, Omar	660	Pettyjohn, Adam	142
Miceli, Dan	654	**N**		Ortiz, Ramon	18	Phelps, Josh	322
Michaels, Jason	592	Nagy, Charles	106	Ortiz, Russ	672	Phillips, J.R.	433
Mientkiewicz, Doug	182	Nannini, Mike	480	Osborne, Donovan	634	Phillips, Jason	613
Mieses, Jose	525	Nathan, Joe	677	Osik, Keith	609	Phillips, Paul	165
Mieske, Matt	478	Nation, Joey	391	Osting, Jimmy	368	Phillips, Tony	227
Millar, Kevin	448	Naulty, Dan	207	Osuna, Antonio	500	Piatt, Adam	231
Miller, Damian	340	Navarro, Jaime	93	Oswalt, Roy	480	Piazza, Mike	559
Miller, Kurt	389	Ndungidi, Ntema	52	Otanez, Willis	320	Pickering, Calvin	51
Miller, Travis	185	Neagle, Denny	400	Owens, Eric	655	Pierre, Juan	436
Miller, Trever	478	Nelson, Jeff	205	Owens, Ryan	345	Pierzynski, A.J.	187
Miller, Wade	480	Nen, Robb	671	Ozuna, Pablo	458	Pineiro, Joel	253
Mills, Alan	498	Network Associates Coliseum	210			Piniella, Lou	233
Millwood, Kevin	357	Neugebauer, Nick	525	**P**		Pisciotta, Marc	163
Milton, Eric	177	Nevin, Phil	649	Pacific Bell Park	661	Pittsley, Jim	523
Minor, Ryan	51	Newhan, David	658	Padilla, Vicente	345	Plesac, Dan	341
Mintz, Steve	27	Newman, Alan	275	Painter, Lance	635	Plunk, Eric	519
Mirabelli, Doug	680	Nicholson, Kevin	660	Palmeiro, Orlando	24	Polanco, Placido	634
Mlicki, Dave	130	Nickle, Doug	592	Palmeiro, Rafael	286	Politte, Cliff	589
Moehler, Brian	131	Nieves, Jose	377	Palmer, Dean	132	Polonia, Luis	139
Mohler, Mike	635	Nilsson, Dave	512	Paniagua, Jose	250	Ponson, Sidney	41
Molina, Ben	27	Nitkowski, C.J.	140	Paquette, Craig	635	Poole, Jim	118
Molina, Gabe	51	Nixon, Otis	366	Park, Chan Ho	489	Porter, Bo	389
Molina, Jose	389	Nixon, Trot	59	Parque, Jim	86	Portugal, Mark	73
Monahan, Shane	252	Noel, Todd	209	Parris, Steve	407	Porzio, Mike	433
Mondesi, Raul	488	Nomo, Hideo	513	Patrick, Bronswell	680	Posada, Jorge	199
Montgomery, Jeff	162	Norris, Ben	345	Patterson, Corey	391	Pose, Scott	163
Montgomery, Steve	587	Norton, Greg	84	Patterson, Danny	297	Pote, Lou	28
Mora, Melvin	567	Norton, Phillip	391	Patterson, John	345	Powell, Dante	343
Morandini, Mickey	376	Nunez, Abraham (Fla)	457	Paul, Josh	97	Powell, Jay	476
Mordecai, Mike	542	Nunez, Abraham (Pit)	609	Pavano, Carl	533	Powell, Jeremy	543
Moreno, Orber	165	Nunez, Franklin	592	Payton, Jay	569	Pratt, Todd	564
Morgan, Mike	297	Nunez, Jorge	502	Peavy, Jacob	660	Prince, Tom	590
Morgan, Scott	120	Nunez, Vladimir	449	Pena, Angel	498	Pritchett, Chris	28
Morman, Alvin	158	Nunnally, Jon	72	Pena, Carlos	299	Pro Player Stadium	437
Morris, Hal	411			Pena, Jesus	95	Prokopec, Luke	502
Morris, Jim	275	**O**		Pena, Juan	75	Pulsipher, Bill	520
Morris, Matt	633	Oates, Johnny	279	Pena, Willy Mo	209		
Morris, Warren	601	O'Brien, Charlie	27	Penny, Brad	458	**Q**	
Mota, Guillermo	543	Ochoa, Alex	519	Peoples, Danny	120	Qualcomm Stadium	639
Mota, Tony	502	Offerman, Jose	60	Percival, Troy	19	Quantrill, Paul	318
Mouton, James	545	Ogea, Chad	587	Perez, Antonio	413	Quevedo, Ruben	391
Mouton, Lyle	523	Ohka, Tomokazu	75	Perez, Carlos	499	Quinn, Mark	165
		Ojala, Kirt	456				

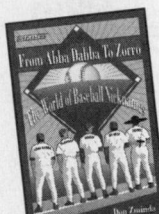

Qty	Product Name	Item Number	Price	Total
	Books (Free first-class shipping for books over $10)			
	STATS Major League Handbook 2000	HB00	$ 19.95	
	STATS Major League Handbook 2000 (Comb-bound)	HC00	$ 24.95	
	The Scouting Notebook 2000	SN00	$ 19.95	
	The Scouting Notebook 2000 (Comb-bound)	SC00	$ 24.95	
	STATS Minor League Handbook 2000	MH00	$ 19.95	
	STATS Minor League Handbook 2000 (Comb-bound)	MC00	$ 24.95	
	STATS Player Profiles 2000	PP00	$ 19.95	
	STATS Player Profiles 2000 (Comb-bound)	PC00	$ 24.95	
	STATS Minor League Scouting Notebook 2000	MN00	$ 19.95	
	STATS Batter Vs. Pitcher Match-Ups! 2000	BP00	$ 24.95	
	STATS Ballpark Sourcebook: Diamond Diagrams	BSDD	$ 24.95	
	STATS Baseball Scoreboard 2000	SB00	$ 19.95	
	STATS Diamond Chronicles 2000	CH00	$ 19.95	
	STATS Pro Football Handbook 2000	FH00	$ 19.95	
	STATS Pro Football Handbook 2000 (Comb-bound)	FC00	$ 24.95	
	STATS Pro Football Scoreboard 2000	SF00	$ 19.95	
	STATS Pro Football Sourcebook 2000	PF00	$ 19.95	
	STATS Hockey Handbook 1999-2000	HH00	$ 19.95	
	STATS Pro Basketball Handbook 1999-2000	BH00	$ 19.95	
	STATS All-Time Major League Handbook, 2nd Edition	ATHB	$ 79.95	
			Total	
	Books Under $10 (Please include $2.00 S&H for each book/magazine)			
	From Abba Dabba to Zorro: The World of Baseball Nicknames	ABBA	$ 9.95	
	STATS Baseball's Terrific 20	KID1	$ 9.95	
	STATS Player Projections Update 2000	PJUP	$ 9.95	
	STATS Fantasy Insider-Pro Football 2000 Edition	IF00	$ 5.95	
			Total	
	Previous Editions (Please Circle appropriate years and include $2.00 S&H for each book)			
	STATS Major League Handbook	'91 '92 '93 '94 '95 '96 '97 '98 '99	$ 9.95	
	The Scouting Notebook/Report	'94 '95 '96 '97 '98 '99	$ 9.95	
	STATS Player Profiles	'93 '94 '95 '96 '97 '98 '99	$ 9.95	
	STATS Minor League Handbook	'92 '93 '94 '95 '96 '97 '98 '99	$ 9.95	
	STATS Minor League Scouting Notebook	'95 '96 '97 '98 '99	$ 9.95	
	STATS Batter Vs. Pitcher Match-Ups!	'94 '95 '96 '97 '98 '99	$ 9.95	
	STATS Diamond Chronicles	'97 '98 '99	$ 9.95	
	STATS Baseball Scoreboard	'92 '93 '94 '95 '96 '97 '98 '99	$ 9.95	
	Pro Football Revealed: The 100-Yard War	'94 '95 '96 '97 '98	$ 9.95	
	STATS Pro Football Handbook	'95 '96 '97 '98 '99	$ 9.95	
	STATS Pro Football Scoreboard	'99	$ 9.95	
	STATS Hockey Handbook	'96-97 '97-98 '98-99	$ 9.95	
	STATS Pro Basketball Handbook	'93-94 '94-95 '95-96 '96-97 '97-98 '98-99	$ 9.95	
	All-Time Major League Handbook (Slightly dinged)	First Edition	$ 45.00	
	All-Time Major League Sourcebook (Slightly dinged)	First Edition	$ 45.00	
			Total	
	Bill James Classic Baseball	BJCB	$ 129.95	
	Bill James Fantasy Baseball	BJFB	$ 89.95	
	STATS Fantasy Football	SFF	$ 49.95	
			Total	

TOTAL [ ]

1st Fantasy Team Name (ex. Colt 45's):_____

Which Fantasy Game is the team for?_____

2nd Fantasy Team Name (ex. Colt 45's):_____

Which Fantasy Game is the team for?_____

Note: $1.00/player is charged for all roster moves and transactions.

STATS INC.®
SPORTS TEAM ANALYSIS & TRACKING SYSTEMS

Phone:
1-800-63-STATS
(847) 677-3322

Mail:
STATS, Inc.
8130 Lehigh Avenue
Morton Grove, IL 60053

Fax:
(847) 470-9140

Bill To:
Company_____
Name_____
Address_____
City_____State_____Zip_____
Phone (   )_____Ext._____Fax (   )_____
E-mail Address_____

Ship To: *(Fill in this section if shipping address differs from billing address)*
Company_____
Name_____
Address_____
City_____State_____Zip_____
Phone (   )_____Ext._____Fax (   )_____
E-mail Address_____

Method of payment:
All prices stated
in U.S. Dollars

❑ Charge to my *(circle one)*
   Visa
   MasterCard
   American Express
   Discover

❑ Check or Money Order
   (U.S. funds only)

Please include credit card number
and expiration date with charge orders!

Exp. Date ┌──────────┐
           │   /   │
           └──────────┘
         Month Year

X_____
  Signature *(as shown on credit card)*

Totals for STATS Products:

Books   [_____]

Books Under $10 *   [_____]

Prior Book Editions *   [_____]

order 2 or more books/subtract: $1.00/book
(Does not include prior editions)   [_____]

Illinois residents add 8.5% sales tax   [_____]

                       Sub Total [_____]

Shipping Costs

Canada   Add $3.50/book   [_____]

* All books under $10   Add $2.00/book   [_____]

Fantasy Games   [_____]

             Grand Total [_____]
         (No other discounts apply)

(Orders subject to availability)

Free First-Class Shipping for Books Over $10